CASES AND MATERIALS ON TORTS

EDITORIAL ADVISORS

ASPEN CASEBOOK SERIES

CASES AND MATERIALS ON TORTS

THIRTEENTH EDITION

RICHARD A. EPSTEIN
Laurence A. Tisch Professor of Law
New York University School of Law
Peter and Kirsten Bedford Senior Fellow
The Hoover Institution
Stanford University
James Parker Hall Distinguished Service Professor of Law
Emeritus and Senior Lecturer
The University of Chicago

CATHERINE M. SHARKEY
Segal Family Professor of Regulatory Law and Policy
New York University School of Law

ASPEN PUBLISHING

To contact Customer Service, e-mail customer.service@aspenpublishing.com, call 1-800-950-5259, or mail correspondence to:

Aspen Publishing
Attn: Order Department
1 Wall Street
Burlington, MA 01803

Printed in the United States of America.

1 2 3 4 5 6 7 8 9 0

ISBN 979-8-8890-6056-7

Library of Congress Cataloging-in-Publication Data

Names: Epstein, Richard Allen, 1943- author. | Sharkey, Catherine M., author.
Title: Cases and materials on torts / Richard A. Epstein, Catherine M. Sharkey.
Description: Thirteenth edition. | Burlington: Aspen Publishing, 2024. | Series: Aspen casebook series | Includes bibliographical references and index. | Summary: "Casebook on Tort law for law students"—Provided by publisher.
Identifiers: LCCN 2023052638 (print) | LCCN 2023052639 (ebook) | ISBN 9798889060567 (hardcover) | ISBN 9798889060581 (ebook)
Subjects: LCSH: Torts—United States.
Classification: LCC KF1250.E655 2024 (print) | LCC KF1250 (ebook) | DDC 346.7303—dc23
LC record available at https://lccn.loc.gov/2023052638
LC ebook record available at https://lccn.loc.gov/2023052639

SUSTAINABLE FORESTRY INITIATIVE Certified Chain of Custody
Promoting Sustainable Forestry
www.forests.org
SFI-01681

SFI label applies to the text stock

About Aspen Publishing

Aspen Publishing is a leading provider of educational content and digital learning solutions to law schools in the U.S. and around the world. Aspen provides best-in-class solutions for legal education through authoritative textbooks, written by renowned authors, and breakthrough products such as Connected eBooks, Connected Quizzing, and PracticePerfect.

The Aspen Casebook Series (famously known among law faculty and students as the "red and black" casebooks) encompasses hundreds of highly regarded textbooks in more than eighty disciplines, from large enrollment courses, such as Torts and Contracts to emerging electives such as Sustainability and the Law of Policing. Study aids such as the *Examples & Explanations* and the *Emanuel Law Outlines* series, both highly popular collections, help law students master complex subject matter.

Major products, programs, and initiatives include:

- **Connected eBooks** are enhanced digital textbooks and study aids that come with a suite of online content and learning tools designed to maximize student success. Designed in collaboration with hundreds of faculty and students, the Connected eBook is a significant leap forward in the legal education learning tools available to students.
- **Connected Quizzing** is an easy-to-use formative assessment tool that tests law students' understanding and provides timely feedback to improve learning outcomes. Delivered through CasebookConnect.com, the learning platform already used by students to access their Aspen casebooks, Connected Quizzing is simple to implement and integrates seamlessly with law school course curricula.
- **PracticePerfect** is a visually engaging, interactive study aid to explain commonly encountered legal doctrines through easy-to-understand animated videos, illustrative examples, and numerous practice questions. Developed by a team of experts, PracticePerfect is the ideal study companion for today's law students.
- The **Aspen Learning Library** enables law schools to provide their students with access to the most popular study aids on the market across all of their courses. Available through an annual subscription, the online library consists of study aids in e-book, audio, and video formats with full text search, note-taking, and highlighting capabilities.
- Aspen's **Digital Bookshelf** is an institutional-level online education bookshelf, consolidating everything students and professors need to ensure success. This program ensures that every student has access to affordable course materials from day one.
- **Leading Edge** is a community centered on thinking differently about legal education and putting those thoughts into actionable strategies. At the core of the program is the Leading Edge Conference, an annual gathering of legal education thought leaders looking to pool ideas and identify promising directions of exploration.

To the next generation

Bella Catherine Pianko
Noah David Pianko
Ethan Saul Pianko
Naomi Alice Zafran-Epstein
Annie Juliette Zafran-Epstein
Ione Pearl Epstein
Caleb Emmett Sharkey
Phoebe Lila Sharkey

SUMMARY OF CONTENTS

CONTENTS

PREFACE

2024 marks the sixty-fifth year since the publication of the first edition of Charles Gregory and Harry Kalven, Jr., *Cases and Materials on Torts*. With our publication of the thirteenth edition, we have arrived at the first revolutionary change in casebook organization. The casebook has now been broken into two separate volumes, a change rendered necessary by the changes in legal education over that sixty-five-year period. The first edition was published at a time when the common law was still the dominant source of law. Law schools typically had full-year or otherwise lengthy courses in torts, contracts, property, and procedure. The first edition fit into that frame by offering materials that could cover that course. In the third edition, 1977, prepared by Epstein with a notable assist from Gregory after Kalven's death in October 1974, new chapters were added on misrepresentation, economic harms, and the various individual and governmental immunities. So conceived, the book had chapters on all tort subjects and, in addition, on the various insurance coverage issues (a big point at the time) and the numerous no-fault systems, starting with workers' compensation and going through the automobile no-fault systems that were among the hottest intellectual debates of the time.

That was then and this is now. Today, the automobile is not the center of attention. Medical malpractice and products liability, areas that came alive in the 1960s and 1970s, have begun to loom larger than before. Since that time, a burst of innovation in tort law and theory took place between the late 1960s and the early 1980s. Many of the principal cases in this book derive from that period, and they are retained because they often contain the most incisive discussion of major issues that are still the leading authorities to this date. By the same token, the emergence of the large administrative state both builds on and displaces traditional common law categories. Thus, the law of nuisance is often supplemented (or displaced) by statutes dealing with various environmental law issues. Matters of product safety are often subject to detailed regulations, especially through the federal Food and Drug Administration. And much of the modern law of securities is based on the principles of misrepresentation that were first developed from the late eighteenth century until the dawn of the twentieth century. The rise of these substantive statutes, coupled with federal regulatory schemes, have had their impact on law school curriculums. The common law courses have been reduced in size and scope, and the first year now commonly has courses in legislation and/or regulation to reflect the change in legal emphasis.

The reduction in the length of the first-year torts curriculum must reflect these institutional changes. We have decided to bite the bullet and, with this thirteenth edition, present a more streamlined casebook appropriate for a comprehensive 1L Torts course. In order to make this transition, we did major surgery on three of the less-taught chapters in the twelfth edition. Material from the old Chapter 10 on Insurance and the No-Fault System and the old Chapter 15 on Torts Immunities has been incorporated into the other chapters of the book. Thus, Chapter 1 on Intentional Torts covers issues relating to intention that relate to insurance coverage on the one hand and immunities for governments on the other. Similarly, material on government immunities for medical malpractice is incorporated into Chapter 3 on Negligence, and material on explosives and public nuisances has been incorporated in Chapter 7 on

Strict Liability, while matters of federal preemption and liability for vaccines has been incorporated into Chapter 8 on Products Liability.

An advanced, companion casebook, *Cases and Materials on Torts Against Nonphysical Interests*, is in development and will be available soon. In that book, matters of privacy, defamation, and misrepresentation have received extensive new treatment, both through case law development and statutory developments, and we have sought to include these new materials in our more limited framework. In the end, we hope that two books work a sensible division between the basic first-year torts course and an advanced, upper division course (or seminar) on torts that deals with defamation, privacy, misrepresentation, and economic harms.

Notwithstanding these new developments, we have strived to preserve the basic character and feel of the book. Accordingly, its basic organization and structure remain consistent with the broad objectives of the first edition of the casebook, which first appeared in 1959 by the late Professors Charles O. Gregory and Harry Kalven, Jr., both exceptional and imaginative scholars. Their second edition followed some ten years later and was in fact the book from which Professor Epstein first taught torts at the University of Southern California in 1969. In 1972, he joined the faculty of the University of Chicago Law School. In January 1974, with Gregory in retirement, Professor Kalven asked Epstein to collaborate with him on the third edition of the casebook. Kalven's tragic death in October 1974 cut short that brief collaboration before it could begin. Thereafter, Professor Gregory re-entered the lists to read and comment on the drafts that Epstein prepared on the third edition, which appeared in 1977, some forty-seven years ago. The preparation for the fourth edition of Epstein, Gregory, and Kalven, which appeared in 1984, was done by Epstein alone. Gregory died in April 1987, after a rich and full life. Epstein was then the sole editor of the fifth (1990), sixth (1995), seventh (2000), eighth (2004), and ninth (2008) editions. Even after so much time and revision, much of the case selection and organization of this book reflect the initial judgments of Gregory and Kalven, whose pioneering spirit and rich imagination brought so much to the study of torts.

The tenth edition (2012) reflected the formation of a new partnership between Epstein and Sharkey, which in turn led to some major changes in content. That edition merged the material on joint and several liability into the chapter on causation. The material on vicarious liability was inserted at the end of the now-Chapter 7 on Strict Liability, to which was also added the materials on trespass to chattels and conversion that had formerly been located in Chapter 1 on Intentional Torts. Extensive references were made to the key provisions of the Third Restatement of Torts: Liability for Physical and Emotional Harm, approved by the American Law Institute in 2011. To these were added the changes in both appearance and organization for the eleventh edition (2016).

As with earlier editions, our intention has been to update the materials while preserving historical and conceptual continuity between the present and the past. In so doing, we have sought to keep one of the distinctive features of this casebook, which is to stress the alternative visions of tort law as they developed in the nineteenth and twentieth centuries, and the ever larger footprint of the twenty-first century. Toward that end, we have retained in the thirteenth edition those great older cases, both English and American, that have proved themselves time and again in the classroom, and which continue to exert great influence on the modern law. We continue to highlight in detail the many major expansionary changes in tort law that took place in the years between 1968 and 1980. Although many of those developments continue to remain important, others have been either modified or rejected in favor of more traditional doctrines. It is no longer likely in 2024 that strict liability rules will exert greater sway in medical malpractice cases, or that market share liability will expand much beyond the original DES cases and other fungible products. By the same token, the Internet has ushered in new challenges across the board, from how to define property torts in this new domain to thorny issues of liability for actors in the "platform economy." We have sought to keep pace with these new developments, which occur both through common law and, increasingly, through legislation and regulation.

Five previous editions of this book were dedicated to the memory of Charles Gregory and Harry Kalven. In 2004, Epstein dedicated the eighth edition of the book to the memory of his contemporary, the late Gary Schwartz, who died in 2001, one of the most insightful, learned, and fair-minded tort professors of any generation. For many years his kindness, generosity, and insight helped improve the earlier editions of the casebook. The ninth edition was dedicated to the late Bernard D. Meltzer, himself a casebook author of great distinction, who passed away at age 92 in 2007. In the tenth edition, we moved from the past to the future, and dedicated jointly this edition to the next generation, our grandchildren and children, respectively. In the thirteenth edition we continue this exercise, now to increased ranks.

Richard A. Epstein
Catherine M. Sharkey

New York
December 2023

ACKNOWLEDGMENTS

In preparing the thirteenth edition of this casebook, we have been fortunate enough to draw on the comments of many teachers and students who have used the book. Over the years we have received additional assistance and suggestions on various points of this volume from Kenneth Abraham, Jennifer Arlen, Vincent Blasi, William Cohen, Michael Corrado, Richard Craswell, Theodore Eisenberg, Robert Ellickson, Cindy Estlund, Stephen Gillers, Rick Hasen, James Henderson, Gail Heriot, Morton Horwitz, Keith Hylton, Jason Johnston, Spencer Kimball, Alvin Klevorick, Stanton Kraus, William Landes, Fred McChesney, Thomas Miles, Marc Miller, Cornelius Peck, Malla Pollock, Richard Posner, Glen Robinson, Howard Sacks, Gary Schwartz, Paul Schwartz, Perry Sentell, Ken Simons, Geoffrey Stone, Alan Sykes, Aaron Twerski, Ernest Weinrib, and Jerry Wiley. We should also like to thank in addition all the unnamed casebook users who have filled in their forms to explain what they did and did not like about earlier editions of the book.

Our largest debt, however, goes to the team of diligent research assistants who helped in the preparation of the thirteenth edition of this book: Tyler Ashman, Joe Kiernan, Randy Quarles, and Stephen Vukovits of the University of Chicago Law School, and Keton Kakkar and Thomas Wiig of NYU School of Law. Keton Kakkar deserves special thanks for proofreading the entire new book.

We also thank Joanne Butler for seeing this project through at Aspen Publishing, and Tom Daughhetee and Dena Kaufman for overseeing production with their team at The Froebe Group. We would also like to thank the authors and copyright holders of the following works:

Articles and Books

American Law Institute. Sections from the Restatement of Torts, Second. Copyright © 1965, 1977, 1979 by the American Law Institute. Reproduced with permission.

American Law Institute. Sections from the Restatement of Torts, Third. Copyright © 2004, 2010, 2011 by the American Law Institute. Reproduced with permission.

Ames, James Barr. "Law and Morals." Harvard Law Review, Vol. 22. Harvard Law School. 1908.

Coase, R.H. "The Problem of Social Cost." The Journal of Law & Economics, Vol. 3. The University of Chicago Press, 1960.

Prosser, William L. "Comparative Negligence." California Law Review, Vol. 41. California Law Review, Inc., 1953.

Ross, H. Laurence. *Settled Out of Court: The Social Process of Insurance Claims Adjustment.* 2nd ed., Transaction Publishers, 1980.

Schwartz, Gary. "Tort Law and the Economy in Nineteenth-Century America: A Reinterpretation." Yale Law Journal, Vol. 90. The Yale Law Journal Company, Inc., 1981.

Seavey, Warren Abner. "Negligence — Subjective or Objective?" Harvard Law Review, Vol. 41. Harvard Law School, 1927.

Thomson, Judith Jarvis. "The Trolley Problem." Yale Law Journal, Vol. 94. The Yale Law Journal Company, Inc., 1985.

Viscusi, W. Kip. *Risk by Choice: Regulating Health and Safety in the Workplace.* Harvard University Press, 1983.

Photographs and Illustrations

1908 Buick Model 10. Photograph. Copyright © PF/Alamy.

1968 Volkswagen Beetle. Photograph. Copyright © Phil Talbot/Alamy.

Albert Sabin. Photograph. Copyright © Bettmann/Corbis via Getty Images.

Benjamin Cardozo. Photograph. Library of Congress via Wikimedia Commons.

Colin Blackburn. Illustration. Harvard University Library via Wikimedia Commons.

Court of Common Pleas (ca. 1460). Illustration. Copyright © Inner Temple Library.

Cover of the first edition of *The Common Law.* Photograph. Wikimedia Commons

"Do you have any picture books?" Illustration. Copyright © Alex Gregory/CartoonStock.

Eden Roc and Fountainebleau hotels. Photograph. Copyright © Jordan Cerruti. Reprinted by permission.

Empire State Building, New York City Blackout of 1977. Photograph. Copyright © Dan Farrell/ New York Daily News Archive via Getty Images.

Erie Railroad "Berkshire" locomotive. Photograph. Bud Laws via Railfan.net.

Exxon Valdez. Photograph. Copyright © Chris Wilkins/AFP/Getty Images.

Fish meal. Photograph. Copyright © Julio Etchart/Alamy.

George William Wilshere Bramwell, 1st Baron Bramwell. Illustration. Via Wikimedia Commons.

Guido Calabresi. Photograph. Copyright © Robert Benson Photography.

Henrietta Lacks. Photograph. Copyright © Obstetrics & Gynaecology/Science Photo Library.

Henry J. Friendly. Photograph. Copyright © The Estate of Fabian Bachrach.

Hugh McCalmont Cairns, 1st Earl Cairns c. 1860. Photograph. Copyright © John Watkins/ National Portrait Gallery, London.

"If you're so enlightened, how come you can't lick that slice?" Illustration. Copyright © Sam Gross/CartoonStock.

"It's a mixed-use facility: retail space." Illustration. Copyright © Sidney Harris/The New Yorker Collection/The Cartoon Bank.

"It's my fault—I wasn't worrying enough." Illustration. Copyright © Tom Cheney/The New Yorker Collection/The Cartoon Bank.

Ken Hamidi. Photograph. Copyright © Ken Hamidi for Governor.

Kenneth Feinberg (2014). Photograph. Copyright © Alex Wong/Getty Images.

Learned Hand. Photograph. Harvard University Library via Wikimedia Commons.

Lemuel Shaw. Photograph. Southworth and Hawes/Museum of Fine Arts, Boston via Wikimedia Commons.

Ortho-Novum Dialpak dispenser. Photograph. Copyright © B Christopher/Alamy.

Liutprand, 712-744 A.D. Via Wikimedia Commons. Licensed under CC BY-SA 2.5 DEED, https://creativecommons.org/licenses/by-sa/2.5/.

Office of the Accident Compensation Commission (ACC) in Palmerston North, New Zealand. Photograph. William Stadtwald Demchick via Wikimedia Commons. Licensed under CC BY 3.0 DEED, https://creativecommons.org/licenses/by/3.0/.

Richard Posner. Photograph. Copyright © University of Chicago Law School.

Roger J. Traynor. Photograph. Copyright © Law School Archives, University of California, Berkeley.

"Safety Last." Illustration. Copyright © Guy & Rodd/Distributed by Universal Uclick for UFS via CartoonStock.com.

"Screens out harmful ultraviolet rays". Illustration. Copyright © Edward Frascino/The New Yorker Collection/The Cartoon Bank.

Sir Nicholas Conyngham Tindal. Illustration. Thomas Philips/National Portrait Gallery, London.

Sir William Blackstone. Illustration. Via Wikimedia Commons.

Tamaroa, United States Coast Guard vessel. Photograph. United States Coast Guard via Wikimedia Commons.

Tugboat John A. Bonker. Copyright © Atomic/Alamy Stock Photo.

"Vioxx?" billboard (2004). Photograph. Copyright © Robert Daemmrich Photography Inc/ Corbis via Getty Images.

Wagon Mound. Photograph. Copyright © Auke Vissier/Bulkers/Photobucket.

"Why carry malpractice insurance if you don't malpractice once in a while?" Illustration. Copyright © Peter Steiner/CartoonStock.

William Prosser. Photograph. Copyright © Law School Archives, University of California, Berkeley.

Wisconsin State Journal staff in 1924. Photograph. Wisconsin State Journal Archive.

INTRODUCTION

The thirteenth edition of this casebook appears, in two separate volumes, four years after the twelfth edition, and some sixty-five years after Charles O. Gregory and Harry Kalven, Jr., published the first edition of this casebook in 1959. Those sixty-five years have been marked by both continuity and change in the law. From the late 1950s until the mid-1980s, these changes tended to move largely in one direction. With the exception of the law of defamation and privacy, tort liability expanded on almost all fronts. Since the mid-1980s, however, the picture has become far more clouded. In some traditional areas of physical injuries, tort liability appeared to have reached its high-water mark but in other areas there is more lack of direction.

In the midst of these ebbs and flows in tort liability, certain questions have remained with us in more or less the same form in which they were faced by the earliest generations of common law lawyers. The tension between the principles of negligence and strict liability in stranger cases surely falls into this class. The debates framed in the nineteenth-century cases have largely shaped the subsequent analysis in important areas of the law, such as those dealing with abnormally dangerous activities and with private and public nuisances, all of which continue to take on additional importance in an age that shows greater preoccupation with environmental harms and toxic torts.

Yet in other areas we have witnessed major transformations, both in the types of cases brought to litigation, and in the choice of legal theories used to decide them. In 1959—the year of the first edition—the paradigmatic tort action was still the automobile collision. When one thought of institutional tort defendants, the railroads came first to mind. The areas of products liability and medical malpractice cases were, when viewed with the benefit of hindsight, still in their early childhood, while mass torts and toxic torts (the two often go together) still lay a decade or more in the future.

The emergence of new types of litigation has taken its toll on traditional tort theory. The question of "proximate cause"—whether a remote consequence could properly be attributed to the wrongful conduct of the defendant—was the dominant issue of causation in 1959 and the major source of contention among academic writers, especially with unique factual situations that resisted easy classification. That is no longer true today. Increasingly modern tort litigation concentrates on two other problems. The first involves the difficult questions of evidence and statistics necessary to establish the factual connection between, for example, the defendant's drug or waste discharge and the medical injuries of the plaintiff. The second involves the rules designed to deal with multiple causation when two or more parties are charged with responsibility for all or part of the same harms, which happens in many nuisance and toxic tort cases. Both of these shifts in emphasis have accelerated in the past generation and continue to be taken into account in this edition.

Notwithstanding the enormous substantive changes, the educational aims of this casebook are much the same as those of the previous twelve editions. The primary goal remains one of giving to you, the student, an accurate sense of both the legal evolution and the current legal position of tort law. In this context, that means incorporating into the book the output of the American Law Institute, which has now published multiple volumes of a Third Restatement dealing with Intentional Harms, Liability for Physical and Emotional Harm, Liability for

Economic Harms, Apportionment of Liability Among Multiple Defendants, Liability Insurance, Products Liability, Remedies, and (the final(?) volume) Miscellaneous Provisions. It also means taking into account repeated rounds of legislative initiatives, which, not by coincidence alone, have taken place in the same areas that have generated the new Restatement output.

This casebook, however, would fail in its essential mission if it did not accomplish two other tasks. First, it should provide you an opportunity to examine the processes of legal method and legal reasoning, with an eye to understanding the judicial evolution of legal rules, their legislative responses, and the huge impact that these changes have had on our social institutions. Second, it should give you some sense of the different systematic and intellectual approaches that have been taken to the law of torts over the years.

The importance of understanding method and historical evolution cannot be underestimated in legal education. A casebook—certainly this casebook—is not a reference book, much less a treatise. Indeed with the rise of the online services, internal case and page references are cut back to a minimum, typically with no explicit indication of omitted citations, in order to improve the flow of the text. The great problem of legal work today does not lie in finding too little law, but in being overwhelmed by too much. A click on a single principal case puts you on a trail that branches off in a thousand directions. Faced with this surfeit of information, the standard legal curriculum, by necessity, touches on only a small fraction of the huge and ever-growing body of judicial decisions, Restatement provisions, statutory material, and academic literature, much of which will change with time. The education of the lawyer of the future therefore rests on an ability to isolate the key documents and doctrines from a mass of legal materials, to identify their underlying assumptions, to determine their possible implications for analogous cases, and, above all, to deal with the persistent uncertainty, ambiguity, and at times downright confusion in the law.

To help with these tasks, it is essential to trace the development of a legal principle over time, through a line of cases that illustrates its application and tests its limits. To that end this casebook contains many cases from the nineteenth century and before, even some that have long ceased to represent the current law. Much of the material in the thirteenth edition does not represent modern cases, but earlier decisions whose intellectual value has survived the passage of decades, or even centuries, including one short but insightful passage from the Lombard laws on comparative negligence that dates from 733 A.D.! Likewise in order to capture the nature of legal debate, in many principal cases we have reproduced not only the opinion of the court but those of concurring or dissenting judges. With Fletcher v. Rylands, *infra* Chapter 2, at 81–86, for example, five separate opinions from three different courts are reproduced, because each adds something to the total picture. These cases are often of exceptional value because their interesting facts invite examination of subtle variations in judicial reasoning. The quality of the judicial arguments has also made these cases focal points for analysis in subsequent judicial opinions. Likewise in legal scholarship, modern treatments of complex issues tend to gravitate to the discussion of the classic cases that have already been studied by previous generations of scholars.

A sound legal education requires more than attention to doctrinal and analytical skills. The law of torts in particular is one of the richest bodies of substantive law, and it has been examined and explored from historical, philosophical, economic, and institutional perspectives by judges and scholars alike. It is essential for all students to gain some sense of the diverse possible analytical approaches to tort law, lest the constant probing with the Socratic method lead to an unhappy form of intellectual nihilism. The materials selected are designed, wherever possible, to allow you to confront torts not only as a collection of discrete rules but also as a systematic intellectual discipline.

For the past five or six decades, judges and scholars have voiced fundamental disagreement about the proper orientation toward the tort law and about the proper choice of its key substantive rules. Speaking first to the question of intellectual orientation, it is possible to identify three major positions. The traditional view—which had unspoken dominance at the time when the first two editions appeared in 1959 and 1969—looked upon the law of torts as a study in corrective justice, that is, as an effort to develop a coherent set of principles to decide whether *this* plaintiff was entitled to compensation or other remedy from *this* defendant as a matter of fairness between the parties. Issues of public policy and social control were of course never absent from the judicial or academic discourse, but they did not dominate judicial or academic attitudes toward either particular cases or general theory. Fairness, justice, and equity, however elusive, were the dominant themes. Most laypeople, and many judges, instinctively approach most tort cases in just this fashion.

Over the past fifty or sixty years, the traditional approach has been under attack from two flanks. On the one hand there is continued insistence, which is sometimes expressly articulated in the cases, that the compensation of injured parties is in itself a valid end of the tort law, such that the doctrines of tort law that frustrate that objective must be hedged with limitations or totally eliminated unless strong justification is given for their retention. The older presumption that the plaintiff had to show "good cause" to hold a defendant liable (roughly speaking) has yielded in some quarters to a new presumption that the defendant who has demonstrably caused harm must show why liability should not be imposed. That shift in presumptions, which is today hotly contested, has two major implications. First, the risk of "inevitable accidents" shifts. These were usually borne by the plaintiff under the dominant view from the late nineteenth to the mid-twentieth century, both for private and institutional defendants. Yet once the presumption shifts, especially with institutional defendants (corporations, hospitals, professional practice groups), the risk of inevitable accidents tends to be shifted to defendants for both physical and emotional harms. Charging institutional defendants with tort liability, it is said, allows for the orderly shift of these individual losses to society at large, either by altering the nature and type of products sold and services provided, or by spreading the risk through liability insurance. Second, in suits against institutional defendants, defenses based on the plaintiff's conduct—notably contributory (or comparative) negligence and assumption of risk—receive a narrower interpretation and rarely bar, but typically reduce, the plaintiff's recovery.

The second critique of the traditional approach comes from a different quarter, that of economic theory. Looking first at tort law as a system of social control, advocates of the economic approach have generally argued that the proper function of tort law is to lay down workable liability rules that create incentives for both individuals and firms to minimize (the sum of) the costs of accidents, the costs of their prevention, and the administrative costs of running the legal system. In this view of the subject, the compensation of individual parties is not an end in itself, but only a means to enlist private parties to help police the harmful activities of others. Tort law is thus understood as part of a complex system that necessarily interacts with legislative and administrative regulation, not to mention contractual and customary limitations on proper conduct. Given its systematic orientation, this economic approach tends to downplay both the importance of corrective justice in the individual case and compensation for individual victims of accidents, treating the first as largely question-begging and the second as better achieved through voluntary first-party arrangements for life, health, or disability insurance. Until fairly recently, its importance was largely academic, but today its influence in the decided cases is increasing. But it would be a mistake to state that current judicial decisions are dominated by the law and economics approach, or that it has displaced the traditional intuitive reliance on fairness—except perhaps with the hardy band of law professors turned judges.

The diversity of opinions on the proper approach to the tort law carries over to disputes about the proper substantive basis of tort liability. From the earliest times until today courts have entertained three main theories—each subject to many variants—for recovery in tort. There is, first, recovery for harms intentionally inflicted by the defendant on the person, property, or emotional wellbeing of the plaintiff. Second, there is recovery for harms negligently inflicted, that is, through the want of reasonable or ordinary care on the part of the defendant. Last, there is recovery under a theory of strict liability—that is, for harms inflicted on the plaintiff by a defendant who acts without negligence and without any intention to harm.

In dealing with these three theories it is important to keep in mind several recurrent themes. One set of issues concerns the relationships between the general approach to the law of torts and the choice of specific theories of liability in particular cases. When does a concern for corrective justice require the use of a strict liability principle, a negligence principle, or an intentional tort principle? What about theories based on the need for individual compensation or on the use of the tort law as a device for minimizing accident costs by channeling scarce resources to their most efficient use? Conversely it is important to ask which *limitations* on recovery are consistent with the basic theories of liability and with their basic orientation to the subject matter. In this connection it is important to ask the extent to which recovery should be denied because of the plaintiff's own conduct—be it called contributory (or comparative) negligence or assumption of risk—the conduct of a third party, or an "act of God" when the plaintiff has otherwise made out a good cause of action.

Finally it is crucial to consider what might conveniently be termed the "boundary" questions in the law of torts. As stated, any of the three theories of liability—strict liability, negligence liability, or liability for intentional harms—could apply to any case involving physical, emotional, reputational, or economic harm. How do these different theories coexist across the full range of tort cases? To anticipate for a moment, does, for example, the commitment to a theory of strict liability in classic trespass cases—those involving the direct application of force on the person or property, both real and personal, of another—require (or allow) the use of a similar theory in cases involving slips and falls on business or residential premises or for the harm caused by those engaged in abnormally dangerous activities or the manufacture of dangerous products? Similarly it must be asked whether the choice of a negligence theory in medical malpractice cases commits us to that theory for routine traffic accidents or whether a theory of intentional harms in assault cases commits us to that theory in defamation cases.

With our major conceptual dimensions identified, it is perhaps desirable to close this introduction with a brief summary about the organization of this book. The subject matter of the law of torts can be approached from a large number of different perspectives, and the order of organization is by no means "neutral," since instructors with one outlook are apt to gravitate to certain materials in one order while those with a different outlook are apt to gravitate to yet another. Here we have tried to adhere to traditional modes of presentation that can, it is hoped, be varied with minimum confusion to suit the tastes of different instructors.

Chapter 1 begins with an exploration of the principles of intentional harms to persons, land, and emotion, with a focus on new provisions from the Third Restatement on Intentional Torts. This study can be conveniently concluded before turning to the bulk of the materials, which deal with physical and emotional harms caused by accident. The chapter covers first and foremost the cases of physical injuries to the person and to land. It also introduces some collateral uses of intention in connection with tort liability and insurance coverage. We have postponed the discussion of conversion and trespass to chattels to Chapter 7, where they are linked with other specific forms of strict liability. Once the analysis of the prima facie case is completed, the book addresses such distinctive defenses as consent, mental disability, defense of self and property, and private and public necessity. Once that is completed the chapter addresses the various harms associated with wrongful imprisonment and the intentional infliction of emotional distress.

Chapter 2 introduces the recurrent tension between negligence and strict liability in the context of accidental physical injuries by examining the two alternatives in both their historical and analytical aspects. The study spans nearly 500 years from the mid-fifteenth to the mid-twentieth century, first in England and then in the United States.

Chapter 3 then undertakes a detailed analysis of the negligence principle, which addresses the different interpretations that can be attached to the idea of unreasonable conduct, the role of custom and statute, and the issues of proof, with special attention to the doctrine of res ipsa loquitur, and to the role of judge and jury in trying negligence cases.

Chapter 4 turns to plaintiff's conduct, including contributory negligence, assumption of risk, and comparative negligence, with both two and more parties. As noted above, new material on workers' compensation and no-fault systems has been folded into this chapter.

Chapter 5 then deals with two of the major issues of causation, cause-in-fact and proximate cause, as seen through both traditional and modern theories. It also covers everything from simple push-pull cases to complex situations where the defendant owes some duty to protect or care for others.

Chapter 6 addresses affirmative duties, most notably the duty to rescue people in distress. It examines this problem both in connection with strangers and then for persons with whom the defendant stands in some special relationship. This latter category includes the full range of entrants onto land from invitees, licensees, and trespassers. It also covers situations in which the defendant exercises some degree of control over other people, including children, students, tenants, and psychiatric patients. Material on affirmative duties in the age of platforms makes a novel appearance here.

Chapter 7 then deals with strict liability torts: animals, trespass to chattels, conversion, abnormally dangerous activities, and nuisance, both private and public, and takes into account the multiple contexts in which public nuisance claims are raised. It concludes with a discussion of the role of strict liability in dealing with vicarious liability, including new material addressing the status of rideshare companies and incorporating the new provision from Third Restatement: Miscellaneous Provisions.

Chapter 8 examines the evolution of products liability from its nineteenth-century preoccupation with privity to its modern applications in dealing with the three major classes of defects: namely those in manufacturing, design, and warning. It also addresses the ever more important question of whether and when federal regulation displaces the private rights of action in duty to warn and design defect cases, which has been the subject of intense litigation in the U.S. Supreme Court in recent years. Finally, it takes on the latest revolutions in product liability concerning dangerous products sold by online platforms.

Chapter 9 completes the exposition of the elements of the basic tort with an analysis of the rules governing damages, both compensatory and punitive, in both its common law and constitutional dimensions. Here, too, we have included new provisions from the Third Restatement: Remedies, with particular consideration of the role of historical bias in calculating damages.

We have consciously edited the materials with an eye toward smoother reading. Unless the context otherwise seems to require, we have followed a loose convention of using the female pronoun for plaintiffs and the male pronoun for defendants. Citations to cases (and to cases within cases), footnotes, and other quoted material have been eliminated or simplified without any special indication, solely to remove clutter and preserve readability. The few footnotes that have been retained keep their original numbering for easier reference to the original materials. Footnotes added by the editors are indicated by an asterisk.

References to W. Prosser and W. Keeton on Torts (5th ed. 1984) are simply to Prosser and Keeton on Torts. References to F. Harper, F. James, and O. Gray, The Law of Torts (3d ed. 2007) are simply to Harper, James & Gray, Torts, unless an earlier edition is explicitly mentioned. Epstein has written a treatise on the law of torts (Torts, Aspen Law & Business 1999); we have refrained from giving citations to it in this volume, lest they appear with monotonous regularity, but we have included a List of Chapters for that book, which indicates its coverage (*infra* at xxxiii).

TORTS: LIST OF CHAPTERS

TORTS
Richard A. Epstein
(Aspen Law & Business, 1999)

LIST OF ABBREVIATIONS

Abbreviation	Full Citation
AC	Appeals Cases (to the House of Lords)
C.F.R.	Code of Federal Regulations
KB	King's Bench
MPC	Model Penal Code
QB	Queen's Bench
RT	Restatement of Torts
RLI	Restatement of the Law, Liability Insurance
RST	Restatement (Second) of Torts
RTT: IT	Restatement (Third) of Torts: Liability for Intentional Torts
RTT: LEH	Restatement (Third) of Torts: Liability for Economic Harm
RTT: LPEH	Restatement (Third) of Torts: Liability for Physical and Emotional Harm
RTT: PL	Restatement (Third) of Torts: Products Liability

CASES AND MATERIALS ON TORTS

CHAPTER 1

INTENTIONAL HARMS: THE PRIMA FACIE CASE AND DEFENSES

SECTION A. INTRODUCTION

It is best to begin our study of tort law with intentional harms to both the person and property. At first blush, these torts are the easiest to comprehend, because no society can survive the war of all against all that would necessarily arise if everyone were free to deliberately kill and maim everyone else whenever they chose. Intuitively, then, controlling deliberate injuries—stopping a Hobbesian war of all against all—is the first order of business for any viable society. However, conceptual and practical complications immediately arise about how this is best done, given the wide number of different mental states that can accompany, say, punching someone in the nose. First, the law often distinguishes between the intent to commit an act that inadvertently causes harm and the intent to cause the harm itself. Why is that distinction important? How does the tort conception of intent differ, if at all, from the criminal conception of *mens rea* (the guilty mind)? Second, once the plaintiff has established her prima facie case, what excuses and justifications are available to the defendant to defeat or diminish his liability, and to what further qualifications are they subject?

Intentional torts have traditionally covered a wide range of interests. Most obviously, the law guards against physical harm to one's person. It also protects people against forcible dispossession, destruction, or damage to their land and against the taking, or conversion, of their personal property by another. Finally, the law extends its protection to imminent threats of the use of force against the person, known as assault, and to affronts to personal dignity and emotional tranquility, the latter more haltingly.

The first part of this chapter discusses physical harms, which include the torts of battery (or trespass to the person) and trespass to real property. In addition, it examines the full range of defenses based on consent, mental disability, defense of person and property, and necessity. The second part of the chapter examines the torts designed to protect dignitary or emotional interests: assault and offensive battery, false imprisonment, and the intentional infliction of emotional distress.

SECTION B. PHYSICAL HARMS

1. Trespass to Person and Land

Vosburg v. Putney

50 N.W. 403 (Wis. 1891)

The action was brought to recover damages for an assault and battery, alleged to have been committed by the defendant upon the plaintiff on February 20, 1889. The answer is a general denial. At the date of the alleged assault the plaintiff was a little more than fourteen years of age, and the defendant a little less than twelve years of age.

The injury complained of was caused by a kick inflicted by defendant upon the leg of the plaintiff, a little below the knee. The transaction occurred in a schoolroom in Waukesha, during school hours, both parties being pupils in the school. A former trial of the cause resulted in a verdict and judgment for the plaintiff for $2,800 [$93,343 in 2023 dollars]. The defendant appealed from such judgment to this court, and the same was reversed for error, and a new trial awarded.

[A more complete statement of the facts is found in the earlier opinion by Orton, J., 47 N.W. 99, 99 (Wis. 1890), on the initial appeal to the Wisconsin Supreme Court: "The plaintiff was about 14 years of age, and the defendant about 11 years of age. On the 20th day of February, 1889, they were sitting opposite to each other across an aisle in the high school of the village of Waukesha. The defendant reached across the aisle with his foot, and hit with his toe the shin of the right leg of the plaintiff. The touch was slight. The plaintiff did not feel it, either on account of its being so slight or of loss of sensation produced by the shock. In a few moments he felt a violent pain in that place, which caused him to cry out loudly. The next day he was sick, and had to be helped to school. On the fourth day he was vomiting, and Dr. Bacon was sent for, but could not come, and he sent medicine to stop the vomiting, and came to see him the next day, on the 25th. There was a slight discoloration of the skin entirely over the inner surface of the tibia an inch below the bend of the knee. The doctor applied fomentations, and gave him anodynes to quiet the pain. This treatment was continued, and the swelling so increased by the 5th day of March that counsel was called, and on the 8th of March an operation was performed on the limb by making an incision, and a moderate amount of pus escaped. [After further difficult surgeries it became clear that] he will never recover the use of his limb. There were black and blue spots on the shin bone, indicating that there had been a blow. On the 1st day of January before, the plaintiff received an injury just above the knee of the same leg by coasting, which appeared to be healing up and drying down at the time of the last injury. The theory of at least one of the medical witnesses was that the limb was in a diseased condition when this touch or kick was given, caused by microbes entering in through the wound above the knee, and which were revivified by the touch, and that the touch was the exciting or remote cause of the destruction of the bone, or of the plaintiff's injury. It does not appear that there was any visible mark made or left by this touch or kick of the defendant's foot, or any appearance of injury until the black and blue spots were discovered by the physician several days afterwards, and then there were more spots than one. There was no proof of any other hurt, and the medical testimony seems to have been agreed that this touch or kick was the exciting cause of the injury to the plaintiff. The jury rendered a verdict for the plaintiff of $2,800. The learned circuit judge said to the jury: 'It is a peculiar case, an unfortunate case, a case, I think I am at liberty to say that ought not to have come into court. The parents of these children ought, in some way, if possible, to have adjusted it between themselves.' We have much of the same feeling about the case."]

The case has been again tried in the circuit court, and the trial resulted in a verdict for plaintiff for $2,500 . . . [$83,342 in 2023 dollars].

On the last trial the jury found a special verdict, as follows: "(1) Had the plaintiff during the month of January, 1889, received an injury just above the knee, which became inflamed, and produced pus? *Answer.* Yes. (2) Had such injury on the 20th day of February, 1889, nearly healed at the point of the injury? *A.* Yes. (3) Was the plaintiff, before said 20th of February, lame, as the result of such injury? *A.* No. (4) Had the tibia in the plaintiff's right leg become inflamed or diseased to some extent before he received the blow or kick from the defendant? *A.* No. (5) What was the exciting cause of the injury to the plaintiff's leg? *A.* Kick. (6) Did the defendant, in touching the plaintiff with his foot, intend to do him any harm? *A.* No. (7) At what sum do you assess the damages of the plaintiff? *A.* $2,500."

The defendant moved for judgment in his favor on the verdict, and also for a new trial. The plaintiff moved for judgment on the verdict in his favor. The motions of defendant were overruled, and that of the plaintiff granted. Thereupon judgment for plaintiff for $2,500 damages and costs of suit was duly entered. The defendant appeals from the judgment.

Lyon, J. The jury having found that the defendant, in touching the plaintiff with his foot, did not intend to do him any harm, counsel for defendant maintain that the plaintiff has no cause of action, and that defendant's motion for judgment on the special verdict should have been granted. In support of this proposition counsel quote from 2 Greenleaf Evidence §83, the rule that "the intention to do harm is of the essence of an assault." Such is the rule, no doubt, in actions or prosecutions for mere assaults. But this is an action to recover damages for an alleged assault and battery. In such case the rule is correctly stated, in many of the authorities cited by counsel, that plaintiff must show either that the intention was unlawful, or that the defendant is in fault. If the intended act is unlawful, the intention to commit it must necessarily be unlawful. Hence, as applied to this case, if the kicking of the plaintiff by the defendant was an unlawful act, the intention of defendant to kick him was also unlawful.

Had the parties been upon the play-grounds of the school, engaged in the usual boyish sports, the defendant being free from malice, wantonness, or negligence, and intending no harm to plaintiff in what he did, we should hesitate to hold the act of the defendant unlawful, or that he could be held liable in this action. Some consideration is due to the implied license of the play-grounds. But it appears that the injury was inflicted in the school, after it had been called to order by the teacher, and after the regular exercises of the school had commenced. Under these circumstances, no implied license to do the act complained of existed, and such act was a violation of the order and decorum of the school, and necessarily unlawful. Hence we are of the opinion that, under the evidence and verdict, the action may be sustained.

Certain questions were proposed on behalf of defendant to be submitted to the jury, founded upon the theory that only such damages could be recovered as the defendant might reasonably be supposed to have contemplated as likely to result from his kicking the plaintiff. The court refused to submit such questions to the jury. The ruling was correct. The rule of damages in actions for torts was held [in a prior case] to be that the wrong-doer is liable for all injuries resulting directly from the wrongful act, whether they could or could not have been foreseen by him. The chief justice and the writer of this opinion dissented from the judgment in that [prior] case, chiefly because we were of the opinion that the complaint stated a cause of action ex contractu [out of contract], and not ex delicto [out of tort], and hence that a different rule of damages—the rule here contended for—was applicable. We did not question that the rule in actions for tort was correctly stated. That case rules this on the question of damages.

[Judgment is reversed, and the case is remanded for a new trial because of a separate error in a ruling on an objection to certain testimony.]

NOTES

1. *Vosburg v. Putney: The Backstory and Aftermath.* For over 130 years, *Vosburg* has remained one of the most storied cases in American law. In *Vosburg v. Putney*: A Centennial Story, 1992 Wis. L. Rev. 877, Professor Zigurds Zile probes every aspect of the legal proceedings and their social setting. The plaintiff, Andrew Vosburg, was a sickly boy from an ordinary farming background, whereas the defendant, George Putney, was the scion of a wealthy and prominent Wisconsin family whose ancestors had arrived in Massachusetts in 1637. Zile further describes the newspaper publicity surrounding the case, its political overtones, the low-level criminal proceedings in justice court brought against the defendant, and the possible medical malpractice action lurking in the background.

And what happened to Andrew Vosburg and George Putney after that fateful encounter at the schoolhouse? Putney finished his education at Union School, graduated from high school, enrolled at the University of Wisconsin, but left during sophomore year. He returned to Waukesha, clerked at his family's general store, got married, moved to Milwaukee, and eventually became a salesman, first of clothing, then of cars. He died on June 13, 1940. Vosburg, in 1900, was hired by the Milwaukee Electric Railroad, rose to foreman, married, had three children, and, along with his wife, made a living buying, refurbishing, and selling homes. Although a laced leather brace limited his activities, he led a satisfying life and died on October 4, 1938, at age 64.

2. *Defendant's Intention and Plaintiff's Conduct.* Which, if any, of the jury's answers to the first six questions may be incorrect in light of the medical evidence? Given the jury's response to the sixth question, can the defendant's act be treated as an intentional tort? Does it make a difference that the teacher had already called the class to order when the kick landed? If pupils typically tapped each other on the leg under the desk to get each other's attention after the class had been called to order, should the defendant's act be excused by the "implied license of the classroom"? Should a defendant's actual malice, wantonness, and negligence all be treated the same way for either playground or classroom injuries? Should the plaintiff have worn a shin guard to protect his leg from further injury? Should he have stayed home from school?

3. *Whither "Unlawful" Intent?* In Garratt v. Dailey, 279 P.2d 1091, 1093–94 (Wash. 1955), and 304 P.2d 681 (Wash. 1956), the plaintiff, an adult woman, brought a battery suit against Brian Dailey, a boy five years and nine months old, who caused her to fracture her hip when he was a guest in her backyard. The defendant claimed that he had tried to help the plaintiff by placing a chair under her as she was about to fall, but that he was too small to move it properly into place. His version was accepted by the judge at the first trial. However, the plaintiff's sister, who was present at the occasion, testified that the plaintiff, an "arthritic woman[,] had begun the slow process of being seated when the defendant quickly removed the chair and seated himself upon it, and that he knew, with substantial certainty at the time, that she would attempt to sit in the place where the chair had been."

The Washington Supreme Court addressed the issue of intent in the tort of battery:

> It is urged that Brian's action in moving the chair constituted a battery. A definition (not all-inclusive but sufficient for our purpose) of a battery is the intentional infliction of a harmful bodily contact upon another. . . .
>
> We have here the conceded volitional act of Brian, i.e., the moving of a chair. Had the plaintiff proved to the satisfaction of the trial court that Brian moved the chair while she was in the act of sitting down, Brian's action would patently have been for the purpose or with the intent of causing the plaintiff's bodily contact with the ground, and she would be entitled to a judgment against him for the resulting damages. Vosburg v. Putney. . . .
>
> A battery would be established if, in addition to plaintiff's fall, it was proved that, when Brian moved the chair, he knew with substantial certainty that the plaintiff would attempt to sit down where the chair had been. . . .

> The mere absence of any intent to injure the plaintiff or to play a prank on her or to embarrass her, or to commit an assault and battery on her would not absolve him from liability if in fact he had such knowledge. Without such knowledge, there would be nothing wrongful about Brian's act in moving the chair and, there being no wrongful act, there would be no liability.

On remand, the trial judge accepted the testimony of the plaintiff's sister and awarded the plaintiff $11,000 [$124,520 in 2023 dollars]. That judgment was upheld on the second appeal. Is removing a chair tantamount to striking the plaintiff?

4. ***The Restatement Account of Intention in Battery Cases.*** The common law of torts was first "codified" in the Restatement of Torts [RT], published in 1934 by the American Law Institute [ALI], an organization founded in 1923. The Restatement of Torts was prepared by a large and distinguished team of judges, practicing lawyers, and academics. Professor Francis H. Bohlen served as its chief reporter. The Restatement, as its name implies, emphasizes "restating" rather than "reforming" the law, but interstitial reform often occurs whenever the law is in flux or some conflict persists among the various states. The Restatement (Second) of Torts [RST] appeared in four volumes, published between 1965 and 1979. Its first 280 sections scrutinize every aspect of intentional torts.

In contrast, the Restatement (Third) of Torts [RTT] has not been organized as a unified project. Instead, different volumes of the RTT dealing with discrete topics have been released at different times. The major volume dealing with physical harms is the Restatement (Third) of Torts: Liability for Physical and Emotional Harm [RTT: LPEH] (2010 and 2012). Additional finished volumes, to date, include Apportionment of Liability (2000) (Reporters William Powers, Jr. and Michael Green); Products Liability (1998) (Reporters James Henderson and Aaron Twerski); and Liability for Economic Harm (2018) (Reporter Ward Farnsworth). Portions of the draft of a fifth volume, Intentional Torts to Persons [RTT: IT] (Tentative Draft 2021) (Reporter Kenneth Simons) have been released. Projects on Remedies (Reporter Douglas Laycock) and Miscellaneous Provisions (Reporters Nora Engstrom and Michael Green) are underway.

It is instructive to compare the definitional provisions of the Second Restatement with those of the Third Restatement. How does the RST square with *Vosburg* and *Garratt?* Both Restatements embrace a "dual definition" of "intent" that includes where "the actor desires to cause consequences of his act, or that he believes that the consequences are substantially certain to result from it." RST §8A; RTT: LPEH §1.

RESTATEMENT OF THE LAW (THIRD) OF TORTS: LIABILITY FOR PHYSICAL AND EMOTIONAL HARM

§1. Intent

A person acts with the intent to produce a consequence if:

(a) the person acts with the purpose of producing that consequence; or

(b) the person acts knowing that the consequence is substantially certain to result.

Illustration 2: Wendy throws a rock at Andrew, someone she dislikes, at a distance of 100 feet, wanting to hit Andrew. Given the distance, it is far from certain Wendy will succeed in this; rather, it is probable that the rock will miss its target. In fact, Wendy's aim is true, and Andrew is struck by the rock. Wendy has purposely, and hence intentionally, caused this harm.

Note also that both the Second and Third Restatements approve of the result in *Vosburg*, which the former describes as follows: "Intending an offensive contact, *A* lightly kicks *B* on the shin." RST §16, comment *a*, illus. 1. Did the court in *Vosburg* treat the incident as one of offensive battery in light of special verdict number six? Compare the analysis of the RST and RTT on the definition of battery and the distinction between "single" and "dual intent."

RESTATEMENT OF THE LAW (SECOND) OF TORTS

§13. Battery: Harmful Conduct

An actor is subject to liability to another for battery if

(a) he acts intending to cause a harmful or offensive contact with the person of the other or a third person, or an imminent apprehension of such a contact, and

(b) a harmful contact with the person of the other directly or indirectly results.

RESTATEMENT OF THE LAW (THIRD) OF TORTS: INTENTIONAL TORTS TO PERSONS (TENTATIVE DRAFT, APPROVED 2021)

§1. Battery: General Definition

An actor is subject to liability to another for battery if:

(a) The actor intends to cause a contact with the person of the other, as provided in §2, or the actor's intent is sufficient under §11 (transferred intent);

(b) The actor's affirmative conduct causes such a contact; and

(c) The contact (i) causes bodily harm to the other or (ii) is offensive, as provided in §3.

§2. Battery: Required Intent

The intent required for battery is the intent to cause a contact with the person of another. The actor need not intend to cause harm or offense to the other.

Comment b. Single Intent v. Dual Intent: . . . The single-intent approach affords greater protection to the plaintiff's interest in bodily integrity, and can be understood as imposing a modest degree of strict liability, insofar as the actor is liable although he might have genuinely and even reasonably believed that the contact he caused would not cause harm or offense. By contrast, the dual-intent approach is more consistent with the view that liability for battery should exist only when the actor is especially culpable—and in particular, more culpable than a negligent or strictly liable actor. . . .

Illustration 2: Stephanie approaches Carol, a new coworker in her office, from behind. "You look tense!" Stephanie declares, and immediately begins giving Carol a vigorous neck massage. When Carol objects, Stephanie promptly ends the massage. The massage injures Carol's neck and requires her to miss several weeks of work. Stephanie is subject to liability to Carol for battery.

However influential, the Second Restatement position is rejected by some courts. In White v. University of Idaho, 797 P.2d 108 (Idaho 1990), the defendant Neher, a music professor, was a social guest in the home of the plaintiff, one of his piano students. While the plaintiff was writing, "Professor Neher walked up behind her and touched her back with both of his hands in a movement later described as one a pianist would make in striking and lifting the fingers from a keyboard." The plaintiff claimed she suffered a strong adverse reaction, which necessitated the removal of a rib, and damage to her brachial plexus nerve that required the severing of her scalenus anterior muscles. The professor claimed he touched Mrs. White to show her the sensation of certain forms of playing but meant no harm. She countered that the touching was nonconsensual. The court accepted her battery claim even though the defendant had not meant either to harm or to offend her. The court brushed aside any attempt to require offensive intent, noting curtly that "we have not previously adopted the Restatement (Second) in Idaho and decline any invitation to do it now." Does the Second Restatement test necessarily entail "dual intent"? How does *White* comport with the Third Restatement?

Dual intent fared better in McElhaney v. Thomas, 405 P.3d 1214, 1216, 1221 (Kan. 2017), where a high school student was injured when another student drove his truck over her feet, momentarily trapping her. In response to her suit for battery, the defendant claimed that he only wanted to come close to the plaintiff to park. A third-party witness said he heard the defendant say that "he only meant to bump into Emma [McElhaney] with his truck." On appeal, Stegall, J., followed the dual intent standard and left it on remand for the jury to decide whether "an intent to bump" was an intent to harm. What should be done with "the nebulous concept of horseplay" in the background in this case?

5. *Battery on the Internet.* The law of battery has been extended to online actions that model forms of physical attacks. In Eichenwald v. Rivello, 318 F. Supp. 3d 766, 775 (D. Md. 2018), the plaintiff, who suffered from chronic epilepsy, was a well-known journalist with anti-Trump views. He received a tweet from the defendant, which "included (and immediately displayed) a Graphic Interchange Format ('GIF')" that contained "an animated strobe image flashing at a rapid speed." In addition to the flashing images, the GIF contained the message "YOU DESERVE A SEIZURE FOR YOUR POSTS." Upon seeing the rapidly flashing GIF, the "[p]laintiff suffered a severe seizure." The defendant was first subject to criminal prosecution, after which the plaintiff brought a suit for battery under Texas law, which adopts the dual definition of intent. Bredar, C.J., concluded:

> Defendant here allegedly chose to use the electronic capabilities of a computer as a weapon—as a means of causing physical harm. Defendant's tweet, activating certain harmful capabilities of the transmitting computer, converted the computer into a weapon to inflict physical injury. The computer and the tweet were no longer merely a mode of communication. Something more, and separate, from mere communication occurred[:] . . . an offensive touching.

6. *Transferred Intent.* In Talmage v. Smith, 59 N.W. 656, 657 (Mich. 1894), the plaintiff was struck in the eye by a stick that the defendant threw at the plaintiff's two companions while they were trespassing upon the defendant's property. The defendant asserted that he did not see the plaintiff, much less intend to hurt him. The court held this contention immaterial:

> The right of the plaintiff to recover was made to depend upon an intention on the part of the defendant to hit somebody, and to inflict an unwarranted injury upon someone. Under these circumstances, the fact that the injury resulted to another than was intended does not relieve the defendant from responsibility.

Does it matter whether the injured plaintiff was trespassing on defendant's property? See RTT: IT §11(a), which holds that intent "is satisfied if the actor intends to cause the relevant tortious consequence to a third party, rather than the plaintiff." Prosser, Transferred Intent, 45 Tex. L. Rev. 650 (1967), claimed that transferred intent was part of tort law by 1869, a conclusion disputed in Kutner, The Prosser Myth of Transferred Intent, 91 Ind. L.J. 1105, 1106 (2016).

Dougherty v. Stepp

18 N.C. 371 (1835)

This was an action of trespass quare clausum fregit [wherefore he broke the close], tried at Buncombe on the last Circuit, before his Honor Judge MARTIN. The only proof introduced by the plaintiff to establish an act of trespass, was, that the defendant had entered on the unenclosed land of the plaintiff, with a surveyor and chain carriers, and actually surveyed a part of it, claiming it as his own, but without marking trees or cutting bushes. This, his Honor held not to be a trespass, and the jury, under his instructions, found a verdict for the defendant, and the plaintiff appealed.

Ruffin, C.J. In the opinion of the Court, there is error in the instructions given to the jury. The amount of damages may depend on the acts done on the land, and the extent of injury to it therefrom. But it is an elementary principle, that every unauthorised, and therefore unlawful entry, into the close of another, is a trespass. From every such entry against the will of the possessor, the law infers some damage; if nothing more, the treading down the grass or the herbage or as here, the shrubbery. Had the locus in quo been under cultivation or enclosed, there would have been no doubt of the plaintiff's right to recover. Now our Courts have for a long time past held, that if there be no adverse possession, the title makes the land the owner's close. Making the survey and marking trees, or making it without marking, differ only in the degree, and not in the nature of the injury. It is the entry that constitutes the trespass. There is no statute, nor rule of reason, that will make a wilful entry into the land of another, upon an unfounded claim of right, innocent, which one, who sat up no title to the land, could not justify or excuse. On the contrary, the pretended ownership aggravates the wrong. Let the judgment be reversed, and a new trial granted.

Judgment reversed.

NOTES

1. ***Traditional Forms of Trespass to Real Property.*** Trespass *quare clausum fregit* (or trespass q.c.f.) has long protected the plaintiff's interest in the exclusive possession of land and its improvements. A trespass to real property takes place not only on the surface, but also with any intrusion above or below the surface of the land. Thus RST §158 provides that a person engages in trespass if he "intentionally (a) enters land in possession of the other, or causes a thing or third person to do so, or (b) remains on the land, or (c) fails to remove from the land a thing which he is under a duty to remove."

Thus in Hutchinson v. Schimmelfeder, 40 Pa. 396, 397 (1861), the Pennsylvania Supreme Court upheld the following jury instruction:

> If two persons own adjoining lots which lie below the grade of the street on which they front, and either wishes to grade his lot up to the street, he must build a wall on his own ground, or in some other way keep the dirt within his own line. He cannot so fill up his own lot as to let the earth pass over his line on the lot of his neighbor.

Should trespass require a direct act? In Smith v. Smith, 110 Mass. 302 (1872), the defendant was held to be a trespasser when the edges of his barn's roof hung over the plaintiff's land.

2. ***Trespass by Overflight.*** In principle, any use of airspace could be regarded as a form of trespass, subject to both damages and an injunction. But the strict application of that suggestion has been displaced in the case of air transport. Thus, in United States v. Causby, 328 U.S. 256, 260–62 (1946), Douglas, J., refused to conclude that the government engages in a taking of real property when it authorizes flights in upper airspace:

> It is ancient doctrine that at common law ownership of the land extended to the periphery of the universe— *Cujus est solum ejus est usque ad coelum.* [Whosoever holds the soil also owns to the heavens.] But that doctrine has no place in the modern world. The air is a public highway, as Congress has declared. Were that not true, every transcontinental flight would subject the operator to countless trespass suits. Common sense revolts at the idea. To recognize such private claims to the airspace would clog these highways, seriously interfere with their control

> and development in the public interest, and transfer into private ownership that to which only the public has a just claim.

The court in *Causby* did, however, find a taking where overflights occurred closer to the ground, an outcome that comported with earlier common law decisions. In Neiswonger v. Goodyear Tire and Rubber Co., 35 F.2d 761 (N.D. Ohio 1929), airplane overflights within 500 feet of the ground, in violation of air traffic rules established by the Department of Commerce, were treated as trespasses. Why the distinction between high-altitude and low-altitude flights?

The modern iteration of this problem arises in connection with the ever-increasing use of drones for a wide range of purposes, including combat, surveillance, and the delivery of goods. The law is still developing, but it is commonly held that unauthorized entries into the lower air space are in the same category as invasions of the surface of the land. Who must give consent when a merchant seeks to deliver goods to a tenant in a large apartment building? Drone deliveries can reduce road congestion, and industry representatives have pressured legislatures to deviate from the *Causby* rule by preventing local governments from blocking drone deliveries. See, for example, Ariz. Rev. Stat. Ann. §13-3729 (2021); Fla. Stat. §330.41(3)(b) (2021). See generally Troy A. Rule, Can Landowners Exclude Drones from Their Low Airspace?, The Ctr. for Growth and Opportunity (April 2023), https://www.thecgo.org/wp-content/uploads/2023/04/Drone-Survey-Report-RIF.pdf.

3. *Intention and Damages in Trespass to Real Property.* Owing to the passive and immovable nature of real property, the courts have generally adopted stringent standards of liability whenever the trespass results in actual harm. In Brown v. Dellinger, 355 S.W.2d 742, 747 (Tex. Civ. App. 1962), two children, aged seven and eight, were held liable for the loss of the plaintiff's $28,000 home ($283,000 in 2023 dollars). The court observed:

> The acts of the minor defendants in bringing matches onto the premises of [plaintiff] and igniting the fire in the charcoal burner in [plaintiff's] garage were all voluntary and purposeful and were acts which they even at their tender years had sufficient capacity to do, as evidenced by the fact that they did do such acts. Undoubtedly they did not intend for the fire to escape from the grill and spread to the curtain canvas and burn and damage the garage, house and contents thereof. However their acts of igniting an unauthorized fire on [plaintiff's] premises made them trespassers, and they must be held civilly liable for the consequences which directly flowed from their unauthorized acts of igniting the fire in question.

If the plaintiff's charcoal burner had been defective and the defendant entrants had used it with all possible care, should the plaintiff still recover? If the defendants had been burned while using the defective burner, could they recover from the plaintiff for their personal injuries? If the defendants had started the fire on their own property, could the plaintiff recover under *Brown* if the fire had spread to his premises?

In Cleveland Park Club v. Perry, 165 A.2d 485, 487–89 (D.C. 1960), the plaintiff operated a social club for the benefit of its members. One day while the defendant, a nine-year-old boy, was using the swimming pool, he dove down to a depth of seven feet, "and thinking there was no suction at the time," removed the drain cover and inserted a rubber ball. The ball was caught in a narrow portion of an attached pipe where it caused extensive damage, requiring the pool to be closed for repairs. The judgment for the defendant at trial was reversed on appeal, and a new trial ordered. The court stressed that in trespass cases "the intent controlling is the intent to complete the physical act and not the intent to cause injurious consequences." Did the defendant intend to place the ball in the mouth of the drain, or in the middle of the pipe? What weight should be given to his mistaken belief that there was no suction? Should it make a difference if the defendant was on the premises with the plaintiff's permission? Could the minors in *Garratt*, *Brown*, and *Cleveland Park* be held liable on a negligence theory? See *infra* Chapter 3, Section A, at 109. How should these cases come out under the standard of intent adopted by RTT: IT §1?

Epstein, Intentional Harms, 4 J. Legal Stud. 391 (1975), provides an account of the role that different understandings of intention play in shaping the substantive tort law.

4. *Intangible Trespasses.* In Public Service Co. of Colorado v. Van Wyk, 27 P.3d 377, 390 (Colo. 2001), the plaintiff sued in trespass for the harm attributable to the noise, radiation, and electromagnetic fields that resulted from an upgrade in Public Service's utility system approved by the state Public Utility Commission. Martinez, J., distinguished this case from physical trespasses in which particulate matter is deposited on the plaintiff's land despite no visible intrusion, and held that, unlike claims for physical invasions,

> an intangible intrusion may give rise to a claim for trespass, but only if an aggrieved party is able to prove physical damage to the property caused by such intangible intrusion.
>
> Our holding here is consistent with the historical requirement of an entry or use that interferes with possession for trespass liability to be established. The requirement that the intangible intrusion be intentional, and that a plaintiff prove physical damage caused by the intrusion, safeguards against the concern that allowing trespass claims against intangible intrusions would produce too much liability. Moreover, a property owner forced to prove damage will be further limited to seeking redress in cases of serious or substantial invasions. The difficulty in proving a connection between a minor damage and an intangible intrusion is too great to support mass litigiousness on the part of pestered property owners.

Liability for intangible trespasses also arose in City of E. St. Louis v. Netflix, Inc., 630 F. Supp. 3d 1003, 1018–19 (S.D. Ill. 2022), which followed *Van Wyk*. The City of East St. Louis, Illinois, alleged that 12 defendant television streaming services, including Netflix, Hulu, and YouTube, trespassed by transmitting video content through the public rights-of-way without first obtaining authorization from the Illinois Commerce Commission and without paying the requisite fees to municipalities. Beatty, M.J., denied the claim:

> Traditionally, trespass law in Illinois and elsewhere only recognized an actual physical invasion by a person or tangible thing. . . . Here, the complaint fails to allege facts demonstrating that Defendants caused a physical intrusion, or that the purported physical intrusion interfered with Plaintiff's possession of the rights-of-way. . . . It is the ISPs' wirelines that are the actual physical intrusion.

5. *Exclusion of Intentional Harm from Insurance Coverage.* Virtually all of the bodily injury and property damage that ordinary individuals tortiously cause is covered, at least prima facie, by either auto or homeowners and renters liability insurance. "Intentional act exclusions" are ubiquitous in insurance policies, not only for homeowners but also for auto and business-related liability, which are covered by auto and Comprehensive General Liability (CGL) policies. Insuring intentional harms creates "moral hazard," which includes not only deliberate wrongdoing, but also increasing the odds that the insured will engage in dangerous activities given that an insurer is on the hook for the tab. Plaintiffs' attorneys typically prefer to take on suits against insured defendants to maximize their payout. For this reason, there are few litigated intentional tort cases.

In general, insurance policies fit well with coverage for accidental harms. The typical CGL policy contains this broad coverage provision that protects the insured

> [f]or all sums which the insured shall become legally obligated to pay as damages because of (a) bodily injury or (b) property damage to which this insurance applies, caused by an occurrence. . . .
>
> The term "occurrence" is defined by the policy as "an accident including continuous or repeated exposure to conditions, which results in bodily injury or property damage *neither expected nor intended* from the standpoint of the insured. . . ." (Emphasis added.)

The term "occurrence" is broader than simple accidents because it includes not just car crashes but also diseases like asbestos and pollution emissions. The term "intended" is meant to cover deliberate releases and those releases that were "expected" by the insured. That last term tends to be construed narrowly because otherwise insurers could say that all harms, including latent ones like those stemming from asbestos or pollutants, were "expected from the standpoint of the insured." Billions of dollars turn on the choice between a broad and narrow reading of this clause.

6. *Intention and Governmental Liability.* The doctrine of sovereign immunity traditionally bars claims of liability against governments. The Federal Tort Claims Act, 28 U.S.C. §2674, starts with a general declaration that removes this total bar with respect to the federal government.

> **§2674. Liability of United States**
>
> The United States shall be liable, respecting the provisions of this title relating to tort claims, in the same manner and to the same extent as a private individual under like circumstances, . . .

But this rule contains a large number of exceptions, including "(h) Any claim arising out of assault, battery, false imprisonment, false arrest, . . ." 28 U.S.C. §2680.

In Sheridan v. United States, 487 U.S. 392, 403 (1988), an obviously intoxicated off-duty serviceman fired several rifle shots that injured the plaintiffs, who were riding in their automobiles. Both sides agreed that the assault and battery exception protected the government for the wrongs committed by the serviceman, given the deliberate nature of the attack. But as is often the case in modern law, the negligence of other government employees who allowed a foreseeable assault and battery to occur may furnish a basis for government liability that is entirely independent of the serviceman's employment status. Thus the Court allowed the plaintiff's further claim that three naval corpsmen were negligent when, having discovered the serviceman "lying face down in a drunken stupor" with a loaded weapon, they failed to take him into custody or to alert the appropriate officials that he was on the prowl, even for malicious wrongdoers. In this case, the government's duty to prevent this foreseeable assault and battery was seemingly defined without regard to whether the drunken serviceman was within or beyond the scope of his employment. See *Ira S. Bushey & Sons, Inc.*, *infra* Chapter 7, at 531.

2. Defenses to Intentional Torts

a. Consensual Defenses

Mohr v. Williams

104 N.W. 12 (Minn. 1905)

BROWN, J. Defendant is a physician and surgeon of standing and character, making disorders of the ear a specialty, and having an extensive practice in the city of St. Paul. He was consulted by plaintiff, who complained to him of trouble with her right ear, and, at her request, made an examination of that organ for the purpose of ascertaining its condition. He also at the same time examined her left ear, but, owing to foreign substances therein, was unable to make a full and complete diagnosis at that time. The examination of her right ear disclosed a large perforation in the lower portion of the drum membrane, and a large polyp in the middle ear, which indicated that some of the small bones of the middle ear (ossicles) were probably diseased. He informed plaintiff of the result of his examination, and advised an operation for the purpose of removing the polyp and diseased ossicles. After consultation with her family physician, and one or two further consultations with defendant, plaintiff decided to submit to the proposed operation. She was not informed that her left ear was in any way diseased, and understood that the necessity for an operation applied to her right ear only. She repaired to the hospital, and was placed under the influence of anaesthetics; and, after being made unconscious, defendant made a thorough examination of her left ear, and found it in a more serious condition than her right one. A small perforation was discovered high up in the drum membrane, hooded, and with granulated edges, and the bone of the inner wall of the middle ear was diseased and dead. He called this discovery to the attention of Dr. Davis—plaintiff's family physician, who attended the operation at her request—who also examined the ear and confirmed defendant in his diagnosis. Defendant also further examined the right ear, and found its condition less serious than expected, and finally concluded that the left, instead of the right, should be operated upon; devoting to the right ear other treatment. He then performed the operation of ossiculectomy on plaintiff's left ear; removing a portion of the drum membrane, and scraping away the diseased portion of the inner wall of the ear. The operation was in every way successful and skillfully performed. It is claimed by plaintiff that the operation greatly impaired her hearing, seriously injured her person, and, not having been consented to by her, was wrongful and unlawful, constituting an assault and battery; and she brought this action to recover damages therefor.

The trial in the court below resulted in a verdict for plaintiff for $14,322.50. [The trial judge set aside the verdict as excessive and ordered a new trial. Both parties appealed from those orders. On appeal Brown, J., first refuses to overturn the jury's finding of no emergency. He then holds that plaintiff's consent to the operation could not be implied, and says in part:]

The last contention of defendant is that the act complained of did not amount to an assault and battery. This is based upon the theory that, as plaintiff's left ear was in fact diseased, in a condition dangerous and threatening to her health, the operation was necessary, and, having been skillfully performed at a time when plaintiff had requested a like operation on the other ear, the charge of assault and battery cannot be sustained; that, in view of these conditions, and the claim that there was no negligence on the part of defendant, and an entire absence of any evidence tending to show an evil intent, the court should say, as a matter of law, that no assault and battery was committed, even though she did not consent to the operation. In other words, that the absence of a showing that defendant was actuated by a wrongful intent, or guilty of negligence, relieves the act of defendant from the charge of an unlawful assault and battery.

We are unable to reach that conclusion, though the contention is not without merit. It would seem to follow from what has been said on the other features of the case that the act of defendant amounted at least to a technical assault and battery. If the operation was performed without plaintiff's consent, and the circumstances were not such as to justify its performance without, it was wrongful; and, if it was wrongful, it was unlawful. As remarked in 1 Jaggard, Torts, 437, every person has a right to complete immunity of his person from physical interference of others, except in so far as contact may be necessary under the general doctrine of privilege; and any unlawful or unauthorized touching of the person of another, except it be in the spirit of pleasantry, constitutes an assault and battery. In the case at bar, as we have already seen, the question whether defendant's act in performing the operation upon plaintiff was authorized was a question for the jury to determine. If it was unauthorized, then it was, within what we have said, unlawful. It was a violent assault, not a mere pleasantry; and, even though no negligence is shown, it was wrongful and unlawful. The case is unlike a criminal prosecution for assault and battery, for there an unlawful intent must be shown. But that rule does not apply to a civil action, to maintain which it is sufficient to show that the assault complained of was wrongful and unlawful or the result of negligence. . . . Vosburg v. Putney, 80 Wis. 523, 50 N.W. 403.

The amount of plaintiff's recovery, if she is entitled to recover at all, must depend upon the character and extent of the injury inflicted upon her, in determining which the nature of the malady intended to be healed and the beneficial nature of the operation should be taken into consideration, as well as the good faith of the defendant.

Orders affirmed.

NOTES

1. ***The Varieties of Consent.*** The chapter of Restatement (Third) of Torts: Intentional Torts to Persons that deals with consent identifies four potential categories of consent: (a) actual consent, (b) apparent consent, (c) presumed consent, and (d) the emergency doctrine.

RESTATEMENT OF THE LAW (THIRD) OF TORTS: INTENTIONAL TORTS TO PERSONS (TENTATIVE DRAFT, APPROVED 2019)

§13. Actual Consent: Definition and Conditions

A person actually consents to an actor's otherwise tortious intentional conduct if:

(a) the person is willing for that conduct to occur, and such willingness may be express or may be inferred from the facts;

(b) the actor's conduct is within the scope of the person's consent, as provided in §14;

(c) the person has the capacity to consent, as provided in §15(a); and

(d) the consent is not given under duress or under substantial mistake, as provided in §15(b) and (c).

§16. Apparent and Presumed Consent

An actor is not liable for otherwise tortious intentional conduct if either apparent or presumed consent exists.

(a) Apparent consent exists if the actor reasonably believes that the other person actually consents to the conduct, without regard to whether the person does actually consent.

(b) Presumed consent exists if:

(1) under prevailing social norms, the actor is justified in engaging in the conduct in the absence of the other person's actual or apparent consent, and

(2) the actor has no reason to believe that the person would not have actually consented to the conduct if the actor had requested the person's consent.

How do these variations play out in the cases?

2. ***Determining the Scope of Consent.*** Did the physician in Mohr v. Williams violently attack or batter his patient solely because he did not obtain the requisite consent to perform the operation? Why didn't the physician face an emergency situation? Should Dr. Davis be treated as the plaintiff's agent? Why did the trial judge conclude that the jury awarded excessive damages? On remand, the jury awarded only nominal damages.

Some modern cases take a less rigid view of the consent requirement. In Kennedy v. Parrott, 90 S.E.2d 754, 759 (N.C. 1956), the defendant surgeon, while performing an appendectomy on the plaintiff, discovered several large cysts on the plaintiff's left ovary. Exercising his best medical judgment, he intentionally punctured the cysts, without negligence. Unfortunately, the puncture cut one of plaintiff's blood vessels, from which she developed a painful phlebitis in her leg. The court rejected her claim for battery even though she did not consent to the puncturing of the cysts, noting that in modern hospital settings surgeons could no longer turn to the guidance of family members. It concluded:

> In major internal operations, both the patient and the surgeon know that the exact condition of the patient cannot be finally and definitely diagnosed until after the patient is completely anesthetized and the incision has been made. In such case the consent—in the absence of proof to the contrary—will be construed as general in nature and the surgeon may extend the operation to remedy any abnormal or diseased condition in the area of the original incision whenever he, in the exercise of his sound professional judgment, determines that correct surgical procedure dictates and requires such an extension of the operation originally contemplated. This rule applies when the patient is at the time incapable of giving consent, and no one with authority to consent for him is immediately available.

Does *Kennedy* support the Second Restatement's view that "the absence of consent is a matter essential to the cause of action [for battery], and it is uniformly held that it must be proved by the plaintiff as a necessary part of his case"? RST §13, comment *d.* The Third Restatement declines to weigh in on which party should bear the burden of persuasion as regards the absence of consent, noting, contra the Second Restatement, that jurisdictions remain split on the issue. RTT: IT §12, comment e.

More recently, in Mayr v. Osborne, 795 S.E.2d 731, 736 (Va. 2017), the patient filed suit against his physician for battery arising out of the surgeon's erroneous fusion of two spinal discs. McCulloch, J., concluded that the case involved an issue of informed consent that sounded in negligence, not battery. The latter tort protects both the interest in bodily integrity and the dignitary right to be free of offensive contact, neither of which was implicated in this case. He also held that the surgeon did not impermissibly exceed the scope of the patient's consent.

No such doubts on the consent issue were found in Rousseau v. Coates, 488 F. Supp. 3d 163 (D. Vt. 2020), when the defendant doctor substituted his own sperm in an artificial insemination procedure for that of an unnamed medical student who resembled the plaintiff's husband. Sessions, J., concluded that the plaintiff gave consent to a particular insemination, but was deceived and received a very different insemination. The defendant's motion for summary judgment with respect to the plaintiff's battery was denied. Why not summary judgment for the plaintiff?

3. *Medical Consent Forms.* To avoid many of the factual issues in cases like *Mohr*, *Kennedy*, and *Mayr*, physicians and hospitals often resort to using consent forms similar to those utilized by the American Medical Association, which often include authorization for procedures in addition to the one requested. See, for example, paragraph two of the sample form, on the next page.

These forms can sometimes be modified in individual cases to prohibit from the outset certain kinds of procedures. In Hoofnel v. Segal, 199 S.W.3d 147, 151 (Ky. 2006), the plaintiff, a woman aged 56 and of limited education, came to the defendant physicians needing the removal of a lesion from her colon. The surgeon, Dr. Galandiuk, recommended that it was best for the plaintiff to remove surgically both her uterus and ovaries, but the plaintiff insisted that she did not want "any of my female parts removed." Nonetheless, she later signed a consent form that authorized both procedures if necessary. During surgery Dr. Galandiuk consulted with Dr. Segal, and both agreed that the organs had to be removed because of their enlarged size and possible cancerous condition. Graves, J., held that the "clear and unambiguous words of the consent form" superseded the prior conversations. "To hold otherwise would negate the legal significance to written consent forms signed by the patient and render the consent form completely unreliable."

A.M.
Date______________ Time________P.M.

1. I authorize the performance upon ______________________
(myself or name of patient)

of the following operation ______________________________
(state nature and extent of operation)

to be performed by or under the direction of Dr.______________.

2. I consent to the performance of operations and procedures in addition to or different from those now contemplated, whether or not arising from presently unforeseen conditions, which the above-named doctor or his associates or assistants may consider necessary or advisable in the course of the operation.

3. I consent to the administration of such anesthetics as may be considered necessary or advisable by the physician responsible

for this service, with the exception of ___________________
(state "none," "spinal anesthesia," etc.)

4. The nature and purpose of the operation, possible alternative methods of treatment, the risks involved, the possible consequences, and the possibility of complications have been explained to me by Dr.______________ and by ______________.

5. I acknowledge that no guarantee or assurance has been given by anyone as to the results that may be obtained.

6. I consent to the photogaphing or televising of the operations or procedures to be performed, including appropriate portions of my body, for medical, scientific or educational purposes, provided my identity is not revealed by the pictures or by descriptive texts accompanying them.

7. For the purpose of advancing medical education, I consent to the admittance of observers to the operating room.

8. I consent to the disposal by hospital authorities of any tissues or body parts which may be removed.

9. I am aware that sterility may rsult from this operation. I know that a sterile person is incapable of becoming a parent.

10. I acknowledge that all blank spaces on this document have been either completed or crossed off prior to my signing.

(Cross Out Any Paragraphs Above Which Do Not Apply)

Witness______________ Signed______________
(Patient or person authorized to consent for patient)

Cooper, J., in dissent, protested the excessive reliance on the consent form relative to the entire "process" that preceded and followed the signing. On the majority view, can anything override the "presumption" that attaches to the form? Compare with the materials on informed consent, *infra* Chapter 3, Section D, at 166.

4. *Emergency Situations as Presumed Consent.* Normally a patient has the right to accept or reject the proffered medical treatment, making an unauthorized operation a technical assault and battery even if no damage ensues. See generally RTT: IT §17, comment *b*. Schloendorff v. Society of New York Hospital, 105 N.E. 92, 93 (N.Y. 1914), stated the general rule:

> Every human being of adult years and sound mind has a right to determine what shall be done with his own body; and a surgeon who performs an operation without his patient's consent, commits an assault, for which he is liable in damages. This is true except in cases of emergency where the patient is unconscious and where it is necessary to operate before consent can be obtained.

It follows that a conscious patient can refuse consent even in an emergency situation. For example, in Cooper v. Lankenau Hospital, 51 A.3d 183, 186 (Pa. 2012), the plaintiff mother, herself a pediatric cardiology anesthesiologist, fell while 27 weeks pregnant. When taken to the hospital, her treating physicians thought that the fetus was suffering from a low heart rate that could lead to fatal consequences. The plaintiff mother testified that she had explicitly refused consent, a fact which was disputed at trial. The jury found that the defendants had not committed a battery. Baer, J., upheld the verdict after approving the following instructions:

> A physician's performance of surgery in a nonemergency without consent, or the performance of surgery in an emergency when the patient has refused consent is considered a battery under the law. A battery is an act done with the intent to cause a harmful or offensive contact with the body of another, and directly results in the harmful or offensive contact with the body of another.
>
> If you find [the defendant] operated on the plaintiff in a nonemergency without consent, or in an emergency where the plaintiff refused consent, then you must find that [the defendant] committed a battery; otherwise no battery occurred.

Is there any need to include the phrase "harmful or offensive contact with the body of another" in the instruction? Whenever actual consent cannot be given, however, "medical treatment also will be lawful under the doctrine of implied consent when a medical emergency requires immediate action to preserve the health or life of the patient." Allore v. Flower Hospital, 699 N.E.2d 560, 564 (Ohio Ct. App. 1997). This implied consent, termed "presumed consent" in the Third Restatement, is a legal fiction, justified by the assumption that the plaintiff, as a rational agent, would have consented to the operation if she could have been asked. This rule thus protects otherwise helpless patients by encouraging others to assist them in times of need. Should the bystander whose quick intervention saves the plaintiff's life receive compensation? What about the surgeon who operates, even if unsuccessful? See Cotnam v. Wisdom, 104 S.W. 164 (Ark. 1907), allowing the action, but only for a successful outcome, while barring higher fees based on the physician's special knowledge of the decedent's wealth. Why are these two conditions attached to the compensation right?

The emergency doctrine is recognized in RTT: IT §17, which applies when the rescuer believes that the gains to life and health outweigh the risk that the rescued party will suffer tortious injury. Note that the privilege is lost if the rescuer thinks that the rescued party would not have consented to the risk. In general, the burden of proving the emergency lies on the provider of the service, "who will normally have greater access to the relevant evidence than will the plaintiff." RTT: IT §17, comment *i*.

RESTATEMENT OF THE LAW (THIRD) OF TORTS: INTENTIONAL TORTS TO PERSONS (TENTATIVE DRAFT APPROVED 2021)

§17. Emergency Doctrine

If an actor engages in otherwise tortious intentional conduct for the purpose of preventing or reducing a risk to the life or health of another, the actor is not liable to the other, provided that:

(a) the actor reasonably believes that:

(i) his or her conduct is necessary in order to prevent or reduce a risk to the life or health of the other that substantially outweighs the other's interest in avoiding the otherwise tortious conduct; and

(ii) it is necessary to act immediately, before it is practicable for the actor to obtain actual consent from the other or from a person empowered to consent for the other, in order to prevent or reduce the risk to life or health; and

(b) the actor has no reason to believe that the other would not have actually consented to the conduct if there had been the opportunity to do so.

5. ***Substitute Consent and Judgment for the Benefit of Others.*** How should physicians treat minors and incompetents who are unable to give consent? The standard rule requires physicians to obtain, except in emergencies, the consent of a guardian. See Bonner v. Moran, 126 F.2d 121, 122 (D.C. Cir. 1941).

Substituted consent is also needed for adult incompetents who lack any capacity to make medical decisions on their own behalf. Generally the law protects the guardian's good-faith decision from any judicial challenge or review. For example, in Brophy v. New England Sinai Hospital, Inc., 497 N.E.2d 626 (Mass. 1986), the court allowed the wife and family of a man left in a permanent vegetative state to cut off all nutrition and hydration over the objections of his treating physicians, when everyone agreed that he would have requested termination if he had been competent. Similarly, in In re Guardianship of Tschumy, 853 N.W.2d 728, 752 (Minn. 2014), Gildea, J., held that a statutory guardian "may consent to remove the ward from life-sustaining treatment when all the interested parties agree that such removal is in the ward's best interests" without first obtaining a court order. Court intervention, however, would be required when interested family members are not in agreement as to what that best interest is. In dissent, Anderson, J., insisted that the statutory powers of a guardian "to enable the ward to receive necessary or medical or other professional care" did not include the power to terminate treatment.

Frequently, someone designates either a family member, religious official, or a close friend to take the role of guardian in these cases. How then should that person proceed? The Substitute Consent form used in the District of Columbia sets out the list of relevant considerations as follows:

> I am willing to provide substituted consent for health care decisions for this individual. . . . I believe that I have had sufficient contact with this individual to be familiar with his/her activities, health care personal beliefs, and that I am thus qualified to make decisions on his/her behalf. I understand that, in making decisions on behalf of this individual, I will consider: the individual's current diagnosis and prognosis with and without the treatment at issue; expressed preferences regarding the type of treatment at issue; relevant religious and moral beliefs and personal values; behavior, attitudes, and past conduct with respect to the treatment at issue and medical treatment generally; reactions to the provision, or withholding or withdrawal of similar treatment to another individual; and expressed concerns about the effect on family or intimate friends of the individual if treatment were provided, withheld or withdrawn.

Available at https://dds.dc.gov/sites/default/files/dc/sites/dds/publication/attachments/New%20Sub%20Decision%20Making%20for%20Non%20Emergency%20Care%20Needs%206%20-%20Consent%20Form.pdf.

What forms of administrative or judicial review, if any, may be used to oversee these decisions?

Substituted judgment becomes more delicate when the proposed treatment or operation is for the benefit of another. In Lausier v. Pescinski, 226 N.W.2d 180, 183 (Wis. 1975), the court held that it did not have the power to permit the removal of one of the incompetent's kidneys, which was needed to save the life of his brother, even though the risk of harm to the incompetent was slight. The incompetent's guardian, his sister, opposed the operation because it "brought back memories of the Dachau concentration camp in Nazi Germany and of medical experiments on unwilling subjects." Similarly, in Curran v. Bosze, 566 N.E.2d 1319, 1326 (Ill. 1990), the court upheld the right of a mother of two 3½-year-old twins to refuse to have her children tested to see if they could make bone marrow transplants to their twelve-year-old half-brother who was dying of leukemia. The court stated that "it is not possible to determine the intent of a 3½-year-old child with regard to consenting to a bone marrow harvesting procedure by examining the child's personal value system." Should the consent of the incompetent's guardian make a difference? How persuasive is the argument that the incompetent will benefit by the survival of his brother?

6. *Constitutional Claims Over Consent to Medical Treatment.* The autonomy principle at work in the medical consent cases does not today compel the constitutional acceptance of the right to voluntary euthanasia. In Cruzan v. Director, Missouri Department of Health, 497 U.S. 261, 281 (1990), Rehnquist, C.J., noted that the sacredness of life under the law of homicide justified using "heightened evidentiary requirements" before cutting off life-sustaining treatment.

At the opposite extreme, how should courts respond to claims that individuals have a right to accept risky treatment, not to end, but to save their lives? In Abigail Alliance for Better Access to Developmental Drugs v. Eschenbach, 495 F.3d 695, 703–07 (D.C. Cir. 2007), Griffith, J., held that claims of personal autonomy did not support a constitutional right to compel the FDA to allow terminally ill cancer patients to use new therapies that had passed Phase I clinical trials—those which establish only that the drugs were not toxic in large doses—but which the FDA had not yet licensed as "safe" and "effective." The dissent of Rogers, J., relied on *Schloendorff, supra* Note 4, to support the conclusion that if every individual has an absolute autonomy right to refuse treatment, every person should have the absolute right knowingly to accept risky treatments.

The decedent Abigail Burroughs, a teenager, was treated by physicians from Johns Hopkins Medical Center, who had recommended the use of either ImClone's Erbitux or AstraZeneca's Iressa, both of which were eventually approved by the FDA. She died before either drug could be obtained. The issue in the case was whether a drug that had gone through Phase I clinical trials but has not received the far more extensive Phase II and Phase III clinical trials, may be used as of right by a person in cases of terminal illness. The right to individual autonomy allows people to refuse drugs for good reason, bad reason, or no reason at all. Should people have the same right to take drugs? Under current law, the answer to that question is no. See United States v. Rutherford, 442 U.S. 544 (1979). Should any such expanded right be dependent on whether other therapies are available? On whether the patient was eligible for participation in ongoing clinical trials?

For a defense of the outcome in *Abigail Alliance*, see Annas, Cancer and the Constitution—Choice at Life's End, 357 New Eng. J. Med. 408 (2007).

7. *Consent Implied in Fact.* Although consent is normally expressed in words, it may also be inferred from conduct. In O'Brien v. Cunard Steamship Co., 28 N.E. 266, 273–75 (Mass. 1891), the plaintiff was an immigrant to the United States whose entry into this

organ donation

marrow donation-children

euthanasia

non FDA risks

country required her to be vaccinated against smallpox. She stood in line with many other female passengers, and held out her arm to the defendant's surgeon, who inspected it and noted the lack of the typical mark found after smallpox vaccinations. Thereafter he told her that she had to be vaccinated, to which she replied that her previous vaccination had left no mark. The physician did not respond further, and the plaintiff held up her arm and allowed the vaccination to take place, after which she received her entry ticket. The alternative to vaccination was detainment and quarantine. The court held that her consent barred her cause of action:

> If the plaintiff's behavior was such as to indicate consent on her part, the surgeon was justified in his act, whatever her unexpressed feelings may have been. In determining whether she consented, he could be guided only by her overt acts and the manifestations of her feelings. . . . [Plaintiff] was one of a large number of women who were vaccinated on that occasion, without, so far as appears, a word of objection from any of them. They all indicated by their conduct that they desired to avail themselves of the provisions made for their benefit. There was nothing in the conduct of the plaintiff to indicate to the surgeon that she did not wish to obtain a card which would save her from detention at quarantine, and to be vaccinated, if necessary, for that purpose.

Would it have been rational for her to refuse treatment? How should we take into account these additional facts found in the record:

> The plaintiff, an Irish immigrant in steerage, was seventeen years old at the time of the vaccination. Signs announcing the vaccinations were posted around the ship, but contained language the plaintiff did not understand. The passengers in steerage were rounded up, divided into lines by gender, and herded down the steps to the doctor. No one was allowed to leave without the doctor's permission.

Vogel, Cases in Context: Lake Champlain Wars, Gentrification and Ploof v. Putnam, 45 St. Louis U. L.J. 791, 796 (2001).

Canterbury v. Spence
464 F.2d 772 (D.C. Cir. 1972)

[The text of the opinion and notes thereto are found *infra* at 166.]

Hudson v. Craft
204 P.2d 1 (Cal. 1949)

Carter, J. [The plaintiff, an 18-year-old boy, was solicited by the defendant promoter to participate in an illegal prize fight for which he received a $5 fee. The fight was neither sanctioned by the State Athletic Commission nor conducted in accordance with its rules. During the fight, the plaintiff sustained personal injuries from a blow by his opponent. Plaintiff sued both his opponent and the promoter but did not serve process on his opponent. The trial court dismissed his complaint against the promoter.]

The basis and theory of liability, if any, in mutual combat cases has been the subject of considerable controversy. Proceeding from the premise that, as between the combatants, the tort involved is that of assault and battery, many courts have held that, inasmuch as each contestant has committed a battery on the other, each may hold the other liable for any injury inflicted although both consented to the contest. [The court cited many cases, including Teeters v. Frost, 292 P. 356 (Okla. 1930).] Being contrary to the maxim volenti non fit injuria [the willing suffer no injury], the courts have endeavored to rationalize the rule by reasoning that the state is a party where there is a breach of the peace, such as occurs in a combat, and that no one may consent to such breach. There are cases expressing a minority view [of no liability] and severe criticism has been leveled at the majority rule, such as, that it ignores the principle of pari delicto [equal wrong] and encourages rather than deters mutual combat. See Hart v. Geysel, 159 Wash. 632[, 294 P. 570]; Bohlen, Consent as Affecting Civil Liability for Breaches of the Peace, 24 Colum. L. Rev. 819 [1924]; . . . The Restatement adopts the minority view. An assent which satisfies the rules stated "prevents an invasion from being tortious and, therefore, actionable, although the invasion assented to constitutes a crime." (Rest., Torts, §60.) An example given thereunder is a boxing match where no license was had as required by law. The only case discovered involving the liability of a third-party promoter of the combat such as we have in the case at bar, is Teeters v. Frost, *supra*, where the court, following the majority position as to the liability of the participants as between themselves, was not confronted with any difficulty in deciding that the instigator was liable as an aider and abettor.

There is an exception to the rule stated in the Restatements, reading: "Where it is a crime to inflict a particular invasion of an interest of personality upon a particular class of persons, irrespective of their assent, and the policy of the law is primarily to protect the interests of such a class of persons from their inability to appreciate the consequences of such an invasion, and it is not solely to protect the interests of the public, the assent of such a person to such an invasion is not a consent thereto." (Rest., Torts, §61.) . . . If liability is predicated on the tort of battery, it might seem to follow that in order to hold the promoter liable, it would be necessary to impose responsibility upon the combatants as to each other on the theory that they are the principals while the instigator is only the aider and abettor. In view of the public policy of this state as expressed by initiative, legislation, rules of the Athletic Commission, and the Constitution, the promoter must be held liable as a principal regardless of what the rule may be as between the combatants.

From the beginning, this state has taken an uncompromising stand against uncontrolled prize fights and boxing matches.

[The court then reviews the extensive history of boxing regulation in California from 1850 through 1942. When this fight took place, the law forbade any person under 18 from participating in a fight; it required all fighters to undergo physical examinations before fighting; it prescribed a maximum number of rounds and a minimum weight for gloves; it required a physician to be in attendance at the fight; and it required that a referee supervise the match and stop the fight if there were "too great a disparity between the boxers." The statute also authorized the boxing commission to adopt rules to set weight classes for fighters, define fouls in the ring, and provide for inspection and physical examination of the premises. Many, if not all, of these requirements were violated in the instant case.]

The foregoing declarations by the people, the Legislature, and the commission evince an unusually strong policy, obviously resting upon a detailed study of the problems relative to boxing matches. While there are other purposes underlying that policy, it is manifest that one of the chief goals is to provide safeguards for the protection of persons engaging in the activity. It may be that the actual participants, as well as the promoter, are liable criminally for a violation of the provisions, but insofar as the purpose is protection from physical harm, the chief offender would be the promoter—the activating force in procuring the occurrence of such exhibitions. It is from his uncontrolled conduct that the combatants are protected. Secondarily, the contestants are protected against their own ill-advised participation in an unregulated match. This is especially true in the case at bar where plaintiff is a lad of 18 years.

The foregoing policy compels the conclusion that the promoter is liable where he conducts boxing matches or prize fights without a license and in violation of the statutory provisions above discussed, regardless of the rights as between the contestants, and that the consent of the combatants does not relieve him of that liability. Manifestly, the doctrine of pari delicto is not pertinent inasmuch as one of the main purposes of the statutes is to protect a class (combatants) of which plaintiff is a member. . . .

It is not necessary in the instant case to state a general rule inasmuch as each situation must have individual consideration. The nature and scope of the legislation here involved and above shown requires liability, especially when we consider that it calls for continuous and "on the spot" supervision of boxing matches.

For the foregoing reasons, the judgment is reversed.

NOTES

1. ***Minority View on Consent to Illegal Acts.*** Why is the fight promoter in *Hudson* responsible for blows inflicted by a third party if the other combatant is entitled to a defense of consent? Should violations of the legislative scheme be sufficient to impose liability per se on the promoter? See *infra* Chapter 3, Section E, at 176.

In Hart v. Geysel, 294 P. 570, 572 (Wash. 1930), the plaintiff's husband was killed by a blow struck in an illegal prizefight in which he consented to participate. A divided court found no liability under the minority view of the (First) Restatement. It first noted that both fighters had violated the criminal statute, and therefore "it is not necessary to reward the one that got the worst of the encounter at the expense of his more fortunate opponent." The *Hart* court relied on two basic legal doctrines that the majority view implicitly rejected: (1) *volenti non fit injuria*, and (2) *ex turpi causa non oritur actio*, or no action shall arise out of an improper or immoral cause. Is the private action for damages a sensible aid to criminal enforcement? Does the denial of a private action encourage or discourage participation in illegal prizefights? Does the action against the promoter discourage prize fighting? Reduce the size of the purses? Both? For an excellent defense of the Restatement's adoption of the minority rule, see Bohlen, Consent as Affecting Civil Liability for Breaches of the Peace, 24 Colum. L. Rev. 819 (1924), reprinted in Studies in the Law of Torts at 577 (1926).

2. ***Private Rights of Action for Statutory Rape.*** In Barton v. Bee Line, Inc., 265 N.Y.S. 284, 285 (App. Div. 1933), an underage plaintiff, age fifteen—where eighteen was the legal age of consent—brought an action for damages even though she had fully consented to sexual intercourse with the defendant's chauffeur, for which he was guilty of statutory rape, a crime then punishable by up to ten years of imprisonment. The court refused to allow her to sue:

> Should a consenting female under the age of eighteen have a cause of action if she has full understanding of the nature of her act? It is one thing to say that society will protect itself by punishing those who consort with females under the age of consent; it is another to hold that knowing the nature of her act, such female shall be rewarded for her indiscretion. Surely public policy—to serve which the statute was adopted—will not be vindicated by recompensing her for willing participation in that against which the law sought to protect her.

Barton was repudiated in Christensen v. Royal School District, 124 P.3d 283, 288 (Wash. 2005), where a thirteen-year-old girl sued both the teacher with whom she had sexual relations and the school district that employed him. A divided court allowed the action on the ground that the girl was "too immature to rationally or legally consent." The majority of courts today follow *Christensen*. Are the statutory rape cases distinguishable from the illegal boxing cases? Note that the RTT: IT §18 takes the position that once

> a person, by word or conduct, expresses to the actor his or her unwillingness to permit any sexual contact, or sexual contact of a specified type, yet the actor proceeds to cause such conduct,

> then as a matter of law, the criteria of actual, apparent, or presumed consent are not satisfied and the actor is subject to liability for battery.

How should risk of miscommunication be handled in these cases? On the general reticence of the Third Restatement to address the role of affirmative consent in sex cases, see Chamallas, The Elephant in the Room: Sidestepping the Affirmative Consent Debate in the Restatement (Third) of Intentional Torts to Persons, 10 J. Tort L. 281 (2017), which states that "affirmative consent" requires explicit verbal consent "to initiate moving to a higher level of sexual intimacy in an interaction."

3. ***Athletic Injuries: Formal Settings.*** The legal remedy for persons deliberately or recklessly injured in professional athletic contests has been frequently litigated. In most sports it is generally held that plaintiffs consent to injury from blows administered in accordance with the rules of the game, but not when the blows are deliberately illegal. In Hackbart v. Cincinnati Bengals, Inc., 601 F.2d 516, 520–21 (10th Cir. 1979), Dale Hackbart, a defensive back for the Denver Broncos, was injured by a blow struck by Charles "Booby" Clark, an offensive halfback for the Bengals. After the Broncos intercepted a pass, Clark, "acting out of anger and frustration, but without a specific intent to injure . . . stepped forward and struck a blow with his right forearm to the back of the kneeling plaintiff's head and neck with sufficient force to cause both players to fall forward to the ground." Although Hackbart suffered no immediate ill effects from the blow, he shortly thereafter experienced severe pains that, after two more brief game appearances, forced him to retire, ending a successful thirteen-year career. The trial court dismissed the action, chiefly on the ground that without legislation it was inappropriate to impose upon one professional football player a duty to care for the safety of another. Doyle, J., reversed:

> Contrary to the position of the court then, there are no principles of law which allow a court to rule out certain tortious conduct by reason of general roughness of the game or difficulty of administering it.
>
> Indeed, the evidence shows that there are rules of the game which prohibit the intentional striking of blows. Thus, Article 1, Item 1, Subsection C, provides that: "All players are prohibited from striking on the head, face or neck with the heel, back or side of the hand, wrist, forearm, elbow or clasped hands." Thus the very conduct which was present here is expressly prohibited by the rule which is quoted above. . . . Therefore, the notion is not correct that all reason has been abandoned, whereby the only possible remedy for the person who has been the victim of an unlawful blow is retaliation.

What would be the result in the absence of a specific rule regulating game conduct? What if the owners of all teams agree that no tort actions should be brought for injuries suffered on the playing field? What about an agreement among the players to the same effect?

Courts have applied similar principles to high school and college athletic contests. In Nabozny v. Barnhill, 334 N.E.2d 258, 261 (Ill. App. Ct. 1975), the plaintiff soccer goalie sustained severe and permanent injuries when kicked in the head inside the penalty area even though the defendant could have easily avoided any contact. The game was played under soccer association rules, under which any contact with the goalkeeper and any attempt to kick a ball in his possession while in the penalty area count as infractions, even if actual contact is unintentional. The court, while concerned about the negative impact of tort liability on legitimate athletic activities, held that

> a player is liable for injury in a tort action if his conduct is such that it is either deliberate, wilful or with a reckless disregard for the safety of the other player so as to cause injury to that player, the same being a question of fact to be decided by a jury.

Today *Nabozny* has spawned the so-called contact sports exception, precluding liability for ordinary negligence. See Karas v. Strevell, 884 N.E.2d 122, 134 (Ill. 2008), arising out of a hard hockey body check from behind, holding that "a participant breaches a duty of care to a coparticipant only if the participant intentionally injures the coparticipant or engages in conduct totally outside the range of the ordinary activity involved in the sport." *Karas* was limited in Pickel v. Springfield Stallions, 926 N.E.2d 877 (Ill. App. 2010), such that a spectator at an indoor football game could maintain an ordinary negligence against the operators of the facility when injured by a player who ran over the wall that separated spectators from participant. No action was brought against the player. Why?

In Avila v. Citrus Community College District, 131 P.3d 383, 392–93 (Cal. 2006), the defendant's pitcher hit the plaintiff, a varsity baseball player, in the head with a pitch, cracking his helmet and causing serious injuries. The plaintiff alleged that "the pitch was an intentional 'beanball' thrown in retaliation for [a] previous hit batter or, at a minimum, was thrown negligently." Werdegar, J., rejected both allegations, holding that the defendant school had a duty "to, at a minimum, not increase the risks inherent in the sport." Even so, the home team was not liable because intentional beanballs were an "inherent risk of the sport." Is throwing beanballs caught by the Third Restatement's definition of recklessness?

RESTATEMENT OF THE LAW (THIRD) OF TORTS: LIABILITY FOR PHYSICAL AND EMOTIONAL HARM

§2. Recklessness

A person acts recklessly in engaging in conduct if:

(a) the person knows of the risk of harm created by the conduct or knows facts that make the risk obvious to another in the person's situation, and

(b) the precaution that would eliminate or reduce the risk involves burdens that are so slight relative to the magnitude of the risk as to render the person's failure to adopt the precaution a demonstration of the person's indifference to the risk.

Comment a. Terminology and Scope: . . . Taken at face value, [gross negligence] simply means negligence that is especially bad. Given this literal interpretation, gross negligence carries a meaning that is less than recklessness.

In Turcotte v. Fell, 502 N.E.2d 964, 969–70 (N.Y. 1986), the plaintiff, a professional jockey, sued for negligence when injured in a race by the defendant, a fellow jockey, who had violated track rules. The court refused to allow the action, contrasting this case with *Hackbart* and *Nabozny* as follows:

> Although the foul riding rule is a safety measure, it is not by its terms absolute for it establishes a spectrum of conduct and penalties, depending on whether the violation is careless or willful and whether the contact was the result of mutual fault. As the rule recognizes, bumping and jostling are normal incidents of the sport. They are not, as were the blows in *Nabozny* and *Hackbart*, flagrant infractions unrelated to the normal method of playing the game and done without any competitive purpose. Plaintiff does not claim that Fell intentionally or recklessly bumped him; he claims only that as a result of carelessness, Fell failed to control his mount as the horses raced for the lead and a preferred position on the track. While a participant's "consent" to join in a sporting activity is not a waiver of all rules infractions, nonetheless a professional clearly understands the usual incidents of competition resulting from carelessness, particularly those which result from the customarily accepted method of playing the sport, and accepts them.

4. *Athletic Injuries: Informal Settings.* In Marchetti v. Kalish, 559 N.E.2d 699, 701–03 (Ohio 1990), the plaintiff and defendant were playing a backyard game called "kick the can" in which players attempt to reach the home base, or can, before they are spotted by the player designated as "it." Once "it" sees another player, he places his foot on the can, and calls out the player's name, yelling "kick the can—one, two, three." (The rules of the game were sufficiently well articulated that the parties set them out in a joint appendix to the opinion.) On this occasion the plaintiff, a thirteen-year-old girl, placed her foot on the ball, used in place of a can, and announced that the defendant, a fifteen-year-old boy, was "it." The defendant continued to run straight at the plaintiff, and collided with her as he was kicking the ball out from under her foot. The plaintiff staggered to the ground and found that she had broken her right leg in two places.

The plaintiff conceded that her injuries were neither intentionally nor recklessly inflicted. The Ohio Supreme Court entered a summary judgment for defendant, relying on both *Nabozny* and *Hackbart.* "[Plaintiff] argues that these cases from other jurisdictions are distinguishable from the present case because we are dealing with children involved in a simple neighborhood game rather than an organized contact sport." But the court held the distinction immaterial so long as the children were "engaging in some type of recreational or sports activity. Whether the activity is organized, unorganized, supervised or unsupervised, is immaterial to the standard of liability. . . . [B]efore a party may proceed with a cause of action involving injury resulted from a recreational or sports activity, reckless or intentional conduct must exist." And in Gentry v. Craycraft, 802 N.E.2d 1116, 1118 (Ohio 2004), the recklessness standard was applied to spectators so long as they were old enough to appreciate the inherent risk in the activity. "To hold otherwise would be to open the floodgates to a myriad of lawsuits involving the backyard games of children." Any liability for the parents for negligent supervision?

b. Mental Disability

McGuire v. Almy

8 N.E.2d 760 (Mass. 1937)

Qua, J. This is an action of tort for assault and battery. The only question of law reported is whether the judge should have directed a verdict for the defendant.

The following facts are established by the plaintiff's own evidence: In August, 1930, the plaintiff was employed to take care of the defendant. The plaintiff was a registered nurse and was a graduate of a training school for nurses. The defendant was an insane person. Before the plaintiff was hired she learned that the defendant was a "mental case and was in good physical condition," and that for some time two nurses had been taking care of her. The plaintiff was on "twenty-four hour duty." The plaintiff slept in the room next to the defendant's room. Except when the plaintiff was with the defendant, the plaintiff kept the defendant locked in the defendant's room. There was a wire grating over the outside of the window of that room. During the period of "fourteen months or so" while the plaintiff cared for the defendant, the defendant "had a few odd spells," when she showed some hostility to the plaintiff and said that "she would like to try and do something to her." The defendant had been violent at times and had broken dishes "and things like that," and on one or two occasions the plaintiff had to have help to subdue the defendant.

On April 19, 1932, the defendant, while locked in her room, had a violent attack. The plaintiff heard a crashing of furniture and then knew that the defendant was ugly, violent and dangerous. The defendant told the plaintiff and a Miss Maroney, "the maid," who was with the plaintiff in the adjoining room, that if they came into the defendant's room, she would kill them. The plaintiff and Miss Maroney looked into the defendant's room, "saw what the defendant had done," and "thought it best to take the broken stuff away before she did any harm to herself with it." They sent for one Emerton, the defendant's brother-in-law. When he arrived the defendant was in the middle of her room about ten feet from the door, holding upraised the leg of a low-boy as if she were going to strike. The plaintiff stepped into the room and walked toward the defendant, while Emerton and Miss Maroney remained in the doorway. As the plaintiff approached the defendant and tried to take hold of the defendant's hand which held the leg, the defendant struck the plaintiff's head with it, causing the injuries for which the action was brought. [After noting that the Massachusetts precedents had not settled the rules governing the liability of an insane person, the court continues:]

Turning to authorities elsewhere, we find that courts in this country almost invariably say in the broadest terms that an insane person is liable for his torts. As a rule no distinction is made between those torts which would ordinarily be classed as intentional and those which would ordinarily be classed as negligent, nor do the courts discuss the effect of different kinds of insanity or of varying degrees of capacity as bearing upon the ability of the defendant to understand the particular act in question or to make a reasoned decision with respect to it, although it is sometimes said that an insane person is not liable for torts requiring malice of which he is incapable. Defamation and malicious prosecution are the torts more commonly mentioned in this connection. A number of illustrative cases appear in the footnote. These decisions are rested more upon grounds of public policy and upon what might be called a popular view of the requirements of essential justice than upon any attempt to apply logically the underlying principles of civil liability to the special instance of the mentally deranged. Thus it is said that a rule imposing liability tends to make more watchful those persons who have charge of the defendant and who may be supposed to have some interest in preserving his property; that as an insane person must pay for his support, if he is financially able, so he ought also to pay for the damage which he does; that an insane person with abundant wealth ought not to continue in unimpaired enjoyment of the comfort which it brings while his victim bears the burden unaided; and there is also a suggestion that courts are loath to introduce into the great body of civil litigation the difficulties in determining mental capacity which it has been found impossible to avoid in the criminal field.

The rule established in these cases has been criticized severely by certain eminent text writers both in this country and in England, principally on the ground that it is an archaic survival of the rigid and formal medieval conception of liability for acts done, without regard to fault, as opposed to what is said to be the general modern theory that liability in tort should rest upon fault. Notwithstanding these criticisms, we think that as a practical matter there is strong force in the reasons underlying these decisions. They are consistent with the general statements found in the cases dealing with the liability of infants for torts. Fault is by no means at the present day a universal prerequisite to liability, and the theory that it should be such has been obliged very recently to yield at several points to what have been thought to be paramount considerations of public good. Finally, it would be difficult not to recognize the persuasive weight of so much authority so widely extended.

But the present occasion does not require us either to accept or to reject the prevailing doctrine in its entirety. For this case it is enough to say that where an insane person by his act does intentional damage to the person or property of another he is liable for that damage in the same circumstances in which a normal person would be liable. This means that in so far as a particular intent would be necessary in order to render a normal person liable, the insane person, in order to be liable, must have been capable of entertaining that same intent and must have entertained it in fact. But the law will not inquire further into his peculiar mental condition with a view to excusing him if it should appear that delusion or other consequence of his affliction has caused him to entertain that intent or that a normal person would not have entertained it.

We do not suggest that this is necessarily a logical stopping point. If public policy demands that a mentally affected person be subjected to the external standard for intentional wrongs, it may well be that public policy also demands that he should be subjected to the external standard for wrongs which are commonly classified as negligent, in accordance with what now seems to be the prevailing view. We stop here for the present, because we are not required to go further in order to decide this case, because of deference to the difficulty of the subject, because full and adequate discussion is lacking in most of the cases decided up to the present time, and because by far the greater number of those cases, however broad their statement of the principle, are in fact cases of intentional rather than of negligent injury.

Coming now to the application of the rule to the facts of this case, it is apparent that the jury could find that the defendant was capable of entertaining and that she did entertain an intent to strike and to injure the plaintiff and that she acted upon that intent. See Am. Law Inst. Restatement: Torts §§13, 14. We think this was enough. [The court then rejects the argument that the plaintiff had consented to or assumed the risk as a matter of law. In its view the risk became "plain and obvious" only after she entered the room, just before the assault, when an emergency sufficient to deny voluntary consent had already been created.]

Judgment for the plaintiff on the verdict.

NOTE

Intention and Mental Disability. What result if Almy had thought she was striking a creature from outer space? That her actions were in self-defense against an imagined assault by McGuire? Looking at the other side of the case, was the court right to reject the defendant's assumption-of-risk defense in light of the elaborate preparations the plaintiff took before entering the defendant's room? In light of her role as a paid caretaker?

The vast majority of the decisions on the so-called insanity defense have hewed to the uncompromising line in *McGuire*. For a justification of this position, see Gould v. American Family Mutual Insurance Co., 543 N.W.2d 282, 285 (Wis. 1996), *infra* Chapter 3 at 125:

> [W]here a loss must be borne by one of two innocent persons, it shall be borne by him who occasioned it, and it has also been held that public policy requires the enforcement of the liability in order that those interested in the estate of the insane person, as relatives or otherwise, may be under inducement to restrain him and that tortfeasors may not simulate or pretend insanity to defend their wrongful acts causing damage to others.

The insanity defense also proved futile on the grisly facts of Polmatier v. Russ, 537 A.2d 468, 472 (Conn. 1988). The defendant Russ and his two-year-old daughter visited his father-in-law's house. The defendant sat astride his father-in-law, beating him over the head with a beer bottle. He then searched two bedrooms in the house, found 30-caliber ammunition and a Winchester rifle, and returned to the living room where he killed his father-in-law with two shots. The defendant was later found naked, sitting on a stump in a wooded area about two miles from the decedent's home, carrying his blood-soaked clothing and cradling his daughter in his arms. He was diagnosed as "suffering from a severe case of paranoid schizophrenia that involved delusions of persecution, grandeur, influence and reference, and also involved auditory hallucinations." The defendant was found unfit to stand for a criminal trial, but was held responsible for an intentional tort:

> We note that we have not been referred to any evidence indicating that the defendant's acts were reflexive, convulsive or epileptic. Furthermore, under the Restatement (Second) of Torts §2, "act" is used "to denote an external manifestation of the actor's will and does not include any of its results, even the most direct, immediate, and intended." Comment b to this section provides

> in pertinent part: "A muscular reaction is always an act unless it is a purely reflexive reaction in which the mind and will have no share." Although the trial court found that the defendant could not form a rational choice, it did find that he could make a schizophrenic or crazy choice. Moreover, a rational choice is not required since "[a]n insane person may have an intent to invade the interests of another, even though his reasons and motives for forming that intention may be entirely irrational." Restatement (Second) of Torts §895J, comment c.

The court rejected any further requirement that the defendant must have "acted for the *purpose* of causing," or with a "desire to cause the resulting injury."

What result in cases of automatism, where the sleepwalking defendant has done *no act* at all and thus cannot have committed any tort, intentional or otherwise? See, for the evolution of the insanity defense, Kelley, Infancy, Insanity and Infirmity in the Law of Torts, 48 Am. J. Juris. 179 (2003).

c. Self-Defense

Courvoisier v. Raymond

47 P. 284 (Colo. 1896)

HAYT, C.J. It is admitted or proven beyond controversy that appellee received a gunshot wound at the hands of the appellant at the time and place designated in the complaint, and that as the result of such wound the appellee was seriously injured. It is further shown that the shooting occurred under the following circumstances:

That Mr. Courvoisier, on the night in question, was asleep in his bed in the second story of a brick building, situated at the corner of South Broadway and Dakota streets in South Denver; that he occupied a portion of the lower floor of this building as a jewelry store. He was aroused from his bed shortly after midnight by parties shaking or trying to open the door of the jewelry store. These parties, when asked by him as to what they wanted, insisted upon being admitted, and upon his refusal to comply with this request, they used profane and abusive epithets toward him. Being unable to gain admission, they broke some signs upon the front of the building, and then entered the building by another entrance, and passing upstairs commenced knocking upon the door of a room where defendant's sister was sleeping. Courvoisier partly dressed himself, and, taking his revolver, went upstairs and expelled the intruders from the building. In doing this he passed downstairs and out on the sidewalk as far as the entrance to his store, which was at the corner of the building. The parties expelled from the building, upon reaching the rear of the store, were joined by two or three others. In order to frighten these parties away, the defendant fired a shot in the air, but instead of retreating they passed around to the street in front, throwing stones and brickbats at the defendant, whereupon he fired a second and perhaps a third shot. The first shot fired attracted the attention of plaintiff Raymond and two deputy sheriffs, who were at the Tramway depot, across the street. These officers started toward Mr. Courvoisier, who still continued to shoot, but two of them stopped when they reached the men in the street, for the purpose of arresting them, Mr. Raymond alone proceeding towards the defendant, calling out to him that he was an officer and to stop shooting. Although the night was dark, the street was well lighted by electricity, and when the officer approached him defendant shaded his eyes, and, taking deliberate aim, fired, causing the injury complained of.

The plaintiff's theory of the case is that he was a duly authorized police officer, and in the discharge of his duties at the time that the defendant was committing a breach of the peace, and that the defendant, knowing him to be a police officer, recklessly fired the shot in question.

The defendant claims that the plaintiff was approaching him at the time in a threatening attitude, and that the surrounding circumstances were such as to cause a reasonable man to believe that his life was in danger, and that it was necessary to shoot in self-defense, and that defendant did so believe at the time of firing the shot. . . .

The next error assigned relates to the instructions given by the court to the jury and to those requested by the defendant and refused by the court. The second instruction given by the court was clearly erroneous. The instruction is as follows: "The court instructs you that if you believe from the evidence, that, at the time the defendant shot the plaintiff, the plaintiff was not assaulting the defendant, then your verdict should be for the plaintiff."

The vice of this instruction is that it excluded from the jury a full consideration of the justification claimed by the defendant. The evidence for the plaintiff tends to show that the shooting, if not malicious, was wanton and reckless, but the evidence for the defendant tends to show that the circumstances surrounding him at the time of the shooting were such as to lead a reasonable man to believe that his life was in danger, or that he was in danger of receiving great bodily harm at the hands of the plaintiff, and the defendant testified that he did so believe. [The court then reviews the injured plaintiff's sworn version of the facts of the case and continues:]

. . . He then adds: "I saw a man come away from the bunch of men and come up towards me, and as I looked around I saw this man put his hand to his hip pocket. I didn't think I had time to jump aside, and therefore turned around and fired at him. I had no doubts but it was somebody that had come to rob me, because some weeks before Mr. Wilson's store was robbed. It is next door to mine."

By this evidence two phases of the transaction are presented for consideration: *First,* was the plaintiff assaulting the defendant at the time plaintiff was shot? *Second,* if not, was there sufficient evidence of justification for the consideration of the jury? The first question was properly submitted, but the second was excluded by the instruction under review. The defendant's justification did not rest entirely upon the proof of assault by the plaintiff. A riot was in progress, and the defendant swears that he was attacked with missiles, hit with stones, brickbats, etc.; that he shot plaintiff, supposing him to be one of the rioters. We must assume these facts as established in reviewing the instruction, as we cannot say what the jury might have found had this evidence been submitted to them under a proper charge.

By the second instruction the conduct of those who started the fracas was eliminated from the consideration of the jury. If the jury believed from the evidence that the defendant would have been justified in shooting one of the rioters had such person advanced towards him as did the plaintiff, then it became important to determine whether the defendant mistook plaintiff for one of the rioters, and if such a mistake was in fact made, was it excusable in the light of all the circumstances leading up to and surrounding the commission of the act? If these issues had been resolved by the jury in favor of the defendant, he would have been entitled to a judgment. Morris v. Platt, 32 Conn. 75.

[Judgment is reversed.]

NOTES

1. *Mistake and Self-Defense.* Note that the *Courvoisier* court held that the defendant could plead self-defense even if he mistakenly thought that he was under attack. In other cases of intentional harms, including cases of trespass and conversion, the risk of an innocent mistake usually falls on the party who makes it. What accounts for the different result in this case?

RESTATEMENT (THIRD) OF TORTS: INTENTIONAL TORTS TO PERSONS (TENTATIVE DRAFT, APPROVED 2021)

§23. Self-Defense by Deadly Force

[A]n actor is privileged to use deadly force for the purpose of defending himself or herself against another only if the actor reasonably believes that:

(1)

(A) the other is intentionally inflicting or about to intentionally inflict unprivileged force upon the actor;

(B) the actor is thereby put in peril of either death, serious bodily harm, or rape by the use or threat of physical force or restraint; and

(C) the actor can safely prevent the peril only by the immediate use of deadly force; or

(2)

(A) the other is committing or about to commit a burglary of the actor'[s] occupied dwelling;

(B) the actor is thereby put in peril of bodily harm; and

(C) the actor can safely prevent such harm only by the immediate use of deadly force.

(b) An actor does not have the privilege stated in Subsection (a) if the actor has a duty to retreat. Such a duty exists only if:

(1) the actor knows or reasonably should know that he or she can with complete safety avoid the need to use deadly force by retreating; and

(2) the other attacks the actor:

(A) in any place other than the actor' dwelling, or

(B) in the actor'[s] dwelling if the other also resides there.

Even though self-defense is universally recognized as a justification for intentionally inflicting harm, there is a persistent debate over whether it can be raised against all actors, regardless of their mental state.

2. ***Self-defense Against Actual Attacks.*** The defense of self-defense is far more secure when the plaintiff has in fact attacked the defendant. But even here critical questions can arise: Who struck the first blow, and was the force excessive under the circumstances? In Boston v. Muncy, 233 P.2d 300, 301, 303 (Okla. 1951), the defendant encountered the plaintiff in a domino parlor after work and asked what had happened to an automobile heater—difficult to obtain because of post–World War II rationing—that he had promised to put aside for the defendant. The plaintiff denied having made such a promise. According to the plaintiff, the defendant then called the plaintiff a liar and, without provocation, struck him over the right eye, causing serious damage. According to the defendant, "when he reminded plaintiff that he had promised to save a heater for him plaintiff called him a liar and made an attempt to hit him with his fist; that he then struck the plaintiff in self-defense." The plaintiff and defendant each had witnesses to support his respective version of the events. The defendant then asked for instructions that provided "the defendant had the right to exercise and use such reasonable force as may have reasonably appeared to him in good faith to be necessary to protect himself from bodily harm, even though he may not have been actually in danger." But the trial court, in instruction No. 8, said:

> [I]f at the time the defendant is alleged to have assaulted and struck the plaintiff the defendant in doing what he did was acting in an effort to protect his own person or life, and the circumstances then surrounding the defendant were such [that] the exercise of reasonable judgment would justify or induce in his mind an honest belief that he was in danger of receiving some great bodily harm, judging from the standpoint of the defendant, then the defendant would be justified in doing what he did, and your verdict should be for the defendant.

The Oklahoma Supreme Court held that instruction No. 8 was prejudicial error because it "too narrowly" limited the right of self-defense. It remanded the case for a new trial, saying:

> The evidence is highly conflicting as to who was the aggressor. The jury might have found that plaintiff was the aggressor, but it also might have further found that defendant was not justified in apprehending or believing that plaintiff intended to inflict upon him some great bodily harm, and under the instruction it might have concluded that the defendant therefore had no right to stand his ground and defend himself against the attack and it was therefore its duty to render a verdict for plaintiff.

Does removing the word "great" from the trial judge's instructions entitle the defendant to use the minimum force necessary to protect himself, even from trivial harm? Should a squeamish and nervous person be held to a standard of "ordinary firmness and courage" that he could not meet in practice? If armed, could he have used a gun when an ordinary man could not have done so? For an excellent discussion of the problem, see Fletcher, Proportionality and the Psychotic Aggressor: A Vignette in Comparative Criminal Theory, 8 Isr. L. Rev. 367 (1973).

3. *Stand-Your-Ground Laws.* Recently, many states have adopted stand-your-ground (SYG) laws that allow people to resist attacks with force even when they have the option to retreat. These laws uniformly apply to attacks that take place within the home, but often are extended to any place where a person has a lawful right to be. Thus Fla. Stat. Ann. §776.032(1) declares one "is immune from . . . civil action for the use or threatened use of such force by the person . . . against whom the force was used or threatened," against anyone except a police officer. The scope of that privilege is then broadly defined by Fla. Stat. Ann. §776.012(2) (2021):

> A person is justified in using or threatening to use deadly force if he or she reasonably believes that using or threatening to use such force is necessary to prevent imminent death or great bodily harm to himself or herself or another or to prevent the imminent commission of a forcible felony. A person who uses or threatens to use deadly force in accordance with this subsection does not have a duty to retreat and has the right to stand his or her ground if the person using or threatening to use the deadly force is not engaged in a criminal activity and is in a place he or she has a right to be.

In Nadell v. Hursey, 363 So. 3d 1135, 1141 (Fla. Dist. Ct. App. 2023), it became clear that SYG laws do not resolve all questions of fact. The altercation in question took place on Nadell's boat. Nadell offered two eyewitnesses who supported his contention that Hursey was the aggressor, even as Hursey testified to the contrary. On appeal, Scales, J., concluded that while the bulk of the testimonial evidence presented supported Nadell's claim, "Hursey's testimony to the contrary constitutes competent, substantial evidence that supports the trial court's legal determination that Nadell is not entitled to SYG immunity."

4. *Defense of Third Parties.* Under what circumstances may a person intervene in defense of a third party? What if he hurts the plaintiff in the mistaken, but reasonable, belief that a third party needs assistance? See RTT: IT §24, which notes that "an actor is privileged to use force to defend a third person against an attack from another to the same extent and under the same conditions" as he would for self-defense, if the actor "reasonably believes that: (a) the circumstances are such that the third person has a privilege of self-defense against the other, and (b) the actor'[s] intervention is immediately necessary for the protection of the third person."

5. *Injury to Innocent Bystanders.* In Morris v. Platt, 32 Conn. 75 (1864), the court held that the accidental harming of an innocent bystander by force reasonably intended in self-defense to repel an attack by a third party is not actionable. Is *Morris* consistent with the trial judge's approach in *Courvoisier*? Does the plaintiff in *Morris* have a cause of action against the defendant's assailant? With *Morris*, contrast the Roman law approach in Justinian's Digest 9.2.45.4:

> Persons who do damage because they cannot otherwise defend themselves are innocent; for all statutes and legal systems allow one to repel force by force. But if in order to defend myself I throw a stone at my adversary, but hit, not him but a passer-by, I shall be liable under the Lex Aquilia [the general Roman tort statute for wrongful damage]; for one is allowed to strike only the person who uses force, and then only when it is done for the purpose of protection and not revenge as well.

Contrast *Morris* and Justinian's Digest with the following Restatement section.

RESTATEMENT (THIRD) OF TORTS: INTENTIONAL TORTS TO PERSONS (TENTATIVE DRAFT, APPROVED 2021)

§26. Liability to Bystander for Intentional Tort or for Negligence

(b) *Liability to bystander for intentional tort.* If an actor, for the purpose of self-defense (or defense of a third person) against an aggressor, intentionally uses force against a bystander, . . . [t]he privilege of the actor is limited as follows:

(1) The actor may not use deadly force against the bystander;

(2) The actor may use force against the bystander if but only if the actor reasonably believes that:

(A) the force that the other person is using or threatening against the actor is substantially greater than the force that the actor uses against the bystander, and

(B) the actor'[s] use of the force against the bystander is immediately necessary to avoid the aggressor'[s] threat or use of force.

d. Defense of Property

Bird v. Holbrook

130 Eng. Rep. 911 (C.P. 1825)

[The defendant had rented and occupied a walled garden in which he grew valuable tulips. The garden was located about a mile from his home, and it contained a single-room summer-house in which he and his wife slept from time to time. Shortly before the present incident, the defendant's garden had been robbed of flowers and roots worth 20 pounds:] in consequence of which, for the protection of his property, with the assistance of another man, he placed in the garden a spring gun, the wires connected with which were made to pass from the door-way of the summer-house to some tulip beds, at the height of about fifteen inches from the ground, and across three or four of the garden paths, which wires were visible from all parts of the garden or the garden wall; but it was admitted by the Defendant, that the Plaintiff had not seen them, and that he had no notice of the spring gun and the wires being there. [The plaintiff, a nineteen-year-old youth, had gone into the garden between six and seven in the afternoon on March 21, 1825, for an innocent purpose—to get back a pea-fowl that had strayed—at the request of the servant of its owner. The plaintiff climbed on the wall at the back of the garden and called out several times before jumping down into the garden. As he approached the summer-house, he triggered the spring gun, which discharged heavy shot that caused a severe wound above the knee.]

A witness to whom the Defendant mentioned the fact of his having been robbed, and of having set a spring gun, proved that he had asked the Defendant if he had put up a notice of such gun being set, to which the Defendant answered, that "he did not conceive that there was any law to oblige him to do so," and the Defendant desired such person not to mention to any one that the gun was set, "lest the villain should not be detected." The Defendant stated to the same person that the garden was very secure, and that he and his wife were going to sleep in the summer-house in a few days. . . .

Merewether, Serjt. [i.e., highest order of counsel] for the defendant. . . . The main ground of the defence, however, is, that the Plaintiff cannot recover for an injury occasioned to him by his own wrongful act. Commodum ex injuria non oritur [an advantage cannot arise out of a wrongful act] and it is equally the principle of our law, that jus ex injuria non oritur [no right arises from a wrong]. If a man place broken glass on a wall, or spikes behind a carriage, one who wilfully encounters them, and is wounded, even though it were by night, when he could have no notice, has no claim for compensation. Volenti non fit injuria [To a willing person, no injury is done]. The Defendant lawfully places a gun on his own property; he leaves the wires visible; he builds a high wall, expressly to keep off intruders; and if, under those circumstances, they are permitted to recover for an injury resulting from their scaling the wall, no man can protect his property at a distance.

Wilde in reply. . . . No illustration can be drawn from the use of spikes and broken glass on walls, & c. These are mere preventives, obvious to the sight,—unless the trespasser *chooses* a time of darkness, when no notice could be available,—mere preventives, injurious only to the persevering and determined trespasser, who can calculate at the moment of incurring the danger the amount of suffering he is about to endure, and who will, consequently, desist from his enterprise whenever the anticipated advantage is outweighed by the pain which he must endure to obtain it.

BEST, C.J. I am of opinion that this action is maintainable. . . .

It has been argued that the law does not compel every line of conduct which humanity or religion may require; but there is no act which Christianity forbids, that the law will not reach: if it were otherwise, Christianity would not be, as it has always been held to be, part of the law of England. I am, therefore, clearly of opinion that he who sets spring guns, without giving notice, is guilty of an inhuman act, and that, if injurious consequences ensue, he is liable to yield redress to the sufferer. But this case stands on grounds distinct from any that have preceded it. In general, spring guns have been set for the purpose of deterring; the Defendant placed his for the express purpose of doing injury; for, when called on to give notice, he said, "If I give notice, I shall not catch him." He intended, therefore, that the gun should be discharged, and that the contents should be lodged in the body of his victim, for he could not be caught in any other way. On these principles the action is clearly maintainable, and particularly on the latter ground. . . . As to the case of Brock v. Copeland, Lord Kenyon proceeded on the ground that the Defendant had a right to keep a dog for the preservation of his house, and the Plaintiff, who was his foreman, knew where the dog was stationed. The case of the furious bull is altogether different; for if a man places such an animal where there is a public footpath, he interferes with the rights of the public. What would be the determination of the court if the bull were placed in a field where there is no footpath, we need not now decide; but it may be observed, that he must be placed somewhere, and is kept, not for mischief, but to renew his species; while the gun in the present case was placed purely for mischief. The case of the pit dug on a common has been distinguished, on the ground that the owner had a right to do what he pleased with his own land, and the Plaintiff could shew no right for the horse to be there.

. . . But we want no authority in a case like the present; we put it on the principle that it is inhuman to catch a man by means which may maim him or endanger his life, and, as far as human means can go, it is the object of English law to uphold humanity and the sanctions of religion. It would be, indeed, a subject of regret, if a party were not liable in damages, who, instead of giving notice of the employment of a destructive engine, or removing it, at least, during the day, expressed a resolution to withhold notice, lest, by affording it, he should fail to entrap his victim.

Burrough, J. The common understanding of mankind shews, that notice ought to be given when these means of protection are resorted to; and it was formerly the practice upon such occasions to give public notice in market towns. But the present case is of a worse complexion than those which have preceded it; for if the Defendant had proposed merely to protect his property from thieves, he would have set the spring guns only by night. The Plaintiff was only a trespasser: if the Defendant had been present, he would not have been authorised even in taking him into custody, and no man can do indirectly that which he is forbidden to do directly.

NOTES

1. *An Economic Interpretation of Bird v. Holbrook.* Writing from an economic perspective, Judge Posner analyzed *Bird* as follows:

> The issue in the case, as an economist would frame it, was the proper accommodation of two legitimate activities, growing tulips and raising peacocks. The defendant had a substantial investment in the tulip garden; he lived at a distance; and the wall had proved ineffective against thieves. In an era of negligible police protection, a spring gun may have been the most cost-effective means of protection for the tulips. But since spring guns do not discriminate between the thief and the innocent trespasser, they deter owners of domestic animals from pursuing their animals onto other people's property and so increase the costs (enclosure costs or straying losses) of keeping animals. The court in *Bird* implied an ingenious accommodation: One who sets a spring gun must post notices that he has done so. Then owners of animals will not be reluctant to pursue their animals onto property not so posted. A notice will be of no avail at night, but animals are more likely to be secured then and in any event few owners would chase their straying animals after dark.

Posner, Economic Analysis of Law 240 (9th ed. 2014). For his more extensive analysis, see Posner, Killing or Wounding to Protect a Property Interest, 14 J.L. & Econ. 201, 208–11 (1971).

Exhibit 1.1 Spring Guns

As Richard Posner notes, "[s]pring guns were something of a *cause célèbre* in early nineteenth century England." Spring guns were often used by large landowners to trap or deter armed bands of poachers. Market gardeners, of whom Holbrook was one, were particularly troubled by the poachers. Their businesses were located on the outskirts of London, and they claimed that an efficient municipal police force had driven London's thieves into their neighborhoods. They viewed spring guns as an easy and inexpensive way to protect their farms. See Posner, Killing or Wounding to Protect a Property Interest, 14 J.L. & Econ. 201, 202 & n.5 (1971).

Parliament enacted strict regulations on the use of spring guns a year before *Bird* was decided. The central provision of the statute stated:

> That from and after the passing of this Act, if any Person shall set or place or cause to be set or placed, any Spring Gun, Man Trap, or other Engine calculated to destroy human Life, or inflict grievous bodily Harm, with the Intent that the same or whereby the same may destroy or inflict grievous bodily Harm upon a Trespasser or other Person coming in contact therewith, the Person so setting or placing, or causing to be so set or placed, such Gun, Trap, or Engine as aforesaid, shall be guilty of a Misdemeanor. . . .

The Act exempted spring guns and similar devices set in dwelling houses between sunset and sunrise. It also "declared and enacted" that the Act did not apply to anything done prior to its passage. Some members of Parliament argued that market gardeners should be allowed to set spring guns to protect their property until they were afforded greater police protection.

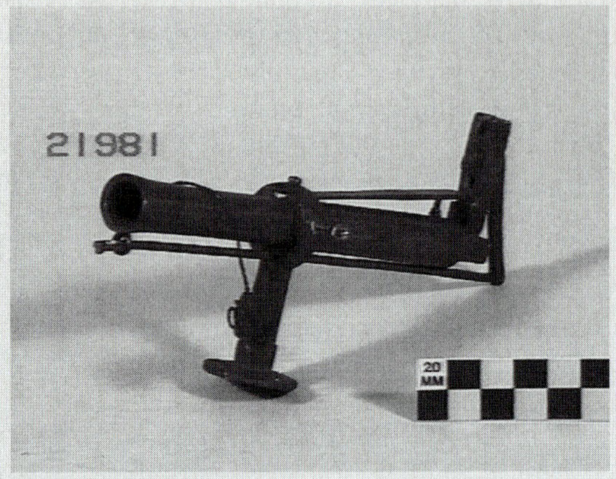

Spring gun – Birmingham, 19th century

Source : Museum Victoria Collections

Suppose a person sets a spring gun in violation of the statute. If the gun is triggered by an individual against whom the application of direct force is warranted (e.g., a would-be assailant who enters a home during the day), does the statute override the homeowner's defense to the intruder's cause of action for personal injuries? Should it excuse the payment of the statutory fine? Note that the statute was repealed in its entirety. 24 & 25 Vict. C. 95 §1 (1861).

What result if an injured child cannot read English? Is it ever proper to use spring guns on property that is not surrounded by a fence or protective wall? Should a landowner be entitled to set spring guns to protect a warehouse as well as a dwelling house? For an affirmative answer, see Scheuermann v. Scharfenberg, 50 So. 335 (Ala. 1909).

2. *The Malicious Use of Spring Guns.* In Katko v. Briney, 183 N.W.2d 657, 659, 663 (Iowa 1971), the defendants owned an old, boarded-up house, located several miles from their home, where they stored various old bottles, fruit jars and the like, which they considered to be antiques. Several times the windows in the house had been broken and the entire place "messed up." The defendants first posted "no trespass" signs, but the break-ins continued. Shortly before the injury to the plaintiff, the defendants placed a "shotgun trap" in one of the bedrooms. The gun was first positioned so as to hit an intruder in the stomach, but Mr. Briney, at his wife's insistence, lowered it to hit at the legs. He said that he set the gun "because I was mad and tired of being tormented," but insisted that he "did not intend to injure anyone." The plaintiff was shot in the legs and permanently injured when he entered the defendants' bedroom shortly after the gun was set. He had been to the place several times before and had intended to steal some of the defendants' possessions. The plaintiff pleaded guilty to a charge of larceny and paid a fine of $50. He also sued the defendants for personal injuries and was awarded $20,000 in actual damages and $10,000 in punitive damages.

At trial the jury was instructed as follows: Instruction No. 5:

> You are hereby instructed that one may use reasonable force in the protection of his property, but such right is subject to the qualification that one may not use such means of force as will take human life or inflict great bodily injury. Such is the rule even though the injured party is a trespasser and is in violation of the law himself.

Instruction No. 6 stated that the rule was not changed even if "the trespasser may be acting in violation of the law," except that "setting a 'spring gun' or a like dangerous device is justified . . . when the trespasser was committing a felony of violence or a felony punishable by death, or where the trespasser was endangering human life by his act."

The Iowa Supreme Court approved these instructions on appeal and affirmed the judgment for the plaintiff without addressing the question of punitive damages, which had not been raised below. Larson, J., protested against awarding large "windfall" damages to a criminal defendant, noting that "where the evidence is sufficient to sustain a finding that the installation was intended only as a warning to ward off thieves and criminals, I can see no compelling reason why the use of such a device alone would create liability as a matter of law."

Katko stirred up great protest in Iowa and throughout the nation. Hundreds of strangers, including prison inmates, sent checks and cash totaling over $10,000 to the Brineys. Mr. Briney remained unrepentant: "They used booby traps in Viet Nam, didn't they? Why can't we use them here to protect our property in this country?" Asked if he would do it again, Briney replied, "There's one thing I'd do different, though, I'd have aimed that gun a few feet higher." See a fuller account in the Chicago Tribune of April 25, 1975, at 1, col. 1.

3. ***Wounding or Killing in Defense of Property.*** The Third Restatement takes a fairly permissive approach toward the use of force in defense of property.

RESTATEMENT OF THE LAW (THIRD) OF TORTS: INTENTIONAL TORTS TO PERSONS (TENTATIVE DRAFT, APPROVED 2021)

§31. Privilege to Defend Land or Personal Property from Intrusion by Use of a Mechanical Device

An actor is privileged to engage in conduct that would otherwise satisfy the elements of battery, assault, purposeful infliction of bodily harm, or false imprisonment by employing a mechanical device for the purpose of preventing or terminating another'[s]intrusion upon the actor'[s]land or personal property only if:

(a) the use of the type of device employed is reasonably necessary to protect the property from intrusion;

(b) the use of the particular device is reasonably proportionate to the value of the interest the actor is protecting;

(c) the device is one customarily used for such a purpose, or reasonable care is taken to make its use known to probable intruders; and

(d) the use of the device is not intended or likely to cause death or serious bodily injury.

Comment c. Most cases of harm from mechanical devices are properly brought as negligence claims, not as intentional torts: . . . [A]lthough mechanical devices might foreseeably contact or harm an intruder, the device is usually not substantially certain to contact or harm anyone in particular or at any particular time.

Comment e. Harm to a bystander: A mechanical device by which the actor intends to deter or harm an intruder might instead or also cause harm to a bystander. So long as such a case satisfies the intent requirements of an intentional tort, the question whether the actor's conduct is privileged is determined pursuant to the Section in combination with the requirements of §33 of this chapter [which decides these cases under principles of negligence.]

Why does it matter that mechanical devices are not substantially likely to cause harm, if every time they are triggered such harm is virtually certain to happen? If a defendant is negligent toward a potential trespasser, does it follow that he is also negligent to some unlikely innocent third party?

What form of force may be used when a defendant is present at the time of the intrusion of the defendant? Should that privilege be broader or narrower than in the spring gun case? In M'Ilvoy v. Cockran, 8 Ky. 271, 275–76 (1820), the defendant, M'Ilvoy, shot and severely wounded the plaintiff, Cockran, while the latter was attempting to tear down a fence on M'Ilvoy's land. The court first held that the defendant did not have to request the plaintiff to leave when he was engaged in the active destruction of property, as he would have to do for a simple entrance. However, the court rejected the defendant's plea that this wounding was justified in defense of property, noting that

> in cases of *actual force*, as breaking open a gate or door, it is lawful to oppose force with force; and if one breaks down a gate, or comes into a close with force and arms, the possessor need not request him to depart, but may lay hands upon him immediately, for it is but returning violence with violence: so if one comes forcibly and takes away my goods, he may be opposed immediately, for there is no time to make a request: but, say the court, where one enters the close without actual force, although his entry will be construed a *force in law*, there must be a request to depart before the possessor can lay hands upon him and turn him out.
>
> But although a wounding cannot be justified barely in defence of possession, yet if, in attempting to remove the intruder, or prevent his forcible entry, he should commit an assault upon the person of the possessor, or his family, and the owner should, in defence of himself or family, wound him, the wounding may, no doubt, be justified; but then, as the personal assault would form the grounds of justification, the plea should set out, specifically, the assault in justification.

The same rules continue to apply today. In People v. Yi Chih Chen, 264 Cal. Rptr. 3d 570 (Ct. App. 2020), a criminal prosecution, the arrestee could not overturn his conviction when he brandished a firearm against his neighbors who were attempting to remove a shared fence without seeking the arrestee's permission. Lethal force was only justified in self-defense when an intruder also threatened death or serious bodily harm, which had not happened here.

4. *Recapture of Chattels or Money.* The rules governing the protection of land and property from invasions by others are covered by RTT: IT §30, which adopts the general approach that requests to leave must be made except in those circumstances where the property occupier or possessor thinks that the warning will be ineffective or create a personal risk of danger. Is it possible to come up with a per se rules in these cases?

In Kirby v. Foster, 22 A. 1111 (R.I. 1891), the plaintiff received from the defendant, his employer, sufficient funds to meet the weekly payroll. The plaintiff believed that the defendant had wrongly docked his pay, so he kept the amount of money he thought he was owed and returned the rest to the defendant. The defendant then seized the plaintiff in order to recover the funds that the latter had retained. Stiness, J., held that the defendant would have had the right to seize any stranger who sought to steal his money, but he could not do so against his employee against whom he could bring a lawsuit to recover the funds. "The law does not permit parties to take the settlement of conflicting claims into their own hands. It gives the right of defence, but not of redress." RTT: IT §32 appears to deviate from this rule when it sometimes allows the right to use reasonable levels of force to recoup the property when the party who took the property refuses to return it and the owner of the property knows that a request for its return is likely to prove futile. What if the party who seeks to retake goods or cash by force knows the name and address of the offending party?

e. Necessity

Ploof v. Putnam

71 A. 188 (Vt. 1908)

MUNSON, J. It is alleged as the ground of recovery that on the 13th day of November, 1904, the defendant was the owner of a certain island in Lake Champlain, and of a certain dock attached thereto, which island and dock were then in charge of the defendant's servant; that the plaintiff was then possessed of and sailing upon said lake a certain loaded sloop, on which were the plaintiff and his wife and two minor children; that there then arose a sudden and violent tempest, whereby the sloop and the property and persons therein were placed in great danger of destruction; that to save these from destruction or injury the plaintiff was compelled to, and did, moor the sloop to defendant's dock; that the defendant by his servant unmoored the sloop, whereupon it was driven upon the shore by the tempest, without the plaintiff's fault; and that the sloop and its contents were thereby destroyed, and the plaintiff and his wife and children cast into the lake and upon the shore, receiving injuries.

This claim is set forth in two counts [tracking the old forms of action, see *infra* Chapter 2 at 70]; one in trespass, charging that the defendant by his servant with force and arms wilfully and designedly unmoored the sloop; the other in case, alleging that it was the duty of the defendant by his servant to permit the plaintiff to moor his sloop to the dock, and to permit it to remain so moored during the continuance of the tempest, but that the defendant by his servant, in disregard of this duty, negligently, carelessly and wrongfully unmoored the sloop. Both counts are demurred to generally.

There are many cases in the books which hold that necessity, and an inability to control movements inaugurated in the proper exercise of a strict right, will justify entries upon land and interferences with personal property that would otherwise have been trespasses. A reference to a few of these will be sufficient to illustrate the doctrine. . . .

In trespass of cattle taken in *A*, defendant pleaded that he was seized of *C*, and found the cattle there damage feasant [causing damage], and chased them toward the pound, and that they escaped from him and went into *A*, and he presently retook them and this was held a good plea. 21 Edw. IV, 64 Vin. Ab. Trespass, H. a. 4 pl. 19. If one have a way over the land of another for his beasts to pass, and the beasts, being properly driven, feed the grass by morsels in passing, or run out of the way and are promptly pursued and brought back, trespass will not lie. See Vin. Ab. Trespass, K. a. pl. 1.

A traveler on a highway, who finds it obstructed from a sudden and temporary cause, may pass upon the adjoining land without becoming a trespasser, because of the necessity.

An entry upon land to save goods which are in danger of being lost or destroyed by water or fire is not a trespass. 21 Hen. VII, 27 Vin. Ab. Trespass, H. a. 4, pl. 24, K. a. pl. 3. In Proctor v. Adams, 113 Mass. 376 (1873), the defendant went upon the plaintiff's beach for the purpose of saving and restoring to the lawful owner a boat which had been driven ashore and was in danger of being carried off by the sea and it was held no trespass.

This doctrine of necessity applies with special force to the preservation of human life. One assaulted and in peril of his life may run through the close of another to escape from his assailant. 37 Hen. VII, pl. 26. One may sacrifice the personal property of another to save his life or the lives of his fellows. In Mouse's Case, 12 Co. 63, the defendant was sued for taking and carrying away the plaintiff's casket and its contents. It appeared that the ferryman of Gravesend took forty-seven passengers into his barge to pass to London, among whom were the plaintiff and defendant; and the barge being upon the water a great tempest happened, and a strong wind, so that the barge and all the passengers were in danger of being lost if certain ponderous things were not cast out, and the defendant thereupon cast out the plaintiff's casket. It was resolved that in case of necessity, to save the lives of the passengers, it was lawful for the defendant, being a passenger, to cast the plaintiff's casket out of the barge; that if the ferryman surcharge the barge the owner shall have his remedy upon the surcharge against the ferryman, but that if there be no surcharge, and the danger accrue only by the act of God, as by tempest, without fault of the ferryman, every one ought to bear this loss, to safeguard the life of a man.

It is clear that an entry upon the land of another may be justified by necessity, and that the declaration before us discloses a necessity for mooring the sloop. But the defendant questions the sufficiency of the counts because they do not negative the existence of natural objects to which the plaintiff could have moored with equal safety. The allegations are, in substance, that the stress of a sudden and violent tempest compelled the plaintiff to moor to defendant's dock to save his sloop and the people in it. The averment of necessity is complete, for it covers not only the necessity of mooring, but the necessity of mooring to the dock; and the details of the situation which created this necessity, whatever the legal requirements regarding them, are matters of proof and need not be alleged. It is certain that the rule suggested cannot be held applicable irrespective of circumstance, and the question must be left for adjudication upon proceedings had with reference to the evidence or the charge. . . .

Judgment affirmed and cause remanded.

NOTES

1. ***Necessity and Self-Help.*** While still at sea, were the plaintiffs entitled to use force to land on the dock if the defendant's servant had resisted them? To keep their boat moored to the dock? Note that under the general common law rules, the defendant's servants, while they may not resist the plaintiff's entry to dock in conditions of necessity, are not obliged to lend a helping hand. See *infra* Chapter 6, Section B, at 404. Why the difference? Why should the employer have to pay for his employee's torts? See *infra* Chapter 7, Section F, at 531.

2. ***General Average Contribution.*** Mouse's Case, (1609) 77 Eng. Rep. 1341 (KB), discussed in cryptic form in *Ploof,* held "that in a case of necessity, for the saving of the lives of the passengers, it was lawful for the defendant, being a passenger, to cast the casket of the plaintiff out of the barge, with other things in it." Mouse's Case hints at the elaboration of the necessity principle in the law of admiralty under the rubric of general average contribution. Suppose a vessel is carrying cargo owned by a number of different parties when its master is confronted with a sudden emergency that jeopardizes the safety of the ship and cargo. Under the law of general average contribution, the master may jettison some of the cargo in order to save the ship and the remaining cargo. In order to prevent any property owners from being relatively disadvantaged by the loss of their cargo, they receive pro rata compensation from other parties, including the owner of the hull, so that the total loss from property damage is prorated across all owners. In effect, in time of emergency all are treated as joint owners of all the property in question. This rule gives the master a desirable incentive to minimize the aggregate loss to all concerned, by throwing over that cargo (often stowed on top) which gives the greatest chance to save the ship at the lowest possible cost. As each owner is placed, as it were, behind a veil of ignorance, he can do best by himself only if he does best by all owners of hull and cargo alike, which means that he has strong incentives to give an accurate valuation of his goods. If he sets it too low, valuable cargo may be overthrown. If he sets it too high, he will have to pay an excessive sum to the common pool. On the complexities of the law of general average contribution, see Gilmore & Black, The Law of Admiralty §§5.1, 5.2 (2d ed. 1975). See also Landes & Posner, Salvors, Finders, Good Samaritans, and Other Rescuers: An Economic Study of Law and Altruism, 7 J. Legal Stud. 83, 106–08 (1978).

Exhibit 1.2 "The Pirates of Lake Champlain"

The official presentation of the facts conveys the impression that Sylvester Ploof was a complete stranger who happened to be traveling on the lake when he was caught in the storm and then just happened to sail to the defendant's island and dock. The local lore about this case is quite different. The Ploofs were a poor, landless family who lived and worked on their boat. They earned their living transporting firewood and other goods on the lake and were well known and disliked by the lakeshore inhabitants. Known as the "pirates" of Lake Champlain, they were often accused of raiding and stealing from vacation homes on the lake. When they were seen in the area, homeowners generally went on the alert and even chased them off with guns. Henry Putnam's caretaker untied the Ploofs' boat because he knew them and he was aware of their reputation as thieves, not simply because the Ploofs were using the dock without the owner's permission.

Photo of a boat similar to one that may have belonged to the Ploofs. The original had its boiler and machinery removed to be used as a houseboat.

Atomic / Alamy

Vogel, Cases in Context: Lake Champlain Wars, Gentrification and Ploof v. Putnam, 45 St. Louis U. L.J. 791, 798 (2001).

Vincent v. Lake Erie Transportation Co.

124 N.W. 221 (Minn. 1910)

O'Brien, J. The steamship Reynolds, owned by the defendant, was for the purpose of discharging her cargo on November 27, 1905, moored to plaintiff's dock in Duluth. While the unloading of the boat was taking place a storm from the northeast developed, which at about ten o'clock P.M., when the unloading was completed, had so grown in violence that the wind was then moving at fifty miles per hour and continued to increase during the night. There is some evidence that one, and perhaps two, boats were able to enter the harbor that night, but it is plain that navigation was practically suspended from the hour mentioned until the morning of the twenty-ninth, when the storm abated, and during that time no master would have been justified in attempting to navigate his vessel, if he could avoid doing so. After the discharge of the cargo the Reynolds signaled for a tug to tow her from the dock, but none could be obtained because of the severity of the storm. If the lines holding the ship to the dock had been cast off, she would doubtless have drifted away; but, instead, the lines were kept fast, and as soon as one parted or chafed it was replaced, sometimes with a larger one. The vessel lay upon the outside of the dock, her bow to the east, the wind and waves striking her starboard quarter with such force that she was constantly being lifted and thrown against the dock, resulting in its damage, as found by the jury, to the amount of $500.

Facts

We are satisfied that the character of this storm was such that it would have been highly imprudent for the master of the Reynolds to have attempted to leave the dock or to have permitted his vessel to drift away from it. One witness testified upon the trial that the vessel could have been warped into a slip, and that, if the attempt to bring the ship into the slip had failed, the worst that could have happened would be that the vessel would have been blown ashore upon a soft and muddy bank. The witness was not present in Duluth at the time of the storm, and, while he may have been right in his conclusions, those in charge of the dock and the vessel at the time of the storm were not required to use the highest human intelligence, nor were they required to resort to every possible experiment which could be suggested for the preservation of their property. Nothing more was demanded of them than ordinary prudence and care, and the record in this case fully sustains the contention of the appellant that, in holding the vessel fast to the dock, those in charge of her exercised good judgment and prudent seamanship.

It is claimed by the respondent that it was negligence to moor the boat at an exposed part of the wharf, and to continue in that position after it became apparent that the storm was to be more than usually severe. We do not agree with this position. The part of the wharf where the vessel was moored appears to have been commonly used for that purpose. It was situated within the harbor at Duluth, and must, we think, be considered a proper and safe place, and would undoubtedly have been such during what would be considered a very severe storm. The storm which made it unsafe was one which surpassed in violence any which might have reasonably been anticipated.

The appellant contends by ample assignments of error that, because its conduct during the storm was rendered necessary by prudence and good seamanship under conditions over which it had no control, it cannot be held liable for any injury resulting to the property of others, and claims that the jury should have been so instructed. An analysis of the charge given by the trial court is not necessary, as in our opinion the only question for the jury was the amount of damages which the plaintiffs were entitled to recover, and no complaint is made upon that score.

The situation was one in which the ordinary rules regulating property rights were suspended by forces beyond human control, and if, without the direct intervention of some act by the one sought to be held liable, the property of another was injured, such injury must be attributed to the act of God, and not to the wrongful act of the person sought to be charged. If during the storm the Reynolds had entered the harbor, and while there had become disabled and been thrown against the plaintiffs' dock, the plaintiffs could not have recovered. Again, if while attempting to hold fast to the dock the lines had parted, without any negligence, and the vessel carried against some other boat or dock in the harbor, there would be no liability upon her owner. But here those in charge of the vessel deliberately and by their direct efforts held her in such a position that the damage to the dock resulted, and, having thus preserved the ship at the expense of the dock, it seems to us that her owners are responsible to the dock owners to the extent of the injury inflicted. . . .

In Ploof v. Putnam, 71 Atl. 188, the Supreme Court of Vermont held that where, under stress of weather, a vessel was without permission moored to a private dock at an island in Lake Champlain owned by the defendant, the plaintiff was not guilty of trespass, and that the defendant was responsible in damages because his representative upon the island unmoored the vessel, permitting it to drift upon the shore, with resultant injuries to it. If, in that case, the vessel had been permitted to remain, and the dock had suffered an injury, we believe the shipowner would have been held liable for the injury done.

Theologians hold that a starving man may, without moral guilt, take what is necessary to sustain life but it could hardly be said that the obligation would not be upon such person to pay the value of the property so taken when he became able to do so. And so public necessity, in times of war or peace, may require the taking of private property for public purposes; but under our system of jurisprudence compensation must be made.

Let us imagine in this case that for the better mooring of the vessel those in charge of her had appropriated a valuable cable lying upon the dock. No matter how justifiable such appropriation might have been, it would not be claimed that, because of the overwhelming necessity of the situation, the owner of the cable could not recover its value.

This is not a case where life or property was menaced by any object or thing belonging to the plaintiffs, the destruction of which became necessary to prevent the threatened disaster. Nor is it a case where, because of the act of God, or unavoidable accident, the infliction of the injury was beyond the control of the defendant, but is one where the defendant prudently and advisedly availed itself of the plaintiffs' property for the purpose of preserving its own more valuable property, and the plaintiffs are entitled to compensation for the injury done.

Order affirmed.

LEWIS, J. I dissent. It was assumed on the trial before the lower court that appellant's liability depended on whether the master of the ship might, in the exercise of reasonable care, have sought a place of safety before the storm made it impossible to leave the dock. The majority opinion assumes that the evidence is conclusive that appellant moored its boat at respondents' dock pursuant to contract, and that the vessel was lawfully in position at the time the additional cables were fastened to the dock, and the reasoning of the opinion is that, because appellant made use of the stronger cables to hold the boat in position, it became liable under the rule that it had voluntarily made use of the property of another for the purpose of saving its own.

In my judgment, if the boat was lawfully in position at the time the storm broke, and the master could not, in the exercise of due care, have left that position without subjecting his vessel to the hazards of the storm, then the damage to the dock, caused by the pounding of the boat, was the result of an inevitable accident. If the master was in the exercise of due care, he was not at fault. The reasoning of the opinion admits that if the ropes, or cables, first attached to the dock had not parted, or if, in the first instance, the master had used the stronger cables, there would be no liability. If the master could not, in the exercise of reasonable care, have anticipated the severity of the storm and sought a place of safety before it became impossible, why should he be required to anticipate the severity of the storm, and, in the first instance, use the stronger cables?

I am of the opinion that one who constructs a dock to the navigable line of waters, and enters into contractual relations with the owner of a vessel to moor the same, takes the risk of damage to his dock by a boat caught there by a storm, which event could not have been avoided in the exercise of due care, and further, that the legal status of the parties in such a case is not changed by renewal of cables to keep the boat from being cast adrift at the mercy of the tempest.

JAGGARD, J., concurs.

NOTES

1. *Private Necessity, Assumption of Risk, and Unjust Enrichment.* Under traditional law, *Vincent* represents a case of "conditional" or "incomplete" privilege. The defendant may use or damage the plaintiff's dock, which he could not do deliberately in the absence of necessity, but, in contrast to self-defense, he must pay for the privilege by tendering reasonable rental value or compensation for lost or damaged property. See RST §197. A case of incomplete privilege usually occurs between strangers, but it may also arise where a business invitee or social guest remains on an owner's property, after being asked to leave, to avoid facing the necessity. Does the majority opinion ever come to grips with the dissent's contention that the case turns on how the mooring contract allocated the risk of loss? How does one decide which risks the shipowner assumed when the contract does not expressly cover the problem? Contrast Epstein, A Theory of Strict Liability, 2 J. Legal Stud. 151, 157–60 (1973) (defending *Vincent*), with Weinrib, Causation and Wrongdoing, 63 Chi.-Kent L. Rev. 407, 425–29 (1987) (criticizing it).

Can the outcome in *Vincent* be justified under a theory of "unjust enrichment," which requires the boat owner to compensate the dock owner for the benefit that he received from the use of the dock? How does that theory work if the shipowner's benefit is $10,000, and the harm to the dock $500? When the figures are reversed? When the ship is lost and the dock damaged? See generally, on unjust enrichment, Keeton, Conditional Fault in the Law of Torts, 72 Harv. L. Rev. 401, 410 (1959).

2. *Necessity and Bilateral Monopoly.* The private necessity issue also has an important contractual dimension. Suppose that a vessel in distress at sea seeks to dock where the normal mooring fee is $100. In a world in which prices are determined solely by private agreement, the dock owner may "hold out" for a far larger fee, perhaps one approaching the value of the boat and cargo. If the boat owner complies with the demand, should he be held to the contractual price when the dock owner practiced neither fraud nor duress? The standard response, both in admiralty and at common law, is to void the contract and restrict the dock owner's recovery to a reasonable fee relative to the cost, as adjusted for risk, of the services rendered.

The point has been made most forcefully with contracts for salvage, or rescue at sea by professional salvors. In Post v. Jones, 60 U.S. 150, 159, 160 (1856), the *Richmond*, laden with oil and whalebone, ran aground in heavy fog in the Bering Sea on a barren shore in an area populated by "few inhabitants, savages and thieves." In distress, its master sold at auction about 800 barrels of oil and large quantities of whalebone to the *Elizabeth Frith* and the *Panama*. On their return home, the owners of the oil and whalebone sought to modify the terms of those sales over claims from the respondents that "this sale was a fair, honest, and valid sale of the property." Grier, J. set aside the transaction, writing:

> The contrivance of an auction sale, under such circumstances, where the master of the Richmond was hopeless, helpless, and passive—where there was no market, no money, no competition—where one party had absolute power, and the other no choice but submission—where the vendor must take what is offered or get nothing—is a transaction which has no characteristic of a valid contract. . . .
>
> It has been contended, also, that the sale was justifiable and valid, because it was better for the interests of all concerned to accept what was offered, than suffer a total loss. But this argument proves too much, as it would justify every sale to a salvor. Courts of admiralty will enforce contracts made for salvage service and salvage compensation, where the salvor has not taken advantage of his power to make an unreasonable bargain; but they will not tolerate the doctrine that a salvor can take advantage of his situation, and avail himself of the calamities of others to drive a bargain; nor will they permit the performance of a public duty to be turned into a traffic of profit. The general interests of commerce will be much better promoted by requiring the salvor to trust for compensation to the liberal recompense usually awarded by the courts for such services.

In practice, the holdout problem at sea is often averted by the common practice of referring salvage awards to arbitration, often through Lloyd's of London, where they are resolved in accordance with standard industry practice. Formerly, the salvor's award had been limited to the rescue of hull and cargo. Now that liability for pollution has become a major economic risk, salvage awards specifically include "liability salvage" for preventing spillage, notwithstanding the obvious measurement problems involved. See Brough, Liability Salvage—By Private Ordering, 19 J. Legal Stud. 95 (1990).

3. *Public Necessity.* When are private or government agents privileged to destroy private property to protect the interests of the community at large? The problem has arisen chiefly in two contexts: first, where property is destroyed in order to prevent the destruction of a city by fire and, second, where weapons and facilities are destroyed to keep them from falling into enemy hands in time of war. In Mayor of New York v. Lord, 18 Wend. 126, 129–30 (N.Y. 1837), the court held that it was "well settled" that the privilege was absolute so that

> in cases of actual necessity, to prevent the spreading of a fire, the ravages of a pestilence, the advance of a hostile army, or any other great public calamity, the private property of an individual may be lawfully taken and used or destroyed, for the relief, protection or safety of the many, without subjecting those, whose duty it is to protect the public interests, by or under whose direction such private property was taken or destroyed, to personal liability for the damage which the owner has thereby sustained.

In the words of Bohlen, "since the benefit is solely social, there is no reason why one who acts as a champion of the public should be required to pay for the privilege of so doing." Bohlen, Incomplete Privilege to Inflict Intentional Invasions of Interests of Property and Personality, 39 Harv. L. Rev. 307, 317–18 (1926). Should the person whose property is converted to the public use be required against his will to become the champion of the public?

To understand the scope of the doctrine, it is important to distinguish two types of public necessity cases. In the first, the property destroyed would have been lost anyway. The city fire would have consumed the homes demolished to prevent its spread; the industrial installations that were blown up would have been taken or destroyed by the enemy. In these cases, the plaintiff loses not because the privilege is complete, but because virtually all the loss is caused by a third party.

In the second type of case, the property would *not* have been destroyed without the defendant's intervention. The fire died out before it reached the demolished homes; the enemy was unable to capture the installations. In these cases, the defendant must rest solely on the privilege. The Pennsylvania Supreme Court in Respublica v. Sparhawk, 1 U.S. (1 Dall.) 357, 363 (Pa. 1788), justified the complete privilege for these cases in this way:

> We find, indeed, a memorable instance of folly recorded in the 3 Vol. of Clarendon's History, where it is mentioned, that the Lord Mayor of London, in 1666, when that city was on fire, would not give directions for, or consent to, the pulling down forty wooden houses, or to the removing the furniture, &c. belonging to the Lawyers of the Temple, then on the Circuit, for fear he should be answerable for a trespass; and in consequence of this conduct half that great city was burnt.

Sparhawk reveals the asymmetrical incentives found in all public necessity cases. The public official who wrongly orders the destruction of property bears all the loss if his prediction that the fire will spread proves false but captures none of the gain if correct. Why then should he act at all? As the official cannot recoup his losses from the owners of the saved property, the only way to balance his incentives is to insulate him from liability, at least when he acts reasonably and in good faith. But this approach, taken alone, does not compensate the individual owners who suffer enormous private losses for the benefit of the community at large. Should an aggrieved landowner be allowed an action for restitution against the benefited landowners? From the government? If so, should it pay out of general revenues, or from special assessments levied against the parties benefited? On the general merits of personal and official immunity, see the Symposium, Civil Liability of Government Officials: Property Rights and Official Accountability, 42 Law & Contemp. Probs. 8 (1978).

4. *Public necessity and Just Compensation.* The complete privilege for public necessity is in constant tension with the basic constitutional principle that requires the government to compensate private owners whose property is taken for public use. For a vivid example that tests the line between the two doctrines during wartime, see United States v. Caltex, Inc., 344 U.S. 149 (1952), where the Court (over the dissent of Black and Douglas, JJ.) refused to order compensation for the demolition of an oil company's terminal facilities in Manila before the Japanese takeover. Likewise, in National Board of Y.M.C.A.s v. United States, 395 U.S. 85 (1969), the Court found no compensable taking when U.S. Army troops occupied the plaintiff's buildings located in the Panama Canal Zone after they had been placed under siege by rioting Panamanians who had already caused substantial damage to the structures.

That position has held firm in the years since. In Brewer v. State, 341 P.3d 1107, 1115–16 (Alaska 2014), major forest fires swept through Fairbanks, Alaska, and threatened to burn the structures of several landowners. The Alaskan Forest Service deliberately set backfires that destroyed the landowners' vegetation but saved their structures. The landowners' tort claim was emphatically rejected on statutory grounds that gave the Forest Service immunity "for the purpose of preventing, suppressing, or controlling a wildland fire." The constitutional takings claim was thereafter rejected under the general police power on grounds of necessity, regardless of whether the fires were intended to save the plaintiff's property or other state lands:

> Public necessity acts as a defense to property torts such as trespass and conversion and allows a person to enter land and destroy property where there is "[a] necessity that involves the public interest." Public necessity "completely excuses the defendant's liability." While the privilege of public necessity is an individual one, state officials can exercise it. Thus, the state generally does not have to pay compensation where "the destruction or damage was, or reasonably appeared to be, necessary to prevent an impending or imminent public disaster from fire, flood, disease, or riot."

Should the Forest Service be entitled to send the landowners a bill for their saved properties?

Judith Jarvis Thomson

The Trolley Problem

94 Yale L.J. 1395 (1985)

Some years ago, Philippa Foot drew attention to an extraordinarily interesting problem. Suppose you are the driver of a trolley. The trolley rounds a bend, and there come into view ahead five track workmen, who have been repairing the track. The track goes through a bit of a valley at that point, and the sides are steep, so you must stop the trolley if you are to avoid running the five men down. You step on the brakes, but alas, they don't work. Now you suddenly see a spur of track leading off to the right. You can turn the trolley onto it, and thus save the five men on the straight track ahead. Unfortunately, Mrs. Foot has arranged that there is one track workman on that spur of track. He can no more get off the track in time than the five can, so you will kill him if you turn the trolley onto him. Is it morally permissible for you to turn the trolley?

Everybody to whom I have put this hypothetical case says, Yes, it is. Some people say something stronger than that it is morally *permissible* for you to turn the trolley: They say that morally speaking, you *must* turn it—that morality requires you to do so. Others do not agree that morality requires you to turn the trolley, and even feel a certain discomfort at the idea of turning it. But everybody says that it is true, at a minimum, that you *may* turn it—that it would not be morally wrong for you to do so.

Now consider a second hypothetical case. This time you are to imagine yourself to be a surgeon, a truly great surgeon. Among other things you do, you transplant organs, and you are such a great surgeon that the organs you transplant always take. At the moment you have five patients who need organs. Two need one lung each, two need a kidney each, and the fifth needs a heart. If they do not get those organs today, they will all die; if you find organs for them today you can transplant the organs and they will all live. But where to find the lungs, the kidneys, and the heart? The time is almost up when a report is brought to you that a young man who has just come into your clinic for his yearly check-up has exactly the right blood type, and is in excellent health. Lo, you have your possible donor. All you need to do is cut him up and distribute *his* parts among the five who need them. You ask, but he says, "Sorry. I deeply sympathize, but no." Would it be morally permissible for you to operate anyway? Everybody to whom I have put this second hypothetical says, No, it would not be morally permissible for you to proceed.

Here then is Mrs. Foot's problem: *Why* is it that the trolley driver may turn his trolley, but the surgeon may not remove the young man's lungs, kidneys, and heart? In both cases, one will die if the agent acts, but five will live who would otherwise die—net saving of four lives. What difference in the other facts of these cases explains the moral difference between them? I fancy that the theorists of tort and criminal law will find this problem as interesting as the moral theorist does.

NOTE

Moral and Legal Theories. Having restated Professor Foot's problem, Professor Thomson then explores some possible responses. If, morally speaking, it is worse to kill than to let die, the surgeon should not act while the trolley driver can turn the wheel because his only choice is between killing one and killing five. But suppose, as Thomson next suggests, a bystander is able to throw a switch that will divert the trolley from its original track, but can choose to do nothing, in which case the trolley will kill five. Is the bystander not justified in doing what the trolley driver may do?

Note that one difference between the two cases rests on the observation that the crisis "suddenly" struck the driver, but not the surgeon. Accordingly, an alternative approach shifts attention to the long-term incentive effects of adopting one rule or the other. So long as the trolley driver is held responsible whether he kills one or five, he faces two separate incentives: The first, which is the subject of the Thomson inquiry, is to minimize the number of deaths *once* the emergency occurs. The second is to check the brakes to prevent the emergency from arising in the first place—an incentive that remains in place so long as the liability rule holds the driver responsible in tort for whatever harm he causes. Quite simply, we should expect fewer brake failures.

The effects on the famous surgeon in the prior period, however, are quite different, for she will never be able to attract patients in the first place if she is intent on cutting them up to help others. Over the long haul, it might be possible to organize a voluntary market for the sale of organs either during life or after death, which does not have the downside of coerced transfers. Yet while organ donations are legal today, their sale is flatly prohibited by federal law. See National Organ Transplant Act (NOTA) §301, 42 U.S.C. §274e (2023), which prohibits the payment or receipt of "valuable consideration," in either cash or kind, in exchange for organs used for human transplantation. For a trenchant critique, see Cohen, Increasing the Supply of Transplant Organs: The Virtues of a Futures Market, 58 Geo. Wash. L. Rev. 1 (1989). The case for a regulated market in organ transplants is made by Williams, Finley &

Rohack, Just Say No to NOTA: Why the Prohibition of Compensation for Human Transplant Organs in NOTA Should Be Repealed and a Regulated Market for Cadaver Organs Instituted, 40 Am. J.L. & Med. 275 (2014). As of June 2023, there were about 106,000 people on the waiting list for an organ, of which about 92,000 (87%) were waiting for kidneys, typically for between three and five years. For continuously updated numbers, see https://www.kidneyfund.org/kidney-donation-and-transplant/transplant-waiting-list. What about a voluntary market especially for kidneys?

SECTION C. EMOTIONAL AND DIGNITARY HARMS

1. Assault

I. de S. and Wife v. W. de S.

At the Assizes, coram Thorpe, C.J., 1348 [or 1349] Year Book, Liber Assisarum, folio 99, placitum 60

I. de S. & M. uxor ejus querunt de W. de S. de eo quod idem W. anno, & c., vi et armis, & c., apud S., in ipsam M. insultum fecit, et ipsam verberavit, & c. [I. de S. and his wife, M., sue W. de S. concerning that which in the year, etc., by force and arms, etc., at S. has made insults of the aforesaid M., and has beat her.] And W. pleaded not guilty. And it was found by verdict of the inquest that the said W. came in the night to the house of the said I., and would have bought some wine, but the door of the tavern was closed; and he struck on the door with a hatchet, which he had in his hand, and the woman plaintiff put her head out at a window and ordered him to stop; and he perceived her and struck with the hatchet, but did not touch the woman. Whereupon the inquest said that it seemed to them that there was no trespass, since there was no harm done.

THORPE, C.J. There is harm, and a trespass for which they shall recover damages, since he made an assault upon the woman, as it is found, although he did no other harm. Wherefore tax his damages, & c. And they taxed the damages at half a mark.

THORPE, C.J., awarded that they should recover their damages, & c., and that the other should be taken. Et sic nota, [And thus it was noted] that for an assault one shall recover damages, & c.

Tuberville v. Savage

(1669) 86 Eng. Rep. 684 (KB)

Action of *assault, battery*, and *wounding*. The evidence to prove a provocation was, that the plaintiff put his hand upon his sword and said, "If *it were not assize-time [i.e., if the judge were not in town], I would not take such language from you.*"—The question was, If that were an assault?—The Court agreed that it was not; for the declaration of the plaintiff was, that he would not assault him, the Judges being in town; and *the intention* as well as *the act* makes an assault. Therefore if one strike another upon the hand, or arm, or breast in discourse, it is no assault, there being no *intention* to assault; but if one intending to assault, strike *at* another and miss him, this is an assault: so if he hold up his hand against another in a threatening manner and say nothing, it is an assault.—In the principal case the plaintiff had judgment.

Exhibit 1.3 Sir William Blackstone

Sir William Blackstone (1723–1780), English jurist and judge, is best known as the author of the Commentaries on the Laws of England, a four-volume treatise that chronicled the state of English law in the eighteenth century. Soon after its publication, the Commentaries became the basis of legal education in England and the United States and continue to be cited by courts to this day. Orphaned by age 12, Blackstone was educated by his uncle, and then at Oxford, where he read classics, logic, and mathematics. He later became a student at Middle Temple, one of the Inns of Court, and was a barrister by 1746. After seven years of practice, he began to concentrate on teaching law, and his lectures on the common law were the first on English law ever delivered in a university. Blackstone combined his academic career with an active public life, which included membership in Parliament, the House of Commons, and a judgeship on the Court of Common Pleas.

Bio source: William Blackstone, *Encyclopaedia Britannica, http://www.britannica.com/biography/William-Blackstone Image source: Wikimedia Commons*

William Blackstone

Commentaries

Vol. 3, p. 120 (1765)

[A]ssault [is] an attempt or offer to beat another, without touching him: as if one lifts up his cane, or his fist, in a threatening manner at another; or strikes at him, but misses him; this is an assault, insultus, which Finch describes to be "an unlawful setting upon one's person." This also is an inchoate violence, amounting considerably higher than bare threats; and therefore, though no actual suffering is proved, yet the party injured may have redress by action of trespass vi et armis [trespass by force and arms]; wherein he shall recover damages as compensation for the injury.

NOTES

1. *The Social Protection Against Assaults.* Does *I. de S.* give uniform protection against mental distress from the threat of assault? Should the defendant be liable for assault when he first struck the door with the hatchet if he knew that the plaintiff was inside? If he thought there was a good chance she was inside? If he thought that she was not inside? Should it matter that the defendant struck the second blow—where? why? how?—only after he "perceived" the plaintiff?

The dangers to the social fabric from threats of force were forcefully stated in Allen v. Hannaford, 244 P. 700, 701 (Wash. 1926). The plaintiff had hired moving men to take her furniture from an apartment she had rented from the defendant. The defendant had placed a lien on the plaintiff's furniture (which gave her the right to seize the furniture, sell it, and apply the proceeds to unpaid back rent). When the defendant discovered that the plaintiff's furniture was being removed, she appeared with a pistol and threatened to shoot the moving men "full of holes" if they took so much as a single piece. Then, "standing only a few feet from [plaintiff], she pointed the pistol at her face and threatened to shoot her." The court rejected the defendant's argument that she could not be guilty of an assault for brandishing an unloaded gun, saying "[w]hether there is an assault in a given case depends more upon the apprehensions created in the mind of the person assaulted than upon what may be the secret intentions of the person committing the assault." The court then affirmed the $750 verdict for the plaintiff (about $13,000 in 2023 dollars), quoting the observations from Beach v. Hancock, 27 N.H. 223 (1853):

> One of the most important objects to be attained by the enactment of laws and the institutions of civilized society is, each of us shall feel secure against unlawful assaults. Without such security society loses most of its value. Peace and order and domestic happiness, inexpressibly more precious than mere forms of government, cannot be enjoyed without the sense of perfect security. We have a right to live in society without being put in fear of personal harm. But it must be a reasonable fear of which we complain. And it surely is not unreasonable for a person to entertain a fear of personal injury, when a pistol is pointed at him in a threatening manner, when, for aught he knows, it may be loaded, and may occasion his immediate death. The business of the world could not be carried on with comfort, if such things could be done with impunity.

If the gun was not pointed toward the plaintiff, did the defendant only make, to use Blackstone's distinction, a "mere threat," or did she commit an act of "inchoate violence"? Is there an assault if the plaintiff knows that the defendant is wielding an unloaded gun?

2. *Mere Words, Conditional Threats, and the Use of Force.* The time-honored common law maxim—"mere words do not amount to an assault"—applies to strong words used during argument. It has been criticized for overlooking the subtle (and not-so-subtle) ways the voice alone can convey threats of the immediate or future use of force. Undoubtedly, this formula is meant to preclude liability in common situations in which intemperate or insulting speech injures feelings or arouses apprehension. In Tuberville v. Savage, why did the court assume that the plaintiff's words gave an accurate rendering of his intention, instead of being a ruse to catch the defendant off guard? What result if it had not been "assize-time," and the plaintiff had said, "If it were not for my generous nature, I would not take such language from you"?

RESTATEMENT OF THE LAW (THIRD) OF TORTS: INTENTIONAL TORTS TO PERSONS (TENTATIVE DRAFT, APPROVED 2019)

§5. Assault

An actor is subject to liability to another for assault if:

(a) (i) the actor intends to cause the other to anticipate an imminent, and harmful or offensive, contact with his or her own person, or

(ii) the actor's intent is sufficient under §11 (transferred intent);

(b) the actor's affirmative conduct causes the other to anticipate an imminent, and harmful or offensive, contact with his or her person.

Does this section provide an adequate summary of the cases discussed? Should cases of harmful and offensive behavior be treated in the same way? If not, should the difference arise from the substantive rules or from the appropriate measure of damages?

Note that RST §21 held that tort law covered any case in which a victim was put in "imminent apprehension" of harm. It then explained the situation as follows:

RESTATEMENT OF THE LAW (SECOND) OF TORTS

§24. What Constitutes Apprehension

In order that the other may be put in the apprehension necessary to make the actor liable for an assault, the other must believe that the act may result in imminent contact unless prevented from so resulting by the other's self-defensive action or by his flight or by the intervention of some outside force.

Comment b. Distinction between apprehension and fright: It is not necessary that the other believe that the act done by the actor will be effective in inflicting the intended contact upon him. It is enough that he believes that the act is capable of immediately inflicting the contact upon him unless something further occurs. Therefore, the mere fact that he can easily prevent the threatened contact by self-defensive measures which he feels amply capable of taking does not prevent the actor's attempt to inflict the contact upon him from being an actionable assault. So too, he may have every reason to believe that bystanders will interfere in time to prevent the blow threatened by the actor from taking effect and his belief may be justified by the event. Bystanders may intervene and prevent the actor from striking him. Nonetheless, the actor's blow thus prevented from taking effect is an actionable assault. The apprehension which is sufficient to make the actor liable may have no relation to fear, which at least implies a doubt as to whether the actor's attempt is capable of certain frustration.

How do these various formulations play out when the claim for assault is brought for threats that the defendant makes at a distance from the plaintiff? In Brower v. Ackerley, 943 P.2d 1141, 1145 (Wash. Ct. App. 1997), the defendants ran a billboard advertising business. The plaintiff, who was active in civic affairs, reported to the Seattle City Council that many of the defendants' billboards were operated without permits and were kept off the tax rolls. When the City did not respond, the plaintiff filed a separate lawsuit against both it and the defendants. Two days later, an anonymous male caller began a campaign of telephone harassment against the plaintiff, which included calling him a "dick" and saying, "I'm going to find out where you live and I am going to kick your ass." After the calls were traced to one of the Ackerleys' sons, the action for assault ensued, in which the plaintiff argued that even though mere words do not constitute an assault, these "spoken threats became assaultive in view of the surrounding circumstances including the fact that the calls were made to his home, at night, creating the impression that the caller was stalking him." But the court denied the action, noting the absence of an immediate threat. Which matters more, the directness of the threat or the probability that it will be carried out?

2. Offensive Battery

Alcorn v. Mitchell

63 Ill. 553 (1872)

Sheldon, J. The ground mainly relied on for the reversal of the judgment in this case is, that the damages are excessive, being $1000.

The case presented is this: There was a trial of an action of trespass between the parties, wherein the appellee was defendant, in the circuit court of Jasper county. At the close of the trial the court adjourned, and, immediately upon the adjournment, in the court room, in the presence of a large number of persons, the appellant deliberately spat in the face of the appellee.

So long as damages are allowable in any civil case, by way of punishment or for the sake of example, the present, of all cases, would seem to be a most fit one for the award of such damages.

The act in question was one of the greatest indignity, highly provocative of retaliation by force, and the law, as far as it may, should afford substantial protection against such outrages, in the way of liberal damages, that the public tranquility may be preserved by saving the necessity of resort to personal violence as the only means of redress.

Suitors, in the assertion of their rights, should be allowed approach to the temple of justice without incurring there exposure to such disgraceful indignities, in the very presence of its ministers.

It is customary to instruct juries that they may give vindictive damages where there are circumstances of malice, wilfulness, wantonness, outrage and indignity attending the wrong complained of. The act in question was wholly made up of such qualities. It was one of pure malignity, done for the mere purpose of insult and indignity.

An exasperated suitor has indulged the gratification of his malignant feelings in this despicable mode. The act was the very refinement of malice. The defendant appears to be a man of wealth; we can not say that he has been made to pay too dearly for the indulgence. . . .

The judgment must be affirmed.

NOTE

Basis of Liability for Offensive Battery. What result in Alcorn v. Mitchell if the appellee spat at the appellant but missed? Does it make a difference whether the appellant knew that the appellee spat at him? RST §18 (not updated as of yet in RTT: IT) takes the position that if there is an intention to either inflict harm or offense, an offensive battery is committed even if no harm results. It also concludes that a defendant is not liable "for a mere offensive contact with the other's person although the act involves an unreasonable risk of inflicting it and, therefore, would be negligent or reckless if the risk threatened bodily harm." Should liability be allowed in these cases if the plaintiff perceived the action as one that carried a threat of physical harm?

There are many reported cases of nonharmful offensive batteries. In Respublica v. De Longchamps, 1 U.S. (1 Dall.) 111, 114 (Pa. 1784), defendant struck the cane of the French ambassador and was prosecuted under the law of nations. The court remarked:

> As to the assault, this is, perhaps, one of that kind, in which the insult is more to be considered than the actual damage; for, though no great bodily pain is suffered by a blow on the palm of the hand, or the skirt of the coat, yet these are clearly within the definition of assault and battery, and among gentlemen too often induce duelling and terminate in murder.

The protection afforded against offensive battery covers not only cases of direct contact with the plaintiff's person, but also contact with "anything so closely attached [to the plaintiff's person] that it is customarily regarded as a part thereof and which is offensive to a reasonable sense of personal dignity." RST §18, comment *c.* An example is the striking of the plaintiff's cane in the *Longchamps* case, *supra*; for other such acts, see Clark v. Downing, 55 Vt. 259 (1882) (striking the horse that plaintiff was riding); Fisher v. Carrousel Motor Hotel, Inc., 424 S.W.2d 627 (Tex. 1967) (grabbing at plaintiff's plate); and Reynolds v. MacFarlane, 322 P.3d 755 (Utah 2014) (taking ten-dollar bill loosely held by plaintiff employee).

3. False Imprisonment

Coblyn v. Kennedy's, Inc.
268 N.E.2d 860 (Mass. 1971)

[The plaintiff, a seventy-year-old man, five feet four inches tall and dressed in a woolen shirt, topcoat, and hat, was shopping in the defendant's store. Around his neck the plaintiff wore an ascot he had previously purchased in Filene's, another department store. While trying on a sportscoat, the plaintiff took off his ascot and put it into his pocket. He purchased the coat, left it for alterations, and, as he was leaving the store, took the ascot out of his pocket and put it on again. At that moment the defendant Goss, an employee of Kennedy's, "loomed up" in front of the plaintiff and demanded that he stop and explain where he had gotten the ascot. As approximately eight to ten people looked on, the plaintiff agreed to return with Goss to the store. On the way up the stairs, the plaintiff experienced chest and back pains and had to stop several times. When they reached the second floor, the salesman who had sold the plaintiff the sportscoat told Goss that the ascot was indeed the plaintiff's. The plaintiff was so upset by the incident that he required the attention of the store's nurse and was consequently hospitalized and treated for a "myocardial infarct." The jury awarded the plaintiff $12,500 for false imprisonment. The defendant appealed.]

SPIEGEL, J. Initially, the defendants contend that as a matter of law the plaintiff was not falsely imprisoned. They argue that no unlawful restraint was imposed by either force or threat upon the plaintiff's freedom of movement. However, "[t]he law is well settled that '[a]ny general restraint is sufficient to constitute an imprisonment . . . ' and '[a]ny demonstration of physical power which, to all appearances, can be avoided only by submission, operates as effectually to constitute an imprisonment, if submitted to, as if any amount of force had been exercised.' 'If a man is restrained of his personal liberty by fear of a personal difficulty, that amounts to a false imprisonment' within the legal meaning of such term."

We think it is clear that there was sufficient evidence of unlawful restraint to submit this question to the jury. Just as the plaintiff had stepped out of the door of the store, the defendant Goss stopped him, firmly grasped his arm and told him that he had "better go back and see the manager." There was another employee at his side. The plaintiff was an elderly man and there were other people standing around staring at him. Considering the plaintiff's age and his heart condition, it is hardly to be expected that with one employee in front of him firmly grasping his arm and another at his side the plaintiff could do other than comply with Goss's "request" that he go back and see the manager. . . .

The defendants next contend that the detention of the plaintiff was sanctioned by G. L. c. 231, §94B, inserted by St. 1958, c. 337. This statute provides as follows:

> In an action for false arrest or false imprisonment brought by any person by reason of having been detained for questioning on or in the immediate vicinity of the premises of a merchant, if such person was detained in a reasonable manner and for not more than a reasonable length of time by a person authorized to make arrests or by the merchant or his agent or servant authorized for such purpose and if there were reasonable grounds to believe that the person so detained was committing or attempting to commit larceny of goods for sale on such premises, it shall be a defence to such action. If such goods had not been purchased and were concealed on or amongst the belongings of a person so detained it shall be presumed that there were reasonable grounds for such belief.

The defendants argue in accordance with the conditions imposed in the statute that the plaintiff was detained in a reasonable manner for a reasonable length of time and that Goss had reasonable grounds for believing that the plaintiff was attempting to commit larceny of goods held for sale.

It is conceded that the detention was for a reasonable length of time. We need not decide whether the detention was effected in a reasonable manner for we are of opinion that there were no reasonable grounds for believing that the plaintiff was committing larceny and, therefore, he should not have been detained at all. However, we observe that Goss's failure to identify himself as an employee of Kennedy's and to disclose the reasons for his inquiry and actions, coupled with the physical restraint in a public place imposed upon the plaintiff, an elderly man, who had exhibited no aggressive intention to depart, could be said to constitute an unreasonable method by which to effect detention. . . .

The defendants assert that the judge improperly instructed the jury in stating that "grounds are reasonable when there is a basis which would appear to the reasonably prudent, cautious, intelligent person." In their brief, they argue that the "prudent and cautious man rule" is an objective standard and requires a more rigorous and restrictive standard of conduct than is contemplated by G. L. c. 231, §94B. The defendants' requests for instructions, in effect, state that the proper test is a subjective one, viz., whether the defendant Goss had an honest and strong suspicion that the plaintiff was committing or attempting to commit larceny. . . .

If we adopt the subjective test as suggested by the defendants, the individual's right to liberty and freedom of movement would become subject to the "honest . . . suspicion" of a shopkeeper based on his own "inarticulate hunches" without regard to any discernible facts. In effect, the result would be to afford the merchant even greater authority than that given to a police officer. In view of the well established meaning of the words "reasonable grounds" we believe that the Legislature intended to give these words their traditional meaning. This seems to us a valid conclusion since the Legislature has permitted an individual to be detained for a "reasonable length of time."

We also note that an objective standard is the criterion for determining probable cause or reasonable grounds in malicious prosecution and false arrest cases. . . .

Exceptions overruled.

NOTES

1. ***Origins of False Imprisonment.*** In Bird v. Jones, (1845) 115 Eng. Rep. 688 (KB), the plaintiff desired to make his way down a public street in order to watch a boat race, for which customers had paid for their seats. The defendant blocked his passage but allowed him to retreat in the direction from which he had come. Coleridge, J., held that so long as the plaintiff was free to go false imprisonment could not be brought, even if the plaintiff could sue under a different writ for the interference with his right of way.

> Some confusion seems to me to arise from confounding imprisonment of the body with mere loss of freedom: it is one part of the definition of freedom to be able to go whithersoever one pleases; but imprisonment is something more than the mere loss of this power; it includes the notion of restraint within some limits defined by a will or power exterior to our own.

Lord Denman, C.J., dissented:

> As long as I am prevented from doing what I have a right to do, of what importance is it that I am permitted to do something else? How does the imposition of an unlawful condition show that I am not restrained? If I am locked in a room, am I not imprisoned because I might effect my escape

through a window, or because I might find an exit dangerous or inconvenient to myself, as by wading through water or by taking a route so circuitous that my necessary affairs would suffer by delay?

He then reverted to the procedural issue: "Must I then sue out a new writ stating that the defendant employed direct force to prevent my going where my business called me, whereby I sustained loss?"

The same theme of partial restriction was evident in Whittaker v. Sandford, 85 A. 399, 403 (Me. 1912), where a woman was given complete freedom of movement on the defendant's palatial yacht, but when she was occasionally allowed on shore, she was not given liberty to roam or to remain there. She was held to have been imprisoned while on the yacht so long as she was denied access to shore by a boat, but damages were reduced to take into account her relative freedom of movement.

RTT: IT covers false imprisonment in §8, where it again makes confinement the centerpiece of the tort. It also makes clear that the defendant is liable for confinement if he "fails to release the other from a confinement despite having a duty to do so." Section 8 places minimal limits on the scope of confinement, as addressed in comment *c*, which reads:

The physical scope of confinement in most cases is relatively small—a room, a house, a prison cell, a moving automobile, a mental institution. But confinement even within a substantial area, such as a city, sufficiently interferes with the other's freedom of movement to warrant liability. Liability should be denied only when the area of confinement is so large that the interference with the other's freedom is de minimis. For example, a court might conclude that confinement within a state is actionable, while confinement within the United States is not. Similarly, it might conclude that a lengthy confinement within a state is actionable, but a brief confinement within a state is not. The area in which a plaintiff is confined need not be stationary. For example, confinement in a moving car or boat is legally sufficient.

2. *Retail Theft.* In cases of false arrest, why should an innocent patron bear the costs of the merchant's *reasonable* mistakes? These shoplifting cases continue to make their way into court with startling regularity, where the pattern is usually similar to that found in *Coblyn*: Customer returns to a shop to exchange goods and is seen leaving without paying for the replacement goods, e.g., Forgie-Buccioni v. Hannaford Bros., Inc., 413 F.3d 175 (1st Cir. 2005), or, owing to a medical condition, engages in odd conduct that excites suspicion, e.g., Dolgencorp, Inc. v. Pounders, 912 So. 2d 523 (Ala. Civ. App. 2005).

In Dill v. Kroger Ltd. P'ship I, 860 S.E.2d 372, 381 (Va. 2021), a grocery store manager observed a customer stealing strawberries and mistook her for the plaintiff, at which point she reported the plaintiff to the police. After the shoplifting charges against the plaintiff were dismissed, the plaintiff sued the grocery store for false imprisonment. Goodwyn, J., upheld dismissal of the plaintiff's tort claim on the ground that the defendants, though mistaken, did not resort to self-help but rather availed themselves of legal process: "Even if the actions of Kroger and Lynch were malicious, and their allegations were not supported by probable cause, Dill's arrest was lawful because it was a consequence of proper legal process." What burden of due diligence should stores have before reporting individuals to the police?

In Zavala v. Wal-Mart, 691 F.3d 527, 545–47 (3d Cir. 2012), the plaintiffs alleged that their minimal command of English made it hard for them to understand that they had been asked to leave the defendant's stores. The court awarded the defendant summary judgment on evidence that the store's doors were locked for security purposes to protect staff and merchandise, that the store had accessible emergency exits that met state and federal law standards, and that managers were "often available to open locked doors." "[F]alse imprisonment cannot occur where there is a safe alternative exit." Could there be occasional instances of false imprisonment given that managers are not always available? Are those claims tenable in a class action context?

3. *Justification for Imprisonment.* Other false imprisonment cases raise the more difficult question whether the defendant's actions are justified as necessary to protect the defendant's person and property, even when the plaintiff suffers serious harm. In Sindle v. New York City Transit Authority, 307 N.E.2d 245, 248 (N.Y. 1973), the defendant operated a school bus carrying between 65 and 70 junior high school students, including the plaintiff. Some of the other students became rowdy, committed acts of vandalism, and remained abusive even when warned by the driver. The driver abandoned his ordinary route, passed several stops, and drove to the police station. On the way, the plaintiff, who had not behaved improperly, jumped out of a side window, only to be run over by the bus's back wheels. The plaintiff abandoned his action for negligence (why?) and pitched the case solely on false imprisonment. The trial judge refused to allow the defendants to introduce any evidence that the imprisonment was reasonable, both in time and manner. The Court of Appeals reversed:

> In view of our determination, it would be well to outline some of the considerations relevant to the issue of justification. In this regard, we note that, generally, restraint or detention, reasonable under the circumstances and in time and manner, imposed for the purpose of preventing another from inflicting personal injuries or interfering with or damaging real or personal property in one's lawful possession or custody is not unlawful. . . . Also, a parent, guardian or teacher entrusted with the care or supervision of a child may use physical force reasonably necessary to maintain discipline or promote the welfare of the child. (Penal Law, §35.10).
>
> Similarly, a school bus driver, entrusted with the care of his student-passengers and the custody of public property, has the duty to take reasonable measures for the safety and protection of both—the passengers and the property. In this regard, the reasonableness of his actions—as bearing on the defense of justification—is to be determined from a consideration of all the circumstances. At a minimum, this would seem to import, a consideration of the need to protect the persons and property in his charge, the duty to aid the investigation and apprehension of those inflicting damage, the manner and place of the occurrence, and the feasibility and practicality of other alternative courses of action.

4. *Consent.* Consent is another defense to an action for false imprisonment. The RTT: IT §7, comment *k*, holds that "apparent consent also precludes liability for false imprisonment. Thus if an actor reasonably believes that a plaintiff actually consents to a confinement, the actor is not liable, even if the plaintiff does not consent."

The RTT: IT also notes that in cases of actual consent, "fact sensitive inquir[ies]" can arise as to whether the defendant's conduct exceeds the scope of the consent given. Such problems may be difficult to resolve when the plaintiff seeks to retract the consent to confinement that was previously given. In Herd v. Weardale Steel, Coal & Coke Co., [1915] AC 67, the plaintiff, a miner, entered the defendant's mine for a shift that normally ended at 4:00 P.M. At 11:00 A.M. plaintiff, with 29 coworkers, asked to be taken to the surface, claiming that unsafe working conditions violated his employment contract and the applicable statutory provisions. An empty elevator was available to take the men up at 1:00 P.M., but was not offered to them until 1:30 P.M. The House of Lords found that the 30-minute delay did not constitute false imprisonment. Haldane, L.C., said:

> The man chose to go to the bottom of the mine under these conditions,—conditions which he accepted. He had no right to call upon the employers to make use of special machinery put there at their cost, and involving cost in its working, to bring him to the surface just when he pleased.

Was there a false imprisonment if the plaintiff had a legitimate safety grievance? What if the delay was not 30 minutes, but until the end of the plaintiff's shift?

Questions of false imprisonment have also arisen when passengers sue for improper confinement when kept on a plane during lengthy delays before takeoff. These cases usually fail for one of two reasons. In Ray v. American Airlines, 609 F.3d 917 (8th Cir. 2010), the defendants were exonerated from liability when they twice offered passengers the opportunity to leave the plane during a nine-hour delay. In Abourezk v. New York Airlines, 895 F.2d 1456 (D.C. Cir. 1990), the plaintiff could not sue for a three-hour confinement because of the absence of exigent circumstances involving matters of either a medical or security risk.

4. The Intentional Infliction of Emotional Distress: Extreme and Outrageous Conduct

Wilkinson v. Downton

[1897] 2 QB 57

[The facts are set forth in the court's opinion. The jury gave a verdict of £100 1*s.* 10½*d.* for transportation money given by the plaintiff to friends to fetch her husband home and £100 for injuries caused by nervous shock. The defendant contended that no recovery should be allowed for the damage caused by nervous shock.]

Wright, J. In this case the defendant, in the execution of what he seems to have regarded as a practical joke, represented to the plaintiff that he was charged by her husband with a message to her to the effect that her husband was smashed up in an accident, and was lying at The Elms at Leytonstone with both legs broken, and that she was to go at once in a cab with two pillows to fetch him home. All this was false. The effect of the statement on the plaintiff was a violent shock to her nervous system, producing vomiting and other more serious and permanent physical consequences at one time threatening her reason, and entailing weeks of suffering and incapacity to her as well as expense to her husband for medical attendance. These consequences were not in any way the result of previous ill-health or weakness of constitution; nor was there any evidence of predisposition to nervous shock or any other idiosyncrasy. . . .

[The court then states that while the 1*s.* 10*d.* is recoverable in fraud and deceit, £100 for mental distress is not "parasitic" upon that action.]

I think, however, that the verdict may be supported upon another ground. The defendant has, as I assume for the moment, wilfully done an act calculated to cause physical harm to the plaintiff—that is to say, to infringe her legal right to personal safety, and has in fact thereby caused physical harm to her. That proposition without more appears to me to state a good cause of action, there being no justification alleged for the act. This wilful injuria is in law malicious, although no malicious purpose to cause the harm which was caused nor any motive of spite is imputed to the defendant.

It remains to consider whether the assumptions involved in the proposition are made out. One question is whether the defendant's act was so plainly calculated to produce some effect of the kind which was produced that an intention to produce it ought to be imputed to the defendant, regard being had to the fact that the effect was produced on a person proved to be in an ordinary state of health and mind. I think that it was. It is difficult to imagine that such a statement, made suddenly and with apparent seriousness, could fail to produce grave effects under the circumstances upon any but an exceptionally indifferent person, and therefore an intention to produce such an effect must be imputed, and it is no answer in law to say that more harm was done than was anticipated, for that is commonly the case with all wrongs. The other question is whether the effect was, to use the ordinary phrase, too remote to be in law regarded as a consequence for which the defendant is answerable. Apart from authority, I should give the same answer and on the same ground as the last question, and say that it was not too remote. . . .

Suppose that a person is in a precarious and dangerous condition, and another person tells him that his physician has said that he has but a day to live. In such a case, if death ensued from the shock caused by the false statement, I cannot doubt that at this day the case might be one of criminal homicide, or that if a serious aggravation of illness ensued damages might be recovered. I think, however, that it must be admitted that the present case is without precedent. . . .

There must be judgment for plaintiff for £100 1*s.* 10½*d.*

NOTES

1. *Nervous Shock and Parasitic Damages.* Note that *Wilkinson* does not involve any form or threat of physical contact and thus does not fall within the Restatement definitions of either assault or battery. Should that make a difference? Why does Wright, J., treat this case as one of physical damages when there has been no physical invasion?

With *Wilkinson*, contrast Bouillon v. Laclede Gaslight Co., 129 S.W. 401, 402 (Mo. Ct. App. 1910). The defendant's meter reader tried to force his way in through the front door of the plaintiff's apartment while the plaintiff was pregnant and at risk for a miscarriage. He had several nasty exchanges with the plaintiff's nurse that the plaintiff overheard through the open front door, which also let in the cold air. That evening the plaintiff suffered chills, and the next day had a miscarriage that her physician attributed to the events of the prior day. The plaintiff was sick for an extended period of time after the incident and suffered permanent impairments to her health. Nortoni, J., allowed the plaintiff's cause of action.

> No one can doubt that the case fails to disclose an assault on plaintiff as the controversy was principally had with, and all the insulting language directed against, another, the nurse. However this may be, the facts reveal a valid ground of liability on the score of trespass, and this is true notwithstanding the damages laid are not for the commission of the initial act of trespass, but relate instead to its consequence alone. Although defendant's agent had a right to enter the basement beneath plaintiff's apartment for the purpose of reading the gas meter, it is entirely clear that he had no authority to enter or pass through plaintiff's flat for that purpose. She was not a consumer of gas and the gas meter was in no sense connected with her household. Plaintiff is assured peaceful repose of her home against unwarranted intrusion from others. A trespasser is liable to respond in damages for such injuries as may result naturally, necessarily, directly, and proximately in consequence of his wrong. This is true for the reason the original act involved in the trespass is unlawful. . . . The doctrine is that though a mere mental disturbance of itself may not be a cause of action in the first instance, fright and mental anguish are competent elements of damage if they arise out of a trespass upon the plaintiff's person or possession and may be included in a suit for the trespass if plaintiff chooses so to do, or, if a physical injury results from such fright, a cause of action accrues from the trespass for compensation as to the physical injury and its consequences alone, which may be pursued even though plaintiff seeks no compensation for the original wrong.

In both *Wilkinson* and *Bouillon*, the defendant committed independent torts, namely, deceit and trespass. Is there any need for a new independent tort when emotional damages are typically "parasitic" on an existing wrong? In 1 Street, Foundations of Legal Liability 466, 470 (1906), the author, in commenting on legal protections against mental distress, observes that "[a] factor which is today recognized as parasitic will, forsooth, tomorrow be recognized as an independent basis of liability."

2. *The Birth of Intentional Infliction of Emotional Distress.* The Restatement formulation of liability turns solely on the defendant's course of conduct, without proof of any other tort such as trespass or deceit. Review the provision that follows.

Exhibit 1.4 William Prosser

Source: Law School Archives, University of California, Berkeley

William Prosser (1898–1972): As Kenneth Abraham and G. Edward White point out in Prosser and His Influence, 6 J. Tort L. 27, 28 (2013), William Prosser, in his Handbook on Torts, "discover[ed] the ['new'] tort[] of Intentional Infliction of Emotional Distress." He did so by "identifying the principles that he sees as linking the cases together" in a not previously understood way. *Id.* at 49–50. When his initial Handbook was published in 1941, Prosser observed that "in recent years the courts have tended to recognize the intentional causing of mental or emotional disturbance as a tort." *Id.* at 51–52. He acknowledged that the law in this area was "in a process of growth," given "tort law's traditional reluctance to redress mental injuries [on account of] difficulties of proof, the evanescence of mental consequences, and the risk of fictitious claims. *Id.* at 52. After an ostensible assessment of the relatively minimal case law in this "growing" field, Prosser concludes that ". . . the rule that seems to be emerging is that there is liability only for conduct exceeding all bounds usually tolerated by society, of a nature which is especially calculated to cause and does cause mental damage of a very serious kind." *Id.* at 54.

RESTATEMENT OF THE LAW (THIRD) OF TORTS: LIABILITY FOR PHYSICAL AND EMOTIONAL HARM

§46. Intentional (or Reckless) Infliction of Emotional Harm

An actor who by extreme and outrageous conduct intentionally or recklessly causes severe emotional harm to another is subject to liability for that emotional harm and, if the emotional harm causes bodily harm, also for the bodily harm.

Comment d. Extreme and outrageous conduct: To be held liable under this Section, an actor must do more than intentionally or recklessly cause emotional harm. The actor must act in a way that is extreme and outrageous. . . . The adjectives "extreme" and "outrageous" are used together in a fashion that might suggest that each merely emphasizes the other, rather than serving a distinct role. However, some conduct that may be outrageous—for example, marital infidelity—is sufficiently common that it could not be characterized as extreme (although today it may also not be outrageous). Similarly, some extreme conduct—climbing Mt. Everest, for example—is not outrageous. Thus, this double limitation, "extreme and outrageous," requires both that the character of the conduct be outrageous and that the conduct be sufficiently unusual to be extreme. . . .

[A]s a matter of policy, even if emotional harm is inflicted for no purpose other than to cause such harm, some degree of emotional harm must be expected in social interaction and tolerated without legal recourse. Under the "extreme and outrageous" requirement, an actor is liable only if the conduct goes beyond the bounds of human decency such that it would be regarded as intolerable in a civilized community. Ordinary insults and indignities are not enough for liability to be imposed, even if the actor desires to cause emotional harm.

Whether an actor's conduct is extreme and outrageous depends on the facts of each case, including the relationship of the parties, whether the actor abused a position of authority over the other person, whether the other person was especially vulnerable and the actor knew of the vulnerability, the motivation of the actor, and whether the conduct was repeated or prolonged. . . .

a. ***Strong-Arm Tactics.*** In State Rubbish Collectors Ass'n v. Siliznoff, 240 P.2d 282, 284–85 (Cal. 1952), the Acme Brewing Company switched its account for the collection of garbage from Abramoff to Kosoff, who in turn assigned the account to Siliznoff. At a stormy meeting representatives of the State Rubbish Collectors Association threatened to beat up Siliznoff, destroy his property, and put him out of business unless he agreed to pay the association part of the proceeds from the Acme account. Siliznoff then promised to pay Abramoff $1,850 for the contract and gave the association a series of notes for that sum.

The association sued on the notes a year later. Siliznoff demanded that the notes be canceled because of duress and lack of consideration. He also filed a cross-complaint praying for "general and exemplary damages because of assaults made by plaintiff and its agents to compel him to join the association and pay Abramoff for the Acme account." Siliznoff recovered $1,250 general and special damages and $4,000 exemplary damages. On appeal, the association contended that "the evidence does not establish an assault against defendant because the threats made all related to action that might take place in the future," and that there was no threat of "immediate physical harm." But the unanimous court, through Traynor, J., concluded that a cause of action was established "when it is shown that one, in the absence of any privilege, intentionally subjects another to mental suffering incident to serious threats to his physical well-being, whether or not the threats are made under such circumstances as to constitute a technical assault."

b. ***Bill Collection.*** In George v. Jordan Marsh Co., 268 N.E.2d 915, 921 (Mass. 1971), the plaintiff alleged that the defendant's bill collectors badgered her with phone calls during the late evening hours, sent her letters marked "account referred to law and collection department," wrote her that her credit was revoked and that she was liable for late charges, and engaged in other dunning tactics. The plaintiff further claimed that she did not owe the disputed sums because she had never guaranteed her son's unpaid debts. As a result of the calls, the plaintiff suffered a heart attack. Her attorney then protested the defendant's "harassing" tactics, but the onslaught continued until the plaintiff suffered a second heart attack. After an exhaustive review of the earlier Massachusetts precedent, the court upheld the sufficiency of her claim for emotional distress.

c. ***Outrageous Professional Conduct.*** In Rockhill v. Pollard, 485 P.2d 28, 32 (Or. 1971), the plaintiff, her mother-in-law, and her ten-month-old daughter, Marla, were all seriously injured in an automobile accident. Both women had serious cuts and bruises, and the daughter was apparently lifeless, with a ghostly pallor to her skin. A passing motorist took them to the office of the defendant physician, who, when summoned, did not examine either woman and gave Marla only a brief examination. When Marla started vomiting, the defendant said it was a result of overeating. He then ordered the women to wait outside in the freezing rain until the plaintiff's husband arrived. The three were then taken to a hospital, where Marla was successfully operated on for a depressed skull fracture.

McAllister, J., found that the evidence supported a finding of conduct outrageous in the extreme, stressing the special duties that physicians owed their patients: "Certainly a physician who is consulted in an emergency has a duty to respect that interest, at least to the extent of making a good-faith attempt to provide adequate treatment or advice. We think a jury could infer . . . that defendant wilfully or recklessly failed to perform that duty." He therefore remanded the case for further findings.

Why does the plaintiff have no action for medical malpractice or breach of contract?

d. ***Harassment.*** Various forms of racial insults have been treated as forms of extreme and outrageous conduct. In Patterson v. McLean Credit Union, 805 F.2d 1143, 1146 (4th Cir. 1986), the plaintiff, who was African American, alleged that her supervisor engaged in racially motivated harassment by "staring" at her for several minutes at a time, by assigning her too many tasks, by making her do sweeping and dusting jobs not assigned to whites, and by saying to her that black people were known to work "slower than" whites. Phillips, J., rejected the tort suit, noting that the allegations fell "far short" of the stringent requirements of North Carolina law. The plaintiff also raised civil rights claims that were rebuffed by the Supreme Court in Patterson v. McLean Credit Union, 491 U.S. 164 (1989), which gave a relatively narrow construction of the scope of the protection afforded to the plaintiff under 42 U.S.C. §1981. Plaintiffs have had more success in bypassing the stringent requirements of intentional infliction of emotional distress (IIED) by arguing sexual harassment. The Supreme Court has held that "Title VII comes into play before the harassing conduct leads to a nervous breakdown. . . . So long as the environment would reasonably be perceived, and is perceived, as hostile or abusive, there is no need for it also to be psychologically injurious." Harris v. Forklift Systems, Inc., 510 U.S. 17, 22 (1993). These cases are sometimes judged by a "reasonable woman standard." See, e.g., Ellison v. Brady, 924 F.2d 872, 879 (9th Cir. 1991).

e. ***Torture.*** IIED has also been invoked in international disputes. In Saberi v. Gov't of the Islamic Republic of Iran, 541 F. Supp. 3d 67, 82 (D.D.C. 2021), "Iran intentionally detained and abused Saberi [an American citizen] for 100 days, and the uncontroverted evidence establishes that Saberi has suffered—and continues to suffer—from severe emotional distress as a result." In addition to IIED, the plaintiff also alleged assault and false imprisonment. How do the three claims interact? A default judgment was entered against Iran. What next?

f. ***University Disciplinary Hearings.*** In Doe v. Brown Univ., 43 F.4th 195, 210–11 (1st Cir. 2022), plaintiff sued his university for IIED for its treatment of him during a disciplinary process. The plaintiff (John), an African American male university student, and a white female student (Jane) met at a bar and then had a brief sexual encounter, after which each accused the other of aggressive behavior. After an internal hearing, John was found responsible and put on probation for a year, during which time he tried to commit suicide by jumping in front of a truck. After a second allegation of sexual assault (which was never formally filed) was made against him, John was told to leave school after finals for an indefinite period of time, at which point he "fell to the floor, rolled into a ball, and cried." On several occasions, John received help from Brown's Counseling and Psychological Services (CAPS). His return to classes the next fall was chaotic, and he was admitted to Rhode Island Hospital for an initial psychiatric examination.

Subsequently, two Brown administrators, a dean and vice president, threatened John with serious consequences (including a possible charge for "vandalizing" the truck he jumped in front of) if he did not immediately go on "voluntary medical leave" from campus. These threats provoked another extreme reaction from John. Eventually, John graduated from Brown and brought suit. Kayatta, J., dismissed John's discrimination claims but, over a dissent, held that his claim for extreme and outrageous conduct could go forward based on the administrative threats to get him to take medical leave, a request that an expert witness claimed had no clinical basis. The key elements of the holding were that:

> First, the parties' relationship required at least some heightened solicitude by Brown. . . . Second, [both the dean and vice president] were aware of John's enhanced susceptibility to extreme emotional distress. . . . Third, the meeting itself did not comport with the reason given for its supposed urgency, [because a simple mention of the new claim did not justify having the meeting when, "or so a jury might find, they attempted to coerce him into withdrawing by piling on threatened claims that need not have been advanced that evening."]

The dissent of Casper, J., concluded that the ultimate question was one of law on which Brown should prevail because the threats Brown made consisted of actions that Brown was legally permitted to "take."

3. *Constitutional Overtones.* The Supreme Court has held that the First Amendment limits the scope of the common law tort of intentional infliction of emotional distress in some contexts. Thus in Hustler Magazine v. Falwell, 485 U.S. 46, 53–54 (1988), Hustler parodied Jerry Falwell by having him state in a mock "interview" that his "first time" was during a drunken incestuous rendezvous with his mother in an outhouse. In small print at the bottom of the page, the ad contains the disclaimer, "ad parody—not to be taken seriously." Rehnquist, C.J., overturned a jury verdict for Falwell of $100,000 in actual damages and $50,000 in punitive damages against both Hustler and its publisher, Larry Flynt, on constitutional grounds. The Court stressed the press's need for "breathing room" under the First Amendment:

> Generally speaking the law does not regard the intent to inflict emotional distress as one which should receive much solicitude, and it is quite understandable that most if not all jurisdictions have chosen to make it civilly culpable where the conduct in question is sufficiently "outrageous." But in the world of debate about public affairs, many things done with motives that are less than admirable are protected by the First Amendment. . . .

Rehnquist, C.J., then noted that cartoonists such as Thomas Nast, who took on the Tweed Ring, which ran New York City in the late nineteenth century, would be at risk under the alternative rule. Is there a slippery slope from Nast to Flynt? Why no action for defamation?

The Court upheld a defense based on the First Amendment against a claim of intentional infliction of emotional distress in Snyder v. Phelps, 562 U.S. 443, 458 (2011). The so-called Westboro Baptist Church, based in Topeka, Kansas, systematically pickets funerals of fallen soldiers to protest the military's tolerance of homosexuality. Phelps and six members of his congregation picketed Lance Corporal Snyder's funeral with signs (among others) reading "God Hates the USA/Thank God for 9/11," "Thank God for Dead Soldiers," and "You're Going to Hell." Snyder's father did not see the slogans on the picket signs at the time of the funeral, but when he saw them broadcast on the news later that evening he became extremely distressed and sued Phelps and Westboro. A jury awarded Snyder's father $2.9 million in compensatory damages and $8 million in punitive damages. The Fourth Circuit overturned the jury's verdict, and the Supreme Court affirmed:

> The jury here was instructed that it could hold Westboro liable for intentional infliction of emotional distress based on a finding that Westboro's picketing was "outrageous." "Outrageousness," however, is a highly malleable standard with "an inherent subjectiveness about it which would allow a jury to impose liability on the basis of the jurors' tastes or views, or perhaps on the basis of their dislike of a particular expression."

4. *Emotional Distress Claims for Terrorist Attacks.* Claims against foreign governments, stemming from deaths overseas in terrorist acts, are governed by the Foreign Sovereign Immunities Act, 28 U.S.C. §§1602–1611 (2023), which generally bars tort actions against foreign governments, subject to a terrorism exception that removes immunity when plaintiffs seek

> money damages . . . against a foreign state for personal injury or death . . . caused by an act of torture, extrajudicial killing, aircraft sabotage, hostage taking, or the provision of material support or resources for such an act if . . . engaged in by an official, employee, or agent of [a] foreign state . . . designated as a state sponsor of terrorism.

28 U.S.C. §1605A(a)(1)–(2)(A)(i)(I).

The scope of that provision was at issue in Republic of Sudan v. Owens, 194 A.3d 38, 39, 42–43 (D.C. 2018), where Fisher, J., wrote:

> Almost simultaneously on August 7, 1998, al Qaeda terrorists detonated powerful truck bombs outside the United States embassies in Dar es Salaam, Tanzania, and Nairobi, Kenya, killing over two hundred people and injuring more than a thousand others. Three years after the attacks, groups of plaintiffs began filing suit in the United States District Court for the District of Columbia, seeking to hold Sudan accountable for its role in the bombings. Eventually, the case reached the United States Court of Appeals for the District of Columbia Circuit and, pursuant to D.C. Code §11-723 (2012 Repl.), it certified the following question of District of Columbia law to this court: "Must a claimant alleging emotional distress arising from a terrorist attack that killed or injured a family member have been present at the scene of the attack in order to state a claim for intentional infliction of emotional distress?" For the reasons that follow, we answer this question "No."

Fisher, J., then held that IIED requires that a plaintiff be "present" when the harm occurred, but found that the general exception to that rule was applicable:

> The presence requirement serves many purposes. It shields defendants from unwarranted liability, tries to ensure that compensation is awarded only to victims with genuine claims of severe emotional distress, and provides a judicially manageable standard that protects courts from a flood of IIED claims. *See* Restatement Second §46 comment *l*. In FSIA terrorism cases, however, the presence requirement is not needed to achieve these goals: the very facts that justify stripping foreign sovereigns of their immunity allay the concerns that the presence requirement was designed to address. As a result, adhering to the rule in this context would serve only to create a high risk that compelling claims will go uncompensated. By establishing the caveat, the Restatement Second sought to prevent such unfair outcomes; by invoking it here, we do just that.

CHAPTER 2

STRICT LIABILITY AND NEGLIGENCE: HISTORIC AND ANALYTIC FOUNDATIONS

SECTION A. INTRODUCTION

We now turn to what historically has perhaps been the most contested topic of tort theory: When is a defendant liable for the physical harm he inadvertently causes to the plaintiff? One approach—traditional strict liability—holds the defendant prima facie liable for any harm that he causes to the plaintiff's person or property, such that the defendant's level of care, be it high or low, is irrelevant to liability. This approach allows for a defense based on assumption of risk and for a range of defenses on causation for harms caused by a natural event, a third party, or an act of the plaintiff herself.

The competing negligence approach allows the plaintiff to recover only if, intentional harms aside, the defendant acted with insufficient care, which could be defined in either objective terms (those that ignore the peculiarities of individual parties), or in subjective terms (those based on the distinctive characteristics of the defendant). As with strict liability, the negligence approach also allows for affirmative defenses, especially those based on plaintiff's conduct.

The integration of both theories is difficult. Must one be used to the exclusion of the other? Is the definition of causation the same in both cases? Is "negligence" a technical term or one of ordinary language? To whom is any duty of care owed? Strangers? Customers? Occupiers? Does the assignment of burdens of proof narrow the gap between the two theories? What about under the rule of res ipsa loquitur, where the defendant's conduct literally "speaks for itself"?

Section B examines the tension between negligence and strict liability in the formative English cases before 1700. Section C traces the influence of the forms of action on the choice of liability rules. Section D follows the nineteenth-century debate over liability rules both in England and the United States after the abolition of the forms of action. Section E examines the same conflict in the twentieth century.

SECTION B. THE FORMATIVE CASES

The Thorns Case (Hull v. Orange)

YB Mich. 6 Ed. 4, f. 7, pl. 18 (1466)

A man brought a writ of Trespass quare vi et armis clausum fregit, etc. et herbam suam pedibus conculcando consumpsit, [Roughly: wherefore by force and arms he broke into the plaintiff's close, and consumed his crops by trampling them with his feet] and alleged the trespass in 5 acres and the defendant said, as to the coming, etc. and as to the trespass in the 5 acres, not guilty and, as to the trespass in the 5 acres, that the plaintiff ought not to have an action for he says that he [the defendant] has an acre of land on which a thorn hedge grows, adjoining the said 5 acres, and that he [the defendant], at the time of the supposed trespass, came and cut the thorns, and that they, against his will, fell on the said acres of the plaintiff, and that he [the defendant] came freshly on to the said acres and took them, which is the same trespass for which he has conceived this action. And on this they demurred and it was well argued, and was adjourned.

One of the earliest known illustrations of the English Court of Common Pleas, c. 1460

Source: The Inner Temple Library

[Oral Arguments:]

And now Catesby says: Sir, it has been said that, if a man does some act, even if it be lawful, and by this act tort and damage are done to another against his will, yet, if he could by any means have eschewed the damage, he shall be punished for this act. Sir, it seems to me that the contrary is true, and, as I understand, if a man does a lawful act and thereby damage comes to another against his will, he shall not be punished. Thus, I put the case that I drive my cattle along the highway, and you have an acre of land lying next the highway, and my beasts enter your land and eat your grass, and I come freshly and chase them out of your land; now here, because the chasing out was lawful and the entry on the land was against my will, you shall not have an action against me. No more shall you have an action here, for the cutting was lawful and the falling on your land was against my will, and so the re-taking was good and lawful. And, Sir, I put the case that I cut my trees and the boughs fall on a man and kill him; in this case I shall not be attainted as of felony, for my cutting was lawful and the falling on the man was against my will. No more here, therefore, etc.

Fairfax: It seems to me that the contrary is true and I say that there is a difference where a man does a thing from which felony ensues and one from which trespass ensues; for in the case which Catesby puts there was no felony, since felony is of malice prepense and, as the act was against his will, it was not animo felonico [with felonious intent]. But if one cuts his trees and the boughs fall on a man and hurt him, in this case he shall have an action of Trespass. So, too, Sir, if a man shoots at the butts and his bow trembles in his hands and he kills a man ipso invito [against his will], this is no felony, as has been said. But if he wounds a man by his shooting, he shall have a good action of Trespass against him, and yet the shooting was lawful and the tort that the other had was against his will. And so here.

Pigot: To the same intent. I put the case that I have a mill and the water which comes to my mill runs past your land, and you have willows growing by the water, and you cut your willows and against your will they fall in the water and stop the water so that I have not sufficient water for my mill, in this case I shall have an action of Trespass, and yet the cutting was lawful and the falling was against my will. And so if a man has a fish-pond in his manor and he empties the water out of the pond to take the fishes and the water floods my land, I shall have a good action, and yet the act was lawful.

Yonge: The contrary seems to me to be true; and in such a case, where a man has dampnum absque injuria [harm without legal injury], he shall have no action, for if he has no tort he has no reason to recover damages. So in this case, when he came on to his close to take the thorns which had fallen on to it, this entry was not tortious, for when he cut them and they fell on his close ipso invito, the property in them was in him and thus it was lawful for him to take them out of his close; wherefore, notwithstanding that he has done damage, he has done no tort.

Brian: I think the contrary. To my intent, when any man does an act, he is bound to do it in such manner that by his act no prejudice or damage is done to others. Thus, in a case where I am building a house and, while the timber is being put up, a piece of it falls on my neighbour's house and damages it, he shall have a good action, and yet the building of the house was lawful and the timber fell me invito [against my will]. So, too, if a man makes an assault upon me and I cannot avoid him, and in my own defence I raise my stick to strike him, and a man is behind me and in raising my stick I wound him, in this case he shall have an action against me, and yet the raising of my stick to defend myself was lawful and I wounded him me invito. So in this case.

[Judicial Opinions:]

Littleton, J. To the same intent. If a man suffers damage, it is right that he be recompensed; and to my intent the case which Catesby has put is not law; for if your cattle come on to my land and eat my grass, notwithstanding you come freshly and drive them out, it is proper for you to make amends for what your cattle have done, be it more or less. . . . And, Sir, if it were law that he could enter and take the thorns, by the same reasoning, if he cut a great tree, he could come with his carts and horses to carry off the tree, which is not reason, for peradventure he has corn or other crops growing, etc. No more here may he do it, for the law is all one in great things and in small and so, according to the amount of the trespass, it is proper that he should make amends.

CHOKE, C.J. I think the same; for when the principal thing is not lawful, then the thing which depends upon it is not lawful. For when he cut the thorns and they fell on to my land, this falling was not lawful, and then his coming to take them away was not lawful. As to what has been said that they fell ipso invito, this is not a good plea; but he should have said that he could not do it in any other manner or that he did all that was in his power to keep them out; otherwise he shall pay damages. And, Sir, if the thorns or a great tree had fallen on his land by the blowing of the wind, in this case he might have come on to the land to take them, since the falling had then been not his act, but that of the wind.

NOTES

1. ***Basis for Liability in Tort.*** In the *Thorns Case,* it is likely that the plaintiff sued for these trifling damages because "the *Case of Thorns* was likely a boundary dispute, where the trespasser was nibbling into his neighbour's land, acting as if the land was his to use." Getzler, Richard Epstein, Strict Liability, and the History of Torts, 3 J. Tort L., Oct. 22, 2010, at 9.

Doctrinally, however, does the *Thorns Case* adopt a theory of strict liability in tort? Initially, that debate seems attenuated given the defendant's deliberate entry onto the plaintiff's land. But could the defendant raise a version of the necessity defense, *supra* Chapter 1, at 37, because the defendant could only retake his thorns by trampling on the plaintiff's land? Should that entry be privileged only if the defendant's original cutting was not tortious? What passages in the *Thorns Case* point to the strict liability rule? To some alternative rule? To negligence? Could trespass be used to settle title under a negligence theory?

The historical basis of tort liability was reviewed in Arnold, Accident, Mistake, and Rules of Liability in the Fourteenth Century Law of Torts, 128 U. Pa. L. Rev. 361, 374–75 (1979), which concludes that "the inference to be drawn from all the available evidence is that in fourteenth-century tort actions civil liability was strict." He points to "a familiar principle in the law of torts that no one was liable to make compensation for injuries that were attributable to some entirely providential cause," such as harms brought about by tempests, earthquakes, or fires of spontaneous origin, commonly grouped as acts of God. Likewise, the plaintiff's own contributory negligence was regarded a good defense because "it is the plaintiff, not the defendant, who is perceived as having 'done' the act resulting in injury." Accordingly, Arnold found only a few cases in which the plaintiff's complaint alleged the defendant's negligence, and fewer still in which the defendant insisted his own lack of negligence as a defense. For Arnold, the substantive issue is closely tied to the logic of pleading:

> To simplify somewhat, a defendant in a writ of trespass was obligated to choose between two kinds of answer: He either had to deny the physical acts he was alleged to have done, or he had to admit them and assign a cause for them. In the case of an assault and battery, for instance, an acceptable "cause" would have been self-defense. Now if a defendant wanted to say that he had hit the plaintiff accidentally (that is, nonnegligently), his story would not technically have fit either of the two modes of responding to complaints. He had, in fact, hit the plaintiff, so a denial was obviously of no use; moreover, he had had no cause, no justification, for hitting him because "cause," as we have seen, was thought of in motivational terms.

2. ***"Best Efforts" as a Means to Avoid Liability.*** In Millen v. Fandrye, (1626) 79 Eng. Rep. 1259 (KB), the plaintiff sued for damage to his sheep when the defendant's dog chased

the sheep off his land, where they had been trespassing, and continued to chase them after the sheep had entered a neighbor's land. Crew, C.J., accepted the defendant's defense:

> It seems to me that he might drive the sheep out with the dog, and he could not withdraw his dog when he would in an instant. . . . [A] man cuts thorns and they fall into another man's land, and in trespass he justified for it; and the opinion was, that notwithstanding this justification trespass lies, because he did not plead that he did his best endeavour to hinder their falling there, yet this was a hard case; but this case is not like [the instant case], for here it was lawful to chase them [the sheep] out of his own land, and he did his best endeavour to recall the dog, and therefore trespass does not lie.

Millen endorses Choke's view in the *Thorns Case*, but *Millen* is also consistent with Littleton's version of strict liability. In *Millen*, the "best efforts" defense arose solely because the defendant tried to drive off the plaintiff's trespassing sheep. The law allowed excessive force when the defendant, in good faith, tried to minimize the damage to the plaintiff's sheep. Compare with the rule that an aggressor takes his victim as he finds him in Vosburg v. Putney, *supra* Chapter 1, at 2. In contrast, the defendant's cutting in the *Thorns Case* was not justified or excused by any prior wrong of the plaintiff, denying there the latitude afforded by the self-defense privilege. Could a third party whose property was trampled by the sheep recover even though the dog's owner tried to call him off? See Morris v. Platt, *supra* Chapter 1, at 30.

3. *Justification in Trespass.* In the *Tithe Case*, YB Trin., 21 Hen. 7, f. 26, 27, 28, pl. 5 (1506), the plaintiff, a local parson, sued for the loss of corn tithed to him by a local farmer, who had placed it in a separate part of his field for the parson. The defendant then moved the corn to the plaintiff's barn, where it perished from unspecified causes. The defendant justified his conduct on the ground that the plaintiff was in danger of losing the corn to beasts that were straying in the field. The court disallowed the justification:

> Kingsmill, J.: Where the goods of another are taken against his will, it must be justified either as a thing necessary for the Commonwealth or through a condition recognized by the law. First, as a thing concerning the Commonwealth, one may justify for goods taken out of a house when it is purely to safeguard the goods, or for breaking down a house to safeguard others; and so in time of war one may justify the entry into another's land to make a bulwark in defence of King and Country; and these things are justifiable and lawful for the maintenance of the Commonwealth. The other cause of justification is where one distrains [i.e., seizes to hold as security] my horse for his rent, and that is justifiable because the land was bound by such a condition of distress; and so in the case of other such conditions. . . . But in this case here we are outside these reasons, . . . and, although it is pleaded that this corn was in danger of being lost, yet it was not in such danger but that the party could have had his remedy. Thus, if I have beasts damage feasant [causing damage on plaintiff's land], I shall not justify my entry to chase them out unless I first tender all amends. So here, when the defendant took the plaintiff's corn that it might not be destroyed, yet this is not justifiable. For if it had been destroyed, the plaintiff would have his remedy against those who destroyed it. And as for his having put it into the plaintiff's barn, yet he must keep it safe against any other mischance; and so no advantage thereby comes to the plaintiff. So this plea is not good.
>
> Rede, C.J.: Although the defendant's intent here was good, yet the intent is not to be construed, though in felony it shall be; as where one shoots at the butts [target] and kills a man, this is not felony, since he had no intent to kill him; and so of a tiler on a house where against his knowledge a stone kills a man, it is not felony. But where one shoots at the butts and wounds a man, although it be against his will, yet he shall be called a trespasser against his will. So it is necessary always to have a good case to justify; as in Trespass, a license is good justification . . . Thus, if my beasts are damage feasant in another's land, I cannot enter to chase them out; and yet it would be a good deed to chase them out, to save them doing more damage. But it is otherwise where a stranger drives my horses into another's land, where they do damage; for here I may justify my entry to drive them out, since this tort has its beginning in the tort of another. But here, . . . it is not like the cases where things are in jeopardy of loss through water or fire and the like, for there the plaintiff has no remedy for the destruction against anyone. So the plea is not good.

The *Tithe Case* raises a variation on the necessity issue raised in *Vincent*, *supra* Chapter 1, at 39. However, the defendant in *Vincent* acted to preserve his own property, whereas the defendant in the *Tithe Case* acted to preserve the plaintiff's property. How valuable is a remedy against a third party who cannot be found? Who has no money? Why should anyone act to benefit a stranger if he must bear the risk of loss? Can that loss be balanced off by a claim in restitution if the corn is in fact saved? Should a system of rewards be introduced? For discussion, see Epstein, Holdouts, Externalities and the Single Owner: One More Salute to Ronald Coase, 36 J.L. & Econ. 553, 579–81 (1993).

Weaver v. Ward

(1616) 80 Eng. Rep. 284 (KB)

Weaver brought an action of trespass of assault and battery against Ward. The defendant pleaded, that he was amongst others by the commandment of the Lords of the Council a trained soldier in London, of the band of one Andrews captain; and so was the plaintiff, and that they were skirmishing with their musquets charged with powder for their exercise in re militari, [on military matters] against another captain and his band; and as they were so skirmishing, the defendant casualiter & per infortunium & contra voluntatem suam, [accidentally, and by misfortune, and against his own will] in discharging of his piece did hurt and wound the plaintiff. And upon demurrer by the plaintiff, judgment was given for him; for though it were agreed, that if men tilt or turney in the presence of the King, or if two masters of defence playing their prizes kill one another, that this shall be no felony; or if a lunatick kill a man, or the like, because felony must be done animo felonico [with felonious intent]: yet in trespass, which tends only to give damages according to hurt or loss, it is not so; and therefore if a lunatick hurt a man, he shall be answerable in trespass: and therefore no man shall be excused of a trespass (for this is the nature of an excuse, and not of a justification, prout ei bene licuit) [as it well appeared to him] except it may be judged utterly without his fault.

As if a man by force take my hand and strike you, or if here the defendant had said, that the plaintiff ran cross his piece when it was discharging, or had set forth the case with the circumstances, so as it had appeared to the Court that it had been inevitable, and that the defendant had committed no negligence to give occasion to the hurt.

NOTES

1. *Inevitable Accident: Conceptual Difficulties.* What counts as an "inevitable accident in *Weaver*? Contra Arnold, *supra* at 66, many commentators regard "inevitable accident" as a backhanded way of saying that the defendant acted neither negligently nor with intent to harm. Thus, Baker, An Introduction to English Legal History 405 (4th ed. 2002), observes that "[w]hat the judges wanted to know was whether the defendant could have taken steps to avoid the accident; in other words, whether it was 'inevitable'—not in the sense of being predestined, but in that there was no reasonable opportunity of avoidance." Similarly, see Brown v. Kendall, *infra* at 78; Holmes, The Common Law, *infra* at 94. For a more nuanced reading, see Gilles, Inevitable Accident in Classical English Tort Law, 43 Emory L.J. 575, 577 (1994), who reads such phrases as "utterly without his fault" and "unavoidable necessity" as asking "not whether the actors had behaved unreasonably—whether they *should* have avoided the accident—but whether they *could* have avoided it by greater practical care."

Apart from the procedural issues raised by Arnold, *supra*, this reading is odd on textual grounds because it renders the last clause in *Weaver* (referring to antecedent negligence) wholly superfluous. In contrast, a literal reading of inevitable accident applies narrowly to those accidents that "had to happen," no matter what the defendant did. Is damage to the dock in *Vincent* inevitable, given that the defendant made efforts to tie its ship to the dock during the storm?

2. *Inevitable Accident: Historical Treatment.* Smith v. Stone, (1647) 82 Eng. Rep. 533 (KB) reads in full:

> Smith brought an action of trespasse against Stone pedibus ambulando [walking by his feet], the defendant pleads this speciall plea in justification, viz. that he was carryed upon the land of the plaintiff by force, and violence of others, and was not there voluntarily, which is the same trespasse, for which the plaintiff brings his action. The plaintiff demurs to this plea: in this case Roll Iustice said, that it is the trespasse of the party that carryed the defendant upon the land, and not the trespasse of the defendant: as he that drives my cattell into another mans land is the trespassor against him, and not I who am owner of the cattell.

Is the denial that he did anything a justification? With *Smith* contrast Gilbert v. Stone, (1647) 82 Eng. Rep. 539 (KB):

> Gilbert brought an action of trespasse quare clausum fregit, and taking of a gelding, against Stone. The defendant pleads that he for fear of his life, and wounding of twelve armed men, who threatened to kill him if he did not [do the act] went into the house of the plaintiff, and took the gelding. The plaintiff demurred to this plea; Roll Iustice, This is no plea to justifie the defendant; for I may not do a trespasse to one for fear of threatnings of another, for by this means the party injured shall have no satisfaction, for he cannot have it of the party that threatned. Therefore let the plaintiff have his judgement.

Dickinson v. Watson, (1682) 84 Eng. Rep. 1218 (KB), also gave a narrow construction to inevitable accident. The defendant, a tax-collector of "hearth-money," discharged his firearm when no one was in view, without intending to harm anyone. Nonetheless he shot the plaintiff who was walking along the road minding his own business. The court upheld a judgment for the plaintiff, "for in trespass the defendant shall not be excused without unavoidable necessity, which is not shewn here. . . ."

In Gibbons v. Pepper, (1695) 91 Eng. Rep. 922 (KB), the defendant was riding a horse on the King's highway. The horse, being frightened, bolted, carrying the defendant along until it struck and injured the plaintiff. The defendant claimed that he called out to the plaintiff to take care, "but that notwithstanding the plaintiff did not go out of the way, but continued there." The defendant pleaded as his justification "that the accident was inevitable, and that the negligence of the defendant did not cause it." Again, on demurrer, judgment was given for the plaintiff ("[o]f which opinion was the whole court"):

> For if I ride upon a horse, and J. S. whips the horse so that he runs away with me and runs over any other person, he who whipped the horse is guilty of the battery, and not me. But if I by spurring was the cause of such accident, then I am guilty. In the same manner, if *A* takes the hand of *B* and with it strikes *C*, *A* is the trespasser and not *B*. And, per Curiam, the defendant might have given this justification in evidence upon the general issue [i.e., a simple denial] pleaded. And therefore judgment was given for the plaintiff.

Was the plaintiff guilty of contributory negligence?

Gibbons treats the defendant's horse as the passive instrument of that third party who incites it to hurt the plaintiff or his property. Yet this equation between animal and inanimate object is far from evident, given that animals have wills of their own. Alternatively, should the owner be (vicariously) responsible for his animal's action, with the right thereafter to sue any third party who rode, spurred, or otherwise caused the animal to do damage? Put in functional terms, who should bear the risk of insolvency of the third party: the owner of the animal or the victim? What if *A* picks *B*'s stick off the ground and uses it to strike *C*? See Scott v. Shepherd, *infra* at 72, and Chapter 7, Section C.

3. *Inevitable Accident: Modern Response.* Modern courts uniformly reject a defendant's rare request for an inevitable accident instruction. In Butigan v. Yellow Cab Co., 320 P.2d 500, 504 (Cal. 1958), the court repudiated its earlier flirtation with that defense in intersection collisions, noting that "an accident may be 'unavoidable or inevitable' where it is caused by a superior or irresistible force or by an absence of exceptional care which the law does not expect of the ordinary prudent man." The court held that no defendant should be held to such a high standard of care, which is now an "obsolete remnant" of the time when liability was always available for injuries to person or property directly caused by a voluntary act of the defendant. Thus under ordinary tort principles "the defendant under a general denial may show any circumstance which militates against either his negligence or its causal effect." At one time *Butigan* was "unique," but "today 21 States and the District of Columbia have abandoned the unavoidable accident instruction and 15 States have severely criticized or limited it." Lenards v. DeBoer, 865 N.W.2d 867, 873 (S.D. 2015) (Kern, J., concurring).

In McWilliams v. Masterson, 112 S.W.3d 314 (Tex. App. 2003), the much-weakened defense of inevitable accident was allowed. The plaintiff was driving his car with his family at night at 65 miles per hour through a severe snowstorm on a four-lane highway. He attempted to pass the defendant's 18-wheeler in the right lane, going about 50 miles per hour. Both drivers were within the speed limit. As the plaintiff attempted to move back to the right, he suddenly saw cattle ahead. He struck one of the animals, which drove him back in front of the truck, resulting in the death of his wife and injuries to the other passengers. The defendant driver received an "unavoidable accident" instruction because of "the truism that some events or injuries may not be proximately caused by the negligence of anyone," but are best attributable to "fate." The defense was also given to the two cattle owners, named Gabels, because they could not restrain the desperate cattle in the face of the storm, even though their fence and gates were in good repair. Thus the absence of all negligence negates liability. A rigorous system of strict liability protects the defendant Masterson, who always had the right of way. But should it protect the Gabels, who chose to keep cattle near the road? Under *Gibbons*?

SECTION C. THE FORMS OF ACTION

1. The Significance of the Forms of Action

The early forms of action exerted a strong, if unintended, influence upon the growth of substantive tort law. To commence a suit in early England, a plaintiff could not simply state facts sufficient to get relief. Instead, she had to further show that her cause of action fell within one of the writs (royal orders used to commence civil actions) recognized at that time. Compare with this with the modern Rule 8(a) of the Federal Rules of Civil Procedure. In the well-known phrase of Henry Maine, "So great is the ascendancy of the Law of Actions in the infancy of Courts of Justice, that substantive law has at first the look of being gradually secreted in the interstices of procedure." Maine, Early Law and Custom 389 (1907).

As Frederic W. Maitland observed in his masterly essay, The Forms of Action at Common Law 4–5 (1936 ed.):

> [T]o a very considerable degree the substantive law administered in a given form of action has grown up independently of the law administered in other forms. Each procedural pigeon-hole

contains its own rules of substantive law, and it is with great caution that we may argue from what is found in one to what will probably be found in another; each has its own precedents. It is quite possible that a litigant will find that his case will fit some two or three of these pigeon-holes. If that be so he will have a choice, which will often be a choice between the old, cumbrous, costly, on the one hand, the modern, rapid, cheap, on the other. Or again he may make a bad choice, fail in his action, and take such comfort as he can from the hints of the judges that another form of action might have been more successful. The plaintiff's choice is irrevocable; he must play the rules of the game that he has chosen. Lastly he may find that, plausible as his case may seem, it just will not fit any one of the receptacles provided by the courts and he may take to himself the lesson that where there is no remedy there is no wrong.

2. Trespass and Case

Two writs—trespass and trespass on the case (or more simply "case")—covered most of the physical harms actionable at common law. Ultimately, trespass lay to redress harm caused by the defendant's direct and immediate application of force against the plaintiff's person or property. Case, in contrast, covered all those "indirect" harms, not involving the use of force. The classic illustration of the difference was given by Fortescue, J., in Reynolds v. Clarke, (1726) 92 Eng. Rep. 410 (KB):

> [I]f a man throws a log into the highway, and in that act it hits me, I may maintain trespass, because it is an immediate wrong; but if as it lies there I tumble over it, and receive an injury, I must bring an action upon the case; because it is only prejudicial in consequence, for which originally I could have no action at all.

How does this distinction apply to "slip and fall" and collision cases?

Fortescue's opinion helps explain the evolution of the substantive tort law. Royal recognition of trespass came first because of the greater threat of the direct use of force. Telltale signs of its original scope are found in two of its Latin phrases: *vi et armis*, by force and arms, and *contra pacem regis*, against the peace of the king. According to one view, case was a much later development that took place toward the middle of the fourteenth century, when the royal courts finally allowed tort actions on the case. Fifoot, History and Sources of the Common Law, Tort and Contract ch. 4 (1949).

Subsequently, however, Professor Milsom decisively challenged this view by demonstrating that the use of a distinct writ for trespass on the case in the fourteenth century did not signal a transformation of the substantive law. Milsom, Historical Foundations of the Common Law ch. 11 (2d ed. 1981). Like the Latin "transgressio," trespass originally meant simply "wrong," and cases brought under that writ in royal courts covered both the use of force and all manner of other actionable harms as well. "If we identify trespass not with a narrow category of wrongs but with wrong generally, with the category of tort rather than a particular tort, we are a good deal closer to thinking fourteenth-century thoughts than we previously were." Arnold, Select Cases of Trespass from the King's Courts—1307–99, at *ix* (Selden Society, vol. 100 (1984)).

This radical change did not alter the substantive law but came about for procedural reasons. The courts no longer required the magic words, *vi et armis* and *contra pacem regis*, in situations to which their ordinary meanings did not apply. To support his thesis, Milsom collected from the old legal records many writs framed in trespass in which the phrases *vi et armis* and *contra pacem regis* were included solely as legal fiction to secure the royal jurisdiction. The writ of trespass was, for example, broad enough to encompass suits brought by lower riparians who suffered flooding when upper riparians failed to make the required repairs to their river walls. Recall that in the *Thorns Case*, Pigot argued that blocking water to a mill by cutting willows was a trespass, even without the direct use of force against the mill owner. Similarly, early trespass actions were used to stop unfair competition by, for example, the owner of a fair against other persons who had sold goods in violation of the plaintiff's exclusive franchise granted by the king. In neither case were the words *vi et armis* or *contra pacem regis* applicable. Finally, an action for professional malpractice brought by the owner of a horse against the smith who cared for his horse also sounded in trespass, because the plaintiff had fictitiously pleaded that the horse had been taken by force and arms in order to sue in royal court. "[W]ere it not for the chinks of a few unusual cases, there would be nothing to make us suspect the truth, except this: the defendants in many such actions for killing horses are named or described as smiths." Milsom, *supra*, at 289.

The royal judges rejected elaborate fictions in the Farrier's Case of 1372, which allowed the plaintiff to sue in royal court without pleading either *vi et armis* or *contra pacem regis*. The emergence of a separate action on the case did not expand the scope of the tort law in the royal courts, but it did require clarification of the boundary between the two distinct writs of trespass and case, for both procedural and substantive reasons. With trespass, the plaintiff could begin his suit with the stringent process of capias, whereby he could seize the defendant's personal property. With case, however, the plaintiff had to commence his action with the less coercive summons and complaint. That distinction was eliminated by statute in 1504. Yet by a statute of 1677 (16 & 17 Car. 2), a second procedural point separated the two writs. In the words of Lord Kenyon in Savignac v. Roome, (1794) 101 Eng. Rep. 470 (KB): "[I]f in an action of trespass the plaintiff recover less than 40 *s.*, he is entitled to no more costs than damages; whereas a verdict with nominal damages only in an action on the case carries all the costs."

The division between trespass and case surfaced again in the famous *Squib Case.*

Scott v. Shepherd

(1773) 96 Eng. Rep. 525 (KB)

Trespass and assault for throwing, casting, and tossing a lighted squib at and against the plaintiff, and striking him therewith on the face, and so burning one of his eyes, that he lost the sight of it, whereby, & c. On Not Guilty pleaded, the cause came on to be tried before Nares, J., last Summer Assizes, at Bridgwater, when the jury found a verdict for the plaintiff with £100 damages, subject to the opinion of the Court on this case: — On the evening of the fair-day at Milborne Port, 28th October, 1770, the defendant threw a *lighted squib*, made of gun powder, &c. from the street into the market-house, which is a covered building, supported by arches, and enclosed at one end, but open at the other and both the sides, where a large concourse of people were assembled; which lighted squib, so thrown by the defendant, fell upon the standing of one Yates, who sold gingerbread, & c. That one Willis instantly, and to prevent injury to himself and the said wares of the said Yates, took up the said lighted squib from off the said standing, and then threw it across the said market-house, when it fell upon another standing there of one Ryal, who sold the same sort of wares, who instantly, and to save his own goods from being injured, took up the said lighted squib from off the said standing, and then threw it to another part of the said market-house, and, in so throwing it, struck the plaintiff then in the said market-house in the face therewith, and the combustible matter then bursting, put out one of the plaintiff's eyes. *Qu.* If this action be maintainable? . . .

"It's my fault—I wasn't worrying enough."

Source: Tom Cheney / The New Yorker Collection / The Cartoon Bank

Nares, J., was of opinion, that trespass would well lie in the present case. That the natural and probable consequence of the act done by the defendant was injury to somebody, and therefore the act was illegal at common law. And the throwing of squibs has by statute W.3, been since made a nuisance. Being therefore unlawful, the defendant was liable to answer for the consequences, be the injury mediate or immediate. 21 Hen. 7, 28, is express that malus animus is not necessary to constitute a trespass. . . .

Blackstone, J., was of opinion, that an action of trespass did not lie for Scott against Shepherd upon this case. He took the settled distinction to be, that where the injury is *immediate*, an action of trespass will lie; where it is only *consequential*, it must be an action on the case: Reynolds and Clarke, Lord Raym. 1401, Stra. 634; . . . The lawfulness or unlawfulness of the original act is not the criterion; though something of that sort is put into Lord Raymond's mouth in Stra. 635, . . . [L]awful or unlawful is quite out of the case; the solid distinction is between direct or immediate injuries on the one hand, and mediate or consequential on the other. And trespass never lay for the latter. If this be so, the only question will be, whether the injury which the plaintiff suffered was immediate, or consequential only; and I hold it to be the latter. The original act was, as against Yates, a trespass; not as against Ryal, or Scott. The tortious act was complete when the squib lay at rest upon Yates's stall. He, or any bystander, had, I allow, a right to protect themselves by removing the squib, but should have taken care to do it in such a manner as not to endamage others. But Shepherd, I think, is not answerable in an action of trespass and assault for the mischief done by the squib in the new motion impressed upon it, and the new direction given it, by either Willis or Ryal; who both were free agents, and acted upon their own judgment. This differs it from the cases put of turning loose a wild beast or a madman. They are only instruments in the hand of the first agent. Nor is it like diverting the course of an enraged ox, or of a stone thrown, or an arrow glancing against a tree; because there the original motion, the vis impressa, is continued, though diverted. Here the instrument of mischief was at rest, till a new impetus and a new direction are given it, not once only, but by two successive rational agents. But it is said that the act is not complete, nor the squib at rest, till after it is spent or exploded. It certainly has a power of doing fresh mischief, and so has a stone that has been thrown against my windows, and now lies still. Yet if any person gives that stone a new motion, and does farther mischief with it, trespass will not lie for that against the original thrower. No doubt but Yates may maintain trespass against Shepherd. And, according to the doctrine contended for, so may Ryal and Scott. Three actions for one single act! nay, it may be extended in infinitum. If a man tosses a football into the street, and, after being kicked about by one hundred people, it at last breaks a tradesman's windows; shall he have trespass against the man who first produced it? Surely only against the man who gave it that mischievous direction. But it is said, if Scott has no action against Shepherd, against whom must he seek his remedy? I give no opinion whether case would lie against Shepherd for the consequential damage; though, as at present advised, I think, upon the circumstances, it would. But I think, in strictness of law, trespass would lie against Ryal, the immediate actor in this unhappy business. Both he and Willis have exceeded the bounds of self-defence, and not used sufficient circumspection in removing the danger from themselves. The throwing it across the market-house, instead of brushing it down, or throwing [it] out of the open sides into the street, (if it was not meant to continue the sport, as it is called), was at least an unnecessary and incautious act. Not even menaces from others are sufficient to justify a trespass against a third person; much less a fear of danger to either his goods or his person—nothing but inevitable necessity; Weaver and Ward, Hob. 134; Gilbert and Stone, Al. 35, Styl. 72. . . . And I admit that the defendant is answerable in trespass for all the direct and inevitable effects caused by his own immediate act. . . . It is said by Lord Raymond, and very justly, in Reynolds and Clarke, "We must keep up the boundaries of actions, otherwise we shall introduce the utmost confusion." . . . I am of opinion, that in this action judgment ought to be for the defendant.

De Grey, C.J. . . . The question here is, whether the injury received by the plaintiff arises from the force of the original act of the defendant, or from a new force by a third person. I agree with my Brother Blackstone as to the principles he has laid down, but not in his application of those principles to the present case. . . . [T]he true question is, whether the injury is the direct and immediate act of the defendant; and I am of opinion, that in this case it is. The throwing the squib was an act unlawful and tending to affright the bystanders. So far, mischief was originally intended; not any particular mischief, but mischief indiscriminate and wanton. Whatever mischief therefore follows, he is the author of it;—Egreditur personam, as the phrase is in criminal cases. And though criminal cases are no rule for civil ones, yet in trespass I think there is an analogy. Every one who does an unlawful act is considered as the doer of all that follows; if done with a deliberate intent, the consequence may amount to murder; if incautiously, to manslaughter. So too a person breaking a horse in Lincoln's Inn Fields hurt a man; held, that trespass lay: and that it need not be laid scienter. I look upon all that was done subsequent to the original throwing as a continuation of the first force and first act, which will continue till the squib was spent by bursting. And I think that any innocent person removing the danger from himself to another is justifiable; the blame lights upon the first thrower. The new direction and new force flow out of the first force, and are not a new trespass. . . . It has been urged, that the intervention of a free agent will make a difference: but I do not consider Willis ad Ryal as free agents in the present case, but acting under a compulsive necessity for their own safety and self-preservation. On these reasons I concur with Brothers Gould and Nares, that the present action is maintainable.

NOTE

Under Which Writ Lies the Cause of Action? In Reynolds v. Clarke, (1726) 92 Eng. Rep. 410 (KB), the plaintiff's action for trespass was dismissed when the defendant fixed a spout in plaintiff's yard from which water leaked, thereby rotting the walls of plaintiff's house. When the invasion is direct, and the harm is consequential, which action should prevail?

What is the proper form of action in the celebrated case of Guille v. Swan, 19 Johns. (N.Y.) 381 (1822)? The defendant Guille flew in a balloon that landed in the garden of the plaintiff Swan. After the balloon landed, it dragged for about 30 feet causing damage to Swan's potatoes and radishes. Given his perilous position, Guille called out to a workman in Swan's field for help, which was heard by the crowd assembled at the boundary line. About 200 people came tearing across plaintiff's land causing additional damage to his vegetables and flowers, for which Swan sued Guille in trespass. Guille sought to limit his liability to the damage that he alone had caused, not that of the crowd. But Spencer, C.J., upheld a jury verdict against Guille for the full $90 in damages because his descent, whose direction was beyond his control,

> would, ordinarily and naturally, draw a crowd of people about him, either from curiosity, or for the purpose of rescuing him from a perilous situation; all this he ought to have foreseen, and must be responsible for. Whether the crowd heard him call for help, or not, is immaterial; he had put himself in a situation to invite help, and they rushed forward, impelled, perhaps, by the double motive of rendering aid, and gratifying a curiosity which he had excited. Can it be doubted, that if the plaintiff in error [i.e., defendant-appellant] had beckoned to the crowd to come to his assistance, that he would be liable for their trespass in entering the enclosure? I think not. In that case, they would have been co-trespassers, and we must consider the situation in which he placed himself, voluntarily and designedly, as equivalent to a direct request to the crowd to follow him. In the present case, he did call for help and may have been heard by the crowd; he is, therefore, undoubtedly, liable for all the injury sustained.

In trespass?

3. The Breakdown of the Forms of Action

Only rarely did American and English courts encounter lighted squibs or falling balloons. The division between the writs, however, was critical in the many cases involving accidents on the highway or the high seas that reached the courts by the 1790s. Yet here the courts failed to make any firm or authoritative choice between trespass and case for both practical and theoretical reasons. Even when the conceptual line between trespass and case was clear in principle, the plaintiff might not know in advance of trial where her case fell. If the plaintiff sued in trespass, the defendant could prevail by showing that his horse, outfitted with too-weak reins, had bolted out of control. If the plaintiff sued in case, the defendant might claim that he had run right over the plaintiff. In collisions at sea, it was always a delicate judgment whether a captain had rammed his ship into another ship, or whether the wind or currents (an act of God) had carried his disabled ship into the other craft. See, e.g., Ogle v. Barnes (1799) 101 Eng. Reg. 1338 (KB).

The twin problems of vicarious liability and joinder of actions complicated matters further. If the plaintiff was run down by the defendant's carriage when driven by his employee, trespass could be brought only against that employee, but not the employer, who could only be held vicariously liable. McManus v. Crickett (1800) 102 Eng. Rep. 580 (KB); Sharrod v. London & N.W. Ry., (1849) 154 Eng. Rep. 1345 (Ex.). Yet suing in case to reach the employer could backfire if the employer had personally driven the coach. Equally important, joinder of actions was not allowed if one action was for trespass and the other in case. Only two separate and expensive actions could cover all possibilities that might emerge at trial.

Illustration of the Court of Common Pleas in Westminster Hall, c. 1808–1810
Source: The British Library

How could the courts break the logjam? The courts were not prepared to buck tradition by allowing a plaintiff to include separate counts of trespass and case in a single writ. The Common Law Procedure Act, 15 & 16 Vict., c. 76, §41 (1852), eventually achieved that reform by statute. The courts also rebuffed a second possibility of letting the plaintiff use trespass against the employer when the employee caused immediate and direct harm.

In the end, the courts adopted a third solution in the watershed case of Williams v. Holland, (1833) 131 Eng. Rep. 848 (CP). There, the Court of Common Pleas held that the plaintiff could sue in case, no matter whether the harm was immediate or consequential, so long as the plaintiff's harm resulted from the defendant's (antecedent) negligence. Trespass was still available for all immediate harms, whether willful or negligent, and only trespass could be brought in cases of willful and immediate harm. Harms directly and negligently caused could be remedied in either trespass or case. Under *Williams*, the plaintiff in virtually all running-down cases would use case because it allowed her, first, to avoid having to guess whether harm was immediate or consequential and, second, to join both employer and employee in a single suit. The only time this solution failed was when the injury inflicted by the employee was both willful and direct, a limitation that hardly mattered for most road accidents. Indeed, in these rare cases, the employer could often defend himself under an early version of the "frolic and detour" exception to the general rule of vicarious liability, applicable to the employee's wrong committed outside the course of employment. See *infra* Chapter 7, Section F.

Williams not only ushered in a procedural revolution, but also shifted the terms of debate in the strict liability/negligence controversy. *Scott* hinted that trespass was proper even in the absence of the defendant's negligence or intent. *Williams* elevated negligence to a more prominent element for recovery in all highway accident cases for either direct or consequential damages. Bramwell, B., in Holmes v. Mather, L.R. 10 Ex. 261, 268–69 (1875), in giving judgment for the defendant, summed up the law as follows:

> As to the cases cited, most of them are really decisions on the form of action, whether case or trespass. The result of them is this, and it is intelligible enough: if the act that does an injury is an act of direct force vi et armis, trespass is the proper remedy (if there is any remedy) where the act is wrongful, either as being wilful or as being the result of negligence. Where the act is not wrongful for either of these reasons, no action is maintainable, though trespass would be the proper form of action if it were wrongful.

The history of trespass and case in England is given here in much abbreviated form. For further materials see Arnold, Select Cases of Trespass from the King's Courts: 1307–99 (Seldon Society, vol. 100, 1984); Fifoot, History and Sources of the Common Law, Tort and Contract ch. 9 (1949); Milsom, Historical Foundations of the Common Law chs. 11, 13 (2d ed. 1981); Epstein, Assumption of Risk in a System of Strict Liability: Conceptual Tangles and Social Consequences 265 (Goudkamp, Wilmot-Smith & Dyson eds., 2015); and Prichard, Trespass, Case and the Rule in Williams v. Holland, 22 Cambridge L.J. 234 (1964) (an excellent article from which much of the account given here is drawn).

SECTION D. STRICT LIABILITY AND NEGLIGENCE IN THE SECOND HALF OF THE NINETEENTH CENTURY

Just as the Common Law Procedure Acts of 1852 removed the last vestiges of the forms of action from English law, the widespread adoption of the so-called Field Codes—named after the reformer David Dudley Field, who championed the adoption of "code pleading" in New York—did the same thing in the United States. See First Report of Commissioners on Practice and Pleading (N.Y. 1848). These reforms abolished the forms of action as procedural devices, with this caveat: "No rule of law, by which rights and wrongs are measured, will be touched, the object and effect of the change being only the removal of old obstructions, in the way of enforcing the rights, and redressing the wrongs." *Id.* at 146–47. Therefore, both the English and American precedents survived this major procedural reform, allowing the choice between negligence and strict liability to be addressed in its most general form. See generally Clark, Code Pleading (2d ed. 1947).

The emergence of negligence as the dominant standard of civil liability in American tort law during the first half of the nineteenth century parallels the English experience. Initially, negligence was a shadowy concept, with a subordinate role in the tort law. In its primary sense, negligence covered the *nonfeasance* of individuals charged either by contract or statute with a duty of care. Smiths and surgeons were, for example, bound by their professional contracts to act carefully, while jailors and keepers of the public highways had similar statutory duties. Negligence, in the sense of carelessness in the performance of some affirmative act that causes harm to a stranger, was not the prevalent conception.

Yet by 1830, the increase in collision cases slowly brought this second sense of negligence to the fore. See Harvey v. Dunlop, Hill & Denio Supp. 193 (N.Y. 1843); Bridge Co. v. Lehigh Coal & Navigation Co., 4 Rawle 8 (Pa. 1833); Sullivan v. Murphy, 2 Miles 298, 2 Law Rep. 246 (1839). See generally Horwitz, The Transformation of American Law: 1780 to 1860, 89–94 (1977).

Brown v. Kendall

60 Mass. 292 (1850)

It appeared in evidence, on the trial, which was before Wells, C.J., in the court of common pleas, that two dogs, belonging to the plaintiff and the defendant, respectively, were fighting in the presence of their masters; that the defendant took a stick about four feet long, and commenced beating the dogs in order to separate them; that the plaintiff was looking on, at the distance of about a rod [= 16.5 feet], and that he advanced a step or two towards the dogs. In their struggle, the dogs approached the place where the plaintiff was standing. The defendant retreated backwards from the dogs, striking them as he retreated; and as he approached the plaintiff, with his back towards him, in raising his stick over his shoulder, in order to strike the dogs, he accidentally hit the plaintiff in the eye, inflicting upon him a severe injury. . . .

Exhibit 2.1 Lemuel Shaw

Lemuel Shaw (1781–1861) was Chief Justice of the Supreme Judicial Court of Massachusetts from 1830 to 1860. After studying at Harvard and reading law privately, he became a successful lawyer in Boston, working on corporate matters in the commercializing Northeast. Before being named to the Massachusetts high court, he served as a justice of the peace and a legislator in both the state house and senate. As chief justice, he penned (quite literally by hand) more than 2,000 opinions.

Much of his output is thought to favor the bustling industrial development of the country at the time, while still deferring to the legislature in economic matters. His harsh (by today's standards) decision in Farwell v. Boston & Worcester Railroad, 45 Mass. 49, 58–59 (1842) (see *infra* Chapter 4, at 245) endorsed the "fellow servant rule" widely followed elsewhere. Shaw repudiated the practice of slavery, even holding that slaves brought into Massachusetts were automatically free, see Commonwealth v. Aves, 18 Pick. 193 (Mass. 1836). Yet he rigorously enforced the fugitive slave laws and upheld the rights of businesses to discriminate against black people. See McCrea v. Marsh, 12 Gray 211 (Mass. 1858).

Bio source: Paul Finkelman, Lemuel Shaw: The Shaping of State Law, in Noble Purposes: Nine Champions of the Rule of Law 33–46 (Gross ed., 2007) Image source: Wikimedia Commons

Shaw, C.J. This is an action of trespass, vi et armis, brought by George Brown against George K. Kendall, for an assault and battery; and the original defendant having died pending the action, his executrix has been summoned in. . . .

The facts set forth in the bill of exceptions preclude the supposition, that the blow, inflicted by the hand of the defendant upon the person of the plaintiff, was intentional. The whole case proceeds on the assumption, that the damage sustained by the plaintiff, from the stick held by the defendant, was inadvertent and unintentional; and the case involves the question how far, and under what qualifications, the party by whose unconscious act the damage was done is responsible for it. We use the term "unintentional" rather than involuntary, because in some of the cases, it is stated, that the act of holding and using a weapon or instrument, the movement of which is the immediate cause of hurt to another, is a voluntary act, although its particular effect in hitting and hurting another is not within the purpose or intention of the party doing the act. . . .

In these discussions, it is frequently stated by judges, that when one receives injury from the direct act of another, trespass will lie. But we think this is said in reference to the question, whether trespass and not case will lie, assuming that the facts are such, that some action will lie. These dicta are no authority, we think, for holding, that damage received by a direct act of force from another will be sufficient to maintain an action of trespass, whether the act was lawful or unlawful, and neither wilful, intentional, nor careless. . . .

We think, as the result of all the authorities, the rule is correctly stated by Mr. Greenleaf, that the plaintiff must come prepared with evidence to show either that the *intention* was unlawful, or that the defendant was *in fault*; for if the injury was unavoidable, and the conduct of the defendant was free from blame, he will not be liable. 2 Greenl. Ev. §§85 to 92. If, in the prosecution of a lawful act, a casualty purely accidental arises, no action can be supported for an injury arising therefrom. . . . In applying these rules to the present case, we can perceive no reason why the instructions asked for by the defendant ought not to have been given; to this effect, that if both plaintiff and defendant at the time of the blow were using ordinary care, or if at that time the defendant was using ordinary care, and the plaintiff was not, or if at that time, both the plaintiff and defendant were not using ordinary care, then the plaintiff could not recover.

In using this term, ordinary care, it may be proper to state, that what constitutes ordinary care will vary with the circumstances of cases. In general, it means that kind and degree of care, which prudent and cautious men would use, such as is required by the exigency of the case, and such as is necessary to guard against probable danger. A man, who should have occasion to discharge a gun, on an open and extensive marsh, or in a forest, would be required to use less circumspection and care, than if he were to do the same thing in an inhabited town, village, or city. To make an accident, or casualty, or as the law sometimes states it, inevitable accident, it must be such an accident as the defendant could not have avoided by the use of the kind and degree of care necessary to the exigency, and in the circumstances in which he was placed.

We are not aware of any circumstances in this case, requiring a distinction between acts which it was lawful and proper to do, and acts of legal duty. There are cases, undoubtedly, in which officers are bound to act under process, for the legality of which they are not responsible, and perhaps some others in which this distinction would be important. We can have no doubt that the act of the defendant in attempting to part the fighting dogs, one of which was his own, and for the injurious acts of which he might be responsible, was a lawful and proper act, which he might do by proper and safe means. If, then, in doing this act, using due care and all proper precautions necessary to the exigency of the case, to avoid hurt to others, in raising his stick for that purpose, he accidentally hit the plaintiff in his eye, and wounded him, this was the result of pure accident, or was involuntary and unavoidable, and therefore the action would not lie. Or if the defendant was chargeable with some negligence, and if the plaintiff was also chargeable with negligence, we think the plaintiff cannot recover without showing that the damage was caused wholly by the act of the defendant, and that the plaintiff's own negligence did not contribute as an efficient cause to produce it.

The court instructed the jury, that if it was not a necessary act, and the defendant was not in duty bound to part the dogs, but might with propriety interfere or not as he chose, the defendant was responsible for the consequences of the blow, unless it appeared that he was in the exercise of extraordinary care, so that the accident was inevitable, using the word not in a strict but a popular sense. This is to be taken in connection with the charge afterwards given, that if the jury believed, that the act of interference in the fight was unnecessary, (that is, as before explained, not a duty incumbent on the defendant), then the burden of proving extraordinary care on the part of the defendant, or want of ordinary care on the part of plaintiff, was on the defendant.

The court is of opinion that these directions were not conformable to law. If the act of hitting the plaintiff was unintentional, on the part of the defendant, and done in the doing of a lawful act, then the defendant was not liable, unless it was done in the want of exercise of due care, adapted to the exigency of the case, and therefore such want of due care became part of the plaintiff's case, and the burden of proof was on the plaintiff to establish it. . . .

Perhaps the learned judge, by the use of the term extraordinary care, in the above charge, explained as it is by the context, may have intended nothing more than that increased degree of care and diligence, which the exigency of particular circumstances might require, and which men of ordinary care and prudence would use under like circumstances, to guard against danger. If such was the meaning of this part of the charge, then it does not differ from our views, as above explained. But we are of opinion, that the other part of the charge, that the burden of proof was on the defendant, was incorrect. Those facts which are essential to enable the plaintiff to recover, he takes the burden of proving. The evidence may be offered by the plaintiff or by the defendant; the question of due care, or want of care, may be essentially connected with the main facts, and arise from the same proof; but the effect of the rule, as to the burden of proof, is this, that when the proof is all in, and before the jury, from whatever side it comes, and whether directly proved, or inferred from circumstances, if it appears that the defendant was doing a lawful act, and unintentionally hit and hurt the plaintiff, then unless it also appears to the satisfaction of the jury, that the defendant is chargeable with some fault, negligence, carelessness, or want of prudence, the plaintiff fails to sustain the burden of proof, and is not entitled to recover.

New trial ordered.

NOTES

1. ***The Ins-and-Outs of Negligence.*** Is *Brown* consistent with the response to the same issue offered by Brian, J., in the *Thorns Case*? Is the defense of assumption of risk available because the plaintiff inched forward to get a better view? Is the defendant entitled to a contributory negligence defense because one of the two dogs was owned by the plaintiff?

2. ***Negligence and Economic Growth.*** The mid-nineteenth century rise of negligence in American tort law has often been viewed as a subsidy for infant industries. Professor Morton Horwitz wrote in The Transformation of American Law, 1780–1860, 99–101 (1977): "One of the most striking aspects of legal change during the antebellum period is the extent to which common law doctrines were transformed to create immunities from legal liability and thereby to provide substantial subsidies for those who undertook schemes of economic development." He argued that subsidies through common law (instead of through taxation) were designed to "more easily disguise underlying political choices. Subsidy through the tax system, by contrast, inevitably involves greater danger of political conflict." In the face of much empirical uncertainty, how should legislatures choose to intervene? "Nevertheless, it does seem fairly clear that the tendency of subsidy through legal change during this period was dramatically to throw the burden of economic development on the weakest and least active elements in the population."

One challenge to the subsidy thesis runs as follows:

> Brown [v. Kendall] itself, after all, did not involve industry; it involved private persons and a dog fight. Rather than simply promoting "General Motors," is it not more accurate to say that Chief Judge Shaw saw the change in moral terms as well, as a sound social policy not only for business but for every man?

Roberts, Negligence: Blackstone to Shaw to ?: An Intellectual Escapade in a Tory Vein, 50 Cornell L.Q. 191, 205 (1965). Is this challenge persuasive, even if Shaw understood the implications of the negligence rule for the growth of industry and trade?

The Horwitz thesis was likewise challenged by Gary Schwartz, Tort Law and the Economy in Nineteenth-Century America: A Reinterpretation, 90 Yale L.J. 1717 (1981). Schwartz shows that many of the early English and especially American cases around 1800 had already adopted the negligence principle. Schwartz also reviewed every nineteenth-century tort case decided in both California and New Hampshire and found no support for the subsidy thesis and no effort by the courts to engage in the "dynamic, utilitarian" calculations that Horwitz attributes to them. Schwartz also noted that it was unlikely that the subsidy question could be kept concealed in the face of explicit legislative debate over subsidies to both railroads and canals.

The Horwitz thesis has also been challenged on theoretical grounds. Most accident cases come out the same way under both negligence and strict liability, meaning that manipulating common law tort rules is a poor way to create interest group subsidies, especially since many large industries often litigated both as plaintiffs and defendants. See Epstein, The Social Consequences of Common Law Rules, 95 Harv. L. Rev. 1717 (1982).

In any event, the same debate over negligence and strict liability also surfaced in the English cases shortly after *Brown*, with dramatically different results.

Fletcher v. Rylands

(1865) 159 Eng. Rep. 737 (Exch.)

Trespass

[The following statement of facts is taken from the opinion of Blackburn, J., in the intermediate appellate court:

"It appears from the statement in the case, that the plaintiff was damaged by his property being flooded by water, which, without any fault on his part, broke out of a reservoir constructed on the defendants' land by the defendants' orders, and maintained by the defendants.

It appears from the statement in the case, that the coal under the defendants' land had, at some remote period, been worked out; but this was unknown at the time when the defendants gave directions to erect the reservoir, and the water in the reservoir would not have escaped from the defendants' land, and no mischief would have been done to the plaintiff, but for this latent defect in the defendants' subsoil. And it further appears, that the defendants selected competent engineers and contractors to make their reservoir, and themselves personally continued in total ignorance of what we have called the latent defect in the subsoil; but that these persons employed by them in the course of the work became aware of the existence of the ancient shafts filled up with soil, though they did not know or suspect that they were shafts communicating with old workings.

It is found that the defendants, personally, were free from all blame, but that in fact proper care and skill was not used by the persons employed by them, to provide for the sufficiency of the reservoir with reference to these shafts. The consequence was, that the reservoir when filled with water burst into the shafts, the water flowed down through them into the old workings, and thence into the plaintiff's mine, and there did the mischief."

This statement should be supplemented by a few additional facts drawn from Lord Cairns' opinion in the House of Lords. (1) the plaintiff had leased his coal mines from the Earl of Wilton; (2) the defendants had constructed their new reservoir upon other land of the Earl of Wilton, with his permission; (3) the reservoir in question was to be used to collect water for the defendants' mill; (4) the defendants had already placed, on their own nearby land, a small reservoir and a mill; (5) the plaintiff in the course of working his mines came across some abandoned shafts and mine passages of unknown origin; and (6) the reservoir burst when it was partially filled with water after one of the vertical shafts beneath it gave way.]

Bramwell, B. . . . Now, what is the plaintiff's right? He had the right to work his mines to their extent, leaving no boundary between himself and the next owner. By so doing he subjected himself to all consequences resulting from natural causes, among others, to the influx of all water naturally flowing in. But he had a right to be free from what has been called "foreign" water, that is, water artificially brought or sent to him directly, or indirectly by its being sent to where it would flow to him. The defendants had no right to pour or send water onto the plaintiff's works. Had they done so knowingly it is admitted an action would lie; and that it would if they did it again. . . . The plaintiff's right then has been infringed; the defendants in causing water to flow to the plaintiff have done that which they had no right to do; what difference in point of law does it make that they have done it unwittingly? I think none, and consequently that the action is maintainable. . . . As a rule the knowledge or ignorance of the damage done is immaterial. The burden of proof of this proposition is not on the plaintiff.

Exhibit 2.2 George William Wilshere Bramwell

George William Wilshere Bramwell, 1st Baron Bramwell (1808–1892), was an English judge who decided Blyth v. Birmingham Water Works, 156 Eng. Rep. 1047 (Ex. 1856), during his first year on the Court of Exchequer. Beginning his career as a clerk in his father's banking business, Bramwell turned to the law and quickly established his legal and procedural acumen. His work on the Common Law Procedure Commission led to the 1852 Common Law Procedure Act. He was also influential in the creation of limited liability for corporate entities in Britain.

Bio source: Herbert Stephen, Bramwell, George William Wilshere, Dictionary of National Biographies 256–57 (1901 supp.)
Image source: Wikimedia Commons
Source: Wikimedia Commons

I proceed to deal with the arguments the other way. It is said there must be a trespass, a nuisance or negligence. I do not agree. . . . But why is this not a trespass? Wilfulness is not material. . . . Why is it not a nuisance? The nuisance is not in the reservoir, but in the water escaping. . . . [T]he act was lawful, the mischievous consequence is a wrong. Where two carriages come in collision, if there is no negligence in either it is as much the act of the one driver as of the other that they meet. The cases of carriers and innkeepers are really cases of contract, and, though exceptional, furnish no evidence that the general law in matters wholly independent of contract is not what I have stated. The old common law liability for fire, created a liability beyond what I contend for here. . . .

MARTIN, B. . . . First, I think there was no trespass. In the judgment of my brother Bramwell, to which I shall hereafter refer, he seems to think the act of the defendants was a trespass, but I cannot concur, and I own it seems to me that the cases cited by him, viz., Leame v. Bray [(1803) 102 Eng. Rep. 724 (KB)], and Gregory v. Piper, 9 B. & C. 591 (E.C.L.R. vol. 17)[, (1829) 109 Eng. Rep. 220 (KB)], prove the contrary. I think the true criterion of trespass is laid down in the judgments in the former case, viz., that to constitute trespass the act doing the damage must be immediate, and that if the damage be mediate or consequential (which I think the present was) it is not a trespass. Secondly, I think there was no nuisance in the ordinary and generally understood meaning of that word, that is to say, something hurtful or injurious to the senses. The making a pond for holding water is a nuisance to no one. The digging a reservoir in a man's own land is a lawful act. It does not appear that there was any embankment, or that the water in the reservoir was ever above the level of the natural surface of the land, and the water escaped from the bottom of the reservoir, and in ordinary course would descend by gravitation into the defendants' own land, and they did not know of the existence of the old workings. To hold the defendants liable would therefore make them insurers against the consequence of a lawful act upon their own land when they had no reason to believe or suspect that any damage was likely to ensue.

No case was cited in which the question has arisen as to real property; but as to personal property the question arises every day, and there is no better established rule of law than that when damage is done to personal property, and even to the person, by collision either upon the road or at sea, there must be negligence in the party doing the damage to render him legally responsible, and if there be no negligence the party sustaining the damage must bear with it. The existence of this rule is proved by the exceptions to it, viz., the cases of the innkeeper and common carrier of goods for hire, who are quasi insurers. These cases are said to be by the custom of the realm, treating them as exceptions from the ordinary rule of law. In the absence of authority to the contrary, I can see no reason why damage to real property should be governed by a different rule or principle than damage to personal property. There is an instance also of damage to real property, when the party causing it was at common law liable upon the custom of the realm as a quasi insurer, viz., the master of a house if a fire had kindled there and consumed the house of another. In such case the master of the house was liable at common law without proof of negligence on his part. This seems to be an exception from the ordinary rule of law, and in my opinion affords an argument that in other cases such as the present there must be negligence to create a liability. For these reasons I think the first question ought to be answered in favour of the defendants. . . .

. . . I entertain no doubt that if the defendants directly and by their immediate act cast water upon the plaintiff's land it would have been a trespass, and that they would be liable to an action for it. But this they did not do. What they did was this, they dug a reservoir in their own land and put water in it, which, by underground openings of which they were ignorant, escaped into the plaintiff's land. I think this a very different thing from a direct casting of water upon the land, and that the legal liabilities consequent upon it are governed by a different principle. . . .

[Pollock, C.B., after stating that the issue was "one of great difficulty, and therefore of much doubt," wrote a brief opinion agreeing with Martin, B.]

rule

Fletcher v. Rylands

[1866] 1 LR Exch. 265

BLACKBURN, J. . . . The plaintiff, though free from all blame on his part, must bear the loss, unless he can establish that it was the consequence of some default for which the defendants are responsible. The question of law therefore arises, what is the obligation which the law casts on a person who, like the defendants, lawfully brings on his land something which, though harmless whilst it remains there, will naturally do mischief if it escape out of his land. It is agreed on all hands that he must take care to keep in that which he has brought on the land and keeps there, in order that it may not escape and damage his neighbours, but the question arises whether the duty which the law casts upon him, under such circumstances, is an absolute duty to keep it in at his peril, or is, as the majority of the Court of Exchequer have thought, merely a duty to take all reasonable and prudent precautions, in order to keep it in, but no more. If the first be the law, the person who has brought on his land and kept there something dangerous, and failed to keep it in, is responsible for all the natural consequences of its escape. If the second be the limit of his duty, he would not be answerable except on proof of negligence, and consequently would not be answerable for escape arising from any latent defect which ordinary prudence and skill could not detect.

Exhibit 2.3 Colin Blackburn

Colin Blackburn, Baron Blackburn (1813–1896), a Scottish judge who served in English courts and delivered the leading opinion in Rylands v. Fletcher, earned a reputation throughout his judicial career as a marvel of common law wisdom. Upon his death, a remembrance in the Harvard Law Review mourned the loss of the "greatest English common law judge of recent years." The notice remarked that in his absence, "one hardly knows yet where to turn for that combination of sound thinking, exact and instructive discrimination, and large, rational, and just exposition by which the law of all English-speaking countries has profited for these many years." Note, 9 Harv. L. Rev. 420–21 (1896).

Source: Wikimedia Commons

Supposing the second to be the correct view of the law, a further question arises subsidiary to the first, viz., whether the defendants are not so far identified with the contractors whom they employed, as to be responsible for the consequences of their want of care and skill in making the reservoir in fact insufficient with reference to the old shafts, of the existence of which they were aware, though they had not ascertained where the shafts went to.

We think that the true rule of law is, that the person who for his own purposes brings on his lands and collects and keeps there anything likely to do mischief if it escapes, must keep it in at his peril, and, if he does not do so, is prima facie answerable for all the damage which is the natural consequence of its escape. He can excuse himself by shewing that the escape was owing to the plaintiff's default; or perhaps that the escape was the consequence of vis major, or the act of God; but as nothing of this sort exists here, it is unnecessary to inquire what excuse would be sufficient. The general rule, as above stated, seems on principle just. The person whose grass or corn is eaten down by the escaping cattle of his neighbour, or whose mine is flooded by the water from his neighbour's reservoir, or whose cellar is invaded by the filth of his neighbour's privy, or whose habitation is made unhealthy by the fumes and noisome vapours of his neighbour's alkali works, is damnified without any fault of his own; and it seems but reasonable and just that the neighbour, who has brought something on his own property which was not naturally there, harmless to others so long as it is confined to his own property, but which he knows to be mischievous if it gets on his neighbour's, should be obliged to make good the damage which ensues if he does not succeed in confining it to his own property. But for his act in bringing it there no mischief could have accrued, and it seems but just that he should at his peril keep it there so that no mischief may accrue, or answer for the natural and anticipated consequences. And upon authority, this we think is established to be the law whether the things so brought be beasts, or water, or filth, or stenches.

[The opinion then exhaustively examines the earlier cases in support of the general proposition, and continues:]

. . . But it was further said by Martin, B., that when damage is done to personal property, or even to the person, by collision, either upon land or at sea, there must be negligence in the party doing the damage to render him legally responsible; and this is no doubt true, and as was pointed out by Mr. Mellish during his argument before us, this is not confined to cases of collision, for there are many cases in which proof of negligence is essential, as for instance, where an unruly horse gets on the footpath of a public street and kills a passenger . . . ; or where a person in a dock is struck by the falling of a bale of cotton which the defendant's servants are lowering . . . ; and many other similar cases may be found. But we think these cases distinguishable from the present. Traffic on the highways, whether by land or sea, cannot be conducted without exposing those whose persons or property are near it to some inevitable risk; and that being so, those who go on the highway, or have their property adjacent to it, may well be held to do so subject to their taking upon themselves the risk of injury from that inevitable danger; and persons who by the licence of the owner pass near the warehouses where goods are being raised or lowered, certainly do so subject to the inevitable risk of accident. In neither case, therefore, can they recover without proof of want of care or skill occasioning the accident; and it is believed that all the cases in which inevitable accident has been held an excuse for what prima facie was a trespass, can be explained on the same principle, viz., that the circumstances were such as to shew that the plaintiff had taken that risk upon himself. But there is no ground for saying that the plaintiff here took upon himself any risk arising from the uses to which the defendants should choose to apply their land. He neither knew what these might be, nor could he in any way control the defendants, or hinder their building what reservoirs they liked, and storing up in them what water they pleased, so long as the defendants succeeded in preventing the water which they there brought from interfering with the plaintiff's property.

The view which we take of the first point renders it unnecessary to consider whether the defendants would or would not be responsible for the want of care and skill in the persons employed by them, under the circumstances stated in the case.

Rylands v. Fletcher

[1868] LR 3 (HL) 330

Cairns, L. C. . . . The Defendants, treating them as the owners or occupiers of the close on which the reservoir was constructed, might lawfully have used that close for any purpose for which it might in the ordinary course of the enjoyment of land be used, and if, in what I may term the natural use of that land, there had been any accumulation of water, either on the surface or underground, and if, by the operation of the laws of nature, that accumulation of water had passed off into the close occupied by the Plaintiff, the Plaintiff could not have complained that that result had taken place. If he had desired to guard himself against it, it would have lain upon him to have done so, by leaving, or by interposing, some barrier between his close and the close of the Defendants in order to have prevented the operation of the law of nature. . . .

On the other hand if the Defendants, not stopping at the natural use of their close, had desired to use it for any purpose which I may term a non-natural use, for the purpose of introducing into the close that which in its natural condition was not in or upon it, for the purpose of introducing water either above or below ground in quantities and in a manner not the result of any work or operation on or under the land,—and if in consequence of their doing so, or in consequence of any imperfection in the mode of their doing so, the water came to escape and to pass off into the close of the Plaintiff, then it appears to me that that which the Defendants were doing they were doing at their own peril and, if in the course of their doing it, the evil arose to which I have referred, the evil, namely, of the escape of the water and its passing away to the close of the Plaintiff and injuring the Plaintiff, then for the consequence of that, in my opinion, the Defendants would be liable. . . .

Lord Cranworth. My Lords, I concur with my noble and learned friend in thinking that the rule of law was correctly stated by Mr. Justice Blackburn in delivering the opinion of the Exchequer Chamber. If a person brings, or accumulates, on his land anything which, if it should escape, may cause damage to his neighbour, he does so at his peril. If it does escape, and cause damage, he is responsible, however careful he may have been, and whatever precautions he may have taken to prevent the damage.

In considering whether a Defendant is liable to a Plaintiff for damage which the Plaintiff may have sustained, the question in general is not whether the Defendant has acted with due care and caution, but whether his acts have occasioned the damage. . . . And the doctrine is founded on good sense. For when one person, in managing his own affairs, causes, however innocently, damage to another, it is obviously only just that he should be the party to suffer. He is bound sic uti suo ut non laedat alienum. . . . [He is bound to use his own property not to harm another.]

The doctrine appears to me to be well illustrated by the two modern cases in the Court of Common Pleas. . . . I allude to the two cases of Smith v. Kenrick[, (1849) 137 Eng. Rep. 205 (CP)], and Baird v. Williamson[, (1863) 143 Eng. Rep. 831 (CP)]. In the former the owner of a coal mine on the higher level worked out the whole of his coal, leaving no barrier between his mine and the mine on the lower level, so that the water percolating through the upper mine flowed into the lower mine, and obstructed the owner of it in getting his coal. It was held that the owner of the lower mine had no ground of complaint. The Defendant, the owner of the upper mine, had a right to remove all his coal. The damage sustained by the Plaintiff was occasioned by the natural flow or percolation of water from the upper strata. There was no obligation on the Defendant to protect the Plaintiff against this. It was his business to erect or leave a sufficient barrier to keep out the water, or to adopt proper means for so conducting the water as that it should not impede him in his workings. The water, in that case, was only left by the Defendant to flow in its natural course.

But in the later case of Baird v. Williamson the Defendant, the owner of the upper mine, did not merely suffer the water to flow through his mine without leaving a barrier between it and the mine below, but in order to work his own mine beneficially he pumped up quantities of water which passed into the Plaintiff's mine in addition to that which would have naturally reached it, and so occasioned him damage. Though this was done without negligence, and in the due working of his own mine, yet he was held to be responsible for the damage so occasioned. It was in consequence of his act, whether skilfully or unskilfully performed, that the Plaintiff had been damaged, and he was therefore held liable for the consequences. The damage in the former case may be treated as having arisen from the act of God; in the latter, from the act of the Defendant.

Applying the principle of these decisions to the case now before the House, I come without hesitation to the conclusion that the judgment of the Exchequer Chamber was right. . . .

Judgment of the Court of Exchequer Chamber affirmed.

NOTES

1. *Rylands v. Fletcher, the Forms of Action, and Common Law Precedent.* The initial exchange between Martin and Bramwell hearkens back to discussions of the forms of action, by asking whether the harm was immediate or consequential, where proof of negligence was required only in the latter case. On this question, does it make a difference that the reservoir was not in fact completely full when its floor gave way? Blackburn, J., sidesteps the disagreement below, first by treating the harm as consequential and then by applying a strict liability rule. Do the earlier precedents on cattle trespass, fire, nuisance, and filth escaping from privies support his decision, or were these all instances of "direct harm"?

The noted English torts scholar Frederick Pollock doubted that *Rylands* was worthy of "universal acceptance." See Pollock, Torts 398–99 (1st ed. 1887), and agreed with the suggestion of Thayer, Liability Without Fault, 29 Harv. L. Rev. 801 (1916), that the principle of res ipsa loquitur (*infra* Chapter 3, Section G, at 199) "which was hardly developed at the date of Rylands v. Fletcher, would suffice to cover the ground for all useful purposes in a simpler and more rational manner." See Pollock, Torts 507 (13th ed. 1929). Holmes, for his part, devoted relatively little attention to *Rylands*, which he treated gingerly:

> It may even be very much for the public good that the dangerous accumulation should be made (a consideration which might influence the decision in some instances, and differently in others): but as there is a limit to the nicety of an inquiry which is possible in a trial, it may be considered that the safest way to secure care is to throw the risk upon the person who decides what precautions shall be taken.

Holmes, The Common Law 117 (1881). Is this point universally true in all negligence cases?

2. *Scope of Rylands v. Fletcher?* Should *Rylands* apply to personal injury cases, or only property damages? In Transco plc v. Stockport Metropolitan Borough Council, [2003] UKHL 61, Lord Bingham treated the matter as a sub-species of nuisance that never applied to personal injury cases, as held by the House of Lords in Read v. J. Lyons & Co., Ltd. [1947] AC 156, and further held that the escape requirement remained fixed. Would Blackburn, J., have denied recovery if a workman had been killed by flooding? Does it make a difference that most reservoirs in England were constructed pursuant to statutory authorizations, given the high risk of dam failure? See Simpson, Legal Liability for Bursting Reservoirs, 13 J. Legal Stud. 209, 244 (1984). See Powell v. Fall, *infra* at 92.

3. *"Non-Natural Use" and Acts of Third Parties.* What importance should be attached to Lord Cairns' "non-natural use" requirement? Is the phrase "natural" read in opposition to "artificial" or "man-made," or in opposition to "unreasonable or inappropriate"? The second reading was adopted in Rickards v. Lothian, [1913] AC 263. The defendant owned a business building with a lavatory on the fourth floor. One night, after the defendant's caretaker had made his usual tour of inspection, an unknown person entered the building, stuffed the lavatory with "various articles such as nails, penholders, string and soap," and opened the faucet all the way. The next morning, the plaintiff discovered that his stock in trade had been damaged and sued the defendant for his losses. The House of Lords held that the case fell outside the scope of Rylands v. Fletcher because

> the provision of a proper supply of water to the various parts of a house is not only reasonable, but has become, in accordance with modern sanitary views, an almost necessary feature of town life. . . . It would be unreasonable for the law to regard those who install and maintain such a system of supply as doing so at their own peril.

Given the stable condition of the privy before the act of the third party, could the defendant have prevailed on causal grounds—the independent act of a third party—even if the lavatory was a non-natural use? If water had leaked into the plaintiff's premises when the lavatory had been used in an ordinary manner, is the defendant liable under *Rylands*? As interpreted in *Rickards*?

Exhibit 2.4 Hugh McCalmont Cairns, 1st Earl Cairns, c. 1860

Source: John Watkins / National Portrait Gallery, London

Hugh McCalmont Cairns, 1st Earl Cairns Privy Council (27 December 1819–2 April 1885), was an Anglo-Irish statesman who served as Lord High Chancellor of Great Britain during the first two ministries of Benjamin Disraeli. He was one of the most prominent Conservative statesmen in the House of Lord during this period Victorian politics. He served as the seventeenth Chancellor of the University of Dublin between 1867 and 1885.

The House of Lords reevaluated the phrase "non-natural use" in Cambridge Water Co. v. Eastern Counties Leather PLC, [1994] 2 AC 264, 309, in which toxic perchloroethenes (P.C.E.s) escaped from the defendant E.C.L.'s tannery and slowly worked their way through an aquifer to the plaintiff's borehole, located some 1.3 miles away in Sawton. Lord Goff rejected defendant's attempt to expand the definition of natural use to do away with the strict liability rule in *Rylands*, "given [that] the storage of chemicals in substantial quantities" could result in contamination that made water undrinkable. He did so even though other establishments posed similar risks, on the ground that "a reasonable supervisor at E.C.L. would not have foreseen, in or before 1976, that such repeated spillages of small quantities of solvent would lead to any environmental hazard or danger." Lord Goff then held that the rule in *Rylands* should not be exempt from the general test of reasonable foresight that in England applies in both nuisance and negligence cases. Why? See *The Wagon Mound, infra* Chapter 5, at 354. On a more functional level, he noted that the solution to the pressing environmental issues rested more on "informed and carefully structured legislation" than the revision of a common law rule. Why not keep the common law rule until the legislature acted? See the discussion of public nuisance, *infra* Chapter 7, at 515. How would the foresight limitation apply to the facts of *Rylands*?

4. *Acts of God under Rylands v. Fletcher.* What distinguishes a mere "escape" from an act of God under *Rylands*? In Nichols v. Marsland, 2 Exch. Div. 1 (1876), the plaintiff's land was flooded when the defendant's "ornamental pools" containing large amounts of water broke their banks during an extraordinary rainfall of unanticipated severity. Bramwell, B., found this storm to be an act of God under Rylands v. Fletcher and accordingly affirmed a judgment for the defendant. The court also found no negligence in the construction or maintenance of the pools. Further, in Carstairs v. Taylor, LR 6 Exch. 217 (1871), the plaintiff, a tenant in the defendant's building, was unable to recover when rats ate through a box containing water that was collected by gutters from the roof of the building. Bramwell, B., noted that the box and gutters had been installed for the mutual benefit of both parties. Hence, *Rylands* did not apply because the defendant did not collect the water for his sole purposes. Compare Brown v. Kendall, *supra* at 78.

More recently, in In re Flood Litigation, 607 S.E.2d 863, 879 (W. Va. 2004), a group of property owners sued a group of defendant coal companies, railroads, landowners, and gas companies, claiming that their joint alteration of the landscape led to flooding damage under *Rylands*. Maynard, C.J., refused to apply *Rylands* because the defendants had not engaged in abnormally dangerous activities. See generally Chapter 7, *infra* at 474. In addressing the act of God defense, he first noted the difficulties in apportioning loss between natural forces and a defendant's activities, and held that

> the defendant is liable only for the damages that are fairly attributable to the defendant's conduct. However, in such a case, a defendant has the burden to show by clear and convincing evidence the character and measure of damages that are not the defendant's responsibility; and if the defendant cannot do so, then the defendant bears the entire liability.

Would this rule require some apportionment of liability in *Nichols* if any water in the ornamental pool escaped in the midst of the storm?

5. *Default of Plaintiff.* What counts as "a default of the plaintiff" to which Blackburn, B., referred? Under Smith v. Kenrick, a plaintiff who removes all the coal up to the boundary of his mine is not in default under *Rylands*, even if that coal had served as a barrier between the plaintiff's and the defendant's properties. In Holgate v. Bleazard, [1917] 1 KB 443, the court held that the plaintiff was not in default in a case of horse trespass when he had not repaired the fence around his own land as required by the covenant with his landlord. How would the case be decided if the covenant to fence had been made with the defendant?

Brown v. Collins

53 N.H. 442 (1873)

Trespass. . . . [The plaintiff owned a stone post with streetlamp. The defendant was waiting by a railroad crossing on his wagon loaded with grain and drawn by two horses.] The horses became frightened by an engine on the railroad near the crossing, and by reason thereof became unmanageable, and ran, striking the post. . . . The shock produced by the collision with the post threw the defendant from his seat in the wagon, and he struck on the ground between horses, but suffered no injury except a slight concussion. The defendant was in the use of ordinary care and skill in managing his team, until they became frightened. . . .

Doe, J. . . . We take the case as one where, without actual fault in the defendant, his horses broke from his control, ran away with him, went upon the plaintiff's land, and did damage there, against the will, intent, and desire of the defendant. [The court then discusses the rule in Rylands v. Fletcher, continuing:]

. . . The rule of such cases is applied, by Blackburn, to everything which a man brings on his land, which will, if it escapes, naturally do damage. One result of such a doctrine is, that every one building a fire on his own hearth, for necessary purposes, with the utmost care, does so at the peril, not only of losing his own house, but of being irretrievably ruined if a spark from his chimney starts a conflagration which lays waste the neighborhood. "In conflict with the rule, as laid down in the English cases, is a class of cases in reference to damage from fire communicated from the adjoining premises. Fire, like water or steam, is likely to produce mischief if it escapes and goes beyond control; and yet it has never been held in this country that one building a fire upon his own premises can be made liable if it escapes upon his neighbor's premises, and does him damage without proof of negligence." Losee v. Buchanan, 51 N.Y. 476, 487 (1873).

Everything that a man can bring on his land is capable of escaping,—against his will, and without his fault, with or without assistance, in some form, solid, liquid, or gaseous, changed or unchanged by the transforming processes of nature or art,—and of doing damage after its escape. Moreover, if there is a legal principle that makes a man liable for the natural consequences of the escape of things which he brings on his land, the application of such a principle cannot be limited to those things: it must be applied to all his acts that disturb the original order of creation or, at least, to all things which he undertakes to possess or control anywhere, and which were not used and enjoyed in what is called the natural or primitive condition of mankind, whatever that may have been. This is going back a long way for a standard of legal rights, and adopting an arbitrary test of responsibility that confounds all degrees of danger, pays no heed to the essential elements of actual fault, puts a clog upon natural and reasonably necessary uses of matter, and tends to embarrass and obstruct much of the work which it seems to be man's duty carefully to do. The distinction made by Lord Cairns—Rylands v. Fletcher, L.R. 3 H.L. 330—between a natural and non-natural use of land, if he meant anything more than the difference between a reasonable use and an unreasonable one, is not established in the law. Even if the arbitrary test were applied only to things which a man brings on his land, it would still recognize the peculiar rights of savage life in a wilderness, ignore the rights growing out of a civilized state of society, and make a distinction not warranted by the enlightened spirit of the common law: it would impose a penalty upon efforts, made in a reasonable, skillful, and careful manner, to rise above a condition of barbarism. . . . "Most of the rights of property, as well as of person, in the social state, are not absolute but relative"—Losee v. Buchanan, 51 N.Y. 485; . . .

It is not improbable that the rules of liability for damage done by brutes or by fire, found in the early English cases, were introduced, by sacerdotal influence, from what was supposed to be the Roman or the Hebrew law. 7 Am. L. Rev. 652, note; . . . It would not be singular if these rules should be spontaneously produced at a certain period in the life of any community. Where they first appeared is of little consequence in the present inquiry. They were certainly introduced in England at an immature stage of English jurisprudence, and an undeveloped state of agriculture, manufactures, and commerce, when the nation had not settled down to these modern, progressive, industrial pursuits which the spirit of the common law, adapted to all conditions of society, encourages and defends. . . . At all events, whatever may be said of the origin of those rules, to extend them, as they were extended in Rylands v. Fletcher, seems to us contrary to the analogies and the general principles of the common law, as now established. To extend them to the present case would be contrary to American authority, as well as to our understanding of legal principles. . . .

[Judgment for defendant.]

NOTES

1. *The Reception of Rylands v. Fletcher into American Common Law.* Should Brown v. Collins be governed by Gibbons v. Pepper, *supra* at 69? Any possible liability for the railroad?

Brown followed Losee v. Buchanan, 51 N.Y. 483, 484–85 (1873), where the plaintiff sued for damages from the defendant's boiler, which, while being operated with all care and skill, exploded and "was projected and thrown onto the plaintiff's premises," causing damage to the buildings located thereon. Judge Earl wrote:

> By becoming a member of civilized society, I am compelled to give up many of my natural rights, but I receive more than a compensation from the surrender by every other man of the same rights, and the security, advantage and protection which the laws give me. So, too, the general rules that I may have the exclusive and undisturbed use and possession of my real estate, and that I must so use my real estate as not to injure my neighbor, are much modified by the exigencies of the social state. We must have factories, machinery, dams, canals and railroads. They are demanded by the manifold wants of mankind, and lay at the basis of all our civilization. If I have any of these upon my lands, and they are not a nuisance and are not so managed as to become such, I am not responsible for any damage they accidentally and unavoidably do my neighbor. He receives his compensation for such damage by the general good, in which he shares, and the right which he has to place the same things upon his lands.

Why does *Losee*'s argument of implicit compensation work only in one direction? Does the greater security obtained under a uniform rule of strict liability supply the compensation to the defendant that justifies imposing liability in the instant case? Note that no matter which starting point or "baseline" is used, a sound decision protocol only displaces it if the new rule generates greater gains across the board than the old one. Can this system work if all people are not situated the same way in some original position? For a further expansion of this theme of "reciprocity," see Fletcher, Fairness and Utility in Tort Law, 85 Harv. L. Rev. 537 (1972), *infra* Chapter 7, at 480. On the fate of *Losee*, see Spano v. Perini, *infra* Chapter 7, at 474.

2. *Damages Versus Injunction?* In Turner v. Big Lake Oil Co., 96 S.W.2d 221, 226 (Tex. 1936), the court rejected Rylands v. Fletcher as inapplicable to Texas, where the storage of water in large cisterns was a "natural" use of the land:

> In Texas we have conditions very different from those which obtain in England. A large portion of Texas is an arid or semi-arid region. West of the 98th meridian of longitude, where the rainfall is approximately 30 inches, the rainfall decreases until finally, in the extreme western part of the State, it is only about 10 inches. This land of decreasing rainfall is the great ranch or livestock region of the state, water for which is stored in thousands of ponds, tanks, and lakes on the surface of the ground. The country is almost without streams and without the storage of water from rainfall in basins constructed for the purpose, or to hold waters pumped from the earth, the great livestock industry of West Texas must perish. No such condition obtains in England. With us the storage of water is a natural or necessary and common use of the land, necessarily within the contemplation of the State and its grantees when grants were made, and obviously the rule announced in Rylands v. Fletcher, predicated upon different conditions, can have no application here.
>
> Again, in England there are no oil wells, no necessity for using surface storage facilities for impounding and evaporating salt waters therefrom. In Texas the situation is different. Texas has many great oil fields, tens of thousands of wells in almost every part of the State. Producing oil is one of our major industries. One of the by-products of oil production is salt water, which must be disposed of without injury to property or the pollution of streams. The construction of basins or ponds to hold this salt water is a necessary part of the oil business.

Does the need for water in Texas require that there be no liability for the occasional case of spillage? Or does it require only that the state not shut down these storage facilities by regulation or an injunction? Given the frequency and severity of these losses, how much would it cost to insure against this risk? See the discussion in Powell v. Fall, *infra*.

After these initial hesitations, *Rylands* gained much U.S. support before 1950. In 1984, Prosser and Keeton, Torts 549, reported that only seven states reject the *Rylands* principle and 30 accept it; that balance continues to swing in favor of the decision. See Abraham, Rylands v. Fletcher: Tort Law's Conscience, *in* Tort Stories 220–24 (Rabin & Sugarman eds., 2003).

Powell v. Fall

(1880) 5 QB 597

MELLOR, J. This was an action tried before me at Devizes without a jury. It was brought by the plaintiffs to recover a sum of £53 6*s.* 8*d.*, in respect of injury done to a rick of hay upon a farm of the plaintiff, John Thomas Powell, adjoining a public highway, and which injury was caused by sparks escaping from the fire of a traction engine belonging to the defendant, which was then being propelled by steam power along the highway. The engine was constructed in conformity with the provisions of 24 & 25 Vict. c.70, and of 28 & 29 Vict. c.83, being the Acts then in force for regulating the use of locomotives on turnpike and other roads.

At the time when the injury was occasioned to the hay stack by the sparks of fire issuing from the defendant's engine, it was not travelling at a greater speed than that prescribed by the Acts referred to, nor was the injury occasioned by any negligence on the part of the defendant's servants conducting or managing the same. . . .

The 13th section of 24 & 25 Vict. c.70, is as follows: "Nothing in this Act contained shall authorize any person to use upon a highway a locomotive engine, which shall be so constructed or used as to cause a public or private nuisance, and every such person so using such engine shall notwithstanding this Act be liable to an indictment or action as the case may be, for such use where, but for the passing of this Act, such indictment or action could be maintained," and by s.12 of 28 & 29 Vict. c.83, [which contained a parallel provision]. And it was further contended on the part of the plaintiffs that whilst the Acts entitled the defendant to use a locomotive properly constructed on the public highway, yet it never was intended by the legislature to exempt him from liability to damages in respect of any injury sustained by third persons in consequence of the use by him of a locomotive, and that it was wholly immaterial to the result that such injury arose from no want of care or negligence on the part of the defendant's servants in the management and use of the same. On the part of the defendant it was contended that the effect of the several statutes being to authorize the use of locomotives on public highways, if constructed and managed according to the provisions of such statutes, was to exempt the owners from liability to make good any injury arising from the use of locomotives, unless some improper construction of the engine, or some act of negligence in the use of it, could be imputed to such owners or their servants. I am of opinion that the contention on the part of the plaintiffs must prevail under Rylands v. Fletcher. . . .

The defendant appealed. . . .

BRAMWELL, L.J. I think that the judgment of Mellor, J., ought to be affirmed. The passing of the engine along the road is confessedly dangerous, inasmuch as sparks cannot be prevented from flying from it. It is conceded that at common law an action may be maintained for the injury suffered by the plaintiffs. The Locomotive Acts are relied upon as affording a defence, but instead of helping the defendant they shew not only that an action would have been maintainable at common law, but also that the right to sue for an injury is carefully preserved. It is just and reasonable that if a person uses a dangerous machine, he should pay for the damage which it occasions; if the reward which he gains for the use of the machine will not pay for the damage, it is mischievous to the public and ought to be suppressed, for the loss ought not to be borne by the community or the injured person. If the use of the machine is profitable, the owner ought to pay compensation for the damage. The plaintiffs are protected by the common law, and nothing adverse to their right to sue can be drawn from the statutes: the statutes do not make it lawful to damage property without paying for the injury. A great deal has been said about the liability of persons who have stored water which has subsequently escaped and done injury, and it has been urged that the emission of sparks from an engine is not so mischievous as the overflow of a large body of water. The arguments which we have heard are ingenious; but I need only say in reply to them that they have hardened my conviction that Rex v. Pease [(1832) 168 Eng. Rep. 216 (KB)] and Vaughan v. Taff Vale Ry. Co. (5 H. & N. 679 29 L. J. (Ex.) 247) were wrongly decided.

NOTES

1. *The Impact of Statute on Common Law Liability.* In Vaughn v. Taff Vale Railway, (1860) 157 Eng. Rep. 1351, 1354 (Exch.), disapproved by Bramwell, J., Cockburn, C.J., held that because the defendant operated the railroad under statutory authorization, the plaintiff had to establish negligence to recover damages:

> Although it may be true, that if a person keeps an animal of known dangerous propensities, or a dangerous instrument, he will be responsible to those who are thereby injured, independently of any negligence in the mode of dealing with the animal or using the instrument; yet when the legislature has sanctioned and authorized the use of a particular thing, and it is used for the purpose for which it was authorized, and every precaution has been observed to prevent injury, the sanction of the legislature carries with it this consequence, that if damage results from the use of such thing independently of negligence, the party using it is not responsible. . . . It is admitted that the defendants used fire for the purpose of propelling locomotive engines, and no doubt they were bound to take proper precaution to prevent injury to persons through whose lands they passed; but the mere use of fire in such engines does not make them liable for injury resulting from such use without any negligence on their part.

The effect of a statute upon a private cause of action was also raised in River Wear Commissioners v. Adamson, [1877] LR 2 App. Cas. 743 (HL) 767 (appeal taken from Eng.), when the applicable statute provided that "the owner of every vessel . . . shall be answerable to the undertakers [plaintiffs] for any damage done by such vessel . . . and the master or person having charge of such vessel through whose wilful act or negligence any such damage is done, shall also be liable to make good the same."

In *Adamson*, the defendant's boat was wrecked in a storm. After the crew abandoned it, the boat crashed into the plaintiff's dock. The owners of the ship were sued under the statute. Lord Blackburn, who wrote Rylands v. Fletcher, concurred in the judgment that the owners were not liable without proof of negligence:

> My Lords, the Common Law is, I think, as follows:—Property adjoining to a spot on which the public have a right to carry on traffic is liable to be injured by that traffic. In this respect there is no difference between a shop, the railings or windows of which may be broken by a carriage on the road, and a pier adjoining to a harbour or a navigable river or the sea, which is liable to be injured by a ship. In either case the owner of the injured property must bear his own loss, unless he can establish that some other person is in fault, and liable to make it good. And he does not establish this against a person merely by shewing that he is owner of the carriage or ship which did the mischief, for the owner incurs no liability merely because he is owner.
>
> But he does establish such a liability against any person who either wilfully did the damage, or neglected that duty which the law casts upon those in charge of a carriage on land, and a ship or a float of timber on water, to take reasonable care and use reasonable skill to prevent it from doing injury, and that this wilfulness or neglect caused the damage.

Is the result consistent with the statute?

2. *The Subsequent History of Powell v. Fall.* "Over the next forty years, Powell v. Fall was repeatedly followed in cases involving traction-engines and steam-rollers which, though driven with due care, had scared horses, crushed water-mains, or started fires." Spencer, Motor-Cars and the Rule in Rylands v. Fletcher*:* A Chapter of Accidents in the History of Law and Motoring, 42 Cambridge L.J. 65, 70 (1983). Nonetheless, *Powell* did not exert enough influence to make strict liability the norm in ordinary highway accidents, even though buses and cars were dangerous, with hard rubber tires and thin wheels prone to skidding. See Wing v. L.G.O.C., [1908] 25 Times L. Rep. 14, for skidding buses, and for ordinary cars, see Park v. L.G.O.C., [1909] 73 J.P. 283.

Oliver Wendell Holmes

The Common Law

77–84, 88–96 (1881)

Cover of the first edition of *The Common Law*, one of the most influential texts in American law. On its first page, it set out an enduring legal aphorism: "The life of the law has not been logic: it has been experience."

Source: Wikimedia Commons

The object of the next two Lectures is to discover whether there is any common ground at the bottom of all liability in tort, and if so, what that ground is. Supposing the attempt to succeed, it will reveal the general principle of civil liability at common law. The liabilities incurred by way of contract are more or less expressly fixed by the agreement of the parties concerned, but those arising from a tort are independent of any previous consent of the wrong-doer to bear the loss occasioned by his act. If *A* fails to pay a certain sum on a certain day, or to deliver a lecture on a certain night, after having made a binding promise to do so, the damages which he has to pay are recovered in accordance with his consent that some or all of the harms which may be caused by his failure shall fall upon him. But when *A* assaults or slanders his neighbor, or converts his neighbor's property, he does a harm which he has never consented to bear, and if the law makes him pay for it, the reason for doing so must be found in some general view of the conduct which every one may fairly expect and demand from every other, whether that other has agreed to it or not.

Such a general view is very hard to find. The law did not begin with a theory. It has never worked one out. . . . But the difficulty of showing [any historical trend] is much enhanced by the circumstances that, until lately, the substantive law has been approached only through the categories of the forms of action. Discussions of legislative principle have been darkened by arguments on the limits between trespass and case, or on the scope of a general issue. . . .

Since the ancient forms of action have disappeared, a broader treatment of the subject ought to be possible. Ignorance is the best of law reformers. People are glad to discuss a question on general principles, when they have forgotten the special knowledge necessary for technical reasoning. . . .

The business of the law of torts is to fix the dividing lines between those cases in which a man is liable for harm which he has done, and those in which he is not. But it cannot enable him to predict with certainty whether a given act under given circumstances will make him liable, because an act will rarely have that effect unless followed by damage, and for the most part, if not always, the consequences of an act are not known, but only guessed at as more or less probable. All the rules that the law can lay down beforehand are rules for determining the conduct which will be followed by liability if it is followed by harm,—that is, the conduct which a man pursues at his peril. The only guide for the future to be drawn from a decision against a defendant in an action of tort is that similar acts, under circumstances which cannot be distinguished except by the result from those of the defendant, are done at the peril of the actor; that if he escapes liability, it is simply because by good fortune no harm comes of his conduct in the particular event.

If, therefore, there is any common ground for all liability in tort, we shall best find it by eliminating the event as it actually turns out, and by considering only the principles on which the peril of his conduct is thrown upon the actor. We are to ask what are the elements, on the defendant's side, which must all be present before liability is possible, and the presence of which will commonly make him liable if damage follows.

The law of torts abounds in moral phraseology. It has much to say of wrongs, of malice, fraud, intent, and negligence. Hence it may naturally be supposed that the risk of a man's conduct is thrown upon him as the result of some moral shortcoming. But while this notion has been entertained, the extreme opposite will be found to have been a far more popular opinion—I mean the notion that a man is answerable for all the consequences of his acts, or, in other words, that he acts at his peril always, and wholly irrespective of the state of his consciousness upon the matter. . . .

The first [theory] is that of Austin, which is essentially the theory of a criminalist. According to him, the characteristic feature of law, properly so called, is a sanction or detriment threatened and imposed by the sovereign for disobedience to the sovereign's commands. As the greater part of the law only makes a man civilly answerable for breaking it, Austin is compelled to regard the liability to an action as a sanction, or, in other words, as a penalty for disobedience. It follows from this, according to the prevailing views of penal law, that such liability ought only to be based upon personal fault; and Austin accepts that conclusion, with its corollaries, one of which is that negligence means a state of the party's mind. These doctrines will be referred to later, so far as necessary.

According to [the second and opposite] view, broadly stated, under the common law a man *acts* at his peril. It may be held as a sort of setoff, that he is never liable for omissions except in consequence of some duty voluntarily undertaken. But the whole and sufficient ground for such liabilities as he does incur outside the last class is supposed to be that he has voluntarily acted, and that damage has ensued. If the act was voluntary, it is totally immaterial that the detriment which followed from it was neither intended nor due to the negligence of the actor.

In order to do justice to this way of looking at the subject, we must remember that the abolition of the common-law forms of pleading has not changed the rules of substantive law.

In the first place, it is said, consider generally the protection given by the law to property, both within and outside the limits of the [trespass] action. If a man crosses his neighbor's boundary by however innocent a mistake, or if his cattle escape into his neighbor's field, he is said to be liable in trespass quare clausum fregit . . . [wherefore he broke into the [plaintiff's] close, i.e., land].

Now suppose that, instead of a dealing with the plaintiff's property, the case is that force has proceeded directly from the defendant's body to the plaintiff's body, it is urged that, as the law cannot be less careful of the persons than of the property of its subjects, the only defences possible are similar to those which would have been open to an alleged trespass on land. You may show that there was no trespass by showing that the defendant did no act; as where he was thrown from his horse upon the plaintiff, or where a third person took his hand and struck the plaintiff with it. In such cases the defendant's body is the passive instrument of an external force, and the bodily motion relied on by the plaintiff is not his act at all. So you may show a justification or excuse in the conduct of the plaintiff himself. But if no such excuse is shown, and the defendant has voluntarily acted, he must answer for the consequences, however little intended and however unforeseen. If, for instance, being assaulted by a third person, the defendant lifted his stick and accidentally hit the plaintiff, who was standing behind him, according to this view he is liable, irrespective of any negligence toward the party injured.

The arguments for the doctrine under consideration are, for the most part, drawn from precedent, but it is sometimes supposed to be defensible as theoretically sound. Every man, it is said, has an absolute right to his person, and so forth, free from detriment at the hands of his neighbors. In the cases put, the plaintiff has done nothing; the defendant, on the other hand, has chosen to act. As between the two, the party whose voluntary conduct has caused the damage should suffer, rather than one who has had no share in producing it. . . .

[Holmes then reviews the historical precedents set out in Section A and continues.]

In spite, however, of all the arguments which may be urged for the rule that a man acts at his peril, it has been rejected by very eminent courts, even under the old forms of action. . . . But we may go further with profit, and inquire whether there are not strong grounds for thinking that the common law has never known such a rule, unless in that period of dry precedent which is so often to be found midway between a creative epoch and a period of solvent philosophical reaction. [Decisions by] Chief Justice Shaw go[] far to prove that the change [away from strict liability] was politic, I think I may assert that a little reflection will show that it was required not only by policy, but by consistency. I will begin with the latter.

The same reasoning which would make a man answerable in trespass for all damage to another by force directly resulting from his own act, irrespective of negligence or intent, would make him answerable in case for the like damage similarly resulting from the act of his servant, in the course of the latter's employment. The discussions of the company's negligence in many railway cases would therefore be wholly out of place, for although, to be sure, there is a contract which would make the company liable for negligence, that contract cannot be taken to diminish any liability which would otherwise exist for a trespass on the part of its employees.

More than this, the same reasoning would make a defendant responsible for all damage, however remote, of which his act could be called the cause. So long, at least, as only physical or irresponsible agencies, however unforeseen, cooperated with the act complained of to produce the result, the argument which would resolve the case of accidentally striking the plaintiff, when lifting a stick in necessary self-defence, adversely to the defendant, would require a decision against him in every case where his act was a factor in the result complained of. The distinction between a direct application of force, and causing damage indirectly, or as a more remote consequence of one's act, although it may determine whether the form of action should be trespass or case, does not touch the theory of responsibility, if that theory be that a man acts at his peril. As was said at the outset, if the strict liability is to be maintained at all, it must be maintained throughout. A principle cannot be stated which would retain the strict liability in trespass while abandoning it in case. It cannot be said that trespass is for acts alone, and case for consequences of those acts. All actions of trespass are for consequences of acts, not for the acts themselves. And some actions of trespass are for consequences more remote from the defendant's act than in other instances where the remedy would be case.

An act is always a voluntary muscular contraction, and nothing else. The chain of physical sequences which it sets in motion or directs to the plaintiff's harm is no part of it, and very generally a long train of such sequences intervenes. An example or two will make this extremely clear.

When a man commits an assault and battery with a pistol, his only act is to contract the muscles of his arm and forefinger in a certain way, but it is the delight of elementary writers to point out what a vast series of physical changes must take place before the harm is done. Suppose that, instead of firing a pistol, he takes up a hose which is discharging water on the sidewalk, and directs it at the plaintiff, he does not even set in motion the physical causes which must cooperate with his act to make a battery. Not only natural causes, but a living being, may intervene between the act and its effect. [Holmes then reviews Gibbons v. Pepper, *supra* at 69, and Scott v. Shepherd, *supra* at 72.]

Now I repeat, that, if principle requires us to charge a man in trespass when his act has brought force to bear on another through a comparatively short train of intervening causes, in spite of his having used all possible care, it requires the same liability, however numerous and unexpected the events between the act and the result. If running a man down is a trespass when the accident can be referred to the rider's act of spurring, why is it not a tort in every case, as was argued in Vincent v. Stinehour [7 Vt. 62 (1835)], seeing that it can always be referred more remotely to his act of mounting and taking the horse out?

Why is a man not responsible for the consequences of an act innocent in its direct and obvious effects, when those consequences would not have followed but for the intervention of a series of extraordinary, although natural, events? The reason is, that, if the intervening events are of such a kind that no foresight could have been expected to look out for them, the defendant is not to blame for having failed to do so. . . .

. . . The difference taken in Gibbons v. Pepper, cited above, is not between results which are and those which are not the consequences of the defendant's acts: it is between consequences which he was bound as a reasonable man to contemplate, and those which he was not. Hard spurring is just so much more likely to lead to harm than merely riding a horse in the street, that the court thought that the defendant would be bound to look out for the consequences of the one, while it would not hold him liable for those resulting merely from the other; because the possibility of being run away with when riding quietly, though familiar, is comparatively slight. If, however, the horse had been unruly, and had been taken into a frequented place for the purpose of being broken, the owner might have been liable, because "it was his fault to bring a wild horse into a place where mischief might probably be done."

To return to the example of the accidental blow with a stick lifted in self-defence, there is no difference between hitting a person standing in one's rear and hitting one who was pushed by a horse within range of the stick just as it was lifted, provided that it was not possible, under the circumstances, in the one case to have known, in the other to have anticipated, the proximity. In either case there is wanting the only element which distinguishes voluntary acts from spasmodic muscular contractions as a ground of liability. In neither of them, that is to say, has there been an opportunity of choice with reference to the consequence complained of,—a chance to guard against the result which has come to pass. A choice which entails a concealed consequence is as to that consequence no choice.

The general principle of our law is that loss from accident must lie where it falls, and this principle is not affected by the fact that a human being is the instrument of misfortune. But relatively to a given human being anything is accident which he could not fairly have been expected to contemplate as possible, and therefore to avoid. In the language of the late Chief Justice Nelson of New York: "No case or principle can be found, or if found can be maintained, subjecting an individual to liability for an act done without fault on his part. . . . All the cases concede that an injury arising from inevitable accident, or, which in law or reason is the same thing, from an act that ordinary human care and foresight are unable to guard against, is but the misfortune of the sufferer, and lays no foundation for legal responsibility." [Harvey v. Dunlop, Lalor 193 (N.Y. Sup. Ct. 1843).] If this were not so, any act would be sufficient, however remote, which set in motion or opened the door for a series of physical sequences ending in damage such as riding the horse, in the case of the runaway, or even coming to a place where one is seized with a fit and strikes the plaintiff in an unconscious spasm. Nay, why need the defendant have acted at all, and why is it not enough that his existence has been at the expense of the plaintiff? The requirement of an act is the requirement that the defendant should have made a choice. But the only possible purpose of introducing this moral element is to make the power of avoiding the evil complained of a condition of liability. There is no such power where the evil cannot be foreseen. . . .

A man need not, it is true, do this or that act,—the term *act* implies a choice,—but he must act somehow. Furthermore, the public generally profits by individual activity. As action cannot be avoided, and tends to the public good, there is obviously no policy in throwing the hazard of what is at once desirable and inevitable upon the actor.

The state might conceivably make itself a mutual insurance company against accidents, and distribute the burden of its citizens' mishaps among all its members. There might be a pension for paralytics, and state aid for those who suffered in person or estate from tempest or wild beasts. As between individuals it might adopt the mutual insurance principle *pro tanto*, and divide damages when both were in fault, as in the *rusticum judicium* [*rough justice*, i.e., an arbitrary rule] of the admiralty, or it might throw all loss upon the actor irrespective of fault. The state does none of those things, however, and the prevailing view is that its cumbrous and expensive machinery ought not to be set in motion unless some clear benefit is to be derived from disturbing the status quo. State interference is an evil, where it cannot be shown to be a good. Universal insurance, if desired, can be better and more cheaply accomplished by private enterprise. The undertaking to redistribute losses simply on the ground that they resulted from the defendant's act would not only be open to these objections, but, as it is hoped the preceding discussion has shown, to the still graver one of offending the sense of justice. Unless my act is of a nature to threaten others, unless under the circumstances a prudent man would have foreseen the possibility of harm, it is no more justifiable to make me indemnify my neighbor against the consequences, than to make me do the same thing if I had fallen upon him in a fit, or to compel me to insure him against lightning.

NOTE

Liability Ex Ante or Ex Post. The Holmes excerpt above represents the most influential theoretical argument on behalf of a negligence rule tied to the principle of reasonable foresight. One key to his argument is the claim that standards of conduct must be known in advance, which is not possible if liability is made to turn exclusively on the outcome of the event. Hence his emphasis on the reasonableness of the defendant's conduct, irrespective of the outcome. Yet why should that be so? The contrary argument for strict liability starts with the premise that no party can take comfort in a standard of conduct that speaks only of reasonable care under the circumstances. But even if no such standard is announced, any party is able to choose some desired level of precautions if instructed from the outset that he or she is responsible for the harms that are caused either by the direct application of force on the one hand or the creation of dangerous conditions (e.g., traps) on the other. Those rules could be extended to hold owners of animals strictly responsible for the damage their animals cause, wholly irrespective of the level of precautions taken. No longer is it necessary to distinguish between ordinary riding and hard spurring. This system, moreover, does not discourage taking precautions. To be sure, the defendant pays the full price for all harms caused. Yet by the same token, the defendant gets the benefit of the reduced level of accidents for which liability should be imposed. The defendant who knows his or her potential liabilities then chooses the appropriate level of care without having to guess in advance what rules of conduct the law might require after the fact.

SECTION E. STRICT LIABILITY AND NEGLIGENCE IN MODERN TIMES

Stone v. Bolton

[1950] 1 KB 201 (CA)

[The plaintiff, Bessie Stone, lived on Beckenham Road, a side street next to a cricket ground. One day, as she had just walked onto the road through the gate in front of her house, she was struck on the head by a cricket ball that had been hit out of the grounds by a visiting player. By all accounts, it was one of the longest balls—travelling about 100 yards before it struck the plaintiff—that had ever been hit out of the grounds during the previous 40 years. The cricket ground was found at trial to be "quite large enough for all practical purposes," even after it was remodeled in 1910 or 1911 to allow for construction of Beckenham Road. The field itself was surrounded by a 12-foot-high fence or hoarding that, owing to a rise in the ground, was about 17 feet above the street on the Beckenham Road side. The southern wicket from which the ball was struck was about 78 yards from Beckenham Road fence. Witnesses testified that over a 30-year period about six to ten balls had been hit onto Beckenham Road, and that several others had landed in the garden of one Brownson, the nearest neighboring house to the cricket grounds. The plaintiff did not sue the batsman or his club but she did sue the home cricket club and all of its members. She first alleged that the grounds constituted a public nuisance. She separately alleged common law negligence, claiming that the defendants had placed the cricket pitch too close to Beckenham Road, that they had failed to erect a fence of sufficient height to prevent balls from being hit onto the road, and that they had otherwise failed to ensure that cricket balls would not be hit into the road. At trial, Oliver, J., gave judgment to the defendants on both the public nuisance and negligence counts. The Court of Appeal reverses the judgment and allows the negligence claim on a two-to-one vote:]

> No doubt as a practical matter the defendants might decide that the double chance of a ball being hit into the road and finding a human target there was so remote that, rather than go to expense in the way of a wire screen or the like, or worse still abandon the ground, they would run the risk of such an occurrence and meet any ensuing claim for damages if and when it arose. But I fail to see on what principle they can be entitled to require people in Beckenham Road to accept the risk, and, if hit by a ball, put up with the possibly very serious harm done to them as damnum sine injuria, unless able to identify, trace, and successfully sue the particular batsman who made the hit.

[The defendants then appealed to the House of Lords.]

Bolton v. Stone

[1951] AC 850

Lord Reid. . . . This case, therefore raises sharply the question what is the nature and extent of the duty of a person who promotes on his land operations which may cause damage to persons on an adjoining highway. Is it that he must not carry out or permit an operation which he knows or ought to know clearly can cause such damage, however improbable that result may be, or is it that he is only bound to take into account the possibility of such damage if such damage is a likely or probable consequence of what he does or permits, or if the risk of damage is such that a reasonable man, careful of the safety of his neighbor, would regard that risk as material? . . .

Counsel for the respondent in this case had to put his case so high as to say that, at least as soon as one ball had been driven into the road in the ordinary course of a match, the appellants could and should have realized that that might happen again and that, if it did, someone might be injured; and that that was enough to put on the appellants a duty to take steps to prevent such an occurrence. If the true test is foreseeability alone I think that must be so [no matter how small the risk]. . . .

It would take a good deal to make me believe that the law has departed so far from the standards which guide ordinary careful people in ordinary life. In the crowded conditions of modern life even the most careful person cannot avoid creating some risks and accepting others. What a man must not do, and what I think a careful man tries not to do, is to create a risk which is substantial. Of course there are numerous cases where special circumstances require that a higher standard shall be observed and where that is recognized by the law. But I do not think that this case comes within any such special category. It was argued that this case comes within the principle in Rylands v. Fletcher, but I agree with your Lordships that there is no substance in this argument. In my judgment the test to be applied here is whether the risk of damage to a person on the road was so small that a reasonable man in the position of the appellants, considering the matter from the point of view of safety, would have thought it right to refrain from taking steps to prevent the danger.

In considering that matter I think that it would be right to take into account not only how remote is the chance that a person might be struck but also how serious the consequences are likely to be if a person is struck; but I do not think that it would be right to take into account the difficulty of remedial measures. If cricket cannot be played on a ground without creating a substantial risk, then it should not be played there *at all.* I think that this is in substance the test which Oliver, J., applied in this case. He considered whether the appellants' ground was large enough to be safe for all practical purposes and held that it was. This is a question not of law but of fact and degree. . . . If this appeal is allowed, that does not in my judgment mean that in every case where cricket has been played on a ground for a number of years without accident or complaint those who organize matches there are safe to go on in reliance on past immunity. I would have reached a different conclusion if I had thought that the risk here had been other than extremely small, because I do not think that a reasonable man considering the matter from the point of view of safety would or should disregard any risk unless it is extremely small.

Lord Radcliffe. My Lords, I agree that this appeal must be allowed. I agree with regret, because I have much sympathy with the decision that commended itself to the majority of the members of the Court of Appeal. I can see nothing unfair in the appellants being required to compensate the respondent for the serious injury that she has received as a result of the sport that they have organized on their cricket ground at Cheetham Hill. But the law of negligence is concerned less with what is fair than with what is culpable, and I cannot persuade myself that the appellants have been guilty of any culpable act or omission in this case. . . .

It seems to me that a reasonable man, taking account of the chances against an accident happening, would not have felt himself called upon either to abandon the use of the ground for cricket or to increase the height of his surrounding fences. He would have done what the appellants did: in other words, he would have done nothing. Whether, if the unlikely event of an accident did occur and his play turn to another's hurt, he would have thought it equally proper to offer no more consolation to his victim than the reflection that a social being is not immune from social risks, I do not say, for I do not think that that is a consideration which is relevant to legal liability.

NOTES

1. ***Negligence, Strict and Vicarious Liability in Bolton v. Stone.*** The plaintiff in Bolton v. Stone might have sued any of three possible defendants: the batsman from the visiting team, the visiting team, or the owner of the home team. Should an action lie against the batsman on a theory of strict liability? After all, he hit Bessie Stone with a batted cricket ball. If so, is the visiting team vicariously liable for the torts of its employee? See *infra* Chapter 7, Section F, at 530. Could vicarious liability also be imposed on the owners of the cricket field? By analogy, at common law an owner was liable for fires set on his land by his guests, but not those set by strangers. See Markham, J., in Beaulieu v. Finglam, *infra* Chapter 5, at 340.

In dealing with the potential negligence of the owner of the field, note that in cricket, unlike baseball, runs are plentiful (a batsman hitting for a century is not uncommon) while outs (of which there are ten per inning) represent major setbacks for the batting team. The astute batsman therefore will try to keep the ball on the ground, knowing that if it crosses the boundary of the field, he will still get four runs. Hitting a fly ball out of the field is worth six runs but carries a substantial risk of being caught. Hence the infrequency of long hits.

Bolton had an uneasy public reception. Professor Goodhart's note, for example, was entitled "Is It Cricket?" 67 Law Q. Rev. 460 (1951). To soften the public criticism, the Cricket Clubs in England wrote to the Law Quarterly Review that they "have done everything that they can to see that Stone does not suffer financially. In fact, so far as they are concerned, she has been left in possession of the damages originally awarded." Note, 68 Law Q. Rev. 1, 3 (1952). Defendants also waived costs of £3,000, to which they were entitled under the English winner-take-all system. Glanville Williams developed the notion of "ethical compensation" to defend this peculiar turn of events in The Aims of the Law of Tort, 4 Current Legal Probs. 137 (1951). Salmond on Torts 30 (13th ed. 1961) notes that "one who is under no legal liability for damage caused to another may yet think it right and proper to offer some measure of compensation." Is ethical compensation needed in a strict liability system? Does it account for the divergence between the legal and the moral duty?

2. ***Cricket Versus Golf?*** With *Bolton*, contrast Rinaldo v. McGovern, 587 N.E.2d 264, 267 (N.Y. 1991). There, one of two defendants—it was not clear who—sliced a golf ball that "soared" off the course and shattered the plaintiff's windshield as she "happened" to drive her car down a public street. Titone, J., rejected the plaintiff's negligence claim for "what amounted to no more than [a] poorly hit tee shot." The defendants had no duty to warn persons who were not in the intended line of flight and who could not have responded to the warning even if they had heard it. The court also rejected any distinction between individuals who chose to live next to the fairway on golf course grounds and strangers who drove along the public street. Titone, J., concluded that a negligence claim could not survive given that "the possibility that the ball will fly off in another direction is a risk inherent in the game," since "even the best professional golfers cannot avoid an occasional 'hook' or 'slice.' " To provide an actionable theory of liability, a person injured by a mishit golf ball must affirmatively show that the golfer failed to exercise due care by adducing proof, for example, that the golfer "aimed so inaccurately as to unreasonably increase the risk of harm."

"If you're so enlightened, how come you can't lick that slice?"

Source: Sam Gross / CartoonStock

What difference would it make if the plaintiff were speeding toward the golf ball when her car was struck? Driving away from it?

In Hennessey v. Pyne, 694 A.2d 691 (R.I. 1997), the defendant's errant shot hit the plaintiff while she was on her condominium grounds. Flanders, J., first denied that the plaintiff could bring either a nuisance or assault and battery claim, but unlike *Rinaldo*, he let negligence claims for a poor shot and an insufficient warning reach the jury, referring to the fact that the hole was constructed to have a dogleg, which gave the golfer a real advantage "if he drove the ball off the tee as closely as possible past Hennessey's condominium (without striking it), thereby maximizing the distance of his shot and the lie of his ball down the fairway." How should a jury distinguish between the hitting and the warning claims?

3. *Corrective Justice and Bolton v. Stone.* Bolton v. Stone raises important questions whether a *corrective justice* approach requires the defendant to *rectify* or *redress* for an invasion of a legal right. Aristotle's Nicomachean Ethics, Book IV (R.W. Browne, translation, 1853), provides an early version of that principle:

> [I]t matters not whether a good man has robbed a bad man, or a bad man a good man, nor whether a good or bad man has committed adultery; the law looks to the difference of the hurt alone, and treats persons, if one commits and the other suffers injury, as equal, and also if one has done and the other suffered hurt.

More recent formulations stress whether the defendant's actions undo the imbalance created by the violation of a preexisting right to exclusive control over one's body and property, solely as a matter of fairness between the parties to a dispute. Explicit concern with long-term incentive effects, on either the wrongdoer or victim, are not part of the basic equation, because corrective justice "provides the immanent critical standpoint informing the law's effort to work itself pure." Weinrib, Corrective Justice in a Nutshell, 52 U. Toronto L.J. 349, 356 (2002).

In Bolton v. Stone, the prima facie causal case against the batsman is simply "he hit me." This causal paradigm has been defended in Epstein, A Theory of Strict Liability, 2 J. Legal Stud. 151, 168–69 (1973):

> Once this simple causal paradigm is accepted, its relationship to the question of responsibility for the harm so caused must be clarified. Briefly put, the argument is that proof of the proposition *A* hit *B* should be sufficient to establish a prima facie case of liability. I do not argue that proof of causation is equivalent to a conclusive demonstration of responsibility. Both the modern and classical systems of law are based upon the development of prima facie cases and defenses thereto. They differ not in their use of presumptions but in the elements needed to create the initial presumption in favor of the plaintiff. The doctrine of strict liability holds that proof that the defendant caused harm creates that presumption because proof of the non-reciprocal source of the harm is sufficient to upset the balance where one person must win and the other must lose. There is no room to consider, as part of the prima facie case, allegations that the defendant intended to harm the plaintiff, or could have avoided the harm he caused by the use of reasonable care. The choice is plaintiff or defendant, and the analysis of causation is the tool which, prima facie, fastens responsibility upon the defendant. Indeed for most persons, the difficult question is often not whether these causal assertions create the presumption, but whether there are in fact any means to distinguish between causation and responsibility, so close is the connection between what a man does and what he is answerable for.

Assumption of the risk is often a defense to a strict liability claim. Is this defense relevant in *Bolton*?

A negligence rule has also been defended on corrective justice grounds with the claim that the defendant's standard of care should be set no higher than the standard the plaintiff could demand from herself. Therefore, the plaintiff who cannot identify any flaw in the defendant's conduct cannot characterize his conduct as *wrongful.* "Corrective justice requires annulling a departure from the preexisting distribution of money or honors in accordance with merit, but only when the departure is the result of *an act of injustice*, causing injury." Posner, The Concept of Corrective Justice in Recent Theories of Tort Law, 10 J. Legal Stud. 187, 200 (1981). Glanville Williams also expressed the same idea in The Aims of the Law of Tort, 4 Current Legal Probs. 137, 151 (1951):

> Finally there is the compensatory or reparative theory, according to which one who has caused injury to another must make good the damage whether he was at fault or not. This is the same as the theory of ethical compensation except that it does not require culpability on the part of the defendant. If valid, it justifies strict liability, which the theory of ethical compensation does not. The difficulty is, however, to state it in such a form as to make it acceptable. If it is said that a person who has been damaged by another ought to be compensated, we readily assent, moved as we are by sympathy for the victim's loss. But what has to be shown is not merely that the sufferer ought to be compensated, but that he ought to be compensated by the defendant. In the absence of any moral blame of the defendant, how is this demonstration possible?

Within a strict liability system, the alternative account of wrongful conduct ties into the system of pleadings outlined by Arnold, *supra* at 66: The blow establishes the prima facie liability, which then (unlike a system of absolute liability) is supplemented by defenses based, for example, on the plaintiff's misconduct or inevitable accident, narrowly construed. Accordingly, strict liability explicates the idea of wrongfulness, not in terms of the lack of negligence or intention, but in terms of these other substantive defenses.

4. ***Economic Efficiency as an Alternative to Corrective Justice.*** Troubled by the ambiguities in corrective justice theories, an alternative economic account of tort liability was articulated in Calabresi & Melamed, Property Rules, Liability Rules and Inalienability: One View of the Cathedral, 85 Harv. L. Rev. 1089, 1093–94 (1972):

> Perhaps the simplest reason for a particular entitlement is to minimize the administrative costs of enforcement. This was the reason Holmes gave for letting the costs lie where they fall in accidents unless some clear societal benefit is achieved by shifting them. By itself this reason will never justify any result except that of letting the stronger win, for obviously that result minimizes enforcement costs. Nevertheless, administrative efficiency may be relevant to choosing entitlements when other reasons are taken into account. This may occur when the reasons accepted are indifferent between conflicting entitlements and one entitlement is cheaper to enforce than the others. It may also occur when the reasons are not indifferent but lead us only slightly to prefer one over another and the first is considerably more expensive to enforce than the second.
>
> But administrative efficiency is just one aspect of the broader concept of economic efficiency. Economic efficiency asks that we choose the set of entitlements which would lead to that allocation of resources which could not be improved in the sense that a further change would not so improve the condition of those who gained by it that they could compensate those who lost from it and still be better off than before. This is often called Pareto optimality. To give two examples, economic efficiency asks for that combination of entitlements to engage in risky activities and to be free from harm from risky activities which will most likely lead to the lowest sum of accident costs and of costs of avoiding accidents. It asks for that form of property, private or communal, which leads to the highest product for the effort of producing.

Technically speaking, what Calabresi and Melamed called Pareto efficiency is known as Kaldor-Hicks efficiency. Pareto efficiency requires that the winners *actually* compensate the losers so that at least some one is better off and no one is worse off than before. Kaldor-Hicks efficiency is satisfied with a demonstration that *hypothetical* compensation was possible. Stated otherwise, so long as the gains to the winner are sufficient to compensate the losers, it does not matter whether such compensation is actually paid. The Pareto standard is less problematic but more demanding; the Kaldor-Hicks standard is the opposite. Note that both standards preclude all social changes that yield systematic losses. Is there a fair distribution of the gains under the Pareto standard if one person gains huge amounts and everyone else is left indifferent? Or, must the gains be distributed pro rata? Can they? For one retrospective on the seminal Calabresi/Melamed article, see Symposium, Property Rules, Liability Rules, and Inalienability: A Twenty-Five Year Retrospective, 106 Yale L.J. 2081, 2081–213 (1997), with articles by, among others, Epstein, Krier and Schwab, Levmore, and Rose. See also Schwab, Property Rules and Liability Rules: The Cathedral in Another Light, 70 N.Y.U. L. Rev. 440 (1995).

Transaction costs, i.e., the costs involved in establishing and enforcing both property rights and contractual arrangements, are critical to the economic analysis. If these could be held to zero, the initial distribution of rights would be of little economic consequence, as private parties could, through repeated, costless, and instantaneous transactions, move all resources to their highest valued use. The end use of any resource would be the same regardless of who was its original owner. Thus, the decisions about property rights would only affect their initial distribution, but not affect their final allocation. See Coase, The Problem of Social Cost, 3 J.L. & Econ. 1 (1960), for the initial elaboration of the Coase theorem. In all real world situations, however, transaction costs are positive, if not prohibitive. Much of the law is designed to create formalities, such as "gap filling" norms in contracts or bright-line rules in tort, to minimize these costs.

In contractual situations, the high costs of transacting can be reduced when either courts or legislatures announce standard "gap-filling" terms for matters on which the parties are silent. Calabresi and Melamed, *supra* at 104, 85 Harv. L. Rev. at 1096–97, tackled this problem as follows:

> (1) that economic efficiency standing alone would dictate that set of entitlements which favors knowledgeable choices between social benefits and the social costs of obtaining them, and between social costs and the social costs of avoiding them; (2) that this implies, in the absence of certainty as to whether a benefit is worth its costs to society, that the cost should be put on the party or activity best located to make such a cost-benefit analysis; (3) that in particular contexts like accidents or pollution this suggests putting costs on the party or activity which can most cheaply avoid them; (4) that in the absence of certainty as to who that party or activity is, the costs should be put on the party or activity which can with the lowest transaction costs act in the market to correct an error in entitlements by inducing the party who can avoid social costs most cheaply to do so; and (5) that since we are in an area where by hypothesis markets do not work perfectly—there are transaction costs—a decision will often have to be made on whether market transactions or collective fiat is most likely to bring us closer to the Pareto optimal result the "perfect" market would reach.

How does a judge or jury determine which party is "best located to make a cost-benefit analysis" if the parties to the accident are not known to each other prior to the accident? Is it better to (presumptively) attach the blame on the party who discharged or released the pollutant? What should be done if the defendant knows more about the probability of harm to another, but the plaintiff knows more about its likely extent?

Hammontree v. Jenner

97 Cal. Rptr. 739 (Ct. App. 1971)

Lillie, J. Plaintiffs Maxine Hammontree and her husband sued defendant for personal injuries and property damage arising out of an automobile accident. The cause was tried to a jury. Plaintiffs appeal from judgment entered on a jury verdict returned against them and in favor of defendant.

The evidence shows that on the afternoon of April 25, 1967, defendant was driving his 1959 Chevrolet home from work; at the same time plaintiff Maxine Hammontree was working in a bicycle shop owned and operated by her and her husband; without warning defendant's car crashed through the wall of the shop, struck Maxine and caused personal injuries and damage to the shop.

Defendant claimed he became unconscious during an epileptic seizure, losing control of his car. He did not recall the accident, but his last recollection before it was leaving a stop light after his last stop, and his first recollection after the accident was being taken out of his car in plaintiffs' shop. Defendant testified he has a medical history of epilepsy and knows of no other reason for his loss of consciousness except an epileptic seizure. [The defendant first learned of his epileptic condition in 1952 and from that time until his accident, he was under the constant care of a neurologist who treated him first with dilantin and then with phelantin. The defendant's last seizure was in 1953, and thereafter he had no trouble at all. His regular physician testified that at all times he was "doing normally," so that it was "safe" for the defendant to drive while medicated, even though it was impossible for the defendant to drive during a seizure.]

In 1955 or 1956 the Department of Motor Vehicles was advised that defendant was an epileptic and placed him on probation under which every six months he had to report to the doctor who was required to advise it in writing of defendant's condition. In 1960 his probation was changed to a once-a-year report. . . .

[The plaintiffs withdrew their negligence count during trial, "electing to stand solely on the theory of absolute liability." But the trial judge nonetheless instructed the jury on negligence and res ipsa loquitur. The jury found for the defendant. The plaintiff then appealed both the denial of the trial court to grant, first, their motion for summary judgment, and second to submit their request for an instruction on absolute liability to the jury.][1]

Under the present state of the law found in appellate authorities beginning with Waters v. Pacific Coast Dairy, Inc., [131 P.2d 588 (Cal. Ct. App. 1942)] (driver rendered unconscious from sharp pain in left arm and shoulder) through Ford v. Carew & English, [200 P.2d 828 (Cal. Ct. App. 1948)] (fainting spells from strained heart muscles), Zabunoff v. Walker, [13 Cal. Rptr. 463 (Ct. App. 1961)] (sudden sneeze), and Tannyhill v. Pacific Motor Trans. Co., [38 Cal. Rptr. 774 (Ct. App. 1964)] (heart attack), the trial judge properly refused the instruction. The foregoing cases generally hold that liability of a driver, suddenly stricken by an illness rendering him unconscious, for injury resulting from an accident occurring during that time rests on principles of negligence. . . .

Appellants seek to have this court override the established law of this state which is dispositive of the issue before us as outmoded in today's social and economic structure, particularly in the light of the now recognized principles imposing liability upon the manufacturer, retailer and all distributive and vending elements and activities which bring a product to the consumer to his injury, on the basis of strict liability in tort expressed first in Justice Traynor's concurring opinion in Escola v. Coca Cola Bottling Co., [150 P.2d 436 (Cal. 1944)]; and then in Greenman v. Yuba Power Products, Inc., [377 P.2d 897 (Cal. 1963)]; Vandermark v. Ford Motor Co., [391 P.2d 168 (Cal. 1964)]; and Elmore v. American Motors Corp., [451 P.2d 84 (Cal. 1969)]. These authorities hold that "A manufacturer [or retailer] is strictly liable in tort when an article he places on the market, knowing that it is to be used without inspection for defects, proves to have a defect that causes injury to a human being." (*Greenman, supra.*) Drawing a parallel with these products liability cases, appellants argue, with some degree of logic, that only the driver affected by a physical condition which could suddenly render him unconscious and who is aware of that condition can anticipate the hazards and foresee the dangers involved in his operation of a motor vehicle, and that the liability of those who by reason of seizure or heart failure or some other physical condition lose the ability to safely operate and control a motor vehicle resulting in injury to an innocent person should be predicated on strict liability.

We decline to superimpose the absolute liability of products liability cases upon drivers under the circumstances here. The theory on which those cases are predicated is that manufacturers, retailers and distributors of products are engaged in the business of distributing goods to the public and are an integral part of the over-all producing and marketing enterprise that should bear the cost of injuries from defective parts. . . . This policy hardly applies here and it is not enough to simply say, as do appellants, that the insurance carriers should be the ones to bear the cost of injuries to innocent victims on a strict liability basis. In Maloney v. Rath, [445 P.2d 513 (Cal. 1968)], followed by Clark v. Dziabas, [445 P.2d 517 (Cal. 1968)], appellant urged that defendant's violation of a safety provision (defective brakes) of the Vehicle Code makes the violator strictly liable for damages caused by the violation. . . . The California Supreme Court refused to apply the doctrine of strict liability to automobile drivers. The situation involved two users of the highway but the problems of fixing responsibility under a

1. "When the evidence shows that a driver of a motor vehicle on a public street or highway loses his ability to safely operate and control such vehicle because of some seizure or health failure, that driver is nevertheless legally liable for all injuries and property damage which an innocent person may suffer as a proximate result of the defendant's inability to so control or operate his motor vehicle. . . . This is true even if you find the defendant driver had no warning of any such impending seizure or health failure."

system of strict liability are as complicated in the instant case as those in Maloney v. Rath, and could only create uncertainty in the area of its concern. As stated in *Maloney*, at 446:

> To invoke a rule of strict liability on users of the streets and highways, however, without also establishing in substantial detail how the new rule should operate would only contribute confusion to the automobile accident problem. Settlement and claims adjustment procedures would become chaotic until the new rules were worked out on a case-by-case basis, and the hardships of delayed compensation would be seriously intensified. Only the Legislature, if it deems it wise to do so, can avoid such difficulties by enacting a comprehensive plan for the compensation of automobile accident victims in place of or in addition to the law of negligence.

The instruction tendered by appellants was properly refused for still another reason. Even assuming the merit of appellants' position under the facts of this case in which defendant knew he had a history of epilepsy, previously had suffered seizures and at the time of the accident was attempting to control the condition by medication, the instruction does not except from its ambit the driver who suddenly is stricken by an illness or physical condition which he had no reason whatever to anticipate and of which he had no prior knowledge.

The judgment is affirmed.

Wood, P.J., and Thompson, J., concurred.

Appellants' petition for a hearing by the Supreme Court was denied on December 16, 1971.

NOTES

1. ***Physician Liability.*** Should the treating physician of an epileptic driver be held responsible to an injured third party if he fails to warn his patients of the relevant risk and erroneously supplies favorable documentation to the Department of Transportation that allows her to obtain a driver's license? In Schmidt v. Mahoney, 659 N.W.2d 552, 555 (Iowa 2003), Carter, J., answered that question in the negative, noting:

> [I]t is highly likely that a consequence of recognizing liability to members of the general public . . . will be that physicians treating patients with seizure disorders will become reluctant to allow them to drive or engage in any other activity in which a seizure could possibly harm a third party. In order to curtail liability, physicians may become prone to make overly restrictive recommendations concerning the activities of their patients and will exercise their role as reporters to the department of transportation in an inflexible manner not in their patient's best interest.

Does insulating the physician from liability strengthen or weaken the case for strict liability against the driver?

2. ***Why the Choice Between Negligence and Strict Liability Is so Difficult.*** For over 200 years courts have vacillated between negligence and strict liability. Why, then, is it unlikely that this tension will resolve itself quickly? The initial premise is often that courts should try to identify some social gain to justify the social costs of litigation. Compensation of the plaintiff, taken alone, is insufficient, so long as first-party insurance is available, which allows each person to tailor coverage on the direct knowledge of her personal needs that no tort defendant could ever obtain.

Since compensation alone does not supply the missing justification, the case for tort liability rests on the need to fashion incentives that reduce the costs of accidents and their prevention. Imposing liability for negligence thus seems unproblematic because that tort rule unambiguously provides incentives to avoid costs that exceed the benefits generated by a particular activity. To see why, think of the optimal level of care as the same amount of care that a single person would take if he himself were the only person at risk for property damage or bodily injury. That individual would prefer to suffer the consequences of some accidents to avoid the greater costs of prevention.

Tort litigation arises only because the victim and injurer are separate parties. Now, intuitions cut in two contrary directions. One impulse imposes liability to force the defendant-injurer to internalize the costs that his conduct would otherwise impose on others. The rival impulse is to dismiss the plaintiff's suit because the defendant acted just as the plaintiff would (and should) have acted under the same circumstances. He took the optimal level of precautions by treating the plaintiff's loss as if it were his own. The law need not intervene because there is no need to correct some defective conduct. Hence the negligence theory imposes liability only when it spots a shortfall in the defendant's basic behavior. How to choose between these options?

One possible way uses the norm of reciprocity encountered in *Losee, supra* at 91. Unfortunately, that norm is consistent with either negligence or strict liability. The incentive effects of the two rules are the same when viewed from the "ex ante" perspective, and no obvious distributional consequences flow from the choice of liability rules. This stalemate tends to make administrative costs the deciding factor in the debate. Yet again, the relevant considerations tug in both directions. The strict liability rule eliminates the need to set the standard of care and determine whether the defendant complied with that standard. But the negligence rule cuts out some expensive lawsuits (since plaintiffs must do more to win), even if the ones that remain are of greater complexity. The tradeoff between these two effects rests on empirical judgments about their relative magnitude: Do we worry more about the cost per suit, or the number of suits?

This inquiry takes us a long way from the principles of fundamental fairness and justice, traditionally and plausibly invoked on *both* sides of the controversy. Yet, if this tradeoff shapes the strict liability/negligence debate, it is easy to see why a consensus has been so slow in developing. While the choice of liability rule has an enormous impact in deciding specific cases, such as Bolton v. Stone, their overall social consequences are less dramatic than first meet the eye. Since both rules create the same basic incentives and have, roughly speaking, the same administrative costs, either rule can provide a workable foundation for tort law. Most cases come out the same way under either rule. It is only when these tort rules are contrasted with radical, system-wide changes, such as no-fault automobile insurance or workers' compensation, that major differences administrative costs and incentive effects emerge. At this point, therefore, it is best to leave the grand question and turn to the more detailed operation of the dominant negligence system.

CHAPTER 3

NEGLIGENCE

Ezra Ripley Thayer

Public Wrong and Private Action

27 Harv. L. Rev. 317, 318 (1914)

In the law of negligence no doctrine is useful or appropriate which cannot be plainly and simply stated, and which, when so stated, does not respond to the test of common sense.

Leon Green

Judge and Jury

185 (1930)

In other words, we may have a process for passing judgment in negligence cases, but practically no "law of negligence" beyond the process itself.

SECTION A. INTRODUCTION

The inconclusive debate between negligence and strict liability theories of the last chapter only affirms the critical—many would say dominant—role of negligence in the law of unintentional harms. This chapter explores how negligence principles, both in theory and practice, determine the scope of a defendant's liability for accidental harms. In dealing with these issues, it is important to draw a preliminary distinction between negligence as a form of subpar conduct and negligence as a separate and distinct tort. The former is an element of the tort of negligence, which in its modern elaboration contains four distinct elements: duty, breach, causation, and damages. A plaintiff must meet all four requirements to establish the prima facie case (which, in turn, is subject to the various defenses discussed *infra* in Chapter 4). These four elements are:

First, ***duty***: Did the defendant owe the plaintiff a duty to conform his conduct to a standard of care necessary to avoid an unreasonable risk of harm to others?

Second, ***breach***: Did the defendant's conduct, whether by way of act or omission, fall below the applicable standard of care?

Third, ***causation***: Was the defendant's failure to meet the applicable standard of care causally connected to the plaintiff's harm? Often this inquiry is divided into two parts: causation in fact and legal (or proximate) causation.

Fourth, ***damages***: Did the plaintiff suffer harm?

This chapter concentrates on the first two elements—whether the defendant breached a duty of care owed to the plaintiff. The issue of causation is addressed in Chapter 5, and that of affirmative duties is the topic of Chapter 6. Damages are discussed in Chapter 9.

The question of negligence spans all of tort law. Its dictates apply not only to ordinary individuals, with the full range of human strengths and frailties, but also to small businesses, large corporations, government entities, unions, and nonprofit associations. This chapter is designed to give some sense of the reach and application of the negligence principle in its various institutional settings. Accordingly, Section B develops the common sense approach to negligence determinations and thereafter the efforts to breathe life into the abstract concept of the reasonable person. The key inquiry asks what allowances, if any, the law should make for the weaknesses of those individuals who are not blessed with the knowledge, skill, or ability to meet the durable, but hypothetical, construct of the reasonable person.

Section C traces the evolution of the reasonable person standard by examining the "balancing of interests" needed to determine whether the risks taken by the defendant are justified by the ends sought. The Restatement (Third) of Torts on Liability for Physical and Emotional Harm simply states that "[c]onduct is negligent if its disadvantages outweigh its advantages, while conduct is not negligent if its advantages outweigh its disadvantages." RTT: LPEH §3, comment *e*. This inquiry in turn delves into the uses and limitations of the various economic interpretations of the negligence principle, which are often couched in "risk-benefit" or "cost-benefit" terms. The term "risk" stresses the probability of harm, without regard to its severity. "Cost" takes into account both the probability of harm and its expected severity. *Id.* Which measure is more accurate from an economic point of view?

Often both tests work at too high a level of abstraction, so skillful lawyers typically supplement that basic approach by pointing to some specific "untaken precaution" that, if taken, could have prevented the accident that actually occurred. See Grady, Untaken Precautions, 18 J. Legal Stud. 139 (1989). At trial, the plaintiff tries to show that some inexpensive precaution (such as a railing, a warning, or an inspection) could have prevented some likely and serious injury. In contrast, the defendant tries to show that the precaution was excessively costly, redundant, ineffective, or downright dangerous and counterproductive in light of the alternative risks created. In hotly contested cases, there is no shortcut for a complete mastery of a case's relevant social and technical facts, often with heavy reliance on expert testimony. Of necessity, skilled negligence lawyers become experts themselves on everything from printing presses to toxic chemicals, from product warnings to complex surgery. Indeed, within law firms, personal injury law is often broken down by subject matter, such as highway accidents, medical malpractice, machine tools, chemicals, athletic injuries, or hunting accidents.

"Why carry malpractice insurance if you don't malpractice once in a while?"

Source: Peter Steiner / CartoonStock

Sometimes, however, the law supplies more concrete guideposts in the featureless landscape dominated by the concept of an unreasonable risk in the form of either customary standards or statutory requirements. Our general analysis of negligence is accordingly supplemented in Section D by looking at the relationship between customary practice relevant to the defendant's actions and negligence determinations. Section D also addresses the central role that professional, business, and industry customs play in setting the standard of care in medical malpractice cases, introduces the heated debate about the efficacy of the medical malpractice system and various reform proposals, and explores the role and scope of the doctrine of informed consent. Section E extends the inquiry to criminal statutes and examines the role of safety regulations in determining whether the parties acted negligently.

The last two sections of the chapter deal with how trials are conducted in negligence cases. Section F examines the allocation of responsibility between judge and jury and explores some aspects of the ongoing debate about the efficacy of the civil jury. Section G then examines the principles governing the proof of negligence at trial, especially the doctrine of res ipsa loquitur—"the thing speaks for itself" (but usually not as clearly as we would like).

SECTION B. THE REASONABLE PERSON

Harry Kalven, Jr.

It is sometimes said that the study of negligence is the study of the mistakes a reasonable man might make.

Vaughan v. Menlove

(1837) 132 Eng. Rep. 490 (CP)

[The plaintiff owned two cottages in the County of Salop. The defendant was a neighbor who had placed a haystack, or rick, on his own property, near the plaintiff's two cottages. The rick caught fire, which spread first to the defendant's nearby wood and thatch buildings and then destroyed the plaintiff's cottages. The plaintiff brought suit, alleging that the defendant negligently constructed and maintained the rick.]

At the trial it appeared that the rick in question had been made by the Defendant near the boundary of his own premises; that the hay was in such a state when put together, as to give rise to discussions on the probability of fire: that though there were conflicting opinions on the subject, yet during a period of five weeks, the Defendant was repeatedly warned of his peril; that his stock was insured; and that upon one occasion, being advised to take the rick down to avoid all danger, he said "he would chance it." He made an aperture or chimney through the rick; but in spite, or perhaps in consequence of this precaution, the rick at length burst into flames from the spontaneous heating of its materials; the flames communicated to the Defendant's barn and stables, and thence to the Plaintiff's cottages, which were entirely destroyed.

Patteson, J., before whom the cause was tried, told the jury that the question for them to consider, was, whether the fire had been occasioned by gross negligence on the part of the Defendant; adding, that he was bound to proceed with such reasonable caution as a prudent man would have exercised under such circumstances.

A verdict having been found for the Plaintiff, a rule nisi for a new trial was obtained [i.e., defendant appealed], on the ground that the jury should have been directed to consider, not, whether the Defendant had been guilty of gross negligence with reference to the standard of ordinary prudence, a standard too uncertain to afford any criterion; but whether he had acted bona fide to the best of his judgment; if he had, he ought not to be responsible for the misfortune of not possessing the highest order of intelligence. The action under such circumstances, was of the first impression....

Talfourd Serjt. and Whately, shewed cause [for plaintiff].

The pleas having expressly raised issues on the negligence of the Defendant, the learned Judge could not do otherwise than leave that question to the jury. . . . And the action, though new in specie, is founded on a principle fully established, that a man must so use his own property as not to injure that of others. On the same circuit a defendant was sued a few years ago, for burning weeds so near the extremity of his own land as to set fire to and destroy his neighbours' wood. The plaintiff recovered damages, and no motion was made to set aside the verdict. Then, there were no means of estimating the defendant's negligence, except by taking as a standard, the conduct of a man of ordinary prudence: that has been the rule always laid down, and there is no other that would not be open to much greater uncertainties.

R. V. Richards, in support of the rule [for defendant].

First, there was no duty imposed on the Defendant, as there is on carriers or other bailees, under an implied contract, to be responsible for the exercise of any given degree of prudence: the Defendant had a right to place his stack as near to the extremity of his own land as he pleased . . . : under that right, and subject to no contract, he can only be called on to act bona fide to the best of his judgment: if he has done that, it is a contradiction in terms, to inquire whether or not he has been guilty of gross negligence. At all events what would have been gross negligence ought to be estimated by the faculties of the individual, and not by those of other men. The measure of prudence varies so with the varying faculties of men, that it is impossible to say what is gross negligence with reference to the standard of what is called ordinary prudence. . . .

Tindal, C.J. I agree that this is a case primae impressionis [of first impression]; but I feel no difficulty in applying to it the principles of law as laid down in other cases of a similar kind. Undoubtedly this is not a case of contract, such as a bailment or the like where the bailee is responsible in consequence of the remuneration he is to receive: but there is a rule of law which says you must so enjoy your own property as not to injure that of another; and according to that rule the Defendant is liable for the consequence of his own neglect: and though the Defendant did not himself light the fire, yet mediately, he is as much the cause of it as if he had himself put a candle to the rick; for it is well known that hay will ferment and take fire if it be not carefully stacked. It has been decided that if an occupier burns weeds so near the boundary of his own land that damage ensues to the property of his neighbour, he is liable to an action for the amount of injury done, unless the accident were occasioned by a sudden blast which he could not foresee: Tuberville v. Stamp (1 Salk. 13 [1697]). But put the case of a chemist making experiments with ingredients, singly innocent, but when combined, liable to ignite if he leaves them together, and injury is thereby occasioned to the property of his neighbour, can any one doubt that an action on the case would lie?

Exhibit 3.1 Sir Nicholas Conyngham Tindal

Sir Nicholas Conyngham Tindal (1776–1846) served as Chief Justice of Common Pleas from 1829 until his death and won great respect from the British public. An obituary of Chief Justice Tindal reported: "As to the merits of Chief Justice Tindal, the bar may be divided, but the public are unanimous. They looked at his summings up as among the most masterly exhibitions of judicial sagacity, and they regarded his calm, thoughtful, and tranquil inflexibility as the impersonation of British justice." Obituary—Lord Chief Justice Tindal, 26 Gentleman's Mag. 199, 200 (1846).

Bio source: Obituary—Lord Chief Justice Tindal, 26 Gentleman's Mag. 199, 200 (1846)

Image source: Thomas Philips / National Portrait Gallery, London

It is contended, however, that the learned Judge was wrong in leaving this to the jury as a case of gross negligence, and that the question of negligence was so mixed up with reference to what would be the conduct of a man of ordinary prudence that the jury might have thought the latter the rule by which they were to decide; that such a rule would be too uncertain to act upon; and that the question ought to have been whether the Defendant had acted honestly and bona fide to the best of his own judgment. That, however, would leave so vague a line as to afford no rule at all, the degree of judgment belonging to each individual being infinitely various: and though it has been urged that the care which a prudent man would take, is not an intelligible proposition as a rule of law . . . yet such has always been the rule adopted in cases of bailment, as laid down in Coggs v. Bernard (2 Ld. Raym. 909 [1703]). Though in some cases a greater degree of care is exacted than in others, yet in "the second sort of bailment, viz. commodatum or lending gratis, the borrower is bound to the strictest care and diligence to keep the goods so as to restore them back again to the lender; because the bailee has a benefit by the use of them, so as if the bailee be guilty of the least neglect he will be answerable; as if a man should lend another a horse to go westward, or for a month; if the bailee put this horse in his stable, and he were stolen from thence, the bailee shall not be answerable for him: but if he or his servant leave the house or stable doors open, and the thieves take the opportunity of that, and steal the horse, he will be chargeable, because the neglect gave the thieves the occasion to steal the horse." The care taken by a prudent man has always been the rule laid down; and as to the supposed difficulty of applying it, a jury has always been able to say, whether, taking that rule as their guide, there has been negligence on the occasion in question.

Instead, therefore, of saying that the liability for negligence should be co-extensive with the judgment of each individual, which would be as variable as the length of the foot of each individual, we ought rather to adhere to the rule which requires in all cases a regard to caution such as a man of ordinary prudence would observe. That was in substance the criterion presented to the jury in this case, and therefore the present rule must be discharged.

Park, J. I entirely concur in what has fallen from his lordship. Although the facts in this case are new in specie, they fall within a principle long established, that a man must so use his own property as not to injure that of others. [Park, J., then recites extensively from Tuberville v. Stamp and concludes:]

As to the direction of the learned judge, it was perfectly correct. Under the circumstances of the case it was proper to leave it to the jury whether with reference to the caution which would have been observed by a man of ordinary prudence, the Defendant had not been guilty of gross negligence. After he had been warned repeatedly during the five weeks as to the consequences likely to happen, there is no colour for altering the verdict, unless it were to increase the damages.

Vaughan, J. The principle on which this action proceeds, is by no means new. It has been urged that the Defendant in such a case takes no duty on himself; but I do not agree in that position: every one takes upon himself the duty of so dealing with his own property as not to injure the property of others. It was, if any thing, too favourable to the Defendant to leave it to the jury whether he had been guilty of gross negligence; for when the Defendant upon being warned as to the consequences likely to ensue from the condition of the rick, said, "he would chance it," it was manifest he adverted to his interest in the insurance office. The conduct of a prudent man has always been the criterion for the jury in such cases: but it is by no means confined to them. . . . Here, there was not a single witness whose testimony did not go to establish gross negligence in the Defendant. He had repeated warnings of what was likely to occur, and the whole calamity was occasioned by his procrastination.

Rule discharged. [Appeal denied.]

NOTES

1. ***Standard of Ordinary Prudence.*** Vaughan v. Menlove speaks not only of the defendant's duty to exercise "ordinary care," but also his "gross negligence" in conducting his own affairs. Does the distinction between ordinary and gross negligence matter? See, in this regard, the famous bon mot of Baron Rolfe, who described gross negligence as the same thing as ordinary negligence "with the addition of a vituperative epithet." Wilson v. Brett, (1843) 152 Eng. Rep. 737 (Exch.). Most of the states have pattern jury instructions that use the concept of the objective "reasonable person," or a variant of the same, to define the duty of ordinary care. Kelley & Wendt, What Judges Tell Juries About Negligence: A Review of Pattern Jury Instructions, 77 Chi.-Kent L. Rev. 587, 594–97 (2002). The common feature of the variously worded pattern instructions "is the device of defining the negligence standard by reference to the conduct of a hypothesized person"—a construct traced to *Vaughan*.

2. ***Conscience of the Community.*** Abraham, The Trouble with Negligence, 54 Vand. L. Rev. 1187, 1196 (2001), disputes the conventional view that in simple negligence cases, such as slip-and-fall or motor vehicle accidents, the finder of fact, given his familiarity with the activity, can simply invoke his conscience and thereby accurately enforce a community norm of appropriate behavior. According to Professor Abraham, *Vaughan*, the classic paradigmatic example, defies this notion:

> The principal issue was whether an aperture should or should not have been built in the stack. One would think that if there were such a thing as a community norm regarding haystack construction, it would encompass whether and when to build apertures. But right at this seminal moment in the development of negligence law, the report of the decision in *Vaughan*—apparently recounting the evidence—makes a deeply revealing statement. The defendant " . . . made an aperture or chimney through the rick; but in spite, or perhaps in consequence of this precaution, the rick at length burst into flames. . . ." Just as in my hypothetical slip-and-fall case, the community norm in *Vaughan*, if there was one, did not come all the way down to the ground. The conscience of the community in *Vaughan* apparently was divided about apertures.

Should that matter if fires were governed by strict liability rules?

3. ***The Standard of Care for Bailments.*** Epstein, The Many Faces of Fault in Contract Law: Or How to Do Economics Right, Without Really Trying, 107 Mich. L. Rev. 1461, 1464 (2009), notes the irony that

> Vaughan v. Menlove is generally credited with introducing the objective standard of care in negligence cases. Yet most suggestively, the defendant in *Vaughan* insisted that the appropriate rules for liability should be drawn from the law of bailments—cases where one party delivers a chattel with a promise for its return at some future date. The unavoidable element of divided control in bailment cases makes the simple boundary-crossing rules used in boundary disputes and highway accidents a poor guide for the ultimate decision.

In the leading case of Coggs v. Bernard, (1704) 92 Eng. Rep. 107 (QB), Holt, C.J., explicitly adopted a classification of six types of bailments (i.e., consensual arrangements under which goods are delivered to another with the intention that they be redelivered at some future time), first articulated in Roman law, each with its distinct standard of care. He categorized them as: (1) gratuitous bailment for safekeeping (depositum); (2) bailment for the bailee's use (commodatum); (3) a simple pawn (vadium); (4) bailment for hire (locatio rei); (5) bailment whereby the bailee agrees for a fee to operate or manage the thing bailed (locatio operis faciendi); and (6) bailment of a thing to be managed (not merely stored) by the bailee without compensation (mandatum). The underlying principle ties the bailee's standard of care to the benefit that he derives from the bailment. He is held liable for the "slightest negligence" where the loan is for his own benefit or use, but for only gross neglect when he undertakes safekeeping for the bailor. If both parties benefit, the usual standard is that of ordinary care. In all cases it is, of course, possible to vary the standard of care by private agreement. How successful is defendant's implicit argument that the law of bailment authorizes the use of a good-faith standard in disputes between neighbors? If both the good-faith and reasonable care standards are used consensually, how can either be too uncertain to be serviceable? Which standard should be used when?

Oliver Wendell Holmes

The Common Law

107–09 (1881)

Supposing it now to be conceded that the general notion upon which liability to an action is founded is fault or blameworthiness in some sense, the question arises, whether it is so in the sense of personal moral shortcoming, . . . Suppose that a defendant were allowed to testify that, before acting, he considered carefully what would be the conduct of a prudent man under the circumstances, and, having formed the best judgment he could, acted accordingly. If the story was believed, it would be conclusive against the defendant's negligence judged by a moral standard which would take his personal characteristics into account. But supposing any such evidence to have got before the jury, it is very clear that the court would say, Gentlemen, the question is not whether the defendant thought his conduct was that of a prudent man, but whether you think it was.

Exhibit 3.2 Oliver Wendell Holmes, Jr.

Oliver Wendell Holmes, Jr. (1841–1935) was a lawyer, scholar, and judge. Before attending Harvard Law School, he fought in the Civil War. He served as a Justice of the United States Supreme Court from 1902 to 1932, and for twenty years before that, sat on the Massachusetts Supreme Judicial Court, from 1882 to 1902. The Common Law, one of his most enduring works, resulted from a series of lectures delivered at Boston's Lowell Institute in 1880 and 1881, in which he declared, "[t]he life of the law has not been logic; it has been experience."

Bio source: Edmund Fuller, Oliver Wendell Holmes, Jr.: The Great Dissenter, Encyclopaedia Britannica (2014)
Image source: Library of Congress

Some middle point must be found between the horns of this dilemma.

The standards of the law are standards of general application. The law takes no account of the infinite varieties of temperament, intellect, and education which make the internal character of a given act so different in different men. It does not attempt to see men as God sees them, for more than one sufficient reason. In the first place, the impossibility of nicely measuring a man's powers and limitations is far clearer than that of ascertaining his knowledge of law, which has been thought to account for what is called the presumption that every man knows the law. But a more satisfactory explanation is, that, when men live in society, a certain average of conduct, a sacrifice of individual peculiarities going beyond a certain point, is necessary to the general welfare. If, for instance, a man is born hasty and awkward, is always having accidents and hurting himself or his neighbors, no doubt his congenital defects will be allowed for in the courts of Heaven, but his slips are no less troublesome to his neighbors than if they sprang from guilty neglect. His neighbors accordingly require him, at his proper peril, to come up to their standard, and the courts which they establish decline to take his personal equation into account.

The rule that the law does, in general, determine liability by blameworthiness, is subject to the limitation that minute differences of character are not allowed for. The law considers, in other words, what would be blameworthy in the average man, the man of ordinary intelligence and prudence, and determines liability by that. If we fall below the level in those gifts, it is our misfortune so much as that we must have at our peril, for the reasons just given. But he who is intelligent and prudent does not act at his peril, in theory of law. On the contrary, it is only when he fails to exercise the foresight of which he is capable, or exercises it with evil intent, that he is answerable for the consequences.

There are exceptions to the principle that every man is presumed to possess ordinary capacity to avoid harm to his neighbors, which illustrate the rule, and also the moral basis of liability in general. When a man has a distinct defect of such a nature that all can recognize it as making certain precautions impossible, he will not be held answerable for not taking them. A blind man is not required to see at his peril; and although he is, no doubt, bound to consider his infirmity in regulating his actions, yet if he properly finds himself in a certain situation, the neglect of precautions requiring eyesight would not prevent his recovering for an injury to himself, and, it may be presumed, would not make him liable for injuring another. So it is held that, in cases where he is the plaintiff, an infant of very tender years is only bound to take the precautions of which an infant is capable; the same principle may be cautiously applied where he is defendant. Insanity is a more difficult matter to deal with, and no general rule can be laid down about it. There is no doubt that in many cases a man may be insane, and yet perfectly capable of taking the precautions, and of being influenced by the motives, which the circumstances demand. But if insanity of a pronounced type exists, manifestly incapacitating the sufferer from complying with the rule which he has broken, good sense would require it to be admitted as an excuse.

Roberts v. Ring

173 N.W. 437 (Minn. 1919)

Hallam, J. Plaintiff brings this action on behalf of his minor son, John B. Roberts, seven years old, to recover damages for injury from collision with defendant's automobile. The jury found for defendant. Plaintiff appeals. Plaintiff assigns as error certain portions of the charge. Defendant contends that the charge was without error and further contends that as a matter of law, defendant was without negligence and that the boy was negligent.

1. Defendant was driving south on a much traveled street in Owatonna. He was seventy-seven years old. His sight and hearing were defective. A buggy was approaching him from the south. There were other conveyances on the street. The travel was practically blocked. The boy ran from behind the buggy across the street to the west and in front of defendant's automobile. There is evidence that he had been riding on the rear of the buggy. He himself testified that he was crossing the street. As he passed in front of defendant's automobile he was struck and injured.

The question of defendant's negligence was a proper one to be submitted to the jury. Defendant was driving from four to five miles an hour, not a negligent rate of speed. If he was negligent, it was in failing to keep a proper lookout and in failing to promptly stop his car. He testified that he saw the boy when he was four or five feet from the automobile. It is a matter of common knowledge that an automobile traveling four or five miles an hour can be stopped within a very few feet, yet defendant knocked the boy down and his car passed clear over him. If defendant saw the boy, as he now claims, he was not alert in stopping his car. If he did not see him as he is alleged to have stated to others he was not keeping a sharp lookout in this crowded street. We are of the opinion that the evidence was such as to raise an issue of fact as to his negligence.

2. The question of the boy's negligence was likewise for the jury. Had a mature man acted as did this boy he might have been chargeable with negligence as a matter of law. But a boy of seven is not held to the same standard of care in self-protection. In considering his contributory negligence the standard is the degree of care commonly exercised by the ordinary boy of his age and maturity. It would be different if he had caused injury to another. In such a case he could not take advantage of his age or infirmities.

As to the negligence of defendant the court charged:

> In determining whether the defendant was guilty of negligence you may take into consideration . . . the age of the defendant . . . and whether or not the defendant had any physical infirmities.

. . . As above indicated, defendant's infirmities did not tend to relieve him from the charge of negligence. On the contrary they weighed against him. Such infirmities, to the extent that they were proper to be considered at all, presented only a reason why defendant should refrain from operating an automobile on a crowded street where care was required to avoid injuring other travelers. When one, by his acts or omissions causes injury to others, his negligence is to be judged by the standard of care usually exercised by the ordinarily prudent normal man.

Order reversed.

NOTES

1. *Old Age.* The Third Restatement follows *Roberts* by refusing to take old age, as such, into account, although it recognizes such infirmities associated with old age by using the standard of a "reasonably careful person with the same disability," meaning physical disabilities or conditions. RTT: LPEH §11, comment *c.* In Estate of Burgess v. Peterson, 537 N.W.2d 115, 119 (Wis. Ct. App. 1995), Cane, J., explained the logic behind this rule: "[W]hile it is impossible to quantify or measure the degree to which age slows thought processes, physical infirmities (e.g., arthritis, osteoporosis, etc.) have physical manifestations that can be objectively observed and measured."

2. *Beginners and Experts.* The question of variable standards of care also arises with different levels of performance that are expected from beginners and experts in certain endeavors. The use of a lower standard of care for beginners encourages them to undertake activities that they might not otherwise attempt, which is often a socially desirable outcome; but it also exacts a subsidy from the people they may hurt in the process, and not from the public at large. Under the Third Restatement, below-average knowledge, skills, and judgment are "generally ignored" in order to discourage excessive risk taking by those with below-average skills, encourage the acquisition of a skill, prevent the multiplication of separate standards, and forestall the risk of fraud. RTT: LPEH §12, comment *b.* One critical exception covers cases in which the plaintiff has assumed the risk that the defendant will exercise a lower standard of care, as happens when an experienced driver agrees to teach a novice how to drive. Holland v. Pitocchelli, 13 N.E.2d 390 (Mass. 1938). The inexperienced driver gets the benefit of the lower standard against her driving instructor (with whom she has a special relationship), but not against an injured pedestrian (a stranger) who did not assume that risk. *Id.*

The converse problem arises when a defendant has greater skills than most people in a particular activity. Here, the Third Restatement favors taking into account above-average skill: "If an actor has skills or knowledge that exceed those possessed by most others, these skills or knowledge are circumstances to be taken into account in determining whether the actor has behaved as a reasonably careful person." RTT: LPEH §12. The Third Restatement holds that the case for applying a higher standard is strongest in three scenarios: (1) when one party "has a clear obligation to acquire special knowledge and skills that relate to that dangerous activity," such as an electric power company; (2) when the parties have a preexisting relationship, where that party "may well have made representations as to a particular set of skills, and the other party . . . may well have relied upon this representation in entering into the relationship"; or (3) when the relationship is an economic one where such skills may be presumably part of the consideration in agreeing to transact. RTT: LPEH §12, comment *a*. But the Third Restatement does not issue any categorical rule, noting that "skills or knowledge are circumstances to be taken into account in determining whether the actor has behaved as a reasonably careful person." Expert testimony may be necessary to determine the standard of care when specialized knowledge, skill, or training is involved. The Third Restatement also expresses some doubt as to whether the skilled skier or skilled driver should be held to a higher standard if sued for a skiing accident or a highway collision, respectively. *Id.*, comment *a*.

As the Third Restatement suggests, using sliding standards of care for different levels of skill becomes particularly pertinent in highway accidents. In Dakter v. Cavallino, 866 N.W.2d 656, 663, 675 (Wis. 2015), the plaintiff automobile driver, heading north, turned left (west) at an intersection when the defendant, the professional driver of an empty 65-foot-long semi tractor-trailer, heading south, came through the intersection behind another car that was either waiting or had just turned left (east), leaving the plaintiff seriously injured in the ensuing collision. The jury instruction required the defendant "to use the degree of care, skill, and judgment which reasonable semi truck drivers would exercise in the same or similar circumstances, having due regard for the state of learning, education, experience, and knowledge possessed by semi truck drivers holding Commercial Driver's Licenses." The plaintiff's expert testified that the defendant should have reduced his speed by a third on a wet and slick road, which he did not do. Abrahamson, C.J., held that, per the Third Restatement, the jury could take into account both

> the superior knowledge rule, which requires an actor with special knowledge or skill to act commensurate with that knowledge or skill, and the profession or trade principle, which requires an actor engaged in a profession or trade to act as a reasonable member of such profession or trade would act under the same or similar circumstances.

By contrast, in Davis v. Brown Loc. Sch. Dist., 131 N.E.3d 431, 445–46 (Ohio Ct. App. 2019), Bartlett, J., refused to hold a commercial bus driver to a heightened standard of care relative to a regular driver, even though the bus driver held a commercial driver's license, the acquisition of which entailed additional training on how to respond to dangers. Otherwise, according to Bartlett, J., "[a] heightened duty of care for commercial drivers in Ohio would place some portion of the responsibility for every accident on a commercial driver, simply because he or she has been instructed to be a defensive driver."

Daniels v. Evans

224 A.2d 63 (N.H. 1966)

[Plaintiff's decedent, a 19-year-old youth, was killed when his motorcycle collided with defendant's automobile. A trial by jury resulted in a verdict for plaintiff, and the only alleged error argued on appeal was the trial court's charge pertaining to the standard of care required of the decedent.]

LAMPRON, J. As to the standard of care to be applied to the conduct of the decedent Robert E. Daniels, 19 years of age, the Trial Court charged the jury in part as follows:

"Now, he is considered a minor, being under the age of twenty-one, and a minor child must exercise the care of the average child of his or her age, experience and stage of mental development. In other words, he is not held to the same degree of care as an adult."

Concededly these instructions substantially reflect the rule by which the care of a minor has been judged heretofore in the courts of our State. Charbonneau v. MacRury[, 153 A. 457 (N.H. 1931)]. However an examination of the cases will reveal that in most the minors therein were engaged in activities appropriate to their age, experience and wisdom. These included being a pedestrian, riding a bicycle, riding a horse, [and] coasting.

We agree that minors are entitled to be judged by standards commensurate with their age, experience, and wisdom when engaged in activities appropriate to their age, experience, and wisdom. Hence when children are walking, running, playing with toys, throwing balls, operating bicycles, sliding or engaged in other childhood activities their conduct should be judged by the rule of what is reasonable conduct under the circumstances among which are the age, experience, and stage of mental development of the minor involved.

However, the question is raised by the defendant in this case whether the standard of care applied to minors in such cases should prevail when the minor is engaged in activities normally undertaken by adults. In other words, when a minor undertakes an adult activity which can result in grave danger to others and to the minor himself if the care used in the course of the activity drops below that care which the reasonable and prudent adult would use, the defendant maintains that the minor's conduct in that instance should meet the same standards as that of an adult.

Many recent cases have held that "when a minor assumes responsibility for the operation of so potentially dangerous an instrument as an automobile, he should . . . assume responsibility for its careful and safe operation in the light of adult standards." 2 Idaho L. Rev., 103, 111 (1965); Dellwo v. Pearson, 107 N.W.2d 859 (Minn. 1961). The rule has been recognized in Restatement (Second), Torts, §283A, comment *c*. . . . In an annotation in 97 A.L.R.2d 872 at page 875 it is said that recent decisions "hold that when a minor engages in such activities as the operation of an automobile or similar power driven device, he forfeits his rights to have the reasonableness of his conduct measured by a standard commensurate with his age and is thenceforth held to the same standard as all other persons."

One of the reasons for such a rule has been stated thusly in Dellwo v. Pearson, *supra*:

> To give legal sanction to the operation of automobiles by teen-agers with less than ordinary care for the safety of others is impractical today, to say the least. We may take judicial notice of the hazards of automobile traffic, the frequency of accidents, the often catastrophic results of accidents, and the fact that immature individuals are no less prone to accidents than adults. . . . [I]t would be unfair to the public to permit a minor in the operation of a motor vehicle to observe any other standards of care and conduct than those expected of all others. A person observing children at play . . . may anticipate conduct that does not reach an adult standard of care or prudence. However, one cannot know whether the operator of an approaching automobile . . . is a minor or an adult, and usually cannot protect himself against youthful imprudence even if warned. . . .

RSA 262-A:2 which establishes rules of the road for the operation of motor vehicles on our highways reads as follows: "Required Obedience to Traffic Laws. It is unlawful and . . . a misdemeanor for *any person* to do any act forbidden or fail to perform any act required in this chapter." (Emphasis supplied.) This is some indication of an intent on the part of our Legislature that all drivers must, and have the right to expect that others using the highways, regardless of their age and experience, will, obey the traffic laws and thus exercise the adult standard of ordinary care. . . .

The rule charged by the Trial Court pertaining to the standard of care to be applied by the jury to the conduct of the minor plaintiff Robert E. Daniels in the operation of the motorcycle was proper in "the bygone days" when children were using relatively innocent contrivances. However in the circumstances of today's modern life, where vehicles moved by powerful motors are readily available and used by many minors, we question the propriety of a rule which would allow such vehicles to be operated to the hazard of the public, and to the driver himself, with less than the degree of care required of an adult.

We are of the opinion that to apply to minors a more lenient standard in the operation of motor vehicles, whether an automobile or a motorcycle, than that applied to adults is unrealistic, contrary to the expressed legislative policy, and inimical to public safety. Furthermore when a minor is operating a motor vehicle there is no reason for making a distinction based on whether he is charged with primary negligence, contributory negligence, or a causal violation of a statute and we so hold.

We hold therefore that a minor operating a motor vehicle, whether an automobile or a motorcycle, must be judged by the same standard of care as an adult and the defendant's objection to the Trial Court's charge applying a different standard to the conduct of plaintiff's intestate was valid. . . .

Exception sustained.

NOTES

1. *Infancy and Childhood.* All U.S. jurisdictions take account of childhood in determinations of negligence. The Third Restatement adheres to the general rule, holding a child to the standard of "a reasonably careful person of the same age, intelligence, and experience." RTT: LPEH §10(a). What explains the differential standard applied to children but not the elderly?

In addition to the exception for dangerous, adult-like activities, the Third Restatement provides that a child under five years of age is incapable of negligence. RTT: LPEH §10(b). Does this confer additional duties on the child's guardian?

2. *Adult and Child Activities.* In Charbonneau v. MacRury, 153 A. 457, 462–63 (N.H. 1931), overruled by Daniels v. Evans, the court justified its use of a variable standard of care for children as follows:

> Unless infants are to be denied the environment and association of their elders until they have acquired maturity, there must be a living relationship between them on terms which permit the child to act as a child in his stage of development. As well expect a boy to learn to swim without experience in the water as to expect him to learn to function as an adult without contact with his superiors. For the law to hold children to the exercise of the care of adults "would be to shut its eyes, ostrich-like to the facts of life and to burden unduly the child's growth to majority." [Shulman, The Standard of Care Required of Children, 37 Yale L.J. 618 (1928).] During the period of his development he must participate in human activities on some basis of reason. Reason requires that indulgence be shown him commensurate with his want of development

> as indicated by his age and experience. Id. 621. Though strictly speaking it is the resultant qualities reasonably attributable to these factors that measure his capacity, it is sufficient, as a practical matter, to speak of age and experience as inclusive of these qualities. . . .

What constitutes an adult-like activity? In Hudson-Connor v. Putney, 86 P.3d 106, 111 (Or. Ct. App. 2004), Brewer, J., held first that it was not an adult activity for a fourteen-year-old child to entrust a golf cart to an eleven-year-old plaintiff, and further, that driving a golf cart on private property was not an adult activity:

> To obtain a license to operate an automobile on the highways, a driver must demonstrate mastery of those skills by passing a knowledge test, a driving skills test, and, if the driver is under the age of 18, a safe driving practices test. No such license is required to operate a motorized golf cart on premises that are not open to the public. Significantly, there is no evidence in the record that the operation of golf carts on private premises and automobiles on premises open to the public requires similar driving skills beyond the most rudimentary level. In short, on the factual record before us, we conclude that the operation of a motorized golf cart on private premises does not require adult qualifications.

By contrast, in Dellwo v. Pearson, 107 N.W.2d 859 (Minn. 1961), discussed in *Daniels*, a twelve-year-old defendant was held to the adult standard of care in the operation of a speed boat, even though there was apparently no licensing statute for such boats. Jackson v. McCuiston, 448 S.W.2d 33 (Ark. 1969), held that a thirteen-year-old farm boy should be judged by the adult standard of care in operating a tractor-propelled stalk cutter, a large piece of machinery with a dangerous cutting blade. By contrast, Johnson v. Johnson, No. 3:17-CV-03001-RAL, 2018 WL 1536320, at *1 (D.S.D. Jan. 16, 2018), held that a twelve-year-old farm boy should be held to the subjective standard applicable to minors, taking into account "his age, intelligence, experience, and capacity" given that the operation of an all-terrain-vehicle on private property is not an activity "normally undertaken only by adults."

The use of firearms presents a particularly vexing application. In Purtle v. Shelton, 474 S.W.2d 123 (Ark. 1971), the Arkansas Supreme Court cut back on *Jackson, supra*, refusing to hold a seventeen-year-old boy to the adult standard of care in using dangerous firearms. It applied a lower standard for minors because deer hunting was not exclusively an adult activity. Byrd, J., dissenting, protested:

> Because a bullet fired from the gun by a minor is just as deadly as a bullet fired by an adult, I'm at a loss to understand why one with "buck fever" because of his minority is entitled to exercise any less care than any one else deer hunting. One killed by a bullet so fired would be just as dead in one instance as the other and without any more warning.

The Third Restatement agrees with the dissent, commenting that "[h]andling firearms is best regarded as a dangerous adult activity. The dangers involved in firearm use are obvious and dramatic." RTT: LPEH §10, comment *f*. But most courts refuse to apply an adult standard of care when a juvenile injures another with a firearm. Is hunting more or less of an inherently adult activity than driving? More or less of a distinctly dangerous activity? Should regional differences be relevant? In Thomas v. Inman, 578 P.2d 399, 403 (Or. 1978), Bryson, J., stated the issue as follows: "In the rural districts of this state, children, or those who have not been licensed to drive automobiles, have always used guns both for target practice and hunting under differing circumstances."

3. *Parental Supervision of Children's Dangerous Activities.* In Becker v. Litzenberger, 989 N.Y.S.2d 823, 825 (Sup. Ct. 2014), the plaintiff, a fifteen-year-old girl, was warming up before her lacrosse team practice when she was struck in the mouth by the nine-year-old son of the assistant coach, himself an experienced lacrosse player, causing the loss of several teeth. The court did not ask whether the activity in question was adult or child, but followed the

New York rule that provides that a "parent owes a duty to protect third parties from harm that is clearly foreseeable from the child's improvident use or operation of a dangerous instrument, where such use is found to be subject to the parent's control," and held as a matter of law that the stick, like a baseball bat, was not a dangerous instrument in light of the "age, maturity, intelligence, and physical characteristics" of the boy. Should the case be resolved on the view that recovery for athletic injuries is governed by a standard of recklessness, wholly without regard to age? What result if the boy had thrown a ball that had hit and injured a bystander?

4. *Reasonable Plaintiff Versus Reasonable Defendant.* In Daniels v. Evans, the court held both child plaintiffs and child defendants to the same standard of care in highway accidents, a view that is widely followed today. See RTT: LPEH §10, comment *e*. While the case law has moved toward the unitary standard of care for all youthful drivers and pedestrians, the case for a general dual standard was advanced in James, The Qualities of the Reasonable Man in Negligence Cases, 16 Mo. L. Rev. 1, 1–2 (1951):

> By and large the law has chosen external, objective standards of conduct. The reasonably prudent man is, to be sure, endowed with some of the qualities of the person whose conduct is being judged, especially where the latter has greater knowledge, skill, or the like, than people generally. But many of the actor's shortcomings such as awkwardness, faulty perception, or poor judgment, are not taken into account if they fall below the general level of the community. This means that individuals are often held guilty of legal fault for failing to live up to a standard which as a matter of fact they cannot meet. Such a result shocks people who believe in refining the fault principle so as to make legal liability correspond more closely to personal moral shortcoming. There has, therefore, been some pressure towards the adoption of a more subjective test. But if the standard of conduct is relaxed for *defendants* who cannot meet a normal standard, then the burden of accident loss resulting from the extra hazards created by society's most dangerous groups (e.g. the young, the novice, the accident prone) will be thrown on the innocent victims of substandard behavior. Such a conclusion shocks people who believe that the compensation of accident victims is a more important objective of modern tort law than a further refinement of the tort principle, and that compensation should prevail when the two objectives conflict. The application of a relaxed subjective standard to the issue of *plaintiff's* contributory negligence, however, involves no such conflict. On this issue the forces of the two objectives combine to demand a subjective test: the refinement of the fault principle furthers the compensation of accident victims by cutting down a defense that would stand in its way. For this reason the writer has elsewhere developed the thesis that there should be an explicit double standard of conduct, namely, an external standard for a defendant's negligence, and a (relaxed) subjective standard for contributory negligence. Even if this thesis is rejected, the same result probably prevails anyhow, because the application of the legal standard is largely left to the jury, and juries, by and large, tend to resolve doubts on both issues in favor of plaintiffs.

Using different standards for the defendant's negligence and the plaintiff's contributory negligence leaves the outcome unclear when both parties are children and both are injured. Should the result depend on whether either or both are insured? Note that the double standard necessarily increases the administrative costs of both settlement and litigation.

Breunig v. American Family Insurance Co.

173 N.W.2d 619 (Wis. 1970)

[Plaintiff brought this action for personal injuries sustained when his car was struck by a car driven by Erma Veith, an insured of the defendant. The accident occurred when Mrs. Veith's car veered across the center of the road into the lane in which plaintiff was traveling. Defendant argued that Mrs. Veith "was not negligent because just prior to the collision she suddenly and without warning was seized with a mental aberration or delusion which rendered her unable to operate the automobile with her conscious mind." The jury returned a verdict finding her causally negligent on the theory she "had knowledge or forewarning of her mental delusions or disability." From the award of $7,000 damages, the defendant insurance company—which under Wisconsin law could be directly sued for the torts of its insured—appeals.]

PH

Hallows, C.J. There is no question that Erma Veith was subject at the time of the accident to an insane delusion which directly affected her ability to operate her car in an ordinarily prudent manner and caused the accident. The specific question considered by the jury under the negligence inquiry was whether she had such foreknowledge of her susceptibility to such a mental aberration, delusion or hallucination as to make her negligent in driving a car at all under such conditions.

. . . The evidence established that Mrs. Veith, while returning home after taking her husband to work, saw a white light on the back of a car ahead of her. She followed this light for three or four blocks. Mrs. Veith did not remember anything else except landing in a field, lying in the side of the road and people talking. She recalled awaking in the hospital.

The psychiatrist testified Mrs. Veith told him she was driving on a road when she believed that God was taking ahold of the steering wheel and was directing her car. She saw the truck coming and stepped on the gas in order to become airborne because she knew she could fly because Batman does it. To her surprise she was not airborne before striking the truck but after the impact she was flying. . . .

The insurance company argues Erma Veith was not negligent as a matter of law because there is no evidence upon which the jury could find that she had knowledge or warning or should have reasonably foreseen that she might be subject to a mental delusion which would suddenly cause her to lose control of the car. Plaintiff argues there was such evidence of forewarning and also suggests Erma Veith should be liable because insanity should not be a defense in negligence cases.

The case was tried on the theory that some forms of insanity are a defense to and preclude liability for negligence under the doctrine of Theisen v. Milwaukee Automobile Mut. Ins. Co.[, 19 N.W.2d 393 (Wis. 1963)]. We agree. Not all types of insanity vitiate responsibility for a negligent tort. The question of liability in every case must depend upon the kind and nature of the insanity. The effect of the mental illness or mental hallucinations or disorder must be such as to affect the person's ability to understand and appreciate the duty which rests upon him to drive his car with ordinary care, or if the insanity does not affect such understanding and appreciation, it must affect his ability to control his car in an ordinarily prudent manner. And in addition, there must be an absence of notice or forewarning to the person that he may be suddenly subject to such a type of insanity or mental illness.

In *Theisen* we recognized one was not negligent if he was unable to conform his conduct through no fault of his own but held a sleeping driver negligent as a matter of law because one is always given conscious warnings of drowsiness and if a person does not heed such warnings and continues to drive his car, he is negligent for continuing to drive under such conditions. But we distinguished those exceptional cases of loss of consciousness resulting from injury inflicted by an outside force, or fainting, or heart attack, or epileptic seizure, or other illness which suddenly incapacitates the driver of an automobile when the occurrence of such disability is not attended with sufficient warning or should not have been reasonably foreseen. . . .

There are authorities which generally hold insanity is not a defense in tort cases except for intentional torts. Restatement, 2 Torts, 2d, p. 16, sec. 283 B, and appendix (1966) and cases cited therein. These cases rest on the historical view of strict liability without regard to the fault of the individual. Prosser, in his Law of Torts (3d ed.), p. 1028, states this view is a historical survival which originated in the dictum in Weaver v. Ward (1616), Hob. 134, 80

English Reports 284 [*supra* Chapter 2, at 68], when the action of trespass still rested upon strict liability. He points out that when the modern law developed to the point of holding the defendant liable for negligence, the dictum was repeated in some cases.

The policy basis of holding a permanently insane person liable for his tort is: (1) Where one of two innocent persons must suffer a loss it should be borne by the one who occasioned it; (2) to induce those interested in the estate of the insane person (if he has one) to restrain and control him and; (3) the fear an insanity defense would lead to false claims of insanity to avoid liability. . . .

We think the statement that insanity is no defense is too broad when it is applied to a negligence case where the driver is suddenly overcome without forewarning by a mental disability or disorder which incapacitates him from conforming his conduct to the standards of a reasonable man under like circumstances. These are rare cases indeed, but their rarity is no reason for overlooking their existence and the justification which is the basis of the whole doctrine of liability for negligence, i.e., that it is unjust to hold a man responsible for his conduct which he is incapable of avoiding and which incapability was unknown to him prior to the accident.

We need not reach the question of contributory negligence of an insane person or the question of comparative negligence as those problems are not now presented. All we hold is that a sudden mental incapacity equivalent in its effect to such physical causes as a sudden heart attack, epileptic seizure, stroke, or fainting should be treated alike and not under the general rule of insanity. . . .

The insurance company argues that since the psychiatrist was the only expert witness who testified concerning the mental disability of Mrs. Veith and the lack of forewarning that as a matter of law there was no forewarning and she could not be held negligent and the trial court should have so held. While there was testimony of friends indicating she was normal for some months prior to the accident, the psychiatrist testified the origin of her mental illness appeared in August, 1965, prior to the accident. In that month Mrs. Veith visited the Necedah Shrine where she was told the Blessed Virgin had sent her to the shrine. She was told to pray for survival. Since that time she felt it had been revealed to her the end of the world was coming and that she was picked by God to survive. Later she had visions of God judging people and sentencing them to Heaven or Hell; she thought Batman was good and was trying to help save the world and her husband was possessed of the devil. Mrs. Veith told her daughter about her visions.

The question is whether she had warning or knowledge which would reasonably lead her to believe that hallucinations would occur and be such as to affect her driving an automobile. Even though the doctor's testimony is uncontradicted, it need not be accepted by the jury. It is an expert's opinion but it is not conclusive. It is for the jury to decide whether the facts underpinning an expert opinion are true. . . . The jury could find that a woman, who believed she had a special relationship to God and was the chosen one to survive the end of the world, could believe that God would take over the direction of her life to the extent of driving her car. Since these mental aberrations were not constant, the jury could infer she had knowledge of her condition and the likelihood of a hallucination just as one who has knowledge of a heart condition knows the possibility of an attack. While the evidence may not be strong upon which to base an inference, especially in view of the fact that two jurors dissented on this verdict and expressly stated they could find no evidence of forewarning, nevertheless, the evidence to sustain the verdict of the jury need not constitute the great weight and clear preponderance.

The insurance company claims the jury was perverse because the verdict is contrary both to the evidence and to the law. We think this argument is without merit.

[Judgment affirmed.]

NOTES

1. ***Mental and Emotional Disabilities.*** According to the Third Restatement, an adult defendant's mental and emotional disability is generally not considered in making negligence determinations. RTT: LPEH §11(c). Notwithstanding the fact that "modern society is increasingly inclined to treat physical disabilities and mental disabilities similarly," courts tend to exonerate defendants for injuries resulting from "a sudden incapacitation or loss of consciousness resulting from *physical* injury" (unless the incapacitating event was foreseeable) but hold them liable if the sudden and unforeseen incapacitation is due to *mental* illness. RTT: LPEH §11(b) & comment *e*. Thus in Sartin v. Estate of McPike, 475 P.3d 522, 530–31 (Wash. Ct. App. 2020), Maxa, C.J., found the driver's loss of consciousness resulting from cardiac arrest not reasonably foreseeable despite high blood pressure, diabetes, sleep apnea, and irregular heartbeat. Whereas in Perez-Rodriguez v. State, 435 P.3d 746, 750 (Or. 2019), Nelson, J., declined to consider mental illness or intellectual capacity in determining reasonableness "because of the problems of administrability that would be encountered in attempting to identify them and assess their significance" (quoting RTT: LPEH §11(b) & comment *e*).

2. ***The Breunig Approach.*** Several courts deviate from the Third Restatement and continue to recognize *Breunig's* apparent exception for sudden and unforeseeable mental incapacity. In Ramey v. Knorr, 124 P.3d 314, 319–20 (Wash. Ct. App. 2005), the defendant Knorr turned her car around on I-405 and rammed headlong into the plaintiff in her attempt to commit suicide. Her defense of sudden mental incapacity was rejected because the record showed that

> in 1994, Knorr had a mental breakdown and was hospitalized for ten days. During that period, Knorr believed the person she worked for was conspiring to steal her and her husband's assets, was going to kill them, and was poisoning her. She also had concerns about her brother being a murderer. . . . Knorr was diagnosed with possible delusional disorder, was put on medication, and was advised to see a psychiatrist. . . . [B]eginning in March 2001, Knorr's delusional thoughts about her brother being a murderer came back. . . . [B]y November 2001, her thoughts escalated and [her husband] tried to get her to agree to go to the hospital. Knorr wanted to wait until after the holidays to go to the hospital and had an appointment scheduled for two days after the accident.

3. ***Institutionalized Mentally Disabled Persons.*** *Breunig* has been narrowed in custodial settings, where courts have not shied away from permitting evidence of an excusing mental or emotional disability. In Gould v. American Family Mutual Insurance, 543 N.W.2d 282 (Wis. 1996), the defendant, an institutionalized patient with Alzheimer's disease, injured his paid caregiver. The court refused to apply *Breunig*.

> In sum, we agree with the Goulds that ordinarily a mentally disabled person is responsible for his or her torts. However, we conclude that this rule does not apply in this case because the circumstances totally negate the rationale [in *Breunig*] behind the rule and would place an unreasonable burden on the negligent institutionalized mentally disabled. When a mentally disabled person injures an employed caretaker, the injured party can reasonably foresee the danger and is not "innocent" of the risk involved. By placing a mentally disabled person in an institution or similar restrictive setting, "those interested in the estate" of that person are not likely to be in need of an inducement for greater restraint. It is incredible to assert that a tortfeasor would "simulate or pretend insanity" over a prolonged period of time and even be institutionalized in order to avoid being held liable for damages for some future civil act. Therefore, we hold that a person institutionalized, as here, with a mental disability, and who does not have the capacity to control or appreciate his or her conduct cannot be liable for injuries caused to caretakers who are employed for financial compensation.

Thereafter, in Jankee v. Clark County, 612 N.W.2d 297, 316 (Wis. 2000), the Wisconsin Supreme Court refused to impose liability on an institution that had not restrained the plaintiff, a mental health patient, who had injured himself while trying to escape by jumping through a window that he had pried open in the county psychiatric hospital. Following *Breunig*, Prosser, J., held the mentally disabled *plaintiff* to an objective standard of care, again to minimize the level of institutionalized care required of mentally disabled people. Prosser, J., distinguished *Gould*, noting the perverse incentive on the psychiatric hospital "to intensify security considerations for the mentally disabled, not to protect the disabled but rather to protect themselves from liability," for example, by "restor[ing] bars to all windows in the facility." Why not resolve these cases (and *McGuire*, *supra* Chapter 1, at 24) with a no-duty rule, leaving the plaintiff with workers' compensation coverage? See generally Light, Note, Rejecting the Logic of Confinement: Care Relationships and the Mentally Disabled Under Tort Law, 109 Yale L.J. 381 (1999).

4. *The Impact on Mentally Disabled Persons.* What effect does the imposition of the "reasonable person" standard have on mentally disabled defendants' liability? See Chriscoe & Lukasik, Re-Examining Reasonableness: Negligence Liability in Adult Defendants with Cognitive Disabilities, 6 Ala. C.R. & C.L. L. Rev. 1 (2015), for a discussion of how "[t]his standard disproportionately burdens adult negligence defendants who have cognitive disabilities. It does so by treating these disabilities as if they do not exist in two key places: in the minds of defendants who have them and in the awareness of most plaintiffs who do not."

Fletcher v. City of Aberdeen

338 P.2d 743 (Wash. 1959)

Foster, J. For the purpose of placing electric wires underground, the city dug a ditch in the parking strip adjacent to the sidewalk at the intersection of Broadway and Fourth streets in the city of Aberdeen. Suitable barricades were erected to protect pedestrians from falling into the excavation, but, unfortunately, at the time of the mishap in question, one of the city's employees had removed the barriers to facilitate his work in the excavation. When he went elsewhere to work, he negligently failed to replace the barricades, which left the excavation unprotected. In approaching the intersection, the respondent husband, who had been blind since his eighth year, had his kit of piano-tuning tools in his left hand and his cane in his right. With the cane he was cautiously feeling his way. Because the protective barriers had been removed, the existence of the excavation was unknown to the respondent. By the use of the cane, the barriers would have protected the respondent if they had been in place. The jury was entitled to find that the city was negligent in removing the barriers without providing other warning.

. . . The city's argument is that it had discharged its duty by the erection of barricades. It may be assumed for present purposes, that the barriers originally erected were sufficient to discharge the city's duty of maintaining its streets and adjacent parking strips in a reasonably safe condition for pedestrian use. However, the city's argument completely ignores the undisputed evidence that its workman had removed the barricades and that the accident in question occurred during this interval. The duty of maintaining the sidewalks and adjacent parking strips is a continuing one. . . .

The city assigns error upon the refusal to instruct as requested that "[t]he fact that the plaintiff is blind does not impose on the City any higher degree of care." . . . The supreme court of Oregon recently commented:

> Public thoroughfares are for the beggar on his crutches as well as the millionaire in his limousine. Neither is it the policy of the law to discriminate against those who suffer physical infirmity. The blind and the halt may use the streets without being guilty of negligence if, in so doing, they exercise that degree of care which an ordinarily prudent person similarly afflicted would exercise under the same circumstances.

Weinstein v. Wheeler, 127 Or. 406 (1928). . . .

The city is charged with knowledge that its streets will be used by those who are physically infirm as well as those in perfect physical condition. . . . The obligations are correlative. The person under a physical disability is obliged to use the care which a reasonable person under the same or similar disability would exercise under the circumstances. The city, on the other hand, is obliged to afford that degree of protection which would bring to the notice of the person so afflicted the danger to be encountered. There was no error, therefore, in the denial of the appellant's requested instruction. . . .

The judgment is, therefore, affirmed.

WEAVER, C.J., and DONWORTH, OTT and HUNTER, JJ., concur.

NOTES

1. *Heightened Duty of Care.* As *Fletcher* demonstrates, a city is obliged to provide use of its streets to the physically disabled. In similar fashion, drivers on the roads should anticipate disabled pedestrians (as well as children) and adjust their level of care accordingly. How do such heightened duties affect the standard of reasonable self-care demanded of these classes of persons? Why is a physical disability relevant for setting the standard of care whereas mental and emotional disabilities are not?

2. *Legal Blindness.* Under the Third Restatement, "the conduct of an actor with a ['significant and objectively verifiable'] physical disability is negligent only if the conduct does not conform to that of a reasonably careful person with the same disability." RTT: LPEH §11(a) & comment *a*. In Kent v. Crocker, 562 N.W.2d 833 (Neb. 1997), a driver with failing eyesight struck and killed a pedestrian. The court found that the defendant's choice to drive with failing eyesight did not conclusively establish negligence, given that medical evidence suggested her eyesight was sufficient for driving. By contrast, in Poyner v. Loftus, 694 A.2d 69 (D.C. 1997), a legally blind plaintiff, capable of seeing about six to eight feet in front of him, was injured as he fell from an incline leading to the defendant's cleaners about four feet above street level. A bush had been removed from the end of the incline, which the plaintiff would have seen had he not been distracted by a call from down the street. The court affirmed summary judgment for the defendant, noting that the plaintiff's testimony conclusively showed his own negligence when "he turned his head, but continued to walk forward," and reasoning that those with poor eyesight must take keener watchfulness in conducting their own affairs. What result if the plaintiff had been totally blind?

3. *Incentive Effects.* In Arroyo v. United States, 656 F.3d 663, 673–74 (7th Cir. 2011), Posner, C.J., commented on *Fletcher* as follows:

> A blind person who, while using the blind person's white cane, is hit at an intersection, when a sighted person would easily have dodged the vehicle hurtling toward him driven by the defendant, is not deemed negligent if he was being as careful as it is reasonable to expect a blind person to be, bearing in mind the cost to the blind of holding them to the same standard of care in crossing streets as sighted persons. Otherwise a blind person would lose the protection of tort law when he ventured to cross a street.
>
> The goal of the average-person rule . . . , in instrumental terms, is to provide an additional incentive, beyond that of moral duty or concern with personal safety, to avoid injuring people (or being injured). A driver who falls below the average of care, and as a result injures someone, is subject to tort liability; it is hoped that the threat will motivate drivers to be careful to avoid injuring others (or themselves).

What result if the blind person crossed against the light?

Denver & Rio Grande R.R. v. Peterson

69 P. 578 (Colo. 1902)

Campbell, C.J. The care required of a warehouseman is the same, whether he be rich or poor. For, if the fact that he is rich requires of him greater care than if he possessed only moderate means or is poor, then, if he were extremely poor, the care required might be such as practically to amount to nothing; and no one would claim that such an uncertain and sliding rule should be the measure of his liability. . . .

NOTE

The Relevance of Wealth to Negligence Liability. *Peterson* suggests that the level of care required of a defendant is constant regardless of his wealth. In Personalizing Negligence Law, 91 N.Y.U. L. Rev. 627, 685–86 (2016), Ben-Shahar and Porat note: "It is sometimes argued that the wealth of the injurer should be factored into the design of negligence standards, perhaps because high-resource injurers can more easily afford greater expenditures on care." However, "income taxes and fiscal policies are thought to be superior tools, in the sense that they achieve redistribution more efficiently and comprehensively." *Id.* Similarly, in Should Legal Rules Favor the Poor? Clarifying the Role of Legal Rules and the Income Tax in Redistributing Income, 20 J. Legal Stud. 821, 823 (2000), Kaplow and Shavell defend the proposition that substantive legal rules should not offer special preference to the poor because

> the income tax system possesses several clear advantages over legal rules as a means of redistribution. Notably, the income tax system affects the entire population and, by its nature treats individuals on the basis of their income. By contrast, the influence of legal rules often is confined to the small fraction of individuals who find themselves involved in legal disputes. Also, legal rules often are very imprecise tools for redistribution because there tends to be substantial income variation within groups of plaintiffs and defendants (so that much of the redistribution will be in the wrong direction). Additionally, many legal rules—such as those of contract, corporate, and commercial law—often leave the distribution of income essentially unchanged because price adjustments negate the distributive effects of the legal rules.

Generally, evidence of a defendant's wealth is not admissible at trial in a tort case, nor is it subject to disclosure during discovery. Evidence regarding insurance is likewise typically not admissible but is discoverable in most states and under Fed. R. Civ. P. 26(a)(1)(A)(iv) and Fed. R. Evid. 411. The relevance of a defendant's wealth to the determination of punitive damages is the subject of current debate; see *infra* Chapter 9, Section D.

5

SECTION C. CALCULUS OF RISK

This section turns to the judicial efforts to fashion and apply an operational standard of reasonable care. Our discussion proceeds on two levels. The first deals with the common sense, intuitive meaning of negligence as it applies to ordinary individuals and corporate or business entities. The second addresses the judicial effort to impart a more precise economic meaning to the term, adopting the language of costs and benefits—the "calculus" of risk. Both approaches have uneasily coexisted throughout the history of the common law.

Blyth v. Birmingham Water Works
(1856) 156 Eng. Rep. 1047 (Exch.)

[The defendants owned a nonprofit waterworks charged by statute with the laying of water mains and fire plugs in the city streets. The pipes were to be buried 18 inches underground. The fireplug in the instant case was built "according to the best known system, and the materials of it were at the time of the accident sound and in good order."]

On the 24th of February, a large quantity of water, escaping from the neck of the main, forced its way through the ground into the plaintiff's house. The apparatus had been laid down 25 years, and had worked well during that time. The defendants' engineer stated, that the water might have forced its way through the brickwork round the neck of the main, and that the accident might have been caused by the frost, inasmuch as the expansion of the water would force up the plug out of the neck, and the stopper being encrusted with ice would not suffer the plug to ascend. One of the severest frosts on record set in on the 15th of January, 1855, and continued until after the accident in question. An incrustation of ice and snow had gathered about the stopper, and in the street all round, and also for some inches between the stopper and the plug. The ice had been observed on the surface of the ground for a considerable time before the accident. A short time after the accident, the company's turncock removed the ice from the stopper, took out the plug, and replaced it.

The judge left it to the jury to consider whether the company had used proper care to prevent the accident. He thought that, if the defendants had taken out the ice adhering to the plug, the accident would not have happened, and left it to the jury to say whether they ought to have removed the ice. The jury found a verdict for the plaintiff for the sum claimed. . . .

Alderson, B. I am of opinion that there was no evidence to be left to the jury. The case turns upon the question, whether the facts proved shew that the defendants were guilty of negligence. Negligence is the omission to do something which a reasonable man, guided upon those considerations which ordinarily regulate the conduct of human affairs, would do, or doing something which a prudent and reasonable man would not do. The defendants might have been liable for negligence, if, unintentionally, they omitted to do that which a reasonable person would have done, or did that which a person taking reasonable precautions would not have done. A reasonable man would act with reference to the average circumstances of the temperature in ordinary years. The defendants had provided against such frosts as experience would have led men, acting prudently, to provide against; and they are not guilty of negligence, because their precautions proved insufficient against the effects of the extreme severity of the frost of 1855, which penetrated to a greater depth than any which ordinarily occurs south of the polar regions. Such a state of circumstances constitutes a contingency against which no reasonable man can provide. The result was an accident, for which the defendants cannot be held liable.

Bramwell, B. The Act of Parliament directed the defendants to lay down pipes, with plugs in them, as safety-valves, to prevent the bursting of the pipes. The plugs were properly made, and of proper material; but there was an accumulation of ice about this plug, which prevented it from acting properly. The defendants were not bound to keep the plugs clear. It appears to me that the plaintiff was under quite as much obligation to remove the ice and snow which had accumulated, as the defendants. However that may be, it appears to me that it would be monstrous to hold the defendants responsible because they did not foresee and prevent an accident, the cause of which was so obscure, that it was not discovered until many months after the accident had happened.

Verdict to be entered for the defendants.

NOTE

The Influence of Blyth. Baron Alderson's definition of negligence continues to exert enormous influence on modern tort litigation. Section 2:10 of the New York Pattern Jury Instructions—Civil (2023) reads:

> Negligence is lack of ordinary care. It is a failure to use that degree of care that a reasonably prudent person would have used under the same circumstances. Negligence may arise from doing an act that a reasonably prudent person would not have done under the same circumstances, or, on the other hand, from failing to do an act that a reasonably prudent person would have done under the same circumstances.

In applying this formula in *Blyth*, should the focus be on the design of the original system or on the failure to remove the ice after the storm? If the former, is it sufficient if the pipes withstand the frost found in "ordinary years"? If the latter, does the formula indicate who has the duty to remove the ice, and why?

Henry Terry

Negligence

29 Harv. L. Rev. 40, 42–44 (1915)

To make conduct negligent the risk involved in it must be unreasonably great; some injurious consequences of it must be not only possible or in a sense probable, but unreasonably probable. It is quite impossible in the business of life to avoid taking risks of injury to one's self or others, and the law does not forbid doing so; what it requires is that the risk be not unreasonably great. The essence of negligence is unreasonableness; due care is simply reasonable conduct. There is no mathematical rule of percentage of probabilities to be followed here. A risk is not necessarily unreasonable because the harmful consequence is more likely than not to follow the conduct, nor reasonable because the chances are against that. A very large risk may be reasonable in some circumstances, and a small risk unreasonable in other circumstances. When due care consists in taking precautions against harm, only reasonable precautions need be taken, not every conceivable or possible precaution. And precautions need not be taken against every conceivable or foreseeable danger, but only against probable dangers. The books are full of cases where persons have been held not negligent for not guarding against a certain harmful event, on the ground that they need not reasonably have expected it to happen. . . .

The reasonableness of a given risk may depend upon the following five factors:

(1) The magnitude of the risk. A risk is more likely to be unreasonable the greater it is.

(2) The value or importance of that which is exposed to the risk, which is the object that the law desires to protect, and may be called the principal object. The reasonableness of a risk means its reasonableness with respect to the principal object.

(3) A person who takes a risk of injuring the principal object usually does so because he has some reason of his own for such conduct,—is pursuing some object of his own. This may be called the collateral object. In some cases, at least, the value or importance of the collateral object is properly to be considered in deciding upon the reasonableness of the risk.

(4) The probability that the collateral object will be attained by the conduct which involves risk to the principal; the utility of the risk.

(5) The probability that the collateral object would not have been attained without taking the risk; the necessity of the risk. The following case will serve as an illustration.

[In Eckert v. Long Island Railroad, 43 N.Y. 502 (1871),] [t]he plaintiff's intestate, seeing a child on a railroad track just in front of a rapidly approaching train, went upon the track to save him. He did save him, but was himself killed by the train. The jury were allowed to find that he had not been guilty of contributory negligence. The question was of course whether he had exposed himself to an unreasonably great risk. Here the above-mentioned elements of reasonableness were as follows:

(1) The magnitude of the risk was the probability that he would be killed or hurt. That was very great.
(2) The principal object was his own life, which was very valuable.
(3) The collateral object was the child's life, which was also very valuable.
(4) The utility of the risk was the probability that he could save the child. That must have been fairly great, since he in fact succeeded. Had there been no fair chance of saving the child, the conduct would have been unreasonable and negligent.
(5) The necessity of the risk was the probability that the child would not have saved himself by getting off the track in time.

Here, although the magnitude of the risk was very great and the principal object very valuable, yet the value of the collateral object and the great utility and necessity of the risk counterbalanced those considerations, and made the risk reasonable. The same risk would have been unreasonable, had the creature on the track been a kitten, because the value of the collateral object would have been small. There is no general rule that human life may not be put at risk in order to save property; but since life is more valuable than property, such a risk has often been held unreasonable in particular cases, which has given rise to dicta to the effect that it is always so. But in the circumstances of other cases a risk of that sort has been held reasonable.

Warren Abner Seavey

Negligence—Subjective or Objective?

41 Harv. L. Rev. 1, 8 n.7 (1927)

We must not assume that we can rely upon any formula in regard to "balancing interests" to solve negligence cases. The phrase is only a convenient one to indicate factors which may be considered and should not connote any mathematical correspondence. Thus I would assume that an actor is liable if, to save his own horse of equal value with the plaintiff's, he were to take a fifty per cent chance of killing the plaintiff's horse, while it would at least be more doubtful whether he might not take a fifty per cent chance of killing another to save his own life. In either event, if the plaintiff's and the defendant's interests are considered of equal value, the defendant would not be liable upon the theory of balancing interests. Upon the same theory one doing an unlawful act or an act in preparation for one, would be liable to any one injured as a consequence, since, by hypothesis, his act has no social value. In the field of negligence, interests are balanced only in the sense that the purposes of the actor, the nature of his act and the harm that may result from action or inaction are elements to be considered. Some of these elements are not considered when the actor knows or desires that his conduct will result in interference with the plaintiff or his property. Thus if, to save his life, *A* intentionally destroys ten cents worth of *B*'s property, *A* must pay; if, however, he takes a ten per cent chance of killing *B* in an effort to save his own life, his conduct might not be found to be wrongful, although obviously *B* would much prefer, antecedently, to lose ten cents worth of property than to submit to a ten per cent chance of being killed.

NOTE

An Economic or Moral Calculus. The *Eckert* decision reveals more complexity than is found in Terry's brief summary of the case. At the time, the defendant's train was running at a "very moderate speed of seven or eight miles per hour," and the evidence suggested that the boy was not located on the tracks over which the train had run. Does that influence any judgment of the reasonableness of the plaintiff's conduct? In addition, the court stressed the predicament in which the plaintiff found himself:

> He had no time for deliberation. He must act instantly, if at all, as a moment's delay would have been fatal to the child. The law has so high a regard for human life that it will not impute negligence to an effort to preserve it, unless made under such circumstances as to constitute rashness in the judgment of prudent persons.

Does that necessity alter the level of care required? Make "rashness" the appropriate standard of care? Was the dissent correct to accept the defense of voluntary assumption of the risk, given that "[h]e was not compelled, or apparently compelled, to take any action to avoid a peril, and harm to himself, from the negligent or wrongful act of the defendant, or the agents in charge of the train"?

Putting these complexities aside, it is perhaps useful to formalize the intuitions that are present in Terry and Seavey as to the balancing of interests in a negligence inquiry. The Terry calculus is as follows: The magnitude of the risk multiplied by the value of the exposed object equals the expected loss from the relevant conduct. The value of the desired, or principal, object multiplied by the *difference* between the probability of success *with* the risk and the probability of success *without* the risk is the expected gain. The action is negligent if the expected loss exceeds the expected gain. Seavey takes a different view, treating the deliberate destruction of ten cents' worth of property as a compensable event, no matter how great the gain, but treating the 50 percent loss of another life as noncompensable, because the expected gain exceeds the expected loss. Why balance in the one case but not in the other?

Osborne v. Montgomery

234 N.W. 372 (Wis. 1931)

On August 30, 1928, the plaintiff Lester Osborne, then a boy of thirteen years of age, was employed by the Wisconsin State Journal in running errands. He was returning to his place of employment on a bicycle. Traveling westerly on East Washington avenue, he turned northerly on Pinckney street and as he proceeded north on Pinckney street he followed a car driven by the defendant. The defendant stopped his car for the purpose of leaving some clothing at a cleaner's. The defendant opened the door to his car intending to step from it on the left-hand side. The defendant's car at the time of the accident stood between a line of cars parked at the curb and the easterly rail of the street car tracks. As the defendant's car stopped and the door opened, and the plaintiff endeavored to pass, the right handle bar of his bicycle came in contact with the outside edge of the door, tipping the bicycle and throwing the plaintiff to the ground, causing the injuries complained of.

There was a jury trial, the jury found the defendant negligent as to lookout and the opening of his car door, but that he was not negligent in stopping his car where he did; that defendant's negligence was the cause of the injury; that the plaintiff was not guilty of contributory negligence; and assessed plaintiff's damages at $2,500, which covered plaintiff's pain and suffering, and the loss of earning capacity he would experience after he turned 21. . . . [The instruction of the trial judge on the definition of negligence read as follows: "1. By ordinary

Staff at the Wisconsin State Journal in 1924, in Madison, Wisconsin

Source : Wisconsin State Journal Archive

care is meant that degree of care which the great mass of mankind, or the type of that mass, the ordinarily prudent man, exercises under like or similar circumstances. 2. Negligence is the want of ordinary care. 3. Every person is negligent when . . . he does such an act, or omits to take such a precaution, that, under the circumstances present, he ought reasonably to foresee that some injury or damage might probably result from his conduct. He is in duty bound to foresee all such natural consequences of his conduct as an ordinarily prudent and intelligent person would ordinarily foresee under the then present circumstances."]

Rosenberry, C.J. Manifestly, not every want of care results in liability. In order to measure care some standards must be adopted. Human beings must live in association with each other, as a consequence of which their rights, duties, and obligations are relative, not absolute. We apply the standards which guide the great mass of mankind in determining what is proper conduct of an individual under all the circumstances and say that he was or was not justified in doing the act in question. While it is true that the standard thus set up is varying and indefinite, it is nevertheless one which may be fairly and justly applied to human conduct. Such a standard is usually spoken of as ordinary care, being that degree of care which under the same or similar circumstances the great mass of mankind would ordinarily exercise.

In a consideration of this subject it is easy to get lost in a maze of metaphysical distinctions, or perhaps it may better be said it is difficult not to be so lost. The defect in the instruction [in paragraph 3] is that it indicates no standard by which the conduct of the defendant is to be measured. In support of the instruction it is argued that the great mass of mankind do not indulge in conduct which results in harm to others; and therefore it must follow that if one does an act which results in injury to another, he departs from the standards which are followed by the great mass of mankind. The argument is based upon an inference not readily drawn, and, in addition to that, the premise is not sound. We are constantly doing acts which result in injury to others which are not negligent and do not result in liability. Many of the cases classified as those damnum absque injuria [harm without legal injury] and cases where the damages are said to be consequential and remote are illustrations of this. While the acts result in injury to others, they are held to be not negligent because they are in conformity to what the great mass of mankind would do under the same or similar circumstances. The statement is true in all situations where liability exists, but it does not exclude situations where liability does not exist.

The fundamental idea of liability for wrongful acts is that upon a balancing of the social interests involved in each case, the law determines that under the circumstances of a particular case an actor should or should not become liable for the natural consequences of his conduct. One driving a car in a thickly populated district on a rainy day, slowly and in the most careful manner, may do injury to the person of another by throwing muddy or infected water upon that person. Society does not hold the actor responsible because the benefit of allowing people to travel under such circumstances so far outweighs the probable injury to bystanders that such conduct is not disapproved. Circumstances may require the driver of a fire truck to take his truck through a thickly populated district at a high rate of speed, but if he exercises that degree of care which such drivers ordinarily exercise under the same or similar circumstances, society, weighing the benefits against the probabilities of damage, in spite of the fact that as a reasonably prudent and intelligent man he should foresee that harm may result, justifies the risk and holds him not liable.

The instruction [in paragraph 3] indicates no standard, but in the present case the court included that element in the instruction in paragraphs 1 and 2.

[Reversed and remanded on the question of damages only.]

Cooley v. Public Service Co.

10 A.2d 673 (N.H. 1940)

Page, J. On November 29, 1935, the telephone company maintained a cable on Taylor Street, Manchester, running north and south. This cable consisted of a lead sheath, inside which were carried a large number of wires connected with the service stations of its subscribers. The cable was supported by rings from a messenger wire strung on the telephone company poles. The construction conformed to standard practices, and the messenger wire was grounded every thousand feet. The sheath of the cable also was grounded. The telephone company further maintained at the station which the plaintiff was using when she received her injuries, two protective devices for grounding foreign currents in order to prevent their entrance to the house and to the subscriber's instrument. There is no evidence that these devices did not operate perfectly.

At a point about a mile distant from the plaintiff's house, the Public Service Company's lines, east and west along Valley Street, crossed the telephone cable at right angles and some eight or ten feet above it. These lines were not insulated.

Shortly after midnight, during a heavy storm, several of the Public Service wires over the intersection of Valley and Taylor Streets broke and fell to the ground. One of them came into contact with the telephone messenger. This particular wire of the defendant carried a voltage of about 2300. Consequently an arc was created, which burned through the messenger and nearly half through the cable before the current was shut off. . . .

When the contact of the wires occurred, the plaintiff was standing at the telephone, engaged in a long-distance conversation. The contact created a violent agitation in the diaphragm of the receiver and a loud explosive noise. The plaintiff fell to the floor. She has since suffered from what her physicians describe as traumatic neurosis, accompanied by loss of sensation on the left side.

[Plaintiff sued the power company and the telephone company. At the trial the jury found for the telephone company but against the power company. The power company appealed, and the judgment was reversed.]

Apparently there is no claim that the negligence of the defendant caused the wires to fall. The plaintiff's sole claim is that the defendant could have anticipated (1) that its wire might fall for a variety of reasons, which is true; (2) that a telephone subscriber in such case might hear a great noise, which also is true; (3) that as a result of fright thereby induced the user of the telephone would suffer physical injuries, which, as we have seen, is a rare contingency, though it may be anticipated. It is urged that the defendant's consequent duty was to maintain such devices at cross-overs as would prevent one of its falling wires from coming into contact with a telephone wire.

The devices suggested are two. The first is a wire-mesh basket suspended from the poles of the defendant at the point of cross-over, above the cable and below the defendant's wires. Two forms were suggested. One would be about six by eight feet. The other would be of an unassigned width and would stretch the full distance between defendant's poles. In either case the basket would be insulated. The theory is that falling wires, though alive, would remain harmless in the basket.

[The court, after detailed examination of these proposals, concludes that each of these suggested devices would have entailed a greater risk of electrocution to people passing on the street, even assuming that they might have reduced the risk of loud noises to those using the telephone. The court then continues, in part:]

There was evidence that baskets and similar devices were used by the telephone company, some years ago, for the protection of their wires at cross-overs. But the verdict establishes its lack of duty thus to protect its customers in this particular instance. There was no evidence that electric light companies ever erected baskets or insulated wires in such situations, and there was positive evidence that standard construction practices do not require either. The plaintiff cannot claim that the defendant maintained a system less carefully devised than one conforming to accepted practice. It is conceded, however, that due care might require some device better than the usual one. If the plaintiff and persons in her situation could be isolated, and duties to others ignored, due care might require the use of such devices as are here urged.

But the same reasoning that would establish a duty to do so raises another duty to the people in the street, not to lessen the protective effect of their circuit-breaking device. . . .

In the case before us, there was danger of electrocution in the street. As long as the telephone company's safety devices are properly installed and maintained, there is no danger of electrocution in the house. The only foreseeable danger to the telephone subscriber is from noise — fright and neuroses. Balancing the two, the danger to those such as the plaintiff is remote, that to those on the ground near the broken wires is obvious and immediate. The balance would not be improved by taking a chance to avoid traumatic neurosis of the plaintiff at the expense of greater risk to the lives of others. To the extent that the duty to use care depends upon relationship, the defendant's duty of care towards the plaintiff is obviously weaker than that towards the man in the street.

The defendant's duty cannot, in the circumstances, be to both. If that were so, performance of one duty would mean non-performance of the other. If it be negligent to save the life of the highway traveler at the expense of bodily injury resulting from the fright and neurosis of a telephone subscriber, it must be equally negligent to avoid the fright at the risk of another's life. The law could tolerate no such theory of "be liable if you do and liable if you don't." The law does not contemplate a shifting duty that requires care towards *A* and then discovers a duty to avoid injury incidentally suffered by *B* because there was due care with respect to *A*. Such a shifting is entirely inconsistent with the fundamental conception that the duty of due care requires precisely the measure of care that is reasonable under all the circumstances. 2 Restatement Torts, §§291–295. . . .

It is not doubted that due care might require the defendant to adopt some device that would afford protection against emotional disturbances in telephone-users without depriving the traveling public of reasonable protection from live wires immediately dangerous to life. Such a device, if it exists, is not disclosed by the record. The burden was upon the plaintiff to show its practicability. Since the burden was not sustained a verdict should have been directed for the defendant.

Other exceptions therefore require no consideration.

Judgment for the defendant. All concurred.

NOTE

Activity Level Versus Care Level. The plaintiff in *Cooley* tried to find fault with how the power company maintained its wires above ground. Accordingly, Page, J., never had to ask whether the power company made a sound decision to place the wires above ground in the first place. If that claim were asserted, should courts and juries examine only the level of care once the defendant has decided to undertake a given activity, such as whether to install a basket or similar device, or should they also examine the type or level of the defendant's activity, like installing above-the-ground wires?

The theoretical point is raised in Shavell, Strict Liability Versus Negligence, 9 J. Legal Stud. 1, 2–3 (1980), which discusses the "unilateral case," "by which it is meant the actions of injurers but not of victims are assumed to affect the probability or severity of losses." Shavell shows that liability for negligence affects an actor's level of care, but not its activity level:

> By definition, under the negligence rule all that an injurer needs to do to avoid the possibility of liability is to make sure to exercise due care if he engages in his activity. Consequently *he will not be motivated to consider the effect on accident losses of his choice of whether to engage in his activity or, more generally, of the level at which to engage in his activity;* he will choose his level of activity in accordance only with the personal benefits so derived. But surely any increase in his level of activity will typically raise expected accident losses (holding constant the level of care). Thus he will be led to choose too high a level of activity; the negligence rule is not "efficient."
>
> Consider by way of illustration the problem of pedestrian-automobile accidents (and, as we are now discussing the unilateral case, let us imagine the behavior of pedestrians to be fixed). Suppose that drivers of automobiles find it in their interest to adhere to the standard of due care but that the possibility of accidents is not thereby eliminated. Then, in deciding how much to drive, they will contemplate only the enjoyment they get from doing so. Because (as they exercise due care) they will not be liable for harm suffered by pedestrians, drivers will not take into account that going more miles will mean a higher expected number of accidents. Hence, there will be too much driving; an individual will, for example, decide to go for a drive on a mere whim despite the imposition of a positive expected cost to pedestrians.

However, under a rule of strict liability, the situation is different. Because an injurer must pay for losses whenever he is causally responsible for an accident, he will be induced to consider the effect on accident losses of *both* his level of care *and* his level of activity. His decisions will therefore be efficient. Because drivers will be liable for losses sustained by pedestrians, they will decide not only to exercise due care in driving but also to drive only when the utility gained from it outweighs expected liability payments to pedestrians.

Does it follow as a matter of definition on Shavell's account that choices of activity level are outside judicial review under a negligence standard? Recall in this context the suggestion made in Bolton v. Stone, *supra* Chapter 2, at 100, that it might have been negligent to play cricket *at all* if the field could not be made safe. Is a jury as competent in making decisions on activity levels as it is on care levels? For an updated version of the activity level point, see Shavell, Liability for Accidents ch. 2 (2007).

United States v. Carroll Towing Co.

159 F.2d 169 (2d Cir. 1947)

L. Hand, J. These appeals concern the sinking of the barge, "*Anna C*," on January 4, 1944, off Pier 51, North River. [The accident occurred when the tug *Carroll* (owned by Carroll Towing Company) attempted a tricky maneuver to move a barge that had been tied up in a tier of barges on the so-called Public Pier just to the north of Pier 52, where the *Anna C* (owned by the Conners Company) was berthed. During the attempt, the fasts directly connecting the *Anna C* to Pier 52 broke. Tides and wind carried the *Anna C* (and the five other barges tied to her) down the Hudson River. The drifting *Anna C* collided with a tanker, and the tanker's propeller punctured a hole near the bottom of the *Anna C*. The barge began to leak, and shortly thereafter "careened," dumped her cargo of flour, and sank. In the admiralty proceeding below, two suits were brought. In the first, the United States sued Carroll Towing Company for the loss of its cargo of flour. In the second, Conners recovered one-half of the damages for the loss of its barge from Carroll Towing. The record revealed that the Conners Company had chartered the *Anna C* to the Pennsylvania Railroad "at a stated hire per diem, by a charter of the kind usual in the Harbor, which included the services of a bargee, apparently limited to the hours 8 A.M. to 4 P.M." In the second suit, the contributory negligence of Conners was raised as a partial defense, as was then allowed in admiralty cases. The gist of the claim of contributory negligence was that "if the bargee had been on board, and had done his duty to his employer, he would have gone below at once, examined the injury, and called for help from the 'Carroll' and [another tug.] . . . [T]he question arises whether a barge owner is slack in the care of his barge if the bargee is absent."]

Exhibit 3.3 Learned Hand

Learned Hand (1872–1961) served as a federal judge for fifty-two years, including thirty-seven years on the United States Court of Appeals for the Second Circuit, covering New York, Connecticut, and Vermont. He is considered by many legal scholars to be among the greatest judges in United States history. His influence extended through myriad areas of the law, including copyright, antitrust, tax, criminal law, and torts. The principle for negligence he announced in *Carroll Towing*, known universally as the "Hand Formula," played a central role in the development of economic frameworks to describe legal rules. He was also known to be tough on the bench, even turning his back on attorneys who appeared before him with weak arguments.

Bio sources: Richard A. Posner, The Learned Hand Biography and the Question of Judicial Greatness, 104 Yale L.J. 511 (1994); Learned Hand, *Encyclopaedia Britannica*
Image Source: Wikimedia Commons

It appears from the foregoing review [of prior case law] that there is no general rule to determine when the absence of a bargee or other attendant will make the owner of the barge liable for injuries to other vessels if she breaks away from her moorings. However, in any cases where he would be so liable for injuries to others, obviously he must reduce his damages proportionately, if the injury is to his own barge. It becomes apparent why there can be no such general rule, when we consider the grounds for such a liability. Since there are occasions when every vessel will break from her moorings, and since, if she does, she becomes a menace to those about her; the owner's duty, as in other similar situations, to provide against resulting injuries is a function of three variables:

(1) The probability that she will break away; (2) the gravity of the resulting injury, if she does; (3) the burden of adequate precautions. Possibly it serves to bring this notion into relief to state it in algebraic terms: if the probability be called *P*; the injury, *L*; and the burden, *B*; liability depends upon whether *B* is less than *L* multiplied by *P*: i.e., whether *B* is less than *PL*. Applied to the situation at bar, the likelihood that a barge will break from her fasts and the damage she will do, vary with the place and time; for example, if a storm threatens, the danger is greater; so it is, if she is in a crowded harbor where moored barges are constantly being shifted about. On the other hand, the barge must not be the bargee's prison, even though he lives aboard; he must go ashore at times. We need not say whether, even in such crowded waters as New York Harbor a bargee must be aboard at night at all; it may be that the custom is otherwise, as Ward, J., supposed in "The Kathryn B. Guinan," [176 F. 301 (2d Cir. 1910)]; and that, if so, the situation is one where custom should control. We leave that question open; but we hold that it is not in all cases a sufficient answer to a bargee's absence without excuse, during working hours, that he has properly made fast his barge to a pier, when he leaves her. In the case at bar the bargee left at five o'clock in the afternoon of January 3rd, and the flotilla broke away at about two o'clock in the afternoon of the following day, twenty-one hours afterwards. The bargee had been away all the time, and we hold that his fabricated story was affirmative evidence that he had no excuse for his absence. At the locus in quo—especially during the short January days and in the full tide of war activity—barges were being constantly "drilled" in and out. Certainly it was not beyond reasonable expectation that, with the inevitable haste and bustle, the work might not be done with adequate care. In such circumstances we hold—and it is all that we do hold—that it was a fair requirement that the Conners Company should have a bargee aboard (unless he had some excuse for his absence), during the working hours of daylight.

NOTES

Exhibit 3.4 Progenitors of Law and Economics

The application of economic analysis to legal rules has a long history, but its influential modern incarnation was largely developed in the latter half of the twentieth century by two noted jurists, Judge Richard A. Posner, left, and Judge Guido Calabresi, right. Judge Posner retired in 2017, after serving on the United States Court of Appeals for the Seventh Circuit for nearly thirty-six years. Judge Calabresi was appointed to the United States Court of Appeals for the Second Circuit in 1994 and continues to serve today.

Sources: Posner – University of Chicago Law School; Calabresi – Robert Benson Photography

1. *The Claims in Carroll Towing.* The sinking of the *Anna C* gave rise to a separate claim brought by the United States against Carroll Towing and Conners for the loss of a load of flour that it was shipping on the *Anna C*. In light of the terms of Conners' charter to the Pennsylvania Railroad, could the United States take advantage of the bargee's absence by claiming to be a third-party beneficiary to the contract between Conners and the Pennsylvania Railroad? Why would either party wish to create any benefit for a stranger to their own contract? For further details on the complex parties and claims, see Gilles, United States v. Carroll Towing Co.: The Hand Formula's Home Port, *in* Tort Stories 11 (Rabin & Sugarman eds., 2003).

2. *An Economic Interpretation of Negligence?* Hand's use of the formula in *Carroll Towing*—whether *B*, the burden of adequate precautions, is less than *PL*, the probability of loss times the magnitude of the loss—spawned a burgeoning academic literature on the economic interpretation of negligence and, by implication, the entire tort law. Posner, A Theory of Negligence, 1 J. Legal Stud. 29, 32–33 (1972), opened the debate by arguing that the Hand formula provides an operational definition of unreasonable risk under the negligence law:

> Hand was adumbrating, perhaps unwittingly, an economic meaning of negligence. Discounting (multiplying) the cost of an accident if it occurs by the probability of occurrence yields a measure of the economic benefit to be anticipated from incurring the costs necessary to prevent the accident. The cost of prevention is what Hand meant by the burden of taking precautions against the accident. It may be the cost of installing safety equipment or otherwise making the activity safer, or the benefit forgone by curtailing or eliminating the activity. If the cost of safety measures or of curtailment—whichever cost is lower—exceeds the benefit in accident avoidance to be gained by incurring that cost, society would be better off, in economic terms, to forgo accident prevention. A rule making the enterprise liable for the accidents that occur in such cases cannot be justified on the ground that it will induce the enterprise to increase the safety of its operations. When the cost of accidents is less than the cost of prevention, a rational profit-maximizing enterprise will pay tort judgments to the accident victims rather than incur the larger cost of avoiding liability. Furthermore, overall economic value or welfare would be diminished rather than increased by incurring a higher accident-prevention cost in order to avoid a lower accident cost. If, on the other hand, the benefits in accident avoidance exceed the costs of prevention, society is better off if those costs are incurred and the accident averted, and so in this case the enterprise is made liable, in the expectation that self-interest will lead it to adopt the precautions in order to avoid a greater cost in tort judgments.

The effort to reduce negligence to the three elements in the Hand formula has been subject to wholesale attacks. Thus Wright, Hand, Posner, and the Myth of the "Hand Formula," 4 Theoretical Inquiries L.145, 273 (2003), examines all of Hand's opinions on negligence, and concludes that only a small fraction of these cases refer to or rely upon his cost-benefit formula. Wright concludes:

> If one then follows the legal realists' advice and looks carefully, in those cases in which the aggregate-risk-utility test is mentioned, at what the courts are actually doing rather than (merely) at what they are saying, one finds that the courts almost never attempt to apply the test; instead, the test is merely trotted out as *dicta* or boilerplate separate from the real analysis. The very few judges who actually try to apply the test either fail in the attempt to do so or end up using the test as window-dressing for results reached on other (justice-based) grounds.

This observation leads Zipursky, Sleight of Hand, 48 Wm. & Mary L. Rev. 1999, 2040 (2007), to suggest that "[n]egligence law is not best understood . . . as a device for deterrence and compensation," but rather as a theory of "civic competency," or an institutionalized set of norms about reasonable and socialized behavior that builds on rights-based and virtue-based theories. Are the two approaches mutually exclusive? Inconsistent? Within the negligence framework, could any system of justice afford to ignore the diminishing marginal value of additional precautions?

3. *The Third Restatement's "Balancing Approach" to Negligence.*

RESTATEMENT OF THE LAW (THIRD) OF TORTS: LIABILITY FOR PHYSICAL AND EMOTIONAL HARM

§3. Negligence

A person acts negligently if the person does not exercise reasonable care under all the circumstances. Primary factors to consider in ascertaining whether the person's conduct lacks reasonable care are the foreseeable likelihood that the person's conduct will result in harm, the foreseeable severity of any harm that may ensue, and the burden of precautions to eliminate or reduce the risk of harm.

Compare to the Hand formula in *Carroll Towing*: ***B < PL***, where "the probability [of injury] be called *P*; the injury, *L*; and the burden, *B*; liability depends upon whether *B* is less than *L* multiplied by *P*: i.e., whether *B* is less than *PL."* Does the Restatement's definition embody the Hand formula? Are the two uses of the term "foreseeable" redundant? If the three elements are only "primary factors," what other elements could be considered? See RTT: LPEH §3, comment *d*. What is the relationship between the Hand formula and the customary account of "ordinary care" or the "reasonably prudent person"?

4. *Measurement Problems Under the Hand Formula.* How precisely can the Hand formula factors be estimated? Grossman, Uncertainty, Insurance and the Learned Hand Formula, 5 L., Probability & Risk 1, 9 (2006), suggests that insurance markets provide a valuable contribution "to the operation of the Learned Hand formula, by providing (if only implicitly) potential tort plaintiffs, defendants and courts with the information about (a) the probabilities and magnitudes of harm from various kinds of accidents and (b) the expected benefits of various precautions in reducing probabilities and magnitudes of harm." Does aggregate data allow for the solution of individual cases? Note when *PL* is uncertain, "parties are likely to either over-invest or under-invest in precaution, B," thus rendering the Hand formula inept to achieve economic efficiency.

In such cases of uncertainty, Judge Hand himself was sensitive to his formula's measurement problem. In Moisan v. Loftus, 178 F.2d 148, 149 (2d Cir. 1949), he wrote:

> The difficulties are in applying the rule. . . . [T]hey arise from the necessity of applying a quantitative test to an incommensurable subject-matter and the same difficulties inhere in the concept of "ordinary" negligence. [Of the three factors, *B*, *P*, and *L*,] care is the only one ever susceptible of quantitative estimate, and often that is not. The injuries are always a variable within limits, which do not admit of even approximate ascertainment and, although probability might theoretically be estimated, if any statistics were available, they never are and, besides, probability varies with the severity of the injuries. It follows that all such attempts are illusory, and, if serviceable at all, are so only to center attention upon which one of the factors may be determinative in any given situation.

What should be done if the estimates of *B*, *P*, and *L* can each vary independently by a factor of 10? If human life (unlike property damage) has no estimable market value? Does the ordinary care formulation eliminate or conceal this problem?

5. *Marginal Precautions and the Hand Formula.* One conceptual problem under the Hand formula involves choosing the correct interval for assessing defendant's conduct. Suppose the jury was presented with evidence that the defendant could take an extra $100 in precautions that would yield $150 in additional benefits. At first blush, the defendant should take these precautions given that *in aggregate* the expected benefits exceed the expected costs.

Nonetheless, a closer analysis reveals that this action could lead to excessive care. The key point is that in economic terms additional precautions should be tested *at the margin* and only taken so long as an additional dollar of precautions reduces the expected costs of injury by at least a dollar. Thus in the example above, suppose that the first $60 in precautions yield $120 in benefits, while the next $40 in precautions yield only $30 in benefits. In principle the lesser precaution is more desirable because it generates $60 in *net* benefits ($120 – $60), while the next $40 in precautions generates *minus* $10 in net benefits ($30 – $40). The lower precaution therefore generates the greater social benefit. On this analysis, therefore, the plaintiff starts by showing a net social gain from taking the proposed precautions. In principle, thereafter, the defendant should be allowed to show that some lower level of precaution would have generated a higher aggregate social return. Assuming this issue can be litigated, how should the burdens of proof be distributed on the question of marginal precautions?

This analysis has important implications for applying the Hand formula in cases of self-risk. As a theoretical matter, the Hand formula is capacious enough to take into account any potential losses that a bargee has either as a potential plaintiff or potential defendant. Thus if the expected loss of a bargee's conduct to some third party (such as the United States for its flour) were $100 and the additional "sinking" damages to the barge itself were $50, then the defendant should be regarded as negligent if the costs of their precautions were less than $150, not $100. Stated otherwise, the avoidance of harm to self reduces the incremental cost in preventing harms to others. Cooter & Porat, Does Risk to Oneself Increase the Care Owed to Others? Law and Economics in Conflict, 29 J. Legal Stud. 19 (2000), concludes that "omitting the injurer's possible harm to himself causes courts to set the legal standard of care too low."

6. *Risk Neutrality.* On its face, the Hand formula treats all individuals as risk neutral. A risk-neutral actor responds to the expected gains or losses of a future uncertain event by simply multiplying the probability of its occurrence by its expected magnitude, as in the Hand formula itself. For example, a 10 percent chance of losing $100 creates an expected loss of $10. In practice, however, sometimes people prefer risk and sometimes they are averse to it. These tastes can vary across persons. In essence, people who prefer risk gain positive satisfaction from taking chances, while people who are averse to risk are prepared to pay to avoid confronting danger. Thus a person who prefers risk would prefer a 10 percent chance of losing $100 to a certainty of losing $10. Conversely the risk-averse person prefers the certainty of losing $10 to a 10 percent chance of losing $100. Risk preference and risk aversion are both matters of degree; it is quite possible that some would pay only $11 to avoid the 10 percent chance of a $100 loss while others might pay as much as $20. For a defense of the risk neutrality assumption in the Hand formula, see Landes & Posner, The Economic Structure of Tort Law 55–57 (1987). Should neutrality be presumed if most individuals and most corporations are risk averse? Note that some modern writers in the field of cognitive biases suggest that individuals may be risk averse in the domain of losses and risk preferrers in the domain of gains. See, e.g., Plous, The Psychology of Judgment and Decision Making 96 (1993). Why do people both gamble and buy liability insurance?

7. *Does Efficiency Require Negligence?* Under the orthodox economic accounts of tort law, the Hand formula is not the only road to social efficiency. Strict liability with contributory negligence, or even a system of negligence without contributory (or comparative) negligence, should also induce (as a first approximation) optimal behavior by *both* parties.

This proposition was demonstrated in Brown, Toward an Economic Theory of Liability, 2 J. Legal Stud. 323 (1973), and extensively considered in Landes & Posner, The Economic Structure of Tort Law ch. 3 (1987), and Shavell, Economic Analysis of Accident Law 26–46 (1987). Let us assume that each (rationally self-interested) party wishes to minimize the sum of its precaution and accident costs. When liability is predicated on proof of defendant's negligence alone, the defendant will take care, even *without* the defense of contributory negligence: The cost of precautions is below that of the anticipated liability. Once the plaintiff knows that the defendant will take care, the plaintiff also knows that all prospect of recovery is thereby precluded. The plaintiff therefore now has (wholly without regard to the contributory negligence defense) an incentive to take the optimal level of care as well. Both parties will behave optimally, even without the contributory negligence defense.

Similarly, under strict liability, the plaintiff will recover unless barred by contributory negligence. Yet, so long as precautions are cheaper than expected accidents, the rational plaintiff will take care in order to preserve the right of action. Once the defendant knows that the plaintiff will not misbehave, even under strict liability, the defendant has an incentive to choose the optimal level of care to minimize the sum of his precaution and accident costs. Again, both sides will take proper care, even though only one party has a duty of care.

Brown's proofs generate a certain paradoxical result: Since all persons are rational, no one can ever be negligent. However, negligence is commonplace, so the question is, why? The most obvious explanation is that error pervades the behavior of both the judges and juries who operate the legal system, making every trial something of a rational gamble. Similar types of error are likely to influence private actors who are ignorant of the rules, and even those who struggle to comply with them. In addition, private actors may fail to comply with the law if they are broke, stressed, demoralized, bored, or fatigued. Moving in the opposite direction, highly sophisticated individuals might choose not to take care because they believe that other persons with whom they may interact will not take care. Each side thus behaves strategically in anticipation of the predicted error of the other side. Note also how the increased possibilities for good care may simply increase the ways to be negligent. The physician who could do nothing to help a patient in 1900 could be found negligent in a thousand ways in 2023 precisely because his increased ability to help patients casts suspicion on his conduct where intervention fails. See generally Grady, Why Are People Negligent? Technology, Nondurable Precautions, and the Medical Malpractice Explosion, 82 Nw. U. L. Rev. 293 (1988).

8. *Discontinuities and the Choice Between Negligence and Strict Liability.* Theories of negligence and strict liability differ in another important respect. Strict liability presents a "smooth slope" of increasing liability relative to care whereas negligence exhibits a "cliff" of liability relative to care, beyond which liability is imposed. As a result, under strict liability, small errors in choosing the optimal level of care will typically generate only small consequences. The defendant is liable for all the accidents he causes, so that small shifts in care levels generate only small changes in either the frequency or severity of harm to others. But under negligence, the defendant who hovers close to the line could find that a small decrease in the level of care results in exposing him to liability for all accidents instead of none. In light of this pronounced discontinuity, one counterintuitive argument holds that the negligence standard induces a somewhat higher level of care than the strict liability rule, especially by defendants anxious to avoid falling off that liability "cliff." See Grady, A New Positive Economic Theory of Negligence, 92 Yale L.J. 799 (1983). Grady's analysis of error has in turn been challenged by Calfee & Craswell, Some Effects of Uncertainty on Compliance with Legal Standards, 70 Va. L. Rev. 965, 982 (1984), which concludes that it is unclear whether a negligence standard will induce too much or too little care by defendants, and may under different circumstances do some of each. They posit that the defendant who takes too little care may not "get caught." The risk of falling off a cliff occurs in only some fraction of the cases, while the savings from taking less care is obtained in all, making it difficult to determine the net effects of error on care levels.

H. Laurence Ross

Settled Out of Court

The Social Process of Insurance Claims Adjustment 98–99 (2d ed. 1980)

The formal law of negligence liability, as stated in casebooks from the opinions of appellate courts, is not easily applied to the accident at Second and Main. It deals with the violation of a duty of care owed by the insured to the claimant and is based on a very complex and perplexing model of the "reasonable man," in this case the reasonable driver. . . . In [insurance adjusters'] day-to-day work, the concern with liability is reduced to the question of whether either or both parties violated the rules of the road as expressed in common traffic laws. Taking the doctrine of negligence per se to an extreme doubtless unforeseen by the makers of the formal law, adjusters tend to define a claim as one of liability or of no liability depending only on whether a rule was violated, regardless of intention, knowledge, necessity, and other such qualifications that might receive sympathetic attention even from a traffic court judge. Such a determination is far easier than the task proposed in theory by the formal law of negligence.

To illustrate, if Car *A* strikes Car *B* from the rear, the driver of *A* is assumed to be liable and *B* is not. In the ordinary course of events, particularly where damages are routine, the adjuster is not concerned with *why A* struck *B*, or with whether *A* violated a duty of care to *B*, or with whether *A* was unreasonable or not. These questions are avoided, not only because they may be impossible to answer, but also because the fact that *A* struck *B* from the rear will satisfy all supervisory levels that a payment is in order, without further explanation. Likewise, in the routine case, the fact that *A* was emerging from a street governed by a stop sign will justify treating this as a case of liability, without concern for whether the sign was seen or not, whether there was adequate reason for not seeing the sign, etc. In short, in the ordinary case the physical facts of the accident are normally sufficient to allocate liability between the drivers. Inasmuch as the basic physical facts of the accident are easily known—and they are frequently ascertainable from the first notice—the issue of liability is usually relatively easy to dispose of.

NOTE

Modern Settlement Procedures and the Routinization of Negligence Determinations. Ross' mid-twentieth century study described the routinization of tort law inside large insurance firms. Issacharoff & Witt, The Inevitability of Aggregate Litigation, 57 Vand. L. Rev. 1571, 1605 (2004), documents that claims settlement has been routinized still further in the decades after Ross' study left off. The emergence of a professional plaintiffs' bar has resulted in the widespread use of "rough and ready" determinations of liability and damages by plaintiffs' lawyers and defense-side insurance adjusters to settle a vast number of tort claims outside of court.

Andrews v. United Airlines

24 F.3d 39 (9th Cir. 1994)

Kozinski, J. We are called upon to determine whether United Airlines took adequate measures to deal with that elementary notion of physics—what goes up, must come down. For, while the skies are friendly enough, the ground can be a mighty dangerous place when heavy objects tumble from overhead compartments.

I

During the mad scramble that usually follows hard upon an airplane's arrival at the gate, a briefcase fell from an overhead compartment and seriously injured plaintiff Billie Jean Andrews. No one knows who opened the compartment or what caused the briefcase to fall, and Andrews doesn't claim that airline personnel were involved in stowing the object or opening the bin. Her claim, rather, is that the injury was foreseeable and the airline didn't prevent it.

The district court dismissed the suit on summary judgment, and we review de novo. This is a diversity action brought in California, whose tort law applies.

II

The parties agree that United Airlines is a common carrier and as such "owe[s] both a duty of utmost care and the vigilance of a very cautious person towards [its] passengers." Acosta v. Southern Cal. Rapid Transit Dist., 465 P.2d 72 (1970). Though United is "responsible for any, even the slightest, negligence and [is] required to do all that human care, vigilance, and foresight reasonably can do under all the circumstances," *Acosta*, 465 P.2d at 72, it is not an insurer of its passengers' safety, Lopez v. Southern Cal. Rapid Transit Dist., 710 P.2d 907 (1985). "[T]he degree of care and diligence which [it] must exercise is only such as can reasonably be exercised consistent with the character and mode of conveyance adopted and the practical operation of [its] business. . . ." Id.

To show that United did not satisfy its duty of care toward its passengers, Ms. Andrews presented the testimony of two witnesses. The first was Janice Northcott, United's Manager of Inflight Safety, who disclosed that in 1987 the airline had received 135 reports of items falling from overhead bins. As a result of these incidents, Ms. Northcott testified, United decided to add a warning to its arrival announcements, to wit, that items stored overhead might have shifted during flight and passengers should use caution in opening the bins. This announcement later became the industry standard.

Ms. Andrews's second witness was safety and human factors expert Dr. David Thompson, who testified that United's announcement was ineffective because passengers opening overhead bins couldn't see objects poised to fall until the bins were opened, by which time it was too late. Dr. Thompson also testified that United could have taken additional steps to prevent the hazard, such as retrofitting its overhead bins with baggage nets, as some airlines had already done, or by requiring passengers to store only lightweight items overhead.

United argues that Andrews presented too little proof to satisfy her burden [to withstand summary judgment]. One hundred thirty-five reported incidents, United points out, are trivial when spread over the millions of passengers travelling on its 175,000 flights every year. Even that number overstates the problem, according to United, because it includes events where passengers merely observed items falling from overhead bins but no one was struck or injured. Indeed, United sees the low incidence of injuries as incontrovertible proof that the safety measures suggested by plaintiff's expert would not merit the additional cost and inconvenience to airline passengers.

III

It is a close question, but we conclude that plaintiff has made a sufficient case to overcome summary judgment. United is hard-pressed to dispute that its passengers are subject to a hazard from objects falling out of overhead bins, considering the warning its flight crews give hundreds of times each day. The case then turns on whether the hazard is serious enough to warrant more than a warning. Given the heightened duty of a common carrier, even a small risk of serious injury to passengers may form the basis of liability if that risk could be eliminated "consistent with the character and mode of [airline travel] and the practical operation of [that] business. . . ." *Lopez*, 710 P.2d at 907. United has demonstrated neither that retrofitting overhead bins with netting (or other means) would be prohibitively expensive, nor that such steps would grossly interfere with the convenience of its passengers. Thus, a jury could find United has failed to do "all that human care, vigilance, and foresight reasonably can do under all the circumstances." *Acosta*, 465 P.2d at 72.

The reality, with which airline passengers are only too familiar, is that airline travel has changed significantly in recent years. As harried travelers try to avoid the agonizing ritual of checked baggage, they hand-carry more and larger items—computers, musical instruments, an occasional deceased relative. The airlines have coped with this trend, but perhaps not well enough. Given its awareness of the hazard, United may not have done everything technology permits and prudence dictates to eliminate it. . . .

Jurors, many of whom will have been airline passengers, will be well equipped to decide whether United had a duty to do more than warn passengers about the possibility of falling baggage. A reasonable jury might conclude United should have done more; it might also find that United did enough. Either decision would be rational on the record presented to the district court which, of course, means summary judgment was not appropriate.

Reversed and remanded.

NOTE

Negligence and the Common Carrier. *Andrews* settled shortly after remand—a reminder of the powerful effect, in terms of inducing private settlement, of a legal decision that plaintiff's evidence withstands summary judgment (or motion to dismiss).

Is the utmost care standard consistent with the Hand formula? If not, how would *Andrews* come out under that test? Historically the utmost care standard has had an uneven reception in common carrier cases. In Kelly v. Manhattan Railway, 20 N.E. 383, 385 (N.Y. 1889), the plaintiff slipped on heavy snow that had accumulated during the night on the stairs leading to the train station. Peckham, J., rejected the utmost care standard in this context, reserving it for those distinctive railroad operations in which the passenger had no control over the operation of the train, as when injury "occurs from a defect in the road-bed, machinery, or in the construction of the cars." He observed that the level of serious injury or death from those "compelled" to use the rails was far higher than those associated with ancillary facilities, such as "platforms, halls, stairways, and the like." In principle, the Hand formula could accommodate these differences, by insisting that greater peril requires greater precaution independent of the utmost care standard.

In light of that observation, Bethel v. New York City Transit Authority, 703 N.E.2d 1214, 1216–17 (N.Y. 1998), rejected a heightened standard of care based upon common carrier status alone. The plaintiff was injured when a movable bus seat collapsed as she attempted to sit down. *Bethel* treated *Kelly* as a bygone response to "the advent of the age of steam railroads in 19th century America. Their primitive safety features resulted in a phenomenal growth in railroad accident injuries and with them, an explosion in personal injury litigation, significantly affecting the American tort system." Levine, J., observed that the earlier development represented a needless departure from the fundamental doctrine of negligence, which relies on a "sliding scale" that makes the level of care commensurate with the level of danger involved in a particular activity. In his view, contemporary negligence jurisprudence has undermined both of the main policy justifications for exacting of common carriers a duty of extraordinary care. The two most often expressed rationales for the duty of highest care were (1) the perceived ultrahazardous nature of the instrumentalities of public rapid transit, and (2) the status of passengers and their relationship to the carrier, notably their total dependency upon the latter for safety precautions.

Why should a broken seat generate one consequence on a bus and another in the bus station? What is wrong with a strict duty to keep seats safe, subject to a defense of assumption of risk when passengers know of the defect before they sit down? How should *Andrews* be decided under *Bethel*?

SECTION D. CUSTOM

The general principles of negligence law leave judges and juries a great deal of latitude in setting the appropriate standard of care. Sometimes that latitude is a sign of the strength of the system, for it supplies the flexibility necessary to apply traditional standards to novel situations without having to fundamentally remake the substantive law. Unfortunately, the "featureless generality" of reasonable care also introduces a large element of uncertainty even into ostensibly routine cases. Using custom to set the standard of care helps reduce this uncertainty. Custom lacks the generality of the basic reasonable care standard, but within its specific area of application it promises greater direction than any broader standard can provide.

This section addresses the role of custom in negligence cases. Does local custom or industry practice provide a decent proxy for a standard of reasonable care? What factors make that more or less likely? Should custom be given the same deference in actions between strangers as in actions arising out of long-term consensual relationships (such as employer-employee, physician-patient)? Should custom carry the same weight when used as a shield (defendant argues that he is not negligent because his conduct conforms to custom), as when used as a sword (plaintiff argues that defendant is negligent because his conduct fails to conform to custom)?

This section also examines the unique role that custom plays in medical malpractice cases, aspects of the modern debate about medical malpractice liability in the health care system, and proposals for reforming it. Finally, the section addresses a subset of malpractice liability, "informed consent" cases, and the relevance of custom in determining the scope of a physician's duty to disclose information to an individual patient.

1. Custom in General

Titus v. Bradford, B. & K. R. Co.
20 A. 517 (Pa. 1890)

[The defendant railroad operated a narrow-gauge railroad track between Bradford and Smethport. This line was connected to the standard-gauge tracks of major lines, and part of the defendant's business was to transfer over its tracks the loaded and unloaded freight cars of major carriers. The transfers were accomplished by means of a "hoist" that lifted car bodies from the standard trucks (bases) used on the major lines and set them down on the narrow trucks used on the defendant's lines. Most of the car bodies from the major lines were designed with flat bottoms, which could be set down relatively easily on the flat trucks in use on the narrow-gauge rails. A substantial portion of the defendant's business, however, involved the transfer of cars from the New York, Pennsylvania and Ohio Railroad. These "Nypano" cars had slightly rounded bottoms, "shaped somewhat like the bottom of a common saucer," which fit into correspondingly shaped trucks when in use on the Nypano lines.

When transferred to the defendant's tracks, however, this car body did not sit securely on its truck, since its bottom was about three inches higher at its edges than at its center. In order to prevent the car bodies from wobbling and toppling when the defendant's train was in motion, the defendant's employees routinely secured them with blocks of hard wood, which were either bolted in place or tied down with telegraph wire.

The decedent had worked on the defendant's railroad with the Nypano cars for nearly two years and was quite familiar with the methods used to secure them to the flat trucks. In the spring of 1888, he became a brakeman on the line. On June 7, 1888, in that capacity, he was riding atop a loaded Nypano freight car. Before setting off, the train's conductor had visually inspected the blocks and believed that they had been properly tied in place with telegraph wire. As the train rounded a curve at a speed of between 7 and 10 miles per hour, it started to sway from side to side. The decedent, who was sitting by the brake wheel on the top rear of the car, tried to run forward over the load to the car in front of him, but could not reach the safety of the next car before his car tipped over. He jumped off onto the track and was killed when struck by the car immediately behind him. A subsequent investigation showed that some of the wire fastening around the blocks of his car had come loose, which allowed the block to become dislodged and the car to wobble and tumble.

"[O]n account of the ill-adaptation of this car body to the truck," the plaintiff contended that "the company was negligent in using on this narrow-gauge road these standard car bodies." The jury returned a verdict for the plaintiff in the amount of $5,325, and the defendant appealed.]

Mitchell, J. We have examined all the testimony carefully, and fail to find any evidence of defendant's negligence. The negligence declared upon is the placing of a broad-gauge car upon a narrow-gauge truck, and the use of "an unsafe, and not the best appliance, to wit, the flat centre plate"; or, as expressed by the learned judge in his charge, in using on the narrow-gauge road the standard car bodies, and particularly the New York, Pennsylvania & Ohio car body described by the witnesses. But the whole evidence, of plaintiff's witnesses as well as of defendant's, shows that the shifting of broad-gauge or standard car bodies on to narrow-gauge trucks for transportation, is a regular part of the business of narrow-gauge railroads, and the plaintiff's evidence makes no attempt to show that the way in which it was done here was either dangerous or unusual. . . . Cazely and Richmond say it was the custom to haul these broad-gauge cars on the narrow-gauge trucks, though most of the broad-gauge were Erie cars, of a somewhat different construction; and Morris says the car in question was put on a Hays truck, fitted for carrying standard-gauge cars on a narrow-gauge road, and that this particular kind of "Nypano" car was so hauled quite often. These are plaintiff's own witnesses, and none of them say the practice was dangerous. The nearest approach to such testimony is by Morris, who says he "had his doubts."

But, even if the practice had been shown to be dangerous, that would not show it to be negligent. Some employments are essentially hazardous, as said by our Brother Green, in North C. Ry. Co. v. Husson, 101 Pa. 1 [(1882)], of coupling railway cars; and it by no means follows that an employer is liable "because a particular accident might have been prevented by some special device or precaution not in common use." All the cases agree that the master is not bound to use the newest and best appliances. He performs his duty when he furnishes those of ordinary character and reasonable safety, and the former is the test of the latter; for, in regard to the style of implement or nature of the mode of performance of any work, "reasonably safe" means safe according to the usages, habits, and ordinary risks of the business. Absolute safety is unattainable, and employers are not insurers. They are liable for the consequences, not of danger but of negligence; and the unbending test of negligence in methods, machinery, and appliances is the ordinary usage of the business. No man is held by law to a higher degree of skill than the fair average of his profession or trade, and the standard of due care is the conduct of the average prudent man. The test of negligence in employers is the same, and however strongly they may be convinced that there is a better or less dangerous way, no jury can be permitted to say that the usual and ordinary way, commonly adopted by those in the same business, is a negligent way for which liability shall be imposed. Juries must necessarily determine the responsibility of individual conduct, but they cannot be allowed to set up a standard which shall, in effect, dictate the customs or control the business of the community. . . .

It is also entirely clear that defendant's third point should have been affirmed. The deceased had been a brakeman on this train for five or six months, during which this mode of carrying broad-gauge cars had been used; cars similar to the one on which the accident occurred had been frequently carried, and that very car at least once, about ten days before. He not only thus had ample opportunity to know the risks of such trains, but he had his attention specially called to the alleged source of the accident, by having worked, just before becoming a brakeman, on the hoist by which the car bodies were transferred to the trucks. It was a perfectly plain case of acceptance of an employment, with full knowledge of the risks.

Judgment reversed.

Mayhew v. Sullivan Mining Co.

76 Me. 100 (1884)

[The plaintiff, an independent contractor, had been hired by the defendant to trace veins of new ore. During the course of his duties, the plaintiff worked on a platform in a mine shaft some 270 feet below ground. Near one corner of the platform was a "bucket-hole," which the plaintiff used in his work. The plaintiff alleged that on the day of the accident the defendant "carelessly and negligently caused a hole three feet in length by twenty-six inches in breadth to be cut for a ladder-hole in the platform near the centre of it directly back of the bucket-hole and twenty inches distant therefrom, without placing any rail or barrier about it, or any light or other warning there, and without giving plaintiff notice that any such dangerous change had been made in the platform; and that without any knowledge of its existence or fault on his part, the plaintiff, in the ordinary course of his business having occasion to go upon the platform fell through this new hole a distance of thirty-five feet, and received serious injury." The ladder-hole was made by one Stanley under the direction of the superintendent. The defendant sought to ask Stanley at trial whether he had "ever known ladder holes at a low level to be railed or fenced around," whether "as a miner" he thought it was "feasible" to use a ladder-hole with a railing around it, or whether he had "ever seen a ladder-hole in a mine, below the surface, with a railing around it." The court refused to allow the questions to be asked. Thereafter, the jury found negligence and returned a verdict for the plaintiff of $2,500.]

Barrows, J. Defendants' counsel claim that the favorable answers to these questions which they had a right to expect would have tended to show that there was no want of "average ordinary care" on the part of the defendants. We think the questions were properly excluded. The nature of the act in which the defendants' negligence was asserted to consist, with all the circumstances of time and place, whether of commission or omission, and its connection with the plaintiff's injury, presented a case as to which the jury were as well qualified to judge as any expert could be. It was not a case where the opinion of experts could be necessary or useful. . . . If the defendants had proved that in every mining establishment that has existed since the days of Tubal-Cain, it has been the practice to cut ladder-holes in their platforms, situated as this was while in daily use for mining operations, without guarding or lighting them, and without notice to contractors or workmen, it would have no tendency to show that the act

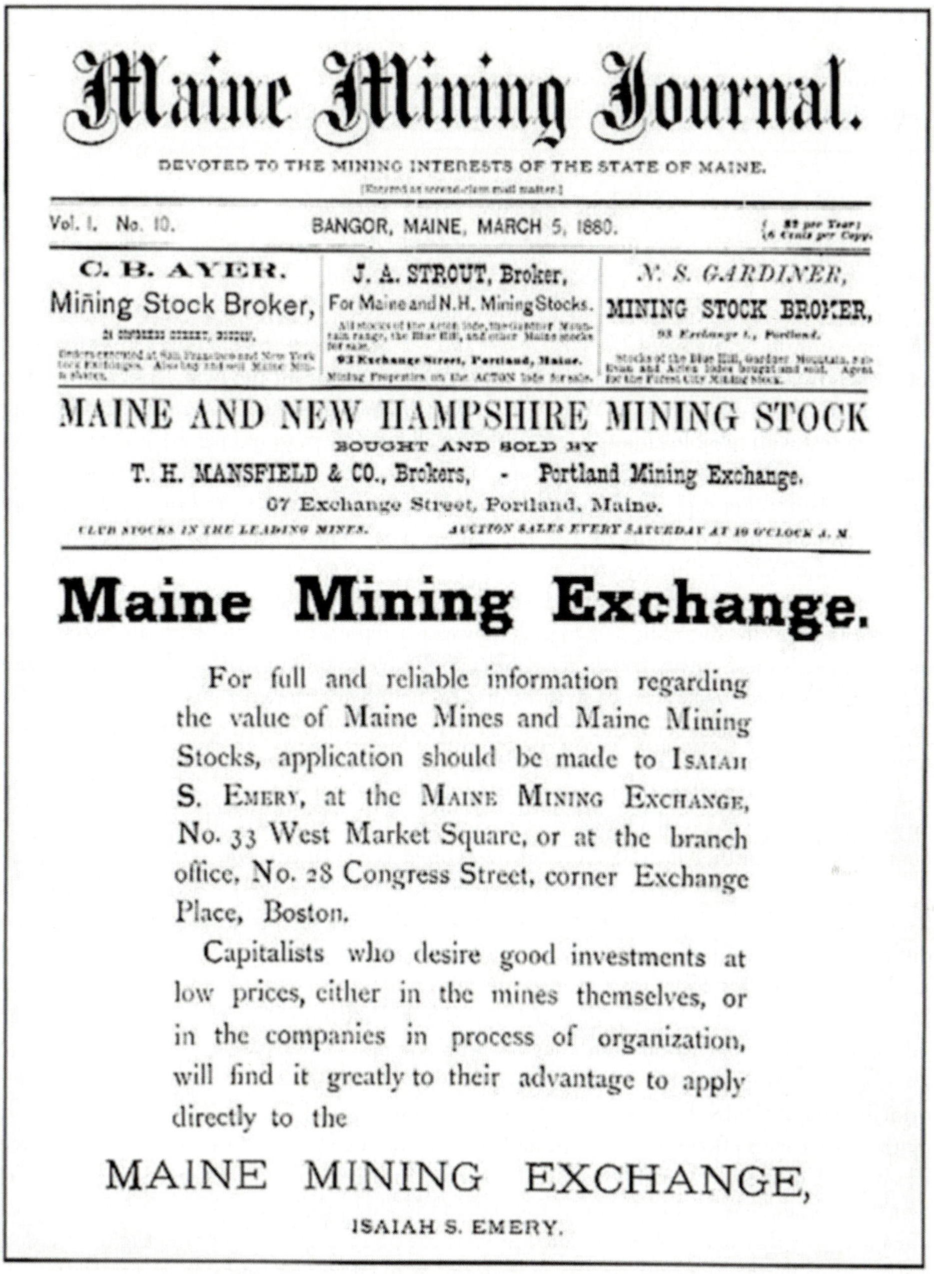

Maine Mining Journal.

DEVOTED TO THE MINING INTERESTS OF THE STATE OF MAINE.

[Entered as second-class mail matter.]

Vol. I. No. 10. BANGOR, MAINE, MARCH 5, 1880. {$2 per Year; 6 Cents per Copy.

C. B. AYER.
Mining Stock Broker,

J. A. STROUT, Broker,
For Maine and N.H. Mining Stocks.
93 Exchange Street, Portland, Maine.

N. S. GARDINER,
MINING STOCK BROKER,
93 Exchange St., Portland.

MAINE AND NEW HAMPSHIRE MINING STOCK
BOUGHT AND SOLD BY
T. H. MANSFIELD & CO., Brokers, - Portland Mining Exchange.
97 Exchange Street, Portland, Maine.

Maine Mining Exchange.

For full and reliable information regarding the value of Maine Mines and Maine Mining Stocks, application should be made to ISAIAH S. EMERY, at the MAINE MINING EXCHANGE, No. 33 West Market Square, or at the branch office, No. 28 Congress Street, corner Exchange Place, Boston.

Capitalists who desire good investments at low prices, either in the mines themselves, or in the companies in process of organization, will find it greatly to their advantage to apply directly to the

MAINE MINING EXCHANGE,

ISAIAH S. EMERY.

Front Page of a Weekly Mining Newspaper During a Notorious Metal Mining Rush That Overtook Parts of Maine from 1879 to 1882. The Accident in *Mayhew* Took Place in December 1881.

Source: Maine Department of Agriculture, Conservation and Forestry

was consistent with ordinary prudence or a due regard for the safety of those who were using their premises by their invitation. The gross carelessness of the act appears conclusively upon its recital. Defendants' counsel argue that "if it should appear that they rarely had railings, then it tends to show no want of ordinary care in that respect," that "if one conforms to custom he is so far exercising average ordinary care." The argument proceeds upon an erroneous idea of what constitutes ordinary care. "Custom" and "average" have no proper place in its definition.

It would be no excuse for a want of ordinary care that carelessness was universal about the matter involved, or at the place of the accident, or in the business generally. . . .

The T.J. Hooper

53 F.2d 107 (S.D.N.Y. 1931)

[The operator of the tugboats *The T.J. Hooper* and the *Montrose* was sued under a towing contract when two barges and their cargo of coal were lost in a gale off the New Jersey coast while in transit from Virginia to New York. The gist of the negligence claim was that neither tug was equipped with reliable radios that would have allowed them to receive the storm warnings broadcast in both the morning and the afternoon of March 8, 1928, by the naval station at Arlington. Four other tugs, the *Mars*, the *Menominee*, *The A.L. Walker*, and the *Waltham*, were on the same northbound route as *The T.J. Hooper.* They had received the messages and put safely into the Delaware breakwater.]

Coxe, District Judge: This raises the question whether the *Hooper* and *Montrose* were required to have effective radio sets to pick up weather reports broadcast along the coast. Concededly, there is no statutory law on the subject applicable to tugs of that type, the radio statute applying only to steamers "licensed to carry, or carrying, fifty or more persons"; and excepting by its terms "steamers plying between ports, or places, less than two hundred miles apart." U.S. Code Annotated, title 46, §484. The standard of seaworthiness is not, however, dependent on statutory enactment, or condemned to inertia or rigidity, but changes "with advancing knowledge, experience, and the changed appliances of navigation." It is particularly affected by new devices of demonstrated worth, which have become recognized as regular equipment by common usage.

Radio broadcasting was no new or untried thing in March, 1928. Everywhere, and in almost every field of activity, it was being utilized as an aid to communication, and for the dissemination of information. And that radio sets were in widespread use on vessels of all kinds is clearly indicated by the testimony in this case. Twice a day the government broadcast from Arlington weather reports forecasting weather conditions. Clearly this was important information which navigators could not afford to ignore.

Captain Powell, master of the *Menominee*, who was a witness for the tugs, testified that prior to March, 1928, his tug, and all other seagoing tugs of his company, were equipped by the owner with efficient radio sets, and that he regarded a radio as part "of the necessary equipment" of every reasonably well-equipped tug in the coastwise service. He further testified that 90 per cent of the coastwise tugs operating along the coast were so equipped. It is, of course, true that many of these radio sets were the personal property of the tug master, and not supplied by the owner. This was so with the *Mars, Waltham*, and *Menominee;* but, notwithstanding that fact, the use of the radio was shown to be so extensive as to amount almost to a universal practice in the navigation of coastwise tugs along the coast. I think therefore there was a duty on the part of the tug owner to supply effective receiving sets.

How have the tugs met this requirement? The *Hooper* had a radio set which belonged to her master, but was practically useless even before the tug left Hampton Roads, and was generally out of order. . . .

I hold therefore . . . (2) that the tugs *T.J. Hooper* and *Montrose* were unseaworthy in failing to have effective radio sets, capable of receiving weather reports on March 8th, . . . [and] (3) that the claims of the cargo owners against the tugs should be allowed. . . .

The T.J. Hooper

60 F.2d 737 (2d Cir. 1932)

[On appeal from the lower court. The court first notes that the evidence supports the claim that *The T.J. Hooper* would have taken shelter if its captain had received the naval broadcasts.]

L. HAND, J. They did not, because their private radio receiving sets, which were on board, were not in working order. These belonged to them personally, and were partly a toy, partly a part of the equipment, but neither furnished by the owner, nor supervised by it. It is not fair to say that there was a general custom among coastwise carriers so to equip their tugs. One line alone did it; as for the rest, they relied upon their crews, so far as they can be said to have relied at all. An adequate receiving set suitable for a coastwise tug can now be got at small cost and is reasonably reliable if kept up; obviously it is a source of great protection to their tows. Twice every day they can receive these predictions, based upon the widest possible information, available to every vessel within two or three hundred miles and more. Such a set is the ears of the tug to catch the spoken word, just as the master's binoculars are her eyes to see a storm signal ashore. Whatever may be said as to other vessels, tugs towing heavy coal laden barges, strung out for half a mile, have little power to manoeuvre, and do not, as this case proves, expose themselves to weather which would not turn back stauncher craft. They can have at hand protection against dangers of which they can learn in no other way.

Is it then a final answer that the business had not yet generally adopted receiving sets? There are, no doubt, cases where courts seem to make the general practice of the calling the standard of proper diligence; we have indeed given some currency to the notion ourselves. Indeed in most cases reasonable prudence is in fact common prudence; but strictly it is never its measure; a whole calling may have unduly lagged in the adoption of new and available devices. It never may set its own tests, however persuasive be its usages. Courts must in the end say what is required; there are precautions so imperative that even their universal disregard will not excuse their omission. But here there was no custom at all as to receiving sets; some had them, some did not; the most that can be urged is that they had not yet become general. Certainly in such a case we need not pause; when some have thought a device necessary, at least we may say that they were right, and the others too slack. The statute [46 U.S.C.A. §484] does not bear on this situation at all. It prescribes not a receiving, but a transmitting set, and for a very different purpose; to call for help, not to get news. We hold the tugs [liable] therefore because had they been properly equipped, they would have got the Arlington reports. The injury was a direct consequence of this unseaworthiness.

Decree affirmed.

NOTES

1. ***The Relationship Between Custom and Negligence.*** The four opinions in the three previous cases express different views on the relationship between custom and negligence. *Mayhew* has gained little following, either in its own time or today, with its conclusion that custom has "no proper place" in the definition of the standard of care. *Titus*, where custom is dispositive, once enjoyed a considerable following, especially in the context of industrial accidents, although the balance of authority was probably against its position even during the nineteenth century. See, e.g., Maynard v. Buck, 100 Mass. 40 (1868), and Wabash Railway v. McDaniels, 107 U.S. 454 (1883). The unrelenting attack on *Titus* often took a strong theoretical turn. Thus Miller, The So-Called Unbending Test of Negligence, 3 Va. L. Rev. 537, 543 (1916), argued that the *Titus* rule would deter new innovations by firms that might

otherwise be prepared to make them, because "the rule of the 'unbending test' constrains him to adopt the unsafe method in order to bring himself within the rule and escape the charge of negligence." Parchomovksy & Stein, Torts and Innovation, 107 Mich. L. Rev. 285, 288 (2008), carries forward the argument that the "custom-based design of our tort law . . . subsidizes producers and users of conventional technologies while taxing innovators." Is this sound? Do firms in a competitive industry have an incentive to improve methods of ensuring worker safety in order to lower wage levels? In a monopolistic industry?

On its facts, *The T.J. Hooper* did not therefore mark a radical break from tradition, although its allusion that "a whole calling may have unduly lagged in the adoption of new and available devices" has allowed wholesale attacks on standard industry policy, not only in admiralty cases but also for industrial accidents and product cases. Some sense of this approach is found in Bimberg v. Northern Pacific Ry., 14 N.W.2d 410, 413 (Minn. 1944), a wrongful death action brought under the Federal Employers' Liability Act. The defendant argued that designing a trestle was "an engineering problem for solution by the railroads and not by the courts," but the court took a different view of the subject:

> Local usage and general custom, either singly or in combination, will not justify or excuse negligence. They are merely foxholes in one of the battlefields of law, providing shelter, but not complete protection against charges of negligence. The generality of its plan of construction for trestles or bridges cannot excuse a railroad company from responsibility for negligence in its construction. Such plan of construction, commonly followed and "fortified," as defendant insists, "by many years of successful railroad operation," may be evidence of due care, but it cannot avail to establish as safe in law that which is dangerous in fact.

Even after these decisions, the precise relationship between custom and negligence remains controversial. Should compliance with custom establish a prima facie case of due care? Or should it only be evidence tending to show that the defendant did not take unreasonable risks of harm to others? On this question, the Third Restatement downgrades the role of custom as relevant to, but not necessarily determinative of, negligence.

RESTATEMENT OF THE LAW (THIRD) OF TORTS: LIABILITY FOR PHYSICAL AND EMOTIONAL HARM

§13. Custom

(a) An actor's compliance with the custom of the community, or of others in like circumstances, is evidence that the actor's conduct is not negligent but does not preclude a finding of negligence.

(b) An actor's departure from the custom of the community, or of others in like circumstances, in a way that increases risk is evidence of the actor's negligence but does not require a finding of negligence.

Comment b. Compliance with custom: rationale: . . . Possibly, the entire community or industry has lagged: all members of the group to which the actor belongs may have been inattentive to new developments or may have been pursuing self-interest in a way that has encouraged the neglect of a reasonable precaution. . . .

Comment c. Departure from custom: rationale: . . . While proof of deviation from custom is only evidence of negligence, this evidence often has significant weight. As a practical matter, the party who has departed from custom can counter the effect of this evidence by questioning the intelligence of the custom, by showing that its operation poses different or less serious risks than those occasioned by others engaging in seemingly similar activities, or by showing that it has adopted an alternative method for reducing or controlling risks that is at least as effective as the customary method. . . .

New York's Pattern Jury Instruction on Customary Business Practices is typical.

NEW YORK PATTERN JURY INSTRUCTION ON CUSTOMARY BUSINESS PRACTICES

CIVIL 2:16. Common Law Standard of Care—Customary Business Practices

. . . Defendant's conduct is not to be considered unreasonable simply because someone else may have used a better [or safer] practice. On the other hand, a general custom, use, or practice by those in the same business or trade may be considered some evidence of what constitutes reasonable conduct in that trade or business. . . . If you find that there is a custom or practice, you may take that general custom or practice into account in considering the care used by defendant in this case. However, a general custom or practice is not the only test; what you must decide is whether, taking all the facts and circumstances into account, defendant acted with reasonable care.

2. *Custom and Cost-Benefit Analysis.* Hand's decision in *The T.J. Hooper* complements his analysis in *Carroll Towing, supra* at 136. While *Carroll Towing* articulates Hand's use of a cost-benefit formula, *The T.J. Hooper* denies any conclusive weight to custom—its major rival in setting the standard of care. Hand's view has received overwhelming acceptance in the courts and among commentators. What should the jury do when custom conflicts with the cost-benefit standard? Abraham, Custom, Noncustomary Practice, and Negligence, 109 Colum. L. Rev. 1784, 1818–20 (2009), insists that when they conflict, "the jury can make its own informed choice between the outcomes dictated by the competing conceptions." Was there such a conflict in *The T.J Hooper*?

A greater respect for custom is found in Epstein, The Path to *The T.J. Hooper*: The Theory and History of Custom in the Law of Tort, 21 J. Legal Stud. 1, 4–5 (1992), which argues:

> [G]iven the imperfections of the legal system, the conventional wisdom that places cost-benefit analysis first and custom second is incorrect in at least two ways. First, in cases that arise out of a consensual arrangement, negligence is often the appropriate standard for liability, and, where it is so, custom should be regarded as conclusive evidence of due care in the absence of any contractual stipulation to the contrary. It is quite possible in some consensual settings no custom will emerge, at which point the negligence inquiry will be inescapably ad hoc. But where consistent custom emerges, regardless of its origins, it should be followed. Second, in stranger cases—that is, those where the harm does not fall on a contracting party or someone with whom the defendant has a special relationship—negligence should normally not be the appropriate standard of care, so that reliance on custom is as irrelevant as the negligence issue to which custom alone is properly directed. But where negligence is adopted in these stranger cases, then custom is normally *not* the appropriate standard because it registers the preferences of the parties to the custom, not those who are victimized by it. It should be taken into account, but given no dispositive weight. . . .

Note that *The T.J. Hooper* arose out of a consensual situation, as does most of the litigation that implicates questions of custom. Accordingly, the choice between the customary and cost-benefit approaches lies at the heart of understanding the distribution of power between the market and the courts in setting the standards of conduct for defendants across many lines of business and endeavors. Here the Hand formula turns out in practice to be far more interventionist than any standard of care based on custom. These cost-benefit tests are used to challenge the rationality of markets, while formulas based on custom accept and rely on some level of implicit rationality in market behavior.

How do customs emerge? Should it make any difference whether we are dealing with customs in a closely knit industry or with those that reach a broad commercial market? Whether we are dealing with parties who have overlapping roles (i.e., transactions between merchants in the same line of business) or with parties having specialized distinctive relationships (e.g., physician/patient or landlord/tenant)? Is it possible to have an accurate picture of the soundness of industry practices if customary evidence is ruled inadmissible, as in *Mayhew*? For a negative answer, see Abraham, *supra* at 153, at 1803–04.

3. *Custom and Private Rules of Conduct.* Can the plaintiff use the defendant's established rules that govern the conduct of his employees as evidence of negligence? In Fonda v. St. Paul City Ry., 74 N.W. 166, 167–70 (Minn. 1898), the plaintiff, an injured pedestrian, sued the defendant for the negligence of its servant in the operation of its train. The plaintiff was "a stranger to and not an employee of" the defendant, so that his "conduct could not have been in any way affected or influenced" by rules of which he had no knowledge. Mitchell, J., differentiated these internal house rules from statutes and municipal ordinances because of the perverse incentives created.

> The effect of it is that, the more cautious and careful a man is in the adoption of rules in the management of his business in order to protect others, the worse he is off, and the higher the degree of care he is bound to exercise. A person may, out of abundant caution, adopt rules requiring of his employees a much higher degree of care than the law imposes. This is a practice that ought to be encouraged, and not discouraged. But, if the adoption of such a course is to be used against him as an admission, he would naturally find it to his interest not to adopt any rules at all.

What if the proprietor can advertise his compliance with higher standards? Does this issue arise in stranger cases brought under a strict liability theory?

More recent cases have shown a willingness to allow the plaintiff to introduce the defendant's own internal rules on the standard of care question. In Lucy Webb Hayes National Training School v. Perotti, 419 F.2d 704, 710 (D.C. Cir. 1969), the plaintiff's decedent had been admitted into the defendant's psychiatric hospital as a mental patient for observation and treatment. Shortly after being admitted, the decedent slipped past the nurses' station that separated the secured portion of the floor, Ward 7-W, into the unsecured area on the same floor. While the defendant's attendant was leading the decedent back to Ward 7-W, the decedent bolted away, jumped through a window, and plunged to his death. The plaintiff argued that the hospital fell short of its own internal standard by allowing the decedent to wander from the closed to the open ward. The court held:

> We think the jury could find negligence upon the part of the hospital from this evidence without the assistance of expert testimony. The jurors might not be able to determine the necessity for a closed ward for mental patients of the type admitted to Ward 7-W, nor to evaluate the need for restrictions upon the movement of patients into and out of the closed ward. But the hospital itself had made these decisions. It could, of course, have presented evidence that the limitations upon patient movement constituted more than due care, or were unrelated to patient safety. Indeed, witnesses did testify for the hospital that the open and closed wards were separated by a locked door chiefly, or only, to isolate the more disturbed patients from those not so acutely ill. On the basis of all the evidence, however, the jury could reasonably conclude that the hospital's failure to observe the standards it had itself established represented negligence.

For the modern equivocation on the question of private standards, see RTT: LPEH §13, comment *f*, which first notes that "allowing the defendant's departure from its own standard to be used against the defendant might seem unfair, since it penalizes the defendant who has voluntarily provided an extra measure of safety." On the other hand, "the plaintiff may well have relied on the defendant's standard (or the defendant's general reputation for safety) in choosing to deal with the defendant; furthermore, the plaintiff may well be paying for at least the general costs of compliance that the standard imposes on the defendant." Should general reputation play the same role as an internal directive?

4. ***Updating Custom.*** How does custom keep pace with technological innovations and evolving standards? In Trimarco v. Klein, 436 N.E.2d 502 (N.Y. 1982), the plaintiff was injured in 1976 when he slipped in his bathroom and received serious lacerations from crashing against a shower door made of ordinary glass estimated to be between 1/16 and 1/4 of an inch thick. The shower door had been installed in the 1950s, when the use of ordinary glass was standard practice. Since the mid-1960s, the common practice in New York City had been to use safer tempered glass "whether to replace broken glass or to comply with the request of a tenant." The plaintiff in this instance did not know that ordinary glass was used in his shower door. Reversing a decision of the Appellate Division, the New York Court of Appeals allowed the plaintiff to reach the jury. Fuchsberg, J., first noted that evidence of custom was admissible because "it reflects the judgment and experience and conduct of many," and because "its relevancy and reliability comes too from the direct bearing it has on feasibility, for its focusing is on the practicability of a precaution in actual operation and the readiness with which it can be employed." Nonetheless, the court refused to give the custom conclusive weight, noting that "[a]fter all, customs and usages run the gamut of merit like anything else." The court then concluded that

> it was also for the jury to decide whether, at the point in time when the accident occurred, the modest cost and ready availability of safety glass and the dynamics of the growing custom to use it for shower enclosures had transformed what once may have been considered a reasonably safe part of the apartment into one which, in light of later developments, no longer could be so regarded.

Nonetheless, Fuchsberg, J., ordered a new trial, holding that it was improper to admit the applicable statutory provisions, which "protected only those tenants for whom shower glazing was installed after the statutory effective date." For the contrary result, see Considine v. City of Waterbury, 905 A.2d 70, 90 (Conn. 2006), where the court held that a building code, which technically does not apply to the defendant's premises, could nonetheless be considered as some evidence of the appropriate standard of care "because it reflects the experience and expertise of what authorities believe to be the safe use of glass in an entryway, albeit for future construction." On either view, must all old shower doors be replaced? Sprinklers and burglar alarms be retrofitted in old buildings?

S

2. Medical Malpractice

Lama v. Borras

16 F.3d 473 (1st Cir. 1994)

Stahl, J. Defendants-appellants Dr. Pedro Borras and Asociación Hospital del Maestro, Inc. (Hospital) appeal from a jury verdict finding them liable for medical malpractice to plaintiffs Roberto Romero Lama (Romero) and his wife, Norma. . . . Finding no error, we affirm.

I. Background

Since the jury found defendants liable, we recount the facts in the light most favorable to plaintiffs, drawing all reasonable inferences in their favor; we do not evaluate the credibility of witnesses or the weight of the evidence. . . .

In 1985, Romero was suffering from back pain and searching for solutions. Dr. Nancy Alfonso, Romero's family physician, provided some treatment but then referred him to Dr. Borras, a neurosurgeon. Dr. Borras concluded that Romero had a herniated disc and scheduled surgery. Prior to surgery, Dr. Borras neither prescribed nor enforced a regime of absolute bed rest, nor did he offer other key components of "conservative treatment."

Although Dr. Borras instructed Romero, a heavy smoker, to enter the hospital one week before surgery in order to "clean out" his lungs and strengthen his heart, Romero was still not subjected to standard conservative treatment.

While operating on April 9, 1986, Dr. Borras discovered that Romero had an "extruded" disc and attempted to remove the extruding material. Either because Dr. Borras failed to remove the offending material or because he operated at the wrong level, Romero's original symptoms returned in full force several days after the operation. Dr. Borras concluded that a second operation was necessary to remedy the "recurrence."

Dr. Borras operated again on May 15, 1986. Dr. Borras did not order pre- or post-operative antibiotics. It is unclear whether the second operation was successful in curing the herniated disc. In any event, as early as May 17, a nurse's note indicates that the bandage covering Romero's surgical wound was "very bloody," a symptom which, according to expert testimony, indicates the possibility of infection. On May 18, Romero was experiencing local pain at the site of the incision, another symptom consistent with an infection. On May 19, the bandage was "soiled again." A more complete account of Romero's evolving condition is not available because the Hospital instructed nurses to engage in "charting by exception," a system whereby nurses did not record qualitative observations for each of the day's three shifts, but instead made such notes only when necessary to chronicle important changes in a patient's condition.

On the night of May 20, Romero began to experience severe discomfort in his back. He passed the night screaming in pain. At some point on May 21, Dr. Edwin Lugo Piazza, an attending physician, diagnosed the problem as discitis—an infection of the space between discs—and responded by initiating antibiotic treatment. Discitis is extremely painful and, since it occurs in a location with little blood circulation, very slow to cure. Romero was hospitalized for several additional months while undergoing treatment for the infection.

After moving from Puerto Rico to Florida, the Romeros filed this diversity tort action in United States District Court for the District of Puerto Rico. Plaintiffs alleged that Dr. Borras was negligent in four general areas: (1) failure to provide proper conservative medical treatment; (2) premature and otherwise improper discharge after surgery; (3) negligent performance of surgery; and (4) failure to provide proper management for the infection. While plaintiffs did not claim that the Hospital was vicariously liable for any negligence on the part of Dr. Borras, they alleged that the Hospital was itself negligent in [its] failure to prepare, use, and monitor proper medical records. . . .

[At trial the jury awarded plaintiffs $600,000, and the district court rejected defendant's motion for a judgment as a matter of law under Fed. R. Civ. P. 50(b), as well as defendant's motion for a new trial under Fed. R. Civ. P. 59. The district court concluded: (1) had Dr. Borras used conservative treatment, he might have obviated all the risks of a complex laminectomy; (2) better record keeping could have allowed hospital personnel to detect the infection at an earlier stage; and (3) the hospital staff could have been negligent in handling the dressings and bandages.]

We find the reasoning of the district court to be substantially sound and therefore affirm the result. . . .

III. Discussion

A. Medical Malpractice Under Puerto Rico Law

We begin our analysis by laying out the substantive law of Puerto Rico governing this diversity suit. To establish a prima facie case of medical malpractice in Puerto Rico, a plaintiff must demonstrate: (1) the basic norms of knowledge and medical care applicable to general practitioners or specialists; (2) proof that the medical personnel failed to follow these basic norms in the treatment of the patient; and (3) a causal relation between the act or omission of the physician and the injury suffered by the patient.

The burden of a medical malpractice plaintiff in establishing the physician's duty is more complicated than that of an ordinary tort plaintiff. Instead of simply appealing to the jury's view of what is reasonable under the circumstances, a medical malpractice plaintiff must establish the relevant national standard of care. . . .

Naturally, the trier of fact can rarely determine the applicable standard of care without the assistance of expert testimony. The predictable battle of the experts then creates a curious predicament for the fact-finder, because an error of judgment regarding diagnosis or treatment does not lead to liability when expert opinion suggests that the physician's conduct fell within a range of acceptable alternatives. While not allowed to speculate, the fact-finder is of course free to find some experts more credible than others.

Proof of causation is also more difficult in a medical malpractice case than in a routine tort case because a jury must often grapple with scientific processes that are unfamiliar and involve inherent uncertainty. A plaintiff must prove, by a preponderance of the evidence, that the physician's negligent conduct was the factor that "most probably" caused harm to the plaintiff. As in the case of duty, however, a jury normally cannot find causation based on mere speculation and conjecture; expert testimony is generally essential. . . .

B. Negligence of Dr. Borras

The Borras Defendants claim that plaintiffs failed to introduce any evidence sufficient to prove either (1) the relevant standards of acceptable medical practice or (2) the causal link between Dr. Borras' conduct and harm to the plaintiffs. While plaintiffs may not have been able to substantiate the broad attack outlined in their complaint, we focus here on only one allegation of negligence: Dr. Borras' failure to provide conservative treatment prior to the first operation.

Defendants argue that plaintiffs failed to prove a general medical standard governing the need for conservative treatment in a case like that of Romero. We disagree. Plaintiffs' chief expert witness, Dr. George Udvarhelyi, testified that, absent an indication of neurological impairment, the standard practice is for a neurosurgeon to postpone lumbar disc surgery while the patient undergoes conservative treatment, with a period of absolute bed rest as the prime ingredient. In these respects, the views of defendants' neurosurgery experts did not diverge from those of Dr. Udvarhelyi. For example, Dr. Luis Guzman Lopez testified that, in the absence of extraordinary factors, "all neurosurgeons go for [conservative treatment] before they finally decide on [an] operation." Indeed, when called by plaintiffs, Dr. Borras (who also testified as a neurosurgery expert) agreed on cross-examination with the statement that "bed rest is normally recommended before surgery is decided in a patient like Mr. Romero," and claimed that he *did* give conservative treatment to Romero.

In spite of Dr. Borras' testimony to the contrary, there was also sufficient evidence for the jury to find that Dr. Borras failed to provide the customary conservative treatment. Dr. Alfonso, Romero's family physician, testified that Dr. Borras, while aware that Romero had not followed a program of absolute bed rest, proceeded with surgery anyway. Although Romero was admitted to the hospital one week before surgery, there was evidence that Dr. Borras neither prescribed nor attempted to enforce a conservative treatment regime. In fact, there was evidence that Dr. Borras' main goal was simply to admit Romero for a week of smoke-free relaxation, not absolute bed rest, because Romero's heavy smoking and mild hypertension made him a high-risk surgery patient. In short, we agree with the district court that the jury could reasonably have concluded that Dr. Borras failed to institute and manage a proper conservative treatment plan.

The issue of causation is somewhat more problematic. There are two potential snags in the chain of causation. First, it is uncertain that premature surgery was the cause of Romero's infection. Second, it is uncertain whether conservative treatment would have made surgery unnecessary. With respect to the first problem, the Puerto Rico Supreme Court has suggested that, when a physician negligently exposes a patient to risk-prone surgery, the physician is liable for the harm associated with a foreseeable risk. In this case, it is undisputed that discitis was a foreseeable risk of lumbar disc surgery.

Turning to the second area of uncertainty, we observe that nearly all of the experts who testified on the subject for both plaintiffs and defendants were of the opinion that conservative treatment would eliminate the need for surgery in the overwhelming majority of cases. Nonetheless, defendants introduced expert testimony that, because Romero suffered from an "extruded" disc, conservative treatment would not have helped. Dr. Udvarhelyi testified, however, that an extruded disc is indeed amenable to conservative treatment. With competent expert testimony in the record, the jury was not left to conjure up its own theories of causation. And certainly, the jury was free to credit some witnesses more than others. The question is admittedly close, but the jury could have reasonably found that Dr. Borras' failure to administer conservative treatment was the "most probable cause" of the first operation.

We conclude that plaintiffs introduced legally sufficient evidence to support each element of at least one major allegation of negligence on the part of Dr. Borras. We therefore hold that the district court properly denied the Borras Defendants' Rule 50 and 59 motions.

C. Negligence of Asociación Hospital del Maestro

While plaintiffs made a number of allegations against the Hospital, we focus on the allegation that the failure of hospital nurses to report on each nursing shift was a negligent cause of the late detection of Romero's infection.

The Hospital cannot seriously dispute that plaintiffs introduced sufficient evidence on the elements of duty and breach. [The court then holds that the jury could properly find that the nursing staff's failure to keep qualitative notes of each nursing shift, as required by regulation, could count as the proximate cause of the harm. It first notes that the sketchy notes could have delayed the diagnosis of plaintiff's excessive bleeding at the site of the wound, which in turn "could have prevented the infection from reaching the disc interspace in the critical period prior to May 20."]

Affirmed.

NOTES

1. ***Unique Role of Custom in Medical Malpractice.*** Custom occupies a privileged position in medical malpractice cases: "Health care professionals must exercise the same care that other professionals customarily exercise. Thus, the duty applied to medical professionals is a purely factual one, unlike the normative 'reasonable care' standard invoked for non-professionals." Cramm & Hartz, Ascertaining Customary Care in Malpractice Cases: Asking Those Who Know, 37 Wake Forest L. Rev. 699, 699–700 (2002).

Why reject *The T.J. Hooper* in medical malpractice cases in favor of deference to custom? One influential explanation is offered in Morris, Custom and Negligence, 42 Colum. L. Rev. 1147, 1164–65 (1942):

> Why should conformity to the practice protect a physician from liability? Drovers [cattle drivers], railroads, merchants, etc., are not so protected. The doctor escapes liability even though he conforms only to the practice in his locality or the practice in similar localities. And treatment need not conform to a general usage, it need only be like that used by some reputable doctors. If all doctors reasonably developed and applied their skill and knowledge, the conformity test might be the equivalent of reasonable care under the circumstances. Doctors as a class may be

> more likely to exert their best efforts than drovers, railroads, and merchants but they are human and subject to the temptations of laziness and unthinking acceptance of traditions. The rationale is: no other standard is practical. Our judges and juries are usually not competent to judge whether or not a doctor has acted reasonably. The conformity test is probably the only workable test available. . . .
>
> The patient who has endured suffering is an appealing plaintiff. Juries are likely to favor him. And it is widely known that doctors usually carry liability insurance. But a doctor who loses a malpractice case stands to lose more than the amount of the judgment — he may also lose his professional reputation and his livelihood. These considerations heighten the need for a test of malpractice that will protect doctors against undeserved liability. The law may be academically deficient in countenancing an excuse that may occasionally be based on the negligence of the other doctors. But the grossly incompetent practitioner will find little comfort in the tests of malpractice. A few negligent doctors may escape, but the quack will not. The reasonably prudent man "test" would enable the ambulance chaser to make a law suit out of any protracted illness.

For a modern critique of Morris' account, see Hetcher, Creating Safe Social Norms in a Dangerous World, 73 S. Cal. L. Rev. 1, 19–22 (1999).

2. ***The Standard of Care in Medical Malpractice Cases.*** Although *Lama* was decided under Puerto Rican law, its basic principles are indistinguishable from those applicable in virtually all common law jurisdictions. Thus in Fay v. Grand Strand Regional Medical Center, 771 S.E.2d 639, 646 (S.C. 2015), the standard was put as follows:

> A plaintiff in a medical malpractice case must present (1) evidence of the generally recognized practices and procedures that would be exercised by competent practitioners in a defendant doctor's field of medicine under the same or similar circumstances, (2) evidence that the defendant doctor departed from the recognized and generally accepted standards, practices, and procedures in the manner alleged by the plaintiff, and (3) evidence that the defendant's departure from the generally accepted standards and practices was the proximate cause of the plaintiff's injuries and damages.

Often, no single custom covers a given medical question. In Jones v. Chidester, 610 A.2d 964, 965, 969 (Pa. 1992), the court described the "two schools" problem as follows:

> A medical practitioner has an absolute defense to a claim of negligence when it is determined that the prescribed treatment or procedure has been approved by one group of medical experts even though an alternate school of thought recommends another approach, or it is agreed among experts that alternative treatments and practices are acceptable. The doctrine is applicable only where there is more than one method of accepted treatment or procedure. In specific terms, however, we are called upon in this case to decide once again whether a school of thought qualifies as such when it is advocated by a "considerable number" of medical experts or when it commands acceptance by "respective, reputable and reasonable" practitioners. The former test calls for a quantitative analysis, while the latter is premised on qualitative grounds.

The court then noted that the precedents left the question unresolved, and continued:

> It is incumbent upon us to settle this confusion. The "two schools of thought doctrine" provides a complete defense to malpractice. It is therefore insufficient to show that there exists a "small minority" of physicians who agree with the defendant's questioned practice. Thus, the Superior Court's "reputable and respected by reasonable medical experts" test is improper. Rather, there must be a considerable number of physicians, recognized and respected in their field, sufficient to create another "school of thought."

On the two schools test, see Bradford, The "Respectable Minority" Doctrine in Missouri Medical Negligence Law, 56 J. Mo. B. 326 (2000).

3. *Setting the Customary Standard.* Expert testimony is generally required to determine the applicable standard of care in medical malpractice cases.

> [A] universal corollary to the professional-standards-based regime of medical negligence law is that testimony by a legally competent medical expert is . . . essential for the plaintiff to make out a prima facie case of professional medical liability. . . . [T]he plaintiff must present [expert] testimony that both identifies the relevant professional standard and also establishes its violation.

King, The Common Knowledge Exception to the Expert Testimony Requirement for Establishing the Standard of Care in Medical Malpractice, 59 Ala. L. Rev. 51, 59 (2007). The "common knowledge rule" is a widely accepted (albeit narrow) exception; when a court determines that the allegedly negligent conduct in a medical malpractice case is "within the understanding of lay members of the public," it generally does not require expert testimony to determine the applicable standard of care. *Id.* at 63.

Other sources are sometimes available but are rarely dispositive. In Morlino v. Medical Center of Ocean County, 706 A.2d 721, 729–30 (N.J. 1998), the defendant emergency room physician, Dr. Dugenio, prescribed Ciprofloxacin to the plaintiff, then eight and one-half months pregnant, when she complained of a serious sore throat. Her fetus was dead the next day. Before prescribing the drug the defendant consulted the Physician's Desk Reference, "a compilation of information about prescription drugs that is published annually and distributed to the medical professional free of charge." The PDR contains a list of indications and contraindications for the use of various drugs, alone and in combination, for treating various conditions. It contained the following warning: "CIPROFLOXACIN SHOULD NOT BE USED IN CHILDREN OR PREGNANT WOMEN," noting that animal studies indicated some fetal risk. Having read this warning, Dr. Dugenio nonetheless prescribed the drug because he was concerned that influenza bacteria, if untreated, could lead to greater patient illness, which in turn could jeopardize the fetus's own welfare. In affirming a jury verdict for the defendants, Pollock, J., had allowed evidence of PDR warnings to establish the applicable standard of care for prescribing medicine, but cautioned:

> Nevertheless, drug manufacturers do not design package inserts and PDR entries to establish a standard of medical care. Manufacturers write drug package inserts and PDR warnings for many reasons including compliance with FDA requirements, advertisement, the provision of useful information to physicians, and an attempt to limit the manufacturer's liability. After a drug has been on the market for a sufficient period of time, moreover, physicians may rely more on their own experience and the professional publications of others than on a drug manufacturer's advertisements, inserts, or PDR entries. . . .
>
> Accordingly, we hold that the package inserts and PDR references alone do not establish the standard of care. It follows that a physician's failure to adhere to PDR warnings does not by itself constitute negligence. Reliance on the PDR alone to establish negligence would both obviate expert testimony on an issue where it is needed and could mislead the jury about the appropriate standard of care.

What result on appeal if the jury found for the plaintiff on this evidence?

4. *The Locality Rule.* If the customary standard has survived, the locality rule, as defended by Morris, has taken a beating in the modern age of national medical standards and accreditation, complete with board-certified physicians. One key transitional decision is Brune v. Belinkoff, 235 N.E.2d 793 (Mass. 1968). There the plaintiff claimed that the defendant anesthesiologist negligently administered a spinal anesthetic during the delivery of plaintiff's baby in October 1958. The defendant, practicing in New Bedford, Massachusetts, gave plaintiff an eight-milligram dosage of pontocaine. Eleven hours later plaintiff attempted to climb out of bed, but slipped and fell, suffering persistent injuries, due to an excessive dosage of pontocaine. Some medical evidence was introduced to show that good medical practice required a dosage of less than five milligrams. Other evidence, including that of defendant, tended to show that the dosage given was customary in New Bedford, and that the smaller dosages given in New York and Boston were appropriate because of the different obstetrical procedures used in those two cities. "The New Bedford obstetricians use supra fundi pressure (pressure applied to the uterus during delivery) which 'requires a higher level of anesthesia.' "

On appeal from judgment for the defendant, Spaulding, J., upheld the plaintiff's exception to that charge importing local custom. He agreed that the traditional locality rule announced in Small v. Howard, 128 Mass. 131 (1880), rightly protected a jack-of-all-trades general practitioner performing difficult surgery in a small country village. But for today's high-powered specialists he opted for a national standard:

> The time has come when the medical profession should no longer be Balkanized by the application of varying geographic standards in malpractice cases. Accordingly, Small v. Howard is hereby overruled. The present case affords a good illustration of the inappropriateness of the "locality" rule to existing conditions. The defendant was a specialist practising in New Bedford, a city of 100,000, which is slightly more than fifty miles from Boston, one of the medical centers of the nation, if not the world. This is a far cry from the country doctor in Small v. Howard, who ninety years ago was called upon to perform difficult surgery. Yet the trial judge told the jury that if the skill and ability of New Bedford physicians were "fifty percent inferior" to those obtaining in Boston the defendant should be judged by New Bedford standards, "having regard to the current state of advance of the profession." This may well be carrying the rule of Small v. Howard to its logical conclusion, but it is, we submit, a reductio ad absurdum of the rule.
>
> The proper standard is whether the physician, if a general practitioner, has exercised the degree of care and skill of the average qualified practitioner, taking into account the advances in the profession. In applying this standard it is permissible to consider the medical resources available to the physician as *one* circumstance in determining the skill and care required. Under this standard some allowance is thus made for the type of community in which the physician carries on his practice. . . .

Under the modern rule, should a rural clinic be required to have the same equipment as a state-of-the-art university hospital? Take costs in general into account? To refer cases to major surgical centers? Should the standard of care vary for residents and fellows who are still in training? For a negative response, see Clark v. University Hospital-UMDNJ, 914 A.2d 838, 843 (N.J. Super. 2006): "Defendants held themselves out as doctors and should be held to the standard of care they claimed to profess." What if they held themselves out as residents in training?

5. ***Government Liability for Medical Malpractice Under the Federal Tort Claims Act.*** Because of sovereign immunity, private citizens who were injured by tortious conduct at the hands of government employees were historically left without a judicial remedy against the federal government. The FTCA, enacted in 1946, waived this sovereign immunity for certain tort claims brought by private citizens against government officials. The basic FTCA contains an exception from tort liability for "(j) [a]ny claim arising out of the combatant activities of the miliary or naval forces, or the Coast Guard, during time of war." That exception was largely put to one side in Feres v. United States, 340 U.S. 135, 145, 146 (1950), which consolidated two cases of medical negligence and one case of occupier's liability. Jackson, J., refused to draw any negative inference by holding that the government could be held liable for military activities when exception (j) did not apply. Instead, Jackson, J., concluded that the phrase "shall be liable . . . in the same manner and to the same extent as a private individual under like circumstances," immunized the federal government from claims brought by soldiers for their service-related injuries:

> We know of no American law which ever has permitted a soldier to recover for negligence, against either his superior officers or the Government he is serving. Nor is there any liability

> "under like circumstances," for no private individual has power to conscript or mobilize a private army with such authorities over persons as the Government vests in echelons of command.
>
> We conclude that the Government is not liable under the Federal Tort Claims Act for injuries to servicemen where the injuries arise out of or are in the course of activity incident to service. Without exception, the relationship of military personnel to the Government has been governed exclusively by federal law. We do not think that Congress, in drafting this Act, created a new cause of action dependent on local law for service-connected injuries or death due to negligence. We cannot impute to Congress such a radical departure from established law in the absence of express congressional command.

Why is the choice of law problem insuperable here when it is not insuperable in highway cases? When the locality rule is rejected? Is the government not capable of meeting ordinary negligence obligations? Is it possible to apply federal common law in these cases? Should liability be allowed at least in those cases where the plaintiff is not entitled to any insurance or other benefit packages given to military personnel?

Murray v. UNMC Physicians

806 N.W.2d 118 (Neb. 2011)

[The decedent, Mary Murray, suffered from pulmonary arterial hypertension, which can lead to a constriction of blood vessels in the lungs, which in turn leads to heart failure. Flolan vasodilator, if administered twenty-four hours per day, can extend life at a cost of about $100,000 per year for the rest of her life. The decedent's physician had written the order for Flolan, "before the catheterization, pending the results of the catheterization and insurance approval." But before the paperwork could be cleared, the decedent returned to the emergency room where she died of cardiac arrest. There was sharply conflicting expert evidence as to the cause of death—was it arterial hypertension, or myocarditis, a heart inflammation caused by bacteria—and whether, if it was cardiac arrest, it could have been prevented by the earlier use of Flolan. The defendant's experts also testified that it would be "devastating" to the patient to discontinue treatment once it had started.]

Gerrard, J. Robert [Mary's husband] moved for a directed verdict on the standard of care, arguing that as a matter of law, insurance coverage cannot dictate what doctors do. UNMC replied that according to its experts, a continuing source for treatment is something that doctors should consider in determining how treatment is to be administered. Robert's motion was overruled. Robert also asked that the jury be instructed that if the standard of care requires prescription of a drug, it is not a defense to a claim the standard of care has been violated that the drug would not be provided until approved by an insurance carrier. That instruction was refused.

[After the jury entered a verdict for the defendants, the trial judge announced]

> . . . that, as a matter of law, a medical standard of care cannot be tied to or controlled by an insurance company or the need for payment. The "bean counters" in an insurance office are not physicians. Medicine cannot reach the point where an insurance company determines the medical standard of care for the treatment of a patient. Nor, can we live in a society where the medical care required is not controlled by the physicians treating the patient. The position advanced by [UNMC's] expert tells us that the standard of care is different for those with money than for those without. This is neither moral nor just. It is wrong. . . .

[On appeal, Gerrard, J., notes that the standard articulation of the customary standard of care is both unitary and wealth-blind. He then notes that it] has been suggested that at a fundamental level, a unitary, wealth-blind standard of care cannot be reconciled with the growth of technology and the stratification of available health care. Custom is increasingly difficult to identify in today's medical marketplace, as resource distinctions produce fragmentation and disintegration. It has also been suggested that maintaining a unitary standard of care disadvantages those who may not be able to pay for health care. Physicians remain free, for the most part, to decline to treat those who cannot pay, and "an outright refusal to treat an indigent patient, in contrast to a decision to treat in a manner inconsistent with the unitary malpractice standard, rarely creates the threat of liability." [Siliciano, Wealth, Equity, and the Unitary Medical Malpractice Standard, 77 Va. L. Rev. 439, 457 (1991).] So, it has been argued that rather than assume the burden of paying for a patient's treatment, or the potential liability of providing some but not all possible care, the unitary standard makes it more likely that "providers will now sidestep the entire problem simply by refusing to accept some, or all, of such patients for treatment." [*Id.*]

On the other hand, it has been argued that permitting physicians to make medical decisions based on resource scarcity would compromise the fiduciary relationship between patient and physician, creating a conflict of interest because the patient's well-being would no longer be the physician's focus. The question is how the value judgments inherent in the development of the standard of care might evolve in response to a societal interest in controlling health care costs. It has been explained that a physician's initial value judgment, in treating a patient, is made in light of conclusions reached about the likely benefits that services would have had for the plaintiff patient. It involves an evaluation as to whether the services should have been provided given their likely benefits, the risk of iatrogenic harm, and the gravity of the problem experienced by the patient. Normally the value judgment does not involve an explicit consideration of the costs of caring for a patient, although economics are implicitly considered. Physicians do not do everything conceivably possible in caring for a patient—they draw what they consider to be reasonable boundary lines. . . .

In short, the traditional ethical norms of the medical profession and the legal demands of the customary standard of care impose significant restrictions on a physician's ability to consider the costs of treatment, despite significant and increasing pressure to contain those costs. Whether the legal standard of care should change to alleviate that conflict, and how it might change, has been the subject of considerable discussion. It has been suggested that the customary standard of care could evolve to permit the denial of marginally beneficial treatment—in other words, when high costs would not be justified by minor expected benefits. Others have suggested that the standard of care should evolve to consider two separate components: (1) a skill component, addressing the skill with which diagnoses are made and treatment is rendered, that would not vary by a patient's financial circumstances and (2) a resource component, addressing deliberate decisions about how much treatment to give a patient, that would vary so as to not demand more of physicians than is reasonable. It has been suggested that physicians should be permitted to rebut the presumption of a unitary standard of care when diminution of care arises by economic necessity instead of negligence. And many have suggested that custom should no longer be the benchmark for the standard of care; instead, practice standards or guidelines could be promulgated that would settle issues of resource allocation.

All of the concerns discussed above are serious, and they present difficult questions that courts will be required to confront in the future. But we do not confront them here, because under the unique facts of this case, they are not presented. Contrary to the district court's belief, this is not a case in which insurance company "bean counters" overrode the medical judgment of a patient's physicians or in which those physicians allowed their medical judgment to be subordinated to a patient's ability to pay for treatment. Nor is this a case in which the parties disputed the cost-effectiveness of the treatment at issue. Rather, UNMC's evidence was that its decision to wait to begin Flolan treatment was not economic—it was a medical decision, based on the health consequences to the patient if the treatment is interrupted.

. . . [M]ore fundamentally, the district court's concerns about health care policy, while understandable, are misplaced in a situation in which the patient's ability to continue to pay for treatment is still a medical consideration. In other words, even when the standard of care is limited to medical considerations relevant to the welfare of the patient, and not economic considerations relevant to the welfare of the health care provider, the standard of care articulated by UNMC's witnesses in this case was still consistent with a medical standard of care.

This case does not involve a conflict of interest between the physician and patient—there was no evidence, for instance, of a financial incentive for UNMC's physicians to control costs . . . because UNMC's physicians were not weighing the risk to Mary's health against the risk to her pocketbook, or UNMC's budget, or even a general social interest in controlling health care costs. UNMC's physicians were weighing the risk to Mary's health of delaying treatment against the risk to Mary's health of potentially interrupted treatment. Stated another way, this was not a case in which a physician refused to provide beneficial care—it was a case in which the physicians determined that the care would not be beneficial if it was later interrupted. In fact, it could be deadly.

[Gerrard, J., then concludes that it is a jury question whether the applicable standard of care "required Flolan to be administered immediately," so it was wrong to order a new trial.]

Reversed.

NOTES

1. ***Revolution in Health Care Provision.*** The traditional fee for service system of payments has been displaced by a complicated array of health care programs—Medicare, Medicaid, the Affordable Care Act of 2010—each with its own elaborate requirements for coverage and reimbursements. As *Murray* indicates, these complex financial constraints are only aggravated in the face of ever more expensive medical treatments of varying effectiveness. Is *Murray* right to leave these questions to the jury in each individual case? Should physicians and medical centers that have no direct financial interest in these cases be held exempt from coverage as a matter of law? For discussions on this question, see Morreim, Cost Containment and the Standard of Medical Care, 75 Calif. L. Rev. 1719 (1987); Henderson & Siliciano, Universal Health Care and the Continued Reliance on Custom in Determining Medical Malpractice, 79 Cornell L. Rev. 1382 (1994).

Financial barriers akin to the ones evident in *Murray* may spur tensions between patients and physicians. In Denver & Rio Grande Railroad v. Peterson, *supra* at 128, the court established that a defendant's wealth does not impact the standard of care that he owes to others. Thus a defendant's liability does not vary based on its financial capacity. Yet does the approach taken by the doctors in *Murray* indicate that a patient's financial ability determines the level of care she is owed, at least in the medical context? Similarly, how does wealth impact the dynamic between physicians and patients? Do financial components—such as medical insurance and health care provider's treatment limitations—create perverse incentives for physicians? See Mehlman, Why Physicians Are Fiduciaries for Their Patients, 12 Ind. Health L. Rev. 1 (2015).

2. ***Empirical Assessment of the Medical Malpractice System.*** How effective is the malpractice system in deterring physician and hospital negligence and in providing compensation to injured patients? What effect does malpractice liability have on health care costs, treatment options, and the way medicine is practiced?

Empirical evidence of a strong deterrent effect from medical malpractice liability is hard to find. One comprehensive review of all tort systems, Dewees & Trebilcock, The Efficacy of the Tort System and Its Alternatives: A Review of the Empirical Evidence, 30 Osgoode

Hall L.J. 57 (1992), notes that Canadian doctors are only 20 percent as likely to be sued as U.S. doctors, and pay insurance premiums around 10 percent of those paid by U.S. doctors, yet "there appears to be no evidence that Canadian physicians are more careless than their U.S. counterparts." Dewees and Trebilcock conclude that the medical malpractice system fares badly, both in absolute terms and in comparison with automobile insurance, in providing compensation to injured parties and in meeting the concerns of corrective justice.

Weiler, Medical Malpractice on Trial 14 (1991), reports on two major studies—one in California during the 1970s, and one in New York from the late 1980s—that between them reviewed the patient records of some 50,000 hospitalizations (some 20,000 in California and 30,000 in New York). Both studies found that the instances of negligent treatment resulting in patient harm far exceeded the number of malpractice claims filed, and, by greater margins, the number of cases in which recovery occurred. The New York investigation (in which Weiler took part), for example, estimated that about one in 100 patients suffered serious injury or death attributable to negligent medical treatment, yet suit was filed for only one in every eight valid claims, with compensation paid in only half those claims. Moreover, "a substantial proportion of the claims actually filed were for cases in which we had concluded on the basis of hospital records that no medical injury at all had occurred, much less one caused by medical negligence." It was not possible to determine whether the compensation actually paid was in the meritorious cases. Stated otherwise, these studies suggest that the liability system picks out the wrong cases for suit.

More recent empirical work by Studdert et al., Claims, Errors, and Compensation Payments in Medical Malpractice Litigation, 354 New Eng. J. Med. 2024, 2024 (2006), suggests that concerns regarding frivolous claims are overstated. Based upon physician review of a random sample of 1,452 closed malpractice claims, including paid claims, from five different liability insurers in 2006, the researchers concluded that "[c]laims that lack evidence of error are not uncommon, but most are denied compensation."

Hyman et al., Does Tort Reform Affect Physician Supply? Evidence from Texas, 43 Int'l Rev. L. & Econ. 203 (2015), examines the impact of the substantial Texas medical malpractice reforms of 2003, and concludes that there is no evidence that these reforms had many effects. "Physician supply was not measurably stunted prior to reform, and it did not measurably improve after reform. This is true for all patient care physicians in Texas, high-malpractice-risk specialties, primary care physicians, and rural physicians." Need the same results apply for the willingness of physicians to take on difficult cases, or alter their fees for services?

Most states have nonetheless responded legislatively to the perceived need to curb malpractice liability. For a comprehensive compendium of the most prevalent tort reforms between 1980 and 2020 in the United States, see Avraham, Database of State Tort Law Reforms (7.1), (U. Tex. L., L. Econ. Rsch. Paper No. e555, 2021), https://ssrn.com/abstract=902711. Hyman & Silver, The Poor State of Health Care Quality in the U.S.: Is Malpractice Liability Part of the Problem or Part of the Solution?, 90 Cornell L. Rev. 893, 895–96 (2005), complains:

> The most popular proposals—damages caps, credits for payments from collateral sources, heightened requirements for expert witnesses, and limits on contingency fees—have more to do with provider and insurer self-interest than with health care quality. Their purpose is to reduce insurance costs in the short run, not to improve delivery systems in ways that address low-quality care or decrease the frequency of harmful errors.

Other more systemic reforms proposed by scholars have not fared well. Mello & Brennan, Deterrence of Medical Errors: Theory and Evidence for Malpractice Reform, 80 Tex. L. Rev. 1595, 1616–17 (2002), concludes that "experience rating"—correlating physicians' medical liability insurance rates to malpractice claims against them—has generally been rejected as "unworkable," given the poor correlation between malpractice claims and negligence, the year-to-year variation in claims, the relatively small rate increases applied, and the ability of physicians simply to switch insurance carriers. Hyman et al., Medical Malpractice and Physician Discipline: The Good, The Bad and The Ugly, 18 J. Legal Empirical Stud. 131 (2021), surveyed 90,000 Illinois physicians over a twenty-five-year period and found that an overwhelming number of paid claims and disciplinary actions are attributable to a small number of repeat offenders.

3. Informed Consent

Peter Schuck

Rethinking Informed Consent

103 Yale L.J. 899, 900–03 (1994)

The doctrine requiring physicians to obtain a patient's informed consent before undertaking treatment is relatively young, having first appeared in a recognizable, relatively robust form only in 1957. Yet the values that underlie the doctrine have an ancient pedigree. The consent norm had occupied a prominent and honored place in our legal thought for many centuries before the courts began to develop a jurisprudence of informed consent in health care. Also well established was the cognate notion that consent must be informed or knowledgeable in some meaningful sense if we are to accord it legal or moral significance. . . .

When Americans think of informed consent, however, they probably think of consent to risks of personal injury from medical treatment and from exposure to dangerous products. In these contexts, informed consent does not simply pursue the contract law goals of individual autonomy, efficiency, and anti-statism; it also advances two related ideas, fault and duty, that pervade and moralize tort law. . . . Informed consent claims arise at the private law intersection of torts and contracts, the laws which govern most workaday activities and choices. It is here that the social meaning of consent becomes most evident.

The doctrine of informed consent in health care shared in the more general expansion of American tort liability that proceeded well into the 1980's and that now appears to have stabilized. Everyone, it seems, favors the principle of informed consent; it is "only" the specific details and applications of the doctrine that arouse serious debate. In order to map and enlarge this debate, it is useful to distinguish three different versions of informed consent doctrine. The first is the letter and spirit of the doctrine as developed primarily by courts—the law "in books." The second is the doctrine as imagined, feared, and often caricatured by some physicians—the law "in the mind." The third version, a consequence both of the gap between the first two and of other situational constraints, is the doctrine as actually practiced by clinicians—the law "in action."

Canterbury v. Spence

464 F.2d 772 (D.C. Cir. 1972)

[The plaintiff-appellant first consulted Dr. Spence, the defendant-appellee, after experiencing severe back pain in December 1958. After a preliminary examination, Dr. Spence had the appellant undergo a myelogram—a procedure in which dye is injected into the spinal column which is then examined for disease or other disorder—that revealed that the appellant suffered from a "filling defect" in the region of his fourth thoracic vertebra. Dr. Spence told the appellant that he needed a laminectomy—an operation on the posterior arch of the vertebra—to correct what he suspected was a ruptured disc. He did not tell the appellant the details of the proposed operation, nor did the appellant inquire about them. Next, Dr. Spence contacted the appellant's mother and told her, when asked, that the operation he proposed was a serious one, but "not any more than any other operation." Dr. Spence performed the operation on February 11, 1959, only to discover that the appellant's spinal cord was swollen and in very poor condition. He did what he could to relieve the pressure on the cord and left the appellant in bed to recuperate in the hospital.

For the first day or so, the appellant's recuperation proceeded normally. However, at least according to appellant's testimony, he was allowed, contrary to Dr. Spence's original instructions, to void unattended. While doing so, he slipped off the side of the bed, there being no one to assist and no side rail to break his fall. Several hours later the appellant had difficulty breathing and suffered near-complete paralysis from the waist down. Dr. Spence performed another emergency operation that night, and the appellant's condition improved thereafter. "Despite extensive medical care, [the appellant] has never been what he was before. Instead of the back pain, even years later, he hobbled about on crutches, a victim of paralysis of the bowels and urinary incontinence. In a very real sense this lawsuit is an understandable search for reasons."]

Robinson, J. Appellant filed suit in the District Court on March 7, 1963, four years after the laminectomy and approximately two years after he attained his majority. The complaint stated several causes of action against each defendant. Against Dr. Spence it alleged, among other things, negligence in the performance of the laminectomy and failure to inform him beforehand of the risk involved. Against the hospital the complaint charged negligent post-operative care in permitting appellant to remain unattended after the laminectomy, in failing to provide a nurse or orderly to assist him at the time of his fall, and in failing to maintain a side rail on his bed. . . .

. . . Appellant introduced no evidence to show medical and hospital practices, if any, customarily pursued in regard to the critical aspects of the case, and only Dr. Spence, called as an adverse witness, testified on the issue of causality. Dr. Spence described the surgical procedures he utilized in the two operations and expressed his opinion that appellant's disabilities stemmed from his pre-operative condition as symptomized by the swollen, nonpulsating spinal cord. He stated, however, that neither he nor any of the other physicians with whom he consulted was certain as to what that condition was, and he admitted that trauma can be a cause of paralysis. Dr. Spence . . . testified that . . . paralysis can be anticipated "somewhere in the nature of one percent" of the laminectomies performed, a risk he termed "a very slight possibility." He felt that communication of that risk to the patient is not good medical practice because it might deter patients from undergoing needed surgery and might produce adverse psychological reactions which could preclude the success of the operation.

At the close of appellant's case in chief, each defendant moved for a directed verdict and the trial judge granted both motions. The basis of the ruling, he explained, was that appellant had failed to produce any medical evidence indicating negligence on Dr. Spence's part in diagnosing appellant's malady or in performing the laminectomy; that there was no proof that Dr. Spence's treatment was responsible for appellant's disabilities; and that notwithstanding some evidence to show negligent post-operative care, an absence of medical testimony to show causality precluded submission of the case against the hospital to the jury. The judge did not allude specifically to the alleged breach of duty by Dr. Spence to divulge the possible consequences of the laminectomy.

We reverse. The testimony of appellant and his mother that Dr. Spence did not reveal the risk of paralysis from the laminectomy made out a prima facie case of violation of the physician's duty to disclose which Dr. Spence's explanation did not negate as a matter of law. . . .

There was also testimony from which the jury could have found that the laminectomy was negligently performed by Dr. Spence, and that appellant's fall was the consequence of negligence on the part of the hospital. The record, moreover, contains evidence of sufficient quantity and quality to tender jury issues as to whether and to what extent any such negligence was causally related to appellant's post-laminectomy condition. These considerations entitled appellant to a new trial. . . .

Suits charging failure by a physician adequately to disclose the risks and alternatives of proposed treatment are not innovations in American law. They date back a good half-century, and in the last decade they have multiplied rapidly. There is, nonetheless, disagreement among the courts and the commentators on many major questions, and there is no precedent of our own directly in point. For the tools enabling resolution of the issues on this appeal, we are forced to begin at first principles.

The root premise is the concept, fundamental in American jurisprudence, that "[e]very human being of adult years and sound mind has a right to determine what shall be done with his own body. . . ." Schloendorff v. Soc'y of N.Y. Hosp., 105 N.E. 92, 93 (N.Y. 1914). True consent to what happens to one's self is the informed exercise of a choice, and that entails an opportunity to evaluate knowledgeably the options available and the risks attendant upon each. The average patient has little or no understanding of the medical arts, and ordinarily has only his physician to whom he can look for enlightenment with which to reach an intelligent decision. From these almost axiomatic considerations springs the need, and in turn the requirement, of a reasonable divulgence by physician to patient to make such a decision possible.[15] . . .

A reasonable revelation in these respects is not only a necessity but, as we see it, is as much a matter of the physician's duty. It is a duty to warn of the dangers lurking in the proposed treatment, and that is surely a facet of due care. It is, too, a duty to impart information which the patient has every right to expect.[27] The patient's reliance upon the physician is a trust of the kind which traditionally has exacted obligations beyond those associated with arms-length transactions. His dependence upon the physician for information affecting his well-being, in terms of contemplated treatment, is well-nigh abject. . . .

Thus the physician has long borne a duty, on pain of liability for unauthorized treatment, to make adequate disclosure to the patient.[36] The evolution of the obligation to communicate

15. In duty-to-disclose cases, the focus of attention is more properly upon the nature and content of the physician's divulgence than the patient's understanding or consent. Adequate disclosure and informed consent are, of course, two sides of the same coin—the former a sine qua non of the latter. But the vital inquiry on duty to disclose relates to the physician's performance of an obligation, while one of the difficulties with analysis in terms of "informed consent" is its tendency to imply that what is decisive is the degree of the patient's comprehension. . . . [T]he physician discharges the duty when he makes a reasonable effort to convey sufficient information although the patient, without fault of the physician, may not fully grasp it.

27. Some doubt has been expressed as to ability of physicians to suitably communicate their evaluations of risks and the advantages of optional treatment, and as to the lay patient's ability to understand what the physician tells him. Karchmer, Informed Consent: . . . We do not share these apprehensions. The discussion need not be a disquisition, and surely the physician is not compelled to give his patient a short medical education; the disclosure rule summons the physician only to a reasonable explanation. That means generally informing the patient in nontechnical terms as to what is at stake: the therapy alternatives open to him, the goals expectably to be achieved, and the risks that may ensue from particular treatment and no treatment. . . . So informing the patient hardly taxes the physician, and it must be the exceptional patient who cannot comprehend such an explanation at least in a rough way.

36. We discard the thought that the patient should ask for information before the physician is required to disclose. Caveat emptor is not the norm for the consumer of medical services. Duty to disclose is more than a call to speak merely on the patient's request, or merely to answer the patient's questions; it is a duty to volunteer, if necessary, the information the patient needs for intelligent decision. The patient may be ignorant, confused, overawed by the physician or frightened by the hospital, or even ashamed to inquire. . . . Perhaps relatively few patients could in any event identify the relevant questions in the absence of prior explanation by the physician. Physicians and hospitals have patients of widely divergent socio-economic backgrounds, and a rule which presumes a degree of sophistication which many members of society lack is likely to breed gross inequities.

for the patient's benefit as well as the physician's protection has hardly involved an extraordinary restructuring of the law.

Duty to disclose has gained recognition in a large number of American jurisdictions, but more largely on a different rationale. The majority of courts dealing with the problem have made the duty depend on whether it was the custom of physicians practicing in the community to make the particular disclosure to the patient. If so, the physician may be held liable for an unreasonable and injurious failure to divulge, but there can be no recovery unless the omission forsakes a practice prevalent in the profession. We agree that the physician's noncompliance with a professional custom to reveal, like any other departure from prevailing medical practice, may give rise to liability to the patient. We do not agree that the patient's cause of action is dependent upon the existence and nonperformance of a relevant professional tradition.

There are, in our view, formidable obstacles to acceptance of the notion that the physician's obligation to disclose is either germinated or limited by medical practice. To begin with, the reality of any discernible custom reflecting a professional consensus on communication of option and risk information to patients is open to serious doubt. We sense the danger that what in fact is no custom at all may be taken as an affirmative custom to maintain silence, and that physician-witnesses to the so-called custom may state merely their personal opinions as to what they or others would do under given conditions. . . . Nor can we ignore the fact that to bind the disclosure obligation to medical usage is to arrogate the decision on revelation to the physician alone. Respect for the patient's right of self-determination on particular therapy demands a standard set by law for physicians rather than one which physicians may or may not impose upon themselves. . . .

. . . We hold that the standard measuring performance of that duty [to disclose] by physicians, as by others, is conduct which is reasonable under the circumstances.

Once the circumstances give rise to a duty on the physician's part to inform his patient, the next inquiry is the scope of the disclosure the physician is legally obliged to make. The courts have frequently confronted this problem but no uniform standard defining the adequacy of the divulgence emerges from the decisions. Some have said "full" disclosure, a norm we are unwilling to adopt literally. It seems obviously prohibitive and unrealistic to expect physicians to discuss with their patients every risk of proposed treatment—no matter how small or remote and generally unnecessary from the patient's viewpoint as well. Indeed, the cases speaking in terms of "full" disclosure appear to envision something less than total disclosure, leaving unanswered the question of just how much.

The larger number of courts, as might be expected, have applied tests framed with reference to prevailing fashion within the medical profession. Some have measured the disclosure by "good medical practice," others by what a reasonable practitioner would have bared under the circumstances, and still others by what medical custom in the community would demand. We have explored this rather considerable body of law but are unprepared to follow it. . . .

In our view, the patient's right of self-decision shapes the boundaries of the duty to reveal. That right can be effectively exercised only if the patient possesses enough information to enable an intelligent choice. The scope of the physician's communications to the patient, then, must be measured by the patient's need, and that need is the information material to the decision. Thus the test for determining whether a particular peril must be divulged is its materiality to the patient's decision: all risks potentially affecting the decision must be unmasked. And to safeguard the patient's interest in achieving his own determination on treatment, the law must itself set the standard for adequate disclosure.

Optimally for the patient, exposure of a risk would be mandatory whenever the patient would deem it significant to his decision, either singly or in combination with other risks. Such a requirement, however, would summon the physician to second-guess the patient, whose ideas on materiality could hardly be known to the physician. That would make an undue demand upon medical practitioners, whose conduct, like that of others, is to be measured in terms of reasonableness. Consonantly with orthodox negligence doctrine, the physician's liability for nondisclosure is to be determined on the basis of foresight, not hindsight; no less than any other aspect of negligence, the issue on nondisclosure must be approached from the viewpoint of the reasonableness of the physician's divulgence in terms of what he knows or should know to be the patient's informational needs. If, but only if, the fact-finder can say that the physician's communication was unreasonably inadequate is an imposition of liability legally or morally justified. . . .

From these considerations we derive the breadth of the disclosure of risks legally to be required. The scope of the standard is not subjective as to either the physician or the patient; it remains objective with due regard for the patient's informational needs and with suitable leeway for the physician's situation. In broad outline, we agree that "[a] risk is thus material when a reasonable person, in what the physician knows or should know to be the patient's position, would be likely to attach significance to the risk or cluster of risks in deciding whether or not to forego the proposed therapy."

The topics importantly demanding a communication of information are the inherent and potential hazards of the proposed treatment, the alternatives to that treatment, if any, and the results likely if the patient remains untreated. The factors contributing significance to the dangerousness of a medical technique are, of course, the incidence of injury and the degree of the harm threatened. A very small chance of death or serious disablement may well be significant; a potential disability which dramatically outweighs the potential benefit of the therapy or the detriments of the existing malady may summon discussion with the patient.[86]

There is no bright line separating the significant from the insignificant; the answer in any case must abide a rule of reason. Some dangers—infection, for example—are inherent in any operation; there is no obligation to communicate those of which persons of average sophistication are aware. Even more clearly, the physician bears no responsibility for discussion of hazards the patient has already discovered, or those having no apparent materiality to patients' decision on therapy. The disclosure doctrine, like others marking lines between permissible and impermissible behavior in medical practice, is in essence a requirement of conduct prudent under the circumstances. Whenever nondisclosure of particular risk information is open to debate by reasonable-minded men, the issue is for the finder of the facts.

Two exceptions to the general rule of disclosure have been noted by the courts. Each is in the nature of a physician's privilege not to disclose, and the reasoning underlying them is appealing. . . . The first comes into play when the patient is unconscious or otherwise incapable of consenting, and harm from a failure to treat is imminent and outweighs any harm threatened by the proposed treatment. When a genuine emergency of that sort arises, it is settled that the impracticality of conferring with the patient dispenses with need for it. Even in situations of that character the physician should, as current law requires, attempt to secure a relative's consent if possible. But if time is too short to accommodate discussion, obviously the physician should proceed with the treatment.

The second exception obtains when risk-disclosure poses such a threat of detriment to the patient as to become unfeasible or contraindicated from a medical point of view. It is recognized that patients occasionally become so ill or emotionally distraught on disclosure as

86. See Bowers v. Talmage, 159 So. 2d 888 (Fla. App. 1963) (3% chance of death, paralysis or other injury, disclosure required); Scott v. Wilson, 396 S.W.2d 532 (Tex. Civ. App. 1965), aff'd, 412 S.W.2d 299 (Tex. 1967) (1% chance of loss of hearing, disclosure required). Compare, where the physician was held not liable: Stottlemire v. Cawood, 213 F. Supp. 897 (D.D.C. 1963) (1/800,000 chance of aplastic anemia); Yeates v. Harms, 393 P.2d 982 (Kan. 1964) (1.5% chance of loss of eye); Starnes v. Taylor, 272 N.C. 386, 158 S.E.2d 339, 344 (1968) (1/250 to 1/500 chance of perforation of esophagus).

to foreclose a rational decision, or complicate or hinder the treatment, or perhaps even pose psychological damage to the patient. Where that is so, the cases have generally held that the physician is armed with a privilege to keep the information from the patient, and we think it clear that portents of that type may justify the physician in action he deems medically warranted. The critical inquiry is whether the physician responded to a sound medical judgment that communication of the risk information would present a threat to the patient's well-being.

The physician's privilege to withhold information for therapeutic reasons must be carefully circumscribed, however, for otherwise it might devour the disclosure rule itself. The privilege does not accept the paternalistic notion that the physician may remain silent simply because divulgence might prompt the patient to forego therapy the physician feels the patient really needs. That attitude presumes instability or perversity for even the normal patient, and runs counter to the foundation principle that the patient should and ordinarily can make the choice for himself.

No more than breach of any other legal duty does nonfulfillment of the physician's obligation to disclose alone establish liability to the patient. . . . [A]s in malpractice actions generally, there must be a causal relationship between the physician's failure to adequately divulge and damage to the patient.

A causal connection exists when, but only when, disclosure of significant risks incidental to treatment would have resulted in a decision against it. The patient obviously has no complaint if he would have submitted to the therapy notwithstanding awareness that the risk was one of its perils. On the other hand, the very purpose of the disclosure rule is to protect the patient against consequences which, if known, he would have avoided by foregoing the treatment. The more difficult question is whether the factual issue on causality calls for an objective or a subjective determination.

It has been assumed that the issue is to be resolved according to whether the fact-finder believes the patient's testimony that he would not have agreed to the treatment if he had known of the danger which later ripened into injury. We think a technique which ties the factual conclusion on causation simply to the assessment of the patient's credibility is unsatisfactory. To be sure, the objective of risk-disclosure is preservation of the patient's interest in intelligent self-choice on proposed treatment, a matter the patient is free to decide for any reason that appeals to him. When, prior to commencement of therapy, the patient is sufficiently informed on risks and he exercises his choice, it may truly be said that he did exactly what he wanted to do. But when causality is explored at a post-injury trial with a professedly uninformed patient, the question whether he actually would have turned the treatment down if he had known the risks is purely hypothetical: "Viewed from the point at which he had to decide, would the patient have decided differently had he known something he did not know?" And the answer which the patient supplies hardly represents more than a guess, perhaps tinged by the circumstance that the uncommunicated hazard has in fact materialized.

In our view, this method of dealing with the issue on causation comes in second-best. It places the physician in jeopardy of the patient's hindsight and bitterness. It places the fact-finder in the position of deciding whether a speculative answer to a hypothetical question is to be credited. It calls for a subjective determination solely on testimony of a patient-witness shadowed by the occurrence of the undisclosed risk.

Better it is, we believe, to resolve the causality issue on an objective basis: in terms of what a prudent person in the patient's position would have decided if suitably informed of all perils bearing significance. If adequate disclosure could reasonably be expected to have caused that person to decline the treatment because of the revelation of the kind of risk or danger that resulted in harm, causation is shown, but otherwise not. The patient's testimony is relevant on that score of course but it would not threaten to dominate the findings. . . .

[The court ordered a new trial because: (1) the appellant testified that he was not told of the hazards of the operation; (2) his mother was told that the laminectomy was no more serious than any other operation; (3) Dr. Spence himself testified about the 1 percent risk of paralysis; and (4) there was no evidence that appellant's "emotional makeup was such that concealment of the risk of paralysis was medically sound.[138]"]

NOTES

1. *The Case on Remand.* What issues were left to be resolved in *Canterbury* on remand? If the risk of paralysis from falling out of bed is common knowledge, does it make a difference that the defendant did not disclose the risk of paralysis from the operation itself? How ought Canterbury's prior condition be taken into account in assessing damages? On retrial the jury found for the defendants on liability. Its decision was affirmed on appeal, without opinion. 509 F.2d 537 (D.C. Cir. 1975).

2. *Materiality of Risk.* Under current law, what level of risk is needed to trigger the duty to disclose? In Kozup v. Georgetown University, 663 F. Supp. 1048, 1053–54 (D.D.C. 1987), the parents of the decedent, Matthew Kozup, brought an informed consent claim against the defendant hospital, which in 1983 transfused Matthew at birth with blood contaminated with the human immunodeficiency virus (HIV), from which he died three years later. Flannery, J., dismissed the suit against the hospital, holding that the risk of AIDS from HIV was not material in 1983. The court stressed that in January 1983, only a single case of possible transfusion-related AIDS had been diagnosed out of the 3.5 million annual blood donations. Moreover, its viral agent HTLV-III would only be identified 15 months later. It then addressed the causation question as follows:

> However, in addition to this flaw in plaintiffs' theory, a second equally fatal problem remains. Even if plaintiffs could show that the risk of AIDS would have been material to their decision regarding Matthew's transfusions, plaintiffs must also show that the hospital's failure to warn of that risk *caused* the injury involved. That is, plaintiffs must show that "disclosure of significant risks incidental to treatment would have resulted in a decision against it." *Canterbury.* No reasonable jury could conclude on the facts of this case that, had the Kozups been informed of a one in 3.5 million possibility of contracting AIDS, they would have declined to permit Georgetown's physicians to transfuse blood into their son. Matthew was premature and his birth was accompanied by many complications including hypovolemia. The transfusions were absolutely necessary to save his life.

On appeal, Kozup v. Georgetown University, 851 F.2d 437 (D.C. Cir. 1988), the court agreed that the informed consent count failed on materiality but remanded the case for a new trial on an alternative battery count, noting that no parental consent had been obtained at all. It rejected, at least for summary judgment purposes, the hospital's theory that "there is no necessity to obtain parent consent for life-saving treatment." If the claim were valid, what would the damages be?

In subsequent cases, expert evidence established that blood banks were negligent in failing to perceive material transfusion risks of AIDS in early 1983. See, e.g., United Blood Services

---

138. Dr. Spence's opinion — that disclosure is medically unwise — was expressed as to patients generally, and not with reference to traits possessed by appellant. His explanation was:

> I think that I always explain to patients the operations are serious, and I feel that any operation is serious. I think that I would not tell patients that they might be paralyzed because of the small percentage, one per cent, that exists. There would be a tremendous percentage of people that would not have surgery and would not therefore be benefited by it, the tremendous percentage that get along very well, 99 per cent.

v. Quintana, 827 P.2d 509 (Colo. 1992). Knowledge advanced so rapidly between January and May of 1983 that the focus of attention at the latter time was not on informed consent but on developing effective institutional safeguards against the transmission of HIV. Note that conformity with professional blood bank testing standards is not an absolute defense after *The T.J. Hooper*. What safeguards, if any, should be introduced to deal with the risk of 20/20 hindsight?

Modern cases rarely involve a repetition of *Canterbury*, as disclosure obligations are now fully internalized into the standard practice of medicine. No longer is disclosure a simple bedside chat between physician and patient on the eve of surgery; it is common for physician groups to prepare standardized material about some planned procedure, which is often communicated by specialists who work with group practices. Signed documents about disclosures are commonplace, and, in some instances, any conversation with a health care provider may be recorded. In addition, the Internet provides extensive materials that give independent sources of information for various conditions. Telemedicine similarly allows for medical updates without hospital or office visits. While the law of informed consent has not changed too much in the last fifty years, the practice of medicine on the disclosure issue has.

3. *Particularity of Disclosure.* Courts have commonly resisted demands for disclosure of the full range of treatment alternatives in complex cases. In Valles v. Albert Einstein Medical Center, 805 A.2d 1232, 1239–40 (Pa. 2002), the decedent, Lope Valles, was admitted into the defendant medical center for treatment of a suspected abdominal aortic aneurysm — a weakness in the wall of the aorta. When surgery was postponed due to subsequent loss of kidney function, the treating physicians recommended the use of a "Permacath" device, suitable for prolonged dialysis. The surgical resident advised Valles of certain risks associated with the insertion of Permacath, "including bleeding, infection, collapsing of a lung and death," but he did not discuss the relative advantages and disadvantages from different placements in veins in the neck, chest, or groin. When one treating physician, Dr. Morros, tried inserting the Permacath in a chest vein, Valles suffered adverse reactions, went into cardiac arrest, and died. The trial court kept the informed consent case from the jury, but the Superior Court reversed and allowed the case to go to the jury, saying that "informed consent applies to the method or manner of surgery and the risks associated therewith." The Pennsylvania Supreme Court rebuffed this position:

> We recently reiterated . . . that "the doctrine of informed consent is a limited one." In light of this limited scope, we find that the manner or method in which the surgeon performs the proposed procedure is not encompassed within the purview of the informed consent doctrine. Although there were several methods of performing the particular surgery, there was only one surgery proposed: the insertion of a Permacath. Appellant does not dispute that Valles was adequately informed of the risks attending the surgery: bleeding, lung collapse, and death. That the subclavian vein [in the chest] may not have been the optimum site is not an issue of informed consent, but of negligence in the physician's decision to place the Permacath at that site.

The dissent insisted that "the patient should be advised of those alternative types of treatment, i.e., the viable locations for the surgery, as well as the risks associated with each location." Who is right?

With *Valles*, contrast Felton v. Lovett, 388 S.W.3d 656 (Tex. 2012), where the defendant, a chiropractor, performed "forceful manipulation" on the plaintiff after which he "suffered a stroke resulting from a vertebral artery dissection." At trial, the plaintiff's expert witness testified that

- vertebral artery dissection is a known risk of neck adjustments but occurs only if the patient's artery is unhealthy or if the adjustment is performed improperly;
- chiropractors have been aware of the risk for a long time;

- there are safer alternatives to manual adjustment that do not run the risk of stroke;
- about 10 to 20% of vertebral dissections are preceded by chiropractic manipulation of the spine. . . .

On the strength of this evidence, Hecht, J., concluded:

> The same kind of injury may occur in other patients undergoing the same kind of treatment. The risk that a patient will not respond well to treatment is clearly one that inheres in the treatment. And as the evidence indicated, and the jury found, the possibility of vertebral artery dissection and stroke is precisely the kind of information a reasonable patient would be expected to want to know before deciding whether to risk such severe consequences in order to alleviate neck pain.

4. *A Subjective or Objective Standard?* *Canterbury*'s objective standard of care (one that considers what a *hypothetical patient* would have done had they been informed of the risk) was picked up in Cobbs v. Grant, 502 P.2d 1 (Cal. 1972), where Mosk J., refused to place the "physician in jeopardy of the patient's bitterness and disillusionment" resulting from "20/20 hindsight." Likewise, Holder, J., in Ashe v. Radiation Oncology Assocs., 9 S.W.3d 119, 123 (Tenn. 1999), commented:

> The objective approach circumvents the need to place the fact-finder in a position of deciding whether a speculative and perhaps emotional answer to a purely hypothetical question shall dictate the outcome of the litigation.

A minority of jurisdictions adopt the subjective standard instead to reinforce individual autonomy. In Pergolizzi v. Bowman, 882 S.E.2d 1, 16–17 (Va. Ct. App. 2022) Lorish, J., explains the rationale:

> A subjective standard . . . adheres to the principles underlying the informed consent doctrine—that every human being of adult years and sound mind has a right to determine what shall be done with his own body. In contrast, an objective standard severely limits the protection granted an injured patient because to the extent the plaintiff, given an adequate disclosure, would have declined the proposed treatment, and a reasonable person in similar circumstances would have consented, a patient's right of self-determination is irrevocably lost.

In Arena v. Gingrich, 748 P.2d 547 (Or. 1988), Linde, J., held that Oregon's informed consent statute, Or. Rev. Stat. §677.097 (2023), precluded the objective standard: "The statute having defined the standard of disclosure without requiring reference to what a prudent patient reasonably would want to know, we shall not reintroduce that hypothetical prudent patient by the back door of 'causation.' " Is it wise to leave it to juries to parse, under a subjective standard, plaintiffs' testimony, which will inevitably be self-serving?

5. *Expert Testimony in Informed Consent Cases.* *Canterbury* held that

> [l]ay witness testimony can competently establish a physician's failure to disclose particular risk information, the patient's lack of knowledge of the risk, and the adverse consequences following the treatment. Experts are unnecessary to a showing of the materiality of a risk to a patient's decision on treatment, or to the reasonably, expectable effect of risk disclosure on the decision.

In Bly v. Rhoads, 222 S.E.2d 783, 787–88 (Va. 1976), the plaintiff sued under an informed consent theory for the adverse consequences of a hysterectomy. The court followed *Canterbury* insofar as it allowed the plaintiff "to establish by lay evidence that his physician did not disclose particular risk information and that he, the patient, had no knowledge of the risk." It also agreed that lay evidence was sometimes admissible "to show the adverse consequences following treatment," and it left open the possibility that infrequently "the duty of disclosure is so obvious that expert testimony should not be required." But it broke with

Canterbury in requiring expert evidence on the full range of complex issues raised by the disclosure question.

> We believe the better rule, which we now adopt, is to require a patient-plaintiff to show by qualified medical experts whether and to what extent information should be disclosed by the physician to his patient. This rule would not, contrary to what *Canterbury* suggests, impose an undue burden upon the patient-plaintiff. After all, in the usual case, the patient unquestionably will have obtained experts to establish the negligent treatment phase of his malpractice action.

Bly represents the majority view on expert evidence, which is often codified. See, e.g., Ark. Code Ann. §16-114-206(b) (2023), which was sustained against a constitutional challenge in Eady v. Lansford, 92 S.W.3d 57, 61 (Ark. 2002), in the absence of any showing "that the legislation is *not* rationally related to achieving any legitimate objective of the government. . . ." Indeed, the court intimated that protecting the medical profession against vexatious litigation justified both requiring expert testimony and adopting the customary care standard rejected in *Canterbury*.

6. *Legislative Response to Informed Consent.* In the wake of *Canterbury*, many legislatures codified the law of informed consent, often at the request of insurance companies and medical organizations. The New York statute, New York Pub. Health Law §2805-d (McKinney 2023), provides that

> [l]ack of informed consent means the failure of the person providing the professional treatment or diagnosis to disclose to the patient such alternatives thereto and the reasonably foreseeable risks and benefits involved as a reasonable medical . . . practitioner under similar circumstances would have disclosed, in a manner permitting the patient to make a knowledgeable evaluation.

Recovery for malpractice "based on a lack of informed consent is limited to those cases involving either (a) non-emergency treatment, procedure or surgery, or (b) a diagnostic procedure which involved invasion or disruption of the integrity of the body." Additionally, a viable defense exists when

> the medical . . . practitioner, after considering all of the attendant facts and circumstances, used reasonable discretion as to the manner and extent to which such alternatives or risks were disclosed to the patient because he reasonably believed that the manner and extent of such disclosure could reasonably be expected to adversely and substantially affect the patient's condition.

How does this statutory regime differ from *Canterbury*? Is the statute preferable to a general good-faith standard whereby doctors make whatever disclosures they regard as appropriate under the circumstances?

Are further legislative reforms sensible in light of modern developments in medical science and health care delivery? Twerski & Cohen, The Second Revolution in Informed Consent: Comparing Physicians to Each Other, 94 Nw. U. L. Rev. 1 (1999), would require managed care organizations to disclose "comparative statistics," which assess the relative risks associated with an individual's *providers* who perform a particular procedure, to plan participants. Comparing informed consent in the treatment and research contexts, Grimm, Informed Consent for All! No Exceptions, 37 N.M. L. Rev. 39 (2007), argues that disclosures in connection with medical research should be significantly more stringent, and permit no exceptions, to ensure sufficient protection for personal autonomy. On the other side, howls of protest have been raised against the excessive delays in experimental research stemming from highly restrictive protocols that drive research away. For a wide range of opinions on this issue, see Symposium, 101 Nw. U. L. Rev. 837 (2007).

7. *The British Rejection of Canterbury.* The duty to disclose, now widely accepted in the United States, has run into strong hostility in England. In Sidaway v. Bethlem Royal Hospital, [1985] All Eng. Rep. 1018, 1030, 1031, the English Court of Appeal explicitly rejected

Canterbury in a case in which the defendant surgeon did tell a patient undergoing an elective laminectomy of the 1 or 2 percent risk of minor nerve damage but decided not to mention the under-one-percent risk of permanent damage to the spinal cord. The dismissal of the plaintiff's suit below was affirmed on appeal with Dunn, L.J., commenting:

> I confess that I reach this conclusion with no regret. The evidence in this case showed that a contrary result would be damaging to the relationship of trust and confidence between doctor and patient, and might well have an adverse effect on the practice of medicine. It is doubtful whether it would be of any significant benefit to patients, most of whom prefer to put themselves unreservedly in the hands of their doctors. This is not in my view "paternalism," to repeat an evocative word used in argument. It is simply an acceptance of the doctor/patient relationship as it has developed in this country. The principal effect of accepting the proposition advanced by the plaintiff would be likely to be an increase in the number of claims for professional negligence against doctors. This would be likely to have an adverse effect on the general standard of medical care, since doctors would inevitably be concerned to safeguard themselves against such claims, rather than to concentrate on their primary duty of treating their patients.

British judges remain more skeptical of informed consent cases. In Pearce v. United Bristol Healthcare NHS Trust, 48 BMLR 118 (1998), Lord Woolf MR reiterated the concerns raised in *Bethlem* only to conclude that "a significant event" did not include an increased risk of one to two in 1,000 that a child might be stillborn if not delivered.

8. *Contracts in Informed Consent Cases.* A more radical approach to the informed consent issue would allow physicians and patients to determine the proper scope of disclosure by private agreement. Arguments supporting that conclusion are found in Epstein, Medical Malpractice: The Case for Contract, 1 Am. B. Found. Res. J. 87, 119–28 (1976). A more bittersweet evaluation is found in Schuck, *supra* at 166, at 957–58, which notes the tension between the defense of autonomous choices and the use of the prudent patient standard for disclosure:

> Like the "reasonable person" standard and other objective standards in tort law, the existing uniform approach to informed consent has two virtues: it is cheaper to know and administer, and it seeks to protect patients against gross inequalities of bargaining power vis-à-vis providers. But a doctrine that treats all patients and physician-patient relationships as essentially homogenous when in fact they are not exacts a price. Specifically, the law requires a level of informed consent that is different from the level that many consumers or groups of consumers want and for which they would be willing to pay if the choice were presented to them. The existing doctrine, then, suffers from an ironic, if endemic vice: it deprives patients of choice in the name of choice.

(5)

SECTION E. STATUTES AND REGULATIONS

This section explores the ways in which statutes can add precision to the general negligence standard of reasonable care. Typically a statute involved in a negligence case provides for the state to administer some penalty in the case of violation, usually a fine, but sometimes incarceration or, occasionally, injunctive relief. The term "statute" is broadly construed to include not only state legislative acts, but also local ordinances, federal laws, and state and federal administrative regulations. RTT: LPEH §14, comment *a*. Traditionally this inquiry was raised in connection with traffic accidents, where violation of motor vehicle laws remains central to the negligence determination. RTT: LPEH §14, comment *d*. Litigation now frequently extends to the full range of health and safety statutes characteristic of the modern administrative state.

A statute can play a role in the determination of negligence in three distinct ways. First, the statute can *create* a private right of action by providing (either expressly or impliedly) that an individual injured by a violation of the statute can sue the offender. Second, the plaintiff can bring a common law negligence suit for her injuries. In that case, the defendant's violation of a relevant statute may constitute "negligence per se." Third, even if the defendant's statutory violation does not constitute negligence per se (usually because the situation does not satisfy criteria that limit the scope of the doctrine), the plaintiff can still argue that the defendant's underlying conduct was negligent.

Anon.

(1703) 87 Eng. Rep. 791 (KB)

Holt, C.J. [F]or wherever a statute enacts anything, or prohibits anything, for the advantage of any person, that person shall have remedy to recover the advantage given him, or to have satisfaction for the injury done him contrary to law by the same statute; for it would be a fine thing to make a law by which one has a right, but no remedy but in equity. . . .

Ezra Ripley Thayer

Public Wrong and Private Action

27 Harv. L. Rev. 317, 321–22 (1914), *reprinted in* Selected Essays on the Law of Torts 276, 280–81 (1924)

Before the ordinance the plaintiff, injured by the runaway horse, must have based his action on negligence. Whether the defendant was negligent in leaving the horse unhitched would have been for the jury to say, unless this was so clear one way or the other that the court must deal with it as a "question of law" (so-called); i.e., as a point on which fair minds could reach but one conclusion. In any situation less extreme the whole matter would have been within the jury's province. And the jury was bound in deciding it to use the test of the "ordinary prudent man." They could not acquit the defendant of negligence without saying that an ordinary prudent man would have left his horse unhitched under these circumstances; that with such a horse as this, and in such a place, the prudent man would have foreseen no danger to others—for the foresight of the prudent man in the defendant's position (in other words, the probability of danger from his standpoint) is the test of negligence. The jury was justified either in accepting or rejecting the theory that he was negligent, for the mere fact of submitting the issue of negligence to them means that a finding either way is warranted by the evidence. The reasonableness of the defendant's conduct was thus in the eye of the law an open question, depending on the circumstances and the inferences fairly to be drawn from them.

Suppose now the situation to be changed by the single circumstance of the ordinance, all other facts remaining the same. Can the issue of negligence any longer be left to the jury? Not unless they would be justified in finding for either party; and what must a finding for the defendant on this issue mean? That an ordinary prudent man, knowing the ordinance—for upon familiar principles he can claim no benefit from his ignorance of the law—would have chosen to break it, "reasonably" believing that damage would not result from his action. It must then, upon this view, be deemed consistent with ordinary prudence for an individual to set his own opinion against the judgment authoritatively pronounced by constituted public authority, for the ordinance has prohibited leaving *all* horses unhitched, without exception, and has done this in order to prevent just such consequences as have occurred. It has thus declared the danger to be so serious and constant that a less sweeping prohibition would be inadequate. And when eminent courts, using familiar phraseology, state that the breach of the ordinance is not "negligence per se," but only "evidence of negligence," and leave the question of negligence as a fact to the jury, they are doing nothing less than informing that body that it may properly stamp with approval, as reasonable conduct, the action of one who has assumed to place his own foresight above that of the legislature in respect of the very danger which it was legislating to prevent.

NOTES

1. ***Thayer in Action.*** Statutory commands still retain the force that Thayer attributed to them more than a century ago. The Third Restatement proclaims that "courts, exercising their common law duty to develop tort doctrine, not only should regard the actor's statutory violation as evidence admissible against the actor, but should treat that violation as actually determining the actor's negligence." RTT: LPEH §14, comment *c.* In Schmitz v. Canadian Pacific Railway, 454 F.3d 678, 684 (7th Cir. 2006), the plaintiff inspector fell into a hole alongside the tracks when the defendant had not cleared away the vegetation as required by federal regulation. The trial judge did not instruct the jury on the mandatory force of the regulation, and his decision was reversed on appeal.

> There can be little doubt that the omission of an instruction on [the regulation] prejudiced Schmitz's case. Canadian Pacific argues that the jury still heard the essence of Schmitz's claim regarding the regulation—that Schmitz alleged the railroad was negligent because it did not keep the vegetation trimmed. But there is a world of difference between telling the jury that Schmitz alleged the railroad should have taken a particular precaution and telling the jury that federal law *required* the railroad to take that very precaution. By not instructing the jury on the federal regulation, the district judge left it up to the jury to decide whether the railroad had a duty to keep the vegetation trimmed. The regulation answers that question in the affirmative—the railroad was required under federal law to keep the vegetation trimmed. The jury should have been deciding only whether the railroad violated the regulation and whether the violation was a cause of Schmitz's injury.

2. ***Defective Statutes as a Source of Duty.*** Thayer relies on the common notion of legislative supremacy to justify the rule that noncompliance with a statute counts as negligence per se. The Third Restatement likewise privileges "the judgment of the legislature, as the authoritative representative of the community" over the jury's assessment of reasonable conduct. RTT: LPEH §14, comment *c.* One test of this thesis examines the role of statutory provisions not currently in force. Assume that an otherwise valid criminal safety statute is invalid because of a technical defect in the enacting procedure. In Thayer's view, could it set the standard of care in a negligence action? Nonetheless, in Clinkscales v. Carver, 136 P.2d 777, 778–79 (Cal. 1943), Traynor, J., held that while the state could not criminally enforce its laws when it erected a stop sign pursuant to a defective statute, nonetheless for a highway user it "was negligence as a matter of law to disregard the stop sign."

> If a through artery has been posted with stop signs by the public authorities in the customary way and to all appearances by regular procedure, any reasonable man should know that the public naturally relies upon their observance. If a driver from a side street enters the ostensibly protected boulevard without stopping, in disregard of the posted safeguards, contrary to what drivers thereon could reasonably have expected him to do, he is guilty of negligence regardless of any irregularity attending the authorization of the signs.

Osborne v. McMasters

41 N.W. 543 (Minn. 1889)

MITCHELL, J. Upon the record in this case it must be taken as the facts that defendant's clerk in his drug-store, in the course of his employment as such, sold to plaintiff's intestate a deadly poison without labeling it "Poison," as required by statute; that she, in ignorance of its deadly qualities, partook of the poison, which caused her death. Except for the ability of counsel and the earnestness with which they have argued the case, we would not have supposed that there could be any serious doubt of defendant's liability on this state of facts. It is immaterial for present purposes whether section 329 of the Penal Code or section 14, c. 147, Laws 1885, or both, are still in force, and constitute the law governing this case. The requirements of both statutes are substantially the same, and the sole object of both is to protect the public against the dangerous qualities of poison. It is now well settled, certainly in this state, that where a statute or municipal ordinance imposes upon any person a specific duty for the protection or benefit of others, if he neglects to perform that duty he is liable to those for whose protection or benefit it was imposed for any injuries of the character which the statute or ordinance was designed to prevent, and which were proximately produced by such neglect. . . .

Defendant contends that this is only true where a right of action for the alleged negligent act existed at common law; that no liability existed at common law for selling poison without labeling it, and therefore none exists under this statute, no right of civil action being given by it. Without stopping to consider the correctness of the assumption that selling poison without labeling it might not be actionable negligence at common law, it is sufficient to say that, in our opinion, defendant's contention proceeds upon an entire misapprehension of the nature and gist of a cause of action of this kind. The common law gives a right of action to every one sustaining injuries caused proximately by the negligence of another. The present is a common-law action, the gist of which is defendant's negligence, resulting in the death of plaintiff's intestate. Negligence is the breach of legal duty. It is immaterial whether the duty is one imposed by the rule of common law requiring the exercise of ordinary care not to injure another, or is imposed by a statute designed for the protection of others. In either case the failure to perform the duty constitutes negligence, and renders the party liable for injuries resulting from it. The only difference is that in the one case the measure of legal duty is to be determined upon common-law principles, while in the other the statute fixes it, so that the violation of the statute constitutes conclusive evidence of negligence, or, in other words, negligence per se. The action in the latter case is not a statutory one, nor does the statute give the right of action in any other sense except that it makes an act negligent which otherwise might not be such, or at least only evidence of negligence. All that the statute does is to establish a fixed standard by which the fact of negligence may be determined. The gist of the action is still negligence, or the non-performance of a legal duty to the person injured.

Judgment affirmed.

NOTES

1. ***Statutory Causes of Action Versus Negligence Per Se.*** *Osborne* rejects the notion that, unless a statute creates an explicit private right of action, it cannot set the relevant standard of care in a common law negligence action. The Second and Third Restatements embrace *Osborne's* position. Relative to custom, where the violation of custom serves only as some evidence of negligence, violations of statutes typically have dispositive force (i.e., negligence per se). Why the difference?

RESTATEMENT OF THE LAW (SECOND) OF TORTS

§286. When Standard of Conduct Defined by Legislation or Regulation will be Adopted

The court may adopt as the standard of conduct of a reasonable man the requirements of a legislative enactment or an administrative regulation whose purpose is found to be exclusively or in part

(a) to protect a class of persons which includes the one whose interest is invaded, and

(b) to protect the particular interest which is invaded, and

(c) to protect that interest against the kind of harm which has resulted, and

(d) to protect that interest against the particular hazard from which the harm results.

RESTATEMENT OF THE LAW (THIRD) OF TORTS: LIABILITY FOR PHYSICAL AND EMOTIONAL HARM

§14. Statutory Violations as Negligence Per Se

An actor is negligent if, without excuse, the actor violates a statute that is designed to protect against the type of accident the actor's conduct causes, and if the accident victim is within the class of persons the statute is designed to protect.

CALIFORNIA EVIDENCE CODE (2023)

§669(A). Due Care; Failure to Exercise

The failure of a person to exercise due care is presumed if:

(1) He violated a statute, ordinance, or regulation of a public entity;

(2) The violation proximately caused death or injury to person or property;

(3) The death or injury resulted from an occurrence of the nature which the statute, ordinance, or regulation was designed to prevent; and

(4) The person suffering the death or the injury to his person or property was one of the class of persons for whose protection the statute, ordinance, or regulation was adopted.

2. *Who Is Protected?* Even where the statute supports a private right of action, the plaintiff must show that she falls within the class of protected individuals, which is easier to do when a single statute is found to serve multiple purposes. In Stimpson v. Wellington Service Corp., 246 N.E.2d 801, 805 (Mass. 1969), the defendant drove a 137-ton rig over city streets without having obtained the necessary statutory permit. The weight of defendant's truck dislocated and broke the pipes in plaintiff's building, flooding the premises. The court found that the statute had a dual purpose.

> Undoubtedly the primary purpose of the statute was to protect the ways themselves from injury from overloaded vehicles. But the Cambridge authorities, in considering an application for a permit under the statute, should have weighed as well other possible effects of the proposal, particularly because of the prohibition of the city ordinance against moving over city streets vehicles so loaded as to be likely to injure property. Failure to apply for a permit meant that the appropriate authority did not have the opportunity to appraise the risks and probabilities and to refuse the permit or impose conditions.

3. *Actions "for any Injuries of the Character Which the Statute or Ordinance Was Designed to Prevent."* In Gorris v. Scott, [1874] LR 9 Exch. 125, 129, the plaintiff had shipped a number of sheep with the defendant shipowner who failed to pen them in accordance with the requirement of the Contagious Disease (Animals) Act of 1869. The animals were washed overboard in a storm and "were lost by reason of the neglect to comply" with administrative orders issued pursuant to the statute. Notwithstanding this causal connection between plaintiff's harm and defendant's breach of statutory duty, Kelly, C.B., denied plaintiff's recovery:

> [I]f we could see that it was the object, or among the objects of this Act, that the owners of sheep and cattle coming from a foreign port should be protected by the means described against the danger of their property being washed overboard, or lost by the perils of the sea, the present action would be within the principle.
>
> But, looking at the Act, it is perfectly clear that its provisions were all enacted with a totally different view; there was no purpose, direct or indirect, to protect against such damage; but, as is recited in the preamble, the Act is directed against the possibility of sheep or cattle being exposed to disease on their way to this country. . . . That being so, if by reason of the default in question the plaintiffs' sheep had been overcrowded, or had been caused unnecessary suffering, and so had arrived in this country in a state of disease, I do not say that they might not have maintained this action. But the damage complained of here is something totally apart from the object of the Act of Parliament, and it is in accordance with all the authorities to say that the action is not maintainable.

Could the plaintiff have maintained an action for breach of the contract of carriage? What about a common law negligence action for not having animal pens, irrespective of the statute?

In Abrahams v. Young & Rubicam, Inc., 79 F.3d 234, 237 (2d Cir. 1996), Winter, J., stressed the difference between statutory claims and common law claims as follows:

> At common law, so long as the plaintiff category is foreseeable, there is no requirement that the risk of injury to the plaintiff, and the risk of the harm that actually occurred, were what made the defendant's actions wrongful in the first place. With statutory claims, the issue is, instead, one of statutory intent: was the plaintiff (even though foreseeably injured) in the category the statute meant to protect, and was the harm that occurred (again, even if foreseeable), the "mischief" the statute sought to avoid.

By contrast, this distinction between common law duties of care and statutory duties was questioned by Posner, J., in Shadday v. Omni Hotels Management Corp., 477 F.3d 511, 517–18 (7th Cir. 2007):

> The violation of a statutory standard of care is negligence; so is a violation of a common law duty of care. In either case, the puzzle of the line of cases that descends from *Gorris* is why the defendant, having been negligent, should get off scot-free just because the harm that would have been averted had he been careful was not foreseeable. No doubt the framers of the Contagious Diseases (Animals) Act made no judgment that the cost of pens was less than the expected cost of a mass drowning of unpenned animals, but that seems irrelevant. Given that the ship-owner was under a legal duty to pen the sheep, why should he not be liable for a disaster that would have been averted if only he had complied with his duty?

4. *Violation of Licensing Requirements.* The question frequently arises whether lack of license—for example, to practice medicine, or to operate a motor vehicle on the highway—alone constitutes negligence. Noting that "the immediate reason for the person's lack of a license is [often] unrelated to the state's general safety purpose," the Third Restatement concludes that the lack of a required license is neither negligence per se, nor evidence of negligence, unless the evidence indicates that the defendant has also violated the "substantive safety standards" enforced by the licensing requirement. RTT: LPEH §14, comment *h*. Michaels v. Avitech, 202 F.3d 746, 752 (2000), involved a plane flown by an unlicensed pilot that crashed and killed all four passengers on board. The Fifth Circuit noted that "the violation of licensing regulations is often an exception to the general rule that the violation of a safety regulation or statute is negligence per se. . . . One reason . . . is that there may be reasons a license has not been renewed that do not relate to the operator's lack of skill."

In Brown v. Shyne, 151 N.E. 197 (N.Y. 1926), the defendant chiropractor, who had no license to practice medicine, held himself out as licensed to practice medicine when he operated on the plaintiff's spine, which led to her paralysis. The plaintiff asked for a jury instruction that said that the physician should be held liable for the accident no matter what level of care was provided because the injury would not have occurred had he not attempted to treat her back at all. That position was rejected by Lehman, J.:

> True, if the defendant had not practiced medicine in this State, he could not have injured the plaintiff, but the protection which the statute was intended to provide was against risk of injury by the unskilled or careless practitioner, and unless the plaintiff's injury was caused by carelessness or lack of skill, the defendant's failure to obtain a license was not connected with the injury.

On this view, the physician who practices without a license may be subject to a fine for a misdemeanor, but his conduct is judged by the same standard of negligence used to evaluate the conduct of a licensed physician. The dissent of Crane, J., took the opposite view:

> The law, to insure against ignorance and carelessness, has laid down a rule to be followed, namely, examinations to test qualifications, and a license to practice. If a man, in violation of this statute, takes his chances in trying to cure disease, and his acts result directly in injury, he should not complain if the law, in a suit for damages, says that his violation of the statute is some evidence of his incapacity.

RTT: LPEH §14, comment *h*, appears to endorse the outcome in *Brown*: "In light, then, of the combination of the statutory-purpose doctrine and ordinary principles of scope of liability, the lack of a license is not negligence per se on the part of the actor, nor is it evidence tending to show the actor's negligence." Compare this view with section 4504 of the New York Civil Practice Law and Rules (McKinney 2023):

> (d) Proof of negligence; unauthorized practice of medicine. In any action for damages for personal injuries or death against a person not authorized to practice medicine . . . for any act or acts constituting the practice of medicine, when such act or acts were a competent producing proximate or contributing cause of such injuries or death, the fact that such person practiced medicine without being so authorized shall be deemed prima facie evidence of negligence.

5. *Private Rights of Action Under Federal Statutes.* In recent times, one vital question is whether plaintiffs may maintain tort actions for defendant's breach of a *federal* statute or regulation under either federal or state law, given the federalism concerns that arise whenever a state court infers a private right of action from a federal statute. See RTT: LPEH §14, comment *c*, Reporter's Note.

At the federal level, the earlier tendency was to freely imply causes of action, as is done in state courts dealing with state statutes. See J.I. Case Co. v. Borak, 377 U.S. 426 (1964). Subsequently, however, the Supreme Court has taken a much more restrictive view of the availability of federal relief. In the watershed case of Cort v. Ash, 422 U.S. 66, 78 (1975), the Court held:

> In determining whether a private remedy is implicit in a statute not expressly providing one, several factors are relevant. First, is the plaintiff "one of the class for whose *especial* benefit the statute was enacted," . . . that is, does the statute create a federal right in favor of the plaintiff? Second, is there any indication of legislative intent, explicit or implicit, either to create such a remedy or to deny one? . . . Third, is it consistent with the underlying purposes of the legislative scheme to imply such a remedy for the plaintiff? . . . And finally, is the cause of action one traditionally relegated to state law, in an area basically the concern of the States, so that it would be inappropriate to infer a cause of action based solely on federal law?

Subsequent Supreme Court decisions confirm the hostile attitude to implying private rights of action in federal statutes. See, e.g., City of Milwaukee v. Illinois, 451 U.S. 304 (1981), where the Court refused to allow a private cause of action for nuisance, which it held was inconsistent with the comprehensive scheme of control imposed by the federal water pollution acts. Assuming the federal statute at issue does not expressly or impliedly preempt state tort law liability (see *infra* Chapter 8, Section F), is the state free to adopt or reject the federal standard as a basis for a private suit?

As the Supreme Court noted in Grable & Sons v. Darue Engineering & Manufacturing, 545 U.S. 308, 318 (2005), even where no private right of action is available, "violation of federal statutes and regulations is commonly given negligence per se effect in state tort proceedings" (quoting Draft No. 1 of the Restatement (Third) of Torts, Reporters' Notes to §14, comment *a*). RTT: LPEH §14, comment *a*, Reporter's Note elaborates:

> One might have expected that some state courts, concerned with protecting state lawmaking prerogatives, would have resisted allowing violation of federal regulations to be given the effect of negligence per se; but that resistance has not materialized.

Lowe v. General Motors Corp., 624 F.2d 1373, 1379 (5th Cir. 1980), illustrates the majority position, by holding that the plaintiff stated a valid state law cause of action when he alleged that the recall and notice practices of the defendant, General Motors, did not comply with the National Traffic and Motor Vehicle Safety Act, 15 U.S.C.A. §1402(a), because Cort v. Ash was inapplicable to a wrongful death action maintained under Alabama law. "This Court has often held that violation of a Federal law or regulation can be evidence of negligence, and even evidence of negligence per se." Contrast with the minority position espoused by Short v. Marvin Keller Trucking, Inc., 570 F. Supp. 3d 459, 466 (E.D. Ky. 2021): "the General Assembly did not intend . . . to embrace the whole of federal laws and the laws of other states and thereby confer a private civil remedy for such a vast array of violations."

Martin v. Herzog

126 N.E. 814 (N.Y. 1920)

[The decedent was killed in a collision between the buggy he was driving and defendant's automobile. The accident occurred after dark, and decedent was driving the buggy without any lights, in violation of a statute. The defendant requested a ruling that the absence of a light on the plaintiff's vehicle was "prima facie evidence of contributory negligence." This request was refused, and the jury was instructed that it might consider the absence of lights as some evidence of negligence, but not conclusive evidence of negligence. The plaintiff next requested a charge that "the fact that the plaintiff's intestate was driving without a light is not negligence in itself," and to this the court acceded. The jury found the defendant liable and the decedent free from contributory negligence and the plaintiff had judgment. The appellate division reversed for error in the instructions. Affirmed.]

Cardozo, J. We think the unexcused omission of the statutory signals is more than some evidence of negligence. It *is* negligence in itself. Lights are intended for the guidance and protection of other travelers on the highway (Highway Law, sec. 329a). By the very terms of the hypothesis, to omit, willfully or heedlessly, the safeguards prescribed by law for the benefit of another that he may be preserved in life or limb, is to fall short of the standard of diligence to which those who live in organized society are under a duty to conform. . . . In the case at hand, we have an instance of the admitted violation of a statute intended for the protection of travelers on the highway, of whom the defendant at the time was one. Yet the jurors were instructed in effect that they were at liberty in their discretion to treat the omission of lights either as innocent or as culpable. They were allowed to "consider the default as lightly or gravely" as they would (Thomas, J., in the court below). They might as well have been told that they could use a like discretion in holding a master at fault for the omission of a safety appliance prescribed by positive law for the protection of a workman. Jurors have no dispensing power by which they may relax the duty that one traveler on the highway owes under the statute to another. It is error to tell them that they have. The omission of these lights was a wrong, and being wholly unexcused was also a negligent wrong. No license should have been conceded to the triers of the facts to find it anything else.

We must be on our guard, however, against confusing the question of negligence with that of the causal connection between the negligence and the injury. A defendant who travels without lights is not to pay damages for his fault unless the absence of lights is the cause of the disaster. A plaintiff who travels without them is not to forfeit the right to damages unless the absence of lights is at least a contributing cause of the disaster. To say that conduct is negligence is not to say that it is always contributory negligence. "Proof of negligence in the air, so to speak, will not do." (Pollock Torts (10th Ed.) p. 472).

We think, however, that evidence of a collision occurring more than an hour after sundown between a car and an unseen buggy, proceeding without lights, is evidence from which a causal connection may be inferred between the collision and the lack of signals. If nothing else is shown to break the connection, we have a case, prima facie sufficient, of negligence contributing to the result.

. . . A statute designed for the protection of human life is not to be brushed aside as a form of words, its commands reduced to the level of cautions, and the duty to obey attenuated into an option to conform.

NOTES

1. ***Negligence Per Se and Excuses.*** Tedla v. Ellman, 19 N.E.2d 987, 989 (N.Y. 1939), offers an instructive contrast with *Martin*. The plaintiff and her deaf, mute brother were walking along a divided highway shortly after dark, pushing baby carriages filled with junk that they had collected for sale as part of their regular business. Instead of walking on the far left-hand side of the double highway, as required by statute so as to face oncoming traffic, they walked on the far right-hand side so that the traffic going in their direction approached them from behind. The defendant struck them with his car, injuring the plaintiff and killing her brother. The defendant's negligence was clearly established at trial and judgment was entered for plaintiff. The only issue on appeal was "whether, as matter of law, disregard of the statutory rule that pedestrians shall keep to the left of the center line of a highway constitutes contributory negligence which bars any recovery by the plaintiff." To answer that question, Lehman, J., noted that prior to the enactment of the statute, the common law custom usually required pedestrians to walk against traffic in order to be alert to dangers from oncoming traffic. The general customary rule, however, also contained a customary exception that required pedestrians to walk with the traffic when the traffic coming from behind was much lighter than the oncoming traffic. The case thus presented a knotty issue of statutory construction: Should the court read a customary exception into a statute that embodied the customary rule? If the statute had defined "specified safeguards against recognized dangers," Lehman, J., would have applied the rule in Martin v. Herzog. But since this statute was designed to "codify, supplement or even change common-law rules," themselves designed to prevent accidents, Lehman, J., implied this exception to the statute for the plaintiff's benefit. In an argument that appears to turn on legislative intent, Lehman, J., rebuffed the defendant as follows:

> Disregard of the statutory rule of the road and observance of a rule based on immemorial custom, it is said, is negligence which as matter of law is a proximate cause of the accident, though observance of the statutory rule might, under the circumstances of the particular case, expose a pedestrian to serious danger from which he would be free if he followed the rule that had been established by custom. If that be true, then the Legislature has decreed that pedestrians must observe the general rule of conduct which it has prescribed for their safety even under circumstances where observance would subject them to unusual risk; that pedestrians are to be charged with negligence as matter of law for acting as prudence dictates. It is unreasonable to ascribe to the Legislature an intention that the statute should have so extraordinary a result, and the courts may not give to a statute an effect not intended by the Legislature.

The one-sentence dissent argued that the plaintiff's action should have been dismissed on the authority of Martin v. Herzog.

The Second Restatement §288A, comment *i*, illus. 6 endorses the court's position in *Tedla*, as does RTT: LPEH §15(e), covering cases in which "the actor's compliance with the statute would involve a greater risk of physical harm to the actor or to others than noncompliance." Both Restatements also provide that violations of a statute may be excused by necessity or emergency, or by reason of incapacity, as is the case with various forms of common law negligence. In addition, the Third Restatement states that statutory causes of action should be judged by negligence, and not strict liability standards, by providing that a statutory violation is excused when "the actor exercises reasonable care in attempting to comply with the statute." RTT: LPEH §15(b). "Accordingly, the common law recognizes that the person can rebut negligence per se by showing that the person made a reasonable effort to comply with the statute," as with the driver who makes reasonable efforts to inspect or maintain brakes that fail. *Id.*, comment *c*.

2. *Dram Shop Statutes.* Causation issues loom large in so-called dram shop litigation. When the basic statute makes it illegal to sell alcoholic beverages to a customer, is the provider of the alcohol responsible if the customer thereafter injures either a third person or himself while driving under the influence? The early common law rule treated the driver as the sole cause of the accident. "The rule was based on the obvious fact that one cannot be intoxicated by reason of liquor furnished him if he does not drink it." Nolan v. Morelli, 226 A.2d 383, 386 (Conn. 1967). In Vesely v. Sager, 486 P.2d 151 (Cal. 1971), the court repudiated the traditional rule and held that the deliberate wrong by a third person did not sever the causal connection between the defendant's breach of statutory duty under California Business and Professions Code §25602(a) not to sell alcoholic beverages "to any habitual or common drunkard or to any obviously intoxicated person is guilty of a misdemeanor" and the injuries suffered by the plaintiff. Dram shop liability did not go down well with California voters, and *Vesely* was overruled by name in 1978.

CALIFORNIA BUSINESS & PROFESSIONS CODE §25602 (2023)

§25602. Sales to Drunkard or Intoxicated Person; Offense; Civil Liability

(a) Every person who sells, furnishes, gives, or causes to be sold, furnished, or given away, any alcoholic beverage to any habitual or common drunkard or to any obviously intoxicated person is guilty of a misdemeanor.

(b) No person who sells, furnishes, gives, or causes to be sold, furnished, or given away, any alcoholic beverage pursuant to subdivision (a) of this section shall be civilly liable to any injured person or the estate of such person for injuries inflicted on that person as a result of intoxication by the consumer of such alcoholic beverage. . . .

Should social hosts be held responsible if commercial hosts are? Local statutory variations in dram shop laws make it almost impossible to state the common law in this area. See generally 3 Harper, James & Gray, Torts §17.5 n.21.

Uhr v. East Greenbush Central School District

720 N.E.2d 886 (N.Y. 1999)

Rosenblatt, J. Education Law §905(1) requires school authorities in the State of New York to examine students between 8 and 16 years of age for scoliosis at least once in each school year. The principal issue on this appeal is whether the statute authorizes a private right of action.

[In the 1992–1993 school year the plaintiff, a pupil in the East Greenbush Central School District, was screened for scoliosis, but the tests were negative. In the following school year, she was not so checked. However, in 1995, as a ninth grader, an examination for scoliosis detected the condition.] Her parents, who are also plaintiffs in this action, then had her examined by an orthopedic doctor who concluded that her scoliosis had progressed to the point that surgery was required instead of the braces that often can be utilized when the condition is diagnosed earlier. The infant [i.e., minor] plaintiff underwent surgery in July 1995. [The plaintiffs then sued both under Education Law §905 and for common law negligence. The lower courts rejected both claims.]

Education Law §905(1) states that "[m]edical inspectors or principals and teachers in charge of schools in this state shall . . . examine all . . . pupils between eight and sixteen years of age for scoliosis, at least once in each school year." Education Law §905(2) provides that "[n]otwithstanding any other provisions of any general, special or local law, the school authorities charged with the duty of making such tests or examinations of pupils for the presence of scoliosis pursuant to this section shall not suffer any liability to any person as a result of making such test or examination, which liability would not have existed by any provision of law, statutory or otherwise, in the absence of this section." Finally, Education Law §911 charges the Commissioner of Education with the duty of enforcing the provisions of sections 901 through 910 of the Education Law and authorizes the Commissioner to "adopt rules and regulations" for such purpose.

The Test for the Availability of a Private Right of Action

As plaintiffs point out, the District's obligation to examine for scoliosis is plain enough. [Given that the statute did not explicitly authorize a private right of action, the court then asks] whether creation of such a right would be consistent with the legislative scheme. . . .

Plaintiffs argue that a private right of action is not only consistent with Education Law §905(1) but also necessary for its operation. They assert that the statute offers no other practical means of enforcement and that a private right of action is imperative, in order to give it life. We disagree and conclude that a private right of action would not be consistent with the statutory scheme. To begin with, the statute carries its own potent official enforcement mechanism. The Legislature has expressly charged the Commissioner of Education with the duty to implement Education Law §905(1) and has equipped the Commissioner with authority to adopt rules and regulations for such purpose. Moreover, the Legislature has vested the Commissioner with power to withhold public funding from noncompliant school districts. Thus, the Legislature clearly contemplated administrative enforcement of this statute. The question then becomes whether, in addition to administrative enforcement, an implied private right of action would be consistent with the legislative scheme.

It would not. The evolution of Education Law §905(2) is compelling evidence of the Legislature's intent to immunize the school districts from any liability that might arise out of the scoliosis screening program. By the language of Education Law §905(2) the Legislature deemed that the school district "shall not suffer any liability to any person as a result of *making* such test or examination" (emphasis added). Plaintiffs contend that by implication, the District is denied immunity for *failing* to perform the examination. In effect, plaintiffs would interpret the statute as conferring immunity for misfeasance but not nonfeasance. On the other hand, the District contends that it would be incongruous for the Legislature to accord immunity for one circumstance but not the other.

Plaintiffs' reading of the statute might have some appeal if we did not have persuasive evidence as to the Legislature's intent to immunize the school districts for both nonfeasance and misfeasance. . . . Revealingly, the Legislature evidently saw no need to amend Education Law §905 in any other way, although obviously aware of [two Appellate Division decisions that had refused to create a private right of action.] Its failure to otherwise amend the statute is strong evidence of the Legislature's conclusion that the Appellate Divisions had correctly interpreted the statute's immunity provision.

There is also the matter of cost to the school districts, as evidenced by the Legislature's expressed sensitivity in that regard. Orthopedists through the New York State Society of Orthopaedic Surgeons and other professionals from the Scoliosis Association, Inc. agreed to volunteer their time and expertise to train existing school personnel on the relatively simple examination procedure. In forecasting its cost, the Legislature anticipated that the program would have minimal financial impact on school districts. Allowing a private right of action against the government as opposed to a private entity has direct and obvious financial consequences to the public.

Given the Legislature's concern over the possible costs to the school districts — as evidenced by the statutory immunity provision and the other legislative statements reflecting those concerns — we conclude that the Legislature did not intend that the districts bear the potential liability for a program that benefits a far wider population. If we are to imply such a right, we must have clear evidence of the Legislature's willingness to expose the governmental entity to liability that it might not otherwise incur. The case before us reveals no such legislative intent.

In sum, we conclude that a private right of action to enforce Education Law §905(1) is inconsistent with the statute's legislative scheme and therefore cannot be fairly implied.

Common-Law Negligence

Plaintiffs contend that the lower courts erred in holding that they failed to state a claim for common-law negligence. Essentially, plaintiffs argue that the District assumed a duty to the infant plaintiff and her parents by creating a special relationship with them in connection with the Education Law §905(1) program and that it breached its duty by failing to perform the examination during the 1993–1994 school year. We agree with the courts below that plaintiffs have failed as a matter of law to state a claim for common-law negligence.

[Affirmed.]

NOTE

Statutory Causes of Action Under Complex Administrative Schemes. *Uhr* represents the modern judicial reluctance to infer private rights of action from the breach of statutory duties imposed as part of complex administrative schemes. An early glimpse of this trend is found in

Lucy Webb Hayes National Training School v. Perotti, *supra* at 154. The decedent killed himself by jumping through a glass window shortly after he was committed to the defendant institution. The 1909 regulations for private hospitals prohibited them from keeping "any delirious or maniacal patient" in a room "not properly barred or closed." The court did not dwell on the question of proximate cause. Rather, it refused to create the private right of action at all:

> The Department of Public Health, which apparently is responsible for the enforcement of the regulation involved, approved the design of Sibley Memorial Hospital, . . . and recommended that the Commissioners of the District of Columbia license its operation, which they did. . . .
>
> Regulations relating to a licensing process are often enacted with the reasonable expectation that the licensing authority will exercise some judgment in applying the general rule to the specific case. To invoke a doctrine of negligence per se in such circumstances robs the regulation of the flexibility that its draftsmen may well have envisioned for it. We conclude that in this case the instruction that violation of the regulation would be negligence per se was erroneous, and requires a new trial. The correct standard . . . is that the hospital's negligence should be "decided on all relevant evidence, including violation of any safety regulation found to be applicable, and consequently admissible in evidence, but including also facts tending to show due care" on the part of the hospital in the construction and operation of [its facilities].

A similar hostility was expressed in Elliot v. City of New York, 747 N.E.2d 760 (N.Y. 2001). The plaintiff fell out of a bleacher seat that was not protected by a guardrail, as required by the city building code. The trial judge had held that the breach of the municipal building code amounted to negligence per se. The Court of Appeals reversed on the ground that a breach of the rules of a "subordinate rule-making body" did not count as negligence per se because only the state had power to pass a statute:

> [C]haracterizing the vast multitude of ordinances that have been adopted by New York City as State statutes would result in considerable fragmentation and uncertainty in the application of the common law of our State. Furthermore, since the City retains the authority to amend or repeal its Administrative Code provisions, including [that applicable here], without the need of State legislative action, we decline to transform the status of this provision from that of a local enactment to a State statute. In the absence of a violation of a statutorily imposed duty in this case, a negligence per se finding was unwarranted and defendants are entitled to a reversal and a new trial.

On the other hand, negligence per se actions have been allowed for violations of Medicare and Medicaid regulations. In McLain v. Mariner Health Care, Inc., 631 S.E.2d 435, 438 (Ga. 2006), Judy McLain alleged that a nursing home's violation of multiple health and safety regulations resulted in the wrongful death of her father. Johnson, J., reversing the lower court, observed that even in the absence of a private cause of action under the federal statute, McLain could assert a claim of negligence per se arising from the violation of regulations:

> It is obvious that as a resident of the nursing home owned by Mariner, McLain's father belonged to the class of persons for whom these statutes and regulations were intended to protect, and that the injuries set forth in the complaint, and which we assume to have occurred for purposes of a motion to dismiss, were among those these same statutes and regulations were designed to prevent. Likewise, the complaint's allegations of violations of the same statutes and regulations would be competent evidence of Mariner's breach of duty under a traditional negligence action.

S

SECTION F. JUDGE AND JURY

The law of negligence (indeed the entire law of tort) does more than articulate standards for liability. It also develops a wide range of legal institutions to apply its basic commands to individual cases. Our legal system divides the responsibility for deciding questions of fact between judge and jury. That divided system necessarily prevents either judge or jury from taking complete control over the individual case, unless both parties to the dispute waive a jury trial. Yet, by the same token, the division of responsibility is not arbitrary, for the jury is not simply told: "You are to decide, on the basis of all you have heard and in terms of your sense of fairness, whether the defendant should pay for the damage sustained by the plaintiff in this case." That total delegation of judicial responsibility has been rejected for two reasons. First, judges fear that the jury might abuse its unlimited power by deciding cases contrary to established principles of law, especially when motivated by obvious passion and prejudice, or even by more subtle forms of class, social, or economic bias. Second, judges believe that unlimited jury discretion repudiates or at least undermines the central principle of distributive justice—that like cases should be treated alike, no matter what substantive principles apply.

Exhibit 3.5 The "Vanishing Trial" Phenomenon

PERCENTAGE OF CIVIL TERMINATIONS DURING OR AFTER TRIAL U.S. DISTRICT COURTS, 1962–2012

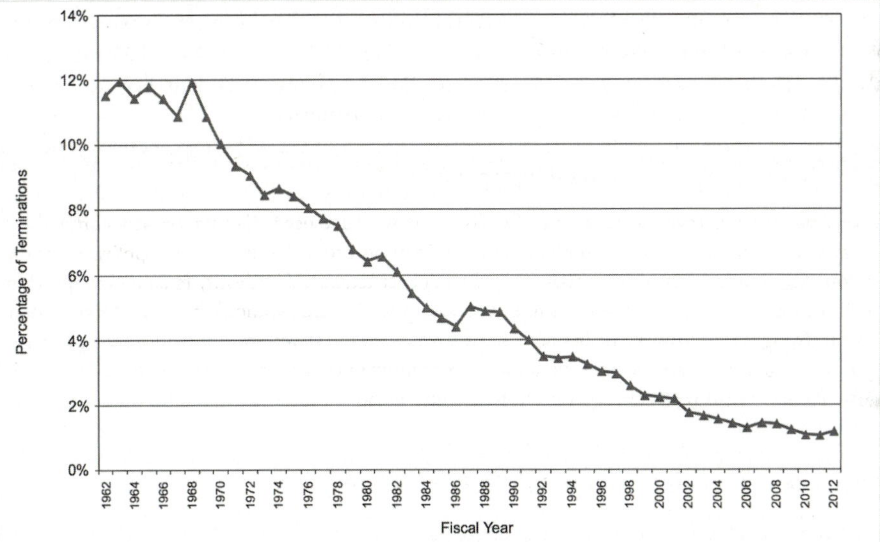

Source: Administrative Office of the U.S. Courts, Annual Report of the Director, Table C-4 (1962–2012).

Yet when juries are empaneled, how are they best controlled? One form of judicial control is found in the judge's instructions to the jury on the relevant principles of substantive law, given at the close of the case. Substantive law is often made when the attorneys for either party challenge those instructions on appeal. Appellate courts set aside jury verdicts based on erroneous and prejudicial instructions precisely because they believe that juries should and do follow their instructions. Sometimes mistakes seem quite minor. In Louisville & Nashville Railroad v. Gower, 3 S.W. 824, 827 (Tenn. 1887), the plaintiff, an employee of the defendant railroad, was hurt while attempting to couple two cars. Snodgrass, J., speaking for the court, reversed a judgment for the plaintiff and ordered a new trial:

> The charge was otherwise incorrect and misleading, particularly in defining the care necessary to have been exercised by Plaintiff Gower in order to entitle him to recovery. The Court, after telling the jury that "it was the duty of the plaintiff to exercise such a degree of care in making

the coupling as a man of ordinary prudence" would have done, adds: "Just such care as one of you, similarly employed, would have exercised under such circumstances. If he exercised that degree of care, and was nevertheless injured, he is entitled to your verdict. If he failed to exercise that degree of care, he cannot recover."

The charge as to the exercise of such care as a man of ordinary prudence would have done was correct, but it was thought not full enough by the judge, who illustrated what he meant by reference to the care which each one of the jurymen would have exercised. His charge, so limited, was erroneous. It does not appear that all or any of the members of the jury were men of ordinary prudence, and yet the judge tells them that what he means by the "exercise of such care as a man of ordinary prudence would have exercised" is that it was the exercise of such care as one of them would have exercised if similarly situated. Under this instruction, if any member of the jury thought he would have done what Gower did in the coupling, he would of course have determined that Gower acted with the care required, and was entitled to recover. This illustration, used to define what he meant by "the care of a man of ordinary prudence" and thereby becoming its definition, was erroneous. The care he was required to exercise was that of a man of ordinary prudence in that dangerous situation, and not "just such care as one of the jury similarly situated" would have done, be that much or little as each member might be very prudent or very imprudent.

A second form of judicial control lies in the court's power to keep certain questions of fact from the jury. In Metropolitan Railway v. Jackson, [1877] 3 AC 193, 197, the issue on appeal was, "Was there at the trial any evidence of negligence by the defendant that ought to have been left to a jury?" Chancellor Cairns remarked as follows:

There was not, at your Lordships' bar, any serious controversy as to the principles applicable to a case of this description. The Judge has a certain duty to discharge, and the jurors have another and a different duty. The Judge has to say whether any facts have been established by evidence from which negligence *may be* reasonably inferred; the jurors have to say whether, from those facts, when submitted to them, negligence *ought to be* inferred. It is, in my opinion, of the greatest importance in the administration of justice that these separate functions should be maintained, and should be maintained distinct. It would be a serious inroad on the province of the jury, if, in a case where there are facts from which negligence may reasonably be inferred, the Judge were to withdraw the case from the jury upon the ground that, in his opinion, negligence ought not to be inferred; and it would, on the other hand, place in the hands of the jurors a power which might be exercised in the most arbitrary manner, if they were at liberty to hold that negligence might be inferred from any state of facts whatever.

As *Metropolitan Railway* suggests, the jury's traditional role is to find the "facts" to which it then applies the "law." In negligence cases, the jury's role fits uneasily into this sharp dichotomy between *law* and *fact.* Is it helpful to think of negligence as a "mixed issue of law and fact," as it is frequently called? Abraham elaborates in The Trouble with Negligence, 54 Vand. L. Rev. 1187, 1190–91 (2001):

[In negligence cases] the task of the finder of fact involves three steps, not just two. In logical order, the finder of fact must (1) find the empirical facts, including what the defendant did; (2) determine how much and what kind of care was reasonable given these facts; and (3) apply the law of negligence to these findings, by deciding whether the defendant behaved in accordance with the norm identified in step (2). It has long been recognized that step (2) involves a very different function than step (1), because the former is entirely empirical, whereas the latter is evaluative. In recognition of this difference, steps (2) and (3) together have been referred to as deciding a "mixed question of fact and law."

This section addresses several questions: What is the role of the jury in law and in actual practice in setting the standard of care? What difference does it make who decides this issue? How does the court limit or control the jury's exercise of discretion? Is there any way to ensure uniformity of jury decisions in similar cases? Are concerns about the objectivity and competence of juries well founded? Do juries ever nullify the legal rules articulated in appellate decisions? See generally James, Functions of Judge and Jury in Negligence Cases, 58 Yale L.J. 667 (1949), and Noah, Civil Jury Nullification, 86 Iowa L. Rev. 1601, 1608–12 (2001).

Oliver Wendell Holmes

The Common Law

110–11, 120–24 (1881)

If, now, the ordinary liabilities in tort arise from failure to comply with fixed and uniform standards of external conduct, which every man is presumed and required to know, it is obvious that it ought to be possible, sooner or later, to formulate these standards at least to some extent, and that to do so must at last be the business of the court. It is equally clear that the featureless generality, that the defendant was bound to use such care as a prudent man would do under the circumstances, ought to be continually giving place to the specific one, that he was bound to use this or that precaution under these or those circumstances. The standard which the defendant was bound to come up to was a standard of specific acts or omissions, with reference to the specific circumstances in which he found himself. If in the whole department of unintentional wrongs the courts arrived at no further utterance than the question of negligence, and left every case, without rudder or compass, to the jury, they would simply confess their inability to state a very large part of the law which they required the defendant to know, and would assert, by implication, that nothing could be learned by experience. But neither courts nor legislatures have ever stopped at that point. . . .

The principles of substantive law which have been established by the courts are believed to have been somewhat obscured by having presented themselves oftenest in the form of rulings upon the sufficiency of evidence. When a judge rules that there is no evidence of negligence, he does something more than is embraced in an ordinary ruling that there is no evidence of a fact. He rules that the acts or omissions proved or in question do not constitute a ground of legal liability, and in this way the law is gradually enriching itself from daily life, as it should. Thus, in Crafter v. Metropolitan Railway Co.[, [1866] LR 1 C.P. 300], the plaintiff slipped on the defendant's stairs and was severely hurt. The cause of his slipping was that the brass nosing of the stairs had been worn smooth by travel over it, and a builder testified that in his opinion the staircase was unsafe by reason of this circumstance and the absence of a hand-rail. There was nothing to contradict this except that great numbers of persons had passed over the stairs and that no accident had happened there, and the plaintiff had a verdict. The court set the verdict aside, and ordered a non-suit. The ruling was in form that there was no evidence of negligence to go to the jury; but this was obviously equivalent to saying, and did in fact mean, that the railroad company had done all that it was bound to do in maintaining such a staircase as was proved by the plaintiff. A hundred other equally concrete instances will be found in the text-books. . . .

Many have noticed the confusion of thought implied in speaking of such cases as presenting mixed questions of law and fact. No doubt, as has been said above, the averment that the defendant has been guilty of negligence is a complex one: first, that he has done or omitted certain things; second, that his alleged conduct does not come up to the legal standard. And so long as the controversy is simply on the first half, the whole complex averment is plain matter for the jury without special instructions, just as a question of ownership would be where the only dispute was as to the fact upon which the legal conclusion was founded. But when a controversy arises on the second half, the question whether the court or the jury ought to judge of the defendant's conduct is wholly unaffected by the accident, whether there is or is not also a dispute as to what that conduct was. If there is such a dispute, it is entirely possible to give a series of hypothetical instructions adapted to every state of facts which it is open to the jury to find. If there is no such dispute, the court may still take their opinion as to the standard. The problem is to explain the relative functions of court and jury with regard to the latter.

When a case arises in which the standard of conduct, pure and simple, is submitted to the jury, the explanation is plain. It is that the court, not entertaining any clear views of public policy applicable to the matter, derives the rule to be applied from daily experience, as it has been agreed that the great body of the law of tort has been derived. But the court further feels that it is not itself possessed of sufficient practical experience to lay down the rule intelligently. It conceives that twelve men taken from the practical part of the community can aid its judgment. Therefore it aids its conscience by taking the opinion of the jury.

But supposing a state of facts often repeated in practice, is it to be imagined that the court is to go on leaving the standard to the jury forever? Is it not manifest, on the contrary, that if the jury is, on the whole, as fair a tribunal as it is represented to be, the lesson which can be got from that source will be learned? Either the court will find that the fair teaching of experience is that the conduct complained of usually is or is not blameworthy, and therefore, unless explained, is or is not a ground of liability; or it will find the jury oscillating to and fro, and will see the necessity of making up its mind for itself. There is no reason why any other such question should not be settled, as well as that of liability for stairs with smooth strips of brass upon their edges. The exceptions would mainly be found where the standard was rapidly changing, as, for instance, in some questions of medical treatment.

If this be the proper conclusion in plain cases, further consequences ensue. Facts do not often exactly repeat themselves in practice; but cases with comparatively small variations from each other do. A judge who has long sat at nisi prius [trial court] ought gradually to acquire a fund of experience which enables him to represent the common sense of the community in ordinary instances far better than an average jury. He should be able to lead and to instruct them in detail, even where he thinks it desirable, on the whole, to take their opinion. Furthermore, the sphere in which he is able to rule without taking their opinion at all should be continually growing.

Baltimore and Ohio R.R. v. Goodman

275 U.S. 66 (1927)

Holmes, J. This is a suit brought by the widow and administratrix of Nathan Goodman against the petitioner for causing his death by running him down at a grade crossing. The defence is that Goodman's own negligence caused the death. At the trial, the defendant asked the Court to direct a verdict for it, but the request, and others looking to the same direction, were refused, and the plaintiff got a verdict and a judgment which was affirmed by the Circuit Court of Appeals. 10 F.(2d) 58.

Goodman was driving an automobile truck in an easterly direction and was killed by a train running southwesterly across the road at a rate of not less than sixty miles an hour. The line was straight, but it is said by the respondent that Goodman "had no practical view" beyond a section house two hundred and forty-three feet north of the crossing until he was about twenty feet from the first rail, or, as the respondent argues, twelve feet from danger, and that then the engine was still obscured by the section house. He had been driving at the rate of ten or twelve miles an hour, but had cut down his rate to five or six miles at about forty feet from the crossing. It is thought that there was an emergency in which, so far as appears, Goodman did all that he could.

We do not go into further details as to Goodman's precise situation, beyond mentioning that it was daylight and that he was familiar with the crossing, for it appears to us plain that nothing is suggested by the evidence to relieve Goodman from responsibility for his own death. When a man goes upon a railroad track he knows that he goes to a place where he will be killed if a train comes upon him before he is clear of the track. He knows that he must stop for the train, not the train stop for him. In such circumstances it seems to us that if a driver cannot be sure otherwise whether a train is dangerously near he must stop and get out of his vehicle, although obviously he will not often be required to do more than to stop and look. It seems to us that if he relies upon not hearing the train or any signal and takes no further precaution he does so at his own risk. If at the last moment Goodman found himself in an emergency it was his own fault that he did not reduce his speed earlier or come to a stop. It is true as said in Flannelly v. Delaware & Hudson Co., 225 U.S. 597 [1912], that the question of due care very generally is left to the jury. But we are dealing with a standard of conduct, and when the standard is clear it should be laid down once for all by the Courts. See Southern Pacific Co. v. Berkshire, 254 U.S. 415 [1921].

Judgment reversed.

Pokora v. Wabash Ry.

292 U.S. 98 (1934)

[The defendant operated four tracks at a level crossing. As plaintiff approached them, these included a switch track, a through track, and then two more switch tracks. Because of the boxcars on the first track, he could not see the main track. Plaintiff stopped, tried to look, and listened, but he heard no bell or whistle. He did not get out of his truck to obtain a better view, as the dictum in Baltimore & Ohio R.R. v. Goodman seemed to require under such circumstances. "Still listening, he crossed the switch, and reaching the main track was struck by a passenger train coming from the north at a speed of twenty-five to thirty miles an hour." The trial court directed a verdict for defendant on its finding that plaintiff had been contributorily negligent and this judgment was affirmed below. Reversed and remanded.]

Cardozo, J. Standards of prudent conduct are declared at times by courts, but they are taken over from the facts of life. To get out of a vehicle and reconnoitre is an uncommon precaution, as everyday experience informs us. Besides being uncommon, it is very likely to be futile, and sometimes even dangerous. If the driver leaves his vehicle when he nears a cut or curve, he will learn nothing by getting out about the perils that lurk beyond. By the time he regains his seat and sets his car in motion, the hidden train may be upon him. . . . Often the added safeguard will be dubious though the track happens to be straight, as it seems that this one was, at all events as far as the station, about five blocks to the north. A train traveling at a speed of thirty miles an hour will cover a quarter of a mile in the space of thirty seconds. It may thus emerge out of obscurity as the driver turns his back to regain the waiting car, and may then descend upon him suddenly when his car is on the track. Instead of helping himself by getting out, he might do better to press forward with all his faculties alert. So a train at a neighboring station, apparently at rest and harmless, may be transformed in a few seconds into an instrument of destruction. At times the course of safety may be different. One can figure to oneself a roadbed so level and unbroken that getting out will be a gain. Even then the balance of advantage depends on many circumstances and can be easily disturbed. Where was Pokora to leave his truck after getting out to reconnoitre? If he was to leave it on the switch, there was the possibility that the box cars would be shunted down upon him before he could regain his seat. The defendant did not show whether there was a locomotive at the forward end, or whether the cars were so few that a locomotive could be seen. If he was to leave his vehicle near the curb, there was even stronger reason to believe that the space to be covered in going back and forth would make his observations worthless. One must remember that while the traveler turns his eye in one direction, a train or a loose engine may be approaching from the other.

Illustrations such as these bear witness to the need for caution in framing standards of behavior that amount to rules of law. The need is the more urgent when there is no background of experience out of which the standards have emerged. They are then, not the natural flowerings of behavior in its customary forms, but rules artificially developed, and imposed from without. Extraordinary situations may not wisely or fairly be subjected to tests or regulations that are fitting for the common-place or normal. In default of the guide of customary conduct, what is suitable for the traveler caught in a mesh where the ordinary safeguards fail him is for the judgment of a jury. The opinion in Goodman's case has been a source of confusion in the federal courts to the extent that it imposes a standard for application by the judge, and has had only wavering support in the courts of the states. We limit it accordingly.

NOTES

1. ***Stop, Look, and Listen.*** *Goodman* and *Pokora* illustrate the difficulty in fashioning a uniform rule for railroad crossing accidents. Notwithstanding *Pokora*'s respectful disapproval of *Goodman*, since 1927, *Goodman* has been cited hundreds of times, often with approval. Most critically, plaintiffs today will have difficulty prevailing in cases involving collisions with trains moving through open country on single tracks. For instance, the court in Ridgeway v. CSX Transportation, Inc., 723 So. 2d 600 (Ala. 1998), emphatically upheld a contributory negligence defense as a matter of law in a single-track wrongful death case. In cases with multiple tracks often flagmen were used to separate the traffic, given all the self-help problems to which *Pokora* referred. See, e.g., Toschi v. Christian, 149 P.2d 848, 851 (Cal. 1944). Flagmen have in turn been replaced by automated gates in the context of ordinary crossings but are still used to protect railway construction crews from oncoming trains.

Pokora is followed by the Third Restatement, which rejects the idea that uniform rules can decide concrete cases:

> [W]hat looks at first to be a constant or recurring issue of conduct in which many parties engage may reveal on closer inspection many variables that can best be considered on a case-by-case basis. Tort law . . . requires that actual moral judgments be based on the circumstances of each individual situation. Tort law's affirmation of this requirement highlights the primary role necessarily fulfilled by the jury.

RTT: LPEH §8, comment *c.*

2. ***Jury Determinations in FELA Cases.*** Juries are given broad discretion in finding negligence for industrial accidents brought under the Federal Employers' Liability Act, 45 U.S.C. §§51–60 (2023). This Act makes every interstate railroad liable in damages for injuries to its employees caused by the negligence of the railroad through any of its officers, agents, or employees, "or by reason of any defect or insufficiency" in any of its premises or equipment. FELA's 1939 amendments eliminated the defense of assumption of risk in all its forms and provided that contributory negligence should not bar an employee's action, but only that "the

damages shall be diminished by the jury in proportion to the amount of negligence attributable to such employee."

In Wilkerson v. McCarthy, 336 U.S. 53, 62–64 (1949), the plaintiff was injured when he slipped on a board covered with oil and grease while taking a shortcut over a pit in the repair shop, even after the railroad had chained off the boardwalk to prevent employees from using it. The Utah Supreme Court overturned the jury verdict for the plaintiff, but a badly fractured Supreme Court reinstated its verdict. Justice Black upheld that jury verdict, by insisting that courts should not assume that "juries will fall short of a fair performance of their constitutional function."

Chief Justice Vinson would have kept the case from the jury, saying in a brief dissent: "In my view of the record, there is no evidence, nor any inference which reasonably may be drawn from the evidence when viewed in the light most favorable to the petitioner, which could sustain a verdict for him." Justice Jackson then offered a fuller defense of the decision of the Utah Supreme Court to take the case from the jury:

> This record shows that both the wheel pit into which plaintiff fell and the board on which he was trying to cross over the pit were blocked off by safety chains strung between posts. Plaintiff admits he knew the chains were there to keep him from crossing over the pit and to require him to go a few feet farther to walk around it. After the chains were put up, any person undertaking to use the board as a cross walk had to complete involved contortions and gymnastics, particularly when, as was the case with petitioner, a car was on the track 23½. A casual examination of the model filed as an exhibit in this Court shows how difficult was such a passage. Nevertheless, the Court holds that if employees succeeded in disregarding the chains and forced passage frequently enough to be considered "customary," and the railroad took no further action, its failure so to do was negligence. The same rule would no doubt apply if the railroad's precautions had consisted of a barricade, or an armed guard.

Subsequent cases have confirmed that so long as the employer's negligence has played "any part, even the slightest" in bringing about the injury, then recovery under the FELA is appropriate. See Rogers v. Missouri Pacific R. Co., 352 U.S. 500 (1957).

3. *Should tort actions be left to the jury?* Why should any negligence case, or indeed any tort action, be tried by juries at all? Does the outcome in *Wilkerson* support the view that the entire FELA system should be displaced by a workers' compensation law? Most civil law countries do not use juries to assess either liability or damages, and even the English courts rely on juries for those functions only in exceptional cases. Ward v. James, [1966] 1 QB 273, 295.

> Whenever a man is on trial for serious crime, or when in a civil case a man's honour or integrity is at stake, or when one or other party must be deliberately lying, then the trial by jury has no equal. But in personal injury cases trial by jury has given place of late to trial by judge alone, the reason being simply this, that in these cases trial by a judge alone is more acceptable to the great majority of people.

In modern times, however, "a striking number of countries have seriously debated or adopted new ways of incorporating ordinary citizens as decision makers in their legal systems." Hans, Jury Systems Around the World, 4 Ann. Rev. L. & Soc. Sci. 9.1, 9.1 (2008). Not all countries adopt the U.S. model; some use "mixed tribunals" of professional judges and laypersons, others are experimenting with tribunals composed of judges and private citizens who possess relevant substantive expertise.

Arguments for and against the use of juries are hotly debated. On the positive side, juries bring the common sense of the community to the difficult estimations of reasonable care required under a negligence system. Tilley, Tort Law Inside Out, 126 Yale L.J. 1320 (2017), highlights the role that tort law plays in reflecting and enforcing local social norms within

American society. Some jury advocates go further to suggest that juries add value to the litigation process by making significant contributions to accuracy in both fact-finding and legal decision making. Juries also provide a check against the domination of the legal system by government officials and professional people. Gifford & Jones, Keeping Cases from Black Juries: An Empirical Analysis of How Race, Income Inequality, and Regional History Affect Tort Law, 73 Wash. & Lee L. Rev. 557 (2016), contends that Southern states were particularly slow to adopt jury-empowering policies due to beliefs that black Americans were overly pro-plaintiff and would engage in wealth redistribution via the tort system.

Jury detractors claim the jury system is expensive and time consuming. Juries may be subject to passion and prejudice, and, even when fair-minded, find themselves overwhelmed with the complex technical issues raised by medical malpractice, patent, or product liability claims. These critics also maintain that juries are pro-plaintiff decision makers, too easily swayed by emotion, and likely to award high amounts in damages.

4. ***Empirical Studies.*** It has proved difficult to assemble hard and reliable empirical data on jury behavior, for it is generally considered unethical to monitor the deliberations of actual juries and too expensive to impanel enough mock juries to obtain a reliable database. The Arizona Jury Project, a small pilot program, did enable a videotaped study of juror behavior in fifty civil cases. See Diamond & Vidmar, Jury Room Rumination on Forbidden Topics, 87 Va. L. Rev. 1857, 1869–72 (2001). Here is an overview of some key empirical findings in some notable studies:

a. ***Judge Versus Jury Decision Making.*** The extensive Kalven and Zeisel Chicago jury study, based upon questionnaires sent to judges presiding over 4,000 state and federal civil jury trials nationwide in the 1950s, yielded data showing a 78 percent agreement between judge and jury on liability. Kalven defended civil juries on the ground that they usually reach the same results as judges sitting as triers of facts, leaving judges themselves generally pleased with their behavior. See Kalven, The Dignity of the Civil Jury, 50 Va. L. Rev. 1055 (1964). This judge-jury correspondence has been replicated in more recent studies. Clermont & Eisenberg, Trial by Jury or Judge: Transcending Empiricism, 77 Cornell L. Rev. 1124 (1992).

But if juries typically reach the same conclusions as judges, do they add anything more to the system other than higher costs? In The Georgia Jury and Negligence: The View from the Trenches, 28 Ga. L. Rev. 1 (1993), Sentelle relied on survey data of trial lawyers and found a significant (but far from unanimous) sentiment that today many judges are more pro-plaintiff than juries, at least on the issue of liability. On damages, however, judges were generally thought less likely to award "runaway verdicts" than a jury. See Clermont & Eisenberg, Litigation Realities, 88 Cornell L. Rev. 119, 145 (2002), which found that, in product liability and medical malpractice cases, plaintiffs prevail "at a much higher rate before judges (48%) than they do before juries (28%)."

b. ***"Deep Pockets."*** Some evidence suggests that, with injuries held constant, the size of the plaintiff's recovery depends largely on the identity of the defendant. Hammitt, Carroll & Relles, Tort Standards and Jury Decisions, 14 J. Legal Stud. 751, 754–56 (1985), found that juries ratcheted up awards against defendants with "deep pockets."

> Compared with individual defendants, our model predicts that corporate defendants pay 34 percent larger awards, after controlling for plaintiffs' injuries and type of legal case. If the plaintiff is permanently and severely injured, the deep-pocket effect is much stronger—a corporate defendant pays almost 4.5 times as much as an individual, on average. Similarly, government defendants are estimated to pay 50 percent more than individuals (averaged over all plaintiff injuries; there were too few cases of permanently and severely injured plaintiffs suing government defendants to analyze these separately). Finally, medical malpractice awards against doctors are almost 2.5 times as great as awards against other individuals in average case types, and awards against hospitals are 85 percent larger. . . .

> There are several plausible explanations for the observed jury behavior. First, jurors may balance the benefit of greater compensation for the plaintiff against the harm to the defendant. While a relatively modest award against an individual defendant might cause him great financial hardship, the same award against a corporation would impose only miniscule losses on each of its stockholders. In addition, it may be impossible for jurors to separate the insult implicit in a tort from the harm to the plaintiff. Thus jurors may require doctors to provide greater compensation to victims of malpractice, not only because doctors are usually heavily insured and are wealthier than other defendants, but also because of the special trust a patient places in his or her doctor.

But see Hans, Business on Trial: The Civil Jury and Corporate Responsibility 23 (2000), which reports juror interviews and experimental studies that failed to detect a "deep pockets" effect.

c. ***Hindsight Bias.*** Individual judgments by jurors (and judges) are often subject to so-called hindsight bias, wherein events that have actually occurred are thought to have been more likely to occur than in fact they really were. The difficulties that hindsight bias poses for the administration of a negligence system are discussed in Rachlinski, A Positive Psychological Theory of Judging in Hindsight, 65 U. Chi. L. Rev. 571, 572 (1998).

> The hindsight bias clearly has implications for the legal system. Consider, for example, the dilemma of a defendant who, despite taking reasonable care, has caused an accident and has been sued. The defendant's level of care will be reviewed by a judge or jury who already knows that it proved inadequate to avoid the plaintiff's injury. Consequently, the defendant's level of care will seem less reasonable in hindsight than it did in foresight. Reasonableness must be determined from the perspective of the defendant at the time that the precautions were taken, but the hindsight bias ensures that subsequent events will influence that determination. The law relies on a process that assigns liability in a biased manner. . . .

Rachlinski notes that hindsight bias in effect moves the negligence standard closer to a "quasi-strict" liability rule, because defendants may be held liable even when they take adequate precautions. Traditional methods for controlling bias, like jury instructions and creating a high burden of persuasion, do not remedy the problem. Although courts are unable to eliminate hindsight bias, Rachlinski argues that they have done a "remarkable job" of creating effective (if second-best) institutional responses. One response is to suppress evidence of information learned, and precautions taken, *after* the relevant time period. *Id.* at 624. Another response is to substitute ex ante standards, like relevant industry custom and regulations, for the standard of reasonable care. *Id.* at 608. What are the costs and benefits of these judicial solutions? Does the answer depend in part on the type of accident involved (e.g., medical malpractice versus highway accident)?

d. ***Anchoring.*** Perhaps the best-documented bias is "anchoring," or the process by which an initial numerical value or "anchor" disproportionately influences the decision maker's ultimate award. See Chapman & Bornstein, The More You Ask For, the More You Get: Anchoring in Personal Injury Verdicts, 10 Applied Cognitive Psychol. 519 (1996); Marti & Wissler, Be Careful What You Ask For: The Effects of Anchors on Personal Injury Damages Awards, 6 J. Exp. Psychol. 91 (2001). Nor does it seem that a defense strategy of offering an alternative damages number could effectively counter the anchoring effect. Campbell et al., Countering the Plaintiff's Anchor: Jury Simulations to Evaluate Damages Arguments, 101 Iowa L. Rev. 543, 564, 565 (2016), suggests nonetheless that anchoring is a mixed blessing for plaintiffs, as requesting higher damages amounts decreased plaintiffs' likelihood of prevailing at trial.

Should we expect judges or juries to be more susceptible to this bias? Guthrie et al., Blinking on the Bench: How Judges Decide Cases, 93 Cornell L. Rev. 1, 20–26, 31

(2007), reminds us that judges are people, too: Judges "generally make intuitive decisions" that expose their decision making to hindsight and anchoring biases, "impressionistic" evaluation of statistical evidence, and the unconscious influence of factors like race and gender. Will concerns about systematic biases make actors take excessive care to avoid large adverse judgments?

e. ***Racial Bias.*** What about the extent to which racial bias infiltrates jury decision making? Cardi et al., Do Black Injuries Matter?: Implicit Bias and Jury Decision Making in Tort Cases, 93 S. Cal. L. Rev. 507 (2019), concludes, on the basis of mock juror assessment using hypothetical cases, that bias may result in higher awards for plaintiffs who sue black defendants and lower awards for black plaintiffs who experience the same injuries as white plaintiffs. How, if at all, should the law respond to such implicit bias?

5. ***Reform Proposals.*** In order to reduce the cost of jury trials, courts have been urged to impanel smaller juries of six or eight instead of twelve jurors. However, the price of reducing the direct costs of jury operation is to decrease the level of community participation, diversity, and reliability of jury efforts. For evaluations of proposals to reduce jury size, see Diamond & Zeisel, "Convincing Empirical Evidence" on the Six-Member Jury, 41 U. Chi. L. Rev. 281 (1974); Vidmar, The Performance of the American Civil Jury: An Empirical Perspective, 40 Ariz. L. Rev. 849 (1998); Saks, The Smaller the Jury, the Greater the Unpredictability, 79 Judicature 263 (1996).

To control for juror bias, "blindfolding" the jury to certain information has been proposed. See generally Diamond & Casper, Blindfolding the Jury to Verdict Consequences: Damages, Experts and the Civil Jury, 26 Law & Soc'y Rev. 513, 557 (1992). Jurors are rarely told whether and how much liability insurance a defendant has, whether other parties to the dispute have settled and for how much, what settlement offers were made and rejected, and whether the court will modify the jury's award (as it does in certain types of cases). Alternatively, jurors may also be instructed to use information for certain purposes only. Diamond & Vidmar, *supra*, are skeptical that such limiting tactics are effective; indeed, the authors suggest withholding such information may be the root cause of wide variability in jury verdicts. Bavli & Mozer, The Effects of Comparable-Case Guidance on Awards for Pain and Suffering and Punitive Damages: Evidence from a Randomized Controlled Trial, 37 Yale L. & Pol'y Rev. 405 (2019), advocates the provision of more information, suggesting that providing juries with historic award information from comparable cases would lead to more "appropriate" awards for plaintiffs.

More drastic proposals call for the removal of certain decisions from the purview of juries. Specialized "health courts" composed of neutral expert panels to adjudicate medical malpractice claims are backed by influential health policy organizations. Peters, Health Courts?, 88 B.U. L. Rev. 227, 230 (2008), describes the procedure:

> Patients seeking to make a claim arising out of a hospital stay would start the process by filing their claim at the hospital or with its liability insurer. . . . A group of medical experts convened by the hospital would then evaluate the claim to decide whether the care given to the patient met the standard of care. . . . In the event of an appeal, an administrative law judge specializing in health court adjudications would review the claim de novo using all available materials, including a live hearing, if requested. After input from a court-appointed medical expert, the health court judge would render a verdict and produce a written opinion with precedential authority.

Engstrom, A Dose of Reality for Specialized Courts: Lessons from the VICP, 163 U. Pa. L. Rev. 1631 (2015), sounds a note of concern regarding such health courts, finding a mixed record from one of these specialty courts (the Vaccine Injury Compensation Program).

(5)

SECTION G. PROOF OF NEGLIGENCE

Success in prosecuting or defending negligence actions typically hinges on what the parties can prove at trial. With respect to offering evidence on the question of negligence, Clarence Morris observed that "the plaintiff has usually exhausted the possibilities of proof once he has shown: (1) what defendant did, (2) how dangerous it was, (3) defendant's opportunity to discern danger, (4) availability of safer alternatives, and (5) defendant's opportunity to know about safer alternatives." Morris, Proof of Negligence, 47 Nw. U. L. Rev. 817, 834 (1953). In most negligence actions, plaintiffs get their cases to juries by proving that defendants failed to take specific precautions that would have averted the accident and resulting harm. Most modern litigation, especially in medical malpractice and products liability cases, also requires expert evidence to address issues such as the proper standard of care or causation. This section, however, is not primarily concerned with these general matters of proof, which are properly taken up in courses on evidence, trial practice, or clinical education.

But one question of proof has a long and close association with the law of tort. The doctrine of res ipsa loquitur—literally, Latin for "the thing speaks for itself"—is frequently invoked when the plaintiff seeks to establish the defendant's negligence by circumstantial evidence. Instead of proving that the defendant committed a specific act of negligence, a plaintiff invoking res ipsa loquitur argues that the jury should *infer* negligence from the very fact of the accident or injury. In some cases, the plaintiff seeks to reach and persuade a jury on the strength of the doctrine itself, relying on the jury's common knowledge. At other times, the plaintiff combines the doctrine with lay and expert testimony. This section traces the development and use of the doctrine, first with ordinary accident cases, and then in medical malpractice cases.

Byrne v. Boadle

(1863) 159 Eng. Rep. 299 (Exch.)

[Plaintiff's complaint stated that he was passing along the highway in front of defendant's premises when he was struck and badly hurt by a barrel of flour that was apparently being lowered from a window above, which was on the premises of the defendant, a dealer in flour. Several witnesses testified that they saw the barrel fall and hit plaintiff. The defendant claimed that there was no evidence of negligence for the jury. The trial court, agreeing, nonsuited plaintiff after the jury had assessed the damages at £50. On appeal in the Court of Exchequer, the plaintiff argued that the evidence was sufficient to support a verdict in his favor. In response, the defendant's lawyer argued that it was consistent with the evidence that the purchaser of the flour or some complete stranger was supervising the lowering of the barrel of flour and that its fall was not attributable in any way to defendant or his servants. Pollock, C.B.: "The presumption is that the defendant's servants were engaged in removing the defendant's flour. If they were not it was competent to the defendant to prove it." Defendant's attorney replied, "Surmise ought not to be substituted for strict proof when it is thought to fix a defendant with serious liability. The plaintiff should establish his case by affirmative evidence. . . . The plaintiff was bound to give affirmative proof of negligence. But there was not a scintilla of evidence, unless the occurrence is of itself evidence of negligence." Pollock, C.B.: "There are certain cases of which it may be said res ipsa loquitur and this seems one of them. In some cases the Court had held that the mere fact of the accident having occurred is evidence of negligence, as, for instance, in the case of railway collisions."]

Pollock, C.B. We are all of opinion that the rule must be absolute [i.e., immediate and unconditional] to enter the verdict for the plaintiff. The learned counsel was quite right in saying that there are many accidents from which no presumption of negligence can arise, but I think it would be wrong to lay down as a rule that in no case can presumption of negligence arise from the fact of an accident. Suppose in this case the barrel had rolled out of the warehouse and fallen on the plaintiff, how could he possibly ascertain from what cause it occurred? It is the duty of persons who keep barrels in a warehouse to take care that they do not roll out, and I think that such a case would, beyond all doubt, afford prima facie evidence of negligence. A barrel could not roll out of a warehouse without some negligence, and to say that a plaintiff who is injured by it must call witnesses from the warehouse to prove negligence seems to me preposterous. So in the building or repairing a house, or putting pots on the chimneys, if a person passing along the road is injured by something falling upon him, I think the accident alone would be prima facie evidence of negligence. Or if an article calculated to cause damage is put in a wrong place and does mischief, I think that those whose duty it was to put it in the right place are prima facie responsible, and if there is any state of facts to rebut the presumption of negligence, they must prove them. The present case upon the evidence comes to this, a man is passing in front of the premises of a dealer in flour, and there falls down upon him a barrel of flour. I think it apparent that the barrel was in the custody of the defendant who occupied the premises, and who is responsible for the acts of his servants who had the control of it; and in my opinion the fact of its falling is prima facie evidence of negligence, and the plaintiff who was injured by it is not bound to show that it could not fall without negligence, but if there are any facts inconsistent with negligence it is for the defendant to prove them. [Judgment below reversed.]

NOTES

1. *Historical Origins.* Baron Pollock's judicial aside in *Byrne* gave the doctrine its enduring Latin tag. Shortly thereafter, Chief Justice Erle supplied one standard account of res ipsa loquitur in Scott v. London & St. Katherine Docks Co., (1865) 159 Eng. Rep. 665 (Exch.).

> There must be reasonable evidence of negligence; but where the thing is shown to be under the management of the defendant or his servants, and the accident is such as in the ordinary course of things does not happen if those who have the management use proper care, it affords reasonable evidence, in the absence of explanation by the defendants, that the accident arose from want of care. . . .

In Wakelin v. London & S.W. Ry., [1886] 12 AC 41 (HL) 45–46 (appeal taken from Eng.), the plaintiff's deceased was struck and killed by one of defendant's trains. The view of the track was unobstructed at the time of the accident, and there was no specific evidence of any negligent act or omission by the defendant. The trial judge allowed the case to go to the jury, which returned a verdict for the plaintiff. The House of Lords overturned the decision, with Lord Halsbury noting:

> In this case I am unable to see any evidence of how this unfortunate calamity occurred. One may surmise, and it is but surmise and not evidence, that the unfortunate man was knocked down by a passing train while on the level crossing; but assuming in the plaintiff's favour that fact to be established, is there anything to shew that the train ran over the man rather than that the man ran against the train? I understand the admission in the answer to the sixth interrogatory to be simply an admission that the death of the plaintiff's husband was caused by contact with the train. If there are two moving bodies which come in contact, whether ships, or carriages, or even persons, it is not uncommon to hear the person complaining of the injury

> describe it as having been caused by his ship, or his carriage, or himself having been run into, or run down, or run upon; but if a man ran across an approaching train so close that he was struck by it, is it more true to say that the engine ran down the man, or that the man ran against the engine? Neither man nor engine were intended to come in contact, but each advanced to such a point that contact was accomplished. . . .

Does res ipsa loquitur as formulated in *Scott* help the plaintiff in *Wakelin*?

The doctrine of res ipsa loquitur is ubiquitous in the United States. Every state has adopted some form of the doctrine with the sole exception of South Carolina. See Snow v. City of Columbia, 409 S.E.2d 797, 803 (S.C. Ct. App. 1991).

2. *From the Terrace, Hotel, etc.* In *Byrne*, was the critical difficulty in establishing negligence in how the barrel was handled, or in showing that the person who dropped the barrel was someone for whom the defendant was responsible? Could the plaintiff have recovered if a thief had dropped the barrel out of the window?

In Larson v. St. Francis Hotel, 188 P.2d 513, 515 (Cal. App. 1948), the plaintiff, while walking on the sidewalk next to the hotel, was hit by a chair apparently thrown out of one of the hotel's windows as "the result of the effervescence and ebullition of San Franciscans in their exuberance of joy on V-J Day, August 14, 1945." Bray, J., refused to apply res ipsa loquitur:

> While, as pointed out by plaintiff, the rule of exclusive control "is not limited to the actual physical control but applies to the right of control of the instrumentality which causes the injury" it is not clear to us how this helps plaintiff's case. A hotel does not have exclusive control, either actual or potential, of its furniture. Guests have, at least, partial control. Moreover, it cannot be said that with the hotel using ordinary care "the accident was such that in the ordinary course of events . . . would not have happened." On the contrary, the mishap would quite as likely be due to the fault of a guest or other person as to that of defendants. The most logical inference from the circumstances shown is that the chair was thrown by some such person from a window. It thus appears that this occurrence is not such as ordinarily does not happen without the negligence of the party charged, but, rather, one in which the accident ordinarily might happen despite the fact that the defendants used reasonable care and were totally free from negligence. To keep guests and visitors from throwing furniture out windows would require a guard to be placed in every room in the hotel, and no one would contend that there is any rule of law requiring a hotel to do that.

Contrast Connolly v. Nicollet Hotel, 95 N.W.2d 657, 669 (Minn. 1959), in which defendant's hotel was "taken over" by a Junior Chamber of Commerce national convention, whose antics gave the management ample notice of drinking, revelry, and hooliganism on the premises. Plaintiff was injured when struck by some unidentified falling object. *Connolly* distinguished *Larson* as a case with a surprise celebration. In an opinion that never used the words "res ipsa loquitur," Murphy, J., reinstated the jury's $30,000 verdict for the plaintiff. Placing heavy reliance on "circumstantial evidence," he reversed the trial judge's judgment notwithstanding the verdict for defendant.

3. *Doctrinal Standards.* How would you characterize the significant differences between the Prosser standard and the Second and Third Restatement formulations? Which standard should courts adopt? The vast majority of modern courts continue to apply the Prosser test or RST §328D. E.g., Estate of Hall v. Akron Gen. Med. Ctr., 927 N.E.2d 1112 (Ohio 2010) (applying a standard derived from RST §328D); Tyndale v. St. Francis Hospital, 65 A.D.3d 1133, 1133 (N.Y. App. Div. 2009) (applying the Prosser test); Linnear v. CenterPoint Energy Entex/Reliant Energy, 966 So. 2d 36, 45 (La. 2007) (applying a standard derived from RST §328D).

PROSSER TEST

(1) the event must be of a kind which ordinarily does not occur in the absence of someone's negligence;

(2) it must be caused by an agency or instrumentality within the exclusive control of the defendant;

(3) it must not have been due to any voluntary action or contribution on the part of the plaintiff.

Prosser and Keeton on Torts §39, at 244 (derived from Wigmore on Evidence §2509 (1st ed. 1905)).

RESTATEMENT OF THE LAW (SECOND) OF TORTS

§328D. Res Ipsa Loquitur

(1) It may be inferred that harm suffered by the plaintiff is caused by negligence of the defendant when

(a) the event is of a kind which ordinarily does not occur in the absence of negligence;

(b) other responsible causes, including the conduct of the plaintiff and third persons, are sufficiently eliminated by the evidence; and

(c) the indicated negligence is within the scope of the defendant's duty to the plaintiff.

(2) It is the function of the court to determine whether the inference may be reasonably drawn by the jury, or whether it must be necessarily drawn.

(3) It is the function of the jury to determine whether the inference is to be drawn in any case where different conclusions may reasonably be reached.

Comment g. Defendant's exclusive control: . . . Usually [plaintiff demonstrates defendant's responsibility] by showing that a specific instrumentality which has caused the event . . . w[as] under the exclusive control of the defendant. Thus the responsibility of the defendant is proved by eliminating that of any other person. . . . [E]xclusive control is merely one way of proving his responsibility.

RESTATEMENT OF THE LAW (THIRD) OF TORTS: LIABILITY FOR PHYSICAL AND EMOTIONAL HARM

§17. Res Ipsa Loquitur

The factfinder may infer that the defendant has been negligent when the accident causing the plaintiff's harm is a type of accident that ordinarily happens as a result of the negligence of a class of actors of which the defendant is the relevant member.

4. *Jury Instructions.* Pattern jury instructions typically advise judges to determine if res ipsa loquitur is appropriate in a given case, and, if so, to explain the doctrine to the jury. Most instructions inform the jury that they are permitted (but not required) to infer the defendant's negligence from the circumstantial evidence presented if they determine that the res ipsa loquitur factors (commonly those listed in RST §328D) are present. E.g., Washington Pattern Jury Instructions—Civil: 22.01 (2023); New York Pattern Jury Instructions—Civil: 2:65 (2023).

WASHINGTON PATTERN JURY INSTRUCTIONS

CIVIL 22.01. Res Ipsa Loquitur—Inference of Negligence

If you find that:

(1) the [accident] [or] [occurrence] producing the [injury] [damage] is of a kind that ordinarily does not happen in the absence of someone's negligence; [and]

(2) the injury was caused by an agency or instrumentality within the exclusive control of the defendant; [and]

[(3) the injury-causing [accident] [or] [occurrence] was not due solely to a voluntary act or omission of the plaintiff;]

then, in the absence of satisfactory explanation, you may infer, but you are not required to infer, that the defendant was negligent [and that such negligence produced the [injury] [damage] complained of by the plaintiff].

5. *Judicial Control.* Consider how judges control juries in res ipsa cases. In Walston v. Lambersten, 349 F.2d 660 (9th Cir. 1965), the defendant's boat disappeared at sea while crab fishing. The ship was in seaworthy condition when it left port and had been seen by other fishermen "going along just like a duck, easy." The plaintiff, the widow of one of the three seaman who died when the boat sank, suggested that the ship might have sunk because of a sudden redistribution of its weight after the catch had been taken aboard. The Ninth Circuit approved the district court's refusal to submit res ipsa loquitur to the jury, noting that "the sea itself contains many hazards, and an inference of liability of the shipowner for the mysterious loss of his vessel should not be lightly drawn." One such hazard mentioned at trial was that of striking "deadheads," such as partially submerged logs. Could it be possible that the decedent's own negligence contributed to the harm?

Conversely, in some cases, a plaintiff presents enough circumstantial evidence to obtain a directed verdict under res ipsa loquitur. In Newing v. Cheatham, 540 P.2d 33 (Cal. 1975), the plaintiff's decedent was killed when a plane owned and piloted by the defendant's decedent crashed in mountainous terrain about thirteen miles east of Tijuana, Mexico. The plaintiff's evidence indicated that the only possible cause of the crash was the negligence of the defendant in running out of fuel while in flight. The defendant had been drinking beer for about an hour on the morning of the crash. When the wreckage of the plane was examined, the smell of alcohol was found on the pilot's breath, as well as on the breath of a second passenger. None was found on plaintiff's decedent's breath. Eight or nine empty beer cans were also uncovered. Visibility was excellent; the weather was calm; there was no evidence of a midair collision; the plane's clock indicated that the crash took place at a time when it could be reasonably expected for the plane's fuel supply to be exhausted; and after the crash the plane's fuel tanks did not contain sufficient fuel to feed the motor. The evidence also pointed to the pilot's exclusive control over the plane. He owned the plane; he was the only licensed pilot on board the aircraft; he was at the controls when the crash took place; and the applicable federal air regulations imposed upon him ultimate responsibility while airborne. Finally, no evidence suggested that the plaintiff's decedent's voluntary conduct could have contributed to the crash, since he did not know how to fly and at the time of the crash was seated in a rear seat, out of reach of the controls. The California Supreme Court upheld the trial court's decision to take the case from the jury and to direct a verdict for the plaintiff.

Why did res ipsa loquitur apply in *Newing* but not in *Walston*? According to Grady, Res Ipsa Loquitur and Compliance Error, 142 U. Pa. L. Rev. 887, 910 (1994), "accidents in areas with the most safety equipment are the strongest res ipsa cases." Better technology reduces the number of accidents, but in the accidents that do occur, it makes it easier to rule out natural events or plaintiff's error.

> Since crab boat technology is so primitive, there are many hazards that will lead to its destruction without anyone having been negligent. Indeed, the cruder safety technology leads to a higher rate of unavoidable accident than there is in the air. Also, with more rudimentary technology, the required rate of precaution is lower than on a commercial aircraft. Hence, the possibilities for compliance error are lower at sea. A strong res ipsa case is one in which the expected rate of compliance error is high relative to the normal rate of unavoidable accident.

Colmenares Vivas v. Sun Alliance Insurance Co.

807 F.2d 1102 (1st Cir. 1986)

Bownes, C.J. Appellants are plaintiffs in a diversity action to recover damages for injuries they suffered in an accident while riding an escalator. After the parties had presented their evidence, the defendants moved for and were granted a directed verdict. The court held that there was no evidence of negligence and that the doctrine of res ipsa loquitur, which would raise a presumption of negligence, did not apply. We reverse the directed verdict and remand the case to the district court because we hold that res ipsa loquitur does apply.

I. Background

The relevant facts are not in dispute. On February 12, 1984, Jose Domingo Colmenares Vivas and his wife, Dilia Arreaza de Colmenares, arrived at the Luis Muñoz Marín International Airport in Puerto Rico. They took an escalator on their way to the Immigration and Customs checkpoint on the second level. Mrs. Colmenares was riding the escalator on the right-hand side, holding the moving handrail, one step ahead of her husband. When the couple was about halfway up the escalator, the handrail stopped moving, but the steps continued the ascent, causing Mrs. Colmenares to lose her balance. Her husband grabbed her from behind with both hands and prevented her from falling, but in doing so, he lost his balance and tumbled down the stairs. Mr. and Mrs. Colmenares filed a direct action against the Sun Alliance Insurance Company (Sun Alliance), who is the liability insurance carrier for the airport's owner and operator, the Puerto Rico Ports Authority (Ports Authority). Sun Alliance brought a third-party contractual action against Westinghouse Electric Corporation (Westinghouse) based on a maintenance contract that required Westinghouse to inspect, maintain, adjust, repair, and replace parts as needed for the escalator and handrails, and to keep the escalator in a safe operating condition....

The trial was conducted on January 30 and 31, 1986. Appellants called four witnesses. The Ports Authority's contract and maintenance supervisor testified about his daily weekday inspections of the escalator, about the maintenance contract with Westinghouse, about inspection and maintenance procedures, and about the accident report and subsequent repair and maintenance of the escalator. The Ports Authority's assistant chief of operations testified about the accident report. Appellants' testimony concerned the accident and their injuries.

... After hearing the parties' arguments, the court ruled that there was no evidence that the Ports Authority had been negligent, and that the case could not go to the jury based on res ipsa loquitur because at least one of the requirements for its application — that the injury-causing instrumentality was within the exclusive control of the defendant — was not met....

II. Res Ipsa Loquitur

Under Puerto Rico law, three requirements must be met for res ipsa loquitur ("the thing speaks for itself") to apply: "(1) the accident must be of a kind which ordinarily does not occur in the absence of someone's negligence; (2) it must be caused by an agency or instrumentality within the exclusive control of the defendant; [and] (3) it must not be due to any voluntary action on the part of the plaintiff." Community Partnership v. Presbyterian Hosp., 88 P.R.R. 379, 386 (1963). If all three requirements are met, the jury may infer that the defendant was negligent even though there is no direct evidence to that effect.

A. The First Requirement: Inference of Negligence

The first requirement that must be met for res ipsa loquitur to apply is that "the accident must be such that in the light of ordinary experience it gives rise to an inference that someone has been negligent." It is not clear to us whether the district court decided that this requirement was met, although the court did suggest that it was giving the benefit of the doubt on this question to the appellants. We hold that this requirement was met because an escalator handrail probably would not stop suddenly while the escalator continues moving unless someone had been negligent.[2]

This requirement would not be met if appellants had shown nothing more than that they had been injured on the escalator, because based on this fact alone it would not be likely that someone other than the appellants had been negligent. Here, it was not disputed that the handrail malfunctioned and stopped suddenly, an event that foreseeably could cause riders to lose their balance and get injured. Thus, the evidence gave rise to an inference that someone probably had been negligent in operating or maintaining the escalator, and the first requirement for the application of res ipsa loquitur was met.

B. The Second Requirement: Exclusive Control

The second requirement for res ipsa loquitur to apply is that the injury-causing instrumentality—in this case, the escalator—must have been within the exclusive control of the defendant. The district court found that this requisite was not met, despite the parties' stipulation that "[t]he escalator in question is property of and is under the control of the Puerto Rico Ports Authority." We agree that this stipulation was not by itself enough to satisfy the res ipsa loquitur requirement. It did not exclude the possibility that someone else also had control over the escalator; indeed, the stipulation said that Westinghouse maintained the escalator. We hold, however, that the Ports Authority effectively had exclusive control over the escalator because the authority in control of a public area had a nondelegable duty to maintain its facilities in a safe condition.

Few courts have required that control literally be "exclusive." . . . The exclusive control requirement, then, should not be so narrowly construed as to take from the jury the ability to infer that a defendant was negligent when the defendant was responsible for the injury-causing instrumentality, even if someone else might also have been responsible. The purpose of the requirement is not to restrict the application of the res ipsa loquitur inference to cases in which there is only one actor who dealt with the instrumentality, but rather "to eliminate the possibility that the accident was caused by a *third party*." It is not necessary, therefore, for the defendant

---

2. In some jurisdictions, the courts have taken the position that escalator operators are common carriers owing the highest degree of care to their passengers. . . . To our knowledge, the Puerto Rico courts have not equated escalators to common carriers, and such a determination is not properly made by this court in the first instance. For the purposes of this appeal, however, it would not matter if the stricter standard did apply, because we hold that an inference of negligence has been raised even under the lower reasonable care standard.

to have had actual physical control; it is enough that the defendant, and not a third party, was ultimately responsible for the instrumentality. Thus, res ipsa loquitur applies even if the defendant shares responsibility with another, or if the defendant is responsible for the instrumentality even though someone else had physical control over it. It follows that a defendant charged with a nondelegable duty of care to maintain an instrumentality in a safe condition effectively has exclusive control over it for the purposes of applying res ipsa loquitur. Unless the duty is delegable, the res ipsa loquitur inference is not defeated if the defendant had shifted physical control to an agent or contracted with another to carry out its responsibilities.

We hold that the Ports Authority could not delegate its duty to maintain safe escalators. There are no set criteria for determining whether a duty is nondelegable; the critical question is whether the responsibility is so important to the community that it should not be transferred to another. The Ports Authority was charged with such a responsibility. It was created for a public purpose, which included the operation and management of the airport. A concomitant of this authority is the duty to keep the facilities it operates in a reasonably safe condition. The public is entitled to rely on the Ports Authority—not its agents or contractors—to see that this is done. The Ports Authority apparently recognized this responsibility, for its maintenance and contract supervisor conducted daily weekday inspections of the escalators despite the maintenance contract with Westinghouse.

Duties have been seen as nondelegable in several analogous situations. For example, a public authority may not delegate to an independent contractor its responsibility to see that work in a public place is done carefully. Also, a government may not delegate its responsibility to maintain safe roads and similar public places. Finally, an owner has a nondelegable duty to keep business premises safe for invitees. These examples demonstrate a general tort law policy not to allow an entity to shift by contract its responsibility for keeping an area used by the public in a safe condition. It would be contrary to this policy to allow the owner and operator of an airport terminal to delegate its duty to keep its facility safe. We hold, therefore, that the district court erred in ruling that the exclusive control requirement was not met.

C. The Third Requirement: The Plaintiff's Actions

The third requirement that must be met for res ipsa loquitur to apply is that the accident must not have been due to the plaintiff's voluntary actions. The district court found, and we agree, that there was no evidence that Mr. and Mrs. Colmenares caused the accident. Indeed, there is no indication that they did anything other than attempt to ride the escalator in the ordinary manner. Therefore, we hold that all three requirements were met and that the jury should have been allowed to consider whether the Ports Authority was liable based on the permissible inference of negligence raised by the application of res ipsa loquitur. . . .

Torruella, C.J. I must regretfully dissent. . . .

In my view, *solely* because the handrail stopped and Mrs. Colmenares fell, without further evidence as to why or how the handrail malfunctioned, does not give rise to an inference of *negligence* by the Ports Authority. . . .

The malfunctioning of an escalator presents an even stronger argument against the raising of an inference of negligence without additional proof as to the cause of the malfunction. Although a court can take notice that an escalator is a complicated piece of machinery, it has no basis of common knowledge for inferring that its malfunction is the result of the operator's negligence. . . .

NOTES

1. *A Difference of Views?* What result in *Colmenares* if both the handrails and the steps had stopped simultaneously? With *Colmenares*, contrast Holzhauer v. Saks & Co., 697 A.2d 89, 93 (Md. 1997), where plaintiff was injured when he tumbled back down the steps after the escalator on which he was riding suddenly stopped. Chasanow, J., refused to allow the plaintiff to use res ipsa loquitur:

> For safety reasons, the escalator in question was equipped with two emergency stop buttons, located at the top and bottom of the escalator, respectively. When either button is pushed, if the escalator is functioning as intended, the escalator will stop. The buttons are safety devices designed to stop the escalator quickly should a hand, foot, or article of clothing become caught; thus, ready accessibility to the buttons is only sensible. We cannot say that the escalator would not stop in the absence of Appellees' negligence because the escalator would also stop whenever any person pushed one of the emergency stop buttons.
>
> The record is silent as to whether anyone did, in fact, push one of the stop buttons, but this is of little concern. The facts need not show that a stop button definitely was pushed to preclude reliance on *res ipsa;* they need only show that something other than Appellees' negligence was just as likely to cause the escalator to stop. The fact that the escalator had never malfunctioned before the day in question, and has not malfunctioned since, makes it equally likely, if not slightly more likely, that the escalator did not malfunction on the day in question but, rather, that it stopped because somebody intentionally or unintentionally pushed an emergency stop button.

In addition, the court held that the plaintiff could not satisfy the exclusive control requirement of res ipsa loquitur, observing: "Hundreds of Saks & Co.'s customers have unlimited access to the emergency buttons each day." Is this case distinguishable from *Colmenares*?

Such disputes over the applicability of res ipsa loquitur also arise with automatic doors. In the leading case of Rose v. New York Port Authority, 293 A.2d 371, 375 (N.J. 1972), the plaintiff claimed damages when he was struck by an automatic glass door while moving about JFK Airport. "Here the occurrence bespeaks negligence. Members of the public passing through automatic doors, whether in an airport, office building or supermarket do so generally without sustaining injury. What happened to the plaintiff here is fortunately unusual and not commonplace. It strongly suggests a malfunction which in turn suggests negligence."

But a similar inference was not drawn in Kmart v. Bassett, 769 So. 2d 282 (Ala. 2000), in which the plaintiff, an eighty-three-year-old woman who used a cane, stepped on a rubber mat outside a Kmart to activate the automatic doors. As she progressed one third of the way, the door closed on her, resulting in a fall that led to a fractured hip. The Alabama Supreme Court reversed a jury verdict of $289,000 for plaintiff. It refused to find negligence in Kmart's decision not to have a regular maintenance contract and to wait for signs of trouble before calling for repairs, and it further rejected the argument that failures of this sort could not happen in the absence of negligence, noting that "a mere malfunction would be insufficient to invoke the doctrine of res ipsa loquitur under Alabama law." Should it make a difference if the door worked after the accident or not? Should the door be designed so as to avoid closing if someone is on the mat, no matter how slowly she moves?

Finally, in Estevez v. SLG 100 Park LLC, 189 N.Y.S.3d 53, 57 (App. Div. 2023), a construction worker was injured when "as the elevator doors started to close parts of his body were inside the elevator, and he was at the midpoint in the process of getting in." The elevator had an infrared sensor installed in the inner cab that should have prevented the elevator door from closing if a person or object was in its path. The court first held that the defendant had "a nondelegable duty to ensure the elevator was kept in a reasonably safe condition," and concluded that the doctrine of res ipsa loquitur could be applied. What if the sensor was determined to have been functioning when the plaintiff was injured?

2. *Exclusive Control.* What should be done when multiple parties are responsible for the safe operation of the dangerous instrumentality? Some courts reject the notion of joint exclusive control. In McGriff v. Gramercy Capital Corp., No. 2:13CV152, 2013 WL 1856233, at *4 (E.D. Va. Apr. 29, 2013), the elevator that the plaintiff had just entered suddenly plunged several floors, causing serious injuries. The court refused to allow the case to go to the jury, noting, "While Virginia will permit a case against multiple defendants to go forward to determine *which* defendant had control, there is no precedent for permitting an action to proceed on the basis of joint exclusive control."

The opposite view was taken in Miles v. St. Regis Paper Co., 467 P.2d 307, 310 (Wash. 1970), which involved the complex interaction between tort and workers' compensation law. In general, the exclusive remedy provision of the workers' compensation statutes prevents an injured party from suing his employer in tort. To meet this challenge, the plaintiff often claims that res ipsa loquitur applies because some third-party defendant has "exclusive" control of the dangerous instrumentality. The decedent, an employee of the "D" Street Rafting Company, was crushed to death by a load of logs that suddenly rolled off the defendant railroad's flatcar while he was releasing one of its binders. Even though the decedent's employer directed the loading operations, a divided court found that the railroad company, which responded to the orders of employees of the rafting company, had "exclusive control" over the movement of the train, observing "the ultimate decision to move the train was made by employees of the railroad." Does a finding of "exclusive control" in *Colmenares* require the same finding here?

3. *Plaintiff's Conduct and Conduct of a Third Party.* In many negligence actions the dangerous instrumentality in question has passed through the hands of a third party, only to cause injury while being used by the plaintiff. In these cases, "the plaintiff's mere possession of a chattel which injures him does not prevent a res ipsa case where it is made clear that he has done nothing abnormal and *has used the thing only for the purpose for which it was intended.*" Prosser, Res Ipsa Loquitur in California, 37 Calif. L. Rev. 183, 201–02 (1949).

Similarly, res ipsa loquitur was invoked in Benedict v. Eppley Hotel Co., 65 N.W.2d 224, 229 (Neb. 1954). The plaintiff-appellee was injured when a folding chair collapsed after she had been sitting on it for some 20 or 30 minutes while participating in a bingo game. After the accident it was discovered that the screws and bolts on one side of the chair were missing.

> [Plaintiff's] acts in reference to the chair were limited to transportation of it from where she first saw it in the hallway connecting the Embassy Room and the ballroom of the Rome Hotel to the table in the latter room where the game was in progress and sitting on it. She occupied the chair as an invitee of appellant. She had no right or duty to examine it for defects. She had a right to assume it was a safe instrumentality for the use she had been invited by appellant to make of it. Appellant had the ownership, possession, and control of the chair under the circumstances of this case and it was obligated to maintain it in a reasonably safe condition for the invited use made of it by the appellee. The fact that the chair when it was being properly used for the purpose for which it was made available gave way permits an inference that it was defective and unsafe and that appellant had not used due care in reference to it.

Why did the plaintiff have "no right" to inspect the chair?

Formerly, res ipsa loquitur was only available when the plaintiff had not contributed in any way to the accident. RTT: LPEH §17, comment *h*, explains the modern rule that plaintiff's conduct only bears on the application of the doctrine when it may have disrupted the alleged causal sequence between the defendant's actions and the harm. Where this is not the case (for example, a plaintiff has been inattentive but cannot possibly have set the accident in motion), the plaintiff's negligence may reduce the amount of damages awarded, but it does not affect the operation of the doctrine in establishing the defendant's negligence. Thus the plaintiff in *Colmenares* can only rely on the doctrine by excluding his own conduct as a source of the escalator malfunction. But the possible contributory negligence of the plaintiff in Byrne v. Boadle does not prevent the use of res ipsa loquitur since the plaintiff had no control whatsoever over the barrel of flour.

What happens when the defendant has acquired the dangerous instrumentality from a third party? The Third Restatement takes a strong stand against the preservation of the exclusive control requirement, noting that it functions as a poor "proxy" for negligence. For example, an injured pedestrian should not normally be able to rely on res ipsa loquitur in a suit against a driver if his car's brakes fail a day after purchase. Although the driver has exclusive control over the car at the time of the accident, there is a high likelihood that the manufacturer is responsible for the brake failure. RTT: LPEH §17, comment *b*.

4. *Assessing the Probabilities of Negligence.* Conceptually the most difficult part of the res ipsa loquitur test comes from attaching a precise meaning to the phrase "ordinarily does not occur in the absence of negligence." Most courts intuit whether this test is satisfied. Thus in McDougald v. Perry, 716 So. 2d 783, 786 (Fla. 1998), the court used res ipsa loquitur when the defendant's 130-pound spare tire fell out from its angled cradle underneath the defendant's tractor-trailer as it was being driven over some railroad tracks. It bounced in the air and struck the plaintiff's jeep. The incident "is the type of accident which, on the basis of common experience and as a matter of general knowledge, would not occur but for the failure to exercise reasonable care by the person who had control of the spare tire."

How strong must the inference of the defendant's negligence be before the plaintiff must introduce evidence to negate the likelihood of alternative causes? The Third Restatement offers a quantitative example:

> . . . [I]f a type of accident is caused by defendant negligence 70 percent of the time, the plaintiff's res ipsa case can proceed even without evidence from the plaintiff negating any of the remaining causes. But for another type of accident, defendant negligence may be implicated only 45 percent of the time; two other causes are 30 percent and 25 percent possibilities. In such cases the plaintiff must offer evidence negating at least one of these causes in order to render the res ipsa claim acceptable.

RTT: LPEH §17, comment *d*.

The Third Restatement shows further sensitivity to this difficulty by requiring the plaintiff to negotiate special hurdles created by issues of compound probabilities. Thus if a given accident of a certain class only occurs two-thirds of the time with negligence, and that negligence is attributable to the defendant only two-thirds of the time, then res ipsa loquitur should not apply. Even if the accident does not ordinarily happen without the occurrence of negligence, it ordinarily happens without the negligence of this defendant, since the evidence establishes that the defendant is likely to be the responsible party only four-ninths (two-thirds multiplied by two-thirds) of the time. RTT: LPEH §17, comment *b*.

The phrase "ordinarily does not occur in the absence of negligence" is fraught with additional difficulties. Linguistically, the expression has generally been taken to signify either

> (1) that the probability of the injury given the exercise of reasonable care is quite small, or (2) that the probability of the injury given reasonable care is smaller than the probability of the injury given negligence, or (3) that the probability of the injury given reasonable care is much smaller than the probability of the injury given negligence.

Kaye, Probability Theory Meets Res Ipsa Loquitur, 77 Mich. L. Rev. 1456, 1465 (1979). However, as Kaye points out, none of these three commonsense statements captures the ultimate issue, namely, whether the probability that the defendant was negligent, given the occurrence of the injury, is greater than 50 percent. The first expression only notes that the probability of accident is quite small when there is reasonable care, but if the defendant exercises reasonable care an overwhelming proportion of the time, it could still prove more likely than not that reasonable care was in fact exercised in the particular case.

To see why this distinction—that the relevant inquiry is whether there is a greater than 50 percent chance of negligence given the occurrence of an injury—is essential, consider this example. Suppose that it is established that a hand grenade has exploded prematurely because it contains a defective fuse. See, e.g., McGonigal v. Gearhart Industries, Inc., 788 F.2d 321 (5th Cir. 1986). Assume further liability turns solely on whether the defective fuse escaped detection because the manufacturer's employees negligently inspected it before shipment. To analyze this situation, consider two scenarios. First, suppose there is a one-in-one-thousand chance of a defective grenade slipping through a reasonable inspection and a one-in-two chance of a defective grenade slipping through a negligent inspection. If the defendant is careful 99.9 percent of the time, then for every one million units produced, 999,000 of them are properly inspected. Of these, we should expect to see 999 instances of failure, none of which are attributable to defendant's negligence. By the same token, we should expect to see 1,000 units that are negligently inspected, yielding an additional 500 failures (half of the negligently inspected 1,000 units). To be sure, any negligently inspected unit is much more likely to be defective than a carefully manufactured one (as in Kaye's proposition (2)), for a 50 percent failure rate is 500 times a 0.1 percent failure rate. Yet—and the point is critical—by the same token it is more likely (by odds of 999 to 500) that any defective unit comes from the group of carefully inspected grenades than from the group of negligently inspected grenades, and thus would not satisfy the "ordinarily does not occur in the absence of negligence" requirement.

Whether negligence is more likely given a defective product, however, is very sensitive to the choice of numbers. Suppose now that the defendant's inspections were careful only 99 percent of the time, and careless 1 percent of the time. If the probability of a bad grenade slipping through the careful inspection remains 0.1 percent, then 990 defective grenades would be produced when care was exercised (one one-thousandth of 990,000). In addition, however, 5,000 defective units (half of 10,000) would be produced with negligence, making it better than five-to-one odds that the grenade came from the badly inspected batch.

These two examples illustrate the problem with inferring negligence from the occurrence of an accident based only on the knowledge that negligence frequently produces accidents like the one that has occurred. Kaye's article contains a formal demonstration, invoking the use of Bayes' theorem, of why in general that inference should be made only in the third situation set out above, namely, the probability of injury when defendant takes due care is much smaller than the probability of injury when the defendant is negligent. On the intricacies of statistical inference, see also Comment, Mathematics, Fuzzy Negligence and the Logic of Res Ipsa Loquitur, 75 Nw. U. L. Rev. 147 (1980).

Given that judges must decide whether a res ipsa instruction is appropriate, how might we expect them to fare with this probabilistic determination? In Guthrie, Rachlinski & Wistrich, Inside the Judicial Mind, 86 Cornell L. Rev. 777, 808–09 (2001), the authors surveyed federal magistrate judges on a variation of this problem that assumed that a barrel (à la *Byrne)* breaks loose only 1 percent of the time if properly handled, but 90 percent of the time if improperly handled, and employees handle the barrels properly 99.9 percent of the time. The judges were asked to state the odds that the fall of the barrel was attributable to negligence. About 41 percent of the judges said that the barrel's fall attributable to negligence fell between zero and 25 percent of the cases; 8.8 percent chose the interval between 25 and 50 percent; 10.1 percent chose the interval between 51 and 75 percent, and 40.3 percent chose 76 and 100 percent. The right answer is 8.3 percent. To calculate this, assume that there are 100,000 lifts. The 99,900 safe lifts result in breakage 999 times (99,900 multiplied by 0.01), while the

100 improper lifts result in breakage 90 times (100 multiplied by 0.9). The 90 breaks due to improper handling constitute roughly 8.3 percent of the 1,089 total breaks (90 divided by (90 plus 990)). Note that the size of the intervals makes it doubtful that the judges who picked the right answer correctly made the correct calculations. But query, if taught the basic insight about base rates first, could they have calculated the right answer?

Ybarra v. Spangard

154 P.2d 687 (Cal. 1944)

Gibson, C.J. This is an action for damages for personal injuries alleged to have been inflicted on plaintiff by defendants during the course of a surgical operation. The trial court entered judgments of nonsuit as to all defendants and plaintiff appealed.

On October 28, 1939, plaintiff consulted defendant Dr. Tilley, who diagnosed his ailment as appendicitis, and made arrangements for an appendectomy to be performed by defendant Dr. Spangard at a hospital owned and managed by defendant Dr. Swift. Plaintiff entered the hospital, was given a hypodermic injection, slept, and later was awakened by Doctors Tilley and Spangard and wheeled into the operating room by a nurse whom he believed to be defendant Gisler, an employee of Dr. Swift. Defendant Dr. Reser, the anesthetist, also an employee of Dr. Swift, adjusted plaintiff for the operation, pulling his body to the head of the operating table and, according to plaintiff's testimony, laying him back against two hard objects at the top of his shoulders, about an inch below his neck. Dr. Reser then administered the anesthetic and plaintiff lost consciousness. When he awoke early the following morning he was in his hospital room attended by defendant Thompson, the special nurse, and another nurse who was not made a defendant.

Plaintiff testified that prior to the operation he had never had any pain in, or injury to, his right arm or shoulder, but that when he awakened he felt a sharp pain about half way between the neck and the point of the right shoulder. He complained to the nurse, and then to Dr. Tilley, who gave him diathermy treatments while he remained in the hospital. The pain did not cease, but spread down to the lower part of his arm, and after his release from the hospital the condition grew worse. He was unable to rotate or lift his arm, and developed paralysis and atrophy of the muscles around the shoulder. He received further treatments from Dr. Tilley until March, 1940, and then returned to work, wearing his arm in a splint on the advice of Dr. Spangard.

Plaintiff also consulted Dr. Wilfred Sterling Clark, who had X-ray pictures taken which showed an area of diminished sensation below the shoulder and atrophy and wasting away of the muscles around the shoulder. In the opinion of Dr. Clark, plaintiff's condition was due to trauma or injury by pressure or strain, applied between his right shoulder and neck.

Plaintiff was also examined by Dr. Fernando Garduno, who expressed the opinion that plaintiff's injury was a paralysis of traumatic origin, not arising from pathological causes, and not systemic, and that the injury resulted in atrophy, loss of use and restriction of motion of the right arm and shoulder.

Plaintiff's theory is that the foregoing evidence presents a proper case for the application of the doctrine of res ipsa loquitur, and that the inference of negligence arising therefrom makes the granting of a nonsuit improper. Defendants take the position that, assuming that plaintiff's condition was in fact the result of an injury, there is no showing that the act of any particular defendant, nor any particular instrumentality, was the cause thereof. They attack plaintiff's action as an attempt to fix liability "en masse" on various defendants, some of whom were not responsible for the acts of others; and they further point to the failure to show which defendants had control of the instrumentalities that may have been involved. Their main defense may be briefly stated in two propositions: (1) that where there are several defendants, and there is a division of responsibility in the use of an instrumentality causing the injury, and the injury might have resulted from the separate act of either one of two or more persons, the rule of res ipsa loquitur cannot be invoked against any one of them; and (2) that where there are several instrumentalities, and no showing is made as to which caused the injury or as to the particular defendant in control of it, the doctrine cannot apply. We are satisfied, however, that these objections are not well taken in the circumstances of this case.

The doctrine of res ipsa loquitur has three conditions: "(1) the accident must be of a kind which ordinarily does not occur in the absence of someone's negligence; (2) it must be caused by an agency or instrumentality within the exclusive control of the defendant; (3) it must not have been due to any voluntary action or contribution on the part of the plaintiff." (Prosser, Torts, p. 295.) It is applied in a wide variety of situations, including cases of medical or dental treatment and hospital care. . . .

There is, however, some uncertainty as to the extent to which res ipsa loquitur may be invoked in cases of injury from medical treatment. This is in part due to the tendency, in some decisions, to lay undue emphasis on the limitations of the doctrine, and to give too little attention to its basic underlying purpose. The result has been that a simple, understandable rule of circumstantial evidence, with a sound background of common sense and human experience, has occasionally been transformed into a rigid legal formula, which arbitrarily precludes its application in many cases where it is most important that it should be applied. If the doctrine is to continue to serve a useful purpose, we should not forget that "the particular force and justice of the rule, regarded as a presumption throwing upon the party charged the duty of producing evidence, consists in the circumstance that the chief evidence of the true cause, whether culpable or innocent, is practically accessible to him but inaccessible to the injured person." (9 Wigmore, Evidence [3d ed. 1940], §2509, p. 382.)

The present case is of a type which comes within the reason and spirit of the doctrine more fully perhaps than any other. The passenger sitting awake in a railroad car at the time of a collision, the pedestrian walking along the street and struck by a falling object or the debris of an explosion, are surely not more entitled to an explanation than the unconscious patient on the operating table. Viewed from this aspect, it is difficult to see how the doctrine can, with any justification, be so restricted in its statement as to become inapplicable to a patient who submits himself to the care and custody of doctors and nurses, is rendered unconscious, and receives some injury from instrumentalities used in his treatment. Without the aid of the doctrine a patient who received permanent injuries of a serious character, obviously the result of someone's negligence, would be entirely unable to recover unless the doctors and nurses in attendance voluntarily chose to disclose the identity of the negligent person and the facts of establishing liability. If this were the state of the law of negligence, the courts, to avoid gross injustice, would be forced to invoke the principles of absolute liability, irrespective of negligence, in actions by persons suffering injuries during the course of treatment under anesthesia. But we think this juncture has not yet been reached, and the doctrine of res ipsa loquitur is properly applicable to the case before us.

The condition that the injury must not have been due to the plaintiff's voluntary action is of course fully satisfied under the evidence produced herein; and the same is true of the condition that the accident must be one which ordinarily does not occur unless someone was negligent. We have here no problem of negligence in treatment, but of distinct injury to a healthy part of the body not the subject of treatment, nor within the area covered by the operation. The decisions in this state make it clear that such circumstances raise the inference of negligence, and call upon the defendant to explain the unusual result. . . .

The argument of defendants is simply that plaintiff has not shown an injury caused by an instrumentality under a defendant's control, because he has not shown which of the several instrumentalities that he came in contact with while in the hospital caused the injury; and he has not shown that any one defendant or his servants had exclusive control over any particular instrumentality. Defendants assert that some of them were not the employees of other defendants, that some did not stand in any permanent relationship from which liability in tort would follow, and that in view of the nature of the injury, the number of defendants and the different functions performed by each, they could not all be liable for the wrong, if any.

We have no doubt that in a modern hospital a patient is quite likely to come under the care of a number of persons in different types of contractual and other relationships with each other. For example, in the present case it appears that Doctors Smith, Spangard and Tilley were physicians or surgeons commonly placed in the legal category of independent contractors and Dr. Reser, the anesthetist, and defendant Thompson, the special nurse, were employees of Dr. Swift and not of the other doctors. But we do not believe that either the number or relationship of the defendants alone determines whether the doctrine of res ipsa loquitur applies. Every defendant in whose custody the plaintiff was placed for any period was bound to exercise ordinary care to see that no unnecessary harm came to him and each would be liable for failure in this regard. Any defendant who negligently injured him, and any defendant charged with his care who so neglected him as to allow injury to occur, would be liable. The defendant employers would be liable for the neglect of their employees and the doctor in charge of the operation would be liable for the negligence of those who became his temporary servants for the purpose of assisting in the operation.

In this connection, it should be noted that while the assisting physicians and nurses may be employed by the hospital, or engaged by the patient, they normally become the temporary servants or agents of the surgeon in charge while the operation is in progress, and liability may be imposed upon him for their negligent acts under the doctrine of respondeat superior. Thus a surgeon has been held liable for the negligence of an assisting nurse who leaves a sponge or other object inside a patient, and the fact that the duty of seeing that such mistakes do not occur is delegated to others does not absolve the doctor from responsibility for their negligence. . . .

It may appear at the trial that, consistent with the principles outlined above, one or more defendants will be found liable and others absolved, but this should not preclude the application of the rule of res ipsa loquitur. The control, at one time or another, of one or more of the various agencies or instrumentalities which might have harmed the plaintiff was in the hands of every defendant or of his employees or temporary servants. This, we think, places upon them the burden of initial explanation. Plaintiff was rendered unconscious for the purpose of undergoing surgical treatment by the defendants; it is manifestly unreasonable for them to insist that he identify any one of them as the person who did the alleged negligent act.

The other aspect of the case which defendants so strongly emphasize is that plaintiff has not identified the instrumentality any more than he has the particular guilty defendant. Here, again, there is a misconception which, if carried to the extreme for which defendants contend, would unreasonably limit the application of the res ipsa loquitur rule. It should be enough that the plaintiff can show an injury resulting from an external force applied while he lay unconscious in the hospital; this is as clear a case of identification of the instrumentality as the plaintiff may ever be able to make.

[The court then discusses a series of precedents.]

In the face of these examples of liberalization of the tests for res ipsa loquitur, there can be no justification for the rejection of the doctrine in the instant case. As pointed out above, if we accept the contention of defendants herein, there will rarely be any compensation for patients injured while unconscious. A hospital today conducts a highly integrated system of activities, with many persons contributing their efforts. There may be, e.g., preparation for surgery by nurses and interns who are employees of the hospital; administering of an anesthetic by a doctor who may be an employee of the hospital, an employee of the operating surgeon, or an independent contractor; performance of an operation by a surgeon and assistants who may be his employees, employees of the hospital, or independent contractors; and post surgical care by the surgeon, a hospital physician, and nurses. The number of those in whose care the patient is placed is not a good reason for denying him all reasonable opportunity to recover for negligent harm. It is rather a good reason for re-examination of the statement of legal theories which supposedly compel such a shocking result.

We do not at this time undertake to state the extent to which the reasoning of this case may be applied to other situations in which the doctrine of res ipsa loquitur is invoked. We merely hold that where a plaintiff receives unusual injuries while unconscious and in the course of medical treatment, all those defendants who had any control over his body or the instrumentalities which might have caused the injuries may properly be called upon to meet the inference of negligence by giving an explanation of their conduct.

The judgment is reversed.

NOTES

1. *Procedural Role of Res Ipsa Loquitur.* The standard justification for res ipsa loquitur is that it offers injured plaintiffs a method of proving defendants' negligence even when there is no way to know (or no evidence to prove) exactly what happened. RTT: LPEH §17, comment *a*. In Morejon v. Rais Construction Co., 851 N.E.2d 1143, 1146, 1146–47, 1149 (N.Y. 2006), Rosenblatt, J., described courts' confusion over the procedural effects of the doctrine: "Courts, including ours, used 'prima face case,' 'presumption of negligence,' and 'inference of negligence' interchangeably even though the phrases can carry different procedural consequences." *Morejon* affirmed the traditional view that the doctrine is "nothing more than a brand of circumstantial evidence." On this view, "only in the rarest of res ipsa loquitur cases may a plaintiff win summary judgment or a directed verdict. That would happen only when the plaintiff's circumstantial proof is so convincing and the defendant's response so weak that the inference of defendant's negligence is inescapable."

Ybarra is one of a number of exceptional cases in which courts shift the burden of production to the defendants. One early defense of the use of res ipsa loquitur in medical malpractice cases was as a tool to overcome the "conspiracy of silence" among physicians.

> One may suspect that the courts are not reluctant to use res ipsa loquitur as a deliberate instrument of policy to even the balance against the professional conspiracy of silence; but with two exceptions the decisions give no hint of anything more than the obvious inference from the circumstantial evidence alone.

Prosser, Selected Topics on the Law of Torts 346 (1954), citing *Ybarra*. The Third Restatement endorses the use of res ipsa loquitur to "smoke out" the culpable defendant in surgery cases, at least when all are simultaneously present in the operating room, noting that one defendant can escape liability by pointing a finger at another. RTT: LPEH §17, comment *f*. Today, however, the rise of modern discovery devices and the active market in expert testimony have quieted these conspiratorial concerns, such that the Third Restatement treats res ipsa loquitur as a doctrine of circumstantial evidence unrelated to any differential of knowledge between the parties. "The plaintiff may invoke res ipsa even though the defendant is as ignorant of the facts of the accident as the plaintiff is." RTT: LPEH §17, comment *i*.

While most states treat res ipsa loquitur as creating only a permissive inference that a jury is entitled to make, a few states treat it as a rebuttable presumption, which requires the defendant to come forward with exonerating evidence or suffer a judgment as a matter of law. See RTT: LPEH §17, comment *j*; see also Cox v. Paul, 828 N.E.2d 907, 912 (Ind. 2005), noting the difference. What defendant would remain silent even if res ipsa loquitur created only a permissive inference of negligence?

On retrial in *Ybarra*, the defendants testified that to their knowledge nothing had gone wrong in the operation. The California Court of Appeal held that the trial judge could still find for the plaintiff on the strength of the circumstantial evidence in the case. *Ybarra* v. Spangard, 208 P.2d 445 (Cal. App. 1949). For criticism of *Ybarra*, see Seavey, Res Ipsa Loquitur: Tabula in Naufragio, 63 Harv. L. Rev. 643 (1950).

2. *Common Knowledge, Expert Testimony, and Res Ipsa Loquitur.* Should *Ybarra* be treated as a pure res ipsa loquitur case given that Dr. Clark testified that he believed that the source of the injury was pressure applied between the shoulder and neck? In fact, modern anesthesiologists guard against just such pressure by cushioning that area, especially in long operations. What result if this risk was not fully understood when the operation took place? In modern practice, many medical malpractice plaintiffs mount a doubled-edged attack, using expert testimony to prove specific negligence, while invoking res ipsa loquitur in the alternative. Most courts will allow this two-front attack to proceed, see RTT: LPEH §17, comment *g*, but the strategy could easily backfire if the plaintiff prevails at trial solely on the alternative theory only for an appellate court to reverse the judgment on the ground that the res ipsa loquitur instruction was improper.

The Third Restatement takes the position that the "better rule, now accepted by most courts, is that expert testimony is admissible in a medical-malpractice res ipsa loquitur case, and indeed is frequently necessary in order to justify submitting the res ipsa claim to the jury." RTT: LPEH §17, comment *c*. A key exception to the modern rule requiring expert testimony arises when the jury has "common knowledge" that the harm would not have occurred without defendant's negligence, as, for example, when a misapplied hot water bottle burns the plaintiff. However, the common knowledge exception rarely applies when complex medical judgments and procedures are at issue.

In Farber v. Olkon, 254 P.2d 520 (Cal. 1953), the plaintiff, who was mentally incompetent, suffered broken bones after being subjected to electroshock therapy. The court explicitly distinguished *Ybarra* as a case where "plaintiff while unconscious on an operating table received injuries to a healthy part of his body, not subject to treatment or within the area covered by his operation." It then refused to apply the common knowledge test given the undisputed testimony by the defendant's experts that "electroshock therapy is designed to have 'an effect upon the entire body' " in the hope that the convulsion will improve the patient's mental condition. Compare Bardessono v. Michels, 478 P.2d 480, 486 (Cal. 1971), in which the plaintiff received a series of injections of cortisone and local anesthetic for the treatment of tendonitis in his shoulder. All the injections caused the plaintiff excruciating pain, and shortly after their completion he developed partial paralysis. The court held that the jury was properly instructed when told that "it could infer negligence from the happening of the accident alone." The court allowed a jury to rely on common knowledge "if the routine medical procedure is relatively commonplace and simple, rather than special, unusual and complex." If the needle damaged one of the plaintiff's nerves, does that establish negligence or only causation? In *Bardessono*, the defendant testified that she had made the same sort of injection hundreds of times without adverse effects. How should the jury have weighed that evidence?

With *Bardessono*, contrast Greenberg v. Michael Reese Hospital, 396 N.E.2d 1088, 1094 (Ill. App. 1979), *aff'd in part and rev'd in part*, 415 N.E.2d 390, 397 (Ill. 1980). Plaintiff had been treated with radiation for enlarged tonsils and adenoids during the 1940s and 1950s, when such treatment was routine at Michael Reese Hospital. The treatment was discontinued when it was discovered that it could result in tumorous growths in or near the thyroid gland.

The court rejected an analogy between these cases and radiation burn cases to which res ipsa loquitur applies:

> In the radiation burn cases, the reasoning takes two steps: first, that there is no medical reason to use radiation sufficient to cause extensive burns and, second, that the doctor in fact used excess radiation and therefore was negligent. Here, however, plaintiffs concede that irradiation of tonsils was a widely used therapeutic treatment, specifically chosen by the referring physician in the light of surgical dangers and poliomyelitic implications. The only possible inference which res ipsa loquitur could provide in the case at bar is that tumors, having resulted in some percentage of cases from either organic or external stimulus, are the result of negligent medical judgment. Res ipsa loquitur arises from a clearly negligent act (i.e., application of excessive doses of radiation) which leads to an almost certain outcome (radiation burns). Unlike these radiation burn cases, the original diagnostic decision to use tonsillar irradiation is at best debatably negligent. Whether or not a medical judgment to use an alternative form of therapy is legally negligent is properly contested at trial, and should not be subject to a presumption of negligence arising solely from the bad result.

The Illinois Supreme Court remanded on the res ipsa question, stating only that "we are unable to say that no set of facts can be proved which will entitle plaintiff to recover," without addressing the difference between excess radiation and tumor cases.

Finally, even in medical malpractice cases, it is possible to find situations where courts will use res ipsa loquitur to give plaintiffs a judgment as a matter of law. In Quinby v. Plumsteadville Family Practice, Inc., 907 A.2d 1061, 1077 (Pa. 2006), the decedent, who had been a quadriplegic for over twenty-five years, was placed on his right side for an operation to remove a small lesion from the left side of his head. When the operation was completed, the decedent, who had been left unattended, somehow fell off the bed, sustaining injuries that led to his death. The trial judge refused to instruct on res ipsa loquitur. On appeal, Baer, J., held that the plaintiff was entitled to a directed verdict on defendant's negligence:

> The only fact that was in dispute during trial was the positioning of Decedent on the table. This fact, however, is inconsequential to assessing Defendants' negligence. Even if Decedent was placed on his back in the center of the table as Defendants maintain, the fact remains that Decedent fell from the table to the floor, and Defendants have not offered any evidence explaining the cause of the fall. Pursuant to the above discussion, this is not the type of event that occurs without negligence; the evidence sufficiently eliminates other causes; and the negligence was within the scope of Defendants' duty to Decedent.

3. ***Statutory Modification of Res Ipsa Loquitur in Medical Malpractice Cases.*** Res ipsa loquitur has led medical groups to fear that the doctrine will become (as it often is in stranger cases) the opening wedge to a doctrine of strict liability that functions poorly in medical malpractice contexts. In order to limit its scope, and that of the use of common knowledge, medical groups have lobbied for statutes, such as Nev. Rev. Stat. §41A.100 (2023). How would this statute apply to the cases discussed in this section?

NEVADA REVISED STATUTES ANNOTATED (2023)

§41A.100. Required Evidence; Exceptions; Rebuttable Presumption of Negligence

1. Liability for personal injury or death is not imposed upon any provider of medical care based on alleged negligence in the performance of that care unless evidence consisting of expert medical testimony, material from recognized medical texts or treatises or the regulations of the licensed medical facility wherein the alleged negligence occurred is presented to demonstrate the alleged deviation from the accepted standard of care

in the specific circumstances of the case and to prove causation of the alleged personal injury or death, except that such evidence is not required and a rebuttable presumption that the personal injury or death was caused by negligence arises where evidence is presented that the personal injury or death occurred in any one or more of the following circumstances:

(a) A foreign substance other than medication or a prosthetic device was unintentionally left within the body of a patient following surgery;

(b) An explosion or fire originating in a substance used in treatment occurred in the course of treatment;

(c) An unintended burn caused by heat, radiation or chemicals was suffered in the course of medical care;

(d) An injury was suffered during the course of treatment to a part of the body not directly involved in the treatment or proximate thereto; or

(e) A surgical procedure was performed on the wrong patient or the wrong organ, limb or part of a patient's body.

4. ***Res Ipsa Loquitur and Multiple Defendants.*** *Ybarra* also has been extended to actions against multiple defendants sued under different substantive theories. In Anderson v. Somberg, 338 A.2d 1, 5, 9–10 (N.J. 1975), the plaintiff suffered serious injuries when the tip of a surgical forceps (a rongeur) broke off in his spinal canal and remained lodged there despite the efforts of defendant physician to remove it. The plaintiff brought actions against four separate defendants: against the physician, for negligence in the operation; against the hospital, for negligently furnishing a defective instrument; against the medical distributor who supplied the rongeur, on a warranty theory; and against the manufacturer of the rongeur, on a strict products liability theory. The jury returned a verdict in favor of each of the four defendants against the plaintiff; the decision was reversed by the appellate division, which held that the jury was obligated to impose liability on at least one of the named defendants. The New Jersey Supreme Court, by a four-to-three vote, applied res ipsa loquitur to this case of multiple defendants, noting that this "development represents a substantial deviation from earlier conceptions of res ipsa loquitur and has more accurately been called 'akin to res ipsa loquitur,' or 'conditional res ipsa loquitur.' " The dissent noted that other surgeons, perhaps numbering twenty, could have created the defect but were not joined as defendants.

The New Jersey Court unanimously reaffirmed *Anderson* in Chin v. St. Barnabas Medical Center, 734 A.2d 778, 783 (N.J. 1999). The decedent, a forty-five-year-old woman, died of a massive air embolism that occurred during a routine "diagnostic hysteroscopy"—a procedure used to determine abnormalities in the uterus. The procedure in question required the cooperation of many physicians and nurses, and the evidence suggested that a hysteroscope had been misused by one of two nurses charged with hooking it up to various devices, so that gas instead of fluid was pumped into her uterus. Because the tubes had been disconnected before an investigation could be made, no one could determine which nurse had erred. Handler, J., held that under *Anderson*, given that Chin "was unconscious, helpless, and utterly blameless," "the air embolism could have been caused only by negligent use of the hysteroscope," and "[a]ll the potential defendants, that is, all those who participated in the chain of events leading up to Ms. Chin's injury, were sued in this case," the jury had to come back with a verdict against at least one defendant. The jury then exonerated the manufacturer, but on the basis of common knowledge, and without expert testimony, divided responsibility between two nurses, the treating physician, and the hospital.

In Johnson v. Armstrong, 211 N.E.3d 355, 361–62, 370 (Ill. 2022), the plaintiff suffered from severe and permanent nerve damage in his leg, which he alleged was caused by a negligently performed hip replacement surgery. The plaintiff sued his surgeon and surgical technicians relying on res ipsa loquitur. Garman, J., concluded that "plaintiff is not required under these circumstances to identify precisely who caused his nerve damage. What plaintiff must establish here is that all parties who were responsible for all reasonable causes of plaintiff's nerve damage are identified."

With *Anderson*, *Chin*, and *Armstrong*, contrast Darrah v. Bryan Memorial Hospital, 571 N.W.2d 783, 786 (Neb. 1998). The plaintiff suffered ulnar nerve damage at the site where an intravenous line was inserted postoperatively. The court upheld summary judgment for the defendant, and affirmed the trial court's refusal to grant a res ipsa loquitur instruction because

> the district court found that the damage to Darrah's ulnar nerve could have occurred during or after surgery while he was hospitalized at BMH. . . . "[T]he requirement of exclusive control cannot be satisfied in view of the absence of the operating surgeons and the anesthesiologist as party defendants. These are parties who control the activities during surgery and they are neither agents [n]or employees of the defendant hospital."

CHAPTER 4

PLAINTIFF'S CONDUCT

SECTION A. INTRODUCTION

This chapter chiefly examines how the plaintiff's own conduct affects her right to recover damages for her physical or emotional harms. This inquiry comes to the fore once the defendant claims that the plaintiff's harm was "her own fault." This commonsense observation contains one key internal ambiguity. Thus, when the plaintiff is the sole cause of her own injury, the defendant may now simply deny his own responsibility by claiming that the plaintiff was the sole cause of her own harm. Without any prima facie case against this defendant, plaintiff's contributory negligence or assumption of risk are not in dispute.

Alternatively, the defendant can remove or reduce recovery by saying her injury was her own fault, even when the defendant's actions were plainly involved in bringing about her harm, as when the defendant negligently runs over the plaintiff who has darted into the street from between two parked cars. Now the key inquiry is whether the plaintiff's conduct reduces or blocks the amount of damages that she can recover for her injury.

This chapter mainly explores the two major versions of the "plaintiff's conduct" defense: contributory (or comparative) negligence and assumption of risk. Contributory negligence is established when the plaintiff has not taken reasonable care for her own safety. If she has not, the further inquiry considers the causal connection between her want of care and her own injuries. At common law, the plaintiff's negligence, if established on the facts, generally barred her from *any* recovery—even if the defendant showed a complete disregard for the appropriate standard of care—subject to an important exception regarding the defendant's "last clear chance" to avoid the harm, or to his willfulness in causing it.

The second key defense is assumption of risk. Unlike contributory negligence, assumption of risk asks whether the plaintiff has *deliberately and voluntarily encountered a known risk* created by the defendant's negligence. If so, the defense bars plaintiff's recovery for her consequent harm. Notwithstanding its intuitive plausibility, the assumption of risk defense has generated protracted analysis and often bitter controversy. Supporters have passionately defended its place in tort law in the name of laissez-faire economics and the autonomy principle. With equal fervor, critics have denounced it as an exploitive doctrine inconsistent with modern social norms of responsibility. The uneasiness with this defense led to the rise of workers' compensation systems that removed the defense while simultaneously limiting the recovery for the injured employee—a development that is briefly covered in this chapter. And for the nonindustrial accidents that remain within the tort system, some scholars have even argued that, properly understood, assumption of risk has no place at all in a mature system of tort law, and is better understood as a variant of comparative negligence. See, e.g., James, Assumption of Risk, 61 Yale L.J. 141 (1952).

With the contours of contributory negligence and assumption of risk thus established, we will investigate the pronounced movement, both by legislation and at common law, toward *comparative negligence*. That principle holds that the plaintiff's negligence should not typically bar her cause of action but should only reduce the amount of damages recoverable. We will have to examine how the various forms of the comparative negligence principle interact with both contributory negligence and assumption of risk, how they mesh with a strict liability system, and how they apply in cases of multiple tortfeasors. And to round off the chapter, we will take a brief look at possible no-fault systems for automobiles, products, and medical injuries, which, if adopted, would also remove both assumption of risk and contributory negligence from the resulting compensation system.

SECTION B. CONTRIBUTORY NEGLIGENCE

1. Basic Doctrine

Butterfield v. Forrester

(1809) 103 Eng. Rep. 926 (KB)

This was an action on the case for obstructing a highway, by means of which obstruction the plaintiff, who was riding along the road, was thrown down with his horse, and injured, &c. At the trial before Bayley, J., at Derby, it appeared that the defendant, for the purpose of making some repairs to his house, which was close by the road side at one end of the town, had put up a pole across this part of the road, a free passage being left by another branch or street in the same direction. That the plaintiff left a public house not far distant from the place in question at 8 o'clock in the evening in August, when they were just beginning to light candles, but while there was light enough left to discern the obstruction at 100 yards distance: and the witness, who proved this, said that if the plaintiff had not been riding very hard he might have observed and avoided it: the plaintiff however, who was riding violently, did not observe it, but rode against it, and fell with his horse and was much hurt in consequence of the accident; and there was no evidence of his being intoxicated at the time. On this evidence Bayley, J., directed the jury, that if a person riding with reasonable and ordinary care could have seen and avoided the obstruction; and if they were satisfied that the plaintiff was riding along the street extremely hard, and without ordinary care, they should find a verdict for the defendant: which they accordingly did.

Vaughan Serjt. now objected to this direction, on moving for a new trial; and referred to Buller's Ni. Pri. 26, where the rule is laid down, that "if a man lay logs of wood across a highway though a person may with care ride safely by, yet if by means thereof my horse stumble and fling me, I may bring an action."

Bayley, J. The plaintiff was proved to be riding as fast as his horse could go, and this was through the streets of Derby. If he had used ordinary care he must have seen the obstruction so that the accident appeared to happen entirely from his own fault.

Lord Ellenborough, C.J. A party is not to cast himself upon an obstruction which has been made by the fault of another, and avail himself of it, if he do not himself use common and ordinary caution to be in the right. In cases of persons riding upon what is considered to be the wrong side of the road, that would not authorise another purposely to ride up against them. One person being in fault will not dispense with another's using ordinary care for himself. Two things must concur to support this action, an obstruction in the road by the fault of the defendant, and no want of ordinary care to avoid it on the part of the plaintiff.

Per Curiam. Rule refused.

Beems v. Chicago, Rock Island & Peoria R.R.

12 N.W. 222 (Iowa 1882)

Beck, J. . . . We will now consider the action of the court in overruling the [railroad's] motion for judgment non-obstante. The intestate met his death in making an attempt to uncouple the tender from a car. The special findings of the jury show that when he went between the cars to uncouple them they were moving at an improper and unusual rate of speed. Counsel for defendant insist that this finding establishes the fact of contributory negligence on the part of the intestate. The petition alleges that defendant's employees in charge of the engine were negligent, in failing to obey a direction given them by a signal made by the intestate to check the speed of the cars. The testimony tends to support this allegation. The jury were authorized to find from the testimony that deceased made two attempts to uncouple the cars while they were moving. After the first attempt he came out from between the cars, and signaled directions to check their speed; he immediately went again between the cars to make the second attempt to uncouple them. His signal was not obeyed. He was authorized to believe that the motion of the car would be checked, and he was not required to wait, before acting, to discover whether obedience would be given to his signal. The jury could have found that after the signal had been given, and after he had gone between the cars, if their speed had been checked, he would not have been exposed to danger. His act, therefore, in going between the cars after having made the signal to check their speed, was not necessarily contributory negligence. . . .

The court instructed the jury that if intestate's foot was caught between the rails and he "was thus held and run over, *without any negligence on the part of the other employees of defendant*, such as is charged in the petition, then the plaintiff cannot recover anything." The defendant asked an instruction, which was refused, to the effect that if the intestate's foot was caught between the rails the defendant is not liable, even though the jury should find the negligence charged in the petition. The instruction given is correct. If intestate was run over by reason of defendant's negligence, surely it cannot be claimed that defendant is not liable, because intestate's foot was caught between the rails. It would be a strange doctrine to hold that defendant could back its trains with unusual speed, without obeying signals to move more slowly, and thus negligently run over a brakesman, and would not be liable, for the reason that the unfortunate man was fastened to the spot by his foot being held between the rails. Whatever was the intestate's condition at the time of the accident, whether free to move, or fastened to the place, the defendant is liable if its cars were negligently driven over him.

Gary Schwartz

Tort Law and the Economy in Nineteenth-Century America: A Reinterpretation

90 Yale L.J. 1717, 1759–62 (1981)

Professor Friedman describes the tort defense of contributory negligence as a "cunning trap" set by courts for nineteenth-century accident victims;[310] Professor Malone argues that nineteenth-century courts frequently were aggressive in withdrawing the contributory negligence

310. Friedman, A History of American Law (1973), at 411–412. According to Professor Levy, nineteenth-century plaintiffs making "a misstep, however slight, from the ideal standard of conduct," were routinely and unfairly denied recoveries. L. Levy, The Law of the Commonwealth and Chief Justice Shaw (1957) at 319. For acceptance of the doctrine of "slight" contributory negligence, see W. Prosser, Law of Torts 421 (4th ed. 1971).

issue from the jury in order carefully to monitor industry liability.[311] These assessments are contradicted, however, by the nineteenth-century experience in New Hampshire and California.

Each state's Supreme Court from an early date accepted the traditional rule of contributory negligence as a complete defense. Both Courts were openly ambivalent about the rule, however. . . .

The California Court placed the contributory-negligence burden of proof on the defendant, and regarded a technical misassignment of the burden of proof as reversible error, even when the defendant was the Central Pacific. . . . When allocating decisionmaking between judge and jury, the New Hampshire Court specified that the contributory negligence issue could be taken away from the jury only in "extraordinary" circumstances; the California Court frequently used language almost as strong.

In administering tort appeals, the two states' Courts developed a variety of maxim-like ideas emphasizing the lenient and forgiving quality of the contributory negligence standard. Thus, a plaintiff was not required to exercise "great care" or to behave in a "very timid or cautious" way; contributory negligence was not proven by an "indiscretion" or a mere "error of judgment," let alone by a "misjudgment" in retrospect. If the plaintiff was "startled and alarmed," that was taken into account in evaluating the reasonableness of his conduct. Momentary distraction is a "most common occurrence" on city streets and "falls far short" of contributory negligence. If the plaintiff forgot what he knew about the particular danger, the Court could say that "people are liable to lapses of memory." Attenuating maxims like these were almost totally lacking in the Courts' opinions dealing with the possible negligence of tort defendants, who were frequently held to a standard of the "utmost care." Whatever, then, the symmetry in form of the doctrines of negligence and contributory negligence, they were administered under an emphatic, if implicit, double standard. . . .[333]

[Professor Schwartz then observes that a detailed analysis of the disposition of all contributory negligence cases in California and New Hampshire is consistent with the impression created by judicial language. Contributory negligence is rarely found as a matter of law; jury verdicts for the plaintiff on the issue are both frequent and usually upheld; jury verdicts for defendants are often set aside, typically because of a defect in jury instructions.]

NOTE

The Scope and Function of Contributory Negligence. Professor Schwartz continues his attack on the proposition that American tort law gave special protection to industry and corporations in Schwartz, The Character of Early American Tort Law, 36 UCLA L. Rev. 641 (1989).

Apart from the history, scholars have had an extensive debate over whether any defense based upon plaintiff's misconduct is needed. To see what is at stake, it is useful to divide cases into stranger cases (including highway accidents) and consensual cases (including both the occupier/visitor and the employer/employee relationships). *Butterfield* illustrates the first class of cases, while *Beems* illustrates the latter class. In the first situation, the ability of each party to act prudently does not depend on its cooperation with the other. In the second situation,

311. Malone, The Formative Era of Contributory Negligence, at 151, 152, 182. Professors Levy and Ursin—supposedly writing about California law specifically—claim that "the nineteenth-century [contributory negligence] doctrine could fairly have been called the rule of railroad and industrial immunity." Levy & Ursin, Tort Law in California: At the Crossroads, 67 Calif. L. Rev. 497, 509 (1979).

333. That is, when the conduct of the defendant and the plaintiff combined to expose the plaintiff to a major risk, the Courts subjected the defendant to a stern negligence obligation even while defining the plaintiff's contributory negligence obligation in a mild and permissive way.

coordination is the order of the day. With the first case, therefore, it becomes more likely that the standards of care imposed on plaintiffs and defendants will be identical, as was the case when infant plaintiffs were charged with contributory negligence measured by objective standards in highway cases.

What rules ought to govern these cases? One possibility is to eliminate the defense of contributory negligence altogether. See Landes & Posner, The Economic Structure of Tort Law 75–76 (1987). Under the Hand formula, they argue, the defendant can always escape liability by showing that he took cost-justified precautions against accidents. The "no-negligence" defense, therefore, provides the rational defendant with all the protection needed against unwarranted suits. Notwithstanding this argument, the defense is retained in practice because the defendant's negligence may be hotly contested even when the plaintiff's negligence is evident. The use of the contributory negligence defense thus buffers against the uncertainties in the basic negligence calculation.

In stranger cases, a strict liability rule could also be adopted. Owing to the greater scope of defendant's potential liability, an affirmative defense based on the plaintiff's conduct now plays a more critical role, lest the plaintiff take great risks at the defendant's expense.

But marrying strict liability with contributory negligence is oddly asymmetrical when both parties start from a position of initial parity. See, e.g., Brown, Toward an Economic Theory of Liability, 2 J. Legal Stud. 323, 351 (1973). Suppose two cars crash head-on when neither driver is negligent. Under strict liability with contributory negligence, each driver must compensate the other for his loss: The relative extent of the two sets of injuries, itself largely a matter of luck, is simply reversed by legal action. Note, however, that a comprehensive system that uses strict standards to judge the conduct of both parties escapes this inelegance. The negligence of both parties is irrelevant, but causation for both parties is not. If the prima facie case was that the defendant struck the plaintiff, then a causal defense arises if other parties were in motion, at which point it is critical to ask whether the plaintiff blocked the defendant's right of way, as by entering an intersection against a red light or the plaintiff crossed the midline. The defendant need not show that the plaintiff was negligent when she violated the rule of the road. See the excerpt from Ross, Settled Out of Court, *supra* Chapter 3, at 143.

For a defense of this strict liability variation, see Friedman, Sharing Responsibility Instead of Allocating Blame: Reforming Torts and Reducing Accidents, 2018 U. Ill. L. Rev. 579, 592: "[T]he comparative negligence rule only leads to liability sharing when a court determines that both parties are at fault. If neither party is at fault, a pure comparative negligence rule allocates the entire loss to the victim. In contrast, the rule I propose views liability sharing as a default." Should liability be shared if one party is negligent and the other is not?

It is of course odd to speak of "strict liability defenses" because a person cannot be liable to himself. Yet once it is recognized that identical causal principles operate on both parties, fairness requires apportioning loss between the causal contributions of the two parties, based on the force at impact and the rights of way of the two vehicles. For an account of joint causation under a thoroughgoing system of strict liability, see Epstein, Defenses and Subsequent Pleas in a System of Strict Liability, 3 J. Legal Stud. 165, 174–85 (1974).

This analysis need not carry over to consensual relationships, because these parties often have differential access to knowledge and different abilities to take care. In *Beems*, the court was clearly moved by the hapless plaintiff's reliance on decisions made by his coworkers who were standing safely above. There was little need to create legal incentives for the plaintiff to do the right thing in light of his evident peril; more so for the defendant's employees who occupied a position of relative safety. But in other cases, the plaintiff's capacity to avoid a known hazard may well be far greater. In those cases, should the level of responsibility be raised to be commensurate with the degree of control? Note the tension between this view and the Hand formula in *Carroll Towing*, *supra* Chapter 3, at 136.

Gyerman v. United States Lines Co.

498 P.2d 1043 (Cal. 1972)

[The plaintiff, a longshoreman employed by the Associated Banning Company, was injured while unloading fishmeal sacks that had just been brought into the warehouse of the defendant, United States Lines. Fishmeal is a very difficult cargo to handle, because it is packaged in sacks that tend to rip and spill. To combat this danger, several common precautions are usually taken: Only eighteen to twenty-two sacks of fishmeal are placed on any one pallet, and then only three or four layers high; the sacks are "bulkheaded," or tied together, to prevent them from falling; and, for maximum stability, they are aligned as are bricks in a wall, with no sack directly on top of another. The plaintiff had been assigned to "break down" the sacks into units that were only two pallets high. Before he began work, he noted that the sacks were not properly arranged. There were 30 sacks per pallet; the sacks were not bulk-headed; and they were not arrayed in brick-like fashion. He complained to Noel, the United States Lines chief marine clerk, that it was dangerous to proceed with the work in question but was told that nothing could be done about it.

Fishmeal, stacked similarly as described in Gyerman

Source: Julio Etchart / Alamy

At no time, however, did the plaintiff speak to his own supervisor, even though the union contract with his employer provided, first, that "Longshoremen shall not be required to work when in good faith they believe that to do so is to immediately endanger health and safety," and established a grievance procedure "to determine whether a condition is safe or unsafe," and, second, that a joint labor-management committee should be immediately convened to resolve any outstanding safety issue. During the first three days of his work, an unusually large number of sacks fell off the forklift, but no harm resulted. On the afternoon of the fourth day, about 12 sacks simultaneously fell off a load that he was moving, and one of them, after bumping into the others, came toward him. Although the exact physical sequence of events was never established, the plaintiff did sustain injuries to his back and legs from the incident. The trial judge, sitting without a jury, found that the defendant, United States Lines, was negligent in its failure to stack the fishmeal sacks in a safe way, conduct that was also a violation of the statutory duty to furnish every employee a "safe" place of employment. He found further that the defendant's negligence was a proximate cause of the plaintiff's harm. But he also found that the plaintiff's negligence in failing to stop work in the face of a known danger barred his cause of action. After disposing of two preliminary procedural points, the California Supreme Court considers the effect of plaintiff's contributory negligence upon his cause of action.]

SULLIVAN, J. . . .

3. Contributory Negligence . . .

"Contributory negligence is conduct on the part of the plaintiff which falls below the standard to which he should conform for his own protection, and which is a legally contributing cause co-operating with the negligence of the defendant in bringing about the plaintiff's harm." (Rest. 2d Torts (1965) §463). The question of contributory negligence is ordinarily one of fact for the determination of the trier of fact.

"A plaintiff is required to exercise only that amount of care which would be exercised by a person of ordinary prudence in the same circumstances." Where a person must work under possibly unsafe or dangerous conditions, the amount of care he must exercise for his own safety may well be less than would otherwise be required by reason of the necessity of his giving attention to his work. The burden of proving that the plaintiff was negligent and that such negligence was a proximate cause of the accident is on the defendant.

In the instant case, absent evidence of the contract governing plaintiff's employment and of the custom and practice affecting stevedoring, we doubt that the record would provide evidentiary support for the finding that plaintiff violated a standard of due care for his own safety. Considered in the light of the realities of his working life, the laborer's duty may become considerably restricted in scope. In some instances he may find himself powerless to abandon the task at hand with impunity whenever he senses a possible danger; in others, he may be uncertain as to which person has supervision of the job or control of the place of employment, and therefore unsure as to whom he should direct his complaint; in still others, having been encouraged to continue working under conditions where danger lurks but has not materialized, he may be baffled in making an on-the-spot decision as to the imminence of harm. All of these factors enter into a determination whether his conduct falls below a standard of due care.

In the case before us the standard of due care required of laborers in general is explicated by evidence of duty imposed by contract and by custom upon the particular type of laborer involved. Custom alone, of course, does not create the standard of proper diligence. "Indeed in most cases reasonable prudence is in fact common prudence but strictly it is never its measure. . . ." (*The T.J. Hooper*). Nevertheless, although custom does not fix the standard of care, evidence of custom is ordinarily admissible for its bearing upon contributory negligence.

[The court then reviewed the facts of the case and concluded that the evidence supported the finding that the plaintiff failed to use ordinary care for his own protection.]

We must now inquire whether defendant sustained its burden of establishing that plaintiff's failure to report the unsafe condition was a "legally contributing cause . . . in bringing about the plaintiff's harm." (Rest. 2d Torts, §463.) As previously noted, the trial court appears to have determined that plaintiff's failure was a proximate cause of his injuries because if plaintiff had reported the condition it would have been corrected. . . .

On this issue the positions of the parties may be summarized thusly: Plaintiff argues that the burden was on defendant to prove that if plaintiff had reported the condition to his own supervisor instead of to defendant's supervisor, the condition would have been corrected or made safer. Defendant asserts that it was not incumbent upon it to prove that the condition complained of was correctable and that in any event there is evidence supporting the trial court's finding.

The burden of proof rests on each party to a civil action as to each fact essential to his claim or defense. A party claiming a person failed to exercise due care has the burden of proof on that issue. The burden of proving all aspects of the affirmative defense of contributory negligence, including causation, rests on the defendant, unless the elements of the defense may be inferred from the plaintiff's evidence. The burden must be met by more than conjecture or speculation. Merely because plaintiff asserts that his own negligence, if any, could not have caused his injury, does not shift to him the burden of proof on the issue. Otherwise denial of any essential element of the defense case would shift the burden of proof on that issue to the plaintiff. . . .

We turn now to the facts of the case before us. It is obvious, of course, from what we have said that plaintiff did not create or maintain the dangerous and unsafe conditions of storage. The trial court found upon substantial evidence that defendant negligently maintained and operated its warehouse under those conditions. It was defendant who had control of the cargo and directed its disposition and high stacking throughout the warehouse. Defendant alone created this risk of harm which materialized in the toppling of the stacks.

Nor did the trial court find that plaintiff was negligent in his operation of the forklift or in his "breaking down" the particular stack of fishmeal whose sacks fell from the top of the load and injured him. In short there is no finding that any negligent conduct of plaintiff, operating with defendant's negligence, brought about the shifting and eventual dislodging of the sacks. According to the trial court's findings, plaintiff's negligence consisted solely in his failure to report the dangerous condition to his own supervisor. Our task then is to find in the record evidence showing, or from which it can be reasonably inferred, that this omission was a substantial factor in bringing about plaintiff's harm.

Defendant's theory of causation is that if plaintiff had reported the dangerous condition to his Associated Banning supervisor, that firm would have made the condition safer. An examination of the record, however, discloses no evidence establishing this theory. Indeed, although defendant vigorously asserts that the record supports a finding of proximate cause, it points to only one page of the extensive record for such evidence. At this part of the record, defendant's witness Hargett [manager of labor relations for Associated Banning, whose "duties were to represent not only Associated Banning but the industry as a whole in negotiations and disputes pertaining to contracts between the longshoremen and the various employers belonging to the Pacific Maritime Association"] responded on direct examination to a question about what a longshoreman should do upon encountering an unsafe condition. Hargett replied that he would have to get another lot to work on or "have supervision called, . . . and we would have sent men there to take care of the situation, if he was in such a condition he couldn't operate."

In our view this testimony does not show that the stacks would have been made safer. Although it indicates that the problem would have received immediate attention, it provides no clue as to what, if anything, could have been done to break down the stacks of fishmeal more safely than by the use of forklifts. Indeed, other than the vague statement as to sending "men there to take care of the situation" no evidence at all was offered as to specific measures that would be taken. Nor does evidence as to the existence of a grievance procedure, formalized in the ILWU-PMA contract constitute proof that in the particular situation culminating in plaintiff's injury, steps would have been taken to make the situation safer. Finally the trial court's suggestions made in its memorandum of decision that the offending bags could have been removed by using ladders or having other forklift drivers remove them one at a time are not based upon evidence in the record and therefore do not support the finding. Indeed such suggestions only point up the complete lack of defense evidence in the record on this critical issue. The record does not establish that plaintiff's failure to report the dangerous condition was a substantial factor in bringing about the fall of the sacks.

In view of the foregoing we conclude that defendant did not meet its burden of proving that plaintiff's contributory negligence was a proximate cause of his injuries.

[The court then remands the case for a retrial on the questions of the plaintiff's contributory negligence and its causal connection to the plaintiff's own harm. It notes that, though the plaintiff's negligence was sufficiently established by evidence below, the court is "not satisfied" that in the instant case the two issues are so "separate and distinct" that the issue of proximate cause could not be tried alone "without such confusion or uncertainty as would amount to a denial of a fair trial."]

The issue of defendant's negligence has been properly determined and we see no reason why it should be relitigated. Retrial should be had on the issue of plaintiff's contributory negligence (including the issue of whether such negligence, if any, was the proximate cause of the accident) and, if such issue is resolved favorably to plaintiff, on the issue of damages.

The judgment is reversed and the cause is remanded with directions for a new trial limited to the issues of plaintiff's contributory negligence and of damages. Each party shall bear his or its own costs on appeal.

Wright, C.J., McComb, Peters, Tobriner, and Burke, JJ., concurred.

NOTES

1. ***Burden of Proof on Contributory Negligence.*** *Gyerman* follows the universal modern rule that the defendant bears the burden of proof on the issues of contributory negligence and its causal relationship to the plaintiff's harm. See RTT: AL §4, comment a: Burden of proof.

Nevertheless, a significant minority of states once required the plaintiff to establish her freedom from contributory negligence as a part of the basic cause of action. The rule probably arose when the intervening negligence of another actor, including the plaintiff, severed the causal connection between the defendant's negligence and the plaintiff's harm. See the discussion of the last clear chance rule, *infra* at 237. Because the plaintiff bore the burden of proof on proximate cause, it was but a small step to say that she bore the burden of proof on contributory negligence. That rule in turn created genuine difficulties in wrongful death actions when the decedent could not defend her own conduct. Initially, the courts shifted that burden back to the defendant in death cases, and over time the exception expanded into the current rule. Today, death cases are often governed by a rule that holds: "[I]n the absence of any evidence as to the conduct of a person who died of injuries received in an accident, there is the presumption that he, acting on the instinct of self-preservation, was in the exercise of ordinary care," and thus a decedent is in a stronger position than an injured plaintiff. Thompson v. Mehlhaff, 698 N.W.2d 512, 526 (S.D. 2005). Is the plaintiff in *Gyerman* in a stronger position than the plaintiff in *Beems*?

2. ***Contributory Negligence and Defendant's Breach of Statutory Duty.*** In *Gyerman*, do the particulars of how best to deal with the stacking of the fishmeal stacks matter if the plaintiff could have refused to work on them as of right under the labor contract? Should the defense of contributory negligence be excluded because the improper stacking of the fishmeal sacks violated the defendant's statutory duty to provide a safe place to work? In Koenig v. Patrick Construction Corp., 83 N.E.2d 133, 135 (N.Y. 1948), the court refused to allow the defenses of either contributory negligence or assumption of risk when the plaintiff was a member of the class of persons for whose benefit a particular statute, the state Scaffold Law, §240(1), was enacted:

> Workmen such as the present plaintiff, who ply their livelihoods on ladders and scaffolds, are scarcely in a position to protect themselves from accident. They usually have no choice but to work with the equipment at hand, though danger looms large. The legislature recognized this and to guard against the known hazards of the occupation required the employer to safeguard the workers from injury caused by faulty or inadequate equipment. If the employer could avoid this duty by pointing to the concurrent negligence of the injured worker in using the equipment, the beneficial purpose of the statute might well be frustrated and nullified.

Is it feasible for workers to decline risky employment? Receive additional compensation for dangerous work? Are individual employees powerless when represented by a union that routinely bargains with the employer over safety issues?

The Scaffold Law in New York has been a source of much contention. Thus in St. Louis v. Town of North Elba, 947 N.E.2d 1169, 1170 (N.Y. 2011), the plaintiff was attempting to clear excess metal from a 20-foot section of snow-making pipe held in place by the jaws of a clamshell bucket attached to a front-end loader. The loader was suspended four feet in the air to allow workers like St. Louis to clear debris from its underside. When the clamshell bucket unexpectedly released, the pipe fell on St. Louis, causing serious injuries to his legs and feet. By its terms, New York Labor Law §241(6) authorizes recovery only if the plaintiff can identify "the specific safety rules and regulations" that the defendant had failed to observe. The section on which the plaintiff relied applied in terms only to "power shovels and backhoes." The defendant claimed that the "front-end loader" fell outside the statute. Lippman, C.J., rejected that claim:

> Further, we agree that the safety requirements of this section appropriately extend to the case of a front-end loader that is enlisted to do the material handling that is otherwise performed by power shovels and backhoes. Although the Code does not enumerate each piece of heavy equipment that can be operated to suspend materials from its bucket or bucket arm, section 23-9.4 (e) was clearly drafted to reduce the threat posed by heavy materials falling from buckets by requiring loads to be fastened with sturdy wire, proportionate to the weight of the load. The same danger that exists for a worker using a power shovel or backhoe with an unsecured load exists for a worker using a front-end loader with an unsecured load.

Smith, J., dissented on the ground that the "purpose based" interpretation was inconsistent with the "plain language" of the explicit statutory command, which should not be disregarded "because the majority does not think the difference between the kinds of equipment justifies different treatment." Which position is more persuasive?

3. *Plaintiff's Breach of Statutory Duty.* Often, safety statutes impose specific requirements on individual workers. When these are breached, the defense of contributory negligence may be established as a matter of law when the *plaintiff* is in breach of statutory duty. Similarly, in Blake v. Securitas Securities Services, 962 F. Supp. 2d 141, 146–47 (D.D.C. 2013), the plaintiff, a seventeen-year-old boy, while attending his high school prom, got high on marijuana and either jumped or fell from a third-story balcony, sustaining serious injuries. Boasberg, J., noted that District of Columbia law made it a misdemeanor for any person, "whether in or on public or private property . . . [to] be intoxicated and endanger the safety of himself, herself, or any other person or property." He then sidestepped the question of whether this statutory breach was contributory negligence as a matter of law, by noting that Blake had also endangered himself when, after smoking the marijuana, he "then proceeded to break away from a school administrator, run down a hallway, and climb under protective cables and over a railing onto the exposed balcony from which he ultimately fell." Boasberg, J., further rejected the claim that the plaintiff was entitled to the lower standard of care normally afforded to children.

4. *Contributory Negligence in Medical Malpractice Cases.* In Cavens v. Zaberdac, 849 N.E.2d 526, 529–30 (Ind. 2006), the decedent suffered from chronic asthma, which the emergency room physician Dr. Cavens attributed in part to her "excessive use of medication and delay in seeking treatment." The defendants asked for this instruction: "A patient may not recover in a malpractice action where the patient is contributorily negligent by failing to follow the defendant physician's instructions if such contributory negligence is simultaneous with and unites with the fault of the defendant to proximately cause the injury." Dickson, J., first acknowledged that "the patient is contributorily negligent by failing to follow the defendant physician's instructions if such contributory negligence is simultaneous with and unites with the fault of the defendant to proximately cause the injury." Thereafter he continued:

> Permitting medical malpractice defendants to assert the defense of contributory negligence by reason of a patient's negligence prior to the defendant physician's treatment of the patient conflicts with a long-standing common law principle: "It is a staple of tort law that the tortfeasor takes her victim as she finds him."
>
> It is people who are sick or injured that most often seek medical attention. Many of these infirmities result, at least in part, from the patients' own carelessness (e.g. negligent driving or other activities, failure to regularly exercise, unhealthy diet, smoking, etc.). To permit healthcare providers to assert their patients' pre-treatment negligent conduct to support a contributory negligence defense would absolve such providers from tort responsibility in the event of medical negligence and thus operate to undermine substantially such providers' duty of reasonable care.

The RTT: Apportionment of Liability, §7, comment *m*, adopts just that view: "In a case involving negligent rendition of a service, including medical services, a factfinder does not consider any plaintiff's conduct that created the condition the service was employed to remedy." Is it possible that any sensible bargain between patient and physician would ever take that antecedent negligence into account? But what happens if the patient ignores the physician's instructions after he is retained? May a physician introduce evidence of excessive use of medication or delay in seeking care to undermine the claim that his negligence, if any, was causally responsible for the plaintiff's loss?

5. *Contributory Negligence and Custodial Care.* What level of care should be required of people who, by virtue of being in custodial care, have demonstrated their inability to act reasonably on their own behalf? In Padula v. State, 398 N.E.2d 548, 551 (N.Y. 1979), the two plaintiffs, inmates at the Iroquois Narcotic Rehabilitation Center, and several of their friends were able, through the negligence of the center's guards, to gain access to the center's printing room. There they found some Ditto fluid, rich in methyl alcohol, which they drank after mixing it "with an orange preparation called Tang." One plaintiff died and the second became blind. The Court of Appeals held that their suit was not barred. The court first held that actions done under an irresistible impulse, even without specific proof of a mental disease, do not sever causal connection. It continued:

> [W]hatever the contributory or comparative negligence rule may ultimately be held to be as to a person under the influence of drugs in a noncustodial situation as to which we express no opinion, we think that in relation to persons in the custody of the State for treatment of a drug problem, contributory (or comparative) negligence should turn not on whether the drug problem or its effects be categorized as a mental disease nor on whether the injured person understood what he was doing, but on whether based upon the entire testimony presented (including objective behavioral evidence, claimant's subjective testimony and the opinions of experts) the trier of fact concludes that the injured person was able to control his actions.

The court was particularly impressed by the clear testimony that "not only Padula and Modaferi [the blind claimant] but six other residents drank the Ditto-Tang concoction notwithstanding that the warning [which spoke of death or blindness] had been read to them." Any action against the supplier of the methyl alcohol? Is there any analogy to the position of the plaintiff in *Beems*? In *Gyerman*?

Just what counts as a custodial situation? In Hendrickson v. Moses Lake School District, 428 P.3d 1197, 1201 (Wash. 2018), the court held that an ordinary school room did not count as a custodial situation, and therefore, the defense of contributory negligence applies given the absence of "context-specific reasons" such as sexual abuse where the defense would not apply.

6. ***Contributory Negligence and Private Necessity.*** Should the defense of contributory negligence be available against a plaintiff who runs into the path of a negligently speeding car on the public highway to escape from a gang attack? In Raimondo v. Harding, 341 N.Y.S.2d 679 (App. Div. 1973), the court reversed the lower court decision, noting that a

> person faced with an emergency and who acts, without opportunity for deliberation, to avoid an accident may not be charged with contributory negligence if he acts as a reasonably prudent person would act under the same emergency circumstances, even though it appears afterwards that he did not take the safest course or exercise the best judgment.

The Third Restatement adopts this basic position, noting, for plaintiffs and defendants alike, that the law of negligence takes into account "an unexpected emergency requiring rapid response." RTT: LPEH §9. The standard caveat to this position is that no party can rely on an emergency created by his prior negligence. *Id.*, comment *d.* Is *Raimondo* consistent with Vincent v. Lake Erie, *supra* Chapter 1, at 39?

7. ***Causation and Contributory Negligence.*** The causal complications with contributory negligence are well illustrated by two famous Connecticut cases. In Smithwick v. Hall & Upson Co., 21 A. 924 (Conn. 1890), the plaintiff was working on a narrow platform erected in front of the defendant's icehouse, about 15 feet above the ground. The defendant's foreman warned plaintiff to stay away from the east side of the platform, which had no railing, because he feared that the plaintiff could slip on the ice. Plaintiff disregarded that instruction but was hurt when the east portion of the icehouse buckled. The defendant's negligence in maintaining the icehouse was conceded, but the plaintiff's contributory negligence was not treated as causally relevant because the resulting harm was "not within the risk," that is, the class of events that made it dangerous for the plaintiff to venture to the east side in the first place. See discussion of *Wagon Mound*, *infra* Chapter 5, at 354. What was the risk of the plaintiff working on the east side of the platform? Would the plaintiff still have been injured if he had followed orders?

In Mahoney v. Beatman, 147 A. 762, 768 (Conn. 1929), plaintiff was driving a Rolls-Royce around 60 miles per hour, while it was still daylight, on a gravel-shouldered, two-lane concrete turnpike, with a clear view in both directions. The defendant was approaching in a Nash from the opposite direction. He turned to speak to somebody in the backseat and thus permitted the Nash to cross over the middle of the highway into the plaintiff's lane. The plaintiff, to avoid a head-on collision, pulled the Rolls-Royce partly off onto the shoulder. Nonetheless, the Nash grazed the Rolls-Royce, causing an estimated $200 worth of damage. The Rolls-Royce proceeded for about 125 feet along the road, and then suddenly turned across the highway, climbed a small bank, and hit a tree and a stone wall, sustaining about $5,650 in additional damage.

The trial court, sitting without a jury, found that the defendant's Nash was on the wrong side of the road, that the speed of the Rolls-Royce was "unreasonable but it did not contribute to the collision which was due entirely to the negligence of the defendant," but that the speed of the Rolls-Royce did "materially hamper plaintiff's chauffeur in controlling the car after the collision and owing to it he completely lost control of it." The trial court then awarded "nominal damages" of $200 to the plaintiff. On appeal, the plaintiff was given judgment for $5,850 for damage to his car. The Supreme Court of Connecticut treated the defendant's negligence as the proximate cause of plaintiff's entire damage. Does this case illustrate the distinction between causation and coincidence? To be sure, the plaintiff's speeding did not contribute to the collision, which could have happened had he been driving at 45 miles per hour at that same location. Yet the plaintiff's speeding did cause the plaintiff to lose control after the collision, thus contributing to the balance of the damage to the Rolls-Royce. What result under comparative negligence?

RESTATEMENT OF THE LAW (THIRD) OF TORTS: APPORTIONMENT OF LIABILITY

§4. Proof of Plaintiff's Negligence and Legal Causation

The defendant has the burden to prove plaintiff's negligence, and may use any of the methods a plaintiff may use to prove defendant's negligence. Except as otherwise provided in Topic 5 [Apportionment of Liability When Damages Can Be Divided by Causation], the defendant also has the burden to prove that the plaintiff's negligence, if any, was a legal cause of the plaintiff's damages.

LeRoy Fibre Co. v. Chicago, Milwaukee & St. Paul Ry.

232 U.S. 340 (1914)

[As part of its business of making flax, the plaintiff stored about 700 tons of straw in 230 stacks located on its own land. The stacks were lined up in two rows. The defendant's right of way ran about seventy feet from the first row and eighty-five feet from the second. One day, a high wind carried sparks from a passing train using the right of way to one of the stacks of flax located in the row farther from the tracks. That fire eventually consumed all the flax. The jury found first that the defendant's servants had negligently operated its locomotive by allowing it to emit large quantities of sparks and live cinders, and second, that this act of negligence was a cause of the plaintiff's harm. Consistent with its instructions, the jury also found the plaintiff guilty of contributory negligence by placing the exposed stacks within 100 feet of the railroad's right of way. The Supreme Court was asked to decide whether there was any question of contributory negligence to leave to the jury.]

McKenna, J. . . . It will be observed, the [plaintiff's] use of the land was of itself a proper use—it did not interfere with nor embarrass the rightful operation of the railroad. It is manifest, therefore, the questions certified . . . are but phases of the broader one, whether one is limited in the use of one's property by its proximity to a railroad or, to limit the proposition to the case under review, whether one is subject in its use to the careless as well as to the careful operation of the road. We might not doubt that an immediate answer in the negative should be given if it were not for the hesitation of the Circuit Court of Appeals evinced by its questions, and the decisions of some courts in the affirmative. That one's uses of his property may be subject to the servitude of the wrongful use by another of his property seems an anomaly. It upsets the presumptions of law and takes from him the assumption and the freedom which comes from the assumption, that the other will obey the law, not violate it. It casts upon him the duty of not only using his own property so as not to injure another, but so to use his own property that it may not be injured by the wrongs of another. How far can this subjection be carried? Or, confining the question to railroads, what limits shall be put upon their immunity from the result of their wrongful operation? In the case at bar, the property destroyed is described as inflammable, but there are degrees of that quality; and how wrongful must be the operation? In this case, large quantities of sparks and "live cinders" were emitted from the passing engine. Houses may be said to be inflammable, and may be, as they have been, set on fire by sparks and cinders from defective or carelessly handled locomotives. Are they to be subject as well as stacks of flax straw, to such lawless operation? And is the use of farms also, the cultivation of which the building of the railroad has preceded? Or is that a use which the railroad must have anticipated and to which it hence owes a duty, which it does not owe to other uses? And why? The question is especially pertinent and immediately shows that the rights of one man in the use of his property cannot be limited by the wrongs of another. The doctrine of contributory negligence is entirely out of place. Depart from the simple requirement of the law, that every one must use his property so as not to injure others, and you pass to refinements and confusing considerations. There is no embarrassment in the principle even to the operation of a railroad. Such operation is a legitimate use of property; other property in its vicinity may suffer inconveniences and be subject to risks by it, but a risk from wrongful operation is not one of them. . . .

Holmes, J., partially concurring. . . . If a man stacked his flax so near to a railroad that it obviously was likely to be set fire to by a well-managed train, I should say that he could not throw the loss upon the railroad by the oscillating result of an inquiry by the jury whether the road had used due care. I should say that although of course he had a right to put his flax where he liked upon his own land, the liability of the railroad for a fire was absolutely conditioned upon the stacks being at a reasonably safe distance from the train. . . .

If I am right so far, a very important element in determining the right to recover is whether the plaintiff's flax was so near to the track as to be in danger from even a prudently managed engine. Here certainly, except in a clear case, we should call in the jury. I do not suppose that anyone would call it prudent to stack flax within five feet of the engines or imprudent to do it at a distance of half a mile, and it would not be absurd if the law ultimately should formulate an exact measure, as it has tended to in other instances; but at present I take it that if the question I suggest be material we should let the jury decide whether seventy feet was too near by the criterion that I have proposed. . . .

I do not think we need trouble ourselves with the thought that my view depends upon differences of degree. The whole law does so as soon as it is civilized. Negligence is all degree—that of the defendant here degree of the nicest sort; and between the variations according to distance that I suppose to exist and the simple universality of the rules in the Twelve Tables or the Leges Barbarorum, there lies the culture of two thousand years.

I am authorized to say that the Chief Justice concurs in the opinion that I express.

"It's a mixed-use facility: retail space, low-rent housing, luxury apartments, and an area set aside for making steel."

Source: Sidney Harris/ The New Yorker Collection/ The Cartoon Bank

NOTE

Reciprocal Causation. *LeRoy Fibre* illustrates the close connection between property rights and causation. Unlike joint causation cases, this case does not involve a collision caused by two moving parties, or by any action of the plaintiff that blocked or hindered the operation of the railroad. In the Court's view, therefore, the issue of contributory negligence cannot arise because the plaintiff (even by stacking his flax close to the tracks, so long as it remains on his own property) has done nothing to invade physically the railroad's right of way. The case is similar to Smith v. Kenrick, *supra* Chapter 2, at 89, which held that a mine owner was under no duty to erect a barrier to keep "foreign" water discharged by the defendant from flooding his mine. Thus it differs sharply from cases of joint causation that arise, say, in highway accidents between two vehicles.

The majority position is nonetheless vulnerable because it gives no incentives for victims to reduce their storage activities to appropriate levels. See Meese, The Externality of Victim Care, 68 U. Chi. L. Rev. 1201, 1218 (2001). That position is hinted at in Holmes' partial concurrence, which stresses less the absence of physical invasion (here by plaintiff of defendant's property) and more the cheaper precautions available to the plaintiff. His position had in fact received a fair bit of support in some of the earlier nineteenth-century cases that imposed duties on farmers to minimize their losses from fires set by passing locomotives, even at distances that Holmes thought were outside the danger zone. Thus, in Kansas Pacific Railway v. Brady, 17 Kan. 380, 386 (1877), the defendant railroad set fire to the plaintiff's hay, which was stacked between one and one-half and two miles away from the tracks. The court first found that there was evidence of the defendant's negligence in the operation of its train, and then turned to the question of contributory negligence:

> If the defendant was negligent at all as against the plaintiffs, it was really as much because said hay was stacked in a dangerous place, and because dry grass was allowed to intervene all the way from the stack to the railway track, as because said fire was permitted to escape. Now as the burning of said hay was the result of the acts and omissions of both the plaintiffs and the defendant, it would seem that the acts and omissions of both parties should have been submitted to the jury. Both parties may have been negligent, and the acts and omissions of both should have been subject to the scrutiny of the jury. But it is claimed that the plaintiffs could not under any circumstances be considered negligent. It is claimed that they had a right to stack their hay as they did stack it, in a dangerous place, with dry grass all around it, and without taking any precautions for its protection. And this is claimed upon the theory that every man has a right to use his own property as he pleases without reference to the great inconvenience he may thereby impose upon others. Is this theory, or rather the plaintiffs' application thereof, correct? . . . Why should any person be allowed to invite the destruction of his own property by his own negligence, so that he might by recovering for the loss thereof lessen the estate of another to that extent? Why should any person be allowed to so use his own property that in the natural course of things he would most likely injure the estate of another to the extent of the value of such property? Or, why should he have it within his power to so use his own property as to make it so hazardous for others to use theirs that such others must necessarily abandon the use of theirs?

Is distance from the track a reliable proxy for safety? In Svea Insurance Co. v. Vicksburg, S. & P. Ry., 153 F. 774 (W.D. La. 1907), the court noted that fire cases required the jury to take into account the "reciprocal duties" of both parties. This theme of reciprocity has received its most famous elaboration in Coase, The Problem of Social Cost, 3 J.L. & Econ. 1, 2 (1960):

> The question is commonly thought of as one in which *A* inflicts harm on *B* and what has to be decided is: how should we restrain *A*? But this is wrong. We are dealing with a problem of a reciprocal nature. To avoid the harm to *B* would inflict harm on *A*. The real question that has to be decided is: should *A* be allowed to harm *B* or should *B* be allowed to harm *A*? The problem is to avoid the more serious harm. I instanced . . . the case of a confectioner the noise and vibrations from whose machinery disturbed a doctor in his work. To avoid harming the doctor would inflict harm on the confectioner. The problem posed by this case was essentially whether it was worth while, as a result of restricting the methods of production which could be used by the confectioner, to secure more doctoring at the cost of a reduced supply of confectionery products. Another example is afforded by the problem of straying cattle which destroy crops on neighbouring land. If it is inevitable that some cattle will stray, an increase in the supply of meat can only be obtained at the expense of a decrease in the supply of crops. The nature of the choice is clear: meat or crops. What answer should be given is, of course, not clear unless we know the value of what is obtained as well as the value of what is sacrificed to obtain it. To give another example, Professor George J. Stigler instances the contamination of a stream. If we assume that the harmful effect of the pollution is that it kills the fish, the question to be decided is: is the value of the fish lost greater or less than the value of the product which the contamination of the stream makes possible.

Is Coase correct to assume that the only question to decide is whether *A* should be allowed to harm *B*, or *B* to harm *A*? What about a rule that allows *A* to harm (i.e., to invade *B*'s premises) only if he compensates *B* for his loss? See Chapter 8, Section E for an elaboration of these themes. Put otherwise, should the railroad be required to purchase an easement to cause fire over the land of the neighboring farmers? Or should the railroad get it for free? For a general discussion of these fire cases, see Grady, Common Law Control of Strategic Behavior: Railroad Sparks and the Farmer, 17 J. Legal Stud. 15 (1988), which attacks the rigid property rights logic of McKenna, J., in *LeRoy Fibre*.

Derheim v. N. Fiorito Co.

492 P.2d 1030 (Wash. 1972)

[The plaintiff's car collided with the defendant's truck when the defendant made a left turn in violation of the rules of the road. The plaintiff was not wearing a seat belt at the time of the accident. The defendant sought to introduce expert evidence at trial to establish that the plaintiff's conduct was a form of contributory negligence, which at the very least should be taken into account to reduce damages under the doctrine of avoidable consequences. The trial judge, however, refused to allow the defendant to raise the seat belt defense in its amended answer. He also refused to allow the defendant's expert to testify that if the plaintiff had worn his seat belt at the time of the accident, he would not have suffered the injuries for which the suit was brought. After a verdict and judgment for the plaintiff, the case was certified for immediate hearing by the Washington Supreme Court.]

Hunter, J. . . . We are thus called upon to determine the rule in this state with respect to the so-called "seat belt defense." No subject in the field of automobile accident litigation, with the possible exception of no-fault insurance, has received more attention in recent years than has the seat or lap belt defense. The question being one of first impression in this state, we have reviewed the published material extensively, concluding that while the research and statistical studies indicate a far greater likelihood of serious injuries in the event of nonuse, nevertheless the courts have been inconsistent in their handling of the defense. This inconsistency seems to result from the fact that the defense does not fit conveniently into the familiar time-honored doctrines traditionally used by the courts in deciding tort cases. Thus, the conduct in question (failure to buckle up) occurs before defendant's negligence, as opposed to contributory negligence which customarily is thought of in terms of conduct contributing to the accident itself. While more precisely, contributory negligence is conduct contributing, with the negligence of the defendant in bringing about the plaintiff's harm, it is a rare case indeed where the distinction need be made. Furthermore, while states with comparative negligence do not have the problem to the same extent, contributory negligence in many states (such as Washington) is a complete bar to any recovery by a plaintiff—an obvious unjust result to apply in seat belt cases. The same result would be reached if the defense were presented in terms of assumption of risk, that is, that one who ventures upon the highway without buckling up is voluntarily assuming the risk of more serious injuries resulting from a possible accident proximately caused by the negligence of another.

The doctrine of avoidable consequences has been suggested as a possible solution to this conceptual dilemma, but here again, the problem is one of appearing to stretch the doctrine to fit an unusual fact pattern. As a legal theory, avoidable consequences is closely akin to mitigation of damages, and customarily is applied when plaintiff's conduct after the occurrence fails to meet the standards of due care. Moreover, courts have traditionally said that a defendant whose negligence proximately causes an injury to plaintiff, "takes the plaintiff as he finds him."

The practical implications of allowing seat belt evidence has also given the courts pause. For example, most automobiles are now manufactured with shoulder straps in addition to seat belts, and medical evidence could be anticipated in certain cases that particular injuries would not have resulted if both shoulder belts and seat belts had been used. Additionally, many automobiles are now equipped with headrests which are designed to protect one from the so-called whiplash type of injury. But to be effective, its height must be adjusted by the occupant. Should the injured victim of a defendant's negligence be penalized in ascertainment of damages for failure to adjust his headrest? Furthermore, the courts are aware that other protective devices and measures are undergoing testing in governmental and private laboratories, or are on the drawing boards. The concern is, of course, that if the seat belt defense is allowed, would not the same analysis require the use of all safety devices with which one's automobile is equipped? A further problem bothers the courts, and that is the effect of injecting the seat belt issue into the trial of automobile personal injury cases. The courts are concerned about unduly lengthening trials and if each automobile accident trial is to provide an arena for a battle of safety experts, as well as medical experts, time and expense of litigation might well be increased.

These problems, legal and practical, are found in reviewing the most recent cases decided by other jurisdictions confronting the issue. . . .

[The court then reviews a series of then recent cases in other jurisdictions, some accepting and some rejecting the "seat belt defense," and continues:]

We believe the cases in those jurisdictions rejecting the "seat belt defense" are the better reasoned cases. It seems extremely unfair to mitigate the damages of one who sustains those damages in an accident for which he was in no way responsible, particularly when, as in this jurisdiction, there is no statutory duty to wear seat belts.

For the reasons heretofore stated, we believe the trial court was correct in refusing admission of evidence on the "seat belt defense."

The judgment of the trial court is affirmed.

NOTES

1. ***The Seat Belt Defense.*** Should the opposite result be reached in *Derheim* if seat belt use were mandated by statute, as it now is (with varying qualifications) in every state except New Hampshire? If it could be shown that overall accident rates and insurance premiums would drop if some seat belt defenses were allowed? Contrast *Derheim* with the observations of Gabrielli, J., in Spier v. Barker, 323 N.E.2d 164, 167–68 (N.Y. 1974):

> We today hold that nonuse of an available [i.e., already installed] seat belt, and expert testimony in regard thereto, is a factor which the jury may consider, in light of all the other facts received in evidence, in arriving at its determination as to whether the plaintiff has exercised due care, not only to avoid injury to himself, but to mitigate any injury he would likely sustain. However, as the trial court observed in its charge, the plaintiff's nonuse of an available seat belt should be strictly limited to the jury's determination of the plaintiff's damages and should not be considered by the triers of fact in resolving the issue of liability. Moreover, the burden of pleading and proving that nonuse thereof by the plaintiff resulted in increasing the extent of his injuries and damages, rests upon the defendant. That is to say, the issue should not be submitted to the jury unless the defendant can demonstrate, by competent evidence, a causal connection between the plaintiff's nonuse of an available seat belt and the injuries and damages sustained. . . .
>
> Since section 383 of the Vehicle and Traffic Law does not require occupants of a passenger car to make use of available seat belts, we hold that a plaintiff's failure to do so does not constitute negligence per se. . . . Likewise, we do not subscribe to the holdings of those cases in which the plaintiff's

failure to fasten his seat belt may be determined by the jury to constitute contributory negligence as a matter of common law. In our view, the doctrine of contributory negligence is applicable only if the plaintiff's failure to exercise due care causes, in whole or in part, *the accident*, rather than when it merely exacerbates or enhances the severity of his injuries. That being the case, holding a nonuser contributorily negligent would be improper since it would impose liability upon the plaintiff for all his injuries though use of a seat belt might have prevented none or only a portion of them.

. . . We concede that the opportunity to mitigate damages prior to the occurrence of an accident does not ordinarily arise, and that the chronological distinction, on which the concept of mitigation damages rest, is justified in most cases. However, in our opinion, the seat belt affords the automobile occupant an unusual and ordinarily unavailable means by which he or she may minimize his or her damages *prior* to the accident. Highway safety has become a national concern; we are told to drive defensively and to "watch out for the other driver." When an automobile occupant may readily protect himself, at least partially, from the consequences of a collision, we think that the burden of buckling an available seat belt may, under the facts of the particular case, be found by the jury to be less than the likelihood of injury when multiplied by its accompanying severity.

Another objection frequently raised is that the jury will be unable to segregate the injuries caused by the initial impact from the injuries caused by the plaintiff's failure to fasten his seat belt. In addition to underestimating the abilities of those trained in the field of accident reconstruction, this argument fails to consider other instances in which the jury is permitted to apportion damages (i.e., as between an original tort-feasor and a physician who negligently treats the original injury).

2. ***Statutory Response to the Seat Belt Defense.*** The availability of the seat belt defense in tort litigation is today heavily regulated by statute, as almost forty states have adopted different regimes, most of which sharply restrict the availability of defense. For a tally, see Schwartz, Comparative Negligence §4.06 (5th ed. 2010). More recent cases have tended to follow *Derheim.* Thus in Siruta v. Siruta, 348 P.3d 549, 553 (Kan. 2015), the court upheld, against a constitutional challenge, Kan. Stat. Ann. §8-1345, which excludes any and all evidence of the failure to use a seat belt or other restraining device for a child as wholly irrelevant to both the question of comparative negligence and mitigation of damages. *Siruta* presented the odd situation where one surviving parent sued the other for the death of their common child. Should the defense of interspousal immunity be applied? Should an insurance company be able to exclude its liability for interspousal suits?

Comment, The Seatbelt Defense: A Doctrine Based in Common Sense, 38 Tulsa L. Rev. 405, 416 n.121, 421 n.156 (2002), reports that of the thirty-nine statutes that deal with the question, twenty-four decline to allow the defense. Some of the remaining states cap the defense at some small fraction of the plaintiff's recovery, e.g., 2 percent. Others require defendant to plead and prove the defense. What is wrong with a rule that reduces the plaintiff's recovery by 25 percent in all cases in which her failure to wear the seat belt contributes to her injury?

Is there any reason to treat a motorcyclist's failure to wear a required helmet differently from her failure to wear a seat belt? McKinley v. Casson, 80 A.2d 618, 626 (Del. 2013), held that in the absence of any statutory or common law duty to wear a helmet, the failure to do so was excluded from the comparative negligence analysis. Could the court have created a common law duty? The following graph plots motorcycle helmet use between 2000 and 2017:

Motorcycle Helmet Use, 2000 – 2017 (Data Source: NOPUS*)

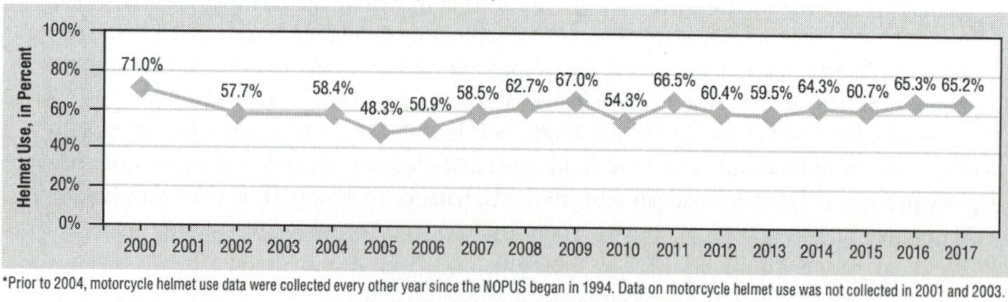

*Prior to 2004, motorcycle helmet use data were collected every other year since the NOPUS began in 1994. Data on motorcycle helmet use was not collected in 2001 and 2003.

https://crashstats.nhtsa.dot.gov/Api/Public/ViewPublication/812512

There have been some substantial year-to-year variations for which it is difficult to find a strong generalization. But it is doubtful that any switch on the question whether the failure to wear a helmet has much to do with the change. Why? There are three possible explanations. First, many motorcycle accidents are one-person affairs for which the rules of contributory negligence do not matter. Second, the risk of death is likely a more powerful influence on conduct than the likelihood of some diminished recovery in the event of injury or death. Third, the use of fines and license suspensions are likely to have a more immediate effect on behavior. Is the same true of the seat belt issue?

5

2. Last Clear Chance

Fuller v. Illinois Central R.R.
56 So. 783 (Miss. 1911)

[Decedent, a man of over seventy, was riding his one-horse wagon on a north-south dirt road that crossed a straight stretch of railroad track that ran perpendicular to it. The decedent had his head down; he did not stop, look, or listen, and did not observe defendant's oncoming train. This train, a light one, came down the tracks thirty minutes late, at around forty miles per hour, faster than usual or appropriate. The decedent was in plain view on the track some 660 feet from the crossing, and the uncontradicted evidence was that the defendant's engineer could have stopped the light train within 200 feet. The record was silent as to what the engineer of the train did or thought when the decedent came into plain view on the tracks, but he did not slow the train down. The only signal he gave was a routine whistle blast some twenty seconds before the train crashed into the wagon. The decedent was instantly killed. In response to contributory negligence, the plaintiff alleged that the defendant's servant had the last clear chance to avoid injury either by braking or promptly sounding a warning whistle. At trial judgment was given for the defendant.]

McLain, J. . . . The rule is settled beyond controversy or doubt, first, that all that is required of the railroad company as against a trespasser is the abstention from wanton or willful injury, or that conduct which is characterized as gross negligence; second, although the injured party may be guilty of contributory negligence, yet this is no defense if the injury were willfully, wantonly, or recklessly done or the party inflicting the injury was guilty of such conduct as to characterize it as gross; and, third, that the contributory negligence of the party injured will not defeat the action if it is shown that the defendant might by the exercise of reasonable care and prudence have avoided the consequence of the injured party's negligence. This last principle is known as the doctrine of the "last clear chance." The origin of this doctrine is found in the celebrated case of Davies v. Mann, 10 Mees & W. 545, [(1842) 152 Eng. Rep. 588 (Exch.)]. The plaintiff in that case fettered the front feet of his donkey, and turned him into the public highway to graze. The defendant's wagon, coming down a slight descent at a "smartish" pace, ran against the donkey, and knocked it down, the wheels of the wagon passing over it, and the donkey was killed. In that case Lord Abinger, C.B., says: "The defendant has not denied that the ass was lawfully in the highway, and therefore we must assume it to have been lawfully there. But, even were it otherwise, it would have made no difference, for, as the defendant might by proper care have avoided injuring the animal and did not, he is liable for the consequences of his negligence, though the animal might have been improperly there." While Park, B., says: "Although the ass might have been wrongfully there, still the defendant was bound to go along the road at such a pace as would be likely to prevent mischief. Were this not so, a man might justify the driving over goods left on the public highway or even a man lying asleep there, or probably running against the carriage going on the wrong side of the road." It is impossible to follow this case through its numerous citations in nearly every jurisdiction subject to Anglo-American jurisprudence. For the present it will be sufficient to say that the principle therein announced has met with practically almost universal favor. It has been severely criticized by some textwriters. The groans, ineffably and mournfully sad, of Davies' dying donkey, have resounded around the earth. The last lingering gaze from the soft, mild eyes of this docile animal, like the last parting sunbeams of the softest day in spring, has appealed to and touched the hearts of men. There has girdled the globe a band of sympathy for Davies' immortal "critter." Its ghost, like Banquo's ghost, will not down at the behest of the people who are charged with inflicting injuries, nor can its groanings be silenced by the rantings and excoriations of carping critics. The law as enunciated in that case has come to stay. The principle has been clearly and accurately stated in 2 Quarterly Law Review, p. 207, as follows: "The party who last has a clear opportunity of avoiding the accident, notwithstanding the negligence of his opponent, is considered solely responsible for it." . . .

. . . The facts in the instant case show that for a distance of six hundred and sixty feet west of the crossing where Mr. Fuller was run over and injured the track was perfectly straight; that there were no obstructions; that there was nothing to prevent those in charge of the train from seeing the perilous position of the plaintiff, and it may be that, if the engineer and fireman were on the lookout, they saw, or by the exercise of reasonable care and diligence might have seen, the perilous position of the plaintiff. No alarm was given. Nothing was done to warn the deceased of the approaching train. He evidently was unconscious of its approach.

The only warning that was given him was too late to be of any benefit whatever, as the train was upon him at the time the two short blasts of the whistle were given. . . . Even if the engineer had not made an effort to stop or check his train, but had contented himself with giving the alarm at the point when he did see, or could have seen by the exercise of reasonable care on his part, the catastrophe in all probability could have been averted.

It must be observed that this is not the case of a pedestrian who approaches or who is on the track. In such cases the engineer has the right ordinarily to act upon the assumption that the party will get out of danger. Mr. Fuller was in a wagon, and the engineer could have seen that he was going to cross the track, and could only with difficulty extricate himself from his perilous position. . . .

Reversed and remanded.

RESTATEMENT OF THE LAW (SECOND) OF TORTS

§479. Last Clear Chance: Helpless Plaintiff

A plaintiff who has negligently subjected himself to a risk of harm from the defendant's subsequent negligence may recover for harm caused thereby if, immediately preceding the harm,

(a) the plaintiff is unable to avoid it by the exercise of reasonable vigilance and care, and

(b) the defendant is negligent in failing to utilize with reasonable care and competence his then existing opportunity to avoid the harm, when he

(i) knows of the plaintiff's situation and realizes or has reason to realize the peril involved in it or

(ii) would discover the situation and thus have reason to realize the peril, if he were to exercise the vigilance which it is then his duty to the plaintiff to exercise.

§480. Last Clear Chance: Inattentive Plaintiff

A plaintiff who, by the exercise of reasonable vigilance, could discover the danger created by the defendant's negligence in time to avoid the harm to him, can recover if, but only if, the defendant

(a) knows of the plaintiff's situation, and

(b) realizes or has reason to realize that the plaintiff is inattentive and therefore unlikely to discover his peril in time to avoid the harm, and

(c) thereafter is negligent in failing to utilize with reasonable care and competence his then existing opportunity to avoid the harm.

Compare to:

RESTATEMENT OF THE LAW (THIRD) OF TORTS: APPORTIONMENT OF LIABILITY

§3. Last Clear Chance: Helpless Plaintiff

. . . Special ameliorative doctrines for defining plaintiff's negligence are abolished.

Comment b. Timing of the plaintiff's and defendant's conduct: last clear chance, mitigation of damages, and avoidable consequences: . . . The timing of the plaintiffs and defendant's conduct may be relevant to the degree of responsibility the factfinder assigns to a plaintiff. . . . It may also be relevant to whether the plaintiff's injury was within the scope of liability of either the plaintiff's or defendant's conduct.

Do rules or standards work better in this context?

NOTES

1. ***Sequential Conduct.*** The doctrine of last clear chance attaches great significance to sequential conduct, that is, situations in which the action of one party takes place after the other person has completed his conduct or has irrevocably committed himself to a given course of conduct, as in *Fuller*. The basic insight in this area is that once the defendant becomes aware of the plaintiff's peril, he then becomes obligated to react to that danger by taking prudent steps to avoid it. The conduct that was optimal without knowledge of the peril is no longer so once that knowledge is acquired or evident to the senses. The problem is in a sense reciprocal to the one in *Gyerman*, where the victim had the last clear chance to avoid the harm. In these sequential cases, should one regard the last party as the cheapest cost avoider, best able to bear the loss? The attractiveness of that position has made the doctrine something of a favorite of law and economics scholars, even though many lawyers regard last clear chance as a transitional doctrine on the road to a comparative negligence regime. See James, Last Clear Chance—Transitional Doctrine, 47 Yale L.J. 704 (1938).

The potential use of the doctrine is conveniently illustrated by Davies v. Mann, (1842) 152 Eng. Rep. 588 (Exch.), so poignantly retold in *Fuller*. The plaintiff first left his donkey in plain view on the highway, only to have it run over by the defendant's wagon. Making contributory negligence an absolute bar reduces the likelihood that the plaintiff will leave his donkey in the road in the first place. Necessarily, however, the contributory negligence defense reduces the defendant's incentive to avoid killing the donkey, even when the defendant knows or has strong reason to know of the danger. Yet the defendant cannot take advantage of that position once either of those two conditions are satisfied. The last clear chance exception applies only in a small fraction of cases, so the plaintiff can hardly count on it to protect her interests in most cases when deciding where to leave her donkey. Thus the exception to the contributory negligence rule only arises when it is likely to be most effective.

For general discussions of this problem, see Shavell, Torts in Which Victim and Injurer Act Sequentially, 26 J.L. & Econ. 589 (1983); Wittman, Optimal Pricing of Sequential Inputs: Last Clear Chance, Mitigation of Damages, and Related Doctrines in the Law, 10 J. Legal Stud. 65 (1981).

2. *Scope of the Last Clear Chance Doctrine.* To make good her case on last clear chance, the plaintiff usually must show that the defendant was guilty of something more than ordinary negligence, which, as the Restatement implied, presupposes either knowledge that the plaintiff is in peril or "negligence so reckless as to betoken indifference to knowledge." Woloszynowski v. New York Central R.R., 172 N.E. 471, 472 (N.Y. 1930). The plaintiff met that burden in the grisly case of Kumkumian v. City of New York, 111 N.E.2d 865, 868 (N.Y. 1953), a wrongful death action in which the City's subway train ran over the decedent, who was lying on the track some 1,400 feet before the station's entrance. The train had halted three times after its tripping device came in contact with something on the tracks. After the first two stops, the brakeman inspected the tracks but found nothing. Only after the third time did the brakeman and engineer discover the decedent's mangled corpse on the track. Some evidence suggested that the fatal injuries were incurred only when the decedent was struck by the tripcocks of the third and fourth cars. Froessel, J., held that the trial judge properly left the case to the jury on a theory of last clear chance:

> Surely we cannot say, as a matter of law, under the last clear chance doctrine, that the motorman and conductor were not negligent in *twice* disregarding the emergency equipment, which is not placed in service to be ignored, and were merely chargeable with an error of judgment. At least it became a question of fact as to whether such conduct constitutes "negligence so reckless as to betoken indifference to knowledge" and whether they "ignored the warning" while there was still opportunity to avoid the accident. It matters not that they received the warning through a faultless mechanical instrumentality rather than a human agency, so long as they had "the requisite knowledge upon which a reasonably prudent man would act." The jury was entitled to find that lack of knowledge on the part of defendant's employees as to decedent's position of danger did not come about through mere lack of vigilance in observing the tracks, but rather as the result of their own willful indifference to the emergency called to their attention by the automatic equipment, to which clear warning they paid no heed. When they did belatedly carry out their plain duty to investigate, they found decedent, and it may be inferred that they would have seen him had they carried out that duty after the second stop—still belatedly, yet in time to have saved his life. We are of the opinion that plaintiff made out at least a prima facie case under the doctrine of last clear chance.

Judge Fuld wrote a brief dissent denying the applicability of last clear chance. "Certainly, neither the motorman nor the conductor knew that any person was in peril in time to have prevented his death, and the evidence is insufficient to support the inference that they *should* have known." Should the doctrine of last clear chance be limited to cases where the defendant knows that the plaintiff is in peril?

SECTION C. IMPUTED CONTRIBUTORY NEGLIGENCE

The cases thus far considered have focused on whether an individual plaintiff could be held responsible in part for the harms that she has suffered. The issue of imputed contributory negligence asks whether the negligence of some other person should be charged or "imputed" to the plaintiff, at which point the traditional rules bar any right to recover.

Traditional nineteenth-century doctrine drew that inference by holding, for example, that the owner of a wagon could be barred from recovery if her servant had carelessly guided the coach. The open question was whether that imputation applied to any other types of relationships between the plaintiff and some third person. In Thorogood v. Bryan, 137 Eng. Rep 452

(1849), the driver of the horse-drawn omnibus stopped in the middle of the road, instead of by the curb. As the decedent stepped off, he was killed when hit by another omnibus that was traveling too fast. The court first held that the driver's negligence should be imputed to the passenger because of the close "identification" between them. The court then further insisted that since the decedent had the choice of omnibuses in which to ride, he could not disclaim the responsibility in question. Initially, *Thorogood* was adopted in most American states, but it was sternly rejected in Little v. Hackett, 116 U.S. 366, 375 (1886), by Field, J.:

> The truth is, the decision in Thorogood v. Bryan rests upon indefensible ground. The identification of the passenger with the negligent driver or the owner, without his personal co-operation or encouragement, is a gratuitous assumption. There is no such identity. The parties are not in the same position. The owner of a public conveyance is a carrier, and the driver or the person managing it is his servant. Neither of them is the servant of the passenger, and his asserted identity with them is contradicted by the daily experience of the world.

Two years later, *Thorogood* was also decisively repudiated in England in Mills v. Armstrong (the *Bernina*), [1888] 13 AC 1. Lord Herschell denounced the doctrine because no one had ever used the identification test to hold the passenger vicariously liable to a stranger for the wrongs of the coach's driver: "[T]he identification appears to be effective only to the extent of enabling another person whose servants have been guilty of negligence to defend himself by the allegation of contributory negligence on the part of the person injured."

The general rejection of *Thorogood's identification test* is subject to a critical exception for "joint enterprise." When the defendant can establish that the passenger and the driver have entered into some relationship that makes the passenger vicariously liable for the driver's torts, as was manifestly not the case in the *Bernina*, some courts impute the negligence of the driver to the passenger. Although such "joint enterprise" could conceivably arise from the simple driver-passenger relationship, most courts have tended to require more, sometimes dwelling on the "community of interest" that such an enterprise presupposes. See RST §491, comments *b* & *g*.

The hostile attitude toward the joint enterprise rule is well illustrated by Dashiell v. Keauhou-Kona Co., 487 F.2d 957, 959–61 (9th Cir. 1973). Mr. Dashiell was injured, jointly through the negligence of his wife, who was driving a golf cart in which he was a passenger, and the negligence of the defendant. By a two-to-one vote, the court reversed the judgment given to the defendant below, holding the joint enterprise defense inapplicable as a matter of law:

> We find that on the facts of this case, at no time did the relationship of joint enterprise or joint venture exist between Mr. and Mrs. Dashiell within the meaning of imputed negligence. This is not a typical case of a business venture of a character similar to a partnership where two or more parties undertake, for some pecuniary purpose, a contractual obligation resulting in the liability of each for the negligence of the other. . . .
>
> Additionally, applying the concept of imputed contributory negligence to the facts of this case would needlessly frustrate some basic policies of tort law. Mr. Dashiell was found by the jury to be blameless, and since negligence law is based on personal fault, it would be both illogical and inequitable to deny him recovery unless he were under a duty to control the actions of Mrs. Dashiell as she drove the golf cart. The record reflects no basis on which to find any duty of control. The original purpose of defining the joint enterprise relationship was vicarious liability, in order to increase the number of those liable to provide a financially responsible person to injured third parties. That purpose is absent when related to the Dashiells; in fact, application of the imputed contributory negligence rule would have the opposite effect of freeing from liability another party who is at fault even though the person denied recovery is blameless.

Dashiell reflects the modern dissatisfaction with the once fashionable "both ways test," which provided that if *A* could be held vicariously liable for the torts of *B*, then the contributory negligence of *B* should be imputed to *A*, barring *A*'s recovery. Despite the uneasiness,

RTT: Apportionment of Liability adopts the "both ways test." See RTT: AL §5 & comment *b*. Should Mr. Dashiell be vicariously liable if Mrs. Dashiell had injured the defendant? What result in the *Bernina* under the "both ways test"?

The doctrine of imputed contributory negligence was also applied in parent-child relationships in the early case of Hartfield v. Roper, 21 Wend. 615, 618–19 (N.Y. 1839). There the court barred the action of a two- or three-year-old infant because of his parents' negligence in allowing him to wander into a roadway, where he was struck and injured by a sleigh driven by defendants Roper and Newall, owing in part to "folly and gross neglect" of the child's parents in allowing him to wander into the road. While conceding that such parental foolishness could not excuse or justify either any deliberate injury or gross neglect of the defendants, the court nonetheless denied the plaintiff's recovery:

> An infant is not *sui juris.* He belongs to another, to whom discretion in the care of his person is exclusively confided. That person is keeper and agent for this purpose; and in respect to third persons, his act must be deemed that of the infant; his neglect, the infant's neglect.

Should the parents also be vicariously liable for the child's tort? *Hartfield* has been repudiated by either common law decision or statute in virtually all jurisdictions. New York, for example, overturned the rule by statute in 1935. N.Y. Dom. Rel. Law §73, now N.Y. Gen. Oblig. Law §3-111 (2023). See generally Gregory, Vicarious Responsibility and Contributory Negligence, 41 Yale L.J. 831 (1932); 2 Harper, James & Gray, Torts ch. 23. Does the parental imputation rule make more sense in a regime of comparative negligence?

SECTION D. ASSUMPTION OF RISK

1. Industrial Accidents

Lamson v. American Axe & Tool Co.

58 N.E. 585 (Mass. 1900)

Tort, under the employers' liability act, St. 1887, c. 270, for personal injuries occasioned to the plaintiff while in the defendant's employ. Trial in the Superior Court, before Lawton, J., who directed the jury to return a verdict for the defendant; and the plaintiff alleged exceptions, which appear in the opinion.

Holmes, C.J. This is an action for personal injuries caused by the fall of a hatchet from a rack in front of which it was the plaintiff's business to work at painting hatchets, and upon which the hatchets were to be placed to dry when painted. The plaintiff had been in the defendant's employment for many years. About a year before the accident new racks had been substituted for those previously in use, and it may be assumed that they were less safe and were not proper, but were dangerous on account of the liability of the hatchets to fall from the pegs upon the plaintiff when the racks were jarred by the motion of machinery near by. The plaintiff complained to the superintendent that the hatchets were more likely to drop off than when the old racks were in use, and that now they might fall upon him, which they could not have done from the old racks. He was answered in substance that he would have to use the racks or leave. The accident which he feared happened, and he brought this suit.

The plaintiff, on his own evidence, appreciated the danger more than any one else. He perfectly understood what was likely to happen. That likelihood did not depend upon the doing of some negligent act by people in another branch of employment, but solely on the permanent conditions of the racks and their surroundings and the plaintiff's continuing to work where he did. He complained, and was notified that he could go if he would not face the chance. He stayed and took the risk. . . . He did so none the less that the fear of losing his place was one of his motives.

Exceptions overruled.

NOTES

1. *Employer Liability Acts.* *Lamson* was brought not at common law, but under the Massachusetts Employers' Liability Act. Based on an English statute of the same name, 43 Vict. c. 42 (1880), the Massachusetts Act, among other things, held employers to a general rule of negligence liability and abolished the fellow servant rule (examined shortly) that all workers assumed the risk of their fellow servants by virtue of their common status as employees. See generally Epstein, The Historical Origins and Economic Structure of Workers' Compensation Law, 16 Ga. L. Rev. 775, 778 (1982). Rejection of the fellow servant rule, however, left behind the common law version of assumption of risk. These claims became primarily governed under the Employers' Liability Act of 1880 (ELA) (as happened in *Lamson*) or under parallel English decisions. See, e.g., Thomas v. Quartermaine (1887) 18 QBD 685; Smith v. Baker, [1891] AC 325.

The surviving version of assumption of risk, however, depended critically on the employee's continued willingness to work in the face of known risks, often after his complaints had been voiced and rejected (as in *Lamson*). In St. Louis Cordage Co. v. Miller, 126 F. 495 (8th Cir. 1903), Sanborn, J., defended assumption of risk as a manifestation of freedom of contract. Lord Bramwell took a similar stance in Smith v. Baker & Sons, [1891] AC 325, 344, in which the plaintiff, while engaged in his employment, was injured when a stone that was being lifted over his head fell and hit him. The House of Lords accepted the plaintiff's contention that he did not assume the risk because he had no specific knowledge that he was about to be struck, but Bramwell, J., a staunch and unreconstructed defender of laissez-faire, dissented, putting his case in the language of the bargain:

> It is a rule of good sense that if a man voluntarily undertakes a risk for a reward which is adequate to induce him, he shall not, if he suffers from the risk, have a compensation for which he did not stipulate. He can, if he chooses, say, "I will undertake the risk for so much, and if hurt, you must give me so much more, or an equivalent for the hurt." But drop the maxim. Treat it as a question of bargain. The plaintiff here thought the pay worth the risk, and did not bargain for a compensation if hurt: in effect, he undertook the work, with its risks, for his wages and no more. He says so. Suppose he had said, "If I am to run this risk, you must give me 6*s.* a day and not 5*s.*," and the master agreed, would he in reason have a claim if he got hurt? Clearly not. What difference is there if the master says, "No I will only give you 5*s.*?" None. I am ashamed to argue it.

How does Bramwell, J., know that this workplace bargain precluded compensation for injury? How could he, or the majority of the House of Lords, find out whether it did?

In one sense, the larger issue in *Smith* was not whether this plaintiff had assumed this risk, but whether as a matter of law he, or any other employee, was allowed under the law to assume it by contract. The legal willingness to ban or limit the assumption of risk defense in industrial accident cases advanced by degrees and culminated in its abolition by a 1939 amendment to the Federal Employers' Liability Act (FELA), 45 U.S.C. §54. The standard workers' compensation statutes adopted in most states shortly after World War I, see *infra* at 247, Note 1, also eliminated the defense. But the defense continues to operate in actions brought against third parties not covered by these statutes. See, e.g., Dullard v. Berkeley Associates Co., 606 F.2d 890 (2d Cir. 1979) (general contractors); Pomer v. Schoolman, 875 F.2d 1262 (7th Cir. 1989) (farmer). For early developments, see Bohlen, Voluntary Assumption of Risk, 20 Harv. L. Rev. 14, 17–18 (1906).

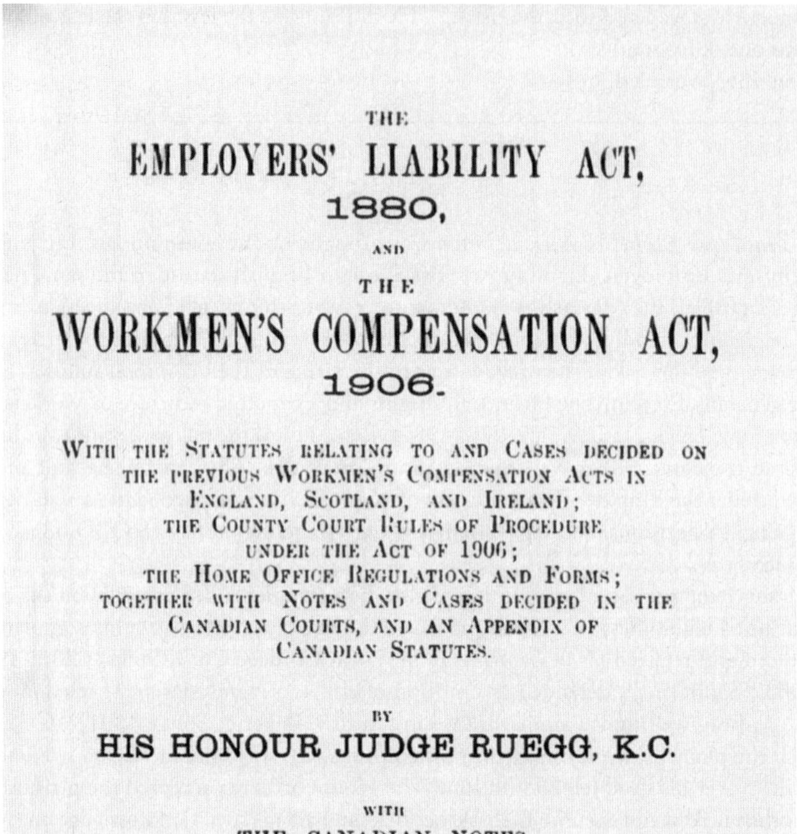

THE

EMPLOYERS' LIABILITY ACT,

1880,

AND

THE

WORKMEN'S COMPENSATION ACT,

1906.

WITH THE STATUTES RELATING TO AND CASES DECIDED ON THE PREVIOUS WORKMEN'S COMPENSATION ACTS IN ENGLAND, SCOTLAND, AND IRELAND; THE COUNTY COURT RULES OF PROCEDURE UNDER THE ACT OF 1906; THE HOME OFFICE REGULATIONS AND FORMS; TOGETHER WITH NOTES AND CASES DECIDED IN THE CANADIAN COURTS, AND AN APPENDIX OF CANADIAN STATUTES.

BY

HIS HONOUR JUDGE RUEGG, K.C.

WITH

THE CANADIAN NOTES

BY

F. A. C. REDDEN,

Of the Ontario Bar.
Solicitor of the Supreme Court, England.

Eighth Edition.

LONDON:
BUTTERWORTH & CO., 11 & 12, BELL YARD, TEMPLE BAR.
Law Publishers.
CANADA LAW BOOK COMPANY, LIMITED, TORONTO, CANADA.
CROMARTY LAW BOOK COMPANY, 1112, CHESTNUT ST., PHILADELPHIA.

1910.

Title page of a leading contemporary treatise on workers' compensation in Britain. Ruegg, The Employers' Liability Act, 1880, and the Workmen's Compensation Act, 1906 (8th ed. 1910).

Source: Internet Archive

2. *The Fellow Servant Rule.* Ironically, the assumption of risk defense found its initial expression in the common employment (or fellow servant) rule, endorsed by Chief Justice

Shaw nearly sixty years before *Lamson.* In Farwell v. Boston & Worcester Railroad Corp., 45 Mass. 49, 58–59 (1842), the defendant employed the plaintiff as a railroad engineer who, while at work, lost his right hand when another of the defendant's servants carelessly threw the wrong switch down the line. The employer had not been negligent in either selecting or supervising the "trusty" switchman. The court refused to charge the railroad for its employee's negligence when sued by that employee's fellow servant, even though a stranger could hold the railroad vicariously liable for his acts. The key difference to Shaw, J., was that the employee had assumed the risk: "[T]he implied contract of the master does not extend to indemnify the servant against the negligence of anyone but himself." He then contrasted the position of an employee with that of a passenger:

> The liability of passenger carriers is founded on similar considerations. They are held to the strictest responsibility for care, vigilance and skill, on the part of themselves and all persons employed by them, and they are paid accordingly. The rule is founded on the expediency of throwing the risk upon those who can best guard against it. Story on Bailments, §590 et seq.

He concluded as follows:

> In applying these principles to the present case, it appears that the plaintiff was employed by the defendants as an engineer, at the rate of wages usually paid in that employment, being a higher rate than the plaintiff had before received as a machinist. It was a voluntary undertaking on his part, with a full knowledge of the risks incident to the employment; and the loss was sustained by means of an ordinary casualty, caused by the negligence of another servant of the company. Under these circumstances, the loss must be deemed to be the result of a pure accident, like those to which all men, in all employments, and at all times, are more or less exposed; and like similar losses from accidental causes, it must rest where it first fell, unless the plaintiff has a remedy against the person actually in default; of which we give no opinion.

The fellow servant rule was, if anything, far more uncompromising than the assumption of risk rule in *Lamson.* In *Farwell,* for example, the risk was assumed by status alone, since the plaintiff was totally ignorant of either the person or the dangerous condition that could cause him harm. In an unavailing effort to escape the fellow servant rule, the plaintiff's counsel in *Farwell* sought to confine it to situations like Priestley v. Fowler, in which the two servants (jointly loading a butcher's wagon) were in face-to-face contact, and not under the immediate supervision of their common employer. Shaw, J., resisted any such compromise by extending the rule to employees who worked in "different departments" of the same business, however defined.

The common employment rule did not long retain its pristine simplicity in *Farwell* as exceptions to the rule mounted. Perhaps its most important refinement was the "vice principal" exception, whereby particular duties of certain supervisory roles were regarded as nondelegable, such as the duty to supply the proper equipment and the duty to furnish a safe workplace. For a comparison to the duties of common carriers, see Kelly v. Manhattan Ry., *supra* Chapter 3, at 145. Applying this exception generated many inconsistent judicial decisions, collected in Labatt, Master & Servant §§1433–1553 (2d ed. 1913). Indeed, Lord Cairns repudiated the whole vice principal exception in England in the celebrated (or infamous) case of Wilson v. Merry, [1868] 1 L.R.-S. & D. App. 326 (HL) (appeal taken from Eng.), which reaffirmed *Priestley* in its original rigor.

These compromises did not, however, satisfy the critics of the fellow-servant rule. In 1 Shearman & Redfield, Negligence vi, vii (5th ed. 1898), the authors denounced the rule in these words:

> A small number of able judges, devoted, from varying motives, to the supposed interests of the wealthy classes, and caring little for any others, boldly invented an exception to the general rule of masters' liability, by which servants were deprived of its protection. Very appropriately,

> this exception was first announced in South Carolina, then the citadel of human slavery. It was eagerly adopted in Massachusetts, then the centre of the factory system, where some decisions were then made in favor of great corporations, so preposterous that they have been disregarded in every other State, without even the compliment of refutation. It was promptly followed in England, which was then governed exclusively by landlords and capitalists. . . .
>
> As the courts, while asserting unlimited power to create new and bad law, denied their power to correct their own errors, the legislature intervened, and to a large extent the whole defence of "common employment" has been taken away in Great Britain. And now, not a single voice is raised in Great Britain in justification of the doctrine once enforced by the unanimous opinions of the English courts. The infallible Chief Justice Shaw and Chancellor Cairns have fallen so low, on *this* point at least, that "there are none so poor as to do them reverence. . . ."

Similarly, twentieth-century scholars uniformly rejected the doctrine. See Friedman, A History of American Law 413, 414 (1973); see also Schwartz, Tort Law and the Economy in Nineteenth-Century America: A Reinterpretation, 90 Yale L.J. 1717, 1768–75 (1981). For a defense of the rule on the contractual grounds originally advanced by Shaw, see Posner, A Theory of Negligence, 1 J. Legal Stud. 29, 67–71 (1972); for an exhaustive account of its origins in Priestley v. Fowler, see Stein, Priestley v. Fowler (1837) and the Emerging Tort of Negligence, 44 B.C. L. Rev. 689 (2003), disputing *Priestley*'s role in the origin of common employment.

2. The Workmen's Compensation Acts

The next chapter in the history of assumption of risk was its general displacement by the adoption of the Workmen's Compensation Acts at the turn of the twentieth century. In England, the pioneering Workmen's Compensation Act, 1897, 60 & 61 Vict. ch. 37, supplanted the ELA in 1897, explicitly banning any contractual waiver of the protection afforded workers. The 1897 Act, in turn, set up an extensive debate in the United States, which culminated in New York enacting the first American workers' compensation statute in 1910, 1910 N.Y. Laws 625, to implement the recommendations of its blue-ribbon Wainwright Commission. The Commission summarized its conclusions as follows:

> First, that the present system in New York rests on a basis that is economically unwise and unfair, and that in operation it is wasteful, uncertain and productive of antagonism between workmen and employers.
>
> Second, that it is satisfactory to none and tolerable only to those employers and workmen who practically disregard their legal rights and obligations, and fairly share the burden of accidents in industries.
>
> Third, that the evils of the system are most marked in hazardous employments, where the trade risk is high and serious accidents frequent.
>
> Fourth, that, as a matter of fact, workmen in the dangerous trades do not, and practically cannot, provide for themselves adequate accident insurance, and therefore, the burden of serious accidents falls on the workmen least able to bear it, and brings many of them and their families to want.

Ives v. S. Buffalo Ry.
94 N.E. 431 (N.Y. 1911)

WERNER, J. The statute, judged by our common-law standards, is plainly revolutionary. Its central and controlling feature is that every employer who is engaged in any of the classified industries shall be liable for any injury to a workman arising out of and in the course of the employment by "a necessary risk or danger of the employment or one inherent in the nature thereof, . . . provided that the employer shall not be liable in respect of any injury to the workman which is caused in whole or in part by the serious and willful misconduct of the workman." This rule of liability, stated in another form, is that the employer is responsible to the employee for every accident in the course of the employment, whether the employer is at fault or not, and whether the employee is at fault or not, except when the fault of the employee is so grave as to constitute serious and willful misconduct on his part. The radical character of this legislation is at once revealed by contrasting it with the rule of the common law, under which the employer is liable for injuries to his employee only when the employer is guilty of some act or acts of negligence which caused the occurrence out of which the injuries arise, and then only when the employee is shown to be free from any negligence which contributes to the occurrence.

[WERNER, J., then addresses the objections to the statute and concludes that it is constitutionally permissible to abolish the employer's "trinity" of common law defenses in personal injury actions: the fellow servant doctrine (whereby the injured party could not recover from the employer for harm caused by the negligence of a fellow servant), assumption of risk, and contributory negligence. Yet in spite of the admittedly impressive economic and sociological brief made on behalf of the statute, the court strikes it down as an impermissible exercise of the police power because it bore no relationship to the health, safety, or morals of employees. The court also finds that the statutory imposition of "liability without fault" worked an unconstitutional deprivation of property without due process of law.]

If the argument in support of this statute is sound we do not see why it cannot logically be carried much further. Poverty and misfortune from every cause are detrimental to the state. It would probably conduce to the welfare of all concerned if there could be a more equal distribution of wealth. Many persons have much more property than they can use to advantage and many more find it impossible to get the means for a comfortable existence. If the legislature can say to an employer, "you must compensate your employee for an injury not caused by you or by your fault," why can it not go further and say to the man of wealth, "you have more property than you need and your neighbor is so poor that he can barely subsist; in the interest of natural justice you must divide with your neighbor so that he and his dependents shall not become a charge upon the State?"

CULLEN, C.J. I know of no principle on which one can be compelled to indemnify another for loss unless it is based upon contractual obligation or fault. It might as well be argued in support of a law requiring a man to pay his neighbor's debts, that the common law requires each man to pay his own debts, and the statute in question was a mere modification of the common law so as to require each to pay his neighbor's debts.

NOTES

1. ***Workers' Compensation Laws Upheld.*** The basic description of the workmen's compensation act is accurate to this very day. The early judicial setback in *Ives* was short-lived. Pursuant to a suggestion made by the court in *Ives,* New York amended its constitution to authorize a workers' compensation statute. In New York Central Railroad v. White, 243 U.S. 188, 202–04, 208 (1916), a unanimous United States Supreme Court upheld the new statute against federal constitutional challenges. Justice Pitney wrote:

> Reduced to its elements, the situation to be dealt with is this: Employer and employee, by mutual consent, engage in a common operation intended to be advantageous to both; the employee is to contribute his personal services, and for these is to receive wages, and ordinarily

nothing more; the employer is to furnish plant, facilities, organization, capital, credit, is to control and manage the operation, paying the wages and other expenses, disposing of the product at such prices as he can obtain, taking all the profits, if any there be, and of necessity bearing the entire losses. [Workplace accidents can impose a terrible toll on workers and their families.] Who is to bear the charge? It is plain that, on grounds of natural justice, it is not unreasonable for the State, while relieving the employer from responsibility for damages measured by common-law standards and payable in cases where he or those for whose conduct he is answerable are found to be at fault, to require him to contribute a reasonable amount, and according to a reasonable and definite scale, by way of compensation for the loss of earning power incurred in the common enterprise, irrespective of the question of negligence, instead of leaving the entire loss to rest where it may chance to fall—that is, upon the injured employee or his dependents, [unless they could prove the employer's negligence and avoid being charged with his own]. Nor can it be deemed arbitrary and unreasonable, from the standpoint of the employee's interest, to supplant a system under which he assumed the entire risk of injury in ordinary cases, and in others had a right to recover an amount more or less speculative upon proving facts of negligence that often were difficult to prove, and substitute a system under which in all ordinary cases of accidental injury he is sure of a definite and easily ascertained compensation, not being obliged to assume the entire loss in any case but in all cases assuming any loss beyond the prescribed scale.

We conclude that the prescribed scheme of compulsory compensation is not repugnant to the provisions of the Fourteenth Amendment....

2. *The Workmen's Compensation Bargain.* As noted in the findings of the Wainwright Commission, the initial scope of workers' compensation law was limited to dangerous employment. The terms of this "workmen's compensation bargain" called for the worker to give up the right to high stakes common law litigation in exchange for a system of broader coverage with a more limited liability. A hidden feature of the system was that its award of incomplete compensation operated as a device to encourage care by workers who were no longer subject to either the assumption of risk or contributory negligence defense. That situation steered individuals who could suffer greater losses (e.g., potential musicians) away from taking employments from which they would suffer disproportionate losses.

One sign of their efficiency in balancing the distribution of losses can be derived from the fact that these compensation systems were adopted for private firms (including union firms) on a voluntary basis. In Griffiths v. Earl of Dudley, [1882] 9 QB 357, and Clements v. London & N.E. Ry., [1894] 2 QB 482, the court upheld the assumption of risk defense after the passage of the English Employer Liability Act (ELA). These cases demonstrate ELA's sophisticated workers' compensation system, which was nonetheless limited to "accidents" (e.g., sudden harms), as opposed to gradual exposures in cumulative trauma, where exposures can take place at different locations and different times (e.g., asbestos or toxic fumes exposure). The agreements found in *Griffiths* set the template for the statutory systems put in place in the 1897 statutes (which lasted until 1948, when Parliament repealed ELA shortly after the adoption of the British National Health Service).

3. *Arising Out of and in the Course of Employment.* These central requirements of the workers' compensation scheme are easily satisfied in the typical industrial accident case. These two terms, "arising out of" and "in the course of" employment, are distinct requirements. "The words 'in the course of' refer to the time, place, and circumstances of the injury. The term 'arising out of' refers to the cause and origin of the injury." Miedema v. Dial Corp., 551 N.W.2d 309 (Iowa 1996). In *Miedema*, the court held that an employee who strained his back after making a trip to the employer's restroom while getting ready for work was injured in the course of employment, but that his injury did not arise out of his employment. Conversely, in Clodgo v. Rentavision, Inc., 701 A.2d 1044 (Vt. 1997), two employees engaged in horseplay by each shooting a staple gun at the other. When the plaintiff was hit in the eye, the injury's occurrence on the employer's premises during working hours was adequate to conclude that the accident arose out of his employment. But this accident was not in the course of employment because the injury did not take place "while fulfilling the duties of the employment contract." Gibson, J., explained:

> Thus the Commissioner did not make any finding about the extent and seriousness of the deviation [from standard work duties]; (2) the completeness of the deviation (i.e., whether the activity was commingled with performance of a work duty or was a complete abandonment of duty); (3) the extent to which the activity had become an accepted part of the employment; and (4) the extent to which the nature of the employment may be expected to include some horseplay.

Accordingly, even though such incidents were commonplace at the workplace, "[c]laimant makes no showing that shooting staples at fellow employees was an accepted part of claimant's employment or furthered [his employer's] interests." Morse, J., in dissent, disagreed on the ground that the claimant had finished all his work duties for the day and thus had engaged in enforced idleness.

4. *Employee Theft.* In Richardson v. Fiedler, 493 N.E.2d 228, 229, 231, 233 (N.Y. 1986), the decedent, a waterproofer and roofing mechanic, fell to his death while attempting to steal copper downspouts from the roof of his job site. Simons, J., held that the death was covered under the workers' compensation law even though the theft was antithetical to the employer's interests. The decisive point was that "it was common practice in the industry for roofers to remove copper downspouts and sell them for scrap. [The Workers' Compensation Board] further found that this employer not only knew of the practice but also frequently had been required to pay for or replace downspouts stolen by its employees." Yet the employer did not discipline or discharge co-employees, nor did it tell its workers in no uncertain terms that illegal conduct on the job would not be tolerated.

For a variation on the theft theme, see Martinez v. Workers' Compensation Appeals Board, 544 P.2d 1350, 1352 (Cal. 1976), where the claimant, after a day of work at a church, confronted some teenagers who he believed had stolen beer from the church. The court determined that the workers' compensation law covered injuries sustained in the ensuing combat because the plaintiff's injuries were emergency actions for the employer's benefit. The law applied because a reasonable employee might "attempt" to prevent theft even if not explicitly hired as a security guard.

5. *Other Marginal Cases: Athletic Injuries, Personal Work, Acts of God, Drunkenness.* The court in Anderton v. WasteAway Services, 880 A.2d 1003, 1007–08 (Conn. App. Ct. 2005) upheld a determination that workers' compensation law can extend to athletic injuries sustained outside an employee's usual job duties. There, the plaintiff tore his left Achilles tendon while playing in a basketball stadium across the street from his place of work during working hours. Because the employee played at the invitation of his supervisor and reasonably thought it would hurt his job prospects to refuse the invitation, the court allowed compensation.

The court in Orsini v. Industrial Commission, 509 N.E.2d 1005, 1008 (Ill. 1987), denied coverage when the plaintiff mechanic used his employer's service bay to repair his own car after hours. According to Clark, C.J., the accident was "personal and noncompensable" for it was not "a risk peculiar to the work or a risk to which the employee is exposed to a greater degree than the general public by reason of his employment." What result if either the firm's workplace or tools were defective?

In Electro-Voice, Inc. v. O'Dell, 519 S.W.2d 395, 397 (Tenn. 1975), the claimant received an award of disability benefits when she suffered a violent allergic reaction after being stung by a bee while working on an assembly line. That injury "arose out of" her employment because plant conditions "increased the risk or hazard" of bee stings given that "bees often entered walls of buildings in the warm summer months and came out later in the year," inducing the employer to treat the building twice in the past two years to kill the embedded bees. *Electro-Voice* adopted the "actual risk" test, whereby the claimant is allowed to recover similarly by showing that the employment increased (perhaps "materially") the risk of the harm beyond the levels to which an ordinary member of the public is exposed. In contrast, the so-called positional risk theory adopted by a minority of jurisdictions allows compensation under a "but for" test if the employer's activities require the employee to work at the place where the injury occurred at the time it occurred.

Section 3600 of the California Labor Code (2023) denies compensation for an injury caused by the intoxication of the injured employee "where the employee has willfully and deliberately caused his own death." What should be done if a worker starts drinking while on the job and is injured by continuing to drink after hours? In Van Vleet v. Montana Ass'n of Counties Workers' Compensation Trust, 103 P.3d 544, 548 (Mont. 2004), the court allowed compensation if the afterhours drinking did not constitute a "substantial deviation" from the drinking while on the job.

6. *Cumulative Trauma Cases.* The cumulative trauma cases excluded from the voluntary nineteenth-century "accident" systems are covered by the modern "occurrence" formula with its far greater administrative difficulties. It is often difficult to decide, for example, whether a heart attack on the job is the product of work-related stresses or the stresses of home life. See Kostamo v. Marquette Iron Mining Co., 274 N.W.2d 411, 415 (Mich. 1979). The *Kostamo* court concluded that compensation cannot be ordered "unless the work has accelerated or aggravated the illness, disease or deterioration and, thus, contributed to it," which could only be established with both the presentation of reliable evidence to that effect and the ruling out of the injuries pre-dating work. N.J. Stat. Ann. §34:15-7.2 (2023), in turn, provides that in cases of "injury or death from cardiovascular or cerebral vascular causes, the claimant shall prove by a preponderance of the credible evidence that the injury or death was produced by the work effort or strain involving a substantial condition, event or happening in excess of the wear and tear of the claimant's daily living."

7. *Going and Coming Cases.* "The 'going and coming' rule provides that workers' compensation does not ordinarily compensate injuries sustained while the employee travels to or from work . . ." Wilson v. Workers' Compensation Appeals Board, 545 P.2d 225, 226 (Cal. 1976). Although most cases are straightforward, many problems arise in cases that involve dual purpose trips. In general, compensation is denied, as in *Wilson*, to the teacher who grades papers at home at night. But the rule is different for workers who commute directly from one work site to another, or who have no fixed site of work. See Hinojosa v. Workmen's Compensation Appeals Board, 501 P.2d 1176, 1181 (Cal. 1972), which awarded compensation to an employee working on multiple ranches after the plaintiff was injured when driven home by a fellow worker. Why not restrict coverage to trips between work sites? Coverage has also been denied to workers injured going to and from a hotel away from home when hit by a car while out socializing after work hours. Atkins v. Webcon, 419 P.3d 1 (Kan. 2018). What should happen if the worker slips and falls in the shower? See Capizzi v. Southern District Reporters, 459 N.E.2d 847, 849 (N.Y. 1984), allowing compensation.

8. *Damages Under Workers' Compensation Systems.* In all states, the benefits payable to the employee are usually calculated in terms of the average weekly wage (AWW). The definition of the AWW provided under N.Y. Workers' Comp. Law §14 (2023) is typical. That statute provides, in the simplest case, that "the average annual earnings shall consist of three hundred times the average daily wage or salary for a six-day worker, and two hundred sixty times the average daily wage or salary for a five-day worker," with appropriate adjustments for part-time and seasonal workers. Injuries are then placed into four general categories:

temporary partial, temporary total, permanent partial, and permanent total. With permanent total injuries, most states set compensation at two-thirds of the worker's weekly wage, subject to various statutory minimums and maximums. In general, greater uncertainty about the severity and duration of temporary disabilities makes the calculations more difficult. For certain specified injuries, the statute delineates a table of scheduled damages, measured as a multiple of the AWW, for specific injuries: arm 312, leg 288, hand 244, foot 205, eye 160, and so on down for lesser injuries, including different rates for different fingers. See N.Y. Workers' Comp. Law §15(3) (April 2023).

9. *Exclusive Remedy.* It is important to note that workers' compensation generally is the exclusive remedy against the employer for any workplace injury. Some important exceptions arise to this exclusive remedy provision: first, when the employer possesses specific intent to harm the employee, and second, when the employee acts in a second capacity under the dual capacity doctrine.

Workers injured "through the deliberate intention of his employer to produce such injury or death" are generally granted an exception to the exclusive remedy. Ky. Rev. Stat. Ann. §342.610(4) (2023). This statute has been read in contrast with the tort definition of intent to *not* include cases "where the employer acts with the knowledge that harm might follow," such that the exception is "viable only when the employer has 'determined to injure an employee and used some means appropriate to that end, and there must be a specific intent.'" In Rainer v. Union Carbide Corp., 402 F.3d 608, 611, 616 (6th Cir. 2005), Gilman, J., using that definition, denied recovery for actual and potential damages to "workers at a uranium-enrichment plant near Paducah, Kentucky [who] were exposed over many years to dangerous radioactive substances without their knowledge."

Source: Guy & Rodd / Distributed by Universal Uclick for UFS via CartoonStock.com

A second important exception to the exclusive remedy provisions is the so-called dual capacity doctrine, which arises when a covered employee interacts with an employer in a second capacity. In Duprey v. Shane, 249 P.2d 8, 15 (Cal. 1952), the defendant chiropractor mistreated his nurse when he treated her work-related injury. The court allowed the tort action because the defendant acted as her doctor and hence as a "person other than the employer." Hendy v. Losse, 819 P.2d 1, 34 (Cal. 1991), distinguished *Duprey* when a professional football player sued the team physician in tort for a misdiagnosis of a knee injury that ended his career, because the physician "did not step out of his coemployee role when he treated plaintiff."

10. *Risk Premium.* Both Shaw, J., in *Farwell* and Bramwell, J., in *Smith* alluded to the possibility that higher wages compensate for riskier employment. Much modern research holds that workers in dangerous employments receive a "risk premium" to cover their added risk before any loss occurs. Measuring the risk premium today is a fraught business at best. Some of the most careful empirical work on this question has been done by Viscusi, Risk by Choice 43–44 (1983), who reports as follows:

> In my study of workers' subjective risk perceptions, I found that workers who believed that they were exposed to dangerous or unhealthy conditions received over $900 annually (1980 prices) [or about $3,333 in 2023 dollars] in hazard pay. It is especially noteworthy that an almost identical figure was obtained when I used an objective industry injury risk measure. . . . The similarity of the findings using subjective and objective measures of risk lends strong empirical support to the validity of the risk premium analysis.
>
> Unfortunately, these results do not enable us to conclude that markets work perfectly. Is the premium less or more than would prevail if workers and employers were fully cognizant of the risks? The size of the premium only implies that compensating differentials are one element of market behavior. A more meaningful index is the wage premium per unit of risk. If it is very likely that a worker will be killed or injured, a $900 risk premium can be seen as a signal that the compensating differential process is deficient. The average blue-collar worker, however, faces an annual occupational death risk of only about 1/10,000 and a less than 1/25 risk of an injury severe enough to cause him to miss a day or more of work. Consequently, the observed premium per unit of risk is quite substantial, with the implicit value of life being [roughly] $2 million . . . for many workers [or about $7.405 million in 2023 dollars].
>
> The safety incentives created by market mechanisms are much stronger than those created by OSHA standards; a conservative estimate of the total job risk premiums for the entire private sector is $69 billion, or almost 3,000 times the total annual penalties now levied by OSHA. Whereas OSHA penalties are only 34 cents per worker, market risk premiums per worker are $925 [or about $3,425 in 2023 dollars] annually.

How does one calculate the value of a life, given that this market has no willing sellers and buyers? One standard approach asks how much money it would take to get a worker to assume some incremental risk of death and then, riskily extrapolate to the case of certain death. Thus, if a person would require $10,000 to take a 0.1 percent risk of death, one thousand times that amount, or $10 million, might cover the case of certain death. Accurate? Some evidence from Viscusi points to a $9 million figure. See Hersch & Viscusi, Assessing the Insurance Role of Tort Liability After Calabresi, 77 Law & Contemp. Probs. 135, 156 (2014). That figure would, moreover, be about 12 percent higher today. For a discussion of damages and the value of a statistical life, see Chapter 9, *infra* at 667.

3. Nonindustrial Accidents

Murphy v. Steeplechase Amusement Co.

166 N.E. 173 (N.Y. 1929)

Cardozo, C.J. The defendant, Steeplechase Amusement Company, maintains an amusement park at Coney Island, New York. One of the supposed attractions is known as "The Flopper." It is a moving belt, running upward on an inclined plane, on which passengers sit or stand. Many of them are unable to keep their feet because of the movement of the belt, and are thrown backward or aside. The belt runs in a groove, with padded walls on either side to a height of four feet, and with padded flooring beyond the walls at the same angle as the belt. An electric motor, driven by current furnished by the Brooklyn Edison Company, supplies the needed power.

Plaintiff, a vigorous young man, visited the park with friends. One of them, a young woman, now his wife, stepped upon the moving belt. Plaintiff followed and stepped behind her. As he did so, he felt what he describes as a sudden jerk, and was thrown to the floor. His wife in front and also friends behind him were thrown at the same time. Something more was here, as every one understood, than the slowly-moving escalator that is common in shops and public places. A fall was foreseen as one of the risks of the adventure. There would have been no point to the whole thing, no adventure about it, if the risk had not been there. The very name above the gate, the Flopper, was warning to the timid. If the name was not enough, there was warning more distinct in the experience of others. We are told by the plaintiff's wife that the members of her party stood looking at the sport before joining in it themselves. Some aboard the belt were able, as she viewed them, to sit down with decorum or even to stand and keep their footing; others jumped or fell. The tumbling bodies and the screams and laughter supplied the merriment and fun. "I took a chance," she said when asked whether she thought that a fall might be expected.

Plaintiff took the chance with her, but, less lucky than his companions, suffered a fracture of a knee cap. He states in his complaint that the belt was dangerous to life and limb in that it stopped and started violently and suddenly and was not properly equipped to prevent injuries to persons who were using it without knowledge of its dangers, and in a bill of particulars he adds that it was operated at a fast and dangerous rate of speed and was not supplied with a proper railing, guard or other device to prevent a fall therefrom. No other negligence is charged.

The Flopper

Source: Courtesy of Kenneth W. Simons, from the Record on Appeal

We see no adequate basis for a finding that the belt was out of order. It was already in motion when the plaintiff put his foot on it. He cannot help himself to a verdict in such circumstances by the addition of the facile comment that it threw him with a jerk. One who steps upon a moving belt and finds his heels above his head is in no position to discriminate with nicety between the successive stages of the shock, between the jerk which is a cause and the jerk, accompanying the fall, as an instantaneous effect. There is evidence for the defendant that power was transmitted smoothly, and could not be transmitted otherwise. If the movement was spasmodic, it was an unexplained and, it seems, an inexplicable departure from the normal workings of the mechanism. An aberration so extraordinary, if it is to lay the basis for a verdict, should rest on something firmer than a mere descriptive epithet, a summary of the sensations of a tense and crowded moment. But the jerk, if it were established, would add little to the case. Whether the movement of the belt was uniform or irregular, the risk at greatest was a fall. This was the very hazard that was invited and foreseen.

Volenti non fit injuria. One who takes part in such a sport accepts the dangers that inhere in it so far as they are obvious and necessary, just as a fencer accepts the risk of a thrust by his antagonist or a spectator at a ball game the chance of contact with the ball. The antics of the clown are not the paces of the cloistered cleric. The rough and boisterous joke, the horseplay of the crowd, evokes its own guffaws, but they are not the pleasures of tranquility. The plaintiff was not seeking a retreat for meditation. Visitors were tumbling about the belt to the merriment of onlookers when he made his choice to join them. He took the chance of a like fate, with whatever damage to his body might ensue from such a fall. The timorous may stay at home.

A different case would be here if the dangers inherent in the sport were obscure or unobserved, or so serious as to justify the belief that precautions of some kind must have been taken to avert them. Nothing happened to the plaintiff except what common experience tells us may happen at any time as the consequence of a sudden fall. Many a skater or a horseman can rehearse a tale of equal woe. A different case there would also be if the accidents had been so many as to show that the game in its inherent nature was too dangerous to be continued without change. The president of the amusement company says that there had never been such an accident before. A nurse employed at an emergency hospital maintained in connection with the park contradicts him to some extent. She says that on other occasions she had attended patrons of the park who had been injured at the Flopper, how many she could not say. None, however, had been badly injured or had suffered broken bones. Such testimony is not enough to show that the game was a trap for the unwary, too perilous to be endured. According to the defendant's estimate, two hundred and fifty thousand visitors were at the Flopper in a year. Some quota of accidents was to be looked for in so great a mass. One might as well say that a skating rink should be abandoned because skaters sometimes fall.

There is testimony by the plaintiff that he fell upon wood, and not upon a canvas padding. He is strongly contradicted by the photographs and by the witnesses for the defendant, and is without corroboration in the testimony of his companions who were witnesses on his behalf. If his observation was correct, there was a defect in the equipment, and one not obvious or known. The padding should have been kept in repair to break the force of any fall. The case did not go to the jury, however, upon any such theory of the defendant's liability, nor is the defect fairly suggested by the plaintiff's bill of particulars, which limits his complaint. The case went to the jury upon the theory that negligence was dependent upon a sharp and sudden jerk.

The judgment of the Appellate Division and that of the Trial Term [for the plaintiff] should be reversed, and a new trial granted, with costs to abide the event.

POUND, CRANE, LEHMAN, KELLOGG and HUBBS, JJ., concur; O'BRIEN, J., dissents.

NOTES

1. *Historical Criticisms of Murphy.* For a strong "dissenting" opinion, see Simons, Murphy v. Steeplechase Amusement Co.: While the Timorous Stay at Home, the Adventurous Ride the Flopper, *in* Tort Stories 179 (Rabin & Sugarman eds., 2003). Simons argues that the Flopper was more dangerous than Cardozo, J., suggested. It was only sixteen inches wide and had to be entered while moving at a speed of seven miles per hour, in contrast to the one to one-and-a-half miles per hour of the standard escalator, and the evidence of the sudden jerk was more persuasive than Cardozo, J., acknowledged. But at the same time, it may have been safer than other rides (e.g., the Whirlpool or Human Roulette Wheel) in standard use at Coney Island, then the amusement capital of the world. Why, on this record, grant a new trial?

2. *Primary and Secondary Assumption of Risk.* In Meistrich v. Casino Arena Attractions, Inc., 155 A.2d 90 (N.J. 1959), the plaintiff fell while skating on the defendant's rink. The plaintiff's evidence showed that "defendant departed from the usual procedure in preparing the ice, with the result that it became too hard and hence too slippery for the patron of average ability using skates sharpened for the usual surface." Weintraub, C.J., speaking for a unanimous court, held that a jury could infer that the defendant's negligence was a proximate cause of the accident. He also held that a "jury could permissibly find [the plaintiff] carelessly contributed to his injury when, with that knowledge, he remained on the ice and skated cross-hand with another." He nonetheless ordered a new trial because of what he regarded as a faulty instruction below on assumption of risk, namely the trial court's instruction "that assumption of risk may be found if plaintiff knew or reasonably should have known of the risk, notwithstanding that a reasonably prudent man would have continued in the face of the risk."

Weintraub, C.J., critically reviewed the history of assumption of risk in industrial accidents, and in the course of his opinion articulated the distinction between primary and secondary assumption of risk as follows:

> [Apart from intentional or contractually addressed harms], assumption of risk has two distinct meanings. In one sense (sometimes called its "primary" sense), it is an alternative expression for the proposition that defendant was not negligent, i.e., either owed no duty or did not breach the duty owed. In its other sense (sometimes called "secondary"), assumption of risk is an affirmative defense to an established breach of duty. In its primary sense, it is accurate to say plaintiff assumed the risk whether or not he was "at fault," for the truth thereby expressed in alternate terminology is that defendant was not negligent. But in its secondary sense, i.e., as an affirmative defense to an established breach of defendant's duty, it is incorrect to say plaintiff assumed the risk whether or not he was at fault. . . .
>
> In applying assumption of risk in its secondary sense in areas other than that of master and servant, our cases have consistently recognized the ultimate question to be whether a reasonably prudent man would have moved in the face of a known risk, dealing with the issue as one of law or leaving it to the jury upon the same standard which controls the handling of the issue of contributory negligence. . . .

One consequence of this definition is that the cases from Chapter 1, *supra* at 22, Note 3, which hold that the plaintiff must show defendant's intentional or reckless behavior to recover from the defendant, are all cases of assumption of risk in its primary sense, as there is no ordinary duty of care. *Meistrich* differs from these cases because the action is brought not against a competitor or participant, but the owner or occupier of established premises who generally owes all patrons a duty of care. In its secondary sense, assumption of risk is only an aspect of contributory negligence. Unlike the situation in *Lamson* or *Murphy*, the plaintiff in *Meistrich* knew that the defendant was in breach of its obligation to provide a safe skating surface before he fell. Why then is he not under an obligation to leave the ice? If he does, can he get his money back? Is *Murphy* a case of primary or secondary assumption of risk?

3. *Assumption of Risk and the Duty to Warn.* One important issue in these amusement park cases is the extent to which assumption of risk can survive the recent expansion of the duty to warn. In Russo v. The Range, Inc., 395 N.E.2d 10, 13–14 (Ill. App. 1979), the plaintiff was injured while riding down the "giant slide" owned and operated by the defendant. Before entering the amusement park, he purchased a ticket that on the reverse side read: "[T]he person using this ticket so assumes all risk of personal injury." At the top of the slide, defendant placed a warning and instructions for its proper use. The plaintiff also admitted that he had taken several similar rides at the amusement park before the accident, but claimed that he had "no knowledge that the slide would cause his body to fly in the air as he rode it—the event which he says caused his injury." The court allowed the plaintiff's case to reach the jury. "From these same facts the Range relies on it is possible to infer that Russo's ride down the slide was an abnormal occurrence caused by some danger unknown to him and a risk he did not assume. It is the presence of this possibility which precludes summary judgment."

Modern providers of rides routinely take aggressive steps to announce the risks, often using bold signs to that effect. Thus in Anderson v. Hedstrom Corp., 76 F. Supp. 2d 422 (S.D.N.Y. 1999), the plaintiff sued for injuries suffered in a trampoline accident. The product came with this warning:

WARNING! MISUSE AND ABUSE OF THIS TRAMPOLINE IS DANGEROUS AND CAN CAUSE SERIOUS INJURIES. DO NOT DO SOMERSAULTS. DO NOT LAND ON NECK OR HEAD. PERMIT ONLY **ONE** PERSON AT A TIME ON THIS TRAMPOLINE. MORE THAN ONE PERSON AT A TIME ON THIS TRAMPOLINE INCREASES THE CHANCE OF INJURY.

Smith, J., denied the defendant's motion for summary judgment saying:

> Whether those warnings should have specified, for example, the specific danger of paralysis from neck injury, rather than only the danger of "serious injuries," is a question upon which reasonable people could disagree. . . . Similarly, in light of defendants' own contention that plaintiff's injuries were caused by his failure to bounce in the center of the trampoline, a jury could reasonably decide that the absence, on the trampoline labels, of any warning to bounce only in the center, constituted a failure to adequately warn, even though a statement in the Owner's Manual did advise, "Avoid bouncing too high. Stay low until you can control your bounce and repeatedly land in the center of the trampoline."

Can any institution draft a warning good enough to support its motion for summary judgment? Should the jury also be instructed to note that many of the risks subject to a warning are also obvious?

4. ***Spectator Sports and Assumption of Risk.*** The assumption of risk defense is commonly used to deny recovery to spectators injured at sporting events. The defense proceeds at two levels. First, at the wholesale level, courts hold that all spectators share the common knowledge of injury from attending these events. Second, at the retail level, particularized evidence tends to confirm that any individual plaintiff has this knowledge, such as the risk of being hit by a hockey puck, Moulas v. PBC Productions, Inc., 570 N.W.2d 739 (Wis. App. 1997), *aff'd by an equally divided court*, 576 N.W.2d 929 (Wis. 1998), a baseball, or a golf ball.

The chinks in the armor of this defense arise in special settings where spectators are said to be induced into letting down their guard. Thus, in Maisonave v. The Newark Bears, Gourmet Services, 852 A.2d 233, 236 (N.J. Super. Ct. App. Div. 2004), the plaintiff spectator was struck in the face by a foul ball as he stood before a vending cart operated by the defendant Gourmet Dining Service, which had a concession contract from the team. The carts were needed because the concession areas were still under construction. By agreement between the defendants, they were positioned close to the field so that customers could continue to watch the game. The plaintiff, himself an experienced baseball player and longtime fan, was hit while reaching into his wallet to pay for his purchase. Building on precedents that require operators of sports facilities to screen high-risk places, Coleman, J., held that the plaintiff was entitled to a jury trial on the question whether the defendants had breached their duty:

> While watching the game, either seated or standing in an unprotected viewing area, spectators reasonably may be expected to pay attention and to look out for their own safety; but the activities and ambiance of a concession area predictably draw the attention of even the most experienced and the most wary fan from the action on the field of play. It is not only foreseeable, but inevitable, that in the process of placing orders or reaching for money or accepting the purchases or striking up conversations with others on line, spectators will be distracted from the action on the field and the risk of injury from flying objects will be increased significantly. The defendants are engaged in a commercial venture which by its nature induces spectators to let down their guard. They have a concomitant duty to exercise reasonable care to protect them during such times of heightened vulnerability. The imposition of a duty under these circumstances, particularly where it involves a temporary arrangement, is not only fair but reasonable.

What result if a fan sitting in the stands is injured while reaching for his wallet to buy a hot dog from a roving vendor?

The assumption of risk defense today remains powerful when people are not in vulnerable positions, including situations where individuals are hurt while working out on their own in unsupervised gyms or health clubs. In Nearhood v. Anytime Fitness-Kingsville, 178 So. 3d 623, 628 (La. Ct. App. 2015), the plaintiff suffered severe injuries

> when he attempted to exit the Precor Smith Squat Machine after hearing what he believed was the sound of his weights clicking back into their secured position. His testimony clearly demonstrates that he is familiar with how to properly secure the weights; however, this simply did not occur. Mr. Nearhood was mistaken, and, unfortunately, his injuries are the consequence of that mistake. The evidence clearly does not support Mr. Nearhood's allegations that his injuries are the result of Fitness Partners' failure to inform him about the equipment's safety stops.

Should it make a difference that the plaintiff made his mistake because the din in the training room distracted him?

5. *Professional Sports and Assumption of Risk.* In Maddox v. City of New York, 487 N.E.2d 553, 556–57 (N.Y. 1985), the plaintiff was an outfielder for the New York Yankees whose professional career was effectively ended after he sustained severe damage to his knee when he slipped in the "wet and muddy" outfield while chasing after a fly ball. He sued the Yankees as his employer, the Mets as lessees of Shea Stadium, and New York City as the stadium's owner. The plaintiff knew about the general condition of the field, and the court held that "[h]is continued participation in the game in light of that awareness constituted assumption of risk as a matter of law, entitling defendants to a summary judgment." The court reasoned as follows:

> There is no question that the doctrine requires not only knowledge of the injury-causing defect but also appreciation of the resultant risk, but awareness of the risk is not to be determined in a vacuum. It is, rather, to be assessed against the background of the skill and experience of the particular plaintiff, and in that assessment a higher degree of awareness will be imputed to a professional than to one with less than professional experience in the particular sport. In that context plaintiff's effort to separate the wetness of the field, which he testified was above the grassline, from the mud beneath it in which his foot became lodged must be rejected for not only was he aware that there was "some mud" in the centerfield area, but also it is a matter of common experience that water of sufficient depth to cover grass may result in the earth beneath being turned to mud. We do not deal here . . . with a hole in the playing field hidden by grass, but with water, indicative of the presence of mud, the danger of which plaintiff was sufficiently aware to complain to the grounds keepers. It is not necessary to the application of assumption of risk that the injured plaintiff have foreseen the exact manner in which his or her injury occurred, so long as he or she is aware of the potential for injury of the mechanism from which the injury results.

Do professional athletes generally have a choice over whether to play in unsafe conditions? How far does the assumption of risk defense extend? In Wright & Ellis, Assumption of Risk in Boat Racing: A Study in Maritime Jurisprudence, 11 Loy. Mar. L.J. 271 (2013), the authors opt in favor of a revived assumption of risk defense in maritime cases, especially boat races.

6. *Assumption of Risk and Abandonment of Rights.* Many cases address assumption of risk in its secondary sense when the defendant has negligently or unlawfully created a dangerous condition that the plaintiff must endure in the exercise of her ordinary rights. In Marshall v. Ranne, 511 S.W.2d 255, 260 (Tex. 1974), the court refused to find that the plaintiff had assumed the risk of being bitten by the defendant's vicious boar, which then bit the plaintiff while the plaintiff was walking from his house to his car:

> We hold that there was no proof that plaintiff had a free and voluntary choice, because he did not have a free choice of alternatives. He had, instead, only a choice of evils, both of which were wrongfully imposed upon him by the defendant. He could remain a prisoner inside his own

> house or he could take the risk of reaching his car before defendant's hog attacked him. Plaintiff could have remained inside his house, but in doing so, he would have surrendered his legal right to proceed over his own property to his car so he could return to his home in Dallas. The latter alternative was forced upon him against his will and was a choice he was not legally required to accept.

See RST §496E, which provides that "[t]he plaintiff's assumption of risk is not voluntary if the defendant's tortious conduct has left him no reasonable alternative course of conduct in order to . . . exercise or protect a right or privilege of which the defendant has no right to deprive him."

The problem of implicit coercion in secondary assumption of risk cases also surfaced in ADM Partnership v. Martin, 702 A.2d 730 (Md. 1997). The plaintiff, Martin, was injured when she fell on a walkway covered with snow and ice while making a delivery to the defendant's premises. The court held that the plaintiff, as a matter of law, had known, appreciated, and voluntarily confronted the risk in question even though she had claimed that she used the walkway "as a result of being coerced by the economic necessity of securing a service contract for her employer and for her continued employment." The court rejected that proposition as a matter of law when the plaintiff could produce no objective evidence that she had ever been threatened with a loss of her job. The court then quoted its earlier decision in Gibson v. Beaver, 226 A.2d 273, 276 (Md. 1967):

> The plaintiff takes a risk voluntarily . . . where the defendant has a right to face him with the dilemma of "take it or leave"—in other words, where [the] defendant is under no duty to make the conditions of their association any safer than they appear to be. In such a case it does not matter that the plaintiff is coerced to assume the risk by some force not emanating from defendant, such as poverty, dearth of living quarters, or a sense of moral responsibility.

Suppose she braved the snow because she was under an employer ultimatum; what then?

7. ***Assumption of Risk: The Fireman's Rule.*** Assumption of risk remains relevant with the so-called fireman's rule, which covers police officers and other public officials who enter private premises in order to maintain public order by responding to a fire or burglar alarm. "[O]ne who has knowingly and voluntarily confronted a hazard cannot recover for injuries sustained thereby." Walters v. Sloan, 571 P.2d 609, 612 (Cal. 1979). The public policy reasons behind this principle were well set out by Weintraub, C.J., shortly after his opinion in *Meistrich*, in Krauth v. Geller, 157 A.2d 129, 130–31 (N.J. 1960):

> [I]t is the fireman's business to deal with that very hazard [the fire] and hence, perhaps by analogy to the contractor engaged as an expert to remedy dangerous situations, he cannot complain of negligence in the creation of the very occasion for his engagement. In terms of duty, it may be said there is none owed the fireman to exercise care so as not to require the special services for which he is trained and paid. Probably most fires are attributable to negligence, and in the final analysis the policy decision is that it would be too burdensome to charge all who carelessly cause or fail to prevent fires with the injuries suffered by the expert retained with public funds to deal with those inevitable, although negligently created, occurrences. Hence, for that risk, the fireman should receive appropriate compensation from the public he serves both in pay which reflects the hazard and in workmen's compensation benefits for the consequences of the inherent risks of the calling.

The basic rule in these cases is subject to exceptions that relate not to the antecedent condition of the premises, but to the conduct of the property owner once the fire has occurred. Thus Sepega v. DeLaura, 167 A.3d 916 (Conn. 2017), declined to apply the fireman's rule when the homeowner refused to unlock his door when the fireman was attempting to kick the door open. Eveleigh, J., held that the standard rationales for the fireman's rule were inapplicable here, because the landowner was not subject to an undue burden when he was asked to honor a simple request to enter. He further concluded that in this, as in other cases, the availability of a workers' compensation remedy against the state did not necessarily preclude a tort action against an independent third party. He further doubted that this rule would discourage anyone from calling for public assistance or would create an excessive litigation burden. The concurring opinion of Robinson, J., took issue with the court on the third point—the effect of liability on the willingness to call for public assistance. Who is right? Why?

Attempts to expand the fireman's rule into caregiving contexts have not been successful. Sanders v. Alger, 394 P.3d 1083, 1088 (Ariz. 2017), arose when an in-home caregiver brought a case against her patient for injuries received on the job. Bales, C.J., allowed the action on the grounds that "a patient owes a duty of reasonable care to a caregiver allegedly injured by the patient's actions" and further that the action was not barred by the fireman's rule, given that the plaintiff had been hired by the Arizona Department of Economic Security. "Unlike firefighters, caregivers generally are not 'public safety employees' who are trained, equipped, and compensated professionally to train others." Could the general assumption of risk defense apply if the plaintiff knew that the defendant was "developmentally disabled and a 'vulnerable' adult"? See Casselman, Re-Examining the Firefighter's Rule in Arizona, 59 Ariz. L. Rev. 263 (2017), arguing both for the abolition of the fireman's rule and, necessarily, against its extension to other areas.

Dalury v. S-K-I Ltd.

670 A.2d 795 (Vt. 1995)

Johnson, J: We reverse the trial court's grant of summary judgment for defendants S-K-I, Ltd. and Killington, Ltd. in a case involving an injury to a skier at a resort operated by defendants. We hold that the exculpatory agreements which defendants require skiers to sign, releasing defendants from all liability resulting from negligence, are void as contrary to public policy.

While skiing at Killington Ski Area, plaintiff Robert Dalury sustained serious injuries when he collided with a metal pole that formed part of the control maze for a ski lift line. Before the season started, Dalury had purchased a midweek season pass and signed a form releasing the ski area from liability. The relevant portion reads:

> **Release from Liability and Conditions of Use**
>
> 1. I accept and understand that Alpine Skiing is a hazardous sport with many dangers and risks and that injuries are a common and ordinary occurrence of the sport. As a condition of being permitted to use the ski area premises, I freely accept and voluntarily assume the risks of injury or property damage and release Killington Ltd., its employees and agents from any and all liability for personal injury or property damage resulting from negligence, conditions of the premises, operations of the ski area, actions or omissions of employees or agents of the ski area or from my participation in skiing at the area, accepting myself the full responsibility for any and all such damage or injury of any kind which may result.

Plaintiff also signed a photo identification card that contained this same language.

Dalury and his wife filed a complaint against defendants, alleging negligent design, construction, and replacement of the maze pole. Defendants moved for summary judgment, arguing that the release of liability barred the negligence action. The trial court, without specifically addressing plaintiffs' contention that the release was contrary to public policy, found that the language of the release clearly absolved defendants of liability for their own negligence. . . .

[W]e hold the agreement is unenforceable. . . .

I

. . . The leading judicial formula for determining whether an exculpatory agreement violates public policy was set forth by Justice Tobriner of the California Supreme Court. Tunkl v. Regents of Univ. of Cal., 383 P.2d 441, 445–46 (Cal. 1963). An agreement is invalid if it exhibits some or all of the following characteristics:

> [1.] It concerns a business of a type generally thought suitable for public regulation. [2.] The party seeking exculpation is engaged in performing a service of great importance to the public, which is often a matter of practical necessity for some members of the public. [3.] The party holds itself out as willing to perform this service for any member of the public who seeks it, or at least for any member coming within certain established standards. [4.] As a result of the essential nature of the service, in the economic setting of the transaction, the party invoking exculpation possesses a decisive advantage of bargaining strength against any member of the public who seeks [the party's] services. [5.] In exercising a superior bargaining power the party confronts the public with a standardized adhesion contract of exculpation, and makes no provision whereby a purchaser may pay additional reasonable fees and obtain protection against negligence. [6.] Finally, as a result of the transaction, the person or property of the purchaser is placed under the control of the seller, subject to the risk of carelessness by the seller or [the seller's] agents.

Applying these factors, the court concluded that a release from liability for future negligence imposed as a condition for admission to a charitable research hospital was invalid. Numerous courts have adopted and applied the *Tunkl* factors. . . .

[Thus i]n Jones [v. Dressel, 623 P.2d 370, 376 (Colo. 1981)], the court concluded, based on the *Tunkl* factors, that no duty to the public was involved in air service for a parachute jump, because that sort of service does not affect the public interest. Using a similar formula, the Wyoming Supreme Court concluded that a ski resort's sponsorship of an Ironman Decathlon competition did not invoke the public interest. Milligan v. Big Valley Corp., 754 P.2d 1063, 1066–67 (Wyo. 1988).

On the other hand, the Virginia Supreme Court recently concluded, in the context of a "Teflon Man Triathlon" competition, that a preinjury release from liability for negligence is void as against public policy because it is simply wrong to put one party to a contract at the mercy of the other's negligence. Hiett v. Lake Barcroft Community Ass'n, 418 S.E.2d 894, 897 (Va. 1992). . . .

II

Defendants urge us to uphold the exculpatory agreement on the ground that ski resorts do not provide an essential public service. They argue that they owe no duty to plaintiff to permit him to use their private lands for skiing, and that the terms and conditions of entry ought to be left entirely within their control. Because skiing, like other recreational sports, is not a necessity of life, defendants contend that the sale of a lift ticket is a purely private matter, implicating no public interest. We disagree.

Whether or not defendants provide an essential public service does not resolve the public policy question in the recreational sports context. The defendants' area is a facility open to the public. They advertise and invite skiers and nonskiers of every level of skiing ability to their premises for the price of a ticket. At oral argument, defendants conceded that thousands of people buy lift tickets every day throughout the season. Thousands of people ride lifts, buy services, and ski the trails. Each ticket sale may be, for some purposes, a purely private transaction. But when a substantial number of such sales take place as a result of the seller's general invitation to the public to utilize the facilities and services in question, a legitimate public interest arises.

The major public policy implications are those underlying the law of premises liability. In Vermont, a business owner has a duty "of active care to make sure that its premises are in safe and suitable condition for its customers." . . . We have already held that a ski area owes its customers the same duty as any other business — to keep its premises reasonably safe.

The policy rationale is to place responsibility for maintenance of the land on those who own or control it, with the ultimate goal of keeping accidents to the minimum level possible. Defendants, not recreational skiers, have the expertise and opportunity to foresee and control hazards, and to guard against the negligence of their agents and employees. They alone can properly maintain and inspect their premises, and train their employees in risk management. They alone can insure against risks and effectively spread the cost of insurance among their thousands of customers. Skiers, on the other hand, are not in a position to discover and correct risks of harm, and they cannot insure against the ski area's negligence.

If defendants were permitted to obtain broad waivers of their liability, an important incentive for ski areas to manage risk would be removed, with the public bearing the cost of the resulting injuries. It is illogical, in these circumstances, to undermine the public policy underlying business invitee law and allow skiers to bear risks they have no ability or right to control. . . .

Defendants argue that the public policy of the state, as expressed in the "Acceptance of inherent risks" statute, 12 V.S.A. 1037,[2] indicates a willingness on the part of the Legislature to limit ski area liability. Therefore, they contend that public policy favors the use of express releases such as the one signed by plaintiff. On the contrary, defendants' allocation of responsibility for skiers' injuries is at odds with the statute. The statute places responsibility for the "inherent risks" of any sport on the participant, insofar as such risks are obvious and necessary. A ski area's own negligence, however, is neither an inherent risk nor an obvious and necessary one in the sport of skiing. Thus, a skier's assumption of the inherent risks of skiing does not abrogate the ski area's duty "to warn of or correct dangers which in the exercise of reasonable prudence in the circumstances could have been foreseen and corrected."

Reversed and remanded.

NOTES

1. *Exculpation Clauses at Ski Resorts.* A different attitude toward exculpation clauses was taken in Chepkevich v. Hidden Valley Resort, L.P., 2 A.3d 1174, 1190 (Pa. 2010). The plaintiff, Lori Chepkevich, was an experienced skier who held a season pass at Hidden Valley Resort. On the day of the injury, she agreed with her other family members that she would take her six-year-old nephew back to the family's condominium when he complained of being cold. The ski lift they used had only one speed, and the plaintiff was afraid that her nephew could not board it safely. She therefore got the lift operator to agree to stop the lift twice, once to let the plaintiff and her nephew get in position to board the lift, and the second time to board it. The first part of the plan was successfully executed, but the second was not. As the plaintiff and her nephew boarded the moving lift, both lost their balance and fell off. The plaintiff sustained a dislocated shoulder and a fractured hip. The plaintiff testified that she took her own seven-year-old son to a variable-speed lift when helping him down the mountain. The release document recited that skiing was "a dangerous sport with inherent risks" from the natural terrain, the manmade structures on the course, and the actions of other skiers, all of which "present

2. "Notwithstanding the provisions of section 1036 of this title, a person who takes part in any sport accepts as a matter of law the dangers that inhere therein insofar as they are obvious and necessary." 12 V.S.A. §1037.

the risk of serious or fatal injury." It concluded by stating: "By accepting this Season Pass I agree to accept all these risks and agree not to sue Hidden Valley Resort or their employees if injured while using their facilities regardless of any negligence on their part." The Pennsylvania Supreme Court held that these contracts could not be regarded as contracts of adhesion because "[t]he signer is under no compulsion, economic or otherwise, to participate, much less to sign the exculpatory agreement, because it does not relate to essential services, but merely governs a voluntary recreational activity." Furthermore, the court stated that public policy supported the exculpation clause given that Pennsylvania statutory law makes it "the clear policy of this Commonwealth . . . to encourage the sport and to place the risks of skiing squarely on the skier." 42 Pa. Con. Stat. §7102(c)(2) (*infra* at 277). Pennsylvania law also applies to negligence actions between patrons (whether they be skiers or snowboarders) of the ski resort or ski area. See Bell v. Dean, 5 A.3d 266, 272 (Pa. Super. Ct. 2010).

Some courts have even gone one step further to enforce exculpation clauses even when they do not explicitly cover negligent conduct. Thus in Sanislo v. Give Kids the World, Inc., 157 So. 3d 256, 259, 270 (Fla. 2015), the plaintiff and her child mounted the rear pneumatic lift attached to a horse-drawn wagon to pose for a family picture. The lift had been added to allow persons in wheelchairs to take the rides offered to other customers. The additional weight caused the vehicle to collapse, inflicting injuries on Ms. Sanislo's left and lower back. The defendant's contract provided that the scope of the release covered "any and all claims and causes of action of every kind arising from any and all physical or emotional injuries and/or damages which may happen to me/us. . . ." The court answered in the affirmative "whether an exculpatory clause's terms 'clearly and unequivocally' release a party of liability for its own negligence or negligent acts when the clause does not contain express language regarding negligence or negligent acts," on the ground that the alternative reading "would not effectuate the intent of the parties and render such contracts, otherwise meaningless." Suppose the exculpation clause was found unenforceable. How successful would the plaintiffs in these cases be in showing that their own conduct was not the sole or dominant cause of the accident? Would the same complications arise in *Lamson*, *supra* at 242, if the defendant was both allowed and entitled to make arguments that the rack was safe and the plaintiff was careless?

2. *Assumption of Risk by Contract: Other Contexts.* The *Tunkl* framework relied on in *Dalury* has been applied outside the medical context. Wagenblast v. Odessa Sch. Dist. No. 105-157-166J, 758 P.2d 968 (Wash. 1988), invoked *Tunkl's* six criteria to strike down an agreement whereby parents released the school district from all liability in negligence related to their children's participation in interscholastic athletics, preferring to examine liability on a case-by-case basis. In contrast, in Zivich v. Mentor Soccer Club, Inc., 696 N.E.2d 201, 205 (Ohio 1998), the court upheld a similar exemption clause when the plaintiff was hurt while swinging from an unanchored soccer goal shortly after winning an intrasquad contest. The court wanted to spare the huge number of volunteer members in such organizations as the Little League and the American Youth Soccer Organization "the risks and overwhelming costs of litigation." A similar result applied in Donahue v. Ledgends, Inc., 331 P.3d 342 (Alaska 2014), where the plaintiff was injured when she fell between 3 and 4½ feet from a rock-climbing wall and injured her tibia. She was barred by an exculpation clause that she read and signed, which stated, "I AM ULTIMATELY RESPONSIBLE for my own safety during my use of or participation in [Rock Gym] facilities, equipment, rentals, or activities." Should different rules apply to schools, nonprofit leagues, and commercial gyms? See generally Developments in the Law: Nonprofit Corporations, 105 Harv. L. Rev. 1578 (1992).

Note too that even if exculpation clauses pass muster on substantive grounds, they can be challenged on the ground that the exculpation clause was not brought clearly to the attention of the plaintiff. The court in Obstetrics & Gynecologists Ltd. v. Pepper, 693 P.2d 1259, 1260 (Nev. 1985), refused to enforce, as an improper contract of adhesion, an arbitration clause that the defendant inserted in all its contracts because the plaintiff testified that she signed the agreement without first having its terms explained to her, and thus "had no opportunity to modify any of its terms; her choices were to sign the agreement as it stood or to forego treatment at the clinic." With *Pepper*, contrast Madden v. Kaiser Foundation Hospitals, 552 P.2d 1178, 1185 (Cal. 1976), which upheld an arbitration clause contained in a contract between a state employee and the defendant foundation—noting that the employer intermediate was able to protect the interest of its employees. But in Engalla v. Permanente Medical Group, Inc., 938 P.2d 903, 909, 911, 912–13 (Cal. 1997), Mosk, J., held that the individual patient could sue to set aside a medical malpractice arbitration plan on grounds of fraud and bias in the selection of the arbitrator.

3. *Contracting Out of Medical Malpractice Liability Generally.* Arbitration clauses represent only the tip of the iceberg in the larger dispute over whether the parties can contract out of the tort rules that now govern medical malpractice litigation. If the procedural obstacles—such as want of notice or bias—can be overcome, should the principle of freedom of contract apply to all issues of liability? Professor Robinson forcefully defends that view:

> In terms of utilitarian efficiency, contractual arrangements allow parties to achieve the most efficient combination of efforts to manage risk in accordance with their respective comparative advantages and their respective risk preferences. The moral argument proceeds along similar lines but emphasizes the fact that contractual allocation promotes individual freedom of choice, constrained only by the need to accommodate the divergent interests of the contracting parties. To justify private ordering one need not suppose that it always yields "good" or "fair" results. It is enough that, in general, private parties are likely to achieve results that are at least as good and fair for themselves as would be achieved by paternalistic intervention.

Robinson, Rethinking the Allocation of Medical Malpractice Risks Between Patients and Providers, 49 Law & Contemp. Probs. 172, 189 (1986). Robinson's article (as well as others by Danzon, Epstein, and Havighurst) provoked the following response from an English scholar in Atiyah, Medical Malpractice and the Contract/Tort Boundary, 49 Law & Contemp. Probs. 287, 296 (1986):

> The real market enthusiasts appear to envisage a situation in which a competitive market offers a range of benefit and risk packages suitable to the individual desires, risk-averseness, and wallets of various patients. If all the bargaining is in practice to be done collectively (by employers and unions whose interests of course are not always identical with those of employees), however, the reality is that the rules which will govern the physician/patient relationship will not be tailored to the individual patient's needs at all. They will be fixed by third parties, just as much as the tort rules are. There may, it is true, be more choice available in the market, but this argument takes us back to our starting point about information, risk evaluation, and bargaining power. If the patient does not understand the differences in the packages offered to him, choice by itself means little, and the presumption of efficiency in outcome is rebutted.

See generally Symposium, Medical Malpractice: Can the Private Sector Find Relief?, 49 Law & Contemp. Probs. 1 (Spring 1986). See also Danzon, Medical Malpractice: Theory, Evidence, and Public Policy 208 (1985), for a qualified endorsement of the contract solution, and Weiler, Medical Malpractice on Trial 113 (1991), for a "highly dubious [view] of the brave new world of no-liability," which Weiler thinks will emerge from any contractual regime. See also Arlen, Contracting over Liability: Medical Malpractice and the Cost of Choice, 158 U. Pa. L. Rev. 957 (2010), who argues against the contract solution as being unable to keep up with the myriad physician actions that could in principle be subject to negligence liability.

SECTION E. COMPARATIVE NEGLIGENCE

1. At Common Law

Lombard Laws, King Liutprand
Law 136.VII. (A.D. 733)

It has likewise been made known to us that a certain man has a well in his courtyard and, according to custom, it has a prop and lift for raising the water. Another man who came along stood under that lift and, when yet another man came to draw water from the well and incautiously released the lift, the weight came down on the man who stood under it, and he was killed. The question then arose over who should pay composition for this death, and it has been referred to us. It seems right to us and to our judges that the man who was killed, since he was not an animal but had the power of reason like other men, should have noticed where he stood or what weight was above his head. Therefore, two-thirds of the amount of his composition shall be assessed to him [the dead man], and one-third of the amount at which he was valued according to law shall be paid as composition by the man who incautiously drew the water. He shall pay the composition to the children or to the near relatives who are the heirs of the dead man, and the case shall be ended without any feud or grievance since it was done unintentionally. Moreover, no blame should be placed on the man who owns the well because if we placed the blame on him, no one hereafter would permit other men to raise water from their wells, and since all men cannot have a well, those who are poor would die and those who are traveling through would also suffer need.

Liutprand (at left), 712–744 A.D.
Source: Wikimedia Commons

Charles Beach

Contributory Negligence
12–13 (2d ed. 1892)

The reasons of the rule which denies relief to a plaintiff guilty of contributory negligence have been previously stated. The common law refuses to apportion damages which arise from negligence. This it does upon considerations of public convenience and public policy, and upon this principle, it is said, depends also the rule which makes the contributory negligence of a plaintiff a complete defense. For the same reason, when there is an action in tort, where injury results from the negligence of two or more persons, the sufferer has a full remedy against any one of them, and no contribution can be enforced between the tort feasors. The policy of the law in this respect is founded upon the inability of human tribunals to mete out exact justice. A perfect code would render each man responsible for the unmixed consequences of his own default; but the common law, in view of the impossibility of assigning all effects to their respective causes, refuses to interfere in those cases where negligence is the issue, at the instance of one whose hands are not free from the stain of contributory fault, and where accordingly the impossibility of apportioning the damage between the parties does not exist, the rule is held not to apply.

William Prosser

Comparative Negligence

41 Calif. L. Rev. 1, 3–4 (1953)

There has been much speculation as to why the rule thus declared found such ready acceptance in later decisions, both in England and in the United States. The explanations given by the courts themselves never have carried much conviction. Most of the decisions have talked about "proximate cause," saying that the plaintiff's negligence is an intervening, insulating cause between the defendant's negligence and the injury. But this cannot be supported unless a meaning is assigned to proximate cause which is found nowhere else. If two automobiles collide and injure a bystander, the negligence of one driver is not held to be a superseding cause which relieves the other of liability; and there is no visible reason for any different conclusion when the action is by one driver against the other. It has been said that the defense has a penal basis, and is intended to punish the plaintiff for his own misconduct; or that the court will not aid one who is himself at fault, and he must come into court with clean hands. But this is no explanation of the many cases, particularly those of the last clear chance, in which a plaintiff clearly at fault is permitted to recover. It has been said that the rule is intended to discourage accidents, by denying recovery to those who fail to use proper care for their own safety; but the assumption that the speeding motorist is, or should be, meditating on the possible failure of a lawsuit for his possible injuries lacks all reality, and it is quite as reasonable to say that the rule promotes accidents by encouraging the negligent defendant. Probably the true explanation lies merely in the highly individualistic attitude of the common law of the early nineteenth century. The period of development of contributory negligence was that of the industrial revolution, and there is reason to think that the courts found in this defense, along with the concepts of duty and proximate cause, a convenient instrument of control over the jury, by which the liabilities of rapidly growing industry were curbed and kept within bounds.

Li v. Yellow Cab Co. of California

532 P.2d 1226 (Cal. 1975)

[The accident in question resulted from the negligence of both parties. The plaintiff had attempted to cross three lanes of oncoming traffic to enter a service station; the defendant's driver was traveling at an excessive speed when he ran a yellow light just before striking the plaintiff's car. The trial court held that the plaintiff was barred from recovery by her own contributory negligence.]

SULLIVAN, J. In this case we address the grave and recurrent question whether we should judicially declare no longer applicable in California courts the doctrine of contributory negligence, which bars all recovery when the plaintiff's negligent conduct has contributed as a legal cause in any degree to the harm suffered by him, and hold that it must give way to a system of comparative negligence, which assesses liability in direct proportion to fault. As we explain in detail infra, we conclude that we should. In the course of reaching our ultimate decision we conclude that: (1) The doctrine of comparative negligence is preferable to the "all-or-nothing" doctrine of contributory negligence from the point of view of logic, practical experience, and fundamental justice; (2) judicial action in this area is not precluded by the presence of section 1714 of the Civil Code, which has been said to "codify" the "all-or-nothing" rule and to render it immune from attack in the courts except on constitutional grounds; (3) given the possibility of judicial action, certain practical difficulties attendant upon the adoption of comparative negligence should not dissuade us from charting a new course—leaving the resolution of some of these problems to future judicial or legislative action; (4) the doctrine of comparative negligence should be applied in this state in its so-called "pure" form under which the assessment of liability in proportion to fault proceeds in spite of the fact that the plaintiff is equally at fault as or more at fault than the defendant and finally; (5) this new rule should be given a limited retrospective application.

I

[The court then notes that the once dominant common law rule treated contributory negligence as an absolute defense subject to a limited last clear chance exception.]

It is unnecessary for us to catalogue the enormous amount of critical comment that has been directed over the years against the "all-or-nothing" approach of the doctrine of contributory negligence. The essence of that criticism has been constant and clear: the doctrine is inequitable in its operation because it fails to distribute responsibility in proportion to fault. Against this have been raised several arguments in justification, but none have proved even remotely adequate to the task [quoting Prosser's 1953 article]. The basic objection to the doctrine—grounded in the primal concept that in a system in which liability is based on fault, the extent of fault should govern the extent of liability—remains irresistible to reason and all intelligent notions of fairness.

Furthermore, practical experience with the application by juries of the doctrine of contributory negligence has added its weight to analyses of its inherent shortcomings: "Every trial lawyer is well aware that juries often do in fact allow recovery in cases of contributory negligence, and that the compromise in the jury room does result in some diminution of the damages because of the plaintiff's fault. But the process is at best a haphazard and most unsatisfactory one." (Prosser, Comparative Negligence.) . . . It is manifest that this state of affairs, viewed from the standpoint of the health and vitality of the legal process, can only detract from public confidence in the ability of law and legal institutions to assign liability on a just and consistent basis. . . .

It is in view of these theoretical and practical considerations that to this date 25 states, have abrogated the "all-or-nothing" rule of contributory negligence and have enacted in its place general apportionment statutes calculated in one manner or another to assess liability in proportion to fault. . . . In 1973 these states were joined by Florida, which effected the same result by judicial decision. (Hoffman v. Jones (Fla. 1973) 280 So. 2d 431.) We are likewise persuaded that logic, practical experience, and fundamental justice counsel against the retention of the doctrine rendering contributory negligence a complete bar to recovery—and that it should be replaced in this state by a system under which liability for damage will be borne by those whose negligence caused it in direct proportion to their respective fault. . . .[6a]

6a. In employing the generic term "fault" throughout this opinion we follow a usage common to the literature on the subject of comparative negligence. In all cases, however, we intend the term to import nothing more than "negligence" in the accepted legal sense. [Footnote 6a did not appear in the original advance sheets. There, the court stated a comparative negligence test that would allocate liability "in direct proportion to the extent of the parties' causal responsibility." 119 Cal. Rptr. 858 (1975), advance sheets only.—Eds.]

II

It is urged that any change in the law of contributory negligence must be made by the Legislature, not by this court. Although the doctrine of contributory negligence is of judicial origin—its genesis being traditionally attributed to the opinion of Lord Ellenborough in Butterfield v. Forrester (K.B. 1809) 103 Eng. Rep. 926—the enactment of section 1714 of the Civil Code in 1872 codified the doctrine as it stood at that date and, the argument continues, rendered it invulnerable to attack in the courts except on constitutional grounds.

[The court then exhaustively examines section 1714 of the California Civil Code, which provides: "Everyone is responsible, not only for the result of his willful acts, but also for an injury occasioned to another by his want of ordinary care or skill in the management of his property or person, except so far as the latter has, willfully or by want of ordinary care, brought the injury upon himself. The extent of liability in such cases is defined by the Title on Compensatory Relief." The court concluded that "it was not the intention of the Legislature in enacting section 1714 of the Civil Code, as well as other sections of that code declarative of the common law, to insulate the matters therein expressed from further judicial development; rather it was the intention of the Legislature to announce and formulate existing common law principles and definitions for purposes of orderly and concise presentation and with a distinct view toward continuing judicial evolution."]

III

We are thus brought to the second group of arguments which have been advanced by defendants and the amici curiae supporting their position. Generally speaking, such arguments expose considerations of a practical nature which, it is urged, counsel against the adoption of a rule of comparative negligence in this state even if such adoption is possible by judicial means.

The most serious of these considerations are those attendant upon the administration of a rule of comparative negligence in cases involving multiple parties. One such problem may arise when all responsible parties are not brought before the court: it may be difficult for the jury to evaluate relative negligence in such circumstances, and to compound this difficulty such an evaluation would not be res judicata in a subsequent suit against the absent wrongdoer. Problems of contribution and indemnity among joint tortfeasors lurk in the background.

A second and related major area of concern involves the administration of the actual process of fact-finding in a comparative negligence system. The assigning of a specific percentage factor to the amount of negligence attributable to a particular party, while in theory a matter of little difficulty, can become a matter of perplexity in the face of hard facts.

The temptation for the jury to resort to a quotient verdict in such circumstances can be great. These inherent difficulties are not, however, insurmountable. Guidelines might be provided the jury which will assist it in keeping focussed upon the true inquiry and the utilization of special verdicts or jury interrogatories can be of invaluable assistance in assuring that the jury has approached its sensitive and often complex task with proper standards and appropriate reverence.

The third area of concern, the status of the doctrines of last clear chance and assumption of risk, involves less the practical problems of administering a particular form of comparative negligence than it does a definition of the theoretical outline of the specific form to be adopted. Although several states which apply comparative negligence concepts retain the last clear chance doctrine, the better reasoned position seems to be that when true comparative negligence is adopted, the need for last clear chance as a palliative of the hardships of the "all-or-nothing" rule disappears and its retention results only in a windfall to the plaintiff in direct contravention of the principle of liability in proportion to fault. As for assumption of risk, we have recognized in this state that this defense overlaps that of contributory negligence to some extent and in fact is made up of at least two distinct defenses. "To simplify greatly, it has been observed . . . that in one kind of situation, to wit, where a plaintiff unreasonably undertakes to encounter a specific known risk imposed by a defendant's negligence, plaintiff's conduct, although he may encounter that risk in a prudent manner, is in reality a form of contributory negligence. . . . Other kinds of situations within the doctrine of assumption of risk are those, for example, where plaintiff is held to agree to relieve defendant of an obligation of reasonable conduct toward him. Such a situation would not involve contributory negligence but rather a reduction of defendant's duty of care." We think it clear that the adoption of a system of comparative negligence should entail the merger of the defense of assumption of risk into the general scheme of assessment of liability in proportion to fault in those particular cases in which the form of assumption of risk involved is no more than a variant of contributory negligence.

Finally there is the problem of the treatment of willful misconduct under a system of comparative negligence. In jurisdictions following the "all-or-nothing" rule, contributory negligence is no defense to an action based upon a claim of willful misconduct (see Rest. 2d Torts, §503), and this is the present rule in California.[19] As Dean Prosser has observed, "[this] is in reality a rule of comparative fault which is being applied, and the court is refusing to set up the lesser fault against the greater." (Prosser, Torts, at §65.) The thought is that the difference between willful and wanton misconduct and ordinary negligence is one of kind rather than degree in that the former involves conduct of an entirely different order,[20] and under this conception it might well be urged that comparative negligence concepts should have no application when one of the parties has been guilty of willful and wanton misconduct. It has been persuasively argued, however, that the loss of deterrent effect that would occur upon application of comparative fault concepts to willful and wanton misconduct as well as ordinary negligence would be slight, and that a comprehensive system of comparative negligence should allow for the apportionment of damages in all cases involving misconduct which falls short of being intentional. The law of punitive damages remains a separate consideration. . . .

The existence of the foregoing areas of difficulty and uncertainty has not diminished our conviction that the time for a revision of the means for dealing with contributory fault in this state is long past due and that it lies within the province of this court to initiate the needed change by our decision in this case. Two of the indicated areas (i.e., multiple parties and willful misconduct) are not involved in the case before us, and we consider it neither necessary nor wise to address ourselves to specific problems of this nature which might be expected to arise. . . .

Our decision in this case is to be viewed as a first step in what we deem to be a proper and just direction, not as a compendium containing the answers to all questions that may be expected to arise. Pending future judicial or legislative developments, we are content for the present to assume the position taken by the Florida court in this matter: "We feel the trial judges of this State are capable of applying [a] comparative negligence rule without our setting guidelines in anticipation of expected problems. The problems are more appropriately resolved at the trial level in a practical manner instead of a theoretical solution at the appellate

19. BAJI No. 3.52 (1971 re-revision) currently provides: "Contributory negligence of a plaintiff is not a bar to his recovery for an injury caused by the wilful or wanton misconduct of a defendant. (¶) Wilful or wanton misconduct is intentional wrongful conduct, done either with knowledge, express or implied, that serious injury to another will probably result, or with a wanton and reckless disregard of the possible results. An intent to injure is not a necessary element of wilful or wanton misconduct. (¶) To prove such misconduct it is not necessary to establish that defendant himself recognized his conduct as dangerous. It is sufficient if it be established that a reasonable man under the same or similar circumstances would be aware of the dangerous character of such conduct."

20. "Disallowing the contributory negligence defense in this context is different from last clear chance; the defense is denied not because defendant had the last opportunity to avoid the accident but rather because defendant's conduct was so culpable it was different in 'kind' from the plaintiff's. The basis is culpability rather than causation." (Schwartz, *supra*, §5.1, p. 100; fn. omitted.)

level. The trial judges are granted broad discretion in adopting such procedures as may accomplish the objectives and purposes expressed in this opinion." (280 So. 2d at pp. 439–440.)

It remains to identify the precise form of comparative negligence which we now adopt for application in this state. Although there are many variants, only the two basic forms need be considered here. The first of these, the so-called "pure" form of comparative negligence, apportions liability in direct proportion to fault in all cases. This was the form adopted by the Supreme Court of Florida in Hoffman v. Jones, supra, and it applies by statute in Mississippi, Rhode Island, and Washington. Moreover it is the form favored by most scholars and commentators. The second basic form of comparative negligence, of which there are several variants, applies apportionment based on fault up to the point at which the plaintiff's negligence is equal to or greater than that of the defendant—when that point is reached, plaintiff is barred from recovery. Nineteen states have adopted this form or one of its variants by statute. The principal argument advanced in its favor is moral in nature: that it is not morally right to permit one more at fault in an accident to recover from one less at fault. Other arguments assert the probability of increased insurance, administrative, and judicial costs if a "pure" rather than a "50 percent" system is adopted, but this has been seriously questioned.

We have concluded that the "pure" form of comparative negligence is that which should be adopted in this state. In our view the "50 percent" system simply shifts the lottery aspect of the contributory negligence rule to a different ground. As Dean Prosser has noted, under such a system "[i]t is obvious that a slight difference in the proportionate fault may permit a recovery and there has been much justified criticism of a rule under which a plaintiff who is charged with 49 percent of the total negligence recovers 51 percent of his damages, while one who is charged with 50 percent recovers nothing at all."[22] (Prosser, Comparative Negligence.) In effect "such a rule distorts the very principle it recognizes, i.e., that persons are responsible for their acts to the extent their fault contributes to an injurious result. The partial rule simply lowers, but does not eliminate, the bar of contributory negligence."

We also consider significant the experience of the State of Wisconsin, which until recently was considered the leading exponent of the "50 percent" system. There that system led to numerous appeals on the narrow but crucial issue whether plaintiff's negligence was equal to defendant's. Numerous reversals have resulted on this point, leading to the development of arcane classifications of negligence according to quality and category. (See cases cited in Vincent v. Pabst Brewing Co., 177 N.W.2d 513, at 513 [(Wis. 1970)] (dissenting opn.).) . . .

[The court then holds its rule should apply in all cases in which the trial has not yet begun. It notes that there is some unfairness in denying the benefits of the comparative negligence rule to other plaintiffs who sought to raise the issue on appeal while granting them to Nga Li, but justifies its result for creating a good incentive in future cases for parties to "raise issues involving renovation of unsound or outmoded legal doctrines." The judgment is reversed. Mosk, J., concurring and dissenting, takes exception to that portion of the opinion that holds the rule of comparative negligence should apply to all cases in which the trial has not yet begun. Clark, J. (with McComb, J., concurring), dissents on the ground that section 1714 of the Civil Code codified the common law rule on contributory negligence, which could only be displaced by other legislation.]

22. This problem is compounded when the injurious result is produced by the combined negligence of several parties. For example in a three-car collision a plaintiff whose negligence amounts to one-third or more recovers nothing; in a four-car collision the plaintiff is barred if his negligence is only one-quarter of the total. [The original 1931 Wisconsin comparative negligence statute contained the words "not as great as" instead of the current words "not greater than."—Eds.]

NOTES

1. ***Historical Origins of the Comparative Negligence System.*** Although comparative negligence has met with widespread favor only since the late 1960s, its origins go earlier. Georgia enacted a comparative negligence statute as early as 1855; Mississippi adopted pure comparative negligence in 1910; and Wisconsin introduced comparative negligence by legislation in 1931. From its humble roots, comparative negligence has become a veritable giant. As recently as 1968, only five states had adopted some form of comparative negligence by statute. Then the dam broke. Between 1969 and 1973, nineteen additional states adopted some form of comparative negligence by legislation so that by the time Hoffman v. Jones and *Li* were decided, the common law rule had been abandoned in about half the states. Today, virtually all states have some form of comparative negligence, usually by legislation and occasionally by judicial decision. As of 2023, the only jurisdictions not to have some form of the doctrine are Alabama, District of Columbia, Maryland, North Carolina, and Virginia. The Maryland court in Coleman v. Soccer Ass'n of Columbia, 69 A.3d 1149 (Md. 2013), refused to adopt comparative negligence by judicial action. Indeed, it appears that no jurisdiction has made its initial shift to comparative negligence after 1992, although many states have modified their doctrines after that date. For detailed tallies, see Schwartz, Comparative Negligence, App. A (5th ed. 2018); Woods & Deere, Comparative Fault, App. (3d ed. 1996 & Supp. 2007).

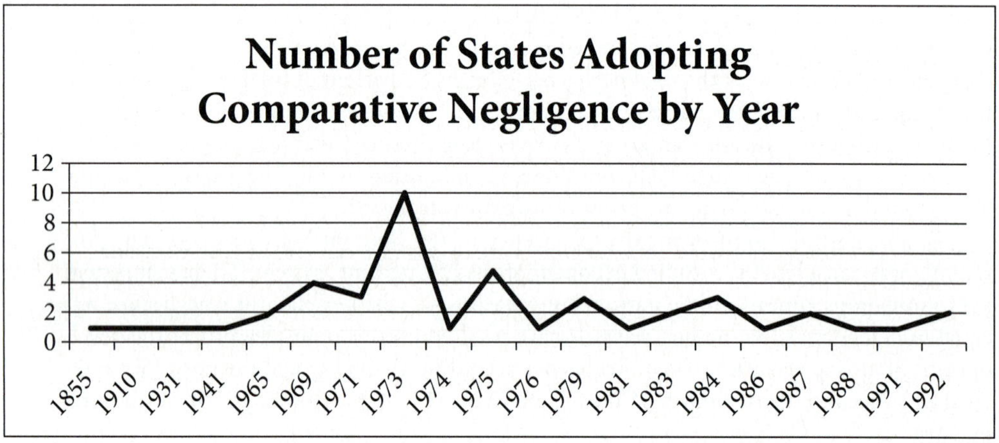

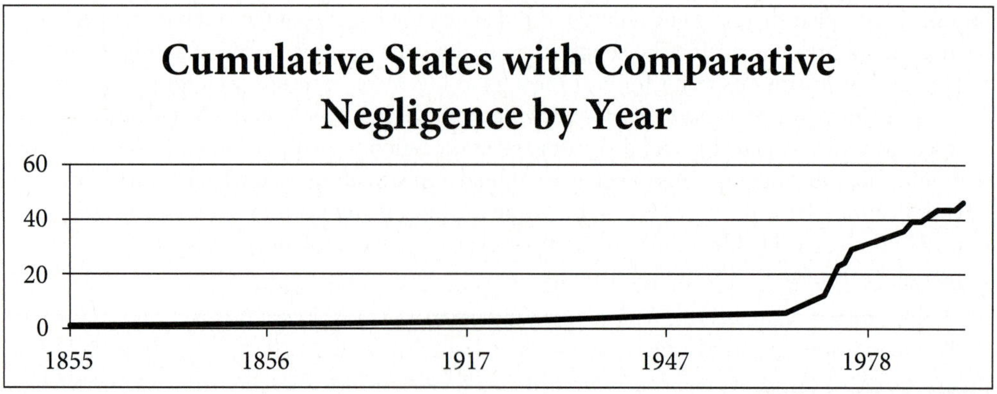

Source: Schwartz & Rowe, Comparative Negligence, Appendix A (5th ed. 2012); data table available from Sam Schoenburg

Table based on following data of when states adopted comparative negligence:

Year	Adopt	Cumulative
1855	1	1
1910	1	2
1931	1	3
1941	1	4
1965	2	6
1969	4	10
1971	3	13
1973	10	23
1974	1	24
1975	5	29

Year	Adopt	Cumulative
1976	1	30
1979	3	33
1981	1	34
1983	2	36
1984	3	39
1986	1	40
1987	2	42
1988	1	43
1991	1	44
1992	2	46

For a post-*Li* endorsement of *Li*, see Fleming, Foreword: Comparative Negligence at Last—by Judicial Choice, 64 Calif. L. Rev. 239 (1976).

2. *Doctrinal Complications—Revisited.* The rise of comparative negligence has forced courts to revisit many of the legal issues that arose when contributory negligence and assumption of risks were absolute defenses. What follows is a sample of reactions to those problems.

a. ***Last Clear Chance.*** An overwhelming majority of cases have followed *Li*'s lead in jettisoning the separate last clear chance doctrine. In Spahn v. Town of Port Royal, 499 S.E.2d 205, 208 (S.C. 1998), the South Carolina Supreme Court, an early holdout, joined the parade, finding that the critical "authorities are persuasive that the rationalization for last clear chance as a matter of proximate cause is simply unnecessary where the jury may compare the parties' negligence." See generally Calabresi & Cooper, New Directions in Tort Law, 30 Val. U. L. Rev. 859, 872 (1996), concluding that "[t]he doctrine of last clear chance, which ameliorated the harshness of the all-or-nothing contributory negligence rule, typically disappears under comparative negligence." In apportioning damages, should the jury be instructed to attach greater weight to defendant's conduct when he has had the last clear chance?

b. ***Assumption of Risk.*** The traditional distinction, endorsed in *Li*, between primary and secondary assumption of risk has held fast. In Knight v. Jewett, 834 P.2d 696 (Cal. 1992), the plaintiff broke her little finger in a casual coed game of touch football after she had cautioned the defendant "not to play so rough," and threatened to quit the game. On the next play, the defendant leaped to intercept a pass; he touched the ball, came down on the plaintiff's back, and fell on the plaintiff's hand, breaking her little finger. The trial judge granted the defendant's motion for summary judgment on the ground that "reasonable implied assumption of risk" continues to operate after *Li*. In upholding that ruling, George, J., treated this case as one of primary assumption of risk because the defendant owed the plaintiff only a duty to avoid reckless misbehavior, but was at most guilty of ordinary negligence, effectively cutting out the plaintiff's cause of action.

Kennard, J., dissented on the ground that the categorical rule should not apply. In her view, it is important to determine assumption of risk on an individual basis. "To establish the defense a defendant must prove that the plaintiff voluntarily accepted a risk with knowledge and appreciation of that risk." One possible way to reconcile the two opinions is to hold that the recklessness rule constitutes the basic default position, which can be displaced if a defendant agreed to observe some higher standard of care in the individual case. Did that displacement of the basic norm take place in *Knight*?

In Sheehan v. The North American Marketing Corp, 610 F.3d 144, 153 (1st Cir. 2010), Saylor, J., likely held something similar to the above, even though in Rhode Island the assumption of risk defense "survives" under the state's pure comparative negligence system. The defendants were the seller and manufacturer of an above ground pool about 18 feet wide and 4 feet deep, which was covered with warnings about the dangers of diving. The plaintiff saw the signs but dove nonetheless. She became a quadriplegic when she hit her head against the bottom. The defendants won a summary judgment on the question of assumption of risk. The plaintiff claimed that she had assumed the risk that "she would scrape the bottom of the pool on a poorly executed dive," but had no sense that she could suffer serious injuries. In response, the court wrote that, "[u]nder Rhode Island law, when the circumstances are such that a person is presumed to know the risks of her dangerous conduct, she is charged with knowing all the ordinary risks associated with that conduct."

The New York Court of Appeals recently reaffirmed the relevance of assumption of risk doctrine for sport and recreation in Grady v. Chenango Valley Central School District, No. 23, No. 24, 2023 WL 3102723, at *1–3, 13–14 (N.Y. Apr. 27, 2023). Garcia, J., while noting that "the assumption of risk doctrine may not 'sit comfortably' within the landscape of comparative fault," nonetheless concluded that primary assumption of risk retains its salience:

> [B]ecause "athletic and recreative activities possess enormous social value, even while they involve significantly heightened risks," we have "employed the notion that these risks may be voluntarily assumed to preserve these beneficial pursuits as against the prohibitive liability to which they would otherwise give rise[.]"

The court came to different conclusions in the pair of cases before it. In the first, where the plaintiff was injured during a basketball drill to retrieve a rebound when he collided with a teammate and fell into the bleachers, the court found the plaintiff had assumed such a risk "inherent in the sport of basketball." By contrast, in the second, where the plaintiff was hit in the face by an errant baseball in a "fast-moving, intricate drill," the court held the defendant hadn't established such an injury was inherent in the sport of baseball. Rivera, J., in partial dissent, advocated for abolishing assumption of the risk entirely, instead folding the doctrine entirely into the pure comparative negligence standard in New York. Does it make sense to distinguish primary from secondary assumption of risk? Are courts up to the task?

c. ***Intentional Torts.*** Intentional tort cases generally do not involve deliberation upon the relative fault of the plaintiff. In Morgan v. Johnson, 976 P.2d 619 (Wash. 1999), the plaintiff and the defendant, never married, had a child some years before, and resumed a stormy and complex relationship after their daughter, who had lived with her mother, became curious about her biological father. One evening, both the plaintiff and the defendant left a bar together while drunk. It appeared that the defendant had threatened the plaintiff with a knife, dragged her to the car, and beat her with the interior rearview mirror. The court rejected the defendant's argument that the plaintiff's intoxication should be a defense to an intentional tort, noting that the term "fault" under Wash. Rev. Code §4.22.015 covered all acts or omissions that were negligent or reckless, or that were the subject of a strict liability or product liability claim. "The statute does not mention intentional torts. Our prior cases interpreting the statute confirm this omission was intentional. . . . The definition is intended to encompass all degrees of fault in tort actions short of intentionally caused harm."

In Blazovic v. Andrich, 590 A.2d 222, 231 (N.J. 1991), a case arising out of a barroom brawl, the court deviated from the majority view:

> [W]e reject the concept that intentional conduct is "different in kind" from both negligence and wanton and willful conduct, and consequently cannot be compared with them. Instead, we view intentional wrongdoing as "different in degree" from either negligence or wanton and willful conduct. To act intentionally involves knowingly or purposefully engaging in conduct "substantially certain" to result in injury to another. In contrast, wanton and willful conduct poses a highly unreasonable risk of harm likely to result in injury. Neither that difference nor the divergence between intentional conduct and negligence precludes comparison by a jury. The different levels of culpability inherent in each type of conduct will merely be reflected in the jury's apportionment of fault. By viewing the various types of tortious conduct in that way, we adhere most closely to the guiding principle of comparative fault—to distribute the loss in proportion to the respective faults of the parties causing that loss.

The court then reduced plaintiff's recovery against the owner of a bar to reflect the intentional wrongs of its patrons who had previously settled with the plaintiff.

d. ***Violation of Safety Act.*** Should violations of safety acts be treated as per se negligence on the part of a plaintiff? In Hardy v. Monsanto Enviro-Chem Systems, Inc., 323 N.W.2d 270, 273–74 (Mich. 1982), the court relied on the advent of Michigan's comparative negligence scheme to reject its earlier view, in Funk v. General Motors Corp., 220 N.W.2d 641 (Mich. 1974), that refused to treat the plaintiff's violation of a safety act as a form of contributory negligence. Ryah, J., held:

> Since the defense of comparative negligence serves not to undermine but to enhance safety in the workplace, we are of the view that comparative negligence is available in those cases where *Funk* . . . formerly prohibited the application of the contributory negligence defense. . . .
>
> [A]t some point a worker must be charged with *some* responsibility for his own safety-related behavior. If a worker continues to work under extremely unsafe conditions when a reasonable worker under all the facts and circumstances would "take a walk," the trier of fact might appropriately reduce the plaintiff's recovery under comparative negligence. Comparative negligence enhances the goal of safety in the workplace under these conditions since it gives the worker some financial incentive to act in a reasonable and prudent fashion.

How should *Gyerman*, *supra* at 224, be decided on this rationale?

e. ***Seat Belt Defense.*** In Nabors Well Services, Ltd. v. Romerop, 456 S.W.3d 553, 555 (Tex. 2015), the Texas Supreme Court reversed its rule that plaintiff's failure to use a seat belt was inadmissible in any car accident case. Brown, J., explained:

> But much has changed in the past four decades. The Legislature has overhauled Texas's system for apportioning fault in negligence cases—a plaintiff's negligence can now be apportioned alongside a defendant's without entirely barring the plaintiff's recovery. And unlike in 1974, seat belts are now required by law and have become an unquestioned part of daily life for the vast majority of drivers and passengers.
>
> These changes have rendered our prohibition on seat-belt evidence an anachronism. The rule may have been appropriate in its time, but today it is a vestige of a bygone legal system and an oddity in light of modern societal norms. Today we overrule it and hold that relevant evidence of use or nonuse of seat belts is admissible for the purpose of apportioning responsibility in civil lawsuits.

In dealing with this issue, must there be an effort to separate harms necessarily caused solely by impact and those which might have been averted by the proper use of a seat belt?

f. ***Imputed Negligence.*** In Clayton v. Morgan County Sheriff's Department, 95 N.E.3d 189, 193 (Ind. Ct. App. 2018), the plaintiffs were a husband and wife whose fifteen-month-old son Kinser had drowned in the family swimming pool. His father had moved the boy from his usual place in the garage into the house, while he did some dangerous work. He kept a line of sight to the boy and went and checked his whereabouts every ten minutes. Nonetheless the boy drowned in the family swimming pool. Both parents sued the sheriff and fire department for their failures to revive their son in a timely fashion. Indiana's general comparative negligence statute contains a carveout for tort claims against government entities and public employees, where contributory negligence still otherwise operates as a complete bar. Baker, J., held that the father was guilty of contributory negligence as a matter of law, given his want of supervision. He further held that the contributory negligence of the father was imputed to the mother, so that both claims were barred as a matter of law, on the ground that the "relationship of husband and wife and of parents and child are so closely and intimately connected that I think it fair to impute to the mother the knowledge and contributory negligence of the father."

Other states have rejected imputed parental (and spousal) negligence by statute. Wash. Rev. Code §4.22.020 (2023) provides:

> The contributory fault of one spouse . . . shall not be imputed to the other spouse . . . or the minor child of the spouse . . . to diminish recovery in an action by the other spouse . . . or the minor child of the spouse . . . , or his or her legal representative, to recover damages caused by fault resulting in death or in injury to the person or property, whether separate or community, of the spouse. . . . In an action brought for wrongful death or loss of consortium, the contributory fault of the decedent or injured person shall be imputed to the claimant in that action.

3. ***Comparative Negligence in Admiralty.*** Traditionally courts of admiralty apportioned damages under a rule of "divided damages," whereby an equal division of property damage was required whenever two ships were guilty of negligence, no matter what their relative degrees of fault. See The Schooner Catharine v. Dickinson, 58 U.S. 170 (1854). In United States v. Reliable Transfer Co., 421 U.S. 397, 405, 411 (1975), the plaintiff's tanker, the *Mary A. Whalen* (which, as the last of its kind, is docked at Red Hook, Brooklyn), crashed into the rocks after its captain attempted dangerous turning maneuvers that failed in part because the Coast Guard had failed to maintain its breakwater lights. "The District Court found that the vessel's grounding was caused 25% by the failure of the Coast Guard to maintain the breakwater light and 75% by the fault of the Whalen," but owing to the admiralty rules, divided damages equally. A unanimous Supreme Court jettisoned the rule of divided damages in favor of the pure form of comparative negligence less than two months before *Li v. Yellow Cab* was decided. Justice Stewart wrote:

> An equal division of damages is a reasonably satisfactory result only where each vessel's fault is approximately equal and each vessel thus assumes a share of the collision damages in proportion to its share of the blame, or where proportionate degrees of fault cannot be measured and determined on a rational basis. The rule produces palpably unfair results in every other case. For example, where one ship's fault in causing a collision is relatively slight and her damages small, and where the second ship is grossly negligent and suffers extensive damage, the first ship must still make a substantial payment to the second. "This result hardly commends itself to the sense of justice any more appealingly than does the common law doctrine of contributory negligence. . . ." G. Gilmore & C. Black, The Law of Admiralty 528 (2d ed. 1975). . . .

Reliable Transfer brought the admiralty rules in United States courts into conformity with those applied by all other leading maritime nations. See the Maritime Conventions Act, 1 & 2 Geo. V., c. 57 (1911), and the comparative negligence rules applicable in personal injury actions under the Jones Act, 46 U.S.C. §30104 (2023).

4. *"Impure" Comparative Negligence by Judicial Action.* In Bradley v. Appalachian Power Co., 256 S.E.2d 879, 885 (W. Va. 1979), the West Virginia Supreme Court adopted comparative negligence by judicial decision but declined to follow *Li* in its choice of the pure form.

> We do not accept the major premise of pure comparative negligence that a party should recover his damages regardless of his fault, so long as his fault is not 100 percent. Without embarking on an extended philosophical discussion of the nature and purpose of our legal system, we do state that in the field of tort law we are not willing to abandon the concept that where a party substantially contributes to his own damages, he should not be permitted to recover for any part of them. We do recognize that the present rule that prohibits recovery to the plaintiff if he is at fault in the slightest degree is manifestly unfair, and in effect rewards the substantially negligent defendant by permitting him to escape any responsibility for his negligence.
>
> Our present judicial rule of contributory negligence is therefore modified to provide that a party is not barred from recovering damages in a tort action so long as his negligence or fault does not equal or exceed the combined negligence or fault of the other parties involved in the accident.

One advantage of this rule is that it knocks out of the system those cases in which the plaintiff bears the huge percentage of the responsibility. But its drawback comes in cases that are more closely decided, for this rule creates a huge discontinuity as the plaintiff who is 49 percent negligent recovers 51 percent of the injury but the one who is 51 percent negligent recovers nothing. Matters are even more strained because on issues this imprecise juries can pick as their focal point a 50/50 split, which could go either way under this rule, depending on whether the applicable states allow the plaintiff to recover if her negligence is no greater than the defendant's or, alternatively, less than the defendant's. Note that under pure comparative negligence, the 49 percent versus 51 percent yields only a 2 percent difference, and the focal 50 percent division just calls for dividing the losses equally. Nonetheless, the impure rule has gained traction. As of 2023, thirty-four states have adopted some version of the 50-percent rule, compared to only eleven states having adopted the pure comparative approach, which is approved of in RTT: AL §7. Does the *Bradley* rule encourage the plaintiff to join as many parties to the suit as possible? What should be done if, for example, a landlord and tenant are joined in a suit arising out of a single incident on common property?

5. *Economic Analysis of Comparative Negligence.* The efficiency analysis of comparative negligence has been, on balance, somewhat more tentative than the fairness arguments made in its favor. Once again, the issue is how to coordinate the behavior of two parties, each of whom will vary the level of care provided as a function of the level of care provided by the other side. In many cases there are statutory or administrative duties that compel compliance with the rules of the road even when no accident occurs.

These duties, however, are usually put to one side in the pure economic analysis, which usually considers the comparative negligence regime as governed exclusively by various permutations of the Hand Formula. When both parties and the court all possess full information, neither party, if fully rational, will behave negligently. Suppose that the expected loss is $100, and the optimal levels of joint precautions are $30 by the plaintiff and $40 by the defendant. If comparative negligence were to leave the plaintiff with 20 percent of the expected loss, it might appear that she would not take the precaution, because her cost of avoidance ($30) is greater than her residual loss ($20). Nonetheless, this analysis ignores the response of the defendant who will prefer to spend $40 on precaution to avoid $80 worth of loss. Yet once that step is taken, the plaintiff may now prefer to take precautions as well, for the $30 spent could avoid a $100 loss that might otherwise occur.

This stylized account is highly sensitive to its initial assumptions. If the defendant thought he would have to spend $50 to avoid a 40 percent chance of a $100 loss, he would not take precautions and thus would be held negligent. But if the plaintiff knew or had reason to believe that the defendant would make this blunder, then she would choose not to take care because the $30 precaution is now more expensive than the $20 in unrecoverable losses. On the other hand, if the precautions taken by the two parties are independent, the defendant's unilateral action could reduce the risk of loss to the point where it no longer makes sense from an economic point of view to make these adjustments. See Posner, Economic Analysis of Law 198, 198–202 (9th ed. 2014). See also Shavell, Economic Analysis of Accident Law 15, 15–16 (1987); Haddock & Curran, An Economic Theory of Comparative Negligence, 14 J. Legal Stud. 49 (1985); Cooter & Ulen, An Economic Case for Comparative Negligence, 61 N.Y.U. L. Rev. 1067 (1986).

The analysis, however, is still more rarified because neither party knows when they choose their level of care whether some other party will be at fault in a future accident. All parties (for there may be more than two) also face the possibility of injuring only themselves or being involved in accidents in which only one party is negligent. Nor do the parties have any reliable information on the relation between the dollar cost of precautions and expected damages when making their initial decisions. Worse still, virtually no actor knows what legal regime applies in any state. Indeed, the differential incentive effects of the various rules are virtually impossible to plot out, in light of practical concerns, such as (a) the risk that the defendant will be insolvent, (b) the possibility of jury error, (c) the payment of contingent fees and other expenses of suit, (d) the lower standard for contributory negligence, (e) the role of fines and other sanctions in influencing behavior, and (f) the internal difficulties of the Hand formula. See generally Schwartz, Contributory and Comparative Negligence: A Reappraisal, 87 Yale L.J. 697 (1978).

How would the analysis be altered under the old admiralty rule of even division? Under the 50 percent negligence threshold, as in Wisconsin and West Virginia?

2. By Legislation

As the decision of the California Supreme Court in *Li v. Yellow Cab* points out, since 1970 there has been a massive legislative move toward comparative negligence. A representative sample of the possible forms of comparative negligence legislation is given below. For a full collection of the statutes, see Schwartz, Comparative Negligence, App. B (5th ed. 2018 cumulative supp.) and Woods & Deere, Comparative Fault, App. (3d ed. 1996 & Supp. 2018). A sampler follows.

Federal Employers' Liability Act

45 U.S.C. §53 (2023)

In all actions on and after April 22, 1908 brought against any such common carrier by railroad under or by virtue of any of the provisions of this chapter to recover damages for personal injuries to an employee, or where such injuries have resulted in his death, the fact that the employee may have been guilty of contributory negligence shall not bar a recovery, but the damages shall be diminished by the jury in proportion to the amount of negligence attributable to such employee: *Provided*, That no such employee who may be injured or killed shall be held to have been guilty of contributory negligence in any case where the violation by such common carrier of any statute enacted for the safety of employees contributed to the injury or death of such employee.

New York

N.Y. Civil Practice Law and Rules §§1411–1412 (McKinney 2023)

§1411. In any action to recover damages for personal injury, injury to property, or wrongful death, the culpable conduct attributable to the claimant or to the decedent, including contributory negligence or assumption of risk, shall not bar recovery, but the amount of damages otherwise recoverable shall be diminished in the proportion which the culpable conduct attributable to the claimant or decedent bears to the culpable conduct which caused the damages.

§1412. Culpable conduct claimed in diminution of damages, in accordance with section fourteen hundred eleven, shall be an affirmative defense to be pleaded and proved by the party asserting the defense.

Pennsylvania

42 Pa. Cons. Stat. Ann. §7102 (2023)

(a) **General rule.** In all actions brought to recover damages for negligence resulting in death or injury to person or property, the fact that the plaintiff may have been guilty of contributory negligence shall not bar a recovery by the plaintiff or his legal representative where such negligence was not greater than the causal negligence of the defendant or defendants against whom recovery is sought, but any damages sustained by the plaintiff shall be diminished in proportion to the amount of negligence attributed to the plaintiff.

(b) **Recovery against joint defendant; contribution.** Where recovery is allowed against more than one defendant, each defendant shall be liable for that proportion of the total dollar amount awarded as damages in the ratio of the amount of his causal negligence to the amount of causal negligence attributed to all defendants against whom recovery is allowed. The plaintiff may recover the full amount of the allowed recovery from any defendant against whom the plaintiff is not barred from recovery. Any defendant who is so compelled to pay more than his percentage share may seek contribution.

(c) **Downhill skiing.**

(1) The General Assembly finds that the sport of downhill skiing is practiced by a large number of citizens of this Commonwealth and also attracts to this Commonwealth large numbers of nonresidents significantly contributing to the economy of this Commonwealth. It is recognized that as in some other sports, there are inherent risks in the sport of downhill skiing.

(2) The doctrine of voluntary assumption of risk as it applies to downhill skiing injuries and damages is not modified by subsections (a) and (b).

Wisconsin

Wis. Stat. Ann. §895.045 (West 2023)

§895.045. (1) Comparative negligence. Contributory negligence shall not bar recovery in an action by any person or the person's legal representative to recover damages for negligence resulting in death or in injury to person or property, if that negligence was not greater than the negligence of the person against whom recovery is sought, but any damages allowed shall be diminished in the proportion to the amount of negligence attributed to the person recovering. The negligence of the plaintiff shall be measured separately against the negligence of each person found to be causally negligent. The liability of each person found to be causally negligent whose percentage of causal negligence is less than 51 percent is limited to the percentage of the total causal negligence attributed to that person. A person found to be causally negligent whose percentage of causal negligence is 51 percent or more shall be jointly and severally liable for the damages allowed. . . .

RESTATEMENT OF THE LAW (THIRD) OF TORTS: APPORTIONMENT OF LIABILITY

§7. Effect of Plaintiff's Negligence when Plaintiff Suffers an Indivisible Injury

Plaintiff's negligence (or the negligence of another person for whose negligence the plaintiff is responsible) that is a legal cause of an indivisible injury to the plaintiff reduces the plaintiff's recovery in proportion to the share of responsibility the factfinder assigns to the plaintiff (or other person for whose negligence the plaintiff is responsible).

NOTES

1. ***PROBLEM: Computational Exercises.*** In examining the respective merits of the principal comparative negligence systems, see how they apply to the following hypothetical five situations, assuming that the negligence of each of the parties contributed causally to the total damage sustained. Does a comparison of the particular numerical results suggest any reason to prefer one system to another?

I. *A*, who is 10 percent negligent, suffers $10,000 damages; *B*, who is 90 percent negligent, suffers no damage.
II. *A*, who is 60 percent negligent, suffers $10,000 damages; *B*, who is 40 percent negligent, suffers no damage.
III. *A*, who is 30 percent negligent, suffers $2,000 damages; *B*, who is 70 percent negligent, suffers $8,000 damages.
IV. *A*, who is approximately 50 percent negligent, suffers $2,000 damages; *B*, who is approximately 50 percent negligent, suffers $8,000 damages.
V. *A* and *B* are equally negligent; *A* suffers $10,000 damages, while *B* suffers no damage.

2. ***Comparative Negligence and the Control of Juries.*** Special verdicts play an important role in administering a comparative negligence system, given that the plaintiff's final damages award depends upon both the extent of her total damages and her degree of negligence. A verdict that states only a dollar figure for the plaintiff's award becomes difficult to interpret after trial. An award of $60,000 to a plaintiff who suffered $150,000 damages could be attacked as inadequate if a finding of contributory negligence totally bars the plaintiff's recovery, since the jury has no valid reason for awarding only partial compensation. Under pure comparative negligence, however, that verdict is consistent with a finding that the plaintiff was 60 percent negligent. General verdicts conceal a jury's thought processes from both the trial judge and the appellate court. Special verdicts promise greater judicial oversight.

Should courts require special verdicts on both the degree of negligence of each party and on the total amount of the plaintiff's damages? Or should special verdicts be ordered only at the request of either party or otherwise be left to the discretion of the court? Note that an Idaho statute allows any party to request the court to "direct the jury to find separate special verdicts determining the amount of damages and the percentage of negligence or comparative responsibility attributable to each party," after which the court makes the appropriate reduction in damages for the successful plaintiff. Idaho Code §6-802 (West 2023). The Idaho statute only allows recovery when the plaintiff's negligence "was not as great as the negligence, gross negligence or comparative responsibility of the person against whom recovery is sought." Idaho Code §6-801 (West 2023). Is there a greater need for the special verdict here or under pure comparative negligence?

3. ***Insurance Complications.*** One collateral complication under comparative negligence concerns the amount of damages that can be recovered when, as so often happens in routine collision cases, each party is a tortfeasor as well as an accident victim. When contributory negligence was an absolute bar, it was difficult, if not impossible, for both parties to obtain judgment, because if both were at fault, typically neither could recover. Accident cases, therefore, resulted in a single judgment against one defendant that was then discharged by the insurance carrier up to its policy limits. Today, comparative negligence makes it possible for each party to recover from the other. Thus, assume that *A* has $100,000 in damages and was 25 percent responsible for her loss, while *B* has $200,000 in damages and was 75 percent responsible for his loss. If *A* alone were injured, she should recover $75,000 in damages from *B*. Likewise, if *B* alone were injured, he should be able to recover $50,000 in damages from *A*. In Jess

v. Herrmann, 604 P.2d 208, 212 (Cal. 1979), the California Supreme Court had to decide whether, as the statute seemed to require, the two damage awards should be set off against each other, so that the insurer of *B* pays *A* $25,000, or whether, in the alternative, *A*'s insurer should pay *B* $50,000 and *B*'s insurer should pay *A* $75,000.

Tobriner, J., held that the statutory setoff was available only when the parties in question were not covered by insurance. In his view, the insurance function would not be well served if the application of the mandatory setoff rule were allowed to produce "the anomalous situation in which a liability insurer's responsibility under its policy depends as much on the extent of injury suffered by its own insured as on the amount of damages sustained by the person its insured has negligently injured." Manual, J., in dissent argued that the court misconstrued the applicable statutory language, and that it did not explain the way in which the rule was to operate in situations in which either or both parties had limited insurance coverage.

SECTION F. MODERN NO-FAULT SYSTEMS

1. Automobile No-Fault Plans

The basic criticism of the common law in industrial accidents had a direct parallel with automobile and railway accidents, where the twin defenses of assumption of risk and contributory negligence migrated from the workers' compensation arena. These no-fault plans are considered briefly here because, in large measure, they sought to eliminate the common law system. This arose from distaste with the twin defenses of assumption of risk and contributory negligence, especially at a time before the advent of comparative negligence when both operated as complete defenses to tort liability.

The initial foray in this direction came just after the workers' compensation laws were fully established. Thus Ballantine, A Compensation Plan for Railway Accident Claims, 29 Harv. L. Rev. 705, 708–09 (1916), identifies the two key elements of the basic no-fault proposal for railway accidents only. First, liability, irrespective of negligence, "is founded upon conviction that the cost of transportation service should include the expense of insuring the passenger against all risks peculiar to the service for which he pays his fare." The second called for a fixed and limited schedule of damages, determined administratively and not through a jury trial since "[e]ach jury flounders about, takes off something from the size of the verdict because of doubts about liability, perhaps averages the estimates of different members, and blunders to a result."

Ballantine's initial no-fault scheme for railway accidents became the template for the early no-fault automobile insurance proposal contained in the Columbia Plan of 1932. See Report of Committee to Study Compensation for Automobile Accidents (Columbia Reports) (1932), which envisioned a system of third-party insurance: "Every owner of a motor vehicle shall pay compensation for disability or death from personal injury caused by the operation of such motor vehicle, without regard to fault as a cause of the injury or death. . . ." The basic rule was then qualified by limited exceptions for intentional wrongs or for persons who drove a vehicle without the owner's permission, express or implied. The plan was extensively discussed and debated in Connecticut, New York, Virginia, and Wisconsin. It was only adopted in some form in Saskatchewan, Canada. See James, The Columbia Study of Compensation for Automobile Accidents, 59 Colum. L. Rev. 408, 410 (1959).

The next wave of no-fault automobile legislation that peaked in the 1960s shifted to a system of first-party coverage. See Keeton & O'Connell, Basic Protection for the Accident Victim (1965). Their "Basic Protection Plan" for personal injuries involved the payment of periodic damages, without the use of scheduled damages found in the workers' compensation cases. The plan also contained a partial exemption provision from the tort system for less serious injuries, while allowing plaintiffs with major injuries to recover from the tort defendant, or, alternatively, from the fund when the defendant was not liable. An extensive government report, U.S. Dep't of Transp., Motor Vehicle Crash Losses and Their Compensation in the United States 51, 94 (1971), defended the first-coverage system on the ground that, first "only 45 percent of those killed or seriously injured in auto accidents benefit[ed] in any way under the tort liability insurance system" and secondly that under the tort system it "would appear to cost in the neighborhood of $1.07 in total system expenses to deliver $1.00 in net benefits to victims."

In response to those charges, then-Professor Posner wrote on behalf of the American Bar Association his explanation as to "why the statistical studies critical of the fault system are fatally flawed." Automobile No-Fault Insurance 13–17 (1978). The gist of his claim was that the 45 percent recovery rate "is meaningless once it is recognized that tort liability is not intended as a system of insurance that can properly be evaluated under a criterion of comprehensiveness" since the tort system is not meant to cover all accidents. Torts are relatively infrequent, which means that the first-party coverages "outside of the tort system—from life, collision, disability, accident, medical, and other first-party insurance, and from wage-replacement sources such as sick leave and workers' compensation," bring total coverage up to 90 percent, as compared with the tort alone figure. Similarly, he notes that the ratio of about $1.07 in administrative expenses for each $1.00 in net benefits only looks high because it ignores the accident prevention function of the tort system, which, while positive, is difficult to measure. A further criticism of the no-fault system is raised in Epstein, Automobile No-Fault Plans: A Second Look at First Principles, 13 Creighton L. Rev. 769, 789–90 (1980), which notes simply the absence of any necessary connection between abolishing the tort system and imposing a *compulsory* state no-fault plan, given that it is possible to adopt a system that

> allows individuals to choose the nature and type of benefits in light of their own estimation of their personal circumstances and needs. Those who wish to buy deep coverage with high deductibles should be allowed to do so, while those who want first dollar coverage with shallow protection should be free to do so as well. Those who want group coverage are free to explore that possibility. It may well be that the case is made for the abolition of all tort liability, but it does not follow that those same arguments require instituting compulsory first party insurance. The real quid pro quo for losing the benefits of being a tort plaintiff is being freed from the burden of being a tort defendant. It is *not* the surrender of a tort claim for the receipt of a set of benefits that are not requested, and which perhaps ill suit the needs of the party to whom they are provided.

Pinnick v. Cleary

271 N.E.2d 592 (Mass. 1971)

Reardon, J: The plaintiff claims that c. 670 [the Massachusetts plan] has impaired a cause of action which is on a higher, more sacrosanct level than the "ordinary" common law cause of action. Two alternative reasons are advanced in support of this contention: first, that the tort action has the status of a "vested property right," and, second, that the function of the cause of action is to safeguard the fundamental "right of personal security and bodily integrity" which, although not mentioned in the Bill of Rights of the United States Constitution, is nonetheless protected by it. We find both grounds unpersuasive.

In arguing that the cause of action affected by c. 670 constitutes a vested property right, the plaintiff seems to ignore the distinction between a cause of action which has accrued and the expectation which every citizen has if a legal wrong should occur to find redress according to the rules of statutory and common law applicable at that time. The Legislature is admittedly restricted in the extent to which it can retroactively affect common law rights of redress which have already accrued. However, there is authority in abundance for the proposition that "[n]o person has a vested interest in any rule of law entitling him to insist that it shall remain unchanged for his benefit." New York Cent. R.R. v. White, 243 U.S. 188, 198 [1916]; Munn v. Illinois, 94 U.S. 113, 134 [1876]. . . .

In the instant case, however, the Legislature has not attempted to abolish the preexisting right of tort recovery and leave the automobile accident victim without redress. On the contrary, as was pointed out above, the statute has affected his substantive rights of recovery only in one respect and has simply altered his method of enforcing them in all others. Therefore, c. 670 may be judged by the stricter test which the plaintiff urges upon us and for which there is considerable authority in workmen's compensation cases: whether the statute provides an adequate and reasonable substitute for preexisting rights. The similarity between c. 670 and the workmen's compensation statutes, in the nature of their purposes and the means chosen to achieve them, also leads us to conclude that the reasonable and adequate substitute test is appropriate to apply here even if its application is not constitutionally required. . . .

In considering the effect of c. 670, we cannot view it from the point of view of plaintiffs and defendants, for these are not preexisting categories as are the employers and employees affected by a workmen's compensation act. Every driver is a potential plaintiff and, equally, a potential defendant. The desired effect of c. 670 on all motorists alike is initially to make available to them compulsory insurance at lower rates due to the savings to insurance companies in administrative expenses and total payments which are expected to follow from c. 670. If injury occurs on the road, motorists are assured of the probability of quick and efficient payment of the first $2,000 of defined losses incurred. In cases of accidents in which the motorist was not negligent, he avoids the uncertainty, delay and cost of a tort proceeding. He still retains the option of recovering more by litigation if he so wishes and the facts so warrant. Although c. 670 may also have the effect of depriving him of his damages for pain and suffering in such an instance, the exchange of rights involved with respect to the driver in an accident in which he was not negligent bears considerable resemblance to that effected by the statute in the *White* case with respect to employees.

NOTES

1. *Reception of No-Fault Plan.* Pinnick v. Cleary has been followed in other states. See Montgomery v. Daniels, 340 N.E.2d 444 (N.Y. 1975); Opinion of the Justices, 304 A.2d 881 (N.H. 1973). Where the no-fault schemes have been struck down, courts have usually relied on the specific language of state constitutions and not on the broad principles of the Due Process or Equal Protection Clauses. In Grace v. Howlett, 283 N.E.2d 474 (Ill. 1972), the Illinois Supreme Court struck down the state's no-fault scheme as offending several state constitutional provisions, including one that required that no "special law" be passed when a "general law" could be made applicable. Likewise, the Florida Supreme Court in Kluger v. White, 281 So. 2d 1, 3–4 (Fla. 1973), invalidated the property no-fault provisions of the Florida law as violating the state constitutional provisions guaranteeing that the courts "shall be open for redress of any injury." This legislation did not provide any "reasonable alternative" remedy to protect the rights of individuals whose property was damaged or destroyed by the acts of another. For a review of the explosive rise to prominence of automobile no-fault plans in the 1960s and 1970s and the absence of more recent no-fault legislative enactments, see Engstrom, An Alternative Explanation for No-Fault's Demise, 61 DePaul L. Rev. 303 (2012).

2. *Tort Thresholds.* The no-fault plans tend to differ in their treatment of limits, deductibles, options, collateral sources, and the like. Some states like New York let individual drivers choose between a "full tort" and a "limited tort" option in which recoverable damages typically vary between $25,000 and $100,000, with various offsets for disability benefits payable either by New York State or by Social Security. Other states rely on a verbal threshold usually couched in terms of a permanent and significant disfigurement. See, e.g., Gillman v. Gillman, 319 So. 2d 165, 166–67 (Fla. App. 1975), treating a permanent scar as a permanent disfigurement. Numerical thresholds act as magnets that encourage parties (as with the workers' compensation system) to inflate their medical costs when bringing tort suits. Verbal thresholds are much more immune from manipulation, but more subject to disputation. The verbal threshold in New York blocks many claims that make it into the tort system in states like California that preserve the traditional tort system. As one measure of the difference, note that in 1989, for every 100 property damage claims there were fifty-six claims for bodily injury in California and only eleven in New York. For discussion of this and similar issues, see O'Connell et al., Consumer Choice in the Auto Insurance Market, 52 Md. L. Rev. 1016 (1993). For a review of the various types of tort thresholds, see Velikova, Theorizing the Automobile No-Fault Tort Threshold, 42 Tort Trial & Ins. Prac. L.J. 1043, 1044 (2007).

3. *The Economic Efficiency of No-Fault Plans.* On theoretical grounds, critics have attacked no-fault plans as inefficient because they allow careless drivers to impose costs on others and induce careful drivers to engage in cautious defensive tactics. Landes observes that no-fault has "produced both an economically and statistically significant increase in fatal accidents: a medical expense threshold of $500 implies about a 4 percent increase in fatal accident rates; a medical expense threshold of $1,500 implies an increase in fatal accidents of *more than 10 percent*!" See Landes, Insurance, Liability, and Accidents: A Theoretical and Empirical Investigation of No-Fault Accidents, 25 J.L. & Econ. 49, 62 (1982). Subsequently, Schwartz, Auto No-Fault and First-Party Insurance: Advantages and Problems, 73 S. Cal. L. Rev. 611 (2000), observed that no-fault systems reverse the premiums for heavy and light vehicles. Thus, in the tort system, the lion's share of the loss goes to drivers of large vehicles owing to the harm they cause; but under a first-party system, this loss is shifted to the lighter vehicles that are hit. Which regime sets the appropriate baseline, and why?

4. *Coverage Disputes.* Unlike workers' compensation litigation, the coverage disputes under automobile no-fault plans have been largely humdrum. The basic Michigan statute, for example, holds that an insurer "is liable to pay benefits for accidental bodily injury arising out of the ownership, operation, maintenance or use of a motor vehicle as a motor vehicle . . ." Mich. Comp. Laws Ann. §500.3105(1) (2023). McKenzie v. Auto Club Insurance Ass'n, 580 N.W.2d 424, 425 (Mich. 1998), denied coverage to two plaintiffs who were nearly asphyxiated by carbon monoxide fumes while sleeping in a camper/trailer because the injury did not arise out of the use of a motor vehicle "as a motor vehicle." Indeed, in Michigan, the major first-party insurance provider sought to cap Personal Insurance Protection (PIP) benefits, or opt out of the system altogether, as suggested in Epstein, *supra* at 280. The single major complaint was that the inflation of PIP benefits made no-fault insurance unaffordable, and the source of the greatest criticism of the system. Since the 1970s, no new system has been enacted.

2. No-Fault Insurance for Medical and Product Injuries

The widespread adoption of automobile no-fault plans in the early 1970s spurred efforts to extend no-fault plans into the medical malpractice and products liability arenas. One such third-party no-fault proposal put forward on an elective or voluntary basis was proposed in O'Connell, Ending Insult to Injury: No-Fault Insurance for Products and Services 97 (1975). O'Connell modeled this approach on workers' compensation such that "elective no-fault liability would be true no-fault insurance, with the fault of neither the injurer nor the injured having a bearing on payment," which would be to out-of-pocket losses when injury results from those risks barring a claim based on fault or a defect against a covered manufacturer.

The idea garnered little support, even from those who favored automobile no-fault insurance. One difficulty was that the manufacturers of component products could not easily notify the ultimate user or consumer that it has elected coverage under the plan. The plan could not apply to bystander injuries. Nor was it obvious how to coordinate this new no-fault coverage with tort liability, workers' compensation, and first-party insurance. Most importantly, the absence of any limiting concept of product defect made it hard to decide, as Professor Blum asked, *which* manufacturer should provide coverage when a worker wearing slippery shoes falls off a well-constructed ladder after drinking a few beers. Blum, Book Review, 43 U. Chi. L. Rev. 217 (1975).

Similar proposals for no-fault schemes have gained modest traction with medical and hospital injuries. As before, the basic no-fault bargain promised broader coverage and lower administrative expenses, in exchange for reduced coverage awards on either an elective or a mandatory basis. And, as before, the central challenge has been to identify a workable definition of a compensable event, in cases of missed medical diagnoses. See Epstein, Medical Malpractice: The Case for Contract, 1 Am. Bar Found. Res. J. 87, 141–47 (1976). If these are covered, the expansion of liability under the medical no-fault system will expose the most skilled physicians to huge liability, leading for a movement to return liability diagnostic errors back to the reasonable care standard. See Weiler, The Case for No-Fault Medical Liability, 52 Md. L. Rev. 908 (1993).

A second form of no-fault liability tries to limit the program by building lists of designated compensable events, or DCEs, in consultation with medical professionals. See Havighurst & Tancredi, "Medical Adversity Insurance"—A No-Fault Approach to Medical Malpractice and Quality Assurance, The Milbank Memorial Fund Quarterly/Health and Society (Spring 1973), *reprinted in* 613 Ins. L.J. 69 (1974), and subsequently in the Commission of Medical Professional Liability of the ABA, Designated Compensable Event System: A Feasibility Study (1979). But no agreement can be found on how to create and update such a list, which if completed might discourage physicians from taking on high-risk patients in the first place. See Danzon, Medical Malpractice: Theory, Evidence and Public Policy 217–19 (1985).

NOTES

1. ***Vaccine Liability.*** One area in which a no-fault scheme has been adopted is through the National Childhood Vaccine Injury Act of 1986 (NCVIA), passed in response to a sharp increase in the price of vaccines that threatened to drive many vaccine manufacturers out of the marketplace. Recovery is based on the deceptively simple question whether the vaccine in question caused the conditions for which the plaintiff seeks damages. In addition, it raises

serious questions of federal preemption. See Bruesewitz v. Wyeth LLC, 562 U.S. 223 (2011), *infra* Chapter 8, at 642. As most vaccines are administered to children, the NCVIA covers a large portion of the overall market. Its basic provisions provide for a complex system of no-fault compensation of up to $250,000 for persons who suffer particular side effects from certain vaccine programs within specified time limits. 42 U.S.C. §300aa (2023). In many cases, the statute employs explicit tests for determining whether compensation is owed. For example, the recipient of a measles vaccine who suffers an anaphylactic shock within twenty-four hours of inoculation can receive payment. The statute also provides that persons who have met the conditions for no-fault recovery may nonetheless choose to reject the payment and sue for tort damages.

According to the Health Resources and Services Administration (HRSA), "[a]ny individual, of any age, who received a covered vaccine and believes he or she was injured as a result, can file a petition. Parents, legal guardians and legal representatives can file on behalf of children, disabled adults, and individuals who are deceased." Covered vaccines include most vaccines routinely administered in the United States, subject to caveats that they must be recommended for use by children or pregnant women. The payouts under the program were summarized by the HRSA as follows:

> According to the CDC, from 2006 to 2017 over 3.4 billion doses of covered vaccines were distributed in the U.S. For petitions filed in this time period, 6,411 petitions were adjudicated by the Court, and of those 4,408 were compensated. This means for every one million doses of vaccine that were distributed, approximately one individual was compensated.
>
> Since 1988, over 20,913 petitions have been filed with the VICP. Over that 30-year time period, 18,070 petitions have been adjudicated, with 6,706 of those determined to be compensable, while 11,364 were dismissed. Total compensation paid over the life of the program is approximately $4.2 billion.

Vaccine compensation has received renewed attention with possible claims of vaccine injury associated with the major vaccines approved for COVID-19—the Pfizer, Moderna, and Johnson & Johnson vaccines. There has been a fierce dispute over the possible side effects for these vaccines, especially with children, but it is generally held that the Secretary of Health and Human Services' January 2020 declaration of a public health emergency pursuant to the Public Health Act, 42 U.S.C. §247(d), provides vaccine manufacturers with immunity from tort liability.

2. *The 9/11 Victim Compensation Fund.* Eleven days after the September 11, 2001, attacks on the World Trade Center, the Pentagon, and United Airlines Flight 93, Congress passed the Air Transportation Safety and System Stabilization Act of 2001, Pub. L. No. 107-42, 115 Stat. 230 (2001) (codified at 49 U.S.C. §40101). Title IV of that Act created the Victim Compensation Fund for any person who was killed or injured in the September 11th terrorist attacks. Pursuant to the Act, President George W. Bush appointed Kenneth Feinberg to administer the victim compensation program. Feinberg set out the rules and regulations for paying compensation without regard to the negligence of any party. To participate in the fund, the claimants had to waive all suits against any airline, airline manufacturer, airport sponsor, or property holder of the World Trade Center. These restrictions were upheld as unambiguous in Virgilio v. City of New York, 407 F.3d 105, 112–13 (2d Cir. 2005), wrongful death actions brought against both New York City and Motorola on behalf of firefighters killed in the burning towers. Tort actions, however, were explicitly preserved against the knowing participants in the hijacking conspiracy. Unlike tort damages, recoveries in question were offset by payments from collateral sources but allowed compensation for all forms of economic and noneconomic losses, without a maximum dollar limitation. These recoveries were not governed by any set rule but were to be based only on the "facts of the claim," including evidence on the extent of harm.

Exhibit 4.1 Kenneth Feinberg

Kenneth Feinberg (b. 1945) is known in many circles as the "compensation czar." Beyond the 9/11 Fund, Feinberg has become a one-man shop for structuring and administering alternate compensation schemes for governments and private corporations. His work has included serving as a special master for the Troubled Asset Relief Program (TARP) Executive Compensation, initiated in the wake of the collapse or near-collapse of major financial institutions in 2008, and overseeing similar funds in the aftermath of the 2007 mass shooting at Virginia Tech, the 2010 Deep Water Horizon oil spill in the Gulf of Mexico, the Boston Marathon bombing in 2013, and in 2014, the injury or death of motorists in General Motors cars due to faulty ignition switches.

Bio sources: Walsh, Kenneth Feinberg to Oversee Cuts in Multiemployer Pension Plans, N.Y. Times, June 17, 2015, http://www.nytimes.com/2015/06/18/business/dealbook/kenneth-feinberg-to-oversee-cuts-in-multiemployer-pension-plans.html; Romero, Compensation Czar Kenneth Feinberg, Time, Oct. 23, 2009, http://content.time.com/time/nation/article/0,8599,1903547,00.html
Image source: Alex Wong / Getty Images

To set these awards, Feinberg created an elaborate grid that allowed claimants to recover under a formula that contained both economic and noneconomic loss components. The economic losses were based on victims' average income between 1998 and 2000, up to $231,000 per year. Noneconomic losses per decedent were set at $250,000 with an additional $100,000 for a spouse and each dependent. These presumptive awards were payable, no questions asked, within 120 days of filing. Alternatively, disappointed claimants could ask for an individual determination. In Colaio v. Feinberg, 262 F. Supp. 2d 273, 301 (S.D.N.Y. 2003), some high-income earners challenged Feinberg's methodology because of "the sharp truncation of potential damage awards at the top of the earnings distribution," which affected financiers whose incomes were far above those amounts. Hellerstein, J., rejected those claims, noting that "[t]he duty of a judge is to give deference to the Department of Justice's regulations and respect to the Special Master's policies to the extent that they are rooted in law." All told, about $7 billion in compensation was paid out, with an average award of $2.1 million to 97 percent of the families that filed claims. Awards to surviving families ranged from a low of $250,000 to a high of $7.1 million. Awards to survivors with personal injuries ranged between $5.0 and $8.6 million. Administrative costs for running the

Office of the Accident Compensation Commission (ACC), the government agency tasked with administering the Accident Compensation Act, in Palmerston North, New Zealand

Source: Wikimedia Commons

system were 1.2 percent of the total awards paid. Of the total claimants, some 1,600 asked for individual hearings. Feinberg personally conducted over 900 of these hearings. For his own reflections, see Feinberg, What Is Life Worth?: The Unprecedented Effort to Compensate the Victims of 9/11 (2005). His bottom line: "There is not one family member I've met who wouldn't gladly give back the check, or, in many cases, their own lives to have that loved one back. 'Happy' never enters into this equation."

3. *The New Zealand Plan.* The New Zealand Accident Compensation Act (as amended by the Accident Compensation Amendment (no. 2) Act of 1973) remains today the most radical no-fault plan in existence. That plan bars virtually all tort actions for personal injuries or death. In exchange, its comprehensive insurance scheme awards benefits to all persons who suffer "personal injury by accident," where the words "by accident" exclude compensation for death or injury caused by sickness. The definition of accident under the Act is generally seen from the point of view of the injured party, so that compensation is awarded to victims of intentional torts (including criminal assaults), as well as those who have been harmed in automobile accidents and product-related injuries. The statute also covers certain occupational diseases, including deafness. But otherwise, sickness and disease were excluded in large measure because of their cost. In 1972, amendments to the original Accident Compensation Act extended coverage to "medical, surgical, dental or first aid misadventure," §2(1)(a)(ii), without further elaboration.

The justifications for the New Zealand plan were outlined in 1967 in the Report of the Royal Commission of Inquiry, Compensation for Personal Injury in New Zealand, more commonly known as the Woodhouse Report after the commission's chairman, Justice Owen Woodhouse. That report criticized the negligence system as a "lottery," and concluded that coverage under workers' compensation and social security was spotty at best in dealing with the 100,000 accidents large and small annually in New Zealand. The Report sought to meet five objectives: community responsibility, comprehensive entitlement, complete rehabilitation, real compensation, and administrative efficiency. The Report insisted on a community responsibility "in urging forward the physical and economic rehabilitation of every adult citizen whose activities bear upon the general welfare. This is the plain answer to any who might query the responsibility of the community in the matter." It also concluded that "Injury, not Cause, is the Issue." Thereby covering all sorts instead of concentrating on any given class of injuries, including those once covered under a workers' compensation act with its restrictions on recovery. The program thus covers the self-employed, independent contractors and women "who as housewives make it possible for the productive work to be done." The plan also sought to create an effective rehabilitation to help individual persons to return to work. And although conscious of potential cost, "the rationalization put forward avoids new large expenditures and yet permits at the same time greatly increased relief where it is needed most—for the losses which are greatest. . . ."

Credit Suisse First Boston, Accident Compensation: Options for Reform 9–12 (1998), concluded that, 30 years in, the program could not meet its expectations. The centralized monopoly structure of the administrative plan could not deal with the onslaught of claims brought because of injured parties and their professional advisors' efforts to game the system. Consequently, there was "a significant tail of long-term claimants," which resulted in "an unfunded liability of $7.5 (NZ) billion," a number which only grew thereafter. Much of the difficulty came from the internal funding methods. Up until 1982, each claim was fully funded in the year of its occurrence. But thereafter, New Zealand shifted to a "pay as you go" system that covered expenses only as they were paid out. Initially, costs were reduced, but in future years they skyrocketed as the fund had to raise new revenues for the earlier big cases. The ACC 2017/2018 Annual Report noted that the surplus in the plan for 2018 was $28 million, down from $602 million in the previous year. Reserves for future claims under the full funding model rose by $2.9 billion to $40.6 billion. The most recent report for 2022 reports major administrative reforms and smaller losses, even when COVID expenses are taken into account. https://www.acc.co.nz/assets/corporate-documents/acc8430-acc-annual-report-2022.pdf.

The New Zealand plan has also generated some tricky coverage disputes over cases of "medical misadventure that were brought within the system." In ACC v. Auckland Hospital Board, [1980] 2 NZLR 748, 751, the court awarded damages to a claimant who became pregnant when a tubal ligation failed because the surgeon, without negligence, had failed to close her fallopian tubes with his then available forceps, subsequently replaced with a more modern variety. The court found medical misadventure because the unsatisfactory outcome was not "within the normal range of medical or surgical failure attendant upon even the most felicitous treatment." Similarly, MacDonald v. Accident Compensation Corp., [1985] 5 NZAR 276, reached a similar conclusion for a leaky bowel suffered during a properly performed operation.

4. *A Final Evaluation.* All current no-fault plans displace the common law rules of negligence with some other definition of compensable event. The new systems eliminate line-drawing under negligence but substitute other boundary conditions, such as a line in workers' compensation cases between workplace and personal injuries, or the line in vaccine cases between injuries caused by vaccines and those caused by natural conditions. At this point, it is possible to introduce more bright-line rules in negligence cases to ease the administrative burden, but as of this writing, there appears to be little major movement in any of the compensation systems now in place. Inertia tends to dominate when there is no clear showing how one system dominates another.

CHAPTER 5

CAUSATION

SECTION A. INTRODUCTION

This chapter examines the topic of causation, which, in one form or another, is an indispensable element in every tort case. Once the plaintiff has established that the defendant has engaged in some wrongful conduct, she must link that wrongful conduct to the harm she suffered. In practice, that requirement of causal linkage generally raises two distinct issues: cause in fact and legal (or proximate) cause.

RESTATEMENT OF THE LAW (THIRD) OF TORTS: LIABILITY FOR PHYSICAL AND EMOTIONAL HARM

§26. Factual Cause

Tortious conduct must be a factual cause of harm for liability to be imposed. Conduct is a factual cause of harm when the harm would not have occurred absent the conduct. . . .

Comment b. "But-for" standard for factual cause: . . . With recognition that there are multiple factual causes of an event, see Comment c, a factual cause can also be described as a necessary condition for the outcome. . . .

Comment c. Tortious conduct need only be one of the factual causes of harm: An actor's tortious conduct need only be *a* [as opposed to *the*] factual cause of the other's harm. . . .

The "cause in fact" rubric addresses the sequence of events that plaintiff claims links the two parties together. In the ordinary highway collision case, for example, the defendant will triumph on the cause in fact question if he can show that the plaintiff's injury occurred before the collision. If so, the defendant did not cause (in fact) any of that preexisting harm; nor is the defendant responsible for any harm attributable to some independent event, such as another automobile or a natural event. A similar analysis carries over to far more complex causal chains, including those involving the drugs and chemicals whose ingestion or exposure may have brought about the plaintiff's disease or disability.

In the modern setting, moreover, issues of cause in fact are no longer confined to the plaintiff's search for some discrete cause of a known and certain harm. Especially thorny issues arise when the plaintiff claims that the defendant's conduct only increased the risk of injury—the so-called lost chance of survival—for harms like cancer that, if wrongfully caused, are themselves compensable. The factual causation inquiry is further complicated when multiple defendants may have contributed to a plaintiff's injury, so that it becomes necessary to apportion damages among them. One important variation on this theme arises when a plaintiff can establish that one of a group of defendants caused her harm, without knowing which one.

How should the law allocate causal responsibility when it is unclear which of a given group of manufacturers produced a fungible product that caused harm to any individual plaintiff? And how should that theory be modified if multiple plaintiffs cannot identify which of a group of defendants either manufactured or supplied the particular product that injured her?

The multiple variations on the theme of factual causation sets up the second inquiry: what actions or omissions count as a "proximate" cause of the harm. The Second Restatement substituted the bland term "legal cause" for proximate cause, but that verbal innovation has never been widely accepted, so the term "proximate cause" has been retained in RTT: LPEH §26, comment *a*, although with evident reluctance. Chapter 6 of the Third Restatement is entitled "Scope of Liability (Proximate Cause)," as the American Law Institute "fervently" hopes that the parenthetical will disappear. In any case, any literal reading of "proximate" as "nearest" misstates the historical operation of the doctrine, which asks whether more distant acts or events, in either time or space, are causally connected to the particular injury. Here, the issues are not factual, but conceptual: Once the facts are laid out, for what harms is the defendant responsible when his own actions are combined, often in long and tortuous chains, with those of other persons and/or natural events?

The traditional account of proximate cause asks whether the defendant's conduct should be regarded as a "substantial factor" in bringing about the plaintiff's harm. But that terminology is disfavored in the Third Restatement. See RTT: LPEH §26, comment *j*, which dismisses the phrase as "confusing" and sticks with the but-for or necessary condition accounts of causation. Nonetheless, the substantial factor phrase continues to be deployed. No matter what the rubric, the much-ingrained substantial factor test asks whether any of the intervening or concurrent human actions or natural events sever the causal connection between the defendant's conduct and the plaintiff's injury. The analysis begins typically in negligence cases but must also be adapted to cases of strict liability. The same issues of causation also arise with the various no-fault systems, already touched on in Chapter 4, Section E.

Analytically, the problem of proximate cause can be addressed in two distinct ways. The forward-looking approach asks whether the chain of events that in fact occurred was sufficiently "foreseeable," "natural," or "probable" for the defendant to be held liable for the ultimate harm. That judgment is made from the standpoint of the defendant *at the time* the tortious act was committed and denies recovery for those harms that are of too low probability or that do not fall "within the risk." This approach has an obvious connection with the negligence standard of liability, which generally refuses to hold a defendant liable for improbable or unforeseeable acts. In contrast, the second approach, dating back to Roman times, starts with the injury and works back toward the wrongful action of the defendant, seeking to determine whether any act or omission of a third party or the plaintiff, or any natural event, severs the causal connection between the harm and the defendant's wrongful conduct. The question of measuring, at least implicitly, antecedent probabilities is wholly irrelevant. Here the question is only whether, when all the evidence is in, it is permissible to say that the defendant "did it," that is, brought about the plaintiff's harm. This approach dominated both Roman law and the early common law, both in strict liability and negligence cases. On this view, the core case of causation is corpore corpori ("by the body to the body"), or, in the English formulation, the direct application of force. Thereafter, the more comprehensive theory sees how far back the connection can go without losing the thread. The interaction between the "foresight" and "directness" perspectives, as they are respectively called, is the subject of Section C of this chapter, which traces its historical evolution from its nineteenth-century origins to its contemporary applications. The first part of this section deals with physical injuries; the second with negligent infliction of emotional distress.

As a rough generalization, the cause in fact issues appear to have gained in importance relative to the proximate cause issues in the past generation. Why might this be so?

SECTION B. CAUSE IN FACT

1. The "But For" Test

New York Central R.R. v. Grimstad

264 F. 334 (2d Cir. 1920)

Action of Elfrieda Grimstad, administratrix of the estate of Angell Grimstad, deceased, against the New York Central Railroad Company. Judgment for plaintiff, and defendant brings error. Reversed.

WARD, C.J. This is an action under the Federal Employers' Liability Act (Comp. St. Sec. 8657–8665) to recover damages for the death of Angell Grimstad, captain of the covered barge *Grayton*, owned by the defendant railroad company. The charge of negligence is failure to equip the barge with proper life-preservers and other necessary and proper appliances, for want of which the decedent, having fallen into the water, was drowned.

The barge was lying on the port side of the steamer *Santa Clara*, on the north side of Pier 2, Erie Basin, Brooklyn, loaded with sugar in transit from Havana to St. John, N.B. The tug *Mary M*, entering the slip between Piers 1 and 2, bumped against the barge. The decedent's wife, feeling the shock, came out from the cabin, looked on one side of the barge, and saw nothing, and then went across the deck to the other side of the barge, and discovered her husband in the water about 10 feet from the barge holding up his hands out of the water. He did not know how to swim. She immediately ran back into the cabin for a small line, and when she returned with it he had disappeared.

It is admitted that the decedent at the time was engaged in interstate commerce. The court left it to the jury to say whether the defendant was negligent in not equipping the barge with life-preservers and whether, if there had been a life-preserver on board, Grimstad would have been saved from drowning.

The jury found as a fact that the defendant was negligent in not equipping the barge with life-preservers. Life-preservers and life belts are intended to be put on the body of a person before getting into the water, and would have been of no use at all to the decedent. On the other hand, life buoys are intended to be thrown to a person when in the water, and we will treat the charge in the complaint as covering life buoys.

Obviously the proximate cause of the decedent's death was his falling into the water, and in the absence of any testimony whatever on the point, we will assume that this happened without negligence on his part or on the part of the defendant. On the second question, whether a life buoy would have saved the decedent from drowning, we think the jury were left to pure conjecture and speculation. A jury might well conclude that a light near an open hatch or rail on the side of a vessel's deck would have prevented a person's falling into the hatch or into the water, in the dark. But there is nothing whatever to show that the decedent was not drowned because he did not know how to swim, nor anything to show that, if there had been a life buoy on board, the decedent's wife would have got it in time, that is, sooner than she got the small line, or, if she had, that she would have thrown it so that her husband could have seized it, or, if she did, that he would have seized it, or that, if he did, it would have prevented him from drowning.

The court erred in denying the defendant's motion to dismiss the complaint at the end of the case.

Judgment reversed.

NOTES

1. ***The Life You Save.*** What are the causal elements in a case where the asserted claim is for a failure to rescue, given the admitted duty to do so? How do these differ from the elements of a simple trespass action? In Ford v. Trident Fisheries Co., 122 N.E. 389, 390 (Mass. 1919), the decedent fell overboard from his shipping vessel and drowned. The plaintiff alleged that the defendant was negligent because its rescue boat was "lashed to the deck instead of being suspended from davits" from which it could be easily lowered. The court held that even if the defendants were negligent,

> there is nothing to show they in any way contributed to Ford's death. He disappeared when he fell from the trawler, and it does not appear that if the boat had been suspended from davits and a different method of propelling it had been used he could have been rescued.

What is the precedential value of *Grimstad*? In Kirincich v. Standard Dredging Co., 112 F.2d 163, 164 (3d Cir. 1940), "the deceased fell off a dredge close to shore and was carried away by the falling tide while shipmates tried to save him with inadequate lifesaving equipment, such inadequacy of equipment being the negligence alleged." The trial judge had dismissed plaintiff's cause of action, but the Third Circuit reversed and remanded for trial. Clark, C.J., observed in part:

> In the light, then, of this logic and these examples, would Kirincich have drowned even if a larger and more buoyant object than the inch heaving line had been thrown within two feet of him? If he could swim, even badly, there would be no doubt. Assuming he could not, we think he might (the appropriate grammatical mood) have saved himself through the help of something which he could more easily grasp. We can take judicial notice of the instinct of self-preservation that at first compensates for lack of skill. A drowning man comes to the surface and clutches at what he finds there—hence the significance of size and buoyancy in life saving apparatus. In other words, we prefer the doctrine of Judge Learned Hand in the case of Zinnel v. United States Shipping Board Emergency Fleet Corp., 10 F.2d 47, 49 [(2d Cir. 1925)]: "There of course remains the question whether they might have also said that the fault caused the loss. About that we agree no certain conclusion was possible. Nobody could, in the nature of things, be sure that the intestate would have seized the rope, or, if he had not, that it would have stopped his body. But we are not dealing with a criminal case, nor are we justified, where certainty is impossible, in insisting upon it. . . . [W]e think it a question about which reasonable men might at least differ whether the intestate would not have been saved, had it been there," to that of his colleague, Judge Hough, dissenting in that case, and concurring in the earlier case of New York Central R. Co. v. Grimstad, 2 Cir., 264 F. 334, 335.

Does it make a difference that the rescue in *Grimstad* was attempted by his wife acting alone, while in *Kirincich* the rescue effort was mounted by the decedent's shipmates? The Third Restatement endorses this hypothetical, or counterfactual, approach, noting the serious factual difficulties in marginal cases where the defendant's deviation from the accepted standard of care is slight. RTT: LPEH §26, comment *e*.

More recent cases explicitly give the jury broad powers of decision in cases of rescue at sea. In Varner v. Celebration Cruise Operator, Inc., No. 0:15-CIV-60867, 2016 WL 7508258 (S.D. Fla. Sept. 30, 2016), the decedent, extremely drunk at an evening party with his fiancée, fell overboard while three nautical miles away from the shore. His body was never recovered. The plaintiffs sued under a variety of negligence theories that pertained to

> (1) Defendant's Alcohol-related Negligence; (2) Inadequate Policies and Procedures for Safety and Security of Passengers; (3) Inadequate Rescue Policies and Procedures; (4) Negligent Rescue Efforts; (5) Inadequate Railings; and (6) Non-compliance with the Cruise Vessel Safety and Security Act of 2010 ("CVSSA").

The defendant denied both any breach of duty and any causal connection between its alleged breach of duty and the plaintiff's death. But Dimitrouleas, J., held that "Defendant is not entitled to summary judgment on whether Defendant failed to promulgate and/or enforce and/or comply with rules and/or policies to rescue passengers who fall overboard." Thus, the plaintiff was allowed to show that the defendant did not begin the rescue effort quickly enough once the decedent fell overboard and failed otherwise to conduct a reasonable search. The defendant asserted that it took "only 15 minutes" to turn the ship turned around, and that it launched the rescue boat with lights, spotlights, flashlights, and "life jackets." Plaintiffs claimed that it took "30 to 45 minutes" to start the rescue. What is the likelihood that the decedent was alive when he hit the water or could have survived at sea at night for even 15 minutes?

2. *Slip-and-Fall Cases.* Difficult questions of cause in fact are also raised in so-called slip-and-fall cases. In Reynolds v. Texas & Pacific Ry., 37 La. Ann. 694, 698 (1885), plaintiff, a 250-pound woman, after hurrying out of a lighted waiting room, fell down the unlighted steps leading to the train platform. The defendant argued that "she might well have made the mis-step and fallen even had it been broad daylight," but the court affirmed judgment for plaintiff, noting:

> We concede that this is possible, and recognize the distinction between post hoc and propter hoc. But where the negligence of the defendant greatly multiplies the chances of accident to the plaintiff, and is of a character naturally leading to its occurrence, the mere possibility that it might have happened without the negligence is not sufficient to break the chain of cause and effect between the negligence and the injury. Courts, in such matters, consider the natural and ordinary course of events, and do not indulge in fanciful suppositions. The whole tendency of the evidence connects the accident with the negligence.

3. *Products Liability Cases: Seat Belts.* In Engberg v. Ford Motor Co., 205 N.W.2d 104, 106 (S.D. 1973), the plaintiff's husband was killed when he drove his newly purchased station wagon off the highway into a ditch—a one-car accident of uncertain origin. The plaintiff claimed that the defendant's seat belt was too weak to withstand the impact of a crash by showing that the belt was found "buckled but broken" after the fatal crash, and that no blood was found inside the car. Her expert witnesses further testified that

> the seat belt severed in this case because the boot and belt were rubbing on the frame of the seat causing them to give way under the pressure of less than expectable force. He also stated that in his opinion, the design of the assembly and the installation of the belt was improper to prevent the rubbing that caused the severance. He further testified, over the defendant's objection, that the absence of internal damage to the vehicle indicated that the fatal injury occurred outside of the car and that had the seat belt remained intact and the decedent remained inside the car, the amount of injury would have been minor.
>
> [The defendant's expert witness in turn] testified that the boot and seat belt could not in any way come into contact with the frame of the seat. [He] also testified that based upon the type and location of the cut, it was his opinion that the seat belt had been severed by the metal capsule that ties together the wires of the seat and that the capsule had been moved from where it was originally installed by the manufacturer.

Additional evidence suggested that the decedent had not properly tightened his seat belt before the crash, leaving ample room for him to slip out under the belt when the crash took place. The court left the case for the jury because defendants could not show that plaintiff's version of the case was "contradicted by its undisputed physical facts," denying that it was pure "speculation" to conclude that the decedent would have survived if the seat belt had remained intact. Could either side introduce evidence to gain a directed verdict?

Seat belt cases continue to raise salient questions of causation. In Long v. TRW Safety Systems, Inc., 796 F. Supp. 2d 1005, 1011–12 (D. Ariz. 2011), a tire tread separation caused a sports utility vehicle to roll over and kill one of seven passengers while injuring a second. The court allowed the plaintiffs to reach the jury on the question of defect without expert testimony. On the causation question, it then held that "there were seven people in the vehicle when it rolled over, but the two most seriously hurt were the only passengers whose seatbelts are alleged to have failed. A jury reasonably could infer that the alleged defective seatbelts 'contributed at least "a little"' to Plaintiffs' injuries." Sound?

4. *Products Liability Cases: Baseball.* In Sanchez v. Hillerich & Bradsby Co., 128 Cal. Rptr. 2d 529, 538–41 (Ct. App. 2002), the plaintiff, a pitcher for California State University, Northridge, was struck by a line-drive hit by Correa, a University of Southern California batter, using an aluminum Air Attack 2 bat, manufactured by the defendant. The bat contained "a pressurized air bladder, which, according to its designer, substantially increases the speed at which the ball leaves the surface of the bat." The trial judge dismissed the case on the ground that "because the speed of the ball leaving the bat was never established, no causation attributed to the increased risk of use of the [bat] could be established." The Court of Appeal held that once the increased speed was established, the plaintiff's case should reach the jury:

> [A]bsent other factors (none are suggested) it follows that the ball must have reached the appellant sooner than if Correa had used a bat other than the Air Attack 2. Dr. Kent [plaintiff's expert] opined that the ball which hit Correa was traveling at a speed of up to 107.8 miles per hour, giving appellant a reaction time of .32 and .37 seconds, below the acceptable minimum time recognized by the NCAA.

Must it also be shown that the plaintiff pitcher could have reacted in time to avoid the injury had the batter been using another bat?

Sanchez was distinguished in Yeaman v. Hillerich & Bradsby Co., 570 Fed. Appx. 728, 737–41 (10th Cir. 2014), where the plaintiff, another star pitcher, was badly hurt when struck by a hit ball. Dr. Kent, the same plaintiff's expert as in *Sanchez*, estimated the ball was traveling at between 100 and 105 miles per hour when it struck the plaintiff. The plaintiff claimed that defendant's 33-inch, 30-ounce Louisville Slugger Exogrid bat, Model No. CB71X, was defective because its design featured a stiff handle and flexible barrel for "maximum trampoline effect" or "rebound." O'Brien, J., upheld the grant of a judgment for the defendant notwithstanding the jury verdict for the plaintiff:

> [W]ithout any objective evidence as to the ball exit speed expected by the ordinary baseball bat consumer or the ball exit speed produced by the Exogrid, there was no basis for a rational jury to reasonably find the Exogrid to be dangerous beyond that expected by the ordinary bat consumer.

The plaintiff's case failed on causation because Kent did not take into account the "numerous variables" that could have influenced the outcome, including "the speed and type of pitch and the ability and swing speed of the batter." The court distinguished *Sanchez* because there "the plaintiffs' evidence included the testimony of the bat's designer who said 'the bat allowed a batter to hit balls at speeds in excess of that which would allow a pitcher sufficient time to react.'" Cannot the same argument be made in *Yeaman*?

Zuchowicz v. United States

140 F.3d 381 (2d Cir. 1998)

Calabresi, J. The defendant, the United States of America, appeals from a judgment of the United States District Court for the District of Connecticut (Warren W. Eginton, Judge). This suit under the Federal Tort Claims Act, 28 U.S.C. §§1346(b), 2671–2680, was originally filed by Patricia Zuchowicz, who claimed to have developed primary pulmonary hypertension, a fatal lung condition, as a result of the defendant's negligence in prescribing an overdose of the drug Danocrine. Following Mrs. Zuchowicz's death in 1991, her husband, Steven, continued the case on behalf of his wife's estate, claiming that the defendant was responsible for her death. After a bench trial, the district court awarded the plaintiff $1,034,236.02 in damages. . . .

I. Background

A. Drug, Illness, and Death

1. The Overdose

The facts, as determined by the district court, are as follows. On February 18, 1989, Mrs. Zuchowicz filled a prescription for the drug Danocrine at the Naval Hospital pharmacy in Groton, Connecticut. The prescription erroneously instructed her to take 1600 milligrams of Danocrine per day, or twice the maximum recommended dosage. The defendant has stipulated that its doctors and/or pharmacists were negligent and violated the prevailing standard of medical care by prescribing this wrong dosage.

Mrs. Zuchowicz took the 1600 milligrams of Danocrine each day for the next month. Thereafter, from March 24 until May 30, she took 800 milligrams per day. While taking Danocrine she experienced abnormal weight gain, bloating, edema, hot flashes, night sweats, a racing heart, chest pains, dizziness, headaches, acne, and fatigue. On May 30, she was examined by an obstetrician/gynecologist in private practice who told her to stop taking the Danocrine. During the summer, she continued to experience severe fatigue and chest tightness and pain, and began having shortness of breath. In October 1989, she was diagnosed with primary pulmonary hypertension ("PPH"), a rare and fatal disease in which increased pressure in an individual's pulmonary artery causes severe strain on the right side of the heart. At the time she was diagnosed with the disease, the median life expectancy for PPH sufferers was 2.5 years. Treatments included calcium channel blockers and heart and lung transplantation.

Mrs. Zuchowicz was on the waiting list for a lung transplant when she became pregnant. Pregnant women are not eligible for transplants, and pregnancy exacerbates PPH. Mrs. Zuchowicz gave birth to a son on November 21, 1991. She died one month later, on December 31, 1991. . . .

B. The Expert Testimony . . .

[Plaintiff's expert] Dr. Matthay testified that he was confident to a reasonable medical certainty that the Danocrine caused Mrs. Zuchowicz's PPH. When pressed, he added that he believed the *overdose* of Danocrine to have been responsible for the disease. His conclusion was based on the temporal relationship between the overdose and the start of the disease and the differential etiology method of excluding other possible causes. While Dr. Matthay did not rule out *all* other possible causes of pulmonary hypertension, he did exclude all the causes of secondary pulmonary hypertension. On the basis of Mrs. Zuchowicz's history, he also ruled out all previously known drug-related causes of primary pulmonary hypertension.

Dr. Matthay further testified that the progression and timing of Mrs. Zuchowicz's disease in relation to her overdose supported a finding of drug-induced PPH. Dr. Matthay emphasized that, prior to the overdose, Mrs. Zuchowicz was a healthy, active young woman with no history of cardiovascular problems, and that, shortly after the overdose, she began experiencing symptoms of PPH such as weight gain, swelling of hands and feet, fatigue, and shortness of breath. He described the similarities between the course of Mrs. Zuchowicz's illness and that of accepted cases of drug-induced PPH, and he went on to discuss cases involving classes of drugs that are known to cause other pulmonary diseases (mainly anti-cancer drugs). He noted that the onset of these diseases, which are recognized to be caused by the particular drugs, was very similar in timing and course to the development of Mrs. Zuchowicz's illness. . . .

II

B. Were the District Court's Factual Findings with Respect to Causation Clearly Erroneous? . . .

4. Was Danocrine a But For Cause of Mrs. Zuchowicz's Illness and Death? . . .

We hold that, on the basis of Dr. Matthay's testimony alone, the finder of fact could have concluded—under Connecticut law—that Mrs. Zuchowicz's PPH was, more likely than not, caused by Danocrine. While it was not possible to eliminate all other possible causes of pulmonary hypertension, the evidence presented showed that the experts had not only excluded all causes of secondary pulmonary hypertension, but had also ruled out all the previously known drug-related causes of PPH. In addition, Dr. Matthay testified, based on his expertise in pulmonary diseases, that the progression and timing of Mrs. Zuchowicz's illness in relationship to the timing of her overdose supported a finding of *drug-induced* PPH to a reasonable medical certainty. In this respect, we note that in the case before us, unlike many toxic torts situations, there was not a long latency period between the onset of symptoms and the patient's exposure to the drug that was alleged to have caused the illness. Rather, as Dr. Matthay testified, the plaintiff began exhibiting symptoms typical of drug-induced PPH shortly after she started taking the Danocrine. Under the circumstances, we cannot say that the fact finder was clearly erroneous in determining that, more probably than not, the Danocrine caused Mrs. Zuchowicz's illness.

5. Was the Overdose a But for Cause of Mrs. Zuchowicz's Illness and Death?

To say that Danocrine caused Mrs. Zuchowicz's injuries is only half the story, however. In order for the causation requirement to be met, a trier of fact must be able to determine, by a preponderance of the evidence, that the defendant's *negligence* was responsible for the injury. In this case, defendant's negligence consisted in prescribing an overdose of Danocrine to Mrs. Zuchowicz. For liability to exist, therefore, it is necessary that the fact finder be able to conclude, more probably than not, that the *overdose* was the cause of Mrs. Zuchowicz's illness and ultimate death. The mere fact that the exposure to Danocrine was likely responsible for the disease does not suffice.

The problem of linking defendant's negligence to the harm that occurred is one that many courts have addressed in the past. A car is speeding and an accident occurs. That the car was involved and was a cause of the crash is readily shown. The accident, moreover, is of the sort that rules prohibiting speeding are designed to prevent. But is this enough to support a finding of fact, in the individual case, that *speeding* was, in fact, more probably than not, the cause of the accident? The same question can be asked when a car that was driving in violation of a minimum speed requirement on a super-highway is rear-ended. Again, it is clear that the car and its driver were causes of the accident. And the accident is of the sort that minimum speeding rules are designed to prevent. But can a fact finder conclude, without more, that the driver's negligence in *driving too slowly* led to the crash? To put it more precisely—the defendant's negligence was strongly causally linked to the accident, and the defendant was undoubtedly a *but for* cause of the harm, but does this suffice to allow a fact finder to say that the defendant's *negligence* was a *but for* cause?

At one time, courts were reluctant to say in such circumstances that the wrong could be deemed to be the cause. They emphasized the logical fallacy of *post hoc, ergo propter hoc*, and demanded some direct evidence connecting the defendant's wrongdoing to the harm. . . .

All that has changed, however. And, as is so frequently the case in tort law, Chief Judge Cardozo in New York and Chief Justice Traynor in California led the way. In various opinions, they stated that: if (a) a negligent act was deemed wrongful *because* that act increased the chances that a particular type of accident would occur, and (b) a mishap of that very sort did happen, this was enough to support a finding by the trier of fact that the negligent behavior caused the harm. Where such a strong causal link exists, it is up to the negligent party to bring in evidence denying *but for* cause and suggesting that in the actual case the wrongful conduct had not been a substantial factor.

Thus, in a case involving a nighttime collision between vehicles, one of which did not have the required lights, Judge Cardozo stated that lights were mandated precisely to reduce the risk of such accidents occurring and that this fact sufficed to show causation unless the negligent party demonstrated, for example, that in the particular instance the presence of very bright street lights or of a full moon rendered the lack of lights on the vehicle an unlikely cause. See Martin v. Herzog [*supra* Chapter 3, at 183]. . . .

The case before us is a good example of the above-mentioned principles in their classic form. The reason the FDA does not approve the prescription of new drugs at above the dosages as to which extensive tests have been performed is because all drugs involve risks of untoward side effects in those who take them. Moreover, it is often true that the higher the dosage the greater is the likelihood of such negative effects. At the approved dosages, the benefits of the particular drug have presumably been deemed worth the risks it entails. At greater than approved dosages, not only do the risks of tragic side effects (known and unknown) increase, but there is no basis on the testing that has been performed for supposing that the drug's benefits outweigh these increased risks. . . . It follows that when a negative side effect is demonstrated to be the result of a drug, and the drug was wrongly prescribed in an unapproved and excessive dosage (*i.e.* a strong causal link has been shown), the plaintiff who is injured has generally shown enough to permit the finder of fact to conclude that the excessive dosage was a substantial factor in producing the harm.

In fact, plaintiff's showing in the case before us, while relying on the above stated principles, is stronger. For plaintiff introduced some direct evidence of causation as well. On the basis of his long experience with drug-induced pulmonary diseases, one of plaintiff's experts, Dr. Matthay, testified that the timing of Mrs. Zuchowicz's illness led him to conclude that the overdose (and not merely Danocrine) was responsible for her catastrophic reaction.

Under the circumstances, we hold that defendant's attack on the district court's finding of causation is meritless. . . .

Affirmed.

NOTES

1. *Incremental Risk and Causal Connections.* As Calabresi, J., stressed, in an overdose case, the plaintiff must prove that the excess dosage caused her injury. In *Zuchowicz*, is it relevant that the current labels list the maximum permissible daily dosage for Danocrine at 400 milligrams for some conditions and 200 milligrams for others, with a strict warning against double dosing if one dose was missed? More concretely, how did Calabresi, J., decide that the excess dosage of Danocrine made the difference? Suppose that the incremental 800 milligram dosage supplied only a 5 percent benefit but increased the risk of death from 10 to 11 percent, and that no one thinks that this extra benefit is worth the extra risk. Does the 1 percent statistical increase suffice to show causation? If not, what level of increase should be required to reach a jury? For a recognition of the different causal inquiry for "incremental risk" in overdose cases, see RTT: LPEH §26, comment *f*, and illustrations 1 & 2.

2. *Switching the Burden of Proof on Causation.* In Haft v. Lone Palm Hotel, 478 P.2d 465, 474–75 (Cal. 1970), the plaintiffs brought wrongful death actions when a father and son drowned in the pool at the defendant's Palm Springs motel. The applicable statute provided that "lifeguard service shall be provided or signs shall be erected clearly indicating that such service is not provided." The defendant neither provided the lifeguard service nor posted the signs, and no evidence explained how the deaths actually took place. The court, through Tobriner, J., first observed that "to hold that a pool owner, who has failed to satisfy either of the section's alternative requirements, may limit his liability to that resulting from his 'lesser' failure to erect a sign, would of course effectively read out of the section the primary requirement of providing lifeguard service." (Is this a reasonable interpretation of the statute?) He then addressed the burden of proof on causation as follows:

> The troublesome problems concerning the causation issue in the instant case of course arise out of the total lack of direct evidence as to the precise manner in which the drownings occurred. Although the paucity of evidence on causation is normally one of the burdens that must be shouldered by a plaintiff in proving his case, the evidentiary void in the instant action results primarily from defendants' failure to provide a lifeguard to observe occurrences within the pool area. The main purpose of the lifeguard requirement is undoubtedly to aid those in danger, but an attentive guard does serve the subsidiary function of witnessing those accidents that do occur. The absence of such a lifeguard in the instant case thus not only stripped decedents of a significant degree of protection to which they were entitled, but also deprived the present plaintiffs of a means of definitively establishing the facts leading to the drownings.
>
> Clearly, the failure to provide a lifeguard greatly enhanced the chances of the occurrence of the instant drownings. In proving (1) that defendants were negligent in this respect, and (2) that the available facts, at the very least, strongly suggest that a competent lifeguard, exercising reasonable care, would have prevented the deaths, plaintiffs have gone as far as they possibly can under the circumstances in proving the requisite causal link between defendants' negligence and the accidents. To require plaintiffs to establish "proximate causation" to a greater certainty than they have in the instant case, would permit defendants to gain the advantage of the lack of proof inherent in the lifeguardless situation which they have created. Under these circumstances the burden of proof on the issue of causation should be shifted to defendants to absolve themselves if they can.

Haft's burden-shifting is one of several solutions proposed by Levmore, Probabilistic Recoveries, Restitution, and Recurring Wrongs, 19 J. Legal Stud. 691, 707–10 (1990), to the "recurring miss" problem—whereby application of the preponderance of the evidence standard leads to systematic underdeterrence in repeat situations where an actor's negligence is less than 50 percent likely to have caused a particular plaintiff's injury, but highly likely to have caused some significant fraction of the total injuries.

Recent cases have tended to confine *Haft* to the instances to which it originally applied, namely those in which there is "an evidentiary void" in direct evidence. Thus in Lopez v. Alroudhan, No. B265996, 2017 WL 1164482, at *5 (Cal. Ct. App. Mar. 29, 2017), the plaintiff was a pedestrian badly injured when struck by the defendant's car. She could not remember any of the details of the accident and sought to rely on *Haft.* Chavez, J., rebuffed that claim, noting:

> Appellant was able to provide testimony regarding the accident and her injuries, as was a police officer on the scene and various medical doctors. There is no reason to shift the burden of proof on causation to respondent. Appellant had the burden to prove her case, and the jury found that she did not succeed.

Even if the burden of proof is not shifted, should plaintiff be entitled to an instruction that the accident partially incapacitated her from giving a full account of the incident?

2. Joint and Several Liability and Multiple Causes

a. Joint and Several Liability

Before discussing multiple and indeterminate causes of a plaintiff's injury, it is useful to understand how the methods for apportioning liability relate to cause in fact determinations. Under a joint liability approach, each of several obligors—any person who bears an obligation—can be held responsible for the entire loss if the others are unable to pay. Under a several liability approach, each person has an obligation to pay only his or her proportionate share, thereby casting onto the plaintiff the risk of the insolvency of any of the codefendants. The traditional method of apportionment for multiple causes is joint and several liability. The second part of the term—"several"—captures the notion that, if all defendants are present, each pays only his proportionate share. The first—"joint"—requires any one of multiple defendants that contributed to the plaintiff's injury to pay for the full amount of the plaintiff's damages, no matter how small his contribution. See Restatement (Third) of Torts: Apportionment of Liability [RTT: AL] §17.

The first common law case to endorse joint liability was Merryweather v. Nixan, (1799) 101 Eng. Rep. 1337 (KB). The plaintiff sued two defendants for conversion of machinery belonging to the plaintiff's mill. The headnote announced: "If *A* recover in tort against two defendants, and levy the whole damages on one, that one cannot recover a moiety against the other for his contribution; aliter, in assumpsit [otherwise in contract]." *Merryweather* offers no explanation for why one defendant has a claim against the other in contract cases but lacks claim for contribution in tort cases. The usual explanation for the difference is that the law of partnership routinely provides for the pro rata division of responsibility among defendants, an objective easily achieved for monetizable obligations. Tort claims, however, do not offer that easy mode of division, so that the hostility toward apportionment in contributory negligence cases carried over to disputes between codefendants based on the common law principle that no wrongdoer could bring suit against another party whose wrong was no greater than its own. It therefore fell to the tort plaintiff to decide if one of two solvent defendants had to shoulder the entire loss: If *A* recovered $100 from *B*, thereafter *B* could not recover $50 from his codefendant, *C*, even if both were equally to blame. As a matter of initial expectations, both defendants look to be equally at risk. But in practice, the plaintiff could extract her full compensation from either defendant to the exclusion of the other. In addition, if one defendant made only partial payment, the plaintiff could then sue the second defendant for the remainder, perhaps enlisting the assistance from the settling plaintiff. Although *Merryweather* only applied to intentional conversions, in time its no-contribution rule was extended to ordinary negligence actions as well.

As a matter of contract law, a defendant saddled with full liability may obtain a partial or total indemnity from his codefendant, see RTT: AL §22. Should indemnification also be allowed in the absence of a contractual agreement? If so, under what circumstances?

Union Stock Yards Co. of Omaha v. Chicago, Burlington, & Quincy R.R.

196 U.S. 217 (1905)

[The plaintiff terminal company was responsible for moving the switching cars for the defendant railroad in its yard. One of the cars under its control had a defective nut, which either the terminal company or the railroad could have discovered by reasonable inspection. Both parties were found negligent in failing to carry out that inspection, consequently injuring the plaintiff's employee. Plaintiff then paid its employee damages, which it sought to recover from the defendant.]

Day, J. . . . Coming to the very question to be determined here, the general principle of law is well settled that one of several wrongdoers cannot recover against another wrongdoer, although he may have been compelled to pay all the damages for the wrong done. In many instances, however, cases have been taken out of this general rule, and it has been held inoperative in order that the ultimate loss may be visited upon the principal wrongdoer, who is made to respond for all the damages, where one less culpable, although legally liable to third persons, may escape the payment of damages assessed against him by putting the ultimate loss upon the one principally responsible for the injury done. These cases have, perhaps, their principal illustration in that class wherein municipalities have been held responsible for injuries to persons lawfully using the streets in a city, because of defects in the streets or sidewalks caused by the negligence or active fault of a property owner. In such cases, where the municipality has been called upon to respond because of its legal duty to keep public highways open and free from nuisances, a recovery over has been permitted for indemnity against the property owner, the principal wrongdoer, whose negligence was the real cause of the injury. . . .

In a case cited and much relied upon at the bar, Gray v. Boston Gas Light Co., 114 Mass. 149 (1873), a telegraph wire was fastened to the plaintiff's chimney without his consent, and, the weight of the wire having pulled the chimney over into the street, to the injury of a passing traveler, an action was brought against the property owner for damages, and notice was duly given to the gas company, which refused to defend. Having settled the damages at a figure which the court thought reasonable, the property owner brought suit against the gas company, and it was held liable. In the opinion the court said:

> When two parties, acting together, commit an illegal or wrongful act the party who is held responsible for the act cannot have indemnity or contribution from the other, because both are equally culpable or *particeps criminis*, and the damage results from their joint offense. This rule does not apply when one does the act or creates the nuisance, and the other does not join therein, but is thereby exposed to liability and suffers damage. He may recover from the party whose wrongful act has thus exposed him. In such cases the parties are not in *pari delicto* as to each other, though, as to third persons, either may be held liable. . . .

Other cases might be cited, which are applications of the exception engrafted upon the general rule of non-contribution among wrongdoers, holding that the law will inquire into the facts of a case of the character shown with a view to fastening the ultimate liability upon the one whose wrong has been primarily responsible for the injury sustained. . . .

The case then stands in this wise: The railroad company and the terminal company have been guilty of a like neglect of duty in failing to properly inspect the car before putting it in use by those who might be injured thereby. We do not perceive that, because the duty of inspection was first required from the railroad company, the case is thereby brought within the class which holds the one primarily responsible, as the real cause of the injury, liable to another less culpable, who may have been held to respond for damages for the injury inflicted. It is not like the case of the one who creates a nuisance in the public streets; or who furnishes a defective dock; or the case of the gas company, where it created the condition of unsafety by its own wrongful act; or the case of the defective boiler, which blew out because it would not stand the pressure warranted by the manufacturer. In all these cases the wrongful act of the one held finally liable created the unsafe or dangerous condition from which the injury resulted. The principal and moving cause, resulting in the injury sustained, was the act of the first wrongdoer, and the other has been held liable to third persons for failing to discover or correct the defect caused by the positive act of the other.

In the present case the negligence of the parties has been of the same character. Both the railroad company and the terminal company failed by proper inspection to discover the defective brake. The terminal company, because of its fault, has been held liable to one sustaining an injury thereby. We do not think the case comes within that exceptional class which permits one wrongdoer who has been mulcted in damages to recover indemnity or contribution from another.

[Judgment for defendant affirmed.]

NOTE

Contribution Versus Indemnity. In *Union Stock Yards*, should an action for contribution or indemnity have been allowed if the cost of inspection was low to the railroad and high to the stockyard? How does *Union Stock Yards* come out if the passive party (the party exposed to liability for setting the stage for the wrongful act of another) may obtain contribution or indemnity from the active one (the party that performed the wrongful act from which liability arises)? Under a rule that allows the party secondarily responsible to obtain contribution or indemnity from the party primarily responsible?

CALIFORNIA CODE OF CIVIL PROCEDURE [ENACTED 1957] §§875–877.5 (2023)

Section 875. Judgment Against Two or More Defendants; Contribution; Subrogation by Insurer; Right of Indemnity; Satisfaction of Judgment in Full.

(a) Where a money judgment has been rendered jointly against two or more defendants in a tort action there shall be a right of contribution among them as hereinafter provided.

(b) Such right of contribution shall be administered in accordance with the principles of equity.

(c) Such right of contribution may be enforced only after one tortfeasor has, by payment, discharged the joint judgment or has paid more than his pro rata share thereof. It shall be limited to the excess so paid over the pro rata share of the person so paying and in no event shall any tortfeasor be compelled to make contribution beyond his own pro rata share of the entire judgment.

(d) There shall be no right of contribution in favor of any tortfeasor who has intentionally injured the injured person.

(e) A liability insurer who by payment has discharged the liability of a tortfeasor judgment debtor shall be subrogated to his right of contribution.

(f) This title shall not impair any right of indemnity under existing law, and where one tortfeasor judgment debtor is entitled to indemnity from another there shall be no right of contribution between them.

(g) This title shall not impair the right of a plaintiff to satisfy a judgment in full as against any tortfeasor judgment debtor.

Section 876. Determination of Pro Rata Share.

(a) The pro rata share of each tortfeasor judgment debtor shall be determined by dividing the entire judgment equally among all of them.

(b) Where one or more persons are held liable solely for the tort of one of them or of another, as in the case of the liability of a master for the tort of his servant, they shall contribute a single pro rata share, as to which there may be indemnity between them.

Section 877. Release of One or More Joint Tortfeasors or Co-Obligors; Effect Upon Liability of Others.

[The section provides inter alia that a release shall not discharge any third party "unless its terms so provide."]

Section 877.5. Sliding Scale Recovery Agreement; Disclosure to Court and Jury; Service of Notice of Intent to Enter.

[This section requires prompt disclosure to the court of any agreement whereby the liability of a party will be reduced if it testifies as a witness for the plaintiff. The court shall disclose to the jury the "existence and content" of that agreement, unless disclosure will cause unfair prejudice or mislead the jury. Unless the judge rules otherwise for good cause, the agreement is only effective if other parties receive notice of an intent to enter an agreement at least 72 hours prior to entering that agreement.]

NOTE

Statutory Repudiation of the Joint and Several Liability Rule. In contrast to the stark all-or-nothing allocations of the common law, the California statute adopted a regime of pro rata liability that allowed each defendant to recover from his codefendants any amount he paid above the share he owed. Thus, if one defendant paid a full $100 judgment, he could recoup $50 in a separate action from the second defendant, so long as judgment had been entered against both. Statutory contribution was not available for intentional harms, nor did it displace any available indemnity actions. Other rules governed cases of vicarious liability. The California statute was initially passed in 1957 before the adoption of pure comparative negligence in Li v. Yellow Cab Co., 532 P.2d 1226 (Cal. 1975), *supra* Chapter 4, at 265. where plaintiff's own negligence reduces rather than bars her ultimate recovery. Does it make sense to have a regime of pure comparative negligence between plaintiffs and defendants and a regime of pro rata apportionment among defendants? How might the differing rules affect each litigant's settlement incentives?

American Motorcycle Association v. Superior Court

578 P.2d 899 (Cal. 1978)

[In this case, the California Supreme Court addresses the proper apportionment of liability in suits against multiple defendants. At the outset, the court states its conclusions as follows:

1. The doctrine subjecting multiple defendants to "joint and several liability" to a single plaintiff was neither abolished nor limited by the decision in *Li.*
2. A doctrine of partial equitable indemnity should be adopted at common law to permit apportionment of loss among codefendants on pure comparative principles.
3. The California contribution statutes do not "preclude" the development of a common law doctrine of comparative indemnity.
4. Under this system of equitable contribution, any defendant may maintain an action against any other party, whether or not joined in the original suit, but that the trial judge may postpone trial of the indemnity action in order "to avoid unduly complicating the plaintiff's suit."]

Tobriner, J. In light of these determinations, we conclude that a writ of mandate should issue, directing the trial court to permit petitioner-defendant to file a cross-complaint for partial indemnity against previously unjoined alleged concurrent tortfeasors.

1. The facts

[The plaintiff, Glen Gregos, was injured in a novice motorcycle race that he claimed was negligently organized and run by two defendants, the American Motorcycle Association (AMA) and the Viking Motorcycle Club (Viking). When he sued the AMA, it sought leave of the court to file a cross-complaint against Gregos' parents, alleging that their negligent improper supervision of their minor son contributed to the injury. It also asked declaratory relief that its portion of the judgment be reduced by the amount of the "allocable negligence" of the parents.]

2. The adoption of comparative negligence in *Li* does not warrant the abolition of joint and several liability of concurrent tortfeasors . . .

In the instant case AMA argues that the *Li* decision, by repudiating the all-or-nothing contributory negligence rule and replacing it by a rule which simply diminishes an injured party's recovery on the basis of his comparative fault, in effect undermined the fundamental rationale of the entire joint and several liability doctrine as applied to concurrent tortfeasors. . . .

AMA argues that after *Li* (1) there *is* a basis for dividing damages, namely on a comparative negligence basis, and (2) a plaintiff is no longer necessarily "innocent," for *Li* permits a negligent plaintiff to recover damages. AMA maintains that in light of these two factors it is logically inconsistent to retain joint and several liability of concurrent tortfeasors after *Li*. As we explain, for a number of reasons we cannot accept AMA's argument.

First, the simple feasibility of apportioning fault on a comparative negligence basis does not render an indivisible injury "divisible" for purposes of the joint and several liability rule. [A] concurrent tortfeasor is liable for the whole of an indivisible injury whenever his negligence is a proximate cause of that injury. In many instances, the negligence of each of several concurrent tortfeasors may be sufficient, in itself, to cause the entire injury; in other instances, it is simply impossible to determine whether or not a particular concurrent tortfeasor's negligence, acting alone, would have caused the same injury. Under such circumstances, a defendant has no equitable claim vis-à-vis an injured plaintiff to be relieved of liability for damage which he has proximately caused simply because some other tortfeasor's negligence may also have caused the same harm. In other words, the mere fact that it may be possible to assign some percentage figure to the relative culpability of one negligent defendant as compared to another does not in any way suggest that each defendant's negligence is not a proximate cause of the entire indivisible injury.

Second, abandonment of the joint and several liability rule is not warranted by AMA's claim that, after *Li*, a plaintiff is no longer "innocent." Initially, of course, it is by no means invariably true that after *Li* injured plaintiffs will be guilty of negligence. In many instances a plaintiff will be completely free of all responsibility for the accident, and yet, under the proposed abolition of joint and several liability, such a completely faultless plaintiff, rather than a wrongdoing defendant, would be forced to bear a portion of the loss if any one of the concurrent tortfeasors should prove financially unable to satisfy his proportioned share of the damages.

Moreover, even when a plaintiff is partially at fault for his own injury, a plaintiff's culpability is not equivalent to that of a defendant. In this setting, a plaintiff's negligence relates only to a failure to use due care for his own protection, while a defendant's negligence relates to a lack of due care for the safety of others. Although we recognized in *Li* that a plaintiff's self-directed negligence would justify reducing his recovery in proportion to his degree of fault for the accident,[2] the fact remains that insofar as the plaintiff's conduct creates only a risk of self-injury, such conduct, unlike that of a negligent defendant, is not tortious.

Finally, from a realistic standpoint, we think that AMA's suggested abandonment of the joint and several liability rule would work a serious and unwarranted deleterious effect on the practical ability of negligently injured persons to receive adequate compensation for their injuries. One of the principal by-products of the joint and several liability rule is that it frequently permits an injured person to obtain full recovery for his injuries even when one or more of the responsible parties do not have the financial resources to cover their liability. In such a case the rule recognizes that fairness dictates that the "wronged party should not be deprived of his right to redress," but that "[t]he wrongdoers should be left to work out between themselves any apportionment." See Summers v. Tice 199 P.2d 1, 5 (1948) [*infra* at 314]. The *Li* decision does not detract in the slightest from this pragmatic policy determination.

[The court then notes that the overwhelming weight of judicial and academic opinion supports its conclusion.]

3. Upon Reexamination of the Common Law Equitable Indemnity Doctrine in Light of the Principles Underlying *Li*, We Conclude that the Doctrine Should be Modified to Permit Partial Indemnity Among Concurrent Tortfeasors on a Comparative Fault Basis . . .

In California, as in most other American jurisdictions, the allocation of damages among multiple tortfeasors has historically been analyzed in terms of two, ostensibly mutually exclusive, doctrines: contribution and indemnification. In traditional terms, the apportionment of loss between multiple tortfeasors has been thought to present a question of contribution; indemnity, by contrast, has traditionally been viewed as concerned solely with whether a loss should be entirely shifted from one tortfeasor to another, rather than whether the loss should be shared between the two. As we shall explain, however, the dichotomy between the two concepts is more formalistic than substantive, and the common goal of both doctrines, the equitable distribution of loss among multiple tortfeasors, suggests a need for a reexamination of the relationship of these twin concepts.

Early California decisions, relying on the ancient law that "the law will not aid a wrongdoer," embraced the then ascendant common law rule denying a tortfeasor any right to contribution whatsoever. [The court then reviews the 1957 legislation set out above.]

[T]he equitable indemnity doctrine originated in the common sense proposition that when two individuals are responsible for a loss, but one of the two is more culpable than the other, it is only fair that the more culpable party should bear a greater share of the loss. Of

---

2. A question has arisen as to whether our *Li* opinion, in mandating that a plaintiff's recovery be diminished in proportion to the plaintiff's negligence, intended that the plaintiff's conduct be compared with each individual tortfeasor's negligence, with the cumulative negligence of all named defendants or with all other negligent conduct that contributed to the injury. The California BAJI Committee, which specifically addressed this issue after *Li*, concluded that "the contributory negligence of the plaintiff must be proportioned to the combined negligence of plaintiff and of all the tortfeasors, whether or not joined as parties . . . whose negligence proximately caused or contributed to plaintiff's injury."

We agree with this conclusion, which finds support in decisions from other comparative negligence jurisdictions. In determining to what degree the injury was due to the fault of the plaintiff, it is logically essential that the plaintiff's negligence be weighed against the combined total of all other causative negligence; moreover, inasmuch as a plaintiff's actual damages do not vary by virtue of the particular defendants who happen to be before the court, we do not think that the damages which a plaintiff may recover against defendants who are joint and severally liable should fluctuate in such a manner.

course, at the time the doctrine developed, common law precepts precluded any attempt to ascertain comparative fault; as a consequence, equitable indemnity, like the contributory negligence doctrine, developed as an all-or-nothing proposition.

Because of the all-or-nothing nature of the equitable indemnity rule, courts were, from the beginning, understandably reluctant to shift the entire loss to a party who was simply slightly more culpable than another. As a consequence, throughout the long history of the equitable indemnity doctrine courts have struggled to find some linguistic formulation that would provide an appropriate test for determining when the relative culpability of the parties is sufficiently disparate to warrant placing the entire loss on one party and completely absolving the other.

A review of the numerous California cases in this area reveals that the struggle has largely been a futile one. . . .

Indeed, some courts, as well as some prominent commentators, after reviewing the welter of inconsistent standards utilized in the equitable indemnity realm, have candidly eschewed any pretense of an objectively definable equitable indemnity test. . . .

If the fundamental problem with the equitable indemnity doctrine as it has developed in this state were simply a matter of an unduly vague or imprecise linguistic standard, the remedy would be simply to attempt to devise a more definite verbal formulation. In our view, however, the principal difficulty with the current equitable indemnity doctrine rests not simply on a question of terminology, but lies instead in the all-or-nothing nature of the doctrine itself. . . .

In order to attain such a system in which liability for an indivisible injury caused by concurrent tortfeasors will be borne by each individual tortfeasor "in direct proportion to [his] respective fault," we conclude that the current equitable indemnity rule should be modified to permit a concurrent tortfeasor to obtain partial indemnity from other concurrent tortfeasors on a comparative fault basis. In reaching this conclusion, we point out that in recent years a great number of courts, particularly in jurisdictions which follow the comparative negligence rule, have for similar reasons adopted, as a matter of common law, comparable rules providing for comparative contribution or comparative indemnity. . . .

Clark, J., dissenting. . . . The majority reject the *Li* principle in two ways. First, they reject it by adopting joint and several liability holding that each defendant—including the marginally negligent one—will be responsible for the loss attributable to his codefendant's negligence. To illustrate, if we assume that the plaintiff is found 30 percent at fault, the first defendant 60 percent, and a second defendant 10 percent, the plaintiff under the majority's decision is entitled to a judgment for 70 percent of the loss against each defendant, and the defendant found only 10 percent at fault may have to pay 70 percent of the loss if his codefendant is unable to respond in damages.

The second way in which the majority reject *Li*'s irresistible principle is by its settlement rules. Under the majority opinion, a good faith settlement releases the settling tortfeasor from further liability, and the "plaintiff's recovery from nonsettling tortfeasors should be diminished only by the amount that the plaintiff has actually recovered in a good faith settlement, rather than by an amount measured by the settling tortfeasor's proportionate responsibility for the injury." The settlement rules announced today may turn *Li*'s principle upside down—the extent of dollar liability may end up in inverse relation to fault.

[Clark, J., then notes that the inversion takes place under the credit rule when a central defendant settles for a small sum. Thus, if P is 30 percent responsible, D_1 is 10 percent responsible, and D_2 60 percent responsible, if D_2 settles for 20 percent, $D1$ could be held responsible for 50 percent of the loss, notwithstanding his 10 percent share of responsibility. Under the carve-out rule, P could pursue D_1 only for 10 percent of the loss no matter how much she obtained from D_2. Clark, J., also argued that if D_2 was insolvent, P could recover only 25 percent of the loss—10 percent from D_1 compared to 30 percent from P].

I do not suggest return to the old contributory negligence system. The true criticism of that system remains valid: one party should not be required to bear a loss which by definition two have caused. However, in departing from the old system of contributory negligence numerous approaches are open, but the Legislature rather than this court is the proper institution in a democratic society to choose the course. . . .

NOTES

1. *Insolvent Defendants in Joint Tortfeasor Cases.* Further complications arise with the insolvency of one or more multiple defendants. *American Motorcycle* seems to hold that the remaining defendants bear *all* of the risk of an insolvent codefendant, but Evangelatos v. Superior Court (Van Waters & Rogers, Inc., RPI), 753 P.2d 585, 590 (Cal. 1988), applied a different rule: "[M]ore recent decisions also make clear that if one or more tortfeasors prove to be insolvent and are not able to bear their fair share of the loss, the shortfall created by such insolvency should be apportioned equitably among the remaining culpable parties—both defendants and plaintiffs."

To revert to Justice Clark's 30/60/10 hypothetical, if the 60 percent defendant is insolvent, *American Motorcycle* placed 70 percent of the loss on the 10 percent defendant. In contrast, *Evangelatos* splits that 60 percent loss between plaintiff and defendant in accordance with their responsibility, so that the plaintiff can recover only 25 percent of her loss from the solvent defendant, representing his own 10 percent responsibility plus one-quarter (10 divided by 40) of the remaining 60 percent of the loss, or 15 percent. The Third Restatement adopts a similar rule: "[I]f a defendant establishes that a judgment for contribution cannot be collected fully from another defendant, the court reallocates the uncollectible portion of the damages to all other parties, including the plaintiff, in proportion to the percentages of comparative responsibility assigned to the other parties." RTT: AL §21(a). The exceptions to this rule cover intentional tortfeasors (*id.* §12), persons acting in concert (*id.* §15), vicarious liability (*id.* §13), and persons who fail to protect plaintiff from the specific risk of an intentional tort (*id.* §14).

2. *Several Liability for Multiple Defendants?* The Restatement's approach of partial reapportionment was not applied in Brown v. Keill, 580 P.2d 867, 873–74 (Kan. 1978), a car accident case involving two parties. In that case, the court held that the Kansas comparative negligence statute, Kan. Stat. Ann. §60-258a (2023), allowing recovery if plaintiff's negligence "was less than" defendant's causal negligence, abrogated the traditional rule of joint and several liability, and created several liability only. Subsection (d) provides:

> Apportioning liability. Where the comparative negligence of the parties in any action is an issue and recovery is allowed against more than one party, each such party shall be liable for that portion of the total dollar amount awarded as damages to any claimant in the proportion that the amount of such party's causal negligence bears to the amount of the causal negligence attributed to all parties against whom such recovery is allowed.

The court first held that the plain language of the statute compelled the result. It then argued that a limitation of losses for defendants was not inconsistent with sound social policy:

> The perceived purpose in adopting K.S.A. 60-258a is fairly clear. The legislature intended to equate recovery and duty to pay to degree of fault. Of necessity, this involved a change of both the doctrine of contributory negligence and of joint and several liability. There is nothing inherently fair about a defendant who is 10% at fault paying 100% of the loss, and there is no social policy that should compel defendants to pay more than their fair share of the loss. Plaintiffs now take the parties as they find them. . . . Previously, when the plaintiff had to be totally without negligence to recover and the defendants had to be merely negligent to incur an obligation

to pay, an argument could be made which justified putting the burden of seeking contribution on the defendants. Such an argument is no longer compelling because of the purpose and intent behind the adoption of the comparative negligence statute.

Under Clark's, J., hypothetical, in the event of the insolvency of the 60 percent defendant, the 10 percent defendant continues to bear 10 percent of the loss, with the rest being borne by the plaintiff. Does joint and several liability make as much sense with 100 defendants in a cumulative trauma case as with two in an accident case?

3. *Statutory Modifications of Joint and Several Liability.* The common law rule of joint and several liability has proved to be a priority for legislative reform. A chief concern has been the marginal defendant whose tiny fraction of responsibility has required it to bear the full damages attributable to more culpable, but wholly or largely insolvent, defendants. One possible response to this problem is to abolish the rule outright, as was done by statute in Colorado, Utah, and Wyoming. See Colo. Rev. Stat. §13-21-111.5 (2023); Utah Code Ann. §78B-5-818 (2023); Wyo. Stat. §1-1-109 (2023).

A second response is to relieve the plight of marginal defendants with ad hoc fixes. Thus, Iowa abolished joint liability for defendants found to be less than 50 percent at fault but retained joint liability for economic damages for defendants 50 percent or more at fault. Iowa Code §668.4 (2023). New Jersey set a 60 percent threshold for joint and several liability for both economic and noneconomic damages. N.J. Stat. §2A:15-5.3 (2023). Finally, New Hampshire allows a judgment for the full amount of damages to be entered against a codefendant found 50 or more percent at fault but allows only for several liability against a codefendant found less than 50 percent at fault. N.H. Rev. Stat. Ann. §507:7-e (2019).

In 1986, New York amended its basic code, N.Y. CPLR 1601(1), to provide that a joint tortfeasor whose culpability is 50 percent or less is not jointly liable for all of plaintiff's noneconomic damages, but only for its proportionate share. That approach was also adopted in 1986, by popular referendum, when California modified its own joint and several liability rule to counteract what the referendum identified as "the deep pocket rule." The current provision reads as follows:

Cal. Civ. Code §1431.2(2023). Several Liability for Noneconomic Damages

(a) In any action for personal injury, property damage, or wrongful death, based upon principles of comparative fault, the liability of each defendant for non-economic damages shall be several only and shall not be joint. Each defendant shall be liable only for the amount of non-economic damages allocated to that defendant in direct proportion to that defendant's percentage of fault, and a separate judgment shall be rendered against that defendant for that amount.

For rules in other states, see the compilation in the Third Restatement, RTT: AL §17, and Matthiesen, Wickert & Lehrer, S.C., Joint and Several Liability and Contribution Laws in All 50 States, available at https://www.mwl-law.com/wp-content/uploads/2018/02/JOINT-AND-SEVERAL-LIABILITY-AND-CONTRIBUTION-LAWS-CHART.pdf. By the most recent tally, seven states and the District of Columbia have pure joint and several liability, while fifteen states have pure several liability. The remaining states are "hybrid" systems, including, first, joint and several liability that places the risk of a tortfeasor's insolvency on all parties who bear responsibility for the plaintiff's damages (including the plaintiff); second, joint and several liability imposed on independent tortfeasors whose percentage of comparative responsibility exceeds a specified threshold; and third, regimes that allow for joint and several liability for economic damages but only several liability for noneconomic damages. See RTT: AL §17, comment *a*.

4. *Contribution: Strict Liability and Negligence.* *American Motorcycle* only addressed the problem of apportionment when both defendants were sued for negligence. Apportionment between the plaintiff and the defendant has, however, been allowed when the plaintiff sues on a strict liability theory. In Safeway Stores, Inc. v. Nest-Kart, 579 P.2d 441, 446 (Cal. 1978), the California Supreme Court adopted the same rule in suits between codefendants. The plaintiff was injured when a supermarket cart collapsed. The plaintiff sued Safeway, the supermarket owner, in negligence, and Nest-Kart, the cart manufacturer, in strict liability. The jury found Safeway 80 percent responsible and Nest-Kart 20 percent responsible.

Safeway's motion to apportion losses evenly between the defendants was granted, and Nest-Kart's appeal followed. On appeal, the court rejected Safeway's contention that the principles of apportionment could not operate with negligence and strict liability theories given the ease with which the jury made the 80/20 apportionment. It continued:

> Finally, we note that a contrary conclusion, which confined the operation of the comparative indemnity doctrine to cases involving solely negligent defendants, would lead to bizarre, and indeed irrational, consequences. Thus, if we were to hold that the comparative indemnity doctrine could only be invoked by a negligent defendant but not a strictly liable defendant, a manufacturer who was actually negligent in producing a product would frequently be placed in a better position than a manufacturer who was free from negligence but who happened to produce a defective product, for the negligent manufacturer would be permitted to shift the bulk of liability to more negligent cotortfeasors, while the strictly liable defendant would be denied the benefit of such apportionment.

Does *Safeway* bear on whether contributory negligence should be allowed as a defense in product liability cases? See Daly v. General Motors, *infra* Chapter 8, at 622.

5. *Choice of Settlement Rules.*

RESTATEMENT OF THE LAW (SECOND) OF TORTS

§886A. Contribution Among Tortfeasors

Comment m. Release: There are three possible solutions for the situation in which one tortfeasor pays a sum to the injured party and takes a release or covenant not to sue that does not purport to be a full satisfaction of the claim. Each has its drawbacks and no one is satisfactory.

(1) The money paid extinguishes any claim that the injured party has against the party released and the amount of his remaining claim against the other tortfeasor is reached by crediting the amount received; but the transaction does not affect a claim for contribution by another tortfeasor who has paid more than his equitable share of the obligation. . . .

(2) The money paid extinguishes both any claims on the part of the injured party and any claim for contribution by another tortfeasor who has paid more than his equitable share of the obligation and seeks contribution. [As in alternative (1), the amount of the injured party's claim against the other tortfeasors is calculated by subtracting the amount of the settlement from the plaintiff's damages.] . . .

(3) The money paid extinguishes any claim that the injured party has against the released tortfeasor and also diminishes the claim that the injured party has against the other tortfeasors by the amount of the equitable share of the obligation of the released tortfeasor. . . .

In McDermott, Inc. v. AmClyde & River Don Castings, Ltd., 511 U.S. 202 (1994), Justice Stevens noted that the first of these rules was "clearly inferior" to the others. It would not be possible to induce any defendant to settle if it knew that it could be liable in contribution to any defendant that remained in the case. At this point, the choice lay between the last two rules, neither of which allows for contribution against settling defendants. Under the credit, or pro tanto, rule, first above, the award against the nonsettling defendant is reduced by the actual amount paid by the settling defendant. Thus, if defendant *A* pays $30,000 in settlement, the plaintiff, who then receives an award of $100,000 against the second defendant, gets to recover $70,000. As Justice Stevens noted, "the settlement figure is likely to be significantly less than the settling defendant's equitable share of the loss, because settlement reflects the uncertainty of trial and provides the plaintiff with a 'war chest' with which to finance the litigation against the remaining defendants." The advantage of the second rule is that it sets out a precise number for the second defendant to pay. Its disadvantage is that it encourages each defendant to settle early so that the other defendant will be left holding the bag, which leads to the inversions between relative culpability and settlement referred to by Justice Clark in his *AMA* dissent.

The third rule, the proportionate share rule, eliminates that incentive. Under this rule, the plaintiff is treated as having two divisible claims, each with its set value. Thus, if each defendant has a 50 percent share of the loss, the initial settlement of $30,000 makes one-half of the claim disappear, so that the second defendant now is only responsible for $50,000 no matter the value of the first defendant's settlement. At this point, neither defendant has any incentive to settle early. Nor is the plaintiff likely to take a discount on either of its claim, knowing that it cannot recover the larger fraction from the second defendant.

The Achilles heel of this proposal is that someone has to determine the relative shares of the two parties to make this system work, and it is not clear when, or by whom, that determination should be made. The administration of the proportionate share rule, however, is easier when each defendant is otherwise liable for a pro rata share of the loss, as was formerly the case in admiralty law. Notwithstanding this difficulty, Justice Stevens opted for the proportionate share rule:

> It seems to us that a plaintiff's good fortune in striking a favorable bargain with one defendant gives other defendants no claim to pay less than their proportionate share of the total loss. In fact, one of the virtues of the proportionate share rule is that, unlike the *pro tanto* rule, it does not make a litigating defendant's liability dependent on the amount of a settlement negotiated by others without regard to its interests.

The *AmClyde* rule continues to gain ground. In a per curiam decision, it was applied to admiralty cases in Foss Maritime Co. v. Corvus Energy Ltd., 878 F.3d 1144, 1146 (9th Cir. 2017), which also noted that "[w]e have held that strict product liability damages are also apportioned by proportionate fault in the personal injury context, and we see no reason why that rule should not extend to property damage."

6. *Bargaining under the Pro Tanto Rule.* How do the strategic bargaining opportunities play out under the pro tanto rule? Kornhauser & Revesz, Settlements Under Joint and Several Liability, 68 N.Y.U. L. Rev. 427, 433 (1993), shows that settlement strategies under the pro tanto method depend on the correlation in the success rates on the two individual claims. One extreme possibility is that the risks of liability for the two defendants are completely *independent* — that is, the success against one defendant "does not depend upon whether the plaintiff prevails against, loses to, or settles with the other defendant." The other extreme occurs when the two risks are perfectly *correlated* — that is, success or failure against one defendant implies the same result against the other. The difference between these two situations matters for the likelihood of settlement. Thus, suppose the plaintiff has two identical

$100 claims, each with a 50 percent chance of prevailing against each defendant, but will only win the one case if she wins the other. Under the pro tanto rule she can settle the first for $25, and then retain a 50 percent chance of winning the second identical claim for $37.50 (50 percent of $75), for a total of $62.50. But if the two claims are wholly independent, settling the first claim for $25 makes that claim disappear entirely, such that the second claim, also worth $50, will also settle for $25, for a total of $50. With the correlated claims, the plaintiff essentially gives up nothing to settle the first claim. But she gives up a great deal in the second case where the claims are not duplicative.

b. Multiple Sufficient Causes

Kingston v. Chicago & N.W. Ry.

211 N.W. 913 (Wis. 1927)

OWEN, J. . . . We therefore have this situation: The northeast fire was set by sparks emitted from defendant's locomotive. This fire, according to the finding of the jury, constituted a proximate cause of the destruction of plaintiff's property. This finding we find to be well supported by the evidence. We have the northwest fire, of unknown origin. This fire, according to the finding of the jury, also constituted a proximate cause of the destruction of the plaintiff's property. This finding we also find to be well supported by the evidence. We have a union of these two fires 940 feet north of plaintiff's property, from which point the united fire bore down upon and destroyed the property. We therefore have two separate, independent, and distinct agencies, each of which constituted the proximate cause of plaintiff's damage, and either of which, in the absence of the other, would have accomplished such result.

It is settled in the law of negligence that any one of two or more joint tortfeasors, or one of two or more wrongdoers whose concurring acts of negligence result in injury, are each individually responsible for the entire damage resulting from their joint or concurrent acts of negligence. This rule also obtains "where two causes, each attributable to the negligence of a responsible person, concur in producing an injury to another, either of which causes would produce it regardless of the other, . . . because, whether the concurrence be intentional, actual, or constructive, each wrongdoer, in effect, adopts the conduct of his co-actor, and for the further reason that it is impossible to apportion the damage or to say that either perpetrated any distinct injury that can be separated from the whole. The whole loss must necessarily be considered and treated as an entirety." Cook v. M., St. P. & S.S.M.R. Co., 74 N.W. 561, 566 (1898). That case presented a situation very similar to this. One fire, originating by sparks emitted from a locomotive, united with another fire of unknown origin and consumed plaintiff's property. There was nothing to indicate that the fire of unknown origin was not set by some human agency. The evidence in the case merely failed to identify the agency. In that case it was held that the railroad company which set one fire was not responsible for the damage committed by the united fires because the origin of the other fire was not identified [and could well have been of natural, not human origins]. . . .

From our present consideration of the subject we are not disposed to criticise the doctrine which exempts from liability a wrongdoer who sets a fire which unites with a fire originating from natural causes, such as lightning, not attributable to any human agency, resulting in damage. It is also conceivable that a fire so set might unite with a fire of so much greater proportions, such as a raging forest fire, as to be enveloped or swallowed up by the greater holocaust, and its identity destroyed, so that the greater fire could be said to be an intervening or superseding cause. But we have no such situation here. These fires were of comparatively equal rank. If there was any difference in their magnitude or threatening aspect, the record indicates that the northeast fire was the larger fire and was really regarded as the menacing agency. At any rate there is no intimation or suggestion that the northeast fire was enveloped and swallowed up by the northwest fire. We will err on the side of the defendant if we regard the two fires as of equal rank.

According to well settled principles of negligence, it is undoubted that if the proof disclosed the origin of the northwest fire, even though its origin be attributed to a third person, the railroad company, as the originator of the northeast fire, would be liable for the entire damage. There is no reason to believe that the northwest fire originated from any other than human agency. It was a small fire. It had traveled over a limited area. It had been in existence but for a day. For a time it was thought to have been extinguished. It was not in the nature of a raging forest fire. The record discloses nothing of natural phenomena which could have given rise to the fire. It is morally certain that it was set by some human agency.

Now the question is whether the railroad company, which is found to have been responsible for the origin of the northeast fire, escapes liability because the origin of the northwest fire is not identified, although there is no reason to believe that it had any other than human origin. An affirmative answer to that question would certainly make a wrongdoer a favorite of the law at the expense of an innocent sufferer. The injustice of such a doctrine sufficiently impeaches the logic upon which it is founded. Where one who has suffered damage by fire proves the origin of a fire and the course of that fire up to the point of the destruction of his property, one has certainly established liability on the part of the originator of the fire. Granting that the union of that fire with another of natural origin, or with another of much greater proportions, is available as a defense, the burden is on the defendant to show that by reason of such union with a fire of such character the fire set by him was not the proximate cause of the damage. No principle of justice requires that the plaintiff be placed under the burden of specifically identifying the origin of both fires in order to recover the damages for which either or both fires are responsible. . . .

While under some circumstances a wrongdoer is not responsible for damage which would have occurred in the absence of his wrongful act, even though such wrongful act was a proximate cause of the accident, that doctrine does not obtain "where two causes, each attributable to the negligence of a responsible person, concur in producing an injury to another, either of which causes would produce it regardless of the other." This is because "it is impossible to apportion the damage or to say that either perpetrated any distinct injury that can be separated from the whole," and to permit each of two wrongdoers to plead the wrong of the other as a defense to his own wrongdoing would permit both wrongdoers to escape and penalize the innocent party who has been damaged by their wrongful acts.

The fact that the northeast fire was set by the railroad company, which fire was a proximate cause of plaintiff's damage, is sufficient to affirm the judgment. This conclusion renders it unnecessary to consider other grounds of liability stressed in respondent's brief.

By the Court.—Judgment affirmed.

NOTES

1. ***Fires: Human and Natural.*** *Kingston* addresses two situations: one in which both fires are set by humans, and a second in which only one such fire is set by humans. Is it wise to adopt a rule of joint and several liability when both fires are of human origin and a rule of no liability when only one fire is set? Why not a rule of several liability that holds the named defendant responsible for half of the damage regardless of how the other fire was set? Which rule gives the railroad the proper incentives to take the optimal level of care?

What weight should be attached when the two fires cause harm to plaintiff at slightly different times? Consider these three situations. Case 1: Fire *A*, of natural origin, burns plaintiff's premises. Minutes later, fire *B*, set by defendant, reaches plaintiff's property. Fire *B* would have destroyed plaintiff's property if fire *A* had not destroyed it first. Case 2: Same sequence of events, only fire *A* is of human origin and *B* is of natural origin. Should the twice-cursed plaintiff be better off in the second case than she is in the first? Case 3: Same as above, only both fires are of human origin.

2. *Restatement Views on the Joint Causation Cases.* The Third Restatement strongly endorses the view that all joint tortfeasors are fully responsible for the undivided consequences of their own actions.

RESTATEMENT OF THE LAW (THIRD) OF TORTS: LIABILITY FOR PHYSICAL AND EMOTIONAL HARM

§27. Multiple Sufficient Causes

If multiple acts occur, each of which under §26 alone would have been a factual cause of the physical harm at the same time in the absence of the other act(s), each act is regarded as a factual cause of the harm.

The Restatement separately discusses a number of different types of cause and conduct:

- **Synergistic cause:** Where two or more causes' combined effect is greater than the sum of their parts. For example, when neither of two fires alone would be sufficient to destroy the plaintiff's property, each defendant's negligence is a factual cause of the harm. *Id.*, comment *a*.
- **Overdetermined cause:** All actors held liable where a subset of them committing that act would have sufficed to cause the harm at issue. For example, if three men combine to push a car over a cliff, all are liable even if the force applied by any two would have been sufficient. *Id.*, comment *f.*

Suppose that the probability of harm given *A*'s acts alone is 40 percent, and that the probability of harm given *B*'s acts alone is 20 percent. When both acts occur, should the losses be allocated by a two-to-one ratio, or divided evenly among defendants? See Rizzo & Arnold, Causal Apportionment in the Law of Torts: An Economic Theory, 80 Colum. L. Rev. 1399 (1980). For an alternative view, see Moore, Causation and Responsibility 410 (2009): "[I]f each of two fires is sufficient for the destruction of a house, then it follows that neither fire is independently necessary for the house's destruction. On the usual counterfactual theory of causation . . . that means that neither fire caused the destruction of the house." If so, then what did?

Yet another influential approach to these joint causation cases is found in Wright, Causation in Tort Law, 73 Calif. L. Rev. 1735, 1775 (1985), which introduces the so-called Necessary Element of a Sufficient Set Test of causation. Under this view, if each of three persons helps push a car over a cliff when the action of any two would suffice, each person counts as cause. If so, how should the losses be apportioned among them?

3. *Apportionment of Damages.* In many cases of multiple causation, no portion of the harm is uniquely attributable to any particular defendant. But what if some causal segregation is possible? On that question, RST §433A, reproduced below, has proved hugely influential. The Third Restatement also endorses apportionment when there is a "reasonable basis for the factfinder to determine . . . the amount of damages separately caused" by each party. See RTT: AL §26(b), also below.

RESTATEMENT OF THE LAW (SECOND) OF TORTS

§433A. Apportionment of Harm to Causes

(1) Damages for harm are to be apportioned among two or more causes where
(a) there are distinct harms, or
(b) there is a reasonable basis for determining the contribution of each cause to a single harm.
(2) Damages for any other harm cannot be apportioned among two or more causes.

Comment d. Divisible harm: . . . [W]here the cattle of two or more owners trespass upon the plaintiff's land and destroy his crop, the aggregate harm is a lost crop, but it may nevertheless be apportioned among the owners of the cattle, on the basis of the number owned by each, and the reasonable assumption that the respective harm done is proportionate to that number. . . .

RESTATEMENT OF THE LAW (THIRD) OF TORTS: APPORTIONMENT OF LIABILITY

§26. Apportionment of Liability When Damages Can Be Divided by Causation

(b) Damages can be divided by causation when the evidence provides a reasonable basis for the factfinder to determine:
(1) that any legally culpable conduct of a party or other relevant person to whom the factfinder assigns a percentage of responsibility was a legal cause of less than the entire damages for which the plaintiff seeks recovery and
(2) the amount of damages separately caused by that conduct.
Otherwise, the damages are indivisible and thus the injury is indivisible. . . .

The cases that address these apportionment problems are legion. In Smith v. J.C. Penney Co., Inc., 525 P.2d 1299, 1305–06 (Or. 1974), the plaintiff was wearing a coat purchased from J.C. Penney made of flammable material supplied, as the jury found, by defendant Bunker-Ramo. The coat was set ablaze by a fire started through the negligence of the employees of another defendant, the Enco Service Station. Bunker-Ramo contended that because "there is no way to segregate the damages as between the various defendants," plaintiff should not recover from any of them. The court, however, thought otherwise:

> There was evidence in this case that as a practical matter plaintiff's injuries were indivisible; that is, the jury could not make any reasonable determination that certain injuries were caused by the gasoline fire and other injuries were caused by the coat.
>
> An employee of the Enco Service Station had gasoline sprayed on his trousers and was engulfed in the same fire as plaintiff, yet suffered only minor burns to his legs. The jury could infer from this that plaintiff would not have incurred severe burns to her lower extremities if she had not been wearing the coat. There was evidence that burning material dripped from the coat, although there was no direct evidence that such dripping material landed on plaintiff's legs or feet. There was evidence that the burning coat radiated such heat that the jury could find it burned plaintiff's lower extremities. There also was testimony that the fierce burning of the coat and the emission of gases in the process would have impeded a wearer from rapidly escaping a fire.

> Most important is that there is evidence that the greatest injury to plaintiff arises out of the totality of her condition. There is testimony that she is physically and psychologically permanently disabled and unable to lead a normal life. This cannot be attributed to a burn on her foot, her head, or her body but only to her entire condition.

Should the Enco Service Station be held liable for the full extent of the damage, given that its employee suffered only minor burns from the same fire?

More recently, the apportionment issues under RST §433A have surfaced on the question whether it is proper to apportion damages for injuries caused by both smoking and asbestos exposure. In Carter v. Wallace & Gale Asbestos Settlement Trust, 96 A.3d 147, 151 (Md. 2014), the plaintiffs sued only asbestos and not tobacco companies. Green, J., refused to allow apportionment, holding on the strength of expert evidence that it was not possible to "differentiate between the two causes because the two exposures 'are not just additive, they are synergistic which means they multiply exposures.' " The decision rested in part on Maryland's continued treatment of contributory negligence as a total bar against recovery, which in turn rests on the difficulty of apportionment in scenarios such as these. On this ground, should the plaintiff be totally barred from all recovery by contributory negligence or assumption of risk? Is apportionment impossible in synergistic cases?

3. Indeterminate Causes

a. Alternative Liability

Summers v. Tice

199 P.2d 1 (Cal. 1948)

Carter, J. Each of the two defendants appeals from a judgment against them in an action for personal injuries. Pursuant to stipulation the appeals have been consolidated.

Plaintiff's action was against both defendants for an injury to his right eye and face as the result of being struck by bird shot discharged from a shotgun. The case was tried by the court without a jury and the court found that on November 20, 1945, plaintiff and the two defendants were hunting quail on the open range. Each of the defendants was armed with a 12 gauge shotgun loaded with shells containing 7-½ size shot. Prior to going hunting plaintiff discussed the hunting procedure with defendants, indicating that they were to exercise care when shooting and to "keep in line." In the course of hunting plaintiff proceeded up a hill, thus placing the hunters at the points of a triangle. The view of defendants with reference to plaintiff was unobstructed and they knew his location. Defendant Tice flushed a quail which rose in flight to a 10-foot elevation and flew between plaintiff and defendants. Both defendants shot at the quail, shooting in plaintiff's direction. At that time defendants were 75 yards from plaintiff. One shot struck plaintiff in his eye and another in his upper lip. Finally it was found by the court that as the direct result of the shooting by defendants the shots struck plaintiff as above mentioned and that defendants were negligent in so shooting and plaintiff was not contributorily negligent.

[The court upholds the findings below on defendants' negligence and plaintiff's lack of contributory negligence and assumption of risk.]

The problem presented in this case is whether the judgment against both defendants may stand. It is argued by defendants that they are not joint tort feasors, and thus jointly and severally liable, as they were not acting in concert, and that there is not sufficient evidence to show which defendant was guilty of the negligence which caused the injuries—the shooting by Tice or that by Simonson. Tice argues that there is evidence to show that the shot which struck plaintiff came from Simonson's gun because of admissions allegedly made by him to third persons and no evidence that they came from his gun. Further in connection with the latter contention, the court failed to find on plaintiff's allegation in his complaint that he did not know which one was at fault—did not find which defendant was guilty of the negligence which caused the injuries to plaintiff.

Considering the last argument first, we believe it is clear that the court sufficiently found on the issue that defendants were jointly liable and that thus the negligence of both was the cause of the injury or to that legal effect. It found that both defendants were negligent and "That as a direct and proximate result of the shots fired by *defendants, and each of them,* a birdshot pellet was caused to and did lodge in plaintiff's right eye and that another birdshot pellet was caused to and did lodge in plaintiff's upper lip." In so doing the court evidently did not give credence to the admissions of Simonson to third persons that he fired the shots, which it was justified in doing. It thus determined that the negligence of both defendants was the legal cause of injury—or that both were responsible. Implicit in such finding is the assumption that the court was unable to ascertain whether the shots were from the gun of one defendant or the other or one shot from each of them. The one shot that entered plaintiff's eye was the major factor in assessing damages and that shot could not have come from the gun of both defendants. It was from one or the other only.

It has been held that where a group of persons are on a hunting party, or otherwise engaged in the use of firearms, and two of them are negligent in firing in the direction of a third person who is injured thereby, both of those so firing are liable for the injury suffered by the third person, although the negligence of only one of them could have caused the injury. (Moore v. Foster, 182 Miss. 15 [(1938)]; Oliver v. Miles, 144 Miss. 852 [(1926)].) These cases speak of the action of defendants as being in concert as the ground of decision, yet it would seem they are straining that concept and the more reasonable basis appears in Oliver v. Miles, supra. There two persons were hunting together. Both shot at some partridges and in so doing shot across the highway injuring plaintiff who was travelling on it. The court stated they were acting in concert and thus both were liable. The court then stated: "We think that . . . each is liable for the resulting injury to the boy, although no one can say definitely who actually shot him. *To hold otherwise would be to exonerate both from liability, although each was negligent, and the injury resulted from such negligence.*" [Emphasis added.]

When we consider the relative position of the parties and the results that would flow if plaintiff was required to pin the injury on one of the defendants only, a requirement that the burden of proof on that subject be shifted to defendants becomes manifest. They are both wrongdoers—both negligent toward plaintiff. They brought about a situation where the negligence of one of them injured the plaintiff, hence it should rest with them each to absolve himself if he can. The injured party has been placed by defendants in the unfair position of pointing to which defendant caused the harm. If one can escape, the other may also and plaintiff is remediless. Ordinarily defendants are in a far better position to offer evidence to determine which one caused the injury. . . .

Cases are cited for the proposition that where two or more tort feasors acting independently of each other cause an injury to plaintiff, they are not joint tort feasors and plaintiff must establish the portion of the damage caused by each, even though it is impossible to prove the portion of the injury caused by each. In view of the foregoing discussion it is apparent that defendants in cases like the present one may be treated as liable on the same basis as joint tort feasors, and hence the last-cited cases are distinguishable inasmuch as they involve independent tort feasors.

In addition to that, however, it should be pointed out that the same reasons of policy and justice shift the burden to each of defendants to absolve himself if he can—relieving the wronged person of the duty of apportioning the injury to a particular defendant, apply here where we are concerned with whether plaintiff is required to supply evidence for the apportionment of damages. If defendants are independent tort feasors and thus each liable for the damage caused by him alone, and, at least, where the matter of apportionment is incapable of proof, the innocent wronged party should not be deprived of his right to redress. The wrongdoers should be left to work out between themselves any apportionment. Some of the cited cases refer to the difficulty of apportioning the burden of damages between the independent tortfeasors, and say that where factually a correct division cannot be made, the trier of fact may make it the best it can, which would be more or less a guess, stressing the factor that the wrongdoers are not in a position to complain of uncertainty. . . .

The judgment is affirmed.

NOTE

Alternative Liability. Prior to *Summers*, some courts were more reluctant to indulge in the fancy footwork needed to apportion harm. In Adams v. Hall, 2 Vt. 9, 11 (1829), the plaintiff's sheep were killed by two dogs, each owned by two separate defendants. Once the evidence showed that the two dogs did not have a common owner, the court refused to allow the plaintiff to recover against either. "Hall was under no obligation to keep the other defendant's dog from killing sheep; nor *vice versa.* Then, shall each become liable for the injury done by the other's dog, merely because the dogs, without the knowledge or consent of the owners did the mischief in company? We think not." Hutchinson, J., then analogized the case to one where two servants of different owners combined to destroy property without the knowledge and consent of their masters, and concluded that there too neither master would be liable.

Summers differs from *Kingston*, in which *both A and B* are causally responsible, because in *Summers either A or B, but not both* is causally responsible for the plaintiff's harm. Is a regime of joint and several liability equally appropriate for both situations? A regime whereby each defendant is liable only for 50 percent of the harm? On the court's reasoning in *Summers*, what result if ten persons were in the hunting party? One hundred? How would the decision look if both defendants were covered by liability insurance issued by the same carrier?

Summers v. Tice has been endorsed by RST §433B(3), and RTT: LPEH §28(b), comment *f*, so long as both defendants acted "tortiously." *Id.*, comment *i*.

RESTATEMENT OF THE LAW (THIRD) OF TORTS: LIABILITY FOR PHYSICAL AND EMOTIONAL HARM

§28. Burden of Proof

(b) When the plaintiff sues all of multiple actors and proves that each engaged in tortious conduct that exposed the plaintiff to a risk of harm and that the tortious conduct of one or more of them caused the plaintiff's harm but the plaintiff cannot reasonably be expected to prove which actor or actors caused the harm, the burden of proof, including both production and persuasion, on factual causation is shifted to the defendants.

Illustration 6: Reed, a pedestrian, was injured by a sofa that was negligently or intentionally thrown from an upper-story hotel room during the celebration of an NCAA basketball championship. Reed sues all of the occupants of the 47 rooms from which the sofa might have been thrown. Reed must prove which of the defendants was responsible for throwing the sofa; the burden shifting provided in this Subsection is unavailable to Reed in his suit because he has not shown that the occupants of each of the 47 rooms acted tortiously. The result would be the same if two sofas fell simultaneously, one thrown negligently or intentionally from one room and the other not due to negligence of the occupant of the other room, and Reed, not knowing from where the sofa that fell on him came, sued the occupants of both rooms. Each of the possible causes of harm must be tortious for this Subsection to be invoked.

b. Market Share Liability

Sindell v. Abbott Laboratories

607 P.2d 924 (Cal. 1980)

Mosk, J. This case involves a complex problem both timely and significant: may a plaintiff, injured as the result of a drug administered to her mother during pregnancy, who knows the type of drug involved but cannot identify the manufacturer of the precise product, hold liable for her injuries a maker of a drug produced from an identical formula?

Plaintiff Judith Sindell brought an action against eleven drug companies . . . on behalf of herself and other women similarly situated.* The complaint alleges as follows:

Between 1941 and 1971, defendants were engaged in the business of manufacturing, promoting, and marketing diethylstilbesterol (DES), a drug which is a synthetic compound of the female hormone estrogen. [After the drug entered the public domain in 1938, perhaps as many as 300 national, regional, and local producers manufactured the identical drug.] The drug was administered to plaintiff's mother and the mothers of the class she represents [other women and girls from California who were exposed to DES in utero], for the purpose of preventing miscarriage. In 1947, the Food and Drug Administration authorized the marketing of DES as a miscarriage preventative, but only on an experimental basis, with a requirement that the drug contain a warning label to that effect. . . .

In 1971, the Food and Drug Administration ordered defendants to cease marketing and promoting DES for the purpose of preventing miscarriages, and to warn physicians and the public that the drug should not be used by pregnant women because of the danger to their unborn children.

During the period defendants marketed DES, they knew or should have known that it was a carcinogenic substance, that there was a grave danger after varying periods of latency it would cause cancerous [adenocarcinoma] and precancerous growths [adenosis] in the daughters of the mothers who took it, and that it was ineffective to prevent miscarriage. Nevertheless, defendants continued to advertise and market the drug as a miscarriage preventative. They failed to test DES for efficacy and safety; the tests performed by others, upon which they relied, indicated that it was not safe or effective. In violation of the authorization of the Food and Drug Administration, defendants marketed DES on an unlimited basis rather than as an experimental drug, and they failed to warn of its potential danger.

Because of defendants' advertised assurances that DES was safe and effective to prevent miscarriage, plaintiff was exposed to the drug prior to her birth. She became aware of the danger from such exposure within one year of the time she filed her complaint. As a result of the DES ingested by her mother, plaintiff developed a malignant bladder tumor which was

* [The California Supreme Court noted that class certification was not discussed in the trial court: "The plaintiff class alleged consists of 'girls and women who are residents of California and who have been exposed to DES before birth and who may or may not know that fact or the dangers' to which they were exposed." — Eds.]

removed by surgery. She suffers from adenosis and must constantly be monitored by biopsy or colposcopy to insure early warning of further malignancy.

The first cause of action alleges that defendants were jointly and individually negligent in that they manufactured, marketed and promoted DES as a safe and efficacious drug to prevent miscarriage, without adequate testing or warning, and without monitoring or reporting its effects.

A separate cause of action alleges that defendants are jointly liable regardless of which particular brand of DES was ingested by plaintiff's mother because defendants collaborated in marketing, promoting and testing the drug, relied upon each other's tests, and adhered to an industry-wide safety standard. DES was produced from a common and mutually agreed upon formula as a fungible drug interchangeable with other brands of the same product; defendants knew or should have known that it was customary for doctors to prescribe the drug by its generic rather than its brand name and that pharmacists filled prescriptions from whatever brand of the drug happened to be in stock. . . .

Each cause of action alleges that defendants are jointly liable because they acted in concert, on the basis of express and implied agreements, and in reliance upon and ratification and exploitation of each other's testing and marketing methods.

Plaintiff seeks compensatory damages of $1 million and punitive damages of $10 million for herself. For the members of her class, she prays for equitable relief in the form of an order that defendants warn physicians and others of the danger of DES and the necessity of performing certain tests to determine the presence of disease caused by the drug, and that they establish free clinics in California to perform such tests. . . .

We begin with the proposition that, as a general rule, the imposition of liability depends upon a showing by the plaintiff that his or her injuries were caused by the act of the defendant or by an instrumentality under the defendant's control. The rule applies whether the injury resulted from an accidental event or from the use of a defective product.

There are, however, exceptions to this rule. Plaintiff's complaint suggests several bases upon which defendants may be held liable for her injuries even though she cannot demonstrate the name of the manufacturer which produced the DES actually taken by her mother. The first of these theories, classically illustrated by Summers v. Tice[, 199 P.2d 1 (Cal. 1948), *supra* at 314] places the burden of proof of causation upon tortious defendants in certain circumstances. The second basis of liability emerging from the complaint is that defendants acted in concert to cause injury to plaintiff. There is a third and novel approach to the problem, sometimes called the theory of "enterprise liability," but which we prefer to designate by the more accurate term of "industry-wide" liability, which might obviate the necessity for identifying the manufacturer of the injury-causing drug. We shall conclude that these doctrines, as previously interpreted, may not be applied to hold defendants liable under the allegations of this complaint. However, we shall propose and adopt a fourth basis for permitting the action to be tried, grounded upon an extension of the *Summers* doctrine.

I

Plaintiff places primary reliance upon cases which hold that if a party cannot identify which of two or more defendants caused an injury, the burden of proof may shift to the defendants to show that they were not responsible for the harm. This principle is sometimes referred to as the "alternative liability" theory.

[The court then discusses Summers v. Tice and Ybarra v. Spangard, 154 P.2d 687 (1944), *supra* Chapter 3, at 211, as seminal cases in the development of "alternative liability."]

Defendants assert that these principles are inapplicable here. First, they insist that a predicate to shifting the burden of proof under *Summers-Ybarra* is that the defendants must have greater access to information regarding the cause of the injuries than the plaintiff, whereas in the present case the reverse appears. . . .

Here, as in *Summers*, the circumstances of the injury appear to render identification of the manufacturer of the drug ingested by plaintiff's mother impossible by either plaintiff or defendants, and it cannot reasonably be said that one is in a better position than the other to make the identification. Because many years elapsed between the time the drug was taken and the manifestation of plaintiff's injuries she, and many other daughters of mothers who took DES, are unable to make such identification. Certainly there can be no implication that plaintiff is at fault in failing to do so—the event occurred while plaintiff was *in utero*, a generation ago.

On the other hand, it cannot be said with assurance that defendants have the means to make the identification. In this connection, they point out that drug manufacturers ordinarily have no direct contact with the patients who take a drug prescribed by their doctors. Defendants sell to wholesalers, who in turn supply the product to physicians and pharmacies. Manufacturers do not maintain records of the persons who take the drugs they produce, and the selection of the medication is made by the physician rather than the manufacturer. Nor do we conclude that the absence of evidence on this subject is due to the fault of defendants. While it is alleged that they produced a defective product with delayed effects and without adequate warnings, the difficulty or impossibility of identification results primarily from the passage of time rather than from their allegedly negligent acts of failing to provide adequate warnings. Thus Haft v. Lone Palm Hotel[, 478 P.2d 465 (Cal. 1970), *supra* at 298], upon which plaintiff relies, is distinguishable.

It is important to observe, however, that while defendants do not have means superior to plaintiff to identify the maker of the precise drug taken by her mother, they may in some instances be able to prove that they did not manufacture the injury-causing substance. In the present case, for example, one of the original defendants was dismissed from the action upon proof that it did not manufacture DES until after plaintiff was born.

Thus we conclude the fact defendants do not have greater access to information which might establish the identity of the manufacturer of the DES which injured plaintiff does not per se prevent application of the *Summers* rule.

Nevertheless, plaintiff may not prevail in her claim that the *Summers* rationale should be employed to fix the whole liability for her injuries upon defendants, at least as those principles have previously been applied. There is an important difference between the situation involved in *Summers* and the present case. There, all the parties who were or could have been responsible for the harm to the plaintiff were joined as defendants. Here, by contrast, there are approximately 200 drug companies which made DES, any of which might have manufactured the injury-producing drug.

Defendants maintain that, while in *Summers* there was a 50 percent chance that one of the two defendants was responsible for the plaintiff's injuries, here since any one of 200 companies which manufactured DES might have made the product which harmed plaintiff, there is no rational basis upon which to infer that any defendant in this action caused plaintiff's injuries, nor even a reasonable possibility that they were responsible.

These arguments are persuasive if we measure the chance that any one of the defendants supplied the injury-causing drug by the number of possible tortfeasors. In such a context, the possibility that any of the five defendants supplied the DES to plaintiff's mother is so remote that it would be unfair to require each defendant to exonerate itself. There may be a substantial likelihood that none of the five defendants joined in the action made the DES which caused the injury, and that the offending producer not named would escape liability altogether. While we propose, *infra*, an adaptation of the rule in *Summers* which will substantially overcome these difficulties, defendants appear to be correct that the rule, as previously applied, cannot relieve plaintiff of the burden of proving the identity of the manufacturer which made the drug causing her injuries.

II

The second principle upon which plaintiff relies is the so-called "concert of action" theory. . . .

. . . The gravamen of the charge of concert is that defendants failed to adequately test the drug or to give sufficient warning of its dangers and that they relied upon the tests performed by one another and took advantage of each others' promotional and marketing techniques. These allegations do not amount to a charge that there was a tacit understanding or a common plan among defendants to fail to conduct adequate tests or give sufficient warnings, and that they substantially aided and encouraged one another in these omissions. . . .

III

[The court rejects an "enterprise theory" of liability in the DES cases.]

IV

If we were confined to the theories of *Summers* and [a case about enterprise theory], we would be constrained to hold that the judgment must be sustained [for the defendant]. Should we require that plaintiff identify the manufacturer which supplied the DES used by her mother or that all DES manufacturers be joined in the action, she would effectively be precluded from any recovery. As defendants candidly admit, there is little likelihood that all the manufacturers who made DES at the time in question are still in business or that they are subject to the jurisdiction of the California courts. There are, however, forceful arguments in favor of holding that plaintiff has a cause of action.

In our contemporary complex industrialized society, advances in science and technology create fungible goods which may harm consumers and which cannot be traced to any specific producer. The response of the courts can be either to adhere rigidly to prior doctrine, denying recovery to those injured by such products, or to fashion remedies to meet these changing needs. Just as Justice Traynor in his landmark concurring opinion in Escola v. Coca Cola Bottling Co.[, 150 P.2d 436 (1944), *infra* Chapter 8, at 557], recognized that in an era of mass production and complex marketing methods the traditional standard of negligence was insufficient to govern the obligations of manufacturer to consumer, so should we acknowledge that some adaptation of the rules of causation and liability may be appropriate in these recurring circumstances. The Restatement comments that modification of the *Summers* rule may be necessary in a situation like that before us.

The most persuasive reason for finding plaintiff states a cause of action is that advanced in *Summers*: as between an innocent plaintiff and negligent defendants, the latter should bear the cost of the injury. Here, as in *Summers*, plaintiff is not at fault in failing to provide evidence of causation, and although the absence of such evidence is not attributable to the defendants either, their conduct in marketing a drug the effects of which are delayed for many years played a significant role in creating the unavailability of proof.

From a broader policy standpoint, defendants are better able to bear the cost of injury resulting from the manufacture of a defective product. As was said by Justice Traynor in *Escola*, "[t]he cost of an injury and the loss of time or health may be an overwhelming misfortune to the person injured, and a needless one, for the risk of injury can be insured by the manufacturer and distributed among the public as a cost of doing business." 150 P.2d at 441. The manufacturer is in the best position to discover and guard against defects in its products and to warn of harmful effects; thus, holding it liable for defects and failure to warn of harmful effects will provide an incentive to product safety. These considerations are particularly significant where medication is involved, for the consumer is virtually helpless to protect himself from serious, sometimes permanent, sometimes fatal, injuries caused by deleterious drugs.

Where, as here, all defendants produced a drug from an identical formula and the manufacturer of the DES which caused plaintiff's injuries cannot be identified through no fault of plaintiff, a modification of the rule of *Summers* is warranted. As we have seen, an undiluted *Summers* rationale is inappropriate to shift the burden of proof of causation to defendants because if we measure the chance that any particular manufacturer supplied the injury-causing product by the number of producers of DES, there is a possibility that none of the five defendants in this case produced the offending substance and that the responsible manufacturer, not named in the action, will escape liability.

But we approach the issue of causation from a different perspective: we hold it to be reasonable in the present context to measure the likelihood that any of the defendants supplied the product which allegedly injured plaintiff by the percentage which the DES sold by each of them for the purpose of preventing miscarriage bears to the entire production of the drug sold by all for that purpose. Plaintiff asserts in her briefs that Eli Lilly and Company and 5 or 6 other companies produced 90 percent of the DES marketed. If at trial this is established to be the fact, then there is a corresponding likelihood that this comparative handful of producers manufactured the DES which caused plaintiff's injuries, and only a 10 percent likelihood that the offending producer would escape liability.[28]

If plaintiff joins in the action the manufacturers of a substantial share of the DES which her mother might have taken, the injustice of shifting the burden of proof to defendants to demonstrate that they could not have made the substance which injured plaintiff is significantly diminished. While 75 to 80 percent of the market is suggested as the requirement by [Comment, DES and a Proposed Theory of Enterprise Liability, 46 Fordham L. Rev. 963, 996 (1978) [hereinafter Fordham Comment]], we hold only that a substantial percentage is required.

The presence in the action of a substantial share of the appropriate market also provides a ready means to apportion damages among the defendants. Each defendant will be held liable for the proportion of the judgment represented by its share of that market unless it demonstrates that it could not have made the product which caused plaintiff's injuries. In the present case, as we have seen, one DES manufacturer was dismissed from the action upon filing a declaration that it had not manufactured DES until after plaintiff was born. Once plaintiff has met her burden of joining the required defendants, they in turn may cross-complaint against other DES manufacturers, not joined in the action, which they can allege might have supplied the injury-causing product.

Under this approach, each manufacturer's liability would approximate its responsibility for the injuries caused by its own products. Some minor discrepancy in the correlation between market share and liability is inevitable; therefore, a defendant may be held liable for a somewhat different percentage of the damage than its share of the appropriate market would justify. It is probably impossible, with the passage of time, to determine market share with mathematical exactitude. But just as jury cannot be expected to determine the

28. The Fordham Comment explains the connection between percentage of market share and liability as follows: "[I]f X Manufacturer sold one-fifth of all the DES prescribed for pregnancy and identification could be made in all cases, X would be the sole defendant in approximately one-fifth of all cases and liable for all the damages in those cases. Under alternative liability, X would be joined in all cases in which identification could not be made, but liable for only one-fifth of the total damages in these cases. X would pay the same amount either way. Although the correlation is not, in practice, perfect [footnote omitted], it is close enough so that defendants' objections on the ground of fairness lose their value." [*Id.* at 994.]

precise relationship between fault and liability in applying the doctrine of comparative fault (Li v. Yellow Cab Co.[, 532 P.2d 1226 (1975), *supra* Chapter 4, at 265]) or partial indemnity (American Motorcycle Ass'n v. Superior Court[, 578 P.2d 899 (Cal. 1978), *supra* at 302]), the difficulty of apportioning damages among the defendant producers in exact relation to their market share does not seriously militate against the rule we adopt. As we said in *Summers* with regard to the liability of independent tortfeasors, where a correct division of liability cannot be made "the trier of fact may make it the best it can." 199 P.2d at 5.

We are not unmindful of the practical problems involved in defining the market and determining market share, but these are largely matters of proof which properly cannot be determined at the pleading stage of these proceedings. Defendants urge that it would be both unfair and contrary to public policy to hold them liable for plaintiff's injuries in the absence of proof that one of them supplied the drug responsible for the damage. Most of their arguments, however, are based upon the assumption that one manufacturer would be held responsible for the products of another or for those of all other manufacturers if plaintiff ultimately prevails. But under the rule we adopt, each manufacturer's liability for an injury would be approximately equivalent to the damages caused by the DES it manufactured.

The judgments are reversed.

Richardson, J., dissenting. . . . With particular reference to the matter before us, and in the context of products liability, the requirement of a causation element has been recognized as equally fundamental. . . . Indeed, an inability to prove this causal link between defendant's conduct and plaintiff's injury has proven fatal in prior cases brought against manufacturers of DES by persons who were situated in positions identical to those of plaintiffs herein. . . . According to the majority, in the present case plaintiffs have openly conceded that they are unable to identify the particular entity which manufactured the drug consumed by their mothers. In fact, plaintiffs have joined only *five* of the approximately *two hundred* drug companies which manufactured DES. Thus, the case constitutes far more than a mere factual variant upon the theme composed in Summers v. Tice, wherein plaintiff joined as codefendants the *only* two persons who could have injured him. . . . In the present case, in stark contrast, it remains wholly speculative and conjectural whether *any* of the five named defendants actually caused plaintiffs' injuries.

The fact that plaintiffs cannot tie defendants to the injury-producing drug does not trouble the majority for it declares that the *Summers* requirement of proof of actual causation by a named defendant is satisfied by a joinder of those defendants who have *together* manufactured "*a substantial percentage*" of the DES which has been marketed. Notably lacking from the majority's expression of its new rule, unfortunately, is any definition or guidance as to what should constitute a "substantial" share of the relevant market. The issue is entirely open-ended and the answer, presumably, is anyone's guess. . . .

In adopting the foregoing rationale the majority rejects over 100 years of tort law which required that before tort liability was imposed a "matching" of defendant's conduct and plaintiff's injury was absolutely essential. Furthermore, in bestowing on plaintiffs this new largess the majority sprinkles the rain of liability upon all the joined defendants alike — those who may be tortfeasors and those who may have had nothing at all to do with plaintiffs' injury — and an added bonus is conferred. Plaintiffs are free to pick and choose their targets. . . .

NOTES

1. ***Calculating Market Shares.*** Calculating market shares has proven difficult because DES was sold for many different uses in many different tablet sizes, making a firm's gross DES sales a poor indicator of its share of the DES market directed to pregnant women. In addition, the plaintiffs were born in different years in which the market composition varied. Half were also born outside of California. *Sindell* settled in September 1983, before discovery was taken on any of these factual issues. The partial information on market shares led the court in McCormack v. Abbott Laboratories, 617 F. Supp. 1521, 1527 (D. Mass. 1985), to proceed as follows: Let each defendant establish its (small) share, and then divide the remainder equally among the remaining defendants. "Assume hypothetically, five prima facie defendants, of whom one shows an actual share of 12%. The four remaining defendants will each be potentially liable for 22%." This system of allocation prevents any plaintiff from charging any defendant the share attributable to absent third parties. "Assume hypothetically, five prima facie defendants who show that their actual shares are, respectively, 5%, 10%, 15%, 20% and 25%. Plaintiff could recover a maximum of 75% of her damages."

Sindell originally held that each defendant could be held liable for the shares of absent or insolvent defendants no matter how small its own share of the market. The California Supreme Court stepped back from that holding in two stages. In Murphy v. E.R. Squibb & Sons, Inc., 710 P.2d 247, 255 (Cal. 1985), it held that the "substantial share" requirement of *Sindell* was not met when the plaintiff sued only one manufacturer, Squibb, with a 10 percent market share. Subsequently in Brown v. Superior Court (Abbott Laboratories, RPI), 751 P.2d 470 (Cal. 1988), Mosk, J., held that defendant was responsible only for its proportionate share of the loss, so that the entire loss could not be thrown on a defendant with an "insignificant" market share.

2. *Exculpatory Evidence?* In Hymowitz v. Eli Lilly & Co., 539 N.E.2d 1069, 1078 (N.Y. 1989), the New York Court of Appeals first noted that *Sindell* based the proportionate liability of each defendant pharmaceutical company on its sales in the "national market" for DES used in pregnancy. *Hymowitz* then concluded that since liability was "based on the over-all risk produced," no exculpatory evidence could be allowed in individual cases. Thus, a defendant could be found liable even if it could demonstrate with certainty that it did not produce the tablets in question. The court reasoned that, while defendant's exculpation evidence, if permitted, would allow it to escape liability in a given case, that evidence would not reduce its overall burden, because its *increased* share of liability for the remaining cases in the pool exactly offsets its saving in the individual case. Since gains and losses net out, it is cheaper administratively in the long run if *no one* can exonerate himself in the individual case. Is the *Hymowitz* approach dependent upon all DES victims' seeking compensation for their injuries? On all jurisdictions adopting the same approach to market share calculation?

3. *Market Share Liability in Lead Cases.* In Skipworth v. Lead Industries Ass'n, 690 A.2d 169, 172, 173 (Pa. 1997), the parents of a child who was treated for lead poisoning five times in three years sued several manufacturers of lead pigment (contained in paint) and a trade association, Lead Industries Association, Inc. (LIA). Plaintiff invoked multiple theories of liability, including market share liability. The trial court granted summary judgment in favor of defendants and the Superior Court affirmed. The Pennsylvania Supreme Court declined to adopt market share liability by distinguishing lead pigment from DES:

> Pennsylvania . . . follows the general rule that a plaintiff, in order to recover, must establish that a particular defendant's negligence was the proximate cause of her injuries. Adoption of the market share liability theory would result in a significant departure from this rule. . . . Application of market share liability to lead paint cases such as this one would lead to a distortion of liability which would be so gross as to make determinations of culpability arbitrary and unfair.

The court focused on two key differences between the lead pigment and DES cases. "First, the relevant time period in question is far more extensive than the relevant time period in a DES case [nine months of pregnancy]." Thus, the plaintiff in *Skipworth* did not know which application of paint in her residence had caused the lead poisoning, and could not narrow the relevant time span from the time the house was built (1870) to the last time paint was applied (1977). Second, "lead paint, as opposed to DES, is not a fungible product."

> [The lack of fungibility] is . . . fatal to [plaintiff's] claim. . . . Market share liability is grounded on the premise that it ensures that "each manufacturer's liability would approximate its responsibility for the injuries caused by its own products." *Sindell*, 607 P.2d at 937. Yet, in this case, apportioning liability based upon a manufacturer defendant's share of the market . . . would not serve to approximate that defendant's responsibility for injuries caused by its lead paint. For example, a manufacturer whose lead product had a lower bioavailability than average would have caused less damage that its market share would indicate. Thus, application of market share to such a manufacturer would impose on it a disproportionately high share of the damages awarded.

The suits against manufacturers of lead pigment, rebuffed in *Skipworth*, received a much warmer reception in Thomas v. Mallett, 701 N.W.2d 523, 562, 563 (Wis. 2005), where Butler, J., allowed an infant plaintiff injured by lead poisoning to sue, in addition to the family landlord, the lead pigment manufacturers under a risk-contribution theory—a variation on *Sindell*'s market-share liability. Butler, J., first held that lead carbonate, the active agent in the defendants' pigment, was a fungible product, as lead pigments differed only in "degree, not function," because "white lead carbonates were produced utilizing 'virtually identical chemical formulas' such that all white lead carbonates were 'identically defective.' " He then held that the risk contribution theory could still apply even though "the record indicates that lead poisoning can stem from the ambient air, many foods, drinking water, soil, and dust," and further that the want of "any signature injury" was no obstacle to the application of the theory. Finally, he concluded the pigment manufacturers actually magnified the risk through their aggressive promotion of white lead carbonate, even despite the awareness of the toxicity of lead. Which of these factors bear on the risk contribution theory? Wilcox, J., dissented on the ground that the majority's theory meant that

> the defendants, lead pigment manufacturers, can be held liable for a product they may or may not have produced, which may or may not have caused the plaintiff's injuries, based on conduct that may have occurred over 100 years ago when some of the defendants were not even part of the relevant market.

In 2013, in response to *Thomas*, the Wisconsin legislature enacted a law that imposed a number of limiting factors—e.g., the manufacturer must have produced the product within twenty-five years of "the date that the claimant's cause of action accrued," and the product in question must have been distributed without any labeling that identified the manufacturer or distributor—which effectively withdrew the risk-contribution theory of liability from the majority of toxic tort cases. See Wis. Stat. Ann. §895.046 (2023).

4. *Market Share: Beyond DES.* A few states have been willing to extend market share liability beyond DES cases. The Hawaii Supreme Court held that market share liability applied against defendant manufacturers of blood products, from which the plaintiff, a hemophiliac, allegedly contracted HIV. Smith v. Cutter Biological, Inc., 823 P.2d 717 (Haw. 1991). A federal district court applying Florida law also imposed market share liability in a blood products case. Ray v. Cutter Laboratories, 754 F. Supp. 193 (M.D. Fla. 1991).

Other courts have taken their cue from *Skipworth*, refusing to extend *Sindell* beyond fungible products like DES. Pooshs v. Philip Morris USA, Inc., 904 F. Supp. 2d 1009, 1032 (N.D. Cal. 2012) refused to apply the theory to cigarettes. Shackil v. Lederle Laboratories, 561 A.2d 511, 523 (N.J. 1989) declined to apply it to diphtheria-pertussis-tetanus (DPT) vaccine, noting that the dangerous pertussis component was prepared in different ways, with different risk levels, by different providers. Finally, Hamilton v. Beretta U.S.A. Corp., 750

N.E.2d 1055, 1067 (N.Y. 2001), refused to extend *Hymowitz* to gun manufacturers, noting that "guns are not identical, fungible products."

In State v. Exxon Mobil Corp., 126 A.3d 266, 298 (N.H. 2015), a truncated version of market share evidence was allowed to establish a causal connection when New Hampshire sued ExxonMobil for the release of Methyl Tertiary Butyl Ether (MTBE) into the state's groundwater system, allegedly causing some $236 million in damages. Dalianis, C.J., held that the trial court had rightly adapted the market share theory to this case:

> [T]he evidence established that MTBE gasoline is a fungible product, that the fungibility of MTBE gasoline allows it to be commingled at nearly every step of the gasoline distribution system, and that commingling prevents the State from tracing a molecule of MTBE gasoline from the refinery to New Hampshire so that the State cannot identify the refiner of the MTBE gasoline that caused the harm. Thus, because the State could not identify the tortfeasor responsible for its injury, under market share liability the burden of identification shifted to Exxon.

Several scholars have endorsed market share liability to apportion liability among fossil fuel companies, based on their share of fossil fuel sales, as a way to deal with climate change. See Burger, Wentz & Horton, The Law and Science of Climate Change Attribution, 45 Colum. J. Envtl. L. 57, 201 (2020); Wentz & Franta, Liability for Public Deception: Linking Fossil Fuel Disinformation to Climate Damages, 52 Envtl. L. Rep. (Envtl. Law Inst.) 10995, 11004 (2022). How might fractions of the impact of climate change be calculated into damages attributable to fossil fuels? See *infra* Chapter 7, on public nuisance.

c. *Loss of Chance of Survival*

Herskovits v. Group Health Cooperative
664 P.2d 474 (Wash. 1983)

Dore, J. This appeal raises the issue of whether an estate can maintain an action for professional negligence as a result of failure to timely diagnose lung cancer, where the estate can show probable reduction in statistical chance for survival but cannot show and/or prove that with timely diagnosis and treatment, decedent probably would have lived to normal life expectancy.

Both counsel advised that for the purpose of this appeal we are to *assume* that the respondent Group Health Cooperative of Puget Sound and its personnel negligently failed to diagnose Herskovits' cancer on his first visit to the hospital and *proximately* caused a 14 percent reduction in his chances of survival. It is undisputed that Herskovits had less than a 50 percent chance of survival at all times herein.

The main issue we will address in this opinion is whether a patient, with less than a 50 percent chance of survival, has a cause of action against the hospital and its employees if they are negligent in diagnosing a lung cancer which reduces his chances of survival by 14 percent.... [The trial judge granted defendant's motion for summary judgment.]

I

... Dr. Ostrow [plaintiff's expert] testified that if the tumor was a "stage 1" tumor in December 1974, Herskovits' chance of a 5-year survival would have been 39 percent. In June 1975, his chances of survival were 25 percent assuming the tumor had progressed to "stage 2." Thus, the delay in diagnosis may have reduced the chance of a 5-year survival by 14 percent....

Plaintiff contends that medical testimony of a reduction of chance of survival from 39 percent to 25 percent is sufficient evidence to allow the proximate cause issue to go to the jury. Defendant Group Health argues conversely that Washington law does not permit such testimony on the issue of medical causation and requires that medical testimony must be at least sufficiently definite to establish that the act complained of "probably" or "more likely than not" caused the subsequent disability. It is Group Health's contention that plaintiff must prove that Herskovits "probably" would have survived had the defendant not been allegedly negligent; that is, the plaintiff must prove there was at least a 51 percent chance of survival. . . .

II

This court has held that a person who negligently renders aid and consequently increases the risk of harm to those he is trying to assist is liable for any physical damages he causes. Brown v. MacPherson's, Inc., 545 P.2d 13 (Wash. 1975). In *Brown*, the court cited Restatement (Second) of Torts §323 (1965), which reads:

> One who undertakes . . . to render services to another which he should recognize as necessary for the protection of the other's person or things, is subject to liability to the other for physical harm resulting from his failure to exercise reasonable care to perform his undertaking, if
>
> (a) his failure to exercise such care increases the risk of such harm, . . .

This court heretofore has not faced the issue of whether, under section 323(a), proof that the defendant's conduct increased the risk of death by decreasing the chances of survival is sufficient to take the issue of proximate cause to the jury. Some courts in other jurisdictions have allowed the proximate cause issue to go to the jury on this type of proof. These courts emphasized the fact that defendants' conduct deprived the decedents of a "significant" chance to survive or recover, rather than requiring proof that with absolute certainty the defendants' conduct caused the physical injury. The underlying reason is that it is not for the wrongdoer, who put the possibility of recovery beyond realization, to say afterward that the result was inevitable.

Other jurisdictions have rejected this approach, generally holding that unless the plaintiff is able to show that it was *more likely than not* that the harm was caused by the defendant's negligence, proof of a decreased chance of survival is not enough to take the proximate cause question to the jury. Cooper v. Sisters of Charity, Inc., 272 N.E.2d 97 (Ohio 1971). These courts have concluded that the defendant should not be liable where the decedent more than likely would have died anyway.

The ultimate question raised here is whether the relationship between the increased risk of harm and Herskovits' death is sufficient to hold Group Health responsible. Is a 36 percent (from 39 percent to 25 percent) reduction in the decedent's chance for survival sufficient evidence of causation to allow the jury to consider the possibility that the physician's failure to timely diagnose the illness was the proximate cause of his death? We answer in the affirmative. To decide otherwise would be a blanket release from liability for doctors and hospitals any time there was less than a 50 percent chance of survival, regardless of how flagrant the negligence.

Conclusion

. . . We reject Group Health's argument that plaintiffs *must show* that Herskovits "probably" would have had a 51 percent chance of survival if the hospital had not been negligent. We hold that medical testimony of a reduction of chance of survival from 39 percent to 25 percent is sufficient evidence to allow the proximate cause issue to go to the jury.

Causing reduction of the opportunity to recover (loss of chance) by one's negligence, however, does not necessitate a total recovery against the negligent party for all damages caused by the victim's death. Damages should be awarded to the injured party or his family based only on damages caused directly by premature death, such as lost earnings and additional medical expenses, etc.

We reverse the trial court and reinstate the cause of action.

Pearson, J., concurring. I agree with the majority that the trial court erred in granting defendant's motion for summary judgment. I cannot, however, agree with the majority's reasoning in reaching this decision.

[Pearson, J., then conducts an exhaustive review of the cases and explicitly adopts the position in King, Causation, Valuation, and Chance in Personal Injury Torts Involving Preexisting Conditions and Future Consequences, 90 Yale L.J. 1353 (1981).]

King's basic thesis is explained in the following passage, which is particularly pertinent to the case before us.

> Causation has for the most part been treated as an all-or-nothing proposition. Either a loss was caused by the defendant or it was not. . . . A plaintiff ordinarily should be required to prove by the applicable standard of proof that the defendant caused the loss in question. *What* caused a loss, however, should be a separate question from what the *nature and extent* of the loss are. This distinction seems to have eluded the courts, with the result that lost chances in many respects are compensated either as certainties or not at all.
>
> To illustrate, consider the case in which a doctor negligently fails to diagnose a patient's cancerous condition until it has become inoperable. Assume further that even with a timely diagnosis the patient would have had only a 30% chance of recovering from the disease and surviving over the long term. There are two ways of handling such a case. Under the traditional approach, this loss of a not-better-than-even chance of recovering from the cancer would not be compensable because it did not appear more likely [than] not that the patient would have survived with proper care. Recoverable damages, if any, would depend on the extent to which it appeared that cancer killed the patient sooner than it would have with timely diagnosis and treatment, and on the extent to which the delay in diagnosis aggravated the patient's condition, such as by causing additional pain. A more rational approach, however, would allow recovery for the loss of the chance of cure even though the chance was not better than even. The probability of long-term survival would be reflected in the amount of damages awarded for the loss of the chance. While the plaintiff here could not prove by a preponderance of the evidence that he was denied a cure by the defendant's negligence, he could show by a preponderance that he was deprived of a 30% chance of a cure. [90 Yale L.J. at 1363–64.]

Under the all-or-nothing approach typified by Cooper v. Sisters of Charity, Inc., a plaintiff who establishes that but for the defendant's negligence the decedent had a 51-percent chance of survival may maintain an action for that death. The defendant will be liable for all damages arising from the death, even though there was a 49-percent chance it would have occurred despite his negligence. On the other hand, a plaintiff who establishes that but for the defendant's negligence the decedent had a 49-percent chance of survival recovers nothing.

[The dissent of Brachtenberg, J., is omitted.]

Dolliver, J., dissenting. . . . I favor the opposing view and believe the reasoning in Cooper v. Sisters of Charity, Inc., also cited by the majority, is more persuasive. In discussing the rule to be adopted the Ohio Supreme Court stated:

> . . . Traditional proximate cause standards require that the trier of the facts, at a minimum, must be provided with evidence that a result was more likely than not to have been caused by an act, in the absence of any intervening cause.
>
> Lesser standards of proof are understandably attractive in malpractice cases where physical well being, and life itself, are the subject of litigation. The strong intuitive sense of humanity tends to emotionally direct us toward a conclusion that in an action for wrongful death an injured person should be compensated for the loss of any chance for survival, regardless of its remoteness. However, we have trepidations that such a rule would be so loose that it would produce more injustice than justice. Even though there exists authority for a rule allowing recovery based upon proof of causation by evidence not meeting the standard of probability, we are not persuaded by their logic. . . .

We consider the better rule to be that in order to comport with the standard of proof of proximate cause, plaintiff in a malpractice case must prove that defendant's negligence, *in probability*, proximately caused the death. (Citations omitted.) *Cooper*, at 251–252.

NOTES

1. ***Judicial Response to the Lost Chance Doctrine.*** The "lost chance" doctrine continues to divide the courts. One tally indicated that twenty-two states have adopted lost chance, sixteen have rejected it, six have deferred on deciding the issue, and six have not yet addressed the issue. Koch, Comment, Whose Loss Is It Anyway? Effects of the "Lost-Chance" Doctrine on Civil Litigation and Medical Malpractice, 88 N.C. L. Rev. 595, 606–11 (2010). If the doctrine is accepted, how should it be applied? More concretely, what is the relevance of the 36 percent "reduction in survival" figure to Dore's, J., analysis? How does the case come out if we posit that the missed diagnosis increased the risk of death from 61 percent to 75 percent, which places the increased risk of death at 14/75, or 18.66 percent? What result if the lost chance reduced the five-year survival rate from 5 percent to 0? Or increased the chance of death from 95 percent to 100 percent?

The lost chance doctrine is addressed in RTT: LPEH §26, comment *n*, in line with recent cases that have invoked it to cover both missed diagnosis and inappropriate or delayed treatment. In Holton v. Memorial Hospital, 679 N.E.2d 1202, 1213 (Ill. 1997), the court embraced the lost chance doctrine, in part out of its concerns with incentives: "Disallowing tort recovery in medical malpractice actions on the theory that a patient was already too ill to survive or recover may operate as a disincentive on the part of health care providers to administer quality medical care to critically ill or injured patients." In most cases, the measure of damages is computed simply by looking at the percentage reduction in the value of life or limb involved in the individual case, allowing for a 14 percent recovery (39 percent minus 25 percent) in *Herskovits*.

RESTATEMENT OF THE LAW (THIRD) OF TORTS: LIABILITY FOR PHYSICAL AND EMOTIONAL HARM

§26. Factual Cause

Comment n. Lost opportunity or lost chance as harm: Concomitant with [the] reconceptualization of the harm for a plaintiff unable to show a probability in excess of 50 percent is an adjustment of the damages to which the plaintiff is entitled. Rather than full damages for the adverse outcome, the plaintiff is only compensated for the lost opportunity. . . . These decisions are a response to inadequate (and unavailable) information about what would have been the course of a specific patient's medical condition if negligence, typically in failing to diagnose, refer, or otherwise provide proper treatment, had not occurred. Lost chance thus serves to ameliorate what would otherwise be insurmountable problems of proof. . . .

Lost chance cases often raise complex factual disputes relating both to whether the defendant was negligent and what kind of lost chance was created. In Dickhoff v. Green, 836 N.W.2d 321 (Minn. 2013), Anderson, J., allowed the lost chance doctrine based upon the defendant's failure to diagnose the newborn plaintiff's cancer when it was a small lump, possibly a cyst, on an early well-baby care visit. An early detection would have allowed for about a 60 percent chance of recovery. The late detection, over a year later, when the tumor was advanced, made it highly likely that the plaintiff would die. The parties differed on how often the plaintiff's mother made reference to the lump, and the plaintiff conceded that painful therapy was needed even with an early diagnosis. But the court concluded that it "should be beyond dispute that a patient regards a chance to survive or achieve a more favorable medical outcome as something of value."

2. *The Incentive Effects of the Lost Chance Doctrine.* The states that still reject the lost chance rule are uneasy about how it fits into the larger system of damage compensation. See Fennell v. Southern Maryland Hospital Center, Inc., 580 A.2d 206, 214 (Md. 1990), in which the court wrote:

> If loss of chance damages are to be recognized, amendments to the wrongful death statute should also be considered. As a class, medical malpractice plaintiffs benefit from the fact that they are entitled to recover 100% of their damages from a defendant whose negligence caused only 51% of their loss because it is more probable than not that the defendant's negligence caused the loss. Reciprocally, a defendant whose negligence caused less than 50% of a plaintiff's loss pays nothing because it is [more] probable that the negligence did not cause the loss. If a plaintiff whose decedent had a 49% chance of survival, which was lost through negligent treatment, is permitted to recover 49% of the value of the decedent's life, then a plaintiff whose decedent had a 51% chance of survival, which was lost through negligent treatment, perhaps ought to have recovery limited to 51% of the value of the life lost. The latter result would require a change in our current wrongful death statute.

For a statutory endorsement of the no lost chance position, see Mich. Comp. Laws Ann. §600.2912a(2) (2023): "In an action alleging medical malpractice . . . the plaintiff cannot recover for loss of an opportunity to survive or an opportunity to achieve a better result unless the opportunity was greater than 50%."

What about other tort actions? *Fennell*'s concern can be recast as an inquiry into the optimal level of deterrence under the tort law. Under the lost chance doctrine, errors in individual cases will not "cancel out" in the long run, so that defendants may be systematically overtaxed for harms that they did *not* cause. Consider a group of 100 cases. Defendant has a 25 percent chance of causing the death in 50 of them and a 75 percent chance of causing the death in the other 50. On balance, the defendant has caused half the deaths [(0.25 × 50) + (0.75 × 50) = 50]. Yet under the *Herskovits* rule, the defendant will be charged for 62.5 deaths [(0.25 × 50) + (1 × 50) = 62.5], which leads to overdeterrence. The *Fennell* rule tends to yield better results because, even though the defendants are undercharged when the chance of loss is less than 50 percent, they are overcharged when it is more. The two errors balance each other out, at least if the losses are symmetrically distributed about a mean of 50 percent probability, in which case the all-or-nothing rule reduces the level of error below what it would be with a proportionate share rule. See Kaye, The Limits of the Preponderance of the Evidence Standard: Justifiably Naked Statistical Evidence and Multiple Causation, 1982 Am. B. Found. Res. J. 487.

This conclusion does not hold, however, in the "recurring miss" situation (see *supra* at 298), which refers to when the defendant undertakes a large number of similar actions that are each less than 50 percent likely to cause harm. The refusal to allow any plaintiff to recover now results in systematic underdeterrence, because a defendant who is, say, 40 percent responsible for loss in each of 100 cases pays nothing at all. See Shavell, Economic Analysis of Accident Law 117 (1987), criticizing the 50 percent threshold on the ground that it "will result in injurers' never being liable for the losses they cause; it may thus provide grossly inadequate incentives to reduce risk." What should be done if the percentage reduction in life chances is uncertain?

3. *Compensation for Future Tortious Risk Only.* The probabilistic tests of causation also can be pressed into service to calculate current awards for tortious risk that has not ripened into actual injury. Suppose a release of radioactive materials increases by 10 percent the expected number of cancers in a community over the next 30 years, from 100 to 110. The

50 percent cutoff denies recovery in all cases, and thus leads to the underdeterrence noted by Levmore (see *supra* at 298) and Shavell. Yet holding the defendant liable in all 110 cancer cases would force the defendant to pay for 100 cancers that he did not cause, thereby inducing him to take excessive precautions.

One way to align the incentives is to require the defendant to compensate the "tortious risk" today, even before the occurrence of actual injury. Professor Robinson so argues in Probabilistic Causation and Compensation for Tortious Risk, 14 J. Legal Stud. 779 (1985). Should, for example, a 10 percent increase in risk trigger 110 actions today, each for about 9 percent of present discounted value, necessarily barring all future claims when they arise? Most courts have avoided this huge administrative hassle when no one can quantify the increase in risk or identify which individuals fall into the exposed class. One variation on this theme was allowed in Jackson v. Johns-Manville Sales Corp., 781 F.2d 394, 413, 414 (5th Cir. 1986), where a plaintiff, who had already contracted asbestosis, was awarded a recovery for "probable future consequences" in light of the 50 percent chance of contracting cancer thereafter.

4. *Enhanced Risk of Injury and Medical Monitoring.* The enhanced risk of future injury has led to many class actions to recover the costs of medical monitoring of potential future diseases. In Friends for All Children, Inc. v. Lockheed Aircraft Corp., 746 F.2d 816, 818 (D.C. Cir. 1984), Starr, J., broke new ground by holding that Lockheed had to supply diagnostic tests to about forty adopted Vietnamese children living in France prior to final judgment because they "faced irreparable injury unless they promptly obtained diagnostic examinations." Allowing costs for medical monitoring was stoutly rejected as a matter of federal common law in Metro-North Commuter Railroad v. Buckley, 521 U.S. 424 (1997). Several states have followed suit. In Henry v. Dow Chemical Co., 701 N.W.2d 684, 690–91 (Mich. 2005), the plaintiffs sought to recover medical monitoring expenses for their exposure to the dioxin component of Agent Orange that Dow manufactured. Noting that a physical injury has long been a part of the negligence claim, Corrigan, J., explained that in his view the physical injury requirement reduced "speculations about the extent to which a plaintiff possesses a cognizable legal claim," and the dangers of fraud. He then noted that it required a legislative function to decide which individuals were class members:

> How far from the Tittibawassee River must a plaintiff live in order to have a cognizable claim? What evidence of exposure to dioxin will be required to support such a claim? What level of medical research is sufficient to support a claim that exposure to dioxin, in contrast to exposure to another chemical, will give rise to a cause of action?

In re NCAA Student-Athlete Concussion Injury Litigation, 314 F.R.D. 580, 585–86 (N.D. Ill. 2016), involved a class action settlement that made these complex arrangements for medical monitoring of athletes suspected of suffering concussion injuries:

> The NCAA and its insurers will pay $70 million to create a Medical Monitoring Fund (the "Fund"). The Fund will be used to pay the expenses associated with the Medical Monitoring Program, including: Screening Questionnaires; Medical Evaluations; Notice and Administrative Costs; Medical Science Committee Costs; approved Attorneys' Fees and Costs; and Class Representatives' Service Awards.
>
> The Medical Monitoring Program (the "Program") will last for a period of fifty years. If the funding for the Medical Monitoring Program is depleted before the fifty-year period ends, the Settlement Class Members may pursue individual *or* class claims seeking medical monitoring, and the statute of limitations will be tolled during the fifty-year period. In addition, as part of the settlement, the NCAA also will provide $5 million in additional funds for concussion-related research over the course of the first ten years of the Medical Monitoring Period.

Dougan v. Sikorsky Aircraft Corp., 251 A.3d 583 (Conn. 2020), took the opposite approach. Employees showing subclinical signs of injury for exposure to asbestos, without having any physical manifestations of actual injury, filed a class action suit seeking medical monitoring. The defendants had started major plant renovations in 2009, but ceased work when small quantities of asbestos were found. Robinson, C.J., affirming summary judgment for the defendants, did not dispute that medical monitoring was appropriate in some cases. Nonetheless, he insisted that, in light of the low probability of injury and the long latency period of asbestos-related harm, it was not appropriate in this case.

S

4. Proof of Factual Causation

General Electric Co. v. Joiner
522 U.S. 136 (1997)

Rehnquist, C.J. delivered the opinion of the court. We granted certiorari in this case to determine what standard an appellate court should apply in reviewing a trial court's decision to admit or exclude expert testimony under Daubert v. Merrell Dow Pharmaceuticals, Inc., 509 U.S. 579 (1993). We hold that abuse of discretion is the appropriate standard. We apply this standard and conclude that the District Court in this case did not abuse its discretion when it excluded certain proffered expert testimony.

I

Respondent Robert Joiner began work as an electrician in the Water & Light Department of Thomasville, Georgia (City) in 1973. This job required him to work with and around the City's electrical transformers, which used a mineral-based dielectric fluid as a coolant. Joiner often had to stick his hands and arms into the fluid to make repairs. The fluid would sometimes splash onto him, occasionally getting into his eyes and mouth. In 1983 the City discovered that the fluid in some of the transformers was contaminated with polychlorinated biphenyls (PCB's). PCB's are widely considered to be hazardous to human health. Congress, with limited exceptions, banned the production and sale of PCB's in 1978.

Joiner was diagnosed with small cell lung cancer in 1991. He sued petitioners in Georgia state court the following year. Petitioner Monsanto manufactured PCB's from 1935 to 1977; petitioners General Electric and Westinghouse Electric manufactured transformers and dielectric fluid. In his complaint Joiner linked his development of cancer to his exposure to PCB's and their derivatives, polychlorinated dibenzofurans (furans) and polychlorinated dibenzodioxins (dioxins). Joiner had been a smoker for approximately eight years, his parents had both been smokers, and there was a history of lung cancer in his family. He was thus perhaps already at a heightened risk of developing lung cancer eventually. The suit alleged that his exposure to PCB's "promoted" his cancer; had it not been for his exposure to these substances, his cancer would not have developed for many years, if at all.

Petitioners removed the case to federal court. Once there, they moved for summary judgment. They contended that (1) there was no evidence that Joiner suffered significant exposure to PCB's, furans, or dioxins, and (2) there was no admissible scientific evidence that PCB's promoted Joiner's cancer. . . .

The District Court ruled that there was a genuine issue of material fact as to whether Joiner had been exposed to PCB's. But it nevertheless granted summary judgment for petitioners because (1) there was no genuine issue as to whether Joiner had been exposed to furans and dioxins, and (2) the testimony of Joiner's experts had failed to show that there was a link between exposure to PCB's and small-cell lung cancer. The court believed that the testimony of respondent's experts to the contrary did not rise above "subjective belief or unsupported speculation." 864 F. Supp. 1310, 1326 (N.D. Ga. 1994). Their testimony was therefore inadmissible.

The Court of Appeals for the Eleventh Circuit reversed. 78 F.3d 524 (1996). It held that "[b]ecause the Federal Rules of Evidence governing expert testimony display a preference for admissibility, we apply a particularly stringent standard of review to the trial judge's exclusion of expert testimony." Id. at 529. Applying that standard, the Court of Appeals held that the District Court had erred in excluding the testimony of Joiner's expert witnesses. . . .

We granted petitioners' petition for a writ of certiorari, and we now reverse. . . .

II

. . . We have held that abuse of discretion is the proper standard of review of a district court's evidentiary rulings. . . . The Court of Appeals suggested that *Daubert* somehow altered this general rule in the context of a district court's decision to exclude scientific evidence. But *Daubert* did not address the standard of appellate review for evidentiary rulings at all. It did hold that the "austere" *Frye* standard of "general acceptance" had not been carried over into the Federal Rules of Evidence. But the opinion also said:

> That the *Frye* test was displaced by the Rules of Evidence does not mean, however, that the Rules themselves place no limits on the admissibility of purportedly scientific evidence. Nor is the trial judge disabled from screening such evidence. To the contrary, under the Rules the trial judge must ensure that any and all scientific testimony or evidence admitted is not only relevant, but reliable.

Thus, while the Federal Rules of Evidence allow district courts to admit a somewhat broader range of scientific testimony than would have been admissible under *Frye*, they leave in place the "gatekeeper" role of the trial judge in screening such evidence. A court of appeals applying "abuse-of-discretion" review to such rulings may not categorically distinguish between rulings allowing expert testimony and rulings disallowing it. We likewise reject respondent's argument that because the granting of summary judgment in this case was "outcome determinative," it should have been subjected to a more searching standard of review. On a motion for summary judgment, disputed issues of fact are resolved against the moving party—here, petitioners. But the question of admissibility of expert testimony is not such an issue of fact, and is reviewable under the abuse-of-discretion standard. . . .

III

We believe that a proper application of the correct standard of review here indicates that the District Court did not abuse its discretion. Joiner's theory of liability was that his exposure to PCB's and their derivatives "promoted" his development of small-cell lung cancer. In support of that theory he proffered the deposition testimony of expert witnesses. . . .

The District Court agreed with petitioners that the animal studies on which respondent's experts relied did not support his contention that exposure to PCB's had contributed to his cancer. The studies involved infant mice that had developed cancer after being exposed to PCB's. The infant mice in the studies had had massive doses of PCB's injected directly into their peritoneums or stomachs. Joiner was an adult human being whose alleged exposure to PCB's was far less than the exposure in the animal studies. The PCB's were injected into the mice in a highly concentrated form. The fluid with which Joiner had come into contact generally had a much smaller PCB concentration of between 0-500 parts per million. The cancer that these mice developed was alveologenic adenomas; Joiner had developed small-cell carcinomas. No study demonstrated that adult mice developed cancer after being exposed to

PCB's. One of the experts admitted that no study had demonstrated that PCB's lead to cancer in any other species.

Respondent failed to reply to this criticism. Rather than explaining how and why the experts could have extrapolated their opinions from these seemingly far-removed animal studies, respondent chose "to proceed as if the only issue [was] whether animal studies can ever be a proper foundation for an expert's opinion." *Joiner*, 864 F. Supp. at 1324. Of course, whether animal studies can ever be a proper foundation for an expert's opinion was not the issue. The issue was whether *these* experts' opinions were sufficiently supported by the animal studies on which they purported to rely. The studies were so dissimilar to the facts presented in this litigation that it was not an abuse of discretion for the District Court to have rejected the experts' reliance on them.

The District Court also concluded that the four epidemiological studies on which respondent relied were not a sufficient basis for the experts' opinions. The first such study involved workers at an Italian capacitor plant who had been exposed to PCB's. The authors noted that lung cancer deaths among ex-employees at the plant were higher than might have been expected, but concluded that "there were apparently no grounds for associating lung cancer deaths (although increased above expectations) and exposure in the plant." Id. at 172. Given that [the authors] were unwilling to say that PCB exposure had caused cancer among the workers they examined, their study did not support the experts' conclusion that Joiner's exposure to PCB's caused his cancer. [The Court then conducts similar reviews of three other studies.]

[Respondent] claims that because the District Court's disagreement was with the conclusion that the experts drew from the studies, the District Court committed legal error and was properly reversed by the Court of Appeals. But conclusions and methodology are not entirely distinct from one another. Trained experts commonly extrapolate from existing data. But nothing in either *Daubert* or the Federal Rules of Evidence requires a district court to admit opinion evidence that is connected to existing data only by the *ipse dixit* of the expert. A court may conclude that there is simply too great an analytical gap between the data and the opinion proffered. That is what the District Court did here, and we hold that it did not abuse its discretion in so doing.

[The Court then remands for a determination of "whether Joiner was exposed to furans and dioxins, and whether if there was such exposure, the opinions of Joiner's experts would then be admissible. . . ."]

Breyer, J., concurring. [M]odern life, including good health as well as economic well-being, depends upon the use of artificial or manufactured substances, such as chemicals. And it may, therefore, prove particularly important to see that judges fulfill their *Daubert* gatekeeping function, so that they help assure that the powerful engine of tort liability, which can generate strong financial incentives to reduce, or to eliminate, production, points toward the right substances and does not destroy the wrong ones. [Justice Breyer then endorses a suggestion from the amici brief of the New England Journal of Medicine that judges "be strongly encouraged to make use of their inherent authority . . . to appoint experts."]

Stevens, J., concurring in part and dissenting in part. Unlike the District Court, the Court of Appeals expressly decided that a "weight of the evidence" methodology was scientifically acceptable. To this extent, the Court of Appeals' opinion is persuasive. It is not intrinsically "unscientific" for experienced professionals to arrive at a conclusion by weighing all available scientific evidence — this is not the sort of "junk science" with which *Daubert* was concerned. After all, as Joiner points out, the Environmental Protection Agency (EPA) uses the same methodology to assess risks, albeit using a somewhat different threshold than that required in a trial. Petitioners' own experts used the same scientific approach as well. And using this methodology, it would seem that an expert could reasonably have concluded that the study of workers at an Italian capacitor plant, coupled with data from Monsanto's study and other studies, raises an inference that PCB's promote lung cancer. . . .

In any event, it bears emphasis that the Court has not held that it would have been an abuse of discretion to admit the expert testimony. . . .

NOTES

1. *Beyond Daubert.* Daubert v. Merrell Dow Pharmaceuticals, Inc., 509 U.S. 579 (1993), discussed at length in *Joiner*, revolutionized proof of causation by setting the standard on what expert testimony is admissible in federal court. Within short order, *Joiner* was expanded in Kumho Tire Co. v. Carmichael, 526 U.S. 137, 148 (1999), extending a district court's gatekeeper function under *Daubert* to technical as well as scientific evidence—there, the engineering testimony about the possible causes of a tire blowout. Justice Breyer noted that

> it would prove difficult, if not impossible, for judges to administer evidentiary rules under which a gatekeeping obligation depended upon a distinction between "scientific" knowledge and "technical" or "other specialized" knowledge. There is no clear line that divides the one from the others. Disciplines such as engineering rest upon scientific knowledge. Pure scientific theory itself may depend for its development upon observation and properly engineered machinery.

These *Daubert* questions tend to give rise to many close cases on two issues: first, whether the expert was qualified to give testimony; and second, whether the theories advanced had sufficient support to allow a case to reach the jury. In Knepfle v. J-Tech Corp., 48 F.4th 1282, 1286–87, 1289 (11th Cir. 2022), plaintiff was riding her motorcycle when she was hit by a car. She was launched into the air, but

> [t]he Z1R Nomad Sinister half-shell helmet she was wearing protected her head as it impacted the Mazda's front passenger side. But according to Knepfle, before landing on the pavement, her helmet came off, and her unprotected skull hit the pavement, causing permanent injuries. . . . [Plaintiff's expert witness] sought to present his novel theory that the Z1R Nomad helmet's double D-ring fasteners—which rest on the side of the wearer's chin, rather than beneath it—make the helmet more prone to losing tension than other types of helmet fasteners.

Branch, J., held that the plaintiff's expert witness had ample professional qualifications, but that his novel theory about the shortness of the helmet's strap was not supported by sufficient evidence to be admissible. She then accepted the defendants' contentions that

> [plaintiff's expert witness] failed to identify a single generally accepted test, peer-reviewed article, or independent study that supported his opinion on the design defect or his theory of events. The defendants also alleged that [the plaintiff's expert witness'] opinion rested on flawed and unreliable methodology. Specifically, they highlighted that, although [plaintiff's expert witness] took measurements of Knepfle's Z1R Nomad helmet's front protective foam liner, he did not conduct any measurements on the rear liner, and instead merely "eyeballed it." Furthermore, the defendants noted that [plaintiff's expert witness] failed to look into whether other similar accidents occurred with other types of D-ring fasteners. Finally, they castigated [the plaintiff's expert witness'] failure to test his design defect theory beyond a simple "demonstration," [by an ad hoc manipulation of the straps that could not occur in practice].

After *Knepfle*, can any plaintiff prevail on a novel theory of causation?

2. *The Bendectin Saga.* In *Daubert*, the defendant obtained summary judgment on the causation issue after the plaintiff's team of eight recognized experts were prepared to testify that Bendectin, a drug once commonly used to control nausea during pregnancy, could cause birth defects, largely by reinterpreting the data contained in peer review studies that had denied this causal association. *Daubert* rejected the traditional test of Frye v. United States, 293 F. 1013, 1014 (D.C. Cir. 1923), which had allowed as admissible only expert testimony that had been "generally accepted" as reliable by the scientific community, in favor of allowing the introduction of relevant scientific testimony that has "a valid scientific connection to the pertinent inquiry." It then remanded the case for further consideration, noting that both lower courts erroneously "focused almost exclusively on 'general acceptance,' as gauged by publication and the decision of other courts," without taking into account sufficiently other measures of reliability and relevance, including the tightness of "fit" between the evidence presented and the charge to be proved.

In a bruising opinion on remand, Kozinski, J., broke with earlier decisions that had freely allowed plaintiff's expert to testify on the relationship between Bendectin and birth defects, see, e.g., Oxendine v. Merrell Dow Pharmaceuticals, Inc., 506 A.2d 1100, 1110 (D.C. 1986), and upheld summary judgment under the revised standard, noting that none of plaintiff's experts "are proposing to testify about matters growing naturally and directly out of research they have conducted independent of the litigation," and far from publishing their results in peer-reviewed journals, "the only place their theories and studies have been published is in the pages of federal and state reporters." See Daubert v. Merrell Dow Pharmaceuticals, Inc., 43 F.3d 1311, 1317, 1318 (9th Cir. 1995). In one sense his decision came too late, because Richardson-Merrell had already pulled Bendectin from the market due to its fear of continued lawsuits. "[W]hile Bendectin usage declined from 1 million new therapy starts in 1979 to zero in 1984, there has been no change in the incidence of birth defects." Lynch v. Merrell-National Laboratories, Inc., 830 F.2d 1190, 1194 (1st Cir. 1987).

3. *The Thimerosal Litigation.* The decision of Kozinski, J., in *Daubert* at the Ninth Circuit proved highly influential in Doe v. Ortho-Clinical Diagnostics, 440 F. Supp. 2d 465, 474 (M.D.N.C. 2006), in which the plaintiff, an autistic child, sued Ortho-Clinical for negligence, breach of warranty, and negligent and intentional misrepresentation. Each claim rested on the assertion that thimerosal, a component in RhoGAM, the defendant's biologic—that is, a complex, large, living molecule often found in blood or vaccines—administered to the plaintiff's mother during pregnancy, caused the plaintiff's autism. That claim depended on showing, first, general causation (namely, that defendant's product was of the type that could have caused the injuries in question) and, second, specific causation (namely, making out that causal connection in the instant case). The court's exhaustive review of the qualifications and proffered testimony of the plaintiff's expert physicians reads like summary judgment for the defendant on both causal issues. For example, Beaty, J., observed that Dr. Geier did not have the formal qualifications as a pediatric neurologist to testify on the relevant causal issues. As did Kozinski, J., in *Daubert*, Beaty, J., also conducted his own extensive review "of a motley assortment of diverse literature" that Dr. Geier presented, noting that it was all "flatly contradicted by all of the epidemiological studies available at this time."

The link between thimerosal and autism also arises in litigation under the National Childhood Vaccine Injury Act of 1986, passed in response to a sharp increase in the price of vaccines that threatened to drive many vaccine makers out of the critical children's marketplace. The NCVIA establishes a complex system of no-fault compensation, paying up to $250,000 for children suffering particular side effects from certain vaccines within specified time limits. 42 U.S.C. §300aa (2023). In some instances, the statute adopts explicit tests for determining whether compensation is owed. For example, the recipient of a measles vaccine who suffers an anaphylactic shock within twenty-four hours of inoculation can receive payment. Also, under the statute, people who meet the conditions for no-fault recovery may nonetheless reject the payment and sue for tort damages. The largest statutory award has been $8.4 million, and the average award has been around $833,000, where autism claims have uniformly been rejected by the Institute of Medicine for the want of any proof of causal connection. A study by the Centers for Disease Control and Prevention (the CDC), Thimerosal in Vaccines, https://www.cdc.gov/vaccinesafety/concerns/thimerosal/index.html, now endorses the use of Thimerosal and notes that the use of Thimerosal is now regarded as safe. Its two central conclusions are:

> **Thimerosal has been shown to be safe when used in vaccines.**
> Thimerosal use in medical products has a record of being very safe. Data from many studies show no evidence of harm caused by the low doses of thimerosal in vaccines.
>
> **Scientific research does not show a connection between thimerosal and autism.**
> Research does not show any link between thimerosal in vaccines and autism, a neurodevelopmental disorder. Many well conducted studies have concluded that thimerosal in vaccines does not contribute to the development of autism. Even after thimerosal was removed from almost all childhood vaccines, autism rates continued to increase, which is the opposite of what would be expected if thimerosal caused autism.

The issue of causation in vaccine cases arises also in other contexts. Thus, in Pafford v. Secretary of Health and Human Services, 451 F.3d 1352 (Fed. Cir. 2006), Rader, C.J., rejected the claim that a suite of vaccines—DTaP (diphtheria, tetanus (commonly known as lockjaw), and pertussis (commonly known as whooping cough)), MMR (measles, mumps, and rubella), and OPV (oral poliovirus)—resulted in the occurrence of systematic juvenile rheumatoid arthritis from a condition known as Still's disease. That condition was not on the "table" of listed events, and it was not a "signature disease" associated with any of the vaccines that the plaintiff took. Her claim was rejected because she could not make out her case on the following three-part causation test identical to that used in tort cases:

> (1) a medical theory causally connecting the vaccination and the injury;
> (2) a logical sequence of cause and effect showing that the vaccination was the reason for the injury; and
> (3) . . . a proximate temporal relationship between the vaccine and injury.

Rader, C.J., then concluded that the plaintiff could not rule out that other contemporaneous events unrelated to the vaccinations might have caused the injury, including "(1) a positive test for mycoplasma (a type of bacteria); (2) x-rays showing a thickening of the sinus membrane consistent with a sinus infection; (3) an earlier bout of tonsillitis; and (4) an earlier cold accompanied by diarrhea.

4. *The Agent Orange litigation.* Proving causation in fact was also the central issue in suits brought mainly by servicemen and their offspring who claimed that Agent Orange (or more specifically, dioxin, a deadly byproduct of its production) caused many serious but undifferentiated illnesses and birth defects. The individual suits were consolidated into a class before Weinstein, J., with individual plaintiffs retaining the right to opt out of the class. The main class settled for $180,000,000, with the funds placed in a trust fund for distribution to the victims. In a subsequent action, Weinstein, J., anticipated *Joiner* and dismissed the suits of the opt-out plaintiffs because the evidence (including animal and epidemiological studies) did not support proof of causal connection. See In re "Agent Orange" Prod. Liab. Litig., 611 F. Supp. 1223, 1241 (E.D.N.Y. 1985). Why should the settlement have provided for any award given the summary judgment that followed? On Agent Orange generally, see Schuck, Agent Orange on Trial: Mass Toxic Disasters in the Courts (1986).

The Agent Orange cases illustrate the three levels of causation relevant in toxic torts cases. These are summarized by Professor Abraham in Individual Action and Collective Responsibility: The Dilemma of Mass Tort Reform, 73 Va. L. Rev. 845, 860, 867–68 (1987):

> To meet traditional burdens of proof in a regime that emphasizes individual responsibility, the plaintiff must show what I shall call *substance, source*, and *exposure* causation. That is, he must prove that the substance for which the defendant is responsible can cause his injury or disease, that the defendant and not someone else was the source of the substance, and that he was in fact exposed to the substance in a way that has caused his disease. In many cases, proof of some of these elements is simple; in some cases, proof of one automatically proves another. For example, when a particular disease is caused almost exclusively by a particular substance, the occurrence of the disease is the substance's "signature." Proof that the plaintiff has the disease, therefore, is also proof of both exposure and substance causation. In many cases, however, meeting the traditional burden of proof as to each of these elements is no minor accomplishment.

Abraham then expressed his doubt that the traditional tort models could work in cases like Agent Orange where no signature disease is found. How does Abraham's framework apply to asbestosis?

5. *The Effectiveness of Daubert and Frye.* In the aftermath of *Daubert*, many states had to choose between *Daubert* and *Frye*. One tabulation suggests that at present about twenty states opt for a *Daubert* and *Kumho Tire* hybrid standard, eight for *Daubert* alone, and eight for *Frye*, with the remaining fourteen using a variety of other tests. Expert Witnesses in Civil Trials §2:54 (2022 ed.). How these different tests play out in practice is more difficult to determine. One study, Cheng & Yoon, Does *Frye* or *Daubert* Matter?: A Study of Scientific Admissibility Standards, 91 Va. L. Rev. 471, 475 (2005), concluded "that the choice between a *Frye* and *Daubert* standard does not make any practical difference."

One lingering question is how effective *either* standard is in dealing with dubious evidence. In a relentless critique of *Daubert*, Giannelli, Forensic Science: *Daubert*'s Failure, 68 Case W. Rsrv. L. Rev. 86 (2018), expresses a deep skepticism that, as administered, *Daubert* is up to the task of excluding dubious forensic evidence dealing with bite marks, hair samples, ballistics, and tire tracks that should never be allowed into evidence. He also cites a National Academy of Science Report, Strengthening Forensic Science in the United States: A Path Forward 100 (2009), which notes the failure of courts to apply *Daubert* with its full rigor:

> The bottom line is simple: In a number of forensic science disciplines, forensic science professionals have yet to establish either the validity of their approach or the accuracy of their conclusions, and the courts have been utterly ineffective in addressing this problem.

However, some judges rigorously apply *Daubert* to exclude dubious evidence. After accepting *Daubert*'s basic contention that judges "must ensure that any and all scientific testimony or evidence admitted is not only relevant, but reliable," Judge Catherine Easterly complained that "[a]s matters currently stand, a certainty statement regarding toolmark pattern matching has the same probative value as the vision of a psychic." Williams v. United States, 130 A.3d 343, 354–55 (D.C. 2016) (Easterly, J., concurring).

For a similar use of *Daubert*, see also Almeciga v. Ctr. for Investigative Reporting, Inc., 185 F. Supp. 3d 401, 415 (S.D.N.Y. 2016), which notes that even after *Daubert*, "[t]here have been too many pseudo-scientific disciplines that have since been exposed as profoundly flawed, unreliable, or baseless for any Court to take this role lightly." What should appellate courts do if district courts fall down in their *Daubert* review?

6. *The Third Restatement on Proof of Factual Causation.* The Third Restatement offers an extended exegesis on proof of causation in toxic substance and disease cases that deliberately skirts the *Daubert* issue. RTT: LPEH §28, comment *c*.

RESTATEMENT OF THE LAW (THIRD) OF TORTS: LIABILITY FOR PHYSICAL AND EMOTIONAL HARM

§28. Factual Cause

Comment c. Toxic substances and disease: . . . A few celebrated cases and case congregations, such as the Agent Orange and Bendectin litigations, led some courts to distrust juries' ability to resolve cases based on conflicting expert-opinion evidence. . . . The high-water mark for this overreliance on scientific thresholds occurred in the Bendectin litigation when one court announced a blanket rule that a plaintiff could not make out a sufficient case without statistically significant epidemiologic evidence.

These courts may be relying on a view that "science" presents an "objective" method of establishing that, in all cases, reasonable minds cannot differ on the issue of factual causation. Such a view is incorrect. First, scientific standards for the sufficiency of evidence to establish a proposition may be inappropriate for the law. . . . Second, scientists report that an evaluation of data and scientific evidence to determine whether an inference of causation is appropriate requires judgment and interpretation. Scientists are subject to their own value judgments and preexisting biases that may affect their view of a body of evidence. . . .

SECTION C. PROXIMATE CAUSE (HEREIN OF DUTY)

1. Physical Injury

Francis Bacon

The Elements of the Common Lawes of England

(1630)

Reg. I. In jure non remota causa sed proxima spectatur. [In law, not the remote, but the proximate cause is to be looked at.] It were infinite for the law to judge the causes, and their impulsions one of another; therefore it contenteth it selfe with the immediate cause, and judgeth of acts by that, without looking to any further degree.

David Hume

An Enquiry Concerning Human Under Standing

Section VII (1740)

[W]e may define a cause to be an object followed by another, and where all the objects, similar to the first, are followed by objects similar to the second. [Or, in other words], where, if the first object had not been, the second never had existed.

Thomas Atkins Street

Foundations of Legal Liability

Vol. I, p. 110 (1906)

The terms "proximate" and "remote" are thus respectively applied to recoverable and non-recoverable damages. . . . It is unfortunate that no definite principle can be laid down by which to determine this question. It is always to be determined on the facts of each case upon mixed considerations of logic, common sense, justice, policy and precedent. . . . The best use that can be made of the authorities on proximate cause is merely to furnish illustrations of situations which judicious men upon careful consideration have adjudged to be on one side of the line or the other.

Ryan v. New York Central R.R.

35 N.Y. 210 (1866)

On the 15th July 1854, in the city of Syracuse, the defendants, by the careless management, or through the insufficient condition, of one of their engines, set fire to their woodshed, and a large quantity of wood therein. The plaintiff's house, situated at a distance of one hundred and thirty feet from the shed, soon took fire from the heat and sparks, and was entirely consumed, notwithstanding diligent efforts were made to save it. A number of other houses were also burned by the spreading of the fire.

These facts having been proved on the part of the plaintiff, the defendants' counsel moved for a nonsuit, which was granted, and an exception taken. And the judgment having been affirmed at general term, the plaintiff appealed to this court.

Hunt, J. [after stating the facts]. The question may be thus stated: A house in a populous city takes fire, through the negligence of the owner or his servant; the flames extend to and destroy an adjacent building: Is the owner of the first building liable to the second owner for the damage sustained by such burning?

It is a general principle, that every person is liable for the consequences of his own acts; he is thus liable in damages for the proximate results of his own acts, but not for remote damages. It is not easy, at all times, to determine what are proximate and what are remote damages. . . .

[After discussing cases of direct ignition of plaintiff's property by defendants' negligence, the court continues:] Thus far the law is settled, and the principle is apparent. If, however, the fire communicates from the house of *A.* to that of *B.*, and that is destroyed, is the negligent party liable for his loss? And if it spreads thence to the house of *C.*, and thence to the house of *D.*, and thence consecutively through the other houses, until it reaches and consumes the house of *Z.*, is the party liable to pay the damages sustained by these twenty-four sufferers? The counsel for the plaintiff does not distinctly claim this, and I think it would not be seriously insisted, that the sufferers could recover in such case. Where, then, is the principle upon which *A.* recovers and *Z.* fails?

It has been suggested, that an important element exists in the difference between an intentional firing and a negligent firing merely; that when a party designedly fires his own house or his own fallow-land, not intending, however, to do any injury to his neighbor, but a damage actually results, that he may be liable for more extended damages than where the fire originated in accident or negligence. It is true, that the most of the cases where the liability was held to exist, were cases of an intentional firing. The case, however, of Vaughan v. Menlove (3 Bing. N.C. 468) [*supra* Chapter 3, at 111] was that of a spontaneous combustion of a hayrick; the rick was burned, the owner's buildings were destroyed, and thence the fire spread to the plaintiff's cottage, which was also consumed; the defendant was held liable.

Without deciding upon the importance of this distinction, I prefer to place my opinion upon the ground, that, in the one case, to wit, the destruction of the building upon which the sparks were thrown by the negligent act of the party sought to be charged, the result was to have been anticipated, the moment the fire was communicated to the building; that its destruction was the ordinary and natural result of its being fired. In the second, third or twenty-fourth case, as supposed, the destruction of the building was not a natural and expected result of the first firing. That a building upon which sparks and cinders fall should be destroyed or seriously injured, must be expected, but that the fire should spread and other buildings be consumed, is not a necessary or a usual result. That it is possible, and that it is not unfrequent, cannot be denied. The result, however, depends, not upon any necessity of a further communication of the fire, but upon a concurrence of accidental circumstances, such as the degree of the heat, the state of the atmosphere, the condition and materials of the adjoining structures and the direction of the wind. These are accidental and varying circumstances; the party has no control over them, and is not responsible for their effects.

My opinion, therefore, is, that this action cannot be sustained, for the reason that the damages incurred are not the immediate but the remote result of the negligence of the defendants. The immediate result was the destruction of their own wood and sheds beyond that, it was remote. . . .

To sustain such a claim as the present, and to follow the same to its legitimate consequences, would subject to a liability against which no prudence could guard, and to meet which no private fortune would be adequate. Nearly all fires are caused by negligence, in its extended sense. In a country where wood, coal, gas and oils are universally used, where men are crowded into cities and villages, where servants are employed, and where children find their home in all houses, it is impossible, that the most vigilant prudence should guard against the occurrence of accidental or negligent fires. A man may insure his own house, or his own furniture, but he cannot insure his neighbor's building or furniture, for the reason that he has no interest in them. To hold that the owner must not only meet his own loss by fire, but that he must guaranty the security of his neighbors on both sides, and to an unlimited extent, would be to create a liability which would be the destruction of all civilized society. No community could long exist, under the operation of such a principle. In a commercial country, each man, to some extent, runs the hazard of his neighbor's conduct, and each, by insurance against such hazards, is enabled to obtain a reasonable security against loss. To neglect such precaution, and to call upon his neighbor, on whose premises a fire originated, to indemnify him instead, would be to award a punishment quite beyond the offence committed. It is to be considered, also, that if the negligent party is liable to the owner of a remote building thus consumed, he would also be liable to the insurance companies who should pay losses to such remote owners. The principle of subrogation would entitle the companies to the benefit of every claim held by the party to whom a loss should be paid.

. . . The remoteness of the damage, in my judgment, forms the true rule on which the question should be decided, and which prohibits a recovery by the plaintiff in this case. Judgment should be affirmed.

NOTES

1. ***Fire!*** The earlier common law cases took a much harder line toward the spread of fire. In Beaulieu v. Finglam, Y.B. 2 Hen. 4, f. 18, pl. 6 (1401), Markham, J., held that liability attached not only for the actions of the owner, but also for all his guests. He was insulated from liability only for fires set by strangers. The following dialogue then ensued: Hornby [the defendant's lawyer]: "The defendant will be undone and impoverished all his days if this action is to be maintained against him; for then twenty other such suits will be brought against him." Thirning, C.J.: "What is that to us? It is better that he should be undone than that the law be changed for him." Why this shift in view in *Ryan*, when the defendant is a railroad, not an individual landowner?

For a contemporary English contrast to *Ryan*, see Smith v. London & South Western Ry., [1870] 6 LRCP 14. A spark from defendant's engine started a fire in some heaps of the railway's cut grass. Fanned by a high wind, the flames spread through a stubble field not owned by the railroad until it consumed plaintiff's cottage. Kelly, C.B., allowed recovery, noting that "there was negligence in the defendants in not removing these trimmings, and that they thus become responsible for all the consequences of their conduct, and that the mere fact of the distance of this cottage from the point where the fire broke out does not affect their liability." The Supreme Court, in Milwaukee & St. Paul Ry. v. Kellogg, 94 U.S. 469, 474 (1876), also rejected *Ryan*'s view, stating,

> [W]hen a building has been set on fire through the negligence of a party, and a second building has been fired from the first, it is a conclusion of law that the owner of the second has no recourse to the negligent wrong-doer, they have not been accepted as authority for such a doctrine, even in the States where the decisions were made.

See generally Schwartz, Tort Law and the Economy in Nineteenth-Century America: A Reinterpretation, 90 Yale L.J. 1717, 1746–47 (1981). See also note to *Leroy Fibre, supra* Chapter 4, at 232.

2. *"Ordinary and Natural Result of Defendant's Negligence."* *Ryan* placed a narrow construction on the phrase "ordinary and natural result" of the defendant's negligence. That phrase must be construed not only with intervening natural events, but also with intervening human conduct. In City of Lincoln, 15 P.D. 15, 18 (1889), the plaintiff's vessel, the *Albatross*, was totally disabled in a collision with the *City of Lincoln*, wholly through the fault of the latter vessel. The *Albatross* lost its compass, log, log glass, and charts, and the captain was unsuccessful in his efforts to bring the ship to port. The court first noted that the "only inquiry in all these cases is whether the damage complained of is the natural and reasonable result of the defendant's act," and found the test satisfied if the damage was "such a consequence as in the ordinary course of things would flow from the act." Lindley, L.J., continued:

> We have then to consider what is the meaning of "the ordinary course of things." Sir Walter Phillimore has asked us to exclude from it all human conduct. I can do nothing of the kind. I take it that reasonable human conduct is part of the ordinary course of things. So far as I can see my way to any definite proposition I should say that the ordinary course of things does not exclude all human conduct, but includes at least the reasonable conduct of those who have sustained the damage, and who are seeking to save further loss. . . . Let us see, then, what occurred in the present case, and what was the real cause of the loss of this vessel. It was the fact that the captain was, by the collision, deprived of the means of ascertaining his position and of properly navigating his ship. He was deprived of his compass, his log-line, and his charts. His ship was not utterly unmanageable but she was in a very bad state, and the necessary consequence of all this was that this captain lost his vessel without any negligence on his part. Under these circumstances the case falls within the rule I have laid down as to the term "ordinary course of things." Therefore, I am of opinion that the owners of the *City of Lincoln* must pay for the loss of the *Albatross*.

3. *Plaintiff's Response to Emergencies.* The problem of intervening actions also arises with sudden emergencies that require the plaintiff's immediate action. In Tuttle v. Atlantic City Railroad, 49 A. 450, 451 (N.J. 1901), Vroom, J., held:

> The true rule governing cases of this character may be stated as follows: That if a defendant, by negligence, puts the plaintiff under a reasonable apprehension of personal physical injury, and plaintiff, in a reasonable effort to escape, sustains physical injury, a right of action arises to recover for the physical injury and the mental disorder naturally incident to its occurrence.

In other words, if the plaintiff acts in good faith to minimize the risk of loss from a dangerous situation of the defendant's making, those actions do not sever causal connection. The defendant cannot complain when the plaintiff has done everything that the defendant would have done for himself to minimize the loss if he had been in the same situation.

In some instances, although now generally disfavored, courts have invoked a foresight limitation to bar recovery in these emergency cases, even when the plaintiff has undertaken a good-faith action. Thus, in Mauney v. Gulf Refining Co., 9 So. 2d 780, 782 (Miss. 1942), the plaintiff, hurrying to fetch her two-year-old child after being warned by neighbors that defendant's delivery truck was on fire and likely to explode, tripped over a chair in her husband's cafe and suffered a miscarriage. The court denied recovery on the ground that if the plaintiff "didn't see a chair in her own place of business, it would impose an inadmissible burden upon the defendants to say that they should have foreseen from across the street and through the walls of a building on another corner what appellant didn't see right at her feet. . . ." What degree of precision is required in working a foreseeability test? See, e.g., Williams, The Risk Principle, 77 Law Q. Rev. 179, 183 (1961): "The test of foreseeability does not require all the details of what happens to be foreseeable; it is enough if it is foreseeable in general outline." Is there any difficulty in holding the defendant liable under a directness standard?

Berry v. Sugar Notch Borough

43 A. 240 (Pa. 1899)

. . . Trespass for personal injuries. Before Woodward, P.J. . . .

Verdict and judgment for plaintiff for $3,162.50. Defendant appealed. . . .

Fell, J. The plaintiff was a motorman in the employ of the Wilkes-Barre and Wyoming Valley Traction Company on its line running from Wilkes-Barre to the borough of Sugar Notch. The ordinance by virtue of which the company was permitted to lay its track and operate its cars in the borough of Sugar Notch contained a provision that the speed of the cars while on the streets of the borough should not exceed eight miles an hour. On the line of the road, and within the borough limits, there was a large chestnut tree, as to the condition of which there was some dispute at the trial. The question of the negligence of the borough in permitting it to remain must, however, be considered as set at rest by the verdict. On the day of the accident the plaintiff was running his car on the borough street in a violent wind-storm, and as he passed under the tree it was blown down, crushing the roof of the car and causing the plaintiff's injury. There is some conflict of testimony as to the speed at which the car was running, but it seems to be fairly well established that it was considerably in excess of the rate permitted by the borough ordinance.

We do not think that the fact that the plaintiff was running his car at a higher rate of speed than eight miles an hour affects his right to recover. It may be that in doing so he violated the ordinance by virtue of which the company was permitted to operate its cars in the streets of the borough, but he certainly was not for that reason without rights upon the streets. Nor can it be said that the speed was the cause of the accident, or contributed to it. It might have been otherwise if the tree had fallen before the car reached it; for in that case a high rate of speed might have rendered it impossible for the plaintiff to avoid a collision which he either foresaw or should have foreseen. Even in that case the ground for denying him the right to recover would be that he had been guilty of contributory negligence, and not that he had violated a borough ordinance. The testimony however shows that the tree fell upon the car as it passed beneath. With this phase of the case in view, it was urged on behalf of the appellant that the speed was the immediate cause of the plaintiff's injury, inasmuch as it was the particular speed at which he was running which brought the car to the place of the accident at the moment when the tree blew down. This argument, while we cannot deny its ingenuity, strikes us, to say the least, as being somewhat sophistical. That his speed brought him to the place of the accident at the moment of the accident was the merest chance, and a thing which no foresight could have predicted. The same thing might as readily have happened to a car running slowly, or it might have been that a high speed alone would have carried him beyond the tree to a place of safety. It was also argued by the appellant's counsel that, even if the speed was not the sole efficient cause of the accident, it at least contributed to its severity, and materially increased the damage. It may be that it did. But what basis could a jury have for finding such to be the case and, should they so find, what guide could be given them for differentiating between the injury done this man and the injury which would have been done a man in a similar accident on a car running at a speed of eight miles an hour or less?

The judgment is affirmed.

NOTES

1. ***Coincidence and Causation.*** In *Berry*, the plaintiff's breach of a safety ordinance was not causally connected with his injuries because the breach did not increase the risk or hazard of his being struck. Is it relevant that the increased speed reduced the time that the plaintiff was exposed to potential injury? Increased the possibility of damage in the event of a collision with a fallen log? With *Berry*, compare Mahoney v. Beatman, *supra* Chapter 4, at 230. The Third Restatement endorses the outcome in *Berry*. RTT: LPEH §30, comment *a*, illus. 1.

The problem of such coincidence between negligence and injury arose in a somewhat different form in Central of Georgia Ry. Co. v. Price, 32 S.E. 77, 77–78 (Ga. 1898). Through its negligence the railroad did not drop the plaintiff off at her station. She spent the night at a hotel to which she had been escorted by the railroad's conductor. At the hotel, she was given a furnished room outfitted with a kerosene lamp, which exploded and set fire to the mosquito netting covering the bed. In her efforts to put out the fire, the plaintiff severely burnt her hands. The court first rejected her argument that the railroad should be liable because the hotel proprietor was its agent. It then held that the plaintiff's harm was too remote from the railroad's negligence:

> The negligence of the company consisted in passing the station where the passenger desired to alight, without giving her an opportunity to get off. Taking her version of the manner in which she was injured, the injury was occasioned by the negligence of the proprietor of the hotel or his servants in giving her a defective lamp. The negligence of the company in passing her station was therefore not the natural and proximate cause of her injury. There was the interposition of a separate, independent agency, the negligence of the proprietor of the hotel, over whom, as we have shown, the railway company neither had nor exercised any control. The injuries to the plaintiff were not the natural and proximate consequences of carrying her beyond her station, but were unusual, and could not have been foreseen or provided against by the highest practicable care. The plaintiff was not entitled to recover for such injuries, and the court erred in overruling the motion for new trial.

In contrast, the defendant railroad was found liable for subjecting the plaintiff passenger to an increased risk in Hines v. Garrett, 108 S.E. 690, 692, 695 (Va. 1921). A railroad conductor negligently carried the 19-year-old plaintiff almost a mile past her stop at night, forcing her to walk back this distance through an area "habitually frequented and infested by hoboes, tramps, and questionable characters." During her walk back she was raped once by a soldier and once by a hobo, both unidentified. Allowing her to recover against the railroad, the court said, in part:

> We do not wish to be understood as questioning the general proposition that no responsibility for a wrong attaches whenever an independent act of a third person intervenes between the negligence complained of and the injury. But . . . this proposition does not apply where the very negligence alleged consists of exposing the injured party to the act causing the injury. It is perfectly well settled and will not be seriously denied that whenever a carrier has reason to anticipate the danger of an assault upon one of its passengers, it rests under the duty of protecting such passenger against the same.

The result in *Hines* was explicitly endorsed in RST §449, illus. 1.

2. *Dependent Causes.* Still another variation on the causal theme arises when each of two successive acts is sufficient to harm the plaintiff, but the plaintiff is exposed to the second cause only because of the prior negligence of a separate actor involved in the first. In these situations, the second act is said to be "dependent" on the first, so that the second defendant is normally responsible only for the incremental damages, if any, brought about by his action. In Dillon v. Twin State Gas & Electric Co., 163 A. 111, 114–15 (N.H. 1932), the plaintiff's decedent, a boy of 14, lost his balance while trespassing on the superstructure of a bridge and grabbed the defendant's high-voltage wires as he fell. The current killed him, and the shock apparently threw his body back onto the girder. The defendant power company owed a duty of care to known trespassers, but that duty was not breached when the boy fell from the girder. However, the defendant was found responsible for the boy's exposure to the uncovered charged wires. The defendant's motion for a directed verdict on the issue of liability was denied, and that decision was affirmed on appeal. Allen, J., wrote:

> In leaning over from the girder and losing his balance he was entitled to no protection from the defendant to keep from falling. Its only liability was in exposing him to the danger of the charged wires. If but for the current in the wires he would have fallen down on the floor of the bridge or into the river, he would without doubt have been either killed or seriously injured. Although he died from electrocution, yet, if by reason of his preceding loss of balance he was bound to fall except for the intervention of the current, he either did not have long to live or was to be maimed. In such an outcome of his loss of balance, the defendant deprived him not of a life of normal expectancy, but of one too short to be given pecuniary allowance, in one alternative, and not of normal but of limited, earning capacity, in the other. . . .
>
> His probable future but for the current thus bears on liability as well as damages. Whether the shock from the current threw him back on the girder or whether he would have recovered his balance, with or without the aid of the wire he took hold of, if it had not been charged, are issues of fact, as to which the evidence as it stands may lead to different conclusions.

What facts justify liability? Which ones do not?

3. *An Apparent Condition of Safety.* Problems of causal intervention also arise when dangerous objects are passed from hand to hand. In Pittsburg Reduction Co. v. Horton, 113 S.W. 647, 648–49 (Ark. 1908), the defendant discarded a dynamite cap on its unenclosed plant premises near a public school. The cap was picked up by Charlie Copple, age ten, who placed it in a tin box with other caps and played with it on several occasions in his house. His mother, who later testified that she did not know what they were, would pick the caps up when Charlie was done playing. About a week after he found the cap, Charlie traded it to Jack Horton, age 13, for some writing paper. Horton thought that "the cap was the shell of a .22 cartridge that had been shot." He was picking the dirt out of the cap with a match when the cap exploded, so injuring his hand that it had to be amputated. Charlie's father, a miner, denied knowing that the cap was in the house until after the accident. Horton sued the defendant company and its foreman, but his claim was denied.

> In the present case the facts are practically undisputed. Charlie Copple's father was an employee of a company engaged in a similar business to that of appellant company. Naturally, his avocation and the proximity of his residence to the mines made both himself and his wife familiar with the nature of explosives. True, Mrs. Copple says that she did not know what the shells contained, but she did know that they were shells for some kind of explosives, that her son brought them home, and that he played with them. She admits that when he would leave them on the floor she would pick them up and lay them away for him. This continued for a week, and then, with her knowledge, he carried them to school. Her course of conduct broke the causal connection between the original negligent act of appellant and the subsequent injury of the plaintiff. It established a new agency, and the possession of Charlie Copple of the caps or shells was thereafter referable to the permission of his parents, and not to the original taking.

> Charlie Copple's parents having permitted him to retain possession of the caps, his further acts in regard to them must be attributable to their permission, and were wholly independent of the original negligence of appellants.

Horton and similar cases were analyzed in great detail in Beale, The Proximate Consequences of an Act, 33 Harv. L. Rev. 633, 650, 651, 656 (1920), which offered the following two generalizations:

> If the defendant's active force has come to rest, but in a dangerous position, creating a new or increasing an existing risk of loss, and the foreseen danger comes to pass, operating harmfully on the condition created by defendant and causing the risked loss, we say that the injury thereby created is a proximate consequence of the defendant's act. . . .
>
> On the other hand, where defendant's active force has come to rest in a position of apparent safety, the court will follow it no longer; if some new force later combines with this condition to create harm, the result is remote from the defendant's act.

With reference to cases like *Horton,* Beale concluded that "if the explosive gets into the hands of an adult the defendant's force has ceased to be an active danger; if the explosive thereafter gets into the hands of a child, defendant is not the proximate cause of anything this child may do with it." Should the result be the same even if the adult, like Charlie's mother, did not know that the cap was dangerous? Or should the active force be seen to come to an end only if the bomb is defused? The outcome in *Horton* has also been defended in Grady, Proximate Cause and the Law of Negligence, 69 Iowa L. Rev. 363, 420 (1984):

> In situations when the last wrongdoer would feel especially disposed to remain at a low level of precaution because of an expectation that the original wrongdoer would be held liable for a lion's share of the expected harm that would result from their joint omissions, the direct-consequences doctrine cuts off the liability of the original wrongdoer and makes the last wrongdoer solely responsible for the damage. This was the result in the *Horton* case.

For a criticism of both Beale and Grady, see Epstein, Toward a General Theory of Tort Law: Strict Liability in Context, 3 J. Tort L., October 22, 2010, at 6, 29. Epstein argues against the Bealean formulation's use of the phrase "active force" because it ties the theory of proximate causation too closely to trespass. For Epstein, the phrase "dangerous condition" better captures the situation. In response to Grady, Epstein urges:

> [T]he flaw in Grady's argument is to assume that once the proximate cause arguments allow the suit against remote actor, all incentives on the intermediate party vanish. This is not the case, however, if the action for contribution or indemnity is allowed for the remote party against the party nearer in control.

For a modern take on this issue that argues for experimentation to reveal the contours of the ordinary concept of causation, see Knobe & Shapiro, Proximate Cause Explained: An Essay in Experimental Jurisprudence, 88 U. Chi. L. Rev. 165 (2021).

Brower v. New York Central & Hudson River R.R.

103 A. 166 (N.J. 1918)

Swayze, J. This is a case of a grade-crossing collision. We are clear that the questions of negligence and contributory negligence were for the jury. If there were nothing else, the testimony of the plaintiff as to signals of the flagman would carry the case to the jury. The only question that has caused us difficulty is that of the extent of the defendant's liability. The complaint avers that the horse was killed, the wagon and harness, and the cider and barrels with which the wagon was loaded, were destroyed. What happened was that as a result of the collision, aside from the death of the horse and the destruction of the wagon, the contents of the wagon, consisting of empty barrels and a keg of cider, were scattered and probably stolen by people at the scene of the accident. The driver, who was alone in charge for the plaintiff, was so stunned that one of the railroad detectives found him immediately after the collision in a fit. There were two railroad detectives on the freight train to protect the property it was carrying against thieves, but they did nothing to protect the plaintiff's property. The controversy on the question of damages is as to the right of the plaintiff to recover the value of the barrels, cider and blanket. . . . It is now argued that the defendant's negligence was not in any event the proximate cause of the loss of this property since the act of the thieves intervened. The rule of law which exempts the one guilty of the original negligence from damage due to an intervening cause is well settled. The difficulty lies in the application. Like the question of proximate cause, this is ordinarily a jury question. . . .

We think these authorities justified the trial judge in his rulings as to the recovery of the value of the barrels, cider and blanket. The negligence which caused the collision resulted immediately in such a condition of the driver of the wagon that he was no longer able to protect his employer's property; the natural and probable result of his enforced abandonment of it in the street of a large city was its disappearance and the wrongdoer cannot escape making reparation for the loss caused by depriving the plaintiff of the protection which the presence of the driver in his right senses would have afforded. "The act of a third person," said the Supreme Judicial Court of Massachusetts, "intervening and contributing a condition necessary to the injurious effect of the original negligence, will not excuse the first wrongdoer, if such act ought to have been foreseen." Lane v. Atlantic Works, 111 Mass. 136 [(1872)]. A railroad company which found it necessary or desirable to have its freight train guarded by two detectives against thieves is surely chargeable with knowledge that portable property left without a guard was likely to be made off with. Again, strictly speaking, the act of the thieves did not intervene between defendant's negligence and the plaintiff's loss; the two causes were to all practical intent simultaneous and concurrent; it is rather a case of a joint tort than an intervening cause. . . . An illustration will perhaps clarify the case. Suppose a fruit vendor at his stand along the street is rendered unconscious by the negligence of the defendant, who disappears, and boys in the street appropriate the unfortunate vendor's stock in trade; could the defendant escape liability for their value? We can hardly imagine a court answering in the affirmative. Yet the case is but little more extreme than the jury might have found the present case. . . .

Garrison, J., dissenting. The collision afforded an opportunity for theft of which a thief took advantage, but I cannot agree that the collision was therefore the proximate cause of loss of the stolen articles. Proximate cause imports unbroken continuity between cause and effect, which, both in law and in logic, is broken by the active intervention of an independent criminal actor. This established rule of law is defeated if proximate cause be confounded with mere opportunity for crime. A maladjusted switch may be the proximate cause of the death of a passenger who was killed by the derailment of the train, or by the fire or collision that ensued, but it is not the proximate cause of the death of a passenger who was murdered by a bandit who boarded the train because of the opportunity afforded by its derailment. This clear distinction is not met by saying that criminal intervention should be foreseen, for this implies that crime is to be presumed and the law is directly otherwise.

NOTES

1. ***The Last Wrongdoer and Beyond.*** The outcome in *Brower* was explicitly endorsed in the Second Restatement §448, illus. 1. In contrast with *Brower*, the earliest tests of proximate causation held the defendant liable only when he was the "last wrongdoer" whose conduct contributed to the loss. Criminal conduct by some third party obviously severed causal connection on this view. More generally, the last actor need not be the last wrongdoer, for his actions could be blameless or even praiseworthy. The efforts of the captain to save his ship in *City of Lincoln, supra* at 341, did not sever causal connection. Likewise, the actions of infants and incompetents do not break the chain of causation, at least in those cases where the law does not regard their actions as tortious. Nevertheless, the test is highly restrictive since it blocks causal recovery not only when the deliberate wrong of a third party intervenes but also when the negligence of a third party intervenes.

Although this "last wrongdoer" test had some early champions (see Beven, Negligence in Law 45 (3d ed. 1908)), it was necessarily circumvented whenever the negligence of one defendant did not sever causal connection to a prior actor. Thus, in Atherton v. Devine, 602 P.2d 634, 636–37 (Okla. 1979), the plaintiff was injured in a road accident attributable to the defendant's negligence. The ambulance that took the plaintiff to the hospital was involved in another collision, aggravating the original injuries. The Oklahoma Supreme Court, reversing the decision below, held that the first collision was a "substantial factor" in causing the subsequent injury, so the harm was not too remote:

> It has long been the rule in Oklahoma that an original wrongdoer, negligently causing injury to another is liable for the negligence of a physician who treats the injured person where the negligent treatment results in the aggravation of injuries, so long as the injured person exercises good faith in the choice of his physician. . . .
>
> As a matter of principle, there would seem to be no material distinction between medical treatment required because of the tortious act, and transportation required to reach an institution where medical treatment is available. The use of an ambulance, like the use of a surgeon's scalpel, is necessitated by the tortfeasor's wrong, and either may be used negligently.

Even after the negligence barrier was overcome, many causal theorists continued to believe that deliberate and malicious acts should in general negate causal connection. Thus, Hart and Honoré offer this general test of causation: "The general principle of the traditional doctrine is that *the free, deliberate and informed act or omission of a human being, intended to exploit the situation created by the defendant, negatives any causal connection.*" Causation in the Law 136 (2d ed. 1985) (italics in original). The commonsense defense of this position rests on the observation that the original actor did not constrain the conduct of the malicious intervenor, but only facilitated his mischief. Yet it was just the creation of unique opportunities for harm that allowed the plaintiff to recover against the railroad in Hines v. Garrett, *supra* at 343, or indeed in *Brower* itself, so this test also is generally regarded as too restrictive on recovery.

2. ***The Second Restatement Approach.*** The Second Restatement establishes a "substantial factor" test for legal, or proximate, causation in RST §431.

RESTATEMENT OF THE LAW (SECOND) OF TORTS

§431. What Constitutes Legal Cause

The actor's negligent conduct is a legal cause of harm to another if

(a) his conduct is a substantial factor in bringing about the harm, and

(b) there is no rule of law relieving the actor from liability because of the manner in which his negligence has resulted in the harm.

Comment a. Distinction between substantial cause and cause in the philosophic sense: In order to be a legal cause of another's harm, it is not enough that the harm would have not occurred had the actor not been negligent. Except as stated in §432(2) [dealing with joint causation], this is necessary, but it is not of itself sufficient. The negligence must also be a substantial factor in bringing about the plaintiff's harm. The word "substantial" is used to denote the fact that the defendant's conduct has such an effect in producing the harm as to lead reasonable men to regard it as a cause, using that word in the popular sense, in which there always lurks the idea of responsibility, rather than in the so-called "philosophic sense," which includes every one of the great number of events without which any happening would not have occurred. Each of these events is a cause in the so-called "philosophic sense," yet the effect of many of them is so insignificant that no ordinary mind would think of them as causes.

3. *Third-Party Intervention under the Second Restatement.* The role of deliberate third-party intervention is taken up in two critical provisions, RST §448 and RST §449.

RESTATEMENT OF THE LAW (SECOND) OF TORTS

§448. Intentionally Tortious or Criminal Acts Done Under Opportunity Afforded by Actor's Negligence

The act of a third person in committing an intentional tort or crime is a superseding cause of harm to another resulting therefrom, although the actor's negligent conduct created a situation which afforded an opportunity to the third person to commit such a tort or crime, unless the actor at the time of his negligent conduct realized or should have realized the likelihood that such a situation might be created, and that a third person might avail himself of the opportunity to commit such a tort or crime.

RESTATEMENT OF THE LAW (SECOND) OF TORTS

§449. Tortious or Criminal Acts the Probability of Which Makes Actor's Conduct Negligent

If the likelihood that a third person may act in a particular manner is the hazard or one of the hazards which makes the actor negligent, such an act whether innocent, negligent, intentionally tortious, or criminal does not prevent the actor from being liable for harm caused thereby.

The Restatement holds that the defendant should be liable precisely because the third party *did* exploit the dangerous condition he created. *Brower* tacitly acknowledges distinct limits to causal responsibility, wholly without reference to foreseeability, even if the malicious acts of a third party do not sever causal connection. The consequences of the defendant's action cease once the railroad gathers up the barrels and places them under a competent guard.

The case law uniformly follows the Second Restatement. In Bigbee v. Pacific Telephone and Telegraph Co., 665 P.2d 947, 952 (Cal. 1983), the plaintiff was trapped in a telephone booth located in a parking lot fifteen feet from a major thoroughfare. The plaintiff saw an oncoming car careening out of control. He was struck by Leona Roberts, a drunk driver, when he was unable to wrestle the door open in time to escape. After holding that the phone company could be found negligent both in its placement and its maintenance of the booth, Bird, C.J., brushed aside the defendant's proximate cause argument, noting that it "is of no consequence that the harm to the plaintiff came about through the negligent or reckless acts of Roberts," citing RST §449.

In Britton v. Wooten, 817 S.W.2d 443, 449 (Ky. 1991), a grocery store, in which the defendant had negligently stacked excessive amounts of flammable trash, was destroyed, possibly by third-party arson. The plaintiff had leased the building to the defendant. Relying on the Second Restatement, the court concluded, "[W]e reject any all-inclusive general rule that, as respondent contends, 'criminal acts of third parties . . . relieve the original negligent party from liability.' " Likewise in Bell v. Board of Education, 687 N.E.2d 1325, 1326 (N.Y. 1998), the defendant school board left the plaintiff behind at a sixth-grade drug awareness fair near her school. On her way back home, she was accosted by three boys and taken to the house of one, where she was raped and sodomized. The court affirmed a jury verdict for the plaintiff, holding that "we cannot say that the intervening act of rape was unforeseeable as a matter of law." Does *Bell* present the same increased risk or hazard as *Hines*, *supra* at 343?

4. ***The Third Restatement Approach.*** The conceptual terminology of the Second Restatement gets a rude reception in the Third Restatement. Typically, the results in particular cases show no difference between the two Restatements, leaving it unclear whether the Third Restatement's preferred language will displace the ingrained usage of the Second.

RESTATEMENT OF THE LAW (THIRD) OF TORTS: LIABILITY FOR PHYSICAL AND EMOTIONAL HARM

§34. Intervening Acts and Superseding Causes

An actor's liability is limited to those harms that result from the risks that made the actor's conduct tortious.

Comment a. History and Introduction: . . . Despite the continuing influence of the Second Restatement of Torts, much of the formalism of its treatment of superseding causes has been supplanted in the latter part of the 20th century with a recognition that there are always multiple causes of an outcome and that the existence of intervening causes does not ordinarily elide a prior actor's liability. . . .

Illustration 3: The Brown Transport Company negligently seals a container truck loaded with a highly flammable liquid. The liquid leaks onto the street, after its driver parks it there while eating lunch. The leaking fluid creates a risk of fire or explosion. A fire does occur when a passerby negligently strikes a match to light her cigar. The flame from the match ignites the vapors produced by the liquid, and the ensuing fire injures Gordon. The harm suffered by Gordon in the fire is within the scope of Brown's liability for its negligence.

Illustration 5: Same facts as Illustration 3, except that the smoker, seeing the liquid and appreciating its flammability, deliberately throws a match onto the liquid. Whether Gordon's harm is within the scope of Brown's liability for its negligence is an issue for the factfinder.

Wagner v. International Ry.

133 N.E. 437 (N.Y. 1921)

Cardozo, J. [After a brief statement of preliminary facts about the electric railway's trestle:] Plaintiff and his cousin Herbert boarded a car at a station near the bottom of one of the trestles. Other passengers, entering at the same time, filled the platform, and blocked admission to the aisle. The platform was provided with doors, but the conductor did not close them. Moving at from six to eight miles an hour, the car, without slackening, turned the curve. There was a violent lurch, and Herbert Wagner was thrown out, near the point where the trestle changes to a bridge. The cry was raised, "Man overboard." The car went on across the bridge, and stopped near the foot of the incline. Night and darkness had come on. Plaintiff walked along the trestle, a distance of four hundred and forty-five feet, until he arrived at the bridge, where he thought to find his cousin's body. He says that he was asked to go there by the conductor. He says, too, that the conductor followed with a lantern. Both these statements the conductor denies. Several other persons, instead of ascending the trestle, went beneath it, and discovered under the bridge the body they were seeking. As they stood there, the plaintiff's body struck the ground beside them. Reaching the bridge, he had found upon a beam his cousin's hat, but nothing else. About him, there was darkness. He missed his footing, and fell.

The trial judge held that negligence toward Herbert Wagner would not charge the defendant with liability for injuries suffered by the plaintiff unless two other facts were found: First, that the plaintiff had been invited by the conductor to go upon the bridge; and second, that the conductor had followed with a light. Thus limited, the jury found in favor of the defendant. Whether the limitation may be upheld, is the question to be answered.

Danger invites rescue. The cry of distress is the summons to relief. The law does not ignore these reactions of the mind in tracing conduct to its consequences. It recognizes them as normal. It places their effects within the range of the natural and probable. The wrong that imperils life is a wrong to the imperiled victim; it is a wrong also to his rescuer. The state that leaves an opening in a bridge is liable to the child that falls into the stream, but liable also to the parent who plunges to its aid. . . . The railroad company whose train approaches without signal is a wrongdoer toward the traveler surprised between the rails, but a wrongdoer also to the bystander who drags him from the path (Eckert v. L.I.R.R. Co., 43 N.Y. 502 [*supra* Chapter 3, at 131]). . . . The rule is the same in other jurisdictions. . . . The risk of rescue, if only it be not wanton, is born of the occasion. The emergency begets the man. The wrongdoer may not have foreseen the coming of a deliverer. He is accountable as if he had. . . .

The defendant says that we must stop, in following the chain of causes, when action ceases to be "instinctive." By this, is meant, it seems, that rescue is at the peril of the rescuer, unless spontaneous and immediate. If there has been time to deliberate, if impulse has given way to judgment, one cause, it is said, has spent its force, and another has intervened. In this case, the plaintiff walked more than four hundred feet in going to Herbert's aid. He had time to reflect and weigh; impulse had been followed by choice; and choice, in the defendant's view, intercepts and breaks the sequence. We find no warrant for thus shortening the chain of jural causes. We may assume, though we are not required to decide, that peril and rescue must be in substance one transaction; that the sight of the one must have aroused the impulse to the other; in short, that there must be unbroken continuity between the commission of the wrong and the effort to avert its consequences. If all this be assumed, the defendant is not aided. Continuity in such circumstances is not broken by the exercise of volition. . . . So sweeping an exception, if recognized, would leave little of the rule. "The human mind," as we have said (People v. Majone, 91 N.Y. 211, 212), "acts with celerity which it is sometimes impossible to measure." The law does not discriminate between the rescuer oblivious of peril and the one who counts the cost. It is enough that the act, whether impulsive or deliberate, is the child of the occasion.

The defendant finds another obstacle, however, in the futility of the plaintiff's sacrifice. [The court then discusses whether or not plaintiff is contributorily negligent, concluding that under the emergency conditions, he is not.]

Whether Herbert Wagner's fall was due to the defendant's negligence, and whether plaintiff in going to the rescue, as he did, was foolhardy or reasonable in the light of the emergency confronting him, were questions for the jury.

NOTE

Danger Invites Rescue? Should the plaintiff's recovery be barred if the conductor had already mounted adequate rescue efforts without the plaintiff's assistance? If he had told the plaintiff to stay in the train? If Herbert were thought to be dead? Whatever its soundness, the "rescue doctrine" is well established today. See Espinoza v. Schulenberg, 129 P.3d 937, 939 (Ariz. 2006) (en banc). See also RTT: LPEH §32, noting that any unreasonable rescue efforts by plaintiff should be covered by comparative negligence and not the doctrine of superseding cause. *Id.*, comment *a.* The functions of the rescue doctrine were described in McCoy v. American Suzuki Motor Corp., 961 P.2d 952, 956 (Wash. 1998), as follows:

> First, it informs a tortfeasor it is foreseeable a rescuer will come to the aid of a person imperiled by the tortfeasor's actions, and, therefore, the tortfeasor owes the rescuer a duty similar to the duty he owes the person he imperils. Second, the rescue doctrine negates the presumption that the rescuer assumed the risk of injury when he knowingly undertook the dangerous rescue, so long as he does not act rashly or recklessly.
>
> To achieve rescuer status one must demonstrate: (1) the defendant was negligent to the person rescued and such negligence caused the peril or appearance of peril to the person rescued; (2) the peril or appearance of peril was imminent; (3) a reasonably prudent person would have concluded such peril or appearance of peril existed; and (4) the rescuer acted with reasonable care in effectuating the rescue.

Is the "danger invites rescue" doctrine justified on economic grounds? According to Hylton, Duty in Tort Law: An Economic Approach, 75 Fordham L. Rev. 1501, 1515 (2006): "By relieving rescuers of the duty to take care for their own safety, courts effectively subsidize rescue attempts. This is justifiable on the theory that the societal benefits of high-stakes altruism are substantial." Is the subsidy needed if the conductor has matters well in hand?

S

In re Polemis & Furness, Withy & Co.

[1921] 3 KB 560

Bankes, L.J. By a time charterparty dated February 21, 1917, the respondents chartered their vessel to the appellants. Clause 21 of the charterparty was in these terms.

["The act of God, the King's enemies, loss or damage from fire on board in hulk or craft, or on shore, arrest and/or restraint of princes, rulers, and people, collision, an act, neglect, or default whatsoever of pilot, master, or crew in the management or navigation of the ship, and all and every of the dangers and accidents of the seas, canals, and rivers, and of navigation of whatever nature or kind always mutually excepted." This charterparty was the agreement whereby the shipowner leased the ship to the "charterers" — the appellants in this case. The "mutually excepted" language meant on its face that each side had to bear its own losses from the stated contingencies. The court first holds that the language of clause 21 did not release the charterers from the consequences of their negligence.]

The vessel was employed by the charterers to carry a cargo to Casablanca in Morocco. The cargo included a quantity of benzine or petrol in cases. While discharging at Casablanca a heavy plank fell into the hold in which the petrol was stowed, and caused an explosion, which set fire to the vessel and completely destroyed her. The owners claimed the value of the vessel from the charterers, alleging that the loss of the vessel was due to the negligence of the charterers' servants. The charterers contended that they were protected by the exception of fire contained in clause 21 of the charterparty, and they also contended that the damages claimed were too remote. The claim was referred to arbitration, and the arbitrators stated a special case for the opinion of the Court. Their findings of fact are as follows.

(a) That the ship was lost by fire.
(b) That the fire arose from a spark igniting petrol vapour in the hold.
(c) That the spark was caused by the falling board coming into contact with some substance in the hold.
(d) That the fall of the board was caused by the negligence of the Arabs (other than the winchman) engaged in the work of discharging.
(e) That the said Arabs were employed by the charterers or their agents the Cie. Transatlantique on behalf of the charterers, and that the said Arabs were the servants of the charterers.
(f) That the causing of the spark could not reasonably have been anticipated from the falling of the board, though some damage to the ship might reasonably have been anticipated.
(g) There was no evidence before us that the Arabs chosen were known or likely to be negligent.

Then they state the damages, £196,165 1*s.* 11*d.* These findings are no doubt intended to raise the question whether the view taken, or said to have been taken, by Pollock, C.B., in Rigby v. Hewitt[, (1850) 155 Eng. Rep. 103 (Exch.),] and Greenland v. Chaplin (5 [Ex.] 243, 155 [Eng. Rep.] 104, [1850]), or the view taken by Channell, B., and Blackburn, J., in Smith v. London & South Western Ry. Co. (3 L. R. 6 C.P. 21 [(1870)]), is the correct one. . . .

Assuming the Chief Baron to have been correctly reported in the Exchequer Reports, the difference between the two views is this: According to the one view, the consequences which may reasonably be expected to result from a particular act are material only in reference to the question whether the act is or is not a negligent act; according to the other view, those consequences are the test whether the damages resulting from the act, assuming it to be negligent, are or are not too remote to be recoverable. [Bankes, L.J., then quoted from H.M.S. London, [1914] P. 72, in part, as follows:] ". . . In Smith v. London and South Western Ry. Co., Channell, B., said: 'Where there is no direct evidence of negligence, the question what a reasonable man might foresee is of importance in considering the question whether there is evidence for the jury of negligence or not . . . but when it has been once determined that there is evidence of negligence, the person guilty of it is equally liable for its consequences, whether he could have foreseen them or not.' And Blackburn, J., in the same case said: 'What the defendants might reasonably anticipate is only material with reference to the question, whether the defendants were negligent or not, and cannot alter their liability if they were guilty of negligence.' " . . .

In the present case the arbitrators have found as a fact that the falling of the plank was due to the negligence of the defendants' servants. The fire appears to me to have been directly caused by the falling of the plank. Under these circumstances I consider that it is immaterial that the causing of the spark by the falling of the plank could not have been reasonably anticipated. The appellants' junior counsel sought to draw a distinction between the anticipation of the extent of damage resulting from a negligent act, and the anticipation of the type of damage resulting from such an act. He admitted that it could not lie in the mouth of a person whose negligent act had caused damage to say that he could not reasonably have foreseen the extent of the damage, but he contended that the negligent person was entitled to rely upon the fact that he could not reasonably have anticipated the type of damage which resulted from his negligent act. I do not think that the distinction can be admitted. Given the breach of duty which constitutes the negligence, and given the damage as a direct result of that negligence, the anticipations of the person whose negligent act has produced the damage appear to me to be irrelevant. I consider that the damages claimed are not too remote.

Warrington, L.J. [referring to a discussion by Beven on Negligence, observes:] . . . The result may be summarised as follows: The presence or absence of reasonable anticipation of damage determines the legal quality of the act as negligent or innocent. If it be thus determined to be negligent, then the question whether particular damages are recoverable depends only on the answer to the question whether they are the direct consequence of the act. Sufficient authority for the proposition is afforded by Smith v. London and South Western Ry. Co., in the Exchequer Chamber, and particularly by the judgments of Channell, B., and Blackburn, J. . . . In the present case it is clear that the act causing the plank to fall was in law a negligent act, because some damage to the ship might reasonably be anticipated. If this is so then the appellants are liable for the actual loss, that being on the findings of the arbitrators the direct result of the falling board. . . .

Scrutton, L.J. . . . The second defence is that the damage is too remote from the negligence, as it could not be reasonably foreseen as a consequence. On this head we were referred to a number of well known cases in which vague language, which I cannot think to be really helpful, has been used in an attempt to define the point at which damage becomes too remote from, or not sufficiently directly caused by, the breach of duty, which is the original cause of action, to be recoverable. For instance, I cannot think it useful to say the damage must be the natural and probable result. This suggests that there are results which are natural but not probable, and other results which are probable but not natural. I am not sure what either adjective means in this connection; if they mean the same thing, two need not be used; if they mean different things, the difference between them should be defined. And as to many cases of fact in which the distinction has been drawn, it is difficult to see why one case should be decided one way and one another. . . . To determine whether an act is negligent, it is relevant to determine whether any reasonable person would foresee that the act would cause damage; if he would not, the act is not negligent. But if the act would or might probably cause damage, the fact that the damage it in fact causes is not the exact kind of damage one would expect is immaterial, so long as the damage is in fact directly traceable to the negligent act, and not due to the operation of independent causes having no connection with the negligent act, except that they could not avoid its results. Once the act is negligent, the fact that its exact operation was not foreseen is immaterial. . . . In the present case it was negligent in discharging cargo to knock down the planks of the temporary staging, for they might easily cause some damage either to workmen, or cargo, or the ship. The fact that they did directly produce an unexpected result, a spark in an atmosphere of petrol vapour which caused a fire, does not relieve the person who was negligent from the damage which his negligent act so directly caused.

NOTES

1. *The Ex Ante Contract.* In light of the contractual exclusion of clause 21, *Polemis* presented a case of an incomplete contract between the owner and charterer because it did not allocate loss in the event of negligence by either party. What result if the contract had provided explicitly that all unforeseeable risks of the charterer's negligence were to be borne by the shipowner? Is that likely to have been the ex ante arrangement between the parties? Could this problem have been averted by taking out an insurance policy on the vessel that covers the loss for both parties?

2. *The Directness Test.* What are the arguments for imposing liability only if the unforeseeable harm results directly, rather than indirectly? Is it enough that this avoids factual problems of causal intervention and thereby simplifies the cause in fact inquiry? Whatever its merits, the *Polemis* approach has long had its American supporters. In Christianson v. Chicago, St. P., M. and O. Ry., 69 N.W. 640, 641 (Minn. 1896), the plaintiff was riding on the rear of a railroad's handcar, moving west. His handcar was being overtaken by a second car, driven by his foreman, going at a faster rate in the same direction. The plaintiff lost his balance and fell off the car, only to be struck and severely injured by the second handcar. Mitchell, J., upheld jury determinations that exonerated the plaintiff from charges of contributory negligence and found the defendant negligent. Thereafter, he rejected the defendant's premise that the workers on the rear car "could not have reasonably anticipated that plaintiff would fall from the car."

> The doctrine contended for by counsel would establish practically the same rule of damages resulting from tort as is applied to damages resulting from breach of contract, under the familiar doctrine of Hadley v. Baxendale, 9 Exch. 341. This mode of stating the law is misleading, if not positively inaccurate. It confounds and mixes the definition of "negligence" with that of "proximate cause."
>
> What a man may reasonably anticipate is important, and may be decisive, in determining whether an act is negligent, but is not at all decisive in determining whether that act is the proximate cause of an injury which ensues. . . . Consequences which follow in unbroken sequence, without an intervening efficient cause, from the original negligent act, are natural and proximate and for such consequences the original wrongdoer is responsible, even though he could not have foreseen the particular results which did follow. Smith v. Railway Co., L. R. 6 C. P. 14.
>
> Tested by this rule, we think that it is clear that the negligence of those on the rear car was the proximate cause of plaintiff's injuries; at least, that the evidence justified the jury in so finding. Counsel admitted on the argument that if, by derailment or other accident, the front car had been suddenly stopped, and a collision and consequent injuries to plaintiff had resulted, the negligence of those on the rear car would have been the proximate cause. But we can see no difference in principle between the case supposed and the present case. The causal connection between the negligent act and the resulting injury would be the same in both cases. The only possible difference is that it might be anticipated that the sudden stoppage of the car was more likely to happen than the falling of one of its occupants upon the track.

What result under a modern foreseeability test? In a famous bon mot, Professor Seavey said, "Prima facie at least, the reasons for creating liability should limit it." Seavey, Mr. Justice Cardozo and the Law of Torts, 39 Colum. L. Rev. 20, 34; 52 Harv. L. Rev. 372, 386; 48 Yale L.J. 390, 404 (1939). How does Seavey's argument apply under a regime of strict liability? As a guide to contractual interpretation?

Overseas Tankship (U.K.) Ltd. v. Morts Dock & Engineering Co., Ltd. (Wagon Mound (No. 1))

[1961] AC 388 (PC) (appeal taken from Austl.)

[The appellants, defendants in the original cause of action, had carelessly discharged oil from their ship while it was berthed in Sydney Harbor. After their ship set sail, the oil was carried by the wind and tide to the plaintiff's wharf, which was used for repair work on other ships in the harbor. Plaintiff's supervisor was concerned about the spread of the oil, and he ordered his workmen to do no welding or burning in the area until further orders. He made some inquiries with the manager of the CalTex Oil Company, where the *Wagon Mound* was berthed, which, coupled with his own knowledge, satisfied him that the oil was not flammable. He accordingly instructed his men to resume their welding operations, and directed them as well to take care that no flammable material should fall off the wharf into the oil.

About two and one-half days later, the plaintiff's wharf was destroyed when the oil caught fire. "The outbreak of fire was due, as the trial judge found, to the fact that there was floating in the oil underneath the wharf a piece of debris on which lay some smouldering cotton waste or rag which had been set on fire by molten metal falling from the wharf: that the cotton waste or rag burst into flames: that the flames from the cotton waste set the floating oil afire either directly or by first setting fire to a wooden pile coated with oil, and that after the floating oil became ignited; the flames spread rapidly over the surface of the oil and quickly developed into a conflagration which severely damaged the wharf." "The trial judge also made the all-important finding, which must be set out in his own words: 'The *raison d'être* of furnace oil is, of course, that it shall burn, but I find the defendant did not know and could not reasonably be expected to have known that it was capable of being set afire when spread on water.' " The trial judge also found that the oil had caused, apart from the conflagration, some slight damage when it mucked up the plaintiff's wharf.]

Wagon Mound
Source: bulkers/photobucket

Viscount Simonds. . . . There can be no doubt that the decision of the Court of Appeal in *Polemis* plainly asserts that, if the defendant is guilty of negligence, he is responsible for all the consequences whether reasonably foreseeable or not. The generality of the proposition is perhaps qualified by the fact that each of the Lords Justices refers to the outbreak of fire as the direct result of the negligent act. There is thus introduced the conception that the negligent actor is not responsible for consequences which are not "direct," whatever that may mean. It has to be asked, then, why this conclusion should have been reached. The answer appears to be that it was reached upon a consideration of certain authorities, comparatively few in number, that were cited to the court. Of these, three are generally regarded as having influenced the decision. [The court then reviews Smith v. London & South Western Railway Co., [1870] 6 LRCP 14, *supra* at 340.] It would perhaps not be improper to say that the law of negligence as an independent tort was then of recent growth and that its implications had not been fully examined.

[The Privy Council then considers the H.M.S. London [1914] P. 72 and Weld Blundell v. Stephens [1970] AC 956, and concludes with a famous passage from the latter case by Lord Sumner:] "What a defendant ought to have anticipated as a reasonable man is material when the question is whether or not he was guilty of negligence, that is, of want of due care according to the circumstances. This, however, goes to culpability, not to compensation." [After discussion of some other English precedents, the opinion continues:]

The impression that may well be left on the reader of the scores of cases in which liability for negligence has been discussed is that the courts were feeling their way to a coherent body of doctrine and were at times in grave danger of being led astray by scholastic theories of causation and their ugly and barely intelligible jargon. . . .

Enough has been said to show that the authority of *Polemis* has been severely shaken though lip service has from time to time been paid to it. In their Lordships' opinion it should no longer be regarded as good law. It is not probable that many cases will for that reason have a different result, though it is hoped that the law will be thereby simplified, and that in some cases, at least, palpable injustice will be avoided. For it does not seem consonant with current ideas of justice or morality that for an act of negligence, however slight or venial, which results in some trivial foreseeable damage the actor should be liable for all consequences however unforeseeable and however grave, so long as they can be said to be "direct." It is a principle of civil liability, subject only to qualifications which have no present relevance, that a man must be considered to be responsible for the probable consequences of his act. To demand more of him is too harsh a rule, to demand less is to ignore that civilized order requires the observance of a minimum standard of behaviour.

This concept applied to the slowly developing law of negligence has led to a great variety of expressions which can, as it appears to their Lordships, be harmonized with little difficulty with the single exception of the so-called rule in *Polemis.* For, if it is asked why a man should be responsible for the natural or necessary or probable consequences of his act (or any other similar description of them) the answer is that it is not because they are natural or necessary or probable, but because, since they have this quality, it is judged by the standard of the reasonable man that he ought to have foreseen them. Thus it is that over and over again it has happened that in different judgments in the same case, and sometimes in a single judgment, liability for a consequence has been imposed on the ground that it was reasonably foreseeable or, alternatively, on the ground that it was natural or necessary or probable. The two grounds have been treated as coterminous, and so they largely are. But, where they are not, the question arises to which the wrong answer was given in *Polemis.* For, if some limitation must be imposed upon the consequences for which the negligent actor is to be held responsible—and all are agreed that some limitation there must be—why should that test (reasonable foreseeability) be rejected which, since he is judged by what the reasonable man ought to foresee, corresponds with the common conscience of mankind, and a test (the "direct" consequence) be substituted which leads to nowhere but the never-ending and insoluble problems of causation. "The lawyer," said Sir Frederick Pollock, "cannot afford to adventure himself with philosophers in the logical and metaphysical controversies that beset the idea of cause." Yet this is just what he has most unfortunately done and must continue to do if the rule in *Polemis* is to prevail. A conspicuous example occurs when the actor seeks to escape liability on the ground that the "chain of causation" is broken by a nova causa or novus actus interveniens. . . .

In the same connection may be mentioned the conclusion to which the Full Court finally came in the present case. Applying the rule in *Polemis* and holding therefore that the unforeseeability of the damage by fire afforded no defence, they went on to consider the remaining question. Was it a "direct" consequence? Upon this Manning, J., said: "Notwithstanding that, if regard is had separately to each individual occurrence in the chain of events that led to this fire, each occurrence was improbable and, in one sense, improbability was heaped upon improbability, I cannot escape from the conclusion that if the ordinary man in the street had been asked, as a matter of common sense, without any detailed analysis of the circumstances, to state the cause of the fire at Morts Dock, he would unhesitatingly have assigned such cause to spillage of oil by the appellant's employees." Perhaps he would, and probably he would have added: "I never should have thought it possible." But with great respect to the Full Court this is surely irrelevant, or, if it is relevant, only serves to show that the *Polemis* rule works in a very strange way. After the event even a fool is wise. But it is not the hindsight of a fool; it is the foresight of the reasonable man which alone can determine responsibility. The *Polemis* rule by substituting "direct" for "reasonably foreseeable" consequence leads to a conclusion equally illogical and unjust.

[Appeal allowed.]

NOTES

1. ***Foresight Versus Directness.*** The abstract debate over the proper standard for remoteness of damage often obscures what is at stake in the two positions. An instructive way to approach this dispute over proximate cause is to ask whether *Wagon Mound (No. 1)* can be reconciled with *In re Polemis* even under the "direct consequences" test. To do so, it is necessary to examine the precise sequence of events between defendant's wrongful conduct and plaintiff's harm. In *Polemis*, no human act intervened between the dropping of the plank and the burning of the ship; the only causal complication was the antecedent presence of fumes in the ship's hold. In *Wagon Mound (No. 1)*, however, the causal chain contained at least two human acts between the oil spill from defendant's ship and the destruction of plaintiff's wharf: first, the consultations by plaintiff's dock supervisor with CalTex's manager and, second, the ignition of the fire by the oxyacetylene torches used by plaintiff's servants. If the conduct of plaintiff's servants amounts to either assumption of risk or contributory negligence, it is possible both to keep the directness test of *Polemis* and to defend the result in *Wagon Mound (No. 1)*. Note also that if either defense is feasible, the plaintiff must proceed gingerly on foreseeability, for if the defendant's servants could have foreseen the harm, so too could the plaintiff's.

The importance of the plaintiff's conduct is illustrated by the Privy Council's subsequent decision in Overseas Tankship (U.K.) Ltd. v. The Miller Steamship Co., [1967] 1 AC 617, 642–43, better known as *Wagon Mound (No. 2)*. The facts in that case were the same as in *Wagon Mound (No. 1)*, except that the plaintiff in *Wagon Mound (No. 2)* was the owner of a ship destroyed by the fire in *Wagon Mound (No. 1)*. The plaintiff shipowner was not, of course, bound by the prior decision; nor was he hampered by possible charges of contributory negligence or assumption of risk. As against the plaintiff, the conduct of the servants of Morts Dock (plaintiff in *Wagon Mound (No. 1)*) only went to the question of causal connection, where in the modern view it could not, as intervening negligence, be decisive. See *supra* at 346. Plaintiff therefore introduced evidence to show that some risk of harm by fire was reasonably foreseeable by defendant's engineer. Lord Reid, speaking for the Privy Council, distinguished *Wagon Mound (No. 1)* and affirmed a judgment for the plaintiff. He noted that the plaintiff lost in Bolton v. Stone, *supra* Chapter 2, at 100, because the risk of harm was small and the activity that caused the harm was lawful, whereas:

> In the present case there was no justification whatever for discharging the oil into Sydney Harbour. Not only was it an offence to do so, but it involved considerable loss financially. If the ship's engineer had thought about the matter, there could have been no question of balancing the advantages and disadvantages. From every point of view it was both his duty and his interest to stop the discharge immediately. . . .
>
> The findings show that he [the ship's engineer] ought to have known that it is possible to ignite this kind of oil on water, and that the ship's engineer probably ought to have known that this had in fact happened before. The most that can be said to justify inaction is that he would have known that this could only happen in very exceptional circumstances. But that does not mean that a reasonable man would dismiss such a risk from his mind and do nothing when it was so easy to prevent it.

Does Lord Reid's argument amount to a repudiation of Bolton v. Stone? An adoption of the Hand formula for negligence? A belated acceptance of the judgment of Nares, J., in Scott v. Shepherd, *supra* Chapter 2, at 72? On the progression from *Polemis* to *Wagon Mound*, see Levmore, *The Wagon Mound Cases*: Foreseeability, Causation, and Mrs. Palsgraf, *in* Torts Stories 129, 142 (Rabin & Sugarman eds., 2003), suggesting that on grounds of causation the outcome of the two cases could easily be reversed.

2. *The Passing of Causation.* The proponents of the foresight test insist that it allows courts to dispense with the technical and nearly insoluble conundrums of causation. Even if the argument is sound (is it?), the foresight test raises unique problems of its own, chiefly in describing the events that led to the plaintiff's harm. Professor Morris discusses this point in Torts 174–77 (1953):

> Once misconduct causes damage, a specific accident has happened in a particular way and has resulted in a discrete harm. When, after the event, the question is asked, "Was the particular accident and the resulting damages foreseeable?", the cases fall into the three classes:

(1) In some cases damages resulting from misconduct are so typical that judge and jurors cannot possibly be convinced that they were unforeseeable. . . .

(2) In some cases freakishness of the facts refuses to be downed and any description that minimizes it is viewed as misdescription. For example, in a recent Louisiana case [Lynch v. Fisher, 41 So. 2d 692 (La. App. 1949)] a trucker negligently left his truck on the highway at night without setting out flares. A car crashed into the truck and caught fire. A passerby came to the rescue of the car occupants—a man and wife. After the rescuer got them out of the car he returned to the car to get a floor mat to pillow the injured wife's head. A pistol lay on the mat the rescuer wanted to use. He picked it up and handed it to the husband. The accident had unbeknownst to the rescuer, temporarily deranged the husband, and he shot rescuer in the leg. Such a consequence of negligently failing to guard a truck with flares is so unarguably unforeseeable that no judge or juror would be likely to hold otherwise. (Incidentally the Louisiana court held the trucker liable to the rescuer on the ground that foreseeability is not a requisite of liability.)

(3) Between these extremes are cases in which consequences are neither typical nor wildly freakish. In these cases unusual details are arguably—but only arguably significant. If they are held significant, then the consequences are unforeseeable; if they are held unimportant then the consequences are foreseeable.

Into which class does *Polemis* fall? *Wagon Mound*? Need the defendant only foresee "in a general way" the consequences of his act, and not the "precise details of its occurrence"?

3. *A Foreseeable Kind of Damage.* In the aftermath of *Wagon Mound (No. 1)*, the English courts struggled to determine whether the harm suffered by the plaintiff was foreseeable. In Doughty v. Turner Manufacturing Co., Ltd., [1964] 1 QB 518, one of the defendant's employees knocked an asbestos cement cover into a vat of extremely hot solution of sodium cyanide—eight times as hot as boiling water. His conduct was negligent since the falling cover might have splashed some of the molten substance on someone standing nearby. In fact, nobody was hurt by the splash, but after a short time the asbestos cement cover caused an explosion in the vat that hurled the molten substance into the air, some of it hurting the plaintiff, who stood nearby. No one had any reason to suspect that the cover, when immersed, would explode. The trial judge allowed recovery given defendant's negligence, but the Court of Appeal reversed because the damage was the consequence of a risk or hazard about which defendant had not been negligent. Does *Doughty* present any problems of causal intervention?

Contrast *Doughty* with Hughes v. Lord Advocate, [1963] AC 837. Defendant's servants were working on an underground cable to which they had access through an open manhole nine feet deep. The manhole was covered by a shelter-tent. When defendant's servants left the work area, they left a ladder near the manhole, pulled a tarpaulin over the entrance to the tent, and lighted four paraffin warning lamps outside the tent. The plaintiff, aged eight, and his uncle, aged ten, came by and started to play with the equipment with a view toward descending into the manhole. Plaintiff tripped over one of the paraffin lamps, which he had brought into the tent, which then fell into the hole. An explosion ensued when, as best as could be determined, "paraffin escaped from the tank, formed vapour and was ignited by the flame." The explosion burned the plaintiff and knocked him into the hole, as a result of which the severity of his burns was greatly increased. The respondents argued that the explosion was unforeseeable even if some harm from burning by the lamp was foreseeable. The House of Lords rejected the argument, holding that the damage was not of a different type from that which was foreseeable given that paraffin lamps were a "known source of danger." Is the distinction between burning and explosion "too fine to warrant acceptance"? If so, why accept the distinction between splashing and exploding? Does *Hughes* present the troublesome questions of causal intervention referred to in *Wagon Mound (No. 1)*? Note that the defendant in *Hughes*, on appeal, did not claim that plaintiff's trespass barred his recovery.

4. *The Thin Skull Rule, or "You Take Your Victim as You Find Him."* One rule of tort law left unshaken by *Wagon Mound (No. 1)* is that the defendant takes his victim as he finds him. In Smith v. Brain Leech & Co. Ltd., [1962] 2 QB 405, plaintiff's decedent was burned on his lip by splashing molten metal because defendant negligently failed to provide an adequate guard. Because of prior exposures of another kind in the past, the decedent had (according to the court) developed a tendency toward cancer. In any event, the burned lip developed a cancer from which he died. The court acknowledged that death by cancer was unforeseeable, but, notwithstanding *Wagon Mound (No. 1)*, it allowed recovery, expressing certainty that the Privy Council had no intention of changing the "take plaintiff as he is" principle or denying recovery to a plaintiff with a thin skull.

On the thin skull rule and its relationship to the problems of causal intervention, see Seavey, Mr. Justice Cardozo and the Law of Torts, 39 Colum. L. Rev. 20, 32–33; 52 Harv. L. Rev. 372, 384–85; 48 Yale L.J. 390, 402–03 (1939):

> [W]here the defendant has negligently struck a person whose skull is so fragile that it is broken by the comparatively slight blow, all courts are agreed that the defendant is liable for the wholly unexpected breaking. This is true not only with reference to physical harm but also other forms of harm. If a person were negligently to incapacitate another who has a yearly earning capacity of a hundred thousand dollars, there is liability for the resulting loss though so great a loss could not have been anticipated. It may be that this is a possible explanation for the reaction of the King's Bench in its famous but doubtful decision of the *Polemis* case, in which the defendant whose workman negligently dropped a plank into the hold of a ship filled with gasoline vapor was made liable for the destruction of the ship resulting from the ensuing explosion. In this, as in other cases, the courts are agreed that the negligent person takes his victims as they are.

The causal complications of the thin skull rule are graphically illustrated by Steinhauser v. Hertz Corp., 421 F.2d 1169, 1172 (2d Cir. 1970). Plaintiff, a 14-year-old child, was a passenger in her parents' car when it was wrongfully struck by the driver of defendant's car. The plaintiff suffered no physical injuries, but shortly thereafter she began to behave strangely; she became "highly agitated," "glassy-eyed," and "nervous." As her condition worsened, she was institutionally treated for schizophrenia. Even after her release she required further medical treatment, with reinstitutionalization a likely prospect. Two years prior to the accident, the plaintiff had suffered a mild concussion. Plaintiff's attorney argued that the accident was a "precipitating cause of a quiescent disease." The trial judge instructed the jury that recovery was permissible only if the plaintiff were normal before the accident, but not if "this plaintiff had this disease all along." Proximate cause was, in the words of the trial judge, "a big word" for what ordinary people call cause. The jury's verdict for defendant was reversed on appeal, with Friendly, J., writing as follows:

> The testimony was that before the accident Cynthia was *neither* a "perfectly normal child" *nor* a schizophrenic, but a child with some degree of pathology which was activated into schizophrenia by an emotional trauma although it otherwise might not have blossomed. Whatever the medical soundness of this theory may or may not be, and there does not seem in fact to have been any dispute about it, plaintiffs were entitled to have it fairly weighed by the jury. They could not properly be pinioned on the dilemma of having either to admit that Cynthia was already suffering from active schizophrenia or to assert that she was wholly without psychotic tendencies.

5. *American Response to Polemis and Wagon Mound (No. 1).* Friendly, J., also commented on the English debate over proximate cause in Petition of Kinsman Transit Co., 338 F.2d 708, 723–25 (2d Cir. 1964). A January thaw on the Buffalo River released large cakes of ice that, because of high water, banged into and loosened a negligently tied and improperly tended ship so that it started downstream, careening into another ship and knocking it loose. Both ships then drifted on and crashed into a drawbridge maintained by the city of Buffalo at a point before the river flows into Lake Erie. The two ships and the drawbridge made an effective dam against which floating ice accumulated, causing flooding for miles. This action was brought against the owner of the first ship and the city. The above events all occurred at night, when no traffic was expected on the river.

The crew tending the drawbridge was, or so the court held, under a statutory duty to raise the drawbridge not only for ships passing by in the course of navigation but also for drifting vessels. If the crew had displayed the requisite alertness by raising the bridge in time, all of the harm at issue could have been avoided. By a two-to-one vote, the court held both defendants jointly liable for plaintiff's damages. Judge Friendly made these observations about the rejection of *Polemis* in *Wagon Mound (No. 1)*:

> [We] find it difficult to understand why one who had failed to use the care required to protect others in the light of expectable forces should be exonerated when the very risks that rendered his conduct negligent produced other and more serious consequences to such persons than were fairly foreseeable when he fell short of what the law demanded. Foreseeability of danger is necessary to render conduct negligent where as here the damage was caused by just those forces whose existence required the exercise of greater care than was taken — the current, the ice, and the physical mass of the Shiras, the incurring of consequences other and greater than foreseen does not make the conduct less culpable or provide a reasoned basis for insulation. The oft-encountered argument that failure to limit liability to foreseeable consequences may subject the defendant to a loss wholly out of proportion to his fault seems scarcely consistent with the universally accepted rule that the defendant takes the plaintiff as he finds him and will be responsible for the full extent of the injury even though a latent susceptibility of the plaintiff renders this far more serious than could reasonably have been anticipated. . . .
>
> The weight of authority in this country rejects the limitation of damages to consequences foreseeable at the time of the negligent conduct when the consequences are "direct," and the damage, although other and greater than expectable, is of the same general sort that was risked. . . . Other American courts, purporting to apply a test of foreseeability to damages, extend that concept to such unforeseen lengths as to raise serious doubt whether the concept is meaningful; indeed, we wonder whether the British courts are not finding it necessary to limit the language of *The Wagon Mound* as we have indicated.
>
> We see no reason why an actor engaging in conduct which entails a large risk of small damage and a small risk of other and greater damage, of the same general sort, from the same forces, and to the same class of persons, should be relieved of responsibility for the latter simply because the chance of its occurrence, if viewed alone, may not have been large enough to require the exercise of care. By hypothesis, the risk of the lesser harm was sufficient to render his disregard of it actionable; the existence of a less likely additional risk that the very forces against whose action he was required to guard would produce other and greater damage than could have been reasonably anticipated should inculpate him further rather than limit his liability.

Why is plaintiff's harm direct damage in *Kinsman*?

Palsgraf v. Long Island R.R.
162 N.E. 99 (N.Y. 1928)

Appeal from a judgment of the Appellate Division of the Supreme Court in the second judicial department, entered December 16, 1927, affirming a judgment in favor of plaintiff entered upon a verdict.

[The following excerpts are from the majority opinion of Seeger, J., in the Appellate Division, 222 App. Div. 166 (1927):]

The defendant contends that the accident was not caused by the negligence of the defendant.

The sole question of defendant's negligence submitted to the jury was whether the defendant's employees were "careless and negligent in the way they handled this particular passenger after he came upon the platform and while he was boarding the train." This question of negligence was submitted to the jury by a fair and impartial charge and the verdict was supported by the evidence. The jury might well find that the act of the passenger in undertaking to board a moving train was negligent, and that the acts of the defendant's employees in assisting him while engaged in that negligent act were also negligent. Instead of aiding or assisting the passenger engaged in such an act, they might better have discouraged and warned him not to board the moving train. It is quite probable that without their assistance the passenger might have succeeded in boarding the train and no accident would have happened, or without the assistance of these employees the passenger might have desisted in his efforts to board the train. In any event, the acts of defendant's employees, which the jury found to be negligent, caused the bundle to be thrown under the train and to explode. It is no answer or defense to these negligent acts to say that the defendant's employees were not chargeable with notice that the passenger's bundle contained an explosive. . . .

It must be remembered that the plaintiff was a passenger of the defendant and entitled to have the defendant exercise the highest degree of care required of common carriers.

[The dissenting opinion of Lazansky, P.J., in the appellate division reads as follows:]

The facts may have warranted the jury in finding the defendant's agents were negligent in assisting a passenger in boarding a moving train in view of the fact that a door of the train should have been closed before the train started, which would have prevented the passenger making the attempt. There was also warrant for a finding by the jury that as a result of the negligence of the defendant a package was thrown between the platform and train, exploded, causing injury to plaintiff, who was on the station platform. In my opinion, the negligence of defendant was not a proximate cause of the injuries to plaintiff. Between the negligence of defendant and the injuries, there intervened the negligence of the passenger carrying the package containing an explosive. This was an independent, and not a concurring act of negligence. The explosion was not reasonably probable as a result of defendant's act of negligence. The negligence of defendant was not a likely or natural cause of the explosion, since the latter was such an unusual occurrence. Defendant's negligence was a cause of plaintiff's injury, but too remote.

[The appellate division split three to two for plaintiff. The Court of Appeals reverses by a four-to-three vote.]

Exhibit 5.1 Benjamin Cardozo

Benjamin Cardozo (1870–1938) was one of the foremost jurists of the early twentieth century, serving on the New York Court of Appeals (1914–1932) and the United States Supreme Court (1932–1938). During his tenure on the Court of Appeals, Cardozo wrote some of the most notable modern tort law decisions, including *Palsgraf*, Murphy v. Steeplechase Amusement Co., and MacPherson v. Buick Motor Co. Cardozo has been praised by Court of Appeals Chief Judge Judith Kaye for "look[ing] beyond the immediate facts to the future course of the law." Cardozo also believed that "there is an accuracy that defeats itself by the overemphasis of details," instead relying on sparse statements of facts to support an opinion's inevitable conclusion (as in *Palsgraf*).

Described as a "legal landmark" by Cardozo biographer Andrew L. Kaufman, *Palsgraf*'s "extraordinary events that linked Helen Palsgraf and Benjamin Cardozo" were not confined to the case itself. Over 60 years after the case was decided, in 1991, Lisa Newell, "the first cousin four times removed of Benjamin Cardozo, married J. Scott Garvey. Mr. Garvey is the great-grandson of Helen Palsgraf." Andrew L. Kaufman, Cardozo 303 (Harvard University Press, 1998).

Bio source: Judith S. Kaye, Benjamin Nathan Cardozo (1870–1938) Court of Appeals 1914–1932 Chief Judge 1927–1932, 6 Jud. Notice 3 (2009)
Image source: Wikimedia Commons

Cardozo, C.J. Plaintiff was standing on a platform of defendant's railroad after buying a ticket to go to Rockaway Beach. A train stopped at the station, bound for another place. Two men ran forward to catch it. One of the men reached the platform of the car without mishap, though the train was already moving. The other man, carrying a package, jumped aboard the car, but seemed unsteady as if about to fall. A guard on the car, who had held the door open, reached forward to help him in, and another guard on the platform pushed him from behind. In this act, the package was dislodged, and fell upon the rails. It was a package of small size, about fifteen inches long, and was covered by a newspaper. In fact it contained fireworks, but there was nothing in its appearance to give notice of its contents. The fireworks when they fell exploded. The shock of the explosion threw down some scales at the other end of the platform, many feet away. The scales struck the plaintiff, causing injuries for which she sues.

The conduct of the defendant's guard, if a wrong in its relation to the holder of the package, was not a wrong in its relation to the plaintiff, standing far away. Relatively to her it was not negligence at all. Nothing in the situation gave notice that the falling package had in it the potency of peril to persons thus removed. Negligence is not actionable unless it involves the invasion of a legally protected interest, the violation of a right. "Proof of negligence in the air, so to speak, will not do" (Pollock, Torts, p. 455 [11th ed.]). The plaintiff as she stood upon the platform of the station might claim to be protected against intentional invasion of her bodily security. Such invasion is not charged. She might claim to be protected against unintentional invasion by conduct involving in the thought of reasonable men an unreasonable hazard that such invasion would ensue. These, from the point of view of the law, were the bounds of her immunity, with perhaps some rare exceptions, survivals for the most part of ancient forms of liability, where conduct is held to be at the peril of the actor. If no hazard was apparent to the eye of ordinary vigilance, an act innocent and harmless, at least to outward seeming, with reference to her, did not take to itself the quality of a tort because it happened to be a wrong, though apparently not one involving the risk of bodily insecurity, with reference to someone else. . . . The plaintiff sues in her own right for a wrong personal to her, and not as the vicarious beneficiary of a breach of duty to another.

A different conclusion will involve us, and swiftly too, in a maze of contradictions. A guard stumbles over a package which has been left upon a platform. It seems to be a bundle of newspapers. It turns out to be a can of dynamite. To the eye of ordinary vigilance, the bundle is abandoned waste, which may be kicked or trod on with impunity. Is a passenger at the other end of the platform protected by the law against the unsuspected hazard concealed beneath the waste? If not, is the result to be any different, so far as the distant passenger is concerned, when the guard stumbles over a valise which a truckman or a porter has left upon the walk? The passenger far away, if the victim of a wrong at all, has a cause of action, not derivative, but original and primary. His claim to be protected against invasion of his bodily security is neither greater nor less because the act resulting in the invasion is a wrong to another far removed. In this case, the rights that are said to have been violated, the interests said to have been invaded, are not even of the same order. The man was not injured in his person nor even put in danger. The purpose of the act, as well as its effect, was to make his person safe. If there was a wrong to him at all, which may very well be doubted, it was a wrong to a property interest only, the safety of his package. Out of this wrong to property, which threatened injury to nothing else, there has passed, we are told, to the plaintiff by derivation or succession a right of action for the invasion of an interest of another order, the right to bodily security. The diversity of interests emphasizes the futility of the effort to build the plaintiff's right upon the basis of a wrong to some one else. The gain is one of emphasis, for a like result would follow if the interests were the same. Even then, the orbit of the danger as disclosed to the eye of reasonable vigilance would be the orbit of the duty. One who jostles one's neighbor in a crowd does not invade the rights of others standing at the outer fringe when the unintended contact casts a bomb upon the ground. The wrongdoer as to them is the man who carries the bomb, not the one who explodes it without suspicion of the danger. Life will have to be made over, and human nature transformed, before prevision so extravagant can be accepted as the norm of conduct, the customary standard to which behavior must conform.

The argument for the plaintiff is built upon the shifting meanings of such words as "wrong" and "wrongful," and shares their instability. What the plaintiff must show is "a wrong" to herself, i.e. a violation of her own right, and not merely a wrong to someone else, nor conduct "wrongful" because unsocial, but not "a wrong" to any one. We are told that one who drives at reckless speed through a crowded city street is guilty of a negligent act and, therefore, of a wrongful one irrespective of the consequences. Negligent the act is, and wrongful in the sense that it is unsocial, but wrongful and unsocial in relation to other travelers, only because the eye of vigilance perceives the risk of damage. If the same act were to be committed on a speedway or a race course, it would lose its wrongful quality. The risk reasonably to be perceived defines the duty to be obeyed, and risk imports relation; it is risk to another or to others within the range of apprehension (Seavey, Negligence, Subjective or Objective, 41 H.L. Rv. 6). This does not mean, of course, that one who launches a destructive force is always relieved of liability if the force, though known to be destructive, pursues an unexpected path. "It was not necessary that the defendant should have had notice of the particular method in which an accident would occur, if the possibility of an accident was clear to the ordinarily prudent eye" (Munsey v. Webb, 231 U.S. 150, 156 [(1913)]). Some acts, such as shooting, are so imminently dangerous to any one who may come within reach of the missile, however unexpectedly, as to impose a duty of prevision not far from that of an insurer. Even today, and much oftener in earlier stages of the law, one acts sometimes at one's peril (Jeremiah Smith, Tort and Absolute Liability, 30 H.L. Rv. 328; Street, Foundations of Legal Liability, vol. 1, pp. 77, 78). Under this head, it may be, fall certain cases of what is known as transferred intent, an act willfully dangerous to *A* resulting by misadventure in injury to *B* (Talmage v. Smith, 101 Mich. 370, 374). These cases aside, wrong is defined in terms of the natural or probable, at least when unintentional (Parrot v. Wells-Fargo Co. [The Nitro-Glycerine Case], [82 U.S.] 15 Wall. [524 (1872)]). The range of reasonable apprehension is at times a question for the court, and at times, if varying inferences are possible, a question for the jury. Here, by concession, there was nothing in the situation to suggest to the most cautious mind that the parcel wrapped in newspaper would spread wreckage through the station. If the guard had thrown it down knowingly and willfully, he would not have threatened the plaintiff's safety, so far as appearances could warn him. His conduct would not have involved, even then, an unreasonable probability of invasion of her bodily security. Liability can be no greater where the act is inadvertent.

Negligence, like risk, is thus a term of relation. Negligence in the abstract, apart from things related, is surely not a tort, if indeed it is understandable at all. . . . The victim does not sue derivatively, or by right of subrogation, to vindicate an interest invaded in the person of another. Thus to view his cause of action [for negligence] is to ignore the fundamental difference between tort and crime. He sues for breach of a duty owing to himself.

The law of causation, remote or proximate, is thus foreign to the case before us. The question of liability is always anterior to the question of the measure of the consequences that go with liability. If there is no tort to be redressed, there is no occasion to consider what damage might be recovered if there were a finding of a tort. We may assume, without deciding, that negligence, not at large or in the abstract, but in relation to the plaintiff, would entail liability for any and all consequences, however novel or extraordinary. There is room for argument that a distinction is to be drawn according to the diversity of interests invaded by the act, as where conduct negligent in that it threatens an insignificant invasion of an interest in property results in an unforeseeable invasion of an interest of another order, as e.g., one of bodily security. Perhaps other distinctions may be necessary. We do not go into the question now. The consequences to be followed must first be rooted in a wrong.

[Reversed.]

ANDREWS, J., dissenting. Assisting a passenger to board a train, the defendant's servant negligently knocked a package from his arms. It fell between the platform and the cars. Of its contents the servant knew and could know nothing. A violent explosion followed. The concussion broke some scales standing a considerable distance away. In falling they injured the plaintiff, an intending passenger.

Upon these facts may she recover the damages she has suffered in an action brought against the master? The result we shall reach depends upon our theory as to the nature of negligence. Is it a relative concept — the breach of some duty owing to a particular person or to particular persons? Or where there is an act which unreasonably threatens the safety of others, is the doer liable for all its proximate consequences, even where they result in injury to one who would generally be thought to be outside the radius of danger? This is not a mere dispute as to words. We might not believe that to the average mind the dropping of the bundle would seem to involve the probability of harm to the plaintiff standing many feet away whatever might be the case as to the owner or to one so near as to be likely to be struck by its fall. If, however, we adopt the second hypothesis we have to inquire only as to the relation between cause and effect. We deal in terms of proximate cause, not of negligence.

Negligence may be defined roughly as an act or omission which unreasonably does or may affect the rights of others, or which unreasonably fails to protect oneself from the dangers resulting from such acts. Here I confine myself to the first branch of the definition. Nor do I comment on the word "unreasonable." For present purposes it sufficiently describes that average of conduct that society requires of its members. . . .

But we are told that "there is no negligence unless there is in the particular case a legal duty to take care, and this duty must be one which is owed to the plaintiff himself and not merely to others." (Salmond, Torts, 24 [6th ed.].) This, I think too narrow a conception. Where there is the unreasonable act, and some right that may be affected there is negligence whether damage does or does not result. That is immaterial. Should we drive down Broadway at a reckless speed, we are negligent whether we strike an approaching car or miss it by an inch. The act itself is wrongful. It is a wrong not only to those who happen to be within the radius of danger but to all who might have been there — a wrong to the public at large. Such is the language of the street. Such is the language of the courts when speaking of contributory negligence. Such is again and again their language in speaking of the duty of some defendant and discussing proximate cause in cases where such a discussion is wholly irrelevant on any other theory. . . . Due care is a duty imposed on each one of us to protect society from unnecessary danger, not to protect *A, B* or *C* alone.

It may well be that there is no such thing as negligence in the abstract. "Proof of negligence in the air, so to speak, will not do." In an empty world negligence would not exist. It does involve a relationship between man and his fellows, but not merely a relationship between man and those whom he might reasonably expect his act would injure; rather, a relationship between him and those whom he does in fact injure. If his act has a tendency to harm some one, it harms him a mile away as surely as it does those on the scene. We now permit children to recover for the negligent killing of the father. It was never prevented on the theory that no duty was owing to them. A husband may be compensated for the loss of his wife's services. To say that the wrongdoer was negligent as to the husband as well as to the wife is merely an attempt to fit facts to theory. An insurance company paying a fire loss recovers its payment of the negligent incendiary. We speak of subrogation — of suing in the right of the insured. Behind the cloud of words is the fact they hide, that the act, wrongful as to the insured, has also injured the company. Even if it be true that the fault of father, wife or insured will prevent recovery, it is because we consider the original negligence not the proximate cause of the injury. (Pollock, Torts, 463 [12th ed.].)

In the well-known *Polemis Case*, Scrutton, L.J., said that the dropping of a plank was negligent for it might injure "workman or cargo or ship." Because of either possibility the owner of the vessel was to be made good for his loss. The act being wrongful the doer was liable for its proximate results. Criticized and explained as this statement may have been, I think it states the law as it should be and as it is.

The proposition is this. Every one owes to the world at large the duty of refraining from those acts that may unreasonably threaten the safety of others. Such an act occurs. Not only is he wronged to whom harm might reasonably be expected to result, but he also who is in fact injured, even if he be outside what would generally be thought the danger zone. There needs be duty due the one complaining but this is not a duty to a particular individual because as to him harm might be expected. Harm to some one being the natural result of the act, not only that one alone, but all those in fact injured may complain. . . . Unreasonable risk being taken, its consequences are not confined to those who might probably be hurt.

If this be so, we do not have a plaintiff suing by "derivation or succession." Her action is original and primary. Her claim is for a breach of duty to herself—not that she is subrogated to any right of action of the owner of the parcel or of a passenger standing at the scene of the explosion.

The right to recover damages rests on additional considerations. The plaintiff's rights must be injured, and this injury must be caused by the negligence. We build a dam, but are negligent as to its foundations. Breaking, it injures property down stream. We are not liable if all this happened because of some reason other than the insecure foundation. But when injuries do result from our unlawful act we are liable for the consequences. It does not matter that they are unusual, unexpected, unforeseen and unforeseeable. But there is one limitation. The damages must be so connected with the negligence that the latter may be said to be the proximate cause of the former.

These two words have never been given an inclusive definition. What is a cause in a legal sense, still more what is a proximate cause, depend in each case upon many considerations, as does the existence of negligence itself. Any philosophical doctrine of causation does not help us. A boy throws a stone into a pond. The ripples spread. The water level rises. The history of that pond is altered to all eternity. It will be altered by other causes also. Yet it will be forever the resultant of all causes combined. Each one will have an influence. How great only omniscience can say. You may speak of a chain, or if you please, a net. An analogy is of little aid. Each cause brings about future events. Without each the future would not be the same. Each is proximate in the sense it is essential. But that is not what we mean by the word. Nor on the other hand do we mean sole cause. There is no such thing.

Should analogy be thought helpful, however, I prefer that of a stream. The spring, starting on its journey, is joined by tributary after tributary. The river, reaching the ocean, comes from a hundred sources. No man may say whence any drop of water is derived. Yet for a time distinction may be possible. Into the clear creek, brown swamp water flows from the left. Later, from the right comes water stained by its clay bed. The three may remain for a space, sharply divided. But at last, inevitably no trace of separation remains. They are so commingled that all distinction is lost.

As we have said, we cannot trace the effect of an act to the end, if end there is. Again, however, we may trace it part of the way. A murder at Serajevo may be the necessary antecedent to an assassination in London twenty years hence. An overturned lantern may burn all Chicago. We may follow the fire from the shed to the last building. We rightly say the fire started by the lantern caused its destruction.

A cause, but not the proximate cause. What we do mean by the word "proximate" is, that because of convenience, of public policy, of a rough sense of justice, the law arbitrarily declines to trace a series of events beyond a certain point. This is not logic. It is practical politics. Take our rule as to fires. Sparks from my burning haystack set on fire my house and my neighbor's. I may recover from a negligent railroad. He may not. Yet the wrongful act as directly harmed the one as the other. We may regret that the line was drawn just where it was, but drawn somewhere it had to be. We said the act of the railroad was not the proximate cause of our neighbor's fire. Cause it surely was. The words we used were simply indicative of our notions of public policy. Other courts think differently. But somewhere they reach the point where they cannot say the stream comes from any one source. . . .

It is all a question of expediency. There are no fixed rules to govern our judgment. There are simply matters of which we may take account. We have in a somewhat different connection spoken of "the stream of events." We have asked whether that stream was deflected—whether it was forced into new and unexpected channels. This is rather rhetoric than law. There is in truth little to guide us other than common sense.

There are some hints that may help us. The proximate cause, involved as it may be with many other causes, must be, at the least, something without which the event would not happen. The court must ask itself whether there was a natural and continuous sequence between cause and effect. Was the one a substantial factor in producing the other? Was there a direct connection between them, without too many intervening causes? Is the effect of cause on result not too attenuated? Is the cause likely, in the usual judgment of mankind, to produce the result? Or by the exercise of prudent foresight could the result be foreseen? Is the result too remote from the cause, and here we consider remoteness in time and space. . . . Clearly we must so consider, for the greater the distance either in time or space, the more surely do other causes intervene to affect the result. When a lantern is overturned the firing of a shed is a fairly direct consequence. Many things contribute to the spread of the conflagration—the force of the wind, the direction and width of streets, the character of intervening structures, other factors. We draw an uncertain and wavering line, but draw it we must as best we can.

Once again, it is all a question of fair judgment, always keeping in mind the fact that we endeavor to make a rule in each case that will be practical and in keeping with the general understanding of mankind. . . .

This last suggestion is the factor which must determine the case before us. The act upon which defendant's liability rests is knocking an apparently harmless package onto the platform. The act was negligent. For its proximate consequences the defendant is liable. If its contents were broken, to the owner; if it fell upon and crushed a passenger's foot, then to him. If it exploded and injured one in the immediate vicinity, to him also. . . . Mrs. Palsgraf was standing some distance away. How far cannot be told from the record—apparently twenty-five or thirty feet. Perhaps less. Except for the explosion, she would not have been injured. We are told by the appellant in his brief "it cannot be denied that the explosion was the direct cause of the plaintiff's injuries." So it was a substantial factor in producing the result—there was here a natural and continuous sequence—direct connection. The only intervening cause was that instead of blowing her to the ground the concussion smashed the weighing machine which in turn fell upon her. There was no remoteness in time, little in space. And surely, given such an explosion as here it needed no great foresight to predict that the natural result would be to injure one on the platform at no greater distance from its scene than was the plaintiff. Just how no one might be able to predict. Whether by flying fragments, by broken glass, by wreckage of machines or structures no one could say. But injury in some form was most probable.

Under these circumstances I cannot say as a matter of law that the plaintiff's injuries were not the proximate result of the negligence. That is all we have before us. The court refused to so charge. No request was made to submit the matter to the jury as a question of fact, even would that have been proper upon the record before us.

The judgment appealed from should be affirmed, with costs.

NOTES

1. *Questions Raised by Palsgraf.* *Palsgraf* has inspired extensive detective work to uncover its facts. Judge Noonan, Persons and Masks of the Law ch. 4 (1976), suggests that the "scales must have been toppled *not by the explosion* of the fireworks, but by the crowd running in panic on the platform." In Cardozo: A Study in Reputation 38–39 (1990), Judge Posner relies on a front-page *New York Times* report of the accident, "Bomb Blast Injures 13 in Station Crowd" (Aug. 25, 1924, at A1), to conclude that the explosion was not only loud enough to cause a stampede, but also violent enough to cause extensive damage to the train station, and to send several of the thirteen people it injured to the hospital with minor injuries. Why didn't the defendant owe the plaintiff the highest duty of care, given that it was a common carrier and she was a passenger? See Prosser, *Palsgraf* Revisited, 52 Mich. L. Rev. 1, 4–5 (1953). Would the conductor have been negligent if he had knocked the package out of the passenger's arm while trying to prevent him from boarding the train while it was in motion? Should Palsgraf have recovered if she stood next to the passenger carrying the package, given that the railroad conductor had no notice of its contents? Should a total stranger, not a patron of the railroad, injured by the blast be able to recover from the railroad if its conductor had innocently set off the bomb? Could the railroad, if held liable, sue the passenger for indemnification if he were solvent?

Exhibit 5.2 What Really Happened on That Train Platform?

- "There was . . . much smoke and a fireball, and the force of the blast ripped up part of the wooden station platform. . . . The explosion shattered the glass in the scale and knocked the scale itself over onto Mrs. Palsgraf, bruising her. It also caused a stampede of the crowd on the platform. There is conjecture that the crowd, rather than the direct force of the explosion, knocked over the scale. . . . Mrs. Palsgraf was one of thirteen people on the platform who were injured by the explosion (or, conceivably, by the stampede that it sparked), none seriously, although several, not including her, were taken to hospitals in ambulances called to the scene."

  Posner, Cardozo: A Study in Reputation 34–35 (1990).

- The "scales must have been toppled *not by the explosion* of the fireworks, but by the crowd running in panic on the platform," and although the plaintiff "had been hit by the scales on the arm, hip and thigh," the chief source of her complaint was "a stammer and a stutter" that appeared about one week after the accident and may have been intensified by the litigation itself.

  Noonan, Persons and Masks of the Law ch. 4 (1976).

- Several large explosions (likely six, but maybe twenty-four . . .) followed [the package at issue being jarred loose]. Panic and pandemonium apparently ensued, resulting in numerous injuries of varying severity. . . . About ten feet away from the explosion, a large penny scale topped on Mrs. Palsgraf, who suffered contusions in the short term, and what we would today call post-traumatic stress disorder (stuttering, nervous fits) in the long term."

  Krauss, Palsgraf*: The Rest of the Story, 9 Green Bag 2d 309, 310 (2006) (reviewing Manz, The* Palsgraf *Case: Courts, Law and Society in 1920s New York (2005)).*

- "No witness saw this [i.e., the facts recounted in Cardozo's opinion]. There was testimony that afterward the scale was found to be 'blown right to pieces and knocked down, the glass was busted and blown—just simply laid down on the platform. . . . Mrs. Palsgraf's . . . daughter said that she heard the scale 'blow apart.' Notwithstanding all this, it is very probable, in line with the original theory of plaintiff's complaint, that the scale was in fact knocked over by the stampede of frightened passengers. There was an appreciable interval after the 'ball of fire' before the 'scale blew.' With the explosion occurring in the pit between the platform and the train, or under the wheels, it is difficult to see how the scale would not be completely protected from it. Although the platform was crowded, there is no indication in the Record that any other damage whatever was done by the explosion itself."

  Source: Prosser, Palsgraf *Revisited, 52 Mich. L. Rev. 1, 3 n.9 (1953) (internal citations to* Palsgraf *record omitted).*

With *Palsgraf*, compare The Nitro-Glycerine Case, Parrot v. Wells, Fargo & Co., 82 U.S. 524 (1872), in which an unmarked package containing nitroglycerine was delivered to the defendant's place of business, which was located in its landlord's building. When the defendant's servants tried to open the package, it exploded, killing them and damaging the building. The Supreme Court noted that different outcomes were required for the servants' wrongful death actions and the landlord's property damage claim. For property damage, the landlord could recover without proof of negligence, basing its case on a covenant in its lease with the defendant. For the death actions, however, the lease was inapplicable, and the cause of action failed for want of proof of negligence, given that the parcel gave no notice of its dangerous contents. For the suggestion that *Palsgraf* should be understood on those "notice" grounds only, see the opinion of Judge Friendly in Petition of Kinsman Transit Co., 338 F.2d 708 (2d Cir. 1964), from which excerpts are reprinted *supra* at 359.

2. *Harm within the Risk.* Note that Second Restatement §281 appears to follow Cardozo on the duty requirement:

> *Comment c. Risk to class of which plaintiff is member.* . . . If the actor's conduct creates such a recognizable risk of harm only to a particular class of persons, the fact that it in fact causes harm to a person of a different class, to whom the actor could not reasonably have anticipated injury, does not make the actor liable to the persons so injured.

How does one decide to which class a particular person belongs? Is this question of duty or causation? For a comprehensive survey, see Cardi, The Hidden Legacy of *Palsgraf*: Modern Duty Law in Microcosm, 91 B.U. L. Rev. 1873, 1890–93 (2011), which reports:

> When faced with the issue, thirty-three (of fifty-one) courts hold with fair consistency that whether the plaintiff was a foreseeable victim is a question to be decided in the duty context. Only four jurisdictions clearly follow Judge Andrews in holding that plaintiff-foreseeability is properly and solely a matter for proximate cause. . . . In the remaining fourteen jurisdictions, the proper doctrinal home for plaintiff-foreseeability remains unclear.

In examining the question of potential liability, Professor Seavey poses a case in which the defendant leaves a ten-pound can of nitroglycerin on a table, which a child then knocks off the table. The can hurts the child's foot but, miraculously, does not explode. If the defendant had left a can of water of similar size on the table, he could not be held negligent: Since the risk that materialized was unrelated to the explosive power of the nitroglycerin, the plaintiff could not recover. See Seavey, Mr. Justice Cardozo and the Law of Torts, 39 Colum. L. Rev. 20, 35; 52 Harv. L. Rev. 372, 385; 48 Yale L.J. 390, 405 (1939); compare RST §281, illus. 2.

A second scenario is put forth in Keeton, Legal Cause in the Law of Torts, 77 Harv. L. Rev. 595 (1963–1964). The defendant "negligently" places unlabeled rat poison on a shelf full of food. The shelf happens to be near a stove that gives off heat, and the heat causes the poison to explode, injuring the plaintiff. Keeton argues that this plaintiff should be denied recovery on grounds that the negligent *aspect* of the defendant's conduct—failure to label—is not the cause of the plaintiff's harm. For a consideration of several other scenarios and an argument that the foreseeable harm test provides the best limits on liability, see Williams, The Risk Principle, 77 Law Q. Rev. 179, 185–90 (1961). Do these examples support Cardozo or Andrews in *Palsgraf*?

The Third Restatement of Torts states its general test for the scope of liability (avoiding the term "proximate cause") in RTT: LPEH §29.

RESTATEMENT OF THE LAW (THIRD) OF TORTS: LIABILITY FOR PHYSICAL AND EMOTIONAL HARM

§29. Limitations on Liability for Tortious Conduct

An actor's liability is limited to those harms that result from the risks that made the actor's conduct tortious.

Comment d. Harm different from the harms risked by the tortious conduct: . . . [T]he jury should be told that, in deciding whether the plaintiff's harm is within the scope of liability, it should go back to the reasons for finding the defendant engaged in negligent or other tortious conduct. If the harms risked by that tortious conduct include the general sort of harm suffered by the plaintiff, the defendant is subject to liability for the plaintiff's harm. . . .

Illustration 3: Richard, a hunter, finishes his day in the field and stops at a friend's house while walking home. His friend's nine-year-old daughter, Kim, greets Richard, who hands his loaded shotgun to her as he enters the house. Kim drops the shotgun, which lands on her toe, breaking it. Although Richard is negligent for giving Kim his shotgun, the risk that makes Richard negligent is that Kim might shoot someone with the gun, not that she would drop it and hurt herself (the gun was neither especially heavy nor unwieldy). Kim's broken toe is outside the scope of Richard's liability, even though Richard's tortious conduct was a factual cause of Kim's harm.

Whatever that answer, the Third Restatement accepts the efforts of both Seavey and Keeton to isolate particular harms that fall outside the risk. Thus it holds as a matter of law that a defendant hunter who carelessly entrusts his loaded gun to a child is not liable if she drops it on her toe, breaking it. RTT: LPEH §29, comment *d*, illus. 3. Note the common thread in all these cases: It turns out after the fact that the aspect of the defendant's behavior that increased the risk of harm to the plaintiff never materialized. The nitroglycerin did not explode; the poison was not consumed; the gun did not go off. Are these cases distinguishable from *Palsgraf*, which involves the materialization of a risk from a dangerous but unknown condition? What about holding the railroad liable for triggering the explosives, with an action over against the person who carried it? For a sustained attack on the harm within the risk test for resulting in too many cases of undercompensation, see Hurd & Moore, Negligence in the Air, 3 Theoretical Inquiries in Law 333 (2002), calling for its abandonment "root and branch."

3. *Jury Instructions on Proximate Causation.* The role of the Second Restatement's substantial factor test, discussed *supra* at 347–48, was examined in Mitchell v. Gonzales, 819 P.2d 872, 877–78 (Cal. 1991). The decedent, 12-year-old Damechie Mitchell, drowned while vacationing with the defendants and their 14-year-old son Luis. Damechie did not know how to swim, but with the Gonzales' permission, he went out on a raft with Luis and his sister Yoshi and drowned; the boys had engaged in horseplay on the raft while Luis's father slept on the beach. The decedent's parents charged Luis with negligence for his conduct on the raft and Luis's parents with negligent supervision. The jury found that the defendants were negligent, but that their negligence was not the proximate cause of the death.

At trial, the judge gave the defendants' requested instruction (BAJI 3.75), a "but for" test of cause in fact, which provided: "A proximate cause of injury is a cause which, in natural and continuous sequence, produces the injury and without which the injury would not have occurred." The test gets its name from the "without which" clause, by adopting the precise language of the Andrews dissent. The rival "substantial factor" instruction (BAJI 3.76), requested by the plaintiff, read: "A legal cause of injury is a cause which is a substantial factor in bringing about the injury."

By a divided vote, the court treated the "but for" instruction as always prejudicial to the plaintiffs. The court also noted its dislike for the term "proximate cause," and adopted Prosser's view that the term was just an unfortunate "legacy of Sir Francis Bacon." It also pointed to experimental studies that indicated subjects interpreted the term as " 'approximate cause,' 'estimated cause,' or some fabrication." The court then adopted the "substantial factor" test because it was largely free of these confusions, was generally intelligible to juries, and helped to clarify issues in joint causation. Accordingly, any but-for instruction was prejudicial error because it "overemphasized the condition temporally closest to the death" (Damechie's inability to swim) and downplayed how the negligent supervision of Mr. and Mrs. Gonzales contributed to the loss. Kennard, J., dissented on the ground that the court should not displace a standard instruction without developing a better alternative, noting that the substantial factor test fails to supply "meaningful guidance" on the proximate cause issue. What is wrong with asking whether the parents could have, to a reasonable certainty, prevented Damechie's death if they had properly watched the children at play? Forbidden them to go out on the raft? Asked the decedent if he knew how to swim?

The Second Restatement's terminology also received a mixed reception for its use of the term "superseding cause" to talk about events occurring after the defendant's negligence that break causal connection. See RST §442. In Barry v. Quality Steel Products, 820 A.2d 258, 266 (Conn. 2003), the court rejected any superseding cause instructions based on the Second Restatement because they only "serve to complicate what is fundamentally a proximate cause analysis." Accordingly, it reversed a directed verdict for the defendant manufacturer and seller of defective brackets. The brackets had failed in part because the plaintiff's employer had improperly installed the roof brackets and did not provide the needed scaffolding to protect the plaintiff from a fall. In the court's view, apportionment under a comparative negligence regime was the proper way to deal with multiple sources of negligence. "The test of proximate cause is whether the defendant's conduct is a substantial factor in bringing about the plaintiff's injuries." What result if sound brackets would have certainly failed given the employer's improper installation?

The substantial factor test rejected in *Barry* was revived in Snell v. Norwalk Yellow Cab, Inc., 158 A.3d 787 (Conn. 2017), where the plaintiff suffered catastrophic injuries when struck by the defendant's car. The car was used for a reckless "joyride" by two drunk teenage boys who had stolen the car after the defendant's driver left the keys in the ignition. The accident occurred after the boy defendants rear-ended the car in front of them. In their attempt to flee they drove the cab over the curb, hit a fire hydrant, and then struck the plaintiff. The defendant asked for and received a superseding cause instruction, and the plaintiff appealed the defendant's verdict. Prescott, J., affirming the decision below, held that the superseding cause doctrine could apply not only for intentional harms, but also for reckless ones.

> "The 'criminal event' at issue was not limited to the theft of the taxicab, which all parties acknowledge was a situation that was foreseeable given [the cab driver's] actions, but included additional criminal acts, which were further removed in both time and distance from the initial theft, and that a jury might reasonably consider unforeseeable."

Why this exception to *Barry*? Is the result consistent with Beale's test, *supra* at 345, which requires that the situation return to a condition of safety?

The Third Restatement rejects all permutations of the substantial factor, intervening cause, and supervening cause language. See RTT: LPEH §26, comment *j*, and §34, comment *b*, dismissing both the phrases "intervening acts" and "superseding causes" as "conclusory labels." Can any single verbal account for causation work for all stranger (including explosion), rescue, malpractice, and supervision cases? If not, how should the causal element of each type of case be addressed? Which set of instructions would be appropriate in *Berry*? *Palsgraf*?

4. *Proximate Causation in FELA Cases.* In CSX Transportation, Inc. v. McBride, 564 U.S. 685, 703, 705 (2011), the Supreme Court held that the proximate cause limitation did not apply in cases brought by injured railroad workers under the Federal Employers' Liability Act (FELA). Quoting the statute, Ginsburg, J., explained: "[R]ailroads are made answerable in damages for an employee's 'injury or death resulting in whole or in part from [carrier] negligence.' " And while reasonable foreseeability of harm . . . is indeed an essential ingredient of [FELA] negligence, . . . [i]f negligence is proved . . . and is shown to have "*played any part,* *even the slightest, in producing the injury,*" then the carrier is answerable in damages even if the extent of the [injury] or the manner in which it occurred was not probable or foreseeable.

Roberts, C.J., criticized the majority for casting aside "the well established principle of [the common] law" and for treating FELA like a no-fault compensation scheme similar to most workers' compensation schemes. Is the rule in *CSX* a return to *In re Polemis*? For a critique of the FELA tests of causation, see Nolan, Are Railroads Liable When Lightning Strikes?, 79 U. Chi. L. Rev. 1513, 1515 (2012), arguing that "the *McBride* Court's statements about the role of foreseeability have led some courts to adopt a form of 'freestanding negligence,' leading to potentially limitless liability." For such an expansive interpretation, see Anderson v. BNSF Ry., 354 P.3d 1248, 1256 (Mont. 2015), noting: "The FELA thus calls for an interpretive approach that is significantly different from that which ordinarily prevails in suits involving common-law negligence claims, and the resulting interpretations often seem anomalous in comparison to the norms of tort law."

Marshall v. Nugent

222 F.2d 604 (1st Cir. 1955)

[A truck owned by the defendant oil company cut the corner as it headed north around a sharp curve on an icy New Hampshire highway, forcing off the road a southbound car driven by the plaintiff's son-in-law, Harriman. Prince, the driver of the truck, offered to help pull Harriman's car back onto the highway and suggested that the plaintiff go around the curve to the south to warn oncoming cars of the unexpected danger. As the plaintiff was getting into position on the west side of the highway, the defendant, Nugent, who was driving north-bound, suddenly saw his way blocked by the oil truck on one side of the road and Prince and Harriman on the other. In an effort to avoid a collision with them, he pulled the car over to the left where it went into a skid, hit a plank guard fence on the west side of the highway, and glanced off it into the plaintiff, severely hurting him.

The jury returned a verdict for Nugent and another for Marshall against the oil company. The second contention of the oil company on appeal was that the wrongful conduct of its driver was not the proximate cause of the plaintiff's injury.]

Magruder, C.J. . . . Coming then to contention (2) above mentioned, this has to do with the doctrine of proximate causation, a doctrine which appellant's arguments tend to make out to be more complex and esoteric than it really is. To say that the situation created by the defendant's culpable acts constituted "merely a condition," not a cause of plaintiff's harm, is to indulge in mere verbiage, which does not solve the question at issue, but is simply a way of stating the conclusions, arrived at from other considerations, that the casual relation between the defendant's act and the plaintiff's injury is not strong enough to warrant holding the defendant legally responsible for the injury.

The adjective "proximate," as commonly used in this connection, is perhaps misleading, since to establish liability it is not necessarily true that the defendant's culpable act must be shown to have been the next or immediate cause of the plaintiff's injury. In many familiar instances, the defendant's act may be more remote in the chain of events and the plaintiff's injury may more immediately have been caused by an intervening force of nature, or an intervening act of a third person whether culpable or not, or even an act by the plaintiff bringing himself in contact with the dangerous situation resulting from the defendant's negligence. Therefore, perhaps, the phrase "legal cause," as used in Am. L. Inst., Rest. of Torts §431, is preferable to "proximate cause"; but the courts continue generally to use "proximate cause," and it is pretty well understood what is meant.

Back of the requirement that the defendant's culpable act must have been a proximate cause of the plaintiff's harm is no doubt the widespread conviction that it would be disproportionately burdensome to hold a culpable actor potentially liable for all the injurious consequences that may flow from his act, i.e., that would not have been inflicted "but for" the occurrence of the act. This is especially so where the injurious consequence was the result of negligence merely. And so, speaking in general terms, the effort of the courts has been, in the development of this doctrine of proximate causation, to confine the liability of a negligent actor to those harmful consequences which result from the operation of the risk, or of a risk, the foreseeability of which rendered the defendant's conduct negligent.

Of course, putting the inquiry in these terms does not furnish a formula which automatically decides each of an infinite variety of cases. Flexibility is still preserved by the further need of defining the risk, or risks, either narrowly, or more broadly, as seems appropriate and just in the special type of case.

Regarding motor vehicle accidents in particular, one should contemplate a variety of risks which are created by negligent driving. There may be injuries resulting from a direct collision between the carelessly driven car and another vehicle. But such direct collision may be avoided, yet the plaintiff may fall and injure himself in frantically racing out of the way of the errant car. Or the plaintiff may be knocked down and injured by a human stampede as the car rushes toward a crowded safety zone. Or the plaintiff may faint from intense excitement stimulated by the near collision, and in falling sustain a fractured skull. Or the plaintiff may suffer a miscarriage or other physical illness as a result of intense nervous shock incident to a hair-raising escape. This bundle of risks could be enlarged indefinitely with a little imagination. In a traffic mix-up due to negligence, before the disturbed waters have become placid and normal again, the unfolding of events between the culpable act and the plaintiff's eventual injury may be bizarre indeed; yet the defendant may be liable for the result. In such a situation, it would be impossible for a person in the defendant's position to predict in advance just how his negligent act would work out to another's injury. Yet this in itself is no bar to recovery.

[Magruder, C.J., then notes that close cases on proximate cause are normally left to the jury.]

Exercising [our] judgment on the facts in the case at bar, we have to conclude that the district court committed no error in refusing to direct a verdict for the defendant Socony on the issue of proximate cause. . . .

Plaintiff Marshall was a passenger in the oncoming Chevrolet car, and thus was one of the persons whose bodily safety was primarily endangered by the negligence of Prince, as might have been found by the jury, in "cutting the corner" with the Socony truck in the circumstances above related. In that view, Prince's negligence constituted an irretrievable breach of duty to the plaintiff. Though this particular act of negligence was over and done with when the truck pulled up alongside of the stalled Chevrolet without having actually collided with it, still the consequences of such past negligence were in the bosom of time, as yet unrevealed. If the Chevrolet had been pulled back onto the highway, and Harriman and Marshall, having got in it again, had resumed their journey and had had a collision with another car five miles down the road, in which Marshall suffered bodily injuries, it could truly be said that such subsequent injury to Marshall was a consequence in fact of the earlier delay caused by the defendant's negligence, in the sense that but for such delay the Chevrolet car would not have been at the fatal intersection at the moment the other car ran into it. But on such assumed state of facts, the courts would no doubt conclude, "as a matter of law," that Prince's earlier negligence in cutting the corner was not the "proximate cause" of this later injury received by the plaintiff. That would be because the extra risks to which such negligence by Prince had subjected the passengers in the Chevrolet car were obviously entirely over; the situation had been stabilized and become normal, and, so far as one could foresee, whatever subsequent risks the Chevrolet might have to encounter in its resumed journey were simply the inseparable risks, no more and no less, that were incident to the Chevrolet's being out on the highway at all. But in the case at bar, the circumstances under which Marshall received the personal injuries complained of presented no such clear-cut situation.

As we have indicated, the extra risks created by Prince's negligence were not all over at the moment the primary risk of collision between the truck and the Chevrolet was successfully surmounted. Many cases have held a defendant, whose negligence caused a traffic tie-up, legally liable for subsequent property damage or personal injuries more immediately caused by an oncoming motorist. This would particularly be so where, as in the present case, the negligent traffic tie-up and delay occurred in a dangerous blind spot, and where the occupants of the stalled Chevrolet, having got out onto the highway to assist in the operation of getting the Chevrolet going again, were necessarily subject to risks of injury from cars in the stream of northbound traffic coming over the crest of the hill. It is true, the Chevrolet car was not owned by the plaintiff Marshall, and no doubt, without violating any legal duty to Harriman, Marshall could have crawled up onto the snowbank at the side of the road out of harm's way and awaited there, passive and inert, until his journey was resumed. But the plaintiff, who as a passenger in this Chevrolet car had already been subjected to a collision risk by the negligent operation of the Socony truck, could reasonably be expected to get out onto the highway and lend a hand to his host in getting the Chevrolet started again, especially as Marshall himself had an interest in facilitating the resumption of the journey in order to keep his business appointment in North Stratford. Marshall was therefore certainly not an "officious intermeddler," and whether or not he was barred by contributory negligence in what he did was a question for the jury, as we have already held. The injury Marshall received by being struck by the Nugent car was not remote, either in time or place, from the negligent conduct of defendant Socony's servant, and it occurred while the traffic mix-up occasioned by defendant's negligence was still persisting, not after the traffic flow had become normal again. In the circumstances presented we conclude that the district court committed no error in leaving the issue of proximate cause to the jury for determination.

NOTE

A Resumption of Normal Conditions. Why shouldn't the plaintiff get a directed verdict on the admitted facts of *Marshall*? Note that Magruder's decision stresses that causation has run its course with the dissipation of the extra risks created by defendant's negligence. In Union Pump Co. v. Allbritton, 898 S.W.2d 773 (Tex. 1995), a pump manufactured by the defendant caught fire in a Texaco Chemical plant in which the plaintiff worked as a trainee employee. The plaintiff assisted her supervisor in putting out the fire and, after it was extinguished, she followed him over an aboveground pipe rack, some two and one-half feet high, to make repairs on a broken valve. Once the valve was fixed, she followed him back over to the pipe rack, where she fell and injured herself. Her supervisor said that his "bad habits" led him to walk over the pipe instead of taking the safer alternative route around it. The plaintiff argued that the defective pump was a cause of her injuries. "But for the pump fire, she asserts, she would never have walked over the pipe rack, which was wet with water or firefighting foam." Owen, J., rejected her argument:

> Even if the pump fire were in some sense a "philosophic" or "but for" cause of Allbritton's injuries, the forces generated by the fire had come to rest when she fell off the pipe rack. The fire had been extinguished, and Allbritton was walking away from the scene. Viewing the evidence in the light most favorable to Allbritton, the pump fire did no more than create the condition

> that made Allbritton's injuries possible. We conclude that the circumstances surrounding her injuries are too remotely connected with Union Pump's conduct or pump to constitute a legal cause of her injuries.

Spector, J., argued in dissent:

> The record reflects that at the time Sue Albritton's injury occurred, the forces generated by the fire in question had *not* come to rest. Rather, the emergency situation was continuing. The whole area of the fire was covered in water and foam; in at least some places, the water was almost knee-deep. Allbritton was still wearing hip boots and other gear, as required to fight the fire. Viewing all the evidence in the light most favorable to Allbritton, . . . the pump defect was both a "but-for" cause and a substantial factor in bringing about Allbritton's injury, and was therefore a cause in fact.

What is the factual dispute in *Union Pump*? Do the conceptual arguments go beyond those advanced by Beale (discussed *supra* at 345, following *Berry*)? Should they?

Virden v. Betts and Beer Construction Co.

656 N.W.2d 805 (Iowa 2003)

Neuman, J., Plaintiff, Ron Virden, worked in the maintenance department of Indianola High School. On the first day of school in 1997, Virden's supervisor asked him to reinstall an angle iron that had fallen from the ceiling of the school's new wrestling room. As Virden was bolting the angle iron into place, he fell from the top of the ten-foot ladder on which he was standing. He sustained severe injuries to his left leg, requiring several surgeries.

Virden sued the contractors, defendants Betts & Beer Construction and Stroh Corporation, who earlier in the year had installed the wrestling room ceiling. Over Virden's objection, the district court granted these defendants summary judgment. It held their negligence, if any, was not the proximate cause of Virden's injuries. Virden appealed and the court of appeals reversed. We granted further review and, now, vacate the court of appeals decision and affirm the judgment of the district court.

I. Scope of Review/Issue on Appeal

[The court notes that summary judgment on the question of proximate cause is granted only in exceptional cases, of which this is one.]

II. Analysis

. . . The summary judgment record makes plain that neither Virden nor his employer contacted the defendants about the fallen angle iron before attempting to effect repairs. Virden also concedes that he sought no help in positioning or securing the ladder, even though several pieces of weight-lifting equipment hampered clear access to the repair site. With this record in mind, we turn to the disputed elements of Virden's claim: duty and causation.

A. Duty

[As a building or construction contractor] the defendants had a duty to Virden, and others using the room, to construct a ceiling that did not fall apart and injure someone.

Virden did not suffer, however, from being hit by the angle iron or tripping over it once it fell from the ceiling. In his words, he was injured when the ladder he stood on to replace the fallen hardware "suddenly kicked out from under [him] and [he] fell." That brings us to the crux of the case.

B. Causation

Defendants' breach of their duty of care only constitutes actionable negligence if it is "also the proximate cause of the injury." There are two components to the proximate-cause inquiry: "(1) the defendant's conduct must have in fact caused the damages; and (2) the policy of the law must require the defendant to be legally responsible for them."

With respect to the first component, a plaintiff must at a minimum prove that the damages would not have occurred *but for* the defendant's negligence. Here, viewing the facts in the light most favorable to Virden, we assume that but for the faulty weld in the angle iron he would not have been perched precariously upon a ladder attempting to fix it. So, minimally, the but-for test of causation would survive defendants' motion for summary judgment.

The but-for test is not the end of the inquiry, however. . . . Virden must also tender proof that defendants' negligent welding of the angle iron was a *substantial factor* in bringing about his injury. . . .

Here, the district court assessed defendants' role in Virden's mishap as remote rather than foreseeable. Its conclusion stemmed from the undisputed fact that the instrumentality causing Virden's injury was a tipping or collapsing ladder, not a defective angle iron. We agree.

. . . [W]e observe that the duty to construct a solid ceiling is not to protect repairmen from perching on tall ladders but to prevent collapsing parts of the ceiling from falling on persons below.

To summarize, the unfortunate outcome of Virden's self-help remedy cannot be said to fall naturally within the scope of the probable risk created by the defendants' failure to properly install the ceiling. Because Virden's fall was not a reasonably foreseeable or probable consequence of *defendants'* negligence, the district court correctly granted judgment in their favor. We therefore vacate the court of appeals' contrary decision and affirm the judgment of the district court.

Hebert v. Enos

806 N.E.2d 452 (Mass. App. 2004)

Kafker, J. The plaintiff William Hebert (Hebert) brought an action to recover for personal injuries he suffered as a result of receiving a severe electric shock while lawfully on the defendant Carl Enos's property to water the defendant's flowers. Hebert claimed that the defendant's faulty repairs of a second-floor toilet caused the toilet to overflow. The flooding water then reacted with the home's electrical system, creating an electrical current that shocked and injured Hebert when he touched the outside water faucet. Hebert asserted a claim for negligence in his complaint, and his wife sought damages for loss of consortium. The defendant moved for summary judgment on the ground that Hebert's injuries were not a reasonably foreseeable consequence of any negligence on the defendant's part. The judge allowed the defendant's motion for summary judgment, finding that "the injury to [Hebert] was highly extraordinary and 'so remote in everyday life' as to preclude a finding that the alleged negligence was a legal cause of [Hebert's] injuries." We affirm.

. . . In their opposition to the defendant's motion for summary judgment, the plaintiffs provided an expert's report prepared by a professional engineer. It was the expert's opinion that "in the several days the water was flowing through the house, the water caused good [or already deteriorated] insulation on wires to break down allowing leakage current to flow into a grounded surface and thence through the water piping system."

When Hebert "came into contact with the water piping system (i.e. the turn-on handle)," he became "part of the electric circuit." Because Hebert was wet from perspiration and from having watered his own flowers, the amount of electricity that would have flowed through him was much greater than it would have been had he been dry. The expert opined to a "reasonable degree of engineering certainty" that the electrical current flowing through Hebert's body and causing his injury was "a direct result of the water overflow and accompanying flooded condition of the house." . . .

Discussion. When the facts and reasonable inferences therefrom are viewed in the light most favorable to the plaintiffs, we conclude that the plaintiffs submitted sufficient evidence to establish that faulty repairs of the toilet by the defendant resulted in flooding and severe electric shock to Hebert when he touched the faucet. Summary judgment is still appropriate, however, if a plaintiff has no reasonable expectation of proving that "the injury to the plaintiff was a foreseeable result of the defendant's negligent conduct."

In the instant case, when we consider the likelihood, character, and location of the harm, we conclude as matter of law that the injuries sustained by Hebert were a "highly extraordinary" consequence of a defective second-floor toilet. . . . We therefore conclude that Hebert's severe and unfortunate injuries were the consequence of the type of unforeseeable accident for which we do not hold the defendant responsible in tort. The harm Hebert suffered, even when the facts and reasonable inferences that could be drawn therefrom are viewed in the light most favorable to him, was so highly extraordinary that the defendant cannot be required to guard against it.

We briefly touch upon various subsidiary arguments raised by the plaintiffs. The plaintiffs argue that water and electricity have distinct places in the law, and that the motion judge should have recognized the foreseeability of the risk of injury due to the mixture of electricity and water "as a matter of common sense." We conclude that the motion judge held the defendant to the "proper standard of care [which] is . . . the usual one of traditional negligence theory: 'to exercise care that was reasonable in the circumstances.' "

Finally, the plaintiffs appear to suggest that so long as the defendant's negligence can be connected in an unbroken causal chain to the resultant harm, and no third party's negligence can be blamed for the injury, the harm is by definition proximate. This is not the law of proximate cause in Massachusetts, nor is it supported by the commentary upon which the plaintiffs rely. Here, the defendant could not have reasonably foreseen the harm that befell Hebert.

Judgment affirmed.

NOTE

A Choice of Theories? *Virden* and *Hebert* both result in summary judgment for the defendant. Yet in a sense they are polar opposites of each other. In *Virden*, the dangerous condition was obvious to the plaintiff who had a wide range of choices on whether, and if so how, to proceed in repairing the angle iron. In *Hebert*, the dangerous condition was wholly concealed from the plaintiff who acted in complete ignorance of the peril created solely by the defendant that befell him. How then do both of these cases result in the same outcome? How should these cases come out if one looks at the question of whether a voluntary and independent act of the plaintiff severed causal connection? If foresight of harm by the defendant is the appropriate test? Should it make a difference in *Hebert* that Hebert was doing a favor for Enos?

2. Emotional Distress

Thus far, the question of proximate causation has been addressed largely with physical injuries. In this section we ask whether other consequences, such as mental shock or emotional distress, can flow from wrongful conduct. As with physical injury claims, the first line of defense simply denies the connection between the distress and the defendant's conduct, blaming some other event for the plaintiff's emotional harm. The second line of defense, however, holds that even if defendant's conduct is the cause in fact of plaintiff's injury, that conduct is not the proximate cause. Over the past century, liability in emotional distress cases has expanded, but the area still retains its distinctive limitations on recovery.

S

Mitchell v. Rochester Ry.

45 N.E. 354 (N.Y. 1896)

MARTIN, J. The facts in this case are few, and may be briefly stated. On the 1st day of April, 1891, the plaintiff was standing upon a cross walk on Main Street, in the city of Rochester, awaiting an opportunity to board one of the defendant's cars which had stopped upon the street at that place. While standing there, and just as she was about to step upon the car, a horse car of the defendant came down the street. As the team attached to the car drew near, it turned to the right, and came close to the plaintiff, so that she stood between the horses' heads when they were stopped. She testified that from fright and excitement caused by the approach and proximity of the team she became unconscious, and also that the result was a miscarriage, and consequent illness. Medical testimony was given to the effect that the mental shock which she then received was sufficient to produce that result. Assuming that the evidence tended to show that the defendant's servant was negligent in the management of the car and horses, and that the plaintiff was free from contributory negligence, the single question presented is whether the plaintiff is entitled to recover for the defendant's negligence which occasioned her fright and alarm, and resulted in the injuries already mentioned. While the authorities are not harmonious upon this question, we think the most reliable and better-considered cases, as well as public policy, fully justify us in holding that the plaintiff cannot recover for injuries occasioned by fright, as there is no immediate personal injury. If it be admitted that no recovery can be had for fright occasioned by the negligence of another, it is somewhat difficult to understand how a defendant would be liable for its consequences. Assuming that fright cannot form the basis of an action, it is obvious that no recovery can be had for injuries resulting therefrom. That the result may be nervous disease, blindness, insanity, or even a miscarriage, in no way changes the principle. These results merely show the degree of right or the extent of the damages. The right of action must still depend upon the question whether a recovery may be had for fright. If it can, then an action may be maintained, however slight the injury. If not, then there can be no recovery, no matter how grave or serious the consequences. Therefore, the logical result of the respondent's concession would seem to be, not only that no recovery can be had for mere fright, but also that none can be had for injuries which are the direct consequences of it. If the right of recovery in this class of cases should be once established, it would naturally result in a flood of litigation in cases where the injury complained of may be easily feigned without detection, and where the damages must rest upon mere conjecture or speculation. The difficulty which often exists in cases of alleged physical injury, in determining whether they exist, and if so, whether they were caused by the negligent act of the defendant, would not only be greatly increased, but a wide field would be opened for fictitious or speculative claims. To establish such a doctrine would be contrary to principles of public policy.

Moreover, it cannot be properly said that the plaintiff's miscarriage was the proximate result of the defendant's negligence. Proximate damages are such as are the ordinary and natural results of the negligence charged, and those that are usual and may, therefore, be expected. It is quite obvious that the plaintiff's injuries do not fall within the rule as to proximate damages. The injuries to the plaintiff were plainly the result of an accidental or unusual combination of circumstances, which could not have been reasonably anticipated, and over which the defendant had no control, and, hence, her damages were too remote to justify a recovery in this action. These considerations lead to the conclusion that no recovery can be had for injuries sustained by fright occasioned by the negligence of another, where there is no immediate personal injury.

[Reversed and dismissed.]

NOTES

1. *Coping with the Physical Injury Rule.* Why should plaintiff's fright count as a superseding cause of the plaintiff's miscarriage? The early opposition to allowing recovery for negligently inflicted emotional distress rested on two distinct grounds. The first was that the damages were too "remote," and the second was the fear that allowing recovery for emotional distress would open the floodgates to fabricated claims. Which argument is stronger for disallowing recovery when fright alone is the cause of the injury?

Historically, however, whenever the plaintiff showed physical impact, courts used that impact, however slight, as the foundation for the plaintiff's damage claim for emotional distress. In effect, courts treated the emotional distress as parasitic damages upon the most nominal of invasions. In Comstock v. Wilson, 177 N.E. 431 (N.Y. 1931), recovery was allowed for a slight jolt in a very minor automobile collision. In Porter v. Delaware, Lackawanna & Western Railroad, 63 A. 860 (N.J. 1906), the plaintiff recovered when "something" slight hit her neck and she got dust in her eyes. In Kenney v. Wong Len, 128 A. 343 (N.H. 1925), the requisite impact was found when a mouse hair in a spoonful of stew touched the roof of the plaintiff's mouth. In Christy Bros. Circus v. Turnage, 144 S.E. 680 (Ga. App. 1928), the hapless plaintiff recovered when one of defendant's horses "evacuated his bowels" in plaintiff's lap, "in full view of many people . . . all of whom laughed at the occurrence." Finally, in Deutsch v. Shein, 597 S.W.2d 141 (Ky. 1980), bombarding the plaintiff with x-rays met the requirements of the impact rule, which only required that the contact be "slight, trifling, or trivial."

2. *Beyond Physical Impact.* While some courts extended the impact rule, other courts reexamined its foundations. In Dulieu v. White & Sons, [1901] 2 KB 669, 677, 681, the court rejected both the proximate cause and floodgates arguments. The plaintiff gave premature birth to her child after nearly being run over by the defendant's team of horses while working behind the counter in her husband's public house. Kennedy, J., rejected *Mitchell*, making these observations about remoteness of damage:

> Why is the accompaniment of physical injury essential? For my own part, I should not like to assume it to be scientifically true that a nervous shock which causes serious bodily illness is not actually accompanied by physical injury, although it may be impossible, or at least difficult, to detect the injury at the time in the living subject. I should not be surprised if the surgeon or the physiologist told us that nervous shock is or may be in itself an injurious affection of the physical organism. Let it be assumed, however, that the physical injury follows the shock, but that the jury are satisfied upon proper and sufficient medical evidence that it follows the shock as its direct and natural effect, is there any legal reason for saying that the damage is less proximate in the legal sense than damage which arises contemporaneously?

Thereafter Kennedy, J., rejected any concern about spurious claims, saying:

> I should be sorry to adopt a rule which would bar all such claims on grounds of policy alone, and in order to prevent the possible success of unrighteous or groundless actions. Such a course involves the denial of redress in meritorious cases, and it necessarily implies a certain degree of distrust, which I do not share, in the capacity of legal tribunals to get at the truth in this class of claim. My experience gives me no reason to suppose that a jury would really have more

> difficulty in weighing the medical evidence as to the effects of nervous shock through fright, than in weighing the like evidence as to the effects of nervous shock through a railway collision or a carriage accident, where, as often happens, no palpable injury, or very slight palpable injury, has been occasioned at the time.

Accordingly, Kennedy, J., nonetheless did impose this limitation:

> [The plaintiff was not] entitled to maintain this action if the nervous shock was produced, not by the fear of bodily injury to herself, but by horror or vexation arising from the sight of mischief being threatened or done either to some other person, or to her own or her husband's property, by the intrusion of the defendant's van and horses.

Is this defensible on proximate cause grounds?

Likewise, in Osborne v. Keeney, 399 S.W.3d 1, 17–18 (Ky. 2012), the Kentucky Supreme Court overruled its past support of the impact rule, declaring that its job was not to "maintain[] the watch as the law ossifies." The court pointed to advances in medical science and mental health treatment, as well as the fact that there had been no flood of litigation in other jurisdictions that had removed the impact requirement, to support its claim that the new standard is "more at home in our current societal and legal landscape."

3. *Empirical Complications.* Is the concern with fraud or error in nervous shock cases understated in *Dulieu*? In 1944, a doctor-lawyer surveyed all cases brought for physical injuries resulting from negligently inflicted fright and concluded:

> On the basis of all available factors, we thought at least 7/10 or 21/30 of the 301 cases examined should have been decided in defendant's favor. . . . [In practice, however], defendants prevailed in only 51 cases or 5/30 of the total series. Taking all cases decided between 1850 and 1944, the net balance of justice would have been greater had all courts denied damages for injury imputed to psychic stimuli alone.

Smith, Relation of Emotions to Injury and Disease: Legal Liability for Psychic Stimuli, 30 Va. L. Rev. 193, 284 (1944). Smith's conclusions are premised on his belief that liability should only result when a plaintiff suffered a normal response; otherwise, he believed that a plaintiff's "preexisting vulnerability" ought to bar recovery. For a critical view, see Chamallas & Kerber, Women, Mothers, and the Law of Fright: A History, 88 Mich. L. Rev. 814, 847–48 (1990), arguing that "Smith's medicalized notions of normality disadvantaged women. He believed that it was proper to classify pregnancy as 'a temporary idiosyncrasy' and that '[a]n actor should not be required to assume that every female in his path is about to become a mother.' "

Dillon v. Legg

441 P.2d 912 (Cal. 1968) (en banc)

[The defendant driver struck and killed Erin Lee Dillon, a child, as she was crossing a public street. Her death precipitated three separate claims. First, decedent's mother and minor sister, Cheryl, sued for wrongful death. Second, her mother sued for nervous shock and serious mental and physical pain suffered in consequence of defendant's negligence. Third, the minor sister, Cheryl, also sued for emotional and physical suffering. The evidence established that the mother was in "close proximity" to Erin Lee at the time of the collision, but that defendant's car never threatened her safety since she was outside the "zone of danger." The trial court dismissed the mother's action for emotional distress under Amaya v. Home Ice, Fuel & Supply Co., 379 P.2d 513 (Cal. 1963), because her fright and distress did not arise out of fear for her own safety. However, Cheryl's parallel action was not dismissed because she might have been in the zone of danger or feared for her own safety. The mother appealed.

Noting that her claim rested on considerations of "natural justice," the court holds it should not be "frustrated" because of judicial fears of fraudulent claims that "would involve the courts in the hopeless task of defining the extent of the tortfeasor's liability." It then critiqued *Amaya*.]

TOBRINER, J.* [W]e can hardly justify relief to the sister for trauma which she suffered upon apprehension of the child's death and yet deny it to the mother merely because of a happenstance that the sister was some few yards closer to the accident. The instant case exposes the hopeless artificiality of the zone-of-danger rule. In the second place, to rest upon the zone-of-danger rule when we have rejected the impact rule becomes even less defensible. We have, indeed, held that impact is not necessary for recovery. The zone-of-danger concept must, then, inevitably collapse because the only reason for the requirement of presence in that zone lies in the fact that one within it will fear the danger of *impact.* At the threshold, then, we point to the incongruity of the rules upon which any rejection of plaintiff's recovery must rest.

We further note, at the outset, that defendant has interposed the defense that the contributory negligence of the mother, the sister, and the child contributed to the accident. If any such defense is sustained and defendant found not liable for the death of the child because of the contributory negligence of the mother, sister or child, we do not believe that the mother or sister should recover for the emotional trauma which they allegedly suffered. In the absence of the primary liability of the tort-feasor for the death of the child, we see no ground for an independent and secondary liability for claims for injuries by third parties. The basis for such claims must be the adjudicated liability and fault of defendant; that liability and fault must be the foundation for the tort-feasor's duty of due care to third parties who, as a consequence of such negligence, sustain emotional trauma.

We turn then to an analysis of the concept of duty, . . .

The history of the concept of duty in itself discloses that it is not an old and deep-rooted doctrine but a legal device of the latter half of the nineteenth century designed to curtail the feared propensities of juries toward liberal awards.

1. This court in the past has rejected the argument that we must deny recovery upon a legitimate claim because other fraudulent ones may be urged. . . .

Indubitably juries and trial courts, constantly called upon to distinguish the frivolous from the substantial and the fraudulent from the meritorious, reach some erroneous results. But such fallibility, inherent in the judicial process, offers no reason for substituting for the case-by-case resolution of causes an artificial and indefensible barrier. Courts not only compromise their basic responsibility to decide the merits of each individually but destroy the public's confidence in them by using the broad broom of "administrative convenience" to sweep away a class of claims a number of which are admittedly meritorious. The mere assertion that fraud is possible, "a possibility [that] exists to some degree in all cases," does not prove a present necessity to abandon the neutral principles of foreseeability, proximate cause and consequential injury that generally govern tort law.

Indeed, we doubt that the problem of the fraudulent claim is substantially more pronounced in the case of a mother claiming physical injury resulting from seeing her child killed than in other areas of tort law in which the right to recover damages is well established in California. For example, a plaintiff claiming that fear for his own safety resulted in physical injury makes out a well recognized case for recovery.

Moreover, damages are allowed for "mental suffering," a type of injury, on the whole, less amenable to objective proof than the physical injury involved here; the mental injury can be in

* [Tobriner, J., while on the California Court of Appeal, wrote the opinion in *Amaya*, later reversed by the California Supreme Court, allowing the plaintiff to recover for nervous shock even though he was beyond the zone of danger. 23 Cal. Rptr. 131 (1962).—EDS.]

aggravation of, or "parasitic to," an established tort. In fact, fear for another, even in the absence of resulting physical injury, can be part of these parasitic damages. And emotional distress, if inflicted intentionally, constitutes an independent tort. The danger of plaintiffs' fraudulent collection of damages for nonexistent injury is at least as great in these examples as in the instant case.

In sum, the application of tort law can never be a matter of mathematical precision. In terms of characterizing conduct as tortious and matching a money award to the injury suffered as well as in fixing the extent of injury, the process cannot be perfect. Undoubtedly, ever since the ancient case of the tavern-keeper's wife who successfully avoided the hatchet cast by an irate customer (I. de S. et ux v. W. de S., Y.B. 22 Edw. iii, f. 99, pl. 60 (1348) [*supra* Chapter 1, at 46]), defendants have argued that plaintiffs' claims of injury from emotional trauma might well be fraudulent. Yet we cannot let the difficulties of adjudication frustrate the principle that there be a remedy for every substantial wrong.

2. The alleged inability to fix definitions for recovery on the different facts of future cases does not justify the denial of recovery on the specific facts of the instant case; in any event, proper guidelines can indicate the extent of liability for such future cases. . . .

Since the chief element in determining whether defendant owes a duty or an obligation to plaintiff is the foreseeability of the risk, that factor will be of prime concern in every case. Because it is inherently intertwined with foreseeability such duty or obligation must necessarily be adjudicated only upon a case-by-case basis. We cannot now predetermine defendant's obligation in every situation by a fixed category; no immutable rule can establish the extent of that obligation for every circumstance of the future. We can, however, define guidelines which will aid in the resolution of such an issue as the instant one.

We note, first, that we deal here with a case in which plaintiff suffered a shock which resulted in physical injury and we confine our ruling to that case. In determining, in such a case, whether defendant should reasonably foresee the injury to plaintiff, or, in other terminology, whether defendant owes plaintiff a duty of due care, the courts will take into account such factors as the following: (1) Whether plaintiff was located near the scene of the accident as contrasted with one who was a distance away from it. (2) Whether the shock resulted from a direct emotional impact upon plaintiff from the sensory and contemporaneous observance of the accident, as contrasted with learning of the accident from others after its occurrence. (3) Whether plaintiff and the victim were closely related, as contrasted with an absence of any relationship or the presence of only a distant relationship.

The evaluation of these factors will indicate the degree of the defendant's foreseeability: obviously defendant is more likely to foresee that a mother who observes an accident affecting her child will suffer harm than to foretell that a stranger witness will do so. Similarly, the degree of foreseeability of the third person's injury is far greater in the case of his contemporaneous observance of the accident than that in which he subsequently learns of it. The defendant is more likely to foresee that shock to the nearby, witnessing mother will cause physical harm than to anticipate that someone distant from the accident will suffer more than a temporary emotional reaction. All these elements, of course, shade into each other; the fixing of obligation, intimately tied into the facts, depends upon each case.

In light of these factors the court will determine whether the accident and harm was *reasonably* foreseeable. Such reasonable foreseeability does not turn on whether the particular defendant as an individual would have in actuality foreseen the exact accident and loss; it contemplates that courts, on a case-to-case basis, analyzing all the circumstances, will decide what the ordinary man under such circumstances should reasonably have foreseen. The courts thus mark out the areas of liability, excluding the remote and unexpected.

In the instant case, the presence of all the above factors indicates that plaintiff has alleged a sufficient prima facie case. Surely the negligent driver who causes the death of a young child may reasonably expect that the mother will not be far distant and will upon witnessing the accident suffer emotional trauma. . . .

The fear of an inability to fix boundaries has not impelled the courts of England to deny recovery for emotional trauma caused by witnessing the death or injury of another due to defendant's negligence. We set forth the holdings of some English cases merely to demonstrate that courts can formulate and apply such limitations of liability.

[The court then reviews the English cases that are favorable to recovery in nervous shock cases.]

Thus we see no good reason why the general rules of tort law, including the concepts of negligence, proximate cause, and foreseeability, long applied to all other types of injury, should not govern the case now before us. . . .

In short, the history of the cases does not show the development of a logical rule but rather a series of changes and abandonments. Upon the argument in each situation that the courts draw a Maginot Line to withstand an onslaught of false claims, the cases have assumed a variety of postures. At first they insisted that there be no recovery for emotional trauma at all. Retreating from this position, they gave relief for such trauma only if physical impact occurred. They then abandoned the requirement for physical impact but insisted that the victim fear for her own safety, holding that a mother could recover for fear for her children's safety if she simultaneously entertained a personal fear for herself. They stated that the mother need only be in the "zone of danger." The final anomaly would be the instant case in which the sister, who observed the accident, would be granted recovery because she was in the "zone of danger," but the *mother*, not far distant, would be barred from recovery.

The successive abandonment of these positions exposes the weakness of artificial abstractions which bar recovery contrary to the general rules. . . .

Yet for some artificial reason this delimitation of liability is alleged to be unworkable in the most egregious case of them all: the mother's emotional trauma at the witnessed death of her child. If we stop at this point, however, we must necessarily question and reject not merely recovery here, but the viability of the judicial process for ascertaining liability for tortious conduct itself. To the extent that it is inconsistent with our ruling here, we therefore overrule Amaya v. Home Ice, Fuel & Supply Co.

To deny recovery would be to chain this state to an outmoded rule of the 19th century which can claim no current credence. No good reason compels our captivity to an indefensible orthodoxy.

The judgment is reversed.

Traynor, C.J. I dissent for the reasons set forth in Amaya v. Home Ice, Fuel & Supply Co. In my opinion that case was correctly decided and should not be overruled.

Burke, J., [dissenting, questions the guidelines set forth in the majority opinion]. . . . What if the plaintiff was honestly *mistaken* in believing the third person to be in danger or to be seriously injured? What if the third person had assumed the risk involved? How "close" must the relationship be between the plaintiff and the third person? I.e., what if the third person was the plaintiff's beloved niece or nephew, grandparent, fiancé, or lifelong friend, more dear to the plaintiff than her immediate family? Next, how "near" must the plaintiff have been to the scene of the accident, and how "soon" must shock have been felt? Indeed, what is the magic in the plaintiff's being actually present? Is the shock any less real if the mother does not know of the accident until her injured child is brought into her home? On the other hand, is it any less real if the mother is physically present at the scene but is nevertheless unaware of the danger or injury to her child until after the accident has occurred? No answers to these questions are to be found in today's majority opinion. Our trial courts, however, will not so easily escape the burden of distinguishing between litigants on the basis of such artificial and unpredictable distinctions.

NOTES

1. ***Foreseeability in Emotional Distress Cases.*** In Tobin v. Grossman, 249 N.E.2d 419, 422–23 (N.Y. 1969), the plaintiff suffered "physical injuries caused by shock and fear" when her two-year-old son was seriously injured in an automobile accident. The plaintiff did not see the accident but heard the screech of brakes and arrived on the scene, from only a few feet away, moments later. In denying recovery for negligent infliction of emotional distress, or NIED, Breitel, J., took direct issue with *Dillon*'s heavy reliance on foreseeability, and predicted that actions, if allowed, could not in principle or practice be confined to close family members who witnessed the accident.

> On foreseeability, it is hardly cogent to assert that the negligent actor if he could foresee injury to the child that he should not also foresee at the same time harm to the mother who, especially in the case of children of tender years, is likely to be present or about. But foreseeability, once recognized, is not so easily limited. Relatives, other than the mother, such as fathers or grandparents, or even other caretakers, equally sensitive and as easily harmed, may be just as foreseeably affected. Hence, foreseeability would, in short order, extend logically to caretakers other than the mother, and ultimately to affected bystanders. . . .
>
> The final and most difficult factor is any reasonable circumscription, within tolerable limits required by public policy, of a rule creating liability. Every parent who loses a child or whose child of any age suffers an injury is likely to sustain grievous psychological trauma, with the added risk of consequential physical harm. Any rule based solely on eyewitnessing the accident could stand only until the first case comes along in which the parent is in the immediate vicinity but did not see the accident. Moreover, the instant advice that one's child has been killed or injured, by telephone, word of mouth, or by whatever means, even if delayed, will have in most cases the same impact. The sight of gore and exposed bones is not necessary to provide special impact on a parent.

Judge Breitel's focus on the foreseeability prong of the *Dillon* test underestimated the resolve of the California courts toward its explicit requirements of a close relationship and direct observation. In Elden v. Sheldon, 758 P.2d 582 (Cal. 1988), the California Supreme Court denied claims for the negligent infliction of emotional distress (and loss of consortium) of an unmarried cohabitant involved in an automobile accident, who not only witnessed his cohabitant's death but was injured himself. The court in *Elden* construed *Dillon*'s third prong—that the plaintiff be "closely related" to the victim—to cover only spouses and siblings. Further, it held that *Dillon*'s general foreseeability language did not include a "close friend" and concluded that unmarried cohabitants stood in no better position than close friends, given the "state's interest in promoting marriage."

In Thing v. La Chusa, 771 P.2d 814, 815 (Cal. 1989), the court refused to buckle on the direct observation requirement when it denied recovery for emotional distress to a mother who had not witnessed the automobile accident that injured her child. Eagleson, J., rejected *Dillon*'s assertion that "foreseeability" was the touchstone of duty, treating the concept as "amorphous." Instead he opted for a "bright line" rule:

> In the absence of physical injury or impact to the plaintiff himself, damages for emotional distress should be recoverable only if the plaintiff: (1) is closely related to the injury victim; (2) is present at the scene of the injury-producing event at the time it occurs and is then aware that it is causing injury to the victim and, (3) as a result suffers emotional distress beyond that which would be anticipated in a disinterested witness.

In defense of creating this "clear rule" for liability, Eagleson, J., reasoned:

> In so doing we balance the impact of arbitrary lines which deny recovery to some victims whose injury is very real against that of imposing liability out of proportion to culpability for negligent acts. We also weigh in the balance the importance to the administration of justice of clear guidelines under which litigants and trial courts may resolve disputes.

2. *Another Maginot Line? Dillon's Reception Outside California.* *Dillon* and its progeny have been subject to intensive examination in other states. One state, Kentucky, subsequently overturned its acceptance of the impact rule in cases of severe or serious emotional distress, noting "that at least forty jurisdictions have either rejected the impact rule or abandoned it." See Osborne v. Keeney, 399 S.W.3d 1, 17–18 (Ky. 2012). One of the holdouts for the older rule is Engler v. Illinois Farmers Insurance Co., 706 N.W.2d 764, 771 (Minn. 2005), which adheres to the zone of danger test in RST §§313 and 436, chiefly because "it provides a bright line to limit recovery." In *Engler* the plaintiff experienced fright because the driver of the other car had threatened both her and her son. Blatz, C.J., allowed her to recover for the fright that she experienced, but not for the post-traumatic distress that she suffered because of the severe injuries to her son. Blatz, C.J., stated that NIED claims were allowable only

> if the plaintiff can prove that she: (1) was in the zone of danger of physical impact; (2) had an objectively reasonable fear for her own safety; (3) had severe emotional distress with attendant physical manifestations; and (4) stands in a close relationship to the third-party victim. In addition, to succeed with such a claim, the plaintiff also must establish that the defendant's negligent conduct—the conduct that created an unreasonable risk of physical injury to the plaintiff—caused serious bodily injury to the third-party victim.

In his concurrence, Anderson, J., claimed that the majority position was too loose insofar as it allowed anyone with a "close relationship" to the injured person to recover, and would have permitted recovery only to a "spouse, parent, child, grandparent, grandchild, or sibling of the plaintiff."

Other courts have read *Dillon* restrictively. Hawaii first adopted the *Dillon* rule in Rodrigues v. State, 472 P.2d 509 (Haw. 1970). However, in Kelley v. Kokua Sales and Supply, Ltd., 532 P.2d 673 (Haw. 1975), a divided court denied recovery when the decedent, a California resident, died of a heart attack shortly after being informed by telephone that his daughter and grandchild had been killed in a road accident. The court, unquestionably motivated by the fear of unlimited liability, invoked the language of "duty of care" and "foresight of consequences" to justify its denial of recovery. In Dziokonski v. Babineau, 380 N.E.2d 1295, 1302 (Mass. 1978), the court held that

> allegations concerning a parent who sustains substantial physical harm as a result of severe mental distress over some peril or harm to his minor child caused by the defendant's negligence state a claim for which relief might be granted, where the parent either witnesses the accident or soon comes on the scene while the child is still there.

More recently in Cardenas v. Swanson, 531 P.3d 917 (Wyo. 2023), the plaintiffs sued for their emotional distress when their dogs died after being entangled in snares set by the defendant. The plaintiffs only discovered the death of their dogs sometime after they were trapped. The court allowed claims for damage for the loss of the dogs and for the personal injuries suffered in seeking to get the dogs out of the snares. However, it drew the line at the emotional distress claim. Gray, J., after showing some affection for the physical impact rule, held:

> Under Wyoming law, dogs are property. While we do not question the Cardenas family's heartache over the deaths of their dogs, [our case law] precludes recovery for emotional distress damages under these facts. See also Steller v. Bischoff (holding that plaintiff could not recover emotional distress damages for the death of his horse in malpractice action against vet).

3. *Proper Plaintiffs in Emotional Distress Cases.* Similarly, the class of eligible plaintiffs has been narrowly construed. In Trombetta v. Conkling, 626 N.E.2d 653, 654 (N.Y. 1993), the court denied an emotional distress claim brought by a niece who witnessed the death of her aunt who had raised her from age 11, concluding baldly: "Recovery of damages by bystanders for the negligent infliction of emotional distress should be limited only to the immediate family." Thompson v. Dhaiti, 103 A.D.3d 711 (N.Y. App. Div. 2013), construed "immediate family" not to include a stepdaughter. In Dunphy v. Gregor, 642 A.2d 372 (N.J. 1994), the New Jersey Supreme Court also split the difference. As in *Dillon*, it required a plaintiff to have observed the death or injury of another person, but it repudiated *Elden*, by extending the concept to an unmarried cohabitant. "The State's interest in marriage would not be harmed if unmarried cohabitants are permitted to prove on a case-by-case basis that they enjoy a steadfast relationship that is equivalent to a legal marriage and thus equally deserves legal protection." *Dunphy* was followed in McDougall v. Lamm, 48 A.3d 312 (N.J. 2012), which disallowed a pet owner an emotional distress claim arising from the death of his pet.

More recently, in Coleson v. City of New York, 24 N.E.3d 1074, 1079 (N.Y. 2014), a child brought an emotional distress claim against the New York City Police Department for injuries suffered when his estranged father stabbed his mother with a knife. The infant plaintiff claimed that he "was in the zone of danger because, although he was in a closet at the time his mother was stabbed, he saw Coleson [his father] with the knife and while in the closet heard his mother's screams." Abdus-Salaam, J., concluded that "the child was not in the zone of danger because he was in a broom closet while his mother was stabbed, and thus neither saw the incident nor was immediately aware of the incident at the time it occurred." The Third Restatement takes much the same hard line in RTT: LPEH §48.

RESTATEMENT OF THE LAW (THIRD) OF TORTS: LIABILITY FOR PHYSICAL AND EMOTIONAL HARM

§48. Negligent Infliction of Emotional Harm Resulting from Bodily Harm to a Third Person

An actor who negligently causes sudden serious bodily injury to a third person is subject to liability for serious emotional harm caused thereby to a person who:

(a) perceives the event contemporaneously, and

(b) is a close family member of the person suffering the bodily injury.

4. *The "At Risk" Plaintiff: of Drugs and Toxic Torts.* One important variation on NIED cases involves individuals who are exposed to dangerous drugs or toxic substances and suffer distress, for fear of future harm to themselves. The Third Restatement notes the powerful judicial sentiment against awarding damages, for example, in cases regarding cancer phobia, in part for the fear of multiple lawsuits—one for the fear and a second for the injury. RTT: LPEH §47, comment *k*. For example, an "at-risk" claim for emotional distress was rejected in Payton v. Abbott Labs, 437 N.E.2d 171, 181 (Mass. 1982), when brought by daughters exposed to DES in utero who stood between 1 in 1,000 and 1 in 10,000 chance of getting adenocarcinoma, a very serious form of cancer. The court insisted that the proper measure of damage was that which would be experienced by "a reasonable person, normally constituted," and then only for physical harm that "must be manifested by objective symptomatology and substantiated by expert medical testimony." Similarly, in Metro-North Commuter Railroad v. Buckley, 521 U.S. 424 (1997), *supra* at 330, the Court disallowed a claim alleging fear of cancer after exposure to asbestos. *Buckley* was distinguished in Norfolk & Western Railway v. Ayers, 538 U.S. 135, 141 (2003), another FELA claim, by allowing mental anguish damages from fear of future cancer for a plaintiff who is actually suffering from asbestosis.

A parallel NIED claim arose in Potter v. Firestone Tire & Rubber Co., 863 P.2d 795, 800, 810, 826 (Cal. 1993), in which the defendant's local employees, in conscious violation of federal and state environmental statutes and internal company policy, dumped certain toxic wastes into an unauthorized dumpsite to cut costs. The defendants sought to limit recovery to persons who manifested some sign of physical injury from the ingested toxic substances.

Baxter, J., required, as in *Payton*, that the plaintiff "pleads and proves that the fear stems from a knowledge, corroborated by reliable medical and scientific opinion, that it is more likely than not that the feared cancer will develop in the future due to the toxic exposure." But owing to the defendant's malicious conduct the court allowed recovery even though plaintiffs' toxic intake from smoking was 2,500 times that found in the defendant's waste. Why credit the plaintiff's fears of the former to the exclusion of the latter?

An NIED claim was also rejected in Weissberger v. Princess Cruise Lines, Ltd., No. 2:20-CV-02328, 2020 WL 3977938 (C.D. Cal. July 14, 2020), where plaintiffs sought recovery for their fear of catching COVID-19 while quarantined aboard the *Grand Princess* in the port of Oakland. Klausner, J., held that the plaintiffs failed to satisfy the zone of danger test. Relying on *Buckley*, *supra*, he wrote: "to recover, a plaintiff must manifest some symptom of the feared disease" and also "must allege that the defendant's negligent conduct placed [the] plaintiff in immediate risk of physical harm." The same administrative worries about separating good from bad claims, of guarding against unlimited liability, and of preventing a flood of unimportant and trivial claims prevailed. How does one prove causation generally in those cases where plaintiffs come down with COVID on (or after they leave) the boat?

5. *Emotional Distress in Medical Malpractice Cases.* In Squeo v. Norwalk Hosp. Ass'n, 113 A.3d 932, 935 (Conn. 2015), the plaintiffs sued a nurse and hospital for negligently discharging their suicidal son after completing an emergency psychiatric examination. The parents claimed that they suffered emotional distress from discovering that their son hung himself in their front yard. Palmer, J., affirmed summary judgment for the defendants concluding:

> [A] bystander to medical malpractice may bring a claim for the resulting emotional distress only when the injuries result from gross negligence such that it would be readily apparent to a lay observer. This additional element reflects our determination that bystander claims should be available in the medical malpractice context only under extremely limited circumstances. [We also] conclude that a bystander must suffer injuries that are severe and debilitating, such that they warrant a psychiatric diagnosis or otherwise substantially impair the bystander's ability to cope with life's daily routines and demands.

A still-developing area of law is that of reproductive harm. In Broadnax v. Gonzalez, 809 N.E.2d 645, 648–49 (N.Y. 2004), the plaintiff was advised by her obstetrician, Dr. Gonzalez, to travel forty-five minutes to a hospital in New York City rather than seek immediate treatment at a suburban hospital. Upon arrival at Columbia Presbyterian Hospital in Manhattan, the plaintiff had to wait an additional forty-five minutes for Dr. Gonzalez to show up, during which time the nurse-midwife who had accompanied the plaintiff from Westchester neglected to contact the on-call doctor. When Dr. Gonzalez arrived, he performed a sonogram that detected fetal heart rate decelerations, but he delayed in performing an emergency cesarean section. Three and a half hours after the plaintiff's initial arrival at the Westchester Birth Center, Dr. Gonzalez finally undertook a cesarean section, delivering a full-term stillborn girl. Reversing the grant of the defendants' summary judgment motion, the Court of Appeals noted the nonsensical nature of the longstanding reluctance to recognize NIED in cases of miscarriage or stillbirth resulting from medical malpractice, absent independent physical injury to the plaintiff:

> [The old rule] exposed medical caregivers to malpractice liability for in utero injuries when the fetus survived, but immunized them against any liability when their malpractice caused a miscarriage or stillbirth. . . . We therefore hold that, even in the absence of an independent injury, medical malpractice resulting in miscarriage or stillbirth should be construed as a violation of a duty of care to the expectant mother, entitling her to damages for emotional distress.

6. *Direct Victims.* The Third Restatement extends liability to "specified categories of activities, undertakings, or relationships in which negligent conduct is especially likely to cause serious emotional harm." RTT: LPEH §47(b). In these cases, there is no requirement of the direct observation of a harm to some third person. "Specifically, courts have imposed liability on hospitals and funeral homes for negligently mishandling a corpse and on telegraph companies for negligently mistranscribing or misdirecting a telegram that informs the recipient, erroneously, about the death of a loved one." *Id.*, comment *b.*

RESTATEMENT OF THE LAW (THIRD) OF TORTS: LIABILITY FOR PHYSICAL AND EMOTIONAL HARM

§47. Negligent Conduct Directly Inflicting Emotional Harm on Another

An actor whose negligent conduct causes serious emotional harm to another is subject to liability to the other if the conduct:

(a) places the other in danger of immediate bodily harm and the emotional harm results from the danger; or

(b) occurs in the course of specified categories of activities, undertakings, or relationships in which negligent conduct is especially likely to cause serious emotional harm.

Comment j. Physical consequences not required: Significant emotional harm may cause physical illness or other bodily harm. Some courts insist that plaintiff present with physical symptoms to ensure that the emotional harm claimed is genuine and serious. The rule stated in this Section, while requiring serious emotional harm, is not limited to cases in which there are physical manifestations. The requirements that the harm be serious, that the circumstances of the case be such that a reasonable person would suffer serious harm, and that there be credible evidence that the plaintiff has suffered such harm better serve the purpose of screening claims than a requirement of physical consequences.

Liability under this provision has also been extended to cover other cases in which the recipient of information is a "direct victim" of the harm. In Molien v. Kaiser Foundation Hospitals, 616 P.2d 813, 817 (Cal. 1980) (en banc), the defendant's employee, Dr. Kilbridge, negligently provided the plaintiff's wife with an erroneous report that she had contracted an infectious type of syphilis. She in turn had to undergo unnecessary medical treatment and became "upset and suspicious that her husband had engaged in extramarital sexual activities." Their marriage broke up from the ensuing tension and hostility, and the husband's suit for emotional distress was allowed, notwithstanding the limitations in *Dillon*, on the ground that the plaintiff was a "direct victim" of the defendant's erroneous report. Mosk, J., wrote:

> In the case at bar the risk of harm to plaintiff was reasonably foreseeable to defendants. It is easily predictable that an erroneous diagnosis of syphilis and its probable source would produce marital discord and resultant emotional distress to a married patient's spouse; Dr. Kilbridge's advice to Mrs. Molien to have her husband examined for the disease confirms that plaintiff was a foreseeable victim of the negligent diagnosis. Because the disease is normally transmitted only by sexual relations, it is rational to anticipate that both husband and wife would experience anxiety, suspicion, and hostility when confronted with what they had every reason to believe was reliable medical evidence of a particularly noxious infidelity.

Post-*Molien,* foresight is no longer the touchstone of duty. Instead, the California court asks whether the defendant has assumed some direct duty to the plaintiff. In Huggins v. Longs Drug Stores California, Inc., 862 P.2d 148, 152–53 (Cal. 1993), the court found that no direct relationship existed between the defendant pharmacy, which dispensed five times the prescribed dosage, and the parents whose child was harmed by the overdose. In Wallace v. Nationstar Mortg. LLC, No. 2:18-CV-02768, 2019 WL 1382499 (E.D. Cal. Mar. 27, 2019), the court ruled that the defendant-lender assumed a duty of care toward the plaintiff-borrower based on a six-factor test, and thus denied defendant's motion to dismiss the plaintiff's NIED claim against the lender for refusing her loan payments and declaring her to be in default on her debt.

Eriksson v. Nunnink, 183 Cal. Rptr. 3d 234, 251–52 (Ct. App. 2015), found no bystander liability based on NIED, where the plaintiffs' child died while participating in an equestrian contest. The plaintiffs' NIED suit against the child's coach was dismissed on the ground that the release signed on behalf of the minor child also bound the parents. King, J., concluded:

> Because the defendant can owe no greater duty to the heirs than to the decedent the release can be asserted against the wrongful death plaintiffs to prove the absence of a duty of ordinary care. The same rationale should apply in bystander NIED cases. Accordingly, just as Nunnink may interpose the defense of express assumption of the risk to the Erikssons' wrongful death suit, she may interpose the same defense to their bystander action for NIED.

CHAPTER 6

AFFIRMATIVE DUTIES

SECTION A. INTRODUCTION

The previous five chapters have been largely, but not exclusively, devoted to understanding the rules for personal injury and property damage that result from the defendant's positive acts, such as hitting another person, or creating dangerous conditions. In this chapter, the focus shifts from liability for misfeasance, or misdeeds, to liability for nonfeasance, or failure to act. The difference between these two types of cases is often articulated in terms of duty.

In misfeasance cases, the basic duty of all individuals is to abstain from hurting other persons, both strangers and persons with whom the defendant has some special relationship. In the stranger setting, any invasion of the plaintiff's person or space by the defendant sets up a prima facie obligation to compensate under strict liability. And in the negligence system, the usual reference to a duty of care is to take care to avoid harm to another person by one's own affirmative acts.

In contrast, for cases of nonfeasance, the idea of negligence is subtly modified. The notion of care no longer refers to taking precautions that allow the defendant to avoid making harmful contact with the plaintiff. Instead, it now requires rendering material aid or support to the plaintiff facing harmful conduct caused either by third parties not under his control or by natural events. That duty of affirmative care is neatly divided in two halves. The first is directed to strangers and the second to individuals with whom the defendant stands in what is commonly termed a special relationship. These two strands of duty are reflected in the Third Restatement, which discusses the question of duty in connection with positive acts in section 7, and the affirmative duties to aid in sections 37–44.

In line with the distinction between affirmative care to strangers and to individuals in a special relationship, the first part of this chapter examines a hardy problem of enduring philosophical interest: When are individuals liable for failing to rescue strangers in imminent peril of life or limb? The so-called Good Samaritan cases are prominent in this area, in which the defendant was in no sense responsible for creating the dangerous condition or situation that brought forth the need to rescue in the first place. Thereafter the discussion is extended to less controversial cases in which the defendant, either tortiously or nontortiously, has created the dangerous situation requiring rescue.

The second set of issues concerns the duties that landowners and occupiers owe to persons who enter their premises. These entries may be unlawful, as with trespassers, or lawful, as with persons who have received permission from the landowner. Despite fluctuations in judicial attitude, the law generally holds that the trespasser takes, at the very least, as against the defendant the risk of purely accidental injuries even if he is entitled to recover for injuries that the defendant deliberately and perhaps recklessly inflicted. In contrast, the landowner clearly owes some duty of care to persons lawfully on the premises. The critical issues are how much care is owed and to which persons. The traditional common law cases distinguished between social guests (called "licensees") and business visitors (called "invitees"), and imposed a lower duty to the former — merely to warn of known latent defects — than it did to the latter — to take reasonable care to both discover danger and to keep the premises safe. Many states today reject this status distinction and impose a uniform duty of reasonable care for the benefit of licensees and invitees alike. In addition, courts have more frequently addressed how far the duties of occupiers extend beyond making the premises safe, such as by providing emergency assistance to persons in various states of distress.

The third set of issues involves gratuitous undertakings by the defendant to benefit or assist the plaintiff. These cases are, in a sense, contractual, as they rest upon the defendant's promise, express or implied, to the plaintiff. But the defendant's undertakings have not been bargained for by the plaintiff, and, for that reason, these cases have historically been treated as part of tort law.

The fourth set of issues arises whenever the defendant owes a duty to prevent harm to the plaintiff's person or property because the defendant stands in some sort of "special relationship" either with the plaintiff or with the person who threatens harm to the plaintiff. The first subclass of special relationship cases is an outgrowth of the premises liability cases and concerns, for example, the duties a landlord owes to his tenant, a hotel to its guests, a club to its members, or a university to its students. In these cases, the defendant may be called upon to guard against various contingencies, ranging from the simple loss or destruction of property entrusted to its care, to the defective conditions of premises under its control, or, in today's most contentious area, to the criminal actions of a third party. The second subclass of special relationship cases arises when prisons and hospitals have charge of persons who, once released, commit acts of violence against third parties. Until recently, contemporary tort law had expanded the range of affirmative duties that large (and not-so-large) social institutions — schools, hotels, hospitals, landlords, common carriers — owe their customers and clients, but today the law shows evidence of stabilization and perhaps modest contraction.

SECTION B. THE DUTY TO RESCUE

Luke 10:30-37 (King James Translation)

A certain man went down from Jerusalem to Jericho, and fell among thieves which stripped him of his raiment, and wounded him, and departed, leaving him half dead. And by chance there came down a certain priest that way: and when he saw him, he passed by on the other side. And likewise a Levite, when he was at the place, came and looked at him, and passed by on the other side. But a certain Samaritan, as he journeyed, came where he was: and when he saw him, he had compassion on him, and went to him, and bound up his wounds, pouring in oil and wine, and set him on his own beast, and brought him to an inn, and took care of him. And on the morrow when he departed, he took out two pence, and gave them to the host and said unto him, Take care of him; and whatsoever thou spendest more, when I come again, I will repay thee. Which of these three, thinkest thou, was neighbour unto him that fell among the thieves. And he said, He that shewed mercy on him. Then said Jesus unto him, Go, do thou likewise.

Vincent van Gogh, "The Good Samaritan" (left) and Rembrandt Harmensz van Rijn, "The Good Samaritan at the Inn" (right)

Source: Public domain

Buch v. Amory Manufacturing Co.

44 A. 809 (N.H. 1897)

[The plaintiff, aged eight years, trespassed in the defendant's mill, where weaving machinery was in operation. An overseer observed him there and told him to leave. The plaintiff did not go because he did not understand English. Nonetheless, the overseer did not put him out, although the running machinery presented an obvious hazard to a child of the plaintiff's age. The plaintiff had his hand crushed in a machine that his brother, age 13 and the defendant's employee, was trying to teach him to run. The trial court denied a motion for a directed verdict for the defendant. The defendant appealed. The verdict for the plaintiff was set aside and judgment was entered for the defendant.]

Carpenter, C.J. Assuming, then, that the plaintiff was incapable either of appreciating the danger or of exercising the care necessary to avoid it, is he, upon the facts stated, entitled to recover? He was a trespasser in a place dangerous to children of his age. In the conduct of their business and management of their machinery the defendants were without fault. The only negligence charged upon, or attributed to, them is that, inasmuch as they could not make the plaintiff understand a command to leave the premises, and ought to have known that they could not, they did not forcibly eject him. Actionable negligence is the neglect of a legal duty. The defendants are not liable unless they owed to the plaintiff a legal duty which they neglected to perform. With purely moral obligations the law does not deal. For example, the priest and Levite who passed by on the other side were not, it is supposed, liable at law for the continued suffering of the man who fell among thieves, which they might and morally ought to have prevented or relieved. Suppose *A*, standing close by a railroad, sees a two-year-old babe on the track and a car approaching. He can easily rescue the child with entire safety to himself, and the instincts of humanity require him to do so. If he does not, he may, perhaps, justly be styled a ruthless savage and a moral monster; but he is not liable in damages for the child's injury, or indictable under the statute for its death. . . .

What duties do the owners owe to a trespasser upon their premises? They may eject him, using such force and such only as is necessary for the purpose. They are bound to abstain from any other or further intentional or negligent acts of personal violence—bound to inflict upon him by means of their own active intervention no injury which by due care they can avoid. They are not bound to warn him against hidden or secret dangers arising from the condition of the premises, or to protect him against any injury that may arise from his own acts or those of other persons. In short, if they do nothing, let him entirely alone, in no manner interfere with him, he can have no cause of action against them for any injury that he may receive. On the contrary, he is liable to them for any damage that he by his unlawful meddling may cause them or their property. What greater or other legal obligation was cast on these defendants by the circumstance that the plaintiff was (as is assumed) an irresponsible infant?

If landowners are not bound to warn an adult trespasser of hidden dangers,—dangers which he by ordinary care cannot discover and, therefore, cannot avoid,—on what ground can it be claimed that they must warn an infant of open and visible dangers which he is unable to appreciate? No legal distinction is perceived between the duties of the owners in one case and the other. The situation of the adult in front of secret dangers which by no degree of care he can discover, and that of the infant incapable of comprehending danger, is in a legal aspect exactly the same. There is no apparent reason for holding that any greater or other duty rests upon the owners in one case than in the other.

There is a wide difference—a broad gulf—both in reason and in law, between causing and preventing an injury; between doing by negligence or otherwise a wrong to one's neighbor, and preventing him from injuring himself; between protecting him against injury by another and guarding him from injury that may accrue to him from the condition of the premises which he has unlawfully invaded. The duty to do no wrong is a legal duty. The duty to protect against wrong is, generally speaking and excepting certain intimate relations in the nature of a trust, a moral obligation only, not recognized or enforced by law. Is a spectator liable if he sees an intelligent man or an unintelligent infant running into danger and does not warn or forcibly restrain him? What difference does it make whether the danger is on another's land, or upon his own, in case the man or infant is not there by his express or implied invitation? If *A* sees an eight-year-old boy beginning to climb into his garden over a wall stuck with spikes and does not warn him or drive him off, is he liable in damages if the boy meets with injury from the spikes? I see my neighbor's two-year-old babe in dangerous proximity to the machinery of his windmill in his yard, and easily might, but do not, rescue him. I am not liable in damages to the child for his injuries, nor, if the child is killed, punishable for manslaughter by the common law or under the statute (P.S., c. 278, S. 8), because the child and I are strangers, and I am under no legal duty to protect him. Now suppose I see the same child trespassing in my own yard and meddling in like manner with the dangerous machinery of my own windmill. What additional obligation is cast upon me by reason of the child's trespass? The mere fact that the child is unable to take care of himself does not impose on me the legal duty of protecting him in the one case more than in the other. Upon what principle of law can an infant by coming unlawfully upon my premises impose upon me the legal duty of a guardian? None has been suggested, and we know of none.

An infant, no matter of how tender years, is liable in law for his trespasses. . . . If, then, the defendants' machinery was injured by the plaintiff's act in putting his hand in the gearing, he is liable to them for the damages in an action of trespass and to nominal damages for the wrongful entry. It would be no answer to such an action that the defendants might by force have prevented the trespass. It is impossible to hold that while the plaintiff is liable to the defendants in trespass, they are liable to him in case for neglecting to prevent the act which caused the injury both to him and them. Cases of enticement, allurement, or invitation of infants to their injury, or setting traps for them, and cases relating to the sufficiency of public ways, or to the exposure upon them of machinery attractive and dangerous to children, have no application here.

Danger from machinery in motion in the ordinary course of business cannot be distinguished from that arising from a well, pit, open scuttle, or other stationary object. The movement of the works is a part of the regular and normal condition of the premises. . . . The law no more compels the owners to shut down their gates and stop their business for the protection of a trespasser than it requires them to maintain a railing about an open scuttle or to fence in their machinery for the same purpose.

Hurley v. Eddingfield

59 N.E. 1058 (Ind. 1901)

Baker, J. Appellant sued appellee for $10,000 damages for wrongfully causing the death of his intestate. The court sustained appellee's demurrer to the complaint; and this ruling is assigned as error.

The material facts alleged may be summarized thus: At and for years before decedent's death appellee was a practicing physician at Mace in Montgomery county, duly licensed under the laws of the State. He held himself out to the public as a general practitioner of medicine. He had been decedent's family physician. Decedent became dangerously ill and sent for appellee. The messenger informed appellee of decedent's violent sickness, tendered him his fees for his services, and stated to him that no other physician was procurable in time and that decedent relied on him for attention. No other physician was procurable in time to be of any use, and decedent did rely on appellee for medical assistance. Without any reason whatever, appellee refused to render aid to decedent. No other patients were requiring appellee's immediate service, and he could have gone to the relief of decedent if he had been willing to do so. Death ensued, without decedent's fault, and wholly from appellee's wrongful act.

The alleged wrongful act was appellee's refusal to enter into a contract of employment. Counsel do not contend that, before the enactment of the law regulating the practice of medicine, physicians were bound to render professional service to every one who applied. The act regulating the practice of medicine provides for a board of examiners, standards of qualification, examinations, licenses to those found qualified, and penalties for practicing without license. The act is a preventive, not a compulsive, measure. In obtaining the State's license (permission) to practice medicine, the State does not require, and the licensee does not engage, that he will practice at all or on other terms than he may choose to accept. Counsel's analogies, drawn from the obligations to the public on the part of innkeepers, common carriers, and the like, are beside the mark.

Judgment affirmed.

NOTE

My Brother's Tormentor. Yania v. Bigan, 155 A.2d 343, 345, 346 (Pa. 1959), manifests a similar hostility toward the creation of affirmative duties. The decedent and defendant were operators of nearby strip mines. One day, Yania was visiting Bigan's land to discuss business. Located on the land was a worked-out strip mine in which about eight to ten feet of water stood in a cut some sixteen or eighteen feet deep. Yania jumped into the cut and drowned, and the complaint in the wrongful death action that ensued charged Bigan

> with three-fold negligence: (1) by urging, enticing, taunting and inveigling Yania to jump into the water; (2) by failing to warn Yania of a dangerous condition on the land; i.e., the cut wherein lay 8 to 10 feet of water; (3) by failing to go to Yania's rescue after he jumped into the water.

Jones, J., dismissed all three parts of the claim. The first count failed because the

> complaint does not allege that Yania slipped or that he was pushed or that Bigan made any *physical* impact on his person. On the contrary, the only inference deducible from the facts alleged in the complaint is that Bigan, by the employment of cajolery and inveiglement, caused such a *mental* impact on Yania that the latter was deprived of his volition and freedom of choice and placed under a compulsion to jump into the water. Had Yania been a child of tender years or a person mentally deficient then it is conceivable that taunting and enticement could constitute actionable negligence if it resulted in harm. However to contend that such conduct directed to an adult in full possession of all his mental faculties constitutes actionable negligence is not only without precedent but completely without merit.

On the second count, Jones, J., held that Yania, as a strip-mine operator, was well aware of the obvious dangers of jumping into the water. The judge addressed the third claim as follows:

> Lastly, it is urged that Bigan failed to take the necessary steps to rescue Yania from the water. The mere fact that Bigan saw Yania in a position of peril in the water imposed upon him no legal, although a moral, obligation or duty to go to his rescue unless Bigan was legally responsible in whole or in part, for placing Yania in the perilous position.

It was his fault for undertaking a dangerous and reckless course of action. How should the law respond to these various situations?

Francis H. Bohlen

The Moral Duty to Aid Others as a Basis of Tort Liability

56 U. Pa. L. Rev. 217, 218–20 (1908)

There is no distinction more deeply rooted in the common law and more fundamental than that between misfeasance and non-feasance, between active misconduct working positive injury to others and passive inaction, a failure to take positive steps to benefit others, or to protect them from harm not created by any wrongful act of the defendant. This distinction is founded on that attitude of extreme individualism so typical of anglo-saxon thought.

James Barr Ames

Law and Morals

22 Harv. L. Rev. 97, 110–13 (1908)

The law is utilitarian. It exists for the realization of the reasonable needs of the community. If the interest of an individual runs counter to this chief object of the law, it must be sacrificed. That is why, in [some cases], the innocent suffer and the wicked go unpunished. . . .

It remains to consider whether the law should ever go so far as to give compensation or to inflict punishment for damage which would not have happened but for the wilful inaction of another. I exclude cases in which, by reason of some relation between the parties like that of father and child, nurse and invalid, master and servant and others, there is a recognized legal duty to act. In the case supposed the only relation between the parties is that both are human beings. As I am walking over a bridge a man falls into the water. He cannot swim and calls for help. I am strong and a good swimmer, or, if you please, there is a rope on the bridge, and I might easily throw him an end and pull him ashore. I neither jump in nor throw him the rope, but see him drown. Or, again, I see a child on the railroad track too young to appreciate the danger of the approaching train. I might easily save the child, but do nothing, and the child, though it lives, loses both legs. Am I guilty of a crime, and must I make compensation to the widow and children of the man drowned and to the wounded child? Macaulay, in commenting upon his Indian Criminal Code, puts the case of a surgeon refusing to go from Calcutta to Meerut to perform an operation, although it should be absolutely certain that this surgeon was the only person in India who could perform it, and that, if it were not performed, the person who required it would die.

We may suppose again that the situation of imminent danger of death was created by the act, but the innocent act, of the person who refuses to prevent the death. The man, for example, whose eye was penetrated by the glancing shot of the careful pheasant hunter, stunned by the shot, fell face downward into a shallow pool by which he was standing. The hunter might easily save him, but lets him drown.

In the first three illustrations, however revolting the conduct of the man who declined to interfere, he was in no way responsible for the perilous situation, he did not increase the peril, he took away nothing from the person in jeopardy, he simply failed to confer a benefit upon a stranger. As the law stands today there would be no legal liability, either civilly or criminally, in any of these cases. The law does not compel active benevolence between man and man. It is left to one's conscience whether he shall be the good Samaritan or not.

But ought the law to remain in this condition? Of course any statutory duty to be benevolent would have to be exceptional. The practical difficulty in such legislation would be in drawing the line. But that difficulty has continually to be faced in the law. We should all be better satisfied if the man who refuses to throw a rope to a drowning man or to save a helpless child on the railroad track could be punished and be made to compensate the widow of the man drowned and the wounded child. We should not think it advisable to penalize the surgeon who refused to make the journey. These illustrations suggest a possible working rule. One who fails to interfere to save another from impending death or great bodily harm, when he might do so with little or no inconvenience to himself, and the death or great bodily harm follows as a consequence of his inaction, shall be punished criminally and shall make compensation to the party injured or to his widow and children in case of death. The case of the drowning of the man shot by the hunter differs from the others in that the hunter, although he acted innocently, did bring about the dangerous situation. Here, too, the lawyer who should try to charge the hunter would lead a forlorn hope. But it seems to me that he could make out a strong case against the hunter on common law grounds. By the early law, as we have seen, he would have been liable simply because he shot the other. In modern times the courts have admitted as an affirmative defense the fact that he was not negligent. May not the same courts refuse to allow a defense, if the defendant did not use reasonable means to prevent a calamity after creating the threatening situation? Be that as it may, it is hard to see why such a rule should not be declared by statute, if not by the courts.

Richard A. Epstein

A Theory of Strict Liability

2 J. Legal Stud. 151, 198–200 (1973)

Under Ames' good Samaritan rule, a defendant in cases of affirmative acts would be required to take only those steps that can be done "with little or no inconvenience." But if the distinction between causing harm and not preventing harm is to be disregarded, why should the difference in standards between the two cases survive the reform of the law? The only explanation is that the two situations are regarded at bottom as raising totally different issues, even for those who insist upon the immateriality of this distinction. Even those who argue, as Ames does, that the law is utilitarian must in the end find some special place for the claims of egoism which are an inseparable byproduct of the belief that individual autonomy—individual liberty—is a good in itself not explainable in terms of its purported social worth. It is one thing to *allow* people to act as they please in the belief that the "invisible hand" will provide the happy congruence of the individual and the social good. Such a theory, however, at bottom must regard individual autonomy as but a means to some social end. It takes a great deal more to assert that men are *entitled* to act as they choose (within the limits of strict liability) even though it is certain that there will be cases where individual welfare will be in conflict with the social good. Only then is it clear that even freedom has its costs: costs revealed in the acceptance of the good Samaritan doctrine.

But are the alternatives more attractive? Once one decides that as a matter of statutory or common law duty, an individual is required under some circumstances to act at his own cost for the exclusive benefit of another, then it is very hard to set out in a principled manner the limits of social interference with individual liberty. Suppose one claims, as Ames does, that his proposed rule applies only in the "obvious" cases where everyone (or almost everyone) would admit that the duty was appropriate: to the case of the man upon the bridge who refuses to throw a rope to a stranger drowning in the waters below. Even if the rule starts out with such modest ambitions, it is difficult to confine it to those limits. Take a simple case first. *X* as a representative of a private charity asks you for $10 in order to save the life of some starving child in a country ravaged by war. There are other donors available but the number of needy children exceeds that number. The money means "nothing" to you. Are you under a legal obligation to give the $10? Or to lend it interest-free? Does $10 amount to a substantial cost or inconvenience within the meaning of Ames' rule? It is true that the relationship between the gift to charity and the survival of an unidentified child is not so apparent as is the relationship between the man upon the bridge and the swimmer caught in the swirling seas. But lest the physical imagery govern, it is clear that someone will die as a consequence of your inaction in both cases. Is there a duty to give, or is the contribution a matter of charity?

Consider yet another example where services, not cash, are in issue. Ames insists that his rule would not require the only surgeon in India capable of saving the life of a person with a given affliction to travel across the subcontinent to perform an operation, presumably because the inconvenience and cost would be substantial. But how would he treat the case if some third person were willing to pay him for all of his efforts? If the payment is sufficient to induce the surgeon to act, then there is no need for the good Samaritan doctrine at all. But if it is not, then it is again necessary to compare the costs of the physician with the benefits to his prospective patient. It is hard to know whether Ames would require the forced exchange under these circumstances. But it is at least arguable that under his theory forced exchanges should be required, since the payment might reduce the surgeon's net inconvenience to the point where it was trivial.

Once forced exchanges, regardless of the levels of payment, are accepted, it will no longer be possible to delineate the sphere of activities in which contracts (or charity) will be required in order to procure desired benefits and the sphere of activity in which those benefits can be procured as of right. Where tests of "reasonableness"—stated with such confidence, and applied with such difficulty—dominate the law of tort, it becomes impossible to tell where liberty ends and obligation begins; where contract ends, and tort begins. In each case, it will be possible for some judge or jury to decide that there was something else which the defendant should have done, and he will decide that on the strength of some cost-benefit formula that is difficult indeed to apply. These remarks are conclusive, I think, against the adoption of Ames' rule by judicial innovation, and they bear heavily on the desirability of the abandonment of the good Samaritan rule by legislation as well. It is not surprising that the law has, in the midst of all the clamor for reform, remained unmoved in the end, given the inability to form alternatives to the current position.

Richard A. Posner

Epstein's Tort Theory: A Critique

8 J. Legal Stud. 457, 460 (1979)

Suppose that if all the members of society could somehow be assembled they would agree unanimously that, as a reasonable measure of mutual protection, anyone who can warn or rescue someone in distress at negligible cost to himself (in time, danger, or whatever) should be required to do so. These mutual promises of assistance would create a contract that Epstein would presumably enforce since he considers the right to make binding contracts a fundamental one. However, there are technical obstacles — in this case insurmountable ones — to the formation of an actual contract among so many people. Transaction costs are prohibitive. If, moved by these circumstances, a court were to impose tort liability on a bystander who failed to assist a person in distress, such liability would be a means of carrying out the original desires of the parties just as if it were an express contract that was being enforced.

The point of this example is that tort duties can sometimes (perhaps, as we shall see, generally) be viewed as devices for vindicating the principles that underlie freedom of contract. It may be argued, however, that the contract analogy is inapplicable because the bystander would not be compensated for coming to the rescue of the person in distress. But this argument overlooks the fact that the consideration for the rescue is not payment when the rescue is effected but a commitment to reciprocate should the roles of the parties some day be reversed. Liability would create a mutual protective arrangement under which everyone was obliged to attempt a rescue when circumstances dictated and, in exchange, was entitled to the assistance of anyone who might be able to help him should he ever find himself in a position of peril.

George Fletcher

Law and Morality: A Kantian Perspective

87 Colum. L. Rev. 533, 548–49 (1987)

Though Kant never squarely addresses a legal duty to render aid to others, his definition of Right readily yields the conclusion that there should be no such duty. Failing to render aid is compatible with the external freedom of the person in distress. There is no violation of his freedom if he is left to cope with his own difficulties. Further, the claim that the Right requires rescue runs afoul of other tenets in Kant's exposition of his legal theory. It would impose an obligation on one person by virtue of the unilateral wants of the other. If promising cannot by itself subject one to a binding legal duty, it is hard to see how the other person's desiring or needing one to perform could have that effect. Also, Kant makes it clear that the law serves to reconcile conflicting assertions of choice. Needs and desires do not amount to acts of choice. They are below the threshold of legal relevance.

Leslie Bender

An Overview of Feminist Torts Scholarship

78 Cornell L. Rev. 575, 580–81 (1993)

"No Duty to Rescue"

Tort law's view of human nature as highly individualistic, autonomous, and self-interested has generated a "no duty to rescue" doctrine. This doctrine states that an actor has no duty to aid or rescue an imperiled person even when the rescue could be performed with no risk to the rescuer, unless the actor directly caused the peril or is in a narrowly defined category of special relationships with the person in danger. Famous cases illustrating this doctrine are taught to most first year law students—stories of "moral monsters" who make no effort to stop young children from being mangled by machinery in factories and business competitors who stand by and watch a man drown in a trench on their property. In challenging that no duty rule, I rely on alternative conceptions of human nature, developed in some feminist theories, in order to transform this doctrine. Applying a feminist ethic of care and responsibility, I [have] argue[d] that "the recognition that we are all interdependent and connected and that we are by nature social beings who must interact with one another should lead us to judge conduct as tortious when it does not evidence responsible care or concern for another's safety, welfare, or health." Utilizing this analysis, the "no duty" doctrine might be transformed into a duty to exercise the "conscious care and concern of a responsible neighbor or social acquaintance," which would impose a duty to aid or rescue within one's capacity under the circumstances. Tort law would no longer condone the inhumane response of doing absolutely nothing to aid or rescue when one could save another person from dying. Finally, . . . feminist theory encourages us to challenge traditional modes of legal analysis and to rethink the questions we ask, including: who are the parties involved, whose interests are protected by tort law, what are appropriate forms of compensation, how should we allocate responsibility for harms and risks, and what assumptions and values underlie various tort doctrines?

NOTES

1. ***An Affirmative Duty to Rescue.*** Judge Posner returned to the Good Samaritan problem in Stockberger v. United States, 332 F.3d 479, 481 (7th Cir. 2003):

> Various rationales have been offered for the seemingly hardhearted common law rule: people should not count on nonprofessionals for rescue; the circle of potentially liable nonrescuers would be difficult to draw (suppose a person is drowning and no one on the crowded beach makes an effort to save him—should all be liable?); altruism makes the problem a small one and liability might actually reduce the number of altruistic rescues by depriving people of credit for altruism (how would they prove they hadn't acted under threat of legal liability?); people would be deterred by threat of liability from putting themselves in a position where they might be called upon to attempt a rescue, especially since a failed rescue might under settled common law principles give rise to liability, on the theory that a clumsy rescue attempt may have interfered with a competent rescue by someone else.

Applying Indiana law, Posner, J., refused to impose liability on coworkers of a hypoglycemic employee at a federal prison for allowing him to undertake his fatal drive home. The coworkers were familiar with the decedent's condition and had supplied him with Ensure, a nutritious liquid food substitute, which made him strong enough to start the drive home. Posner, J., treated this essentially as a stranger case, because otherwise "the exceptions to the rule that there is no 'good Samaritan' liability would have to be enlarged, to encompass the case in which an employee becomes ill at the workplace for reasons unrelated to his work and the employer fails to use due care to treat the illness."

Why shouldn't the employer be liable?

On the complications of creating a generalized duty of rescue, see Epstein, Causation and Corrective Justice, A Reply to Two Critics, 8 J. Legal Stud. 477, 490–92 (1979). For the affirmative case for the duty of easy rescue, see Weinrib, The Case for a Duty to Rescue, 90 Yale L.J. 247 (1980); Hasen, The Efficient Duty to Rescue, 15 Int'l Rev. L. & Econ. 141 (1995).

2. *Restitution and Rescue.* As a common law matter, is it better to approach the rescue problem with restitution instead of tort doctrines? Restitution imposes on the party rescued an obligation to compensate the rescuer for his costs. Whereas the tort solution requires a large judgment against the able defendant who does not rescue, the restitution solution gives a much smaller payment to the enterprising person who does rescue. The restitution scheme reduces the level of legal intervention, and it eliminates the vexing problems of multiple causation that arise whenever many persons are in a position to undertake a rescue (or to call the police) and none in fact does. Yet how are the levels of compensation to be fixed? Should an award be limited to out-of-pocket costs, without allowance for time spent or personal risk incurred? Is it sound policy to pay rescuers out of public funds? Dawson, Rewards for the Rescue of Human Life, *in* The Good Samaritan and the Law (Ratcliffe ed., 1966), takes a cautious attitude toward creating restitution remedies. Note that restitution remedies have been allowed for professional rescuers who might be discouraged by the threat of tort suits from making the heavy investments necessary to carry out rescues at sea. See Landes & Posner, Salvors, Finders, Good Samaritans, and Other Rescuers: An Economic Study of Law and Altruism, 7 J. Legal Stud. 83, 119–27 (1978). For a broad exploration of other reward and penalty incentive structures to promote rescue, see Levmore, Waiting for Rescue, 72 Va. L. Rev. 879, 882–929 (1986).

3. *Legislation and the Good Samaritan.* Legislative responses to the Good Samaritan problem have typically been designed either to induce rescue by insulating the rescuer against liability for ordinary negligence or by imposing affirmative duties to rescue, subject to the payment of fines. Similar immunities for similar reasons have been extended to laypersons who supply emergency care, such as driving injured people to the hospital. See, e.g., Swenson v. Waseca Mutual Insurance Co., 653 N.W.2d 794, 798 (Minn. App. 2002).

KANSAS STATUTES ANNOTATED (2023)

§65-2891. Emergency Care by Healthcare Providers; Liability; Standards of Care Applicable

(a) Any healthcare provider who in good faith renders emergency care or assistance at the scene of an emergency or accident including treatment of a minor without first obtaining the consent of the parent or guardian of such minor shall not be liable for any civil damages for acts or omissions other than damages occasioned by gross negligence or by willful and wanton acts or omissions by such person in rendering such emergency care. . . .

(d) Except as otherwise provided, the ordinary standards of care and rules of negligence shall apply in those cases wherein emergency care and assistance is rendered in any physician's or dentist's office, clinic, emergency room or hospital with or without compensation.

NEW JERSEY STATUTES ANNOTATED (2023)

§2A:62A-1. Emergency Care

Any individual, including a person licensed to practice any method of treatment of human ailments, disease, pain, injury, deformity, mental or physical condition, or licensed to render services ancillary thereto, or any person who is a volunteer member of a duly incorporated first aid and emergency or volunteer ambulance or rescue squad association, who in good faith renders emergency care at the scene of an accident or emergency to the victim or victims thereof, or while transporting the victim or victims thereof to a hospital or other facility where treatment or care is to be rendered, shall not be liable for any civil damages as a result of any acts or omissions by such person in rendering the emergency care.

A very different approach to the Good Samaritan problem was adopted in Vermont.

VERMONT STATUTES ANNOTATED (2023)

12 V.S.A. §519. Emergency Medical Care

(a) A person who knows that another is exposed to grave physical harm shall, to the extent that the same can be rendered without danger or peril to himself or herself or without interference with important duties owed to others, give reasonable assistance to the exposed person unless that assistance or care is being provided by others.

(b) A person who provides reasonable assistance in compliance with subsection (a) of this section shall not be liable in civil damages unless his or her acts constitute gross negligence or unless he or she will receive or expects to receive remuneration. Nothing contained in this subsection shall alter existing law with respect to tort liability of a practitioner of the healing arts for acts committed in the ordinary course of his or her practice.

(c) A person who willfully violates subsection (a) of this section shall be fined not more than $100.00.

In Velazquez ex rel. Velazquez v. Jiminez, 798 A.2d 51, 52 (N.J. 2002), the court held the New Jersey statute "cannot be invoked to immunize a hospital physician who assists a patient at the hospital during a medical emergency." Does the statute compel that result?

Does the Vermont statute adopt a straight negligence approach in rescue cases? Does it authorize the creation of a private cause of action? See Franklin, Vermont Requires Rescue: A Comment, 25 Stan. L. Rev. 51 (1972). Litigation under this section does not reveal any application of a duty to rescue strangers. In Lewis v. Bellows Falls Congregation of Jehovah's Witnesses, No. 1:14-cv-205, 2015 WL 13501874, at *5 (D. Vt. 2015), the plaintiff alleged that the defendant congregation had failed to protect her when she was sexually abused as a child by Norton True, a ministerial servant of the church. The court held that the "[Vermont] statute creates no duty in the present case, as Lewis nowhere alleges the Congregation was aware she was in contact with True." Other section 519 cases involve suits against government agencies. See Sabia v. State of Vermont, 669 A.2d 1187 (Vt. 1995), where section 519 was used to help create a cause of action in another sexual abuse case in which the defendants were already under a statutory duty to protect the plaintiff.

4. *Empirical Study of Duty to Rescue.* The movement for statutory duties to rescue provoked this response in Hyman, Rescue Without Law: An Empirical Perspective on the Duty to Rescue, 84 Tex. L. Rev. 653, 712 (2006):

> During the past decade, there have been an average of 1.6 documented cases of non-rescue each year in the entire United States. Every year, Americans perform at least 946 non-risky rescues and 243 risky rescues. Every year, at least sixty-five times as many Americans die while attempting to rescue someone else as die from a documented case of non-risky non-rescue. If a few isolated (and largely unverified and undocumented) cases of non-rescues have been deemed sufficient to justify legislative reform, one would think a total of approximately 1,200 documented cases of rescue every year should point rather decisively in the opposite direction. When it comes to the duty to rescue, leaving well enough alone is likely to be sufficient unto the day.

Uneasiness with the current law of rescue elicited a proposal to remove rescue cases from the tort liability system altogether by allowing injured rescuers to "recover compensatory damages under either a renter's or homeowner's insurance policy." See White, No Good Deed Goes Unpunished: The Case for Reform of the Rescue Doctrine, 97 Nw. U. L. Rev. 507 (2002). Why can't insurance companies just voluntarily supply the coverage?

Montgomery v. National Convoy & Trucking Co.
195 S.E. 247 (S.C. 1937)

[The defendants' trucks had stalled on an icy highway without their fault, blocking the road completely. About fifteen minutes later, the plaintiff's car came over a hill and started down toward the trucks before either the plaintiff-respondent or his driver could see them. The trucks were about fifty feet away, but they were not previously visible because they were obscured by the hill. In view of the icy condition of the road, the plaintiff's chauffeur could not stop the car in time. "The agents of the [defendants] operating the trucks knew, or had every reason to know, that once a car had passed the crest of the hill and started down the decline, . . . it would be impossible to stop such automobile or motor vehicle due to the icy condition of the highway, regardless of the rate of speed at which such automobile may be traveling." The defendants' drivers had ample time to place a warning signal at the top of the hill, where it could have been observed by the plaintiff's chauffeur who, well aware of the dangerous condition of the road, could have stopped before the collision that injured the plaintiff. The defendants' motion for a directed verdict was refused, and the jury awarded the plaintiff the full amount demanded, $3,000 ($64,122 in 2023 dollars). The defendants appealed.]

Baker, J. One may be negligent by acts of omission as well as of commission, and liability therefor will attach if the act of omission of a duty owed another, under the circumstances, is the direct, proximate and efficient cause of the injury. It is only where the evidence is susceptible of but one reasonable inference that the Court may declare what that inference is and take the case from the consideration of the jury. . . .

One of the acts of negligence alleged in the complaint is the failure of the appellants to warn approaching vehicles of the conditions existing, and this necessarily means that the warning should be given at a point where it would be effective. That appellants recognized that they owed a duty to others using the highway cannot be questioned, since they at some time put out flares and left the lights on their trucks. But if appellants owed a duty to others using the highway, and this cannot be disputed, the performance of such duty was not met by merely having lights at the point where the trucks blocked the highway, but it was incumbent on the appellants to take such precautions as would reasonably be calculated to prevent injury.

For the moment let us repeat some of the facts. There is a curve in the highway at the crest of a long hill. A short distance to the south of the curve and crest of the hill two trucks are stalled and block the entire road. It is a much-traveled highway. Respondent's chauffeur testified that due to the curve in the road and the hill, the lights of an automobile approaching from the north would not focus on the trucks until the automobile was within a little over fifty feet from the trucks. Once a car passed the crest of the hill and commenced to descend on the south side, it could not be stopped due to the ice on the highway — the slippery condition thereof, which was known or should have been known to appellants. No flagman nor warning of any description was placed at the crest of the hill to warn approaching cars. That a warning at the crest of the hill would have been effective and prevented the injury is fully demonstrated from other evidence had upon the trial. The danger of the situation was so self-evident that a jury could have concluded that the omission to warn approaching travelers from the north at a point where the warning would be effective, amounted not only to negligence, but to willfulness. However, the jury in this case have vindicated their intelligence and freedom from passion when they found only inadvertence.

NOTES

1. *Misfeasance and Nonfeasance.* The distinction between misfeasance and nonfeasance articulated with such confidence by Bohlen, *supra* at 394, is more difficult to draw when the defendant fails to neutralize a dangerous condition that he has created, as in *Montgomery* when the defendants' stalled trucks, without fault, blocked the icy highway. How would Bohlen treat the case? What result if the defendants' drivers did not have time to place the flares at the top of the hill? Was the defendant Socony Oil Company in Marshall v. Nugent, *supra* Chapter 5, at 371, under an obligation to post a warning before the curve in the road?

A similar situation arose in Newton v. Ellis, (1855) 119 Eng. Rep. 424 (KB). The defendant, while under contract with the local board of health, dug a hole in a public highway that he left unlighted at night. Shortly thereafter the plaintiff, while driving, fell into the hole. The three judges who heard the case denied that the plaintiff's action was for nonfeasance. Coleridge, J., remarked: "This is not a case of not doing: the defendant does something, omitting to secure protection for the public. He is not sued for not putting up a light, but for the complex act." Erle, J., agreed, saying:

> Here the cause of action is the making the hole, compounded with the not putting up a light. When these two are blended, the result is no more than if two positive acts were committed, such as digging the hole and throwing out the dirt: the two would make up one act.

Suppose that *A*, while driving, hits *B* because *A* has failed to apply the brakes. Can *A* argue that this is a simple case of nonfeasance for which he is not responsible? Why not? See Abraham & Kendrick, No Such Thing as Affirmative Duty, 104 Iowa L. Rev. 1649, 1667, 1683 (2019), which offers a conceptual framework for the situations arising in *Montgomery* and *Newton*: "In fact, there are three relevant categories here: not only misfeasance, which waives the liberty to be left alone, and nonfeasance, which the courts assumed did not, but also what might be called 'feasance' — non-negligent, waiver-generating conduct."

Consider into which of these categories you would place the following case. In Louisville & Nashville Railroad v. Scruggs, 49 So. 399 (Ala. 1909), the defendant's freight train was stopped, blocking a fire engine as it drove up to extinguish a fire in the plaintiff's house just across the tracks. The defendant's employees refused to move the train except on the dispatcher's orders and, by the time the firemen arrived, the plaintiff's house was destroyed. Because the defendant's use of its land was "merely passive," the Alabama Supreme Court denied recovery, adding that "[t]he law imposes no duty on one man to aid another in the preservation of the latter's property, but only the duty not to injure another's property in the use of his own." The court conceded that the defendant could be held liable for the loss of the plaintiff's home if its engineer deliberately or negligently ran over a hose that already was laid across the tracks. One judge dissented, thinking the attitude of the defendant's employees showed "an indifference to the situation and emergency that was little short of shocking." What if the local rules of the road give fire engines the right of way over all other traffic?

Scruggs provoked the following response in Hale, Prima Facie Torts, Combination, and Non-Feasance, 46 Colum. L. Rev. 196, 214 (1946):

> Perhaps judicial reluctance to recognize affirmative duties is based on one or both of two inarticulate assumptions. One of these is that a rugged, independent individual needs no help from others, save such as they may be disposed to render him out of kindness, or such as he can induce them to render by the ordinary process of bargaining, without having the government step in to make them help. All he is supposed to ask of the government is that it interfere to prevent others from doing him positive harm. The other assumption is that when a government *requires* a person to act, it is necessarily interfering more seriously with his liberty than when it places limits on his freedom to act—to make a man serve another is to make him a slave, while to forbid him to commit affirmative wrongs is to leave him still essentially a freeman. Neither of these assumptions is universally true. Neither was true in [*Scruggs*]. No matter how rugged the owner of the burning building, his property depended for its preservation on the affirmative acts of the railroad employees—acts which they were evidently not disposed to render out of kindness, and which he was in no position to induce them to perform by bargaining. Nor would a legal duty to move the train have subjected either the employees or the railroad company itself to anything having the slightest resemblance to slavery.

The Third Restatement has codified the rule in *Montgomery* in RTT: LPEH §39.

RESTATEMENT OF THE LAW (THIRD) OF TORTS: LIABILITY FOR PHYSICAL AND EMOTIONAL HARM

§39. Duty Based on Prior Conduct Creating A Risk of Physical Harm

When an actor's prior conduct, even though not tortious, creates a continuing risk of physical harm of a type characteristic of the conduct, the actor has a duty to exercise reasonable care to prevent or minimize the harm.

Could this duty attach if the defendant had no knowledge, or reason to know, of the risk of physical injury to others? Is there any reason, if the defendant does have knowledge, to limit the continuing duty of care to cases of "physical harm of a type characteristic of the conduct"? Note that the parallel provision in the Second Restatement only applied to a plaintiff who was rendered "helpless and in danger of further harm." RST §322. Any reason for the helpless limitation? Many state statutes impose particular obligations on motorists to render "reasonable assistance" to other persons involved in an accident, and to exchange information, names, and registration to facilitate subsequent resolution of any future litigation. See, e.g., Cal. Veh. Code §20003 (2023).

In Podias v. Mairs, 926 A.2d 859, 866 (N.J. Super. Ct. App. Div. 2007), two teenage defendants who were passengers in a vehicle were held liable in tort after they abandoned the severely injured decedent who had been struck by their car on the public highway. They did not provide or call for help. Several minutes later, the decedent was killed by a third-party driver. On appeal, Parrillo, J.A.D., overturned a summary judgment for these defendants on the ground that these two defendants' duty "to summon help or take other precautionary measures was readily and clearly foreseeable . . . [because they were] aware of the risk of harm created by their own inaction [and] were in a unique position to know of the risk of harm" posed to the helpless decedent.

2. *Aid to the Helpless: Once Begun, Then Undone.* In Zelenko v. Gimbel Bros., 287 N.Y.S. 134, 135 (Sup. Ct. 1935), Lauer, J., wrote:

> . . . Plaintiff's intestate was taken ill in defendant's store. We will assume that the defendant owed her no duty at all; that defendant could have let her be and die. But if a defendant undertakes a task, even if under no duty to undertake it, the defendant must not omit to do what an ordinary man would do in performing the task.
>
> Here the defendant undertook to render medical aid to the plaintiff's intestate. Plaintiff says that defendant kept his intestate for six hours in an infirmary without any medical care. If defendant had left plaintiff's intestate alone, beyond doubt some bystander, who would be influenced more by charity than by legalistic duty, would have summoned an ambulance. Defendant segregated this plaintiff's intestate where such aid could not be given and then left her alone.
>
> The plaintiff is wrong in thinking that the duty of a common carrier of passengers is the same as the duty of this defendant. The common carrier assumes its duty by its contract of carriage. This defendant assumed its duty by meddling in matters with which legalistically it had no concern. The plaintiff is right in arguing that when the duty arose, the same type of neglect is actionable in both cases.

Does RTT: LPEH §44 prefer lofty indifference to honest but inept efforts to aid? Compare the following two cases: In the first, *A*, coming upon the scene of an accident, picks up *B*, who is helpless, and starts to drive him to a hospital. En route she drives negligently and has a collision, aggravating *B*'s injuries. In the second, *A* comes upon the scene of an accident and picks up *B*, who is helpless, and starts to drive him to a hospital. A moment later, *A* changes her mind and returns *B* to the scene of the accident. What result in each case if prompt medical care would have greatly reduced the harm to *B* and that this was obvious to *A*?

RESTATEMENT OF THE LAW (THIRD) OF TORTS: LIABILITY FOR PHYSICAL AND EMOTIONAL HARM

§44. Duty to Another Based on Taking Charge of the Other

(a) An actor who, despite no duty to do so, takes charge of another who reasonably appears to be:

(1) imperiled; and

(2) helpless or unable to protect himself or herself

has a duty to exercise reasonable care while the other is within the actor's charge.

(b) An actor who discontinues aid or protection is subject to a duty of reasonable care to refrain from putting the other in a worse position than existed before the actor took charge of the other and, if the other reasonably appears to be in imminent peril of serious physical harm at the time of termination, to exercise reasonable care with regard to the peril before terminating the rescue.

3. *Cracks in the Good Samaritan Doctrine.* In Soldano v. O'Daniels, 190 Cal. Rptr. 310 (Ct. App. 1983), the decedent was in imminent danger of being shot at Happy Jack's Saloon. Another patron ran across the street to the defendant's restaurant. In the age before cell phones, he asked the defendant's bartender either to use the defendant's phone to call the police or, alternatively, to make the emergency call. The bartender refused both requests, and the decedent was killed. The court rebuffed the defendant's argument that there was no duty to aid or assist the plaintiff. It first agreed with Prosser that the common law rule denying the duty to rescue violates "common decency" and is "revolting to any moral sense." It then held that the defendant, while not required to rescue, was required "to permit the patron from

Happy Jack's to place a call to the police or to place the call himself." Restatement (Second) of Torts §327 renders any person who "knows or has reason to know that a third person is giving or is ready to give another aid necessary to prevent physical harm to [an endangered person]" tortiously liable if he "negligently prevents or disables the third person from giving such aid." Should it matter that the bartender in *Soldano* only prevented the third party from using his own phone, and did not block the use of any third person's phone? Eric J. v. Betty M., 90 Cal. Rptr. 2d 549, 560 (Ct. App. 1999), criticized *Soldano* for not distinguishing between "[i]nterference and refusal to allow one's property to be commandeered, even for a good purpose." Should *Soldano* be governed by the doctrine of private necessity as in Vincent v. Lake Eric Transportation Co., *supra* Chapter 1, at 39?

SECTION C. DUTIES OF OWNERS AND OCCUPIERS

Robert Addie & Sons (Collieries), Ltd. v. Dumbreck

[1929] AC 358 (appeal taken from Scot.)

[The defendant colliers (coal miners) operated a haulage system in their fields near a public road in order to remove coal ashes from the pithead, where mining operations were going on. The haulage system employed a continuous wire cable; at one end of the system, near the mouth of the mine, there was an eight-horsepower engine used intermittently to operate the system. At the other end, which was not visible to anyone working the electrical motor, was a large, heavy horizontal wheel around which the cable passed at a rate of two to two and one-half miles per hour when the system was in use. The wheel in question was protected only by four boards placed upon its top, leaving a space of eight or nine inches between the boards and the bed of ashes beneath the wheel. The court below found that the wheel was dangerous and attractive to children.

The haulage system was located in a field surrounded by a hedge that contained a number of gaps, making it inadequate for keeping little children away from the wheel. In fact, many people used the field as a shortcut and many children played there. Though the defendant's servants from time to time warned children to stay out of the field and admonished adults not to cross, they knew their warnings had little or no effect. The defendant's servants did maintain a watch over the field, but to protect the defendant's property, not the persons who trespassed on it. There were two gates to the field, at one of which was posted a notice that read "Trespassers will be prosecuted."

The plaintiff's son was a four-year-old boy whom the plaintiff had warned not to go into the field and not to play with the wheel. The exact circumstances of his death were not determined, but it appeared that he had either been "sitting on the cover of the wheel or in a position in front of and in close proximity to the pulley and rope, being caught and drawn into the mechanism when it was set in motion by the defendant's servants."

The court below awarded the plaintiff judgment on the ground that the accident was due to the fault of the defendant in not taking suitable precautions to avoid accidents to persons using the fields before activating the haulage system.

The defendant appealed.]

Hailsham, L.C. . . . The first and in my opinion the only question which arises for determination is the capacity in which the deceased child was in the field and at the wheel on the occasion of the accident. There are three categories in which persons visiting premises belonging to another person may fall; they may go

1. By the invitation, express or implied, of the occupier;
2. With the leave and license of the occupier; and
3. As trespassers.

It was suggested in argument that there was a fourth category of persons who were not on the premises with the leave or license of the occupier, but who were not pure trespassers. I cannot find any foundation for this suggestion either in English or Scotch law, and I do not think that the category exists.

The duty which rests upon the occupier of premises towards the persons who come on such premises differs according to the category into which the visitor falls. The highest duty exists towards those persons who fall into the first category, and who are present by the invitation of the occupier. Towards such persons the occupier has the duty of taking reasonable care that the premises are safe.

In the case of persons who are not there by invitation, but who are there by leave and licence, express or implied, the duty is much less stringent — the occupier has no duty to ensure that the premises are safe, but he is bound not to create a trap or allow a concealed danger to exist upon the said premises, which is not apparent to the visitor, but which is known — or ought to be known — to the occupier.

Towards the trespasser the occupier has no duty to take reasonable care for his protection or even to protect him from concealed danger. The trespasser comes on to the premises at his own risk. An occupier is in such a case liable only where the injury is due to some wilful act involving something more than the absence of reasonable care. There must be some act done with the deliberate intention of doing harm to the trespasser, or at least some act done with reckless disregard of the presence of the trespasser. . . .

The only question, therefore, that remains for decision in this case is whether, upon the findings of fact of the Court of Session (which are not open to review), the respondent's son may properly be regarded as having been at the wheel at the time of the accident with the leave and license of the appellants. If this had been proved, I should have been prepared to hold that the wheel, which was at times stationary and which was started without any warning, and which was, in the words of the Court of Session, "dangerous and attractive to children and insufficiently protected at the time of the accident," amounted to a trap, and that the respondent would therefore have been entitled to recover. But in my opinion, the findings of fact effectually negative that view. It is found that the appellants warned children out of the field and reproved adults who came there, and all that can be said is that these warnings were frequently neglected and that there was a gap in the hedge through which it was easy to pass on to the field. I cannot regard the fact that the appellants did not effectively fence the field or the fact that their warnings were frequently disregarded as sufficient to justify an inference that they permitted the children to be on the field, and, in the absence of such a permission, it is clear that the respondent's child was merely a trespasser. The sympathy which one cannot help feeling for the unhappy father must not be allowed to alter one's view of the law, and I have no doubt that in law the respondent's son was a mere trespasser, and that as such the appellants owed him no duty to protect him from injury. On these grounds I am of opinion that this appeal succeeds and must be allowed with costs, and I move your Lordships accordingly.

Viscount Dunedin . . . What I particularly wish to emphasize is that there are the three different classes — invitees, licensees, trespassers. . . .

Now the line that separates each of these three classes is an absolutely rigid line. There is no half-way house, no no-man's land between adjacent territories. When I say rigid, I mean rigid in law. When you come to the facts it may well be that there is great difficulty — such difficulty as may give rise to difference of judicial opinion — in deciding into which category a particular case falls, but a judge must decide and, having decided, then the law of that category will rule and there must be no looking to the law of the adjoining category. I cannot help thinking that the use of epithets, "bare licensees," "pure trespassers" and so on, has much to answer for in obscuring what I think is a vital proposition that, in deciding cases of the class we are considering, the first duty of the tribunal is to fix once and for all into which of the three classes the person in question falls. . . .

Something has been said about fencing. There is no duty on a proprietor to fence his land against the world under sanction that, if he does not, those who come over it become licensees. Of course, a proprietor may do nothing at all to prevent people coming over his lands and they may come so often that permission will be held to be implied, or he may do something, but that something so half-heartedly as to be equivalent to doing nothing. For instance, a mere putting up of a notice "No Trespassers Allowed" or "Strictly Private," followed, when people often come, by no further steps, would, I think, leave it open for a judge or jury to hold implied permission. But when a proprietor protests and goes on protesting, turning away people when he meets them, as he did here, and giving no countenance in anything that he does to their presence there, then I think no Court has a right to say that permission must be implied. As I have said, circumstances vary infinitely and you cannot ab ante furnish a test which will fit every case; but it is permission that must be proved, not tolerance, though tolerance in some circumstances may be so pronounced as to lead to a conclusion that it was really tantamount to permission. I, therefore, find that the child who met with an accident in this case was a trespasser.

[Appeal allowed.]

NOTES

1. ***Willful and Wanton Exception.*** The three categories of land entrants outlined in *Addie* still organize the American law on the subject, which also accepts its central proposition that a trespasser is not owed a duty of ordinary care but is only protected from willful and wanton conduct by the landowner. In Excelsior Wire Rope Co., Ltd. v. Callan, [1930] AC 404 (HL), decided the year after *Addie*, the House of Lords upheld a judgment on behalf of two child plaintiffs whose hands had been crushed when caught between the wire rope and the pulley used to operate the defendant's haulage system. The House of Lords treated the plaintiffs as trespassers, but distinguished *Addie* by holding that the defendant's servants had acted in reckless disregard of the plaintiffs' welfare. The haulage system was located in an open field next to a playground run by the local town corporation for the benefit of its children. The field was constantly "swarming" with children, who left the playground to play games on and about the defendant's machinery. The defendant's servants knew that the children constantly played upon the machinery. The House of Lords found them in reckless disregard of their duty even though they first cleared the area of children, because "they started the machinery without being clear that the wire was free from children." In distinguishing *Addie*, Lord Buckmaster held that the defendants were in breach of their duty because it was "well known" to them "that when this machine was going to start it was extremely likely that children would be there and, with the wire in motion, would be exposed to grave danger."

The "willful and wanton" exception was also invoked in Gould v. DeBeve, 330 F.2d 826 (D.C. Cir. 1964). The plaintiff, Jacques DeBeve, a two-year-old infant, and his mother were staying temporarily with a Mrs. Dodd, under an arrangement whereby Mrs. DeBeve reimbursed Mrs. Dodd for half of the rent owed to the landlord. The defendant landlord, who operated the premises, did not know of this arrangement, which was contrary to an express provision in Mrs. Dodd's lease that restricted occupation of her apartment to herself and to members of her immediate family. On the day of the accident, the two women had left a bedroom window open because of the extreme heat, even though its screen was warped and cracked, rendering it defective. The plaintiff, while playing by the open window, knocked out the loose screen and fell to the ground three stories below, sustaining injuries. The court expressed an obvious distaste for a rule that treats alike all trespassers, from guileless infants to persistent poachers. While it did not upset the finding below that the plaintiff was a trespasser in the apartment, it held that the jury could properly find the defendants guilty of "wilful and wanton misconduct" in ignoring their statutory obligation to replace the defective screen after receiving urgent requests from Mrs. Dodd to do so. Although the statute only provided that the screens "be so maintained as to prevent effectively the entrance of flies and mosquitoes into the building," the court found that the defendant's statutory obligation "certainly comprehends, in the Washington summer when windows must be raised, screens which keep flies out and young children in."

But in routine railroad cases, the willful and wanton standard continues to hold just as it does in the last clear chance cases, *supra* Chapter 4, at 237. Thus, in Quiroz v. Chicago Transit Auth., 211 N.E.3d 437 (Ill. 2022), a pedestrian was killed by an oncoming train after he slipped and fell while trespassing into a restricted subway tunnel reserved for transit authority personnel. His estate claimed that train operators failed to monitor security cameras or otherwise keep a lookout for objects and persons who might be in the subway tunnel. Theis, J., rejected these claims because, under the willful and wanton standard, the allegations of negligence necessarily failed in the absence of any independent duty of care.

2. *Attractive Nuisance Doctrine: Origins.* The rigors of the common law rules regarding trespassers were at one time eased when a person was lured onto the defendant's premises by some tempting condition created and maintained by the defendant, such as railway turntables, explosives, electrical conduits, smoldering fires, and rickety structures. That doctrine tended to exclude "rivers, creeks, ponds, wagons, axes, plows, woodpiles, haystacks," and the like. Franich v. Great Northern Ry., 260 F.2d 599, 600 (9th Cir. 1958). In the nineteenth century, that doctrine was rejected by Mitchell, J., in Twist v. Winona & St. Peter Railroad, 39 N.W. 402, 404 (Minn. 1888), who wrote that for "the average boy there is no limit to the objects which can be made attractive playthings" and thus with the doctrine in place "it would be unsafe for a man to own property." Yet most courts, including the New Hampshire court in *Buch, supra* at 391 followed the Supreme Court in Sioux City & Pacific Railroad v. Stout, 84 U.S. 657, 661 (1873), which allowed the plaintiff, a six-year-old child, to recover when his foot was caught between the fixed rail of the roadbed and the turning rail of a turntable while playing with friends. The Court wrote that

> if from the evidence given it might justly be inferred by the jury that the defendant, in the construction, location, management, or condition of its machine had omitted that care and attention to prevent the occurrence of accidents which prudent and careful men ordinarily bestow, the jury was at liberty to find for the plaintiff.

3. *Restatement Reformulation of the Attractive Nuisance Doctrine.* Thereafter, the Second Restatement long exerted enormous influence on the law of attractive nuisance with its effort in section 339 to reconcile "[t]he public interest in the possessor's free use of his land for his own purposes" (comment *n*) with the general law of negligence, by applying the doctrine only to "artificial conditions on the land."

RESTATEMENT OF THE LAW (SECOND) OF TORTS

§339. Artificial Conditions Highly Dangerous to Trespassing Children

A possessor of land is subject to liability for physical harm to children trespassing thereon caused by an artificial condition upon the land if

(a) the place where the condition exists is one upon which the possessor knows or has reason to know that children are likely to trespass, and

(b) the condition is one of which the possessor knows or has reason to know and which he realizes or should realize will involve an unreasonable risk of death or serious bodily harm to such children, and

(c) the children because of their youth do not discover the condition or realize the risk involved in intermeddling with it or in coming within the area made dangerous by it, and

(d) the utility to the possessor of maintaining the condition and the burden of eliminating the danger are slight as compared with the risk to children involved, and

(e) the possessor fails to exercise reasonable care to eliminate the danger or otherwise to protect the children.

The Second Restatement excluded from recovery under the doctrine persons on the premises with the permission of the landowner, who are treated as licensees, protected from latent defects. In addition, it cabined attractive nuisance only to places that the owner knew that children were likely to trespass, without being able to know or discover that condition, so long as it was not too costly to eliminate that risk in a timely fashion. The owner had no duty to discover any dangerous condition that was not well known, and was not responsible whenever a child assumed an obvious risk, as when a nine-year-old boy was injured while jumping trains. See, e.g., Holland v. Baltimore & Ohio R.R., 431 A.2d 597 (D.C. 1981). The Second Restatement formulation did allow the case to reach the jury when a two-year-old drowned in a canal, which could not be made inaccessible to children. Carmona v. Hagerman Irrigation Co., 957 P.2d 44, 49 (N.M. 1998). A similar result obtained when a five-year-old child drowned in a swimming pool left unused for three years, filled with six feet of rainwater and covered with algae. Bennett v. Stanley, 748 N.E.2d 41 (Ohio 2001). At the same time RST §343B extended the duties found in section 339 to child licensees and invitees. Why is this extension necessary when the property owner assumes at least some duties by allowing the child onto the land?

Nonetheless, the entire doctrine contained in RST §339 was formally eliminated in RTT: LPEH §51 & comment *l*. Compare the above excerpts of RST §339 with the following provisions.

RESTATEMENT OF THE LAW (THIRD) OF TORTS

§51. General Duty of Land Possessors

Subject to §52, a land possessor owes a duty of reasonable care to entrants on the land with regard to:

(a) conduct by the land possessor that creates risks to entrants on the land;

(b) artificial conditions on the land that pose risks to entrants on the land;

(c) natural conditions on the land that pose risks to entrants on the land; and

(d) other risks to entrants on the land when any of the affirmative duties provided in Chapter 7 is applicable.

Comment l. Child trespassers: Section 339 of the Restatement Second of Torts, another special trespasser rule, provided a duty of reasonable care to foreseeable child trespassers in the case of especially dangerous artificial conditions. Section 339 is superseded by this Section, as is §343B of the Second Restatement, which extended the duty contained in §339 to child licensees and invitees.

The principle behind §339 remains relevant in determining whether a land possessor exercised reasonable care. Foreseeable risk is a function of the number and kind of persons who may be exposed to a dangerous condition. That some of the persons likely to be exposed are children who are particularly vulnerable because of their immaturity is relevant to the extent of the precaution required of the land possessor.

Although not explicit, a number of limitations on the scope of §339 were influenced by the prevailing rule on a plaintiff's contributory negligence, which barred any recovery. However, the adoption of comparative fault affects the instances in which recovery is appropriate by child (and other) trespassers. This Section thus begins with a default duty of reasonable care to all trespassers. A child trespasser who is aware of a danger and unreasonably confronts it may have his or her damages reduced, but recovery is not barred under this Section.

At least in theory, §339 may not be fully subsumed by this Section. Thus, there may be the rare child who not only fits the model of the immature, innocent, and impetuous youth contemplated by §339 of the Second Restatement but whose entrance onto the land occurs with sufficient violence to the land possessor's rights that the child might also come within the scope of §52, comment *a*, which defines flagrant trespassers. In such a case, §§ 51 and 52 are sufficiently flexible to permit a court to resolve the tension between employing a duty of reasonable care or denying it.

§52. Duty of Land Possessors to Flagrant Trespassers

(a) The only duty a land possessor owes to flagrant trespassers is the duty not to act in an intentional, willful, or wanton manner to cause physical harm.

(b) Notwithstanding Subsection (a), a land possessor has a duty to flagrant trespassers to exercise reasonable care if the trespasser reasonably appears to be imperiled and

(1) helpless; or

(2) unable to protect him- or herself.

Though comment *l* formally eliminates the attractive nuisance doctrine, note the imperfect continuity. In one sense, comment *l* is the tip of the iceberg, for the entire thrust of the RTT: LPEH is in general to downgrade the tripartite classification found in *Robert Addie & Sons*.

4. *Licensees Versus Invitees.* Even though classical common law devoted considerable ingenuity to refining the difference between a licensee and an invitee, a host of marginal cases remained. Professor Harper observed:

> When a customer goes into a store to buy something and actually makes the purchase, the problem is easy. But how about the person who is merely "shopping" or who accompanies a friend who makes a purchase or children who accompany their parents or one who drops into a hotel or store to go to the toilet or use the telephone, or to mail a letter? And what of a worker looking for a job which he may or may not get? Then there is the problem of public officials of one kind or another who enter another's premises, not with his permission, but because they have legal authority to do so in the discharge of their duties.

Harper, Laube v. Stevenson: A Discussion: Licensor-Licensee, 25 Conn. B.J. 123, 131 (1951).

One response to these difficulties focuses not on the purpose of the plaintiff's visit but on the nature of the defendant's premises. Those who run business premises, or premises to which the public generally is invited, are treated as invitees; those who maintain private or residential premises are not. See Prosser, Business Visitors and Invitees, 26 Minn. L. Rev. 573 (1942), defending this position, which has been adopted in RST §332.

RESTATEMENT OF THE LAW (SECOND) OF TORTS

§332. Invitee Defined

(1) An invitee is either a public invitee or a business visitor.

(2) A public invitee is a person who is invited to enter or remain on land as a member of the public for a purpose for which the land is held open to the public.

(3) A business visitor is a person who is invited to enter or remain on land for a purpose directly or indirectly connected with business dealings with the possessor of the land.

Even under this view, private understandings might alter this background standard of care. In Lemon v. Busey, 461 P.2d 145 (Kan. 1969), a five-year-old child was brought to the defendant church by her grandmother, a part-time church employee. The arrangement was "for the convenience of her grandmother and parents" and the church at no time supervised the child. While her grandmother was busy at work, the child wandered off and fell to her death from a roof that she had probably reached through an unlocked elevator door or fire escape. The court held that she was a licensee and denied recovery.

In Olier v. Bailey, 164 So. 3d 982, 987–88 (Miss. 2015), the defendant Bailey maintained a garden in which she allowed geese to run free, even though she knew of their tendency to bite people. The garden was posted with a sign: "Beware—Attack Geese." The defendant also maintained a row of five-gallon water buckets for the geese that formed a protective barrier behind which anyone could stand. When the plaintiff Olier first ventured into the garden, a goose came close to her, and she retreated behind the buckets, after which she was told by the defendant that she could venture forth again if she defended herself with a stick. When the plaintiff went out a second time, she panicked when a goose attacked her in the "crotch area," dropped her stick, and injured herself when she tripped over one of the buckets while attempting to flee. Kitchen, J., held that the plaintiff was a licensee as a matter of law because "Olier came at Bailey's invitation to view Bailey's plants. She did not assist Bailey with housework, help her move, take her somewhere, or do anything to benefit Bailey. Instead, she came entirely for her own benefit to look at Bailey's plants and perhaps take a sample home with her." Should the defendant be liable for ordinary negligence? The plaintiff for contributory negligence?

With *Lemon* and *Olier* contrast Post v. Lunney, 261 So. 2d 146 (Fla. 1972). The plaintiff bought a ticket for five dollars from a club for its tour of several estates in the area, including the defendant Marjorie Merriweather Post's home. While touring the Post estate, she "tripped on a piece of transparent vinyl which had been placed over a valuable oriental rug, and she fractured her hip." The trial judge categorized the plaintiff as a licensee because the visit was not, as the older conception of invitee required, to their mutual economic advantage because the defendant received nothing for letting the plaintiff into her house. The Florida Supreme Court rejected that contention and treated the plaintiff as a public invitee, since Ms. Post had opened up her home for a paid public tour. Should it make any difference whether the vinyl was placed over the oriental rug solely in preparation for the tour? Does Ms. Post have an action over against the tour organizer?

In Depuis v. Eastern Idaho Health Services, Inc., 485 P.3d 144, 150 (2021), the Idaho Supreme Court adopted a standard for indirect business connections similar to that of RTT §322 where the plaintiff slipped on black ice in the parking lot of a hospital while visiting his wife who was in treatment there. The court determined that hospital visitors are invitees, writing:

> [E]stablishing invitee status does not require that an entrant be on the premises for the same purpose as the business conducted on the land; instead, the entrant must be on the premises for a purpose connected with the business conducted on the land. [Plaintiff's] purpose was closely connected to [the hospital's] business—that is, [he] was only present because his wife was being treated there as a patient.

5. *Duties to Licensees and Invitees in Slip-and-Fall Cases.* Slip-and-fall cases offer a vivid contrast between the duties to licensees and invitees. The sources of danger in slip-and-fall cases are typically short-lived phenomena, such as spilled fluids. A licensor typically has no knowledge of these evanescent conditions and no duty to inspect for them, but lives instead in a self-help regime.

An invitee, by contrast, can "show the proprietor had actual knowledge of a dangerous condition, *or* the dangerous condition existed for a sufficient amount of time to establish constructive knowledge, in that the proprietor should have known of the condition . . ." Thomas v. Boyd Biloxi LLC, 360 So. 3d 204, 213, 214 (Miss. 2023) (en banc). Thus, in *Thomas*, where plaintiff fell on the stairs of a spa near a pool, and evidence showed the defendant proprietor had notice of two prior falls occurring in the same area, Randolph, C.J., overturned a grant of summary judgment for the defendant, holding "based on the time between the prior falls and [the plaintiff's] fall, a reasonable jury could find that [the defendant] had sufficient time to correct the condition." Contrast Zuppardi v. Wal-Mart Stores, 770 F.3d 644 (7th Cir. 2014), in which the plaintiff slipped in a clear puddle of water on a concrete floor as she walked down a busy "action aisle" used by Wal-Mart employees for restocking shelves. There were no footprints or other signs of danger near the puddle. Wal-Mart's standard policy tasked all employees to carry "a towel in pocket" to clean up any spill they encountered. There were no personal witnesses to or video footage of the accident. On appeal, Kendall, J., affirmed the summary judgment for the defendant. There was no evidence that the defendant caused the spill given that there "were no trails, tracks, or footprints leading to or from the puddle to any store display or freezer." Nor did Wal-Mart have constructive notice of the puddle given that plaintiff "present[ed] next to no evidence of how much time elapsed between the spill and the fall."

Rowland v. Christian

443 P.2d 561 (Cal. 1968)

[On November 30, 1963, the defendant, Nancy Christian, invited James Rowland to her apartment. While he was using the bathroom fixtures, the porcelain handle on one of the water faucets broke, severing the nerves and tendons of his right hand. The defendant knew of the crack in the faucet, and two weeks before the incident she had asked her landlord to repair it, but she did not warn the plaintiff of the danger. The defendant's affidavits did not show that the defect was "obvious or even nonconcealed" or that the plaintiff knew or had reason to know of the defect. The defendant moved for a summary judgment, alleging first that the plaintiff was a social guest and, second, that the twin defenses of assumption of risk and contributory negligence barred the action. The trial court granted the motion. Reversed.]

Peters, J. . . . Section 1714 of the Civil Code provides: "Every one is responsible, not only for the result of his willful acts, but also for an injury occasioned to another by his want of ordinary care or skill in the management of his property or person, except so far as the latter has, willfully or by want of ordinary care, brought the injury upon himself. . . ." This code section, which has been unchanged in our law since 1872, states a civil law and not a common law principle.

Nevertheless, some common law judges and commentators have urged that the principle embodied in this code section serves as the foundation of our negligence law. Thus in a concurring opinion, Brett, M.R., in Heaven v. Pender (1883) 11 Q.B.D. 503, 509, states: "whenever one person is by circumstances placed in such a position with regard to another that every one of ordinary sense who did think would at once recognise that if he did not use ordinary care and skill in his own conduct with regard to those circumstances he would cause danger of injury to the person or property of the other, a duty arises to use ordinary care and skill to avoid such danger."

Although it is true that some exceptions have been made to the general principle that a person is liable for injuries caused by his failure to exercise reasonable care in the circumstances, it is clear that in the absence of statutory provision declaring an exception to the fundamental principle enunciated by section 1714 of the Civil Code, no such exception should be made unless clearly supported by public policy.

A departure from this fundamental principle involves the balancing of a number of considerations; the major ones are the foreseeability of harm to the plaintiff, the degree of certainty that the plaintiff suffered injury, the closeness of the connection between the defendant's conduct and the injury suffered, the moral blame attached to the defendant's conduct, the policy of preventing future harm, the extent of the burden to the defendant and consequences to the community of imposing a duty to exercise care with resulting liability for breach, and the availability, cost, and prevalence of insurance for the risk involved. Biakanja v. Irving, 320 P.2d 16 (Cal. 1958).

One of the areas where this court and other courts have departed from the fundamental concept that a man is liable for injuries caused by his carelessness is with regard to the liability of a possessor of land for injuries to persons who have entered upon that land. It has been suggested that the special rules regarding liability of the possessor of land are due to historical considerations stemming from the high place which land has traditionally held in English and American thought, the dominance and prestige of the landowning class in England during the formative period of the rules governing the possessor's liability, and the heritage of feudalism.

The departure from the fundamental rule of liability for negligence has been accomplished by classifying the plaintiff either as a trespasser, licensee, or invitee and then adopting special rules as to the duty owed by the possessor to each of the classifications. Generally speaking a trespasser is a person who enters or remains upon land of another without a privilege to do so; a licensee is a person like a social guest who is not an invitee and who is privileged to enter or remain upon land by virtue of the possessor's consent, and an invitee is a business visitor who is invited or permitted to enter or remain on the land for a purpose directly or indirectly connected with business dealings between them.

Although the invitor owes the invitee a duty to exercise ordinary care to avoid injuring him, . . . the general rule is that a trespasser and licensee or social guest are obliged to take the premises as they find them insofar as any alleged defective condition thereon may exist, and that the possessor of the land owes them only the duty of refraining from wanton or willful injury. The ordinary justification for the general rule severely restricting the occupier's liability to social guests is based on the theory that the guest should not expect special precautions to be made on his account and that if the host does not inspect and maintain his property the guest should not expect this to be done on his account.

An increasing regard for human safety has led to a retreat from this position, and an exception to the general rule limiting liability has been made as to active operations where an obligation to exercise reasonable care for the protection of the licensee has been imposed on the occupier of land. . . . In an apparent attempt to avoid the general rule limiting liability, courts have broadly defined active operations, sometimes giving the term a strained construction in cases involving dangers known to the occupier.

Thus in Hansen v. Richey, 46 Cal. Rptr. 909 [1965], an action for wrongful death of a drowned youth, the court held that liability could be predicated not upon the maintenance of a dangerous swimming pool but upon negligence "in the active conduct of a party for a large number of youthful guests in the light of knowledge of the dangerous pool." . . .

Another exception to the general rule limiting liability has been recognized for cases where the occupier is aware of the dangerous condition, the condition amounts to a concealed trap, and the guest is unaware of the trap. In none of these cases, however, did the court impose liability on the basis of a concealed trap; in some liability was found on another theory, and in others the court concluded that there was no trap. A trap has been defined as a "concealed" danger, a danger with a deceptive appearance of safety. It has also been defined as something akin to a spring gun or steel trap. . . . [I]t is pointed out that the lack of definiteness in the application of the term "trap" to any other situation makes its use argumentative and unsatisfactory.

The cases dealing with the active negligence and the trap exceptions are indicative of the subtleties and confusion which have resulted from application of the common law principles governing the liability of the possessor of land. Similar confusion and complexity exist as to the definitions of trespasser, licensee, and invitee.

In refusing to adopt the rules relating to the liability of a possessor of land for the law of admiralty, the United States Supreme Court stated: "The distinctions which the common law draws between licensee and invitee were inherited from a culture deeply rooted to the land, a culture which traced many of its standards to a heritage of feudalism. In an effort to do justice in an industrialized urban society, with its complex economic and individual relationships, modern common-law courts have found it necessary to formulate increasingly subtle verbal refinements, to create subclassifications among traditional common-law categories, and to delineate fine gradations in the standards of care which the landowner owes to each. Yet even within a single jurisdiction, the classifications and subclassifications bred by the common law have produced confusion and conflict. As new distinctions have been spawned, older ones have become obscured. Through this semantic morass the common law has moved, unevenly and with hesitation, towards 'imposing on owners and occupiers a single duty of reasonable care in all circumstances.'" (Footnotes omitted.) (Kermarec v. Compagnie Generale, 358 U.S. 625, 630–631 (1959). . . .

There is another fundamental objection to the approach to the question of the possessor's liability on the basis of the common law distinctions based upon the status of the injured party as a trespasser, licensee, or invitee. Complexity can be borne and confusion remedied where the underlying principles governing liability are based upon proper considerations. Whatever may have been the historical justifications for the common law distinctions, it is clear that those distinctions are not justified in the light of our modern society and that the complexity and confusion which has arisen is not due to difficulty in applying the original common law rules—they are all too easy to apply in their original formulation—but is due to the attempts to apply just rules in our modern society within the ancient terminology.

Without attempting to labor all of the rules relating to the possessor's liability, it is apparent that the classifications of trespasser, licensee, and invitee, the immunities from liability predicated upon those classifications, and the exceptions to those immunities, often do not reflect the major factors which should determine whether immunity should be conferred upon the possessor of land. Some of those factors, including the closeness of the connection between the injury and the defendant's conduct, the moral blame attached to the defendant's conduct, the policy of preventing future harm, and the prevalence and availability of insurance, bear little, if any, relationship to the classifications of trespasser, licensee, and invitee and the existing rules conferring immunity.

Although in general there may be a relationship between the remaining factors and the classifications of trespasser, licensee, and invitee, there are many cases in which no such relationship may exist. Thus, although the foreseeability of harm to an invitee would ordinarily seem greater than the foreseeability of harm to a trespasser, in a particular case the opposite may be true. The same may be said of the issue of certainty of injury. The burden to the defendant and consequences to the community of imposing a duty to exercise care with resulting liability for breach may often be greater with respect to trespassers than with respect to invitees, but it by no means follows that this is true in every case. In many situations, the burden will be the same, i.e., the conduct necessary upon the defendant's part to meet the burden of exercising due care as to invitees will also meet his burden with respect to licensees and trespassers. The last of the major factors, the cost of insurance, will, of course, vary depending upon the rules of liability adopted, but there is no persuasive evidence that applying ordinary principles of negligence law to the land occupier's liability will materially reduce the prevalence of insurance due to increased cost or even substantially increase the cost.

Considerations such as these have led some courts in particular situations to reject the rigid common law classifications and to approach the issue of the duty of the occupier on the basis of ordinary principles of negligence. (E.g., Gould v. DeBeve, 330 F.2d 826, 829–830 (1964).) And the common law distinctions after thorough study have been repudiated by the jurisdiction of their birth. (Occupiers' Liability Act, 1957, 5 and 6 Eliz. 2, ch. 31.) [which abolished the distinction between invitees and licensees, but left untouched the common law rules as applied to trespassers. — Eds.]

A man's life or limb does not become less worthy of protection by the law nor a loss less worthy of compensation under the law because he has come upon the land of another without permission or with permission but without a business purpose. Reasonable people do not ordinarily vary their conduct depending upon such matters, and to focus upon the status of the injured party as a trespasser, licensee, or invitee in order to determine the question whether the landowner has a duty of care, is contrary to our modern social mores and humanitarian values. The common law rules obscure rather than illuminate the proper considerations which should govern determination of the question of duty. . . .

We decline to follow and perpetuate such rigid classifications. The proper test to be applied to the liability of the possessor of land in accordance with section 1714 of the Civil Code is whether in the management of his property he has acted as a reasonable man in view of the probability of injury to others, and, although the plaintiff's status as a trespasser, licensee, or invitee may in the light of the facts giving rise to such status have some bearing on the question of liability, the status is not determinative.

Once the ancient concepts as to the liability of the occupier of land are stripped away, the status of the plaintiff relegated to its proper place in determining such liability, and ordinary principles of negligence applied, the result in the instant case presents no substantial difficulties. As we have seen, when we view the matters presented on the motion for summary judgment as we must, we must assume defendant Miss Christian was aware that the faucet handle was defective and dangerous, that the defect was not obvious, and that plaintiff was about to come in contact with the defective condition, and under the undisputed facts she neither remedied the condition nor warned plaintiff of it. Where the occupier of land is aware of a concealed condition involving in the absence of precautions an unreasonable risk of harm to those coming in contact with it and is aware that a person on the premises is about to come in contact with it, the trier of fact can reasonably conclude that a failure to warn or to repair the condition constitutes negligence. Whether or not a guest has a right to expect that his host will remedy dangerous conditions on his account, he should reasonably be entitled to rely upon a warning of the dangerous condition so that he, like the host, will be in a position to take special precautions when he comes in contact with it. . . .

The judgment is reversed.

TRAYNOR, C.J., and TOBRINER, MOSK, and SULLIVAN, JJ., concur.

Burke, J., dissenting. I dissent. In determining the liability of the occupier or owner of land for injuries, the distinctions between trespassers, licensees and invitees have been developed and applied by the courts over a period of many years. They supply a reasonable and workable approach to the problems involved, and one which provides the degree of stability and predictability so highly prized in the law. The unfortunate alternative, it appears to me, is the route taken by the majority in their opinion in this case that such issues are to be decided on a case by case basis under the application of the basic law of negligence, bereft of the guiding principles and precedent which the law has heretofore attached by a virtue of the relationship of the parties to one another.

Liability for negligence turns upon whether a duty of care is owed, and if so, the extent thereof. Who can doubt that the corner grocery, the large department store, or the financial institution owes a greater duty of care to one whom it has invited to enter its premises as a prospective customer of its wares or services than it owes to a trespasser seeking to enter after the close of business hours and for a nonbusiness or even an antagonistic purpose? I do not think it unreasonable or unfair that a social guest (classified by the law as a licensee, as was plaintiff here) should be obliged to take the premises in the same condition as his host finds them or permits them to be. Surely a homeowner should not be obliged to hover over his guests with warnings of possible dangers to be found in the condition of the home (e.g., waxed floors, slipping rugs, toys in unexpected places, etc., etc.). Yet today's decision appears to open the door to potentially unlimited liability despite the purpose and circumstances motivating the plaintiff in entering the premises of another, and despite the caveat of the majority that the status of the parties may "have some bearing on the question of liability . . . ," whatever the future may show that language to mean.

In my view, it is not a proper function of this court to overturn the learning, wisdom and experience of the past in this field. Sweeping modifications of tort liability law fall more suitably within the domain of the Legislature, before which all affected interests can be heard and which can enact statutes providing uniform standards and guidelines for the future.

I would affirm the judgment for defendant.

NOTES

1. ***California's Response to Rowland v. Christian.*** Is it necessary to abolish the distinction between licensees and invitees in order to deny the defendant's motion for summary judgment? Should Burke's, J., opinion properly have been a concurrence? Note that prior to *Rowland*, California had not accepted the standard view stated in RST §342 that the possessor of real property was under a duty to warn a licensee of concealed dangerous conditions but instead used the same rule of liability for trespassers and social guests. See, e.g., Fisher v. General Petroleum Corp., 267 P.2d 841 (Cal. App. 1954); Hansen v. Richey, 46 Cal. Rptr. 909 (Ct. App. 1965). On remand in *Rowland*, will the plaintiff be able to prevail if the defendant can show that the defect was obvious? Will the defendant escape liability if the defect was concealed? Does it make a difference if Rowland's apartment was a pigsty when she moved in so that the crack in the faucet was concealed under grime? For a discussion of the origins and influence of the case, see Rabin, Rowland v. Christian: Hallmark of an Expansionary Era, *in* Torts Stories 73 (Rabin & Sugarman eds., 2003). For an argument that, in recent years, "[t]he categorical approach to questions of duties owed to entrants onto real property is quietly being resurrected" by California courts, see Esper & Keating, Abusing "Duty," 79 S. Cal. L. Rev. 265, 322 (2006).

Within California, *Rowland* has governed the duty question in tort law outside the specific area of occupier's liability. The *Biakanja* exceptions to section 1714 (referenced in *Rowland*, *supra*) have controlled many other forms of special relationships. See, e.g., *Tarasoff*, *infra* at 441.

2. ***Response to Rowland Elsewhere.*** *Rowland* has received a somewhat mixed response elsewhere. In Mallet v. Pickens, 522 S.E.2d 436, 444–45 (W. Va. 1999), West Virginia abandoned the invitee/licensee distinction, while preserving the traditional common law rules for trespassers. It summarized the current state of authority as follows:

> Broad generalizations about the state of premises liability law in other jurisdictions are always subject to caveats and limitations. Several states have special rules for invited social guests; others limit landowner liability via recreational use statutes, or employ a distinction between "active" and "passive" negligence. Having said that, our research reveals that at least 25 jurisdictions have abolished or largely abandoned the licensee/invitee distinction. Among these 25 jurisdictions that have broken with past tradition, at least 17 have eliminated or fundamentally altered the distinction. Another eight of the 25 have eliminated even the trespasser distinction. And, of those retaining the old scheme, judges in at least five of those states have authored vigorous dissents or concurrences arguing for change.

In Demag v. Better Power Equipment, Inc., 102 A.3d 1101, 1110 (Vt. 2014), Vermont joined the ranks, holding "that a landowner owes the same duty of care to a licensee as to an invitee."

Hylton, Tort Duties of Landowners: A Positive Theory, 44 Wake Forest L. Rev. 1049, 1061 (2009), takes a stab at providing an economic justification for the common law categories. Drawing upon traditional assumption-of-risk theory, Hylton argues that "[l]icensees, typically social guests, are likely to know more about the landowner than would the typical invitee," and are thus able to foresee and protect against possible dangers.

Critics of the traditional rules have been more vocal. Thus, in Koenig v. Koenig, 766 N.W.2d 635, 643–45 (Iowa 2009), the court wrote:

> The primary advantage of abolishing the invitee-licensee distinction is to avoid confusion. . . . [The cases are] replete with examples of the difficulties appellate courts have experienced in attempting to fit modern human interaction into rigid categories developed three centuries ago. Such confusion is likely to only increase in the future. . . . As a result, retention of the common-law system has not fulfilled its goal of predictability, but rather has "produced confusion and conflict." . . . The fungible and unpredictable nature of the classifications makes it impossible for landowners to conform their behavior to current community standards. . . . Contrary to courts that have upheld the trichotomy, there is nothing to fear about jury involvement. . . . [B]oth logic and almost forty years of practice suggest that there is no reason to question a jury's ability to perform in the area of premises liability as opposed to any other area of tort law. . . . Finally, abandonment of this common-law distinction recognizes a higher valuation of public safety over property rights.

Many of these difficulties may be eased by Prosser's claim, *supra* at 410, that the nature of the premises and not the intentions of the visitor should inform the distinction between licenses and invitees. Still, hard cases remain. In Ward v. K-Mart Corp., 554 N.E.2d 223, 230–31, 233 (Ill. 1990), the plaintiff sustained injuries to his face and partial loss of vision when he walked into a concrete post located about nineteen inches from the rear wall of the K-Mart store. On entering the store, the plaintiff had noticed the post, but he had forgotten about it momentarily while leaving the store carrying a large bathroom mirror that obscured his view. The trial judge overruled a jury verdict for the plaintiff for $68,000 ($160,135 in 2023 dollars), but the Illinois Supreme Court reinstated the verdict. Ryan, J., refused to hold that the defendant had automatically discharged its duty of care for dangerous conditions that are open and obvious, saying:

> [I]n the case at bar it was reasonably foreseeable that a customer would collide with the post while exiting defendant's store carrying merchandise which could obscure view of the post. . . . It should be remembered that the post was located immediately outside the entrance to the Home Center section of defendant's store. Defendant had every reason to expect that customers

> would carry large, bulky items through that door, particularly where, as here, the large overhead door was closed. The burden on the defendant of protecting against this danger would be slight. A simple warning or a relocation of the post may have sufficed. It is also relevant that there were no windows or transparent panels on the customer entrance doors to permit viewing of the posts from the interior of the store.

Could this defect be treated as latent to the plaintiff even if obvious to the world? Note that *Ward* was decided under an earlier version of 740 Ill. Comp. Stat. 130/2, which read in pertinent part:

> §2. The distinction under the common law between invitees and licensees as to the duty owed by an owner or occupier of any premises to such entrants is abolished.
>
> The duty owed to such entrants is that of reasonable care under the circumstances regarding the state of the premises or acts done or omitted on them.

3. *Duties to Trespassers After Rowland v. Christian.* As noted above, *Rowland* has been met with greater resistance on its extension of the ordinary duty of care to trespassers. Thus the Minnesota Supreme Court, in Peterson v. Balach, 199 N.W.2d 639, 642 (Minn. 1972), observed:

> [T]he considerations governing a landowner's or occupant's liability to trespassers may be fundamentally different from his duty to those whom he has expressly or by implication invited onto his property. Burglars are trespassers; vandals are trespassers. We have criminal statutes governing trespassers. Minn. St. 609.605. Sweeping away all distinction between trespassers and social guests and business invitees is a drastic step to take because there may be, and often is, good reason to distinguish between a trespasser and a social guest. There is little or no reason to distinguish between a social guest and a business invitee.

The Massachusetts Supreme Judicial Court, however, cast its lot with *Rowland* in Pridgen v. Boston Housing Authority, 308 N.E.2d 467, 476–77 (Mass. 1974). The plaintiff, an eleven-year-old boy, lifted an escape hatch in the ceiling of an elevator and climbed into the elevator shaft. He slipped off the elevator roof and became trapped. His mother, having learned of her son's predicament, asked one of the defendant's servants to turn off "the lights" to keep her son from being injured, but he failed to shut down the power in time to prevent the boy's legs from being crushed by the moving elevator. The court, much troubled by the influence of the Good Samaritan doctrine on the common law, observed:

> In the context of the relationship between an owner or occupier (owner) of the property and a trapped, imperiled and helpless trespasser thereon, we reject any rule which would exempt the owner from liability if he knowingly refrains from taking reasonable action which he is in a position to take and which would prevent injury or further injury to the trespasser. It should not be, it cannot be, and surely it is not now the law of this Commonwealth that the owner in such a situation is rewarded with immunity from liability as long as he ignores the plight of the trapped trespasser and takes no affirmative action to help him. Thus, in the case before us it is unthinkable to have a rule which would hold the authority liable if one of its employees, acting in the course of his employment, pushed the "go" button on the elevator although he knew Joseph Pridgen was trapped in the elevator shaft, but would not hold it liable if, being reasonably able to do so, the employee knowingly failed or refused to turn off the switch to the electrical power for the same elevator.

How would *Pridgen* be decided under Addie v. Dumbreck or under Excelsior Wire Rope Ltd. v. Callan? Does *Pridgen* deal with the condition of the premises or with the actions of the defendant's employees?

4. *Recreational Land Statutes.* Many states have also passed statutes that relax the liability of owners for recreational or rural lands. N.J. Stat. Ann. §2A:42A-3 (2023) provides:

> a. An owner, lessee or occupant of premises, whether or not posted . . . and whether or not improved or maintained in a natural condition, or used as part of a commercial enterprise, owes no duty to keep the premises safe for entry or use by others for sport and recreational activities, or to give warning of any hazardous condition of the land or in connection with the use of any structure or by reason of any activity on such premises to persons entering for such purposes;
>
> b. An owner, lessee or occupant of premises who gives permission to another to enter upon such premises for a sport or recreational activity or purpose does not thereby (1) extend any assurance that the premises are safe for such purpose, or (2) constitute the person to whom permission is granted an invitee to whom a duty of care is owed, or (3) assume responsibility for or incur liability for any injury to person or property caused by any act of persons to whom the permission is granted.

"Sport and recreational activities" as statutory terms are to "be liberally construed to serve as an inducement to the owners, lessees and occupants of property, that might otherwise be reluctant to do so for fear of liability, to permit persons to come onto their property for sport and recreational activities." *Id.* §2A:42A-5.1. This statute did not, however, protect a landowner against suit by a Good Samaritan who drowned while trying to rescue two fifteen-year-old boys who had fallen through thin ice on the defendant's reservoir on the first day of the skating season, because the rescuer was not engaged in recreational activities. Harrison v. Middlesex Water Co., 403 A.2d 910, 914 (N.J. 1979).

Some jurisdictions retain more explicit exceptions in their recreational use statutes for invitees. Thus, in California, "if an owner expressly invites someone onto the property and the person is injured while using the land for a recreational purpose, then the general release from liability [of the recreational statute] is abrogated." Hoffman v. Young, 515 P.3d 635, 642 (Cal. 2022).

See generally Carroll et al., Recreational User Statutes and Landowner Immunity: A Comparison Study of State Legislation, 17 J. Legal Aspects Sport 163 (2007).

5. *Duties to Strangers After Rowland v. Christian.* Should *Rowland* also impact the liability of owners and occupiers to persons who have not entered their land but who are injured by either natural or artificial conditions on the defendant's land? Most American cases refuse to impose liability for natural conditions, except harm caused by falling trees. See, e.g., Taylor v. Olsen, 578 P.2d 779 (Or. 1978). See also Noel, Nuisances from Land in Its Natural Condition, 56 Harv. L. Rev. 772, 796–97 (1943), which observed: "Where a planted tree has become dangerous to persons on the highway or on adjoining land, and causes harm, the fault lies not in the planting of the tree but in permitting it to remain after it has become unsafe."

The no-liability regime for natural conditions has been challenged, at least in urban settings. In Sprecher v. Adamson Co., 636 P.2d 1121, 1125–26, 1136 (Cal. 1981), the court demonstrated a willingness to impose an affirmative duty on one Malibu landowner to prevent a mudslide after heavy rains that would damage the home of his downhill neighbor. Bird, C.J., showcased hostility to the misfeasance-nonfeasance distinction at common law and placed heavy reliance upon *Rowland*, noting the

> inherent injustice . . . in allowing a landowner [to] escape all liability for serious damage to his neighbors [or those using a public highway], merely by allowing nature to take its course. . . . Whatever the rule may once have been, it is now clear that a duty to exercise due care can arise out of possession alone.

Richardson, J., concurred in the reversal of summary judgment but found it "exceedingly difficult to imagine what respondents *reasonably* could have done to prevent or reduce the damage caused by the natural condition here present."

Sprecher was relied on in Contra Costa County v. Pinole Point Properties, LLC, 186 Cal. Rptr. 3d 109, 122 (Ct. App. 2015), to impose liability on a landowner for failing to take affirmative action to prevent debris buildup in a drainage channel. "Although this latter situation is less common, liability can be based on an *omission* or *inaction* when the failure to act is an *unreasonable* use of the property." Is *Contra Costa* an example of the "compound act" in Newton v. Ellis, *supra* at 402?

Sprecher was relied on outside California in Whitt v. Silverman, 788 So. 2d 210 (Fla. 2001), when one pedestrian was killed and another injured when struck by a driver leaving the defendant's gas station. The driver's view of the highway was obscured by heavy foliage located exclusively on the defendant's property. The court refused to follow the so-called agrarian rule, whereby a landowner owes no duty of care to a stranger for harm caused by the natural condition of his land. The owners of ordinary businesses have specific knowledge of the "continuous flow of traffic entering and exiting the premises for the commercial benefit of the landowners," where their control over their own premises undercuts any claim "that it would have been unduly burdensome for the landowners to have maintained this foliage consistent with the safe egress and ingress of vehicles attracted to the business and persons affect thereby."

SECTION D. GRATUITOUS UNDERTAKINGS

Coggs v. Bernard

(1703) 92 Eng. Rep. 107 (KB)

[The action was brought in *assumpsit* —Latin for "he has undertaken,"—which allowed for the recovery of damages for breach of a simple contract. The defendant had moved casks of brandy owned by the plaintiff from one cellar to another. Through the defendant's negligence, some of the casks were split open and great quantities of brandy were lost. The defendant sought to overturn the judgment in the plaintiff's favor because the plaintiff had not alleged either that the defendant was a common porter or that he had received any reward or consideration. Notwithstanding, the plaintiff had judgment.]

Gould, J. I think this is a good declaration [complaint]. The objection that has been made is, because there is not any consideration laid. But I think it is good either way, and that any man, that undertakes to carry goods, is liable to an action, be he a common carrier, or whatever he is, if through his neglect they are lost, or come to any damage: and if a praemium be laid to be given, then it is without question so. The reason of the action is, the particular trust reposed in the defendant, to which he has concurred by his assumption, and in the executing which he has miscarried by his neglect. But if a man undertakes to build a house, without any thing to be had for his pains, an action will not lie for non-performance, because it is nudum pactum. . . .

Holt, C.J. . . .

[After his review of the six different types of bailments in Roman law, discussed *supra* Chapter 3, at 114, he continues]: If it had appeared that the mischief happened by any person that met the cart in the way, the bailee had not been chargeable. As if a drunken man had come by in the streets, and had pierced the cask of brandy; in this case the defendant had not been answerable for it, because he was to have nothing for his pains. Then the bailee having undertaken to manage the goods and having managed them ill, and so by his neglect a damage had happened to the bailor, which is the case in question, what will you call this?

In Bracton, lib. 3,100, it is called *mandatum*. It is an obligation which arises *ex mandato*. It is what we call in English an acting commission. And if a man acts by his commission for another and in executing his commission behaves himself negligently, he is answerable. . . . [I]t is supported by good reason and authority. The reasons are, first, because in such a case, a neglect is a deceit to the bailor. For when he intrusts the bailee upon his undertaking to be careful, he has put a fraud upon the plaintiff by being negligent, his pretence of care being the persuasion that induced the plaintiff to trust him. And a breach of a trust undertaken voluntarily will be a ground for an action. . . .

But secondly it is objected, that there is no consideration to ground this promise upon, and therefore the undertaking is but *nudum pactum*. But to this I answer, that the owner's trusting him with the goods is a sufficient consideration to oblige him to a careful management. Indeed if the agreement had been executory, to carry these brandies from the one place to the other such a day, the defendant had not been bound to carry them. But this is a different case, for *assumpsit* does not only signify a future agreement, but in such a case as this, it signifies an actual entry upon the thing, and taking the trust upon himself. And if a man will do that, and miscarries in the performance of his trust, an action will lie against him for that, though no body could have compelled him to do the thing.

NOTES

1. ***Contract Without Consideration.*** *Coggs*, also discussed *supra* Chapter 3, at 114, on the issue of degrees of negligence, bears as well on the question whether gratuitous promises can be a source of affirmative duties. Holt, C.J., attacks this point in two ways. He first claims that the case has overtones of deceit and pretense, both of which seem to be unlikely on the facts on the case. He next claims that consideration can be "found" in this essentially gratuitous transaction, given that the general formula requires a benefit to the promisor or a detriment to the promisee. Note too that civil law treats these cases as contract cases without invoking the idea of consideration. In Roman law, these gratuitous arrangements were called "real" contracts, which became binding only after the goods in question were delivered to the bailee. Thus the plaintiff may recover on contractual grounds for the improper performance of the duty even though the promisor can withdraw from his engagement if he changes his mind before performance was due. The doctrine of consideration functions in the civil law mainly as the test for enforceability of fully executory agreements, not as the test of whether the parties formed any contract at all.

The interaction between tort and contract is illustrated again by the famous early case of Thorne v. Deas, 4 Johns. 84 (N.Y. Sup. Ct. 1809). The plaintiff was captain of a ship and, as he was about to leave on a voyage, he suggested to his co-owner, the defendant, that they insure the ship before leaving. The defendant told the plaintiff to go ahead and sail—that he would insure the ship on the plaintiff's departure. Relying on the defendant's promise, the plaintiff left port. The defendant failed to insure the ship, which was subsequently wrecked. On his return home, the plaintiff sued the defendant for his loss. The court denied recovery. Kent, C.J., following the rule announced by Gould, J., *supra*, noted that this was "an action on the case, for a *non-feasance*" and that it could not lie because of "the want of a consideration for the promise," even though the plaintiff's case was good under Roman contract law under the contract of mandate—essentially a gratuitous agency.

Because the contract option was foreclosed by the English consideration rules, the plaintiff tried to frame his action in tort. Kent refused to first deny recovery for breach of a promise unsupported by consideration, only to turn around and allow recovery by calling the defendant's conduct a tort. However, the plaintiff could recover, according to Kent, by showing that the defendant had engaged in misfeasance—i.e., he had actually started to perform and had done so negligently. Would the actions (incorrectly filling out papers) of the defendant have been tortious without reference to the former promise? If not, why does the ineffective promise make these ministerial mishaps actionable? What if the defendant fails to finish the job he started, as by failing to supply the insurer with a certificate of title?

2. *Promissory Estoppel.* Section 90 of the Restatement (Second) of Contracts provides:

§90. Promise Reasonably Inducing Action or Forbearance

(1) A promise which the promisor should reasonably expect to induce action or forbearance on the part of the promisee or a third person and which does induce such action or forbearance is binding if injustice can be avoided only by enforcement of the promise. The remedy granted for breach may be limited as justice requires.

Does this section help the plaintiff in *Coggs* or *Thorne*? On section 90 and this area in general, see Seavey, Reliance upon Gratuitous Promises or Other Conduct, 64 Harv. L. Rev. 913, 926–27 (1951), who observed:

> The colloquial explanation for the rule of the section is that it creates "promissory estoppel." Estoppel is basically a tort doctrine and the rationale of the section is that justice requires the defendant to pay for the harm caused by foreseeable reliance upon the performance of his promise. The wrong is not primarily in depriving the plaintiff of the promised reward but in causing the plaintiff to change position to his detriment. . . . In a case like Thorne v. Deas, however, the continuing representation becomes fraudulent when the promisor decides not to perform and does not inform the plaintiff, knowing that he still relies upon performance.

What if the defendant simply forgot his promise? How does reliance on voluntary undertakings work for promises made to the public at large?

Erie R.R. v. Stewart

40 F.2d 855 (6th Cir. 1930)

Hickenlooper, C.J. Stewart, plaintiff below, was a passenger in an automobile truck, sitting on the front seat to the right of the driver, a fellow employee of the East Ohio Gas Company. He recovered a judgment in the District Court for injuries received when the truck was struck by one of the defendant's trains at the 123d Street crossing in the city of Cleveland. Defendant maintained a watchman at this crossing, which was admittedly heavily traveled, but the watchman was either within the shanty or just outside of it as the train approached, and he gave no warning until too late to avoid the accident. . . .

The second contention of appellant presents the question whether the court erred in charging the jury that the absence of the watchman, where one had been maintained by the defendant company at a highway crossing over a long period of time to the knowledge of the plaintiff, would constitute negligence as a matter of law. In the present case it is conceded that the employment of the watchman by the defendant was voluntary upon its part, there being no statute or ordinance requiring the same, and that plaintiff had knowledge of this practice and relied

An Erie Railroad "Berkshire" locomotive

Source: Wikimedia Commons

upon the absence of the watchman as an assurance of safety and implied invitation to cross. We are not now concerned with the extent of the duty owing to one who had no notice of the prior practice, nor, in this aspect of the case, with the question of contributory negligence and the extent to which the plaintiff was relieved from the obligation of vigilance by the absence of the watchman. The question is simply whether there was any positive duty owing to the plaintiff in respect to the maintenance of such watchman, and whether a breach of such duty is so conclusively shown as to justify a peremptory charge of negligence. The question whether such negligence was the proximate cause of the injury was properly submitted to the jury.

Where the employment of a watchman or other precaution is required by statute, existence of an absolute duty to the plaintiff is conclusively shown, and failure to observe the statutory requirement is negligence per se. . . . Conversely, where there is no duty prescribed by statute or ordinance, it is usually a question for the jury whether the circumstances made the employment of a watchman necessary in the exercise of due care. Where the voluntary employment of a watchman was unknown to the traveler upon the highway, the mere absence of such watchman could probably not be considered as negligence toward him as a matter of law, for in such case there is neither an established duty positively owing to such traveler as a member of the general public, nor had he been led into reliance upon the custom. The question would remain simply whether the circumstances demanded such employment. But where the practice is known to the traveler upon the highway, and such traveler has been educated into reliance upon it, some positive duty must rest upon the railway with reference thereto. The elements of invitation and assurance of safety exist in this connection no less than in connection with contributory negligence. The company has established for itself a standard of due care while operating its trains across the highway, and, having led the traveler into reliance upon such standard, it should not be permitted thereafter to say that no duty required, arose from or attached to these precautions.

This duty has been recognized as not only actual and positive, but as absolute, in the sense that the practice may not be discontinued without exercising reasonable care to give warning of such discontinuance, although the company may thereafter do all that would otherwise be reasonably necessary. Conceding for the purposes of this opinion that, in cases where a watchman is voluntarily employed by the railway in an abundance of precaution, the duty is not absolute, in the same sense as where it is imposed by statute, still, if there be some duty, it cannot be less than that the company must use reasonable care to see that reliance by members of the educated public upon its representation of safety is not converted into a trap. Responsibility for injury will arise if the service be negligently performed or abandoned without other notice of that fact. . . .

So, in the present case, the evidence conclusively establishes the voluntary employment of a watchman, knowledge of this fact and reliance upon it by the plaintiff, a duty, therefore, that the company, through the watchman, will exercise reasonable care in warning such travelers as plaintiff, the presence of the watchman thereabouts, and no explanation of the failure to warn. Therefore, even though the duty be considered as qualified, rather than absolute, a prima facie case was established by plaintiff, requiring the defendant to go forward with evidence to rebut the presumption of negligence thus raised, or else suffer a verdict against it on this point. . . . No such evidence was introduced by defendant. No other inference than that of negligence could therefore be drawn from the evidence. If, perhaps, the rule was stated more broadly than this in the charge, the error, if any, was harmless as applied to the present case. . . .

[Affirmed.]

Tuttle, J. I concur in the result reached by the opinion of the majority of the court. I cannot, however, concur in the views, expressed in that opinion, which would make the actionable negligence of the defendant dependent upon the knowledge of the plaintiff, previous to his injury, of the custom of the defendant in maintaining a watchman at the crossing where such injury occurred. It is settled law that a railroad company operating trains at high speed across a public highway owes to travelers properly using such highway the duty to exercise reasonable care to give such warning of approaching trains as may be reasonably required by the particular circumstances. It is equally well settled that the standard of duty thus owed to the public, at least where not otherwise prescribed by statutory law, consists of that care and prudence which an ordinarily prudent person would exercise under the same circumstances. I am satisfied that where, as here, a railroad company has established a custom, known to the general public, of maintaining a watchman at a public crossing with instructions to warn the traveling public of the approach of trains, such railroad company, in the exercise of that reasonable care which it owes to the public, should expect, and is bound to expect, that any member of the traveling public approaching such crossing along the public highway is likely to have knowledge of and to rely upon the giving of such warning. Such knowledge, with the consequent reliance, may be acquired by a traveler at any time, perhaps only a moment before going upon the crossing, and this also the railroad company is bound to anticipate. Having, in effect, given notice to the public traveling this highway that it would warn them of trains at this crossing, I think that it was bound to assume (at least in the absence of knowledge to the contrary) that every member of such public would receive, and rely on, such notice. Under such circumstances such a railroad company, in my opinion, owes to every traveler so approaching this crossing a duty to give such a warning, if reasonably possible, and a reasonably prudent railroad company would not fail, without sufficient cause, to perform that duty. It follows that the unexplained failure, as in the present case, of the defendant to give this customary warning to the plaintiff, a traveler on the highway approaching this crossing, indicates, as a matter of law, actionable negligence for which it is liable. While undoubtedly lack of reliance by plaintiff upon the custom of the defendant has an important bearing and effect upon the question whether the plaintiff was guilty of contributory negligence, it seems to me clear that the knowledge or lack of knowledge of the plaintiff, unknown to the defendant, concerning such customs cannot affect the nature or extent of the duty owed to the plaintiff by the defendant or the performance of such duty. As therefore the conclusions expressed in the opinion of a majority of the court are, to the extent which I have thus indicated, not in accord with my own views in this connection, I have felt it my duty to briefly state such views in this separate concurring opinion.

NOTES

1. ***The Scope of Voluntary Undertakings.*** What exactly is the point of disagreement between Judges Hickenlooper and Tuttle? If reliance is required in cases where promises or representations are made to a single person, should any member of the public who is injured be required to show that she was aware of the prior practice in order to make good her claim for "negative" reliance?

The limits of *Erie Railroad* are evident in Martin v. Twin Falls School District #411, 59 P.3d 317, 320 (Idaho 2002). There the plaintiff children were struck by a pick-up truck driven by one Ryan Canoy as they were walking through a designated school crossing, properly equipped with signs and flashing lights, located about two blocks from their school. The plaintiffs claimed that the school district had a duty to supply crossing guards at this intersection because it had provided crossing guards at other intersections. Eismann, J., rejected that contention, noting: "By providing crossing guards at certain intersections or pedestrian crossings, the school district did not thereby assume the duty to provide guards at any other intersections or crossings." This decision is approved in the Third Restatement, which notes: "The scope of an undertaking can be determined only from the facts and circumstances of the case. When reasonable minds can differ about whether the risk or negligence was within the scope of the undertaking, it is a question of fact for the factfinder." RTT: LPEH §42, comment *g*.

The reluctance to recognize special relationships beyond situations in which the defendant has direct charge of the plaintiff is evident in Beers v. Corporation of President of Church of Jesus Christ of Latter-Day Saints [COP], 316 P.3d 92, 100–01 (Idaho 2013). Heidi Beers, a thirteen-year-old girl, who had attended a church retreat without her parents, was severely injured when she jumped off a bridge. At that time, she was with several adults who had marked out a place safe for jumping. Heidi jumped in at an uninspected location. In affirming a grant of summary judgment for the defendants below, Horton, J., first denied that there was a special relationship between the plaintiff and COP that generated a duty of protection under RST §315(b), *infra* at 432:

> Here, the COP's only affirmative actions were extending an open invitation to all Ward members to attend a campout and planning two meals and a devotional. These actions do not reflect the assumption of a duty by the Ward to supervise Heidi jumping from a bridge a mile away from the location of the Ward campout upon which she could reasonably rely.

Horton, J., further held that the individual church members who were at the bridge supervising their own children did not assume a duty to supervise Heidi.

Contrast with Dent v. NFL, 968 F.3d 1126, 1131, 1134 (9th Cir. 2020), where the plaintiff football players sued the NFL for failing to "regulat[e] the manner in which [pain] [m]edications were administered and distributed." The plaintiffs alleged that the pain medication administered to them by their respective football teams exacerbated their injuries by encouraging them to get back on the field before they were healthy. Tallman, J., reversed dismissal on the plaintiffs' voluntary undertakings claim:

> [T]he [complaint] paints a picture of the NFL's "mandated" and "required" audits, oversight, and procedures regarding drug distribution across member Clubs, as well as the NFL's failure to enforce rules that it knows are necessary to avoid further injury to players. These allegations support Plaintiffs' theory that the NFL undertook "the duty of overseeing [the] administration" of the distribution of pain medications to players and is aware that it should be providing protections.

Why might it be difficult to hold sports leagues responsible for ordinary negligence?

2. *Special Precautions for Rabies Inspections.* In Marsalis v. LaSalle, 94 So. 2d 120, 126 (La. App. 1957), the plaintiff had been bitten or scratched by the defendant's cat in the defendant's store. After the bite, the plaintiff asked the defendant to keep the cat "under observation" and "locked up" for two weeks until it could be determined whether or not it had rabies. The defendants, despite agreeing to this, took no special precautions to keep the cat in. About four days later the cat escaped. It was found about one month later, free of any rabies symptom. In the interim, the plaintiff, on the advice of her neighbor, a neurologist, received rabies shots, to which she developed a severe allergic reaction. The shots would have been completely unnecessary if the cat had been properly held in. The court recognized (soundly?) that the plaintiff could not recover for the simple cat bite or scratch, but adopted the rule "that one who voluntarily undertakes to care for, or to afford relief or assistance to, an ill, injured, or helpless person is under a legal obligation to use reasonable care and prudence in what he does." It then explained:

> Perhaps the defendant, LaSalle, initially owed no duty whatever to Mrs. Marsalis, but when he once agreed to restrain and keep the cat under observation, he was bound to use reasonable care and prudence in doing so and to assume and exercise reasonable care and common humanity. It may be that Mrs. Marsalis had open to her some other course by which she could have had the cat incarcerated and examined in order to determine if it was rabid, but she unquestionably and in good faith relied upon defendant to carry out the agreement which he voluntarily made, thus foregoing such other possible available protection. It was of extreme importance to know if the cat had rabies so she could regulate her course of conduct with reference to the injury. . . .

In light of the decision in *Montgomery* and RTT: LPEH §39, *supra* at 403, is the voluntary undertaking necessary to impose the duty of care on the LaSalles? What result in *Marsalis* if the defendant's cat had in fact been rabid? How does the case come out on a strict liability theory?

The Third Restatement's principle of duty based on undertaking is frequently invoked today in suits against the government for breach of its various regulatory duties. In the leading case of Indian Towing v. United States, 350 U.S. 61, 64–65 (1955), the U.S. Coast Guard operated a lighthouse whose light was negligently allowed to go out, whereupon the plaintiff's barge ran aground. The plaintiff brought suit under the Federal Tort Claims Act, which imposes upon the government the duties of a private party acting under like circumstances. Frankfurter, J., allowed the cause of action, noting that "it is hornbook tort law that one who undertakes to warn the public of danger and thereby induces reliance must perform his 'good Samaritan' task in a careful manner."

RESTATEMENT (THIRD) OF TORTS: LIABILITY FOR PHYSICAL AND EMOTIONAL HARM

§42. Duty Based on Undertaking

An actor who undertakes to render services to another that the actor knows or should know reduce the risk of physical harm to the other has a duty of reasonable care to the other in conducting the undertaking if:

(a) the failure to exercise such care increases the risk of harm beyond that which existed without the undertaking, or

(b) the person to whom the services are rendered or another relies on the actor's exercising reasonable care in the undertaking.

Moch Co. v. Rensselaer Water Co.

159 N.E. 896 (N.Y. 1928)

Cardozo, C.J. The defendant, a water works company under the laws of this State, made a contract with the city of Rensselaer for the supply of water during a term of years. Water was to be furnished to the city for sewer flushing and street sprinkling; for service to schools and public buildings; and for service at fire hydrants, the latter service at the rate of $42.50 [$765 in 2023 dollars] a year for each hydrant. Water was to be furnished to private takers within the city at their homes and factories and other industries at reasonable rates, not exceeding a stated schedule. While this contract was in force, a building caught fire. The flames, spreading to the plaintiff's warehouse near by, destroyed it and its contents. The defendant according to the complaint was promptly notified of the fire, "but omitted and neglected after such notice, to supply or furnish sufficient or adequate quantity of water, with adequate pressure to stay, suppress or extinguish the fire before it reached the warehouse of the plaintiff, although the pressure and supply which the defendant was equipped to supply and furnish, and had agreed by said contract to supply and furnish, was adequate and sufficient to prevent the spread of the fire to and the destruction of the plaintiff's warehouse and its contents." By reason of the failure of the defendant to "fulfill the provisions of the contract between it and the city of Rensselaer," the plaintiff is said to have suffered damage, for which judgment is demanded. A motion, in the nature of a demurrer, to dismiss the complaint, was denied at Special Term. The Appellate Division reversed by a divided court.

Liability in the plaintiff's argument is placed on one or other of three grounds. The complaint, we are told, is to be viewed as stating: (1) A cause of action for breach of contract within Lawrence v. Fox (20 N.Y. 268 [1859]); (2) a cause of action for a common-law tort, within MacPherson v. Buick Motor Company (217 N.Y. 382 [1916]); or (3) a cause of action for the breach of a statutory duty. These several grounds of liability will be considered in succession.

(1) We think the action is not maintainable as one for breach of contract.

No legal duty rests upon a city to supply its inhabitants with protection against fire. That being so, a member of the public may not maintain an action under Lawrence v. Fox against one contracting with the city to furnish water at the hydrants, unless an intention appears that the promisor is to be answerable to individual members of the public as well as to the city for any loss ensuing from the failure to fulfill the promise. No such intention is discernible here. On the contrary, the contract here is significantly divided into two branches: One a promise to the city for the benefit of the city in its corporate capacity, in which branch is included the service at the hydrants; and the other a promise to the city for the benefit of private takers, in which branch is included the service at their homes and factories. In a broad sense it is true that every city contract, not improvident or wasteful, is for the benefit of the public. More than this, however, must be shown to give a right of action to a member of the public not formally a party. The benefit, as it is sometimes said, must be one that is not merely incident and secondary. It must be primary and immediate in such a sense and to such a degree as to bespeak the assumption of a duty to make reparation directly to the individual members of the public if the benefit is lost. The field of obligation would be expanded beyond reasonable limits if less than this were demanded as a condition of liability. A promisor undertakes to supply fuel for heating a public building. He is not liable for breach of contract to a visitor who finds the building without fuel, and thus contracts a cold. . . .

[Cardozo then notes that the overwhelming authority treats the benefit to the public under these contracts as incidental and secondary.] An intention to assume an obligation of indefinite extension to every member of the public is seen to be the more improbable when we recall the crushing burden that the obligation would impose. . . . If the plaintiff is to prevail, one who negligently omits to supply sufficient pressure to extinguish a fire started by another assumes an obligation to pay the ensuing damage, though the whole city is laid low. A promisor will not be deemed to have had in mind the assumption of a risk so overwhelming for any trivial reward. . . .

(2) We think the action is not maintainable as one for a common-law tort.

"It is ancient learning that one who assumes to act, even though gratuitously, may thereby become subject to the duty of acting carefully, if he acts at all" (Glanzer v. Shepard, 233 N.Y. 236, 239 [1922]). The plaintiff would bring its case within the orbit of that principle. The hand once set to a task may not always be withdrawn with impunity though liability would fail if it had never been applied at all. A time-honored formula often phrases the distinction as one between misfeasance and nonfeasance. Incomplete the formula is, and so at times misleading. Given a relation involving in its existence a duty of care irrespective of a contract, a tort may result as well from acts of omission as of commission in the fulfillment of the duty thus recognized by law. What we need to know is not so much the conduct to be avoided when the relation and its attendant duty are established as existing. What we need to know is the conduct that engenders the relation. It is here that the formula, however incomplete, has its value and significance. If conduct has gone forward to such a stage that inaction would commonly result, not negatively merely in withholding a benefit, but positively or actively in working an injury, there exists a relation out of which arises a duty to go forward. So the surgeon who operates without pay is liable though his negligence is in the omission to sterilize his instruments; the engineer, though his fault is in the failure to shut off steam; the maker of automobiles, at the suit of some one other than the buyer, though his negligence is merely in inadequate inspection (*MacPherson*). The query always is whether the putative wrongdoer has advanced to such a point as to have launched a force or instrument of harm, or has stopped where inaction is at most a refusal to become an instrument for good.

The plaintiff would have us hold that the defendant, when once it entered upon the performance of its contract with the city, was brought into such a relation with every one who might potentially be benefited through the supply of water at the hydrants as to give to negligent performance, without reasonable notice of a refusal to continue, the quality of a tort. . . . We are satisfied that liability would be unduly and indeed indefinitely extended by this enlargement of the zone of duty. The dealer in coal who is to supply fuel for a shop must then answer to the customers if fuel is lacking. The manufacturer of goods, who enters upon the performance of his contract, must answer, in that view, not only to the buyer, but to those who to his knowledge are looking to the buyer for their own sources of supply. Everyone making a promise having the quality of a contract will be under a duty to the promisee by virtue of the promise, but under another duty, apart from contract, to an indefinite number of potential beneficiaries when performance has begun. The assumption of one relation will mean the involuntary assumption of a series of new relations, inescapably hooked together. Again we may say in the words of the Supreme Court of the United States: "The law does not spread its protection so far" (Robins Dry Dock & Repair Co. v. Flint, 275 U.S. 303 [1927]; cf. Byrd v. English, 117 Ga. 191 [1903]). We do not need to determine now what remedy, if any, there might be if the defendant had withheld the water or reduced the pressure with a malicious intent to do injury to the plaintiff or another. We put aside also the problem that would arise if there had been reckless and wanton indifference to consequences measured and foreseen. Difficulties would be present even then, but they need not now perplex us. What we are dealing with at this time is a mere negligent omission, unaccompanied by malice or other aggravating elements. The failure in such circumstances to furnish an adequate supply of water is at most the denial of a benefit. It is not the commission of a wrong.

(3) We think the action is not maintainable as one for the breach of a statutory duty.

The defendant, a public service corporation, is subject to the provisions of the Transportation Corporations Act. The duty imposed upon it by that act is in substance to furnish water, upon demand by the inhabitants, at reasonable rates, through suitable connections at office, factory or dwelling, and to furnish water at like rates through hydrants or in public buildings upon demand by the city, all according to its capacity. We find nothing in these requirements to enlarge the zone of liability where an inhabitant of the city suffers indirect or incidental damage through deficient pressure at the hydrants. The breach of duty in any case is to the one to whom service is denied at the time and at the place where services to such one is due. The denial, though wrongful, is unavailing without more to give a cause of action to another. We may find a helpful analogy in the law of common carriers. A railroad company is under a duty to supply reasonable facilities for carriage at reasonable rates. It is liable, generally speaking, for breach of a duty imposed by law if it refuses to accept merchandise tendered by a shipper. The fact that its duty is of this character does not make it liable to some one else who may be counting upon the prompt delivery of the merchandise to save him from loss in going forward with his work. If the defendant may not be held for a tort at common law, we find no adequate reason for a holding that it may be held under the statute.

The judgment should be affirmed with costs.

NOTES

1. ***The Privity Limitation and the Waterworks Cases.*** *Moch* represents an uneasy mixture of a gratuitous and a commercial transaction. On the one hand, the contract required

the city to reimburse the water company for the services it provided. On the other hand, the plaintiff, a stranger to the contract, did not pay for any services even as a taxpayer of the local community that funded the contract. Cardozo addresses both sides of the dilemma. He first refuses to treat the plaintiff as a third-party beneficiary. He then refuses as a matter of tort or statutory law to impose upon the defendant a duty to act carefully toward the plaintiff in what is, as to it, a gratuitous undertaking.

The decision has met with divided reviews. It was criticized in Seavey, Reliance upon Gratuitous Promises or Other Conduct, 64 Harv. L. Rev. 913, 920–21 (1951), on the ground that

> it is difficult to differentiate this type of case from that where a person has negligently broken a water main and is held responsible for harm caused by the consequent lack of pressure. The earlier cases, however, were decided at a time when nonfeasance and lack of privity were sufficient to prevent liability and the subsequent cases have followed these precedents. Even Cardozo, in what is perhaps his most unsatisfactory opinion in the field of torts, rested his decision, in part, upon the nonfeasance of the waterworks company.

Similarly, Abraham & Kendrick, There's No Such Thing as Affirmative Duty, 104 Iowa L. Rev. 1649, 1671 (2019), questions *Moch*'s distinction between misfeasance and nonfeasance:

> One way [*Moch*] has been justified is to argue that plaintiff was no worse off than he would have been in the absence of defendant: "Had the defendant water company never existed—had there been no water promised to the city—plaintiff's building would have burned just the same." . . . Those justifying *Moch* seem to assume that the relevant counterfactual is a city with no water service. But why is that the relevant comparison? It is not even a plausible one. This explanation does not provide a neutral basis for determining when a duty of care exists and when it does not or for distinguishing misfeasance from mere nonfeasance.

In contrast, Gregory, Gratuitous Undertakings and the Duty of Care, 1 DePaul L. Rev. 30, 59–60 (1951), defended *Moch* on the grounds that it placed the burden of the loss on the fire insurance companies who would otherwise assert their subrogation rights—which allow them to stand in the shoes of their insureds after paying the underlying claims—against the water company. "Cardozo thought the sum of $42.50 [$765 in 2023 dollars] insufficient to warrant the conclusion that a negligent water company should be made to relieve a fire insurance company from bearing the ultimate risk of loss by fire. . . ." Would Gregory's logic preclude liability even if the water company's own employee accidentally broke the water main while making repairs?

Should the plaintiff in *Moch* be able to recover on the strength of RTT: LPEH §42(a) or (b), *supra*, given that the breakdown in services was in the water supply to the plaintiff's neighbor? RTT: LPEH §42, comment *f* observes: "This [reliance] requirement is often met because the plaintiff or another relied on the actor's performing the undertaking in a nonnegligent manner and declined to pursue an alternative means for protection."

Note that the comments to the Third Restatement explicitly question *Moch's* nonfeasance rationale:

> The difficulty with [*Moch*] is that the provision of utilities fundamentally changes the landscape, creating an expectation of and reliance on continued service. When the utility ceases to supply service, the omission is much like ceasing to provide warning signals at a railroad crossing. Put another way, reliance on the utility's continuing to provide its services is a cause of the harm. Moreover, the policies supporting the no-duty-to-rescue rule do not apply to a commercial enterprise that is engaged in the business of supplying services to customers.
>
> The better explanation for limitations on the duty of public utilities is concern about the huge magnitude of liability to which a utility might be exposed from a single failure to provide service that affects hundreds, thousands, or, in the case of an electrical blackout, millions of people. In addition, when the harm is property damage, often the plaintiff will have first-party insurance that covers the loss.

2. ***Judicial Developments Since Moch.*** Judicial developments since *Moch* largely anticipated the uneasiness now expressed in the Third Restatement. Most notably, in Doyle v. South Pittsburgh Water Co., 199 A.2d 875, 878 (Pa. 1964), Musmanno, J., held that waterworks cases fell

New York City blackout of 1977

Source: Dan Farrell / New York Daily News Archive via Getty Images

> squarely within the rule that where a party to a contract assumes a duty to the other party to the contract, and it is foreseeable that a breach of that duty will cause injury to some third person not a party to the contract, the contracting party owes a duty to all those falling within the foreseeable orbit of risk of harm.

New York courts, however, have followed *Moch*. Strauss v. Belle Realty Co., 482 N.E.2d 34, 38 (N.Y. 1985), arose out of the great New York City power failure of 1977, for which the defendant, Consolidated Edison, had been found grossly negligent. The power failure cut off the pumps used to circulate water upstairs in the defendant Belle Realty's building. The plaintiff, a seventy-seven-year-old tenant in Belle's building, was injured when he fell in the dark on some defective basement stairs in search of water. Both the plaintiff and Belle were customers of Con Ed, but only Belle had a contract with the utility. The court refused to extend the utility's liability in negligence to the plaintiff tenant:

> [W]e deal here with a system-wide power failure occasioned by what has already been determined to be the utility's gross negligence. If liability could be found here, then in logic and fairness the same result must follow in many similar situations. For example, a tenant's guests and invitees, as well as persons making deliveries or repairing equipment in the building, are equally persons who must use the common areas, and for whom they are maintained. Customers of a store and occupants of an office building stand in much the same position with respect to Con Edison as tenants of an apartment building. In all cases the numbers are to a certain extent limited and defined, and while identities may change, so do those of apartment dwellers. While limiting recovery to customers in this instance can hardly be said to confer immunity from negligence on Con Edison, permitting recovery to those in plaintiff's circumstances would, in our view, violate the court's responsibility to define an orbit of duty that places controllable limits on liability. . . .

3. ***Affirmative Duties and the Role of Insurance.*** The availability of insurer's subrogation rights led to a partial retreat from Cardozo's no-duty rule in Weinberg v. Dinger, 524 A.2d 366, 378 (N.J. 1987). The court first noted its concern with the high insurance costs that water companies might have to bear, and wrote as follows:

> We believe that the imposition on a water company of liability for subrogation claims of carriers who pay fire losses caused by the company's negligent failure to maintain adequate water pressure would inevitably result in higher water rates paid by the class of consumers that paid for the fire insurance. The result of imposing subrogation-claim liability on water companies in such cases would be to shift the risk from the fire-insurance company to the water company, and, ultimately, to the consumer in the form of increased water rates. Thus, the consumer

would pay twice—first for property insurance premiums, and then in the form of higher water rates to fund the cost of the water company's liability insurance. We find this result contrary to public policy.

Accordingly, we abrogate the water company's immunity for losses caused by the negligent failure to maintain adequate water pressure for fire fighting only to the extent of claims that are uninsured or underinsured. To the extent that such claims are insured and thereby assigned to the insurance carrier as required by statute, *N.J.S.A.* 17:36-5:20, we hold that the carrier's subrogation claims are unenforceable against the water company.

Note that the water company contract at issue in *Weinberg* provided as follows:

> 8. The Company will use due diligence at all times to provide continuous service of the character or quality proposed to be supplied but in case the service shall be interrupted or irregular or defective or fail, the Company shall be liable and obligated only to use reasonably diligent efforts in light of the circumstances then existing to restore or correct its characteristics. . . .
>
> 10. The standard terms and conditions contained in this tariff are a part of every contract for service entered into by the Company and govern all classes of service where applicable.

What should be the result if homeowner fire insurance contracts are redrafted to deny coverage for fires that the water company could avoid by exercising due care?

The tariff limitation referred to above played a prominent role in Los Angeles Cellular Telephone Company v. Superior Court (Spielholz RPI), 76 Cal. Rptr. 2d 894 (Ct. App. 1998). Spielholz could not get a connection on the defendant's cellular system to call 911 as she was pursued by two men, one of whom subsequently shot her. The defendant company interposed its tariff that had been approved by the state's Public Utility Commission. That tariff explicitly and unambiguously limited the defendant's liability to $5,000 ($9,441 in 2023 dollars) per incident. The court, without resort to common law principles of nonfeasance, unhesitatingly applied the damage limitation noting: "A condition imposed by a tariff binds a utility's customers without regard to whether a contract is signed by the customer and without regard to the customer's actual knowledge of the tariff." Would *Moch* have come out the same way if its tariff had contained a similar dollar maximum?

In Laprocina v. Lourie, 250 A.3d 1281, 1289 (R.I. 2021), the court upheld a tariff limitation on liability to deny recovery where the plaintiff pedestrian was struck by a car on a road made unduly dark by an inoperable streetlight. The utility's tariff, in addition to disclaiming injury liability, further outsourced the duty to inspect streetlights onto the city. Goldberg, J., wrote:

> If [the utility] were to be held liable to third parties for incidents allegedly caused, in part, by inoperable streetlights, then it would be required to alter its business operations by inspecting, maintaining, and replacing thousands of streetlights on hundreds of streets in the city. . . . At night, motor vehicles generally are driven with headlights illuminating the way; therefore, it is unlikely that a single inoperable streetlight will be a substantial factor in causing a collision[.]

By contrast, Tyus v. Indianapolis Power & Light Co., 134 N.E.3d 389, 395 (Ind. Ct. App. 2019), allowed a negligence claim against a utility to proceed despite a tariff limitation. There, a fallen tree cut off power to an intersection resulting in disrupted service to its stop lights. "[E]ight hours after the traffic signals initially went black, the Intersection and its surrounding street lights were still completely without power and there was no traffic control at the Intersection," which resulted in the plaintiff's vehicle getting "t-boned" there. Kirsch, J., wrote, "[P]rivatization of a governmental service is not a farce in which the privatized entity enjoys the benefits both of not being the state and so being freed from the regulations that constrain state agencies, and of being the state and so being immune from suit."

SECTION E. SPECIAL RELATIONSHIPS

RESTATEMENT (SECOND) OF TORTS

§315. General Principle

There is no duty so to control the conduct of a third person as to prevent him from causing physical harm to another unless

(a) a special relation exists between the actor and the third person which imposes a duty upon the actor to control the third person's conduct, or

(b) a special relation exists between the actor and the other which gives the other a right to protection.

NOTE

On the Borderland of Nonfeasance. In Weirum v. RKO General Inc., 539 P.2d 36, 40–41 (Cal. 1975), the defendant's disk jockey, the Real Don Steele, staged a novel promotional contest. He drove around town announcing that he "had bread to spread" and gave his street location on the air. The first contestant to reach that location and answer some simple quiz questions correctly won small prizes. Two teenage drivers got into an eighty-miles-per-hour drag race in an effort to reach Steele at his new location and forced decedent's car off the highway, where it overturned, killing him. The California Court of Appeal, over a dissent, reversed the plaintiff's judgment against the radio station, holding that the station "had no control, or right to control, over the conduct of the drivers of other cars on the highway." 119 Cal. Rptr. 468 (Ct. App. 1975). The California Supreme Court unanimously reinstated the plaintiff's judgment, insisting that imposing liability here did not open up a Pandora's box:

> We are not persuaded that the imposition of a duty here will lead to unwarranted extensions of liability. Defendant is fearful that entrepreneurs will henceforth be burdened with an avalanche of obligations: an athletic department will owe a duty to an ardent sports fan injured while hastening to purchase one of a limited number of tickets; a department store will be liable to injuries incurred in response to a "while-they-last" sale. This argument, however, suffers from a myopic view of the facts presented here. The giveaway contest was no commonplace invitation to an attraction available on a limited basis. It was a competitive scramble in which the thrill of the chase to be the one and only victor was intensified by the live broadcasts which accompanied the pursuit. In the assertedly analogous situations described by defendant, any haste involved in the purchase of the commodity is an incidental and unavoidable result of the scarcity of the commodity itself. In such situations there is no attempt, as here, to generate a competitive pursuit on public streets, accelerated by repeated importuning by radio to be the very first to arrive at a particular destination. Manifestly the "spectacular" bears little resemblance to daily commercial activities.

The court then rebuffed an effort to limit liability under RST §315, noting that its main purpose was to codify the common law "Good Samaritan rule" applicable to cases of nonfeasance only:

> Here, there can be little doubt that we review an act of misfeasance to which section 315 is inapplicable. Liability is not predicated upon defendant's failure to intervene for the benefit of decedent but rather upon its creation of an unreasonable risk of harm to him. Defendant's reliance upon cases which involve the failure to prevent harm to another is therefore misplaced. . . .

Kline v. 1500 Massachusetts Avenue Apartment Corp.

439 F.2d 477 (D.C. Cir. 1970)

Wilkey, J. The appellee apartment corporation states that there is "only one issue presented for review . . . whether a duty should be placed on a landlord to take steps to protect tenants from foreseeable criminal acts committed by third parties." The District Court as a matter of law held that there is no such duty. We find that there is, and that in the circumstances here the applicable standard of care was breached. We therefore reverse and remand to the District Court for the determination of damages for the appellant.

I

The appellant, Sarah B. Kline, sustained serious injuries when she was criminally assaulted and robbed at approximately 10:15 in the evening by an intruder in the common hallway of an apartment house at 1500 Massachusetts Avenue. This facility, into which the appellant Kline moved in October 1959, is a large apartment building with approximately 585 individual apartment units. It has a main entrance on Massachusetts Avenue, with side entrances on both 15th and 16th Streets. At the time the appellant first signed a lease a doorman was on duty at the main entrance twenty-four hours a day, and at least one employee at all times manned a desk in the lobby from which all persons using the elevators could be observed. The 15th Street door adjoined the entrance to a parking garage used by both the tenants and the public. Two garage attendants were stationed at this dual entranceway; the duties of each being arranged so that one of them always was in position to observe those entering either the apartment building or the garage. The 16th Street entrance was unattended during the day but was locked after 9:00 p.m.

By mid-1966, however, the main entrance had no doorman, the desk in the lobby was left unattended much of the time, the 15th Street entrance was generally unguarded due to a decrease in garage personnel, and the 16th Street entrance was often left unlocked all night. The entrances were allowed to be thus unguarded in the face of an increasing number of assaults, larcenies, and robberies being perpetrated against the tenants in and from the common hallways of the apartment building. These facts were undisputed. . . . The landlord had notice of these crimes and had in fact been urged by appellant Kline herself prior to the events leading to the instant appeal to take steps to secure the building.

Shortly after 10:00 p.m. on November 17, 1966, Miss Kline was assaulted and robbed just outside her apartment on the first floor above the street level of this 585 unit apartment building. This occurred only two months after Leona Sullivan, another female tenant, had been similarly attacked in the same commonway.

II

At the outset we note that of the crimes of violence, robbery, and assault which had been occurring with mounting frequency on the premises at 1500 Massachusetts Avenue, the assaults on Miss Kline and Miss Sullivan took place in the hallways of the building, which were under the exclusive control of the appellee landlord. Even in those crimes of robbery or assault committed in individual apartments, the intruders of necessity had to gain entrance through the common entry and passageways. These premises fronted on three heavily traveled streets, and had multiple entrances. The risk to be guarded against therefore was the risk of unauthorized entrance into the apartment house by intruders bent upon some crime of violence or theft.

While the apartment lessees themselves could take some steps to guard against this risk by installing extra heavy locks and other security devices on the doors and windows of their respective apartments, yet this risk in the greater part could only be guarded against by the landlord. No individual tenant had it within his power to take measures to guard the garage entranceways, to provide scrutiny at the main entrance of the building, to patrol the common hallways and elevators, to set up any kind of a security alarm system in the building, to provide additional locking devices on the main doors, to provide a system of announcement for authorized visitors only, to close the garage doors at appropriate hours, and to see that the entrance was manned at all times.

The risk of criminal assault and robbery on a tenant in the common hallways of the building was thus entirely predictable; that same risk had been occurring with increasing frequency over a period of several months immediately prior to the incident giving rise to this case; it was a risk whose prevention or minimization was almost entirely within the power of the landlord; and the risk materialized in the assault and robbery of appellant on November 17, 1966.

III

In this jurisdiction, certain duties have been assigned to the landlord because of his *control* of common hallways, lobbies, stairwells, etc., used by all tenants in multiple dwelling units. This Court in Levine v. Katz, 407 F.2d 303, 304 (D.C. Cir. 1968), pointed out that:

> It has long been well settled in this jurisdiction that, where a landlord leases separate portions of property and reserves under his own control the halls, stairs, or other parts of the property for use in common by all tenants, he has a duty to all those on the premises of legal right to use ordinary care and diligence to maintain the retained parts in a reasonably safe condition.

While Levine v. Katz dealt with a physical defect in the building leading to the plaintiff's injury, the rationale as applied to predictable criminal acts by third parties is the same. The duty is the landlord's because by his control of the areas of common use and common danger he is the only party who has the *power* to make the necessary repairs or to provide the necessary protection.

As a general rule, a private person does not have a duty to protect another from a criminal attack by a third person. We recognize that this rule has sometimes in the past been applied in landlord-tenant law, even by this court. Among the reasons for the application of this rule to landlords are: judicial reluctance to tamper with the traditional common law concept of the landlord-tenant relationship; the notion that the act of a third person in committing an intentional tort or crime is a superseding cause of the harm to another resulting therefrom; the oftentimes difficult problem of determining foreseeability of criminal acts; the vagueness of the standard which the landlord must meet; the economic consequences of the imposition of the duty; and conflict with the public policy allocating the duty of protecting citizens from criminal acts to the government rather than the private sector.

But the rationale of this very broad general rule falters when it is applied to the conditions of modern day urban apartment living, particularly in the circumstances of this case. The rationale of the general rule exonerating a third party from any duty to protect another from a criminal attack has no applicability to the landlord-tenant relationship in multiple dwelling houses. The landlord is no insurer of his tenants' safety, but he certainly is no bystander. And where, as here, the landlord has notice of repeated criminal assaults and robberies, has notice that these crimes occurred in the portion of the premises exclusively within his control, has every reason to expect like crimes to happen again, and has the exclusive power to take preventive action, it does not seem unfair to place upon the landlord a duty to take those steps which are within his power to minimize the predictable risk to his tenants. . . .

In the case at bar we place the duty of taking protective measures guarding the entire premises and the areas peculiarly under the landlord's control against the perpetration of criminal acts upon the landlord, the party to the lease contract who has the effective capacity to perform these necessary acts.

[The court then notes that innkeepers were held liable to their guests for assaults and molestations by third parties, "be they innkeeper's employees, fellow guests or intruders."] Other relationships in which similar duties have been imposed include landowner-invitee, businessman-patron, employer-employee, school district-pupil, hospital-patient, and carrier-passenger. In all, the theory of liability is essentially the same: that since the ability of one of the parties to provide for his own protection has been limited in some way by his submission to the control of the other, a duty should be imposed upon the one possessing control (and thus the power to act) to take reasonable precautions to protect the other one from assaults by third parties which, at least, could reasonably have been anticipated. However, there is no liability normally imposed upon the one having the power to act if the violence is sudden and unexpected provided that the source of the violence is not an employee of the one in control.

We are aware of various cases in other jurisdictions following a different line of reasoning, conceiving of the landlord and tenant relationship along more traditional common law lines, and on varying fact situations reaching a different result from that we reach here. Typical of these is a much cited (although only a 4-3) decision of the Supreme Court of New Jersey, Goldberg v. Housing Authority of Newark [186 A.2d 291 (N.J. 1962)], relied on by appellee landlord here. There the court said:

> Everyone can foresee the commission of crime virtually anywhere and at any time. If foreseeability itself gave rise to a duty to provide "police" protection for others, every residential curtilage, every shop, every store, every manufacturing plant would have to be patrolled by the private arm of the owner. And since hijacking and attack upon occupants of motor vehicles are also foreseeable, it would be the duty of every motorist to provide armed protection for his passengers and the property of others. Of course, none of this is at all palatable.

This language seems to indicate that the court was using the word *foreseeable* interchangeably with the word *possible.* In that context, the statement is quite correct. It would be folly to impose liability for mere possibilities. But we must reach the question of liability for attacks which are foreseeable in the sense that they are *probable* and *predictable*. . . . As between tenant and landlord, the landlord is the only one in the position to take the necessary acts of protection required. He is not an insurer, but he is obligated to minimize the risk to his tenants. Not only as between landlord and tenant is the landlord best equipped to guard against the predictable risk of intruders, but even as between landlord and the police power of government, the landlord is in the best position to take the necessary protective measures. Municipal police cannot patrol the entryways and the hallways, the garages and the basements of private multiple unit apartment dwellings. They are neither equipped, manned, nor empowered to do so. In the area of the predictable risk which materialized in this case, only the landlord could have taken measures which might have prevented the injuries suffered by appellant.

We note that in the fight against crime the police are not expected to do it all; every segment of society has obligations to aid in law enforcement and to minimize the opportunities for crime. . . .

IV

We now turn to the standard of care which should be applied in judging if the landlord has fulfilled his duty of protection to the tenant. Although in many cases the language speaks as if the standard of care itself varies, in the last analysis the standard of care is the same—reasonable care in all the circumstances. . . .

We therefore hold in this case that the applicable standard of care in providing protection for the tenant is that standard which this landlord himself was employing in October 1959 when the appellant became a resident on the premises at 1500 Massachusetts Avenue. The tenant was led to expect that she could rely upon this degree of protection. While we do not say that the precise measures for security which were then in vogue should have been kept up (e.g., the number of people at the main entrances might have been reduced if a tenant-controlled intercom-automatic latch system had been installed in the common entryways), we do hold that the same relative degree of security should have been maintained.

V

[The court then holds that liability was "clear" on the face of the record and remanded the case to the district court on the issue of damages only.]

Having said this, it would be well to state what is *not* said by this decision. We do not hold that the landlord is by any means an insurer of the safety of his tenants. His duty is to take those measures of protection which are within his power and capacity to take, and which can reasonably be expected to mitigate the risk of intruders assaulting and robbing tenants. The landlord is not expected to provide protection commonly owed by a municipal police department; but as illustrated in this case, he is obligated to protect those parts of his premises which are not usually subject to periodic patrol and inspection by the municipal police. We do not say that every multiple unit apartment house in the District of Columbia should have those same measures of protection which 1500 Massachusetts Avenue enjoyed in 1959, nor do we say that 1500 Massachusetts Avenue should have precisely those same measures in effect at the present time. Alternative and more up-to-date methods may be equally or even more effective.

Granted, the discharge of this duty of protection by landlords will cause, in many instances, the expenditure of large sums for additional equipment and services, and granted, the cost will be ultimately passed on to the tenant in the form of increased rents. This prospect, in itself, however, is no deterrent to our acknowledging and giving force to the duty, since without protection the tenant already pays in losses from theft, physical assault and increased insurance premiums.

The landlord is entirely justified in passing on the cost of increased protective measures to his tenants, but the rationale of compelling the landlord to do it in the first place is that he is the only one who is in a position to take the necessary protective measures for overall protection of the premises, which he owns in whole and rents in part to individual tenants.

Reversed and remanded to the District Court for the determination of damages.

MacKinnon, J., dissenting. [The dissent first argues that liability was not established on the record, so that the case should, even on the court's view of the substantive law, be retried de novo, because the evidence on the number and frequency of previous criminal attacks was insufficient, given that only one of the 20 incidents involved both an assault and robbery. It also argues that the notice to the landlord was only of theft, and that there was no evidence in the record that the landlord knew of the previous assault upon Leona Sullivan. It continues:]

The evidence introduced by the plaintiff is also deficient in my opinion in not proving that the alleged negligence was the proximate cause of the assault or that it contributed to it in any way. Plaintiff's evidence did not negate that it was a tenant, guest or person properly on the property who committed the offense, and while the panel opinion throughout asserts that an "intruder" committed the offense, there is no proof of that fact. So plaintiff's evidence failed to prove a nexus between the alleged deficiencies of the appellee and the cause of any damage to appellant. . . .

As for the claim that appellant was led to believe she would get the same standard of protection in 1966 that was furnished in 1959, there is obviously nothing to this point. She was not led to expect that. She personally observed the changes which occurred in this respect. They were obvious to her each day of her life. And since her original lease had terminated and her tenancy in 1966 was on a month to month basis, whatever contract existed was created at the beginning of the month and since there was no evidence of any alteration in the security precautions during the current month, there is no basis for any damage claim based on contract. . . .

In my opinion the decision in Goldberg v. Housing Authority of Newark, 186 A.2d 291 (N.J. 1962), answers all appellant's arguments. It is just too much, absent a contractual agreement, to require or expect a combination office-apartment building such as is involved here to provide police patrol protection or its equivalent in the block-long, well-lighted passageways. Yet nothing short of that will meet the second guessing standard of protection the panel opinion practically directs. If tenants expect such protection, they can move to apartments where it is available and presumably pay a higher rental, but it is a mistake in my judgment to hold an office-apartment building to such a requirement when the tenant knew for years that such protection was not being afforded.

NOTES

1. ***Contract or Special Relationship?*** If the defendant landlord could have taken effective steps to prevent crimes in common areas at a lower cost than its tenants, why didn't it assume that liability in its standard residential lease? If it made that promise voluntarily, could it impose a cap on damages similar to that upheld in *Los Angeles Cellular*, *supra* at 431? In dealing with the contract alternative, should the court in *Kline* take into account administrative costs? Contributory negligence? Error rates in litigation?

Whatever the correct answer to these questions, *Kline* has been met with widespread approval insofar as it reverses the older common law rule that imposed no duty on a landlord to shield tenants from criminal attacks. Nonetheless, with stepped-up security precautions, it is now more difficult for plaintiffs to avoid summary judgment under the *Kline* rule.

2. ***Heightened Foreseeability.*** One key issue in *Kline* involves the necessary specificity of the foresight requirement. It is agreed on all sides that the test is far more stringent than it was in the *Wagon Mound* line of cases, *supra* Chapter 5, at 354, where the defendants did cause or create the dangerous condition that resulted in harm. In Sigmund v. Starwood Urban Retail VI, LLC, 617 F.3d 512, 516 (D.C. Cir. 2010), the defendant operated a garage in an office building in which a car was parked that was owned by the plaintiff's father. The plaintiff's half-brother, Prescott, who had the keys to the car, had plotted to kill the plaintiff's father with a car bomb in order to gain an inheritance of some $300,000. One day, Prescott sensed the "opportunity he had been looking for" when the overhead garage door was locked in the open position. Prescott snuck into the garage and planted the bomb in the car. When the plaintiff, instead of his father, came to retrieve the car, the bomb exploded and caused the injuries for which the plaintiff sued. Prescott was sentenced to thirty-two years in prison.

In disallowing the plaintiff's claim, Garland, J., distinguished *Kline*:

> Sigmund cannot satisfy the heightened foreseeability standard required by the D.C. Court of Appeals. Although he need not show previous occurrences of the particular type of harm that befell him, he must show the defendants' increased awareness of the danger of a particular criminal act. In the context of an intervening criminal act involving the discharge of a weapon — and, a fortiori, of a pipe bomb — the requirement of precise proof of a heightened showing of foreseeability is particularly demanding. Sigmund must establish that [the defendants] had an increased awareness of the risk *of a violent, armed assault* in the parking garage.

> Needless to say, there is no history of car bombings at 5225 Wisconsin Avenue. Nor is there any history of homicides, or assaults with intent to kill on the premises. In fact, in the six-and-a-half years preceding the bombing, there were only four crimes reported in the garage, none of which involved an assault of any kind. And, of all of the crimes reported at the building during that period, only four were crimes against persons, none involving a violent, armed assault resulting in any serious injury to the victim. . . . In 2001 and 2002, there were no crimes against persons reported at the building at all.

3. *Proximate Causation.* The issues of proximate causation stressed in MacKinnon's, J., dissent explicitly surfaced in Burgos v. Aqueduct Realty Corp., 706 N.E.2d 1163, 1166 (N.Y. 1998). The plaintiff was leaving her apartment unit when she was forced back into it by two men who beat and robbed her. In her action against the landlord for inadequate security, Kaye, C.J., held:

> [T]he necessary causal link between a landlord's culpable failure to provide adequate security and a tenant's injuries resulting from a criminal attack in the building can be established only if the assailant gained access to the premises through a negligently maintained entrance. . . . Without such a requirement, landlords would be exposed to liability for virtually all criminal activity in their buildings. By the same token, because victims of criminal assaults often cannot identify their attackers, a blanket rule precluding recovery whenever the attacker remains unidentified would place an impossible burden on tenants.

Kaye, C.J., then held that the plaintiff could satisfy her burden of proof on the causation issue by testifying first that the assailants did not wear masks and then that none of the building's entrances had functioning locks. What about the possibility that friends of tenants had assaulted the plaintiff?

4. *The Expansion of Liability.* The new liability first raised in *Kline* has generated a flood of subsequent litigation about institutional responsibilities to protect against criminal acts.

a. ***Colleges and Universities.*** In Peterson v. San Francisco Community College District, 685 P.2d 1193, 1197 (Cal. 1984), the California Supreme Court held that a community college district had a duty to protect a college student against a foreseeable criminal assault that took place in broad daylight on campus—here, on a stairway in a parking lot—on the strength of its special relationship with the student. The plaintiff reached the jury on two counts of negligence: first, had the defendant properly trimmed the hedge and foliage that concealed the perpetrator before he committed the crime and, second, did the school have a duty to warn the plaintiff about the hazards it left uncorrected. How might such a warning be given? Be updated?

Peterson was applied in Regents of Univ. of California v. Superior Court, 413 P.3d 656, 660, 665 (Cal. 2018), where a hallucinatory student, Damon Thompson, stabbed a female student in a chemistry lab. Thompson had constant run-ins with university officials over academic and behavioral issues in classes and dormitories. Corrigan, J., wrote:

> Considering the unique features of the college environment, we conclude postsecondary schools *do* have a special relationship with students while they are engaged in activities that are part of the school's curriculum or closely related to its delivery of educational services. . . . Along with educational services, colleges provide students social, athletic, and cultural opportunities. Regardless of the campus layout, colleges provide a discrete community for their students. For many students, college is the first time they have lived away from home.

In contrast, Helfman v. Northeastern Univ., 149 N.E.3d 758, 767 (Mass. 2020), tightened the requirements for suit against universities in the context of sexual assaults. There, the plaintiff and a male student got drunk at a party hosted by a university residential assistant in the university dorms. The male student walked the plaintiff freshman back to her dorm. The plaintiff alleged that he then initiated unwanted sexual contact, for which she sought to hold the university liable. Lenk, J., recognized the special student-university relationship only to dismiss the claim: "Northeastern had no duty to take steps to prevent the alleged sexual assault, because it was not reasonably foreseeable that the plaintiff would suffer a criminal act by a third party or other imminent physical harm due to her intoxication at the time of the incident." Is that correct? How would an average college student foresee this event occurring?

b. ***Common Carriers.*** In Lopez v. Southern California Rapid Transit District, 710 P.2d 907, 910–11 (Cal. 1985), the California Supreme Court held that a duty of care in favor of public transit passengers would not impose a "colossal financial burden" on a public transportation district. Even without demanding "an armed security guard on every bus," the district could train drivers to eject unruly passengers who did not heed warnings to quiet down, to radio the police for assistance, or to equip buses with alarm lights to warn of threatened or actual criminal activity. Might such a duty threaten the safety of public transit personnel? More recently in Preston v. Greyhound Lines, Inc., No. C082571, 2018 WL 2676558, at *6 (Cal. Ct. App. 2018), the court reiterated that common carriers owe "a duty of utmost care" to protect passengers from assaults by fellow passengers, without becoming insurers of their safety.

c. ***Condominiums.*** In Frances T. v. Village Green Owners Association, 723 P.2d 573 (Cal. 1986), the plaintiff was "molested, raped and robbed" by an unidentified assailant who entered her condominium unit at night after the condominium board refused to allow the plaintiff to install lights by her unit for her own self-protection. The court extended the liability imposed on landlords in *Kline* to condominium boards and to their individual members who functioned as the de facto landlords of the premises. In dissent, Mosk, J., rejected any parallels between a condominium board and an ordinary landlord and denied the existence of special relationship between a condominium association and its unit members. Will potential liability deter association members from serving gratis on condominium boards? In yet another context, Desernio v. Ardelean, 188 A.D.3d 992 (N.Y. App. Div. 2020), read a condominium's bylaws to establish that it owed the plaintiff tenant a duty of care for personal injuries caused by exposure to toxic mold.

d. ***Shopping Malls.*** In Ann M. v. Pacific Plaza Shopping Center, 863 P.2d 207, 210, 215–16 (Cal. 1993), the court refused to allow the plaintiff, who had been raped inside her place of employment in the defendant's shopping mall, to sue her employer's landlord. The plaintiff's employer had signed a lease that gave the defendant exclusive control over all common areas. The plaintiff was raped when she was alone in her shop at around 8:00 A.M. by a customer who entered the store from the mall. There was some evidence that the tenants in the shopping mall had complained of lack of security and the presence of transients, but the merchants association decided not to hire walking guards because the tenants could not afford the prohibitive rent increases needed to fund the expenditures. Instead alternative arrangements were made for another security company to drive by three or four times a day. Panelli, J., concluded that

> a high degree of foreseeability is required in order to find that the scope of a landlord's duty of care includes the hiring of security guards. We further conclude that the requisite degree of foreseeability rarely, if ever, can be proven in the absence of prior similar incidents of violent crime on the landlord's premises. To hold otherwise would be to impose an unfair burden upon landlords and, in effect, would force landlords to become the insurers of public safety, contrary to well established policy in this state.

What if the tenants balked at rent increases after violent incidents were reported?

In Williams v. Fremont Corners, Inc., 250 Cal. Rptr. 3d 46 (Ct. App. 2019), a musician was assaulted in the parking lot of a shopping center after performing at a bar there. The court followed *Ann M.*'s high standard of foreseeability by denying that general knowledge of the possibility of violent crime met the standard, even after prior occurrences of a burglary and a broken window.

e. ***Off-Premises Liability.*** In twin cases, Delgado v. Trax Bar & Grill, 113 P.3d 1159 (Cal. 2005), and Morris v. De La Torre, 113 P.3d 1182, 1188 (Cal. 2005), restaurant patrons were attacked while leaving the premises in plain view of the restaurant employees. In *Delgado*, the defendant's bouncer did not accompany the plaintiffs to their car, and in *Morris*, the employees did not call 911 after a criminal assailant broke into the restaurant to steal a knife that he used to stab one of the plaintiffs. The court allowed both cases to go to the jury. In *Morris*, George, J., explicitly distinguished *Ann M.* by holding that, even if there is no special duty to provide security guards, under the heightened foreseeability standard "such a proprietor nevertheless owes a special-relationship-based duty to undertake reasonable and minimally burdensome measures to assist customers or invitees who face danger from imminent or ongoing criminal assaultive conduct occurring upon the premises."

In HNMC, Inc. v. Chan, 637 S.W.3d 919, 930–31 (Tex. App. 2021) (en banc), the court upheld a jury verdict in favor of a plaintiff whose decedent, upon crossing the public road separating the defendant's facility from its parking lot, was struck by a vehicle at a poorly maintained crosswalk. Poissant, J., explained:

> The record indicates that [the defendant] had superior knowledge of the risk because [it] was aware that [the] County abandoned the crosswalk where Chan was struck prior to Chan's injury. . . . The risk was increased by the design of HNMC's premises on both sides of the street. . . . [The defendant's] design included a concrete pad on both sides of the street from the sidewalk to the curb, directly aligning with . . . the faded but marked abandoned crosswalk where [the decedent] was killed.

Jewell, J., dissented from the majority's focus on the design of premises adjacent to the site of the accident: "The majority's mischaracterization of the hazard distorts Texas's traditional approach to identifying unreasonably dangerous 'conditions.' When referencing a 'condition' of a premises, we speak of the 'state of being' of the property itself." He continued, "As to the utility, burden, and consequences of imposing a duty on the defendant, creating a duty to protect pedestrians from dangers inherent in crossing a street would impose a vast and substantial burden on millions of Texas property owners, which is not easily or reasonably justified."

But there are limits, as in Toomer v. United States, 615 F.3d 1233 (9th Cir. 2010), where a navy sailor who fought with another club patron at a dance club on his base was owed no duty of protection when he was shot and killed by that other patron when both parties were across the street from the base.

f. ***Other Duties on Occupiers and Service Providers.*** Other cases have been reluctant to extend *Kline* in new directions. In Verdugo v. Target Corp., 327 P.3d 774 (Cal. 2014), the court held that Target was under no duty to obtain and make available a defibrillator to a customer who died of a sudden cardiac arrest. The court noted that less than 10 percent of the persons treated for cardiac arrest before they reach a hospital survive. Similarly, in Sells v. CSX Transportation, Inc., 170 So. 3d 27 (Fla. Dist. Ct. App. 2015), the court concluded that "it would be a radical departure from the common law to require employers to ensure that their employees are available, capable, and willing to perform CPR on an injured co-employee while under the instruction of a 911 operator."

Most recently in Jane Doe No. 1 v. Uber Techs., Inc., 294 Cal. Rptr. 3d 664, 668 (Ct. App. 2022), several female passengers were abducted and sexually assaulted upon leaving nightclubs by assailants who, though not affiliated with Uber, had obtained Uber decals from the Uber website and affixed them to their vehicles to pose as authorized drivers and lure passengers into their vehicles. The plaintiffs sought to impose liability on the ground that respondent Uber had been warned by the authorities of this scheme occurring at venues similar to the plaintiffs' pickup locations yet still "negligently failed to warn the Jane Does about the fake Uber scheme, failed to implement additional safety precautions to protect them against third parties employing the fake Uber scheme, and concealed instances of sexual assault via the fake Uber scheme." Rothschild, P.J., rebuffed the claims:

> The complaint thus did not allege actionable nonfeasance. Nor does the complaint allege actionable misfeasance, because the Uber entities' alleged actions did not *create* the risk that criminals would take advantage of the existence of the Uber app to abduct and rape women trying to use it. Although it is foreseeable that third parties could abuse the platform in this way, such crime must be a "necessary component" of the Uber app or the Uber entities' actions in order for the Uber entities to be held liable, absent a special relationship between the parties.

Would the plaintiffs' assaults have happened if Uber had given them warning of the scheme upon fulfilling their ride requests?

g. ***Liability of Oversight Bodies.*** In Brown v. USA Taekwondo, 483 P.3d 159 (Cal. 2021), three female plaintiffs were training for the Olympic sport of taekwondo when they were repeatedly sexually abused by their coach Marc Gitelman, who upon discovery was first banned from coaching and then convicted of many felonies. The plaintiffs sued both USA Taekwondo (USAT) and the United States Olympic Committee (USOC) for negligence. Kruger, J., split the difference and held that the plaintiffs had a special relationship with USAT but not the USOC, which was one step further removed. The issue ultimately turned on control, which the USAT had over the coach but the USOC did not, making extensive reliance on the list of relevant factors for special relationships set out in *Rowland* and *Biakanja*, *supra* at 412–13, as reasons to depart from section 1714 of the California Civil Code. Both sources of liability have been extended far beyond the premise liability issue in *Rowland* itself, as further refined and applied in *Tarasoff*, the following case.

Tarasoff v. Regents of University of California
551 P.2d 334 (Cal. 1976)

Tobriner, J. On October 27, 1969, Prosenjit Poddar killed Tatiana Tarasoff. Plaintiffs, Tatiana's parents, allege that two months earlier Poddar confided his intention to kill Tatiana to Dr. Lawrence Moore, a psychologist employed by the Cowell Memorial Hospital at the University of California at Berkeley. They allege that on Moore's request, the campus police briefly detained Poddar, but released him when he appeared rational. They further claim that Dr. Harvey Powelson, Moore's superior, then directed that no further action be taken to detain Poddar.

[Elsewhere in the opinion, Tobriner, J., notes: "Poddar had persuaded Tatiana's brother to share an apartment with him near Tatiana's residence; shortly after her return from Brazil, Poddar went to her residence and killed her." By way of additional background, Poddar was an "untouchable" Bengali who at that time had little or no contact with women in India. He had come to Berkeley to study naval architecture and found it difficult to adapt to American mores. Tatiana was of Russian heritage, born in China and raised in Brazil, with a much more liberal upbringing. The trouble began when she kissed Poddar on New Year's Eve 1968, but thereafter was unresponsive to his attentions. She in turn had sexual relations with other men, which sent Poddar into a tailspin until his personal life and university work unraveled. He saw Dr. Moore some seven times, who diagnosed his condition as "paranoid schizophrenic reaction, acute and severe." Moore recommended that he be involuntarily committed for the safety of others. Moore's superior may have ordered him not to get further involved in the case. It is clear that no one took any steps to warn Tatiana of any danger. She returned from Brazil in September 1969, making Poddar's pain all the more acute. In late October 1969, Poddar tracked her to her family home, shot her with a pellet gun, and stabbed her seventeen times with a kitchen knife.*] No one warned plaintiffs of Tatiana's peril.

Concluding that these facts set forth causes of action against neither therapists and policemen involved, nor against the Regents of the University of California as their employer, the superior court sustained defendants' demurrers to plaintiffs' second amended complaints without leave to amend. This appeal ensued. . . .

Plaintiffs' complaints predicate liability on two grounds: defendants' failure to warn plaintiffs of the impending danger and their failure to bring about Poddar's confinement pursuant to the Lanterman-Petris-Short Act (Welf. & Inst. Code, §5000ff.). Defendants, in turn, assert that they owed no duty of reasonable care to Tatiana and that they are immune from suit under the California Tort Claims Act of 1963 (Gov. Code, §810ff.). . . .

2. Plaintiffs Can State a Cause of Action Against Defendant Therapists for Negligent Failure to Protect Tatiana

The second cause of action can be amended to allege that Tatiana's death proximately resulted from defendant's negligent failure to warn Tatiana or others likely to apprise her of her danger. Plaintiffs contend that as amended, such allegations of negligence and proximate causation, with resulting damages, establish a cause of action. Defendants, however, contend that in the circumstances of the present case they owed no duty of care to Tatiana or her parents and that, in the absence of such duty, they were free to act in careless disregard of Tatiana's life and safety.

In analyzing this issue, we bear in mind that legal duties are not discoverable facts of nature, but merely conclusory expressions that, in cases of a particular type, liability should be imposed for damage done. As stated in Dillon v. Legg, 441 P.2d 912, 916 (Cal. 1968): "The assertion that liability must . . . be denied because defendant bears no 'duty' to plaintiff 'begs the essential question—whether the plaintiff's interests are entitled to legal protection against the defendant's conduct. . . . [Duty] is not sacrosanct in itself, but only an expression of the sum total of those considerations of policy which lead the law to say that the particular plaintiff is entitled to protection.' (Prosser, Law of Torts [3d ed. 1964] at pp. 332-333.)"

[Tobriner, J., then explicitly relies on the general statements on duties to care from the landmark cases of Rowland v. Christian, *supra* at 412, and Heaven v. Pender, *supra* at 413, to conclude]: We depart from "this fundamental principle" only upon the "balancing of a number of considerations" major ones "are the foreseeability of harm to the plaintiff, the degree of certainty that the plaintiff suffered injury, the closeness of the connection between the defendant's conduct and the injury suffered, the moral blame attached to the defendant's conduct, the policy of preventing future harm, the extent of the burden to the defendant and consequences to the community of imposing a duty to exercise care with resulting liability for breach, and the availability, cost and prevalence of insurance for the risk involved."

The most important of these considerations in establishing duty is foreseeability. As a general principle, a "defendant owes a duty of care to all persons who are foreseeably endangered by his conduct, with respect to all risks which make the conduct unreasonably dangerous."

* These and other details are contained in Schuck & Givelber, *Tarasoff v. Regents of the University of California:* The Therapist's Dilemma, *in* Tort Stories 99 (Rabin & Sugarman eds., 2003).

As we shall explain, however, when the avoidance of foreseeable harm requires a defendant to control the conduct of another person, or to warn of such conduct, the common law has traditionally imposed liability only if the defendant bears some special relationship to the dangerous person or to the potential victim. Since the relationship between a therapist and his patient satisfies this requirement, we need not here decide whether foreseeability alone is sufficient to create a duty to exercise reasonable care to protect a potential victim of another's conduct.

Although, as we have stated above, under the common law, as a general rule, one person owed no duty to control the conduct of another the courts have carved out an exception to this rule[5] in cases in which the defendant stands in some special relationship to either the person whose conduct needs to be controlled or in a relationship to the foreseeable victim of that conduct. Applying this exception to the present case, we note that a relationship of defendant therapists to either Tatiana or Poddar will suffice to establish a duty of care [under RST §315, *supra* at 432].

Although plaintiff's pleadings assert no special relation between Tatiana and defendant therapists, they establish as between Poddar and defendant therapists the special relation that arises between a patient and his doctor or psychotherapist. Such a relationship may support affirmative duties for the benefit of third persons. Thus, for example, a hospital must exercise reasonable care to control the behavior of a patient which may endanger other persons.[7] A doctor must also warn a patient if the patient's condition or medication renders certain conduct, such as driving a car, dangerous to others.

Although the California decisions that recognize this duty have involved cases in which the defendant stood in a special relationship *both* to the victim and to the person whose conduct created the danger,[9] we do not think that the duty should logically be constricted to such situations. Decisions of other jurisdictions hold that the single relationship of a doctor to his patient is sufficient to support the duty to exercise reasonable care to protect others against dangers emanating from the patient's illness. The courts hold that a doctor is liable to persons infected by his patient if he negligently fails to diagnose a contagious disease, or, having diagnosed the illness, fails to warn members of the patient's family.

Since it involved a dangerous mental patient, the decision in Merchants Nat. Bank & Trust Co. of Fargo v. United States, 272 F. Supp. 409 (D.N.D. 1967) comes closer to the issue. The Veterans Administration arranged for the patient to work on a local farm, but did not inform the farmer of the man's background. The farmer consequently permitted the

5. This rule derives from the common law's distinction between misfeasance and nonfeasance, and its reluctance to impose liability for the latter. (See Harper & Kime, The Duty to Control the Conduct of Another (1934) 43 Yale L.J. 886, 887). Morally questionable, the rule owes its survival to "the difficulties of setting any standards of unselfish service to fellow men, and of making any workable rule to cover possible situations where fifty people might fail to rescue. . . ." (Prosser, Torts (4th ed. 1971) §56, p. 341). Because of these practical difficulties, the courts have increased the number of instances in which affirmative duties are imposed not by direct rejection of the common law rule, but by expanding the list of special relationships which will justify departure from that rule.

7. When a "hospital has notice or knowledge of facts from which it might reasonably be concluded that a patient would be likely to harm himself *or others* unless preclusive measures were taken, then the hospital must use reasonable care in the circumstances to prevent such harm." (Vistica v. Presbyterian Hospital, 432 P.2d 193, 196 (Cal. 1967).) (Emphasis added.) A mental hospital may be liable if it negligently permits the escape or release of a dangerous patient. Greenberg v. Barbour (E.D. Pa. 1971) 322 F. Supp. 745, upheld a cause of action against a hospital staff doctor whose negligent failure to admit a mental patient resulted in that patient assaulting the plaintiff.

9. Ellis v. D'Angelo, 253 P.2d 675 (Cal. App. 1953), upheld a cause of action against parents who failed to warn a babysitter of the violent proclivities of their child; Johnson v. State of California, 447 P.2d 352 (Cal. 1968), upheld a suit against the state for failure to warn foster parents of the dangerous tendencies of their ward; Morgan v. City of Yuba, 41 Cal. Rptr. 508 (Cal. App. 1964), sustained a cause of action against a sheriff who had promised to warn decedent before releasing a dangerous prisoner, but failed to do so.

patient to come and go freely during nonworking hours; the patient borrowed a car, drove to his wife's residence and killed her. Notwithstanding the lack of any "special relationship" between the Veterans Administration and the wife, the court found the Veterans Administration liable for the wrongful death of the wife. . . .

Defendants contend, however, that imposition of a duty to exercise reasonable care to protect third persons is unworkable because therapists cannot accurately predict whether or not a patient will resort to violence. In support of this argument amicus representing the American Psychiatric Association and other professional societies cites numerous articles which indicate that therapists, in the present state of the art, are unable reliably to predict violent acts; their forecasts, amicus claims, tend consistently to overpredict violence, and indeed are more often wrong than right. Since predictions of violence are often erroneous, amicus concludes, the courts should not render rulings that predicate the liability of therapists upon the validity of such predictions. . . .

We recognize the difficulty that a therapist encounters in attempting to forecast whether a patient presents a serious danger of violence. Obviously we do not require that the therapist, in making that determination, render a perfect performance; the therapist need only exercise "that reasonable degree of skill, knowledge, and care ordinarily possessed and exercised by members of [that professional specialty] under similar circumstances." Within the broad range of reasonable practice and treatment in which professional opinion and judgment may differ, the therapist is free to exercise his or her own best judgment without liability; proof, aided by hindsight, that he or she judged wrongly is insufficient to establish negligence.

In the instant case, however, the pleadings do not raise any question as to failure of defendant therapists to predict that Poddar presented a serious danger of violence. On the contrary, the present complaints allege that defendant therapists did in fact predict that Poddar would kill, but were negligent in failing to warn.

Amicus contends, however, that even when a therapist does in fact predict that a patient poses a serious danger of violence to others, the therapist should be absolved of any responsibility for failing to act to protect the potential victim. In our view, however, once a therapist does in fact determine, or under applicable professional standards reasonably should have determined, that a patient poses a serious danger of violence to others, he bears a duty to exercise reasonable care to protect the foreseeable victim of that danger. While the discharge of this duty of due care will necessarily vary with the facts of each case,[11] in each instance the adequacy of the therapist's conduct must be measured against the traditional negligence standard of the rendition of reasonable care under the circumstances. . . .

The risk that unnecessary warnings may be given is a reasonable price to pay for the lives of possible victims that may be saved. We would hesitate to hold that the therapist who is aware that his patient expects to attempt to assassinate the President of the United States would not be obligated to warn the authorities because the therapist cannot predict with accuracy that his patient will commit the crime. . . .

We recognize the public interest in supporting effective treatment of mental illness and in protecting the rights of patients to privacy, and the consequent public importance of safeguarding the confidential character of psychotherapeutic communication. Against this interest, however, we must weigh the public interest in safety from violent assault. The Legislature has undertaken the difficult task of balancing the countervailing concerns. In Evidence Code

11. Defendant therapists and amicus also argue that warnings must be given only in those cases in which the therapist knows the identity of the victim. We recognize that in some cases it would be unreasonable to require the therapist to interrogate his patient to discover the victim's identity, or to conduct an independent investigation. But there may also be cases in which a moment's reflection will reveal the victim's identity. The matter thus is one which depends upon the circumstances of each case, and should not be governed by any hard and fast rule.

section 1014, it established a broad rule of privilege to protect confidential communications between patient and psychotherapist. In Evidence Code section 1024, the Legislature created a specific and limited exception to the psychotherapist-patient privilege: "There is no privilege . . . if the psychotherapist has reasonable cause to believe that the patient is in such mental or emotional condition as to be dangerous to himself or to the person or property of another and that disclosure of the communication is necessary to prevent the threatened danger."

We realize that the open and confidential character of psychotherapeutic dialogue encourages patients to express threats of violence, few of which are ever executed. Certainly a therapist should not be encouraged routinely to reveal such threats; such disclosures could seriously disrupt the patient's relationship with his therapist and with the persons threatened. To the contrary, the therapist's obligations to his patient require that he not disclose a confidence unless such disclosure is necessary to avert danger to others, and even then that he do so discreetly, and in a fashion that would preserve the privacy of his patient to the fullest extent compatible with the prevention of the threatened danger. (See Fleming & Maximov, The Patient or His Victim: The Therapist's Dilemma (1974) 62 Cal. L. Rev. 1025, 1065–1066).

The revelation of a communication under the above circumstances is not a breach of trust or a violation of professional ethics as stated in the Principles of Medical Ethics of the American Medical Association (1957) section 9: "A physician may not reveal the confidence entrusted to him in the course of medical attendance . . . *unless he is required to do so by law or unless it becomes necessary in order to protect the welfare of the individual or of the community.*" (Emphasis added). We conclude that the public policy favoring protection of the confidential character of patient-psychotherapist communications must yield to the extent to which disclosure is essential to avert danger to others. The protective privilege ends where the public peril begins.

Our current crowded and computerized society compels the interdependence of its members. In this risk-infested society we can hardly tolerate the further exposure to danger that would result from a concealed knowledge of the therapist that his patient was lethal. If the exercise of reasonable care to protect the threatened victim requires the therapist to warn the endangered party or those who can reasonably be expected to notify him, we see no sufficient societal interest that would protect and justify concealment. The containment of such risks lies in the public interest. For the foregoing reasons, we find that plaintiffs' complaints can be amended to state a cause of action against defendants Moore, Powelson, Gold, and Yandell and against the Regents as their employer, for breach of a duty to exercise reasonable care to protect Tatiana.

[The court then holds that the defendant therapists are not immune from liability for their failure to warn under the discretionary function exception to the California Tort Claims Act. It further holds that both the defendant therapists and the defendant police officers are immune from liability for failure to confine Poddar. Finally, the court concludes that the police defendants "do not have any such special relationship to either Tatiana or to Poddar sufficient to impose upon such defendants a duty to warning respecting Poddar's violent intentions."]

Wright, C.J., and Sullivan and Richardson, JJ., concur.

Mosk, J., concurring in part and dissenting in part. I concur in the result in this instance only because the complaints allege that defendant therapists did in fact predict that Poddar would kill and were therefore negligent in failing to warn of that danger. Thus the issue here is very narrow: we are not concerned with whether the therapists, pursuant to the standards of their profession, "should have" predicted potential violence; they allegedly did so in actuality. Under these limited circumstances I agree that a cause of action can be stated. . . .

Clark, J., dissenting. Until today's majority opinion, both legal and medical authorities have agreed that confidentiality is essential to effectively treat the mentally ill, and that imposing a duty on doctors to disclose patient threats to potential victims would greatly impair treatment. Further, recognizing that effective treatment and society's safety are necessarily intertwined, the Legislature has already decided effective and confidential treatment is preferred over imposition of a duty to warn.

The issue whether effective treatment for the mentally ill should be sacrificed to a system of warnings is, in my opinion, properly one for the Legislature, and we are bound by its judgment. Moreover, even in the absence of clear legislative direction, we must reach the same conclusion because imposing the majority's new duty is certain to result in a net increase in violence.

NOTES

1. *Tarasoff's California Aftermath.* The duty of reasonable care announced in *Tarasoff* has been widely accepted, and codified in RTT: LPEH §41.

RESTATEMENT (THIRD) OF TORTS: LIABILITY FOR PHYSICAL AND EMOTIONAL HARM

§41. Duty to Third Persons Based on Special Relationship with Person Posing Risks

(a) An actor in a special relationship with another owes a duty of reasonable care to third persons with regard to risks posed by the other that arise within the scope of the relationship.

(b) Special relationships giving rise to the duty provided in Subsection (a) include:

(1) a parent with dependent children,

(2) a custodian with those in its custody,

(3) an employer with employees when the employment facilitates the employee's causing harm to third parties, and

(4) a mental-health professional with patients.

Under the Third Restatement's rationale, is the plaintiff's case easier or more difficult because the defendants were medical professionals instead of ordinary individuals? Should we focus on the competence of psychiatrists to detect dangerous persons or the need for confidentiality in patient-psychiatrist relationships? How should the law reflect the differences between dangerous persons who are or who are not in custody?

Tarasoff's limits were tested in Beauchene v. Synanon Foundation, Inc., 151 Cal. Rptr. 796 (Ct. App. 1979), which held that a *private* rehabilitation center owed no duty of care to members of the public at large when it accepted convicted individuals referred to it by the state criminal justice system as an alternative to incarceration. The court held that the absence of a duty of care was fatal to both of the plaintiff's claims, to wit, that the assailant had been improperly admitted into the program, and that he had been improperly supervised once admitted. Should the same result apply when a private institution treats patients without a criminal conviction?

In the subsequent California Supreme Court case of Thompson v. County of Alameda, 614 P.2d 728, 736 (Cal. 1980), a juvenile with a long and sorrowful personal history of violence and sexual abuse was released into the custody of his mother, even though the county knew that the youth had "indicated that he would, if released, take the life of a young child residing in the neighborhood." Although no particular person was identified, the released juvenile in fact murdered the plaintiff's son in the plaintiff's mother's garage within twenty-four hours of his release. The plaintiffs argued that warnings should have been issued to (a) the police, (b) the parents in the neighborhood, and/or (c) the juvenile's mother. The contention was rejected by the court:

> Unlike members of the general public, in *Tarasoff*. . . the potential victims were specifically known and designated individuals. The warnings which we therein required were directed at making those individuals aware of the danger to which they were uniquely exposed. The threatened targets were precise. In such cases, it is fair to conclude that warnings given discreetly and to a limited number of persons would have a greater effect because they would alert those particular targeted individuals of the possibility of a specific threat pointed at them. In contrast, the warnings sought by plaintiffs would of necessity have to be made to a broad segment of the population and would be only general in nature. In addition to the likelihood that such generalized warnings when frequently repeated would do little as a practical matter to stimulate increased safety measures . . . such extensive warnings would be difficult to give.

Tobriner, J., dissented on the ground that warnings should have been given to the mother, who "might" have taken additional steps to control the conduct of her son.

The issue of the therapist's care in California is today governed by Cal. Civ. Code §43.92 (2023), which provides:

> (a) There shall be no monetary liability on the part of, and no cause of action shall arise against, any person who is a psychotherapist . . . in failing to protect from a patient's threatened violent behavior or failing to predict and protect from a patient's violent behavior except if the patient has communicated to the psychotherapist a serious threat of physical violence against a reasonably identifiable victim or victims.
>
> (b) There shall be no monetary liability on the part of, and no cause of action shall arise against, a psychotherapist who . . . discharges his or her duty to protect by making reasonable efforts to communicate the threat to the victim or victims and to a law enforcement agency.

2. *Beyond California.* *Tarasoff's* influence has extended far beyond California. The duties are especially strict on defendants whose steps facilitate attacks by persons within their care on innocent plaintiffs. One particularly chilling example is Lundgren v. Fultz, 354 N.W.2d 25, 29 (Minn. 1984), in which a psychiatrist interceded on behalf of his patient, Fultz, who had been diagnosed and committed as a paranoid schizophrenic, to secure the return of his guns that had been confiscated by the police. Fultz proceeded to shoot Lundgren in "an unprovoked and random attack." The court noted that

> a jury could conclude that the psychiatrist's letter caused the police to return these guns and, thus, materially increased the danger that Fultz posed. . . . There is a limit to the protection given the discretion in a professional relationship. That limit is exceeded where a psychiatrist places the gun in a potential assassin's hand under the guise of fostering trust between patient and psychiatrist.

Liability is more closely contested when a psychiatrist has only limited interactions with psychiatric individuals on an outpatient basis. In Long v. Broadlawns Medical Center, 656 N.W.2d 71, 83 (Iowa 2002), the decedent, Jillene Long, was killed by her husband, Gerald, a psychiatric patient who had been released from the defendant medical center. The husband had a long history of spousal abuse. During his commitment, the decedent agreed with hospital officials that she would remain at the marital residence, but that Broadlawns would call her on the day of her husband's discharge. That call was never made, and Cady, J., after extensive consideration of *Tarasoff*, held that the basic issue was "whether Broadlawns failed to exercise reasonable care in performing a promise to warn Jillene of Gerald's discharge thereby increasing the risk of harm to her or resulting in harm to her because of her reliance on the promised warning." The court continued: "[S]ubstantial evidence exists to support a finding that Jillene would not have been at the marital residence had she known Gerald was discharged and essentially free to return there himself." Gerald's conduct did not count as a superseding cause because his acts fell "squarely within the scope of the original risk."

For an exhaustive bibliography on these issues, see RTT: LPEH §41, comment *g* and its Reporter's Note.

3. *Should Online Platforms Have a Tarasoff Duty?* In Goodwin v. Facebook, 160 N.E.3d 372, 376, 377, 382, 388 (Ohio Ct. App. 2020), the plaintiff's father was sitting peaceably in a local park when he was murdered by a stranger. Prior to the murder, the perpetrator had made the following post to his followers on Facebook:

> FB my life for the pass [sic] year has really been [expletive] up!!! lost everything [sic] ever had due to gambling at the Cleveland Jack casino and Erie casino . . . I [sic] not going to go into details but I'm at my breaking point [sic] I'm really on some murder shit . . . FB you have 4 minutes to tell me why I shouldn't be on deathrow!!!! [sic] dead serious #teamdeathrow.

Seeking an extension of Ohio's *Tarasoff* rule, the plaintiff sued Facebook "based on the failure to warn [the victim] of [the perpetrator's] dangerous propensity of which Facebook was aware through its data-mining practices." Gallagher, J., upheld dismissal of the claim: "[Plaintiff] has not cited any authority for the proposition that a social media company 'takes charge' of its users to the same extent that a medical or mental health professional takes charge of her patient. . . ." Blackmon, J., concurring, expressed concern over the development of the laws governing social media companies:

> As a matter of policy, public safety should be of primary concern, which is why we have tort law. I truly do not see Facebook's issue. It had information of a potential crime. By acting it might have saved a life. . . . Only when legal and moral duty diverge can courts hear a call for movement and reform.

Was Facebook's information of a possible crime sufficient to warn the authorities? What if the advent of sophisticated natural language processing technology renders it capable of parsing posts in real time? Should the inquiry differ for smart devices? Haber, The Digital Samaritans, 77 Wash. & Lee L. Rev. 1559, 1623 (2020), argues that "[t]he cost-benefit analysis of imposing duties to report on [artificial intelligence] devices currently tilts in the direction of not imposing artificial Samaritan duties." Why?

4. *A Tarasoff Retrospective.* One reason *Tarasoff* has always raised difficult problems is that it is not amenable to easy contractual solutions because, unlike in *Long*, the three parties are not in privity with each other. Hence, no one doubts the legitimate state interest in seeking to prevent death or serious injury by imposing some form of liability on the psychiatrists and institutions who provide care for seriously deranged patients. Disturbed persons are not easily deterred, and they have few if any resources to answer tort claims. At the same time, the fear that potential disclosure will drive disturbed individuals from the care they so desperately need has placed a brake on the liability. Rosenhan et al., Warning Third Parties: The Ripple Effects of *Tarasoff*, 24 Pac. L.J. 1165, 1185–89 (1993), reported that, of 872 surveyed therapists: (i) 50 percent believed they had lost a patient as a result of discussing the need to breach confidentiality should the patient threaten harm; (ii) 18 percent avoided counseling dangerous patients at least in part because of *Tarasoff*; and (iii) 37 percent focused disproportionately on the potential dangerousness of their patients due to *Tarasoff*. Edwards, Doing Their Duty: An Empirical Analysis of the Unintended Effect of Tarasoff v. Regents on Homicidal Activity, 57 J.L. & Econ. 321, 344 (2014), confirms the thrust of this survey evidence with statistical analysis:

> [A]ll else being equal, mandatory duty-to-warn laws cause an increase in homicides of 5 percent. . . . Duty-to-warn laws change the incentives of both the patient and the doctor. The original intention of the law was to deter dangerous patients from committing heinous crimes, but what may actually have happened was that the law changed the incentives to the patient and the doctor such that the patient has an incentive to withhold homicidal tendencies, and the doctor has an incentive to not explore homicidal tendencies.

When *Tarasoff* came down in 1976 there were many predictions of systematic professional doom, but these have, on the whole, moderated with time. Alan Stone, an expert in law and psychiatry, first denounced *Tarasoff*. Stone, The *Tarasoff* Decision: Suing Psychotherapists to Safeguard Society, 90 Harv. L. Rev. 358 (1976). But on reflection he later wrote "the duty to warn is not as unmitigated a disaster for the enterprise of psychotherapy as it once seemed to critics like myself." Stone, Law Psychiatry and Morality: Essays and Analysis 181 (1984). In fact Ginsberg, *Tarasoff* at Thirty: Victim's Knowledge Shrinks the Psychotherapist's Duty to Warn and Protect, 21 J. Contemp. Health L. & Pol'y 1, 2 (2004), endorses *Tarasoff*:

> In particular, a recent but persistent line of cases has limited the so-called "*Tarasoff* duty" when the victim had prior knowledge of the patient-attacker's violent tendencies. This has quelled some of the controversy stemming from the sweeping breadth of the original 1974 and 1976 decisions. This limitation has also appeased those therapists who viewed the courts as shifting the public protection burden from the realm of law enforcement to the realm of psychotherapy.
>
> Also, psychotherapists have re-examined *Tarasoff* for themselves, to very interesting ends. To wit, some contemporary psychiatric commentators have presented anecdotal evidence suggesting that the act of issuing a "*Tarasoff* warning" might be a valuable clinical tool, particularly when done by the patient himself.
>
> In short, thirty years of reflection and empirical observation have cast *Tarasoff* in a more optimistic, evolving light.

Nonetheless, much uneasiness remains among therapists about the scope and application of the *Tarasoff* rule. In his 2013 presidential address before the American Psychological Association, Dr. Donald Bersoff described the decision as "bad law, bad social science, and bad social policy." His main concern was understanding what triggered the duty. How high did the risk have to be to trigger the duty — 50 percent? Higher? Lower? There is even greater uncertainty when the potential threat involves lesser violence to some other person or oneself.

Consider whether these concerns also apply to the following situations: (1) where the potential target has been identified by the disturbed person, as in *Tarasoff* itself; (2) where the psychiatrist has somehow facilitated the commission of the crime, as in *Lundgren*; and (3) where the psychiatrist or institution has breached some explicit promise to the future victim, as in *Long*.

CHAPTER 7

STRICT LIABILITY

SECTION A. INTRODUCTION

One major theme of this casebook concerns the recurrent tension between negligence and strict liability. This chapter pursues one facet of that theme by looking in detail at those areas of tort law that resisted incorporation into a general negligence framework even when its influence was at its peak. Torts to personal property, including trespass to chattels and conversion, apply a version of strict liability principles that only requires the tortfeasor's intent to exercise control over the property, even when he mistakenly believes, while acting reasonably and in good faith, that the property of another is his own. Additional primary historical bastions of strict liability, grouped together in this chapter, involve liability for animals, ultrahazardous or abnormally dangerous activities, and nuisance. These theories of tort liability are quite ancient and were, it will be recalled, treated by Judge Blackburn as instances of the "true rule" (of strict liability for bringing, keeping, and collecting) that he announced in Fletcher v. Rylands, *supra* Chapter 2, at 83. The second head of liability—ultrahazardous activities—developed in the United States as part of an effort to rationalize and generalize from *Rylands*. Thus *Rylands* provides the most convenient point of departure for determining how these rules relate to each other and to *Rylands* itself. In order to place the subject matter in perspective, it is helpful at this point to reread all the *Rylands* opinions. Finally, this chapter explores vicarious liability, which in most typical cases holds employers liable for the torts of their employees that arise out of and in the course of their employment.

SECTION B. TRESPASS TO CHATTELS AND CONVERSION

1. Trespass to Chattels

In many respects the law of trespass to chattels parallels that of trespass to land, discussed *supra* in Chapter 1. One point of possible difference concerns the availability of damages or injunctions for the unauthorized use of chattels that does not result in harm. The Restatement resists the award of damages in these cases. See RST §218, comment *e.*

RESTATEMENT OF THE LAW (SECOND) OF TORTS

§218. Liability to Person in Possession

Comment e: The interest of a possessor of a chattel in its inviolability, unlike the similar interest of a possessor of land, is not given legal protection by an action for nominal damages for harmless intermeddlings with the chattel. In order that an actor who interferes with another's chattel may be liable, his conduct must affect some other and more important interest of the possessor. Therefore, one who intentionally intermeddles with another's chattel is subject to liability only if his intermeddling is harmful to the possessor's materially valuable interest in the physical condition, quality, or value of the chattel, or if the possessor is deprived of the use of the chattel for a substantial time, or some other legally protected interest of the possessor is affected as stated in Clause (c) [relating to the deprivation of use for a substantial time]. Sufficient legal protection . . . of his chattel is afforded by his privilege to use reasonable force to protect his possession against even harmless interference.

Illustration 2: *A*, a child, climbs upon the back of *B*'s large dog and pulls its ears. No harm is done to the dog, or to any other legally protected interest of *B*. *A* is not liable to *B*.

With the Restatement's view, compare Blondell v. Consolidated Gas Co., 43 A. 817, 819 (Md. 1899). A large group of gas company customers sought to attach governors to the company's gas meters. The meters measured the flow of gas. The governors regulated that flow. The plaintiff gas company insisted that attaching governors to the meters could increase the danger of explosion. The defendants denied these allegations. The court sidestepped the question of possible future damage by asking only whether the defendants had made unauthorized use of the plaintiff's property:

> Now it seems to us that the large mass of testimony contained in the record showing, on the one hand, that the affixing of the governor was, and on the other hand that it was not, injurious to the meter and its connections, is entirely beside the question. For whether the alleged acts were or were not productive of injury, they were in the eye of the law trespasses, if, as we have said, the meters are the plaintiff's property, and if the acts were unauthorized, there is a legal injury for which the plaintiff could recover, at least, nominal damages; and the continuation of which would be enjoined by a Court of Equity.

Should it make a difference whether the pipes are regarded as real or personal property?

The next case examines how the tort of trespass to chattels applies to less tangible rights of possession. While reading *Hamidi*, ask yourself whether the court's approach sufficiently protects the right at issue.

Intel Corp. v. Hamidi

71 P.3d 296 (Cal. 2003)

Werdegar, J. Intel Corporation (Intel) maintains an electronic mail system, connected to the Internet, through which messages between employees and those outside the company can be sent and received, and permits its employees to make reasonable nonbusiness use of this system. On six occasions over almost two years, Kourosh Kenneth Hamidi, a former Intel employee, sent e-mails criticizing Intel's employment practices to numerous current employees [up to 35,000 in number per occasion] on Intel's electronic mail system. Hamidi breached no computer security barriers in order to communicate with Intel employees. He offered to, and did, remove from his mailing list any recipient who so wished. Hamidi's communications to individual Intel employees caused neither physical damage nor functional disruption to the company's computers, nor did they at any time deprive Intel of the use of its computers. The contents of the messages, however, caused discussion among employees and managers. [On several occasions, Intel sent notice to Hamidi by registered mail, asking him to cease and desist use of all its equipment.]

On these facts, Intel brought suit, claiming that by communicating with its employees over the company's e-mail system Hamidi committed the tort of trespass to chattels. The trial court granted Intel's motion for summary judgment and enjoined Hamidi from any further mailings. A divided Court of Appeal affirmed.

Ken Hamidi
Source: Ken Hamidi for Governor

After reviewing the decisions analyzing unauthorized electronic contact with computer systems as potential trespasses to chattels, we conclude that under California law the tort does not encompass, and should not be extended to encompass, an electronic communication that neither damages the recipient computer system nor impairs its functioning. Such an electronic communication does not constitute an actionable trespass to personal property, i.e., the computer system, because it does not interfere with the possessor's use or possession of, or any other legally protected interest in, the personal property itself. The consequential economic damage Intel claims to have suffered, i.e., loss of productivity caused by employees reading and reacting to Hamidi's messages and company efforts to block the messages, is not an injury to the company's interest in its computers—which worked as intended and were unharmed by the communications—any more than the personal distress caused by reading an unpleasant letter would be an injury to the recipient's mailbox, or the loss of privacy caused by an intrusive telephone call would be an injury to the recipient's telephone equipment.

[Werdegar, J., then notes that the ruling did not block remedies for interference with contract or economic relations, intentional infliction of emotional distress, defamation, or publication of private facts.]

Nor does our holding affect the legal remedies of Internet service providers (ISP's) against senders of unsolicited commercial bulk e-mail (UCE), also known as "spam." A series of federal district court decisions, beginning with CompuServe, Inc. v. Cyber Promotions, Inc. 962 F. Supp. 1015 (S.D. Ohio 1997), has approved the use of trespass to chattels as a theory of spammers' liability to ISP's, based upon evidence that the vast quantities of mail sent by spammers both overburdened the ISP's own computers and made the entire computer system harder to use for recipients, the ISP's customers. . . .

Discussion

I. Current California Tort Law

Dubbed by Prosser the "little brother of conversion," the tort of trespass to chattels allows recovery for interferences with possession of personal property "not sufficiently important to be classed as conversion, and so to compel the defendant to pay the full value of the thing with which he has interfered."

Though not amounting to conversion, the defendant's interference must, to be actionable, have caused some injury to the chattel or to the plaintiff's rights in it. Under California law, trespass to chattels "lies where an intentional interference with the possession of personal property *has proximately caused injury*." . . .

The Restatement, too, makes clear that some actual injury must have occurred in order for a trespass to chattels to be actionable. Under Section 218 of the Restatement Second of Torts, dispossession alone, without further damages, is actionable, but other forms of interference require some additional harm to the personal property or the possessor's interests in it. [The court quotes the passage set out *supra* at 451.]

Intel suggests that the requirement of actual harm does not apply here because it sought only injunctive relief, as protection from future injuries. But as Justice Kolkey, dissenting below, observed, "[t]he fact the relief sought is injunctive does not excuse a showing of injury, whether actual or threatened." Indeed, in order to obtain injunctive relief the plaintiff must ordinarily show that the defendant's wrongful acts threaten to cause *irreparable* injuries, ones that cannot be adequately compensated in damages. . . . A fortiori, to issue an injunction without a showing of likely irreparable injury in an action for trespass to chattels, in which injury to the personal property or the possessor's interest in it *is* an element of the action, would make little legal sense.

[The court reiterates the absence of damage to the plaintiff's computer system itself, as happened in eBay, Inc. v. Bidder's Edge, Inc. See *infra* Note 2 at 457 and CompuServe, Inc. v. Cyber Promotions, Inc.]

In addition to impairment of system functionality, *CompuServe* and its progeny also refer to the ISP's loss of business reputation and customer goodwill, resulting from the inconvenience and cost that spam causes to its members, as harm to the ISP's legally protected interests in its personal property. Intel argues that its own interest in employee productivity, assertedly disrupted by Hamidi's messages, is a comparable protected interest in its computer system. We disagree. . . .

CompuServe's customers were annoyed because the system was inundated with unsolicited commercial messages, making its use for personal communication more difficult and costly. Their complaint, which allegedly led some to cancel their CompuServe service, was about *the functioning of CompuServe's electronic mail service.* Intel's workers, in contrast, were allegedly distracted from their work not because of the frequency or quantity of Hamidi's messages, but because of assertions and opinions the messages conveyed. Intel's complaint is thus about *the contents of the messages* rather than the functioning of the company's e-mail system. Even accepting *CompuServe*'s economic injury rationale, therefore, Intel's position represents a further extension of the trespass to chattels tort, fictionally recharacterizing the allegedly injurious effect of a communication's *contents* on recipients as an impairment to the device which transmitted the message.

This theory of "impairment by content" threatens to stretch trespass law to cover injuries far afield from the harms to possession the tort evolved to protect. . . .

Nor may Intel appropriately assert a *property* interest in its employees' time.

. . . We conclude, therefore, that Intel has not presented undisputed facts demonstrating an injury to its personal property, or to its legal interest in that property, that support, under California tort law, an action for trespass to chattels.

II. Proposed Extension of California Tort Law

We next consider whether California common law should be *extended* to cover, as a trespass to chattels, an otherwise harmless electronic communication whose contents are objectionable. We decline to so expand California law. . . .

Writing on behalf of several industry groups appearing as amici curiae, Professor Richard A. Epstein of the University of Chicago urges us to excuse the required showing of injury to personal property in cases of unauthorized electronic contact between computers, "extending the rules of trespass to real property to all interactive Web sites and servers." The court is thus urged to recognize, for owners of a particular species of personal property, computer servers, the same interest in inviolability as is generally accorded a possessor of land. In effect, Professor Epstein suggests that a company's server should be its castle, upon which any unauthorized intrusion, however harmless, is a trespass.

Epstein's argument derives, in part, from the familiar metaphor of the Internet as a physical space, reflected in much of the language that has been used to describe it: "cyberspace," "the information superhighway," e-mail "addresses," and the like. Of course, the Internet is also frequently called simply the "Net," a term, Hamidi points out, "evoking a fisherman's chattel." A major component of the Internet is the World Wide "Web," a descriptive term suggesting neither personal nor real property, and "cyberspace" itself has come to be known by the oxymoronic phrase "virtual reality," which would suggest that any real property "located" in "cyberspace" must be "virtually real" property. Metaphor is a two-edged sword.

Indeed, the metaphorical application of real property rules would not, by itself, transform a physically harmless electronic intrusion on a computer server into a trespass. That is because, under California law, intangible intrusions on land, including electromagnetic transmissions, are not actionable as trespasses (though they may be as nuisances) unless they cause physical damage to the real property. Since Intel does not claim Hamidi's electronically transmitted messages physically damaged its servers, it could not prove a trespass to land even were we to treat the computers as a type of real property. Some further extension of the conceit would be required, under which the electronic signals Hamidi sent would be recast as tangible intruders, perhaps as tiny messengers rushing through the "hallways" of Intel's computers and bursting out of employees' computers to read them Hamidi's missives. But such fictions promise more confusion than clarity in the law.

The plain fact is that computers, even those making up the Internet, are—like such older communications equipment as telephones and fax machines—personal property, not realty. Professor Epstein observes that "[a]lthough servers may be moved in real space, they cannot be moved in cyberspace," because an Internet server must, to be useful, be accessible at a known address. But the same is true of the telephone: to be useful for incoming communication, the telephone must remain constantly linked to the same number. . . . Does this suggest that an unwelcome message delivered through a telephone or fax machine should be viewed as a trespass to a type of real property? We think not. . . .

More substantively, Professor Epstein argues that a rule of computer server inviolability will, through the formation or extension of a market in computer-to-computer access, create "the right social result." In most circumstances, he predicts, companies with computers on the Internet will continue to authorize transmission of information through e-mail, Web site searching, and page linking because they benefit by that open access. When a Web site owner does deny access to a particular sending, searching, or linking computer, a system of "simple one-on-one negotiations" will arise to provide the necessary individual licenses.

Other scholars are less optimistic about such a complete propertization of the Internet. Professor Mark Lemley of the University of California, Berkeley, writing on behalf of an amici curiae group of professors of intellectual property and computer law, observes that under a property rule of server inviolability, "each of the hundreds of millions of [Internet] users must get permission in advance from anyone with whom they want to communicate and anyone who owns a server through which their message may travel." The consequence for e-mail could be a substantial reduction in the freedom of electronic communication, as the owner of each computer through which an electronic message passes could impose its own limitations on message content or source. . . . A leading scholar of Internet law and policy, Professor Lawrence Lessig of Stanford University, has criticized Professor Epstein's theory of the computer server as quasi-real property, previously put forward in the *eBay* case, on the ground that it ignores the costs to society in the loss of network benefits: "eBay benefits greatly from a network that is open and where access is free. It is this general feature of the Net that makes the Net so valuable to users and a source of great innovation. And to the extent that individual sites begin to impose their own rules of exclusion, the value of the network as a network declines. If machines must negotiate before entering any individual site, then the costs of using the network climb." (Lessig, The Future of Ideas: The Fate of the Commons in a Connected World (2001) p. 171. . . .)

We discuss this debate among the amici curiae and academic writers only to note its existence and contours, not to attempt its resolution. [The court notes that legislative solutions are possible in both this situation and with spam.]

III. Constitutional Considerations

[The court then declines to address the First Amendment claims that would arise if Intel had stated a claim for common law trespass. It concludes:] Hamidi himself had no tangible presence on Intel property, instead speaking from his own home through his computer. He no more invaded Intel's property than does a protester holding a sign or shouting through a bullhorn outside corporate headquarters, posting a letter through the mail, or telephoning to complain of a corporate practice.

The judgment of the Court of Appeal is reversed.

KENNARD, J., concurring. Does a person commit the tort of trespass to chattels by making occasional personal calls to a mobile phone despite the stated objection of the person who owns the mobile phone and pays for the mobile phone service? Does it matter that the calls are not made to the mobile phone's owner, but to another person who ordinarily uses that phone? Does it matter that the person to whom the calls are made has not objected to them? Does it matter that the calls do not damage the mobile phone or reduce in any significant way its availability or usefulness? . . .

Intel has my sympathy. . . . [However, b]ecause plaintiff Intel has not shown that defendant Hamidi's occasional bulk e-mail messages to Intel's employees have damaged Intel's computer system or impaired its functioning in any significant way, Intel has not established the tort of trespass to chattels.

This is not to say that Intel is helpless either practically or legally. As a practical matter, Intel need only instruct its employees to delete messages from Hamidi without reading them and to notify Hamidi to remove their workplace e-mail addresses from his mailing lists. . . .

BROWN, J., dissenting. . . . Intel has invested millions of dollars to develop and maintain a computer system. It did this not to act as a public forum but to enhance the productivity of its employees. Kourosh Kenneth Hamidi sent as many as 200,000 e-mail messages to Intel employees. The time required to review and delete Hamidi's messages diverted employees from productive tasks and undermined the utility of the computer system. . . .

The majority repeatedly asserts that Intel objected to the hundreds of thousands of messages solely due to their content, and proposes that Intel seek relief by pleading content-based speech torts. This proposal misses the point that Intel's objection is directed not toward Hamidi's message but his use of Intel's property to display his message. Intel has not sought to prevent Hamidi from expressing his ideas on his Web site, through private mail (paper or electronic) to employees' homes, or through any other means like picketing or billboards. But as counsel for Intel explained during oral argument, the company objects to Hamidi's using Intel's property to advance his message.

Of course, Intel deserves an injunction even if its objections are based entirely on the e-mail's content. Intel is entitled, for example, to allow employees use of the Internet to check stock market tables or weather forecasts without incurring any concomitant obligation to allow access to pornographic Web sites. A private property owner may choose to exclude unwanted mail for any reason, including its content. Rowan v. U.S. Post Office Dept., 397 U.S. 728, 738 (1970). . . .

MOSK, J., dissenting. . . . The majority fail to distinguish open communication in the public "commons" of the Internet from unauthorized intermeddling on a private, proprietary intranet. Hamidi is not communicating in the equivalent of a town square or of an unsolicited "junk" mailing through the United States Postal Service. His action, in crossing from the public Internet into a private intranet, is more like intruding into a private office mailroom, commandeering the mail cart, and dropping off unwanted broadsides on 30,000 desks. Because Intel's security measures have been circumvented by Hamidi, the majority leave Intel, which has exercised all reasonable self-help efforts, with no recourse unless he causes a malfunction or systems "crash."

NOTES

1. *Trespass in Cyberspace.* How persuasive are the analogies between the telephone and the Internet? Do telemarketing phone calls made to persons who have enrolled on the National Do Not Call Registry, https://www.donotcall.gov, count as trespasses to chattels? If repeated, should they be enjoined? Is an unsolicited phone call to a single person a fair analogy to an email blast to 35,000 people? Is the plaintiff's claim in *Hamidi* a protest against the content of the emails or the unauthorized use of its servers? If the plaintiff is entitled to use self-help to keep the defendant off its servers, why encourage a game of "cat-and-mouse" by denying the injunction? Would the result have been different if the defendant had, without disruption of service, used the plaintiff's servers to transfer information to third parties for profit?

In Casillas v. Berkshire Hathaway Homestate Insurance Co., 294 Cal. Rptr. 3d 841, 841, 849 (Ct. App. 2022), the plaintiffs alleged that the defendants "copied thousands of electronic litigation files, which had been uploaded to the system by workers' compensation and personal injury attorneys and their clients . . . and transmitted the copies to insurers and insurance defense law firms for use in litigation." Following *Hamidi*, Manella, P.J., affirmed dismissal of the trespass to chattels claim "[b]ecause the copying did not affect the files or appellants' ability to use them." Grimmelmann & Mulligan, Data Property, 72 Am. U. L. Rev. 829 (2023), claims that someone possesses data when he controls at least one copy of the data. Thus, deleting a copy of someone's file, even when there is a backup copy, interferes with that person's possessory interest. Does this view of trespass to chattels for digital data undermine *Casillas*?

Hamidi generated an extensive cottage industry on the role of metaphor in connecting trespasses in real space and cyberspace. What weight, if any, should be given to speaking of Internet sites as addresses located along an Internet highway? For an early warning against the use of trespass in cyberspace, see Burk, The Trouble with Trespass, 4 J. Small & Emerging Bus. L. 27 (2000). For an extensive criticism of the potential abuse in moving across contexts, see Hunter, Cyberspace as Place and the Tragedy of the Digital Anticommons, 91 Calif. L. Rev. 439 (2003), in which the term "anticommons" refers to the destructive fragmentation of a unified space by the creation of arbitrary boundaries that impede communication. For a defense of the explicit translation of the relative spheres of private and common property from real space to cyberspace, see Epstein, Intel v. Hamidi: The Role of Self-Help in Cyberspace, 1 J.L. Econ. & Pol'y 147 (2005); McGowan, The Trespass Trouble and the Metaphor Muddle, 1 J.L. Econ. & Pol'y 109 (2005).

2. *Modern Forms of Trespass.* *Hamidi* is only one of many cases that apply traditional common law trespass rules to cyberspace. In eBay, Inc. v. Bidder's Edge, Inc., 100 F. Supp. 2d 1058 (N.D. Cal. 2000), eBay sued Bidder's Edge for trespass to chattels. Bidder's Edge was an auction aggregator whose software enabled its customers to compare bids for similar items sold on different online sites. To obtain the needed information, Bidder's Edge deployed Internet "spiders" to search eBay's online auction database thousands of times per hour to post bidding updates on its own website. Although eBay's database was publicly accessible, its stated policies forbade anyone from probing its space with spiders. When Bidder's Edge refused to discontinue its "spidering," the court granted eBay a preliminary injunction against Bidder's Edge's activities, finding that its repeated searches amounted to trespass to chattels, capable of impairing the operation of its site because the use of "BE's web crawlers exceeded the scope of [eBay's] consent when they began acting like robots by making repeated queries." Note that eBay had been prepared to allow Bidder's Edge access to its site under its standard licensing agreement, under which eBay would pay Bidder's Edge for any customers referred to its site. Should it matter that Bidder's Edge allowed customers to enter eBay's site through a secondary portal where they would not see eBay's advertisements, given the consequent loss of revenue?

The post-*Hamidi* cases have generally followed the basic decision. Microsoft could recover for "lost time and money" and "tarnished . . . business goodwill" where Russian operatives committed trespass to chattels by accessing Microsoft's computers and servers and directing search engine results to their chosen websites. See Microsoft Corp. v. Does 1-18, No.1:13CV139 LMB/TCB, 2014 WL 1338677, at *10 (E.D. Va. Apr. 2, 2014). On the other hand, in In re Jetblue Airways Corp. Privacy Litigation, 379 F. Supp. 2d 299, 328–29 (E.D.N.Y. 2005), Amon, J., refused to apply a trespass to chattels theory to prevent the defendant from taking key passenger name records off JetBlue's computers, on the ground that "even if their privacy interests were indeed infringed by the data transfer, such a harm does not amount to a diminishment of the quality or value of a materially valuable interest in their personal information." What result if customer lists are regarded as a trade secret? Is there any serious hold-up problem if the property rule is adopted? If the presumption is that anyone may enter (like a store or restaurant) unless explicitly excluded? See Lemley & Weiser, Should Property or Liability Rules Govern Information?, 85 Tex. L. Rev. 783, 786–90 (2007). Is there any reason to think that Intel's effort to protect itself posed any threat to the interconnectivity of the Internet?

2. Conversion

Poggi v. Scott

139 P. 815 (Cal. 1914)

Henshaw, J. Plaintiff sued to recover from defendant the sum of two thousand dollars damages suffered by him by reason of the unlawful conversion by defendant of some two hundred barrels of plaintiff's wine. A nonsuit was granted upon the ground that plaintiff had failed to prove a sufficient case for the jury and from the judgment which followed he appeals.

[The plaintiff stored his wine barrels in a basement under lock and key in a room that he rented initially from Judge Mouser and thereafter from his lessee, the Sanitary Laundry Company. The plaintiff visited his storeroom about twice a month. Mouser sold the building to the defendant, Scott, and had informed Scott of the plaintiff's lease with the Laundry Company. Mouser did not tell the plaintiff that the premises had been sold. Later the plaintiff discovered that his wine barrels had been carted off. It seems as though two men, Bernardini and Ricci, knew that the wine was valuable. They called on Scott and told him that they wanted to buy some broken barrels stored in the basement. Scott located the barrels in the basement, tapped them to see if they were filled, and sold the allegedly empty barrels for $15 ($461 in 2023 dollars) on the condition that the men clean out the basement, which they did. Bernardini and Ricci were arrested for the theft of the wine, and Poggi brought this conversion action against Scott.]

In support of the nonsuit respondent argues that Scott thought he was disposing of so much junk or rubbish in the form of barrels, that, therefore, he cannot be held for the conversion of full barrels of wine or for the value of wine in barrels. Further it is said that it is fallacious to argue that the loss of the wine was the consequence of any act of Scott, or that any act of Scott produced it, or that there was any chain of connection, broken or unbroken, between Scott's act and the injury to Poggi, or that the loss to Poggi of his wine was the result, proximate or otherwise, of any act of Scott, or that Scott's act caused it in any sense at all.

If respondent's premises, as here stated, are correct, the conclusion of his nonliability is unassailable. But are they correct? The foundation for the action of conversion rests neither in the knowledge nor the intent of the defendant. It rests upon the unwarranted interference by defendant with the dominion over the property of the plaintiff from which injury to the latter results. Therefore, neither good nor bad faith, neither care nor negligence, neither knowledge nor ignorance, are of the gist of the action. "The plaintiff's right of redress no longer depends upon his showing, in any way, that the defendant did the act in question from wrongful motives, or generally speaking, even intentionally; and hence the want of such motives, or of intention, is no defense. Nor, indeed, is negligence any necessary part of the case. Here, then, is a class of cases in which the tort consists in the breach of what may be called an absolute duty; the act itself (in some cases it must have caused damage) is unlawful and redressible as a tort." (1 Bigelow on Torts, p.6.) And says Judge Cooley (Cubit v. O'Dett, 51 Mich. 347, [46 Atl. 679]): "Absence of bad faith can never excuse a trespass, though the existence of bad faith may sometimes aggravate it. Every one must be sure of his legal right when he invades the possession of another."

In consonance with the principles of law thus declared no question can arise of the defendant's responsibility under the evidence. Conceding all that may be argued as to the absence of improper motives on the part of the defendant, the all important fact yet remains, under his own testimony, that he sold barrels that did not belong to him and which did with their contents belong to the plaintiff. That he did not know that the barrels contained wine did not excuse his conduct. He had no legal right to sell the barrels whether or not they contained wine. He was exercising an unjustifiable and unwarranted dominion and control over the property of another and from his acts great loss resulted to that other. . . .

[Reversed.]

NOTES

1. ***The Reach of Conversion.*** As in cases of trespass to land and chattels, the intent requirement also arises in conversion cases, whereby the defendant takes, or, as in *Poggi*, sells, property belonging to the plaintiff. Without question, the defendant claims ownership or dominion over the chattels that are taken or stolen. Yet as in cases of trespass to chattels or real property, neither the lack of an intention to harm nor the existence of material mistake about the ownership or condition of the property excuses the conversion. Instead the defendant is obliged to pay for the value of the goods taken, even if, as in *Poggi*, he did not pocket the proceeds from that conversion or sale. More generally, conversion can be committed by dealing with goods in the role of an owner, whether by buying, selling, using, altering, or delivering the chattel, or, most critically, refusing to surrender the chattel to its proper owner. See RST §222A & §223, comment *b*.

RESTATEMENT OF THE LAW (SECOND) OF TORTS

§222A. What Constitutes Conversion

(1) Conversion is an intentional exercise of dominion or control over a chattel which so seriously interferes with the right of another to control it that the actor may justly be required to pay the other the full value of the chattel.

(2) In determining the seriousness of the interference and the justice of requiring the actor to pay the full value, the following factors are important:

(a) the extent and duration of the actor's exercise of dominion or control;

(b) the actor's intent to assert a right in fact inconsistent with the other's right of control;

(c) the actor's good faith;

(d) the extent and duration of the resulting interference with the other's right of control;

(e) the harm done to the chattel;

(f) the inconvenience and expense caused to the other.

§223. Ways of Committing Conversion

Comment b. Necessity of intent: Conversion is always an intentional exercise of dominion or control over the chattel. Mere non-feasance or negligence, without such an intent, is not sufficient for conversion. (See §224.) If the actor has the intent to do the act exercising dominion or control, however, he is not relieved from liability by his mistaken belief that he has possession of the chattel or the right to possession, or that he is privileged to act. (See §244.)

Under the Restatement formulation, the chief difficulty lies in setting the boundaries between conversion and trespass to chattels. Trespass to chattels requires the plaintiff to show that the defendant carried off goods that were in the plaintiff's *possession*. The Latin name for the wrong is *de bonis asportatis* (or trespass d.b.a.) — the asportation (carrying away) of chattels. Since the trespass is solely an offense to possession alone, the plaintiff can maintain the action even if some third party has a title paramount to both the plaintiff's and the defendant's. In contrast, conversion can be brought by any party who claims either ownership rights in the thing or some right to its immediate possession.

Clearly most cases of trespass to chattels are also conversions, and vice versa. But the overlap is not complete in either direction. Thus only conversion was available to *A* against *C* when *C* had taken the property from *B*, who had previously taken it from *A*. Trespass to chattels was inappropriate because at the time of *C*'s wrong, *B* had possession of the goods. See Ames, Lectures in Legal History 60–61 (1913). For the complications created when chattels were bailed, mortgaged, leased, or subject to contract of sale, see The Winkfield, [1902] P 42 (CA). Conversely only trespass would lie when the defendant had taken possession of the plaintiff's goods without claiming ownership of them. For example, in Fouldes v. Willoughby, (1841) 151 Eng. Rep. 1153 (Ex.), the plaintiff brought an action in conversion against a ferryman who removed the plaintiff's horses from the ferry before setting sail. In dismissing the action, Lord Abinger, C.B., said that "a simple asportation of a chattel, without any intention of making any further use of it, although it may be a sufficient foundation for an action of trespass, is not sufficient to establish a conversion." The defendant in *Fouldes* tried to justify his conduct by saying that he removed the animals in order to induce the plaintiff, who was misbehaving, to leave the ferry. Should the success of that defense depend upon the choice of the original action? On trespass and conversion, see generally Pollock & Wright, Possession in the Common Law (1888); 1 Harper, James & Gray, Torts (3d ed.) §§2.14–2.15. On the earlier history of the various writs, see Maitland, The Forms of Action at Common Law, Lectures V and VI (1936).

2. *Good and Bad Faith Conversions.* Maye v. Yappan, 23 Cal. 306, 307–08 (1863), reconfirms the tough standard used in conversion cases. The defendant dug up gold-bearing earth from the plaintiffs' land after the plaintiffs mistakenly, but in good faith, told the defendant that he owned the land. The court awarded the plaintiffs damages equal to the value of the gold, less the cost of its extraction and refinement, holding it "immaterial" "whether the defendants acted willfully and maliciously, or ignorantly and innocently, in digging up and taking away the gold-bearing earth."

Oliver Wendell Holmes defended that result in his classic book, The Common Law 97 (1881):

> When a man goes upon his neighbor's land, thinking it is his own, he intends the very act or consequence complained of. He means to intermeddle with a certain thing in a certain way, and it is just that intended intermeddling for which he is sued. . . . One who diminishes the value of property by intentional damage knows it belongs to somebody. If he thinks it belongs to himself, he expects whatever harm he may do to come out of his own pocket. It would be odd if he were to get rid of the burden by discovering that it belonged to his neighbor.

Can you "intermeddle" with property you think you own?

Unlike determinations of liability, the measure of damages for conversion depends on the defendant's mental state. Neither party in *Maye* thought the plaintiff intended to make a gift of his gold deposit when he said that he thought that the defendant owned it. Such mistakes are common in mining territory. Allowing the defendant to obtain a credit for the cost of extraction returns the situation to how matters would have stood if the defendant had not made the mistake in the first place. The defendant need not make a gift of services to the plaintiff. But if he takes ore or cuts the plaintiff's trees in bad faith (that is, with knowledge that they belong to another), he receives no offset for the labor expended, which discourages his conscious violation of the plaintiff's rights, for now he is left worse off than he would have been if he had not taken the gold at all.

3. ***Trespass Versus Conversion: The Measure of Damage.*** Notwithstanding the different theories for trespass and conversion, many wrongs fall within the scope of both. From the early 1600s, it was settled that the plaintiff could elect the more advantageous action when both were available. Originally conversion was treated as a "forced sale," under which the defendant, now designated as the owner of the plaintiff's property, was now made to buy it at the full market price—even if the defendant was willing to return it. In Munier v. Zachary, 114 N.W. 525–26 (Iowa 1908), the court put the point emphatically: "After the conversion of property has become complete the wrongdoer cannot escape liability, nor lessen the actual damage recoverable, by a tender back of the property." Today, that rule has been relaxed in most jurisdictions, so that the innocent converter may generally return the property taken, at least if it has not suffered substantial damage or alteration, conditional upon payment for the loss of interim use or for repairs. See RST §922.

Historically, for trespass to chattels, damages were limited to the reduction in value of the chattel. The defendant was therefore able to force the plaintiff to take the chattel back, so that the full price was awarded only in cases of complete destruction. For an exchange on the proper remedies for conversion, see Ayres, Protecting Property with Puts, 32 Val. U. L. Rev. 793, 813–18 (1998); Epstein, Protecting Property Rights with Legal Remedies: A Common Sense Reply to Professor Ayres, 32 Val. U. L. Rev. 833, 845–52 (1998).

Moore v. Regents of the University of California

793 P.2d 479 (Cal. 1990)

Panelli, J. We granted review in this case to determine whether plaintiff has stated a cause of action against his physician and other defendants for using his cells in potentially lucrative medical research without his permission. Plaintiff alleges that his physician failed to disclose preexisting research and economic interests in the cells before obtaining consent to the medical procedures by which they were extracted. The superior court sustained all defendants' demurrers to the third amended complaint, and the Court of Appeal reversed. We hold that the complaint states a cause of action for breach of the physician's disclosure obligations, but not for conversion.

The plaintiff is John Moore (Moore), who underwent treatment for hairy-cell leukemia at the Medical Center of the University of California at Los Angeles (UCLA Medical Center). The five defendants are: (1) Dr. David W. Golde (Golde), a physician who attended Moore at UCLA Medical Center; (2) the Regents of the University of California (Regents), who own and operate the university; (3) Shirley G. Quan, a researcher employed by the Regents; (4) Genetics Institute, Inc. (Genetics Institute); and (5) Sandoz Pharmaceuticals Corporation and related entities (collectively Sandoz).

[Moore first visited UCLA Medical Center in 1976, shortly after he learned that he had hairy-cell leukemia. Dr. Golde confirmed the earlier diagnosis, and Moore's fourteen-pound-plus spleen was removed, with his consent, to save his life. Even before the operation, Golde and Quan knew that Moore's blood products could have great commercial uses unrelated to his medical care. But neither Golde nor Quan informed Moore of their research plan, nor did they ask for his permission to use his spleen for their medical research. Moore also flew in from Seattle to UCLA several times between 1976 and 1983, having been told falsely that these visits, which were designed to collect more research materials, were "necessary and required for his well-being." "On each of these visits Golde withdrew additional samples of 'blood, blood serum, skin, bone marrow aspirate, and sperm.'"]

Sometime before August 1979, Golde established a cell line from Moore's T-lymphocytes, white blood cells that regulate the immune system. In 1981, the Regents applied for a patent on the cell line, listing Golde and Quan as inventors. "[B]y virtue of an established policy . . . , [the] Regents, Golde, and Quan would share in any royalties or profits . . . arising out of [the] patent." The patent issued on March 20, 1984, naming Golde and Quan as the inventors of the cell line and the Regents as the assignee of the patent.

[With the Regents' assistance, Golde negotiated agreements for commercial development of the cell line and products to be derived from it. Under an agreement with Genetics Institute, Golde became a paid consultant with stock options, and Quan continued to work largely on the project. Sandoz joined the group in 1982. Sometime during 1983 Moore received a new consent form that read: "I (do, do not) voluntarily grant to the University of California all rights I, or my heirs, may have in any cell line or any other potential product which might be developed from the blood and/or bone marrow obtained from me." At the time he received the form, Moore had no knowledge of the patent. Nonetheless, he refused to sign the form, which he then turned over to his lawyer whose investigations uncovered the Golde and Quan patent.

Panelli, J., first concludes that nondisclosure of collateral research motives was a violation of the physicians' duties of disclosure.] Accordingly, we hold that a physician who is seeking a patient's consent for a medical procedure must, in order to satisfy his fiduciary duty and to obtain the patient's informed consent, disclose personal interests unrelated to the patient's health, whether research or economic, that may affect his medical judgment.

B. Conversion

Moore also attempts to characterize the invasion of his rights as a conversion—a tort that protects against interference with possessory and ownership interests in personal property. He theorizes that he continued to own his cells following their removal from his body, at least for the purpose of directing their use, and that he never consented to their use in potentially lucrative medical research. Thus, to complete Moore's argument, defendants' unauthorized use of his cells constitutes a conversion. As a result of the alleged conversion, Moore claims a proprietary interest in each of the products that any of the defendants might ever create from his cells or the patented cell line.

No court, however, has ever in a reported decision imposed conversion liability for the use of human cells in medical research. While that fact does not end our inquiry, it raises a flag of caution. In effect, what Moore is asking us to do is to impose a tort duty on scientists to investigate the consensual pedigree of each human cell sample used in research. To impose such a duty, which would affect medical research of importance to all of society, implicates policy concerns far removed from the traditional, two-party ownership disputes in which the law of conversion arose. Invoking a tort theory originally used to determine whether the loser or the finder of a horse had the better title, Moore claims ownership of the results of socially important medical research, including the genetic code for chemicals that regulate the functions of every human being's immune system.

1. Moore's Claim Under Existing Law

"To establish a conversion, plaintiff must establish an actual interference with his *ownership* or *right of possession*. . . . Where plaintiff neither has title to the property alleged to have been converted, nor possession thereof, he cannot maintain an action for conversion."

Since Moore clearly did not expect to retain possession of his cells following their removal,[20] to sue for their conversion he must have retained an ownership interest in them. But there are several reasons to doubt that he did retain any such interest. First, no reported judicial decision supports Moore's claim, either directly or by close analogy. Second, California statutory law drastically limits any continuing interest of a patient in excised cells. Third, the subject matters of the Regents' patent — the patented cell line and the products derived from it — cannot be Moore's property.

Neither the Court of Appeal's opinion, the parties' briefs, nor our research discloses a case holding that a person retains a sufficient interest in excised cells to support a cause of action for conversion. We do not find this surprising, since the laws governing such things as human tissues, transplantable organs, blood, fetuses, pituitary glands, corneal tissue, and dead bodies deal with human biological materials as objects sui generis, regulating their disposition to achieve policy goals rather than abandoning them to the general law of personal property. It is these specialized statutes, not the law of conversion, to which courts ordinarily should and do look for guidance on the disposition of human biological materials. . . .

2. Should Conversion Liability Be Extended?

There are three reasons why it is inappropriate to impose liability for conversion based upon the allegations of Moore's complaint. First, a fair balancing of the relevant policy considerations counsels against extending the tort. Second, problems in this area are better suited to legislative resolution. Third, the tort of conversion is not necessary to protect patients' rights. For these reasons, we conclude that the use of excised human cells in medical research does not amount to a conversion.

Of the relevant policy considerations, two are of overriding importance. The first is protection of a competent patient's right to make autonomous medical decisions. That right, as already discussed, is grounded in well-recognized and long-standing principles of fiduciary duty and informed consent. This policy weighs in favor of providing a remedy to patients when physicians act with undisclosed motives that may affect their professional judgment. The second important policy consideration is that we not threaten with disabling civil liability innocent parties who are engaged in socially useful activities, such as researchers who have no reason to believe that their use of a particular cell sample is, or may be, against a donor's wishes.

To reach an appropriate balance of these policy considerations is extremely important. . . .

We need not, however, make an arbitrary choice between liability and nonliability. Instead, an examination of the relevant policy considerations suggests an appropriate balance: Liability based upon existing disclosure obligations, rather than an unprecedented extension of the conversion theory, protects patients' rights of privacy and autonomy without unnecessarily hindering research.

---

20. In his complaint, Moore does not seek possession of his cells or claim the right to possess them. This is consistent with Health and Safety Code section 7054.4, which provides that "human tissues . . . following conclusion of scientific use shall be disposed of by interment, incineration, or any other method determined by the state department [of health services] to protect the public health and safety."

To be sure, the threat of liability for conversion might help to enforce patients' rights indirectly. This is because physicians might be able to avoid liability by obtaining patients' consent, in the broadest possible terms, to any conceivable subsequent research use of excised cells. Unfortunately, to extend the conversion theory would utterly sacrifice the other goal of protecting innocent parties. Since conversion is a strict liability tort, it would impose liability on all those into whose hands the cells come, whether or not the particular defendant participated in, or knew of, the inadequate disclosures that violated the patient's right to make an informed decision. In contrast to the conversion theory, the fiduciary-duty and informed-consent theories protect the patient directly, without punishing innocent parties or creating disincentives to the conduct of socially beneficial research.

To expand liability by extending conversion law into this area would have a broad impact. [The court then concludes that the creation of tort liability would dull the incentives for medical innovation.] If the use of cells in research is a conversion, then with every cell sample a researcher purchases a ticket in a litigation lottery. Because liability for conversion is predicated on a continuing ownership interest, "companies are unlikely to invest heavily in developing, manufacturing, or marketing a product when uncertainty about clear title exists."

If the scientific users of human cells are to be held liable for failing to investigate the consensual pedigree of their raw materials, we believe the Legislature should make that decision.

Finally, there is no pressing need to impose a judicially created rule of strict liability, since enforcement of physicians' disclosure obligations will protect patients against the very type of harm with which Moore was threatened. So long as a physician discloses research and economic interests that may affect his judgment, the patient is protected from conflicts of interest. Aware of any conflicts, the patient can make an informed decision to consent to treatment, or to withhold consent and look elsewhere for medical assistance. . . .

For these reasons, we hold that the allegations of Moore's third amended complaint state a cause of action for breach of fiduciary duty or lack of informed consent, but not conversion.

Lucas, C.J., and Eagleson and Kennard, JJ., concur.

[The concurring opinion of Arabian, J., is omitted.]

Broussard, J., concurring and dissenting. . . .

II

. . . I dissent from the majority's conclusion that the facts alleged in this case do not state a cause of action for conversion.

If this were a typical case in which a patient consented to the use of his removed organ for general research purposes and the patient's doctor had no prior knowledge of the scientific or commercial value of the patient's organ or cells, I would agree that the patient could not maintain a conversion action. In that common scenario, the patient has abandoned any interest in the removed organ and is not entitled to demand compensation if it should later be discovered that the organ or cells have some unanticipated value. I cannot agree, however, with the majority that a patient may *never* maintain a conversion action for the unauthorized use of his excised organ or cells, even against a party who knew of the value of the organ or cells before they were removed and breached a duty to disclose that value to the patient. Because plaintiff alleges that defendants wrongfully interfered with his right to determine, prior to the removal of his body parts, how those parts would be used after removal, I conclude that the complaint states a cause of action under traditional, common law conversion principles. . . .

Mosk, J., dissenting.

[Mosk, J., first argues that an acceptance of legislative dominance does not require judicial passivity in applying traditional common law principles of conversion to "the recent explosive growth in the commercialization of biotechnology." Next he argues that the current legislative schemes do not preclude the sale of human organs removed for medical reasons. He then turns to a comparison of conversion with the informed consent action. After noting the difficulties of proving causation in informed consent cases, he continues:]

The second reason why the nondisclosure cause of action is inadequate for the task that the majority assign to it is that it fails to solve half the problem before us: it gives the patient only the right to *refuse* consent, i.e., the right to prohibit the commercialization of his tissue; it does not give him the right to *grant* consent to that commercialization on the condition that he share in its proceeds. . . .

Reversing the words of the old song, the nondisclosure cause of action thus accentuates the negative and eliminates the positive: the patient can say no, but he cannot say yes and expect to share in the proceeds of his contribution. . . .

Third, the nondisclosure cause of action fails to reach a major class of potential defendants: all those who are outside the strict physician-patient relationship with the plaintiff. . . .

To the extent that a plaintiff such as Moore is unable to plead or prove a satisfactory theory of secondary liability, the nondisclosure cause of action will thus be inadequate to reach a number of parties to the commercial exploitation of his tissue. Such parties include, for example, any physician-researcher who is not personally treating the patient, any other researcher who is not a physician, any employer of the foregoing (or even of the treating physician), and any person or corporation thereafter participating in the commercial exploitation of the tissue. Yet some or all of those parties may well have participated more in, and profited more from, such exploitation than the particular physician with whom the plaintiff happened to have a formal doctor-patient relationship at the time.

Exhibit 7.1 Henrietta Lacks

Henrietta Lacks (1920–1951) was an African American woman who died of a cervical cancerous tumor at the age of thirty-one. Unbeknownst to her, some of her cancer cells were cultured by the scientist George Otto Gey to start an "immortal line" of cells, the HeLa cell line, which does not die off in a few days like ordinary cancer cells. Since their original cultivation, more than 74,000 studies have used HeLa cells, shedding light on wide areas of the life sciences, including cell biology, cancer, and vaccinations. In 2013, the Lacks family reached an agreement with the National Institute of Health after Henrietta's genome was published by European researchers, an act that had raised privacy concerns for the family. The agreement gives the Lacks family some control over how their forebear's genome is used but does not give them any right to future profits that may result from HeLa cells. Skloot, The Immortal Life of Henrietta Lacks (2010), extensively covers the story behind this remarkable cell line.

Source: Science Photo Library

NOTES

1. ***Voluntary Donation of Blood Samples for Medical Research.*** What are the different consequences of the nondisclosure and conversion theories? This inquiry breaks down into two parts. The first part looks backward to the case at bar: What damages could Moore recover under the conversion theory that he could not recover under the nondisclosure theory? Under both theories what allowance should be made for the value added by the work of the research scientists?

The second part of the inquiry looks forward to future transactions. Once disclosures are made to patients, can they hold out for a royalty on future invention? Demand that the organ be destroyed? Go overseas to an establishment that will pay for the organ use? Moore died in 2001 at age fifty-six. Before his death, he negotiated what he termed a "token" settlement with UCLA covering his legal fees on the theory that he had not agreed to participate in the research of whose nature he was not informed. For the details of Moore's personal history, see Skloot, The Immortal Life of Henrietta Lacks 199–206 (2010).

In Greenberg v. Miami Children's Hospital Research Institute, Inc., 264 F. Supp. 2d 1064, 1074, 1075–76 (S.D. Fla. 2003), the plaintiffs were parents of Ashkenazi Jewish children afflicted with Canavan's disease, a fatal genetic affliction. In 1987, the plaintiff group approached Dr. Reuben Matalon, then in Chicago, with offers to provide him voluntarily with blood samples needed to isolate the gene for Canavan's disease. Matalon's research, first in Chicago and later in Miami, identified the key gene. At the time, Matalon and his group patented the gene, which enabled them to restrict others' research access to the gene. They also threatened suit against medical centers that offered Canavan testing. The plaintiffs claimed that they had collected the samples with the specific "understanding and expectations" that their use in research on the disease and the results of that research "would remain in the public domain." Their claim that the defendants failed to make appropriate disclosures, in breach of the duty of informed consent, was dismissed on the ground that all collection efforts took place outside any treatment relationship between physician and patient. Relying on *Moore*, Moreno, J., also rejected the count for conversion:

> First, Plaintiffs have no cognizable property interest in body tissue and genetic matter donated for research under a theory of conversion. . . .
>
> The Court finds that Florida statutory and common law do not provide a remedy for Plaintiffs' donations of body tissue and blood samples under a theory of conversion liability. Indeed, the Complaint does not allege that the Defendants used the genetic material for any purpose but medical research. Plaintiffs claim that the *fruits* of the research, namely the patented material, was commercialized. This is an important distinction and another step in the chain of attenuation that renders conversion liability inapplicable to the facts as alleged. If adopted, the expansive theory championed by Plaintiffs would cripple medical research as it would bestow a continuing right for donors to possess the results of any research conducted by the hospital. At the core, these were donations to research without any contemporaneous expectations of return.

The court did hold that the plaintiffs' count for unjust enrichment, a remedy in restitution, survived summary judgment. Why not allow a damage claim against any or all defendants?

In August 2023, the estate of Henrietta Lacks (discussed in Exhibit 7.1, *supra*) settled its claim for unjust enrichment against Thermo Fisher Scientific, a biotech company that profits from the use of HeLa cells. See Holpuch, Family of Henrietta Lacks Settles with Biotech Company That Used Her Cells, N.Y. Times, Aug. 1, 2023, https://www.nytimes.com/2023/08/01/science/henrietta-lacks-cells-lawsuit-settlement.html. Similar claims are forthcoming. See Civil Complaint & Request for Jury Trial, Lacks v. Ultragenyx Pharmaceutical, Inc, No. 1:23-cv-02171 (D. Md. Aug. 10, 2023), ECF No. 1. Does recognizing a claim for unjust enrichment yield conversion liability by another name?

How should future donors proceed at the outset to make sure that the results of their funded research remain in the public domain? For the contentious issues that have arisen in connection with the patenting of the BRCA genes (associated with breast cancer) for cancer research, see Association for Molecular Pathology v. Myriad, 569 U.S. 576 (2013), where the Supreme Court refused to allow anyone to patent a gene, because it remains a product of nature (and not an invention) even after it is isolated. Yet, the Court also held that cDNA (or complementary DNA) can be patented because it is a creation of man. For statutory modification of genetic testing protocols, see Fla. Stat. Ann. §760.40 (2023).

FLORIDA STATUTES ANNOTATED

§760.40. Genetic Testing; Informed Consent; Confidentiality; Penalties; Notice of Use of Results

(1) As used in this section, the term "DNA analysis" means the medical and biological examination and analysis of a person to identify the presence and composition of genes in that person's body. The term includes DNA typing and genetic testing.

(2) Except for [criminal prosecution and investigation], a person or entity may only perform DNA analysis with express consent. The results of such DNA analysis, whether held by a public or private entity, are the exclusive property of the person tested, are confidential, and may not be disclosed without express consent. . . .

2. *Conversion of Intangible Property.* In Kremen v. Cohen, 337 F.3d 1024, 1032–35 (9th Cir. 2003), the plaintiff, Kremen, registered the domain name "sex.com" with the defendant, Internet domain registrar Network Solutions. He did not engage in any active development of the site. His company, Online Classifieds, was listed as the owner of the domain name, with Kremen as the contact person. Shortly thereafter, Cohen, a long-time swindler, sent a letter to Network Solutions telling it that Online Classifieds had dismissed Kremen, had decided to abandon the use of the domain name sex.com, and had no objection if Cohen used that name. Cohen promptly used the name to create "a lucrative online porn empire." His letter was a total fabrication, but Network Solutions never checked with Kremen to verify Cohen's claims. Once aware of the fraud, Kremen sued Cohen and won a judgment for about $64 million ($109 million in 2023 dollars), after which Cohen fled to Mexico to avoid payment. Kremen also sued Network Solutions for conversion. Network Solutions first claimed that, under RST §242, conversion for intangibles was only available if the intangible had been "merged" into a document. Kozinski, J., rebuffed that claim:

> On the contrary, courts routinely apply the tort to intangibles without inquiring whether they are merged in a document and, while it's often possible to dream up *some* document the intangible is connected to in some fashion, it's seldom one that represents the owner's property interest. . . . [The strict merger] rule cannot be squared with a jurisprudence that recognizes conversion of music recordings, radio shows, customer lists, regulatory filings, confidential information and even domain names.

Kozinski, J., then held that, even if California law had such a requirement, it had been met because Kremen's name was stored in the defendant's Domain Name System, which counted as "a document (or perhaps more accurately a collection of documents). That it is stored in electronic form rather than on ink and paper is immaterial." Finally, he addressed the question of liability:

> The [district] court was reluctant to apply the tort of conversion because of its strict liability nature. This concern rings somewhat hollow in this case because the district court effectively exempted Network Solutions from liability to Kremen altogether, whether or not it was negligent. Network Solutions made no effort to contact Kremen before giving away his domain name, despite receiving a facially suspect letter from a third party. A jury would be justified in finding it was unreasonably careless.
>
> We must, of course, take the broader view, but there is nothing unfair about holding a company responsible for giving away someone else's property even if it was not at fault. Cohen is obviously the guilty party here, and the one who should in all fairness pay for his theft. But he's skipped the country, and his money is stashed in some offshore bank account. Unless Kremen's luck with his bounty hunters improves, Cohen is out of the picture. The question becomes whether Network Solutions should be open to liability for its decision to hand over Kremen's

domain name. Negligent or not, it was Network Solutions that gave away Kremen's property. Kremen never did anything. It would not be unfair to hold Network Solutions responsible and force it to try to recoup its losses by chasing down Cohen. This, at any rate, is the logic of the common law, and we do not lightly discard it.

On a historical note, the scam in *Kremen* took place in 1994 when the Web was just getting started. The early standard form contract contained no limitation against recovery of consequential damages (i.e., those flowing from breach) for the improper assignment of domain names that are today inserted in every such contract. Given that Network Classifieds received no compensation, why not judge its conduct under the contractual standard that asked whether or not it was acting in good faith? See Epstein, The Roman Law of Cyberconversion, 2005 Mich. St. L. Rev. 103. For a competing view, see Hancock, Note, You Can Have It But Can You Hold It? Treating Domain Names as Tangible Property, 99 Ky. L.J. 185 (2010).

Jurisdictions remain divided on the nature of property rights in domain names. Nevada followed Kozinski's, J., liberal interpretation of RST §242 in M.C. Multi-Family Development, LLC v. Crestdale Associates, Ltd., 193 P.3d 536, 538 (Nev. 2008), whereas Maryland and the District of Columbia hew to a stricter requirement that intangible property can only be the object of conversion if its rights have been merged into an actual document. See Pan 4 Am., LLC v. Tito & Tita Food Truck, LLC, No. DLB-21-401, 2022 WL 622234, at *9 (D. Md. Mar. 3, 2022). Should property be defined by whether it is tangible or rather by the set of permissions and obligations it signals to others? For embrace of the latter, see Marinotti, Possessing Intangibles, 116 Nw. U. L. Rev. 1227, 1232–33 (2022).

What about conversion liability for deletion of data on an online account? Compare Sims v. Little Rock Plastic Surgery, No. 4:19-cv-653, 2020 WL 4514572 (E.D. Ark. Aug. 5, 2020), answering in the affirmative, where the defendant deleted the plaintiff's Instagram posts, with Universal Meridian E-Commerce v. Puchalsky, No. 4:21-cv-357 RWS, 2021 WL 4775476, at *3 n.2 (E.D. Mo. Oct. 13, 2021), answering in the negative, where the defendant deleted the plaintiff's emails, when the underlying data was "easily retrievable."

SECTION C. ANIMALS

Gehrts v. Batteen

620 N.W.2d 775 (S.D. 2001)

Gilbertson, J. Gehrts was bitten by a St. Bernard owned by Nielsen. Gehrts sued Nielsen in strict liability and in negligence. The trial court granted summary judgment as to both claims. Gehrts appeals and we affirm.

Facts and Procedure

On July 29, 1995, Cindy Nielsen (Nielsen) visited the home of [fourteen-year-old] Jessica Gehrts (Gehrts) to pick up a wreath made by Gehrts' mother. Nielsen had come directly from dog obedience school with her eight-month-old dog, Wilbur, a St. Bernard. Wilbur was secured in the back of Nielsen's pickup by a harness attached to a restraining device that had been installed in the pickup box. This device allowed Wilbur to move freely between the sides of the box, but limited his movement between the front and back. While the parties were near the truck, Gehrts asked Nielsen if she could pet Wilbur. Nielsen allowed her to do so. As Gehrts reached up to pet Wilbur, he bit her in the face, causing injuries to her nose and forehead. Gehrts received extensive medical treatment as a result of those injuries.

Gehrts sued Nielsen and her husband, Jon Batteen, to recover for her injuries. In her complaint, Gehrts alleged that Nielsen was negligent in failing to restrain or control her dog. Nielsen moved for summary judgment, which was granted. Gehrts appeals the trial court's ruling and we affirm.

Analysis and Decision

1. Negligence

When wild animals, such as a bear or wolf, are kept as pets, an owner is liable for injuries caused by the animal. This results even if the owner had no prior knowledge of the animal's propensity to cause harm, and even if the owner has exercised the utmost care in preventing harm.

Owners of domesticated animals may also be held liable for harm caused by their pet if the owner knows or has reason to know that the animal has abnormally dangerous propensities. Again, this liability attaches regardless of the amount of care exercised by the owner. However, this liability is not strict liability. Rather, the failure to act upon the knowledge of an animal's abnormally dangerous propensities establishes a breach of the duty of care owed by the owner to those that come in contact with the animal. As it is a cause of action sounding in negligence, the defenses of contributory negligence and assumption of the risk are available to temper this liability. Before this breach of duty will affix to an owner, the plaintiff must establish that the owner knew or should have known of that animal's dangerous propensities. This knowledge is generally imputed to the owner when there is evidence of at least one attack by the animal.[1] In the case of a dog, evidence of the owner's knowledge that it constantly barked, bared its teeth, and strained at its leash is sufficient to establish dangerous propensities, absent an actual attack.

However, in certain instances a cause of action for negligence can survive without the owner's actual knowledge of an animal's dangerous propensities. When the owner does not know of the animal's dangerous propensities, the ordinary negligence standard of foreseeability will still be applied. To recover, the plaintiff must establish that a duty existed between the owner and the victim and that there was a breach of that duty. Thus, when no actual knowledge of dangerousness exists, the plaintiff must establish that as an ordinary, prudent person, the owner should have foreseen the event that caused the injury and taken steps to prevent the injury. Such liability may arise "depending upon the kind and character of the particular animal concerned, the circumstances in which it is placed, and the purposes for which it is employed or kept."

In the present action, there has been no evidence presented that Nielsen had any knowledge that Wilbur had dangerous propensities. The parties agree that, by nature, St. Bernards are gentle dogs. Nielsen and her husband testified in their depositions that Wilbur had never previously growled, bared his teeth, tried to bite or act aggressively toward any person. In addition, Gehrts admitted that she did not know of any incidents that would have alerted Nielsen to any dangerous propensities. Gehrts argues that the act of an unprovoked biting is evidence of the animal's dangerous propensity. While other jurisdictions may allow juries to determine after the fact whether the animal had dangerous propensities, such reasoning has been expressly rejected in South Dakota.

Nevertheless, Gehrts will still be allowed to recover if she can show that Nielsen failed to use reasonable care in the circumstances in that Nielsen as a prudent person should have foreseen the danger. In support of this claim, Gehrts produced an affidavit from a dog expert

1. There is no requirement that the attack cause injury to the victim to establish dangerous propensities. The common law "one free bite rule" was expressly rejected in Ross v. Hanson, 200 N.W.2d 255, 256 (S.D. 1972).

who concluded that Nielsen acted in an unreasonable manner when she failed to properly restrain Wilbur. This affidavit was based largely on the fact that the Gehrts family kept a dog at their home, its scent would be on Gehrts, and Nielsen should have known that the smell of a strange dog would make Wilbur act aggressively. However, there is no evidence in the record that Nielsen was aware that Gehrts owned a dog or that the scent of the dog would be on Gehrts. Beyond the assertions in the affidavit, there is no evidence or reason to believe that Nielsen knew, or as a prudent person should have known, that the scent of a strange dog would cause Wilbur to attack Gehrts.

Gehrts also claims that Nielsen was negligent in failing to restrain and have control over Wilbur while he was being petted by Gehrts. Wilbur was attached to a harness in the back of the pickup. This harness was specifically designed to secure a large dog. Gehrts claims that Nielsen should have released Wilbur from the harness, taken him out of the truck bed and allowed Gehrts to pet him while Nielsen held the leash. Whether this would have prevented the injury is speculative. It may actually have exacerbated the situation. If Wilbur had become sufficiently agitated to pull free of Nielsen's control, Gehrts' injuries may have been much more severe. . . .

There is simply no evidence that Nielsen violated the reasonable person standard of care in her handling of Wilbur. Therefore, Gehrts' cause of action for negligence cannot survive.

2. Strict Liability

[Gehrts] also urges us to follow the lead of the South Carolina Supreme Court by judicially adopting a strict liability standard for injuries caused by dogs. See Hossenlopp v. Cannon, 329 S.E.2d 438 (S.C. 1985). We decline to do so. The overwhelming majority of states that impose strict liability for injuries caused by dogs have done so through legislative mandate. See . . . Cal. Civil Code §3342 (West 1997). . . . Our legislature has already imposed strict liability on dog owners for damages inflicted upon "poultry or domestic animal[s]." SDCL 40-34-2. While one may question the application of strict liability for damages to livestock, but not for injuries to children, the legislature is the proper place to decide such public policy issues.

[Affirmed.]

Sabers, J., dissenting.

I disagree with the premature conclusion that the facts of this case warrant summary judgment for Nielsen. "This Court has stated on numerous occasions that summary judgment is generally not appropriate in negligence actions." . . .

Whether Nielsen was negligent: 1) in restraining the dog, 2) allowing the fourteen year old girl to pet the dog, 3) failing to release the dog from the harness, or 4) whether Nielsen knew that her co-worker, Gehrts' mother, owned a dog at that house are genuine issues of material fact that should be resolved by a jury. The facts of this case can not be resolved by summary judgment or rubber stamped by appellate review. The majority opinion's finding that Nielsen was not negligent for failing to release the dog from the harness is a function best left to the jury.

NOTES

1. *Basis of Liability for Animals.* *Gehrts* states the dominant English and U.S. view that the liability rules tend to be strict, at least for animals classified as dangerous by nature, often called *animals ferae naturae* in the older cases. For wild animals, the Third Restatement subjects the owner or possessor to strict liability for physical harm. RTT: LPEH §22. The category "wild animals" includes most of the obvious suspects such as lions and tigers but has also been extended to cover elephants, monkeys, and camels. By contrast, "wild animals" do not include iguanas or manatees. *Id.*, comment *b*. The Third Restatement treats as wild any animal "that belongs to a category of animals that have not been generally domesticated and that are likely, unless restrained, to cause personal injury." What about property damage?

For animals tame by nature (animals *mansuetae naturae*), the rules are a bit more complex. Normally the owner is only liable for negligence, but a strict liability rule applies to domestic animals that individually have shown dangerous propensities even if they have not bitten. The common statement that every dog is entitled to "one free bite" is not an accurate reflection of the general law; a demonstrated tendency to bite is enough. RTT: LPEH §23. When the common law is uncertain, the one free bite rule is often rejected by statute. See, e.g., N.H. Rev. Stat. Ann. §466:19 (2023). Why should the line between wild and tame matter? Should pit bulls be put on the wild side of the line based on their perceived genetic characteristics? The invitation to create this subcategory of dangerous animals was rejected in Ferrara v. Marra, 823 A.2d 1134, 1137 (R.I. 2003). For a time, many jurisdictions passed laws prohibiting certain breeds within cities. These ordinances have mostly been relaxed to allow for conditional permits, or otherwise superseded entirely by state law. See, e.g., Denver, Colo., Rev. Mun. Code §8-67 (2023) (allowing residents to acquire a permit to keep pit bulls, relaxing a previous municipal ban); S.B. 942, 2023 Leg., 125th Reg. Sess. (Fla. 2023) (overriding Miami ordinance prohibiting pit bulls).

2. *Vicarious Liability for Dangerous Animals.* What is wrong with a unified prima facie case that holds that "your dog (or other animal) bit me"? In that case, should the battleground switch to the defense of assumption of risk, given that Jessica approached the dog? Would a strict liability rule be appropriate if the defendant's St. Bernard escaped and attacked an innocent stranger? In any event, the Third Restatement rejects the vicarious liability intuition behind this approach by noting that "the language of trespass is analytically imperfect; a cow is obviously incapable of committing a tort. For that reason, any idea of vicarious liability is also inapt; there is no tort on the part of the cow that can be imputed to the owner." RTT: LPEH §21, comment *b*.

Historically, cattle trespass was one of the oldest branches of the law of animals, where the first writ for cattle trespass was issued in the reign of King John (1199–1216). Why reject that view today? Is it because cattle cannot form intentions? Understand the significance of boundary lines? Note that following the Restatement lead, it is often said the strict liability cause of action rests not on the biting or kicking of the animal as such, but on the breach of an absolute duty of the owner or possessor to keep it contained. These different formulations can result in different outcomes, especially when the animal is in the custody of someone who is not the owner.

In Baker v. Snell, [1908] 2 KB 825, the defendant owned a dog known to be vicious, which he entrusted to his potman, or servant, to take care of each morning. While in the kitchen with the plaintiff, the potman, "presumably by way of a foolish practical joke, said, 'I will bet the dog will not bite any one,' and then, 'Go it, Bob,' whereupon the dog bit the plaintiff." The county court judge dismissed the cause of action "on the ground that the conduct of the barman who had the dog in charge amounted to an assault by him." At the first stage of appeal, a new trial was ordered on the question of scope of the potman's employment. Channell, J., said that the key question about the incitement by the potman was

> whether the man's wrongful act was done in the course of his employment, or whether it was done for purposes of his own. If it could be shewn that the man did it maliciously to gratify some grudge against the plaintiff, his master would not be liable. But there was no evidence of that. In my view the potman's act amount to nothing more than a foolish and wanton act done in neglect of his duty to keep the dog safe; and if that is the right view, the defendant would be responsible. But the question is one of fact which ought to have been left to the jury.

Cozens-Hardy, M.R., accepted that position but made it clear that he did not think that the characterization of the potman's act was decisive.

> If a man keeps an animal whose nature is ferocious, or an animal of a class not generally ferocious, but which is known to the owner to be dangerous, is the owner of that animal liable only if he neglects his duty of keeping it safe or is negligent in the discharge of that duty, or is he bound to keep it secure at his peril? In my opinion the latter is the correct proposition of law. . . .

What result if lightning breaks the chains restraining the dog, who gets free and does mischief to a stranger? If the dog is in the custody of someone who is not the defendant's employee?

Compare the view on causation under RTT: LPEH §23.

RESTATEMENT OF THE LAW (THIRD) OF TORTS: LIABILITY FOR PHYSICAL AND EMOTIONAL HARM

§23. Abnormally Dangerous Animals

An owner or possessor of an animal that the owner or possessor knows or has reason to know has dangerous tendencies abnormal for the animal's category is subject to strict liability for physical harm caused by the animal if the harm ensues from that dangerous tendency.

When the animal's owner entrusts it to someone else for safekeeping, as in *Baker*, the Third Restatement concludes: "Both the owner and the possessor are sufficiently responsible for the animal as to make their [joint] liability appropriate. Further, the owner and the possessor remain free to work out between themselves the ultimate allocation of liability." *RTT: LPEH §21*, comment *f.* The position is otherwise if the possessor has taken the animal without the owner's consent. *Id.* The possessor is then manifestly liable.

3. *Affirmative Defenses for Wild Animals.* The strict liability principle works best when wild animals attack or injure strangers. However, this rule has been relaxed in a variety of controlled settings. In City & County of Denver v. Kennedy, 476 P.2d 762 (Colo. App. 1970), the court held that its state's general rule of strict liability did not apply to animals kept in public zoos. It agreed in general that the keeping or harboring of a wild animal is "in defiance of the safety and desires of the surrounding society." Nonetheless, it concluded that it would be improper to apply that strict liability rule to a zoo, which is maintained and operated "in response to the public's obvious desires," and "unrealistic" to hold that the operation of the zoo "exposes the public to an inordinate risk" of harm. It therefore applied negligence principles. On appeal, the state supreme court held that the plaintiff made out a jury case in negligence by showing that the defendant's zebra pit was constructed so that a person could easily reach over the barriers and come in direct physical contact with the animals. Kennedy v. City & County of Denver, 506 P.2d 764 (Colo. 1972).

In Rubenstein v. United States, 338 F. Supp. 654 (N.D. Cal. 1972), *aff'd*, 488 F.2d 1071 (9th Cir. 1973), the court reached the same conclusion for animals in national parks. The plaintiff, while sleeping in his tent in Yellowstone Park, was attacked and mauled by a bear. Before the incident took place, the plaintiff had received written warnings from the park authorities about the dangers of camping out in the park. The court held that the defendants had not been negligent, having discharged their duty to warn. The same result follows on strict liability, since the written warnings compel the finding that the plaintiff assumed the risk of injury.

Strict liability principles were applied, however, in City of Dallas v. Heard, 252 S.W.3d 98 (Tex. App. 2008), in which an adolescent lowland gorilla escaped from an outdoor exhibit at a city zoo and attacked three people. The court found that a state statute waived government immunity, and attached no weight to the public policy in maintaining a zoo. The situation often changes with respect to livestock, which can easily wander off their own lands. In general, the owner or possessor of the animal is responsible for any damage it does to the plaintiff's real property and to animals peacefully grazing there. See, e.g., Lee v. Riley (1865) 144 Eng. Rep. 629 (CB). See also RTT §21, which keeps the strict liability rule. But in many cases that liability attaches only after deciding whether certain harms fall within the class of those that make the animal dangerous. See RST §504(3)(a). Thus section 504, comment *g*, notes that "any trespassing bull may be expected to attack and gore any other animal, or any person who gets in his way."

4. *Distress Damage Feasant.* "Distress damage feasant" refers to "the taking of chattels, whether animate or inanimate, that are doing damage to or (perhaps) encumbering land, or depasturing chattels, and the retaining of them by way of security until compensation is paid." Williams, Liability for Animals 7 (1939). This self-help remedy was critical in most disputes between farmers arising from trespassing cattle, which helps explain the dominance of the strict liability rule for trespassing animals. In Marshall v. Welwood, 38 N.J.L. 339, 341 (1876), Beasley, C.J., argued that

> the right to plead that the escape had occurred by inevitable accident would have seriously impaired, if it did not entirely frustrate, the process of distress damage feasant. Custom has had much to do in giving shape to the law, and what is highly convenient readily runs into usage, and is accepted as a rule. It would but rarely occur that cattle would escape from a vigilant owner. . . .

Note also that in England, a proposal to govern cattle trespass by negligence rules, Report of the Committee on the Law of Civil Liability for Damage Done by Animals, CMD 8746, & ¶3 (1953), was rejected in large measure because of the protests of the farmers themselves. As the report stated, "This class of liability is of interest only to farmers and landowners and the general public are not affected thereby." That position was modified in England by section 7(1) of the Animals Act 1971 c. 22, so that now the sale of animals so detained is conducted by public authorities.

5. *"Fencing in" and "Fencing Out": Historical, Economic, and Social Complications.* In Garcia v. Sumrall, 121 P.2d 640, 644 (Ariz. 1942), Lockwood, C.J., said:

> Under the common law it was presumed to be the duty of the owners of animals to keep the same properly enclosed and under control, and if they failed to do so and the animals trespassed upon the property of another, fenced or unfenced, the owners of the animals were liable for damages. This rule, however, has been greatly modified in America, and particularly in what is commonly referred to as the grazing states. The situation in these states may be briefly stated as follows:
>
> A very large percentage of the land therein is owned by the United States government, only an extremely small portion being under private ownership. Much of this land is valuable only for the pasturage of meat animals. The federal government for many years recognized the custom existing of allowing such animals to run at large upon the land and acquiesced therein, but forbade its enclosure by fences. The result was that if the old common law rule of trespass was applied, it would have been practically impossible to use these federal lands for grazing, for the animals running at large thereon, due to their natural instincts, would be practically certain to trespass upon any privately owned lands lying adjacent to the open range. For this reason many, if not most, of the western states adopted statutes similar to ours above referred to. The obvious purpose and effect of these statutes was to change the common law rule and to make the owner of private premises fence his land to keep animals out, rather than to compel the owner of the

> animals to fence the land upon which they were grazing in order to keep them in. But notwithstanding this, it was practically universally held in the states having such laws that they did not have the effect of permitting those grazing animals upon the public domain to commit acts of willful trespass by deliberately and intentionally causing their animals to trespass upon private property.

"Fencing out" statutes depart from the usual principles of property law by requiring a plaintiff to take affirmative action to protect the exclusive use of her land. RTT: LPEH §21, comments *c* and *d* explore in some depth the diversity of positions on the fencing out question. These comments note that use of the English fencing in rule is more common when farmers outnumber ranchers, especially since fencing in helps the cattle owner protect his herd against a variety of perils ranging from rustlers and snakes to unwanted insemination. Should the private landowners receive some compensation for the fencing that they are now required to construct in defense of their property?

The issue lies at the tail end of fierce political conflicts during much of the nineteenth century. This early history has been well documented. See, e.g., Ellickson, Order Without Law: How Neighbors Settle Disputes chs. 2 & 3 (1991); Vogel, The Coase Theorem and California Animal Trespass Law, 16 J. Legal Stud. 149 (1987). Open-range regimes requiring landowners to fence out have slowly given way to the closed-range alternatives now favored in the Third Restatement.

This choice between open and closed range not only has dramatic economic consequences for both ranchers and farmers, but also influences bargaining over land use. As Vogel points out, moving from open-range rules (favoring the rancher) to closed-range rules (favoring the farmer) reduces the costs of negotiating a change in the patterns of land use. Under an open-range system, a single landowner cannot in practice buy off some ranchers and hope to preserve his land for agricultural uses, given that those ranchers not bound by the agreement could still let their cattle roam at will. Yet, when the rights to exclude belong to the farmer, a voluntary agreement can allow some ranchers limited grazing rights, without opening the land up to all ranchers. Placing exclusive rights in the farmer facilitates consensual reassignments of rights better than the open-range rules. In practice, land remains open range when virtually all its users are cattle ranchers who benefit when animals can run freely. But once land is more intensively cultivated, the advantage shifts to the closed-range system, which encourages more specialized land uses. See also RTT: LPEH §21, comment *d*, which notes that coordination costs tend to favor open-range regimes when ranchers dominate and closed-range regimes when they do not.

SECTION D. ULTRAHAZARDOUS OR ABNORMALLY DANGEROUS ACTIVITIES

Spano v. Perini Corp.

250 N.E.2d 31 (N.Y. 1969)

Fuld, C.J. The principal question posed on this appeal is whether a person who has sustained property damage caused by blasting on nearby property can maintain an action for damages without a showing that the blaster was negligent. Since 1893, when this court decided the case of Booth v. Rome, W. & O.T.R.R. Co., [35 N.E. 592 (N.Y. 1893),] it has been the law of this State that proof of negligence was required unless the blast was accompanied by an actual physical invasion of the damaged property—for example, by rocks or other material being cast upon the premises. We are now asked to reconsider that rule.

The plaintiff Spano is the owner of a garage in Brooklyn which was wrecked by a blast occurring on November 27, 1962. There was then in that garage, for repairs, an automobile owned by the plaintiff Davis which he also claims was damaged by the blasting. Each of the plaintiffs brought suit against the two defendants who, as joint venturers, were engaged in constructing a tunnel in the vicinity pursuant to a contract with the City of New York. . . .

It is undisputed that, on the day in question (November 27, 1962), the defendants had set off a total of 194 sticks of dynamite at a construction site which was only 125 feet away from the damaged premises. Although both plaintiffs alleged negligence in their complaints [in this nonjury case], no attempt was made to show that the defendants had failed to exercise reasonable care or to take necessary precautions when they were blasting. Instead, they chose to rely, upon the trial, solely on the principle of absolute liability either on a tort theory or on the basis of their being third-party beneficiaries of the defendants' contract with the city. At the close of the plaintiff Spano's case, when defendants' attorney moved to dismiss the action on the ground, among others, that no negligence had been proved, the trial judge expressed the view that the defendants could be held liable even though they were not shown to have been careless. The case then proceeded, with evidence being introduced solely on the question of damages and proximate cause. Following the trial, the court awarded damages of some $4,400 [$36,800 in 2023 dollars] to Spano and of $329 [$2,752 in 2023 dollars] to Davis.

On appeal, a divided Appellate Term reversed that judgment, declaring that it deemed itself concluded by the established rule in this State requiring proof of negligence. Justice Markowitz, who dissented, urged that the *Booth* case should no longer be considered controlling precedent.

The Appellate Division affirmed; it called attention to a decision in the Third Department in which the court observed that "[i]f *Booth* is to be overruled, 'the announcement thereof should come from the authoritative source and not in the form of interpretation or prediction by an intermediate appellate court.' "

In our view, the time has come for this court to make that "announcement" and declare that one who engages in blasting must assume responsibility, and be liable without fault, for any injury he causes to neighboring property.

The concept of absolute liability in blasting cases is hardly a novel one. The overwhelming majority of American jurisdictions have adopted such a rule. . . .

We need not rely solely, however, upon out-of-state decisions in order to attain our result. Not only has the rationale of the *Booth* case been overwhelmingly rejected elsewhere but it appears to be fundamentally inconsistent with earlier cases in our own court which had held, long before *Booth* was decided, that a party was absolutely liable for damages to neighboring property caused by explosions. (See, e.g., Hay v. Cohoes Co., 2 N.Y. 159 [(1849)]; Heeg v. Licht, 80 N.Y. 579 [(1880).]) In the *Hay* case, for example, the defendant was engaged in blasting an excavation for a canal and the force of the blasts caused large quantities of earth and stones to be thrown against the plaintiff's house, knocking down his stoop and part of his chimney. The court held the defendant *absolutely* liable for the damage caused, stating:

> It is an elementary principle in reference to private rights, that every individual is entitled to the undisturbed possession and lawful enjoyment of his own property. The mode of enjoyment is necessarily limited by the rights of others—otherwise it might be made destructive of their rights altogether. Hence the maxim sic utere tuo, &c. [Latin for "use your own property as to not injure that of another."] The defendants had the right to dig the canal. The plaintiff the right to the undisturbed possession of his property. If these rights conflict, the former must yield to the latter, as the more important of the two, since, upon grounds of public policy, it is better that one man should surrender a particular use of his land, than that another should be deprived of the beneficial use of his property altogether, which might be the consequence if the privilege of the former should be wholly unrestricted. The case before us illustrates this

> principle. For if the defendants in excavating their canal, in itself a lawful use of their land, could, in the manner mentioned by the witnesses, demolish the stoop of the plaintiff with impunity, they might, for the same purpose, on the exercise of reasonable care, demolish his house, and thus deprive him of all use of his property.

Although the court in *Booth* drew a distinction between a situation—such as was presented in the *Hay* case—where there was "a physical invasion" of, or trespass on, the plaintiff's property and one in which the damage was caused by "setting the air in motion, or in some other unexplained way," it is clear that the court, in the earlier cases, was not concerned with the particular manner by which the damage was caused but by the simple fact that any explosion in a built-up area was likely to cause damage. Thus, in Heeg v. Licht the court held that there should be absolute liability where the damage was caused by the accidental explosion of stored gunpowder, even in the absence of a physical trespass:

> The defendant had erected a building and stored materials therein, which from their character were liable to and actually did explode, causing injury to the plaintiff. The fact that the explosion took place tends to establish that the magazine was dangerous and liable to cause damage to the property of persons residing in the vicinity. . . . The fact that the magazine was liable to such a contingency, which could not be guarded against or averted by the greatest degree of care and vigilance, evinces its dangerous character, . . . In such a case, the rule which exonerates a party engaged in a lawful business, when free from negligence, has no application.

Such reasoning should, we venture, have led to the conclusion that the *intentional* setting off of explosives—that is, blasting—in an area in which it was likely to cause harm to neighboring property similarly results in absolute liability. However, the court in the *Booth* case rejected such an extension of the rule for the reason that "[t]o exclude the defendant from blasting to adapt its lot to the contemplated uses, at the instance of the plaintiff, would not be a compromise between conflicting rights, but an extinguishment of the right of the one for the benefit of the other." The court expanded on this by stating, "This sacrifice, we think, the law does not exact. Public policy is promoted by the building up of towns and cities and the improvement of property. Any unnecessary restraint on freedom of action of a property owner hinders this."

This rationale cannot withstand analysis. The plaintiff in *Booth* was not seeking, as the court implied, to "exclude the defendant from blasting" and thus prevent desirable improvements to the latter's property. Rather, he was merely seeking compensation for the damage which was inflicted upon his own property as a result of that blasting. The question, in other words, was not *whether* it was lawful or proper to engage in blasting but *who* should bear the cost of any resulting damage—the person who engaged in the dangerous activity or the innocent neighbor injured thereby. Viewed in such a light, it clearly appears that *Booth* was wrongly decided and should be forthrightly overruled.

In more recent cases, our court has already gone far toward mitigating the harsh effect of the rule laid down in the *Booth* case [by allowing the force of the blast to establish negligence]. . . .

Indeed, the defendants devote but brief argument in defense of the *Booth* rule. The principal thrust of their argument is directed not to the requisite standard of care to be used but, rather, to the sufficiency of the plaintiffs' pleadings and the proof adduced on the issue of causation. [The court then disposes of both these points in the plaintiff's favor.]

[Reversed and remanded.]

NOTE

Influence of the Forms of Action. The rule in Booth v. Rome, discussed in *Spano*, rested in part on the distinction between trespass and case, discussed *supra* in Chapter 2, Section C.

The argument there was that the physical entry of rocks or other materials upon the plaintiff's land was a direct invasion by the defendant and thus a trespass, to which strict liability applied. In contrast to blasting, damage caused only by vibration or concussion was "indirect" and thus fell under trespass on the case, with a negligence requirement. Fuld's, C.J., opinion echoes Holmes' argument in The Common Law, *supra* Chapter 2, at 94, that the substantive ground for relief should not turn on the procedural niceties of the forms of action. Note how history has afforded Holmes only partial vindication of his views because the uniform theory is one of strict liability and not of negligence. To what extent does Fuld's argument anticipate the highly influential treatment of the subject in the Second and Third Restatements?

RESTATEMENT OF THE LAW (SECOND) OF TORTS

§519. General Principle

(1) One who carries on an abnormally dangerous activity is subject to liability for harm to the person, land or chattels of another resulting from the activity, although he has exercised the utmost care to prevent the harm.

(2) This strict liability is limited to the kind of harm, the possibility of which makes the activity abnormally dangerous.

Comment c: The word "care" includes care in preparation, care in operation and skill both in operation and preparation.

Comment on Subsection (2): e. Extent of protection: The rule of strict liability stated in Subsection (1) applies only to harm that is within the scope of the abnormal risk that is the basis of the liability. One who carries on an abnormally dangerous activity is not under strict liability for every possible harm that may result from carrying it on. For example, the thing that makes the storage of dynamite in a city abnormally dangerous is the risk of harm to those in the vicinity if it should explode. If an explosion occurs and does harm to persons, land or chattels in the vicinity, the rule stated in Subsection (1) applies. If, however, there is no explosion and for some unexpected reason a part of the wall of the magazine in which the dynamite is stored falls upon a pedestrian on the highway upon which the magazine abuts, the rule stated in Subsection (1) has no application. In this case the liability, if any, will be dependent upon proof of negligence in the construction or maintenance of the wall. So also, the transportation of dynamite or other high explosives by truck through the streets of a city is abnormally dangerous for the same reason as that which makes the storage of the explosives abnormally dangerous. If the dynamite explodes in the course of the transportation, a private person transporting it is subject to liability under the rule stated in Subsection (1), although he has exercised the utmost care. On the other hand, if the vehicle containing the explosives runs over a pedestrian, he cannot recover unless the vehicle was driven negligently.

RESTATEMENT OF THE LAW (SECOND) OF TORTS

§520. Abnormally Dangerous Activities

In determining whether an activity is abnormally dangerous, the following factors are to be considered:

(a) existence of a high degree of risk of some harm to the person, land or chattels of others;

(b) likelihood that the harm that results from it will be great;

(c) inability to eliminate the risk by the exercise of reasonable care;

(d) extent to which the activity is not a matter of common usage;

(e) inappropriateness of the activity to the place where it is carried on; and

(f) extent to which its value to the community is outweighed by its dangerous attributes.

Comment d. Purpose of activity: In the great majority of the cases that involve abnormally dangerous activities the activity is carried on by the actor for purposes in which he has a financial interest, such as a business conducted for profit. This, however, is not necessary for the existence of such an activity. The rule here stated is equally applicable when there is no pecuniary benefit to the actor. Thus a private owner of an abnormally dangerous body of water who keeps it only for his own use and pleasure as a swimming pool is subject to the same liability as one who operates a reservoir of water for profit.

Comment e. Not limited to the defendant's land: In most of the cases to which the rule of strict liability is applicable the abnormally dangerous activity is conducted on land in the possession of the defendant. This, again, is not necessary to the existence of such an activity. It may be carried on in a public highway or other public place or upon the land of another. . . .

Comment on Clause (c): h. Risk not eliminated by reasonable care: Another important factor to be taken into account in determining whether the activity is abnormally dangerous is the impossibility of eliminating the risk by the exercise of reasonable care. Most ordinary activities can be made entirely safe by the taking of all reasonable precautions; and when safety cannot be attained by the exercise of due care there is reason to regard the danger as an abnormal one. . . .

Comment on Clause (d): i. Common usage: An activity is a matter of common usage if it is customarily carried on by the great mass of mankind or by many people in the community. It does not cease to be so because it is carried on for a purpose peculiar to the individual who engages in it. Certain activities, notwithstanding their recognizable danger, are so generally carried on as to be regarded as customary. Thus automobiles have come into such general use that their operation is a matter of common usage. This, notwithstanding the residue of unavoidable risk of serious harm that may result even from their careful operation, is sufficient to prevent their use from being regarded as an abnormally dangerous activity. On the other hand, the operation of a tank or any other motor vehicle of such size and weight as to be unusually difficult to control safely, or to be likely to damage the ground over which it is driven, is not yet a usual activity for many people, and therefore the operation of such a vehicle may be abnormally dangerous.

Although blasting is recognized as a proper means of excavation for building purposes or of clearing woodland for cultivation, it is not carried on by any large percentage of the population, and therefore it is not a matter of common usage. Likewise the manufacture, storage, transportation and use of high explosives, although necessary to the construction of many public and private works, are carried on by only a comparatively small number of persons and therefore are not matters of common usage. So likewise, the very nature of oil lands and the essential interest of the public in the production of oil require that oil wells be drilled, but the dangers incident to the operation are characteristic of oil lands and not of lands in general, and relatively few persons are engaged in the activity. . . .

Comment on Clause (f): k. Value to the community: Even though the activity involves a serious risk of harm that cannot be eliminated with reasonable care and it is not a matter of common usage, its value to the community may be such that the danger will not be regarded as an abnormal one. . . .

Comment l. Function of court: Whether the activity is an abnormally dangerous one is to be determined by the court, upon consideration of all the factors listed in this Section, and the weight given to each that it merits upon the facts in evidence. In this it differs from questions of negligence [in which questions of liability are typically left to the jury].

RESTATEMENT OF THE LAW (THIRD) OF TORTS: LIABILITY FOR PHYSICAL AND EMOTIONAL HARM

§20. Abnormally Dangerous Activities

(a) An actor who carries on an abnormally dangerous activity is subject to strict liability for physical harm resulting from the activity.

(b) An activity is abnormally dangerous if:

(1) the activity creates a foreseeable and highly significant risk of physical harm even when reasonable care is exercised by all actors; and

(2) the activity is not one of common usage.

Comment b. Relationship to negligence: . . . [A] prerequisite for the strict-liability rule identified in this Section is not merely a highly significant risk associated with the activity itself, but a highly significant risk that remains with the activity even when all actors exercise reasonable care. Accordingly, at least at a general level, the issue of strict liability emerges at about the point at which the assignment of liability and losses in accordance with all actors' apparent negligence leaves off. . . .

NOTES

1. ***Definition of Abnormally Dangerous Activities.*** There is a peculiar progression on strict liability for abnormally dangerous activities. Sections 519 and 520 of the Second Restatement modify provisions of the First Restatement that in 1934 endorsed strict liability for all "ultrahazardous activities." The Second Restatement adds a set of elaborate conditions under section 520, most of which are excised from section 20 of the Third Restatement. For all their differences, these three sections do have at least some points in common. They all make judgments about *classes* of activities, such as drilling for oil, see Green v. General Petroleum Corp., 270 P. 952 (Cal. 1928); fumigation, see Luthringer v. Moore, 190 P.2d 1 (Cal. 1948); and gasoline storage, see Bowers v. Wurzburg, 528 S.E.2d 475 (W. Va. 1999), that are covered by the provisions. See also RTT: LPEH §20, comment *e*, reaffirming strict liability for blasting. The scorecard in In re Hanford Nuclear Reservation Litigation, 350 F. Supp. 2d 871, 876 (E.D. Wash. 2004), reads:

> In Washington, an assessment of the §520 factors has resulted in the imposition of strict liability for fire work displays; pile driving where injury occurred to the property on an adjacent lot; for aerial spraying of crops; and for a common carriers' transportation of large quantities of gasoline. . . . Washington courts have [also] held that the following activities are not abnormally dangerous including the transmission of electricity; the selling of handguns; ground damage caused by the crash landing of aircraft; and the transmission of natural gas.

Why is a categorical approach adopted for strict liability when negligence liability is usually determined on a case-by-case basis? Does the distinction collapse depending on how the relevant activity is characterized? Thus, in Schuck v. Beck, 497 P.3d 395, 426 (Wash. Ct. App. 2021), Fearing, J., held that selling a chlorine tank to a recycling facility was an abnormally dangerous activity subject to strict liability. In a sharp dissent, Staab, J., insisted that the relevant activity was the broader category of selling scrap metal and forewarned that, "[b]y including the particular elements of negligence into the definition of the activity [namely, the defendant's inadvertent inclusion of a container of chlorine gas in scrap metal], the majority's decision will, in effect, enable plaintiffs to invoke strict liability for all negligently-conducted activity." Why is not the correct target for abnormally dangerous activity only the recycling facility?

How successful are the authors of either the Second or Third Restatements in distinguishing between ordinary and "abnormally dangerous" activities? Is there any ordinary activity that can be made *entirely* safe by taking all *reasonable* precautions? More generally, should the general Hand formula for negligence apply to all abnormally dangerous activities? Henderson, Why Negligence Dominates Tort, 50 UCLA L. Rev. 377, 393 (2002), insists that strict liability has to pick limited spots, as "broad-based strict liability would not be viable because it would generate unadjudicable disputes." Why?

2. *Common Usage.* What is the function of the common usage requirement set out in RST §520(d)? If it is taken seriously, how can blasting, fumigating, or the manufacturing of explosives not be matters of common usage? One notable effort to make sense out of the Second Restatement's common usage requirement is found in Fletcher, Fairness and Utility in Tort Theory, 85 Harv. L. Rev. 537, 541–42, 547–48 (1972):

> I shall propose a specific standard of risk that makes sense of the Restatement's emphasis on uncommon, extra-hazardous risks, but which shows that the Restatement's theory is part of a larger rationale of liability that cuts across negligence, intentional torts, and numerous pockets of strict liability. The general principle expressed in all of these situations governed by diverse doctrinal standards is that a victim has a right to recover for injuries caused by a risk greater in degree and different in order from those created by the victim and imposed on the defendant—in short, for injuries resulting from nonreciprocal risks. Cases of liability are those in which the defendant generates a disproportionate, excessive risk of harm, relative to the victim's risk-creating activity. . . .
>
> The rationale of nonreciprocal risk-taking accounts as well for pockets of strict liability outside the coverage of the Restatement's sections on extra-hazardous activities. For example, an individual is strictly liable for damage done by a wild animal in his charge, but not for damage committed by his domesticated pet. Most people have pets, children, or friends whose presence creates some risk to neighbors and their property. These are risks that offset each other; they are, as a class, reciprocal risks. Yet bringing an unruly horse into the city goes beyond the accepted and shared level of risks in having pets, children, and friends in one's household. If the defendant creates a risk that exceeds those to which he is reciprocally subject, it seems fair to hold him liable for the results of his aberrant indulgence. Similarly, according to the [Second] Restatement, airplane owners and pilots are strictly liable for ground damage, but not for mid-air collisions. Risk of ground damage is nonreciprocal; homeowners do not create risks to airplanes flying overhead. The risks of mid-air collisions, on the other hand, are generated reciprocally by all those who fly the air lanes. Accordingly, the threshold of liability for damage resulting from mid-air collisions is higher than mere involvement in the activity of flying.

Fletcher's norm of reciprocity works well with repeated, low-level interferences that might be characterized as reciprocal, but it works less well with personal injuries, in which the harms are both infrequent and substantial. Often, as with dangerous animals, both actions are allowed instead of neither. How do we decide whether two actions or none is superior? In some cases, however, the outcome seems clear. In In re Hanford Nuclear Reservation Litigation, 350 F. Supp. 2d 871, 881 (E.D. Wash. 2004), the defendants' nuclear product process required complex forms of chemical separation, which released radioactive I-131 (iodine, with atomic weight of 131) into the atmosphere. The plaintiffs relied on a strict liability theory against the defendants after being diagnosed with thyroid disease that could stem from the radioactive iodine. Nielsen, J., applied the strict liability theory of the Second Restatement. On common usage, he wrote:

> Plaintiffs argue that the production process certainly was not a common usage during the time period at issue in this case. In response, the Defendants argue that while the production of plutonium for use in atomic weapons was not a common activity, the chemical separation and air dilution and venting through a tall stack were common endeavors based on the science of the time. As to I-131, the Defendants argue also that existing knowledge was used to make the

> emissions safe. . . . Although radiation had seen medical usage and chemical separation had been used before, it is still undisputed that the weapons grade plutonium production which included chemical separation that released I-131 was an activity in which few people were engaged. As such it was not one of common usage and this factor weighs in favor of a finding of an abnormally dangerous activity.

Nielsen, J., then concluded that each factor under section 520 favored the abnormally dangerous classification.

3. *Social Utility of the Defendant's Activity.* The Second Restatement's willingness to consider the social value of an activity in determining whether it is abnormally dangerous was ably criticized in Koos v. Roth, 652 P.2d 1255, 1261–62 (Or. 1982). Linde, J., upholding a strict liability action for fire damage, observed:

> There are at least two reasons not to judge civil liability for unintended harm by a court's views of the utility or value of the harmful activity. One reason lies in the nature of the judgment. Utility and value often are subjective and controversial. They will be judged differently by those who profit from an activity and those who are endangered by it, and between one locality and another. The use of explosives to remove old buildings for a new highway or shopping center may be described as slum clearance or as the destruction of historic landmarks and neighborhoods. On a smaller scale, it may celebrate a traditional holiday which some may value more highly than either buildings or roads. Highly toxic materials may be necessary to the production of agricultural pesticides, or of drugs, or of chemical or bacteriological weapons, or of industrial products of all sorts; does liability for injury from their storage or movement depend on the utility of these products? Judges, like others, may differ about such values; they can hardly be described as conclusions of law. . . .
>
> The second reason why the value of a hazardous activity does not preclude strict liability for its consequences is that the conclusion does not follow from the premise. In the prior cases, the court did not question the economic value of blasting, cropdusting, or storing natural gas. In an action for damages, the question is not whether the activity threatens such harm that it should not be continued. The question is who shall pay for harm that has been done. The loss has occurred. It is a cost of the activity whoever bears it. To say that when the activity has great economic value the cost should be borne by others is no more or less logical than to say that when the costs of an activity are borne by others it gains in value.

The Third Restatement responded to the criticism in *Koos* by scratching the social utility factor from the list of relevant factors for determining abnormally dangerous activities. See RTT: LPEH §20, Reporter's Note to comment *k*. In regard to the manufacturing of nuclear weapons, Nielsen, J., tartly remarked on factor (f) that "the benefit accrued to the entire nation but the risk and the potential harm was endured only by the people downwind of Hanford." *In re Hanford*, 350 F. Supp. 2d at 883.

Nonetheless, the social utility factor still continues to have weight in the litigated cases. Cadena v. Chicago Fireworks Manufacturing Co., 697 N.E.2d 802, 814 (Ill. App. Ct. 1998), held that fireworks displays were *not* abnormally dangerous in part because under factor (f) "the general public enjoys fireworks displays to celebrate every July 4, [and] they are of some social utility to communities." Similarly, in Toms v. Calvary Assembly of God, 132 A.3d 866, 881 (Md. 2016), a church that put on a fireworks display was not held liable for the damage to livestock and property when neighboring cattle stampeded. Greene, J., concluded: "This Court recognizes that not all segments of the population may enjoy fireworks displays, especially those with noise sensitivities[;] however, we conclude that the social desirability of fireworks appear to outweigh their dangerous attributes." Consistent with *Koos*? Would the court come out the same way if the fireworks had killed a bystander?

In Burchett v. Global Supertanker Services, No. 2:19-CV-01812-MCE-JDP, 2021 WL 1614397, at *8 (E.D. Cal. Apr. 23, 2021), the operator of a Very Large Air Tanker (VLAT) dropped fire retardant at such a height that, instead of misting, it killed a firefighter upon impact. England, J., allowed the plaintiff to proceed on a strict liability for abnormally dangerous activities claim. With regard to factor (f), he pointed to "allegations that the U.S. Forest Service does not approve of the VLAT's use in these instances." Should courts defer to agency views when determining the social utility of abnormally dangerous activities? Is there any avenue to defend a dangerous product that seriously malfunctions?

4. ***Government Execution of Abnormally Dangerous Activities.*** Often dangerous activities are undertaken by the government itself or by private parties pursuant to government authorization. Dalehite v. United States, 346 U.S. 15, 30, 35–36, 50–51 (1953), was a test case that arose out of a huge explosion in Texas City on April 16 and 17, 1947 when 880 tons of ammonium nitrate fertilizer were being loaded and stored on French vessels in the harbor, destined for Europe to ease a major food shortage after World War II. The fierce flames from the explosion spread to other vessels, causing the death of 560 persons, the injury of 3,000 more, and many millions of dollars of property damage. A private defendant would at that time have been treated as engaging in an ultrahazardous or abnormally dangerous activity. Nonetheless in this case the government escaped all liability by relying on the discretionary function exception to the Federal Tort Claims Act, 28 U.S.C. §§2671–2680 (2023). The Act's general command holds the United States liable "in the same manner and to the same extent as a private individual under like circumstances," but excludes claims "based upon the exercise or performance or the failure to exercise or perform a discretionary function or duty on the part of a federal agency or an employee of the Government, whether or not the discretion involved be abused." Reed, J., then gave a broad reading to this exception:

> It is unnecessary to define, apart from this case, precisely where discretion ends. It is enough to hold, as we do, that the "discretionary function or duty" that cannot form a basis for suit under the Tort Claims Act includes more than the initiation of programs and activities. It also includes determinations made by executives or administrators in establishing plans, specifications or schedules of operations. Where there is room for policy judgment and decision there is discretion. It necessarily follows that acts of subordinates in carrying out the operations of government in accordance with official directions cannot be actionable.

Jackson, J., expressed in dissent his frustration about "an unfortunate trend toward relaxation of private as well as official responsibility in making, vending or transporting inherently dangerous products." Is there any reason why a no-liability regime should be adopted to cover the procedures used for loading and storing explosives on sea-bound vessels?

Indiana Harbor Belt R.R. v. American Cyanamid Co.

916 F.2d 1174 (7th Cir. 1990)

POSNER, J.

[The American Cyanamid Company, a large diversified chemical manufacturer, leased from the North American Car Company a railroad car, which it filled with 20,000 gallons of liquid acrylonitrile, a highly toxic chemical, possibly carcinogenic, flammable at thirty degrees Fahrenheit. The car was routed to a Cyanamid plant in New Jersey through the Blue Island Yard, located on the outskirts of Chicago and run by the Indiana Harbor Belt Railroad, which specialized in shifting cars between major railroad lines. Several hours after the car arrived in the plaintiff's Blue Island yard, several of its employees noted a leak from the Cyanamid car. Local authorities, fearing that all 20,000 gallons may have leaked, ordered an evacuation of the yard, which lasted for several hours. When the car was moved to another portion of the lot, it was discovered that only about a quarter of its load had leaked. Nonetheless, the Illinois

Department of Environmental Protection ordered decontamination measures that cost the plaintiff close to $1 million ($2.4 million in 2023 dollars). The plaintiff brought an action against Cyanamid to recover its clean-up costs, and it won in the district court on summary judgment. On review, Posner, J., first notes that the district court's conclusion of law received no deference and continues:]

The roots of [Second Restatement] section 520 are in nineteenth-century cases. The most famous one is Rylands v. Fletcher[, [1868] LR 3 (HL) 330, *supra* Chapter 2, at 85], but a more illuminating one in the present context is Guille v. Swan, 19 Johns. (N.Y.) 381 (1822)[, *supra* Chapter 2, at 75]. A man took off in a hot-air balloon and landed, without intending to, in a vegetable garden in New York City. A crowd that had been anxiously watching his involuntary descent trampled the vegetables in their endeavor to rescue him when he landed. The owner of the garden sued the balloonist for the resulting damage, and won. Yet the balloonist had not been careless. In the then state of ballooning it was impossible to make a pinpoint landing.

Guille is a paradigmatic case for strict liability. (a) The risk (probability) of harm was great, and (b) the harm that would ensue if the risk materialized could be, although luckily was not, great (the balloonist could have crashed into the crowd rather than into the vegetables). The confluence of these two factors established the urgency of seeking to prevent such accidents. (c) Yet such accidents could not be prevented by the exercise of due care; the technology of care in ballooning was insufficiently developed. (d) The activity was not a matter of common usage, so there was no presumption that it was a highly valuable activity despite its unavoidable riskiness. (e) The activity was inappropriate to the place in which it took place—densely populated New York City. The risk of serious harm to others (other than the balloonist himself, that is) could have been reduced by shifting the activity to the sparsely inhabited areas that surrounded the city in those days. (f) Reinforcing (d), the value to the community of the activity of recreational ballooning did not appear to be great enough to offset its unavoidable risks.

These are, of course, the six factors in section 520. They are related to each other in that each is a different facet of a common quest for a proper legal regime to govern accidents that negligence liability cannot adequately control. . . . Shavell, Strict Liability versus Negligence, 9 J. Legal Stud. 1 (1980). By making the actor strictly liable—by denying him in other words an excuse based on his inability to avoid accidents by being more careful—we give him an incentive, missing in a negligence regime, to experiment with methods of preventing accidents that involve not greater exertions of care, assumed to be futile, but instead relocating, changing, or reducing (perhaps to the vanishing point) the activity giving rise to the accident. The greater the risk of an accident ((a)) and the costs of an accident if one occurs ((b)), the more we want the actor to consider the possibility of making accident-reducing activity changes; the stronger, therefore, is the case for strict liability. Finally, if an activity is extremely common ((d)), like driving an automobile, it is unlikely either that its hazards are perceived as great or that there is no technology of care available to minimize them; so the case for strict liability is weakened.

The largest class of cases in which strict liability has been imposed under the standard codified in the Second Restatement of Torts involves the use of dynamite and other explosives for demolition in residential or urban areas. Restatement, *supra*, §519, comment d. Explosives are dangerous even when handled carefully, and we therefore want blasters to choose the location of the activity with care and also to explore the feasibility of using safer substitutes (such as a wrecking ball), as well as to be careful in the blasting itself. Blasting is not a commonplace activity like driving a car, or so superior to substitute methods of demolition that the imposition of liability is unlikely to have any effect except to raise the activity's costs.

Against this background we turn to the particulars of acrylonitrile. Acrylonitrile is one of a large number of chemicals that are hazardous in the sense of being flammable, toxic, or both; acrylonitrile is both, as are many others. [Posner, J., then summarizes a list of 125 such substances, some more and some less dangerous than acrylonitrile. He then notes that under plaintiff's theory,] [e]very shipper of any of these materials would therefore be strictly liable for the consequences of a spill or other accident that occurred while the material was being shipped through a metropolitan area. . . .

No cases recognize so sweeping a liability. Several reject it, though none has facts much like those of the present case. [A discussion of some cases not following the Restatement rule is omitted.]

Siegler v. Kuhlman, 502 P.2d 1181 (Wash. 1972), also imposed strict liability on a transporter of hazardous materials, but the circumstances were again rather special. A gasoline truck blew up, obliterating the plaintiff's decedent and her car. The court emphasized that the explosion had destroyed the evidence necessary to establish whether the accident had been due to negligence; so, unless liability was strict, there would be no liability—and this as the very consequence of the defendant's hazardous activity. . . .

So we can get little help from precedent, and might as well apply section 520 to the acrylonitrile problem from the ground up. To begin with, we have been given no reason, whether the reason in *Siegler* or any other, for believing that a negligence regime is not perfectly adequate to remedy and deter, at reasonable cost, the accidental spillage of acrylonitrile from rail cars. Acrylonitrile could explode and destroy evidence, but of course did not here, making imposition of strict liability on the theory of the *Siegler* decision premature. More important, although acrylonitrile is flammable even at relatively low temperatures, and toxic, it is not so corrosive or otherwise destructive that it will eat through or otherwise damage or weaken a tank car's valves although they are maintained with due (which essentially means, with average) care. No one suggests, therefore, that the leak in this case was caused by the inherent properties of acrylonitrile. It was caused by carelessness—whether that of the North American Car Corporation in failing to maintain or inspect the car properly, or that of Cyanamid in failing to maintain or inspect it, or that of the Missouri Pacific when it had custody of the car, or that of the switching line itself in failing to notice the ruptured lid, or some combination of these possible failures of care. Accidents that are due to a lack of care can be prevented by taking care; and when a lack of care can (unlike *Siegler*) be shown in court, such accidents are adequately deterred by the threat of liability for negligence.

It is true that the district court purported to find as a fact that there is an inevitable risk of derailment or other calamity in transporting "large quantities of anything." This is not a finding of fact, but a truism: anything can happen. The question is, how likely is this type of accident if the actor uses due care? For all that appears from the record of the case or any other sources of information that we have found, if a tank car is carefully maintained the danger of a spill of acrylonitrile is negligible. If this is right, there is no compelling reason to move to a regime of strict liability, especially one that might embrace all other hazardous materials shipped by rail as well. . . .

The district judge and the plaintiff's lawyer make much of the fact that the spill occurred in a densely inhabited metropolitan area. Only 4,000 gallons spilled; what if all 20,000 had done so? Isn't the risk that this might happen even if everybody were careful sufficient to warrant giving the shipper an incentive to explore alternative routes? Strict liability would supply that incentive. But this argument overlooks the fact that, like other transportation networks, the railroad network is a hub-and-spoke system. And the hubs are in metropolitan areas. Chicago is one of the nation's largest railroad hubs. In 1983, the latest year for which we have figures, Chicago's railroad yards handled the third highest volume of hazardous-material shipments in the nation. East St. Louis, which is also in Illinois, handled the second highest volume. With most hazardous chemicals (by volume of shipments) being at least as hazardous as acrylonitrile, it is unlikely—and certainly not demonstrated by the plaintiff—that they can be rerouted around all the metropolitan areas in the country, except at prohibitive cost. Even if it were feasible to reroute them one would hardly expect shippers, as distinct from carriers, to be the firms best situated to do the rerouting. Granted, the usual view is that common carriers are not subject to strict liability for the carriage of materials that make the transportation of them abnormally dangerous, because a common carrier cannot refuse service to a shipper of a lawful commodity. Restatement, *supra*, §521. Two courts, however, have rejected the common carrier exception. If it were rejected in Illinois, this would weaken still further the case for imposing strict liability on shippers whose goods pass through the densely inhabited portions of the state.

The difference between shipper and carrier points to a deep flaw in the plaintiff's case. Unlike *Guille*, and unlike *Siegler*, and unlike the storage cases, beginning with *Rylands* itself, here it is not the actors — that is, the transporters of acrylonitrile and other chemicals — but the manufacturers, who are sought to be held strictly liable. A shipper can in the bill of lading designate the route of his shipment if he likes, 49 U.S.C. §11710(a)(1), but is it realistic to suppose that shippers will become students of railroading in order to lay out the safest route by which to ship their goods? Anyway, rerouting is no panacea. Often it will increase the length of the journey, or compel the use of poorer track, or both. When this happens, the probability of an accident is increased, even if the consequences of an accident if one occurs are reduced; so the expected accident cost, being the product of the probability of an accident and the harm if the accident occurs, may rise. It is easy to see how the accident in this case might have been prevented at reasonable cost by greater care on the part of those who handled the tank car of acrylonitrile. It is difficult to see how it might have been prevented at reasonable cost by a change in the activity of transporting the chemical. This is therefore not an apt case for strict liability. . . .

The relevant activity is transportation, not manufacturing and shipping. . . . It is no more realistic to propose to reroute the shipment of all hazardous materials around Chicago than it is to propose the relocation of homes adjacent to the Blue Island switching yard to more distant suburbs. It may be less realistic. Brutal though it may seem to say it, the inappropriate use to which land is being put in the Blue Island yard and neighborhood may be, not the transportation of hazardous chemicals, but residential living. The analogy is to building your home between the runways at O'Hare. . . .

At argument . . . the plaintiff's lawyer invoked distributive considerations by pointing out that Cyanamid is a huge firm and the Indiana Harbor Belt Railroad a fifty-mile-long switching line that almost went broke in the winter of 1979, when the accident occurred. Well, so what? A corporation is not a living person but a set of contracts the terms of which determine who will bear the brunt of liability. Tracing the incidence of a cost is a complex undertaking which the plaintiff sensibly has made no effort to assume, since its legal relevance would be dubious. We add only that however small the plaintiff may be, it has mighty parents: it is a jointly owned subsidiary of Conrail and the Soo line. . . .

The judgment is reversed (with no award of costs in this court) and the case remanded for further proceedings, consistent with this opinion, on the plaintiff's claim for negligence.

Reversed and remanded, with directions.

NOTES

1. *The Strict Liability Alternative.* Under a strict liability system, must a court make judgments as to the proper choice of routes and equipment, or can it leave those responsibilities to the parties to allocate by contract among themselves? In Siegler v. Kuhlman, 502 P.2d 1181, 1184–85 (Wash. 1972), discussed in *Indiana Harbor*, the court defended relying on Rylands v. Fletcher for gasoline transported on public highways:

> In many respects, hauling gasoline as freight is no more unusual, but more dangerous, than collecting water. When gasoline is carried as cargo—as distinguished from fuel for the carrier vehicle—it takes on uniquely hazardous characteristics, as does water impounded in large quantities. Dangerous in itself, gasoline develops even greater potential for harm when carried as freight—extraordinary dangers deriving from sheer quantity, bulk and weight, which enormously multiply its hazardous properties. And the very hazards inhering from the size of the load, its bulk or quantity and its movement along the highways presents another reason for application of the Fletcher v. Rylands rule not present in the impounding of large quantities of water—the likely destruction of cogent evidence from which negligence or want of it may be proved or disproved. It is quite probable that the most important ingredients of proof will be lost in a gasoline explosion and fire. Gasoline is always dangerous whether kept in large or small quantities because of its volatility, inflammability and explosiveness. But when several thousand gallons of it are allowed to spill across a public highway—that is, if, while in transit as freight, it is not kept impounded—the hazards to third persons are so great as to be almost beyond calculation.

Do the different properties of acrylonitrile justify a different response? Note that in *Indiana Harbor* the action was brought against the shipper but not the carrier. How does the Second Restatement rule apply to transporters? How should *Indiana Harbor* come out under the Third Restatement? How does the analysis change if the bottom of the car was punctured by debris left on the track? If vandals damaged the car? See Sykes, Strict Liability versus Negligence in *Indiana Harbor*, 74 U. Chi. L. Rev. 1911 (2007).

2. *Back to Negligence?* The refusal to treat the shipment of dangerous chemicals as an abnormally dangerous activity still leaves the plaintiff with a negligence cause of action. Should the railroad be joined in the suit as a codefendant, and if so, does res ipsa loquitur apply?

In Gonzalez v. O & G Industries, 267 A.3d 766, 775, 783 (Conn. 2021), the Supreme Court of Connecticut, for the first time since the publication of the Restatement (Second) of Torts, addressed the standard for abnormally dangerous activities. In a case arising out of an explosion at a power plant, the court leaned heavily on factor (c). Following *Indiana Harbor*, McDonald, J., wrote:

> When determining whether a claim is well suited to the strict liability framework, it is crucial to inquire whether the exercise of reasonable care would have materially reduced the risk of harm, the severity of any resulting harm, or the otherwise dangerous attributes of the activity or instrumentality. If so, then the claim is better suited to the negligence framework so that liability hinges on whether the actor actually employed reasonable care.

Similarly, in Foster v. City of Keyser, 501 S.E.2d 165, 175 (W. Va. 1997), the defendant excavating company dug around the pipeline of the defendant gas company, such that the movement of the soil "contributed to the failure of a compression coupling joining two sections of the gas line, which in turn led to the line's separation." The court declined to treat the ordinary transmission of gas as an abnormally dangerous activity, noting its judgment was "largely predicated upon our conclusion that other principles of law—a high standard of care and *res ipsa loquitur*—can sufficiently address the concerns that argue for strict liability in gas transmission line leak/explosion cases." Are we back to Booth v. Rome? With or without res ipsa?

3. *Liability Rules and Information Production.* In *Indiana Harbor*, Posner, J., concedes that strict liability can be appropriate when, as in Siegler v. Kuhlman, the accident has destroyed the evidence necessary to prove negligence. What role should information production play in choosing liability rules? Jacob & Shapira, An Information-Production Theory of Liability Rules, 89 U. Chi. L. Rev. 1113, 1113 (2022), defends a default rule of negligence on information-forcing grounds:

> Litigation under negligence produces granular information on whether the defendant could have reasonably avoided the harm, how she fares relative to others in her profession, and so on. Such information, to the extent it becomes public, allows outside observers to infer whether the past accident is indicative of the defendant's future behavior or not, which in turn affects their willingness to do business with her going forward. A physician found negligent may lose future patients, a seller failing the consumer-expectations test in products liability may lose future consumers, and so on. Litigation under strict liability produces much coarser information—namely, that a harm occurred as a result of the defendant's activity. It rarely provides outside observers with information on the competence or integrity of the defendant vis-à-vis her peers. The efficiency rationale for negligence thus stems from facilitating more robust market discipline.

What about situations where there is no market? How about situations in which agencies offer contemporaneous ratings information that does not depend on the resolution of a case years after the accident occurs?

4. ***Abnormally Dangerous Activities: Causal Complications and Affirmative Defenses.*** Even if strict liability principles apply to abnormally dangerous activities, the plaintiff still must negotiate hurdles on proximate causation, as well as a full range of potential affirmative defenses. The Second Restatement sets forth these possibilities.

RESTATEMENT OF THE LAW (SECOND) OF TORTS

§522. Contributing Actions of Third Persons, Animals and Forces of Nature

One carrying on an abnormally dangerous activity is subject to strict liability for the resulting harm, although it is caused by the unexpectable

(a) innocent, negligent or reckless conduct of a third person, or
(b) action of an animal, or
(c) operation of a force of nature.

§523. Assumption of Risk

The plaintiff's assumption of the risk of harm from an abnormally dangerous activity bars his recovery for the harm.

§524. Contributory Negligence

(1) Except as stated in Subsection (2), the contributory negligence of the plaintiff is not a defense to the strict liability of one who carries on an abnormally dangerous activity.

(2) The plaintiff's contributory negligence in knowingly and unreasonably subjecting himself to the risk of harm from the activity is a defense to the strict liability.

§524A. Plaintiff's Abnormally Sensitive Activity

There is no strict liability for harm caused by an abnormally dangerous activity if the harm would not have resulted but for the abnormally sensitive character of the plaintiff's activity.

The Third Restatement takes a somewhat different approach in its exceptions to when strict liability applies.

RESTATEMENT OF THE LAW (THIRD) OF TORTS: LIABILITY FOR PHYSICAL AND EMOTIONAL HARM

§24. Scope of Strict Liability

Strict liability . . . does not apply

(a) if the person suffers physical or emotional harm as a result of making contact with or coming into proximity to the defendant's animal or abnormally dangerous activity for the purpose of securing some benefit from that contact or that proximity; or

(b) if the defendant maintains ownership or possession of the animal or carries on the abnormally dangerous activity in pursuance of an obligation imposed by law.

§25. Comparative Responsibility

If the plaintiff has been contributorily negligent in failing to take reasonable precautions, the plaintiff's recovery in a strict-liability claim . . . for physical or emotional harm is reduced in accordance with the share of comparative responsibility assigned to the plaintiff.

Comment d. Assigning proportionate shares: The apportionment of responsibility under this Section is best described as an ad hoc evaluation about the facts of a particular case; that evaluation is treated as though it were an instance of factfinding as such, and it is therefore entrusted primarily to the jury. . . . Obviously, applying the principle of comparative responsibility in a strict-liability action is somewhat more difficult than applying it in an action in which the defendant is held liable under a theory of negligence. . . . When the defendant is held liable under a theory of strict liability, no literal comparison of the fault of the two parties may be possible. . . . [The comment explains that the factors listed in the Restatement (Third) of Torts: Apportionment of Liability §8 should be taken into account in allocating fault.]

Have the difficulties that arise in these cases been encountered elsewhere?

In Madsen v. East Jordan Irrigation Co., 125 P.2d 794, 795 (Utah 1942), the plaintiff's farm was used for breeding and raising mink for sale. One hundred yards north of the farm, the defendant blasted with explosives in order to repair its irrigation ditch. The noise from the blast so frightened the mother mink that it "caused 108 of them to kill 230 of their 'kittens' (offspring)." Pratt, J., conceded that blasting was governed by an absolute liability rule, but held that the damages were too remote, observing:

> [H]e who fires explosives is not liable for every occurrence following the explosion which has a semblance of connection to it. Jake's horse might become so excited that he would run next door and kick a few ribs out of Cy's jersey cow, but is such a thing to be anticipated from an explosion? Whether the cases are concussion or nonconcussion, the results chargeable to the nonnegligent user of explosives are those things ordinarily resulting from an explosion. Shock, air vibrations, thrown missiles are all illustrative of the anticipated result of explosives; they are physical as distinguished from mental in character. The famous *Squib* case[, *supra* Chapter 2, at 72,] does not mitigate what has been said in the preceding lines. That was a case where the mental reaction was to be anticipated as an instinctive matter of self-preservation. In the instant case, the killing of their kittens was not an act of self-preservation on the part of the mother mink but a peculiarity of disposition which was not within the realm of matters to be anticipated. Had a squib been thrown and suddenly picked up by a dog, in fun, and carried near another, it is ventured that we would not have had a famous *Squib* case, as such a result would not have been within the realm of anticipation.

Does it matter that military aircraft are routinely cautioned about flying over mink farms? The result in *Madsen* was endorsed in RST §519, illus. 1.

Human intervention often prompts a different response. In Yukon Equipment v. Fireman's Fund Insurance Co., 585 P.2d 1206, 1211 (Alaska 1978), the defendants were sued for damage caused by the explosion of their storage magazine, located in suburban Anchorage. The damage was caused by four young thieves who set off the explosives in order to conceal evidence of their theft. The court held that strict liability applied to the storage of explosives under the leading case of Exner v. Sherman Power Construction Co., 54 F.2d 510 (2d Cir. 1931), whose application was not defeated by the petitioners' decision to locate their plant in a remote part of town nearly one mile from the nearest public highway.

The petitioners also claimed that the conduct of the four thieves was a superseding cause that negated their tortious liability. That argument was rejected because "incendiary destruction of premises by thieves to cover evidence of theft is not so uncommon an occurrence that it can be regarded as highly extraordinary." Is this decision consistent with *Madsen*?

SECTION E. NUISANCE

The law of nuisance is of vast significance in both ordinary private disputes and in connection with larger social harms. In the past several years, the law of private nuisance has not much altered, but there has been an explosive growth in the law of public nuisance. A recent spate of litigation throughout the country has seen public nuisance claims brought against those who advertised lead paint 100 years ago to pay for lead paint abatement in buildings constructed before 1950 (see, e.g., People v. ConAgra Grocery Prod. Co., 227 Cal. Rptr. 3d 499 (Ct. App. 2017)), against oil companies to provide relief against sea-level rise allegedly attributable to global warming (e.g., City of New York v. Chevron Corp., 993 F.3d 81 (2d Cir. 2021)), and against opioid manufacturers for marketing, advertising, and sales practices that fueled the enduring opioid abuse public health crisis (e.g., State ex rel. Hunter v. Johnson & Johnson, 499 P.3d 719 (Okla. 2021)). In a set of coordinated bellwether cases in Ohio, a jury found CVS, Walmart, and Walgreens defendants liable on a public nuisance theory for contributing to the opioid crisis. In a subsequent bench trial, the defendants were ordered to pay $650.6 million to an abatement fund. County of Lake v. Purdue Pharma, L.P. (In re Nat'l Prescription Opiate Litig.), 622 F. Supp. 3d 584, 592 (N.D. Ohio 2022). In the spring of 2022, Johnson & Johnson and distributors AmerisourceBergen, Cardinal Health, and McKesson reached a settlement of $26 billion with states and municipalities. See Hoffman, Companies Finalize $26 Billion Deal with States and Cities to End Opioid Lawsuits, N.Y. Times, Feb. 25, 2022, https://www.nytimes.com/2022/02/25/health/opioids-settlement-distributors-johnson.html.

In this section, we begin with private nuisance and then turn to public nuisance, tracing the evolution of the doctrine from its sixteenth-century historical origins to the expansion of the doctrine over the last several years.

1. Private Nuisance

Vogel v. Grant-Lafayette Electric Cooperative

548 N.W.2d 829 (Wis. 1996)

Bradley, J. The following background facts are undisputed. The Vogels were dairy farmers and members of GLEC, a cooperative association that distributes electricity to its members. Shortly after the Vogels built a new milking facility in 1970, they noticed problems with their herd. Many cows exhibited violent or erratic behavior while in the facility. The herd also suffered from excessive and chronic mastitis. As a result, the Vogels suffered a decline in their herd's milk production and cows were repeatedly culled from the herd. Despite the fact that the Vogels made various changes with their equipment and in the facility itself, these problems persisted in varying degrees over subsequent years.

In March of 1986, the Vogels contacted GLEC because they suspected that the cows were suffering from the effects of excessive stray voltage. The Vogels received their electricity via a distribution system referred to as a multi-grounded neutral system, based on the fact that neutral wires in both the provider's primary system and the farm's secondary wiring system are connected to metal grounding rods driven into the earth. Because the neutral wires in a typical farm's electrical system are connected to metal work in the barn for safety purposes in order to provide a path for electrical current to flow to earth, a cow that contacts grounded metal objects may provide a path for this "stray voltage" traveling on the farm's secondary system.

GLEC responded to the Vogels' concerns about possible stray voltage by installing an "isolator" at its transformer on the Vogel farm, which is intended to reduce the risk of excessive stray voltage. After the isolator was properly installed, the behavior of the herd and the other problems began to improve immediately. GLEC subsequently visited the farm on numerous occasions to conduct tests and respond to other concerns raised by the Vogels.

In 1992, the Vogels filed suit against GLEC on theories of negligence and nuisance [for the "annoyance and inconvenience" caused by the stray voltage.]

The case was tried to a jury, which found that GLEC was negligent and that it had created a nuisance. It awarded the Vogels $240,000 [$470,000 in 2023 dollars] in economic damages on their negligence claim and $60,000 [$117,000 in 2023 dollars] for annoyance and inconvenience damages on their nuisance claim. The jury also found that the Vogels were one-third causally negligent.

[The trial judge entered a verdict for $200,000 [$391,000 in 2023 dollars]. GLEC appealed, claiming that stray voltage could not be a private nuisance. The Vogels appealed, claiming that the defendant committed an "intentional nuisance" not subject to reduction for contributory negligence. The Wisconsin Court of Appeals held that the trial judge erred in submitting the nuisance claim to the jury and "struck the $60,000 [$117,000 in 2023 dollars] in damages awarded for annoyance and inconvenience attributed to the nuisance."]

I. Private Nuisance Action for Stray Voltage

. . . This court has previously adopted the definition of private nuisance set forth in the Restatement (Second) of Torts (1979). The Restatement defines nuisance as "a nontrespassory invasion of another's interest in the private use and enjoyment of land." Restatement (Second) of Torts §821D.

GLEC argues that the concept of invasion in the Restatement necessarily involves a "unilateral encroachment." It contends that a nuisance is produced by an activity under the defendant's control to which the plaintiff objects, and not by activity which the plaintiff has requested and facilitated. According to GLEC, the Vogels' act of requesting electrical service and cooperating in the receipt of electricity by connecting its system to GLEC's distribution system negates the concept of unilateral invasion and thus defeats a claim for nuisance.

The court of appeals agreed with GLEC and concluded as a matter of law that the provision of electricity to the Vogels' farm cannot be considered a nuisance because it does not constitute the type of invasion on which nuisance liability is typically predicated. According to the court of appeals, "[a]s users of an instrumentality they invited onto their land, and have in many ways benefited from over the years, we do not think they now may be heard to claim that the instrumentality has illegally 'invaded' their property."[3] . . .

We agree with the Vogels that their request for electric service itself does not negate the invasion element of nuisance. Both GLEC and the court of appeals fail to distinguish between electrical service generally and excessive levels of stray voltage which may accompany it. While the Vogels requested electric service, they did not request excessive stray voltage to flow through their farm. Similarly, while they received benefit from the electrical service generally, the evidence presented at trial indicates that they hardly benefited from excessive stray voltage. . . .

We also disagree with the court of appeals that previous nuisance cases in Wisconsin compel the conclusion that stray voltage does not constitute the type of invasion on which nuisance liability is predicated. The court of appeals erroneously focuses on private nuisance as an invasion of land. . . .

Although some of the nuisance cases identified by the court of appeals involve a physical invasion of land, the Restatement uses the phrase "interest in the use and enjoyment of land" broadly to include more than freedom from detrimental change in the physical condition of the land itself: [It "comprehends the pleasure, comfort and enjoyment that a person normally derives from the occupancy of land." RST §821D, comment *b*.]

. . . This court has previously characterized the common law doctrine of private nuisance as being both "broad" to meet the wide variety of possible invasions, and "flexible" to adapt to changing social values and conditions. An interpretation of nuisance as only arising from a unilateral action and a physical invasion of land restricts the essential flexibility of the nuisance doctrine. We decline to do so here.

We conclude that nuisance law is applicable to stray voltage claims because excessive levels of stray voltage may invade a person's private use and enjoyment of land. Although excessive levels of stray voltage may be found to constitute a nuisance in certain circumstances, we do not hold that it constitutes a nuisance under all circumstances. The determination of whether stray voltage unreasonably interferes with a person's interest in the private use and enjoyment of land is reserved for the trier of fact.

II. "Intentional Invasion" Nuisance

. . .

The Vogels argue that the uncontradicted testimony of their expert was that GLEC knew that a portion of its electric current would travel to the earth through the farm and its structures based on its use of the multi-grounded system with interconnected neutrals. They assert that although GLEC may not have intended to cause harm, the invasion is intentional under §825(b) because GLEC knew that the stray voltage was substantially certain to result from its conduct by application of basic laws of electricity. GLEC contends that even if it was substantially certain that some level of current would travel through the farm's structures, there is no evidence that any interference with the Vogels' use and enjoyment was certain to result.

3. The court of appeals and GLEC cite the following cases to support the propositions that the invasion must be unilateral and not be requested by the plaintiffs: Fortier v. Flambeau Plastics Co., 476 N.W.2d 593 (Wis. App. 1991) (toxic chemicals deposited in a landfill which seeped or leached onto the plaintiffs' property and contaminated their well water was the type of "invasion" that would subject the defendants to nuisance liability); Crest Chevrolet-Oldsmobile-Cadillac, Inc. v. Willemsen, 384 N.W.2d 692 (Wis. 1986) (diversion of surface water onto the plaintiff's property); Krueger v. Mitchell, 332 N.W.2d 733 (Wis. 1983) (excessive noise from an airport interfering with the operation of a neighboring business); . . . Jost v. Dairyland Power Coop., 172 N.W.2d 647 (Wis. 1969) (discharge of sulphur dioxide gases from an electrical generating plant onto adjoining cropland).

We agree with GLEC that the mere fact that the systems were interconnected does not create an intentional invasion. . . . It is the unreasonable levels of stray voltage that may give rise to liability for an intentional invasion, not the use of a multi-grounded delivery system with interconnecting neutrals. The Vogels fail to identify any evidence in the record that GLEC had knowledge prior to March of 1986 that its system was imposing unreasonable levels of stray voltage onto the Vogels' farm.

The Vogels also argue that GLEC's conduct constitutes an intentional invasion because it was a continuing invasion of which they had knowledge. . . . [RST §825, comment *d.*] The Vogels maintain that in this case, stray voltage arising from a multi-grounded distribution system necessarily involves a continuing invasion because the utility knows that a portion of its current is going to the earth through the farm's structures and the cows.

This argument fails in part for the same reason stated above. Intentionally supplying electrical current with the resulting stray voltage may be an invasion of the land but it does not constitute a legal cause of action in nuisance. In order for a nuisance to exist in this fact situation, there must be an unreasonable amount of stray voltage that affects the person's interest in the private use and enjoyment of land. Therefore, GLEC may be liable for an intentional invasion under the continuing invasion rationale expressed in the Restatement if it continued to impose excessive levels of stray voltage onto the Vogels' farm that might endanger their cows after it had knowledge of the problem. However, that is not the case here. In fact, the record indicates the opposite [in light of the many steps, stated above, that GLEC took as of March 1986 to contain the nuisance.]

Based on the record in this case, we conclude as a matter of law that the trial court did not err by construing the nuisance action as an unintentional invasion and otherwise actionable under negligence, and by not submitting the question of intentional invasion to the jury. . . .

The decision of the court of appeals ordering the circuit court to strike nuisance-related damages from the judgment is reversed.

NOTES

1. ***Nuisance Generally.*** Stray voltage cases are a subset of the larger class of nuisances, which have both the common definition offered in *Vogel* and its statutory variations. Compare the Restatement definition of a nuisance given in *Vogel* with that provided by the California Civil Code (2023).

§3479. Nuisance Defined

Anything which is injurious to health, including, but not limited to, the illegal sale of controlled substances, or is indecent or offensive to the senses, or an obstruction to the free use of property, so as to interfere with the comfortable enjoyment of life or property, or unlawfully obstructs the free passage or use, in the customary manner, of any navigable lake, or river, bay, stream, canal, or basin, or any public park, square, street, or highway, is a nuisance.

The reference to the sale of controlled substances was added in 1996. The rest of the statute dates from 1872. What prompted the change?

In some cases, the key question is not whether the defendant's conduct is actionable, but whether it is actionable as a trespass or a nontrespassory nuisance. In Martin v. Reynolds Metals Co., 342 P.2d 790 (Or. 1959), the defendants had released quantities of fluoride gas that became airborne and settled on adjacent land, rendering it unfit for cattle grazing and watering. The defendants claimed that the plaintiff's cause of action sounded in nuisance, with a two-year statute of limitations. The court, however, ruled that the defendant's conduct amounted to an actionable trespass, to which a six-year statute of limitations applied. The court also noted that the question of trespass or nuisance could be important on substantive issues as well, pointing out that the defense of "coming to the nuisance," *infra* at 506, Note 1, is, almost by definition, inapplicable to a trespass case. If trespass involves the direct and immediate application of force against the person or property of another, can the court's position in *Martin* be defended? See Merrill, Trespass, Nuisance, and the Costs of Determining Property Rights, 14 J. Legal Stud. 13 (1985). How does *Martin* come out under the California statute?

2. *Reasonableness in the Law of Nuisance.* Like *Vogel*, most accounts of nuisance law provide that the defendant's invasive conduct is actionable only if it constitutes an "unreasonable" interference with the plaintiff's use and enjoyment of her property. See RST §822.

One view is that this reasonableness language imports general negligence principles into the law of nuisance, so that the ultimate question is whether the expected benefits of the challenged activities exceed their expected costs. See RST §826.

RESTATEMENT OF THE LAW (SECOND) OF TORTS

§822. General Rule [of Nuisance]

One is subject to liability for a private nuisance if, but only if, his conduct is a legal cause of an invasion of another's interest in the private use and enjoyment of land, and the invasion is either

(a) intentional and unreasonable, or

(b) unintentional and otherwise actionable under the rules controlling liability for negligent or reckless conduct, or for abnormally dangerous conditions or activities.

RESTATEMENT OF THE LAW (SECOND) OF TORTS

§826. Unreasonableness of Intentional Invasion

An intentional invasion of another's interest in the use and enjoyment of land is unreasonable if

(a) the gravity of the harm outweighs the utility of the actor's conduct, or

(b) the harm caused by the conduct is serious and the financial burden of compensating for this and similar harm to others would not make the continuation of the conduct not feasible.

This view appears to have been adopted in Copart Industries, Inc. v. Consolidated Edison Co. of New York, Inc., 362 N.E.2d 968, 971 (N.Y. 1977). There the plaintiff, an operator of a new car storage and preparation business, alleged that the emissions from the smokestacks of a nearby Con Ed plant damaged the finishes on his and his customers' cars, forcing him out of business. The Court of Appeals affirmed the judgment for the defendant below, noting the limited basis of liability in nuisance cases:

> Despite early private nuisance cases, which apparently assumed that the defendant was strictly liable, today it is recognized that one is subject to liability for a private nuisance if his conduct is a legal cause of the invasion of the interest in the private use and enjoyment of land and such invasion is (1) intentional and unreasonable, (2) negligent or reckless, or (3) actionable under the rules governing liability for abnormally dangerous conditions or activities.

Does option (3) on abnormally dangerous activities reintroduce strict liability through the back door?

A more hostile reception to negligence principles in nuisance cases is found in Jost v. Dairyland Power Cooperative, 172 N.W.2d 647, 650–52 (Wis. 1969), cited in *Vogel*, in which discharges of sulfur dioxide resulted in substantial damage to the plaintiff's land. The court adopted a strict liability rule for damages, which the jury had found "substantial":

> Plaintiffs' attorney from the outset made it clear that liability was predicated on the *fact* that sulphur dioxide gases were emitted into the atmosphere, despite complaints over a period of several years. There was no attempt to hinge plaintiffs' case on the theory that the defendant was not exercising due care. Under the plaintiffs' theory, which we deem to be a correct one, it is irrelevant that defendant was conforming to industry standards of due care if its conduct created a nuisance.

Could the same result be reached through a negligence per se standard? Through res ipsa loquitur?

3. *Actual Harm Under Nuisance Law.* The traditional cases of nuisance were often directed at physical invasions that were harmful to the senses, rather than invasions that caused obvious damage to real property.

In recent years, many nuisance claims have been brought for forms of physical contamination that have not produced any overt signs of harm. In Smith v. Carbide & Chemicals Corp., 298 F. Supp. 2d 561 (W.D. Ky. 2004), the district court held, applying Kentucky law, that the plaintiff's nuisance and trespass claims foundered when they could not show that the low levels of radioactive waste from the defendant's Paducah Gaseous Diffusion Plant operations, which caused a decline in the market value of their properties, created a significant health risk to the occupants. But on appeal, the decision was reversed in Smith v. Carbide & Chemicals Corp., 507 F.3d 372, 379–81 (6th Cir. 2007), which concluded that while unfounded fears of the *presence of contamination* may not support a nuisance claim, once the plaintiff proves that his land was contaminated he may recover for diminished property value caused by unfounded fears that the contamination poses health risks. The court in Cook v. Rockwell International Corp., 618 F.3d 1127, 1145 (10th Cir. 2010), disagreed, holding that "a scientifically unfounded risk cannot rise to the level of an unreasonable and substantial interference" with the plaintiff's use or enjoyment of his land to support a nuisance claim. If trace elements of nuclear wastes can spark a clean-up under Superfund, why shouldn't the defendant have to pay damages under tort law?

Similarly, in Golen v. Union Corp., 718 A.2d 298 (Pa. Super. Ct. 1998), the court denied a nuisance action to a plaintiff who was unable to sell his property because the defendant's nearby contaminated property was listed on the Superfund National Priority List. Fearing that it might open the "floodgates" of litigation, the court held that fluctuations in market value did not matter as the plaintiff's use and enjoyment were unchanged. Is that result correct if future contamination were a real possibility? If possible contamination deterred the plaintiff from improving her property? What about probable contamination?

Michalson v. Nutting

175 N.E. 490 (Mass. 1931)

Wait, J. The plaintiffs brought this bill in equity alleging that roots from a poplar tree growing upon the land of the defendants had penetrated the plaintiffs' land and had filled up sewer and drain pipes there, causing expense in digging them up and clearing them, and also had grown under the cement cellar of the plaintiffs' house, causing the cement to crack and crumble and threatening seriously to injure the foundation of the dwelling. They sought a mandatory injunction compelling the removal of the roots, a permanent injunction restraining the defendants from allowing the roots to encroach on the plaintiffs' land, and damages. . . . [The trial judge dismissed the complaint and the plaintiff appealed.]

There is no error. The law of Massachusetts was stated in Bliss v. Ball, 99 Mass. 597, 598 [1868], by Chapman, C.J., to be "As against adjoining proprietors, the owner of a lot may plant shade trees upon it, or cover it with a thick forest, and the injury done to them by the mere shade of the trees is *damnum absque injuria.* It is no violation of their rights." We see no distinction in principle between damage done by shade, and damage caused by overhanging branches or invading roots. The principle involved is that an owner of land is at liberty to use his land, and all of it, to grow trees. Their growth naturally and reasonably will be accompanied by the extension of boughs and the penetration of roots over and into adjoining property of others. . . .

The neighbor, though without right of appeal to the courts if harm results to him, is, nevertheless, not without remedy. His right to cut off the intruding boughs and roots is well recognized. His remedy is in his own hands. The common sense of the common law has recognized that it is wiser to leave the individual to protect himself, if harm results to him from this exercise of another's right to use his property in a reasonable way, than to subject that other to the annoyance, and the public to the burden, of actions at law, which would be likely to be innumerable and, in many instances, purely vexatious. . . .

Decree affirmed.

NOTES

1. *Does the Law of Nuisance Contain an Act Requirement?* For ordinary torts, the defendant must normally have taken some positive action before liability can be imposed. What about nuisance cases? Is that requirement satisfied in the tree cases? See *supra* Chapter 2, at 63. If the defendant planted the tree? Decided not to trim it?

The act requirement is controversial in other contexts. In Puritan Holding Co. v. Holloschitz, 372 N.Y.S.2d 500 (Sup. Ct. 1975), the court held the defendant liable in nuisance when she abandoned and left in disrepair a building she owned in an urban renewal area in which property values had shown a marked increase. The court noted that her conduct violated the local administrative ordinance that required vacant buildings to be guarded or sealed. It further stated that her conduct might not constitute a nuisance in an area that had already deteriorated, and measured the plaintiff's damages by the loss in market value attributable to the defendant's nuisance.

The act requirement was also tested in Merriam v. McConnell, 175 N.E.2d 293 (Ill. App. 1961), in which the court held that the bugs infesting the plaintiff's trees did not constitute a nuisance because the defendant had not placed them there. Similarly, the court in Robinson v. Whitelaw, 364 P.2d 1085, 1085 (Utah 1961), denied an action for damage caused by sand and dirt deposited on the plaintiff's property after the defendant cut the sagebrush and natural growth off his land to make way for future cultivation he never undertook. Henriod, J., noted that the "defendant would have difficulty in stopping the wind or replacing the sagebrush." What result if he had cleared the land to vex the plaintiff? Similarly, in Carvalho v. Wolfe, 140 P.3d 1161, 1164 (Or. App. 2006), Brewer, C.J., held that the defendants did not commit an actionable nuisance when the roots of trees on their land crossed the boundary and damaged the foundation of the plaintiff's house. "Plaintiffs also allege that defendants have not taken any action to ensure that the trees have been killed and the growth of their roots permanently stopped, but they do not allege either that the growth is continuing or that defendants know or should know that it is continuing." How could the plaintiffs not know of the growth? How does this rationale differ from that in *Michalson*?

2. *Absolute Property Rights?* *Michalson* sidesteps the question whether the defendant caused the nuisance by treating the harm as *damnum absque injuria* (Latin for harm without legal injury). The phrase is odd because the poplar tree did cause real harm. But the court offered two powerful justifications for why this harm should not be actionable. First, each landowner had the right of self-help even if cutting the roots kills the trees. Is that sufficient if undetected trees cause damage to the plaintiff's house or driveway? Second, the harms in question may be *reciprocal* if each landowner has trees on his property that encroach on a neighbor's land. Was that the case here?

More generally, the rhetoric of absolute property rights, often dominant in the law of trespass to land, is muted in the law of nuisance. Sharp property boundaries are softened to accommodate the high frequency of low-level nuisance invasions, which make it quite undesirable to give universal redress for all these events. For an elaboration of this argument, see Epstein, Nuisance Law: Corrective Justice and Its Utilitarian Constraints, 8 J. Legal Stud. 49, 74–79, 82–90 (1979), which looks at these considerations to explain why from an ex ante perspective all landowners may often be better off with the relaxation of the otherwise absolute common law right to be wholly free from physical interference:

1. High administrative costs for claim resolution;
2. High transaction costs for voluntary reassignment of rights;
3. Low value to the interested parties of the ownership rights whose rearrangement is mandated by the public rule; and
4. Presence of implicit in-kind compensation from all to all that precludes any systematic redistribution of wealth among the interested parties.

3. *Live and Let Live.* One discrete application of Epstein's approach is found in the "live and let live" rule as articulated by Bramwell, B., in Bamford v. Turnley, (1862) 122 Eng. Rep. 27, 32–33 (Ex.):

> The instances put during the argument, of burning weeds, emptying cesspools, making noises during repairs, and other instances which be nuisances if done wantonly or maliciously, nevertheless may be lawfully done. It cannot be said that such acts are not nuisances, because, by the hypothesis they are; and it cannot be doubted that, if a person maliciously and without cause made close to a dwelling-house the same offensive smells as may be made in emptying a cesspool, an action would lie. . . .
>
> There must be, then, some principle on which such cases must be excepted. It seems to me that that principle may be deduced from the character of these cases, and is this, viz., that those acts necessary for the common and ordinary use and occupation of land and houses may be done, if conveniently done, without submitting those who do them to an action. . . . There is an obvious necessity for such a principle as I have mentioned. It is as much for the advantage of one owner as of another for the very nuisance the one complains of, as the result of the ordinary use of his neighbour's land, he himself will create in the ordinary use of his own, and the reciprocal nuisances are of a comparatively trifling character. The convenience of such a rule may be indicated by calling it a rule of give and take, live and let live. . . .
>
> The public consists of all the individuals of it, and a thing is only for the public benefit when it is productive of good to those individuals on the balance of loss and gain to all. So that if all the loss and all the gain were borne and received by one individual, he on the whole would be the gainer. But whenever this is the case,—whenever a thing is for the public benefit, properly understood,—the loss to the individuals of the public who lose will bear compensation out of the gains of those who gain. It is for the public benefit there should be railways, but it would not be unless the gain of having the railway was sufficient to compensate the loss occasioned by the use of the land required for its site; and accordingly no one thinks it would be right to take an individual's land without compensation to make a railway.

Bramwell's endorsement of the "live and let live" principle shows the link between the requirement of just compensation and the principle of reciprocity. Since all these common interferences are "reciprocal" in character, virtually *all* parties are left better off under the regime of "live and let live" for minimal harms. As stated, moreover, the rule contains its own limitations. Substantial damages make it more likely, first, that the parties will not suffer inconveniences of equal magnitude and, second, that the administrative costs of dispute resolution will shrink relative to the amount in controversy. In those cases, as with taking a land for a railway, explicit compensation helps ensure that the taking operates for the benefit of all.

For the classic discussion of the impact of transaction costs on market transactions, see Coase, The Problem of Social Cost, 3 J.L. & Econ. 1 (1960). For the connection between Bramwell's general views and the modern tests of social welfare, see Coleman, Efficiency, Utility and Wealth Maximization, 8 Hofstra L. Rev. 509 (1980). For the connection between nuisance law and eminent domain, see Epstein, Takings: Private Property and the Power of Eminent Domain 199–202, 229–38 (1985).

4. *Locality Rule.* Reciprocity also helps explain another feature of nuisance law with no parallel in the law of trespass, the so-called locality rule. Its underpinnings are well articulated by Earl, J., in Campbell v. Seaman, 63 N.Y. 568, 576–77 (1876), when the fumes from the defendant's brick factory destroyed the trees and vegetation upon the plaintiff's land.

> Persons living in organized communities must suffer some damage, annoyance and inconvenience from each other. For these they are compensated by all the advantages of civilized society. If one lives in the city he must expect to suffer the dirt, smoke, noisome odors, noise and confusion incident to city life. . . .
>
> . . . As to what is a reasonable use of one's own property cannot be defined by any certain general rules, but must depend upon the circumstances of each case. A use of property in one locality and under some circumstances may be lawful and reasonable, which, under other circumstances, would be unlawful, unreasonable and a nuisance. To constitute a nuisance, the use must be such as to produce a tangible and appreciable injury to neighboring property, or such as to render its enjoyment specially uncomfortable or inconvenient.
>
> Within the rules thus referred to, that defendant's brick burning was a nuisance to plaintiffs cannot be doubted.

Fontainebleau Hotel Corp. v. Forty-Five Twenty-Five, Inc.
114 So. 2d 357 (Fla. App. 1959)

Per Curiam. This is an interlocutory appeal from an order temporarily enjoining the appellants from continuing with the construction of a fourteen-story addition to the Fontainebleau Hotel, owned and operated by the appellants. Appellee, plaintiff below, owns the Eden Roc Hotel, which was constructed in 1955, about a year after the Fontainebleau, and adjoins the Fontainebleau on the north. Both are luxury hotels, facing the Atlantic Ocean. The proposed addition to the Fontainebleau is being constructed twenty feet from its north property line, 130 feet from the mean high water mark of the Atlantic Ocean, and 76 feet 8 inches from the ocean bulkhead line. The 14-story tower will extend 160 feet above grade in height and is 416 feet long from east to west. During the winter months, from around two o'clock in the afternoon for the remainder of the day, the shadow of the addition will extend over the cabana, swimming pool, and sunbathing areas of the Eden Roc, which are located in the southern portion of its property.

In this action, plaintiff-appellee sought to enjoin the defendants-appellants from proceeding with the construction of the addition to the Fontainebleau (it appears to have been roughly eight stories high at the time suit was filed), alleging that the construction would interfere with the light and air on the beach in front of the Eden Roc and cast a shadow of such size as to render the beach wholly unfitted for the use and enjoyment of its guests, to the irreparable injury of the plaintiff; further, that the construction of such addition on the north side of defendant's property, rather than the south side, was actuated by malice and ill will on the part of the defendants' president toward the plaintiff's president; and that the construction was in violation of a building ordinance requiring a 100-foot setback from the ocean. It was also alleged that the construction would interfere with the easements of light and air enjoyed by plaintiff and its predecessors in title for more than twenty years and "impliedly granted by virtue of the acts of the plaintiff's predecessors in title, as well as under the common law and the express recognition of such rights by virtue of Chapter 9837, Laws of Florida 1923. . . ." Some attempt was also made to allege an easement by implication in favor of the plaintiff's property, as the dominant, and against the defendants' property, as the servient, tenement.

The defendants' answer denied the material allegations of the complaint, pleaded laches and estoppel by judgment.

The chancellor heard considerable testimony on the issues made by the complaint and the answer and, as noted, entered a temporary injunction restraining the defendants from continuing with the construction of the addition. His reason for so doing was stated by him, in a memorandum opinion, as follows:

> In granting the temporary injunction in this case the Court wishes to make several things very clear. The ruling is not based on any alleged presumptive title nor prescriptive right of the plaintiff to light and air nor is it based on any deed restrictions nor recorded plats in the title of the plaintiff nor of the defendant nor of any plat of record. It is not based on any zoning ordinance nor on any provision of the building code of the City of Miami Beach nor on the decision of any court, nisi prius or appellate. It is based solely on the proposition that no one has a right to use his property to the injury of another. In this case it is clear from the evidence that the proposed use by the Fontainebleau will materially damage the Eden Roc. There is evidence indicating that the construction of the proposed annex by the Fontainebleau is malicious or deliberate for the purpose of injuring the Eden Roc, but it is scarcely sufficient, standing alone, to afford a basis for equitable relief.

This is indeed a novel application of the maxim sic utere tuo ut alienum non laedas. This maxim does not mean that one must never use his own property in such a way as to do any injury to his neighbor. It means only that one must use his property so as not to injure the lawful *rights* of another. . . .

No American decision has been cited, and independent research has revealed none, in which it has been held that—in the absence of some contractual or statutory obligation—a landowner has a legal right to the free flow of light and air across the adjoining land of his neighbor. Even at common law, the landowner had no legal right, in the absence of an easement or uninterrupted use and enjoyment for a period of 20 years, to unobstructed light and air from the adjoining land. And the English doctrine of "ancient lights" has been unanimously repudiated in this country.

There being, then, no legal right to the free flow of light and air from the adjoining land, it is universally held that where a structure serves a useful and beneficial purpose, it does not give rise to a cause of action, either for damages or for an injunction under the maxim sic utere tuo ut alienum non laedas, even though it causes injury to another by cutting off the light and air and interfering with the view that would otherwise be available over adjoining land in its natural state, regardless of the fact that the structure may have been erected partly for spite.

We see no reason for departing from this universal rule. If, as contended on behalf of plaintiff, public policy demands that a landowner in the Miami Beach area refrain from constructing buildings on his premises that will cast a shadow on the adjoining premises, an amendment of its comprehensive planning and zoning ordinance, applicable to the public as a whole, is the means by which such purpose should be achieved. (No opinion is expressed here as to the validity of such an ordinance, if one should be enacted pursuant to the requirements of law. But to change the universal rule—and the custom followed in this state since its inception—that adjoining landowners have an equal right under the law to build to the line of their respective tracts and to such a height as is desired by them (in the absence, of course, of building restrictions or regulations) amounts, in our opinion, to judicial legislation. . . .)

[Reversed.]

NOTES

1. *Cast a Giant Shadow: An Easement of Light.* As *Fontainebleau* states, American courts traditionally rejected a common law easement for the light and air that pass over a neighbor's property because that easement would inhibit the growth of both towns and industry. The height restrictions often imposed by legislation have, however, uniformly been sustained against challenges under the Takings Clause of the Constitution. See Welch v. Swasey, 214 U.S. 91 (1909). On the vexed relationship between the law of nuisance and the law of eminent domain, see generally Michelman, Property, Utility, and Fairness: Comments on the Ethical Formulations of "Just Compensation" Law, 80 Harv. L. Rev. 1165 (1967); see also Miller v. Schoene, 276 U.S. 272 (1928).

The Eden Roc Strikes Back. The Fontainebleau (left) and Eden Roc (right) hotels in Miami in December 2007.

Source: Jordan Cerruti, with permission of the photographer

A very different approach to the easement of light was taken in Prah v. Maretti, 321 N.W.2d 182, 189–91 (Wis. 1982). There the plaintiff and the defendant owned adjoining plots in a subdivision, with the defendant's land located to the south of the plaintiff's. The defendant wished to construct a house on his plot that conformed to all applicable subdivision and zoning restrictions. The plaintiff sought to enjoin the proposed construction until the defendant relocated it on the site, claiming that the defendant's proposed house would impair the efficiency of the plaintiff's solar heating system by blocking off the sunlight during part of the year.

The Wisconsin Supreme Court overturned the defendant's summary judgment in trial court, explicitly repudiating *Fontainebleau*, by holding that an "unreasonable obstruction of access to sunlight might be a private nuisance." The court observed that easements of light could be acquired by prescription under the English doctrine of "ancient lights" and everywhere by express grant. It justified the judicial recognition of solar easements by noting the sharp rise in land use regulation, and by insisting that "the policy of favoring unhindered private development in an expanding economy is no longer in harmony with the realities of our society." The court then concluded that summary judgment was inappropriate:

> The application of the reasonable use standard in nuisance cases normally requires a full exposition of all underlying facts and circumstances. Too little is known in this case of such matters as the extent of the harm to the plaintiff, the suitability of solar heat in that neighborhood, the availability of remedies to the plaintiff, and the costs to the defendant of avoiding the harm.

A lengthy dissent insisted, first, that there was no "invasion" by the defendant, second, that solar energy had not proved itself in the marketplace, and third, that the elaborate legislative scheme in place should not be displaced by a parallel judicial innovation. Why wouldn't the original developer of the common tract have the right incentives to decide whether to grant solar easements to individual tract owners?

Tenn v. 889 Associates, Ltd., 500 A.2d 366, 371 (N.H. 1985), steered a middle course between *Fontainebleau* and *Prah.* It first rejected the hardline proposition that the doctrine of ancient lights could never limit a neighbor's right to build and stated that "there is no reason in principle why the law of nuisance should not be applied to claims for the protection of a property owner's interests in light and air." Nonetheless, on the facts of the case, it refused to enjoin the defendant's plans to construct a six-story office building at the property line just south of the plaintiff's own six-story building.

> The sites were in the downtown commercial area of Manchester, where buildings commonly buttress and block the sides of adjacent structures. Moreover, the defendant proposed to do no more than the plaintiff's own predecessor-in-title had done, by building right to the lot line and to a height of six stories. If, as the plaintiff claimed, this would require expenditures for additional artificial lighting and ventilation systems, she failed to present any evidence that the costs would exceed what was customarily necessary for such buildings.

Given that courts seem wary of enforcing height restrictions in nuisance actions, how might property owners respond? Brady, Turning Neighbors into Nuisances, 134 Harv. L. Rev. 1609 (2021), details efforts by property owners to enforce various building restrictions by enacting nuisance covenants that at one time were directed toward particular common law nuisances, but later were extended to attack the construction of apartment houses in single-family home neighborhoods.

2. *Protecting Views by Contract.* A very different approach toward the protection of views took place in the upscale Chelsea area in New York City. A group of loft owners (average size apartment 5,000 feet) in a twelve-story building learned that a developer had plans to build a large tower next door that would block their light and their view of the Empire State building. Instead of going to the local zoning authorities, the loft owners banded together to pay the developer $11 million to not build at all. Among themselves the loft-owners developed by contract an allocation system that required larger payments for the owners on the higher floors. The owners have no intention to build with their air rights. See Goodman, How Much Is a View Worth in Manhattan? Try $11 Million, N.Y. Times, July 22, 2019, https://www.nytimes.com/2019/07/22/nyregion/manhattan-real-estate-views-air-rights.html. Keeping the land empty may well work to the benefit of other neighbors by increasing their air, light, and views. Should the buyers of air rights have claims against these neighbors? For a cautious answer in the affirmative, see Porat, Private Production of Public Goods: Liability for Unrequested Benefits, 108 Mich. L. Rev. 189, 195 (2009), which advocates a relaxation of the standard requirement for restitution in cases of unjust enrichment that allow compensation only "[w]hen a benefactor *voluntarily* confers benefits *at the recipient's request.*" For a defense of the traditional requirements, see Epstein, Positive and Negative Externalities in Real Estate Development, 102 Minn. L. Rev. 1493, 1511–13 (2018).

3. *Projections on Private Property.* Today a wide assortment of artists, businesses, protesters, and civil groups take advantage of modern technologies to project their desired images on buildings owned by other individuals. In these situations, several courts have held that the property owner is not entitled to any remedy under a theory of either trespass or nuisance, given that the beams of light have caused no harm to the property on which they are projected. Thus in International Union of Painters and Allied Trades v. Great Wash Park, LLC, No. 67453, 2016 WL 4499940 (Nev. Ct. App. Aug. 18, 2016), the defendant union projected a message on the façade of the plaintiff's property to note several health code violations on the property. The plaintiff claimed irreparable harm on the ground that the message reduced the revenues of the restaurant, which in turn diminished the amount that the plaintiff was owed as the landlord based on a percentage lease with the restaurant. The court denied a preliminary injunction on the grounds that there was no trespass of either a tangible or intangible variety. Brady, Property and Projection, 133 Harv. L. Rev. 1143, 1190 (2020), takes issue with that result, claiming that the full recognition of the dignitary and privacy interests of the landowner should provide greater protection for the "communicative uses in property."

> Whether textual or aesthetic, these communications provide information about the owner's beliefs and values; property is itself an image that the owner creates through labor or inaction. Just as it was with the other torts, these nonpecuniary interests of the owner are recognized across legal areas, but the forms of action have simply not caught up.

How is the privacy of the landowner invaded if the dignitary harms are to the restaurant tenant who has no interest in the wall? Is it possible to turn this case around by seeking restitution because the defendant has unjustly enriched itself by using the plaintiff's wall to its advantage? Compare with *Hamidi*, *supra* at 452.

4. ***Spite Fences.*** It has often been held that "a fence erected maliciously, and with no other purpose than to shut out the light and air from a neighbor's window, is a nuisance." Flaherty v. Moran, 45 N.W. 381, 381 (Mich. 1890). This proposition tracks the logic of the live-and-let-live rule insofar as it rests on the belief that all individuals are better off if each is denied the right to construct fences solely out of malice. Yet even those courts that regard spite fences as actionable nuisances are quick to qualify their conclusions. Thus, in Kuzniak v. Kozminski, 65 N.W. 275 (Mich. 1895), the defendant moved his coal and wood shed close to the plaintiff's property line, where it blocked the light and air to the plaintiff's windows, partly out of malice. Nonetheless, the court refused to extend the spite fence doctrine because the shed served some "useful purpose." What about spite fences with useful functions? How might *Prah* be distinguished from the spite fence cases?

5. ***Noninvasive Nuisances: of Ugly Things and Beautiful Views.*** Is it a nuisance if the defendant paints his house the most horrendous shade of pink, thereby driving down the value of the neighboring houses? May aesthetic blight be so inconsistent with the character of a neighborhood that it becomes a nuisance? In Mathewson v. Primeau, 395 P.2d 183 (Wash. 1964), the court was willing to enjoin the raising of hogs on the defendant's land because their odors reached the plaintiff's property, but it nonetheless refused to require the defendant to remove the collection of junk from his land. It flatly held the law of nuisance was not concerned with aesthetics. Similarly, the court in Bansbach v. Harbin, 728 S.E.2d 533, 538 (W. Va. 2012), denied recovery to homeowners whose neighbors created "an eyesore" by constructing a junkyard and posting offensive signs on their property. According to McHugh, J., "unsightliness alone is an insufficient basis" for nuisance liability.

A tougher attitude toward aesthetic nuisances was taken in Rattigan v. Wile, 841 N.E.2d 680, 691–92 (Mass. 2006). A long struggle began when the defendant outbid the plaintiffs to purchase a 2.9-acre beachfront lot next to the plaintiffs' own luxurious Edgewater property. The plaintiffs then sought unsuccessfully to block the defendant's efforts to get building permits and access rights. In retaliation, the defendant conducted a set of harassing activities sporadically for a period of years, including piloting a low-flying helicopter, and piling unsightly objects higher than the six-foot fence that the plaintiffs had erected to block out the view of junk previously left on the ground near the boundary line. The trial judge found that the local community was "intolerant" of the defendant's activities, awarded plaintiffs $532,035.05 ($810,260 in 2023 dollars) in damages, including lost rentals, and issued an injunction, which when modified on appeal, provided that

> the defendant shall not leave unattended any objects more than six feet in height within forty feet of the plaintiffs' boundary line, such as tents, portable toilets, construction and industrial materials, trailers, and warning signs, except reasonable vegetation. The defendant shall not operate, or cause to be operated, a helicopter on his property or within the zone of interest above the property.

And in Sowers v. Forest Hills Subdivision, 294 P.3d 427, 430 (Nev. 2013), the court upheld an injunction against a neighbor who planned to erect a wind turbine. While "aesthetics alone" (in this case, "the large proportions of the turbine") could not support a nuisance finding, the injunction was justified because the plaintiff could also show "the noise and shadow flicker it would create, and its potential to diminish surrounding property values."

Note that condominium associations often impose extensive aesthetic restrictions. Should zoning laws be allowed to do the same?

Rogers v. Elliott

15 N.E. 768 (Mass. 1888)

[The defendant operated a large church bell in a small Massachusetts town, which he rang regularly each day. The plaintiff was recovering from a serious case of sunstroke in a house located not far from the church. One Saturday the plaintiff suffered severe convulsions attributed by his physician to the bell's noise. After the Saturday episode the physician informed the defendant of his patient's condition and predicted that the plaintiff would have further convulsions if the defendant rang the bell the next day. After receiving this warning, the defendant said he would ring his bell as usual the next day because "[the] bell is more musical than the rest of the bells in town." He added that the plaintiff had previously had him arrested, but he said that he would ring it even if his sister or brother were ill. The next day the defendant rang his bell and the plaintiff suffered further damage, for which he brought this action.]

Knowlton, J. The defendant was the custodian and authorized manager of property of the Roman Catholic Church used for religious worship. The acts for which the plaintiff seeks to hold him responsible were done in the use of this property, and the sole question before us is whether or not that use was unlawful. The plaintiff's case rests upon the proposition that the ringing of the bell was a nuisance. The consideration of this proposition involves an inquiry into what the defendant could properly do in the use of the real estate which he had in charge, and what was the standard by which his rights were to be measured.

It appears that the church was built upon a public street in a thickly settled part of the town, and if the ringing of the bell on Sundays had materially affected the health or comfort of all in the vicinity, whether residing or passing there, this use of the property would have been a public nuisance, for which there would have been a remedy by indictment. Individuals suffering from it in their persons or their property could have recovered damages for a private nuisance.

In an action of this kind, a fundamental question is, by what standard, as against the interests of a neighbor, is one's right to use his real estate to be measured. In densely populated communities the use of property in many ways which are legitimate and proper necessarily affects in greater or less degree the property or persons of others in the vicinity. In such cases the inquiry always is, when rights are called in question, what is reasonable under the circumstances. If a use of property is objectionable solely on account of the noise which it makes, it is a nuisance, if at all, by reason of its effect upon the health or comfort of those who are within hearing. The right to make a noise for a proper purpose must be measured in reference to the degree of annoyance which others may reasonably be required to submit to. In connection with the importance of the business from which it proceeds, that must be determined by the effect of noise upon people generally, and not upon those, on the one hand, who are peculiarly susceptible to it, or those, on the other, who by long experience have learned to endure it without inconvenience; not upon those whose strong nerves and robust health enable them to endure the greatest disturbances without suffering, nor upon those whose mental or physical condition makes them painfully sensitive to everything about them.

That this must be the rule in regard to public nuisances is obvious. It is the rule as well, and for reasons nearly if not quite as satisfactory, in relation to private nuisances. Upon a question whether one can lawfully ring his factory bell, or run his noisy machinery, or whether the noise will be a private nuisance to the occupant of a house near by, it is necessary to ascertain the natural and probable effect of the sound upon ordinary persons in that house,—not how it will affect a particular person, who happens to be there to-day, or who may chance to come tomorrow. St. Helen's Smelting Co. v. Tipping, [(1865) 11 Eng. Rep. 1485 (HL) (appeal taken from Eng.)]. In the case of Westcott v. Middleton, 43 N.J. Eq. 478 (1887), it appeared that the defendant carried on the business of an undertaker, and the windows of the plaintiff's house looked out upon his yard, where boxes which had been used to preserve the bodies of the dead were frequently washed, and where other objects were visible and other work was going on, which affected the tender sensibilities of the plaintiff, and caused him great discomfort. Vice-Chancellor Bird, in dismissing the bill for an injunction against carrying on the business there, said: ". . . A wide range has indeed been given to courts of equity in dealing with these matters; but I can find no case where the court has extended aid unless the act complained of was, as I have above said, of a nature to affect all reasonable persons, similarly situated, alike."

If one's right to use his property were to depend upon the effect of the use upon a person of peculiar temperament or disposition, or upon one suffering from an uncommon disease, the standard for measuring it would be so uncertain and fluctuating as to paralyze industrial enterprises. The owner of a factory containing noisy machinery, with dwelling-houses all about it, might find his business lawful as to all but one of the tenants of the houses, and as to that one, who dwelt no nearer than the others, it might be a nuisance. The character of his business might change from legal to illegal, or illegal to legal, with every change of tenants of an adjacent estate or with an arrival or departure of a guest or boarder at a house near by or even with the wakefulness or the tranquil repose of an invalid neighbor on a particular night. Legal rights to the use of property cannot be left to such uncertainty. When an act is of such a nature as to extend its influence to those in the vicinity, and its legal quality depends upon the effect of that influence, it is as important that the rightfulness of it should be tried by the experience of ordinary people, as it is, in determining a question as to negligence, that the test should be the common care of persons of ordinary prudence, without regard to the peculiarities of him whose conduct is on trial.

In the case at bar it is not contended that the ringing of the bell for church services in the manner shown by the evidence materially affected the health or comfort of ordinary people in the vicinity, but the plaintiff's claim rests upon the injury done him on account of his peculiar condition. However his request should have been treated by the defendant upon considerations of humanity, we think he could not put himself in a place of exposure to noise, and demand as of legal right that the bell should not be used.

The plaintiff, in his brief, concedes that there was no evidence of express malice on the part of the defendant, but contends that malice was implied in his acts. In the absence of evidence that he acted wantonly, or with express malice, this implication could not come from his exercise of his legal rights. How far and under what circumstances malice may be material in cases of this kind, it is unnecessary to consider.

Judgment on the verdict.

NOTE

Extrasensitive Plaintiffs Under the Law of Nuisance. Can the result in Rogers v. Elliott be reconciled with the general rule, applicable in trespass and negligence cases, that the defendant takes his victim as he finds him? If it had been found in *Rogers* that an ordinary person would have suffered substantial discomfort but no physical injuries from the ringing of the bells, could the plaintiff have recovered for the full extent of his injuries? Could the defendant claim a prescriptive easement, based on long use, against the public at large? *Rogers* is explicitly approved in RST §821F.

RESTATEMENT OF THE LAW (SECOND) OF TORTS

§821F. Significant Harm

There is liability for a nuisance only to those to whom it causes significant harm, of a kind that would be suffered by a normal person in the community or by property in normal condition and used for a normal purpose.

Illustration 2: *A* operates a race track, which is illuminated at night by flood lights directed downward. *B* operates next door an open-air motion picture theater, screened off from the highway. The reflection of *A*'s lights, equivalent to the light of the full moon, would be harmless and unobjectionable to anyone making a normal use of adjoining land, but so seriously interferes with the operation of *B*'s motion pictures that *B* loses customers. *B* cannot recover from *A* for a private nuisance.

The extrasensitivity issue in nuisance cases arises not only with personal injuries, but also with property damage. In Belmar Drive-In Theater Co. v. Illinois State Toll Highway Commission, 216 N.E.2d 788 (Ill. 1966), the defendants operated a toll-road service center adjacent to the plaintiff's outdoor movie theater. The charge in the complaint was that the "brilliant artificial lights" used in the service area "dispelled" the darkness, making it impossible for the plaintiff to exhibit outdoor movies, reducing the value of his theater. The court denied the plaintiff's cause of action, relying on the extrasensitivity test. *Belmar* is endorsed in RST §821F, illus. 2, *supra*. What if the defendant could have constructed its tollway service center so as not to cast light on the plaintiff's theater? Suppose the defendant was not a governmental agency?

Belmar, which is widely followed today, see Blue Ink, Ltd. v. Two Farms, Inc., 96 A.3d 810 (Md. Ct. Spec. App. 2014), was expressly distinguished in Page County Appliance Center v. Honeywell, Inc., 347 N.W.2d 171, 175–76 (Iowa 1984). The defendant Honeywell installed a computer in a local travel agency as part of the defendant ITT's plan to lease computers to retail travel outlets nationwide. The computer leaked extensive amounts of radiation, which interfered with the images on the television sets on display in the plaintiff's nearby appliance store. Honeywell's efforts to fix the computers were to no avail because the "interference-causing radiation was a design and not a service problem." The jury awarded the plaintiff $221,000 ($653,000 in 2023 dollars) in damages ($71,000 compensatory, $150,000 punitive), and the judge required Honeywell to make full indemnity to ITT. The judgment was affirmed on appeal by Reynoldson, C.J.:

> In the case before us, ITT asserts the Appliance Center's display televisions constituted a hypersensitive use of its premises as a matter of law, and equates this situation to cases involving light thrown on outdoor theater screens in which light-throwing defendants have carried the day. *See Belmar*. . . .

> We cannot equate the rare outdoor theater screen with the ubiquitous television that exists, in various numbers in almost every home. Clearly, the presence of televisions on any premises is not such an abnormal condition that we can say, as a matter of law, that the owner has engaged in a *peculiarly* sensitive use of the property.

On extrasensitivity, see generally Ellickson, Alternatives to Zoning: Covenants, Nuisance Rules, and Fines as Land Use Controls, 40 U. Chi. L. Rev. 681, 751–57 (1973).

Ensign v. Walls

34 N.W.2d 549 (Mich. 1948)

Carr, J. Defendant herein has for some years past carried on at 13949 Dacosta Street, in the City of Detroit, the business of raising, breeding and boarding St. Bernard dogs. Plaintiffs are property owners and residents in the immediate neighborhood. Claiming that the business conducted by defendant constituted a nuisance as to them and their property, plaintiffs brought suit for injunctive relief. The bill of complaint alleged that obnoxious odors came from defendant's premises at all times, that the continual barking of the dogs interfered with and disturbed plaintiffs in the use and enjoyment of their respective properties, that the premises were infested with rats and flies, and that on occasions dogs escaped from defendant's premises and roamed about the neighborhood. Defendant in her answer denied that her business was conducted in such a manner as to constitute a nuisance, and claimed further that she had carried on the business at the premises in question since 1926, that she had invested a considerable sum of money in the purchase of the property and in the subsequent erection of buildings thereon, and that under the circumstances plaintiffs were not entitled to the relief sought. . . .

[The court concludes that the evidence supported the finding that the defendant's business constituted a nuisance to the plaintiffs and that the defendant had not acquired by prescriptive use the right to continue the nuisance.]

The record discloses that the plaintiffs, or the majority of them at least, have moved into the neighborhood in recent years. In view of this situation it is claimed by defendant that, inasmuch as she was carrying on her business of raising, breeding and boarding dogs on her premises at the time plaintiffs established their residences in the neighborhood, they cannot now be heard to complain. Such circumstance may properly be taken into account in a proceeding of this nature in determining whether the relief sought ought, in equity and good conscience, to be granted. Doubtless under such circumstances courts of equity are more reluctant to restrain the continued operation of a lawful business than in instances where it is sought to begin in a residential district a business of such character that it will constitute a nuisance. The Supreme Court of Pennsylvania in Wier's Appeal, 74 Pa. 230 [(1873)], declared the commonly accepted rule as follows:

> There is a very marked distinction to be observed in reason and equity between the case of a business long established in a particular locality, which has become a nuisance from the growth of population and the erection of dwellings in proximity to it, and that of a new erection threatened in such a vicinity. Carrying on an offensive trade for any number of years in a place remote from buildings and public roads, does not entitle the owner to continue it in the same place after houses have been built and roads laid out in the neighborhood, to the occupants of which and travellers upon which it is a nuisance. As the city extends, such nuisances should be removed to the vacant grounds beyond the immediate neighborhood of the residences of the citizens. This, public policy, as well as the health and comfort of the population of the city, demand. It certainly ought to be a much clearer case, however, to justify a court of equity in

> stretching forth the strong arm of injunction to compel a man to remove an establishment in which he has invested his capital and been carrying on business for a long period of time, from that of one who comes into a neighborhood proposing to establish such a business for the first time, and who is met at the threshold of his enterprise by a remonstrance and notice that if he persists in his purpose, application will be made to a court of equity to prevent him. . . .

Defendant cites and relies on prior decisions of this court in each of which consideration was given to the circumstance that the parties seeking relief had established residences near the business the operation of which was sought to be enjoined. That such a circumstance may properly be considered in any case of this character in determining whether equitable relief should be granted is scarcely open to question. However it is not necessarily controlling. Looking to all the facts and circumstances involved, the question invariably presented is whether the discretion of the court should be exercised in favor of the parties seeking relief. In the case at bar the trial court came to the conclusion that the nuisance found by him to exist ought to be abated, and that such action was necessary in order to protect the plaintiffs in their rights and in the use and enjoyment of their homes. It may be assumed that new residences will be built in the community in the future, as they have been in the past, and that in consequence the community will become more and more thickly populated. This means of course that the injurious results of the carrying on of defendant's business, if the nuisance is not abated, will be greater in the future than it has been in the past. Such was obviously the view of the trial judge, and we cannot say that he abused his discretion in granting relief. On the contrary we think his conclusions were fully justified by the record. . . .

The decree of the Circuit Court is affirmed. Plaintiffs may have costs.

NOTES

1. ***Coming to the Nuisance.*** Ensign v. Walls adopts the general view that it is no categorical defense to show that the plaintiff came to the nuisance, so trial courts do not abuse their discretion by issuing injunctions in these cases. The majority position finds its basis in the plaintiff's right to the exclusive use and control of her own land and holds that the defendant is not entitled to acquire by his unilateral conduct an easement to cause damage to the plaintiff's property. The case, briefly put, is that an acceptance of the coming to the nuisance defense allows the "theft" of an incorporeal interest in real property. Why not mandate the injunction in all cases?

The minority view on the coming to the nuisance question usually rests on some version of assumption of risk. In Bove v. Donner-Hanna Coke Corp., 258 N.Y.S. 229, 234 (App. Div. 1932), the plaintiff sought to enjoin the operation of the defendant's coke oven, which was located on the opposite side of the street. The region was industrialized when the plaintiff moved into it, but a hickory grove was located on the site of the defendant's coke oven. The court rejected the plaintiff's request for an injunction because the plaintiff moved into the area "with full knowledge that this region was especially adapted for industrial rather than residential purposes, and that factories would increase in the future." The opinion concluded with a marked deference to local zoning authorities, by noting that it was inappropriate for a court to "condemn as a nuisance a business which is being conducted in an approved and expert manner, at the very spot where the council said it might be located."

The Second Restatement equivocates. Section 840C provides that assumption of risk should be a defense in nuisance actions "to the same extent as in other tort actions." Thereafter, section 840D puts this gloss on coming to the nuisance: "The fact that the plaintiff has acquired or improved his land after a nuisance interfering with it has come into existence is not in itself sufficient to bar his action, but is a factor to be considered in determining whether the nuisance is actionable."

The limits of the coming to the nuisance doctrine were tested in Amaral v. Cuppels, 831 N.E.2d 915, 919 (Mass. App. Ct. 2005), which held that the coming to the nuisance defense was not available to the owner of a golf course who was sued for a continuing trespass when players near the ninth hole bombarded landowners' homes, which were subsequently built nearby. Green, J., held that the discretionary principles applicable to coming to the nuisance cases did not apply because there is "no cognate notion of 'coming to a trespass.'" Why the difference?

2. *"Right to Farm" Laws.* All fifty states today have abridged the coming to the nuisance doctrine by passage of right to farm laws. Representative of this group is Illinois Farm Nuisance Suit Act, 740 Ill. Comp. Stat. 70/3 (2023), whose "declared policy" is "to conserve and protect and encourage the development and improvement of its agricultural land for the production of food and other agricultural products." Its key operative provision states:

> No farm or any of its appurtenances shall be or become a private or public nuisance because of any changed conditions in the surrounding area occurring after the farm has been in operation for more than one year, when such farm was not a nuisance at the time it began operation, provided, that the provisions of this Section shall not apply whenever a nuisance results from the negligent or improper operation of any farm or its appurtenances.

In Toftoy v. Rosenwinkel, 983 N.E.2d 463 (Ill. 2012), the court held that the Illinois statute barred suits from anyone who came to the nuisance more than one year after the farm went into operation. The limitations period runs from the time that the farm first went into operation even against a plaintiff who first bought her house only several years after the farm was established. The upshot was that the plaintiff could obtain no injunction against an infestation of flies coming from the defendant's longstanding farming operations.

3. *Economic Analysis and the Coming to the Nuisance Rule.* A spirited attack on the coming to the nuisance rule is found in Baxter & Altree, Legal Aspects of Airport Noise, 15 J.L. & Econ. 1 (1972), which claims that a law and economics approach suggests that the optimal use of land will be achieved with the following liability rule: "of two incompatible land uses the one which had but did not take the opportunity to avoid creating costs of incompatibility should bear the costs." From this premise it follows in general that the first party to invest in a given area should be protected and, to use the authors' phrase, "the unavoidable reciprocal costs" that arise when a second party makes an incompatible use of his own land should be borne by the second party. The temporal element is given dominance under this formulation that under the traditional nuisance law was reserved for the spatial element.

The Baxter-Altree rule is meant to discourage any wasteful investment that the second user might otherwise make if he knew he could collect full damages or enjoin the prior use. But it does not indicate what restrictions, if any, should be placed on the *initial* land use decision by the first user. If their proposal is followed, the plaintiff is left without a remedy in the standard coming to the nuisance case, which gives any landowner a strong incentive to develop quickly if only to preserve legal rights. Further, the second use could prove more beneficial to society, but be blocked by the incompatible land uses. The coming to the nuisance rule is therefore understood as an implicit bargain between two landowners in which the first allows the second to operate on the condition that the second waives any statute of limitations objection should the former develop his land. That rule postpones any litigation and holds open the prospect that the initial builder will abandon his obnoxious use when the developed region makes other uses more attractive. Note that the statute of limitations played an important role in Sturges v. Bridgman, (1879) 11 Ch D 852, in which Jessel, M.R., enjoined an established confectioner from the use of his mortar and pestle when the plaintiff physician built his examining room on the opposite side of the shared wall.

Essentially, there are many more degrees of freedom in locating businesses before the conflicts arise. How does this situation compare with the purchase of view rights in New York City, *supra* at 500, Note 2?

For accounts of *Sturges*, see Simpson, *Coase v. Pigou* Reexamined, 25 J. Legal Stud. 53 (1996); Coase, Law and Economics and A.W. Brian Simpson, 25 J. Legal Stud. 103 (1996); and in reply, Simpson, An Addendum, 25 J. Legal Stud. 99 (1996); Epstein, Principles of a Free Society: Reconciling Individual Liberty with the Common Good 202–06 (1998).

Boomer v. Atlantic Cement Co.

257 N.E.2d 870 (N.Y. 1970)

Bergan, J. Defendant operates a large cement plant near Albany. These are actions for injunction and damages by neighboring land owners alleging injury to property from dirt, smoke and vibration emanating from the plant. A nuisance has been found after trial, temporary damages have been allowed; but an injunction has been denied.

The public concern with air pollution arising from many sources in industry and in transportation is currently accorded ever wider recognition accompanied by a growing sense of responsibility in State and Federal Governments to control it. Cement plants are obvious sources of air pollution in the neighborhoods where they operate.

But there is now before the court private litigation in which individual property owners have sought specific relief from a single plant operation. The threshold question raised by the division of view on this appeal is whether the court should resolve the litigation between the parties now before it as equitably as seems possible; or whether, seeking promotion of the general public welfare, it should channel private litigation into broad public objectives. . . .

Effective control of air pollution is a problem presently far from solution even with the full public and financial powers of government. In large measure adequate technical procedures are yet to be developed and some that appear possible may be economically impracticable.

[The court then notes that the scientific, financial, and political implications are not easily addressed, and lie in] an area beyond the circumference of one private lawsuit. It is a direct responsibility for government and should not thus be undertaken as an incident to solving a dispute between property owners and a single cement plant—one of many—in the Hudson River valley.

The cement making operations of defendant have been found by the court at Special Term to have damaged the nearby properties of plaintiffs in these two actions. That court, as it has been noted, accordingly found defendant maintained a nuisance and this has been affirmed at the Appellate Division. The total damage to plaintiffs' properties is, however, relatively small in comparison with the value of defendant's operation and with the consequences of the injunction which plaintiffs seek.

The ground for the denial of injunction, notwithstanding the finding both that there is a nuisance and that plaintiffs have been damaged substantially, is the large disparity in economic consequences of the nuisance and of the injunction. This theory cannot, however, be sustained without overruling a doctrine which has been consistently reaffirmed in several leading cases in this court and which has never been disavowed here, namely that where a nuisance has been found and where there has been any substantial damage shown by the party complaining an injunction will be granted.

The rule in New York has been that such a nuisance will be enjoined although marked disparity be shown in economic consequence between the effect of the injunction and the effect of the nuisance.

The problem of disparity in economic consequence was sharply in focus in Whalen v. Union Bag & Paper Co.[, 101 N.E. 805 (N.Y. 1913)]. A pulp mill entailing an investment of more than a million dollars polluted a stream in which plaintiff, who owned a farm, was "a lower riparian owner." The economic loss to plaintiff from this pollution was small. This court, reversing the Appellate Division, reinstated the injunction granted by the Special Term against the argument of the mill owner that in view of "the slight advantage to plaintiff and the great loss that will be inflicted on defendant" an injunction should not be granted. "Such a balancing of injuries cannot be justified by the circumstances of this case," Judge Werner noted. He continued: "Although the damage to the plaintiff may be slight as compared with the defendant's expense of abating the condition, that is not a good reason for refusing an injunction."

Thus the unconditional injunction granted at Special Term was reinstated. The rule laid down in that case, then, is that whenever the damage resulting from a nuisance is found not "unsubstantial," viz., $100 [$3,100 in 2023 dollars] a year, injunction would follow. This states a rule that had been followed in this court with marked consistency.

Although the court at Special Term and the Appellate Division held that injunction should be denied, it was found that plaintiffs had been damaged in various specific amounts up to the time of the trial and damages to the respective plaintiffs were awarded for those amounts. The effect of this was, injunction having been denied, plaintiffs could maintain successive actions at law for damages thereafter as further damage was incurred.

The court at Special Term also found the amount of permanent damage attributable to each plaintiff, for the guidance of the parties in the event both sides stipulated to the payment and acceptance of such permanent damage as a settlement of all the controversies among the parties. The total of permanent damages to all plaintiffs thus found was $185,000 [$1,460,000 in 2023 dollars]. This basis of adjustment has not resulted in any stipulation by the parties.

This result at Special Term and at the Appellate Division is a departure from a rule that has become settled; but to follow the rule literally in these cases would be to close down the plant at once. This court is fully agreed to avoid that immediately drastic remedy; the difference in view is how best to avoid it.*

One alternative is to grant the injunction but postpone its effect to a specified future date to give opportunity for technical advances to permit defendant to eliminate the nuisance; another is to grant the injunction conditioned on the payment of permanent damages to plaintiffs which would compensate them for the total economic loss to their property present and future caused by defendant's operations. For reasons which will be developed the court chooses the latter alternative.

If the injunction were to be granted unless within a short period—e.g., 18 months—the nuisance be abated by improved methods, there would be no assurance that any significant technical improvement would occur.

The parties could settle this private litigation at any time if defendant paid enough money and the imminent threat of closing the plant would build up the pressure on defendant. If there were no improved techniques found, there would inevitably be applications to the court at Special Term for extensions of time to perform on showing of good faith efforts to find such techniques.

Moreover, techniques to eliminate dust and other annoying by-products of cement making are unlikely to be developed by any research the defendant can undertake within any short period, but will depend on the total resources of the cement industry nationwide and throughout the world. The problem is universal wherever cement is made.

* Respondent's investment in the plant is in excess of $45,000,000 [$356,000,000 in 2023 dollars]. There are over 300 people employed there.

For obvious reasons the rate of the research is beyond control of defendant. If at the end of 18 months the whole industry has not found a technical solution a court would be hard put to close down this one cement plant if due regard be given to equitable principles.

On the other hand, to grant the injunction unless defendant pays plaintiffs such permanent damages as may be fixed by the court seems to do justice between the contending parties. All of the attributions of economic loss to the properties on which plaintiffs' complaints are based will have been redressed.

The nuisance complained of by these plaintiffs may have other public or private consequences, but these particular parties are the only ones who have sought remedies and the judgment proposed will fully redress them. The limitation of relief granted is a limitation only within the four corners of these actions and does not foreclose public health or the public agencies from seeking proper relief in a proper court.

It seems reasonable to think that the risk of being required to pay permanent damages to injured property owners by cement plant owners would itself be a reasonable effective spur to research for improved techniques to minimize nuisance.

The power of the court to condition on equitable grounds the continuance of an injunction on the payment of permanent damages seems undoubted. . . .

Thus it seems fair to both sides to grant permanent damages to plaintiffs which will terminate this private litigation. The theory of damage is the "servitude on land" of plaintiffs imposed by defendant's nuisance. (See United States v. Causby, 328 U.S. 256, 261, 262, 267 (1946), where the term "servitude" addressed to the land was used by Justice Douglas relating to the effect of airplane noise on property near an airport.)

The judgment, by allowance of permanent damages imposing a servitude on land, which is the basis of the actions, would preclude future recovery by plaintiffs or their grantees.

This should be placed beyond debate by a provision of the judgment that the payment by defendant and the acceptance by plaintiffs of permanent damages found by the court shall be in compensation for a servitude on the land. . . .

The orders should be reversed, without costs, and the cases remitted to Supreme Court, Albany County to grant an injunction which shall be vacated upon payment by defendant of such amounts of permanent damage to the respective plaintiffs as shall for this purpose be determined by the court.

Jasen, J., dissenting. I agree with the majority that a reversal is required here, but I do not subscribe to the newly enunciated doctrine of assessment of permanent damages, in lieu of an injunction, where substantial property rights have been impaired by the creation of a nuisance.

It has long been the rule in this State, as the majority acknowledges, that a nuisance which results in substantial continuing damage to neighbors must be enjoined. To now change the rule to permit the cement company to continue polluting the air indefinitely upon the payment of permanent damages is, in my opinion, compounding the magnitude of a very serious problem in our State and Nation today.

In recognition of this problem, the Legislature of this State has enacted the Air Pollution Control Act (Public Health Law, §§1264–1299-m) declaring that it is the State policy to require the use of all available and reasonable methods to prevent and control air pollution.

The harmful nature and widespread occurrence of air pollution have been extensively documented. Congressional hearings have revealed that air pollution causes substantial property damage, as well as being a contributing factor to a rising incidence of lung cancer, emphysema, bronchitis and asthma.

The specific problem faced here is known as particulate contamination because of the fine dust particles emanating from defendant's cement plant. The particular type of nuisance is not new, having appeared in many cases for at least the past 60 years. It is interesting to note that cement production has recently been identified as a significant source of particulate contamination in the Hudson Valley. This type of pollution, wherein very small particles escape and stay in the atmosphere, has been denominated as the type of air pollution which produces the greatest hazard to human health. We have thus a nuisance which not only is damaging to the plaintiffs, but also is decidedly harmful to the general public.

I see grave dangers in overruling our long-established rule of granting an injunction where a nuisance results in substantial continuing damage. In permitting the injunction to become inoperative upon the payment of permanent damages, the majority is, in effect, licensing a continuing wrong. It is the same as saying to the cement company, you may continue to do harm to your neighbors so long as you pay a fee for it. Furthermore, once such permanent damages are assessed and paid, the incentive to alleviate the wrong would be eliminated, thereby continuing air pollution of an area without abatement.

It is true that some courts have sanctioned the remedy here proposed by the majority in a number of cases, but none of the authorities relied upon by the majority are analogous to the situation before us. In those cases, the courts, in denying an injunction and awarding money damages, grounded their decision on a showing that the use to which the property was intended to be put was primarily for the public benefit. Here, on the other hand, it is clearly established that the cement company is creating a continuing air pollution nuisance primarily for its own private interest with no public benefit.

This kind of inverse condemnation may not be invoked by a private person or corporation for private gain or advantage. Inverse condemnation should only be permitted when the public is primarily served in the taking or impairment of property. The promotion of the interests of the polluting cement company has, in my opinion, no public use or benefit.

Nor is it constitutionally permissible to impose servitude on land, without consent of the owner, by payment of permanent damages where the continuing impairment of the land is for a private use. This is made clear by the State Constitution (art. I, §7, subd. [a]) which provides that "[p]rivate property shall not be taken for *public* use without just compensation" (emphasis added). It is, of course, significant that the section makes no mention of taking for a *private* use. . . .

I would enjoin the defendant cement company from continuing the discharge of dust particles upon its neighbors' properties unless, within 18 months, the cement company abated this nuisance.

NOTES

1. ***Damages and Injunctions: Complements or Substitutes?*** The assumption of both the majority and dissent is that, within the familiar Calabresi-Melamed framework, the choice is between *either* damages or injunctions, without regard to the clean-up rule: using injunctions for the most serious invasions and damages to "clean-up" the remainder.

> [U]nlike the oversimplified model of damages *versus* injunctive relief developed by Professors Guido Calabresi and Douglas Melamed, the use of injunctions and damages are more often complements than substitutes. The injunctive side of the equation allows for conditional injunctions, bound by levels and time of emissions. The damage side picks up the slack where the injunctive relief backs off. By starting with the former and moving cautiously to the latter, the total level of dislocations is far lower than moving to a corner position in which one of these remedies is adopted to the exclusion of the other. The exact remedial mix is not easy to determine, but the traditional locality rule in nuisance cases suggests where levels of interference from similar activities are reciprocal, higher levels of pollution are allowable, so long as the emissions are confined to a particular area. But for lower-level nuisances, a more universal

> live-and-let-live rule takes over, so that *neither* damages nor injunctive relief is allowed, given the freedom of action that arises from allowing these low-level nuisances is universally beneficial, especially since everyone saves on administrative costs.

Epstein, Positive and Negative Externalities in Real Estate Development, 102 Minn. L. Rev. 1493, 1509 (2018).

2. *Discretion to Issue Injunctions: Undue Hardship.* One recurrent issue in working this analysis involves the role of "the undue-hardship defense to injunctive relief—often referred to simply as 'balancing the equities'—[which] enables a right violator to rebut a prima facie case for an injunction by showing that an injunction will inflict on its target hardship that is 'disproportionate to any benefit plaintiff will derive.' " Gergen et al., The Supreme Court's Accidental Revolution? The Test for Permanent Injunctions, 112 Colum. L. Rev. 203, 226 (2012). That defense is heavily associated with Whalen v. Union Bag & Paper, 101 N.E. 805 (N.Y. 1913), discussed in *Boomer.*

Even though, as both *Ensign* and *Boomer* suggest, courts do not follow an inflexible rule that requires an immediate injunction in all cases, they are typically cautious in denying injunctive relief, which proves valuable whenever there is a serious risk of the defendant's insolvency, or a need to protect innocent third parties from nontrivial losses. See Menell, A Note on Private Versus Social Incentives to Sue in a Costly Legal System, 12 J. Legal Stud. 41 (1983).

Yet in cases of extreme disparity, injunctions are often denied. Thus, in Madison v. Ducktown Sulphur, Copper & Iron Co., 83 S.W. 658, 666, 667 (Tenn. 1904), the plaintiffs were all owners of "thin mountain lands, of little agricultural value." The defendants operated two large copper smelting plants that the plaintiffs sought to shut down. The court refused to close the plants, worth nearly $2 million, in order to protect property worth $1,000. The injunction would ultimately "destroy half of the taxable values of a county, and drive more than 10,000 people from their homes."

Madison, in particular, offers a graphic illustration of strategic bargaining behavior in cases of enormous disparity between a defendant's loss and a plaintiff's gain. More specifically, granting the unconditional injunction gives both parties incentives to renegotiate the deal. Since the defendants' property was worth $2 million and the plaintiffs' lots $1,000, any bargain to dissolve the injunction that paid the plaintiffs more than $1,000 but less than $2 million would leave both sides better off. The huge bargaining range ($1,999,000) invites the plaintiffs to hold out for a large portion of the gain as the price for letting the defendants resume their activities.

Unqualified injunctive relief thus poses two major risks: First, parties might waste enormous resources in bargaining over the surplus and, second, they might not be able to reach any agreement at all given the tendency to bluff and bluster. (Recall the private necessity cases in Chapter 1.) The damage remedy forestalls these risks because the plaintiffs are at most entitled to $1,000, which the defendants would happily pay. Could the use of an equitable clean-up rule obviate these difficulties? On the proper mix between injunctions and damages, see Polinsky, Resolving Nuisance Disputes: The Simple Economics of Injunctive and Damage Remedies, 32 Stan. L. Rev. 1075 (1980).

The limits of injunctive relief arose in the important Supreme Court decision eBay v. MercExchange LLC, 547 U.S. 388, 391 (2006), which announced an oft-used four-part test for issuing an injunction under which a plaintiff must show:

> (1) that it has suffered an irreparable injury; (2) that remedies available at law, such as monetary damages, are inadequate to compensate for that injury; (3) that, considering the balance of hardships between the plaintiff and defendant, a remedy in equity is warranted; and (4) that the public interest would not be disserved by a permanent injunction.

Would the *eBay* test be serviceable in dealing with injunctions in private nuisance cases? Gergen et al. critique the four-part *eBay* test in both patent and nuisance law.

3. *Conditional Injunctions.* The law on injunctions is still more complicated because courts, in the exercise of their undeniable power to enjoin nuisances, may, at their discretion, either deny the injunction or, in the alternative, grant it only if certain conditions are attached. In Pendoley v. Ferreira, 187 N.E.2d 142 (Mass. 1963), the court delayed injunctive relief against the continued operation of the defendants' piggery to allow the defendants time to engage in "an orderly, rather than a hurried, liquidation of their pigs," and to have an "opportunity to find new premises." It is also possible to permit a defendant to continue in business, but only if it takes specific measures to eliminate the objectionable features of its enterprise. Thus, in Quinn v. American Spiral Spring & Manufacturing Co., 141 A. 855 (Pa. 1928), the defendant was allowed to continue using its factory, but only on the condition that it rearrange its heavy machinery in order to reduce the inconvenience to the plaintiff. Similarly in Hansen v. Independent School District No. 1, 98 P.2d 959 (Idaho 1939), the defendant school board could continue to schedule night baseball games on the school's athletic fields, but only if it controlled the illumination of its lights, terminated the games at a reasonable hour, and limited the parking in the neighborhood. Finally, in Mirabella at ASU v. Peacocks Unlimited LLC, No. CV 2021-016159, 2022 WL 18144980, at *3 (Ariz. Super. Ct. Apr. 13, 2022), *vacated and remanded* at No. 1 CA-CV 22-0318, 2022 WL 17983430, at *4 (Ariz. Ct. App. Dec. 29, 2022), a restaurant located across the street from a retirement home complex in Tempe hosted electronic dance music concerts frequented by Arizona State University students. According to a neighbor, "the bass from the concerts penetrate[d] the walls of her apartment and [shook] her bed." The trial court limited the hours and volume of the concerts and required that the defendants make available to the plaintiffs "a method for live-monitoring of the sound level measurements." On appeal, the court vacated the injunction, holding that the hours limitation "burdens more speech than necessary" under the First Amendment. How far should the First Amendment protect one's right to disturb one's neighbors?

4. *Purchased Injunctions.* The three common remedies in nuisance cases are damages, injunctions (permanent or temporary), and, of course, no remedy at all. A fourth solution, often missed by courts and commentators alike, is a "purchased injunction." The plaintiff may enjoin the defendant, but only if she is prepared to compensate the defendant for the loss incurred. The rule first surfaced in Calabresi & Melamed, Property Rules, Liability Rules, and Inalienability: One View of the Cathedral, 85 Harv. L. Rev. 1089, 1115–23 (1972), which proposed the following: "Marshall [the plaintiff] may stop Taney [the defendant] from polluting, but if he does he must compensate Taney." Does the rule make sense if Taney is hitting Marshall?

Almost simultaneously, Spur Industries, Inc. v. Del E. Webb Development Co., 494 P.2d 700, 707–08 (Ariz. 1972), proposed a variation of this rule. The defendants operated a cattle feedlot on the outskirts of Phoenix. The plaintiff development corporation purchased land in the vicinity of the defendant's feedlot that it developed into a tract of private homes. The initial houses were not near the defendant's feedlot, but its later homes were. The odors and flies from the feedlot made it impossible for the new residents to enjoy the outdoor amenities promised by the plaintiff, rendering unmarketable the plaintiff's unsold homes near the defendant's feedlot. The court held that the defendant's activities constituted an actionable nuisance and enjoined its operation. The court noted, however, that it would have accepted the coming to the nuisance defense if the plaintiff had not sold some of the units to individual purchasers. It continued:

> There was no indication in the instant case at the time Spur and its predecessors located in western Maricopa County that a new city would spring up, full-blown, alongside the feeding

> operation and that the developer of that city would ask the court to order Spur to move because of the new city. Spur is required to move not because of any wrongdoing on the part of Spur, but because of a proper and legitimate regard of the courts for the rights and interests of the public.
>
> Del Webb, on the other hand, is entitled to the relief prayed for (a permanent injunction), not because Webb is blameless, but because of the damage to the people who have been encouraged to purchase homes in Sun City. It does not equitably or legally follow, however, that Webb, being entitled to the injunction, is then free of any liability to Spur if Webb has in fact been the cause of the damage Spur has sustained. It does not seem harsh to require a developer, who has taken advantage of the lesser land values in a rural area as well as the availability of large tracts of land on which to build and develop a new town or city in the area, to indemnify those who are forced to leave as a result.
>
> Having brought people to the nuisance to the foreseeable detriment of Spur, Webb must indemnify Spur for a reasonable amount of the cost of moving or shutting down.

Should Spur be allowed to recover for lost profits? Should the purchasers of the individual units be required to help pay for Spur's closing and relocation costs?

5. ***Bargaining After Injunctions.*** One theoretical argument in favor of injunctions is that they allow the parties thereafter to use private bargains to correct any uneconomic assignment of property rights made by judicial decree. One empirical examination of the question suggests that these after-the-fact corrections never take place, even when renegotiation involves only two parties in low-transaction costs environments. Farnsworth, Do Parties to Nuisance Cases Bargain After Judgment? A Glimpse Inside the Cathedral, 66 U. Chi. L. Rev. 373, 421–22 (1999), reports as follows:

> A study of twenty old-fashioned nuisance cases litigated to judgment revealed no bargaining after judgment in any of them. Nor did any of the lawyers contacted believe that bargaining after judgment would have occurred if the loser had won. They attributed the lack of bargaining after judgment to acrimony between the parties and to attitudes the parties held toward their rights that made them reluctant to bargain. . . .
>
> These results raise a number of questions worthy of further exploration. Why might parties have the attitudes toward cash exchanges that the lawyers in these cases describe? To what extent do similar attitudes toward cash exchanges exist in other nonmarket contexts? What stance should the law take toward the parties' feelings in cases like these? . . .
>
> [I]f it turns out that parties do not bargain over their rights when transaction costs are low (or if we know they wouldn't because we see them refusing to bargain for reasons that have nothing to do with transaction costs in the sense of feasibility problems), then the broad project of using law to create bargains for parties when transaction costs are high becomes more complicated to defend.

Does the conclusion follow? Does the premise? Perhaps the set of litigants whose disputes last until judgment consists of extreme personalities, unable to resolve issues through simple give-and-take.

6. ***Permanent and Temporary Damages.*** If injunctions (at long last) are put to one side, plaintiffs may seek damages in a nuisance action. If so, frequently the court must decide between periodic payments or a single lump sum to cover the plaintiff's loss. As might be expected, both approaches have their advantages and disadvantages. Temporary damages allow the court to make more accurate assessments of actual harm without having to speculate about the course of future events. But they impose high administrative costs and burden the plaintiff with the inconvenience of having to bring multiple actions to redress one continuing wrong. Permanent damages raise the converse problem, given the risk of a single inaccurate valuation leading to economic distortions in multiple follow-on cases. In contrast, permanent damages do not offer a once and for all solution if the defendant increases its interference with the plaintiff's land beyond its previous or expected levels. How does one measure damages in such a case? Determine when the statute of limitations starts to run? Given the difficulties in choosing between permanent and temporary damages, should the plaintiff be given an election of remedies?

7. ***Mitigation of Damages.*** With either permanent or temporary damages, the plaintiff is under a duty to mitigate damages. In Belkus v. City of Brockton, 184 N.E. 812 (Mass. 1933), the plaintiff's land had been flooded at various times in the six years prior to suit. The court allowed the plaintiff to recover the costs of raising the level of his basement in order to prevent its repeated flooding from a culvert that the defendant municipality improperly maintained. Should the costs of extensive renovations be allowed after a single flooding? In Stratford Theater, Inc. v. Town of Stratford, 101 A.2d 279 (Conn. 1953), the plaintiff's theater had been "frequently" flooded from a broken sewer line. The plaintiff recovered the expense, not of altering his own property, but of repairing the defendant's broken line. If the plaintiff had refused to make the repairs, could it recover for anticipated future losses, even if greater than the cost of repairs?

A hostile attitude toward mitigation is forcefully asserted in an oft-quoted, but little-followed, passage in Wood, The Law of Nuisances §844, 435 (3d ed. 1893):

> A person injured by a nuisance, is not precluded from a recovery by the fact that he might, by small exertion and a small expenditure, have prevented the injury, the rule being, that as it was the defendant's duty to abstain from the creation of the nuisance, and having created it adjoining owners are not bound to guard against the consequences ensuing therefrom, when in order to do so they are required to expend time or money. . . . A party is not bound to expend a dollar, or to do any act to secure for himself the exercise or enjoyment of a legal right of which he is deprived by reason of the wrongful acts of another.

Is this position consistent with the clean-up rule? Any balance of equities test?

2. Public Nuisance

Anonymous

Y.B. Mich. 27 Hen. 8, f. 27, pl. 10 (1536)

One brought a Writ sur son cas [on his case] against another. He alleged that, whereas the plaintiff had used to have a way from his house to a close over the King's highway for carriage and re-carriage, etc., the defendant had stopped the King's highway, so that the plaintiff could not go to his aforesaid close, to his tort and damage.

Baldwin, C.J. It seems to me that this action does not lie to the plaintiff for the stopping of the highway; for the King has the punishment of that, and he has his plaint in the Leet and there he has his redress, because it is a common nuisance to all the King's lieges, and so there is no reason for a private particular person to have an accion sur son cas; for if one person shall have an action for this, by the same reason every person shall have an action, and so he will be punished a hundred times on the same case.

Fitzherbert, J., to the contrary. I agree well that each nuisance done in the King's highway is punishable in the Leet and not by an action, unless it be where one man has suffered greater hurt or inconvenience than the generality have; but he who has suffered such greater displeasure or hurt can have an action to recover the damage which he has by reason of this special hurt. So if one makes a ditch across the highway, and I come riding along the way in the night and I and my horse are thrown into the ditch so that I have great damage and displeasure thereby, I shall have an action here against him who made this ditch across the highway, because I have suffered more damage than any other person. So here the plaintiff had more convenience by this highway than any other person had, and so when he is stopped he suffers more damage because he has no way to go to his close. Wherefore it seems to me that he shall have this action pour ce special matiere [for his special harm]: but if he had not suffered greater damage than all others suffered, then he would not have the action. Quod Nota. [Which was noted.]

NOTE

Public Nuisances. S.C. Code Ann. §49-1-10 (2023) treats all navigable streams as common highways and defines their obstruction as a public nuisance. But that section says nothing about what private actions could be maintained in the event of breach. In Overcash v. South Carolina Electric & Gas Co., 614 S.E.2d 619, 621 (S.C. 2005), the plaintiff was seriously injured in a boating accident involving a dock obstruction in public waters. Burnett, J., denied the cause of action:

> The dissent by Justice Fitzherbert in a 1536 King's Bench decision [*supra*] derailed the course of nuisance law as a branch of the common law, which once dealt only with harm to real property.* Justice Fitzherbert argued against the contemporaneous understanding of the law in advocating an individual's action for special or particular damage, including personal injury, should be recognized under a cause of action for public nuisance. Although Justice Fitzherbert's view has been widely followed by other courts, we decline to recognize a common law cause of action under the doctrine of public nuisance for purely personal injuries.

Why not an ordinary tort action?

RESTATEMENT OF THE LAW (SECOND) OF TORTS

§821B. Public Nuisance

(1) A public nuisance is an unreasonable interference with a right common to the general public.

(2) Circumstances that may sustain a holding that an interference with a public right is unreasonable include the following:

(a) Whether the conduct involves a significant interference with the public health, the public safety, the public peace, the public comfort or the public convenience, or

(b) whether the conduct is proscribed by a statute, ordinance or administrative regulation, or

(c) whether the conduct is of a continuing nature or has produced a permanent or long-lasting effect, and, as the actor knows or has reason to know, has a significant effect upon the public right.

Comment i. Action for damages distinguished from one for injunction: In determining whether to award damages, the court's task is to decide whether it is unreasonable to engage in the conduct without paying for the harm done. Although a general activity may have great utility it may still be unreasonable to inflict the harm without compensating for it. In an action for injunction the question is whether the activity itself is so unreasonable that it must be stopped. It may be reasonable to continue an important activity if payment is made for the harm it is causing, but unreasonable to continue it without paying.

---

* [Fitzherbert's decision was in fact the majority decision, even though the Chief Justice spoke first.—Eds.]

§821C. Who Can Recover for Public Nuisance

(1) In order to recover damages in an individual action for a public nuisance, one must have suffered harm of a kind different from that suffered by other members of the public exercising the right common to the general public that was the subject of interference.

(2) In order to maintain a proceeding to enjoin to abate a public nuisance, one must

(a) have the right to recover damages, as indicated in Subsection (1), or

(b) have authority as a public official or public agency to represent the state or a political subdivision in the matter, or

(c) have standing to sue as a representative of the general public, as a citizen in a citizen's action or as a member of a class in a class action.

Burgess v. M/V Tamano

370 F. Supp. 247 (D. Me. 1973)

Gignoux, J. Plaintiffs in these class actions seek to recover damages incurred as a result of the discharge into the waters of Casco Bay of approximately 100,000 gallons of Bunker C oil from the tanker M/V TAMANO early on the morning of July 22, 1972, when she struck an outcropping of "Soldier Ledge" while passing through Hussey Sound en route to the port of Portland. Variously named as defendants or third-party defendants are the TAMANO, her owners, her captain, her pilot and the local pilots' association, her charterer, Texaco, Inc., the State of Maine, and the United States of America. Liability is asserted on theories of negligence, unseaworthiness, trespass and nuisance. . . .

Presently before the Court are defendants' motions to dismiss the claims of three of the plaintiff classes: the commercial fishermen . . . ; the commercial clam diggers . . . ; and . . . the owners of motels, trailer parks, camp grounds, restaurants, grocery stores, and similar establishments in Old Orchard Beach, whose businesses are dependent on tourist trade. . . . [D]efendants contend that the economic interests (loss of profits and impairment of earning capacity) which these classes of plaintiffs assert to have been damaged by the oil spill are not legally cognizable because none of the classes had any property interest in the coastal waters and marine life or shores claimed to have been injured by the spill. For reasons to be briefly stated, the Court holds that the motions to dismiss the claims of the commercial fishermen and clam diggers must be denied, but that the motions to dismiss the claims of the Old Orchard Beach businessmen, other than those who owned shore property physically injured by the spill, must be granted. . . .

First, as to the claims of the commercial fishermen and clam diggers, it is not disputed that title to its coastal waters and marine life, including the seabeds and the beds of all tidal waters, is vested in the State of Maine and that individual citizens have no separate property interest therein. It is also uncontroverted that the right to fish or to harvest clams in Maine's coastal waters is not the private right of any individual, but is a public right held by the State "in trust for the common benefit of the people." Moulton v. Libbey, 37 Me. 472, 488 (1854). Since the fishermen and clam diggers have no individual property rights with respect to the waters and marine life allegedly harmed by the oil spill, their right to recover in the present action depends upon whether they may maintain private actions for damages based upon the alleged tortious invasion of public rights which are held by the State of Maine in trust for the common benefit of all the people. As to this issue, the long standing rule of law is that a private individual can recover in tort for invasion of a public right only if he has suffered damage particular to him — that is, damage different in kind, rather than simply in degree, from that sustained by the public generally. Prosser, Law of Torts, §88 at 586–87 (4th ed. 1971); . . . Restatement (Second) of Torts §821C(1) (Tent. Draft No. 17, 1971). Concededly, the line between damages different in kind and those different only in degree from those suffered by the public at large has been difficult to draw. But the Court is persuaded that the commercial fishermen and clam diggers have sufficiently alleged "particular" damage to support their private actions.

The commercial fishermen and clam diggers in the present cases clearly have a special interest, quite apart from that of the public generally, to take fish and harvest clams from the coastal waters of the State of Maine. The injury of which they complain has resulted from defendants' alleged interference with their direct exercise of the public right to fish and to dig clams. It would be an incongruous result for the Court to say that a man engaged in commercial fishing or clamming, and dependent thereon for his livelihood, who may have had his business destroyed by the tortious act of another, should be denied any right to recover for his pecuniary loss on the ground that his injury is no different in kind from that sustained by the general public. Indeed, in substantially all of those cases in which commercial fishermen using public waters have sought damages for the pollution or other tortious invasion of those waters, they have been permitted to recover [citing myriad cases]. These cases are no more than applications of the more general principle that pecuniary loss to the plaintiff will be regarded as different in kind "where the plaintiff has an established business making a commercial use of the public right with which the defendant interferes. . . ." Prosser, Law of Torts, In the view of this Court, to the extent their pecuniary losses can be established, the commercial fishermen and clam diggers should be entitled to recover for the same.

Unlike the commercial fishermen and clam diggers, the Old Orchard Beach businessmen do not assert any interference with their direct exercise of a public right. They complain only of loss of customers indirectly resulting from alleged pollution of the coastal waters and beaches in which they do not have a property interest. Although in some instances their damage may be greater in degree, the injury of which they complain, which is derivative from that of the public at large, is common to all businesses and residents of the Old Orchard Beach area.

In such circumstances, the line is drawn and the courts have consistently denied recovery. In the view of this Court, the Old Orchard Beach businessmen can show no such distinct harm from the oil spill as to support their present action.

[The defendants' motions to dismiss the claims of the commercial fisherman and clam diggers are denied. Motions to dismiss the claims of the businessmen are granted.]

NOTES

1. *"Special" Injury Requirement.* General damages from public nuisances are controlled exclusively by direct public action, usually administrative regulation or criminal prosecution. The private action is maintainable only for "special," "peculiar," or "disproportionate" harm to the individual plaintiff. The reasons for this division lie less in matters of justice and more in matters of administration. General damages are of low intensity and are widely diffused across an extended population. Private actions for admitted grievances are therefore simply too costly to maintain. The enforcement function is centralized to preserve the deterrent and control objectives of the tort law, even though direct compensation to aggrieved parties is necessarily abandoned. When, however, the harms are "special," private actions may again be maintained, as in all ordinary tort situations, for now the administrative burdens are far smaller relative to the size of the stakes. See generally Epstein, Nuisance Law: Corrective Justice and Its Utilitarian

Constraints, 8 J. Legal Stud. 49, 98–102 (1979). What is the relationship between public nuisances and the live and let live doctrine in the law of private nuisances?

Sharkey, Public Nuisance as Modern Business Tort: A New Unified Framework for Liability for Economic Harms, 70 DePaul L. Rev. 431, 448–50 (2020), elaborates the enforcement rationale, whereby the special injury rule deputizes a subclass of impacted individuals or entities to sue to force the tortfeasor to internalize the social costs of its activities. Courts have struggled to articulate what amounts to private harms that are "different in kind" from those of the general public. Consider Mills v. Hall & Richards, 9 Wend. 315–16 (N.Y. Sup. Ct. 1832), where the defendant had built a dam that created a pool of water that attracted malarial mosquitoes, and "after the rebuilding of the dam, the fever and ague was more common in that section of the country than it had been before." The plaintiff and his family suffered health effects. Sutherland, J., wrote: "a man may overflow his own land; but if such overflow spread disease and death through the neighborhood, it may be abated, and he must respond in damages for the special injury which any individual may have sustained from it."

Contrast *Mills* with Palmer v. Amazon.com, Inc., 51 F.4th 491, 519–21 (2d Cir. 2022), where workers at an 840,000-square-foot Amazon fulfillment center warehouse on Staten Island claimed that Amazon's workplace policies prevented workers from engaging in COVID-19 preventative social distancing or basic hygiene and sanitation practices. Nardini, J., concluded that "although Plaintiffs may plead a harm that is different *in degree* from the community at large, they fail to plead a harm that is different *in kind*, thereby failing to allege the special injury required to state a claim for public nuisance under New York law." Chin, J., dissented:

> Plaintiffs faced heightened COVID-19 risks due to the conditions of their employment. The harms here . . . are different in kind because they resulted from Amazon's affirmative decisions not to implement any sufficient measures to mitigate the high risk of COVID-19 transmission inherent in warehouse work.

What is the violation of the public right alleged by the workers in *Palmer*? Which position aligns with *Mills*?

2. *Public Nuisance and Environmental Harms.* When a multitude of municipalities sued fossil-fuel companies for polluting groundwater with the gasoline additive MBTE, public nuisance claims survived a motion to dismiss, resulting in a settlement for over $400 million ($570 million in 2023 dollars). See In re Methyl Tertiary Butyl Ether Prods. Liab. Litig., 578 F. Supp. 2d 519 (S.D.N.Y. 2008); In re Methyl Tertiary Butyl Ether Prods. Liab. Litig., 379 F. Supp. 2d 348 (S.D.N.Y. 2005). In State ex rel. Jennings v. Monsanto Co., 299 A.3d 372, 376 (Del. 2023), the state of Delaware was allowed to bring public nuisance claims forward against Monsanto for the manufacture of PCB chemicals, which persist indefinitely when released into the environment and pose serious health risks. Seitz, C.J., wrote:

> [E]ven though Monsanto did not control the PCBs after sale, it substantially participated in creating the public nuisance . . . by actively misleading the public and continuing to supply PCBs to industry and consumers knowing that PCBs were hazardous, would escape into the environment after sale to third parties, and would lead to widespread and lasting contamination of Delaware's lands and waters.

What if the extent of the releases depends on the activities of downstream users? Must Monsanto have a minimum share of the market for the action to survive? Does it have any actions over against end users? Distributors?

In smaller-scale disasters, public nuisance has proven vital to providing relief to those whose property and livelihoods have been harmed by such disasters as oil spills. More recently, cities, counties, and states have brought public nuisance actions for large-scale climate harm as well, seeking to recover damages that they allege will come from sea-level rise attributable to global warming.

City of New York v. Chevron Corp.

993 F.3d 81 (2d Cir. 2021)

Sullivan, J. The question before us is whether municipalities may utilize state tort law to hold multinational oil companies liable for the damages caused by global greenhouse gas emissions. Given the nature of the harm and the existence of a complex web of federal and international environmental law regulating such emissions, we hold that the answer is "no."

Global warming presents a uniquely international problem of national concern. It is therefore not well-suited to the application of state law. Consistent with that fact, greenhouse gas emissions are the subject of numerous federal statutory regimes and international treaties. These laws provide interlocking frameworks for regulating greenhouse gas emissions, as well as enforcement mechanisms to ensure that those regulations are followed.

The City of New York has sidestepped those procedures and instead instituted a state-law tort suit against five oil companies to recover damages caused by those companies' admittedly legal commercial conduct in producing and selling fossil fuels around the world. In so doing, the City effectively seeks to replace these carefully crafted frameworks—which are the product of the political process—with a patchwork of claims under state nuisance law. [W]e cannot condone such an action and we AFFIRM the dismissal of the City's complaint.

I. Background

Global warming is one of the greatest challenges facing humanity today. Among the scientific community, there is near universal consensus that global warming is primarily caused, or at least accelerated, by the burning of fossil fuels, which emits greenhouse gases like carbon dioxide and methane into the atmosphere. Once released, those gases can remain in the atmosphere for hundreds of years, where they trap heat that would otherwise radiate into space.

According to the complaint, New York City "is exceptionally vulnerable" to the effects of global warming, such as rising sea levels, because of its "520-mile coastline." So, in the aftermath of Hurricane Sandy, the City "launched a $20 billion-plus multilayered investment program in climate resiliency across all five boroughs." These preparations have included constructing seawalls and other coastal armaments, enlarging and augmenting the City's storm and wastewater infrastructure, and implementing public-health programs designed to tackle the effects of heatwaves, among other measures meant to protect the public and City property.

Even though every single person who uses gas and electricity—whether in travelling by bus, cab, Uber, or jitney, or in receiving home deliveries via FedEx, Amazon, or UPS—contributes to global warming, the City asserts that its taxpayers should not have to shoulder the burden of financing the City's preparations to mitigate the effects of global warming. Rather, the City suggests that a group of large fossil fuel producers are primarily responsible for global warming and should bear the brunt of these costs. Included among that group are Defendants Chevron Corporation, ConocoPhillips, Exxon Mobil Corporation (together, the "Domestic Producers"), BP p.l.c., and Royal Dutch Shell plc (together with BP, the "Foreign Producers" and, collectively with the Domestic Producers, the "Producers"). The Producers "are, respectively, the first (Chevron), second (Exxon), fourth (BP), sixth (Shell), and ninth (ConocoPhillips) largest cumulative producers of fossil fuels worldwide" since the mid-nineteenth century.

As the City sees it, the Producers have known for decades that their fossil fuel products pose a severe risk to the planet's climate. The City alleges that, despite that knowledge, the Producers downplayed the risks and continued to sell massive quantities of fossil fuels, which has caused and will continue to cause significant changes to the City's climate and landscape.

The City freely admits that it is not able to halt the Producers' conduct under any federal statute or international agreement. Indeed, it acknowledges that the Producers' conduct is "lawful . . . commercial activit[y]." Nonetheless, the City believes that it is appropriate to "shift the costs of protecting the City from climate change impacts back onto the companies that have done nearly all they could to create this existential threat."

Understanding the context of this dispute requires some background knowledge about our nation's regulatory framework concerning environmental issues. The Clean Air Act . . . "is an intricate regulatory regime intended to 'protect and enhance the quality of the [n]ation's air resources so as to promote the public health and welfare and the productive capacity of its population.' "

Consistent with that mandate, the Environmental Protection Agency (EPA) was established in 1970 to implement programs to regulate pollution from both mobile and stationary sources under the Clean Air Act and other related statutes, a role which was later interpreted to include the regulation of carbon dioxide and other greenhouse gases. . . .

III. Discussion

A. The City's State-Law Tort Claims Are Displaced by Federal Common Law

1. What Is Federal Common Law?

In the aftermath of Erie Railroad Co. v. Tompkins, 304 U.S. 64 (1938), "[f]ederal courts, unlike state courts, . . . do not possess a general power to develop and apply their own rules of decision." But *Erie* was not a death knell to all federal common law. . . .

In a nutshell, federal common law exists in only the "few and restricted" enclaves, where a federal court is "compelled to consider federal questions [that] cannot be answered from federal statutes alone." And once Congress speaks directly to those questions, "the need for such an unusual exercise of lawmaking by federal courts disappears." In that sense, federal common law functions much like legal duct tape—it is a "necessary expedient" that permits federal courts to address issues of national concern until Congress provides a more permanent solution.

Despite its utility, however, courts have been quick to declare that our constitutional architecture restricts federal common law to a "modest role." And for good reason. Where federal common law exists, it "pre-empt[s] and replace[s]" state law. It thus threatens a potent mix of judicial lawmaking and encroachment on our federalist structure. . . .

2. Does Federal Common Law Apply Here?

. . . Stripped to its essence, then, the question before us is whether a nuisance suit seeking to recover damages for the harms caused by global greenhouse gas emissions may proceed under New York law. Our answer is simple: no.

For over a century, a mostly unbroken string of cases has applied federal law to disputes involving interstate air or water pollution. This is because such quarrels often implicate two federal interests that are incompatible with the application of state law: (i) the "overriding . . . need for a uniform rule of decision" on matters influencing national energy and environmental policy, and (ii) "basic interests of federalism." The City's lawsuit is no different.

To state the obvious, the City does not seek to hold the Producers liable for the effects of emissions released in New York, or even in New York's neighboring states. Instead, the City intends to hold the Producers liable, under New York law, for the effects of emissions made around the globe over the past several hundred years. In other words, the City requests damages for the cumulative impact of conduct occurring simultaneously across just about every jurisdiction on the planet.

Such a sprawling case is simply beyond the limits of state law. To start, a substantial damages award like the one requested by the City would effectively regulate the Producers' behavior far beyond New York's borders. Since "[g]reenhouse gases once emitted 'become well mixed in the atmosphere,' " "emissions in [New York or] New Jersey may contribute no more to flooding in New York than emissions in China." Any actions the Producers take to mitigate their liability, then, must undoubtedly take effect across every state (and country). And all without asking what the laws of those other states (or countries) require. Because it therefore "implicat[es] the conflicting rights of [s]tates [and] our relations with foreign nations," this case poses the quintessential example of when federal common law is most needed. . . .

The City disagrees, positing that because it seeks damages—not abatement or the imposition of pollution standards—its claims do not threaten to regulate emissions at all, let alone beyond New York's borders. But this ignores economic reality. As the Supreme Court has long recognized, " 'regulation can be effectively exerted through an award of damages,' and 'the obligation to pay compensation can be, indeed is designed to be, a potent method of governing conduct and controlling policy.' "

Thus, while the City is not expressly seeking to impose a standard of care or emission restrictions on the Producers, the goal of its lawsuit is perhaps even more ambitious: to effectively impose strict liability for the damages caused by fossil fuel emissions no matter where in the world those emissions were released (or who released them). If the Producers want to avoid all liability, then their only solution would be to cease global production altogether. And even if some level of ongoing liability were deemed palatable, a significant damages award would no doubt "compel[ ]" the Producers to develop new "means of pollution control." [citing Boomer v. Atl. Cement Co., 257 N.E.2d 870 (N.Y. 1970) (acknowledging that nuisance damages "effective[ly] spur" a change in behavior).] . . . Consequently, though the City's lawsuit would regulate cross-border emissions in an indirect and roundabout manner, it would regulate them nonetheless.

B. The Clean Air Act, in Turn, Displaces the City's Federal Common Law Claims Where Domestic Emissions Are Involved

Having concluded that the City's claims must be brought under federal common law, we see that those federal claims immediately run headlong into a problem of their own. For many of the same reasons that federal common law preempts state law, the Clean Air Act displaces federal common law claims concerned with domestic greenhouse gas emissions. . . .

That Congress chose to preempt the federal common law of nuisance with a well-defined and robust statutory and regulatory scheme of environmental law is by no means surprising. Numerous courts have bemoaned the "often . . . 'vague' and 'indeterminate' " standards attached to nuisance law. . . . Such an elastic standard is especially ill-suited to address "the technically complex area of environmental law," particularly since it would be administered by federal judges who "lack the scientific, economic, and technological resources" to "cop[e] with issues of this order." By contrast, it makes far more sense to "entrust[ ] [the] complex balancing" of interests that climate change demands to an "expert agency" such as the EPA.

At bottom, it is enough to say that the issues raised in this dispute concerning domestic emissions are squarely addressed by the Clean Air Act. As a result, we affirm the district court's conclusion that the City's federal common law claims concerning domestic greenhouse gas emissions are displaced by statute.

C. The Clean Air Act's Displacement of Federal Common Law Does Not Resuscitate the City's State-Law Claims

As its final volley on this issue, the City argues that if the Clean Air Act displaced federal common law, then the City's state law nuisance claims may snap back into action unless specifically preempted by statute. In other words, the City sees the Clean Air Act as having vaporized any preemptive effect that federal common law had on state law, thereby requiring us to engage in a traditional statutory preemption analysis. But while the caselaw on this point is admittedly not a model of clarity, the City's position is difficult to square with the fact that federal common law governed this issue in the first place.

IV. Conclusion

For the reasons stated above, we AFFIRM the judgment of the district court.

NOTES

1. ***Evaluating the Torts Claims.*** There are two classes of potential defendants — the actual emitters and the more remote suppliers of fossil fuels, including crude oil, which has a wide range of alternative uses. Which is the better class of defendants? Which are the cheapest cost avoiders? If it is downstream producers, just how much of the harm can be attributed to five oil companies? Saad, Attribution for Climate Torts, 64 B.C. L. Rev. 867, 903–07 (2023), situates the causation problems in climate suits within the framework of scientific and legal techniques developed in the toxic torts context, which similarly involved the problems of latency periods, additive effects, fungible products, and noise induced by concurrent natural contributions and contributory behavior.

In addition to the causal inquiry, how does one measure the losses attributable to global warming, including potential sea rise? The background rate of sea-level rise has been about five inches per century for about 10,000 years. How can one predict its levels in 2050? Should one take those potentials into account now? Note too that the City of New York makes extensive use of fossil fuels in its own activities. Does that count as a form of comparative negligence that reduces recovery?

2. ***Federal Displacement of Federal Common Law Public Nuisance Claims.*** To date, the use of public nuisance suits has been frustrated by Supreme Court determinations that federal common law public nuisance claims are displaced by the comprehensive systems of direct federal regulation. Thus, in City of Milwaukee v. Illinois, 451 U.S. 304, 317 (1981), the Court held that public nuisance suits brought by Illinois were blocked by the explicit effluent limitations set out in the 1972 amendments to the Federal Water Pollution Control Act. Rehnquist, J., wrote: "Congress has not left the formulation of appropriate federal standards to the courts through application of often vague and indeterminate nuisance concepts and maxims of equity jurisprudence, but rather has occupied the field through the establishment of a comprehensive regulatory program supervised by an expert administrative agency."

Subsequently, in American Electric Power Co. v. Connecticut, 564 U.S. 410, 415, 424 (2011), the Court was asked "whether the plaintiffs (several States, the city of New York, and three private land trusts) can maintain federal common law public nuisance claims against carbon-dioxide emitters (four private power companies and the federal Tennessee Valley Authority)," with an eye toward setting emissions levels for each outfit. A unanimous Court, speaking through Ginsburg, J., held that to the extent that these claims rested on federal common law they were blocked. Citing *Milwaukee*, she concluded that "the Clean Air Act and the EPA actions it authorizes displace any federal common law right to seek abatement of carbon-dioxide emissions from fossil-fuel fired power plants."

For criticism of *AEP*, see Ewing & Kysar, Prods and Pleas: Limited Government in an Era of Unlimited Harm, 121 Yale L.J. 350 (2011). For a response, see Epstein, Beware of Prods and Pleas: A Defense of the Conventional Views on Tort and Administrative Law in the Context of Global Warming, 121 Yale L.J. Online 317 (2011).

3. *State Law Public Nuisance Claims?* *AEP* left open the question whether *state* common law causes of action were similarly preempted. Nor did *City of New York* tackle it head-on. Rather, it read the city's state law claims as necessarily arising under federal common law (on what basis?) and then found those claims displaced under *AEP*. Contrast County of San Mateo v. Chevron Corp., 32 F.4th 733, 747 (9th Cir. 2022), where the court affirmed the remand of the plaintiff's state law tort theories, including public nuisance, failure to warn, design defect, private nuisance, negligence, and trespass, to state court. Ikuta, J., rebuffed the defendants' argument that the plaintiff's global-warming claims arise under federal law and, as such, are removable to federal court.

> [E]ven if we assume that the Counties' complaints "could give rise to a cognizable claim" under federal common law, the global-warming-related tort claims do not "require resolution of a substantial question of federal law" because they do not require any interpretation of a federal statutory or constitutional issue, and are "displaced by the Clean Air Act."

The question whether federal law preempts state climate nuisance claims is before a state supreme court in City & County of Honolulu v. Sunoco LP, No. SCAP-22-0000429 (Haw. argued Aug. 17, 2023), a decision that might influence the future trajectory of climate nuisance litigation.

Is there any meaningful difference between the state and federal public nuisance claims? Epstein, The Private Law Connections to Public Nuisance Law: Some Realism About Today's Intellectual Nominalism, 17 J.L. Econ. & Pol'y 282, 297 (2022), sees no role for such state tort actions. "[T]he power of a state in a federal system is only to tax and regulate those activities solely within its borders. It cannot be allowed, and should not be allowed, to do so with respect to activities that take place elsewhere with local consequences." Adler, Displacement and Preemption of Climate Nuisance Claims, 17 J.L. Econ. & Pol'y 217 (2022), argues that preemption of state tort claims is unwarranted. Sharkey, Common Law Tort as a Transitional Regulatory Regime: A New Perspective on Climate Change Litigation, *in* Climate Liberalism: Perspectives on Liberty, Property and Pollution 103 (Adler ed., 2023), posits that tort claims can serve a valuable information-production role, especially in areas that pose emerging and incompletely understood health and safety risks. Is litigation the cheapest way to produce such information in the climate context?

4. *Regulatory Solutions.* If private lawsuits fail, what system of regulation should be put in their place? Should there be a tax on carbon dioxide emissions, tied to the level of anticipated harm? How would such a tax work for goods that are made outside the United States with carbon dioxide intensive processes? How should the tax be adjusted with changes, up or down, in the perception of the relationship of carbon dioxide levels to global warming? Alternatively, should there be emissions quotas for carbon dioxide? If so, should they be transferrable between parties? For discussions of these questions, compare Muresianu, Carbon Taxes in Theory and Practice, May 2023, https://taxfoundation.org/research/all/eu/carbon-taxes-in-practice/, which argues that existing carbon taxes around the world "reduc[e] emissions at a relatively low economic cost, with a substantial portion of revenue being returned to taxpayers or replacing other tax increases," with Zycher, Against a Carbon Tax, June 16, 2022, https://www.aei.org/articles/against-a-carbon-tax/, which argues that "a greenhouse gases tax, like almost all seemingly plausible climate policies, would be all costs and no benefits."

City & County of San Francisco v. Purdue Pharma L.P.
620 F. Supp. 3d 936 (N.D. Cal. 2022)

Breyer, J. The opioid epidemic has plagued San Francisco for over twenty years. The number of individuals who die annually from opioid overdoses continues to climb. Thousands of city residents, from all walks of life, struggle with addiction. Widespread opioid use has strained the city's hospitals. It has forced streets, parks, and public spaces to close. It has exacerbated crime and homelessness. Every year, San Francisco devotes significant resources to a multi-prong fight against the opioid epidemic. That fight includes this case.

This case is part of a nationwide multidistrict litigation stemming from the ongoing opioid epidemic. Cities, counties, and states across the country have filed claims against manufacturers, distributors, and dispensers of prescription opioids. While the facts of each case vary, the claims center on the contention that each defendant has contributed to the opioid epidemic that has engulfed the country. . . .

At trial, Plaintiff brought a single public nuisance claim against Walgreens. The question for the Court is whether Plaintiff proffered sufficient evidence at trial to prove this claim. To carry its burden of proof, Plaintiff had to establish that it is more likely than not that Walgreens knowingly engaged in unreasonable conduct that was a substantial factor in contributing to the opioid epidemic in San Francisco. After careful consideration of the evidence, the Court finds that Plaintiff carried its burden. . . .

I. Findings of Fact

. . . For over two decades, San Francisco has been battling an opioid epidemic, defined by high rates of opioid abuse and addiction throughout the city. . . .

San Franciscans grapple with the effects of the opioid epidemic every day. City workers, including park rangers, street cleaners, fire fighters, paramedics, doctors, and librarians, respond to overdoses, clean up opioid debris, and work to help those suffering from opioid addiction. Neighborhoods across the city have been devastated. Residents' use of public areas — like parks, sidewalks, and libraries — has been significantly impaired and, in some cases, ruined. Even right outside this courthouse, people suffering from severe opioid addiction buy, sell, and use opioids in plain sight. The impact on the city has been "worse than catastrophic." . . .

[Breyer, J., discusses at length trial evidence to support its findings of fact:

"Walgreens is the largest retail pharmacy chain in San Francisco. Between 2006 and 2020, Walgreens distributed and dispensed over one hundred million prescription opioid pills in the city. The Controlled Substances Act ('CSA') and its implementing regulations impose duties on distributors and dispensers of prescription opioids. In exchange for the privilege of distributing and dispensing prescription opioids, Walgreens has regulatory obligations to take reasonable steps to prevent the drugs from being diverted and harming the public. The evidence at trial established that Walgreens breached these obligations.

The evidence at trial established that from 2006 to 2020, Walgreens pharmacies in San Francisco dispensed hundreds of thousands of red flag opioid prescriptions without performing adequate due diligence. Tens of thousands of these prescriptions were written by doctors with suspect prescribing patterns. The evidence showed that Walgreens did not provide its pharmacists with sufficient time, staffing, or resources to perform due diligence on these prescriptions. Pharmacists experienced constant pressure to fill prescriptions as quickly as possible, and a shortage of resources to review them before dispensing. As a result of Walgreens' fifteen-year failure to perform adequate due diligence, Plaintiff proved that it is more likely than not that Walgreens pharmacies dispensed large volumes of medically illegitimate opioid prescriptions that were diverted for illicit use and that substantially contributed to the opioid epidemic in San Francisco."]

II. Conclusions of Law

Plaintiff proved that Walgreens is liable for substantially contributing to the public nuisance—the ongoing opioid epidemic—in San Francisco. . . .

Plaintiff is authorized to bring this action for abatement of a public nuisance existing within San Francisco. To succeed on its public nuisance claim at trial, Plaintiff had the burden of proving by a preponderance of the evidence that Walgreens had knowledge that its unreasonable conduct caused a substantial interference with a right common to the public. Plaintiff carried its burden.

A. Unreasonable Conduct with Knowledge

1. Unreasonable Conduct

Conduct encompasses any action that "assist[s] in creating a system that causes" an interference with a public right. [Citing cases and Restatement (Second) of Torts §821B.] Conduct is unreasonable if it violates a statute, ordinance, or administrative regulation. Conduct is also unreasonable if "the gravity of the harm outweighs the social utility of the defendant's conduct." . . .

At trial, Plaintiff proved that Walgreens pharmacies violated 21 C.F.R. §1306.04(a) for fifteen years. [Section 1306.04(a) states that "[t]he responsibility for the proper prescribing and dispensing of controlled substances is upon the prescribing practitioner, but a corresponding responsibility rests with the pharmacist who fills the prescription." That responsibility in turn "requires pharmacists and pharmacies to identify and resolve objective signs 'arising during the presentation of a prescription' that create 'a reasonable suspicion that the prescription is not, on its face, legitimate.' "]

This is unreasonable conduct sufficient to support a public nuisance claim. The CSA and its implementing regulations strike a bargain with registrants. In exchange for the privilege of dispensing powerful controlled substances, pharmacies are required to take reasonable steps to prevent those substances from being diverted and harming the public. [Breyer, J., then addresses the evidence set out above on Walgreen's systematic neglect of its duties.]

2. Knowledge

California's public nuisance claim has a knowledge requirement. But the California Supreme Court has not squarely addressed the extent to which a plaintiff must prove that a defendant has knowledge of the harm resulting from its unreasonable conduct. The California Court of Appeal articulated the knowledge requirement clearly in People v. ConAgra Grocery Prod. Co., 17 Cal. App. 5th 51, 83–86 (2017). . . .

In *ConAgra*, the court held that the plaintiff presented sufficient evidence to establish that the defendants acted with the requisite level of knowledge because the record "indicated that the defendants had learned about the harms and hazards of lead exposure by the 1920s, yet still promoted its lead products." *ConAgra*, 17 Cal. App. 5th at 85. . . .

Applying *ConAgra* here, Plaintiff proved that Walgreens "must have known" of the harms that would result from violating its regulatory duties for over a decade. The CSA and its implementing regulations reflect the dangers posed by the controlled substances that Walgreens dispenses. The regulations that apply to Walgreens were put in place precisely because of the harms that result when opioids are diverted. Based on the regulatory scheme alone, it is reasonable to infer that Walgreens "must have known" that failing to prevent diversion of opioids would result in harm in San Francisco. . . .

B. Factual and Legal Causation

[Breyer, J., holds that the elements of factual causation ("defendant's conduct was a 'substantial factor in bringing about' the nuisance") and legal causation ("the defendant's wrongful conduct was not 'too remote from the current hazard to be its "legal cause,"' i.e., proximate causation") were satisfied. With regard to factual causation, the court credits "circumstantial evidence of sufficient substantiality" to permit reasonable inferences that "support a finding of causation in fact."

With regard to proximate causation, Breyer, J., holds that "Plaintiff proved that the numerous forms of harm resulting from Walgreens' unlawful dispensing of illegitimate opioid prescriptions were foreseeable." Indeed, "[a] lack of reasonable care in the handling, distribution, and administration of controlled substances can foreseeably harm the individuals who take them. That's why they're controlled in the first place — overuse or misuse can lead to addictions and long-term health problems."]

C. Substantial Interference with Public Rights

Public nuisance law "protect[s] the quality of organized social life." "A public nuisance is one which affects at the same time an entire community or neighborhood, or any considerable number of persons, although the extent of the annoyance or damage inflicted up individuals may be unequal." Cal. Civ. Code §3480. "[P]ublic nuisances are offenses against, or interferences with, the exercise of rights common to the public." The California Supreme Court has recognized five categories of public rights that can give rise to a claim for a public nuisance — "the public health, the public safety, the public peace, the public comfort or the public convenience."

Throughout this case, Walgreens has argued that a public nuisance claim requires Plaintiff to identify discrete conduct or conditions that are abatable. Walgreens contends that "every California public nuisance decision" involves "well-defined conduct" like "emitting noxious odors" or "a well-defined hazardous condition" like water pollution or lead paint in home. Walgreens argues that to be actionable, a nuisance claim must involve discrete conduct or conditions that can be remedied through abatement.

California courts have repeatedly rejected Walgreens' "ability to abate" argument. "[L]iability for nuisance does not hinge on whether the defendant owns, possesses or controls the property, nor on whether he is in a position to abate the nuisance; the critical question is whether the defendant created or assisted in the creation of the nuisance."

Consistent with the case law, California statute broadly defines a nuisance as:

> *Anything* which is injurious to health, including, but not limited to, the illegal sale of controlled substances, or is indecent or offensive to the senses, or an obstruction to the free use of property, so as to interfere with the comfortable enjoyment of life or property, or unlawfully obstructs the free passage or use, in the customary manner, of any navigable lake, or river, bay, stream, canal, or basin, or any public park, square, street, or highway, is a nuisance.

Cal. Civ. Code §3479 (emphasis added).

At trial, Plaintiff proved that the opioid epidemic, defined by high rates of opioid abuse, addiction, and overdoses, constitutes a public nuisance. Plaintiff further proved that the opioid epidemic interferes with all five categories of public rights recognized by the California Supreme Court — "the public health, the public safety, the public peace, the public comfort or the public convenience." And Plaintiff proved that Walgreens substantially contributed to the opioid epidemic in San Francisco, which has caused widespread harm across the city and interfered with public peace, comfort and convenience.

III. Conclusion

For the foregoing reasons, Plaintiff has proven by a preponderance of the evidence that Walgreens substantially contributed to the public nuisance in San Francisco. A subsequent trial will be held to determine the extent to which Walgreens must abate the public nuisance that it helped to create.

NOTES

1. ***"Traditional" Public Nuisance Claims.*** *City & County of San Francisco* is one of the bellwether trials in a larger multi-district litigation, which is consolidated before Polster, J., in Ohio and likely constitutes the largest civil action in American history. The bulk of the actions have settled, often for billions of dollars. To what extent is Walgreens responsible for opioid addiction in persons who acquired their opioids elsewhere or illegally? If various social policies of the city exacerbated the problem, should its conduct give rise to a contributory negligence defense?

Courts in several jurisdictions have expressed grave concerns about extending public nuisance to the sale or distribution of opioids. One concern raised is that nuisance law traditionally applies only "in the context of conduct that interferes with public property or resources." See City of Huntington v. AmerisourceBergen Drug Corp., 609 F. Supp. 3d 408, 472 (S.D. W. Va. 2022); State ex rel. Hunter v. Johnson & Johnson, 499 P.3d 719, 727 (Okla. 2021) (overturning a $465 million trial verdict).

Epstein, The Private Law Connections to Public Nuisance Law: Some Realism About Today's Intellectual Nominalism, 17 J.L. Econ. & Pol'y 282, 285 (2022), calls for a return to a land-based view of public nuisance, grounded in private nuisance. Merrill, Public Nuisance as Risk Regulation, 17 J.L. Econ. & Pol'y 347 (2022), disagrees, as a historical matter, that public nuisance must be land-based, but argues, more radically, that public nuisance is not a tort but rather a public action to regulate prospective harms. Now that legislative and regulatory bodies can define proscribed conduct in advance, Merrill argues the use of public nuisance for tort should be curtailed.

A second concern is that applying "the law of public nuisance to the sale, marketing and distribution of products would invite litigation against any product with a known risk of harm." *City of Huntington*, 609 F. Supp. 3d at 474. But recall that liability in *City & County of San Francisco* is premised on a knowing violation of a regulation, 21 C.F.R. §1306.04(a). Is this akin to negligence per se?

2. ***Public Nuisance Remedies.*** Abatement is typically the only remedy available to public entities in a traditional public nuisance suit. See, e.g., Cal. Civ. Proc. Code §731 (2023). The abatement remedy sought in *City & County of San Francisco*, however, includes monetary sums awarded to the plaintiff to reduce not the defendant's continuing actions but rather

the ongoing effect of its past ones, in this case the ongoing impact of the opioids crisis on the city. Merrill, The New Public Nuisance: Illegitimate and Dysfunctional, 132 Yale L.J.F. 985 (2023), sharply criticizes the practice of granting monetary remedies in public nuisance actions, arguing that it incentivizes municipal plaintiffs to partner with private firms on a contingency-fee basis to pursue defendants with deep pockets, as opposed to those most responsible for the harm. Kendrick, The Perils and Promise of Public Nuisance, 132 Yale L.J. 702 (2023), sets forth a defense of contemporary public nuisance suits, including those seeking monetary damages.

Should public entities seeking damages be required to show special injury? Is there any functional difference between damages and an abatement fund?

3. *Guns and Public Nuisances.* The contemporary advent of public nuisance suits to address large-scale societal ills began with the tobacco litigation in the 1990s. Subsequently, local governments sought to bring public nuisance suits for the public costs needed to combat local criminal use of hand guns. In City of Cincinnati v. Beretta U.S.A. Corp., 768 N.E.2d 1136 (Ohio 2002), the city alleged that the gun manufacturers created a nuisance "through their ongoing conduct of marketing, distributing, and selling firearms in a manner that facilitated their flow into the illegal market." Although the manufacturers did not control the actual use of firearms that cause injury, Sweeney, J., held: "Just as the individuals who fire the guns are held accountable for the injuries sustained, appellees can be held liable for creating the alleged nuisance."

By contrast, in Camden County Board of Chosen Freeholders v. Beretta U.S.A. Corp., 273 F.3d 536 (3d Cir. 2001), the court rejected the claim that selling guns was a public nuisance simply because some fraction of them ended up in the hands of criminals. The court noted that gun distribution takes place through several channels from manufacture, to sale to distributors, and to the diversion of guns into the hands of potential criminals, and concluded that "[t]his causal chain is simply too attenuated to attribute sufficient control to the manufacturers to make out a public nuisance claim." In City of Philadelphia v. Beretta U.S.A. Corp., 277 F.3d 415, 424 (3d Cir. 2002), the plaintiffs tried to shorten the causal chain by arguing that the "thriving illegal market . . . injures [them], even before any guns acquired in the illegal market are actually used in the commission of a crime." But Greenberg, J., held that even an efficient resale market acquired guns through the same pattern of distribution as in *Camden County Board.*

Washington State recently passed a statute deeming it a public nuisance to market firearms products without "reasonable controls" to prevent the risk of downstream illegal sale or inventory theft. 2023 Wash. Sess. Laws ch. 163. The statute is substantially similar to statutes passed in Hawaii, Act 28, 2023 Haw. Sess. Laws __; California, 2022 Cal. Stat. ch. 98; New York, 2021 N.Y. Sess. ch. 237; New Jersey, 2022 N.J. Laws ch. 56; and Delaware, 83 Del. Laws ch. 332 (2022). The National Shooting Sports Foundation (NSSF) has challenged these statutes as preempted by the Protection of Lawful Commerce in Arms Act, 15 U.S.C. §§7901–7903. A federal district court in New York rejected the NSSF's challenge, and that case is currently on appeal in the Second Circuit. Nat'l Shooting Sports Found., Inc. v. James, 604 F. Supp. 3d 48 (N.D.N.Y. 2022). By contrast, a federal district court in New Jersey granted a preliminary injunction preventing implementation of the New Jersey law. Nat'l Shooting Sports Found. v. Platkin, No. 22-6646, 2023 WL 1380388 (D.N.J. Jan. 31, 2023). And, on appeal, the Third Circuit dismissed the plaintiff's pre-enforcement challenge as premature. Nat'l Shooting Sports Found. v. Att'y Gen. of N.J., 80 F.4th 215 (3d Cir. 2023). For a broad overview of the litigation, see Raji, The Brewing Gun-Control Fight That Could Be Headed to the Supreme Court, Wash. Post, Feb. 21, 2023, https://www.washingtonpost.com/politics/2023/02/21/gun-manufacturer-shooting-lawsuits-supreme-court/.

Academic views on treating gun sales as a public nuisance are divided. Hylton, The Economics of Public Nuisance Law and the New Enforcement Actions, 18 Sup. Ct. Econ. Rev. 43, 73–76 (2010), supports treating initial gun sales as a public nuisance, given their inherent dangers. In sharp contrast, Professor Merrill claims that the public nuisance doctrine has "gone off the rails," and that these issues are better dealt with by the criminal law. See Merrill, Is Public Nuisance a Tort?, J. Tort L., Sept. 1, 2011 at 5.

SECTION F. VICARIOUS LIABILITY

Vicarious liability refers to rules whereby one person is held responsible for the wrongful acts of another by virtue of some status connection between them. This principle, which often goes under the Latin label respondeat superior ("let the superior answer"), enjoys an unquestioned acceptance in all common law jurisdictions. Nonetheless, controversy surrounds the contours of the doctrine. The American Law Institute is restating the law of vicarious liability for the first time in Restatement of the Law (Third) of Torts: Miscellaneous Provisions, excerpts of which are included below. Compare these provisions to the cases that follow.

RESTATEMENT OF THE LAW (THIRD) OF TORTS: MISCELLANEOUS PROVISIONS (TENTATIVE DRAFT, RELEASED 2023)

§3. Respondeat Superior—General Rule

An employer is subject to vicarious liability for a tort committed by its employee (as defined in §4) acting within the scope of employment (as defined in §5).

§4. Respondeat Superior—Definition of "Employee"

For purposes of respondeat superior, an "employee" is an agent whose principal controls or has the right to control the manner and means of the agent's performance of work.

Comment i. Nontraditional forms of business organization: Recent years have seen a proliferation of businesses such as Uber and Lyft, whose business model involves connecting customers over the internet with the services of drivers and other service providers whose contractual relationship with the business is stated to be that of independent contractors rather than employees. Other businesses have also made increasing use of independent contractors. Whether such businesses are liable under the doctrine of respondeat superior for the torts of their drivers or other service providers is determined by the same test that is used in respondeat superior cases generally: whether the businesses control or have the right to control the manner and means of performance of the drivers or other service providers.

§5. Respondeat Superior—Scope of Employment

For purposes of respondeat superior, an employee acts within the scope of employment when both of the following conditions are satisfied:

(a) The employee is performing work assigned by the employer or engaging in a course of conduct subject to the employer's control; and

(b) The employee's conduct is intended by the employee in any way to serve any purpose of the employer.

Ira S. Bushey & Sons, Inc. v. United States

398 F.2d 167 (2d Cir. 1968)

United States Coast Guard cutter *Tamaroa* in 1990. The ship was commissioned by the United States Navy in 1943 and sailed for the Coast Guard from 1946 until 1994, when she was decommissioned.
Source: Wikimedia Commons

Friendly, J. While the United States Coast Guard vessel *Tamaroa* was being overhauled in a floating drydock located in Brooklyn's Gowanus Canal, a seaman [named Lane] returning from shore leave late at night, in the condition for which seamen are famed, turned some wheels on the drydock wall. He thus opened valves that controlled the flooding of the tanks on one side of the drydock. Soon the ship listed, slid off the blocks and fell against the wall. Parts of the drydock sank, and the ship partially did — fortunately without loss of life or personal injury. The drydock owner [Bushey] sought and was granted compensation by the District Court for the Eastern District of New York in an amount to be determined, 276 F. Supp. 518; the United States appeals. . . .

Exhibit 7.3 Henry J. Friendly

Henry J. Friendly (1903–1986) was a universally respected judge who served on the United States Court of Appelas for the Second Circuit for twenty-seven years. During his time on the appellate bench, every Supreme Court Justice who served five years or more cited from his opinions at least once. His influence extended through disparate areas of the law, including securities and trademark, privacy, and federal jurisdiction. While never receiving the nod for the high court himself, Friendly left an indelible mark on the federal judiciary, penning more than 1,000 opinions, most of them by himself, and most in less than a day. Before his judicial career, he attended Harvard College and Harvard Law School, clerked for Supreme Court Justice Louis Brandeis, and served for many years in private practice at law firms and as corporate counsel for Pan American World Airways. For an exhaustive account of Friendly's legacy and jurisprudence, see Dorsen, Henry Friendly: Greatest Judge of His Era (2012).

Bio sources: David M. Dorsen, Henry Friendly: Greatest Judge of His Era (2012); Bill Mears, Biography Tells of Greatest Judge You Never Knew, CNN, Apr. 18, 2012
Image source: The Estate of Fabian Bachrach

The Government attacks imposition of liability on the ground that Lane's acts were not within the scope of his employment. It relies heavily on section 228(1) of the Restatement of Agency 2d which says that "conduct of a servant is within the scope of employment if, but only if: . . . (c) it is actuated, at least in part by a purpose to serve the master." Courts have gone to considerable lengths to find such a purpose, as witness a well-known opinion in which Judge Learned Hand concluded that a drunken boatswain who routed the plaintiff out of his bunk with a blow, saying "Get up, you big son of a bitch, and turn to," and then continued to fight, might have thought he was acting in the interest of the ship. Nelson v. American-West African Line, 86 F.2d 730 (2d Cir. 1936). It would be going too far to find such a purpose here; while Lane's return to the *Tamaroa* was to serve his employer, no one has suggested how he could have thought turning the wheels to be, even if—which is by no means clear—he was unaware of the consequences.

In light of the highly artificial way in which the motive test has been applied, the district judge believed himself obliged to test the doctrine's continuing vitality by referring to the larger purposes respondeat superior is supposed to serve. He concluded that the old formulation failed this test. We do not find his analysis so compelling, however, as to constitute a sufficient basis in itself for discarding the old doctrine. It is not at all clear, as the court below suggested, that expansion of liability in the manner here suggested will lead to a more efficient allocation of resources. As the most astute exponent of this theory has emphasized, a more efficient allocation can only be expected if there is some reason to believe that imposing a particular cost on the enterprise will lead it to consider whether steps should be taken to prevent a recurrence of the accident. Calabresi, The Decision for Accidents: An Approach to Non-Fault Allocation of Costs, 78 Harv. L. Rev. 713, 725–34 (1965). And the suggestion that imposition of liability here will lead to more intensive screening of employees rests on highly questionable premises.[5] The unsatisfactory quality of the allocation of resource rationale is especially striking on the facts of this case. It could well be that application of the traditional rule might induce drydock owners, prodded by their insurance companies, to install locks on their valves to avoid similar incidents in the future, while placing the burden on shipowners is much less likely to lead to accident prevention.[7] It is true, of course, that in many cases the plaintiff will not be in a position to insure, and so expansion of liability will, at the very least, serve respondeat superior's loss spreading function. But the fact that the defendant is better able to afford damages is not alone sufficient to justify legal responsibility, see Blum & Kalven, Public Law Perspectives on a Private Law Problem (1965), and this overarching principle must be taken into account in deciding whether to expand the reach of respondeat superior.

A policy analysis thus is not sufficient to justify this proposed expansion of vicarious liability. This is not surprising since respondeat superior, even within its traditional limits, rests not so much on policy grounds consistent with the governing principles of tort law as in a deeply rooted sentiment that a business enterprise cannot justly disclaim responsibility for accidents which may fairly be said to be characteristic of its activities. It is in this light that the inadequacy of the motive test becomes apparent. Whatever may have been the case in the past, a doctrine that would create such drastically different consequences for the actions of the drunken boatswain in *Nelson* and those of the drunken seaman here reflects a wholly unrealistic attitude toward the risks characteristically attendant upon the operation of a ship.

5. We are not here speaking of cases in which the enterprise has negligently hired an employee whose undesirable propensities are known or should have been. See Koehler v. Presque-Isle Transp. Co., 141 F.2d 490 (2d Cir. 1943).

7. Although it is theoretically possible that shipowners would demand that drydock owners take appropriate action, see Coase, The Problem of Social Cost, 3 J.L. & Economics 1 (1960), this would seem unlikely to occur in real life.

We concur in the statement of Mr. Justice Rutledge in a case involving violence injuring a fellow-worker, in this instance in the context of workmen's compensation:

> Men do not discard their personal qualities when they go to work. Into the job they carry their intelligence, skill, habits of care and rectitude. Just as inevitably they take along also their tendencies to carelessness and camaraderie, as well as emotional make-up. In bringing men together, work brings these qualities together, causes frictions between them, creates occasions for lapses into carelessness, and for fun-making and emotional flare-up. . . . These expressions of human nature are incidents inseparable from working together. They involve risks of injury and these risks are inherent in the working environment.

Hartford Accident & Indemnity Co. v. Cardillo, 112 F.2d 11, 15 (D.C. Cir. 1940). . . .

Put another way, Lane's conduct was not so "unforeseeable" as to make it unfair to charge the Government with responsibility. . . . Here it was foreseeable that crew members crossing the drydock might do damage, negligently or even intentionally, such as pushing a Bushey employee or kicking property into the water. Moreover, the proclivity of seamen to find solace for solitude by copious resort to the bottle while ashore has been noted in opinions too numerous to warrant citation. Once all this is granted, it is immaterial that Lane's precise action was not to be foreseen. . . . Consequently, we can no longer accept our past decisions that have refused to move beyond the *Nelson* rule, since they do not accord with modern understanding as to when it is fair for an enterprise to disclaim the actions of its employees.

One can readily think of cases that fall on the other side of the line. If Lane had set fire to the bar where he had been imbibing or had caused an accident on the street while returning to the drydock, the Government would not be liable; the activities of the "enterprise" do not reach into areas where the servant does not create risks different from those attendant on the activities of the community in general. We agree with the district judge that if the seaman "upon returning to the drydock, recognized the Bushey security guard as his wife's lover and shot him," 276 F. Supp. at 530, vicarious liability would not follow; the incident would have related to the seaman's domestic life, not to his seafaring activity, and it would have been the most unlikely happenstance that the confrontation with the paramour occurred on a drydock rather than at the traditional spot. Here Lane had come within the closed-off area where his ship lay, to occupy a berth to which the Government insisted he have access, and while his act is not readily explicable, at least it was not shown to be due entirely to facets of his personal life. The risk that seamen going and coming from the *Tamaroa* might cause damage to the drydock is enough to make it fair that the enterprise bear the loss. It is not a fatal objection that the rule we lay down lacks sharp contours in the end, as Judge Andrews said in a related context, "it is all a question [of expediency,] . . . of fair judgment, always keeping in mind the fact that we endeavor to make a rule in each case that will be practical and in keeping with the general understanding of mankind." Palsgraf v. Long Island R.R. Co., 162 N.E. 99, 104 (N.Y. 1928) (dissenting opinion). . . .

[Affirmed.]

NOTES

1. *Respondeat Superior: History.* Notwithstanding the overall acceptance of vicarious liability, there remains an undercurrent of academic dissatisfaction with the rule, stemming perhaps from an inability to identify its precise rationale. Thus Holmes, in his famous articles on agency, 4 Harv. L. Rev. 345 (1891); 5 Harv. L. Rev. 1 (1891), treated respondeat superior as an anomaly that "must be explained by some cause not manifest to common sense alone. . . . I assume that common-sense is opposed to making one man pay for another man's wrong, unless he has actually brought the wrong to pass. . . . I therefore assume that common-sense is opposed to the fundamental theory of agency. . . ." For a sustained attack on vicarious liability as a doctrine that "has attained its luxuriant growth through carelessness and false analogy," see Baty, Vicarious Liability (1916).

What made respondeat superior so remarkable was that its strict liability foundations withstood the late-nineteenth-century onslaught of negligence liability. While typically respondeat superior only applied when the employee negligently discharged his duties, the defendant employer did not have to be similarly negligent in selecting or supervising the employee. To the contrary, an unbroken line of cases invoked vicarious liability against employers who had expressly forbidden the very conduct that constituted employee negligence. See Limpus v. London Gen. Omnibus Co. (1862) 158 Eng. Rep. 993 (Ex.). Thus from 1700 on, vicarious liability turned on whether the tort arose out of the employee's employment, not on whether the employer was negligent in selection or supervision, or whether he had authorized, expressly or impliedly, the commission of the tort for which he was vicariously charged. Hern v. Nichols (1708) 91 Eng. Rep. 256 (Ex.). Blackstone explained in 1 Bl. Comm. 418–19 (1765), using the historical terms servant and master in lieu of employee and employer:

> If a servant, lastly, by his negligence does any damage to a stranger, the master shall answer for his neglect; if a smith's servant lames a horse while shoeing him, an action lies against the master, and not against the servant. But in these cases, the damage must be done, while his actually employed in the master's service; otherwise the servant shall answer for his own misbehaviour.

The law today holds *both* employer and employee liable for torts that arise out of and in the course of employment. One explanation for that dual system of liability involves the deep pocket of the employer. In River Wear Commissioners v. Adamson, [1876] 2 AC 743 (HL) (appeal taken from Eng.), Blackburn, L., was explicit:

> In the great majority of cases the servant actually guilty of the negligence is poor, and unable to make good the damage, especially if it is considerable, and the master is at least comparatively rich, and consequently it is generally better to fix the master with liability; but there is also concurrent liability in the servant, who is not discharged from liability because his master also is liable.

A similar conclusion is reached in Smith, Frolic and Detour, 23 Colum. L. Rev. 444, 455–56 (1923), which, following Baty's work on vicarious liability, lists the nine traditional rationales for vicarious liability: control, profit, revenge, carefulness and choice, identification, evidence, indulgence, danger, and satisfaction. Having concluded that none of these could fully account for the doctrine, Smith offers his own explanation:

> A reason which occurs to the writer is that which has been offered in justification of workmen's compensation statutes. In substance it is the belief that it is socially more expedient to spread or distribute among a large group of the community the losses which experience has taught are inevitable in the carrying on of industry, than to cast the loss upon a few.

Why isn't loss spreading more cheaply accomplished through first-party insurance?

2. *Efficiency Arguments.* Modern scholarship defends vicarious liability on efficiency grounds by placing greater stress on loss prevention. Sykes, The Economics of Vicarious Liability, 93 Yale L.J. 1231 (1984), explicitly compares two possible legal regimes. Under pure personal liability, the injured third party has recourse only against the employee, who in turn can seek an indemnity against the employer. Under vicarious liability, the employer (along with the employee) is directly liable, and in turn enjoys possible rights of indemnity against the erring employee. As between the employer and the employee, Sykes observes that the employer is usually the superior risk bearer because of its greater access to insurance markets, especially when the employer is a public corporation whose shareholders are able to diversify their individual portfolios by investing in many different firms. Vicarious liability also reduces the risk that the insolvency of a particular employee will impose an uncompensated risk on a third party. In addition, the doctrine reduces the need to create an extensive network of voluntary contracts between employees and employers to make the employer the ultimate risk bearer when the employee is actually solvent. Finally, vicarious liability protects third parties who know that some firm employee is responsible for the loss but cannot determine which employee is responsible, given the hundreds of designers and artisans that work, say, on any automobile.

3. *Frolic and Detour: Traditional Applications.* Vicarious liability requires a legal determination of which acts fall within the scope of employment. Employees do not always act as employees when they are supposed to be on the job. Difficulties on this score frequently arise when the employee deviates from the driving route set by his employer for personal reasons. The general rule today, roughly, is that respondeat superior covers small deviations but not large ones. For example, in Riley v. Standard Oil Co., 132 N.E. 97 (N.Y. 1921), the court recognized that "[n]o hard and fast rule on the subject either in space or time can be applied," and then held that driving four blocks out of the way on a personal errand did not take the employee out of his employer's business. Similarly, in Hinkle Metals & Supply Co. v. Feltman, 280 So. 3d 1031, 1037 (Ala. 2019), the court upheld a jury verdict holding an air conditioning company liable when its employee struck a pedestrian while on a personal errand, saying it was up to the jury to decide "[i]n cases where an employee combines personal activities with the employer's business" whether the employee was acting within the scope of employment. Always?

In principle, it is unclear whether the frolic and detour rule tends to increase or reduce the number of accidents. Imposing vicarious liability creates a strong incentive for the employer to monitor the behavior of the employee. If the deviation is effectively curtailed, the employee might undertake the same mission outside of work, having to travel a greater distance and probably creating a higher accident rate. Alternatively the errand may become so burdensome that the employee will not undertake it at all. In the first case, using an expansive vicarious liability rule will tend to increase the number of accidents. In the second case, the expansive rule will reduce the accident level. Often it is not clear which effect will dominate. It is therefore not surprising that no hard and fast rule covers these cases. See generally Sykes, The Boundaries of Vicarious Liability: An Economic Analysis of the Scope of Employment Rule and Related Legal Doctrines, 101 Harv. L. Rev. 563 (1988).

4. *The "Borrowed Employee."* When a given person works for two employers, which should be held vicariously liable for his tort? The problem of divided authority arises in the construction industry, for example, when a general contractor hires a crane operator from a crane company for specialized work. The crane company retains the general power to hire, fire, and impose safety regulations, work rules, and the like; the construction company designates the operator's particular tasks on the job. Which firm is ultimately responsible for the wrongful acts of the employee? Cardozo, J., gave this answer in Charles v. Barrett, 135 N.E. 199, 200 (N.Y. 1922):

> The rule now is that, as long as the employee is furthering the business of his general employer by the service rendered to another, there will be no inference of a new relation unless command has been surrendered, and no inference of its surrender from the mere fact of its division.

More recent cases, however, tend to hold both employers responsible for the torts of the borrowed employee. In Morgan v. ABC Manufacturer, 710 So. 2d 1077, 1081 (La. 1998), the court rejected any effort to partition responsibility between the general and special employer, holding both jointly liable for the employee's tort: "Since liability is based on the *right* of control, rather than actual control of the employee at the time of the accident, it is unreasonable to choose between the two employers when each shares the *right* to control the employee's actions." See generally Note, Borrowed Servants and the Theory of Enterprise Liability, 76 Yale L.J. 807 (1967).

5. *Employer's Indemnification.* May an employer, as the passive and innocent party, recoup his losses against the individual employee whose active negligence caused the original accident and, therefore, the employer's loss? That right of indemnification has been nearly universally adopted in all American courts. See, e.g., Fireman's Fund Am. Ins. Co. v. Turner, 488 P.2d 429 (Or. 1971); and in England, see Lister v. Romford Ice & Cold Storage, [1957] AC 555. However, often the employee is financially unable to answer for the loss, and, commonly, the employer takes out insurance to cover both parties, making actions for indemnification rare and unpopular. See, e.g., James, Indemnity, Subrogation, and Contribution and the Efficient Distribution of Accident Losses, 21 NACCA L.J. 360 (1958).

Search v. Uber Technologies, Inc.

128 F. Supp. 3d 222 (D.D.C. 2015)

Boasberg, J. For generations, parents have admonished their children not to get into cars with strangers. See, e.g., Forrest Gump (Paramount Pictures 1994) ("Mama said not to be taking rides from strangers."). But in today's "sharing economy," that warning is an anachronism: every day, millions of Americans summon unknown drivers with the press of a button. At the same time, the danger of taking a ride from a stranger has not entirely disappeared. As with other growing pains of twenty-first-century economics, courts must now determine what is to be done about the risk of that old-fashioned danger in a market shaped by new players and new technologies.

Plaintiff Erik Search filed this lawsuit against Uber Technologies, Inc., claiming that it is liable for an alleged knife attack by one of its drivers, Yohannes Deresse. Search has asserted, *inter alia*, claims of negligent hiring, training, and supervision; negligence under *respondeat superior* and apparent-agency theories; and violations of the D.C. Code. Whether Uber is liable for many of these depends on whether it was—or presented itself as—Deresse's employer.

In now moving to dismiss, Uber argues that Deresse was instead merely an independent contractor. It maintains that it "is not a transportation company," but rather "a technology company that acts as a conduit between transportation providers and passengers." Search responds that Defendant now seeks to disavow, for its own legal expediency, the promotional language and promises that helped it amass a broad consumer base and multi-billion-dollar valuation—in his view, Uber's is a classic corporate case of trying to have one's cake and eat it, too. . . .

I. Background

. . . Defendant Uber "is a car service that provides drivers to customers on demand through a cell phone application, or 'app,' in cities around the world." In its app—which is free to download and install on any smartphone—the company markets itself to consumers as "your private driver in more than 50 countries." . . .

On September 8, 2013, Plaintiff Erik Search and three of his friends required transportation from 3030 K Street, NW, in the District of Columbia. As he had on multiple past occasions, Search used the Uber app on his phone to request a pick-up at that location. On that evening, Uber driver Yohannes Deresse accepted Plaintiff's request and arrived shortly thereafter.

Immediately following the group's entry into the car, Deresse "began to act erratically." Uncomfortable with Deresse's behavior, Search and his companions exited the vehicle and began walking away. According to Plaintiff, Deresse followed them out of the car and began to verbally harass them. In response, Search told the driver "to leave them alone," and that "they did not feel safe riding in an Uber car with him."

At that point, the verbal dispute escalated into physical violence. As Search recounts, Deresse pulled out a knife and stabbed him at least six times in his chest and left arm. Plaintiff sustained severe injuries during the course of the brutal attack, requiring him to undergo "CT scans, x-rays, surgical exploration of the chest wound, diagnostic laparoscopy, cauterization, and muscle reconstruction with sutures and staples." In addition, Plaintiff suffered "pain, mental anguish, humiliation, and indignity" as a result of the assault.

Naming Deresse and Uber as Defendants, Plaintiff filed suit in D.C. Superior Court, alleging a variety of state-law tort claims and one violation of the D.C. Consumer Protection Procedures Act, codified at D.C. Code §28-3905(k). Uber, in turn, removed the suit to federal court on diversity grounds and now moves to dismiss all causes of action lodged against it. (Deresse has not yet been served.)

III. Analysis

In the instant Motion, Uber moves to dismiss. . . .

[The court first dismisses the negligent hiring, training, and supervision claim. All parties agree that Uber has a duty to take reasonable care in hiring, training, and supervising its drivers. "[T]o state a claim for negligent hiring, a plaintiff must allege specific facts from which an inference can be drawn that the employer did not conduct a reasonable background investigation, and that such an investigation would have uncovered a reason not to hire the alleged tortfeasor." Here, the plaintiff Search quoted from Uber's website that it promised to conduct "a rigorous background check" of "[a]ll Uber ridesharing and livery partners," but did not allege that Uber did not conduct a background check prior to hiring Deresse or that any "red flag" existed in Deresse's past. Nor did the plaintiff Search "identify any particular measures that Uber did not take that could have prevented the hiring of Deresse." The court concludes that the plaintiff's allegations about Uber's supervisory negligence are "conclusory" and "devoid of any factual matter."]

Respondeat Superior

Search . . . seeks to hold Uber vicariously liable for Deresse's actions. It is hornbook law that "[u]nder the doctrine of *respondeat superior*, an employer may be held liable for the acts of his employees committed within the scope of their employment." A claim for vicarious liability under a *respondeat superior* theory consists, therefore, of two prongs: an employer-employee relationship and a tortious act committed by the employee within the scope of his employment. The Court addresses each in turn.

1. Employer-Employee Relationship

The parties agree that in the District of Columbia, the question of whether an employer-employee relationship exists is governed by a five-factor test that examines: (1) involvement in the selection and engagement of the employee; (2) payment of wages; (3) power to discharge; (4) power to control the employee's conduct; and (5) whether the employee's work is part of the regular business of the employer. Under this test, the fourth factor—"the right to control an employee . . . and not the actual exercise of control or supervision"—is usually "the determinative factor." "Whether a master-servant (or principal-agent) relationship exists in a given situation depends on the particular facts of each case[.]"

Plaintiff asserts that Deresse was "an employee, agent, and/or servant" of Uber at the time of the incident at issue in this case. He alleges a number of facts that, he believes, establish this employer-employee relationship: For instance, Uber screens new drivers, dictates the fares they may charge, and pays such drivers weekly. Search claims that "[u]pon threat of termination, Uber subjects its drivers to a host of specific requirements," including, *inter alia*, the use of the Uber app, standards for the cleanliness and mechanical functioning of their cars, rules regarding tipping, minimum timeframes and acceptance rates for ride requests, and display of the Uber logo. According to Plaintiff, these facts establish the first four factors of the aforementioned test. Search maintains that the fifth factor, whether Deresse's work is part of Uber's regular business, is satisfied by his allegation that "Uber is a car service" for which Deresse was a driver.

The Court agrees, for the most part. The Amended Complaint sets forth facts illustrating Uber's involvement in the selection process of new drivers (by way of its screening procedures); payment of wages (by paying drivers weekly rather than permitting them to collect payment or tips directly from passengers); and termination of employees (by enjoying broad latitude to terminate employees who fail to comply with the company's standards). As to the question whether driving is Uber's regular business, Defendant simply disagrees with Plaintiff's factual allegation that the company is a "car service." It does not argue—for good reason—that even if Uber is a car service, as alleged, Deresse's driving is not its regular work.

This leaves the fourth and "determinative" factor: whether Uber controlled Deresse's day-to-day operations or merely exercised general supervision over his activities. Uber contends that an entity that monitors, evaluates, and improves the results of a worker's performance is not necessarily an employer. . . .

Uber is correct that "the right to inspect [and] the right to set standards" are not necessarily "indicia of control," but may be "indicative of a contractual relationship" between an employer and independent contractor. However, "the parties' *actual* relationship, in spite of contractual language, may be the conclusive factor."

The District of Columbia Court of Appeals' opinion in Schecter [v. Merchants Home Delivery, Inc., 892 A.2d 415, 431 (D.C. 2006)] is instructive for this issue. The court there examined a number of facts in determining whether a home deliveryman who stole jewelry and other valuables from a customer was employed by the delivery company for which he worked. The company made most decisions as to the routes, deliveries, clothing, and morning start times of the deliveryman, accommodating some route preferences but "not relinquishing control" over routes. Like Uber drivers, the deliverymen enjoyed a "right to decline any" delivery requests, but only up to a point, for the retail chain could mandate some deliveries. And, like Uber drivers, deliverymen were granted some flexibility with regard to timeliness; the delivery company afforded them delivery windows, but it measured their performance based on timely deliveries and terminated those whose performance was unsatisfactory. Effectively, the delivery company "controlled in some detail the manner in which a driver made each delivery." Based on these facts, the court concluded, "An impartial juror could reasonably find" that the delivery company placed "substantial limitation[s] upon the independence of those who wished to make deliveries" for the company, "consistent with their being servants or employees, rather than independent contractors." For that reason, the court reversed the trial court's directed verdict for the defendant.

Here, Plaintiff has alleged that Uber controls the rate of refusal of ride requests, the timeliness of the drivers' responses to requests, the display on vehicles of its logo, the frequency with which drivers may contact passengers, the drivers' interactions with passengers (including how they accept tips and collect fares), and the quality of drivers via its rating system. Taking these allegations as true, a reasonable factfinder could conclude that Uber exercised control over Deresse in a manner evincing an employer-employee relationship.

[The court distinguishes a prior case, Ames v. Yellow Cab of D.C., No. 00-3116, 2006 WL 2711546 (D.D.C. Sept. 21, 2006), which Uber sought to rely on. In *Ames*, the court held that Yellow Cab operated a scheme to license its name and logo, not a cab service, and that individual cab drivers were not its employees. But, "Yellow Cab could not terminate any of its employees but could only cancel the licensing arrangement; Yellow Cab did not set a driver's fares; Yellow Cab did not pay its drivers wages or any other form of compensation; Yellow Cab did not require cab drivers to acquire rides through its dispatch service at all, meaning that it had no limits on a driver's refusal rate; Yellow Cab did not impose other restrictions on drivers' interactions with their passengers (*i.e.*, relating to tipping or cash payments); and Yellow Cab did not 'hire the drivers,' but rather set minimum requirements for licensees of its logo and name."]

2. Scope of Employment

Even if the Court does determine that an employer-employee relationship may exist between Deresse and Uber, Defendant contends that it is nevertheless not liable for his alleged assault on Search, as the stabbing occurred outside the scope of his employment. If an employee's conduct "is different in kind from that authorized, far beyond the authorized time or space limits, or too little actuated by a purpose to serve" his employer, that conduct falls outside the scope of employment. . . .

Uber appears to believe that "a violent attack . . . could not conceivably be one of a limousine driver's job duties," and it is therefore always outside the scope of his employment. But the "scope of employment" inquiry in the District of Columbia is not as narrow as Defendant would like to imagine. In fact, if "there is evidence that the assault grew out of a job-related controversy," an assault may very well fall within the scope of the perpetrator's employment. . . . Here, Plaintiff has alleged facts suggesting that the dispute giving rise to Deresse's attack grew out of an encounter related to Uber's business. . . . This is sufficient to survive a 12(b)(6) motion[.] . . . "Scope of employment is ordinarily a question for the jury," and here the Court cannot conclude that, as a matter of law, Deresse's alleged stabbing was an act outside such employment.

Apparent Agency

Even if Deresse and Uber are not bound by an *actual* employer-employee relationship, Plaintiff argues in the alternative that Uber represented to customers, including Search, that its drivers were its agents, and that it screened and managed them accordingly. The District of Columbia recognizes "apparent authority" as a basis for imputing liability for the tortious acts of independent contractors to those who hired them "when the principal places the agent in such a position as to mislead third persons into believing that the agent is clothed with the authority which in fact he does not possess." Apparent authority "depends upon the third-party's perception of the agent's authority," which "may be based upon written or spoken words or any other conduct of the principal which, reasonably interpreted, causes the third person to believe that the principal consents to have the act done on her behalf" by the apparent agent. An inquiry into the existence of such authority operates something like the hoary legal principle known as the "duck test": "[I]f it walks like a duck, swims like a duck, and quacks like a duck, it's a duck." The doctrine, at bottom, "prevents [Defendant] from denying any liability for the torts of its independent contractors while it profits from the image and good will created by the company's general business reputation."

Search alleges that Uber, "[t]hrough several forms of media" such as its mobile app and its website, represented to customers that it is "your private driver," "that it subjects its drivers to rigorous screening procedures" before hiring them, and that it "continues to monitor" those drivers after they are hired. Uber responds that it "could not have been clearer that Mr. Deresse was not its agent, and it was unreasonable for Plaintiff to believe" otherwise. For this rebuttal, however, Uber relies entirely on its User Agreement, in which it "included an exculpatory provision whereby Uber clearly, unequivocally and specifically stated that Mr. Deresse was not [its] agent." The parties spill considerable ink over the meaning and effect of the User Agreement and on how it was perceived by Uber customers. Yet, whatever its exculpatory effect, the User Agreement is material *outside* the Complaint, offered to disprove the facts as alleged therein, and the Court thus cannot consider it in resolving the 12(b)(6) motion at hand.

IV. Conclusion

[The court grants Uber's Motion to Dismiss with regard to the negligent hiring, training and supervising claims and denies it as to the respondeat superior and apparent agency claims.]

NOTES

1. *Independent Contractors in the Gig Economy.* Key employment benefits turn on the classification of drivers as employees or independent contractors. See Dynamex Operations West v. Superior Court, 416 P.3d 1, 5, 7 (Cal. 2018), where Dynamex was a firm that hired drivers as part of its nationwide network of couriers and delivery services for its clients. Cantil-Sakauye, C.J., observed first that the stakes on the classification question were enormous in that

> if a worker should properly be classified as an employee, the hiring business bears the responsibility of paying federal Social Security and payroll taxes, unemployment insurance taxes and state employment taxes, providing worker's compensation insurance, and, most relevant for the present case, complying with numerous state and federal statutes and regulations governing the wages, hours, and working conditions of employees.

She then noted "the potentially substantial economic incentives that a business may have in mischaracterizing some workers as independent contractors," in order to gain an unfair competitive advantage over their competitors. Finally, she adopted the so-called ABC test to classify members of the plaintiff class as employees. That test defines independent contractor as:

> (a) The person is free from the control and direction of the hiring entity in connection with the performance of the work, both under the contract for the performance of the work and in fact.
>
> (b) The person performs work that is outside the usual course of the hiring entity's business.
>
> (c) The person is customarily engaged in an independently established trade, occupation, or business of the same nature as that involved in the work performed.

Is there any reason why the contract should be ignored *as between the parties* when all the apparent authority issues are no longer in the case? Whatever the answer to that question, in 2019 California passed Assembly Bill 5, which incorporated the ABC test, followed with an exhaustive list of professions, including physicians, attorneys, and accountants, that fell outside the classification; rideshare companies were thus assumed to fall within the classification. In 2020, California voters passed by ballot initiative Proposition 22, an act that allows rideshare companies to classify their drivers as independent contractors instead of employees. A state constitutional challenge to Proposition 22 is currently pending before the California Supreme Court. See Castellanos v. State of California (Protect App-Based Drivers & Services), 309 Cal. Rptr. 3d 725 (Cal. 2023).

Elsewhere, the case law remains in flux. Compare Saleem v. Corporate Transportation Group, Ltd., 854 F.3d 131, 140 (2d Cir. 2017), where Livingston, J., determined that the plaintiff black car drivers in New York were independent contractors not entitled to overtime pay under either the federal Fair Labor Standards Act or state's labor law, with Razak v. Uber Technologies, Inc., 951 F.3d 137, 142–43 (3d Cir. 2020), where Greenaway, J., overturned a grant of summary judgment to Uber for similar claims under the FSLA and Pennsylvania law, given disputed facts regarding whether the plaintiff UberBLACK drivers were "operating within Uber's system and under Uber's rules, and whether Plaintiffs or their corporations contracted directly with Uber."

Who benefits if Lyft and Uber require their drivers to pick a single firm for which they must work explicit shifts?

2. *Independent Contractors with "Apparent Authority" in Medical Malpractice Cases.* It is uniformly accepted that physician practice groups are vicariously liable for the torts of their members. But much controversy arises as to how much further that liability should extend. In Gilbert v. Sycamore Municipal Hospital, 622 N.E.2d 788 (Ill. 1993), a patient suffered a heart attack after being treated and released by a physician at a hospital emergency room (ER). Unbeknownst to the patient, the ER was owned by a corporation that operated independently of the hospital. The court nonetheless held that the principles of respondeat superior applied because the hospital "held out" the ER as though it were its own.

A much more controversial application of vicarious liability arose in Petrovich v. Share Health Plan of Illinois, Inc., 719 N.E.2d 756, 760, 766, 770 (Ill. 1999), where a patient sued her health maintenance organization (HMO), claiming that "the plaintiff's HMO may be held vicariously liable for the negligence of its independent-contractor physicians under agency law," when her physician failed to make a timely diagnosis of her oral cancer. Bilandic, J., held that she could proceed on both theories of apparent and implied authority.

> To establish apparent authority against an HMO for physician malpractice, the patient must prove (1) that the HMO held itself out as the provider of health care, without informing the patient that the care is given by independent contractors, and (2) that the patient justifiably relied upon the conduct of the HMO by looking to the HMO to provide health care services, rather than to a specific physician. Apparent agency is a question of fact.

On implied authority, he held that

> [t]he cardinal consideration for determining the existence of implied authority is whether the alleged agent retains the right to control the manner of doing the work. Where a person's status as an independent contractor is negated, liability may result under the doctrine of *respondeat superior*. Plaintiff contends that the facts and circumstances of this case show that Share exerted sufficient control over [the plaintiff's physicians] because it used a capitation system for compensation.

The treating physicians testified that their professional judgment was not influenced by Share in this particular case.

To what extent could Share have avoided liability by clearly disclosing in its individual subscriber contracts its full business arrangements with its physicians, and then disclaiming all liability for their wrongs? Would a theory of vicarious liability be necessary if Share had actually limited the tests that the physician could have ordered for the plaintiff? Why would a patient want to sue the HMO if the physician is insured, given that the practice group is also liable? For an argument against the extension of liability, see Epstein & Sykes, The Assault of Managed Care: Vicarious Liability, ERISA Preemption, and Class Actions, 30 J. Legal Stud. 625, 638 (2001):

> When physicians establish independent practices and carry substantial malpractice insurance on their own, . . . the case for vicarious liability [of Managed Care Organizations (MCOs)] is much weaker. The physicians' personal assets, including malpractice coverage, become considerable, and the problem of potential insolvency greatly diminishes. Further, the ability of hospitals or MCOs to monitor these independent physicians is extremely limited, as there is no one with greater medical expertise in the hierarchy regularly overseeing their work. We thus doubt that vicarious liability for independent physicians with their own malpractice coverage will accomplish much beyond adding a party to litigation, which is of course costly in itself and opens the prospect of side deals between plaintiffs and physician defendants.

RESTATEMENT OF THE LAW (THIRD) OF TORTS: MISCELLANEOUS PROVISIONS (TENTATIVE DRAFT, RELEASED 2023)

§6. Vicarious Liability of Principals for Torts Committed by Actors With Apparent Authority

A principal is subject to vicarious liability for a tort committed by an actor in dealing or communicating with a third party when the third party reasonably believes that the actor is acting and has authority to act on behalf of the principal and that belief is traceable to the principal's manifestations.

3. *Intentional Torts Within "Scope of Employment.* In *Bushey*, Friendly, J., referred to "responsibility for accidents which may fairly be said to be characteristic of its activities." How does that approach apply to the employee's intentional torts? Today, many cases clearly reject in this context the "characteristic risk" approach to discerning the scope of employment, as does the Restatement (Third) of Torts: Miscellaneous Provisions §5, comment *l*. In Doe v. Fulton-DeKalb Hospital Authority, 628 F.3d 1325, 1333 (11th Cir. 2010), a substance abuse counselor employed by the defendant-hospital sexually harassed three patients during the course of their drug rehabilitation treatment. Tjoflat, J., explained Georgia's rejection of vicarious liability for employee sexual misconduct: "These types of torts, being purely personal in nature, are unrelated to the employee's duties and, therefore, are outside the scope of employment because they are not in furtherance of the master's business." The general bar on vicarious liability for intentional torts extends beyond sexual assaults committed by employees. For example, vicarious liability did not attach in Kephart v. Genuity, Inc., 38 Cal. Rptr. 3d 845, 855 (Ct. App. 2006), when the defendant's employee, Graham, in a prolonged fit of road rage, forced the plaintiff's car off the highway. The plaintiff's car overturned, leaving her a quadriplegic. Scotland, P.J., held "the jury reasonably could find that Graham left his home at least five hours earlier than was required by his business trip and that, as he testified, he did so entirely for personal reasons."

By contrast, in Jane IL Doe v. Brightstar Residential Inc., 291 Cal. Rptr. 3d 279, 290 (Ct. App. 2022), where a patient in a residential facility for mentally disabled individuals was sexually abused by an independent contractor handyman, Wiley, J., held the facility liable on account of its ability to "control [the handyman] in pertinent ways[,]" e.g., by "determin[ing] whether and when [the handyman] would work at the property and under what conditions and supervision." What role should attention to prevention of harm play in vicarious liability?

4. *Punitive Damages Against an Employer.* In Lake Shore & Michigan Southern Railway v. Prentice, 147 U.S. 101, 107 (1893), the sole question before the Court was "whether a railroad corporation can be charged with punitive or exemplary damages for the illegal, wanton and oppressive conduct of a conductor of one of its trains towards a passenger." Gray, J., answered that question in the negative:

> Exemplary or punitive damages, being awarded, not by way of compensation to the sufferer, but by way of punishment of the offender, and as a warning to others, can only be awarded against one who has participated in the offence. A principal, therefore, though of course liable to make compensation for injuries done by his agent within the scope of his employment, cannot be held liable for exemplary or punitive damages, merely by reason of wanton, oppressive or malicious intent on the part of the agent.

What result if the railroad suspected but did not know of any improper conduct by its conductor?

5. *Negligent Hiring.* Sometimes employers may be held responsible for negligent hiring or supervision, even for intentional wrongs that fall outside the employee's scope of employment. In Schechter v. Merchants Home Delivery, Inc., 892 A.2d 415, 432 (D.C. 2006), cited above in *Uber Technologies*, two workers hired by the defendant MHD robbed Ms. Schechter, an 80-year-old widow, while installing a new washing machine in her house. Schwelb, J., allowed the plaintiff to reach a jury solely on the theory of negligent hiring, on the question whether "[MHD] utterly failed in its duty to supervise, train and maintain . . . its delivery personnel." In *Schechter*, one of the employees had a criminal record for burglary. Should that suffice to grant the plaintiff summary judgment on a negligent hiring claim?

But often (as in *Uber Technologies*) it is a formidable hurdle for the plaintiff to identify with sufficient particularity the specific preventative measures that would have prevented (or reduced) the harm. Sharkey, Institutional Liability for Employees' Intentional Torts: Vicarious Liability as a Quasi-Substitute for Punitive Damages, 53 Val. U. L. Rev. 1, 32 (2018), suggests that vicarious liability steps in to address the under-detection problem that inheres in the high burden of pleading a prima facie case for negligent hiring: "[S]trict liability could thus promote as-yet-unimagined and currently untaken preventative measures. [A] motivated and innovative employer could find ways to investigate employees' past conduct more thoroughly and supervise their present conduct more comprehensively."

6. *Vicarious Liability in the Modern Regulatory State.* In recent years, the Supreme Court has grappled with the extent to which the common law principles of vicarious liability survive in the modern regulatory state. In Vance v. Ball State University, 570 U.S. 421, 431, 451 (2013), the Court examined the bipartite standard for employer liability that has emerged in sexual harassment cases under Title VII of the Civil Rights Act. For harassment by coworkers, the employer must be negligent in the supervision of the workplace. But for harassment by supervisors a strict regime of vicarious liability applies. Alito, J., held that an employee counts as a supervisor "only when the employer has empowered that employee to take tangible employment actions against the victim, *i.e.*, to effect a significant change in employment status, such as hiring, firing, failing to promote, reassignment with significantly different responsibilities, or a decision causing a significant change in benefits." The four dissenters, led by Ginsburg, J., adopted the broader definition propounded by the Equal Opportunity Employment Commission: "(1) an individual authorized 'to undertake or recommend tangible employment decisions affecting the employee,' including 'hiring, firing, promoting, demoting, and reassigning the employee'; *or* (2) an individual authorized 'to direct the employee's daily work activities.' "

CHAPTER 8

PRODUCTS LIABILITY

SECTION A. INTRODUCTION

Products liability law has become so important that it is virtually a legal field unto itself. This field is conveniently defined in contrast to the abnormally dangerous activities examined in Chapter 7, which explored the liability of defendants who exercised direct control over dangerous instrumentalities at the time they caused injury. Products liability law, on the other hand, governs the activities of manufacturers, distributors, and sellers who have placed a product in the stream of commerce and are *no longer* in possession of it when it causes damage.

As befits its complexity, products liability law has a rich and dense history, which can be roughly divided into four periods. The first period ran from approximately the mid-nineteenth century to the early twentieth century, when the major debate was whether to allow an injured party to sue either product manufacturers or sellers. Courts often held that the "privity" limitation prevented the injured party—whether consumer, user, or bystander—from suing the "remote" supplier of the product in question, that is, one who has no direct contractual relationship with the injured party. Instead an injured consumer or user could sue only the immediate vendor of the product; an injured bystander could sue only the party in possession of the product just before the injury occurred.

The last half of the nineteenth century witnessed a gradual erosion of this privity limitation, as exceptions were created for products known to hold hidden dangers that manifested themselves when either the plaintiff or some third party put them to ordinary use. This second period began when MacPherson v. Buick Motor Co., 111 N.E. 1050 (N.Y. 1916), rejected the privity limitation outright by imposing liability for negligence on a remote seller.

The third stage of products liability law was inaugurated by the famous concurring opinion of Justice Traynor in Escola v. Coca Cola Bottling Co., 150 P.2d 436, 440 (Cal. 1944), which argued that strict liability, not negligence principles, should govern the manufacturer's liability. Traynor's view steadily gained adherents and became the dominant view by 1965, when the American Law Institute incorporated a general principle of strict liability into section 402A of the Second Restatement. For a discussion of the early development of strict liability through the Second Restatement, see Epstein, Modern Products Liability Law (1980); Prosser, The Assault Upon the Citadel (Strict Liability to the Consumer), 69 Yale L.J. 1099 (1960).

Soon after the Second Restatement was adopted, products liability law entered a period of rapid expansion. The three dominant themes in debates leading up to the Second Restatement focused on the role of manufacturers: their market power, their capacity to obtain insurance, and their ability to internalize the costs of accidents associated with their products. Taken together, these three issues pointed to placing nearly "absolute liability" on the manufacturer, and perhaps others in the chain of distribution. As Priest, The Invention of Enterprise Liability: A Critical History of the Intellectual Foundations of Modern Tort Law, 14 J. Legal Stud. 461, 527 (1985), laments "[t]he presuppositions themselves do not incorporate any conceptual limit to manufacturer's liability."

The fourth and present stage of products liability law began in the decade following the 1965 Restatement with a series of important decisions in "defective design" and "failure to warn" cases, as they are now commonly known. These cases, which somewhat ironically have expanded liability within the traditional negligence framework, form the centerpiece of modern products liability law.

In 1998, in response to these major developments, the American Law Institute issued a separate volume of the Third Restatement devoted exclusively to products liability law. "This [Third] Restatement is . . . an almost total overhaul of Restatement Second as it concerns the liability of commercial sellers of products." RTT: PL at 3. The Third Restatement has received a rather chilly reception in the courts and mixed reviews in the academy. Courts are still reacting unevenly to various provisions of the Third Restatement, and it remains unclear whether the longer Third Restatement will displace or supplement the earlier, but more concise, Second Restatement. It is therefore necessary to study both Restatements throughout this chapter. In any event, it is now evident that the fourth period has been a period of doctrinal consolidation, if not some modest retrenchment. The steady string of plaintiffs' breakthroughs that were par for the course between 1965 and 1980—the rise of crashworthiness theories, the decline of the open and obvious defense, and the expansive definitions of product defect—has slowed markedly. See Henderson & Eisenberg, The Quiet Revolution in Products Liability: An Empirical Study of Legal Change, 37 UCLA L. Rev. 479, 481 (1990); Schwartz, The Beginning and the Possible End of the Rise of Modern American Tort Law, 26 Ga. L. Rev. 601, 604 (1992).

The newest developments in this field go beyond the traditional contours of the tort law. Consider, for example, the emergence of autonomous vehicles. Autonomous vehicles hold the promise of dramatically reducing automobile accident rates, roughly 98 percent of which are caused by human error. But what about crashes due to software glitches? Should these be handled under strict products liability? Also of immediate relevance is the question of whether online suppliers of goods (like Amazon.com) should be subject to the products liability legal regime when they act as an aggregator and conduit between other product sellers and their customers. These questions have momentous implications for the safety of products and the business models of sellers and distributors.

Another fast-developing area in tort law comes from government regulatory oversight. Today it is common for government agencies to launch extensive investigations of product defects, which can lead to major fines or criminal prosecutions, activities that are largely beyond the scope of this chapter. Relatedly, however, this chapter considers the extent to which direct forms of federal regulation can supersede private rights of action under state tort law, a legal concept known as preemption. The stakes here are enormous, as federal regulation affects products as varied as motor vehicles, pharmaceuticals, medical devices, and toxic chemicals. Without question, the major developments in products liability since 2000 have concerned the preemption question, which forces tort lawyers to negotiate the treacherous shoals of federalism and administrative law. See Sharkey, Products Liability Preemption: An Institutional Approach, 76 Geo. Wash. L. Rev. 449 (2008).

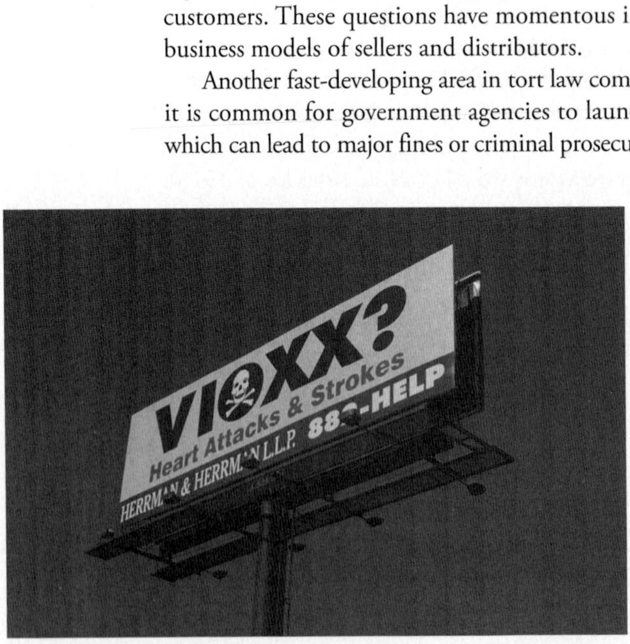

A billboard for a Texas law firm that sought plaintiffs after Vioxx was removed from the market

Source: Bob Daemmrich / Corbis

Products liability law is also inevitably bound up with mass tort litigation, including, but not limited to, class actions. Major class action suits dominate the headlines, and capture the attention of political, corporate, and consumer actors. The 3M multidistrict litigation provides a high-profile example. Numerous federal cases that allege that 3M's dual-ended Combat Arms earplugs are defective and caused the plaintiffs to develop hearing loss are consolidated in a multidistrict litigation in Northern Florida under Judge M. Casey Rodgers. See In re 3M Combat Arms Earplug Products Liability, Case No. 3:19-md-2885. In a 2022 bellwether trial, a jury awarded a plaintiff $72 million in damages after concluding 3M was liable for defective design and failure to warn, among other claims. Verdict Form, Beal v. 3M Co., No. 7:20-cv-00006 (N.D. Fla. May 20, 2022), ECF No. 176.

These multifaceted legal developments demonstrate that products liability law is big business. In 2020, some 241,438 products liability tort suits were filed in U.S. federal district courts, a dramatic increase from the previous peak of 64,367 in 2010. This spike, likely a result of the COVID-19 pandemic, has tapered off a bit, with the numbers for 2022 reverting to 61,712, only slightly above pre-COVID levels. See Admin. Office of the U.S. Courts, 2022 Annual Report of the Director: Judicial Business of the United States Courts tbl. C-11 (Sept. 30, 2022), https://www.uscourts.gov/sites/default/files/data_tables/jb_c11_0930.2022.pdf. From these numbers, it should come as no surprise that personal injury products liability actions now constitute over 20 percent of the docket of new civil filings in federal district courts, up from under 5 percent in 1980.

Interestingly, the rapid increase in the overall level of products litigation has been matched by a long and steady decline in accident levels. From 1945 to 2021, fatal workplace accidents declined from 33 per 100,000 to 3.6 per 100,000, with home and vehicular accident rates falling dramatically as well. See Bureau of Labor Stat., U.S. Dep't of Labor, USDL-22-2309, National Census of Fatal Occupation Injuries (2022). On this issue, the relationship between the improved accident picture and the changes in the tort liability arena is unclear. The decline in accident rates started before the expansion in tort liability and has continued uniformly even as the doctrinal expansion in the field slowed around 1990. See generally Priest, Products Liability Law and the Accident Rate, *in* Liability: Perspectives and Policy (Litan & Winston eds., 1988).

Today, intense battles rage on about whether tort claims exert a positive influence in promoting safety and deterring accidents. Some scholars argue that the headline-grabbing pharmaceutical and medical-device cases of the past twenty years have highlighted the insufficiency of federal regulation; others claim that tort suits undermine the careful balancing done by the federal regulators, thereby exposing manufacturers to excessive risk. To understand the contemporary state of products liability, it is helpful to trace its origins back to the mid-nineteenth century.

SECTION B. EXPOSITION

Winterbottom v. Wright
(1842) 152 Eng. Rep. 402 (Ex.)

[The plaintiff brought an action on the case, i.e., in tort, based on the following undisputed facts. The defendant contracted with the Postmaster-General to supply coaches to carry mail and to see that the coaches would "be kept in a fit, proper, safe, and secure state and condition for said purpose." Under this contract the defendant assumed "the sole and exclusive duty, charge, care, and burden of the repairs, state, and condition" thereof. Atkinson, knowing of this contract, personally contracted with the Postmaster-General to supply horses and drivers for the defendant's coaches. The plaintiff, one of Atkinson's drivers, was driving a coach serviced by the defendant, and was hurt when a latent defect caused the coach to break down, throwing him to the ground and injuring him. The defendant demurred to the plaintiff's action.]

ABINGER, C.B. I am clearly of opinion that the defendant is entitled to our judgment. We ought not to permit a doubt to rest upon this subject, for our doing so might be the means of letting in upon us an infinity of actions. This is an action of the first impression, and it has been brought in spite of the precautions which were taken, in the judgment of this Court in the case of Levy v. Langridge, [(1836) 150 Eng. Rep. 863 (Ex.)], a case of fraudulent representation by the seller to the purchaser, to obviate any notion that such an action could be maintained. We ought not to attempt to extend the principle of that decision, which, although it has been cited in support of this action, wholly fails as an authority in its favour; for there the gun was bought for the use of the son, the plaintiff in that action, who could not make the bargain himself, but was really and substantially the party contracting. Here the action is brought simply because the defendant was a contractor with a third person; and it is contended that thereupon he became liable to everybody who might use the carriage. If there had been any ground for such an action, there certainly would have been some precedent of it; but with the exception of actions against innkeepers, and some few other persons, no case of a similar nature has occurred in practice. That is a strong circumstance, and is of itself a great authority against its maintenance. It is however contended, that this contract being made on the behalf of the public by the Postmaster-General, no action could be maintained against him, and therefore the plaintiff must have a remedy against the defendant. But that is by no means a necessary consequence—he may be remediless altogether. There is no privity of contract between these parties; and if the plaintiff can sue, every passenger, or even any person passing along the road, who was injured by the upsetting of the coach, might bring a similar action. Unless we confine the operation of such contracts as this to the parties who entered into them, the most absurd and outrageous consequences, to which I can see no limit, would ensue. Where a party becomes responsible to the public, by undertaking a public duty, he is liable, though the injury may have arisen from the negligence of his servant or agent. So, in cases of public nuisances, whether the act was done by the party as a servant, or in any other capacity, you are liable to an action at the suit of any person who suffers. Those, however, are cases where the real ground of the liability is the public duty, or the commission of the public nuisance. There is also a class of cases in which the law permits a contract to be turned into a tort; but unless there has been some public duty undertaken, or public nuisance committed, they are all cases in which an action might have been maintained upon the contract. Thus, a carrier may be sued either in assumpsit [contract] or case [tort]; but there is no instance in which a party, who was not privy to the contract entered into with him, can maintain any such action. The plaintiff in this case could not have brought an action on the contract; if he could have done so, what would have been his situation, supposing the Postmaster-General had released the defendant? That would, at all events, have defeated his claim altogether. By permitting this action, we should be working this injustice, that after the defendant had done everything to the satisfaction of his employer, and after all matters between them had been adjusted, and all accounts settled on the footing of their contract, we should subject them to be ripped open by this action of tort being brought against him.

NOTE

The American Reception of Winterbottom v. Wright. During the nineteenth century, Winterbottom v. Wright was a leading—albeit controversial—case both in England and in the United States. Negotiating the line between contracts and torts, *Winterbottom*'s requirement of privity between the parties provided a clear rule that limited the scope of tort duties owed to third persons who were not parties to the underlying contract, in this instance to repair the coach. According to one explanation, the result in *Winterbottom* had as much to do with procedure as with substance:

> The dominant focus of the pre-negligence era [before 1850 at the earliest] was fixed upon the different and difficult problem of concurrence [between tort and contract remedies]. The early common law was traditionally hostile to double remedies, and this attitude, though less intense in the 19th century, was still alive.

Palmer, Why Privity Entered Tort—An Historical Reexamination of Winterbottom v. Wright, 27 Am. J. Legal Hist. 85, 89 (1983).

Would this problem be so severe if the court in *Winterbottom* had limited tort remedies to defective products? That concept came to the fore in several late nineteenth-century cases, which carved out significant exceptions to *Winterbottom*'s categorical prohibition. The overall position in the United States was summarized by Sanborn, J., in Huset v. J.I. Case Threshing Machine Co., 120 F. 865, 866–71 (8th Cir. 1903):

> [T]he natural and probable effect of the negligence of the contractor or manufacturer will generally be limited to the party for whom the article is constructed, or to whom it is first sold, and, perhaps more than all this, for the reason that a wise and conservative public policy has impressed the courts with the view that there must be a fixed and definite limitation to the liability of manufacturers and vendors for negligence in the construction and sale of complicated machines and structures which are to be operated or used by the intelligent and the ignorant, the skillful and the incompetent, the watchful and the careless, parties that cannot be known to the manufacturers or vendors, and who use the articles all over the country hundreds of miles distant from the place of their manufacture or original sale, a general rule has been adopted and has become established by repeated decisions of the courts of England and of this country that in these cases the liability of the contractor or manufacturer for negligence in the construction or sale of the articles which he makes or vends is limited to the persons to whom he is liable under his contracts of construction or sale. The limits of the liability for negligence and for breaches of contract in cases of this character are held to be identical. The general rule is that a contractor, manufacturer, or vendor is not liable to third parties who have no contractual relations with him for negligence in the construction, manufacture, or sale of the articles he handles. But while this general rule is both established and settled, there are, as is usually the case, exceptions to it as well defined and settled as the rule itself. There are three exceptions to this rule.
>
> The first is that an act of negligence of a manufacturer or vendor which is imminently dangerous to the life or health of mankind, and which is committed in the preparation or sale of an article intended to preserve, destroy, or affect human life, is actionable by third parties who suffer from the negligence. . . .
>
> The second exception is that an owner's act of negligence which causes injury to one who is invited by him to use his defective appliance upon the owner's premises may form the basis of an action against the owner. . . .
>
> The third exception to the rule is that one who sells or delivers an article which he knows to be imminently dangerous to life or limb to another without notice of its qualities is liable to any person who suffers an injury therefrom which might have been reasonably anticipated, whether there were any contractual relations between the parties or not.

The court then held that the plaintiff's complaint alleged a cause of action under the third exception: that the defendant's threshing machine was constructed so that the cylinder covering upon which its operator had to walk could not support his weight, that the defect was latent in that it could not be discovered by ordinary inspection, and that this defective condition was known by the defendant. The court remanded the case for trial, noting that it was "perhaps improbable" that the defendant had knowledge of the imminently dangerous character of the machine at the time of delivery.

Some cases did succeed under this third exception. In Kuelling v. Roderick Lean Manufacturing Co., 75 N.E. 1098, 1101 (N.Y. 1905), the defendants sold a roller to a dealer who then resold it to the plaintiff. The roller was made out of weak wood and contained a knot that prevented a safe hook-up of the roller to the team of horses that pulled it. The defect was deliberately concealed by putty and paint. Bartlett, J., allowed the action:

> In the case at bar we have, not only fraudulent deceit and concealment, but what amounts to an affirmative representation that the tongue of the roller was sound, as the manufacturer by filling the defect with putty and painting the entire surface so that the eye could not detect any weakness by reason of the knot, knothole filled up, the kind of wood employed and the fact that it was cross-grained, must be held to have represented that the roller as offered for sale was in a perfectly marketable condition.

MacPherson v. Buick Motor Co.

111 N.E. 1050 (N.Y. 1916)

Cardozo, J. The defendant is a manufacturer of automobiles. It sold an automobile to a retail dealer. The retail dealer resold to the plaintiff. While the plaintiff was in the car, it suddenly collapsed. He was thrown out and injured. One of the wheels was made of defective wood, and its spokes crumbled into fragments. The wheel was not made by the defendant; it was bought from another manufacturer. There is evidence, however, that its defects could have been discovered by reasonable inspection, and that inspection was omitted. There is no claim that the defendant knew of the defect and willfully concealed it. The case, in other words, is not brought within the rule of Kuelling v. Lean Mfg. Co. The charge is one, not of fraud, but of negligence. The question to be determined is whether the defendant owed a duty of care and vigilance to any one but the immediate purchaser.

Exhibit 8.1 1910 Buick Model 10

"The Buick Model 10 was introduced in 1908. The Gentlemen's Light Four-cylinder Roadster body-style soon became the company's best seller. Over 4,000 examples were created during its first year and that figure doubled the following year to 8,100. The last year was in 1910, with production approaching 11,000 units." 1910 Buick Model 10, Conceptcarz, http://www.conceptcarz.com/vehicle/z7409/Buick-Model-10.aspx.

Source: PF / Alamy

The foundations of this branch of the law, at least in this state, were laid in Thomas v. Winchester (6 N.Y. 397 (1852)). A poison was falsely labeled. The sale was made to a druggist, who in turn sold to a customer. The customer recovered damages from the seller who affixed the label. "The defendant's negligence," it was said, "put human life in imminent danger." A poison falsely labeled is likely to injure anyone who gets it. Because the danger is to be foreseen, there is a duty to avoid the injury. . . .

Thomas v. Winchester became quickly a landmark of the law. In the application of its principle there may at times have been uncertainty or even error. There has never in this state been doubt or disavowal of the principle itself. The chief cases are well known, yet to recall some of them will be helpful. Loop v. Litchfield (42 N.Y. 351 (1870)) is the earliest. It was the case of a defect in a small balance wheel used on a circular saw. The manufacturer pointed out the defect to the buyer, who wished a cheap article and was ready to assume the risk. The risk can hardly have been an imminent one, for the wheel lasted five years before it broke. In the meanwhile the buyer had made a lease of the machinery. It was held that the manufacturer was not answerable to the lessee. Loop v. Litchfield was followed in Losee v. Clute (51 N.Y. 494 (1873)), the case of the explosion of a steam boiler. That decision has been criticised but it must be confined to its special facts. It was put upon the ground that the risk of injury was too remote. The buyer in that case had not only accepted the boiler, but had tested it. The manufacturer knew that his own test was not the final one. The finality of the test has a bearing on the measure of diligence owing to persons other than the purchaser.

These early cases suggest a narrow construction of the rule. Later cases, however, evince a more liberal spirit. First in importance is Devlin v. Smith (89 N.Y. 470 (1882)). The defendant, a contractor, built a scaffold for a painter. The painter's servants were injured. The contractor was held liable. He knew that the scaffold, if improperly constructed, was a most dangerous trap. He knew that it was to be used by the workmen. He was building it for that very purpose. Building it for their use, he owed them a duty, irrespective of his contract with their master, to build it with care.

From Devlin v. Smith we pass over intermediate cases and turn to the latest case in this court in which Thomas v. Winchester was followed. That case is Statler v. Ray Mfg. Co. (195 N.Y. 478, 480 (1909)). The defendant manufactured a large coffee urn. It was installed in a restaurant. When heated, the urn exploded and injured the plaintiff. We held that the manufacturer was liable. We said that the urn "was of such a character inherently that, when applied to the purposes for which it was designed, it was liable to become a source of great danger to many people if not carefully and properly constructed."

It may be that Devlin v. Smith and Statler v. Ray Mfg. Co. have extended the rule of Thomas v. Winchester. If so, this court is committed to the extension. The defendant argues that things imminently dangerous to life are poisons, explosives, deadly weapons — things whose normal function it is to injure or destroy. But whatever the rule in Thomas v. Winchester may once have been, it has no longer that restricted meaning. A scaffold (Devlin v. Smith, *supra*) is not inherently a destructive instrument. It becomes destructive only if imperfectly constructed. A large coffee urn . . . may have within itself, if negligently made, the potency of danger, yet no one thinks of it as an implement whose normal function is destruction. What is true of the coffee urn is equally true of bottles of aerated water (Torgeson v. Schultz, 192 N.Y. 156 (1908)). We have mentioned only cases in this court. But the rule has received a like extension in our courts of intermediate appeal. . . .

[Cardozo, J., then reviews the parallel English decisions.]

We hold, then, that the principle of Thomas v. Winchester is not limited to poisons, explosives, and things of like nature, to things which in their normal operation are implements of destruction. If the nature of a thing is such that it is reasonably certain to place life and limb in peril when negligently made, it is then a thing of danger. Its nature gives warning of the consequences to be expected. If to the element of danger there is added knowledge that the thing will be used by persons other than the purchaser, and used without new tests, then, irrespective of contract, the manufacturer of this thing of danger is under a duty to make it carefully. That is as far as we are required to go for the decision of this case. There must be knowledge of a danger, not merely possible, but probable. It is *possible* to use almost anything in a way that will make it dangerous if defective. That is not enough to charge the manufacturer with a duty independent of his contract. Whether a given thing is dangerous may be sometimes a question for the court and sometimes a question for the jury. There must also be knowledge that in the usual course of events the danger will be shared by others than the buyer. Such knowledge may often be inferred from the nature of the transaction. But it is possible that even knowledge of the danger and of the use will not always be enough. The proximity or remoteness of the relation is a factor to be considered. We are dealing now with the liability of the manufacturer of the finished product, who puts it on the market to be used without inspection by his customers. If he is negligent, where danger is to be foreseen, a liability will follow. We are not required at this time to say that it is legitimate to go back of the manufacturer of the finished product and hold the manufacturers of the component parts. To make their negligence a cause of imminent danger, an independent cause must often intervene; the manufacturer of the finished product must also fail in *his* duty of inspection. It may be that in those circumstances the negligence of the earlier members of the series is too remote to constitute, as to the ultimate user, an actionable wrong. . . . We leave that question open. We shall have to deal with it when it arises. The difficulty which it suggests is not present in this case. There is here no break in the chain of cause and effect. In such circumstances, the presence of a known danger, attendant upon a known use, makes vigilance a duty. We have put aside the notion that the duty to safeguard life and limb, when the consequences of negligence may be foreseen, grows out of contract and nothing else. We have put the source of the obligation where it ought to be. We have put its source in the law.

From this survey of the decisions, there thus emerges a definition of the duty of a manufacturer which enables us to measure this defendant's liability. Beyond all question, the nature of an automobile gives warning of probable danger if its construction is defective. This automobile was designed to go fifty miles an hour. Unless its wheels were sound and strong, injury was almost certain. It was as much a thing of danger as a defective engine for a railroad. The defendant knew the danger. It knew also that the car would be used by persons other than the buyer. This was apparent from its size; there were seats for three persons. It was apparent also from the fact that the buyer was a dealer in cars, who bought to resell. The maker of this car supplied it for the use of purchasers from the dealer just as plainly as the contractor in Devlin v. Smith supplied the scaffold for use by the servants of the owner. The dealer was indeed the one person of whom it might be said with some approach to certainty that by him the car would not be used. Yet the defendant would have us say that he was the one person whom it was under a legal duty to protect. The law does not lead us to so inconsequent a conclusion. Precedents drawn from the days of travel by stage coach do not fit the conditions of travel today. The principle that the danger must be imminent does not change, but the things subject to the principle do change. They are whatever the needs of life in a developing civilization require them to be.

In reaching this conclusion, we do not ignore the decisions to the contrary in other jurisdictions. . . . The earlier cases are summarized by Judge Sanborn in Huset v. J. I. Case Threshing Machine Co. (120 Fed. Rep. 865). . . . Judge Sanborn says . . . that the contractor who builds a bridge, or the manufacturer who builds a car, cannot ordinarily foresee injury to other persons than the owner as the probable result. We take a different view. We think that injury to others is to be foreseen not merely as a possible, but as an almost inevitable result. Indeed,

Judge Sanborn concedes that his view is not to be reconciled with our decision in Devlin v. Smith. The doctrine of that decision has now become the settled law of this state, and we have no desire to depart from it.

[Cardozo, J., then reviews the English cases from *Winterbottom* onward and continues:] From these cases a consistent principle is with difficulty extracted. The English courts, however, agree with ours in holding that one who invites another to make use of an appliance is bound to the exercise of reasonable care. That at bottom is the underlying principle of Devlin v. Smith. The contractor who builds the scaffold invites the owner's workmen to use it. The manufacturer who sells the automobile to the retail dealer invites the dealer's customers to use it. The invitation is addressed in the one case to determinate persons and in the other to an indeterminate class, but in each case it is equally plain, and in each its consequences must be the same. . . .

. . . Subtle distinctions are drawn by the defendant between things inherently dangerous and things imminently dangerous, but the case does not turn upon these verbal niceties. If danger was to be expected as reasonably certain, there was a duty of vigilance, and this whether you call the danger inherent or imminent. In varying forms that thought was put before the jury. We do not say that the court would not have been justified in ruling as a matter of law that the car was a dangerous thing. If there was any error, it was none of which the defendant can complain.

We think the defendant was not absolved from a duty of inspection because it bought the wheels from a reputable manufacturer. It was not merely a dealer in automobiles. It was a manufacturer of automobiles. It was responsible for the finished product. It was not at liberty to put the finished product on the market without subjecting the component parts to ordinary and simple tests. Under the charge of the trial judge nothing more was required of it. The obligation to inspect must vary with the nature of the thing to be inspected. The more probable the danger, the greater the need of caution. . . .

The judgment should be affirmed with costs.

Bartlett, C.J., dissenting. . . . [In Thomas v. Winchester,] Chief Judge Ruggles, who delivered the opinion of the court, distinguished between an act of negligence imminently dangerous to the lives of others and one that is not so, saying: "If A. build a wagon and sell it to B., who sells it to C. and C. hires it to D., who in consequence of the gross negligence of A. in building the wagon is overturned and injured, D. cannot recover damages against A., the builder. A.'s obligation to build the wagon faithfully, arises solely out of his contract with B. The public have nothing to do with it. . . . So, for the same reason, if a horse be defectively shod by a smith, and a person hiring the horse from the owner is thrown and injured in consequence of the smith's negligence in shoeing the smith is not liable for the injury." . . .

I do not see how we can uphold the judgment in the present case without overruling what has been so often said by this court and other courts of like authority in reference to the absence of any liability for negligence on the part of the original vendor of an ordinary carriage to any one except his immediate vendee. The absence of such liability was the very point actually decided in the English case of Winterbottom v. Wright, and the illustration quoted from the opinion of Chief Judge Ruggles in Thomas v. Winchester assumes that the law on the subject was so plain that the statement would be accepted almost as a matter of course. In the case at bar the defective wheel on an automobile moving only eight miles an hour was not any more dangerous to the occupants of the car than a similarly defective wheel would be to the occupants of a carriage drawn by a horse at the same speed; and yet unless the courts have been all wrong on this question up to the present time there would be no liability to strangers to the original sale in the case of the horse-drawn carriage.

NOTES

1. *A Landmark Case.* The *MacPherson* trial record yields a somewhat different view of the facts of this case. The eyewitnesses all testified that MacPherson was traveling (in 1911) at over thirty miles per hour when the accident took place, not the leisurely eight miles per hour stated in the dissent. As James Henderson notes,

> [t]he problem with MacPherson's story was that it was premised on a physical impossibility. Uncontradicted expert testimony from defendant's experts showed that, at such a low speed in high gear, the Buick would have stalled in its tracks—the engine could not possibly have continued to operate in four inches of gravel—and the car would have come to a stop almost immediately.

Henderson, *MacPherson v. Buick Motor Company*: Simplifying the Facts While Reshaping the Law, *in* Tort Stories 45–46 (Rabin & Sugarman eds., 2003).

The nature of the collision offers a compelling explanation as to why the wheel broke as it did. If the defect had been built in from the beginning, the wheel surely would have collapsed sooner under the pressure of driving on back country roads. None of these details came out in the appellate litigation, as Buick preferred to concentrate on the privity defense on the appeal in the hopes of securing a categorical defense that did not turn on the condition of the wheel at the time of the accident. If the facts had come out, would the case for the privity limitation have been stronger or weaker? On its actual facts, could MacPherson get to the jury today?

Exhibit 8.2 *MacPherson's* Facts: Not as Simple as Cardozo Suggests

The few facts recited in Cardozo's *MacPherson* decision are "starkly simple" and "give[] no hint of the inherently controversial nature of the conclusions reached at trial." Henderson, *MacPherson v. Buick Motor Company*: Simplifying the Facts While Reshaping the Law, *in* Torts Stories 41, 51 (Rabin & Sugarman eds., 2003). By the time the case reached the Court of Appeals, the underlying facts of *MacPherson* had already been manipulated; Cardozo then altogether elided them in the course of reshaping the law of products liability. For instance:

- *Car Not New*. MacPherson's Buick Model 10 runabout "was not new, or even nearly new; the MacPhersons had owned it for over a year and had put it to hard use. . . . [They] had driven the car all over . . . upstate New York . . . on all kinds of surfaces, including rough country roads." Henderson, *supra*, at 41–42. They had used it, moreover, "with a lot of weight aboard," to carry grave stones and markers, in connection with the family's gravestone and marker business. *Id.*
- *MacPherson No Novice*. By the time of the accident, MacPherson had "owned and operated several other automobiles . . . and was an experienced driver." *Id.*
- *Travel at High Gear*. The accident occurred on a "paved state road," on which MacPherson, according to "several disinterested eyewitnesses," "shifted the Buick into high gear and pushed the speed up to over 30 miles an hour." *Id.* at 42, 45. MacPherson testified that he was only going eight miles per hour—a speed at which the accident would have been, according to uncontradicted expert testimony, a "physical impossibility." *Id.* at 45.
- *When Did That Wheel Break?* The Buick ran into a "stretch of loose gravel" on the paved road, at which time MacPherson "lost control" of the car, which slid off the road to the right, and "struck a telephone pole with the front right bumper, spun around 180 degrees from its own momentum, and fell . . . into a three-foot ditch. When the automobile landed in the ditch, the left rear wheel broke under the sudden force of the impact. . . ." *Id.* at 43. MacPherson however testified that "the left rear wheel suddenly collapsed while the car was being driven," *id.* at 47—a rendition ostensibly endorsed in full by Cardozo. ("While the plaintiff was in the car, it suddenly collapsed. He was thrown out and injured. One of the wheels was made of defective wood, and its spokes crumbled into fragments." *MacPherson*, 111 N.E. at 1051.)

As argued on appeal, *MacPherson* counts as a landmark decision in the history of our law. Before *MacPherson*, Sanborn, J., in Huset v. J.I. Case, *supra* at 549, stated the law as it stood in virtually all jurisdictions, including New York. After *MacPherson*, one jurisdiction after another abandoned the privity rule in cases involving physical injuries caused by defective products. Subsequent cases incrementally extended the scope of *MacPherson*. Thus in Smith v. Peerless Glass Co., 181 N.E. 576 (N.Y. 1932), the court allowed a direct action for negligence to be brought against the manufacturer of a component part, such as the wheel maker in *MacPherson*. Today, every jurisdiction in the United States follows the *MacPherson* rule. Great Britain eventually abandoned *Winterbottom* as well in Donoghue v. Stevenson, [1932] AC 562, 580, 599 (appeal taken from Scot.), in which the plaintiff was allowed to sue, even without privity, the maker of a ginger beer bottle for the physical harm sustained when she drank the remains of a decomposed snail left in an opaque bottle of its brew. While the House of Lords went out of its way to avoid explicitly overruling Winterbottom v. Wright, it took exception to its view of privity:

> [A] manufacturer of products which he sells in such a form as to show that he intends them to reach the ultimate consumer in the form in which they left him, with no reasonable possibility of intermediate examination, and with the knowledge that the absence of reasonable care in the preparation or putting up of the products is likely to result in injury to the consumer's life or property, owes a duty to the consumer to take that reasonable care.

Could MacPherson have recovered under this formulation of the rule in light of his ability to inspect the wheel?

2. *Privity in Contract Law: The Warranty Side of the Line.* In *Huset*, Sanborn, J., noted that products liability claims frequently sounded in contract as well as in negligence. Often the plaintiff's strategy is to claim that the defendant made an express or implied warranty that the product sold was fit for its intended purpose. These contract theories must surmount two obstacles: privity and the intrinsic limitations of warranty law.

First, could the plaintiff rely on a warranty theory if she did not purchase the product directly from the defendant? In Chysky v. Drake Brothers Co., 139 N.E. 576, 577 (N.Y. 1923), the plaintiff, a waitress, was given a piece of the defendant's cake for lunch. She bit on a concealed nail that had been baked into the cake and suffered injuries to her mouth. Section 96 of the New York Personal Property Code provided that

> there is no implied warranty or condition as to the quality or fitness for any particular purpose of goods supplied under a contract to sell or a sale, except as follows: 1. Where the buyer, expressly or by implication, makes known to the seller the particular purpose for which the goods are required, and it appears that the buyer relies on the seller's skill or judgment (whether he be the grower or manufacturer or not), there is an implied warranty that the goods shall be reasonably fit for such purpose.

Even after *MacPherson*, the New York Court of Appeals held that the plaintiff's cause of action failed under this section, stating that

> [t]he general rule is that a manufacturer or seller of food, or other articles of personal property, is not liable to third persons, under an implied warranty, who have no contractual relations with him. The reason for this rule is that privity of contract does not exist between the seller and such third persons, and unless there be privity of contract, there can be no implied warranty.

Chysky, 139 N.E. at 578.

The privity barrier was overcome in Baxter v. Ford Motor Co., 12 P.2d 409, 412 (Wash. 1932). The plaintiff was injured in the eye when a small rock shattered the front windshield of his car, which was manufactured by Ford and sold to the plaintiff by the defendant dealer, St. John Motors. The Washington Supreme Court allowed the dealer to escape liability under a provision in the contract of sale that excluded all warranties. But relying on Thomas v.

Winchester, the court held that Ford could be responsible for its representations in catalogues and printed materials that St. John distributed to customers about the car's "Tri-plex shatter-proof glass windshield."

> The rule in such cases does not rest upon contractual obligations, but rather on the principle that the original act of delivering an article is wrong, when, because of the lack of those qualities which the manufacturer represented it as having, the absence of which could not be readily detected by the consumer, the article is not safe for the purposes for which the consumer would ordinarily use it.
>
> Since the rule of *caveat emptor* was first formulated, vast changes have taken place in the economic structures of the English speaking peoples. Methods of doing business have undergone a great transition. Radio, bill boards and the products of the printing press have become the means of creating a large part of the demand that causes goods to depart from factories to the ultimate consumer. It would be unjust to recognize a rule that would permit manufacturers of goods to create a demand for their products by representing that they possess qualities which they, in fact, do not possess; and then, because there is no privity of contract existing between the consumer and the manufacturer, deny the consumer the right to recover if damages result from the absence of those qualities, when such absence is not readily noticeable.

Dealer liability on an implied warranty theory was also at issue in McCabe v. L.K. Liggett Drug Co., 112 N.E.2d 254, 256–57 (Mass. 1953), where the plaintiff was injured by a metal coffee maker, the "Lucifer Lifetime," sold (but not manufactured) by the defendant in a sealed cardboard box and assembled by the plaintiff in accordance with the instructions. The plaintiff's expert testified that the "notches" in the coffee maker's filtration system were "inadequate to provide for the release of the pressure which developed from the boiling water," especially if they became clogged by the "congealing" of the coffee grounds. As a result, the coffee maker blew up and injured the plaintiff. Williams, J., brushed aside other defenses as follows:

> The sale carried an implied warranty by the seller that the appliance was a coffee maker of merchantable quality. G. L. (Ter. Ed.) c. 106, §17 (2). Merchantable quality means that goods are reasonably suitable for the ordinary uses for which goods of that description are sold. . . .
>
> The fact that the apparatus violently burst apart in the manner described showed that the accumulating pressure was not being released and in the absence of explanation was itself evidence of a defective condition. The jury could find that the explosion was caused by the failure of the water to rise into the upper bowl and from an examination of the notches in the filter that this failure was due to an inadequate outlet and the clogging effect of coffee grounds which would collect around the notches.
>
> If the coffee maker was so imperfect in design that it could not be used without the likelihood of an explosion it could be found that the appliance was not reasonably fit for making coffee and therefore not merchantable. The plaintiff was not deprived of her right to rely upon the implied warranty either by a failure to inspect or by an inspection before use, as it could have been found that the defect in design would not be obvious to an ordinary person on inspection.
>
> The judge was not justified in entering the verdict for the defendant on the ground that, as contended by the defendant, the notice required by G. L. (Ter. Ed.) c.106, §38, was insufficient, in not stating the exact date of the purchase or the name of the purchaser. Information as to the exact date of the sale was here of little if of any importance to the seller. The defendant had been selling these coffee makers over a period of a week. Presumably all were constructed alike. No claim was made that there was a defect in the particular appliance which was not common to all. The notice indicated a date of purchase within the period when they were being sold and was sufficient to enable the defendant to examine into any fault in their common design. The name of the person who actually made the purchase did not enter into the transaction with the defendant and the failure to state it did not invalidate the notice.

After *MacPherson*, how would a defense lawyer attack a plaintiff's story? Is there any difference between a defective and an unmerchantable appliance? Why shouldn't this action be brought against the manufacturer? How do the parallel lines of warranty and tort evolve?

Escola v. Coca Cola Bottling Co. of Fresno

150 P.2d 436 (Cal. 1944)

[The plaintiff was a waitress. As part of her job, she was placing into the restaurant's refrigerator bottles of Coca-Cola that had been delivered to the restaurant at least 36 hours earlier. As she put the fourth bottle into the refrigerator, it exploded in her hand, causing severe injuries. The plaintiff alleged that the defendant had been negligent in selling "bottles containing said beverage which on account of excessive pressure of gas or by reason of some defect in the bottle was dangerous . . . and likely to explode."

The jury entered a verdict for the plaintiff that was affirmed on appeal. Gibson, J., wrote as follows: "The bottle was admittedly charged with gas under pressure, and the charging of the bottle was within the exclusive control of the defendant. As it is a matter of common knowledge that an overcharge would not ordinarily result without negligence, it follows under the doctrine of res ipsa loquitur that if the bottle was in fact excessively charged an inference of defendant's negligence would arise."]

TRAYNOR, J. I concur in the judgment, but I believe the manufacturer's negligence should no longer be singled out as the basis of a plaintiff's right to recover in cases like the present one. In my opinion it should now be recognized that a manufacturer incurs an absolute liability when an article that he has placed on the market, knowing that it is to be used without inspection, proves to have a defect that causes injury to human beings. MacPherson v. Buick Motor Co. established the principle, recognized by this court, that irrespective of privity of contract, the manufacturer is responsible for an injury caused by such an article to any person who comes in lawful contact with it. In these cases the source of the manufacturer's liability was his negligence in the manufacturing process or in the inspection of component parts supplied by others. Even if there is no negligence, however, public policy demands that responsibility be fixed wherever it will most effectively reduce the hazards to life and health inherent in defective products that reach the market. It is evident that the manufacturer can anticipate some hazards and guard against the recurrence of others, as the public cannot. Those who suffer injury from defective products are unprepared to meet its consequences. The cost of an injury and the loss of time or health may be an overwhelming misfortune to the person injured, and a needless one, for the risk of injury can be insured by the manufacturer and distributed among the public as a cost of doing business. It is to the public interest to discourage the marketing of products having defects that are a menace to the public. If such products nevertheless find their way into the market it is to the public interest to place the responsibility for whatever injury they may cause upon the manufacturer, who, even if he is not negligent in the manufacture of the product, is responsible for its reaching the market. However intermittently such injuries may occur and however haphazardly they may strike, the risk of their occurrence is a constant risk and a general one. Against such a risk there should be general and constant protection and the manufacturer is best situated to afford such protection.

The injury from a defective product does not become a matter of indifference because the defect arises from causes other than the negligence of the manufacturer, such as negligence of a submanufacturer of a component part whose defects could not be revealed by inspection, or unknown causes that even by the device of res ipsa loquitur cannot be classified as negligence of the manufacturer. The inference of negligence may be dispelled by an affirmative showing of proper care. If the evidence against the fact inferred is "clear, positive, uncontradicted, and of such a nature that it cannot rationally be disbelieved, the court must instruct the jury that the nonexistence of the fact has been established as a matter of law." An injured person, however, is not ordinarily in a position to refute such evidence or identify the cause of the defect, for he can hardly be familiar with the manufacturing process as the manufacturer himself is. In leaving it to the jury to decide whether the inference has been dispelled, regardless of the evidence against it, the negligence rule approaches the rule of strict liability. It is needlessly circuitous to make negligence the basis of recovery and impose what is in reality liability without negligence. If public policy demands that a manufacturer of goods be responsible for their quality regardless of negligence there is no reason not to fix that responsibility openly.

Exhibit 8.3 Roger Traynor

Justice Roger Traynor (1900–1983), whose thirty-year tenure on the California Supreme Court encompassed twenty-four years as an associate justice (1940–1964) and six as chief justice (1964–1970), is the subject of a chapter in White, Tort Law in America: An Intellectual History ch. 6 (2003). According to White, the Traynor years were marked by "a strong interest in academic literature as source material; an effort to preserve, where possible, the lawmaking power of courts [in the face of "an increasingly detailed legislative apparatus"], and a search for a harmony of result and doctrine in his opinions." White, *supra*, at 182.

Source: Law School Archives, University of California, Berkeley

White further explains: "The basis for Traynor's faith in the judiciary as a lawmaking force . . . was his conviction that rationality could be achieved through enlightened judging." *Id.* at 188. Traynor, who "never departed from his belief that rationality was an achievable judicial goal . . . was not disturbed by the 'activist judge' label often attached to him." *Id.*

Indeed, and as shown by his concurrence in *Escola* and decision in *Greenman v. Yuba Power Products*, Inc., Traynor, "[i]n his activist conception of judging . . . was one of the pioneers of his time and one of the precursors of a 'policymaking' role for judges in tort cases. . . . Traynor was committed to using his powers as fully as possible to promote social policies in which he believed and to reorient the common law of California in directions he thought rational and desirable." *Id.* at 208.

In the case of foodstuffs, the public policy of the state is formulated in a criminal statute. . . . Statutes of this kind result in a strict liability of the manufacturer in tort to the member of the public injured.

The statute may well be applicable to a bottle whose defects cause it to explode. In any event it is significant that the statute imposes criminal liability without fault, reflecting the public policy of protecting the public from dangerous products placed on the market, irrespective of negligence in their manufacture. While the Legislature imposes criminal liability only with regard to food products and their containers, there are many other sources of danger. It is to the public interest to prevent injury to the public from any defective goods by the imposition of civil liability generally.

The retailer, even though not equipped to test a product, is under an absolute liability to his customer, for the implied warranties of fitness for proposed use and merchantable quality include a warranty of safety of the product. This warranty is not necessarily a contractual one; see 1 Williston on Sales, 2d ed., §§197–201, for public policy requires that the buyer be insured at the seller's expense against injury. The courts recognize, however, that the retailer cannot bear the burden of this warranty, and allow him to recoup any losses by means of the warranty of safety attending the wholesaler's or manufacturer's sale to him. . . . Such a procedure, however, is needlessly circuitous and engenders wasteful litigation. Much would be gained if the injured person could base his action directly on the manufacturer's warranty.

The liability of the manufacturer to an immediate buyer injured by a defective product follows without proof of negligence from the implied warranty of safety attending the sale. Ordinarily, however, the immediate buyer is a dealer who does not intend to use the product himself, and if the warranty of safety is to serve the purpose of protecting health and safety it must give rights to others than the dealer. In the words of Judge Cardozo in the *MacPherson* case: "The dealer was indeed the one person of whom it might be said with some approach to certainty that by him the car would not be used. Yet, the defendant would have us say that he was the one person whom it was under a legal duty to protect. The law does not lead us to so inconsequent a solution." While the defendant's negligence in the *MacPherson* case made it unnecessary for the court to base liability on warranty, Judge Cardozo's reasoning recognized the injured person as the real party in interest and effectively disposed on the theory that the liability of the manufacturer incurred by his warranty should apply only to the immediate purchaser. It thus paves the way for a standard of liability that would make the manufacturer guarantee the safety of his product even when there is no negligence.

This court and many others have extended protection according to such a standard to consumers of food products, taking the view that the right of a consumer injured by unwholesome food does not depend "upon the intricacies of the law of sales" and that the warranty of the manufacturer to the consumer in absence of privity of contract rests on public policy. Dangers to life and health inhere in other consumers' goods that are defective and there is no reason to differentiate them from the dangers of defective food products.

In the food products cases the courts have resorted to various fictions to rationalize the extension of the manufacturer's warranty to the consumer: that a warranty runs with the chattel; that the cause of action of the dealer is assigned to the consumer; that the consumer is a third party beneficiary of the manufacturer's contract with the dealer. They have also held the manufacturer liable on a mere fiction of negligence: "Practically he must know [the product] is fit, or bear the consequences if it proves destructive." Such fictions are not necessary to fix the manufacturer's liability under a warranty if the warranty is severed from the contract of sale between the dealer and the consumer and based on the law of torts as a strict liability. Warranties are not necessarily rights arising under a contract. An action on a warranty "was, in its origin, a pure action of tort," and only late in the historical development of warranties was an action in assumpsit allowed. (Ames, The History of Assumpsit, 2 Harv. L. Rev. 1, 8; 4 Williston on Contracts (1936) §970.) . . .

As handicrafts have been replaced by mass production with its great markets and transportation facilities, the close relationship between the producer and consumer of a product has been altered. Manufacturing processes, frequently valuable secrets, are ordinarily either inaccessible to or beyond the ken of the general public. The consumer no longer has means or skill enough to investigate for himself the soundness of a product, even when it is not contained in a sealed package, and his erstwhile vigilance has been lulled by the steady efforts of manufacturers to build up confidence by advertising and marketing devices such as trademarks. (See Thomas v. Winchester, 6 N.Y. 697; Baxter v. Ford Motor Co.[, 12 P.2d 409 (Wash. 1932)].) Consumers no longer approach products warily but accept them on faith, relying on the reputation of the manufacturer or the trademark. Manufacturers have sought to justify that faith by increasingly high standards of inspection and a readiness to make good on defective products by way of replacements and refunds. (See Bogert and Fink, Business Practices Regarding Warranties in the Sale of Goods, 25 Ill. L. Rev. 400.) The manufacturer's obligation to the consumer must keep pace with the changing relationship between them; it cannot be escaped because the marketing of a product has become so complicated as to require one or more intermediaries. Certainly, there is greater reason to impose liability on the manufacturer than on the retailer who is but a conduit of a product that he is not himself able to test.

The manufacturer's liability should, of course, be defined in terms of the safety of the product in normal and proper use, and should not extend to injuries that cannot be traced to the product as it reached the market.

NOTES

1. ***Rationales.*** At a factual level, does the switch to a theory of strict liability resolve the question of whether the Coca-Cola bottles were excessively charged in the factory or were mishandled by subsequent parties? As a theoretical matter, how sound are the various rationales for strict liability that Traynor, J., offers?

a. ***Loss Minimization.*** One rationale offered is that the manufacturer, rather than the unwitting consumer, is most knowledgeable and is therefore in the best position to minimize the losses that arise out of the general use of its product. If correct, should we also require strict liability for defective premises owned by commercial enterprises, or for that matter, strict liability for automobile accidents, at least when business enterprises are defendants? Recall Hammontree v. Jenner, *supra* Chapter 2, at 105. On this rationale, what adjustments should be made if the plaintiff or some downstream third party is in a better position to take the desired precautions? What if the plaintiff shook the bottle in use, or stored it in a hot place? Is it consistent with the loss minimization rationale to allow the manufacturer to contract out of liability with the consumer? Does a negligence rule fail to create the necessary incentives for the manufacturer to take appropriate cost-justified precautions?

b. ***Loss Spreading.*** A second defense of the strict liability rule in *Escola* rests upon the ability of the defendant producer to spread the damages among many consumers, thus cushioning the "overwhelming misfortune" of the injured person or her family. This risk-spreading rationale for strict liability was challenged in Wights v. Staff Jennings, Inc., 405 P.2d 624, 628 (Or. 1965), where the court observed:

> The rationale of risk spreading and compensating the victim has no special relevancy to cases involving injuries resulting from the use of defective goods. The reasoning would seem to apply not only in cases involving personal injuries arising from the *sale* of defective goods, but equally to any case where an injury results from the risk creating conduct of the seller in any stage of the production and distribution of goods. Thus a manufacturer would be strictly liable even in the absence of fault for any injury to a person struck by one of the manufacturer's trucks being used in transporting his goods to market. It seems to us that the enterprise liability rationale employed in the *Escola* case proves too much and that if adopted would compel us to apply the principle of strict liability in all future cases where the loss could be distributed.

c. ***Elimination of Proof Complications.*** Traynor, J., also defends strict liability in *Escola* because it simplifies the law by eliminating the need to resort to res ipsa loquitur—the same reason used to defend strict liability in Rylands v. Fletcher. See Chapter 2, *supra* at 85. In all contexts, a strict liability rule switches the residual risk of unavoidable accidents from the plaintiff to the defendant. With exploding soda bottles, that risk is generally quite small given the stringent quality control and inspection devices incorporated into the manufacturing process. How does res ipsa loquitur apply when misconduct by the plaintiff or a third party is also at issue? Should it make any difference that the plaintiff in *Escola* could not produce the pieces of the broken bottle for inspection and examination?

d. ***The Foodstuffs Analogy.*** A fourth defense of strict liability rests on the analogy between adulterated foodstuffs and product defects. In this regard, the law after *MacPherson* and before *Escola* drew a distinction between foodstuffs that were sold in sealed containers and those that were not. For goods sold in sealed containers, the law exempted the retailer from liability but allowed a direct suit against the manufacturer, albeit on a negligence theory. See, e.g., Richenbacher v. California Packing Corp., 145 N.E. 281 (Mass. 1924), sustaining the use of res ipsa loquitur when the plaintiff's mouth was cut by glass found in a container of spinach. In contrast, when goods were not packaged, the general rule imposed negligence liability, if at all, on the retailer, but not on the original food supplier. Is *Richenbacher* an easier case for res ipsa loquitur than *Escola*? Why?

e. ***Corrective Justice.*** Another argument for strict liability in products cases—one not pressed by Traynor—is that the loss should be placed upon the party who created the dangerous condition, not the party who suffered from it. This reasoning is similar to the argument for strict liability in ordinary trespass cases, or even under the rule in Rylands v. Fletcher: Once the plaintiff establishes the causal connection to the defendant's act (in *Escola*, the defective bottling under pressure that caused harm), then, prima facie, the defendant should be held liable. Note, however, one structural difference between the two types of cases. With abnormally dangerous activities, the defendant is virtually always in possession of the dangerous instrumentality just before it causes the accident, so the class of defenses based upon plaintiff's conduct remains quite small. See *supra* Chapter 2, Note 2, at 66, and Chapter 7, Note 4, at 487. With products liability, the defendant is never in possession of the dangerous product when it causes injury, so that the older privity limitation might be a sensible way for liability to track possession (and hence control), except in those few cases in which a party out of possession is in a better position to avoid the loss. See Epstein, The Historical Origins and Economic Structure of Workers' Compensation Law, 16 Ga. L. Rev. 775, 806–08 (1982), defending privity for workplace injuries on the ground that employer's liability is both cheaper and more efficient than manufacturer's liability.

2. *Criticisms.* For an early criticism of strict liability in products cases, see Plant, Strict Liability of Manufacturers for Injuries Caused by Defects in Products—An Opposing View, 24 Tenn. L. Rev. 938, 945 (1957), in which it is noted that "[t]he element which is most disturbing to manufacturers is not the potential judgment of legal liability but the injury which is done to the reputation of the product and its producers." Note that modern "event studies" establish that the decline in the value of the shares of a publicly traded company after a major product incident is greater than the anticipated amount of the liability. For evidence of the impact of these studies, see Prince & Rubin, The Effects of Product Liability Litigation on the Value of Firms, 45 Am. L. & Econ. Rev. 44 (2002):

> [F]irms facing lawsuits for their products suffer capital market losses approximately equal to a worst-case scenario associated with the litigation. Thus, it appears that individual firms may suffer reputation costs as a consequence of product liability lawsuits but that these reputation losses are smaller than losses from government actions such as recall.

See also Dranove, Delivering Bad News: Market Responses to Negligence, 55 J.L. & Econ. 1, 2 (2012), which notes some "anecdotal evidence" that points to some reputational effect:

> For example, sales of Johnson & Johnson's Tylenol plummeted in 1982 after the product was tainted by tampering, and ValuJet lost customers and even changed its name after the 1996 crash of flight 592. More recently, the spate of vehicle recalls faced by Toyota over allegedly defective acceleration put the automaker under intense public scrutiny and caused its U.S. market share to plummet. . . .

To what extent should the negative effect depend on the perceived fault of the defendant in bringing about the incident? The promptness of its corrective actions? The willingness to remove product from the market? Is the perception of fault likely to be greater for airline crashes and brake failures than for contaminations known to be caused downstream by malicious third parties?

3. *Implied Warranty: Elimination of Privity in Contract Law.* The early privity limitation in Chysky v. Drake, *supra* at 555, was overruled thirty-eight years later in Greenberg v. Lorenz, 173 N.E.2d 773 (N.Y. 1961). There the plaintiff was injured when she ate canned salmon that contained sharp metal slivers, sold by the defendant retail food dealer to her father. The court below dismissed the plaintiff's complaint because the plaintiff had not purchased the salmon herself. The Court of Appeals reversed. Just about that time, the warranty provisions of the law of sales were reworked under a new Uniform Commercial Code, which offers three possible approaches to the scope of the warranty.

UNIFORM COMMERCIAL CODE

§2-318. Third Party Beneficiaries of Warranties Express or Implied

Alternative A

A seller's warranty whether express or implied extends to any natural person who is in the family or household of his buyer or who is a guest in his home if it is reasonable to expect that such person may use, consume or be affected by the goods and who is injured in person by breach of the warranty. A seller may not exclude or limit the operation of this section.

Alternative B

A seller's warranty whether express or implied extends to any natural person who may reasonably be expected to use, consume or be affected by the goods and who is injured in person by breach of the warranty. A seller may not exclude or limit the operation of this section.

Alternative C

A seller's warranty whether express or implied extends to any person who may reasonably be expected to use, consume or be affected by the goods and who is injured by breach of the warranty. A seller may not exclude or limit the operation of this section with respect to injury to the person of an individual to whom the warranty extends.

New York originally adopted alternative A. In 1975, however, it adopted alternative B (N.Y. U.C.C. Law §2-318 (2023)). If *X* steals a roll from *Y*, who had purchased it from *Z*, should *X* recover from *Z* under the variations of section 2-318 when injured by a piece of sharp metal baked into the roll? Why should the parties, unlike the dealer in *Baxter*, *supra* at 555, be unable to contract out of this provision?

4. *Henningsen: Implied Warranty with a Vengeance.* In Henningsen v. Bloomfield Motors, Inc., 161 A.2d 69 (N.J. 1960), Henningsen purchased a new Plymouth automobile, manufactured by the defendant Chrysler Corporation, from the defendant Bloomfield Motors, Inc. Henningsen gave the car to his wife, after indicating to the dealer his intention to make it a gift. The contract of sale between Mr. Henningsen and the two defendants expressly disclaimed all warranties by the dealer or manufacturer, except one that limited the liability of the defendants to the original purchaser and only then for replacement of defective parts within ninety days or 4,000 miles, whichever occurred first. Shortly after the car was purchased, the plaintiff, Mrs. Henningsen, was driving along a clear road when the steering mechanism suddenly went awry. The car went out of control and veered off the road and into a wall, injuring her. She sued on theories of negligence and warranty. After the trial court dismissed the negligence claim, the jury found for the plaintiff against both defendants on the warranty claim and the defendants appealed. In a very lengthy opinion, Francis, J., examined how the courts had extended the implied warranty of merchantability to individuals who were not party to the original sales agreement, a development he found absolutely necessary as manufacturers increasingly distanced themselves from sales act liability to consumers by a complex web of contracts. He insisted that the limited protection to the plaintiff under this express warranty was a "sad commentary" on the marketing practices of automobile manufacturers.

Although he thought the ordinary warranty of merchantability might technically survive this disclaimer clause, Francis, J., did not rely on any interpretative techniques. Instead he voided the disclaimer clause on the ground that it "was not fairly obtained." It followed that the benefit of the implied warranty ran to the plaintiff, even in the absence of privity, so long as the defendant "puts a new automobile in the stream of trade and promotes its purchase by the public."

A breakthrough for its time, *Henningsen*'s importance appears to have waned somewhat, not because courts have rejected its outcome, but because, ironically, its implied warranty theory tied products liability actions too closely to the law of sales. Modern cases, however, still occasionally allow a jury to find liability under a warranty theory while denying recovery under a tort theory. In Denny v. Ford Motor Co., 662 N.E.2d 730, 736 (N.Y. 1995), the plaintiff was injured when her Ford Bronco, owing to its high center of gravity, rolled over after she slammed on the brakes. The jury found that the vehicle was not "defective" but awarded her $1,200,000 in damages ($2,423,535 in 2023 dollars) on an implied warranty theory. The court rejected Ford's contention that tort had "completely subsumed" warranty theory, noting that the "negligence-like risk/benefit component of the defect element differentiates strict products liability claims from U.C.C.-based breach of implied warranty claims in cases involving design defects."

Can a product without a defect flunk the merchantability test? In Castro v. QVC Network, 139 F.3d 114, 118 (2d Cir. 1998), the plaintiff was badly burned when a twenty-five-pound Thanksgiving turkey fell on her legs and ankles. It caused second- and third-degree burns after it slipped out of a roaster manufactured by defendant U.S.A. T-Fal Corp. and sold by defendant QVC over its home-shopping network. The trial judge refused to offer separate instructions on both strict liability and warranty counts, but after the jury found for the defendants, Calabresi, J., relied on *Denny* to grant a new trial: "The imposition of strict liability for an alleged design 'defect' is determined by a risk-utility standard. The notion of 'defect' in a U.C.C.-based breach of warranty claim focuses, instead, on consumer expectations." Here, according to Calabresi, J., the purpose for which the product was marketed (cooking a large turkey) was different from its designed-for use (cooking low-volume baked goods). Will all "dual-purpose" goods henceforth require separate jury instructions?

What if a product component is unfit for its ordinary purpose? In Nemes v. Dick's Sporting Goods, Inc., 521 F. Supp. 3d 328, 343–44 (S.D.N.Y. 2021), a case about a crossbow with an allegedly-defective finger guard, Roman, J., distinguished *Castro*:

> That holding does not reflect that a product's component parts, e.g., the handle of the pan, define the ordinary purpose of that product. . . . [T]he ordinary purpose of a good is not usually defined by the individual function of an ancillary component. . . . Instead, the implied warranty is breached where the product in question is not fit for the ordinary purpose for which it is to be used.

Is the court's holding sound given that consumers expect product components to serve the functions for which they are designed?

5. *Strict Liability in Torts: The Greenman Reformulation.* Shortly after *Henningsen*, the tort side of products liability also gravitated toward strict liability. In Greenman v. Yuba Power Products, Inc., 377 P.2d 897, 900–01 (Cal. 1963), the plaintiff's wife gave him a Shopsmith combination power tool, manufactured by the defendant, that could be used as a saw, a drill, and a wood lathe. The plaintiff read the manufacturer's brochure, which contained the following statements: "(1) WHEN SHOPSMITH IS IN HORIZONTAL POSITION—Rugged construction of frame provides rigid support from end to end. Heavy centerless-ground steel tubing insures perfect alignment of components. (2) SHOPSMITH maintains its accuracy because every component has positive locks that hold adjustments through rough or precision work." In the course of working the lathe, a piece of wood "suddenly flew out of the machine and struck him on the forehead, inflicting serious injury." There was substantial evidence that the plaintiff's injuries were caused by the defective construction of the Shopsmith, whose set screws were of insufficient strength to hold the wood in place while the lathe was being operated. The plaintiff recovered damages from the manufacturer for negligence and breach of both express and implied warranties.

One of the defendant's contentions on appeal was that the plaintiff's cause of action was barred because he failed to give notice of his injury within a "reasonable time" as required by section 1769 of the California Civil Code. Traynor, J., speaking for the entire court, sidestepped the "intricacies" of the warranty provisions by opting for strict liability in tort:

> A manufacturer is strictly liable in tort when an article he places on the market, knowing that it is to be used without inspection for defects, proves to have a defect that causes injury to a human being. Recognized first in the case of unwholesome food products, such liability has now been extended to a variety of other products that create as great or greater hazards if defective.
>
> Although in these cases strict liability has usually been based on the theory of an express or implied warranty running from the manufacturer to the plaintiff, the abandonment of the requirement of a contract between them, the recognition that the liability is not assumed by agreement but imposed by law, and the refusal to permit the manufacturer to define the scope of its own responsibility for defective products make clear that the liability is not one governed by the law of contract warranties but by the law of strict liability in tort. Accordingly, rules defining and governing warranties that were developed to meet the needs of commercial transactions cannot properly be invoked to govern the manufacturer's liability to those injured by their defective products unless those rules also serve the purposes for which such liability is imposed.
>
> We need not recanvass the reasons for imposing strict liability on the manufacturer. The purpose of such liability is to insure that the costs of injuries resulting from defective products are borne by the manufacturers that put such products on the market rather than by the injured persons who are powerless to protect themselves. Sales warranties serve this purpose fitfully at best. In the present case, for example, plaintiff was able to plead and prove an express warranty only because he read and relied on the representations of the Shopsmith's ruggedness contained in the manufacturer's brochure. Implicit in the machine's presence on the market, however, was a representation that it would safely do the jobs for which it was built. Under these circumstances, it should not be controlling whether plaintiff selected the machine because of the statements in the brochure, or because of the machine's own appearance of excellence that belied the defect lurking beneath the surface, or because he merely assumed that it would safely do the jobs it was built to do. It should not be controlling whether the details of the sales from manufacturer to retailer and from retailer to plaintiff's wife were such that one or more of the implied warranties of the sales act arose. (Civ. Code, §1735.) "The remedies of injured consumers ought not to be made to depend upon the intricacies of the law of sales." To establish the manufacturer's liability it was sufficient that plaintiff proved that he was injured while using the Shopsmith in a way it was intended to be used as a result of a defect in design and manufacture of which plaintiff was not aware that made the Shopsmith unsafe for its intended use.

SECTION C. THE RESTATEMENTS

1. A Tale of Two Texts

RESTATEMENT (SECOND) OF TORTS

§402A. Special Liability of Seller of Product for Physical Harm to User or Consumer

(1) One who sells any product in a defective condition unreasonably dangerous to the user or consumer or to his property is subject to liability for physical harm thereby caused to the ultimate user or consumer, or to his property, if

(a) the seller is engaged in the business of selling such a product, and

(b) it is expected to and does reach the user or consumer without substantial change in the condition in which it is sold.

(2) The rule stated in Subsection (1) applies although

(a) the seller has exercised all possible care in the preparation and sale of his product, and

(b) the user or consumer has not bought the product from or entered into any contractual relation with the seller.

Caveat: The Institute expresses no opinion as to whether the rules stated in this Section may not apply

(1) to harm to persons other than users or consumers

(2) to the seller of a product expected to be processed or otherwise substantially changed before it reaches the user or consumer or

(3) to the seller of a component part of a product to be assembled.

Comment f. Business of Selling: The rule stated in this Section applies to any person engaged in the business of selling products for use or consumption. It therefore applies to any manufacturer of such a product, to any wholesale or retail dealer or distributor, and to the operator of a restaurant. . . .

The rule does not, however, apply to the occasional seller of food or other such products who is not engaged in that activity as a part of his business. Thus it does not apply to the housewife who, on one occasion, sells to her neighbor a jar of jam or a pound of sugar. Nor does it apply to the owner of an automobile who, on one occasion, sells it to his neighbor, or even sells it to a dealer in used cars, and this even though he is fully aware that the dealer plans to resell it. The basis for the rule is the ancient one of the special responsibility for the safety of the public undertaken by one who enters into the business of supplying human beings with products which may endanger the safety of their persons and property, and the forced reliance upon that undertaking on the part of those who purchase such goods. This basis is lacking in the case of the ordinary individual who makes the isolated sale, and he is not liable to a third person, or even to his buyer, in the absence of his negligence. . . .

Comment g. Defective Condition: The rule stated in this Section applies only where the product is, at the time it leaves the seller's hands, in a condition not contemplated by the ultimate consumer, which will be unreasonably dangerous to him. The seller is not liable when he delivers the product in a safe condition, and subsequent mishandling or other causes make it harmful by the time it is consumed. The burden of proof that the product was in a defective condition at the time that it left the hands of the particular seller is upon the injured plaintiff; and unless evidence can be produced which will support the conclusion that it was then defective, the burden is not sustained.

Safe condition at the time of delivery by the seller will, however, include proper packaging, necessary sterilization, and other precautions required to permit the product to remain safe for a normal length of time when handled in a normal manner.

Comment h: A product is not in defective condition when it is safe for normal handling and consumption. If the injury results from abnormal handling, as where a bottled beverage is knocked against a radiator to remove the cap, or from abnormal preparation for use, as where too much salt is added to food, or from abnormal consumption, as where a child eats too much candy and is made ill, the seller is not liable. . . .

The defective condition may arise not only from harmful ingredients, not characteristic of the product itself either as to presence or quantity, but also from foreign objects contained in the product, from decay or deterioration before sale, or from the way in which the product is prepared or packed. No reason is apparent for distinguishing between the product itself and the container in which it is supplied; and the two are purchased by the user or consumer as an integrated whole. Where the container is itself dangerous, the product is sold in a defective condition. Thus a carbonated beverage in a bottle which is so weak, or cracked, or jagged at the edges, or bottled under such excessive pressure that it may explode or otherwise cause harm to the person who handles it, is in a defective and dangerous condition. . . .

Comment i. Unreasonably Dangerous: The rule stated in this Section applies only where the defective condition of the product makes it unreasonably dangerous to the user or consumer. Many products cannot possibly be made entirely safe for all consumption, and any food or drug necessarily involves some risk of harm, if only from over-consumption. Ordinary sugar is a deadly poison to diabetics, and castor oil found use under Mussolini as an instrument of torture. That is not what is meant by "unreasonably dangerous" in this Section. The article sold must be dangerous to an extent beyond that which would be contemplated by the ordinary consumer who purchases it, with the ordinary knowledge common to the community as to its characteristics. Good whiskey is not unreasonably dangerous merely because it will make some people drunk, and is especially dangerous to alcoholics; but bad whiskey, containing a dangerous amount of fusel oil, is unreasonably dangerous. Good tobacco is not unreasonably dangerous merely because the effects of smoking may be harmful; but tobacco containing something like marijuana may be unreasonably dangerous. Good butter is not unreasonably dangerous merely because, if such be the case, it deposits cholesterol in the arteries and leads to heart attacks; but bad butter, contaminated with poisonous fish oil, is unreasonably dangerous.

Comment j. Directions or Warning: In order to prevent the product from being unreasonably dangerous, the seller may be required to give directions or warning, on the container, as to its use. The seller may reasonably assume that those with common allergies, as for example to eggs or strawberries, will be aware of them, and he is not required to warn against them. Where, however, the product contains an ingredient to which a substantial number of the population are allergic, and the ingredient is one whose danger is not generally known, or if known is one which the consumer would reasonably not expect to find in the product, the seller is required to give warning against it, if he has knowledge, or by the application of reasonable, developed human skill and foresight should have knowledge, of the presence of the ingredient and the danger. Likewise in the case of poisonous drugs, or those unduly dangerous for other reasons, warning as to use may be required.

But a seller is not required to warn with respect to products, or ingredients in them, which are only dangerous or potentially so, when consumed in excessive quantity, or over a long period of time, when the danger, or potentiality of danger, is generally known and recognized. Again the dangers of alcoholic beverages are an example, as are also those of foods containing such substances as saturated fats, which may over a period of time have a deleterious effect upon the human heart.

Where warning is given, the seller may reasonably assume that it will be read and heeded; and a product bearing such a warning, which is safe for use if it is followed, is not in defective condition, nor is it unreasonably dangerous.

Comment k. Unavoidably Unsafe Products: There are some products which, in the present state of human knowledge, are quite incapable of being made safe for their intended and ordinary use. These are especially common in the field of drugs. An outstanding example is the vaccine for the Pasteur treatment of rabies, which not uncommonly leads to very serious and damaging consequences when it is injected. Since the disease itself invariably leads to a dreadful death, both the marketing and the use of the vaccine are fully justified, notwithstanding the unavoidable high degree of risk which they involve. Such a product, properly prepared, and accompanied by proper directions and warning, is not defective, nor is it *unreasonably* dangerous. The same is true of many other drugs, vaccines, and the like, many of which for this very reason cannot legally be sold except to physicians, or under the prescription of a physician. It is also true in particular of many new or experimental drugs as to which, because of lack of time and opportunity for sufficient medical experience, there can be no assurance of safety, or perhaps even of purity of ingredients, but such experience as there is justifies the marketing and use of the drug notwithstanding a medically recognizable risk. The seller of such products, again with the qualification that they are properly prepared and marketed, and proper warning is given, where the situation calls for it, is not to be held to strict liability for unfortunate consequences attending their use, merely because he has undertaken to supply the public with an apparently useful and desirable product, attended with a known but apparently reasonable risk.

Comment m. "Warranty": The rule stated in this Section does not require any reliance on the part of the consumer upon the reputation, skill, or judgment of the seller who is to be held liable, nor any representation or undertaking on the part of that seller. The seller is strictly liable although, as is frequently the case, the consumer does not even know who he is at the time of consumption. The rule stated in this Section is not governed by the provisions of the Uniform Sales Act, or those of the Uniform Commercial Code, as to warranties; and it is not affected by limitations on the scope and content of warranties, or by limitation to "buyer" and "seller" in those statutes. Nor is the consumer required to give notice to the seller of his injury within a reasonable time after it occurs, as is provided by the Uniform Act. . . .

Comment n. Contributory Negligence: Since the liability with which this Section deals is not based upon negligence of the seller, but is strict liability, the rule applied to strict liability cases (see §524) applies. Contributory negligence of the plaintiff is not a defense when such negligence consists merely in a failure to discover the defect in the product, or to guard against the possibility of its existence. On the other hand the form of contributory negligence which consists in voluntarily and unreasonably proceeding to encounter a known danger, and commonly passes under the name of assumption of risk, is a defense under this Section as in other cases of strict liability. If the user or consumer discovers the defect and is aware of the danger, and nevertheless proceeds unreasonably to make use of the product and is injured by it, he is barred from recovery.

NOTES

1. ***Second Restatement §402A.*** Until the adoption of the Restatement (Third) of Torts: Products Liability, section 402A and its comments formed the basic text of modern products liability law. At its inception, section 402A was noted for its adoption of a broad strict liability rule for product defects. Its early drafts were originally confined to foodstuffs and products intended for intimate bodily use, but by 1965 the strict liability rule was extended to all products. This broad application made it more difficult to devise a single rule to cover an endless diversity of products, for example, the unique issues raised by pharmaceuticals. Accordingly, Prosser and other drafters of the Second Restatement addressed many difficult questions in the comments to the basic text, which, over time, have become as important as the basic provision itself. Even today, the Third Restatement has not displaced the Second across the board, so it is critical to gain mastery over both. On the adoption of section 402A, see Epstein, Modern Products Liability Law ch. 6 (1980); Priest, The Invention of Enterprise Liability: A Critical History of the Intellectual Foundations of Modern Tort Law, 14 J. Legal Stud. 461, 505–19 (1985).

The Second Restatement also contains section 402B, "Misrepresentation by Seller of Chattels to Consumer," which adopts a strict liability standard for a product seller, proclaiming that one "who, by advertising, labels, or otherwise, makes to the public a misrepresentation of a material fact concerning the character or quality of a chattel sold by him is subject to liability for physical harm to a consumer of the chattel caused by justifiable reliance upon the misrepresentation." Section 402B has been swallowed up in litigation by section 402A. Does it provide a superior basis for liability in *Henningsen*? *Greenman*?

2. ***Bystander's Recovery.*** Current case law has gone beyond the Second Restatement by allowing injured bystanders to sue the original manufacturer. The initial hesitation regarding bystander cases rested in part on the uncertainty of whether any implied warranty or misrepresentation theory could hold the defendant accountable to anyone outside the chain of contracts. The bystander is not lured into using the product by the defendant's representations. Neither is she an immediate or ultimate beneficiary of any seller or manufacturer warranty. The bystander's case for strict liability in tort is far stronger: As with abnormally dangerous activities, the bystander has been hurt by a process that was in no sense her making because she never used the product at all. Though in practice bystander injuries are relatively infrequent compared to the numerous injuries to product consumers or users, today the liability of the manufacturer or seller to the bystander is universally allowed. See, e.g., Elmore v. Am. Motors Corp., 451 P.2d 84 (Cal. 1969); Codling v. Paglia, 298 N.E.2d 622 (N.Y. 1973); Noel, Defective Products: Extension of Strict Liability to Bystanders, 38 Tenn. L. Rev. 1 (1970).

RESTATEMENT (THIRD) OF TORTS: PRODUCTS LIABILITY

§1. Liability of Commercial Seller or Distributor for Harm Caused by Defective Products

One engaged in the business of selling or otherwise distributing products who sells or distributes a defective product is subject to liability for harm to persons or property caused by the defect.

§2. Categories of Product Defects

[For purposes of determining liability under section 1:]

A product is defective when, at the time of sale or distribution, it contains a manufacturing defect, is defective in design, or is defective because of inadequate instructions or warnings. A product:

(a) contains a manufacturing defect when the product departs from its intended design even though all possible care was exercised in the preparation and marketing of the product;

(b) is defective in design when the foreseeable risks of harm posed by the product could have been reduced or avoided by the adoption of a reasonable alternative design by the seller or other distributor, or a predecessor in the commercial chain of distribution, and the omission of the alternative design renders the product not reasonably safe;

(c) is defective because of inadequate instructions or warnings when the foreseeable risks of harm posed by the product could have been reduced or avoided by the provision of reasonable instructions or warnings by the seller or other distributor, or a predecessor in the commercial chain of distribution, and the omission of the instructions or warnings renders the product not reasonably safe.

NOTES

1. ***Into the Next Generation.*** The Third Restatement reflects the transformation of products liability law after 1965. Most significantly, it adopts the now dominant tripartite classification of manufacturing, design, and warning defects, and establishes a distinct liability rule for each class. It keeps the original strict liability rule for products with manufacturing defects but imposes only the more limited obligation to make product designs, warnings, and instructions "reasonably safe." Although the Third Restatement rejects RST §402A's caveat on bystander liability, many of the old rules still carry over, such as the exclusion of "casual sellers." See RTT: PL §1, comment *c.* Subsequent provisions of the Third Restatement examine each class of defects, and contain additional provisions to deal with prescription drugs, issues of causation, and affirmative defenses. For an early discussion of the revisions of the Second Restatement, by the joint reporters for the Third Restatement, see Henderson & Twerski, A Proposed Revision of Section 402A of the Restatement (Second) of Torts, 77 Cornell L. Rev. 1512 (1992). For an acceptance of the Third Restatement over the Second, see Evans v. Lorillard Tobacco Co., 990 N.E.2d 997, 1013–14 (Mass. 2013); for a continued preference for the Second Restatement over the Third, see Tincher v. Omega Flex, Inc., 104 A.3d 328, 335 (Pa. 2014), *infra* at 596.

2. ***Who Chooses to Adopt the Third Restatement?*** The Pennsylvania Supreme Court in *Tincher* wrestled with whether the courts, rather than the legislature, should play an active role in deciding whether to adopt the Third Restatement. While the court in *Tincher* believed this decision should be left to the democratically elected General Assembly, is it ever justified to leave this decision to the courts?

2. The Theory of Products Liability: Tort or Contract

The early history of products liability law reveals a consistent tension between the contract-based theory of implied warranty and the tort theory sounding either in negligence or strict liability. The adoption of the Second Restatement in 1965 largely endorsed the tort theory for personal injuries, while the treatment of damage to property remained less clear, as the Second Restatement intimated that matters of "economic loss" were best left to voluntary agreement between the parties. But how are those losses defined? Everyone agrees that disappointed expectations about product performance are outside section 402A, as when a truck constantly stalls out on the highway, causing its owner to make late deliveries. But do these losses also cover economic losses that flow from physical damage to the product sold? The following materials explore the difficulties that arise in policing the line between products liability and contract law respectively.

Casa Clara Condominium Association, Inc. v. Charley Toppino & Sons, Inc.

620 So. 2d 1244 (Fla. 1993)

McDonald, J. . . . The issue is whether a homeowner can recover for purely economic losses from a concrete supplier under a negligence theory. We agree with the district court that such a recovery cannot be had. . . .

Charley Toppino & Sons, Inc., a dissolved corporation, supplied concrete for numerous construction projects in Monroe County. Apparently, some of the concrete supplied by Toppino contained a high content of salt that caused the reinforcing steel inserted in the concrete to rust, which, in turn, caused the concrete to crack and break off. The petitioners own condominium units and single-family homes built with, and now allegedly damaged by, Toppino's concrete. In separate actions the homeowners sued numerous defendants and included claims against Toppino for breach of common law implied warranty, products liability, negligence, and violation of the building code. The circuit court dismissed all counts against Toppino in each case. On appeal the district court applied the economic loss rule and held that, because no person was injured and no other property damaged, the homeowners had no cause of action against Toppino in tort. The district court also held that Toppino, a supplier, had no duty to comply with the building code.

Plaintiffs find a tort remedy attractive because it often permits the recovery of greater damages than an action on a contract and may avoid the conditions of a contract. The distinction between "tort recovery for physical injuries and warranty recovery for economic loss" rests

> on an understanding of the nature of the responsibility a manufacturer must undertake in distributing his products. He can appropriately be held liable for physical injuries caused by defects by requiring his goods to match a standard of safety defined in terms of conditions that create unreasonable risks of harm. *He cannot be held liable for the level of performance of his products in the consumer's business unless he agrees that the product was designed to meet the consumer's demands.*

Seely v. White Motor Co., 403 P.2d 145, 151 (Cal. 1965) (emphasis supplied). An individual consumer, on the other hand,

> should not be charged at the will of the manufacturer with bearing the risk of physical injury when he buys a product on the market. He can, however, be fairly charged with the risk that the product will not match his economic expectations unless the manufacturer agrees that it will.

Id. Seely sets out the economic loss rule, which prohibits tort recovery when a product damages itself, causing economic loss, but does not cause personal injury or damage to any property other than itself. E.g., East River Steamship Corp. v. Transamerica Delaval, Inc., 476 U.S. 858 (1986). . . .

Casa Clara Condominiums in Key Colony Beach, Florida

Source: Google Maps

Economic loss has been defined as "damages for inadequate value, costs of repair and replacement of the defective product, or consequent loss of profits—without any claim of personal injury or damage to other property." Note, Economic Loss in Products Liability Jurisprudence, 66 Colum. L. Rev. 917, 918 (1966). It includes "the diminution in the value of the product because it is inferior in quality and does not work for the general purposes for which it was manufactured and sold." Comment, Manufacturers' Liability to Remote Purchasers for "Economic Loss" Damages—Tort or Contract?, 114 U. Pa. L. Rev. 539, 541 (1966). In other words, economic losses are "disappointed economic expectations," which are protected by contract law, rather than tort law. This is the basic difference between contract law, which protects expectations, and tort law, which is determined by the duty owed to an injured party. For recovery in tort "there must be a showing of harm above and beyond disappointed expectations. A buyer's desire to enjoy the benefit of his bargain is not an interest that tort law traditionally protects." Redarowicz v. Ohlendorf, 441 N.E.2d 324, 327 (Ill. 1982).

The homeowners are seeking purely economic damages—no one has sustained any physical injuries and no property, other than the structures built with Toppino's concrete, has sustained any damage. They argue that holding them to contract remedies is unfair and that homeowners in general should be excepted from the operation of the economic loss rule. We disagree.

In tort a manufacturer or producer of goods "is liable whether or not it is negligent because 'public policy demands that responsibility be fixed wherever it will most effectively reduce the hazards to life and health inherent in defective products that reach the market.'" *East River*, 476 U.S. at 866 (quoting Escola v. Coca Cola Bottling Co. (Traynor, J., concurring)). . . . The purpose of a duty in tort is to protect society's interest in being free from harm, and the cost of protecting society from harm is borne by society in general. Contractual duties, on the other hand, come from society's interest in the performance of promises. When only economic harm is involved, the question becomes "whether the consuming public as a whole should bear the cost of economic losses sustained by those who failed to bargain for adequate contract remedies."

We are urged to make an exception to the economic loss doctrine for homeowners. Buying a house is the largest investment many consumers ever make, and homeowners are an appealing, sympathetic class. If a house causes economic disappointment by not meeting a purchaser's expectations, the resulting failure to receive the benefit of the bargain is a core concern of contract, not tort, law. There are protections for homebuyers, however, such as statutory warranties, the general warranty of habitability, and the duty of sellers to disclose defects, as well as the ability of purchasers to inspect houses for defects. Coupled with homebuyers' power to bargain over price, these protections must be viewed as sufficient when compared with the mischief that could be caused by allowing tort recovery for purely economic losses. Therefore, we again "hold contract principles more appropriate than tort principles for recovering economic loss without an accompanying physical injury or property damage." *Florida Power & Light*, 510 So. 2d at 902. If we held otherwise, "contract law would drown in a sea of tort." *East River*. We refuse to hold that homeowners are not subject to the economic loss rule.

The homeowners also argue that Toppino's concrete damaged "other" property because the individual components and items of building material, not the homes themselves, are the products they purchased. We disagree. The character of a loss determines the appropriate remedies, and, to determine the character of a loss, one must look to the product purchased by the plaintiff, not the product sold by the defendant. Generally, house buyers have little or no interest in how or where the individual components of a house are obtained. They are content to let the builder produce the finished product, i.e., a house. These homeowners bought finished products—dwellings—not the individual components of those dwellings. They bargained for the finished products, not their various components. The concrete became an integral part of the finished product and, thus, did not injure "other" property.

We also disagree with the homeowners that the mere possibility that the exploding concrete will cause physical injury is sufficient reason to abrogate the economic loss rule. This argument goes completely against the principle that injury must occur before a negligence action exists. Because an injury has not occurred, its extent and the identity of injured persons is completely speculative. Thus, the degree of risk is indeterminate, with no guarantee that damages will be reasonably related to the risk of injury, and with no possibility for the producer of a product to structure its business behavior to cover that risk. Agreeing with the homeowners' argument would make it difficult "to maintain a realistic limitation on damages." *East River*.

[Affirmed.]

Barkett, C.J., concurring in part, dissenting in part.

If the allegations of the homeowners in this case are true, their homes are literally crumbling around them because the concrete supplied by Toppino was negligently manufactured. The homeowners assert that the concrete is now cracking and breaking apart and poses a danger of serious injury. The courts, including this one, have said "too bad."

I find that answer unacceptable in light of the principle underlying Florida's access to courts provision: that absent compelling, countervailing public policies, wrongs must have remedies. Art. I, §21, Fla. Const. I understand and accept that sometimes the remedies provided cannot be in the full measure that pure justice unfettered by pragmatism can provide. Thus, some applications of the economic loss doctrine may have acceptable viability. But surely it stretches reason to apply the doctrine in this context to deny these homeowners any remedy.

Their claim for breach of implied warranty has been denied (they lack privity with Toppino); their claim that Toppino violated the Florida Building Codes Act has been denied (Toppino, as a material supplier, is not governed by the Standard Building Code); and now their claim in tort has been denied because, notwithstanding their alleged ability to prove that their houses are falling down around them, they have not suffered any damage to their property on the basis that homes are "products."

A key premise underlying the economic loss rule is that parties in a business context have the ability to allocate economic risks and remedies as part of their contractual negotiations. That premise does not exist here. Moreover, I cannot subscribe to the majority's view that the defective concrete has not damaged "other property" in the form of the houses' individual components. . . .

Shaw, J., concurring and dissenting . . .

While I agree with the majority opinion that parties who have freely bargained and entered a contract relative to a particular subject matter should be bound by the terms of that contract including the distribution of loss, I feel that the theory is stretched when it is used to deny a cause of action to an innocent third party who the defendant knew or should have known would be injured by the tortious conduct. Toppino knew that the concrete that was the subject matter of the bargain between Toppino and the general contractor would be incorporated into homes that would be bought and occupied by innocent third parties.

When the concrete proved to be contaminated, damages were not limited to simply the loss of concrete; innocent third parties suffered various degrees of damage to structures using the concrete. In my mind, the economic loss theory was never intended to defeat a tort cause of action that would otherwise lie for damages caused to a third party by a defective product.

NOTES

1. ***Tort or Contract: The Minority View and Intermediate Approaches.*** The economic loss rule in *Casa Clara* represents the majority position in the United States, and controls in admiralty cases as well. Thus in East River Steamship Corp. v. Transamerica Delaval, Inc., 476 U.S. 858 (1986), the Supreme Court refused to allow a tort action against the manufacturer of turbine engines that malfunctioned once installed into oil-transporting supertankers.

Casa Clara poses a provocative question: Why should the logic of contract apply only to economic losses but not personal injury or property damage? If contractual solutions bind parties for economic losses of $1,000,000, why do they break down for physical damage worth $1,000? Does it make a difference if the transactions are between merchants? With consumers? Conversely, if the bargaining impediments for physical damage justify overriding disclaimers for liability for physical injury, then why not for economic loss? Peters, J., dissenting in *Seely*, 403 P.2d at 153–54, so argued:

> Given the rationale of Greenman v. Yuba Power Products, Inc., it cannot properly be held that plaintiff may not recover the value of his truck and his lost profits on the basis of strict liability. The nature of the damage sustained by the plaintiff is immaterial, so long as it proximately flowed from the defect. What *is* important is not the nature of the damage but the relative roles played by the parties to the purchase contract and the nature of their transaction. . . .
>
> In *Greenman* we allowed recovery for "personal injury" damages. It is well established that such an award may include compensation for past loss of time and earnings due to the injury, for loss of future earning capacity, and for increased living expenses caused by the injury. There is no logical distinction between these losses and the losses suffered by plaintiff here. All involve economic loss, and all proximately arise out of the purchase of a defective product. I find it hard to understand how one might, for example, award a traveling salesman lost earnings if a defect in his car causes his *leg* to break in an accident but deny that salesman his lost earnings if the defect instead disables only his *car* before any accident occurs. The losses are exactly the same; the chains of causation are slightly different, but both are "proximate." Yet the majority would allow recovery under strict liability in the first situation but not in the second. This, I submit, is arbitrary.

The Third Restatement follows *Casa Clara*. Section 1 limits the scope of the Restatement to "harms to persons or property," which are defined in section 21 to include only "the plaintiff's property other than the defective product itself." See RTT: PL §21(a). In Saratoga Fishing Co. v. J.M. Martinac & Co., 520 U.S. 875, 877 (1997), the Supreme Court treated the loss of "extra equipment (a skiff, a fishing net, spare parts) added by the initial user after the first sale and then resold as part of the ship" as "other property" for which a tort action was appropriate. Justice Breyer argued that the contractual remedy was ineffective in the context of resale after initial use "because, as other courts have suggested, the Subsequent User does not contract directly with the Manufacturer (or distributor)."

RESTATEMENT OF THE LAW (THIRD) OF TORTS: PRODUCTS LIABILITY

§21. Definition of "Harm to Persons or Property": Recovery for Economic Loss

For purposes of this Restatement, harm to persons or property includes economic loss if caused by harm to: . . .

(c) the plaintiff's property other than the defective product itself.

Comment a. Rationale: . . . Some categories of loss, including those often referred to as "pure economic loss," are more appropriately assigned to contract law and the remedies set forth in Articles 2 and 2A of the Uniform Commercial Code. When the Code governs a claim, its provisions regarding such issues as statutes of limitation, privity, notice of claim, and disclaimer ordinarily govern the litigation.

Casa Clara represents the high-water mark of the economic loss rule. Subsequent cases have widened the exceptions to the economic loss rule, thereby extending the role of tort law. In Florida, the scope of the rule was explicitly limited to products liability cases in Tiara Condominium Association v. Marsh & McLennan Co., 110 So. 3d 399 (Fla. 2013), in which the court held that Tiara could maintain a suit for negligence seeking purely economic losses against its insurance broker, Marsh, which had procured for it a windstorm coverage contract of $50 million. Marsh had assured Tiara that the $50 million limit was per occurrence, but the insurer, Citizens Property, had claimed that the policy contained a single aggregate limit that covered the damages suffered from both Hurricanes Frances and Jeanne in 2004. Is there any reason why freedom of contract should not apply when the two parties are in privity? Why it should be disregarded when, as in *Casa Clara*, the injured party has an explicit contract with the condominium developer?

2. ***Tort or Warranty: The Statute of Limitations.*** Claims for breach of warranty are subject to the statute of limitations of U.C.C. §2-725, which runs four years from the date of sale. In contrast, the tort statute of limitations may run much longer, starting at the earliest from the date of the injury and in most jurisdictions only from the date at which the plaintiff has discovered, or through the exercise of reasonable diligence could have discovered, that injury. Today, the tort rule trumps the U.C.C. In Victorson v. Bock Laundry Machine Co., 335 N.E.2d 275, 279 (N.Y. 1975), the court opted for the tort approach on the ground that "it is all but unthinkable that a person should be time-barred from prosecuting a cause of action before he ever had one."

> One can observe that while passage of time may work a deterioration of the manufacturer's capability to defend, by similar token it can be expected to complicate the plaintiff's problem of proving, as he must, that the alleged defect existed at the time the product left the manufacturer's plant. In any event this consideration, of varying weight from case to case, cannot be accorded such significance as to dictate the outcome.

The concern with long-lived products that cause damage years after their initial sale has led many states to adopt so-called statutes of repose. Ohio Rev. Code §2305.10 bars all products liability suits for injuries sustained more than ten years after the seller delivers it to its first purchaser. The court in Groch v. General Motors Co., 883 N.E.2d 377, 402 (Ohio 2008), sustained this provision against various constitutional challenges by holding that "[i]t is not this court's role to establish legislative policies or to second-guess the General Assembly's policy choices." A majority of the courts with statutes of repose follow the Ohio approach.

3. ***Limitations on Damages in Express Warranties.*** In Collins v. Uniroyal, Inc., 315 A.2d 16 (N.J. 1974), the defendant tire company sold its Royal Master Tire with a guarantee against "blowouts, cuts, bruises, and similar injury rendering the tire unserviceable," covering the tires as long as they were not "punctured or abused." The guarantee went on to exclude, in italics, all liability for "consequential damage," obligating the tire company only to repair or replace the tire. The decedent was killed in an unexplained tire blowout, and the plaintiff's tort recovery was blocked by the inability to identify any tire defect. The court, however, allowed the plaintiff to sue for full damages on the broad warranty coverage and denied defendant the benefit of the limitation of liability contained in the italicized clause.

The court relied in part upon U.C.C. §2-719, which provides: "Consequential damages may be limited or excluded unless the limitation or exclusion is unconscionable. Limitation of consequential damages for injury to the person in the case of consumer goods is prima facie unconscionable, but limitation of damages where the loss is commercial is not." What is the force of the words "prima facie unconscionable"? Should the presumption be overridden here given that Uniroyal had no obligation to provide any comprehensive guarantee for its product at all? For criticism of *Collins* and of the general unconscionability doctrine, see Epstein, Unconscionability: A Critical Reappraisal, 18 J.L. & Econ. 293 (1975).

3. Proper Defendants Under Section 402A

Second Restatement §402A only applies to sellers who are "engaged in the business of selling . . . a product."

Loomis v. Amazon.com LLC

277 Cal. Rptr. 3d 769 (Ct. App. 2021)

Ohta, J. Kisha Loomis brought suit against Amazon.com LLC (Amazon) for injuries she suffered from an allegedly defective hoverboard. The hoverboard was sold by a third party seller named TurnUpUp through the Amazon website. The trial court granted summary judgment in favor of Amazon. The primary issue on appeal is whether Amazon may be held strictly liable for Loomis's injuries from the defective product. . . . We reverse and remand with directions.

Facts

Loomis ordered a hoverboard on Amazon's website on November 28, 2015. The listing identified the seller to be TurnUpUp, a name used by SMILETO to sell its products on Amazon's marketplace. SMILETO is allegedly a company based in China. . . . Loomis gifted the hoverboard to her son. On New Year's Eve, he plugged it into an outlet in Loomis's bedroom to charge. Loomis's boyfriend later discovered a fire burning in her bedroom. Her bed and the hoverboard were on fire. Loomis suffered burns to her hand and foot as a result of fighting the fire. . . .

Amazon.com is an online marketplace where Amazon and third party sellers list their products for sale. Amazon describes its marketplace as "an online mall" which provides an "online storefront" to third party sellers. Where Amazon is the seller of a product, it is identified as the seller on the product detail page, and it sources the product, sets the price, and holds title to it. This case does not involve an Amazon-listed product. Where a third party is the seller, it is identified as such on the product detail page and again on the order confirmation page before the user places the order. The third party sources the product, sets the price, and holds title to it.

All third party sellers operate under the Amazon services business solutions agreement (BSA). . . .

Analysis

Vertical Chain of Distribution

As technology advances, innovation is paving the way to new business practices. Amazon is on the leading edge of e-commerce. Based on our review of Amazon's third party business model under the BSA, we are persuaded that Amazon's own business practices make it a direct link in the vertical chain of distribution under California's strict liability doctrine.

Contrary to Amazon's assertion that it merely provided an online storefront for TurnUpUp and others to sell their wares, it is undisputed Amazon placed itself squarely between TurnUpUp, the seller, and Loomis, the buyer, in the transaction at issue. When Loomis wanted to buy a hoverboard for her son, she perused product listings on Amazon's website. Amazon took Loomis's order and processed her payment. It then transmitted the order to TurnUpUp, who packaged and shipped the product to Loomis. . . . TurnUpUp was not allowed to communicate with Loomis directly. If Loomis had wanted to return the hoverboard, the return would have been routed through Amazon.

Amazon remitted Loomis's payment to TurnUpUp after deducting its fees, including a 15 percent referral fee based on the total sale price. These facts undermine Amazon's characterization of its marketplace as an online mall providing online storefronts for sellers. Owners of malls typically do not serve as conduits for payment and communication in each transaction between a buyer and a seller. Moreover, they do not typically charge a per-item fee rather than a fixed amount to rent their storefronts. Instead, these actions—(1) interacting with the customer, (2) taking the order, (3) processing the order to the third party seller, (4) collecting the money, and (5) being paid a percentage of the sale—are consistent with a retailer or a distributor of consumer goods.

Stream of Commerce Approach

Although we conclude Amazon is a link in the vertical chain of distribution, we nevertheless recognize e-commerce may not neatly fit into a traditional sales structure. The stream of commerce approach or market enterprise theory offers an alternative basis for strict liability. . . . [A] defendant may be strictly liable under the stream of commerce approach if:

(1) the defendant received a direct financial benefit from its activities and from the sale of the product;
(2) the defendant's role was integral to the business enterprise such that the defendant's conduct was a necessary factor in bringing the product to the initial consumer market; and
(3) the defendant had control over, or a substantial ability to influence, the manufacturing or distribution process.

[The court then holds that the 15 percent referral fee satisfied the first condition; it holds that the second issue was triable because "it has presented no evidence of its role in bringing TurnUpUp's hoverboards to market." It then holds that the third factor was satisfied because Amazon could exert influence over the process thanks to its "ability to require safety certification, indemnification, and insurance before it agrees to list any product."]

Policy Considerations Underlying the Doctrine Are Furthered by Imposing Strict Products Liability in This Case

In analyzing whether strict liability is appropriate in new circumstances, courts assess whether relevant public policy goals are furthered by its application. . . . [T]he relevant public policy considerations are:

(1) Whether Amazon may play a substantial part in insuring that the product is safe or may be in a position to exert pressure on the manufacturer to that end;
(2) Whether Amazon may be the only member in the distribution chain reasonably available to the injured plaintiff; and
(3) Whether Amazon is in a position to adjust the costs of compensating the injured plaintiff amongst various members in the distribution chain.

We address each in turn.

[Ohta, J., holds that the limited steps that Amazon could take satisfied the first test, and predicts that a strict liability rule will encourage Amazon to "expand its safety compliance requirement, and to use its "gatekeeper" rule to pressure upstream suppliers to take additional precautions.]

As to consumer compensation, Amazon may be the only member of the distribution chain reasonably available for an injured consumer to recover damages. Amazon contends there is no evidence to show how frequently an injured plaintiff is truly left without recourse. The record shows, however, that Forrinx, the only other defendant in this matter, failed to appear and a default was taken against it. . . .

As to loss spreading, Amazon can adjust the costs of consumer protection between it and third party sellers through its fees, indemnity requirements, and insurance. . . .

Accordingly, we hold the application of strict liability to Amazon's third party seller business model is supported by the relevant public policy considerations[.]

Wiley, J., concurring. [W]e have an easy case that beautifully illustrates the deep structure of modern tort law: a judicial quest to minimize the social costs of accidents—that is, the sum of the cost of accidents and the cost of avoiding accidents. Judges have been applying this social cost-benefit analysis as a felt instinct for a long time. . . . That deep structure makes this case simple to decide. When efforts to minimize accident costs are relatively inexpensive and apt to be effective, courts impose tort duties. Amazon has cost-effective options for minimizing accident costs. Amazon therefore has a duty in strict liability to the buyers from its site, including Kisha Loomis. . . .

Amazon's options are practical and cost-effective; indeed, Amazon says it is *already* taking these actions. Amazon thus must face strict liability for Loomis's fiery encounter with the hoverboard she bought from Amazon's site. Imposing this duty on Amazon creates financial incentives that back up Amazon's good words about its concern for customer safety.

Some suggest considerations of moral justice can compete with tort law's calculus of social benefit. . . . If they ever do, moral justice and cost-benefit analyses do not conflict in this case.

NOTES

1. *Online Platforms: The Fifth Stage of Products Liability?* Sharkey, Products Liability in the Digital Age: Online Platforms as "Cheapest Cost Avoiders," 73 Hastings L.J. 1327 (2022), heralds the arrival of a new stage of products liability in the digital age. Moreover, *Loomis* fits the pattern that, at each new juncture,

> judges have relied explicitly on deterrence, or prevention of harm, rationales to address new forms of risks and prevent them from materializing into harms. This is no less true as we enter a new stage of digital e-commerce risks faced by society in the 21st century.

Sharkey, The Irresistible Simplicity of Preventing Harm, 16 J. Tort L. 143, 151 (2023). Twerski & Janger, The Heavy Hand of Amazon: A Seller Not a Neutral Platform, 14 Brook. J. Corp. Fin. & Com. L. 259, 267 (2020), likewise prods courts to recognize how "Amazon itself controls access to the site, the manner in which the items are displayed, and receives compensation at every stage. In fact, except for the formality of title, the level of integration in Amazon's supply chain is comparable to that of a standard brick-and-mortar seller."

Whereas *Loomis* relied on the common law evolution of products liability in California, other jurisdictions have declined to find liability under their respective product liability statutes. E.g., Amazon.com, Inc. v. McMillan, 625 S.W.3d 101 (Tex. 2021); Stiner v. Amazon.com, Inc., 164 N.E.3d 394 (Ohio 2020). Given the volume and diversity of merchant offerings, is Amazon in the best position to eliminate the unsafe character of products in the first instance? Would adding a vetting process for merchants hinder the business prospects of new or small merchants? What about requiring foreign sellers to designate domestic parties who could then bear liability?

2. *Liability of Retailers and Distributors.* Products liability law has long applied uniformly to all ordinary product retailers and distributors in the initial chain of distribution. Traynor, J., made this case in Vandermark v. Ford Motor Co., 391 P.2d 168, 171–72 (Cal. 1964), holding an automobile dealer strictly liable for product defects:

> Retailers like manufacturers are engaged in the business of distributing goods to the public. They are an integral part of the overall producing and marketing enterprise that should bear the cost of injuries resulting from defective products. In some cases the retailer may be the only member of that enterprise reasonably available to the injured plaintiff. In other cases the retailer himself may play a substantial part in insuring that the product is safe or may be in a position

> to exert pressure on the manufacturer to that end; the retailer's strict liability thus serves as an added incentive to safety. Strict liability on the manufacturer and retailer alike affords maximum protection to the injured plaintiff and works no injustice to the defendants, for they can adjust the costs of such protection between them in the course of their continuing business relationship.

Does *Vandermark* require liability in *Loomis*?

The Third Restatement follows the Second, as product sellers include "nonmanufacturing sellers and distributors such as wholesalers and retailers," RTT: PL §1, comment *e*, even when they act as mere conduits that do nothing to make the products dangerous. In addition, section 20, comment *f*, treats commercial lessors and bailors as product sellers, such that a dealer will be held to the same rules when he allows a test drive as when he sells a car. Section 2, comment *o*, acknowledges that nonmanufacturing sellers "often are not in a good position feasibly to adopt safer product designs or better instructions or warnings." But it reiterates that nonmanufacturing sellers are nonetheless subject to the same standards applicable to manufacturers: "As long as the plaintiff establishes that the product was defective when it left the hands of a given seller in the distributive chain, liability will attach to that seller." §2, comment *c*. Should a retailer be liable if it has no control over the manufacture, design, or warnings associated with a given product? What might the safety implications be?

In Defries v. Yamaha Motor Corp., 300 Cal. Rptr. 3d 670, 678 (Ct. App. 2022), Raphael, J., over a strong dissent, extended *Vandermark* and section 2, comment *c*, to hold that an upstream distributor "had a nondelegable duty to deliver a dirt bike to [the plaintiff] free from dangerous defects, regardless of whether those defects were caused by . . . one of [its] dealers in the final assembly." How is a distributor of partially unassembled products to monitor the quality of a downstream dealer's assembly? Is there an indemnity over?

Some cases have imposed liability on parties involved in only a fraction of the production cycle. In Sprung v. MTR Ravensburg, Inc., 788 N.E.2d 620, 623 (N.Y. 2003), Kaye, J., applied a strict liability regime to a custom fabricator for General Motors, arguing:

> Like other manufacturers, custom fabricators engaged in the regular course of their business hold themselves out as having expertise in manufacturing their custom products, have the opportunity and incentive to ensure safety in the process of making those products, and are better able to shoulder the costs of injuries caused by defective products than injured consumers or users.

Feinman, J., followed suit in Matter of Eighth Jud. Dist. Asbestos Litig., 129 N.E.3d 891 (N.Y. 2019), holding that the manufacture of a coke oven that was custom-fabricated for a steel plant had a duty to warn. Who was in the better position to warn end users about asbestos dangers? Does it matter that tort claims against employers are often precluded by workers' compensation schemes?

3. *Sales Versus Services.* Inevitably questions arise about whether a particular seller is providing a product or a service. One concern is that the broad definition of a seller in products liability cases could allow its strict liability rules to spill over into areas that have traditionally been governed under negligence law. In Cafazzo v. Central Medical Health Services, Inc., 668 A.2d 521, 525, 526, 527 (Pa. 1995), that concern led Montemuro, J., to reject an attempt to hold a hospital and physician strictly liable for the defects in a mandibular prosthesis used during an operation. Montemuro, J., held that supplying the product was "ancillary" to the provision of medical services, even if there happened to be a surcharge on the medical product:

> [I]t must be noted that the "seller" need not be engaged solely in the business of selling products such as the defective one to be held strictly liable. An example supporting this proposition appears in comment *f* of the Restatement (Second) of Torts, §402A and concerns the owner of a

> motion picture theater who offers edibles such as popcorn and candy for sale to movie patrons. The analogue to the instant case is valid in one respect only: both the candy and the . . . implant are ancillary to the primary activity, viewing a film or undergoing surgery respectively. However, beyond that any comparison is specious. A movie audience is free to purchase or not any food items on offer, and regardless of which option is exercised the primary activity is unaffected. On the other hand, while the implant was incidental to the surgical procedure here, it was a necessary adjunct to the treatment administered, as were the scalpel used to make the incision, and any other material objects involved in performing the operation, all of which fulfill a particular role in provision of medical service, the primary activity.

Montemuro, J., reasoned that strict liability would not provide an incentive for hospitals and doctors to choose different services, as they rely on the FDA's stamp of approval. He warned against allowing the "selection of the wrong product [to] become[] a matter of professional negligence for which recovery is available." Nor did he think strict liability was needed to compensate the injured party, finding that the "net effect of this cost spreading would further endanger the already beleaguered health care system."

The Third Restatement follows the Second by holding that "[s]ervices, even when provided commercially, are not products," RTT: PL §19(b), including those services to inspect, repair, and maintain machinery of the original product seller. A replacement part therefore is subject to products liability, but its installation is not.

4. *Information as a Product.* Does products liability law apply to information? The Third Restatement defines products as "tangible personal property distributed commercially for use or consumption." RTT: PL §19. The Restatement generally excludes intangible property like information contained in books or media due to free speech concerns: "Most courts, expressing concern that imposing strict liability for the dissemination of false and defective information would significantly impinge on free speech have, appropriately, refused to impose strict products liability in these cases." This reluctance to extend liability to intangible products presents new complications in our increasingly digital world. Consumers engage with intangible products like computer software and smartphone apps constantly, raising questions as to whether the owners of these platforms can be held liable for the information disseminated through them.

Section 230(c)(1) of the Communications Decency Act of 1996 (CDA) has been broadly construed to immunize online companies from liability arising from third-party information content. Its text reads: "No provider or user of an interactive computer service shall be treated as the publisher or speaker of any information provided by another information content provider." 47 U.S.C. §230(c)(1). If these providers can't be held liable for the content on their platforms, can they be held liable under a products liability theory for the algorithms that bring content to consumers' attention?

In Twitter v. Taamneh, 143 S. Ct. 1206 (2023), plaintiffs sued Twitter for damages under the Antiterrorism Act, 18 U.S.C. §2333, alleging, inter alia, that its recommendation algorithms helped ISIS recruit members, which contributed to a terrorist attack that harmed plaintiffs. A unanimous Supreme Court held that plaintiffs failed to state a claim for aiding and abetting as required under the statute. In Gonzalez v. Google, 143 S. Ct. 1191 (2023), a parallel case, the Court heard arguments challenging the Ninth Circuit's determination that CDA §230 barred similar claims against Google, regardless of whether liability could be found under the Antiterrorism Act. The Court punted on this question, remanding the case in light of *Taamneh* given that, without liability under the Antiterrorism Act, plaintiff stated no independent claim for relief. *Gonzalez* thus left for a further day resolution of the scope of CDA §230 immunity in the context of algorithms. What result if plaintiffs cast their claim as a product liability theory?

In Maynard v. Snapchat, Inc., 870 S.E.2d 739, 743 (Ga. 2022), the plaintiff sued Snapchat after being rear-ended by a car going 107 miles per hour, driven by a Snapchat user who told her passengers prior to the accident that she was " 'just trying to get the car to 100 m.p.h. to post it on Snapchat' using Snapchat's Speed Filter." Colvin, J., held:

> [T]he Maynards asserted a conventional design-defect claim based on the ordinary design duty recognized under our decisional law. . . . [They] alleged that . . . Snap knew that other drivers were using the Speed Filter while speeding at 100 miles per hour or more as part of "a game," purposefully designed its products to encourage such behavior, [and] knew of at least one other instance in which a driver who was using Snapchat while speeding caused a car crash. . . .

What result in *Maynard* if the Speed Filter had been designed by another user?

The court in a recent multidistrict litigation crafted a test to determine when platforms are subject to products liability. In re Soc. Media Adolescent Addiction, No. 4:22-MD-3047, 2023 WL 7524912 (N.D. Cal. Mar. 10, 2023). Evaluating whether specific "functionalities" of platforms are analogous to physical products, Rogers, J., allowed design defect claims for platforms' omissions of parental and screen-time controls, among others, to survive a motion to dismiss.

5. *Used and Reconditioned Products.* How does products liability law apply to the sale of used or reconditioned products? In Tillman v. Vance Equipment Co., 596 P.2d 1299, 1303–04 (Or. 1979), the court refused to apply the strict liability rule of section 402A to a defendant who sold a good on an "as is" basis, noting that "it would work a significant change in the very nature of used goods markets"; parties who want warranties typically bargain for them.

Roughly speaking, the Third Restatement (see RTT: PL §8) follows cases like *Tillman* by limiting liability of the seller of used products to those defects that it created, or those created by predecessors in the same commercial chain of distribution. The Third Restatement also requires the reseller of used products to comply with all applicable regulations in force at the time of resale. *Id.* §8(d). In some states, legislation addresses the issue. See, e.g., Kan. Stat. Ann. §60-3306(b)(3) (2023), which explicitly offers sellers of used products protection against liability in a products liability claim when "the product was sold in substantially the same condition as it was when it was acquired for resale" and judgment against the manufacturer is "reasonably certain of being satisfied."

6. *Successor Liability.* Can a corporation that acquires either the assets or shares of an original product seller be sued for its predecessor's torts after the original corporation liquidates? The leading case in support of successor liability is Ray v. Alad Corp., 560 P.2d 3, 9 (Cal. 1977), where the new defendant corporation simply took over the business of the prior corporation and exploited its goodwill without any change in operation or control. The court rested its case for successor liability on three separate grounds:

> (1) the virtual destruction of the plaintiff's remedies against the original manufacturer caused by the successor's acquisition of the business, (2) the successor's ability to assume the original manufacturer's risk-spreading role, and (3) the fairness of requiring the successor to assume a responsibility for defective products that was a burden necessarily attached to the original manufacturer's good will being enjoyed by the successor in the continued operation of the business.

A majority of courts, however, decline to recognize the product line exception. In Semenetz v. Sherling & Walden, Inc., 851 N.E.2d 1170, 1174 (N.Y. 2006), the New York Court of Appeals expressed a common concern that small businesses with limited assets face "economic annihilation" if burdened with the liabilities of their predecessors in ways that could deter the resale of existing assets, even though the liquidation of that corporation also cuts off tort liability for the user of its products. Accordingly, RTT: PL §12 allows successor liability only when the acquisition

> (a) is accompanied by an agreement for the successor to assume such liability; or (b) results from a fraudulent conveyance to escape liability for the debts or liabilities of the predecessor; or (c) constitutes a consolidation or merger with the predecessor; or (d) results in the successor becoming a continuation of the predecessor.

For a proposal that all corporations wishing to go out of business by either sale or liquidation be required to get asset insurance, see Green, Successor Liability: The Superiority of Statutory Reform to Protect Products Liability Claimants, 72 Cornell L. Rev. 17 (1986). For a defense of using successor liability to induce corporate purchasers to exact greater diligence in their asset acquisitions, see Cupp, Redesigning Successor Liability, 1999 Ill. L. Rev. 845.

SECTION D. PRODUCT DEFECTS

1. Manufacturing Defects

RESTATEMENT OF THE LAW (THIRD) OF TORTS: PRODUCTS LIABILITY

§3. Circumstantial Evidence Supporting Inference of Product Defect

It may be inferred that the harm sustained by the plaintiff was caused by a product defect existing at the time of sale or distribution, without proof of a specific defect, when the incident that harmed the plaintiff:

(a) was of a kind that ordinarily occurs as a result of product defect; and

(b) was not, in the particular case, solely the result of causes other than product defect existing at the time of sale or distribution.

Speller v. Sears, Roebuck and Co.

790 N.E.2d 252 (N.Y. 2003)

Graffeo, J. In this products liability case, defendants — a product manufacturer and retailer — were granted summary judgment dismissing plaintiffs' complaint. Because we conclude that plaintiffs raised a triable issue of fact concerning whether a defective refrigerator caused the fire that resulted in plaintiffs' injuries, we reverse and reinstate the complaint against these defendants.

Plaintiffs' decedent Sandra Speller died in a house fire that also injured her seven-year-old son. It is undisputed that the fire originated in the kitchen. Plaintiffs commenced this action against Sears, Roebuck & Co., Whirlpool Corporation and the property owner alleging negligence, strict products liability and breach of warranty. Relevant to this appeal, plaintiffs asserted that the fire was caused by defective wiring in the refrigerator, a product manufactured by Whirlpool and sold by Sears.

A party injured as a result of a defective product may seek relief against the product manufacturer or others in the distribution chain if the defect was a substantial factor in causing the injury. . . .

In this case, plaintiffs' theory was that the wiring in the upper right quadrant of the refrigerator was faulty, causing an electrical fire which then spread to other areas of the kitchen and residence. Because that part of the refrigerator had been consumed in the fire, plaintiffs noted that it was impossible to examine or test the wiring to determine the precise nature of the defect. Thus, plaintiffs sought to prove their claim circumstantially by establishing that the refrigerator caused the house fire and therefore did not perform as intended. [The defendant's experts claimed that the fire started on the stove, but they conceded "that a fire would not occur in a refrigerator unless the product was defective."]

Of course, if a plaintiff's proof is insufficient with respect to either prong of this circumstantial inquiry, a jury may not infer that the harm was caused by a defective product unless plaintiff offers competent evidence identifying a specific flaw.

Here, in their motion for summary judgment, defendants focused on the second prong of the circumstantial inquiry, offering evidence that the injuries were not caused by their product but by an entirely different instrumentality—a grease fire that began on top of the stove. This was the conclusion of the Fire Marshall who stated during deposition testimony that his opinion was based on his interpretation of the burn patterns in the kitchen, his observation that one of the burner knobs on the stove was in the "on" position, and his conversation with a resident of the home who apparently advised him that the oven was on when the resident placed some food on the stovetop a few hours before the fire.

In order to withstand summary judgment, plaintiffs were required to come forward with competent evidence excluding the stove as the origin of the fire. To meet that burden, plaintiffs offered three expert opinions: the depositions of an electrical engineer and a fire investigator, and the affidavit of a former Deputy Chief of the New York City Fire Department. Each concluded that the fire originated in the refrigerator and not on the stove.

In his extensive deposition testimony, the electrical engineer opined that the fire started in the top-right-rear corner of the refrigerator, an area that housed the air balancing unit, thermostat, moisture control and light control. He stated that the wiring in this part of the appliance had been destroyed in the fire, making it impossible to identify the precise mechanical failure and, thus, he could only speculate as to the specific nature of the defect. He testified that the "most logical probability" was that a bad connection or bad splice to one of the components in that portion of the unit caused the wire to become "red hot" and to ignite the adjacent plastic. He tested the combustibility of the plastic and confirmed that the "plastic lights up very easily, with a single match" and continues to burn like candle wax. The engineer observed that the doors of the refrigerator were "slightly bellied out," indicating they were blown out from the expanding hot gases inside the refrigerator. The wall behind the refrigerator was significantly damaged and the upper right quadrant was burned to such a degree that it was not likely to have been caused by an external fire. Interpreting the burn patterns differently from the Fire Marshall, the electrical engineer found that the cabinets above the stove, although damaged, were not destroyed to the extent he expected to find if there had been a stovetop grease fire.

Plaintiffs' fire investigator similarly opined that the fire originated in the refrigerator's upper right corner, in part basing his conclusion on his observations of the scene three days after the fire and his examination of the appliances. He also interviewed a witness to the fire. He testified that he eliminated the stove as the source of the fire after his examination of that appliance and the cabinets above it. Contrary to the testimony of the Fire Marshall, he observed that all of the burner knobs on the stove were in the same position, either all "off" or all "on." He further examined the burn patterns, noting that if the blaze had been caused by a grease fire on the stove, the cabinets directly above would have been consumed in the fire. Instead, they were merely damaged. He acknowledged that he did not know exactly how the fire started inside the refrigerator but indicated he suspected there had been a poor connection in the wiring that caused the wire to smolder until it ignited the highly combustible foam insulation inside the unit.

The former Deputy Chief of the New York City Fire Department asserted in his affidavit that the "fire damage to the area around the refrigerator when compared to that of the stove clearly shows the longer and heavier burn at the refrigerator," indicating the fire originated there. He also stated that he had ruled out all other possible origins of the fire.

Upon review of these expert depositions and affidavit, we conclude that plaintiffs raised a triable question of fact by offering competent evidence which, if credited by the jury, was sufficient to rebut defendants' alternative cause evidence. In other words, based on plaintiffs' proof, a reasonable jury could conclude that plaintiffs excluded all other causes of the fire.

We therefore disagree with the Appellate Division's characterization of plaintiffs' submissions as equivocal. Plaintiffs' experts consistently asserted that the fire originated in the upper right quadrant of the refrigerator and each contended the stove was not the source of the blaze. Both parties supported their positions with detailed, non-conclusory expert depositions and other submissions which explained the bases for the opinions.

Defendants contend that after they came forward with evidence suggesting an alternative cause of the fire, plaintiffs were foreclosed from establishing a product defect circumstantially but were then required to produce evidence of a specific defect to survive summary judgment. We reject this approach for two reasons. First, such an analysis would allow a defendant who offered minimally sufficient alternative cause evidence in a products liability case to foreclose a plaintiff from proceeding circumstantially without a jury having determined whether defendant's evidence should be credited. Second, it misinterprets the court's role in adjudicating a motion for summary judgment, which is issue identification, not issue resolution. . . . [P]laintiffs directly rebutted defendants' submissions with competent proof specifically ruling out the stove as the source of the blaze. Because a reasonable jury could credit this proof and find that plaintiff excluded all other causes of the fire not attributable to defendants, this case presents material issues of fact requiring a trial.

[Reversed.]

NOTES

1. ***Proof of Manufacturing Defect.*** What role, if any, did the decedent or her son play in bringing about the fire? Even if the fire started in the refrigerator, did the plaintiffs introduce any evidence of an original defect in the equipment? If so, was it a manufacturing (construction) defect or a design defect? As should be evident, the switch from negligence to strict liability in manufacturing defect cases does not eliminate difficult causal questions that arise when the plaintiff's conduct occupies an uncertain place in the chain of causation, a problem exemplified by long-lived products subject to intensive and protracted use. Indeed many states have adopted statutes of repose that limit the availability of products liability suits to a certain number of years after purchase.

In Jagmin v. Simonds Abrasive Co., 211 N.W.2d 810 (Wis. 1973), the plaintiff was struck in the face by a grinding wheel that broke into pieces while he was operating it. The plaintiff established that the wheel was manufactured by the defendant. He further testified that he had used the wheel in the proper manner, that he had not placed undue stress on it, that he had no evidence suggesting that any other person had used the wheel while he was away from his job, and that the wheel had several hours of useful life left at the time the accident took place. The wheel itself was destroyed after it broke. The trial court refused to allow the case to go to the jury, ruling that there was insufficient evidence on the question of "defect." The Wisconsin Supreme Court reversed, allowing an "exceedingly close" case to reach the jury on a modified version of res ipsa loquitur. The plaintiff's evidence tended to exclude the possibility of any responsible cause of the injury apart from an original product defect even if that defect could not be identified. Does the plaintiff's evidence negate the possibility that the wheel was damaged in shipment or in installation? Does the plaintiff's evidence explain why the wheel worked as long as it did? Does

Henderson's account of the *MacPherson* facts, *supra* at 554, argue in favor of requiring a specific identification of a product defect in manufacturing cases? Does the information-forcing rationale for res ipsa loquitur put forth in *Ybarra*, *supra* Chapter 3, at 211, apply here? Do modern discovery rules mitigate any information disparities between the consumer and the product manufacturer?

In a modern twist on *Speller*, the plaintiff in Red Hed Oil, Inc. v. H.T. Hackney Co., 292 F. Supp. 3d 764, 775, 778 (E.D. Ky. 2017), sued the distributor and manufacturers of e-cigarettes that allegedly caught fire and caused extensive damage to the plaintiff's convenience store. The plaintiff's manufacturing and design defect claims failed on similar causation issues as those originally raised in *Speller*. According to Hood, J.:

> Plaintiffs fail to provide factual allegations that these e-cigarettes did, in fact, cause this fire. Plaintiffs blame it on a defect, but they do not specify what defect, which product was defective, or how the defect sparked the fire. . . .
>
> The plaintiffs do not allege an alternative design, how the products deviated from the intended design, how the e-cigarettes were assembled wrong, or how the e-cigarettes fail the risk-utility test. Plaintiffs cannot rely on general assertions that the e-cigarettes were dangerous; they must make at least some factual allegations as to *how*.

2. *Manufacturing Defects in Food Cases.* In *Escola*, food cases were one of the original battlegrounds for a theory of strict liability. In particular, the early common law held manufacturers strictly liable for any "foreign object" that was found within the food, be it a sliver of tin or some waste impurities from animals. By the same token, the earlier cases refused to hold manufacturers liable under any theory for substances "natural" to the product served. Thus the leading case of Mix v. Ingersoll Candy Co., 59 P.2d 144, 148 (Cal. 1936), held that "[b]ones which are natural to the type of meat served cannot legitimately be called a foreign substance, and a consumer who eats meat dishes ought to anticipate and be on his guard against the presence of such bones."

Modern cases have uniformly rejected this approach in favor of a reasonable expectations test. In Schafer v. JLC Food Systems, 695 N.W.2d 570, 575 (Minn. 2005), the plaintiff took a bite from a pumpkin muffin served at the defendant's restaurant only to experience a sharp pain in her throat, which later turned into a serious infection. Page, J., wrote:

> Under the [Third] Restatement approach, consumer expectations are based on culturally defined, widely shared standards allowing a seller's liability to be resolved by judges and triers of fact based on their assessment of what consumers have a right to expect from preparation of the food in question. §7 cmt. b. . . .
>
> Instead of drawing arbitrary distinctions between foreign and natural substances that caused harm, relying on consumers' reasonable expectations is likely to yield a more equitable result. After all, an unexpected natural object or substance contained in a food product, such as a chicken bone in chicken soup, can cause as much harm as a foreign object or substance, such as a piece of glass in the same soup.

Page, J., next allowed the plaintiff to get to the jury even though she could not "present evidence identifying the object that cause the alleged harm," relying again on the strict liability analog to res ipsa loquitur, whereby, as in *Jagmin*, the plaintiff's task is to exclude all other causes of harm. Should this test be adopted in cases of food poisoning that manifest themselves a day after eating in the restaurant?

Berkheimer v. REKM, LLC, 206 N.E.3d 90, 94 (Ohio Ct. App. 2023), denied recovery to a plaintiff who could have reasonably expected to find a bone in a "boneless chicken wing." Hendrickson, J., reasoned that "reasonable expectations" depend on whether a part is a natural to the food at issue. Is this a return to the foreign-natural test by another name?

2. Design Defects

Campo v. Scofield
95 N.E.2d 802 (N.Y. 1950)

Fuld, J. Plaintiff, working on his son's farm, was engaged in feeding onions into an "onion topping" machine, when his hands became caught in its revolving steel rollers and were badly injured. . . .

If a manufacturer does everything necessary to make the machine function properly for the purpose for which it is designed, if the machine is without any latent defect, and if its functioning creates no danger or peril that is not known to the user, then the manufacturer has satisfied the law's demands. We have not yet reached the state where a manufacturer is under the duty of making a machine accident proof or foolproof. Just as the manufacturer is under no obligation, in order to guard against injury resulting from deterioration, to furnish a machine that will not wear out, so he is under no duty to guard against injury from a patent peril or from a source manifestly dangerous.

To illustrate, the manufacturer who makes, properly and free of defects, an axe or a buzz saw or an airplane with an exposed propeller, is not to be held liable if one using the axe or the buzz saw is cut by it, or if some one working around the airplane comes in contact with the propeller. In such cases, the manufacturer has the right to expect that such persons will do everything necessary to avoid such contact, for the very nature of the article gives notice and warning of the consequences to be expected, of the injuries to be suffered.

2 Harper and James, Torts §28.5
(1956)

The bottom does not logically drop out of a negligence case against the maker when it is shown that the purchaser knew of the dangerous condition. Thus if the product is a carrot-topping machine with exposed moving parts, or an electric clothes wringer dangerous to the limbs of the operator, and if it would be feasible for the maker of the product to install a guard or safety release, it should be a question for the jury whether reasonable care demanded such a precaution, though its absence is obvious. Surely reasonable men might find here a great danger, even to one who knew the condition and since it was so readily avoidable they might find the maker negligent.

John W. Wade

On the Nature of Strict Tort Liability for Products
44 Miss. L.J. 825, 836–37 (1973)

If there is agreement that the determination of whether a product is unreasonably dangerous, or is not duly safe, involves the necessary application of a standard, it will, like the determination of negligence or of strict liability for an abnormally dangerous activity, require the consideration and weighing of a number of factors. I offer here a revised list of factors which seem to me to be of significance in applying the standard.

(1) The usefulness and desirability of the product—its utility to the user and to the public as a whole.
(2) The safety aspects of the product—the likelihood that it will cause injury, and the probable seriousness of the injury.
(3) The availability of a substitute product which would meet the same need and not be as unsafe.
(4) The manufacturer's ability to eliminate the unsafe character of the product without impairing its usefulness or making it too expensive to maintain its utility.
(5) The user's ability to avoid danger by the exercise of care in the use of the product.
(6) The user's anticipated awareness of the dangers inherent in the product and their availability, because of general public knowledge of the obvious condition of the product, or of the existence of suitable warnings or instructions.
(7) The feasibility, on the part of the manufacturer, of spreading the loss by setting the price of the product or carrying liability insurance.

NOTE

Two (or Is It Three?) Views of Design Defect. The passages quoted above set up the possible approaches to design defect litigation. The open and obvious test of *Campo* dominated the law until the adoption of the Second Restatement, in which a design defect was determined by the consumer expectations test. RST §402A, comments *g* & *i*. Contrary to *Campo*, Professors Harper and James insisted that a negligence cause of action was not necessarily defeated by the obvious nature of the defect. Professor Wade's influential formulation of the risk-utility standard offers a strict liability version of the relevant cost benefit analysis. The Third Restatement requires a modified risk-utility test, in which the plaintiff is charged with showing that a "reasonable alternative design" exists that would make the product less dangerous. Judicial embrace of these different versions of design defect liability have ebbed and flowed over the past sixty years. The next case deals with the rise of the negligence standard in design defect cases dealing with the crashworthiness of automobiles.

a. Development of the Negligence Test

Volkswagen of America, Inc. v. Young

321 A.2d 737 (Md. 1974)

[The decedent had stopped his 1968 Volkswagen Beetle at a red light when he was hit from behind by a 1967 Ford, negligently driven by William Benson. As a result, the decedent's car was pushed forward. The seat bracketing pieces and seat adjustment mechanisms broke away from the body of the car. In the ensuing "second collision" the decedent was hurled into the rear of the car and was killed by head and torso injuries sustained on impact. The plaintiff sued Volkswagen in federal district court. She alleged that the Beetle was "defectively designed, manufactured, and marketed with defects which rendered it structurally hazardous, not merchantable, and not fit for the purpose intended" in that its entire seat assembly was "unreasonably vulnerable to separation from the floor upon collision." The district court certified this question to the Maryland Court of Appeals, the highest state court:

> Whether or not, under Maryland law, the definition of the "intended use" of a motor vehicle includes the vehicle's involvement in a collision; and thus in turn, whether a cause of action is

stated against the manufacturer or importer of said vehicle in breach of warranty or negligence or absolute liability or misrepresentation by allegations that the design and manufacture of the vehicle unreasonably increased the risk of injury to occupants following a collision not caused by any defect of the vehicle.

The Maryland court answers the question in the affirmative, holding that the "intended use" of an automobile was not only to provide transportation but also reasonably safe transportation, and that the plaintiff's complaint stated a cause of action in negligence under Maryland law.]

A 1968 Volkswagen Beetle Type 1, the model of the decedent's car in *Young*

Source: Phil Talbot / Alamy

Eldridge, J. . . . This is the first case to reach this Court concerning the extent of an automobile manufacturer's liability for a design defect resulting in enhanced injuries in a motor vehicle accident, where the defect did not cause the initial impact or movement of the injured person. Such cases are often called "second collision" cases or "automobile crashworthiness" cases. They differ from other products liability cases involving defective automobiles by the combination of two factors. First, the alleged defect is in the design of the automobile rather than a negligent deviation during the construction or assembly process from the manner in which the vehicle was supposed to be made. The latter is usually called a "construction defect." Second, the defect is not the cause of the initial impact. Typically, the actions of the driver of the car in which the plaintiff is riding, or the actions of the driver of another vehicle, or the actions of some third person, cause an initial disruption or impact which in turn results in the plaintiff's colliding with the interior (or occasionally the exterior) of the car. The plaintiff's collision with the car is the so-called "second collision." The issue of whether the automobile manufacturer has a duty to take reasonable steps to design its vehicles so as to minimize the injuries caused by "second collisions" has engendered much controversy and comment throughout the nation.

The principal case holding that an automobile manufacturer has no duty to design its cars so as to minimize the injuries suffered in automobile accidents is Evans v. General Motors Corporation, 359 F.2d 822 (7th Cir. 1966). The plaintiff in *Evans* was killed when his 1961 Chevrolet station wagon was struck broadside by another car. He claimed that General Motors was negligent in designing the frame of his car, inasmuch as an "X" type frame rather than a box or perimeter type frame was used, contrary to the construction of some other cars. The claim was that an "X" type frame without side rails would not adequately protect occupants during a side impact collision, and that the defendant manufacturer had created an unreasonable risk of serious injury. The trial court, applying Indiana law, dismissed the complaint for failure to state a claim on which relief could be granted, and the dismissal was affirmed by the United States Court of Appeals for the Seventh Circuit. The Court of Appeals held that the critical question was the nature of the manufacturer's duty. It went on to conclude that a manufacturer has a duty only to design a car reasonably fit for its intended purpose, and that "[t]he intended purpose of an automobile does not include its participation in collisions with other objects, despite the manufacturer's ability to foresee the possibility that such collisions may occur. As defendant argues, the defendant also knows that its automobiles may be driven into bodies of water, but it is not suggested that defendant has a duty to equip them with pontoons." (*Id.* at 825.)

The Court of Appeals for the Seventh Circuit also stated as grounds for its decision that a "manufacturer is not under a duty to make his automobile accident-proof or fool-proof" and that requiring "manufacturers to construct automobiles in which it would be safe to collide . . . [is] a legislative function. . . ."

The seminal case on the other side of the issue is Larsen v. General Motors Corporation, 391 F.2d 495 (8th Cir. 1968). The plaintiff in *Larsen* suffered severe bodily injuries while driving a 1963 Corvair which collided head-on with another car. The impact caused the steering mechanism to thrust forward into the plaintiff's head. The suit against General Motors charged negligence in the design of the steering assembly and the placement of the component parts of the steering assembly into the structure of the car. It was alleged that General Motors was also negligent in not warning the user of this latent condition. The specific defect relied upon by the plaintiff was that the solid steering shaft was so designed as to extend "without interruption from a point 2.7 inches in front of the leading surface of the front tires to a position directly in front of the driver," exposing him "to an unreasonable risk of injury from the rearward displacement of that shaft in the event of a left-of-center head-on collision. So positioned it receives the initial impact of forces generated by a left-of-center head-on collision. The unabsorbed forces of the collision in this area are transmitted directly toward the driver's head, the shaft acting as a spear aimed at a vital part of the driver's anatomy." *Id.* at 497, n.2. The plaintiff also pointed out that other cars were designed so as to protect against such rearward displacement, in that the steering column did not protrude beyond the forward surface of the front tires. The lower court in *Larsen* granted General Motors' motion for summary judgment on the theory that the manufacturer had no duty to design a vehicle which would protect the plaintiff from injury in a collision. On appeal, the United States Court of Appeals for the Eighth Circuit reversed, holding that the plaintiff had made out a sufficient case for consideration by the jury.

[The court in *Larsen* gave a broad interpretation to "intended use," stating:]

> Automobiles are made for use on the roads and highways in transporting persons and cargo to and from various points. This intended use cannot be carried out without encountering in varying degrees the statistically proved hazard of injury-producing impacts of various types. The manufacturer should not be heard to say that it does not intend its product to be involved in any accident when it can easily foresee and when it knows that the probability over the life of its product is high, that it will be involved in some type of injury-producing accident. . . .

The Court of Appeals concluded that an automobile manufacturer "is under a duty to use reasonable care in the design of its vehicle to avoid subjecting the user to an unreasonable risk of injury in the event of a collision." (*Id.* at 502.)

The *Larsen* court then emphasized the limitations of its holding that it was not making automobile manufacturers "insurers"; that it was merely applying common law principles of negligence; that the standard for manufacturers was "reasonable care"; and that an automobile did not have to be absolutely crash-proof but only designed to provide "a reasonably safe vehicle in which to travel." (*Id.* at 503.)*

In our view, Larsen v. General Motors Corporation, *supra*, and the cases following it, are more in accord with traditional negligence principles than Evans v. General Motors Corporation, *supra*. . . .

* [The defendant in *Larsen* received a unanimous verdict after a three-week trial, having introduced scientific evidence that the plaintiff had not been hit by the steering column. For a discussion of the expert evidence introduced at trial, see Bowman, Defense of an Auto Design Negligence Case, 10 For the Defense, No. 5, May 1969.—Eds.]

That the design defect does not cause the initial collision should make no difference if it is a cause of the ultimate injury. Where the injuries to an occupant of a motor vehicle resulted from both the negligence of a driver as well as a negligent condition created by some other entity, this Court has held that both negligent actors may be liable. . . .

In sum, "traditional rules of negligence" lead to the conclusion that an automobile manufacturer is liable for a defect in design which the manufacturer could have reasonably foreseen would cause or enhance injuries on impact, which is not patent or obvious to the user, and which in fact leads to or enhances the injuries in an automobile collision. . . .

While the intended purpose of an automobile may not be to participate in collisions, the intended purpose includes providing a reasonable measure of safety when, inevitably, collisions do occur. For many years automobiles have been equipped with safety glass, bumpers, windshield wipers, etc. More recently, and largely as a result of governmental action, automobiles are equipped with additional safety devices such as seat belts, shoulder harnesses, padded dashboards, padded visors, non-protruding knobs, etc. Frequent collisions are foreseeable, and the intended purpose of all of these parts of the vehicle is to afford reasonable safety when those collisions occur.

The arguments that there is no duty to design "accident-proof" or "injury-proof" vehicles, and that automobile manufacturers are not insurers, are "straw men." No case has ever held that an automobile manufacturer must design an "accident-proof" or "injury-proof" vehicle or that the manufacturer is an insurer. Concerning two of the examples most often used by the advocates of non-liability for design defects, no one has suggested that an automobile must be designed to withstand a high speed head-on collision with a truck or to float if it leaves the road and goes into a body of water. . . .

The standard to be applied is the traditional one of reasonableness.

The contention that the design of automobiles involves a legislative function and not a judicial function, similarly furnishes no sound reason for exempting automobile "second collision" cases from the normal principles of tort liability. Legislative or administrative requirements that persons or businesses conduct their operations in a particular manner, and adhere to specified standards, have never been viewed as supplanting tort liability. On the contrary, such statutory or regulatory requirements are deemed to furnish standards by which courts or juries determine, along with other circumstances, whether or not conduct is negligent. Failure to adhere to those standards is evidence of negligence for the court or jury to consider. Moreover, the most significant legislation dealing with motor vehicle safety standards makes it clear that Congress did not view the question of safe motor vehicle design as solely a legislative problem. The National Traffic and Motor Vehicle Safety Act of 1966 specifically provided that "Compliance with any Federal motor vehicle safety standard issued under this subchapter does not exempt any person from any liability under common law." 15 U.S.C. 1397(c). . . .

In addition, there can be no recovery if the danger inherent in the particular design was obvious or patent to the user of the vehicle. . . .

[The court then refuses to apply the strict liability theory of section 402A to design defect cases.] Consequently, the tort liability under Maryland law of a manufacturer or supplier of a motor vehicle, for a defective design which enhances injuries in a collision, depends upon traditional principles of negligence.

NOTES

1. *Determining Standards for Design Defects.* As *Young* indicates, design defect liability grew up under the aegis of negligence. As such, can the court accept the negligence doctrine and allow a complete defense for any dangers that were "obvious or patent" to the user of the vehicle? Could a jury regard a Volkswagen van, with its engine in the rear, as defective?

A convertible? A cigarette lighter? For a negative answer on the first query, see Dreisonstok v. Volkswagenwerk A.G., 489 F.2d 1066 (4th Cir. 1974); for a negative answer on the second, see Delvaux v. Ford Motor Co., 764 F.2d 469 (7th Cir. 1985); and for a negative answer on the third, see Todd v. Societe Bic, S.A., 21 F.3d 1402, 1407 (7th Cir. 1994). When the defects are obvious, how should the cost-benefit analysis be conducted?

Conversely, how would *Young* play out under section 402A of the Second Restatement? Note that traditional strict liability works well to protect strangers against a defendant's use of force, as with abnormally dangerous activities, but it seems inappropriate to require any defendant to protect the plaintiff against any use (or misuse) of force initiated by either the plaintiff, a third party, or an act of God. A motorcycle gasoline tank might be made "totally" safe against impact, but its weight and unwieldiness would make the motorcycle unmovable. Once absolute protection is rejected as unworkable, reasonableness standards take over. In some instances, standards are set by legislation. See, e.g., The National Traffic and Motor Vehicle Safety Act, 49 U.S.C. §§30101–30170, wherein, for example, 49 C.F.R. §571.216 (2023) ("Roof Crush Resistance") provides that a force equal to 1.5 times a car's unloaded weight or 22,240 newtons (5,000 pounds), whichever is less, should not move the roof more than 127 millimeters (five inches) when applied to either of its front corners. Because statutory compliance does not provide an absolute defense in a design defect case, courts typically turn to cost-benefit tests to determine the applicable design standard. But how? For an early skeptical response, see Henderson, Judicial Review of Manufacturers' Conscious Design Choices: The Limits of Adjudication, 73 Colum. L. Rev. 1531, 1540 (1973), stressing the "polycentric nature" of design decisions, which requires a design engineer to find the proper balance of "such factors as market price, functional utility, and aesthetics, as well as safety." Henderson insisted these matters could not be adequately reexamined in litigation because courts are not "institutionally suited to establishing safety standards." For the early impetus on liability for design defects, see Nader & Page, Automobile Design and Judicial Process, 55 Calif. L. Rev. 645 (1967).

2. *Enhancement of Injury.* The defendant in a crashworthiness case is not responsible for the unavoidable injuries associated with the original impact, but only for those harms that were "enhanced or aggravated" by the defective design. In light of the implicit division on causation, who bears the burden of proof on the issue of enhancement? One view is that the plaintiff must prove that "it is more probable than not that the alleged defect aggravated or enhanced the injuries resulting from the initial collision." See Caiazzo v. Volkswagenwerk A.G., 647 F.2d 241, 251 (2d Cir. 1981). *Caiazzo* was promptly rejected in Mitchell v. Volkswagenwerk A.G., 669 F.2d 1199, 1204–05 (8th Cir. 1982):

> The primary difficulty we have with this analysis is that it forces not only the parties but the jury as well to try a hypothetical case. Liability and damage questions are difficult enough within orthodox principles of tort law without extending consideration to a case of a hypothetical victim. More realistically, the parties and juries should direct their attentions to what actually happened rather than what might have happened.
>
> By placing the burden of proof on a plaintiff to prove that the designer was the sole cause of not only an enhanced indivisible injury, but, in addition, that he would not otherwise have received injuries absent a defect, the injured victim is relegated to an almost hopeless state of never being able to succeed against a defective designer. The public interest is little served. We write to reaffirm that *Larsen* was not intended to create a rule which requires the plaintiff to assume an impossible burden of proving a negative fact.

Is the defendant ever the sole responsible party in any crashworthiness case? How can a jury avoid trying a "hypothetical case" once the defendant introduces evidence that the alleged defect did not cause all or some of the harms? Does the burden of production ever switch back to the plaintiff? Whatever the force of these objections, the Third Restatement takes the same view. Even though the theory of proximate causation holds the defendant liable only for the "increased harm," the full loss falls on the defendant "[i]f proof does not support a determination . . . of the harm that would have resulted in the absence of the product defect." RTT: PL §16(c).

Egbert v. Nissan Motor Co., Ltd., 228 P.3d 737, 746 (Utah 2010), rejected the Restatement view and both *Mitchell* and *Caiazzo* by taking its cue from Utah Code Ann. §78B-5-818(3) (2023), which provides: "No defendant is liable to any person seeking recovery for any amount in excess of the proportion of fault attributed to that defendant. . . ." Durham, C.J., concluded that fault, broadly defined under the statute, should always be apportioned between two parties when the jury has "sufficient" evidence of the culpability of each.

> [B]ecause all injuries, as a matter of Utah law, can and must be apportioned, there is no shifting of burden — informal or formal — to a defendant product seller to prove apportionment. The plaintiff bears the burden of proof in an enhanced-injury case. Finally, because of the nature of an enhanced-injury claim and the abolition of joint and several liability, a defendant product seller cannot become liable for the entire injury merely by virtue of being a codefendant.

3. *Crashworthiness Cases: Acceptance, Disquiet, and Reform?* The crashworthiness doctrine of *Larsen* and *Young* is today the law in every state and explicitly embraced in the Third Restatement. See RTT: PL §16, comment *a.* But some courts have expressed misgivings about its potential scope. In Dawson v. Chrysler Corp., 630 F.2d 950, 962–63 (3d Cir. 1980), the plaintiff, a police officer, was hurrying to answer a burglar alarm when his Dodge Monaco patrol car slipped off a rain-soaked highway into an "unyielding" steel pole some fifteen inches in diameter. The pole ripped through the side of the car, crushed the plaintiff, and left him a quadriplegic. The plaintiff argued the car was defective because it did not have "a full continuous steel frame extending through the door panels," which would have kept the pole from penetrating the passenger space. The defendant's expert testified that the plaintiff's proposed changes would have added between 200 and 250 pounds of weight to the car and cost some $300 ($1,120 in 2023 dollars). He also noted that "deformation" of a car in a crash is in general desirable because it absorbs the impact that would otherwise be transmitted to the occupant. Adams, J., uneasily affirmed the plaintiff's jury verdict under New Jersey law:

> The result of such arrangement is that while the jury found Chrysler liable for not producing a rigid enough vehicular frame, a factfinder in another case might well hold the manufacturer liable for producing a frame that is too rigid. Yet, as pointed out at trial, in certain types of accidents — head-on collisions — it is desirable to have a car designed to collapse upon impact because the deformation would absorb much of the shock of the collision, and divert the force of deceleration away from the vehicle's passengers. In effect, this permits individual juries applying varying laws in different jurisdictions to set nationwide automobile safety standards and to impose on automobile manufacturers conflicting requirements. It would be difficult for members of the industry to alter their design and production behavior in response to jury verdicts in such cases, because their response might well be at variance with what some other jury decides is a defective design. Under these circumstances, the law imposes on the industry the responsibility of insuring vast numbers of persons involved in automobile accidents.

The level of cynicism about this "damned-if-you-do-damned-if-you-don't" problem surfaced in Blankenship v. General Motors Corp., 406 S.E.2d 781, 783–84 (W. Va. 1991). Neely, J., joined the crashworthiness parade for reasons that had little to do with the intrinsic merits of the doctrine:

> West Virginia is a small rural state with .66 percent of the population of the United States. Although some members of this court have reservations about the wisdom of many aspects of the tort law, as a court we are utterly powerless to make the *overall* tort system for cases arising in interstate commerce more rational: Nothing that we do will have any impact whatsoever on

> the set of economic trade-offs that occur in the *national* economy. And, ironically, trying unilaterally to make the American tort system more rational through being uniquely responsible in West Virginia will only punish our residents severely without, in any regard, improving the system for anyone else.

So long as West Virginians have to pay premiums on General Motors cars sold around the world, it would be "foolish and irresponsible," according to Neely, J., not to allow West Virginians to collect on their implicit insurance policies for accidents to them.

4. *The Decline of Open and Obvious.* Automobiles were not the only product for which liability expanded dramatically in the 1970s. The design liability for machine tools and other equipment exploded as well. *Campo* was explicitly overruled in Micallef v. Miehle Co., 348 N.E.2d 571, 577–78 (N.Y. 1976). There the plaintiff sought to "chase a hickie" (that is, remove a foreign object) that had made its way onto a high-speed printing press manufactured by the defendant. Without shutting down the press (which would have cost valuable production time), he tried to remove the hickie with an eight-inch piece of plastic, and his finger got caught in the nip-point of the machine. The plaintiff tried to turn off the press, but the shut-off button was beyond his reach. Cooke, J., rejected the open and obvious rule in *Campo*:

> Apace with advanced technology, a relaxation of the *Campo* stringency is advisable. A casting of increased responsibility upon the manufacturer, who stands in a superior position to recognize and cure defects, for improper conduct in the placement of finished products into the channels of commerce furthers the public interest. To this end, we hold that a manufacturer is obligated to exercise that degree of care in his plan or design so as to avoid any unreasonable risk of harm to anyone who is likely to be exposed to the danger when the product is used in the manner for which the product was intended as well as an unintended yet reasonably foreseeable use.
>
> What constitutes "reasonable care" will, of course, vary with the surrounding circumstances and will involve "a balancing of the likelihood of harm, and the gravity of harm if it happens, against the burden of the precaution which would be effective to avoid the harm." Under this approach, "the plaintiff endeavors to show the jury such facts as that competitors used the safety device which was missing here, or that a 'cotter pin costing a penny' could have prevented the accident. The defendant points to such matters as cost, function, and competition as narrowing the design choices. He stresses 'trade-offs.' If the product would be unworkable when the alleged missing feature was added, or would be so expensive as to be priced out of the market, that would be relevant defensive matter." (Rheingold, Expanding Liability of the Product Supplier: A Primer, 2 Hofstra L. Rev. 521, 537.)

The Third Restatement endorses *Micallef.* See RTT: PL §2, illus. 3. This now dominant position is articulated in section 2, comment *d*: "The fact that a danger is open and obvious is relevant to the issue of defectiveness, but does not necessarily preclude a plaintiff from establishing that a reasonable alternative design should have been adopted that would have reduced or prevented injury to the plaintiff." States have generally followed suit in adopting open and obvious as a factor in determining defectiveness under a risk-utility or reasonable alternative design standard, rather than as a standalone defense. Thus in Genie Indus., Inc. v. Matak, 462 S.W.3d 1, 17 (Tex. 2015), Boyd, J., explained:

> We have rejected such absolute rules [of open and obvious] in favor of the more fluid risk-utility analysis because that analysis provides a more effective way to encourage manufacturers to reach an optimum level of safety in designing their products. A design that eliminates a risk is safer than a design that retains the risk, even if the risk is open and obvious or warned against.

But there are nevertheless some limits to liability. In Linegar v. Armour of America, Inc., 909 F.2d 1150, 1154 (8th Cir. 1990), the decedent, a highway trooper, wore a standard-issue Armour bullet-proof vest that, as he knew, did not wrap around his torso. He was killed in a routine traffic stop. His vest stopped all bullets that hit it but did not prevent a bullet from entering his body near his armpit and penetrating his heart. More extensive vests were available, but these were both uncomfortable to wear and somewhat less maneuverable. After citing RST §402A, comment *i*, Bowman, J., held that "[a]n otherwise completely effective protective vest cannot be regarded as dangerous, much less unreasonably so, simply because it leaves some parts of the body obviously exposed." The Third Restatement endorses *Linegar*. See RTT: PL §2, illus. 10.

b. Consumer Expectations versus Risk-Utility Tests

Barker v. Lull Engineering Co.

573 P.2d 443 (Cal. 1978)

Tobriner, C.J. In August 1970, plaintiff Ray Barker was injured at a construction site at the University of California at Santa Cruz while operating a high-lift loader manufactured by defendant Lull Engineering Co. and leased to plaintiff's employer by defendant George M. Philpott Co., Inc. Claiming that his injuries were proximately caused, inter alia, by the alleged defective design of the loader, Barker instituted the present tort action seeking to recover damages for his injuries. The jury returned a verdict in favor of defendants, and plaintiff appeals from the judgment entered upon that verdict, contending primarily that in view of this court's decision in Cronin v. J. B. E. Olson Corp. 501 P.2d 1153 (Cal. 1972), the trial court erred in instructing the jury "that strict liability for a defect in design of a product is based on a finding that the product was unreasonably dangerous for its intended use. . . ."

As we explain, we agree with plaintiff's objection to the challenged instruction and conclude that the judgment must be reversed. . . .

[W]e have concluded from this review that a product is defective in design either (1) if the product has failed to perform as safely as an ordinary consumer would expect when used in an intended or reasonably foreseeable manner, or (2) if, in light of the relevant factors discussed below, the benefits of the challenged design do not outweigh the risk of danger inherent in such design. In addition, we explain how the burden of proof with respect to the latter "risk-benefit" standard should be allocated.

This dual standard for design defect assures an injured plaintiff protection from products that either fall below ordinary consumer expectations as to safety, or that, on balance, are not as safely designed as they should be. At the same time, the standard permits a manufacturer who has marketed a product which satisfies ordinary consumer expectations to demonstrate the relative complexity of design decisions and the tradeoffs that are frequently required in the adoption of alternative designs. Finally, this test reflects our continued adherence to the principle that, in a product liability action, the trier of fact must focus on the *product*, not on the *manufacturer's conduct*, and that the plaintiff need not prove that the manufacturer acted unreasonably or negligently in order to prevail in such an action. . . .

1. The facts of the present case

[Barker, a substitute driver, was injured while using a Lull High-Lift Loader, which was designed to be kept level on a sloping terrain. He had received only limited instruction in the use of the loader. While attempting to lift a load of lumber eighteen-or-so feet on uneven ground, he tried to maneuver the forks on the base of the load to compensate for sloping ground. As he lost control of the loader, he attempted to jump away from it, and was struck and seriously injured by some falling timber.

Barker claimed that the loader was defective in several respects: first, that it was not equipped with seat belts or a roll-bar; second, that it was not equipped with "outriggers" that might have given it greater lateral stability; third, that it was not equipped with an automatic locking device on its leveling mechanism; and, fourth, that it was not equipped with a separate park gear. In response to this assignment of defects, the defendant argued as follows: first, that seat belts or roll-bars were in fact dangerous because they prevented any quick escape from the loader; second, that the outriggers were not needed if the loader was operated on level terrain as was intended, that none of the defendant's competitors had such outriggers, and that a regular crane should have been called in if work on uneven terrain was required; third, that the leveling device used was the most convenient and safe for the operator; and, fourth, that none of the transmissions manufactured for loaders incorporated a park position. The defendant also argued that the plaintiff's inexperience and panic were the sole source of his injury.

The jury returned a verdict for the defendant by a vote of ten to two.] . . .

3. A trial court may properly formulate instructions to elucidate the "defect" concept in varying circumstances. In particular, in design defect cases, a court may properly instruct a jury that a product is defective in design if (1) the plaintiff proves that the product failed to perform as safely as an ordinary consumer would expect when used in an intended or reasonably foreseeable manner, or (2) the plaintiff proves that the product's design proximately caused injury and the defendant fails to prove, in light of the relevant factors, that on balance the benefits of the challenged design outweigh the risk of danger inherent in such design. . . .

As this court has recognized on numerous occasions, the term defect as utilized in the strict liability context is neither self-defining nor susceptible to a single definition applicable in all contexts.[8] . . . [T]he concept of defect raises considerably more difficulties in the design defect context than it does in the manufacturing or production defect context.

In general, a manufacturing or production defect is readily identifiable because a defective product is one that differs from the manufacturer's intended result or from other ostensibly identical units of the same product line. For example, when a product comes off the assembly line in a substandard condition it has incurred a manufacturing defect. . . . A design defect, by contrast, cannot be identified simply by comparing the injury-producing product with the manufacturer's plans or with other units of the same product line, since by definition the plans and all such units will reflect the same design. Rather than applying any sort of deviation-from-the-norm test in determining whether a product is defective in design for strict liability purposes, our cases have employed two alternative criteria in ascertaining, in Justice Traynor's words, whether there is something "wrong, if not in the manufacturer's manner of production, at least in his product." (Traynor, The Ways and Meanings of Defective Products and Strict Liability, 32 Tenn. L. Rev. 363, 366 [1965].)

First, our cases establish that a product may be found defective in design if the plaintiff demonstrates that the product failed to perform as safely as an ordinary consumer would expect when used in an intended or reasonably foreseeable manner. This initial standard, somewhat analogous to the Uniform Commercial Code's warranty of fitness and merchantability (Cal. U. Com. Code, §2314), reflects the warranty heritage upon which California product liability doctrine in part rests. As we noted in *Greenman*, "implicit in [a product's] presence on the market . . . [is] a representation that it [will] safely do the jobs for which it was built." When a product fails to satisfy such ordinary consumer expectations as to safety in its intended or reasonably foreseeable operation, a manufacturer is strictly liable for resulting injuries. . . .

8. One commentator has observed that, in addition to the deficiencies in the "unreasonably dangerous" terminology noted in *Cronin*, the Restatement's language is potentially misleading because "[i]t may suggest an idea like ultrahazardous, or abnormally dangerous, and thus give rise to the impression that the plaintiff must prove that the product was unusually or extremely dangerous." (Wade, On the Nature of Strict Tort Liability for Products, 44 Miss. L.J. 825, 832 (1973).) We agree with this criticism and believe it constitutes a further reason for refraining from utilizing the "unreasonably dangerous" terminology in defining a defective product.

As Professor Wade has pointed out, however, the expectations of the ordinary consumer cannot be viewed as the exclusive yardstick for evaluating design defectiveness because "[i]n many situations . . . the consumer would not know what to expect, because he would have no idea how safe the product could be made." . . . Numerous California decisions have implicitly recognized this fact and have made clear, through varying linguistic formulations, that a product may be found defective in design, even if it satisfies ordinary consumer expectations, if through hindsight the jury determines that the product's design embodies "excessive preventable danger," or, in other words, if the jury finds that the risk of danger inherent in the challenged design outweighs the benefits of such design. . . .

A review of past cases indicates that in evaluating the adequacy of a product's design pursuant to this latter standard, a jury may consider, among other relevant factors, the gravity of the danger posed by the challenged design, the likelihood that such danger would occur, the mechanical feasibility of a safer alternative design, the financial cost of an improved design, and the adverse consequences to the product and to the consumer that would result from an alternative design. . . .

Although our cases have thus recognized a variety of considerations that may be relevant to the determination of the adequacy of a product's design, past authorities have generally not devoted much attention to the appropriate allocation of the burden of proof with respect to these matters. . . . The allocation of such burden is particularly significant in this context in as much as this court's product liability decisions, from *Greenman* to *Cronin*, have repeatedly emphasized that one of the principal purposes behind the strict product liability doctrine is to relieve an injured plaintiff of many of the onerous evidentiary burdens inherent in a negligence cause of action. Because most of the evidentiary matters which may be relevant to the determination of the adequacy of a product's design under the "risk-benefit" standard—e.g., the feasibility and cost of alternative designs—are similar to issues typically presented in a negligent design case and involve technical matters peculiarly within the knowledge of the manufacturer, we conclude that once the plaintiff makes a prima facie showing that the injury was proximately caused by the product's design, the burden should appropriately shift to the defendant to prove, in light of the relevant factors, that the product is not defective. Moreover, inasmuch as this conclusion flows from our determination that the fundamental public policies embraced in *Greenman* dictate that a manufacturer who seeks to escape liability for an injury proximately caused by its product's design on a risk-benefit theory should bear the burden of persuading the trier of fact that its product should not be judged defective, the defendant's burden is one affecting the burden of proof, rather than simply the burden of producing evidence. . . .

Because the jury may have interpreted the erroneous instruction given in the instant case as requiring plaintiff to prove that the high-lift loader was ultrahazardous or more dangerous than the average consumer contemplated, and because the instruction additionally misinformed the jury that the defectiveness of the product must be evaluated in light of the product's "intended use" rather than its "reasonably foreseeable use" . . . , we cannot find that the error was harmless on the facts of this case. In light of this conclusion, we need not address plaintiff's additional claims of error, for such issues may not arise on retrial.

The judgment in favor of defendants is reversed.

NOTES

1. *What Is a Design Defect?* Some jurisdictions today follow *Barker* and allow either the consumer expectations test or the risk-utility test to prove a design defect. Other jurisdictions adopt just one of the two tests. In Aubin v. Union Carbide Corp., 177 So. 3d 489, 510 (Fla. 2015), the plaintiff alleged he developed mesothelioma from exposure to asbestos contained in defendant's construction products. The jury found in favor of the plaintiff, but the intermediate appellate court reversed on the ground that the trial court failed to instruct the jury using the Third Restatement's reasonable alternative design test for design defect claims. Pariente, J., in turn reversed the intermediate court. In so doing he rejected the Third Restatement's view on alternative design while extolling the virtues of the consumer expectations test:

> The important aspect of strict products liability that led to our adoption [of the consumer expectations test] remains true today: the burden of compensating victims of unreasonably dangerous products is placed on the manufacturers, who are most able to protect against the risk of harm, and not on the consumer injured by the product. Increasing the burden for injured consumers to prove their strict liability claims for unreasonably dangerous products that were placed into the stream of commerce is contrary to the policy reasons behind the adoption of strict liability. . . .

Other design defect tests were propounded during the late 1970s but have receded in recent years as most courts have adopted the *Barker* test. For example, Azzarello v. Black Bros. Co., Inc., 391 A.2d 1020, 1027 (Pa. 1978), held that even though the supplier was not "an insurer of all injuries caused by the product," it nonetheless was cast "in the role of a guarantor of his product's safety," under which the words "unreasonably dangerous" had no part. Instead "the jury may find a defect where the product left the supplier's control lacking any element necessary to make it safe for its intended use or possessing any feature that renders it unsafe for the intended use." Pennsylvania retreated from the *Azzarello* test in Tincher v. Omega Flex, Inc., 104 A.3d 328, 335 (Pa. 2014), but refused to adopt the Third Restatement reasonable alternative design test. In *Tincher*, the plaintiff sought to show that corrugated stainless-steel tubing used to transport natural gas to the Tinchers' first floor fireplace was defective because it was punctured by a lightning strike. Castille, C.J., reversed a jury verdict and announced this test for product defect:

> [W]e conclude that a plaintiff pursuing a cause upon a theory of strict liability in tort must prove that the product is in a "defective condition." The plaintiff may prove defective condition by showing either that (1) the danger is unknowable and unacceptable to the average or ordinary consumer, or that (2) a reasonable person would conclude that the probability and seriousness of harm caused by the product outweigh the burden or costs of taking precautions. The burden of production and persuasion is by a preponderance of the evidence.

An approach to design defects more restrictive than *Barker*'s was taken in Wilson v. Piper Aircraft Corp., 577 P.2d 1322, 1327–28 (Or. 1978), a wrongful death action brought by the representatives of two passengers who died in the crash of a Piper Cherokee airplane manufactured by the defendants. The plaintiffs claimed that the defective design was the engine's susceptibility to icing, in part because the aircraft was not equipped with a state-of-the-art injection-type fuel system. Holman, J., parted with *Barker* by imposing stringent requirements that the plaintiff present evidence "from which the jury could find the suggested alternatives are not only technically feasible but also practicable in terms of cost and the over-all design and operation of the product." Further the Federal Aviation Administration (FAA) had awarded the defendant a certificate of airworthiness, which in its own terms set only minimum design standards. The court concluded that

> in a field as closely regulated as aircraft design and manufacture, it is proper to take into consideration, in determining whether plaintiffs have produced sufficient evidence of defect to go to the jury, the fact that the regulatory agency has approved the very design of which they complain after considering the dangers involved.

2. *State of the Art: Time of Sale or Time of Trial?* In setting the appropriate design standard for product safety, many judicial decisions look in part to the state of the art in the product supplier's trade or business. The state of the art refers to something more stringent than the "common practice" in the industry and embraces the scientific, technological, and safety standards that are reasonably feasible at the time of product design. Thus in Kim v. Toyota Motor Corp., 424 P.3d 290, 296 (Cal. 2018), Kruger, J., distinguished industry custom—"the use of the challenged design within the relevant industry," i.e., "what is done"—from state of the art evidence—"what can be done under present technological capacity." See also RTT: PL §2, comment *d.*

Most courts today do not allow compliance with the state of the art to resolve the design defect question in the defendant's favor but nonetheless treat it as a factor to consider, which "is both necessary and probative on the issue of 'unreasonably dangerous.' " Reed v. Tiffin Motor Homes, Inc., 697 F.2d 1192, 1197 (4th Cir. 1982). In Bruce v. Martin-Marietta Corp., 544 F.2d 442, 447 (10th Cir. 1976), the court measured the state of the art at the time the defendant's airplane seats entered the stream of commerce in 1952, not at the time of the crash in 1970. The record showed that the seats met all FAA standards as well as the applicable state of the art for 1952. In the court's view, the crucial test was the "expectation of the ordinary consumer," who "would not expect a Model T to have safety features which are incorporated in automobiles today." See *The T.J. Hooper, supra* Chapter 3, at 150. Contrast with City of Pomona v. SQM North America Corp., 801 Fed. App'x. 488, 489–90, 492 (9th Cir. 2020), which involved "Pomona's strict product liability claim that fertilizer manufactured by SQM contaminated the city's water supply with a toxic chemical called perchlorate." Under *Barker* "the jury must determine 'through hindsight' whether 'the risk of danger inherent in the challenged design outweighs the benefits of such design.' " Accordingly, in an action for current harm, the court allowed "jurors to consider risks that were not, and could not have been, known to the manufacturer at the time of manufacture." This prompted a vigorous dissent from Lee, J.:

> Notably, the City conceded at oral argument that it has not located a single California state court ruling—in the forty years since *Barker*'s issuance—that applied *Barker* to hold a party liable based on scientific knowledge that was unknowable at the time of the incident but known at the time of trial.

3. *Subsequent Improvements.* The substantive disputes in state of the art cases frequently raise evidentiary inquiries: Can evidence of subsequent design changes be introduced to show the defectiveness of the defendant's basic design? In Ault v. International Harvester Co., 528 P.2d 1148, 1152 (Cal. 1974), the California Supreme Court allowed such evidence, saying:

> The contemporary corporate mass producer of goods, the normal products liability defendant, manufactures tens of thousands of units of goods; it is manifestly unrealistic to suggest that such a producer will forego making improvements in its product, and risk innumerable additional lawsuits and the attendant adverse effect upon its public image, simply because evidence of adoption of such improvement may be admitted in an action founded on strict liability for recovery on an injury that preceded the improvement.

Nonetheless, a strong majority of courts have refused to admit the evidence in both negligence and strict liability cases. See Cann v. Ford Motor Co., 658 F.2d 54, 60 (2d Cir. 1981). Federal Rule of Evidence 407 provides:

> When measures are taken that would have made an earlier injury or harm less likely to occur, evidence of the subsequent measures is not admissible to prove:
>
> - negligence;
> - culpable conduct;
> - a defect in a product or its design; or
> - a need for a warning or instruction.

Or, as Baron Bramwell put it, the rule rejects the notion that "because the world gets wiser as it gets older, therefore it was foolish before." Hart v. Lancashire & Yorkshire Ry. Co. (1869) 21 LT 261, 263 (quoted in Note of Advisory Committee on Proposed Rule 407).

4. *Product Modification.* Much litigation has focused on the question whether a product alteration made after a manufacturer has shipped goods constitutes a superseding cause sufficient to relieve the original manufacturer of liability for design defects. Young v. Aeroil Products Co., 248 F.2d 185 (9th Cir. 1957), represents the traditional view of protecting manufacturers from liability based on subsequent alterations. There the decedent had been crushed to death when the portable elevator he had been operating toppled. The decedent's employer had previously added additional equipment to the elevator, causing its imbalance. Even though the defendant had sold the elevator with the express warranty that it was balanced, the court held that the warranty was unavailing because "[t]he thing being used was not the thing sold."

In Hoover v. New Holland North America, Inc., 11 N.E.3d 693 (N.Y. 2014), the plaintiff, a 16-year-old girl, was badly injured when "she was caught and dragged into the rotating driveline of a tractor-driven post hole digger distributed by defendant-appellant CNH America LLC (CNH) and sold by defendant-appellant Niagara Frontier Equipment Sales, Inc. (Niagara) (collectively, defendants)." The manufacturer of the device, Alamo/SMC Corporation (SMC), was not joined as a defendant in the suit. "The jury returned a verdict in favor of plaintiff in the amount of $8,811,587.29 and apportioned liability as follows: 35 percent to CNH, 30 percent to SMC, 30 percent to Smith [the owner of the digger], 3 percent to Gary Hoover [the plaintiff's stepfather], and 2 percent to Niagara."

The defendant's product had been distributed with extensive warnings, including: "DANGER! SHIELD MISSING DO NOT OPERATE!" and "KEEP ALL SHIELDS IN PLACE AND IN GOOD CONDITION." Smith was aware of these warnings but nonetheless decided not to replace the key shields on the device after they incurred damage over several years from installing between 1,000 and 2,000 posts per year. Smith testified that he removed the guard and continued to use the machine without replacing the guard, "because it was only going to break again."

Abdus-Salaam, J., rejected the defendant's motion for summary judgment on the ground that

> Smith did not modify the digger in order to "circumvent[]" the utility of the shield or to "adapt" the digger to suit his own needs. Rather, Smith removed the shield because its "functional utility" had already been destroyed, and his testimony raised a question of fact whether removal of the broken shield was to blame for plaintiff's injuries. Plaintiff also proffered Berry's expert affidavit, in which the engineer averred that the shield was "not reasonably safe" because it was not "designed to last the life" of the digger, and that defendants' failure to incorporate a safer yet feasible alternative design, such as an integral guard or metal shield, was "a substantial factor" in causing plaintiff's injuries.

Smith, J., dissented, arguing that the full liability should rest on Smith because "[h]e chose not to get a replacement shield—which would have cost $40 and taken no more than half an hour to install—because 'it's only going to get bent up and broke again.' " How does the case come out under the open and obvious defense?

In Singh v. Gemini Auto Lifts, Inc., 27 N.Y.S.3d 637, 638–39 (App. Div. 2016), the court extended *Hoover* to reach a situation where the plaintiff caught his hand in a hole on an automotive lift, from which the plastic cover had been removed. The court held that the plaintiff had raised triable issues of fact "as to whether the lift was intended to be used without the cover in place." Does it make sense for courts to resolve liability in the face of post-sale modifications in terms of design defect? What about liability for failure to warn? See *infra* at 616, Note 1.

The Third Restatement recognizes that product alteration and modification may defeat or diminish defendant's responsibility, but develops no specialized rules to deal with them, treating them (along with product misuse) as parts of the broader questions of product defect, causation, and plaintiff's conduct. RTT: PL §2, comment *p*.

c. *The Third Restatement Reasonable Alternative Design Test*

The Third Restatement rejected the consumer expectations test as part of its attempt to rein in what was perceived to be excessive liability arising out of the *Barker* dual-pronged standard.

RESTATEMENT OF THE LAW (THIRD) OF TORTS: PRODUCTS LIABILITY

§2. Categories of Product Defect

A product: . . .

(b) is defective in design when the foreseeable risks of harm posed by the product could have been reduced or avoided by the adoption of a reasonable alternative design by the seller or other distributor, or a predecessor in the commercial chain of distribution, and the omission of the alternative design renders the product not reasonably safe. . . .

Comment a. Rationale: . . . The emphasis is on creating incentives for manufacturers to achieve optimal levels of safety in designing and marketing products. Society does not benefit from products that are excessively safe—for example, automobiles designed with maximum speeds of 20 miles per hour—any more than it benefits from products that are too risky. Society benefits most when the right, or optimal, amount of product safety is achieved.

Illustration 5: ABC Co. manufactures novelty items. One item, an exploding cigar, is made to explode with a loud bang and the emission of smoke. Robert purchased the exploding cigar and presented it to his boss, Jack, at a birthday party arranged for him at the office. Jack lit the cigar. When it exploded, the heat from the explosion lit Jack's beard on fire causing serious burns to his face. . . . [T]he finder of fact might find ABC liable for the defective design of the exploding cigar even if no reasonable alternative design was available that would provide similar prank characteristics. The utility of the exploding cigar is so low and the risk of injury is so high as to warrant a conclusion that the cigar is defective and should not have been marketed at all.

Does an alternative design test ensure optimal product-design safety?

NOTES

1. *Alternative Designs.* The reasonable alternative design test in the Third Restatement was developed largely in response to the New Jersey case of O'Brien v. Muskin Corp., 463 A.2d 298, 302–03, 305–06 (N.J. 1983). Muskin sold a pool to Arthur Henry, which, when assembled, had an embossed vinyl bottom and a depth of about three feet. The plaintiff, twenty-three years old, dove into the pool from either a nearby platform or from the eight-foot-high roof of the Henrys' garage. "As his outstretched hands hit the vinyl-lined pool bottom, they slid apart, and O'Brien struck his head on the bottom of the pool, thereby sustaining injuries." The plaintiff's expert claimed that the pool design was dangerous because wet vinyl was more than twice as slippery as the rubber latex used to line in-ground pools.

The trial court excluded that testimony when the expert admitted that he knew of no above-ground pool lined with a material other than vinyl. On appeal the court allowed the design defect count to go to the jury on Professor Wade's risk-utility test, noting that for the plaintiff to reach the jury under such a test, "it was not necessary for plaintiff to prove the existence of alternative, safer designs."

In New Jersey, *Muskin* was altered by statute, which provided, among other things, that "the manufacturer or seller shall not be liable if: (1) At the time the product left the control of the manufacturer, there was not a practical and technically feasible alternative design that would have prevented the harm without substantially impairing the reasonably anticipated or intended function of the product. . . ." N.J. Stat. Ann. §2A:58C-3(a) (West 2023). The Third Restatement takes much the same line by requiring "that the plaintiff show a reasonable alternative design . . . even though the plaintiff alleges that the category of product sold by the defendant is so dangerous that it should not have been marketed at all." RTT: PL §2, comment *d*. It explicitly disapproved of *Muskin* because "the vinyl pool liner that [the manufacturer] utilized was the best and safest liner available and that no alternative, less slippery liner was feasible." RTT: PL §2, illus. 4. Is it appropriate for a jury to decide that, absent a reasonably feasible alternative design, above-ground pools should not be marketed at all? In dealing with its alternative design conception, section 2, comment *f* of the Third Restatement observes:

> A broad range of factors may be considered in determining whether an alternative design is reasonable and whether its omission renders a product not reasonably safe. The factors include, among others, the magnitude and probability of the foreseeable risks of harm, the instructions and warnings accompanying the product, and the nature and strength of consumer expectations regarding the product, including expectations arising from product portrayal and marketing. The relative advantages and disadvantages of the product as designed and as it alternatively could have been designed may also be considered. Thus, the likely effects of the alternative design on production costs; the effect of alternative design on product longevity, maintenance, repair, and esthetics; and the range of consumer choice among products are factors that may be taken into account.

2. *Judicial Reception of the Third Restatement.* The reasonable alternative design requirement has received a mixed reception. In Potter v. Chicago Pneumatic Tool Co., 694 A.2d 1319, 1332, 1334–35 (Conn. 1997), Katz, J., noted that a majority of states did not impose the Third Restatement's alternative design requirement, and refused to do so, lest the law place an "undue burden" on plaintiffs by requiring them to use expert evidence in every design defect case. In *Tincher*, 104 A.3d at 395, *supra* at 596, Castille, J., likewise resisted the move to the Third Restatement's "evidence-bound standard of proof," on the ground that "[t]he approach suggests *a priori* categorical exemptions for some products—such as novel products with no alternative design—but not others." He elaborated this rationale:

> Neither courts, nor the American Law Institute for that matter, are in the business of articulating general principles tailored to anoint special "winners" and "losers" among those who engage in the same type of conduct. In our view, the question of "special tort-insulated status" for certain suppliers—for example, manufacturers of innovative products with no comparable alternative design—optimally "requires an assessment and balancing of policies best left to the General Assembly."

The necessity for a reasonable alternative design was, however, embraced in Casey v. Toyota Motor Engineering & Manufacturing North America Inc., 770 F.3d 322, 332–34 (5th Cir. 2014), in which the plaintiff claimed that the defective design of Toyota's side curtain airbag resulted in his wife's death in a one-car accident in which she had been driving at excessive speed. The plaintiff's expert witness testified that a different material (elastomer) mentioned in an unrelated patent application was safer than the nylon material then used by Toyota. Higginson, J., first noted that the plaintiff's "reliance on the patent application's tests was not evidence of the alternative design's superior safety because the testing did not involve similar forces and factors as involved in Mrs. Casey's rollover accident." He continued:

> In addition, there is no evidence in the record that the baseline material to which the patent applicants compared their invention was the same as the airbag used in the airbag installed in Mrs. Casey's vehicle. While both used nylon, there is no evidence that the weave, coating, or other construction of the Toyota airbag was the same as the baseline used in the patent's tests. In sum, because the patent application did not test the alternative material under similar accident conditions, Casey has failed to show that using that material would have prevented or reduced the risk of injury in Mrs. Casey's accident.

Higginson, J., then noted that the plaintiff had not shown that the new design would not "inject any new risks into the vehicle or diminish its usefulness or safety in any way," or "that the alternative design could have been implemented in the 2010 Toyota Highlander, has been implemented in any vehicle, or could possibly be implemented." Lastly, he noted that the "economic feasibility" of the alternative design had not been proven.

Twerski, An Essay on the Quieting of Products Liability Law, 105 Cornell L. Rev. 1211, 1211 (2020), argues that the reasonable alternative design test has become the de facto norm:

> In fifteen of the seventeen states that allow recovery based on consumer expectations the author could not find a single case in which the plaintiff did not introduce a reasonable alternative design. And in all jurisdictions but one, a defendant is free to introduce risk-utility evidence as relevant to the issue of whether the product disappoints consumer expectations. Thus, whether a reasonable alternative design is required de jure, it is de facto a staple in almost all design defect cases.

Should the plaintiff ever be able to invoke a design that has never been put to commercial use as the appropriate alternative design?

3. *"Unavoidably Unsafe" Products.* The "comment k" defense, derived from RST §402A, *supra* at 567, precludes certain "unavoidably unsafe products," notably prescription drugs and medical devices, from being classified as defective merely because they are, at the time of distribution, incapable of being made safe. States differ in terms of whether they apply a "blanket" or "case-by-case" (i.e., product-by-product) approach to comment *k*. The "blanket" approach exempts from strict liability design defect certain categories of products deemed "unavoidably unsafe." For example, the California Supreme Court deemed all prescription drugs categorically exempt from strict liability for design defect in Brown v. Superior Court, 751 P.2d 470, 477 (Cal. 1988):

> (1) a drug manufacturer's liability for a defectively designed drug should not be measured by the standards of strict liability; (2) because of the public interest in the development, availability, and reasonable price of drugs, the appropriate test for determining responsibility is the test stated in comment k; and (3) for these same reasons of policy, we disapprove the holding . . . that only those prescription drugs found to be "unavoidably dangerous" should be measured by the comment k standard and that strict liability should apply to drugs that do not meet that description.

A large majority of states, however, reject the blanket approach in favor of a "case-by-case" approach that requires the defendant to establish that the product is "unavoidably unsafe." For example, the New Jersey Supreme Court held in Feldman v. Lederle Laboratories, 479 A.2d 374, 382–83 (N.J. 1984), that only certain drugs—namely those proven to be "unavoidably unsafe" on a case-by-case basis—qualify for comment *k*'s protection:

> [W]e see no reason to hold as a matter of law and policy that all prescription drugs that are unsafe are unavoidably so. Drugs, like any other products, may contain defects that could have been avoided by better manufacturing or design. Whether a drug is unavoidably unsafe should be decided on a case-by-case basis. . . .

To meet this burden, the defendant must show that no feasible alternative design exists that would accomplish the same purpose with a lesser risk and that the drug's overall benefits outweigh the risks it presents to individual safety.

4. *Modern Defective Drug Design Litigation.* In Benefield v. Pfizer Inc., 103 F. Supp. 3d 449, 462 (S.D.N.Y. 2015), the plaintiff brought a design defect claim over conditions allegedly developed from taking Tygacil, a brand-name, antibacterial drug that she was prescribed for an abdominal infection. Pfizer argued that the design defect claims should be dismissed because the plaintiff failed to allege "better alternatives." Oetken, J., rejected Pfizer's contention:

> Several factors figure in the risk-utility test, but the "heart" of the analysis is about "whether the design chosen was a reasonable one from among the feasible choices of which the manufacturer was aware or should have been aware." . . . At this stage, Plaintiffs must merely "set forth sufficient facts from which the Court can reasonably infer that the design was defective." . . . Plaintiffs have done so. They have plausibly alleged that Tygacil brought about [plaintiff's] injuries.

How does the plaintiff's assertion of injury demonstrate that risk outweighs utility?

RESTATEMENT OF THE LAW (THIRD) OF TORTS: PRODUCTS LIABILITY

§6. Liability of Commercial Product Seller or Distributor for Harm Caused by Defective Prescription Drugs and Medical Devices

(c) A prescription drug or medical device is not reasonably safe due to defective design if the foreseeable risks of harm posed by the drug or medical device are sufficiently great in relation to its foreseeable therapeutic benefits that reasonable health-care providers, knowing of such foreseeable risks and therapeutic benefits, would not prescribe the drug or medical device for any class of patients.

Comment b. Rationale: . . . The traditional refusal by courts to impose tort liability for defective designs of prescription drugs and medical devices is based on the fact that a prescription drug or medical device entails a unique set of risks and benefits. What may be harmful to one patient may be beneficial to another. Under Subsection (c) a drug is defectively designed only when it provides no net benefit to any class of patients. . . .

Criticism of the Third Restatement's design defect test was voiced in Bryant v. Hoffman-LaRoche, 585 S.E.2d 723, 727–28 (Ga. Ct. App. 2003), in which the plaintiff sued the defendant on the ground that his wife died as a result of the heart medication, Posicor, which he alleged was defectively designed and thus interacted poorly with other drugs she had taken. The defendant manufacturer urged that the case be governed by RTT §6(c). The court rejected this view in favor of comment *k* to the Second Restatement, noting:

> [Section] 6(c) has been criticized for its failure to reflect existing case law, its lack of flexibility with regard to drugs involving differing benefits and risks, its unprecedented application of a reasonable physician standard, and the fact that a consumer's claim could easily be defeated by expert opinion that the drug had some use for someone, despite potentially harmful effects on a large class of individuals. [Freeman v. Hoffman-LaRoche, 618 N.W.2d 827 (Neb. 2000).] To

> date, no court has adopted the Third Restatement's strict liability test for prescription drugs, and one court [*Freeman*] has explicitly refused to adopt the test. . . .
>
> Moreover, we agree with the majority of courts that Comment *k* serves as an affirmative defense and that the defense has no application to claims of manufacturing defect or failure to warn.

Does section 6(c) functionally grant absolute immunity to all FDA-approved drugs?

For further criticism of the "complete overhaul" of the design defect provisions in the Third Restatement, see Conk, Is There a Design Defect in the Restatement (Third) of Torts: Products Liability?, 109 Yale L.J. 1087 (2000). But Professors Henderson and Twerski insist:

> A claim that seeks to find a given drug design defective because the manufacturer should have developed a safer alternative drug is inappropriate because courts are incapable of sensibly deciding whether the alternative proposed by the plaintiff would have met with FDA approval. Since any drug marketed in the United States must be approved by the FDA, a court must be able to determine that the FDA would have approved the drug. Given the many-year duration of the FDA approval process, which involves testing of thousands of patients, no court could rationally determine that an alternative drug would have been approved.

Twerski & Henderson Jr., Drug Design Liability: Farewell to Comment k, 67 Baylor L. Rev. 521, 577 (2015). Does this argument preclude the claim in *Bryant*? A malpractice action against the treating physician? Require federal preemption of state law? Sharkey, Field Preemption: Opening the "Gates of Escape" from Tort Law, 50 J. Legal Stud. S27, S47–50 (2021), argues that federal preemption, *infra* at 629, stunted the development of 6(c).

3. The Duty to Warn

Implicit in many design defect decisions is the view that it is better to design out certain dangerous conditions than it is to warn consumers and users of their dangers. Although that rule works well for many forms of equipment, it poses significant challenges for pharmaceutical and chemical products for which small changes in molecular composition can negate the effectiveness of the product for its intended purpose, or require a new round of approvals from, for example, the Food and Drug Administration or the Environmental Protection Agency. In these cases, the use of product warnings instead of design alterations may offer a sensible compromise, especially when the potential harms are not apparent to a product user from the appearance of the product or from common knowledge about its lurking dangers. What legal standards should apply in these warning cases?

MacDonald v. Ortho Pharmaceutical Corp.

475 N.E.2d 65 (Mass. 1985)

Abrams, J. This products liability action raises the question of the extent of a drug manufacturer's duty to warn consumers of dangers inherent in the use of oral contraceptives. The plaintiffs brought suit against the defendant, Ortho Pharmaceutical Corporation (Ortho), for injuries allegedly caused by Ortho's birth control pills, and obtained a jury verdict in their favor. The defendant moved for a judgment notwithstanding the verdict. The judge concluded that the defendant did not owe a duty to warn the plaintiffs, and entered judgment for Ortho. The plaintiffs appealed. We transferred the case to this court on our own motion and reinstate the jury verdict.

We summarize the facts. In September, 1973, the plaintiff Carole D. MacDonald (MacDonald), who was twenty-six years old at the time, obtained from her gynecologist a prescription for Ortho-Novum contraceptive pills, manufactured by Ortho. As required by the then effective regulations promulgated by the United States Food and Drug Administration (FDA), the pill dispenser she received was labeled with a warning that "oral contraceptives are powerful and effective drugs which can cause side effects in some users and should not be used at all by some women," and that "[t]he most serious known side effect is abnormal blood clotting which can be fatal." The warning also referred MacDonald to a booklet which she obtained from her gynecologist, and which was distributed by Ortho pursuant to FDA requirements. The booklet contained detailed information about the contraceptive pill, including the increased risk to pill users that vital organs such as the brain may be damaged by abnormal blood clotting. [The warning supplied listed the death and injury rates to women of various ages from taking the pill and noted "that women who have had blood clots in the legs, lungs, or brain [should] not use oral contraceptives."] The word "stroke" did not appear on the dispenser warning or in the booklet.

MacDonald's prescription for Ortho-Novum pills was renewed at subsequent annual visits to her gynecologist. The prescription was filled annually. On July 24, 1976, after approximately three years of using the pills, MacDonald suffered an occlusion of a cerebral artery by a blood clot, an injury commonly referred to as a stroke [or a "cerebral vascular accident"]. The injury caused the death of approximately twenty per cent of MacDonald's brain tissue, and left her permanently disabled. She and her husband initiated an action in the Superior Court against Ortho, seeking recovery for her personal injuries and his consequential damages and loss of consortium.

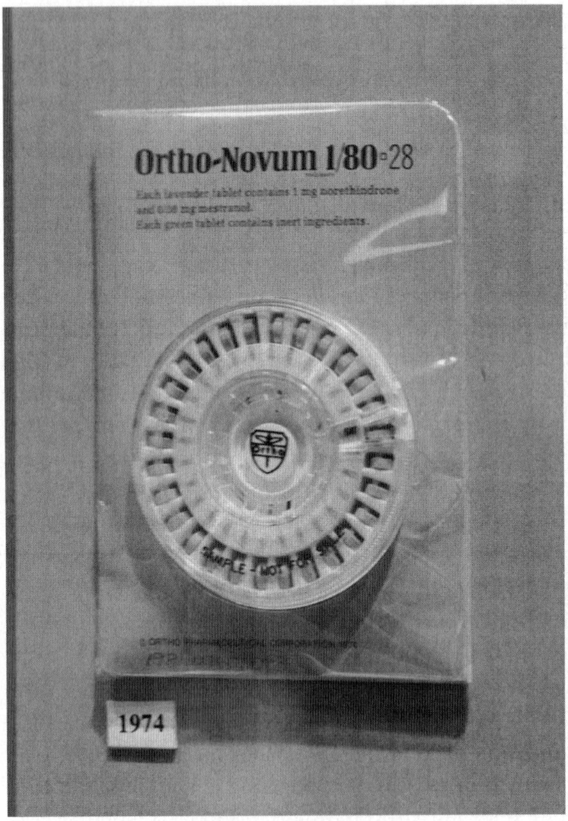

Ortho-Novum Dialpak dispenser
Source: B Christopher / Alamy

MacDonald testified that, during the time she used the pills, she was unaware that the risk of abnormal blood clotting encompassed the risk of stroke, and that she would not have used the pills had she been warned that stroke is an associated risk. [The court notes that the amended FDA regulations listed " 'the serious side effects of oral contraceptives, such as thrombophlebitis, pulmonary embolism, myocardial infarction, retinal artery thrombosis, *stroke*, benign hepatic adenomas, induction of fetal abnormalities, and gallbladder disease' (emphasis added). See 21 C.F.R. §310.501(a)(2)(iv) (1984)."] The case was submitted to a jury on the plaintiffs' theories that Ortho was negligent in failing to warn adequately of the dangers associated with the pills and that Ortho breached its warranty of merchantability. These two theories were treated, in effect, as a single claim of failure to warn. The jury returned a special verdict, finding no negligence or breach of warranty in the manufacture of the pills. The jury also found that Ortho adequately advised the gynecologist of the risks inherent in the pills;[7] the jury found, however, that Ortho was negligent and in breach of warranty because it failed to give MacDonald sufficient warning of such dangers. The jury further found that MacDonald's injury was caused by Ortho's pills, that the inadequacy of the warnings to MacDonald was the proximate cause of her injury, and that Ortho was liable to MacDonald and her husband.

After the jury verdict, the judge granted Ortho's motion for judgment notwithstanding the verdict, concluding that, because oral contraceptives are prescription drugs, a manufacturer's duty to warn the consumer is satisfied if the manufacturer gives adequate warnings to the prescribing physician, and that the manufacturer has no duty to warn the consumer directly.

The narrow issue, on appeal, is whether, as the plaintiffs contend, a manufacturer of birth control pills owes a direct duty to the consumer to warn her of the dangers inherent in the use of the pill. We conclude that such a duty exists under the law of this Commonwealth.

1. Extent of Duty to Warn . . .

[The court first notes that the general rule was that the defendant must warn all "persons who it is foreseeable will come in contact with, and consequently be endangered by, that product." It then recognizes a "narrow" exception, as set out in Restatement (Second) of Torts §388, comment *n*, when warnings have been given to a responsible intermediary "so that the manufacturer has no duty directly to warn the consumer." It continues:]

The rule in jurisdictions that have addressed the question of the extent of a manufacturer's duty to warn in cases involving prescription drugs is that the prescribing physician acts as a "learned intermediary" between the manufacturer and the patient, and "the duty of the ethical drug manufacturer is to warn the doctor, rather than the patient, [although] the manufacturer is directly liable to the patient for a breach of such duty." McEwen v. Ortho Pharmaceutical Corp., 528 P.2d 522 (Or. 1974). Oral contraceptives, however, bear peculiar characteristics which warrant the imposition of a common law duty on the manufacturer to warn users directly of associated risks. Whereas a patient's involvement in decision-making concerning use of a prescription drug necessary to treat a malady is typically minimal or nonexistent, the healthy, young consumer of oral contraceptives is usually actively involved in the decision to use "the pill," as opposed to other available birth control products, and the prescribing physician is relegated to a relatively passive role.

Furthermore, the physician prescribing "the pill," as a matter of course, examines the patient once before prescribing an oral contraceptive and only annually thereafter. At her annual checkup, the patient receives a renewal prescription for a full year's supply of the pill. Thus, the patient may only seldom have the opportunity to explore her questions and concerns about the medication with the prescribing physician. Even if the physician, on those occasions, were scrupulously to remind the patient of the risks attendant on continuation of the oral contraceptive, "the patient cannot be expected to remember all of the details for a protracted period of time." 35 Fed. Reg. 9002 (1970).

Last, the birth control pill is specifically subject to extensive Federal regulation [which, inter alia, requires that "users of these drugs should, without exception, be furnished with written information telling them of the drug's benefits and risks."]

7. MacDonald stated at trial that her gynecologist had informed her only that oral contraceptives might cause bloating, and had not advised her of the increased risk of stroke associated with consumption of birth control pills. The physician was not joined as a defendant in this action, and no questions relating to any potential liability on his part are before us. MacDonald further testified at trial that she had read both the warning on the Dialpak tablet dispenser as well as the booklet which she received from her gynecologist.

The oral contraceptive thus stands apart from other prescription drugs in light of the heightened participation of patients in decisions relating to use of "the pill"; the substantial risks affiliated with the product's use; the feasibility of direct warnings by the manufacturer to the user; the limited participation of the physician (annual prescriptions); and the possibility that oral communications between physicians and consumers may be insufficient or too scanty standing alone fully to apprise consumers of the product's dangers at the time the initial selection of a contraceptive method is made as well as at subsequent points when alternative methods may be considered. We conclude that the manufacturer of oral contraceptives is not justified in relying on warnings to the medical profession to satisfy its common law duty to warn, and that the manufacturer's obligation encompasses a duty to warn the ultimate user. Thus, the manufacturer's duty is to provide to the consumer written warnings conveying reasonable notice of the nature, gravity, and likelihood of known or knowable side effects, and advising the consumer to seek fuller explanation from the prescribing physician or other doctor of any such information of concern to the consumer.[13]

2. Adequacy of the Warning

Because we reject the judge's conclusion that Ortho had no duty to warn MacDonald, we turn to Ortho's separate argument, not reached by the judge, that the evidence was insufficient to warrant the jury's finding that Ortho's warnings to MacDonald were inadequate. Ortho contends initially that its warnings complied with FDA labeling requirements, and that those requirements preempt or define the bounds of the common law duty to warn. We disagree. The regulatory history of the FDA requirements belies any objective to cloak them with preemptive effect. In response to concerns raised by drug manufacturers that warnings required and drafted by the FDA might be deemed inadequate by juries, the FDA commissioner specifically noted that the boundaries of civil tort liability for failure to warn are controlled by applicable State law. 43 Fed. Reg. 4214 (1978). Although the common law duty we today recognize is to a large degree coextensive with the regulatory duties imposed by the FDA, we are persuaded that, in instances where a trier of fact could reasonably conclude that a manufacturer's compliance with FDA labeling requirements or guidelines did not adequately apprise oral contraceptive users of inherent risks, the manufacturer should not be shielded from liability by such compliance. Thus, compliance with FDA requirements, though admissible to demonstrate lack of negligence, is not conclusive on this issue, just as violation of FDA requirements is evidence, but not conclusive evidence, of negligence. We therefore concur with the plaintiffs' argument that even if the conclusion that Ortho complied with FDA requirements were inescapable, an issue we need not decide, the jury nonetheless could have found that the lack of a reference to "stroke" breached Ortho's common law duty to warn.

The common law duty to warn, like the analogous FDA "lay language" requirement, necessitates a warning "comprehensible to the average user and . . . convey[ing] a fair indication of the nature and extent of the danger to the mind of a reasonably prudent person."

Whether a particular warning measures up to this standard is almost always an issue to be resolved by a jury; few questions are "more appropriately left to a common sense lay judgment than that of whether a written warning gets its message across to an average person." Ferebee v. Chevron Chem. Co., 552 F. Supp. 1293, 1304 (D.D.C. 1982). A court may, as a matter of law, determine "whether the defendant has conformed to that standard, in any case in which

13. This opinion does not diminish the prescribing physician's duty to "disclose in a reasonable manner all significant medical information that the physician possesses or reasonably should possess that is material to an intelligent decision by the patient whether to" take "the pill." Harnish v. Children's Hosp. Medical Center, 439 N.E.2d 240 (Mass. 1982).

the jury may not reasonably come to a different conclusion," Restatement (Second) of Torts §328B(d) and Comment *g* (1965), but judicial intrusion into jury decision-making in negligence cases is exceedingly rare. Further, we must view the evidence in the light most favorable to the plaintiffs. The test is whether "anywhere in the evidence, from whatever source derived, any combination of circumstances could be found from which a reasonable inference could be drawn in favor of the plaintiff."

Ortho argues that reasonable minds could not differ as to whether MacDonald was adequately informed of the risk of the injury she sustained by Ortho's warning that the oral contraceptives could cause "abnormal blood clotting which can be fatal" and further warning of the incremental likelihood of hospitalization or death due to blood clotting in "vital organs, such as the brain." We disagree. . . . We cannot say that this jury's decision that the warning was inadequate is so unreasonable as to require the opposite conclusion as a matter of law. The jury may well have concluded, in light of their common experience and MacDonald's testimony, that the absence of a reference to "stroke" in the warning unduly minimized the warning's impact or failed to make the nature of the risk reasonably comprehensible to the average consumer. Similarly, the jury may have concluded that there are fates worse than death, such as the permanent disablement suffered by MacDonald, and that the mention of the risk of death did not, therefore, suffice to apprise an average consumer of the material risks of oral contraceptive use.

We reverse the judgment, which the judge ordered notwithstanding the verdict, and remand the case to the Superior Court for the entry of judgment for the plaintiffs.

So ordered.

O'Connor, J., dissenting. . . . I would hold that, as a matter of law, by adequately informing physicians of the risks associated with its product and by complying with applicable FDA regulations, a contraceptive pill manufacturer fulfils the duty to warn that it owes consumers. . . .

I believe that the "prescription drug" rule, combined with the *Harnish* rule most fairly and efficiently allocates among drug manufacturers, physicians, and drug users, the risks and responsibilities involved with the use of prescription drugs. Furthermore, I believe that those rules best ensure that a prescription drug user will receive in the most effective manner the information that she needs to make an informed decision as to whether to use the drug. The rules place on drug manufacturers the duty to gather, compile, and provide to doctors data regarding the use of their drugs, tasks for which the manufacturers are best suited, and the rules place on doctors the burden of conveying those data to their patients in a useful and understandable manner, a task for which doctors are best suited. Doctors, unlike printed warnings, can tailor to the needs and abilities of an individual patient the information that that patient needs in order to make an informed decision whether to use a particular drug. Manufacturers are not in position to give adequate advice directly to those consumers whose medical histories and physical conditions, perhaps unknown to the consumers, make them peculiarly susceptible to risk. Prescription drugs — including oral contraceptives — differ from other products because their dangers vary widely depending on characteristics of individual consumers. Exposing a prescription drug manufacturer to liability based on a jury's determination that, despite adequately informing physicians of the drug's risks and complying with FDA regulations, the manufacturer failed reasonably to warn a particular plaintiff-consumer of individualized risks is not essential to reasonable consumer protection and places an unfair burden on prescription drug manufacturers.

NOTES

1. *Physicians as Learned Intermediaries.* Why did the plaintiffs not join the treating physician? To what extent is the decision in *MacDonald* strengthened or weakened by the wide availability of all forms of product warnings on the Internet? The learned intermediary rule held firm in Harrison v. American Home Products Corp. (AHP), 165 F.3d 374, 379 (5th Cir. 1999), when the plaintiffs complained of adverse side effects from the contraceptive Norplant, a long-term birth control method. Jolly, J., stressed the "significant role" that physicians played "in prescribing Norplant and in educating their patients about the benefits and disadvantages to using it." He also rejected the view that AHP's aggressive direct-to-consumer marketing campaign undercut the physicians' duty to warn in the absence of any evidence that the plaintiffs "actually saw, let alone relied, on" any AHP marketing materials. What result if they had so relied?

Consider Perez v. Wyeth Laboratories, 734 A.2d 1245 (N.J. 1999), where the court imposed a direct duty to warn the plaintiff patient on Wyeth, the drug manufacturer, because of its "massive advertising campaign for Norplant in 1991, which it directed at women rather than at their doctors" through such women's magazines as *Glamour, Mademoiselle*, and *Cosmopolitan*. The *Perez* rule, however, has not caught on. In 2022, Owens, J., surveyed the landscape and noted that "only New Jersey has adopted a direct-to-consumer exception, but that decision has not been subsequently relied on." Dearinger v. Eli Lilly & Co., 510 P.3d 326, 331 (Wash. 2022) (en banc). Recently, Hunte v. Abbott Laboratories, Inc., 569 F. Supp. 3d 115 (D. Conn. 2021), certified to the Connecticut Supreme Court the question whether a direct-to-consumer marketing exception applies to infant formula for premature babies.

RESTATEMENT OF THE LAW (THIRD) OF TORTS: PRODUCTS LIABILITY

§6. Liability of Commercial Seller or Distributor for Harm Caused by Defective Prescription Drugs and Medical Devices

(d) A prescription drug or medical device is not reasonably safe due to inadequate instructions or warnings if reasonable instructions or warnings regarding foreseeable risks of harm are not provided to:

(1) prescribing and other health-care providers who are in a position to reduce the risks of harm in accordance with the instructions or warnings; or

(2) the patient when the manufacturer knows or has reason to know that health-care providers will not be in a position to reduce the risks of harm in accordance with the instructions or warnings.

On the status of the learned intermediary defense in birth control and mass vaccination cases, the Third Restatement takes a studious pass: "The Institute leaves to developing case law whether exceptions to the learned intermediary rule in these or other situations should be recognized." RTT: PL §6, comment *e*.

How does *MacDonald* come out under the Third Restatement test? In 2021, the United States Court of Appeals for the Eighth Circuit determined Nebraska "would follow what has become an 'overwhelming majority' rule" in adopting the Third Restatement's version of the learned intermediary doctrine, finding that Massachusetts in *MacDonald* "stands alone in unequivocally adopting" a prescription-contraceptives exception. Ideus v. Teva Pharms. United States, Inc., 986 F.3d 1098, 1102 (8th Cir. 2021).

Should drug manufacturers' direct promotional activities for other drugs be factored into the mix under section 6(d)(2)? For a sharp criticism of drug marketing practices, see Vukadin, Failure-to-Warn: Facing Up to the Real Impact of Pharmaceutical Marketing on the Physician's Decision to Prescribe, 50 Tulsa L. Rev. 75, 75, 104 (2014), insisting that "[f]ailure-to-warn jurisprudence should stop relying on empty paper compliance and recognize present-day pharmaceutical marketing as a compelling and driving force in the decision to prescribe." Nonetheless, successful overpromotion cases are difficult to win, given the requirement that "such overpromotion caused the physician to initiate or maintain the prescription at issue. General claims of overpromotion are not sufficient." In re Zyprexa Prods. Liab. Litig., 649 F. Supp. 2d 18, 33 (E.D.N.Y. 2009). See also DiBartolo v. Abbott Labs., 914 F. Supp. 2d 601 (S.D.N.Y. 2012).

2. *Pharmacists' Duty to Warn.* A pharmacist's education and training justify the imposition of a set of standard duties: (1) a duty to fill a prescription correctly, (2) a duty to remedy inadequacies on the face of the prescription, (3) and a duty to take reasonable care in preparing or dispensing the medicine.

The vast majority of states retain the general common law rule that pharmacists do not have a duty to warn patients of the risks of medication. Under the learned intermediary doctrine, a court "could not place a greater burden on pharmacists" than on drug manufacturers because it is within the discretion of the physician, as the party who prescribes the drug, to warn the patient. Fakhouri v. Taylor, 618 N.E.2d 518, 519 (Ill. App. Ct. 1993). The Third Restatement §6(e) also restricts the liability of retail sellers of drugs and medical devices to cases of manufacturing defects (why?) or for failing "to exercise reasonable care and such failure causes harm to persons." Nonetheless some courts have required pharmacists to (1) inform a doctor of a contraindication or of an abnormally high dosage, (2) provide a detailed warning where, through advertising, the pharmacy claims to have an enhanced warning or safety system in place, and (3) provide a warning where the pharmacist knows or has reason to know a customer's allergies. Thus in Happel v. Wal-Mart Stores, Inc., 766 N.E.2d 1118, 1124 (Ill. 2002), the defendant maintained a registry that warned of possible adverse drug interactions or allergic reactions for all of its customers. A duty to warn was imposed because "[t]he burden on defendant of imposing this duty is minimal. All that is required is that the pharmacist telephone the physician and inform him or her of the contraindication. Alternatively, the pharmacist could provide the same information to the patient."

Dr. Albert Sabin

Source: Bettmann / Corbis

3. *Mass Vaccination Cases.* The dissemination and adequacy of warnings has proved critically important to mass immunization programs. Davis v. Wyeth Laboratories, Inc., 399 F.2d 121, 129–31 (9th Cir. 1968), and Reyes v. Wyeth Laboratories, Inc., 498 F.2d 1264 (5th Cir. 1974), are the watershed cases involving liability for the Sabin live-virus polio vaccine. In *Davis*, the plaintiff contracted polio after being vaccinated as part of a mass immunization program administered by the local pharmacist, when no physician was available to do the job. The program for immunization was promoted by one of the defendant's representatives whose expenses were reimbursed by the local medical organization. The court held that the defendant did not meet its duty to warn when it failed to inform the plaintiff of the one-in-a-million chance that the vaccine could cause polio, even when properly prepared and administered.

> Ordinarily in the case of prescription drugs warning to the prescribing physician is sufficient. . . .
>
> Here, however, although the drug was denominated a prescription drug it was not dispensed as such. It was dispensed to all comers at mass clinics without an individualized balancing by a physician of the risks involved. In such cases (as in the case of over-the-counter sales of nonprescription drugs) warning by the manufacturer to its immediate purchaser will not suffice. . . . In such cases, then, it is the responsibility of the manufacturer to see that warnings reach the consumer, either by giving warning itself or by obligating the purchaser to give warning. . . .
>
> This duty does not impose an unreasonable burden on the manufacturer. When drugs are sold over the counter to all comers warnings normally can be given by proper labeling. Such method of giving warning was not available here, since the vaccine came in bottles never seen by the consumer. But other means of communication such as advertisements, posters, releases to be read and signed by recipients of the vaccine, or oral warnings were clearly available and could easily have been undertaken or prescribed by appellee.

In *Reyes*, the court then let the jury decide whether the vaccine was the physical cause of the injury and whether an adequate warning would have led the plaintiff to change his behavior. Is this a higher or lower standard than in *MacDonald*? Note that the standard used is akin to the informed consent test. Is that an appropriate duty for the manufacturer? Does that duty change if a learned intermediary is involved?

The *Reyes* court continued: "In the absence of evidence rebutting the presumption, a jury finding that the defendant's product was the producing cause of the plaintiff's injury would be sufficient to hold him liable." Does this presumption make sense if the background rate of infection from the "wild strain" is known on average to be ten or one hundred times as great as that from vaccines?

Reyes and *Davis* were first-generation cases in which no warnings had been provided. Subsequent litigation focused on the adequacy of the warnings. In Givens v. Lederle, 556 F.2d 1341, 1343 (5th Cir. 1977), another Sabin vaccine case, the defendant Lederle's warning to physicians stated in full:

> Paralytic disease following the ingestion of live polio virus vaccines has been reported in individuals receiving the vaccine, and in some instances, in persons who were in close contact with subjects who had been given live oral polio virus vaccine. Fortunately, such occurrences are rare, and it could not be definitely established that any such case was due to the vaccine strain and was not coincidental with infection due to naturally occurring poliomyelitis, or other enteroviruses.

The package insert also noted that the risk, if any, was one in three million. The physician who had inoculated the plaintiff's daughter gave the plaintiff no warning of the risk because he thought that the insert was too "nebulous" to require it. On appeal, the court held that his testimony, together with evidence showing that such infections had occurred, supported the jury's verdict that the warning was inadequate, especially because the warning denied any definite connection between the vaccine and the disease. Dr. Sabin had testified for the defendant that his vaccine could not possibly cause polio.

The number of large damage awards in the late 1970s and 1980s substantially increased the costs of vaccines. See Manning, Changing Rules of Tort Law and the Market for Childhood Vaccines, 37 J.L. & Econ. 247, 248 (1994), whose econometric analysis shows that the price of the DPT vaccine between 1975 and 1990 increased by over 2,000 percent, and of that increase over 96 percent went to litigation costs.

In response to the crisis, Congress passed the National Childhood Vaccine Injury Act of 1986 (NCVIA), which provides for a complex system of no-fault compensation of up to

$250,000 for persons who suffer particular side effects from certain vaccine programs within specified time limits. 42 U.S.C. §300aa (2023). The statute raises many of the hard issues of proof of causation found in other products liability settings.

4. ***Federal Liability for Bad Vaccines Under the Federal Tort Claims Act (FTCA).*** The FDA has extensive regulatory authority of the general approval of new vaccines and the power to approve or withhold the release of particular vaccines to the marketplace. At the same time, like other federal agencies, it receives the protection of the discretionary function exception to the FTCA, which insulates the government from liability if the action challenged in the case involves the permissible exercise of policy judgment. In Berkovitz v. United States, 486 U.S. 531, 542, 546 (1988), the infant plaintiff suffered a severe case of polio after ingesting a dose of Orimune manufactured by Lederle Laboratories, which settled with the plaintiff. The case involved a two-step process. First the Division of Biologic Standards (DBS) gave general licensing approval for production of the vaccine, after which the Bureau of Biologics (BoB) had responsibility for releasing particular lots of the vaccine. Marshall, J., first rejected the government's position that the discretionary function exception precludes liability for any and all acts arising out of the regulatory programs of federal agencies. He then concluded that the DBS was not protected by that exception when "the DBS issued a product license without first receiving data that the manufacturer must submit showing how the product, at the various stages of the manufacturing process, matched up against regulatory safety standards" because the DBS has "no discretion to issue a license without first receiving the required test data." But with respect to the release of a particular lot, Marshall, J., held that "the discretionary function exception bars any claims that challenge the Bureau's formulation of policy as to the appropriate way in which to regulate the release of vaccine lots." Does that make sense if there are standard protocols that the BoB should use to decide whether or not to release vaccines? Or should the FDA receive a broader protection to encourage it to reduce erroneous releases by remaining in the inspection business, given the strict liability of the drug manufacturers?

5. ***Standardized Warnings.*** The decisions in both *MacDonald* and *Givens* that allow juries to treat FDA warnings as statutory minimums have prompted some legislative reform. Consider the Michigan Revised Judicature Act of 1961, Mich. Comp. Laws §600.2946(5) (2023), which allows for FDA warnings to be an absolute defense in duty to warn cases for drugs lawfully on the market unless the drug manufacturer during the drug approval process "intentionally withholds from or misrepresents" to the FDA information about the drug that results in it obtaining an approval that would have been denied if accurate information had been supplied. When the Michigan statute applies, a defendant can typically obtain summary judgment in a duty to warn case. Defenders of the statute point to the excessive risk aversion that the FDA has on the question of new drug approval. Opponents of the statute point to the serious gaps in the FDA approval process. For a review of the huge literature on this topic, see Struve, The FDA and the Tort System: Postmarketing Surveillance, Compensation, and the Role of Litigation, 5 Yale J. Health Pol'y L. & Ethics 587 (2005) (critical of the statute); Noah, Rewarding Regulatory Compliance: The Pursuit of Symmetry in Products Liability, 88 Geo. L.J. 2147 (2000) (supportive of the statute).

Vassallo v. Baxter Healthcare Corp.

696 N.E.2d 909 (Mass. 1998)

Greaney, J. In this products liability case, the plaintiff Florence Vassallo claimed that the defendants, Baxter Healthcare Corporation and Baxter International, Inc., were liable to her for damages because silicone breast implants, manufactured by a predecessor company to the defendants (Heyer-Schulte Corporation), that had been implanted in her were negligently designed, accompanied by negligent product warnings, and breached the implied warranty of merchantability, with the consequence that she was injured. [The plaintiff underwent breast implant surgery in 1977, and her implants ruptured in 1992, and were replaced with saline implants in 1993. In 1976, the defendant's Dear Doctor letter did not address all possible adverse consequences that leakage could have on an implant user, including "risks of chronic inflammation, permanent tissue scarring, or possible effects on the immune system." The court reviews the plaintiff's expert evidence on the harm caused by the slow release of silicone gel. It also examines extensive testimony that Heyer-Schulte knew of the risk of rupture and of its adverse consequences. The plaintiff alleged that had she known of the true state of affairs, she would never have consented to the implants.] Plaintiff Vincent Vassallo claimed a loss of consortium. The plaintiffs also asserted a claim for violation of G.L. c. 93A, §§2(a) and 9. [The court affirms the judgment for the plaintiffs below on the negligence and statutory claims.]

We conclude, however, that we should change our products liability law to conform to the clear majority rule regarding what has to be shown to recover in a breach of warranty claim for failure to warn of risks associated with a product. . . .

We take this opportunity . . . to consider the defendants' argument that we should change our products liability law concerning the implied warranty of merchantability from what is stated in Hayes v. Ariens Co., 462 N.E.2d 273 (Mass. 1984), and that the law should be reformulated to adopt a "state of the art" standard that conditions a manufacturer's liability on actual or constructive knowledge of the risks.

Our current law, regarding the duty to warn under the implied warranty of merchantability, presumes that a manufacturer was fully informed of all risks associated with the product at issue, regardless of the state of the art at the time of the sale, and amounts to strict liability for failure to warn of these risks. This rule has been justified by the public policy that a defective product, "unreasonably dangerous due to lack of adequate warning[s], [is] not fit for the ordinary purposes for which [it is] used regardless of the absence of fault on [a defendant's] part."

At trial, [the judge followed *Hayes* by refusing to issue a "jury instruction that a manufacturer need only warn of risks 'known or reasonably knowable in light of the generally accepted scientific knowledge available at the time of the manufacture and distribution of the device.' "] While the judge's instruction was a correct statement of our law, we recognize that we are among a distinct minority of States that applies a hindsight analysis to the duty to warn.[17] . . .

The thin judicial support for a hindsight approach to the duty to warn is easily explained. The goal of the law is to induce conduct that is capable of being performed. This goal is not advanced by imposing liability for failure to warn of risks that were not capable of being known.

The Restatement (Third) of Torts: Products Liability §2(c) (1998), approved by the American Law Institute, reaffirms the principle expressed in Restatement (Second) of Torts, *supra* at §402A comment *j*, by stating that a product "is defective because of inadequate instructions or warnings when the foreseeable risks of harm posed by the product could have been reduced or avoided by the provision of reasonable instructions or warnings . . . and the omission of the instructions or warnings renders the product not reasonably safe." The rationale behind the principle is explained by stating that "[u]nforeseeable risks arising from foreseeable product use . . . by definition cannot specifically be warned against." Restatement (Third) of Torts:

17. The Reporters' Note to the Restatement (Third) of Torts: Products Liability §2(c) comment *m*, at 106 (1998), lists four States taking the position that a manufacturer is charged with a duty to warn of risks without regard to whether the manufacturer knew or reasonably should have known of the risks, including Massachusetts; Hawaii; Pennsylvania; Washington.

Products Liability, *supra* at §2 comment *m*, at 34. However, comment *m* also clarifies the manufacturer's duty "to perform reasonable testing prior to marketing a product and to discover risks and risk-avoidance measures that such testing would reveal. A seller is charged with knowledge of what reasonable testing would reveal." *Id*. . . .

In recognition of the clear judicial trend regarding the duty to warn in products liability cases, and the principles stated in Restatement (Third) of Torts: Products Liability, *supra* at §2 and comment *m*, we hereby revise our law to state that a defendant will not be held liable under an implied warranty of merchantability for failure to warn or provide instructions about risks that were not reasonably foreseeable at the time of sale or could not have been discovered by way of reasonable testing prior to marketing the product. A manufacturer will be held to the standard of knowledge of an expert in the appropriate field, and will remain subject to a continuing duty to warn (at least purchasers) of risks discovered following the sale of the product at issue. In accordance with the usual rule governing retroactivity in this type of action, the standard just expressed will apply to all claims on which a final judgment has not been entered, or as to which an appeal is pending or the appeal period has not expired, and to all claims on which an action is commenced after the release of this opinion. [The court notes that the defendant could not take advantage of this change in law because of the adverse jury verdict on the negligence count, and the jury's apparent conclusion that defendant did have actual or constructive notice of the risks associated with their silicone implants.]

[Affirmed.]

NOTES

1. ***Post-Sale Duty to Warn.*** *Vassallo* recognizes a continuing duty to warn, even as it rejects a hindsight duty to warn. Assuming a company learns of a latent risk that had gone undiscovered despite reasonable pre-market testing, should it now have a duty to notify past buyers of the product of the newly discovered risk? See RTT: PL §10.

RESTATEMENT OF THE LAW (THIRD) OF TORTS: PRODUCTS LIABILITY

§10. Liability of Commercial Product Seller or Distributor for Harm Caused by Post-Sale Failure to Warn

(a) One engaged in the business of selling or otherwise distributing products is subject to liability for harm to persons or property caused by the seller's failure to provide a warning after the time of sale or distribution of a product if a reasonable person in the seller's position would provide such a warning.

(b) A reasonable person in the seller's position would provide a warning after the time of sale if:

(1) the seller knows or reasonably should know that the product poses a substantial risk of harm to persons or property; and

(2) those to whom a warning might be provided can be identified and can reasonably be assumed to be unaware of the risk of harm; and

(3) a warning can be effectively communicated to and acted on by those to whom a warning might be provided; and

(4) the risk of harm is sufficiently great to justify the burden of providing a warning.

Comment j. Distinguishing post-sale failures to warn from defects existing at the time of sale: When a product is defective at the time of sale, liability can be established without reference to a post-sale duty to warn. A seller who discovers after sale that its product was defective at the time of sale within the meaning of this Restatement cannot generally absolve itself of liability by issuing a post-sale warning.

RTT: PL §11 details the circumstances under which a manufacturer can be liable for a failure to recall. The Reporters delimited these sections as additional duties—not as a way for manufacturers to immunize themselves against liability for time-of-sale defects by issuing post-sale warnings. RTT: PL §10, comment *j*.

2. ***Unavoidably Dangerous Products.*** Closely related to RST §402A, comment *j*, is comment *k*, which deals with products known to be unavoidably dangerous, typically drugs. See *supra* at 567. In these cases, it is impractical to remove the product from the market or to alter its design or composition because mitigating the adverse side effects would undermine the effectiveness of the product. Consequently, a warning that allows informed consumer choice is the only workable alternative. Thus, in Nolen v. C.R. Bard Inc., 533 F. Supp. 3d 584, 592 (M.D. Tenn. 2021), Trauger, J., opined that, while defendant "may ultimately be entitled to the protection of Comment k," the "availability of that protection" depends on whether defendant "adequately warned physicians regarding the heightened risks" of the product.

Similarly, in the case of blood transfusions, jurisdictions have rejected the strict liability position for contaminated blood so long as adequate warning is provided. In Brody v. Overlook Hospital, 317 A.2d 392, 395 (N.J. Super. Ct. App. Div. 1974), the court reasoned that donor blood is a medical necessity, and without the capacity to cheaply test it for diseases, it is unavoidably unsafe. More than forty states have enacted legislation adopting the negligence standard in blood transfusion cases, including Illinois. 745 Ill. Comp. Stat. 40/3 (2023).

Hood v. Ryobi America Corp.

181 F.3d 608 (4th Cir. 1999)

Wilkinson, C.J. Wilson M. Hood lost part of his thumb and lacerated his leg when he removed the blade guards from his new Ryobi miter saw and then used the unguarded saw for home carpentry. Hood sued Ryobi, alleging that the company failed adequately to warn of the saw's dangers and that the saw was defective. Applying Maryland products liability law, the district court granted summary judgment to Ryobi on all claims.

The saw and owner's manual bore at least seven clear, simple warnings not to operate the tool with the blade guards removed. The warnings were not required to spell out all the consequences of improper use. Nor was the saw defective—Hood altered and used the tool in violation of Ryobi's clear warnings. Thus we affirm the judgment.

I

Hood purchased a Ryobi TS-254 miter saw in Westminster, Maryland on February 25, 1995, for the purpose of performing home repairs. The saw was fully assembled at the time of purchase. It had a ten-inch diameter blade mounted on a rotating spindle controlled by a finger trigger on a handle near the top of the blade. To operate the saw, the consumer would use that handle to lower the blade through the material being cut.

Two blade guards shielded nearly the entire saw blade. A large metal guard, fixed to the frame of the saw, surrounded the upper half of the blade. A transparent plastic lower guard covered the rest of the blade and retracted into the upper guard as the saw came into contact with the work piece.

A number of warnings in the operator's manual and affixed to the saw itself stated that the user should operate the saw only with the blade guards in place. For example, the owner's manual declared that the user should "KEEP GUARDS IN PLACE" and warned: "ALWAYS USE THE SAW BLADE GUARD. Never operate the machine with the guard removed"; "NEVER operate this saw without all guards in place and in good operating condition"; and "WARNING: TO PREVENT POSSIBLE SERIOUS PERSONAL INJURY, NEVER PERFORM ANY CUTTING OPERATION WITH THE UPPER OR LOWER BLADE GUARD REMOVED." The saw itself carried several decals stating "DANGER: DO NOT REMOVE ANY GUARD. USE OF SAW WITHOUT THIS GUARD WILL RESULT IN SERIOUS INJURY"; "OPERATE ONLY WITH GUARDS IN PLACE"; and "WARNING . . . DO NOT operate saw without the upper and lower guards in place."

The day after his purchase, Hood began working with the saw in his driveway. While attempting to cut a piece of wood approximately four inches in height Hood found that the blade guards prevented the saw blade from passing completely through the piece. Disregarding the manufacturer's warnings, Hood decided to remove the blade guards from the saw. Hood first detached the saw blade from its spindle. He then unscrewed the four screws that held the blade guard assembly to the frame of the saw. Finally, he replaced the blade onto the bare spindle and completed his cut.

Rather than replacing the blade guards, Hood continued to work with the saw blade exposed. He worked in this fashion for about twenty minutes longer when, in the middle of another cut, the spinning saw blade flew off the saw and back toward Hood. The blade partially amputated his left thumb and lacerated his right leg.

Hood admits that he read the owner's manual and most of the warning labels on the saw before he began his work. He claims, however, that he believed the blade guards were intended solely to prevent a user's clothing or fingers from coming into contact with the saw blade. He contends that he was unaware that removing the blade guards would permit the spinning blade to detach from the saw. But Ryobi, he claims, was aware of that possibility. In fact, another customer had sued Ryobi after suffering a similar accident in the mid-1980s. . . .

II

A manufacturer may be liable for placing a product on the market that bears inadequate instructions and warnings or that is defective in design. Hood asserts that Ryobi failed adequately to warn of the dangers of using the saw without the blade guards in place. Hood also contends that the design of the saw was defective. We disagree on both counts.

A

Hood first complains that the warnings he received were insufficiently specific. Hood admits that Ryobi provided several clear and conspicuous warnings not to operate the saw without the blade guards. He contends, however, that the warnings affixed to the product and displayed in the operator's manual were inadequate to alert him to the dangers of doing so. In addition to Ryobi's directive "never" to operate a guardless saw, Hood would require the company to inform of the actual consequences of such conduct. Specifically, Hood contends that an adequate warning would have explained that removing the guards would lead to blade detachment.

We disagree. Maryland does not require an encyclopedic warning. Instead, "a warning need only be one that is reasonable under the circumstances." Levin v. Walter Kidde &

Co., 248 A.2d 151, 153 (Md. 1968). A clear and specific warning will normally be sufficient—"the manufacturer need not warn of every mishap or source of injury that the mind can imagine flowing from the product." Liesener v. Weslo, Inc., 775 F. Supp. 857, 861 (D. Md. 1991); see *Levin*, 248 A.2d at 154 (declining to require warning of the danger that a cracked syphon bottle might explode and holding "never use cracked bottle" to be adequate as a matter of law). In deciding whether a warning is adequate, Maryland law asks whether the benefits of a more detailed warning outweigh the costs of requiring the change.

Hood assumes that the cost of a more detailed warning label is minimal in this case, and he claims that such a warning would have prevented his injury. But the price of more detailed warnings is greater than their additional printing fees alone. Some commentators have observed that the proliferation of label detail threatens to undermine the effectiveness of warnings altogether. As manufacturers append line after line onto product labels in the quest for the best possible warning, it is easy to lose sight of the label's communicative value as a whole. Well-meaning attempts to warn of every possible accident lead over time to voluminous yet impenetrable labels—too prolix to read and too technical to understand.

By contrast, Ryobi's warnings are clear and unequivocal. Three labels on the saw itself and at least four warnings in the owner's manual direct the user not to operate the saw with the blade guards removed. Two declare that "serious injury" could result from doing so. This is not a case where the manufacturer has failed to include any warnings at all with its product. Ryobi provided warnings sufficient to apprise the ordinary consumer that it is unsafe to operate a guardless saw—warnings which, if followed, would have prevented the injury in this case.

It is apparent, moreover, that the vast majority of consumers do not detach this critical safety feature before using this type of saw. Indeed, although Ryobi claims to have sold thousands of these saws, Hood has identified only one fifteen-year-old incident similar to his. Hood has thus not shown that these clear, unmistakable, and prominent warnings are insufficient to accomplish their purpose. Nor can he prove that increased label clutter would bring any net societal benefit. We hold that the warnings Ryobi provided are adequate as a matter of law.

B

Hood's defective design claim is likewise unpersuasive [on the ground that the product alterations defeat liability].

Affirmed.

NOTES

1. ***Warnings, Design Modification, and the Heeding Presumption.*** In Liriano v. Hobart Corp., 700 N.E.2d 303, 308 (N.Y. 1998), the seventeen-year-old plaintiff caught his right hand and lower arm in a commercial meat grinding machine from which the employer had removed the safety guard. Unlike *Hood*, no warnings stated that it was dangerous to remove the guard. On an advisory opinion of a certified question from the Second Circuit, Ciparick, J., held that a duty to warn cause of action could survive even in cases where a product modification blocked liability under a design defect theory. The court noted that if the injured person is

> fully aware of the hazard through general knowledge, observation or common sense, or participated in the removal of the safety device whose purpose is obvious, lack of a warning about that danger may well obviate the failure to warn as a legal cause of an injury resulting from that

> danger. . . . Similarly, a limited class of hazards need not be warned of as a matter of law because they are patently dangerous or pose open and obvious risks.

Nonetheless the court then returned the failure to warn cause of action for a "fact-specific" inquiry in the Second Circuit.

Next, in Liriano v. Hobart Corp., 170 F.3d 264 (2d Cir. 1999), Calabresi, J., upheld a jury verdict for the plaintiff (subject to a one-third reduction for comparative negligence) because the youthful plaintiff had only recently immigrated to the United States; had worked for his employer — Super grocery store — for only a week, and had never been given instructions on how to operate the grinder, which he had used only two or three times. In light of the variation in product users, some users might not discover dangers that others find obvious. Accordingly, Calabresi, J., held that the

> jury could reasonably find that there exist people who are employed as meat grinders and who do not know (a) that it is feasible to reduce the risk with safety guards, (b) that such guards are made available with grinders, and (c) that the grinders should be used only with the guards.

Calabresi, J., further held that, on the question of causation, the burden of proof shifted to the defendant:

> When a defendant's negligent act is deemed wrongful precisely because it has a strong propensity to cause the type of injury that ensued, that very causal tendency is evidence enough to establish a *prima facie* case of cause-in-fact. The burden then shifts to the *defendant* to come forward with evidence that its negligence was *not* such a but-for cause.

The heeding presumption received an extensive analysis in Foster v. Ethicon, Inc., 529 F. Supp. 3d 992, 1002 (D.S.D. 2021), where the plaintiff brought claims for complications resulting from the installation of Ethicon's pelvic mesh, a medical device that aims to repair defective tissue in the pelvis. In this case, the plaintiffs argued that the warnings given to the physicians were insufficient to convey the seriousness of the risk. Lange, C.J., regarded that as beside the point, for, as the defendant argued, "Ms. Foster cannot show causation because Dr. Ferrell [the treating physician] did not rely on the TVT's [implanted device] warnings and would have prescribed the TVT for Ms. Foster even if he had received an adequate warning." Lange, C.J., continued, "Ms. Foster is entitled to a rebuttable presumption that Dr. Ferrell would have read and heeded an adequate warning. As explained below, however, Ethicon has rebutted the presumption and Ms. Foster has failed to show a material question of fact on causation."

2. *When Must a Warning Be Given? Latent Defects.* In Ayers v. Johnson & Johnson Co., 818 P.2d 1337, 1341 (Wash. 1991) (en banc), David Ayers, then aged fifteen months, had taken an unmarked bottle of Johnson's baby oil out of the purse of his thirteen-year-old sister. Just as he began to drink the oil, his mother yelled at him, causing him to gasp and inhale the oil in his lungs. Once there, the baby oil coated his air sacs and quickly led to oxygen deprivation that resulted in serious injuries: His leg motions became spastic; he had limited control over his head movements; and he suffered brain impairment, seizures, and lost any ability to speak.

Both sides agreed that once David inhaled the baby oil, no medical attention could have prevented these injuries. The plaintiff contended that a warning on the bottle was needed to alert users of this risk in order to keep baby oil out of the reach of infants in the first place. The plaintiff's mother testified that she read warnings, and kept dangerous products away from her young children, and instructed her teenage daughters to do the same. Both mother and daughters testified that they thought baby oil could cause diarrhea or stomach upset, but not more serious injuries. Johnson & Johnson argued that it was rank speculation to claim that the additional knowledge would have led to different conduct since all members of the Ayers family knew that the baby oil was only for external use and was dangerous if taken internally. The jury found for the plaintiff, and its verdict was sustained on appeal:

> On the basis of this evidence, the jury was entitled to infer that if the Ayerses had known of the dangers of aspiration, they would have treated the baby oil with greater care; that they would have treated it with the caution they used in relation to items they recognized as highly dangerous, like cleaning products; and that had they done so, the accident would have never occurred. We conclude that the evidence of causation presented to the jury was sufficient to sustain the jury's verdict.

Should Johnson & Johnson change the warnings on its bottles? On its package inserts? If a warning should be included, what should it say?

3. *Duty to Warn: Patent Defects.* The risks in *Ayers* were both latent and remote. What ought to be done with respect to generic properties of common substances known to cause harm, such as alcohol? In Garrison v. Heublein, Inc., 673 F.2d 189, 189 (7th Cir. 1982), the court rejected the plaintiff's claim for "physical and mental injuries as a result of consuming the defendant's product [Smirnoff vodka] over a twenty-year period," holding that the defendant had no duty to warn of risks that were common knowledge.

"Screens out harmful ultraviolet rays, conditions skin, repels insects, won't wash off while swimming, will not stain most fabrics. Warning: Contact with eyes, ears, nose, or mouth may be fatal."

Source: Edward Frascino / The New Yorker Collection / The Cartoon Bank

Common knowledge, however, did not allow the defendant to obtain a summary judgment in Hon v. Stroh Brewery Co., 835 F.2d 510, 511 (3d Cir. 1987). The plaintiff's husband had died of pancreatitis that the plaintiff alleged had resulted mainly from his consumption of about eight to twelve cans of the defendant's beer each week over a period of several years. The court accepted the plaintiff's claim that a warning was required because it was not common knowledge that "*either* excessive *or* prolonged, even though moderate, use of alcohol may result in diseases of many kinds, including pancreatic disease." The court rejected the defendant's comment *j* defense in part because the jury could find that Stroh's advertising campaign linked the consumption of large quantities of beer to the "good life." It found that "comment *j* does not say that whenever alcohol is consumed over a long period of time the dangers are necessarily generally known. Rather it says that *when* the danger is generally known, no warning is required." Note that federal regulations, 27 C.F.R. §16.21 (2023), now require the following warning label to be attached conspicuously to containers of alcoholic beverages sold:

> GOVERNMENT WARNING: (1) According to the Surgeon General, women should not drink alcoholic beverages during pregnancy because of the risk of birth defects. (2) Consumption of alcoholic beverages impairs your ability to drive a car or operate machinery, and may cause health problems.

Air & Liquid Systems Corp. v. DeVries

139 S. Ct. 986 (2019)

KAVANAUGH, J.

In maritime tort cases, we act as a common-law court, subject to any controlling statutes enacted by Congress. This maritime tort case raises a question about the scope of a manufacturer's duty to warn. The manufacturers here produced equipment such as pumps, blowers, and turbines for three Navy ships. The equipment required asbestos insulation or asbestos parts in order to function as intended. When used on the ships, the equipment released asbestos fibers into the air. Two Navy veterans who were exposed to asbestos on the ships developed cancer and later died. The veterans' families sued the equipment manufacturers, claiming that the manufacturers were negligent in failing to warn of the dangers of asbestos.

II

. . . Maritime law has likewise recognized common-law principles of products liability for decades. See East River S. S. Corp., 476 U.S. at 865[, *supra* at 573].

In this negligence case, we must decide whether a manufacturer has a duty to warn when the manufacturer's product requires later incorporation of a dangerous part—here, asbestos—in order for the integrated product to function as intended.

We start with basic tort-law principles. Tort law imposes "a duty to exercise reasonable care" on those whose conduct presents a risk of harm to others. Restatement (Third) of Torts: Liability for Physical and Emotional Harm §7, p. 77 (2005). For the manufacturer of a product, the general duty of care includes a duty to warn when the manufacturer "knows or has reason to know" that its product "is or is likely to be dangerous for the use for which it is supplied" and the manufacturer "has no reason to believe" that the product's users will realize that danger. Restatement (Second) of Torts §388, p. 301 (1963–1964).

In tort cases, the federal and state courts have not reached consensus on how to apply that general tort-law "duty to warn" principle when the manufacturer's product requires later incorporation of a dangerous part in order for the integrated product to function as intended. Three approaches have emerged.

The first approach is the more plaintiff-friendly foreseeability rule that the Third Circuit adopted in this case: A manufacturer may be liable when it was foreseeable that the manufacturer's product would be used with another product or part, even if the manufacturer's product did not require use or incorporation of that other product or part.

The second approach is the more defendant-friendly bare-metal defense that the manufacturers urge here: If a manufacturer did not itself make, sell, or distribute the part or incorporate the part into the product, the manufacturer is not liable for harm caused by the integrated product—even if the product required incorporation of the part and the manufacturer knew that the integrated product was likely to be dangerous for its intended uses.

The third approach falls between those two approaches. Under the third approach, foreseeability that the product may be used with another product or part that is likely to be dangerous is not enough to trigger a duty to warn. But a manufacturer does have a duty to warn when its product requires incorporation of a part and the manufacturer knows or has reason to know that the integrated product is likely to be dangerous for its intended uses. Under that approach, the manufacturer may be liable even when the manufacturer does not itself incorporate the required part into the product.

We conclude that the third approach is the most appropriate for this maritime tort context.

To begin, we agree with the manufacturers that a rule of mere foreseeability would sweep too broadly. See generally Restatement (Third) of Torts: Liability for Physical and Emotional Harm §7, Comment j, at 82; Restatement (Second) of Torts §395, Comment j, at 330. Many products can foreseeably be used in numerous ways with numerous other products and parts. Requiring a product manufacturer to imagine and warn about all of those possible uses—with massive liability looming for failure to correctly predict how its product might be used with other products or parts—would impose a difficult and costly burden on manufacturers, while simultaneously overwarning users. In light of that uncertainty and unfairness, we reject the foreseeability approach for this maritime context.

That said, we agree with the plaintiffs that the bare-metal defense ultimately goes too far in the other direction. In urging the bare-metal defense, the manufacturers contend that a business generally has "no duty" to "control the conduct of a third person as to prevent him from causing physical harm to another." *Id.*, §315, at 122. That is true, but it is also beside the point here. After all, when a manufacturer's product is dangerous in and of itself, the manufacturer "knows or has reason to know" that the product "is or is likely to be dangerous for the use for which it is supplied." *Id.*, §388, at 301. The same holds true, we conclude, when the manufacturer's product requires incorporation of a part that the manufacturer knows or has reason to know is likely to make the integrated product dangerous for its intended uses. As a matter of maritime tort law, we find no persuasive reason to distinguish those two similar situations for purposes of a manufacturer's duty to warn. See Restatement (Third) of Torts: Products Liability §2, Comment i, p. 30 (1997) ("[W]arnings also may be needed to inform users and consumers of nonobvious and not generally known risks that unavoidably inhere in using or consuming the product").

Importantly, the product manufacturer will often be in a better position than the parts manufacturer to warn of the danger from the integrated product. See generally G. Calabresi, The Costs of Accidents 311–318 (1970). The product manufacturer knows the nature of the ultimate integrated product and is typically more aware of the risks associated with that integrated product. By contrast, a parts manufacturer may be aware only that its part could conceivably be used in any number of ways in any number of products. A parts manufacturer may not always be aware that its part will be used in a way that poses a risk of danger.

To be sure, as the manufacturers correctly point out, issuing a warning costs time and money. But the burden usually is not significant. Manufacturers already have a duty to warn of the dangers of their own products. That duty typically imposes a light burden on manufacturers. Requiring a manufacturer to also warn when the manufacturer knows or has reason to know that a required later-added part is likely to make the integrated product dangerous for its intended uses should not meaningfully add to that burden. . . .

The manufacturers further assert that requiring a warning in these circumstances will lead to excessive warning of consumers. Again, however, we are not aware of substantial overwarning problems in those jurisdictions that have adopted this approach. And because the rule we adopt here applies only in certain narrow circumstances, it will not require a plethora of new warnings. . . .

In the maritime tort context, we hold that a product manufacturer has a duty to warn when (i) its product requires incorporation of a part, (ii) the manufacturer knows or has reason to know that the integrated product is likely to be dangerous for its intended uses, and (iii) the manufacturer has no reason to believe that the product's users will realize that danger.

[Affirmed.]

Gorsuch, J., dissenting:

. . . [T]he traditional common law rule still makes the most sense today. The manufacturer of a product is in the best position to understand and warn users about its risks; in the language of law and economics, those who make products are generally the least-cost avoiders of their risks. By placing the duty to warn on a product's manufacturer, we force it to internalize the full cost of any injuries caused by inadequate warnings—and in that way ensure it is fully incentivized to provide adequate warnings. By contrast, we dilute the incentive of a manufacturer to warn about the dangers of its products when we require other people to share the duty to warn and its corresponding costs.

NOTES

1. ***"Third Wave" of Asbestos Litigation?*** Asbestos fits within the category of "unavoidably dangerous products," *supra* at 614, because it is both highly useful as an insulation product and because it undeniably causes many fatal conditions—chief among them asbestosis, mesothelioma, and bronchogenic carcinoma. Manufacturers have a duty to warn, even though they may be shielded from design defect liability. The watershed case is Borel v. Fibreboard Paper Products Corp., 493 F.2d 1076 (5th Cir. 1973), which affirmed a jury verdict against asbestos manufacturers on behalf of an insulation worker who had extensive contact with asbestos for more than thirty years. Wisdom, J., in an exhaustive opinion, found sufficient evidence of the dangers of asbestos in the medical literature to impose upon manufacturers—here held to the standard of "experts" in the field—a duty to warn all workers coming in contact with the product to allow them to make an informed choice of whether to expose themselves to asbestos.

Prior to *Borel* no plaintiff had ever recovered from an asbestos manufacturer. The decision unleashed an avalanche of suits against asbestos suppliers. The first generation of asbestos cases was brought against the manufacturers of asbestos products, virtually all of whom were driven into bankruptcy. One early case suggested that manufacturers could have been held responsible for unknowable defects. See Beshada v. Johns-Manville Prods. Corp., 447 A.2d 539 (N.J. 1982). But this push for strict liability for asbestos was rejected, just as it was for medical products in *Vassallo*. See, e.g., Anderson v. Owens-Corning Fiberglas Corp., 810 P.2d 549, 558–59 (Cal. 1991). In both cases, however, plaintiffs consistently won on negligence theories and often obtained hefty punitive damages.

The second wave of litigation, which began in the late 1990s, pushed further with suits against second-tier defendants, such as firms that operated premises on which asbestos products were used or which incorporated asbestos into their own products, e.g., brake linings. Typically, these cases did not involve asbestosis, but rather evidence of pleural plaque. "Pleural plaques have been described as 'discrete, elevated, opaque, shiny, rounded lesions, . . . diffuse or nodular,' of the parietal pleura or diaphragm. They strongly indicate asbestos exposure." Schuck, The Worst Should Go First: Deferral Registries in Asbestos Litigation, 15 Harv. J.L. & Pub. Pol'y 541, 545 (1992). Although these plaques illustrate exposure, they do not increase the risk of deadly asbestosis or any other deadly disease. See Weiss, Asbestos-Related Pleural Plaques and Lung Cancer, 103 Chest. 1854 (1993).

An effort to forge a class action settlement of these cases was rejected in Amchem Products, Inc. v. Windsor, 521 U.S. 591 (1997), partly on the ground that it did not provide adequate safeguards for future injured persons. See also Ortiz v. Fibreboard Corp., 527 U.S. 815 (1999). The matter has now spilled over into the political arena, but Congress thus far has been unable to fashion any solution that satisfies the plaintiffs, the various asbestos defendants, and their insurers.

2. ***Warnings and Consumer Behavior.*** Paredes, Blinded by the Light: Information Overload and Its Consequences for Securities Regulation, 81 Wash. U. L.Q. 417, 440–43 (2003), argues that consumers tend to make poorer choices as the amount of available information increases: "[A]s more information becomes available, a person might use less information, on net, as the information search and processing costs increase. Making matters worse, studies show that people do not always focus on the most relevant information but might become distracted by less relevant information." Posner, J., took Paredes' message to heart in Robinson v. McNeil Consumer Healthcare, 615 F.3d 861, 869 (7th Cir. 2010), which rejected the plaintiff's claim against the manufacturer of an ibuprofen drug for failing to warn against SJS/TEN, a very rare but serious skin disease that caused blindness in one eye and the loss of 60 percent of the plaintiff's skin:

> [T]he label would have had to describe as well every other serious disease that might, however infrequently, be caused, or even just arguably caused (for it is unclear whether ibuprofen can cause SJS/TEN), by ibuprofen. And it would have to recite the symptoms of the disease if it was rare. The resulting information overload would make label warnings worthless to consumers.

The impatience with warnings received a very different spin in Latin, Good Warnings, Bad Products, and Cognitive Limitations, 41 UCLA L. Rev. 1193 (1994). Latin rejects the "Rational Risk Calculator Model" of human behavior, often championed by economists, in favor of the rival "Mistake and Momentary Inattention" model. This model draws more heavily on psychological and sociological literature to support the view that even cautious actors are subject to momentary lapses in judgment or attention. Latin strongly supports this second perspective, which clearly implies that even "good" warnings should not be respected when cheap design alternatives are available to protect the users of products from the disastrous consequences of not heeding a warning. Latin's object of attack is Restatement §402A, comment *j*: "Where warning is given, the seller may reasonably assume that it will be read and heeded." If the Mistake and Momentary Inattention Model is correct, Latin argues the law should require design changes no matter how strong or "good" the warnings are.

Latin's prescriptions were followed in Uniroyal Goodrich Tire Co. v. Martinez, 977 S.W.2d 328, 337 (Tex. 1998), in which the plaintiff mechanic was injured when a 16-inch tire exploded while he sought to mount it on a 16.5-inch wheel in the face of stern "NEVERS," beginning with "NEVER MOUNT A 16" SIZE DIAMETER TIRE ON A 16.5" RIM. Mounting a 16" tire on a 16.5" rim can cause severe injury or death." Phillips, C.J., rejected the test of section 402A, comment *j*, and, citing Latin, adopted the position of the Third Restatement §2, comment *l*, "that warnings and safer alternative designs are factors, among others, for the jury to consider in determining whether the product as designed is reasonably safe." Who is right? Does Latin's approach work for dangerous drugs, or only consumer products? As a variation on the warnings question, what should be done with Q-Tips or other cotton swabs whose standard warnings instruct people never to insert them into the ear? Is the correct remedy to redesign the Q-Tip, strengthen the warning, take the product off the market, or keep the status quo?

SECTION E. PLAINTIFF'S CONDUCT

Daly v. General Motors Corp.
575 P.2d 1162 (Cal. 1978)

Richardson, J. The most important of several problems which we consider is whether the principles of comparative negligence expressed by us in Li v. Yellow Cab Co., apply to actions founded on strict products liability. We will conclude that they do. . . .

[The decedent was driving his Opel southbound on the Harbor Freeway between 50 and 70 miles per hour when it struck the metal divider. The car spun around and the decedent was forcibly thrown from the car, sustaining fatal head injuries. The plaintiffs alleged that the door lock was defectively designed because of its exposed push button, which, it was claimed, was forced open during the original collision.]

Over plaintiffs' objections, defendants were permitted to introduce evidence indicating that: (1) the Opel was equipped with a seat belt-shoulder harness system, and a door lock, either of which if used, it was contended, would have prevented Daly's ejection from the vehicle; (2) Daly used neither the harness system nor the lock; (3) the 1970 Opel owner's manual contained warnings that seat belts should be worn and doors locked when the car was in motion for "accident security"; and (4) Daly was intoxicated at the time of collision, which evidence the jury was advised was admitted for the limited purpose of determining whether decedent had used the vehicle's safety equipment. After relatively brief deliberations the jury returned a verdict favoring all defendants, and plaintiffs appeal from the ensuing adverse judgment.

Strict Products Liability and Comparative Fault . . .

Those counseling against the recognition of comparative fault principles in strict products liability cases vigorously stress, perhaps equally, not only the conceptual, but also the semantic difficulties incident to such a course. The task of merging the two concepts is said to be impossible, that "apples and oranges" cannot be compared, that "oil and water" do not mix, and that strict liability, which is not founded on negligence or fault, is inhospitable to comparative principles. The syllogism runs, contributory negligence was only a defense to negligence, comparative negligence only affects contributory negligence, therefore comparative negligence cannot be a defense to strict liability. . . . While fully recognizing the theoretical and semantic distinctions between the twin principles of strict products liability and traditional negligence, we think they can be blended or accommodated.

The inherent difficulty in the "apples and oranges" argument is its insistence on fixed and precise definitional treatment of legal concepts. In the evolving areas of both products liability and tort defenses, however, there has developed much conceptual overlapping and interweaving in order to attain substantial justice. The concept of strict liability itself, as we have noted, arose from dissatisfaction with the wooden formalisms of traditional tort and contract principles in order to protect the consumer of manufactured goods. Similarly, increasing social awareness of its harsh "all or nothing" consequences led us in *Li* to moderate the impact of traditional contributory negligence in order to accomplish a fairer and more balanced result. We acknowledged an intermixing of defenses of contributory negligence and assumption of risk and formally effected a type of merger. . . .

Furthermore, the "apples and oranges" argument may be conceptually suspect. It has been suggested that the term "contributory negligence," one of the vital building blocks upon which much of the argument is based, may indeed itself be a misnomer since it lacks the first element of the classical negligence formula, namely, a duty of care owing to another. . . .

Given all of the foregoing, we are, in the wake of *Li*, disinclined to resolve the important issue before us by the simple expedient of matching linguistic labels which have evolved either for convenience or by custom. Rather, we consider it more useful to examine the foundational reasons underlying the creation of strict products liability in California to ascertain whether the purposes of the doctrine would be defeated or diluted by adoption of comparative principles. We imposed strict liability against the manufacturer and in favor of the user or consumer in order to relieve injured consumers "from *problems of proof* inherent in pursuing negligence . . . and warranty . . . remedies. . . ." As we have noted, we sought to place the burden of loss on manufacturers rather than " . . . injured persons *who are powerless to protect themselves . . .* " (["*protection of otherwise defenseless victims* of manufacturing defects and the spreading throughout society of the cost of compensating them"] italics added).

The foregoing goals, we think, will not be frustrated by the adoption of comparative principles. Plaintiffs will continue to be relieved of proving that the manufacturer or distributor was negligent in the production, design, or dissemination of the article in question. Defendant's liability for injuries caused by a defective product remains strict. The principle of protecting the defenseless is likewise preserved, for plaintiff's recovery will be reduced *only* to the extent that his own lack of reasonable care contributed to his injury. The cost of compensating the victim of a defective product, albeit proportionately reduced, remains on defendant manufacturer, and will, through him, be "spread among society." However, we do not permit plaintiff's own conduct relative to the product to escape unexamined, and as to that share of plaintiff's damages which flows from his own fault we discern no reason of policy why it should, following *Li*, be borne by others. Such a result would directly contravene the principle announced in *Li*, that loss should be assessed equitably in proportion to fault.

We conclude, accordingly, that the expressed purposes which persuaded us in the first instance to adopt strict liability in California would not be thwarted were we to apply comparative principles. What would be forfeit is a degree of semantic symmetry. However, in this evolving area of tort law in which new remedies are judicially created, and old defenses judicially merged, impelled by strong considerations of equity and fairness we seek a larger synthesis. If a more just result follows from the expansion of comparative principles, we have no hesitancy in seeking it, mindful always that the fundamental and underlying purpose of *Li* was to promote the equitable allocation of loss among all parties legally responsible in proportion to their fault.

A second objection to the application of comparative principles in strict products liability cases is that a manufacturer's incentive to produce safe products will thereby be reduced or removed. While we fully recognize this concern we think, for several reasons, that the problem is more shadow than substance. First, of course, the manufacturer cannot avoid its continuing liability for a defective product even when the plaintiff's own conduct has contributed to his injury. The manufacturer's liability, and therefore its incentive to avoid and correct product defects, remains; its exposure will be lessened only to the extent that the trier finds that the victim's conduct contributed to his injury. Second, as a practical matter a manufacturer, in a particular case, cannot assume that the user of a defective product upon whom an injury is visited will be blameworthy. Doubtless, many users are free of fault, and a defect is at least as likely as not to be exposed by an entirely innocent plaintiff who will obtain full recovery. In such cases the manufacturer's incentive toward safety both in design and production is wholly unaffected. Finally, we must observe that under the present law, which recognizes assumption of risk as a complete defense to products liability, the curious and cynical message is that it profits the manufacturer to make his product so defective that in the event of injury he can argue that the user had to be aware of its patent defects. To that extent the incentives are inverted. We conclude, accordingly, that no substantial or significant impairment of the safety incentives of defendants will occur by the adoption of comparative principles.

In passing, we note one important and felicitous result if we apply comparative principles to strict products liability. This arises from the fact that under present law when plaintiff sues in negligence his own contributory negligence, however denominated, may diminish but cannot wholly defeat his recovery. When he sues in strict products liability, however, his "assumption of risk" *completely bars* his recovery. Under *Li*, as we have noted, "assumption of risk" is merged into comparative principles. . . . The consequence is that after *Li* in a negligence action, plaintiff's conduct which amounts to "negligent" assumption of risk no longer defeats plaintiff's recovery. Identical conduct, however, in a strict liability case acts as a complete bar under rules heretofore applicable. Thus, strict products liability, which was developed to free injured consumers from the constraints imposed by traditional negligence and warranty theories, places a consumer plaintiff in a worse position than would be the case were his claim founded on simple negligence. This, in turn, rewards adroit pleading and selection of theories. The application of comparative principles to strict liability obviates this bizarre anomaly by treating alike the defenses to both negligence and strict products liability actions. In each instance the defense, if established, will reduce but not bar plaintiff's claim.

A third objection to the merger of strict liability and comparative fault focuses on the claim that, as a practical matter, triers of fact, particularly jurors, cannot assess, measure, or compare plaintiff's negligence with defendant's strict liability. We are unpersuaded by the argument and are convinced that jurors are able to undertake a fair apportionment of liability. . . . [The court then notes that comparative principles have functioned smoothly in the unseaworthiness cases tried in admiralty, even though unseaworthiness is a strict liability concept.]

We find equally unpersuasive a final objection that the merger of the two principles somehow will abolish or adversely affect the liability of such intermediate entities in the chain of distribution as retailers . . . and bailors. . . . We foresee no such consequence. Regardless of the identity of a particular defendant or of his position in the commercial chain the basis for his liability remains that he has marketed or distributed a defective product. If, as we believe, jurors are capable of assessing fully and fairly the legal responsibility of a manufacturer on a strict liability basis, no reason appears why they cannot do likewise with respect to subsequent distributors and vendors of the product.

We note that the majority of our sister states which have addressed the problem, either by statute or judicial decree, have extended comparative principles to strict products liability.

Our research discloses that of the more than 30 states which have adopted some form of comparative negligence, three (including California) have done so judicially. . . . [The court notes that its position enjoys considerable academic support, and that the proposed Uniform Comparative Fault Act embraces a comparative fault principle in strict liability actions. It concludes that it also covers assumption of risk, to the extent that it is a form of contributory negligence.]

JEFFERSON, J., concurring and dissenting. . . . What the majority envisions as a fair apportionment of liability to be undertaken by the jury will constitute nothing more than an *unfair reduction* in the plaintiff's total damages suffered, resulting from a jury process that necessarily is predicated on speculation, conjecture and guesswork. . . .

MOSK, J., dissenting. I dissent.

This will be remembered as the dark day when this court, which heroically took the lead in originating the doctrine of products liability [in *Greenman*] and steadfastly resisted efforts to inject concepts of negligence into the newly designed tort (Cronin v. J. B. E. Olson Corp.), inexplicably turned 180 degrees and beat a hasty retreat almost back to square one. The pure concept of products liability so pridefully fashioned and nurtured by this court for the past decade and a half is reduced to a shambles.

The majority inject a foreign object—the tort of negligence—into the tort of products liability by the simple expedient of calling negligence something else: on some pages their opinion speaks of "comparative fault," on others reference is to "comparative principles," and elsewhere the term "equitable apportionment" is employed, although this is clearly not a proceeding in equity. But a rose is a rose and negligence is negligence; thus the majority find that despite semantic camouflage they must rely on Li v. Yellow Cab Co., even though *Li* is purely and simply a negligence case which merely rejects contributory negligence and substitutes therefor comparative negligence.

. . . [I]n *Cronin* we stressed that "the very purpose of our pioneering efforts in this field was to relieve the plaintiff from problems of proof inherent in pursuing negligence." And in Luque v. McLean, 501 P.2d 1163 (Cal. 1972), this court unanimously declared that "contributory negligence does not bar recovery in a strict liability action." . . .

The bench and bar have abided by this elementary rule. They have learned to avoid injecting negligence—whether of the defendant or the plaintiff—into a products liability case. And they have understood the reason behind the distinction between negligence of any party and products liability. It was expressed over three decades ago by Justice Traynor in his concurring opinion in Escola v. Coca Cola Bottling Co.[, *supra* at 557]. . . .

Transferring the liability, or part of the liability, from the party responsible for putting the article in the stream of commerce to the consumer is precisely what the majority propose to do. They do this by employing a euphemism: the victim's recovery is to be "proportionately reduced." The result, however delicately described, is to dilute the defect of the article by elevating the conduct of the wounded consumer to an issue of equal significance. We can be as certain as tomorrow's daylight that every defendant charged with marketing a defective product will hereafter assert that the injured plaintiff did something, anything, that conceivably could be deemed contributorily negligent: he drove the vehicle with a defective steering mechanism 56 miles an hour instead of 54; or he should have discovered a latent defect hidden in the machinery; or perhaps he should not have succumbed to the salesman's persuasion and purchased the defective object in the first instance. I need no crystal ball to foresee that the pleading of affirmative defenses alleging contributory negligence—or the currently approved substitute terminology—will now become boilerplate. . . .

The defective product is comparable to a time bomb ready to explode; it maims its victims indiscriminately, the righteous and the evil, the careful and the careless. Thus when a faulty design or otherwise defective product is involved, the litigation should not be diverted to consideration of the negligence of the plaintiff. The liability issues are simple: was the product or its design faulty, did the defendant inject the defective product into the stream of commerce, and did the defect cause the injury? The conduct of the ultimate consumer-victim who used the product in the contemplated or foreseeable manner is wholly irrelevant to those issues. . . .

The majority note one "felicitous result" of adopting comparative negligence to products liability: the merger of assumption of risk—which they term a "bizarre anomaly"—into their innovative defense. I find that result neither felicitous nor tenable. In Barker v. Lull Engineering Co., we defined a defective product as one which failed to perform safely when used in an intended or foreseeable manner. If a consumer elects to use a product patently defective when other alternatives are available, or to use a product in a manner clearly not intended or foreseeable, he assumes the risks inherent in his improper utilization and should not be heard to complain about the condition of the object. One who employs a power saw to trim his fingernails—and thereafter finds the number of his fingers reduced—should not prevail to any extent whatever against the manufacturer even if the saw had a defective blade. I would retain assumption of risk as a total defense to products liability, as it always has been.

I would affirm the judgment.

NOTES

1. *Foreseeable Misuse.* In most crashworthiness cases, the plaintiff's misconduct goes far beyond the "normal and proper use" contemplated in *Escola*. In LeBouef v. Goodyear Tire & Rubber Co., 623 F.2d 985, 989 (5th Cir. 1980), the decedent purchased "a new, 1976 Mercury Cougar equipped with a 460 cubic-inch, a 425-horsepower engine, and with Goodyear HER78-15 Custom Polysteel Radial Tires." The car was capable of going 100 miles per hour, but Goodyear had tested the tires for safety only for speeds of eighty-five miles per hour. Ford's only warning was "a statement in the Cougar owner's manual that '[c]ontinuous driving over 90 mph requires using high-speed-capability tires'; the manual did not state whether the tires in question were or were not of high-speed-caliber." The decedent was driving while intoxicated at speeds of 100 to 105 miles per hour and was killed when the car veered off the road. The trial court, sitting without a jury, found that the tire, although properly manufactured, was defective because of its insufficient warnings about the risk of tread separation at high speeds. It also found that "while [the decedent's] excessive speed was a contributory cause of the accident, his intoxication was not." It also rejected the contributory negligence and assumption of risk defenses. On appeal, the decision was affirmed, and the court had this to say about the misuse defense:

> Certainly the operation of the Cougar in excess of 100 miles per hour was not "normal" in the sense of being a routine or intended use. "Normal use," however, is a term of art in the parlance of Louisiana products liability law, delineating the scope of a manufacturer's duty and consequent liability; it encompasses all *reasonably foreseeable* uses of a product. . . . The sports car involved here was marketed with an intended and recognized appeal to youthful drivers. The 425 horsepower engine with which Ford had equipped it provided a capability of speeds over 100 miles per hour, and the car's allure, no doubt exploited in its marketing, lay in no small measure in this power and potential speed. It was not simply foreseeable, but was to be readily expected, that the Cougar would, on occasion, be driven in excess of the 85 miles per hour proven maximum safe operating speed of its Goodyear tires. Consequently, Ford cannot, on the basis of abnormal use, escape its duty either to provide an adequate warning of the specific danger of tread separation at such high speeds or to ameliorate the danger in some other way.

The foreseeable misuse standard has been criticized as creating a "moral hazard" problem by sanctioning reckless behavior and increasing the probability of accidents. In addition, foreseeable misuse creates an implicit transfer of wealth from careful to careless drivers because the manufacturer cannot differentiate in price charged between a retiree and a traveling salesman, or between the careful driver who has never had a ticket and the teenage hot-rodder. Epstein, Products Liability as an Insurance Market, 14 J. Legal Stud. 645 (1985), notes that first-party insurers routinely make these risk classifications in selling automobile insurance.

2. *The Restatement Position.* The Third Restatement follows *Daly* in what has become the majority position. See RTT: PL §17. In essence, the Third Restatement declines to treat product misuse, alteration, or assumption of risk as independent defenses. Rather, to the extent that these are traced to the plaintiff's conduct, they are governed by the comparative fault system in effect within the jurisdiction, usually pure comparative negligence or the 50 percent cut-off rule. Prior to the Third Restatement many states followed a rule that provided that the plaintiff was under no duty to discover latent defects contained in the defendant's product. Under the influence of comparative negligence, this defense may be allowed, at least in some cases: "[W]hen the defendant claims that the plaintiff failed to discover a defect, there must be evidence that the plaintiff's conduct in failing to discover a defect did, in fact, fail to meet a standard of reasonable care." RTT: PL §17, comment *d.*

RESTATEMENT OF THE LAW (THIRD) OF TORTS: PRODUCTS LIABILITY

§17. Apportionment of Responsibility Between or Among Plaintiff, Sellers and Distributors of Defective Products, and Others

(a) A plaintiff's recovery of damages for harm caused by a product defect may be reduced if the conduct of the plaintiff combines with the product defect to cause the harm and the plaintiff's conduct fails to conform to generally applicable rules establishing appropriate standards of care.

(b) The manner and extent of the reduction under Subsection (a) and the apportionment of plaintiff's recovery among multiple defendants are governed by generally applicable rules apportioning responsibility.

3. *Contractual Defenses to Products Liability Actions.* The Waiver Society Project, https://www.waiversociety.org/, is an ongoing project that tracks "the ubiquity of waivers in our world." Such express assumption of risk by contract is a complete defense to a tort action in some settings. One vital question is whether product sellers should be able, directly or through intermediaries, to contract out of their liability with potential product users and consumers. The contractual regime could redefine product defect, cap damages, or eliminate liability altogether. Since *Henningsen*, courts have uniformly rejected that approach, which also receives a chilly reception in the Third Restatement. See RTT: PL §18. The rule does not apply to cases of purely economic loss usually covered under the U.C.C., nor does it necessarily apply whenever product users and consumers are "represented by informed and economically powerful consumer groups or intermediaries." See RTT: PL §18, comment *d.* Does a reduction in price or increase in product or service access count as the necessary quid pro quo? How would the law of products liability have to be rewritten if the contractual waivers were freely accepted in all cases of physical injury or property damage?

RESTATEMENT OF THE LAW (THIRD) OF TORTS: PRODUCTS LIABILITY

§18. Disclaimers, Limitations, Waivers, and Other Contractual Exculpations as Defenses to Products Liability Claims for Harm to Persons

Disclaimers and limitations of remedies by product sellers or other distributors, waivers by product purchasers, and other similar contractual exculpations, oral or written, do not bar or reduce otherwise valid products-liability claims against sellers or other distributors of new products for harm to persons.

Comment a. Effects of contract defenses on products liability tort claims for harm to persons: . . . It is presumed that the ordinary product user or consumer lacks sufficient information and bargaining power to execute a fair contractual limitation of rights to recover. . . .

Comment d. Waiver of rights in contractual settings in which product purchasers possess both adequate knowledge and sufficient economic power: . . . This Section does not address whether consumers, especially when represented by informed and economically powerful consumer groups or intermediaries, with full information and sufficient bargaining power, may contract with product sellers to accept curtailment of liability in exchange for concomitant benefits, or whether such consumers might be allowed to agree to substitute alternative dispute resolution mechanisms in place of traditional adjudication. When such contracts are accompanied by alternative nontort remedies that serve as an adequate quid pro quo for reducing or eliminating rights to recover in tort, arguments may support giving effect to such agreements. Such contractual arrangements raise policy questions different from those raised by this Section and require careful consideration by the courts.

§21. Comment f. Harm to other property: disclaimers and limitations of remedies: . . . When a defective product causes harm to property owned by third persons, the contractual arrangements between the contracting parties should not shield the seller from liability to the third party. However, contractual limitations on tort liability for harm to property, when fairly bargained for, may provide an effective way for the contracting parties efficiently to allocate risks of such harm between themselves.

SECTION F. FEDERAL PREEMPTION

A major fraction of tort litigation addresses the interaction between direct forms of federal regulation and the state-based common law of products liability. The debate over federal preemption implicates the policy debate over the relative desirability of ex ante regulation by federal agencies versus ex post litigation by injured parties in ensuring optimal health and safety standards. Rabin, Reassessing Regulatory Compliance, 88 Geo. L.J. 2049, 2068–70 (2000), argues that even with the presence of federal regulators, tort litigation is beneficial because the process involves the collection of information about post-market use and defects that might not otherwise come to light, particularly in the case of fraud on the part of the manufacturer. Tort liability, in Rabin's account, effectively complements regulation, by providing independent incentives for product safety. In contrast, Epstein has argued that the imposition of tort liability will only make matters worse if the regulatory system already embodies safety standards that are too strict. "Where the FDA incorrectly blocks a drug from entering the market, litigation can do nothing to correct that error. Where the regulatory process lets drugs correctly on the market, litigation remains costly even if it vindicates the defendant." Epstein, The Case for Field Preemption of State Laws in Drug Cases, 103 Nw. U. L. Rev. 463, 470 (2009).

At its core, federal preemption is not just a question of public policy, but also a question of statutory interpretation with constitutional overtones. The Supremacy Clause, Article VI, §2, of the U.S. Constitution, provides that any federal statute or regulation trumps any inconsistent state law:

> This Constitution, and the Laws of the United States which shall be made in Pursuance thereof; and all Treaties made, or which shall be made, under the Authority of the United States, shall be the supreme Law of the Land: and the Judges in every State shall be bound thereby, any Thing in the Constitution or Law of any State to the contrary notwithstanding.

In some instances, the federal statute explicitly displaces state law. Express preemption by Congress is often the exception, not the rule. More often real or apparent conflicts between federal and state laws give rise to complex matters of statutory construction. Early on, in Rice v. Santa Fe Elevator Corp., 331 U.S. 218, 230–31 (1947), the Supreme Court set out the basic presumption against federal preemption when it wrote:

> [W]e start with the assumption that the historic police powers of the States [to regulate safety and health] were not to be superseded by the Federal Act unless that was the clear and manifest purpose of Congress. Such a purpose may be evidenced in several ways. The scheme of federal regulation may be so pervasive as to make reasonable the inference that Congress left no room for the States to supplement it. Or the Act of Congress may touch a field in which the federal interest is so dominant that the federal system will be assumed to preclude enforcement of state laws on the same subject. Likewise, the object sought to be obtained by the federal law and the character of obligations imposed by it may reveal the same purpose. Or the state policy may produce a result inconsistent with the objective of the federal statute.

After *Rice*, implied preemption takes on three different guises. So-called field preemption arises when the federal statute is sufficiently comprehensive to "occupy the field," thereby precluding any state standards in that substantive area. Field preemption is virtually nonexistent in products liability. Most products cases involve "conflict preemption," which comes in two varieties: (1) the state law is flatly inconsistent with the federal statute ("impossibility preemption"), and (2) the enforcement of the state law frustrates or presents an obstacle to the federal scheme ("obstacle preemption"). Working out the implications of this basic system is challenging given the modern proliferation of design, warning, and liability theories at the state law level.

Geier v. American Honda Motor Co.

529 U.S. 861 (2000)

Breyer, J. This case focuses on the 1984 version of a Federal Motor Vehicle Safety Standard promulgated by the Department of Transportation under the authority of the National Traffic and Motor Vehicle Safety Act of 1966, 80 Stat. 718, 15 U.S.C. §1381 et seq. (1988 ed.). The standard, FMVSS 208, required auto manufacturers to equip some but not all of their 1987 vehicles with passive restraints. We ask whether the Act pre-empts a state common-law tort action [for a design defect] in which the plaintiff claims that the defendant auto manufacturer, who was in compliance with the standard, should nonetheless have equipped a 1987 automobile with airbags. We conclude that the Act, taken together with FMVSS 208, pre-empts the lawsuit.

I

In 1992, petitioner Alexis Geier, driving a 1987 Honda Accord, collided with a tree and was seriously injured. The car was equipped with manual shoulder and lap belts which Geier had buckled up at the time. The car was not equipped with airbags or other passive restraint devices.

1987 Honda Accord
Source: Wikimedia Commons

[Breyer, J., outlines the procedural history of the case and notes the sharp split of opinion in the lower federal and state courts.]

We granted certiorari to resolve these differences. We now hold that this kind of "no airbag" lawsuit conflicts with the objectives of FMVSS 208, a standard authorized by the Act, and is therefore pre-empted by the Act.

In reaching our conclusion, we consider three subsidiary questions. First, does the Act's express pre-emption provision pre-empt this lawsuit? We think not. Second, do ordinary pre-emption principles nonetheless apply? We hold that they do. Third, does this lawsuit actually conflict with FMVSS 208, hence with the Act itself? We hold that it does.

II

We first ask whether the Safety Act's express pre-emption provision pre-empts this tort action. The provision reads as follows:

> "Whenever a Federal motor vehicle safety standard established under this subchapter is in effect, no State or political subdivision of a State shall have any authority either to establish, or to continue in effect, with respect to any motor vehicle or item of motor vehicle equipment[,] any safety standard applicable to the same aspect of performance of such vehicle or item of equipment which is not identical to the Federal standard." 215 U.S.C. §1392(d) (1988 ed.).

American Honda points out that a majority of this Court has said that a somewhat similar statutory provision in a different federal statute—a provision that uses the word "requirements"—may well expressly pre-empt similar tort actions. Petitioners reply that this statute speaks of pre-empting a state-law "safety *standard*," not a "requirement," and that a tort action does not involve a safety *standard*. Hence, they conclude, the express pre-emption provision does not apply.

We need not determine the precise significance of the use of the word "standard," rather than "requirement," however, for the Act contains another provision, which resolves the disagreement. That provision, a broad "savings" clause, says that "[c]ompliance with" a federal safety standard "does not exempt any person from any liability under common law." 15 U.S.C. §1397(k) (1988 ed.). The saving clause assumes that there are some significant number of common-law liability cases to save. And a reading of the express pre-emption provision that excludes common-law tort actions gives actual meaning to the saving clause's literal language, while leaving adequate room for state tort law to operate — for example, where federal law creates only a floor, *i.e.*, a minimum safety standard. See, *e.g.*, Brief for United States as Amicus Curiae 21 (explaining that common-law claim that a vehicle is defectively designed because it lacks antilock brakes would not be pre-empted by 49 CFR §571.105 (1999), a safety standard establishing minimum requirements for brake performance). Without the saving clause, a broad reading of the express pre-emption provision arguably might pre-empt those actions, for, as we have just mentioned, it is possible to read the pre-emption provision, standing alone, as applying to standards imposed in common-law tort actions, as well as standards contained in state legislation or regulations. And if so, it would pre-empt all nonidentical state standards established in tort actions covering the same aspect of performance as an applicable federal standard, even if the federal standard merely established a minimum standard. On that broad reading of the pre-emption clause little, if any, potential "liability at common law" would remain. And few, if any, state tort actions would remain for the saving clause to save. We have found no convincing indication that Congress wanted to pre-empt, not only state statutes and regulations, but also common-law tort actions, in such circumstances. Hence the broad reading cannot be correct. The language of the pre-emption provision permits a narrow reading that excludes common-law actions. Given the presence of the saving clause, we conclude that the pre-emption clause must be so read.

III

We have just said that the saving clause at least removes tort actions from the scope of the express pre-emption clause. Does it do more? In particular, does it foreclose or limit the operation of ordinary pre-emption principles insofar as those principles instruct us to read statutes as pre-empting state laws (including common-law rules) that "actually conflict" with the statute or federal standards promulgated thereunder? . . .

Nothing in the language of the saving clause suggests an intent to save state-law tort actions that conflict with federal regulations. The words "[c]ompliance" and "does not exempt," sound as if they simply bar a special kind of defense, namely, a defense that compliance with a federal standard automatically exempts a defendant from state law, whether the Federal Government meant that standard to be an absolute requirement or only a minimum one. See Restatement (Third) of Torts: Products Liability §4(b), Comment *e* (1997) (distinguishing between state-law compliance defense and a federal claim of pre-emption). It is difficult to understand why Congress would have insisted on a compliance-with-federal-regulation precondition to the provision's applicability had it wished the Act to "save" all state-law tort actions, regardless of their potential threat to the objectives of federal safety standards promulgated under that Act. . . .

Why, in any event, would Congress not have wanted ordinary pre-emption principles to apply where an actual conflict with a federal objective is at stake? Some such principle is needed. In its absence, state law could impose legal duties that would conflict directly with federal regulatory mandates, say, by premising liability upon the presence of the very windshield retention requirements that federal law requires. . . .

IV

The basic question, then, is whether a common-law "no airbag" action like the one before us actually conflicts with FMVSS 208. We hold that it does.

In petitioners' and the dissent's view, FMVSS 208 sets a minimum airbag standard. As far as FMVSS 208 is concerned, the more airbags, and the sooner, the better. But that was not the Secretary's view. The Department of Transportation's (DOT's) comments, which accompanied the promulgation of FMVSS 208, make clear that the standard deliberately provided the manufacturer with a range of choices among different passive restraint devices. Those choices would bring about a mix of different devices introduced gradually over time; and FMVSS 208 would thereby lower costs, overcome technical safety problems, encourage technological development, and win widespread consumer acceptance—all of which would promote FMVSS 208's safety objectives.

A

[A review of the history of the regulation is omitted.]

B

Read in light of this history, DOT's own contemporaneous explanation of FMVSS 208 makes clear that the 1984 version of FMVSS 208 reflected the following significant considerations. First, buckled up seatbelts are a vital ingredient of automobile safety. . . . Second, despite the enormous and unnecessary risks that a passenger runs by not buckling up manual lap and shoulder belts, more than 80% of front seat passengers would leave their manual seatbelts unbuckled. Third, airbags could make up for the dangers caused by unbuckled manual belts, but they could not make up for them entirely.

Fourth, passive restraint systems had their own disadvantages, for example, the dangers associated with, intrusiveness of, and corresponding public dislike for, nondetachable automatic belts. Fifth, airbags brought with them their own special risks to safety, such as the risk of danger to out-of-position occupants (usually children) in small cars. . . .

Sixth, airbags were expected to be significantly more expensive than other passive restraint devices, raising the average cost of a vehicle price $320 for full frontal airbags over the cost of a car with manual lap and shoulder seatbelts (and potentially much more if production volumes were low). And the agency worried that the high replacement cost—estimated to be $800—could lead car owners to refuse to replace them after deployment. . . .

FMVSS 208 reflected these considerations in several ways. Most importantly, that standard deliberately sought variety—a mix of several different passive restraint systems. It did so by setting a performance requirement for passive restraint devices and allowing manufacturers to choose among different passive restraint mechanisms, such as airbags, automatic belts, or other passive restraint technologies to satisfy that requirement. And DOT explained why FMVSS 208 sought the mix of devices that it expected its performance standard to produce. DOT wrote that it had *rejected* a proposed FMVSS 208 "all airbag" standard because of safety concerns (perceived or real) associated with airbags, which concerns threatened a "backlash" more easily overcome "if airbags" were "not the only way of complying." It added that a mix of devices would help develop data on comparative effectiveness, would allow the industry time to overcome the safety problems and the high production costs associated with airbags, and would facilitate the development of alternative, cheaper, and safer passive restraint systems. And it would thereby build public confidence, necessary to avoid another interlock-type fiasco.

The 1984 FMVSS 208 standard also deliberately sought a *gradual* phase-in of passive restraints. . . .

In effect, petitioners' tort action depends upon its claim that manufacturers had a duty to install an airbag when they manufactured the 1987 Honda Accord. Such a state law—*i.e.*, a rule of state tort law imposing such a duty—by its terms would have required manufacturers of all similar cars to install airbags rather than other passive restraint systems, such as automatic belts or passive interiors. It thereby would have presented an obstacle to the variety and mix of devices that the federal regulation sought.

[Affirmed.]

STEVENS, J., dissenting.

Airbag technology has been available to automobile manufacturers for over 30 years. There is now general agreement on the proposition "that, to be safe, a car must have an airbag." Indeed, current federal law imposes that requirement on all automobile manufacturers. The question raised by petitioners' common-law tort action is whether that proposition was sufficiently obvious when Honda's 1987 Accord was manufactured to make the failure to install such a safety feature actionable under theories of negligence or defective design. The Court holds that an interim regulation motivated by the Secretary of Transportation's desire to foster gradual development of a variety of passive restraint devices deprives state courts of jurisdiction to answer that question. I respectfully dissent from that holding, and especially from the Court's unprecedented extension of the doctrine of pre-emption. . . .

NOTES

1. *State Law "Requirements" and Common Law Duties.* *Geier* was one of many cases that struggled to set the boundaries of the preemption doctrine. Nine years earlier, in Cipollone v. Liggett Group, Inc., 505 U.S. 504, 521, 524 (1992), the Supreme Court set the stage for the modern developments when, for the first time, it interpreted federal statutory preemptive "requirements" to include common law tort actions. More specifically, the Court held that plaintiff's duty to warn claims against cigarette manufacturers were preempted under the Public Health Cigarette Smoking Act, 15 U.S.C. §§1331–1340, which in section 5(b) provided:

> No requirement or prohibition based on smoking and health shall be imposed under State law with respect to the advertising or promotion of any cigarettes the packages of which are labeled in conformity with the provisions of this Act.

The Court rejected plaintiff's claim that this provision only preempted claims based on state statutes and administrative rules, holding that "those words easily encompass obligations that take the form of common law rules." Thereafter, the Court concluded that plaintiff's failure to warn claims insofar as they "require a showing that respondents' post-1969 advertising or promotions should have included additional, or more clearly stated, warnings . . . are preempted." But this ruling did not preempt, for example, design defect, express warranty, or fraud claims.

The Court turned its back on both *Cipollone* and *Geier* by giving a narrow reading to federal preemption in Bates v. Dow Agrosciences LLC, 544 U.S. 431, 442, 445, 454 (2005). There the petitioners, Texas peanut farmers, sued Dow claiming that their crops were damaged during the 2000 growing season when treated with Dow's Strongarm pesticide, which they claimed stunted their crops and did not kill weeds. Strongarm was marketed with a warning that said: "Use of Strongarm is recommended in all areas where peanuts are grown." The plaintiffs alleged that Strongarm was only appropriate in soils with a pH below 7.0, and not in Texas where the soil had a pH of 7.2. After the initiation of the plaintiffs' suit, Dow changed its warning to read: "Do not apply Strongarm to soils with a pH of 7.2 or greater."

Stevens, J., held that the Federal Insecticide, Fungicide, and Rodenticide Act (FIFRA), 7 U.S.C. §136 (2023), did not preempt the plaintiff's claim. Its preemption provision provided in section 136v(b): "Such State shall not impose or continue in effect any requirements for labeling or packaging in addition to or different from those required under this subchapter."

Stevens, J., first held that the states have "ample authority" to impose additional sanctions "for violating state rules that merely duplicate federal requirements." He then denied that petitioners' claims for defective design, defective manufacture, negligent testing, and breach of express warranty were preempted, but he remanded the case to see if the plaintiff's duty to warn claims were preempted.

Would any of these claims have survived if Strongarm had been originally marketed with a warning that said the product was not to be used in soil whose pH was over 7.2? If not, then why doesn't the comprehensive federal control over warnings trigger the application of conflict preemption?

2. *Deference to the Regulating Federal Agency.* In Sprietsma v. Mercury Marine, 537 U.S. 51, 54, 60 (2002), a unanimous Supreme Court held that the Federal Boat Safety Act of 1971, 46 U.S.C. §§4301–4311 (2023), and the regulations promulgated under it, did not preempt a state tort action brought on behalf of a decedent who was killed when she fell overboard from "an 18-foot ski boat equipped with a 115-horsepower outboard motor manufactured by [defendant]." As in *Geier*, the FBSA contained a preemption clause that forbade the state imposition of requirements that were not "identical" to those contained in the federal regulation. That clause was coupled with a savings clause for common law actions. As in *Geier*, the Secretary of Transportation conducted an exhaustive safety study, but refused to issue any regulations that mandated propeller guards because the data were insufficient to resolve the key tradeoff: "[G]iven current technology, feasible propeller guards might prevent penetrating injuries but increase the potential for blunt trauma caused by collision with the guard, which enlarges the boat's underwater profile." Stevens, J., allowed the action to go forward out of deference to the agency's explanation of its decision not to regulate:

> The agency is likely to have a thorough understanding of its own regulation and its objectives and is "uniquely qualified" to comprehend the likely impact of state requirements. In the case before us today, the Solicitor General, joined by counsel for the Coast Guard, has informed us that the agency does not view the 1990 refusal to regulate or any subsequent regulatory actions by the Coast Guard as having any pre-emptive effect.

Should it matter that the Coast Guard waited until after the Supreme Court granted certiorari in *Sprietsma* to elaborate its view? Sharkey, Products Liability Preemption: An Institutional Approach, 76 Geo. Wash. L. Rev. 449 (2008), highlights the influence of the underlying federal regulator in preemption disputes.

3. *Geier Revisited.* The continued vitality of *Geier* was tested in Williamson v. Mazda Motor of America, Inc., 562 U.S. 323, 332 (2011). Thanh Williamson was a passenger in the rear aisle seat of a Mazda minivan. While wearing a lap belt, she was killed when the minivan was struck head-on by another car. FMVSS 208 requires auto manufacturers to install lap-and-shoulder belts on those seats located next to the doors or frames of any vehicle. But with respect to the inside rear seats, including Williamson's aisle seat, the regulation gave the manufacturers the choice of installing either lap belts or lap-and-shoulder belts. Willamson's estate claimed that Mazda should have installed lap-and-shoulder belts, not lap belts, on all rear inner seats. The trial court dismissed the tort claim; the California appellate court affirmed, concluding that, as in *Geier*, the choice explicitly reserved to the manufacturer under federal regulation preempted the state tort suit. The Supreme Court unanimously allowed the state tort claim to proceed. Breyer, J., explained: "Like the regulation in *Geier*, the regulation here leaves the manufacturer with a choice. And, like the tort suit in *Geier*, the tort suit here would restrict that choice. But unlike *Geier*, we do not believe here that choice is a significant regulatory objective," as the agency's choice did not involve the timing of the introduction of a new technology, such as air bags, into the market. Continuing the Court's trend of agency deference, Breyer, J., was swayed by "the promulgating agency's contemporaneous explanation of its objectives, and the agency's current views of the regulation's pre-emptive effect." Should an agency be required to state in advance whether it attaches preemptive weight to its regulation?

Following cues from *Sprietsma* and *Williamson*, the Supreme Court of Arizona recently held that the National Highway Traffic Safety Administration had not established clear policy objectives sufficient to preempt state tort claims alleging failure to install automatic emergency braking technologies. Varela v. FCA US LLC, 505 P.3d 244 (Ariz. 2022). Is it ever safe for a manufacturer to take advantage of any low-cost option left to it under federal regulation?

Wyeth v. Levine

555 U.S. 555 (2009)

Stevens, J. Directly injecting the drug Phenergan into a patient's vein creates a significant risk of catastrophic consequences. A Vermont jury found that petitioner Wyeth, the manufacturer of the drug, had failed to provide an adequate warning of that risk and awarded damages to respondent Diana Levine to compensate her for the amputation of her arm. The warnings on Phenergan's label had been deemed sufficient by the federal Food and Drug Administration (FDA) when it approved Wyeth's new drug application in 1955 and when it later approved changes in the drug's labeling. The question we must decide is whether the FDA's approvals provide Wyeth with a complete defense to Levine's tort claims. We conclude that they do not.

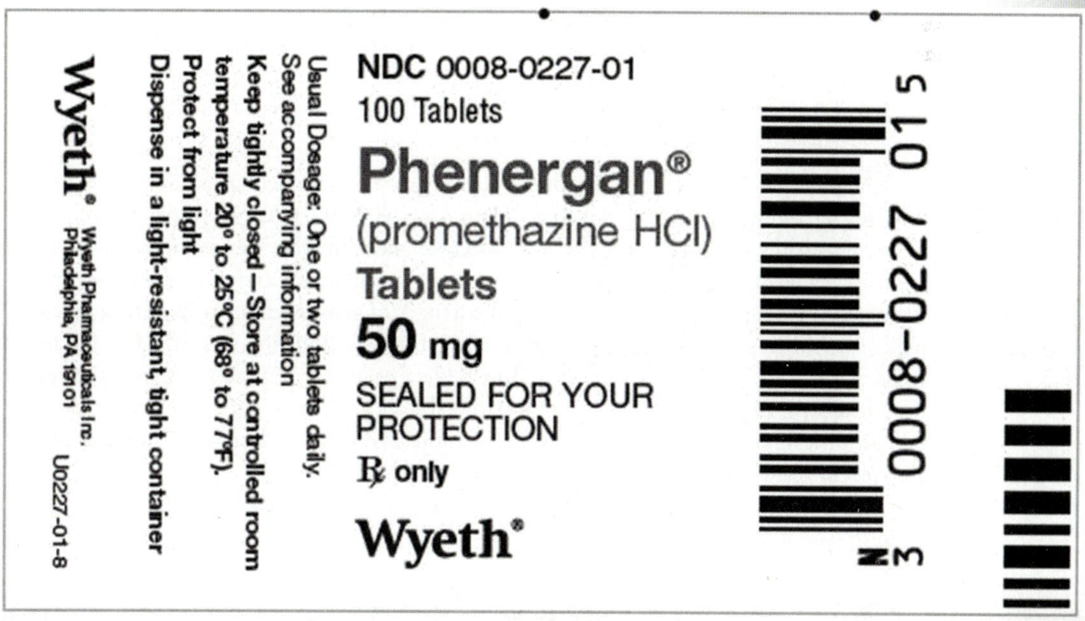

Phenergan label

Source: National Institutes of Health

I

Phenergan is Wyeth's brand name for promethazine hydrochloride, an antihistamine used to treat nausea. The injectable form of Phenergan can be administered intramuscularly or intravenously, and it can be administered intravenously through either the "IV-push" method, whereby the drug is injected directly into a patient's vein, or the "IV-drip" method, whereby the drug is introduced into a saline solution in a hanging intravenous bag and slowly descends through a catheter inserted in a patient's vein. The drug is corrosive and causes irreversible gangrene if it enters a patient's artery.

Levine's injury resulted from an IV-push injection of Phenergan. On April 7, 2000, as on previous visits to her local clinic for treatment of a migraine headache, she received an intramuscular injection of Demerol for her headache and Phenergan for her nausea. Because the combination did not provide relief, she returned later that day and received a second injection of both drugs. This time, the physician assistant administered the drugs by the IV-push method, and Phenergan entered Levine's artery, either because the needle penetrated an artery directly or because the drug escaped from the vein into surrounding tissue (a phenomenon called "perivascular extravasation") where it came in contact with arterial blood. As a result, Levine developed gangrene, and doctors amputated first her right hand and then her entire forearm. In addition to her pain and suffering, Levine incurred substantial medical expenses and the loss of her livelihood as a professional musician.

[In part the warning provided:

> Due to the close proximity of arteries and veins in the areas most commonly used for intravenous injection, extreme care should be exercised to avoid perivascular extravasation or inadvertent intra-arterial injection. Reports compatible with inadvertent intra-arterial injection of Phenergan Injection, usually in conjunction with other drugs intended for intravenous use, suggest that pain, severe chemical irritation, severe spasm of distal vessels, and resultant gangrene requiring amputation are likely under such circumstances. . . . Phenergan Injection should be given in a concentration no greater than 25 mg per mL and at a rate not to exceed 25 mg per minute. When administering any irritant drug intravenously, it is usually preferable to inject it through the tubing of an intravenous infusion set that is known to be functioning satisfactorily. In the event that a patient complains of pain during intended intravenous injection of Phenergan Injection, the injection should be stopped immediately to provide for evaluation of possible arterial placement or perivascular extravasation.

The physician's assistant injected the Phenergan into an artery at a rate of 100 mg per minute. She did not use any tubing and did not stop when the patient complained of pain.]

After settling claims against the health center and clinician, Levine brought an action for damages against Wyeth, relying on common-law negligence and strict-liability theories. Although Phenergan's labeling warned of the danger of gangrene and amputation following inadvertent intra-arterial injection, Levine alleged that the labeling was defective because it failed to instruct clinicians to use the IV-drip method of intravenous administration instead of the higher risk IV-push method. More broadly, she alleged that Phenergan is not reasonably safe for intravenous administration because the foreseeable risks of gangrene and loss of limb are great in relation to the drug's therapeutic benefits. . . .

[The jury awarded the plaintiff $7,400,000, which was reduced by the $700,000 the plaintiff had obtained in settlement from the health clinic.]

II

. . . Our [analysis] must be guided by two cornerstones of our pre-emption jurisprudence. First, "the purpose of Congress is the ultimate touchstone in every pre-emption case." Second, "[i]n all pre-emption cases, and particularly in those in which Congress has 'legislated . . . in a field which the States have traditionally occupied,' . . . we 'start with the assumption that the historic police powers of the States were not to be superseded by the Federal Act unless that was the clear and manifest purpose of Congress.' "

[A review of the history of federal regulation of drugs and drug labeling is omitted.]

III

Wyeth first argues that Levine's state-law claims are pre-empted because it is impossible for it to comply with both the state-law duties underlying those claims and its federal labeling duties. The FDA's premarket approval of a new drug application includes the approval of the exact text in the proposed label. Generally speaking, a manufacturer may only change a drug label after the FDA approves a supplemental application. There is, however, an FDA regulation that permits a manufacturer to make certain changes to its label before receiving the agency's approval. Among other things, this "changes being effected" (CBE) regulation provides that if a manufacturer is changing a label to "add or strengthen a contraindication, warning, precaution, or adverse reaction" or to "add or strengthen an instruction about dosage and administration that is intended to increase the safe use of the drug product," it may make the labeling change upon filing its supplemental application with the FDA; it need not wait for FDA approval.

. . . Levine . . . present[ed] evidence of at least 20 incidents prior to her injury in which a Phenergan injection resulted in gangrene and an amputation. After the first such incident came to Wyeth's attention in 1967, it notified the FDA and worked with the agency to change Phenergan's label. In later years, as amputations continued to occur, Wyeth could have analyzed the accumulating data and added a stronger warning about IV-push administration of the drug.

. . . Wyeth suggests that the FDA, rather than the manufacturer, bears primary responsibility for drug labeling. Yet through many amendments to the FDCA and to FDA regulations, it has remained a central premise of federal drug regulation that the manufacturer bears responsibility for the content of its label at all times. It is charged both with crafting an adequate label and with ensuring that its warnings remain adequate as long as the drug is on the market. . . .

Of course, the FDA retains authority to reject labeling changes made pursuant to the CBE regulation in its review of the manufacturer's supplemental application, just as it retains such authority in reviewing all supplemental applications. But absent clear evidence that the FDA would not have approved a change to Phenergan's label, we will not conclude that it was impossible for Wyeth to comply with both federal and state requirements. . . .

Impossibility pre-emption is a demanding defense. On the record before us, Wyeth has failed to demonstrate that it was impossible for it to comply with both federal and state requirements. The CBE regulation permitted Wyeth to unilaterally strengthen its warning, and the mere fact that the FDA approved Phenergan's label does not establish that it would have prohibited such a change.

IV

Wyeth also argues that requiring it to comply with a state-law duty to provide a stronger warning about IV-push administration would obstruct the purposes and objectives of federal drug labeling regulation. Levine's tort claims, it maintains, are pre-empted because they interfere with "Congress's purpose to entrust an expert agency to make drug labeling decisions that strike a balance between competing objectives." We find no merit in this argument, which relies on an untenable interpretation of congressional intent and an overbroad view of an agency's power to pre-empt state law.

Wyeth contends that the FDCA establishes both a floor and a ceiling for drug regulation: Once the FDA has approved a drug's label, a state-law verdict may not deem the label inadequate, regardless of whether there is any evidence that the FDA has considered the stronger warning at issue. The most glaring problem with this argument is that all evidence of Congress' purposes is to the contrary. Building on its 1906 Act, Congress enacted the FDCA to bolster consumer protection against harmful products. Congress did not provide a federal remedy for consumers harmed by unsafe or ineffective drugs in the 1938 statute or in any subsequent amendment. Evidently, it determined that widely available state rights of action provided appropriate relief for injured consumers. It may also have recognized that state-law remedies further consumer protection by motivating manufacturers to produce safe and effective drugs and to give adequate warnings.

If Congress thought state-law suits posed an obstacle to its objectives, it surely would have enacted an express pre-emption provision at some point during the FDCA's 70-year history. . . . Its silence on the issue, coupled with its certain awareness of the prevalence of state tort litigation, is powerful evidence that Congress did not intend FDA oversight to be the exclusive means of ensuring drug safety and effectiveness. . . .

[Justice Stevens then rejects the argument that a 2006 preamble to an FDA regulation is sufficient to interpret the FDCA as setting "both a 'floor' and a 'ceiling,' " so that "FDA approval of labeling . . . preempts conflicting or contrary State law." He then held that the preamble is "at odds with what evidence we have of Congress' purposes, and . . . reverses the FDA's own longstanding position without providing a reasoned explanation, including any discussion of how state law has interfered with the FDA's regulation of drug labeling during decades of coexistence."]

In short, Wyeth has not persuaded us that failure-to-warn claims like Levine's obstruct the federal regulation of drug labeling. Congress has repeatedly declined to pre-empt state law, and the FDA's recently adopted position that state tort suits interfere with its statutory mandate is entitled to no weight. Although we recognize that some state-law claims might well frustrate the achievement of congressional objectives, this is not such a case.

[Affirmed.]

Alito, J., dissenting.

I

The court frames the question presented as a "narro[w]" one—namely, whether Wyeth has a duty to provide "an adequate warning about using the IV-push method" to administer Phenergan. But that ignores the antecedent question of who—the FDA or a jury in Vermont—has the authority and responsibility for determining the "adequacy" of Phenergan's warnings. Moreover, it is unclear how a "stronger" warning could have helped respondent; after all, the physician's assistant who treated her disregarded at least six separate warnings that are already on Phenergan's labeling, so respondent would be hard pressed to prove that a seventh would have made a difference.

More to the point, the question presented by this case is not a "narrow" one, and it does not concern whether Phenergan's label should bear a "stronger" warning. Rather, the real issue is whether a state tort jury can countermand the FDA's considered judgment that Phenergan's FDA-mandated warning label renders its intravenous (IV) use "safe." Indeed, respondent's amended complaint alleged that Phenergan is "not reasonably safe for intravenous administration," respondent's attorney told the jury that Phenergan's label should say, " 'Do not use this drug intravenously,' "; respondent's expert told the jury, "I think the drug should be labeled 'Not for IV use,' " and during his closing argument, respondent's attorney told the jury, "Thank God we don't rely on the FDA to . . . make the safe[ty] decision. You will make the decision. . . . The FDA doesn't make the decision, you do."

Federal law, however, *does* rely on the FDA to make safety determinations like the one it made here. The FDA has long known about the risks associated with IV push in general and its use to administer Phenergan in particular. Whether wisely or not, the FDA has concluded—over the course of extensive, 54-year-long regulatory proceedings—that the drug is "safe" and "effective" when used in accordance with its FDA-mandated labeling. The unfortunate fact that respondent's healthcare providers ignored Phenergan's labeling may make this an ideal medical malpractice case. But turning a common-law tort suit into a "frontal assault" on the FDA's regulatory regime for drug labeling upsets the well-settled meaning of the Supremacy Clause and our conflict pre-emption jurisprudence.

II

A

To the extent that the purpose of Congress is the ultimate touchstone in every preemption case, Congress made its "purpose" plain in authorizing the FDA—not state tort juries—to determine when and under what circumstances a drug is "safe." "[T]he process for approving new drugs is at least as rigorous as the premarket approval process for medical devices," Riegel v. Medtronic, Inc., 552 U.S. 312, 343 (2008) (Ginsburg, J., dissenting), and we held that the latter pre-empted a state-law tort suit that conflicted with the FDA's determination that a medical device was "safe." [Alito, J., sets forth the lengthy FDCA approval process.]

III

[Part A provides a detailed account of the FDA's regulatory oversight of the Phenergan warning. Alito, J., argues that the FDA did in fact consider the costs and benefits associated with IV push.]

B

Given the "balance" that the FDA struck between the costs and benefits of administering Phenergan via IV push, *Geier* compels the pre-emption of tort suits (like this one) that would upset that balance. The contrary conclusion requires turning yesterday's dissent into today's majority opinion. . . .

Geier does not countenance the use of state tort suits to second-guess the FDA's labeling decisions. And the Court's contrary conclusion has potentially far-reaching consequences.

C

By their very nature, juries are ill-equipped to perform the FDA's cost-benefit-balancing function. . . . [J]uries tend to focus on the risk of a particular product's design or warning label that arguably contributed to a particular plaintiff's injury, not on the overall benefits of that design or label; "the patients who reaped those benefits are not represented in court." Indeed, patients like respondent are the only ones whom tort juries ever see, and for a patient like respondent—who has already suffered a tragic accident—Phenergan's risks are no longer a matter of probabilities and potentialities.

In contrast, the FDA has the benefit of the long view. Its drug-approval determinations consider the interests of all potential users of a drug, including "those who would suffer without new medical [products]" if juries in all 50 States were free to contradict the FDA's expert determinations. And the FDA conveys its warnings with one voice, rather than whipsawing the medical community with 50 (or more) potentially conflicting ones. After today's ruling, however, parochialism may prevail.

• • •

To be sure, state tort suits can peacefully coexist with the FDA's labeling regime, and they have done so for decades. But this case is far from peaceful coexistence. The FDA told Wyeth that Phenergan's label renders its use "safe." But the State of Vermont, through its tort law, said: "Not so."

The state-law rule at issue here is squarely pre-empted. Therefore, I would reverse the judgment of the Supreme Court of Vermont.

NOTES

1. ***Drug and Medical Device Preemption.*** *Levine* forms a key part in a succession of high-stakes litigation over the extensive federal regulatory scheme for new drugs and medical devices. The saga starts with Medtronic, Inc. v. Lohr, 518 U.S. 470, 489 (1996), in which the plaintiff sued on a variety of failure to warn and design defect theories when her pacemaker failed, requiring emergency surgery. The Medical Device Amendment Act (MDA), 21 U.S.C. §360k(a), reads:

> [N]o State or political subdivision of a State may establish or continue in effect with respect to a device intended for human use any requirement (1) which is different from, or in addition to, any requirement applicable under [the MDA] to the device, and (2) which relates to the safety or effectiveness of the device or to any other matter included in a requirement applicable to the device under [the MDA].

The pre-market notification process is an abbreviated review of the product lasting an average of twenty hours, under which the FDA undertakes no tests or systematic review of product safety but allows for the marketing of the product as long as it is "substantially equivalent" to a pre-1976 product already on the market, at least until the earlier product is required to undergo a pre-market approval (PMA) process. Stevens, J., relied on *Rice*'s presumption against preemption to hold that the pre-market notification process did not preempt either the duty to warn or manufacturing defect claims, but only prohibited those design defect actions that specifically targeted medical devices for special treatment. "Given the ambiguities in the statute and the scope of the preclusion that would occur otherwise, we cannot accept Medtronic's argument that by using the term 'requirement,' Congress clearly signaled its intent to deprive States of any role in protecting consumers from the dangers inherent in many medical devices."

The preemptive effect of the MDA was back before the Supreme Court in Riegel v. Medtronic, Inc., 552 U.S. 312 (2008). There the plaintiff was injured when a cardiologist used Medtronic's FDA-approved Evergreen Balloon Catheter to perform an angioplasty—designed to clear clogged arteries—at a pressure of ten atmospheres when it was only rated for use at eight atmospheres. The overinflated balloon ruptured inside the plaintiff, causing serious injuries. The question before the Supreme Court was not the state law tort question whether the overinflation counted as a product misuse that severed causal connection. Rather it was whether, in light of *Lohr*, the Medical Device Act "preempts state-law claims seeking damages for injuries caused by medical devices that received premarket approval from the Food and Drug Administration." Unlike pre-market notification, the PMA process involves an exhaustive review of product design and data, because the balloon catheter was classified as a potentially dangerous, or Class III, device that required intensive scrutiny because of the serious risk its use posed to human life and health. As in *Lohr*, the Court assumed that the "requirements" under state law included private law actions. Scalia, J., in an eight-to-one decision (with Ginsburg, J., dissenting) found that the "rigorous process" of FDA review, which required an average of 1,200 hours per submission, dictated preemption. He noted that a jury should not be allowed to second guess the explicit decision of the agency, which included extensive post-market surveillance and regulated product advertisement.

To what extent does preemption protection for medical device manufacturers increase pressure upon physicians subject to malpractice claims? Gentry & McMichael, Responses to Liability Immunization: Evidence from Medical Devices, 17 J. Empirical Legal Stud. 789 (2020), provides some evidence that "physicians in high-malpractice-pressure states change their treatment plans to reduce the use of medical devices, relative to physicians in low-malpractice-pressure states."

To avoid express preemption under the MDA, plaintiffs have brought forward novel claims based on the manufacturer's failure to warn the FDA of risks that emerge post-approval. In Glover v. Bausch & Lomb, Inc., 6 F.4th 229, 239 (2d Cir. 2021), the plaintiff, who suffered pain and loss of vision after she was implanted with Trulign Toric intraocular lenses in both of her eyes to correct her vision following cataract surgery, alleged that the defendant Bausch & Lomb failed to warn the FDA of known safety risks and failed to comply with the FDA's post-approval safety requirements. Thus framed, the plaintiff contended that her negligence and failure-to-warn claims should "proceed under traditional tort law and are not a veiled attempt to enforce federal requirements that Congress has not provided a private right of action to enforce." Lynch, J., certified to the Connecticut Supreme Court the question whether Connecticut recognized such a state law claim. The Connecticut Supreme Court responded in the affirmative, holding that "defendants had a duty under the [Connecticut Product Liability Act] to comply with federal statutes and regulations requiring them to report adverse events . . . to the FDA and to comply with the FDA's postapproval requirements in a timely manner." Glover v. Bausch & Lomb, Inc., 275 A.3d 168, 172 (Conn. 2022).

Academic writing has taken varying positions on FDA preemption. Nagareda, FDA Preemption: When Tort Law Meets the Administrative State, J. Tort L., Dec. 4, 2006, at 1, proposes that FDA preemption be conditioned on the willingness of drug companies to supply further information about their products to the public at large. In response, see Epstein, Why the FDA Must Preempt Tort Litigation: A Critique of *Chevron* Deference and a Response to Richard Nagareda, J. Tort L., Dec. 4, 2006, at 1, urging a return to the field preemption doctrine. Sharkey, Products Liability Preemption: An Institutional Approach, *supra* at 634, suggests that the court should scrutinize the agency record and give deference to the agency only to the extent that the agency considered the precise risk at issue in the suit.

2. *Levine's "Clear Evidence" Rule Revisited.* In Merck Sharp & Dohme Corp. v. Albrecht, 139 S. Ct. 1668, 1668, 1680 (2019), the Supreme Court clarified the "clear evidence" standard articulated in *Levine*, explaining:

> "Clear evidence" . . . is evidence that shows the court that the drug manufacturer fully informed the FDA of the justifications for the warning required by state law and that the FDA, in turn, informed the drug manufacturer that the FDA would not approve a change to the drug's label to include that warning.

The Court also held that judges, rather than juries, should determine what constitutes "clear evidence." Breyer, J., explained:

> The complexity of the . . . law helps to illustrate why we answer this question by concluding that the question is a legal one for the judge, not a jury. The question often involves the use of legal skills to determine whether agency disapproval fits facts that are not in dispute. Moreover, judges, rather than lay juries, are better equipped to evaluate the nature and scope of an

> agency's determination. Judges are experienced in [t]he construction of written instruments, such as those normally produced by a federal agency to memorialize its considered judgments. And judges are better suited than are juries to understand and to interpret agency decisions in light of the governing statutory and regulatory context. To understand the question as a legal question for judges makes sense given the fact that judges are normally familiar with principles of administrative law. Doing so should produce greater uniformity among courts; and greater uniformity is normally a virtue when a question requires a determination concerning the scope and effect of federal agency action.

3. *Vaccines and Preemption.* The case for preemption of tort law claims is stronger for vaccines than for other pharmaceutical drugs. First, the National Childhood Vaccine Injury Act of 1986 includes an express preemption provision:

> No vaccine manufacturer shall be liable in a civil action for damages arising from a vaccine-related injury or death associated with the administration of a vaccine . . . if the injury or death resulted from side effects that were unavoidable even though the vaccine was properly prepared and was accompanied by proper directions and warnings.

42 U.S.C. §300aa-22(b)(1) (2023).

Second, Congress established a no-fault vaccine injury compensation fund to provide substitute remedies.

In Bruesewitz v. Wyeth LLC, 562 U.S. 223, 239, 251 (2011), Hannah, a seemingly healthy infant, suffered violent seizures following her injection with Tri-Immunol, a "whole cell" diphtheria, tetanus, and pertussis (DTP) vaccine manufactured by Wyeth. The Bruesewitzes claimed that Tri-Immunol was defective and that Wyeth had, at the relevant time, an approved license for Tri-Solgen, an alternative, safer "fractionated" DTP vaccine.

Scalia, J., writing for a five-member majority, engaged in a close textualist reading of the "concessive subordinate clause," to conclude that the statute categorically preempts liability for design defects, while leaving intact liability for manufacturing defects and failure to warn claims. According to Scalia, J., Congress intended to impose this "quid pro quo": "The vaccine manufacturers fund from their own sales an informal, efficient compensation program for vaccine injuries; in exchange they avoid costly tort litigation and the occasional disproportionate jury verdict." And (sounding a theme similar to that of Alito, J., in his *Levine* dissent) Congress expressed a preference, "a sensible choice to leave complex epidemiological judgments about vaccine design to the FDA and the National Vaccine Program rather than juries." Sotomayor, J., dissented on the ground that "Congress must . . . have intended a vaccine manufacturer to demonstrate in each civil action that the particular side effects of a vaccine's design were 'unavoidable[,]' " and the majority's alternative reading "leaves a regulatory vacuum in which no one ensures that vaccine manufacturers adequately take account of scientific and technological advancements when designing or distributing their products." How should this preemption provision apply to "avoidable" side effects? Does the provision do any work if the FDA warnings are not deemed proper in all cases?

4. *Generic Drugs and Preemption.* Should the fact that generic drugs are subject to a different regulatory framework from brand-name drugs affect the preemption analysis? Instead of a lengthy pre-market approval process used for brand-name drugs, generics go through an abbreviated review process that tests the product only for bioequivalence with its branded counterpart. The packaging for the generic must also be sent to the FDA, 21 U.S.C. §355(j)(2)(A)(v), and the label for the generic must match the label for the branded drug. 21 C.F.R. §314.127(a)(7).

In PLIVA, Inc. v. Mensing, 564 U.S. 604, 623–24 (2011), Gladys Mensing and Julie Demahy sued the generic drug manufacturers of metoclopramide for failing to adequately warn of the danger that long-term use of the drug could result in tardive dyskinesia, a severe neurological disorder. The manufacturers raised preemption as a defense, arguing that, because the federal statutes and FDA regulations required them to use the same labeling as their brand-name counterparts, it was impossible for them to comply with both federal law and any state tort law duty that required them to use a different label. In a sharply divided five-to-four decision, Thomas, J., upheld the impossibility preemption defense. Thomas, J., recognized that immunizing generic but not brand-name drug manufacturers from state tort liability "makes little sense" insofar as afflicted individuals who took generics drugs are denied the remedies available to persons who receive brand-name drugs. But he insisted that it was not the Court's role to correct or reinterpret statutory schemes established by Congress that clearly preempted claims against the generic manufacturers. Sotomayor, J., again wrote in dissent, claiming that the majority opinion had cut back on the burden to receive the otherwise narrow impossibility defense of *Levine*, given that "generic manufacturers of metoclopramide (Manufacturers) have shown only that they *might* have been unable to comply with both federal law and their state-law duties to warn respondents Gladys Mensing and Julie Demahy."

Thereafter, in Mutual Pharmaceutical Co., Inc. v. Bartlett, 570 U.S. 472 (2013), Alito, J., held (in another sharply divided five-to-four decision) "that [the New Hampshire] state-law design-defect claims that turn on the adequacy of a drug's warnings are pre-empted by federal law under *PLIVA*." In so doing, he noted that impossibility preemption was appropriate because it precluded actions that required the generic drug manufacturer either to redesign the drug or to strengthen its warning. Breyer, J., dissented on the ground that the state law litigation could properly "supplement" the FDA's regulatory activities.

Should it make a difference that generic manufacturers may market their drugs if they meet a statutory requirement that they be "the same" as the branded drug? Is uniformity in warnings important? Can it be preserved if each of ten or more generic manufacturers has an independent duty to update warnings?

In the wake of *PLIVA* and *Bartlett*, plaintiffs have sought to hold manufacturers of brand-name drugs liable for failing to warn of harms suffered by using generics, whose labels copied that of the brand-name drugs. In T.H. v. Novartis Pharmaceuticals Corp., 407 P.3d 18, 31 (Cal. 2017), Cuéllar, J., imposed such "innovator liability" on the brand-name manufacturer:

> Time and again we have recognized how " '[t]he overall policy of preventing future harm is ordinarily served, in tort law, by imposing the costs of negligent conduct upon those responsible.' " A brand-name drug manufacturer is not only in the best position to warn of a drug's harmful effects: It is also the only manufacturer with the unilateral authority under federal law to issue such a warning for the brand-name drug or its generic bioequivalent.

The Third Restatement has recently embraced such claims under the somewhat forgotten theory of negligent misrepresentation. RTT: Miscellaneous Provisions Ch. 3. §18A, comment *q* (Tentative Draft 2023).

RESTATEMENT OF THE LAW (THIRD) OF TORTS: MISCELLANEOUS PROVISIONS (TENTATIVE DRAFT 2023)

§18A. Negligent Misrepresentation Causing Physical Harm

(a) An actor who negligently furnishes false information is subject to liability for any physical harm factually caused by another's reliance on the information that is within the actor's scope of liability.

CHAPTER 9

DAMAGES

Sullivan v. Old Colony Street Ry.

83 N.E. 1091, 1092 (Mass. 1908)

Rugg, C.J. The rule of damages is a practical instrumentality for the administration of justice. The principle on which it is founded is compensation. Its object is to afford the equivalent in money for the actual loss caused by the wrong of another. Recurrence to this fundamental conception tests the soundness of claims for the inclusion of new elements of damage.

Zibbell v. Southern Pacific Co.

116 P. 513, 520 (Cal. 1911)

Henshaw, J. No rational being would change places with the injured man for an amount of gold that would fill the room of the court, yet no lawyer would contend that such is the legal measure of damages.

SECTION A. INTRODUCTION

Proof of damages is an essential element of the plaintiff's cause of action in most civil litigation. Section B introduces compensatory damages, which serve as the primary mechanism of compensating the plaintiff and deterring the defendant. Compensatory damages are comprised of pecuniary (economic) damages and nonpecuniary (noneconomic) damages, with the former including so-called hard damages such as lost wages and medical expenses and the latter including "soft" damages like pain and suffering and (sometimes) loss of enjoyment of life. When liability is clear, both sides will judge their success by the size of the damages verdict. The plaintiff will suffer a major defeat if she receives a low verdict when a high one was expected. The converse is true for the defendant. In this day of potential million-dollar verdicts, it is routine for both sides to retain medical and economic experts to testify on three critical elements of damages: pain and suffering, medical expenses, and lost earnings attributable to the harm. For each head of damages, a jury must take into account both past and future losses. Often substantial, concrete evidence is available for past losses, but for future losses only estimates—frequently verging on guesswork—are available, for which the duration and severity may be unknown.

The difficulties in making damage calculations should not cause us to lose sight of their essential function within the tort system, whether as an expression of justice or a mechanism for deterrence. Within a system of corrective justice, damages are meant, as Rugg, C.J., suggests, to place the plaintiff in the position that she would have enjoyed if the tort had never been committed. Over a wide range of cases, that standard works fairly well, but in extreme cases (of which death is paramount) no amount of money can serve that substitution function, even though some amount must be chosen by a jury and ratified by a court. Damages are also crucial to the deterrence function of tort law because they set the "prices" defendants must pay for engaging in their chosen activities. If damage awards are set too low, defendants do not fully internalize the losses they create. Thus they will not be induced to take adequate care, and they may engage in excessively risky activities. Yet if damage awards are set too high, defendants will be overly cautious and may be discouraged from engaging in activities that promise private and social benefits. To be sure, too much can be made of the deterrent and control function of damages, given the host of other sanctions—injunctions, licenses, inspections, fines, and even imprisonment—that serve to curb harmful behavior. But even though these sanctions from time to time intrude, the tort damage remedy remains one constant feature in our system of social control for large and discrete personal injuries and property damages. Does the ideal amount of damages in, say, a wrongful death case compute the same way under a compensatory and a deterrence theory? If not, which approach should be followed and why? How might conflicts between the goal to do justice between the parties and the desire to achieve larger societal aims arise within the question of damages?

The topic of damages also has some distinctive features. There are special rules governing the loss of consortium (i.e., the services to the decedent's spouse) and wrongful death, as addressed in Section C. The rules covering punitive damages, discussed in Section D, have ever greater constitutional overtones. Punitive damages focus on the misconduct of the defendant, as opposed to the harm suffered by the plaintiff, and the added deterrent effects to avoid the repetition of such conduct. Finally, Section E points to the many cases that also raise questions of mitigation of damages and setoffs for payments from collateral sources, such as first-party health plans, in an age of expanding public and private benefits programs.

SECTION B. COMPENSATORY DAMAGES

1. Nonpecuniary Damages

McDougald v. Garber

536 N.E.2d 372 (N.Y. 1989)

WACHTLER, C.J. This appeal raises fundamental questions about the nature and role of nonpecuniary damages in personal injury litigation. By nonpecuniary damages, we mean those damages awarded to compensate an injured person for the physical and emotional consequences of the injury, such as pain and suffering and the loss of the ability to engage in certain activities. Pecuniary damages, on the other hand, compensate the victim for the economic consequences of the injury, such as medical expenses, lost earnings and the cost of custodial care.

The specific questions raised here deal with assessment of nonpecuniary damages and are (1) whether some degree of cognitive awareness is a prerequisite to recovery for loss of enjoyment of life and (2) whether a jury should be instructed to consider and award damages for loss of enjoyment of life separately from damages for pain and suffering. We answer the first question in the affirmative and the second question in the negative.

I

On September 7, 1978, plaintiff Emma McDougald, then 31 years old, underwent a Caesarean section and tubal ligation at New York Infirmary. Defendant Garber performed the surgery; defendants Armengol and Kulkarni provided anesthesia. During the surgery, Mrs. McDougald suffered oxygen deprivation which resulted in severe brain damage and left her in a permanent comatose condition. This action was brought by Mrs. McDougald and her husband, suing derivatively, alleging that the injuries were caused by the defendants' acts of malpractice.

A jury found all defendants liable and awarded Emma McDougald a total of $9,650,102 in damages, including $1,000,000 for conscious pain and suffering and a separate award of $3,500,000 for loss of the pleasures and pursuits of life. The balance of the damages awarded to her were for pecuniary damages—lost earnings and the cost of custodial and nursing care. Her husband was awarded $1,500,000 on his derivative claim for the loss of his wife's services. On defendants' posttrial motions, the Trial Judge reduced the total award to Emma McDougald to $4,796,728 by striking the entire award for future nursing care ($2,353,374) and by reducing the separate awards for conscious pain and suffering and loss of the pleasures and pursuits of life to a single award of $2,000,000. Her husband's award was left intact. On cross appeals, the Appellate Division affirmed and later granted defendants leave to appeal to this court.

II

We note at the outset that the defendants' liability for Emma McDougald's injuries is unchallenged here.

Also unchallenged are the awards in the amount of $770,978 for loss of earnings and $2,025,750 for future custodial care—that is, the pecuniary damage awards that survived defendants' posttrial motions.

What remains in dispute, primarily, is the award to Emma McDougald for nonpecuniary damages. At trial, defendants sought to show that Mrs. McDougald's injuries were so severe that she was incapable of either experiencing pain or appreciating her condition. Plaintiffs, on the other hand, introduced proof that Mrs. McDougald responded to certain stimuli to a sufficient extent to indicate that she was aware of her circumstances. Thus, the extent of Mrs. McDougald's cognitive abilities, if any, was sharply disputed.

The parties and the trial court agreed that Mrs. McDougald could not recover for pain and suffering unless she were conscious of the pain. Defendants maintained that such consciousness was also required to support an award for loss of enjoyment of life. The court, however, accepted plaintiffs' view that loss of enjoyment of life was compensable without regard to whether the plaintiff was aware of the loss. Accordingly, because the level of Mrs. McDougald's cognitive abilities was in dispute, the court instructed the jury to consider loss of enjoyment of life as an element of nonpecuniary damages separate from pain and suffering. . . .

We conclude that the court erred, both in instructing the jury that Mrs. McDougald's awareness was irrelevant to their consideration of damages for loss of enjoyment of life and in directing the jury to consider that aspect of damages separately from pain and suffering.

III

We begin with the familiar proposition that an award of damages to a person injured by the negligence of another is to compensate the victim, not to punish the wrongdoer. The goal is to restore the injured party, to the extent possible, to the position that would have been occupied had the wrong not occurred. To be sure, placing the burden of compensation on the negligent party also serves as a deterrent, but purely punitive damages—that is, those which have no compensatory purpose—are prohibited unless the harmful conduct is intentional, malicious, outrageous, or otherwise aggravated beyond mere negligence.

Damages for nonpecuniary losses are, of course, among those that can be awarded as compensation to the victim. This aspect of damages, however, stands on less certain ground than does an award for pecuniary damages. An economic loss can be compensated in kind by an economic gain; but recovery for noneconomic losses such as pain and suffering and loss of enjoyment of life rests on "the legal fiction that money damages can compensate for a victim's injury." We accept this fiction, knowing that although money will neither ease the pain nor restore the victim's abilities, this device is as close as the law can come in its effort to right the wrong. We have no hope of evaluating what has been lost, but a monetary award may provide a measure of solace for the condition created.

Our willingness to indulge this fiction comes to an end, however, when it ceases to serve the compensatory goals of tort recovery. When that limit is met, further indulgence can only result in assessing damages that are punitive. The question posed by this case, then, is whether an award of damages for loss of enjoyment of life to a person whose injuries preclude any awareness of the loss serves a compensatory purpose. We conclude that it does not.

Simply put, an award of money damages in such circumstances has no meaning or utility to the injured person. An award for the loss of enjoyment of life "cannot provide [such a victim] with any consolation or ease any burden resting on him. . . . He cannot spend it upon necessities or pleasures. He cannot experience the pleasure of giving it away."

We recognize that, as the trial court noted, requiring some cognitive awareness as a prerequisite to recovery for loss of enjoyment of life will result in some cases "in the paradoxical situation that the greater the degree of brain injury inflicted by a negligent defendant, the smaller the award the plaintiff can recover in general damages." The force of this argument, however—the temptation to achieve a balance between injury and damages—has nothing to do with meaningful compensation for the victim. Instead, the temptation is rooted in a desire to punish the defendant in proportion to the harm inflicted. However relevant such retributive symmetry may be in the criminal law, it has no place in the law of civil damages, at least in the absence of culpability beyond mere negligence.

Accordingly, we conclude that cognitive awareness is a prerequisite to recovery for loss of enjoyment of life. We do not go so far, however, as to require the fact finder to sort out varying degrees of cognition and determine at what level a particular deprivation can be fully appreciated. With respect to pain and suffering, the trial court charged simply that there must be "some level of awareness" in order for plaintiff to recover. We think that this is an appropriate standard for all aspects of nonpecuniary loss. No doubt the standard ignores analytically relevant levels of cognition, but we resist the desire for analytical purity in favor of simplicity. A more complex instruction might give the appearance of greater precision but, given the limits of our understanding of the human mind, it would in reality lead only to greater speculation.

We turn next to the question whether loss of enjoyment of life should be considered a category of damages separate from pain and suffering.

IV

There is no dispute here that the fact finder may, in assessing nonpecuniary damages, consider the effect of the injuries on the plaintiff's capacity to lead a normal life. [The court reviews the movement, within and outside of New York, to treat loss of enjoyment of life as a separate category, in part to facilitate the appellate review of damage awards.]

We do not dispute that distinctions can be found or created between the concepts of pain and suffering and loss of enjoyment of life. If the term "suffering" is limited to the emotional response to the sensation of pain, then the emotional response caused by the limitation of life's activities may be considered qualitatively different. But suffering need not be so limited—it can easily encompass the frustration and anguish caused by the inability to participate in activities that once brought pleasure. Traditionally, by treating loss of enjoyment of life as a permissible factor in assessing pain and suffering, courts have given the term this broad meaning.

If we are to depart from this traditional approach and approve a separate award for loss of enjoyment of life, it must be on the basis that such an approach will yield a more accurate evaluation of the compensation due to the plaintiff. We have no doubt that, in general, the total award for nonpecuniary damages would increase if we adopted the rule. That separate awards are advocated by plaintiffs and resisted by defendants is sufficient evidence that larger awards are at stake here. But a larger award does not by itself indicate that the goal of compensation has been better served.

The advocates of separate awards contend that because pain and suffering and loss of enjoyment of life can be distinguished, they must be treated separately if the plaintiff is to be compensated fully for each distinct injury suffered. We disagree. Such an analytical approach may have its place when the subject is pecuniary damages, which can be calculated with some precision. But the estimation of nonpecuniary damages is not amenable to such analytical precision and may, in fact, suffer from its application. Translating human suffering into dollars and cents involves no mathematical formula; it rests, as we have said, on a legal fiction. The figure that emerges is unavoidably distorted by the translation. Application of this murky process to the component parts of nonpecuniary injuries (however analytically distinguishable they may be) cannot make it more accurate. If anything, the distortion will be amplified by repetition.

[The court orders a] new trial on the issue of nonpecuniary damages to be awarded to plaintiff Emma McDougald. . . .

Titone, J., dissenting.

The majority's holding represents a compromise position that neither comports with the fundamental principles of tort compensation nor furnishes a satisfactory, logically consistent framework for compensating nonpecuniary loss. Because I conclude that loss of enjoyment of life is an objective damage item, conceptually distinct from conscious pain and suffering, I can find no fault with the trial court's instruction authorizing separate awards and permitting an award for "loss of enjoyment of life" even in the absence of any awareness of that loss on the part of the injured plaintiff. Accordingly, I dissent. . . .

[T]he compensatory nature of a monetary award for loss of enjoyment of life is not altered or rendered punitive by the fact that the unaware injured plaintiff cannot experience the pleasure of having it. The fundamental distinction between punitive and compensatory damages is that the former exceed the amount necessary to replace what the plaintiff lost. . . .

NOTES

1. ***Recovery for Pain and Suffering.*** In *McDougald*, the majority and dissent agreed, in principle, that recovery for pain and suffering is generally proper in tort actions. In practice, however, the calculation of how much a plaintiff is entitled to recover is far less straightforward for pain and suffering than for categories like medical expenses or lost wages. Typically, the elements of pain and suffering include worry, anguish, and grief—all notoriously difficult

to quantify. Even for a conscious plaintiff, there is typically extensive disagreement as to how to present the issue of pain and suffering to the jury. In Rounds v. Rush Trucking Corp., 211 F.3d 185, 190 (2d Cir. 2000), the plaintiff suffered serious and permanent injuries when her pick-up truck was rammed in the rear by one of defendant's tractor-trailers. The jury awarded the plaintiff $350,000 for past and future mental suffering and $350,000 for past and future emotional distress. On appeal, Walker, J., struck the second award on the ground that *McDougald* embraces both forms of loss under a single heading.

> Despite our ability to distinguish between loss of enjoyment of life and the emotional distress at issue in this case, we follow the reasoning of the New York Court of Appeals and find that emotional distress is no more amenable to analytical precision than loss of enjoyment of life. There is no plausible basis for limiting *McDougald* to its facts and holding, as Rounds urges, that pain and suffering does not also encompass emotional distress, which is just as difficult to measure.

Accordingly, Walker, J., ordered a new trial unless the plaintiff agreed to a reduction of $350,000 in damages in light of the duplicative instructions. What if the jury already reduced the award for pain and suffering precisely because a separate head was allowed for emotional distress? "If Rounds is convinced that a properly charged jury would award in excess of $350,000 for pain and suffering, including emotional distress, she is free to reject remittitur and re-present the case to a jury." The original liability determination would remain undisturbed.

McDougald and *Rounds* raise the larger question whether the difficulties in arriving at a valuation of appropriate damages should preclude any recovery for pain and suffering, no matter how packaged. The most famous critique of this sort is Jaffe, Damages for Personal Injury: The Impact of Insurance, 18 Law & Contemp. Probs. 219, 224–25 (1953):

> But why we may ask *should* the plaintiff be compensated in money for an experience which involves no financial loss? It cannot be on the principle of returning what is his own. Essentially that principle rests on an economic foundation: on maintaining the integrity of the economic arrangements which provide the normally expectable basis for livelihood in our society. Pain is a harm, an "injury," but neither past pain nor its compensation has any consistent economic significance. The past experience is not a loss except in so far as it produced present deterioration. . . .
>
> I am aware, however, that though the premise may elude detection, some deep intuition may claim to validate this process of evaluating the imponderable. One who has suffered a violation of his bodily integrity may feel a sense of continuing outrage. This is particularly true where there has been disfigurement or loss of a member (even though not giving rise to economic loss). Because our society sets a high value on money it uses money or price as a means of recognizing the worth of non-economic as well as economic goods. If, insists the plaintiff, society really values my personality, my bodily integrity, it will signify its sincerity by paying me a sum of money. Damages thus may somewhat reestablish the plaintiff's self-confidence, wipe out his sense of outrage. Furthermore, though money is not an equivalent it may be a consolation, a solatium. . . .

With the Jaffe excerpt's expressive approach to nonpecuniary harms, compare Kwasny v. United States, 823 F.2d 194, 197 (7th Cir. 1987), where Posner, J., argues that nonpecuniary damages are essential for a properly functioning deterrence regime. *Kwasny* involved the death of a sixty-three-year-old man suffering from severe rheumatoid arthritis from an allegedly negligently performed intubation. Although the government "[came] close to arguing that . . . the hospital did [Kwasny] and his wife a favor by shortening his life" in its appeal from the pain and suffering award, Posner, J., noted:

> We disagree with those students of tort law who believe that pain and suffering are not real costs and should not be allowable items of damages in a tort suit. No one likes pain and suffering and most people would pay a good deal of money to be free from them. If they were not recoverable

in damages, the cost of negligence would be less to the tortfeasors and there would be more negligence, more accidents, more pain and suffering, and hence higher social costs. . . .

In Smith By and Through Lundy-Smith v. Northern Manhattan Nursing Home, Inc., 140 N.Y.S.3d 350, 354 (Sup. Ct. 2020), the court affirmed a $2.5 million award for pain and suffering (including lost enjoyment of life) to the widow of a nursing home resident who suffered hypoglycemia leading to anoxic encephalopathy that destroyed his brain function, as a result of the home's failure to monitor him. Billings, J., pointed out that *McDougald* limited the cognitive awareness prerequisite for recovery of pain and suffering to "the absence of culpability beyond mere negligence." Thus, regardless of whether decedent was conscious of his suffering or not, the award was justified given that the nursing home's culpability "extended beyond mere negligence," and was necessary "to achieve a balance between injury and damages."

Critics of nonpecuniary damages point to the elimination of damages for pain and suffering in various first-party insurance schemes (i.e., plans that directly cover the insured individual), including Social Security Disability Income as well as Medicare and Medicaid. These omissions in first-party markets have been treated as evidence that injured parties are generally unwilling to purchase insurance against possible future pain and suffering. See Danzon, Tort Reform and the Role of Government in Private Insurance Markets, 13 J. Legal Stud. 517 (1984). Why? Would anyone sell this insurance? Even if Danzon's point is true, does it follow that damages in tort actions should ignore pain and suffering, given that the deterrence function is irrelevant to first-party payment schemes? Croley & Hanson, The Nonpecuniary Costs of Accidents: Pain-and-Suffering Damages in Tort Law, 108 Harv. L. Rev. 1785 (1995), points to limited examples of insurance that specifically include pain and suffering damages, such as uninsured motorist coverage and airport flight insurance. If the recovery of damages is allowable for torts that involve no physical contact or tangible injury (e.g., assault), is there a reason for treating awards for pain and suffering differently? For a discussion of pain and suffering awards in light of the historical context of awarding damages for intangible losses, and a reminder that pecuniary losses may be nearly as susceptible to inaccuracy as pain and suffering awards, see Rabin, Pain and Suffering and Beyond: Some Thoughts on Recovery for Intangible Loss, 55 DePaul L. Rev. 359 (2006).

2. *Hedonic Damages.* The Restatement (Third) of Torts: Remedies takes the view, contra *McDougald*, that loss of enjoyment of life ("hedonic damages") should be compensable for cognitively impaired victims, but cautions that "care should be taken to craft instructions explaining to the jury the nature of a claim for this harm as compared to a claim for conscious pain and suffering." RTT: Remedies §20, comment *i* (Tentative Draft No. 2, approved 2023). Apart from victims who have lost all ability to sense pleasure or pain, loss of enjoyment is generally compensable. *Id.*; see also comment *c*. Nevertheless, an extensive literature casts some doubt on the practice of awarding hedonic damages that go beyond conscious pain and suffering, on the ground that individuals are sufficiently adaptive that these awards may overestimate the situation on the ground. Indeed "[a] rich psychological literature demonstrates that disability does not inherently limit enjoyment of life to the degree that these courts suggest. Rather, people who experience disabling injuries tend to adapt to their disabilities." Bagenstos & Schlanger, Hedonic Damages, Hedonic Adaptation, and Disability, 60 Vand. L. Rev. 745, 749 (2007). Is survey evidence that seriously disabled people report higher levels of happiness than expected enough to clinch this case? What if disabled people spend, when possible, large sums to eliminate their disabilities? For a skeptical response to such adaptation arguments, see DePianto, Tort Damages and the (Misunderstood) Money-Happiness Connection, 44 Ariz. St. L.J. 1385 (2012), which argues that countervailing distortions—such as an inflated view of how much happiness or satisfaction a dollar award can provide—further complicate the award of hedonic damages.

3. *The "Per Diem" Rule.* Even if attention is concentrated on pain and suffering, how is that information translated into dollars? One ingenious suggestion about how to solve these valuation difficulties—the per diem rule—was first advanced in Belli, The Use of Demonstrative Evidence in Achieving "The More Adequate Award" 33–35 (1952):

> This is the key: You must break up the 30-year life expectancy into *finite* detailed periods of time. You must take these small periods of time, seconds and minutes, and determine in dollars and cents what each period is worth. You must start with the seconds and minutes rather than at the other end of thirty years. You cannot stand in front of a jury and say, "Here is a man horribly injured, permanently disabled, who will suffer excruciating pain for the rest of his life, he is entitled to a verdict of $225,000 [$2.6 million in 2023 dollars]."
>
> You must start at the beginning and show that pain is a continuous thing, second by second, minute by minute, hour by hour, year after year for thirty years. You must interpret one second, one minute, one hour, one year of pain and suffering into dollars and cents and then multiply to your absolute figure to show how you have achieved your result of an award approaching adequacy at $225,000. If you throw a novel figure at a jury or an appellate court of $225,000, without breaking it down, you are going to frighten both your trier of facts and your reviewer of facts. . . .

Belli's approach to valuation still retains much of its punch. Does it work for hedonic damages?

The propriety of Belli's argument has been much debated in the appellate courts. The use of the per diem argument was initially prohibited in Botta v. Brunner, 138 A.2d 713 (N.J. 1958), and several other jurisdictions followed suit, e.g., Ramirez v. City of Chicago, 740 N.E.2d 1190 (Ill. App. Ct. 2000). Today, however, a majority of jurisdictions allow the jury to hear per diem calculations, subject to a cautionary instruction that this approach is argument, not evidence, or leave the decision to the discretion of the trial judge. See, e.g., Campbell, Chao & Robertson, Time Is Money: An Empirical Assessment of Non-Economic Damages Arguments, 95 Wash. U. L. Rev. 1, 6 (2017); Swift v. Wesco Ins. Co., No. CV-18-01531, 2021 WL 717252 (D. Ariz. Feb. 24, 2021); Collazo v. Progressive Select Ins. Co., No. 20-25302, 2022 WL 4483436 (S.D. Fla. Sept. 27, 2022). Other courts have condemned per diem instructions to the jury but have permitted the trial judge to allow the plaintiff to use that approach in closing argument. E.g., Manning v. Lunda Constr. Co., 953 F.2d 1090, 1093 (8th Cir. 1992).

4. *Increased Risk of Future Injury.* The proper treatment of probabilistic assessments of future pain and suffering divided the court in DePass v. United States, 721 F.2d 203, 210 (7th Cir. 1983). There, the plaintiff suffered a traumatic amputation of his left leg below the knee. In addition to the usual elements of pain and suffering, plaintiff's expert testified, largely on the strength of an extensive National Institute of Health study of World War II veterans, that there was "a statistical connection between traumatic limb amputations and future cardiovascular problems and decreased life expectancy." The expert estimated an eleven-year reduction in plaintiff's life expectancy. The government did nothing to counter that evidence, but the trial judge rejected these potential losses as speculative damages. Flaum, J., affirmed on the ground that the study was "inconclusive" and that "Illinois law is not settled as to whether increased risk of future injury is compensable." A spirited dissent by Posner, J., argued that it was clearly erroneous to refuse to award damages for this type of loss:

> The district judge's rejection of such evidence, if widely followed, would lead to systematically undercompensating the victims of serious accidents and thus to systematically underdeterring such accidents. Accidents that require the amputation of a limb, particularly a leg, are apparently even more catastrophic than one had thought. They do not just cause a lifetime of disfigurement and reduced mobility; they create a high risk of premature death from heart disease. The goal of awarding damages in tort law is to put the tort victim as nearly as possible in the position he would have occupied if the tort had not been committed. This goal cannot be

attained or even approached if judges shut their eyes to consequences that scientists have found are likely to follow from particular types of accident, merely because the scientists' evidence is statistical.

Should the decision to award damages for increased risk depend on the certainty of the increased risk? On a particular threshold of increased risk? In Cudone v. Gehret, 821 F. Supp. 266, 271 (D. Del. 1993), a physician's alleged failure to timely diagnose a patient's breast cancer increased the probability that she would suffer a recurrence within ten years from under 25 to 30 percent to 50 to 60 percent. The court distinguished *DePass* as involving "less compelling circumstances," and held that the failure to provide a jury instruction on increased risk would produce "an absurd result." How should damages based on increased risk be calculated?

2. Pecuniary Damages

O'Shea v. Riverway Towing Co.

677 F.2d 1194 (7th Cir. 1982)

Posner, J. This is a tort case under the federal admiralty jurisdiction. We are called upon to decide questions of contributory negligence and damage assessment. . . .

On the day of the accident, Margaret O'Shea was coming off duty as a cook on a towboat plying the Mississippi River. A harbor boat operated by the defendant, Riverway Towing Company, carried Mrs. O'Shea to shore and while getting off the boat she fell and sustained the injury complained of. The district judge found Riverway negligent and Mrs. O'Shea free from contributory negligence, and assessed damages in excess of $150,000. Riverway appeals only from the finding that there was no contributory negligence and from the part of the damage award that was intended to compensate Mrs. O'Shea for her lost future wages. [The court holds that the plaintiff was free of contributory negligence.]

The more substantial issues in this appeal relate to the computation of lost wages. Mrs. O'Shea's job as a cook paid her $40 a day, and since the custom was to work 30 days consecutively and then have the next 30 days off, this comes to $7200 a year although, as we shall see, she never had earned that much in a single year. She testified that when the accident occurred she had been about to get another cook's job on a Mississippi towboat that would have paid her $60 a day ($10,800 a year). She also testified that she had been intending to work as a boat's cook until she was 70—longer if she was able. An economist who testified on Mrs. O'Shea's behalf used the foregoing testimony as the basis for estimating the wages that she lost because of the accident. He first subtracted federal income tax from yearly wage estimates based on alternative assumptions about her wage rate (that it would be either $40 or $60 a day); assumed that this wage would have grown by between six and eight percent a year; assumed that she would have worked either to age 65 or to age 70; and then discounted the resulting lost-wage estimates to present value, using a discount rate of 8.5 percent a year. These calculations, being based on alternative assumptions concerning starting wage rate, annual wage increases, and length of employment, yielded a range of values rather than a single value. The bottom of the range was $50,000. This is the present value, computed at an 8.5 percent discount rate, of Mrs. O'Shea's lost future wages on the assumption that her starting wage was $40 a day and that it would have grown by six percent a year until she retired at the age of 65. The top of the range was $114,000, which is the present value (again discounted at 8.5 percent) of her lost future wages assuming she would have worked till she was 70 at a wage that would have started at $60 a day and increased by eight percent a year. The judge awarded a figure—$86,033—near the midpoint of this range. . . .

There is no doubt that the accident disabled Mrs. O'Shea from working as a cook on a boat. The break in her leg was very serious: it reduced the stability of the leg and caused her to fall frequently. It is impossible to see how she could have continued working as a cook, a job performed mostly while standing up, and especially on a boat, with its unsteady motion. But Riverway argues that Mrs. O'Shea (who has not worked at all since the accident, which occurred two years before the trial) could have gotten some sort of job and that the wages in that job should be deducted from the admittedly higher wages that she could have earned as a cook on a boat.

The question is not whether Mrs. O'Shea is totally disabled in the sense, relevant to social security disability cases but not tort cases, that there is no job in the American economy for which she is medically fit. It is whether she can by reasonable diligence find gainful employment, given the physical condition in which the accident left her. Here is a middle-aged woman, very overweight, badly scarred on one arm and one leg, unsteady on her feet, in constant and serious pain from the accident, with no education beyond high school and no work skills other than cooking, a job that happens to require standing for long periods which she is incapable of doing. It seems unlikely that someone in this condition could find gainful work at the minimum wage. True, the probability is not zero; and a better procedure, therefore, might have been to subtract from Mrs. O'Shea's lost future wages as a boat's cook the wages in some other job, discounted (i.e., multiplied) by the probability — very low — that she would in fact be able to get another job. But the district judge cannot be criticized for having failed to use a procedure not suggested by either party. The question put to him was the dichotomous one, would she or would she not get another job if she made reasonable efforts to do so? This required him to decide whether there was a more than 50 percent probability that she would. We cannot say that the negative answer he gave to that question was clearly erroneous.

Riverway argues next that it was wrong for the judge to award damages on the basis of a wage not validated, as it were, by at least a year's employment at that wage. Mrs. O'Shea had never worked full time, had never in fact earned more than $3600 in a full year, and in the year preceding the accident had earned only $900. But previous wages do not put a cap on an award of lost future wages. If a man who had never worked in his life graduated from law school, began working at a law firm at an annual salary of $35,000, and was killed the second day on the job, his lack of a past wage history would be irrelevant to computing his lost future wages. The present case is similar if less dramatic. Mrs. O'Shea did not work at all until 1974, when her husband died. She then lived on her inheritance and worked at a variety of part-time jobs till January 1979, when she started working as a cook on the towboat. According to her testimony, which the trial judge believed, she was then working full time. It is immaterial that this was her first full-time job and that the accident occurred before she had held it for a full year. Her job history was typical of women who return to the labor force after their children are grown or, as in Mrs. O'Shea's case, after their husband dies, and these women are, like any tort victims, entitled to damages based on what they would have earned in the future rather than on what they may or may not have earned in the past.

If we are correct so far, Mrs. O'Shea was entitled to have her lost wages determined on the assumption that she would have earned at least $7200 in the first year after the accident and that the accident caused her to lose that entire amount by disabling her from any gainful employment. And since Riverway neither challenges the district judge's (apparent) finding that Mrs. O'Shea would have worked till she was 70 nor contends that the lost wages for each year until then should be discounted by the probability that she would in fact have been alive and working as a boat's cook throughout the damage period, we may also assume that her wages would have been at least $7200 a year for the 12 years between the date of the accident and her seventieth birthday. . . .

[Posner, J., then discusses the method used to account for inflation in the assessment of the plaintiff's lost future wages. He upholds the award, notwithstanding some questionable assumptions in the economist's methodology, and concludes that the calculation of lost earnings "can and should be an analytical rather than an intuitive undertaking," and, "for the future," asks "the district judges in this circuit to indicate the steps by which they arrive at damage awards for lost future earnings."]

Judgment affirmed.

NOTES

1. ***Work-Life Expectancy.*** In *O'Shea*, Posner, J., discussed the plaintiff's work and wage history, and criticized the economist's failure to discount the suggested damage award based on the probability that the plaintiff would not have remained in the job market for the entire length of her work-life expectancy. Any award for future earnings should take into account the possibility of the plaintiff's death or disability before retirement in order not to overstate systematically lost future earnings. The proper procedure thus asks (1) the expected (discounted) earnings of each future year, and (2) the probability that the plaintiff will actually be in the workforce in that year. While the probability that the plaintiff would have worked the next year may be close to 100 percent, the same cannot be said of employment ten or twenty years later. The results achieved by this annualized methodology differ from the results achieved by assuming that a person will, in all cases, live exactly to her life expectancy.

2. ***Potential Bias in Work-Life Expectancy Calculations.*** Work-life expectancy calculations have come under increased scrutiny given the use of historical tables that incorporate race and gender-based differences. The Restatement (Third) of Torts: Remedies has adopted the position that courts should not "allow expert testimony or other evidence or argument that a plaintiff's earning capacity is higher or lower based on average earnings or average working-life expectancy for workers of the plaintiff's race, ethnicity, or sex." See RTT: Remedies §18, comment *e* (Tentative Draft No. 2, approved 2023). The Restatement cites approvingly Sharkey, Valuing Black and Female Lives: A Proposal for Incorporating Agency VSL into Tort Damages, 96 Notre Dame L. Rev. 1479, 1486–87 (2021), which argues:

> The use of such gender- and race-based tables reifies and perpetuates structural inequities. To the extent that the lower wage estimates for women and members of minority racial/ethnic groups reflect, at least to some degree, structural inequities and historical injustices, these are incorporated into tort damage estimates. Similarly, to the extent that minority patients receive inferior healthcare treatment, this affects not only expected medical expenses, but also life expectancy, that likewise will be incorporated into depressed tort damages estimates.
>
> Moreover, such gender- and race-based tables are inaccurate predictors of the future. The table figures are static, meaning they reflect a snapshot of the time period from which the data were collected without accounting for trends that were evolving over that time period. The use of static figures rests on the assumption that whatever discrepancies exist between demographic groups will not only persist but also remain constant into the future. Specifically, such figures do not capture the emerging legal, professional, and social norms that favor workplace equality and increase the likelihood that discrepancies in employment data between demographic groups will diminish in the future. Young female and minority tort victims bear the particular brunt of the effects of discriminatory and inaccurate data, given that their expected wages cannot be extrapolated from past earning history but instead must be based on the gender- and race-based historical tables.

In McMillan v. City of New York, 253 F.R.D. 247, 256 (E.D.N.Y. 2008), Weinstein, J., refused to use race-based statistics to calculate the life expectancy of the African American male plaintiff who was rendered a quadriplegic in the crash of a negligently operated ferryboat. He also noted the inconsistency of using race-based statistics to shorten the life expectancy of the plaintiff for the purposes of assessing future medical expenses when "the damages awarded are designed to extend claimant's life by providing him with the best medical and other care—more than the equivalent of what the average American quadriplegic could expect."

The difficulties that arise in the calculation of a plaintiff's lost future earnings and work-life expectancy are compounded when a plaintiff is very young. In G.M.M. v. Kimpson, 116 F. Supp. 3d 126, 129 (E.D.N.Y. 2015), Weinstein, J., extended *McMillan* and rejected the use of statistics based on ethnicity to project the likelihood that a three-year-old Hispanic child would have obtained higher education had he not suffered from lead poisoning due to his landlord's negligence in failing to remove lead paint from the apartment. Weinstein, J., explained: "Based upon his specific family background, had the child not been injured, there was a high probability of superior educational attainment and corresponding high earnings. Treated by experts as a 'Hispanic,' his potential, based on the education and income of 'average "Hispanics" in the United States,' was relatively low." Similarly, in CivA 10064/02 Migdal Insurance Co. Ltd. v. Abu-Hanna, (3) TakSC 3932 (2005) (Isr.), the Israeli Supreme Court considered how best to calculate the lost earning potential of a five-month-old girl injured in a road accident. The Court took a strong stand against consideration of typical factors such as the child's gender, race, ethnic origin, and socioeconomic status:

> In the absence of specific circumstances to prove the contrary, every boy and girl in Israel—whether from a rich or a poor home, and regardless of origin—has an opportunity of finding their way into the various economic circles. . . . Giving less compensation for identical injuries, merely because of the gender, socio-economic status or ethnic origin of the injured person . . . fails to restore the damage caused by the tort[i]ous act . . . [and] perpetuates a historical reality. . . .
>
> Compensation that relies on data concerning the ethnicity, social status or race of the plaintiff may lead to an absurd result, where the expected damage to injured individuals with a low expected income is less than the expected damage to those with a higher one; consequently, the precautions that a tortfeasor will take—will be different according to the potential victims (a man or a woman; people of different religious affiliations; a resident of a high-class neighborhood or a resident of a poor city). In so far as the tortfeasor has control of the situation, and sometimes he does have such control, the risks he takes will be directed towards the weaker sectors of society. . . .

Is the Israeli approach, which uses a national average wage statistic to assess damages for the lost earning capacity of children, preferable to more individualized approaches? The Israeli court noted that individual evidence of higher than average ability (e.g., in sports or academia) could be used to increase the damages assessment. What should be done with lower than average ability? What if use of the tables benefits the plaintiff? See Banda v. Herc Rentals, Inc., No. 18-CV-05329, 2020 WL 353461, at *4 (N.D. Cal. Jan. 21, 2020), where the plaintiff wished to be compared to other Hispanic males with no high school education, given that they have a longer work-life expectancy than others with a similar level of education. Note that Kenneth Feinberg, the Special Master of the September 11th Victim Compensation Fund, used the same tables (based on white males) for all victims of the disaster. See Chamallas, The September 11th Victim Compensation Fund: Rethinking the Damages Element in Injury Law, 71 Tenn. L. Rev. 51, 69–73 (2003). How would the various calculations affect potential tortfeasors? Are corrective justice goals served? Deterrence goals?

3. ***Imputed Income.*** Imputed income from nonmarket activities (e.g., lost household labor) is another element of pecuniary damages, in addition to market losses (e.g., lost wages or medical expenses). The benefits are said to be "imputed" because there is no explicit market transaction to give direct evidence of their worth. In the law of damages, the most important aspect of imputed income applies to serious personal injuries to a spouse not working outside the home, which may disable him or her from performing services of great value to the family, thus requiring hiring replacement services. See, e.g., Shepard v. Capitol Foundry of Virginia, Inc., 554 S.E.2d 72, 73–74 (Va. 2001), in which the court reinstated a $1.7 million award for nonpecuniary damages for a husband whose wife was killed in an automobile accident. Virginia's wrongful death statute provides recovery for "[s]orrow, mental anguish, and solace which may include society, companionship, comfort, guidance, [and] kindly offices and advice of the decedent. . . ." Va. Code Ann. §8.01-52 (2023). The sixty-seven-year-old decedent had been married to her husband for forty-four years. She was the "primary caregiver" of their six children. Moreover, when her husband's thirty-year military career took him away from home, she "handled the family's business matters and continued to do so after he retired." Is the proper measure of damages what she could have earned in the marketplace, less the taxes paid thereon? For a development of this theme, see Komesar, Toward a General Theory of Personal Injury Loss, 3 J. Legal Stud. 457 (1974).

4. ***Mitigation of Damages.*** In tort law, as in contract law, the plaintiff normally has a duty to mitigate damages; that is, to take steps that minimize her expected losses from an accident. Hence the inquiry in *O'Shea* as to whether the plaintiff could find a suitable alternative that was not so onerous as to leave her worse off than before.

The mitigation issue raises even more serious challenges with medical interventions. In principle, it seems easy to conclude that the plaintiff should spend $1,000 on medical treatment to save the defendant $10,000. The plaintiff is no worse off from mitigation so long as she receives the $1,000 from the defendant, who is still left better off by $9,000. Thus, mitigation operates as a barrier against waste by making the plaintiff a fiduciary of sorts for the defendant. However, the outcome of a surgical intervention, for example, is often highly uncertain. Thus, if an operation costing $1,000 turns out to be a success, the defendant could save $9,000. But if the patient dies or is permanently injured, the plaintiff has incurred large losses if the defendant must compensate for the inferior outcome. The defendant faces either large potential gains or losses whenever the patient elects risky treatment. Sensing this conflict of interest, most courts give the plaintiff the benefit of the doubt so long as she acts in good faith in deciding whether to accept or reject treatment. See, e.g., Flemings v. State, 19 So. 3d 1220 (La. Ct. App. 2009), in which the court held that the plaintiff did not have to undergo a third surgical procedure to improve the appearance and increase the extension of his thumb after he had undertaken two unsuccessful procedures. What result if the plaintiff accepts the surgery and has a bad outcome? A good one? For a detailed discussion of the requirement to mitigate tort damages, see Shipley, Annotation, Duty of Injured Person to Submit to Surgery to Minimize Tort Damages, 62 A.L.R.3d 9 (2023).

5. ***Taxation of Tort Damage Awards.*** The Internal Revenue Code does not tax damage awards received in compensation for personal injuries stemming from physical harm, even when they substitute for lost taxable income. However, damages received in compensation for personal injuries stemming from emotional harms are taxable. I.R.C. §104(a). Complicated questions arise when physical and emotional harms occur simultaneously. In Parkinson v. Commissioner, 99 T.C.M. (CCH) 1583 (2010), the court had to determine the tax status of damages awarded for a heart attack that had both serious physical and emotional components. The court excluded from gross income the half of the damages award for the petitioner's heart

attack, but not the half attributable to the petitioner's emotional distress. What justifies this different tax treatment?

Another recurrent question is whether actual damage awards for lost earnings should be reduced to offset their tax-free status. In Norfolk & Western Railway. v. Liepelt, 444 U.S. 490, 494 (1980), Justice Stevens allowed these tax issues into evidence in FELA cases, reasoning:

> Admittedly there are many variables that may affect the amount of a wage earner's future income-tax liability. The law may change, his family may increase or decrease in size, his spouse's earnings may affect his tax bracket, and extra income or unforeseen deductions may become available. But future employment itself, future health, future personal expenditures, future interest rates, and future inflation are also matters of estimate and prediction. Any one of these issues might provide the basis for protracted expert testimony and debate. But the practical wisdom of the trial bar and the trial bench has developed effective methods of presenting the essential elements of an expert calculation in a form that is understandable by juries that are increasingly familiar with the complexities of modern life. We therefore reject the notion that the introduction of evidence describing a decedent's estimated after-tax earnings is too speculative or complex for a jury.

Justice Blackmun's dissent supported the older practice of ignoring taxes in torts cases:

> In my view, by mandating adjustment of the award by way of reduction for federal income taxes that would have been paid by the decedent on his earnings, the Court appropriates for the tortfeasor a benefit intended to be conferred on the victim or his survivors. And in requiring that the jury be instructed that a wrongful-death award is not subject to federal income tax, the Court opens the door for a variety of admonitions to the jury not to "misbehave," and unnecessarily interjects what is now to be federal law into the administration of a trial in a state court.

The administrative complexities of taking taxes into account provoked a different response in New York, where by statute, in medical malpractice cases, evidence of the federal, state, and local taxation of lost earnings "shall be admissible for consideration by the court, outside of the presence of the jury. . . ." N.Y. C.P.L.R. §4546 (2023). Why not a simplified alternative that reduces all damage awards for lost income by a fixed figure, say, 20 percent? Is the loss in precision offset by the consistency in results and the reduction in administrative costs?

6. *Discounting to Present Value and Inflation.* Future benefits from all sources need to be discounted to present value, whether lost earnings or medical expenses. The requirement for discounting future income streams can be justified by a single proposition: A dollar today is worth more than a dollar next year. The reason for the difference should be apparent: If a person has a dollar today, he will enjoy both the dollar and the interest earned on it, paid by the party who in the interim used that dollar, at the end of the year. The value of that one year's use of the dollar is, ignoring uncertainty, a function of the going rate of interest for the use of money. As interest rates increase, the demand for immediate cash, relative to future payments, increases as well. Accordingly the discount rate will be steeper. The formula for discounting to present value is:

$$PV_{\$1.00} = \$1.00 \div (1 + i)^n$$

where $PV_{\$1.00}$ equals the present value of the future payment of \$1.00, n equals the number of years until this payment is made, and i equals the interest rate applicable during the period. Inspection of the formula reveals that the discount for a future payment depends both on the interest rate and on the length of time before payment is due. The longer a creditor must wait for payment, the greater its discounted value today. The inflation-free rate of interest is generally estimated at somewhere between 1.5 and 3.0 percent, with 2 percent perhaps the most common value. Should future pain and suffering be discounted to present value? For a negative answer, see Brant v. Bockholt, 532 N.W.2d 801 (Iowa 1995), following RST §913A.

Not all courts require that the parties engage in methodical, individualized calculations to set the time value of money. In Kaczkowski v. Bolubasz, 421 A.2d 1027, 1038–39 (Pa. 1980), the court held that "future inflation shall be presumed equal to future interest rates with these factors offsetting. Thus the courts of this Commonwealth are instructed to abandon the practice of discounting lost future earnings." Even if discounting is done, is there any reason not to use the same rate in all contexts? For a defense of fixed rates, see Bowers, Courts, Contracts, and the Appropriate Discount Rate: A Quick Fix for the Legal Lottery, 63 U. Chi. L. Rev. 1099 (1996). For extensive judicial discussion, see Ammar v. United States, 342 F.3d 133, 148–49 (2d Cir. 2003).

Duncan v. Kansas City Southern Ry.

773 So. 2d 670 (La. 2000)

JOHNSON, J. This case arises out of a collision between a locomotive and a church van at a railroad crossing in Beauregard Parish. There were three passengers, all sisters, riding in the church van. As a result of the collision, one sister [Amanda, aged twelve] was killed, a second [Rachel, aged eleven] was rendered a quadriplegic, and the third [Myranda, aged seven] suffered less serious injuries. Plaintiffs, parents of the three passengers, filed suit to recover damages. A jury found the driver of the van and the railroad liable for the accident, apportioning fault between the two. The decision was affirmed by the court of appeal. We granted certiorari to review the correctness of this decision. . . .

The plaintiffs were awarded damages totaling $27,876,813.31. Included in the award were future medical expenses in the amount of $17,000,000.00 and general damages for physical pain and suffering, mental anguish, and loss of enjoyment of life in the amount of $8,000,000.00 to Rachel Duncan. . . .

EXCESSIVE DAMAGES

Finally, we turn our attention to the last assignment of error raised by KCS [defendant Kansas City Southern Railway], whether the jury's award of damages was so excessive as to be set aside. . . .

General Damages

General damages are those which may not be fixed with pecuniary exactitude; instead, they "involve mental or physical pain or suffering, inconvenience, the loss of intellectual gratification or physical enjoyment, or other losses of life or life-style which cannot be definitely measured in monetary terms." Vast discretion is accorded the trier of fact in fixing general damage awards. This vast discretion is such that an appellate court should rarely disturb an award of general damages. Thus, the role of the appellate court in reviewing general damage awards is not to decide what it considers to be an appropriate award, but rather to review the exercise of discretion by the trier of fact. . . .

The initial inquiry, in reviewing an award of general damages, is whether the trier of fact abused its discretion in assessing the amount of damages. Only after a determination that the trier of fact has abused its "much discretion" is a resort to prior awards appropriate and then only for the purpose of determining the highest or lowest point which is reasonably within that discretion.

Rachel Duncan

In the present case, the trial court awarded $8 million in general damages to Rachel Duncan for her physical pain and suffering, mental anguish, and loss of enjoyment of life. According to KCS, this award far exceeds the highest reasonable awards in cases involving similar injuries. However, our initial determination is not guided by awards for similar injuries; rather, our initial inquiry is whether the instant award is beyond that which a reasonable trier of fact could assess for the effects of the particular injury to the particular plaintiff under the particular circumstances. KCS contends the jury's award was based on sympathy for Rachel, who was brought in and out of the courtroom during the trial in a special, self-propelled wheelchair. While the sight of Rachel in her self-propelled wheelchair may have elicited some sympathetic feelings from the jury, the evidence presented more than amply demonstrates the effects of this accident on Rachel Duncan.

Prior to the accident, Rachel was an active eleven-year-old girl, she enjoyed outdoor activities, she was excelling academically in her sixth-grade class, she had many friends, and she was planning to attend college someday. As a result of the accident, Rachel's whole life has changed. The injuries she sustained when she was thrown from the church van have left her a quadriplegic who is totally dependent on others for all her care needs. Rachel's medical diagnosis and impairments include C5 ASIA A tetraplegia, traumatic brain injury, scoliosis, a tracheostomy, neurogenic bladder, neurogenic bowel, muscle spasms, contractures of upper and lower extremities, pulmonary insufficiency, a non-functioning left lung, left-sided hearing loss, severe headaches, anorexia, severe malnutrition and depression. She also suffers from recurrent pulmonary infections, recurrent bladder infections, and is in constant danger of developing decubitus ulcers and autonomic dysreflexia.

In addition to having to cope with the injuries she sustained in the accident, Rachel is also coping with the fact that her older sister was killed in the accident and her younger sister was injured in the accident. She is no longer able to attend school with her friends, she spends the majority of her day in either her bed or her wheelchair, she can no longer go on the family fishing and camping trips she enjoyed before the accident, and she is aware of the effect her injuries have had on her family. While Rachel still plans on attending college, she will not be able to go off to college like other college freshmen. Even if she decides to move out of her parents' home when she becomes an adult, she will require a specially designed home and 24-hour care. Even when all these factors are considered, we find that the general damage award of $8,000,000 is excessive and the trial court abused its discretion in fixing the general damage award to Rachel Duncan. A review of cases involving similar injuries reveals that the highest amount that could reasonably be awarded under the facts of this case is $6,000,000. Therefore, we reduce the general damage award from $8,000,000 to $6,000,000.

[Other assignments of error are omitted.]

Lastly, KCS contends that the $17 million award for Rachel's future medical care is clearly excessive. According to KCS, if this award is invested conservatively so as to obtain only a five percent return, it would still produce an annual interest income of $850,000. Future medical expenses must be established with some degree of certainty. Awards will not be made in the absence of medical testimony that they are indicated and setting out their probable cost.

In the matter at hand, the jury was presented with medical testimony by plaintiffs', as well as, defendant's experts. [T]he [plaintiffs' expert's] plan provides for a treatment program with individual counseling, family counseling, occupational therapy, physical therapy, speech therapy, weekly review by a registered nurse ("RN"), and 24-hour attendant care by either a licensed practical nurse ("LPN") or a RN. The LPN or RN would be provided by a home health agency, and their activities would be supervised by a case manager. [The plan is based] on Rachel having the same life expectancy as persons her age without spinal cord injuries, that is 81 years. . . .

[Defendant's expert's] plan . . . recommends evaluations by physicians specializing in physical medicine and rehabilitation, pulmonology, urology, internal medicine, orthopedics, and psychiatry. [This plan] further recommends educational counseling, physical therapy, and occupational therapy, as well as, 16 to 24 hour attendant care by a home health aide.

[The court reviews the different mixes of attendant care, either registered nurses or home health aides, on either 16-hour or 24-hour cycles. It further discusses what life expectancy should be used: a 57-year life expectancy, based on statistics for people with spinal cord injuries, or an 81-year life expectancy based on general actuarial tables.]

Rachel Duncan has been diagnosed as a C5 tetraplegic and her age at the time of trial was 14.6 years. [A] 15-year old in the C5 neurologic category has a life expectancy of 42.6 years. The record does include accurate evidence with reference to Rachel's life expectancy. Dr. Zidek's [Rachel's treating physician] predicted 57-year life expectancy for Rachel is more realistic than the 81-year life expectancy predicted by Dr. Voogt [plaintiffs' expert]. Furthermore, the 57-year life expectancy is also the more scientifically accurate prediction. [The court reduces the recovery for future medical expenses from $17 million to $10,528,722, based on the jury's estimate of the cost of annual care for the 57-year life expectancy instead of the longer life expectancy erroneously introduced.]

NOTES

1. ***Excessive Damages as an Abuse of Discretion.*** If the standard for the appellate review of damage awards is abuse of discretion, on what basis does the court in *Duncan* decide that $8 million is too much and $6 million is about right? Cases involving serious injury routinely give rise to the questions raised in *Duncan*. Historically, most courts applied some variation of the "shock the conscience" standard, which offers a very limited power to review jury awards, such as to avoid a clear "miscarriage of justice." See, e.g., Johnson v. Parrish, 827 F.2d 988 (4th Cir. 1987). Under this deferential standard, most courts have sustained large verdicts for gruesome injuries. See, e.g., Phipps v. Copeland Corp. LLC, 278 Cal. Rptr. 3d 688 (Ct. App. 2021) (upholding $26 million products liability and loss of consortium award to technician and wife for mesothelioma resulting from asbestos exposure); Kimble v. Laser Spine Inst., LLC, 264 A.3d 782 (Pa. Super. Ct. 2021) (sustaining award of $20 million following patient's death after operation); Morga v. FedEx Ground Package Sys., Inc., 512 P.3d 774 (N.M. 2022) (denying new trial and affirming $165 million verdict to four plaintiffs for wrongful death, loss of consortium, and personal injuries sustained in traffic accident).

2. ***Remittitur and Additur.*** One common way that courts have exercised some control over damage awards in personal injury cases in state court is through remittitur or additur. Under remittitur, the court does not simply lower the award below what the jury had provided. Rather, it gives the plaintiff the option to avoid the cost and expense of a new trial by accepting a reduction in the size of the jury award. Under additur, the defendant can avoid the cost of a new trial by consenting to a larger verdict equal, perhaps, to the smallest verdict the court would sustain against a charge of inadequacy.

Both remittitur and additur—which involve judges' exercising their power to reshape jury decisions—are limited in federal courts by the Seventh Amendment, which provides that "no fact tried by a jury, shall be otherwise reexamined in any Court of the United States, than according to the rules of the common law." Additur is constitutionally prohibited as "a bald addition of something which in no sense can be said to be included in the verdict." Dimick v. Schiedt, 293 U.S. 474, 486 (1935). Remittur is permitted so long as an appellate court does not reduce the size of an award on its own motion. Instead, it must remand the case and allow the plaintiff the option of a new trial if it finds the reduced amount too small. See Hetzel v. Prince William County, 523 U.S. 208, 211 (1998).

Different states have experimented with different modes of controlling jury verdicts. In Firestone v. Crown Center Redevelopment Corp., 693 S.W.2d 99 (Mo. 1985), the Missouri Supreme Court abolished the practice of remittitur as an invasion of the province of the jury that has "been fraught with confusion and inconsistency." In contrast, the New York legislature increased the judicial power to trim excessive damage awards, and incidentally, to boost up inadequate ones by displacing a "shock the conscience" standard with N.Y. C.P.L.R. §5501(c) (2023), which reads:

> In reviewing a money judgment . . . in which it is contended that the award is excessive or inadequate and that a new trial should have been granted unless a stipulation is entered to a different award, the appellate division shall determine that an award is excessive or inadequate if it deviates materially from what would be reasonable compensation.

In Consorti v. Armstrong World Industries, Inc., 9 F. Supp. 2d 307, 313 (S.D.N.Y. 1998), the plaintiff contracted incurable mesothelioma, from which he eventually died at age fifty-one. The jury awarded him $12 million for pain and suffering—$8 million to cover about twenty-three months of past pain and suffering, and $4 million to cover the anticipated pain and suffering for the estimated nine remaining months of his life. The trial judge remitted the jury award to $5 million, after surveying the pool of mesothelioma cases to see if the award was within the "reasonable" range, and concluding that the jury's verdict reflected a consistent upward push in awards for pain and suffering from $100,000 per month in 1990, to $129,000 by the mid-1990s, to $156,000 per month in 1998. For a defense of comparative verdict review in advancing both reasonableness and uniformity, see Baldus et al., Improving Judicial Oversight of Jury Damages Assessments: A Proposal for the Comparative Additur/Remittitur Review of Awards for Nonpecuniary Harms and Punitive Damages, 80 Iowa L. Rev. 1109 (1995).

3. *Structured Settlements.* One way to reduce the pressure of large verdicts is through the use of structured settlements, which pay the plaintiff's damages in periodic installments rather than in a single lump sum. The structured settlement reduces the need for the parties to make a once-and-for-all joint estimate of future inflation rates since future payments can be geared to inflation if and when it occurs. They can also allow for annual payments for expenses as they accrue, funded by an annuity that takes into account uncertainties in life expectancy. Structured settlements in big cases help reduce the uncertainty in projecting sizeable lost earnings and future medical expenses. Their use in smaller cases is, however, sharply limited because of their high administrative costs.

Structured settlements may be used by mutual agreement of the parties even if the common law rule provides only for lump sum damages. The more controversial question is whether one party may demand them as of right over the opposition of the other. For example, legislation may allow one side to require their use. A California law (Cal. Civ. Proc. Code §667.7 (2023)), states that when future damages awarded against any "provider of health care services" exceed $50,000, either party may request that it be paid in whole or in part in periodic payments and not in lump sum. Deocampo v. Ahn, 125 Cal. Rptr. 2d 79, 89 (Ct. App. 2002), construed the provision as follows:

> Section 667.7 is intended to enable courts to provide for the needs of injured plaintiffs and their dependents for the length of time such monetary compensation is necessary. The goal is to prevent early dissipation of an award, and ensure that when the plaintiff incurs losses or expenses in the future, the money awarded to him will be there. While a precise match between future needs and the periodic payments is not necessary, there must be evidence to support the payment schedule developed by the court.

> Section 667.7 also addresses plaintiffs who die prematurely after entry of a judgment providing for such periodic payments. Section 667.7 prevents such a plaintiff's survivors from receiving the periodic payments that the plaintiff would have received for his or her future care if he or she had not died prematurely, thus preventing the survivors from receiving a windfall of such money which would no longer be needed for the plaintiff's care. Section 667.7 does not place such a blanket restriction, however, on the periodic payments for the future lost *wages* awarded to the plaintiff.

Why the difference between wages and medical expenses? For a defense of the lump-sum common law system of payments, see Rea, Lump-Sum Versus Periodic Damage Awards, 10 J. Legal Stud. 131 (1981).

4. *Caps on Damages.* The dramatic increase in the level of damages awarded to successful plaintiffs in tort actions has brought forth a strong legislative response in many states: capping damages, especially in medical malpractice cases. This reform, in its many variations, has met with a mixed fate when subjected to constitutional challenges.

For an early acquiescence to these limits, see Fein v. Permanente Medical Group, 695 P.2d 665, 683 (Cal. 1985), in which the California Supreme Court upheld section 3333.2 of the California Civil Code, which limited recovery for pain and suffering to $250,000. The court adopted the deferential "rational basis" standard of review and noted that the statute placed no restrictions on recovery for economic losses:

> The choice between reasonable alternative methods of achieving a given objective is generally for the Legislature, and there are a number of reasons why the Legislature may have made the choice it did. One of the problems identified in the legislative hearing was the unpredictability of the size of large noneconomic damage awards, resulting from the inherent difficulties in valuing such damages and the great disparity in the price tag which different juries placed on such losses. The Legislature could reasonably have determined that an across-the-board limit would provide a more stable base on which to calculate insurance rates. Furthermore . . . the Legislature may have felt that the fixed $250,000 limit would promote settlements by eliminating "the unknown possibility of phenomenal awards for pain and suffering that can make litigation worth the gamble." Finally, the Legislature simply may have felt that it was fairer to malpractice plaintiffs in general to reduce only the very large noneconomic damage awards. . . . Each of these grounds provides a sufficient rationale for the $250,000 limit.

Unlike California, several courts have struck down caps on damages on constitutional grounds. For example, the Georgia Supreme Court struck down Georgia's $350,000 cap on pain and suffering damages in medical malpractice cases in Atlanta Oculoplastic Surgery, P.C. v. Nestlehutt, 691 S.E.2d 218, 223 (Ga. 2010), on the theory that it violated litigants' constitutional right to have a jury fully determine damages, including noneconomic damages, by "clearly nullif[ying] the jury's findings of fact regarding damages and thereby undermin[ing] the jury's basic function." See also Estate of McCall v. United States, 134 So. 3d 894, 901 (Fla. 2014), where the Florida Supreme Court struck down a statutory cap on wrongful death noneconomic damages on equal protection grounds because "medical malpractice claimants do not receive the same rights to full compensation because of arbitrarily diminished compensation for legally cognizable claims."

5. *Scheduled Damages.* Damages schedules are an alternative reform proposed in lieu of damages caps, simplifying the calculation of damages while also providing greater consistency for a given injury. Bovbjerg, Sloan & Blumstein, Valuing Life and Limb in Tort: Scheduling "Pain and Suffering," 83 Nw. U. L. Rev. 908, 923–24 (1989), documents the high variation in pain and suffering awards for individuals rated as having approximately the same level of severity:

> Within an individual severity level, the highest valuation can be scores of times larger than the lowest. Awards for the most serious permanent injuries [such as those involving quadriplegia] . . . range in value from a low of $147,000 to a high of $18,100,000. Even considering only the spread between the top and bottom quartiles, the range is great. All the awards in the top 25% of [permanent significant injury cases, such as deafness, loss of limb, loss of eye, or loss of one kidney or lung], for example, are at least six times larger than any of the bottom 25%; the ranges are even larger for lower severity cases. Very large awards are also disproportionately present; the distributions skew to the high end of values, as mean values always far exceed medians.

"Do you have any picture books that could help a child understand tort reform?"

Source: Alex Gregory / CartoonStock

Given the high variation in awards for similar injuries, the authors urge courts to use "scheduled" damages for pain and suffering and other forms of noneconomic loss, preferably by developing a matrix that classifies injuries by severity and age. A second approach to reducing jury variation informs the jury of the range of awards in past similar cases as nonbinding benchmarks for recovery. Bavli & Mozer, The Effects of Comparable-Case Guidance on Awards for Pain and Suffering and Punitive Damages: Evidence from a Randomized Controlled Trial, 37 Yale L. & Pol'y Rev. 405 (2019), finds evidence that prior-award information significantly reduces the variability of awards. A third approach sets floors and ceilings to constrain awards.

6. *Empirical Estimation of the Effects of Medical Malpractice Reform.* Studies attempting to measure the effects of tort reforms are complex, for reasons including the outcome of interest (e.g., malpractice premiums, number of malpractice claims, payouts per claim, total payouts by insurers, health care spending/defensive medicine, and the number of physicians in the state), limited availability of data (only a few states have closed claims databases, and the National Practitioner Databank does not contain comprehensive information), the heterogeneity of the tort reforms adopted (although roughly thirty states have caps on noneconomic or total damages, there is considerable variation in the caps that are adopted), and the importance of controlling for other factors that influence claiming and payouts (e.g., inflation and population growth). The consensus from the vast literature is that damages caps can have a very substantial effect on claim frequency, and a more modest but still material impact on severity (payouts per claim), with the precise impact varying based on the strictness of the cap and the distribution of damages. See, e.g., Liu & Hyman, The Impact of Medical Malpractice Reforms, 16 Ann. Rev. L. & Soc. Sci. 405 (2020). DeVito & Jurs, "Doubling-Down" for Defendants: The Pernicious Effects of Tort Reform, 118 Penn St. L. Rev. 543, 543 (2014), concluded in a study of several states that imposing a cap produces on average "a statistically significant drop of 23 percent in medical malpractice filings," which in turn is matched by an increase in filings of 29 percent once the cap is struck down.

SECTION C. WRONGFUL DEATH AND LOSS OF CONSORTIUM

The close connection between claims for wrongful death and loss of consortium justifies treating them together. Unlike typical tort actions in which an injured party seeks to redress an injury personally suffered, both wrongful death and loss of consortium actions address the relational interest of the plaintiff to the person injured or killed. This relational interest rests on the evident social fact that individuals have obligations of duty and support to other persons: spouses to one another, parents to children, and (historically) servants to employers. The protection of relational interests adds another layer of complexity to the law, for now the legal system must coordinate the actions of the injured party with those who bring derivative claims through that party.

The common law protected relational interests in two distinct ways: loss of consortium and wrongful death actions. The consortium action, *quod servitium amisit* ("because the service has been lost"), was given historically only to a man whenever the defendant injured the man's wife, child, or servant, thereby preventing them from rendering him valuable services. 3 Bl. Comm. 142; Kendrick v. McCrary, 11 Ga. 603 (1852).

The basic action was subject to two limitations. First, the action for loss of services could not be brought by a wife or a child. Second, the action for loss of services did not cover cases of wrongful death. The efforts to overcome these two limitations did not proceed in an orderly fashion. Accordingly, we turn first to the history of actions for wrongful death and its measure of damages. Thereafter, we consider the history of survival of actions. Finally, we will study the expansion of actions for loss of consortium to women and children, and the appropriate measure of damages.

1. Wrongful Death

a. History

The orderly development of wrongful death actions at common law in England was stymied by Baker v. Bolton, (1808) 170 Eng. Rep. 1033 (KB), which held that a husband suffered no damage when his wife was not merely injured, but killed, by the defendant's wrongful conduct. The plaintiff could recover damages for the loss of his wife's services and consortium only for the month between injury and death but was denied damages for both lost after her death. The situation stood unchanged in England until the passage of Lord Campbell's Act of 1846 (Fatal Accidents Act, 9 & 10 Vict. C. 93 (1846)). The statutory preamble treated Baker v. Bolton as decisive authority against allowing the action at the common law. Its operative provision then provided that

> whenever the death of a person is caused by the wrongful act, neglect or default of another, such as would (if death had not ensued) have entitled the injured person to sue and recover damages in respect thereof, then the person who would have been liable if death had not ensued shall be liable to an action for damages, although the death shall have been caused under circumstances as amount to a felony.

The last clause was inserted to make it clear that the plaintiff in the wrongful death action did not have to first prosecute the defendant for any possible felony. The statute designated the class of dependents (since expanded by the Fatal Accidents Act, 1959 §1(1)) entitled to the action: husband, wife, parent, child, grandparent, or grandchild of the deceased.

After passage of Lord Campbell's Act, some plaintiffs sued at common law to recover elements of damages not listed in the wrongful death statutes, but to no avail. Thus in Osborn v. Gillett, (1873) 8 Ex. 88 (LR), the plaintiff was denied recovery for burial expenses, then not provided for under the statute. In Admiralty Commissioners v. S.S. Amerika, [1917] AC 38, the plaintiffs failed to recover the ex gratiae pensions they had paid out to the relatives of crew members lost when the defendant ship sank an admiralty submarine. Baker v. Bolton loomed large in both cases, where it effectively foreclosed any common law development in England long after its errors were openly acknowledged. The courts declined to tread where Parliament had intervened, partly out of deference to Parliament and partly out of fear of the complications that a dual scheme for wrongful death actions could create.

The history of wrongful death in the United States mirrors the same complex interaction between common law foreclosure of wrongful death actions and legislation expressly providing for such actions. In the early colonial period, particularly in Massachusetts, local tribunals probably made awards for wrongful death that were not sanctioned by statute or at common law. Even after Baker v. Bolton, some courts seemed prepared to develop wrongful death actions on their own. See, e.g., Plummer v. Webb, 19 Fed. Cas. 894 (No. 11234) (1825); Ford v. Monroe, 20 Wend. 210 (N.Y. Sup. Ct. 1838). But the rarity of such actions suggests that they were not well established. Indeed Baker v. Bolton was not even cited in an American court until 1848. In that year, the Massachusetts Supreme Judicial Court, in Carey v. Berkshire R.R., 55 Mass. 475 (1848), relied on Baker v. Bolton to deny the plaintiff a common law action for wrongful death. The companion case of Skinner v. Housatonic Railroad, 55 Mass. 475 (1848), refused to allow a wrongful death action to a father for the loss of services of his deceased son. Eight years before *Carey*, Massachusetts had passed a statute that authorized wrongful death actions for between $500 and $5,000 to the families of deceased railway passengers whose death was caused by the negligence of the railroad. The deceased in *Carey* was an employee, not a passenger, and thus not covered by the statute. He lost because the court did not wish to create its own wrongful death action in parallel with the legislature's. State after state followed *Carey's* logic, with only Georgia willing to face the problems of policing and coordinating two different systems of wrongful death actions. See Shields v. Yonge, 15 Ga. 349 (1854).

Beginning in 1847, states all across the United States enacted versions of Lord Campbell's Act. Unlike Lord Campbell's Act, most of the American statutes excluded dependent husbands from the class of eligible statutory beneficiaries. In the twentieth century, workers' compensation statutes and New Deal social insurance legislation reproduced the asymmetry established in the wrongful death statutes. Only in the 1970s and 1980s were the provisions excluding widowers from death benefits in statutory accident claims struck down as unconstitutional. See Wengler v. Druggists Mutual Insurance Co., 446 U.S. 142 (1980); Witt, From Loss of Services to Loss of Support: The Wrongful Death Statutes, the Origins of Modern Tort Law, and the Making of the Nineteenth-Century Family, 25 Law & Soc. Inquiry 717, 734–37 (2000). For an excellent history of the early evolution of wrongful death actions, see Malone, The Genesis of Wrongful Death, 17 Stan. L. Rev. 1043 (1965).

b. Measure of Damages

Most early wrongful death statutes placed stringent ceilings on the amount of damages permitted the surviving plaintiff, largely out of fear of the jury's passion and sympathy for the aggrieved plaintiff, but these limitations fell out of favor over time. Twenty-two states had ceilings on wrongful death claims in 1893. By 1965 that number dropped to twelve, and by 1974 the number had dwindled to four. Today, no state has a hard dollar cap on damages in wrongful death actions, although a few states retain special limitations for certain types of cases.

But what measure of damages is appropriate? No state attempts the impossible, which is to put the decedent in the position that she would have enjoyed if the tort had never happened. And no state is able to overcome the profound irony—and puzzle for the economic theory of tort law—that it is cheaper for a defendant to kill his victim than it is to maim her for life. Medical expenses are not part of a wrongful death action per se. That said, most statutes fall into one of two camps: loss to survivors and loss to the decedent's estate. Under a loss-to-survivors standard, the defendant must pay damages only to some beneficiary who depended upon the decedent for support. Under the loss-to-estate standard, damages will be awarded against the defendant even if the decedent had no dependents at the time of death. Most jurisdictions have adopted a loss-to-survivors test as the measure of damages. See Schap

& Thompson, Recoverable Damages for Wrongful Death in the States: A 2015 Review of Statutory Law, 22 J. Legal Econ. 143 (2015), for a survey of the methodology used to calculate wrongful death damages in each state. Which standard is better from the point of view of deterrence?

Calculating damages in wrongful death cases is fraught with many of the same administrative difficulties found in serious personal injury cases. The pure wrongful death action awards nothing for the decedent's pain and suffering or medical expenses. Nonetheless, enormous controversy can arise over both the suffering of the survivors and the estimation of lost earnings, especially for children who were never old enough to assume any definable niche in life. Thus in Wycko v. Gnodtke, 105 N.W.2d 118, 122 (Mich. 1960), the court allowed the parents of a reliable and trustworthy boy of fourteen to recover $15,000 in damages, dismissing the objection that the parents were entitled to recover only for their pecuniary loss. The court noted the general progress in the social treatment of children since the passage of Lord Campbell's Act in 1846, but rejected "as prayed by appellant, the child-labor measure of the pecuniary loss suffered through the death of a minor child, namely, his probable wages less the cost of his keep." The court then awarded two types of damages. First, on analogy to the costs of maintenance service and repairs for machinery, it allowed the parents damages for the "expenses of birth, of food, of clothing, of medicines, of instruction, of nurture and of shelter." Second, by treating the family as a functioning social unit, it allowed "the value of mutual society and protection, in a word, companionship." Michigan law now provides:

> [T]he court or jury may award damages as the court or jury shall consider fair and equitable, under all the circumstances including reasonable medical, hospital, funeral, and burial expenses for which the estate is liable; reasonable compensation for the pain and suffering, while conscious, undergone by the deceased during the period intervening between the time of the injury and death; and damages for the loss of financial support and the loss of the society and companionship of the deceased.

Mich. Comp. Laws Ann. §600.2922(6) (2023).

Cooter, Hand Rule Damages for Incompensable Losses, 40 San Diego L. Rev. 1097, 1120 (2003), proposes using the Hand formula to calculate damages for incompensable losses (i.e., those for which a reasonable person could not assign a monetary value), such as the death of a child; the measure is based on "a reasonable person's point of indifference between the cost of more precaution and the resulting reduction in risk of an incompensable loss." For an account of the deviation between the evaluation of a lost life in tort and administrative law, see E. Posner & Sunstein, Dollars and Death, 72 U. Chi. L. Rev. 537 (2005), urging major reforms in the tort law, including granting damages for the welfare loss to the decedent. Viscusi, The Devaluation of Life, 3 Reg. & Governance 103 (2009), proposes that administrative agencies rely on the recommendations of a peer-reviewed scientific advisory panel when setting the statistical value of human life, and Sharkey, Valuing Black and Female Lives: A Proposal for Incorporating Agency VSL into Tort Damages, 96 Notre Dame L. Rev. 1479 (2021), extends the case for use of value of statistical life to calibrate incentives and simultaneously reduce bias.

2. Survival of Personal Injury Actions

From at least the fifteenth century, the common law maxim *actio personalis moritur cum persona*—a personal action dies with the person—provided that any tort action, including one for personal injuries or property damage (but not to recover real or personal property), was extinguished by the death of either the plaintiff or the defendant. The right of action created by the defendant's wrong was treated as exclusively personal between the two original parties; as death severed that personal relationship, so it destroyed any cause of action predicated upon it.

Abandonment of the early position came slowly. Today, survival of actions is well-nigh universal—except, perhaps, for actions for deceit or defamation, and even these actions pass in a few states. Under the typical survivor statute, compensation is allowed for the pain and suffering of the decedent before her death, as that item of damages is not covered under the wrongful death statutes proper. See Leebron, Final Moments: Damages for Pain and Suffering Prior to Death, 64 N.Y.U. L. Rev. 256 (1989), which concludes that the primary justification for such awards must be deterrence and not compensation. Leebron notes that, empirically, the variation in awards under this head of damages is exceptionally high and recommends more judicial supervision to iron out the anomalies in the area.

3. Actions for Loss of Consortium

a. History

The historical development of the action for loss of consortium has not followed the course of wrongful death actions. Unlike wrongful death, which is largely administered through statutes, loss of consortium is a common law claim. After early acceptance of the doctrine, the English courts came to regard all actions for loss of consortium as misconceived. In Best v. Samuel Fox & Co. Ltd, [1952] AC 716, the House of Lords, with evident discomfort, refused to grant the action to the wife for her loss of the services and comfort of her husband. In 1982, Parliament finished the job by abolishing the action for loss of consortium for husbands, parents, children, and menial servants. 30 & 31 Eliz. 2 §2 (1982).

The American cases, however, took the opposite course, universally allowing wives as well as husbands to sue for loss of consortium following widespread adoption of Hitaffer v. Argonne Co., 183 F.2d 811, 813–814 (D.C. Cir. 1950). In a self-conscious break with the past, the court in *Hitaffer* first argued that although the element of lost services was important in a consortium case, elements of "companionship, love, felicity and sexual relations" were of equal if not greater importance. It then rejected arguments that the wife's action should be barred because her injuries were too "indirect," too "remote," or too "consequential." See RTT: Remedies §25 (Tentative Draft No. 2, approved 2023), which provides for "compensation for lost services and for loss of society, including affection, comfort, companionship, love, support, and, in the case of a marital relationship, sexual relations, resulting from the physical or emotional harm suffered by an injured family member." Should such claims be barred on the grounds that persons deprived of society and services can adapt to their change of circumstances?

b. Parents and Children

The debate over the action for loss of consortium has now shifted from suits by the spouse (spousal consortium) to suits by children whose parents have been injured or killed (parental consortium) or to suits by parents whose children have been injured or killed (child consortium). The Restatement (Second) of Torts recognized both spousal consortium (RST §693) and child consortium (RST §703), but denied parental consortium (RST §707A). The Restatement (Third) Torts: Remedies recognizes all three claims. See RTT: Remedies §25, comment *a* (Tentative Draft No. 2, approved 2023). Wrongful death actions are allowed to children in part because of the forcible disruption of their advantageous relationships with their parents. The same type of relational loss, albeit of different extent, also exists when the parent is not killed but injured. If one spouse may sue when the other is killed or injured, and children may sue (for wrongful death) when parents are killed, why shouldn't children be able to sue when their parents are injured? Note, however, substantial administrative costs are entailed by the recognition of such actions. Although the decedent had only one spouse, he or she could have many children (not to mention grandchildren and more distant relations). It is easy to envision severe difficulties in estimating damages owed to each claimant and in coordinating the recovery of the injured party with that of the dependents. The leading case against the child's consortium action is Borer v. American Airlines, Inc., 563 P.2d 858, 860–61 (Cal. 1977), in which Tobriner, J., rejected the damage claims of the injured party's nine children:

> Loss of consortium is an intangible injury for which money damages do not afford an accurate measure or suitable recompense; recognition of a right to recover for such losses in the present context, moreover, may substantially increase the number of claims asserted in ordinary accident cases, the expense of settling or resolving such claims, and the ultimate liability of the defendants. Taking these considerations into account, we shall explain why we have concluded that the payment of damages to persons for the lost affection and society of a parent or child neither truly compensates for such loss nor justifies the social cost in attempting to do so.

Subsequent cases have been mixed. A divided Connecticut court initially refused to recognize in children an action for loss of parental consortium, even though they can recover for emotional distress if they witness the death of a parent. See Mendillo v. Bd. of Educ. of E. Haddam, 717 A.2d 1177 (Conn. 1998). However, in Campos v. Coleman, 123 A.3d 854, 866–68 (Conn. 2015), the Supreme Court of Connecticut overruled this decision, stating that as of 2015, forty-six states either recognized for children an action for loss of parental consortium arising from a parent's wrongful death or recognized in children an action for loss of parental consortium arising from a parent's injury—and this is still the case in 2023.

A similar debate has arisen among courts over whether a child consortium action in the parents for the loss of filial companionship of their children should be recognized. The court in Sizemore v. Smock, 422 N.W.2d 666, 666 (Mich. 1988), held that Michigan "does not recognize a parent's action for the loss of a child's society and companionship, and that any decision to further extend a negligent tortfeasor's liability for consortium damages should be determined by the Legislature." A somewhat different pattern emerged in other states, such as Arizona and Montana, which now freely allow both children and parents to bring actions for loss of consortium. See, e.g., Hern v. Safeco Ins. Co. of Ill., 125 P.3d 597 (Mont. 2005); Villareal v. Arizona, 774 P.2d 213 (Ariz. 1989). These states, moreover, allow parents to recover for the loss of companionship of their adult children, even though the parents were not dependent upon those adult children for financial support. See, e.g., *Hern*, 125 P.3d 597; Howard Frank, M.D., P.C. v. Superior Court, 722 P.2d 955, 960 (Ariz. 1986). In *Frank*, the court brushed aside the defendant's objections that the new action would "spawn increased litigation," noting that courts could deal with these administrative complications as they arise without heeding "the fabled cry of wolf." However, some jurisdictions that recognize a parent's action for the loss of companionship of minor children do not allow action for the loss of companionship of adult children. See, e.g., Benda v. Roman Catholic Bishop of Salt Lake City, 384 P.3d 207, 212 (Utah 2016). In *Benda*, the court justifies this by comparing parent-minor relationships to spousal relationships, reasoning that, "[l]ike the relationship between spouses, the relationship between parents and a minor child is a legally recognized relationship involving legal obligations. Like the relationship between spouses, it also tends to be a particularly close relationship highly valued in society."

c. *Nontraditional Families*

Many courts have balked at extending actions for loss of consortium to unmarried couples who are living together. See, e.g., Toledo v. St. Vincent's Med. Ctr., 71 Conn. L. Rptr. 41 (Super. Ct. 2021) (seeking to draw a "clear distinction" between cohabitation and marriage by granting greater rights and protections only for married couples). In Elden v. Sheldon, 758 P.2d 582, 269, 279 (Cal. 1988), the plaintiff's female partner died as the result of a car accident in which he too was injured. Plaintiff sought to introduce evidence that their "unmarried cohabitation relationship . . . was both stable and significant and parallel to marriage," so that he could recover for loss of consortium. The California Supreme Court upheld the trial court's preclusion of this evidence and summary judgment, stressing "the state's interest in promoting the responsibilities of marriage and the difficulty of assessing the emotional, sexual and financial relationship of cohabiting parties to determine whether their arrangement was the equivalent of marriage." Justice Broussard noted in dissent that the decision would create an injustice by precluding any recovery for loss of consortium by same-sex couples unable (at that time) to choose marriage. The Supreme Court's decision in Obergefell v. Hodges, 575 U.S. 994 (2015), puts that issue to rest and likewise ensures that same-sex spouses can recover for loss of consortium.

Courts may nonetheless refuse to recognize actions for loss of consortium even between spouses if the injury that caused the loss occurred before marriage. See, e.g., Philip Morris USA, Inc. v. Rintoul, 342 So. 3d 656, 666–67 (Fla. Dist. Ct. App. 2022); Mason v. United States, 2022 WL 2898909, at *10 (M.D. Tenn. July 20, 2022). Some states have nonetheless made an exception for same-sex couples who would have been married at the time of injury but for state law prohibitions on same-sex marriage. See, e.g., Mueller v. Tepler, 95 A.3d 1011 (Conn. 2014). Another exception was found in Lozoya v. Sanchez, 66 P.3d 948, 958 (N.M. 2003), for common law marriages. The plaintiff and her husband were unmarried at the time of his first accident but had lived together for about fifteen years in a home they had jointly purchased, and had three children together. The first accident disrupted their social and sexual arrangements, but they nonetheless married before their second accident. Minzner, J., held that the action for loss of consortium was proper.

> They held themselves out as a married couple. Further, they testified as to their mutual dependence on each other in their day to day lives. Every single factor we have enunciated for determining whether they had an intimate familial relationship also appears to cut in their favor. We believe that the evidence presented demonstrates that Sara may be able to present a cognizable claim for loss of consortium. She should therefore be allowed to present this claim to the jury.

d. Damages in Consortium Cases

Once the right to sue for loss of consortium is established, how should the damages be calculated? In principle these should be kept separate and apart from the losses to the primary party. But in the absence of any physical injury, courts have not found any obvious way to measure these damages. One effort to short-circuit this problem is to treat damages for loss of consortium as a fixed fraction of the damages awarded to the primary plaintiff. Defending this solution in Arpin v. United States, 521 F.3d 769, 777 (7th Cir. 2008), Posner, J., first looked to some mathematical formula, such as treble damages in antitrust actions or the more fluid standards in punitive damage cases, which are typically limited to some single-digit multiple of actual damages. He then continued:

> The first step in taking a ratio approach to calculating damages for loss of consortium would be to examine the average ratio in wrongful-death cases in which the award of such damages was upheld on appeal. The next step would be to consider any special factors that might warrant a departure from the average in the case at hand. Suppose the average ratio is 1.5—that in the average case, the damages awarded for loss of consortium are 20 percent of the damages awarded to compensate for the other losses resulting from the victim's death. The amount might then be adjusted upward or downward on the basis of the number of the decedent's children, whether they were minors or adults, and the closeness of the relationship between the decedent and his spouse and children.

SECTION D. PUNITIVE DAMAGES

Kemezy v. Peters
79 F.3d 33 (7th Cir. 1996)

POSNER, C.J. Jeffrey Kemezy sued a Muncie, Indiana policeman named James Peters under 42 U.S.C. §1983, claiming that Peters had wantonly beaten him with the officer's nightstick in an altercation in a bowling alley where Peters was moonlighting as a security guard. The jury awarded Kemezy $10,000 in compensatory damages and $20,000 in punitive damages. Peters' appeal challenges only the award of punitive damages, and that on the narrowest of grounds: that it was the plaintiff's burden to introduce evidence concerning the defendant's net worth for purposes of equipping the jury with information essential to a just measurement of punitive damages.

[Posner, C.J., notes that a majority of courts have rejected Peters' contention.] [W]e think the majority rule, which places no burden of production on the plaintiff, is sound, and we take this opportunity to make clear that it is indeed the law of this circuit.

The standard judicial formulation of the purpose of punitive damages is that it is to punish the defendant for reprehensible conduct and to deter him and others from engaging in similar conduct. . . . A review of the reasons [for awarding punitive damages] will point us toward a sound choice between the majority and minority views.

1. Compensatory damages do not always compensate fully. Because courts insist that an award of compensatory damages have an objective basis in evidence, such awards are likely to fall short in some cases, especially when the injury is of an elusive or intangible character. If you spit upon another person in anger, you inflict a real injury but one exceedingly difficult to quantify. If the court is confident that the injurious conduct had no redeeming social value, so that "overdeterring" such conduct by an "excessive" award of damages is not a concern, a generous award of punitive damages will assure full compensation without impeding socially valuable conduct.

2. By the same token, punitive damages are necessary in such cases in order to make sure that tortious conduct is not underdeterred, as it might be if compensatory damages fell short of the actual injury inflicted by the tort. . . .

3. Punitive damages are necessary in some cases to make sure that people channel transactions through the market when the costs of voluntary transactions are low. We do not want a person to be able to take his neighbor's car and when the neighbor complains tell him to go sue for its value. We want to make such expropriations valueless to the expropriator and we can do this by adding a punitive exaction to the judgment for the market value of what is taken. . . .

4. When a tortious act is concealable, a judgment equal to the harm done by the act will underdeter. Suppose a person who goes around assaulting other people is caught only half the time. Then in comparing the costs, in the form of anticipated damages, of the assaults with the benefits to him, he will discount the costs (but not the benefits, because they are realized in every assault) by 50 percent, and so in deciding whether to commit the next assault he will not be confronted by the full social cost of his activity.

5. An award of punitive damages expresses the community's abhorrence at the defendant's act. We understand that otherwise upright, decent, law-abiding people are sometimes careless and that their carelessness can result in unintentional injury for which compensation should

be required. We react far more strongly to the deliberate or reckless wrongdoer, and an award of punitive damages commutes our indignation into a kind of civil fine, civil punishment.

Some of these functions are also performed by the criminal justice system. Many legal systems do not permit awards of punitive damages at all, believing that such awards anomalously intrude the principles of criminal justice into civil cases. . . .

6. Punitive damages relieve the pressures on the criminal justice system. They do this not so much by creating an additional sanction, which could be done by increasing the fines imposed in criminal cases, as by giving private individuals—the tort victims themselves—a monetary incentive to shoulder the costs of enforcement.

7. If we assume realistically that the criminal justice system could not or would not take up the slack if punitive damages were abolished, then they have the additional function of heading off breaches of the peace by giving individuals injured by relatively minor outrages a judicial remedy in lieu of the violent self-help to which they might resort if their complaints to the criminal justice authorities were certain to be ignored and they had no other legal remedy.

What is striking about the purposes that are served by the awarding of punitive damages is that none of them depends critically on proof that the defendant's income or wealth *exceeds* some specified level. The more wealth the defendant has, the smaller is the relative bite that an award of punitive damages not actually geared to that wealth will take out of his pocketbook, while if he has very little wealth the award of punitive damages may exceed his ability to pay and perhaps drive him into bankruptcy. To a very rich person, the pain of having to pay a heavy award of damages may be a mere pinprick and so not deter him (or people like him) from continuing to engage in the same type of wrongdoing. What in economics is called the principle of diminishing marginal utility teaches, what is anyway obvious, that losing $1 is likely to cause less unhappiness (disutility) to a rich person than to a poor one. . . . But rich people are not famous for being indifferent to money, and if they are forced to pay not merely the cost of the harm to the victims of their torts but also some multiple of that cost they are likely to think twice before engaging in such expensive behavior again. Juries, rightly or wrongly, think differently, so plaintiffs who are seeking punitive damages often present evidence of the defendant's wealth. The question is whether they *must* present such evidence—whether it is somehow unjust to allow a jury to award punitive damages without knowing that the defendant really is a wealthy person. The answer, obviously, is no. . . .

It ill becomes *defendants* to argue that plaintiffs *must* introduce evidence of the defendant's wealth. Since most tort defendants against whom punitive damages are sought are enterprises rather than individuals, the effect of such a rule would be to encourage plaintiffs to seek punitive damages whether or not justified, in order to be able to put before the jury evidence that the defendant has a deep pocket and therefore should be made to pay a large judgment regardless of any nice calculation of actual culpability. . . . Individual defendants, as in the present case, are reluctant to disclose their net worth in any circumstances, so that compelling plaintiffs to seek discovery of that information would invite a particularly intrusive and resented form of pretrial discovery and disable the defendant from objecting. Since, moreover, information about net worth is in the possession of the person whose net wealth is in issue, the normal principles of pleading would put the burden of production on the defendant—which, as we have been at pains to stress, is just where defendants as a whole would want it. . . .

Affirmed.

NOTES

1. *Punitive Damages: Common Law Origins and Theoretical Basis.* Punitive damages have long been awarded at common law. In Day v. Woodworth, 54 U.S. 363, 371 (1852), the plaintiff brought a trespass action against the defendants for tearing down and destroying his mill-dam, more than was necessary to protect the operation of their own mill-dam. Grier, J., affirmed an award of punitive damages, noting:

> In actions of trespass, where the injury has been wanton and malicious, or gross and outrageous, courts permit juries to add to the measured compensation of the plaintiff that he would have been entitled to recover, had the injury been inflicted without design or intention, something farther by way of punishment or example, which has sometimes been called "smart money." This has been always left to the discretion of the jury, as the degree of punishment to be thus inflicted must depend on the peculiar circumstances of each case.

An extensive academic literature has examined the theoretical basis and practical operation of punitive damages in tort cases. Polinsky & Shavell, Punitive Damages: An Economic Analysis, 111 Harv. L. Rev. 869 (1998), proposes a strict efficiency model, stressing the need for a damage multiplier to take into account the risk that a wrongdoer will escape punishment. That rationale seems to apply with equal force in cases of negligent infliction of harm when it is hard to identify the wrongdoer, and thus tends not to comport with the standard mental requirements for punitive damages. It received some judicial backing from Calabresi, J., in Ciraolo v. City of New York, 216 F.3d 236, 243 (2d Cir. 2000), who noted: "Punitive damages can ensure that a wrongdoer bears all the costs of its actions, and is thus appropriately deterred from causing harm, in those categories of cases in which compensatory damages alone result in systematic underassessment of costs, and hence in systematic underdeterrence." This theory does not, however, systematically take into account the risk of overdeterrence from the repetitive use of these multipliers. Hylton, Punitive Damages and the Economic Theory of Penalties, 87 Geo. L.J. 421 (1998), suggests an alternative economic framework, focusing on using punitive damages awards to eliminate defendants' wrongful gains to accomplish complete deterrence of offensive conduct.

The efficiency boomlet nonetheless did not carry the day in the Supreme Court. In Cooper Industries, Inc. v. Leatherman Tool Group, Inc., 532 U.S. 424, 438 (2001), Stevens, J., wrote, first, that "[h]owever attractive such an approach to punitive damages might be as an abstract policy matter, it is clear that juries do not normally engage in such a finely tuned exercise of deterrence calibration when awarding punitive damages." Second, he stated that "[c]itizens and legislators may rightly insist that they are willing to tolerate some loss in economic efficiency in order to deter what they consider morally offensive conduct, albeit cost-beneficial morally offensive conduct," quoting Galanter & Luban, Poetic Justice: Punitive Damages and Legal Pluralism, 42 Am. U. L. Rev. 1393, 1449 (1993). For his initial point, Stevens, J., relied on Sunstein, Schkade & Kahneman, Do People Want Optimal Deterrence?, 29 J. Legal Stud. 237 (2000), disputing the Polinsky and Shavell position that jurors increase punitive damages in hard-to-detect events. The authors instead note a wide consensus across social, geographical, and racial boundaries on the determinants of "shared outrage" in punitive damage cases. They then suggest that the wide variation in punitive damage awards given this apparent consensus stems from a common inability to translate moral judgments into dollar amounts. See Schkade, Sunstein & Kahneman, Deliberating About Dollars: The Severity Shift, 100 Colum. L. Rev. 1139 (2000).

Punitive damages awards often present a catch-22, especially in products liability cases. First, a court demands that a manufacturer make an explicit cost-benefit analysis in designing products. Second, juries then infer that a correct cost-benefit analysis shows the callous quantification of human life that calls for punitive damages. See Viscusi, Pricing Lives for Corporate Risk Decisions, 68 Vand. L. Rev. 1117, 1133–43 (2015), detailing how corporations have been "vilified" for making required cost-benefit analyses, triggering increases in punitive damage awards. One instance of conscious design choices was Grimshaw v. Ford Motor Co., 174 Cal. Rptr. 348 (Ct. App. 1981), in which the jury awarded the plaintiff $125,000,000 in punitive damages against Ford. In designing the Pinto, Ford had made a number of cost-benefit calculations that involved estimating the value of a human life. In dealing with that issue, should it make a difference if the changes proposed (such as a bladder inside the gas tank of the Pinto) had never been used commercially in cars sold at any price? If the Pinto had a rate of burn deaths or injuries no greater than that of other comparably priced and sized cars? For an exhaustive analysis of the case, see Schwartz, The Myth of the Ford Pinto Case, 43 Rutgers L. Rev. 1013 (1991).

2. *Evidence of Defendant's Wealth.* Whereas compensatory damages focus on the loss to the plaintiff, punitive damages instead focus on the defendant's conduct. Should a defendant's wealth be taken into account on either a retributive- or deterrence-based theory of punitive damages? Abraham & Jeffries, Punitive Damages and the Rule of Law: The Role of Defendant's Wealth, 18 J. Legal Stud. 415, 419–23 (1989), argues that consideration of a defendant's wealth cannot be justified on either retributive or deterrence grounds:

> First, there is no logical, necessary, or even plausible connection between the extent of the defendant's wealth and the amount of underenforcement. The amount of underenforcement in mass tort cases, for example, is likely to depend on factors completely unrelated to the extent of the defendant's wealth. . . .
>
> Second, even if the wealth of the defendant were related to the probability of underenforcement of its tort liabilities, no additional liability should be imposed absent specific proof of underenforcement in the case at hand. Otherwise, the defendant would be held liable for punitive damages, in potentially ruinous amounts, without the opportunity to disprove the facts on which such liability is based.
>
> The only rational deterrence explanation for taking defendant's wealth into account is . . . the speculation that a wealthy defendant, usually a large corporation, may have engaged in a *pattern* of misconduct, of which any given case is merely illustrative. . . . [However,] [p]unishment cannot fairly be based on unaided speculation about what the defendant might or might not have done in various unspecified circumstances not then before the court. Yet that is exactly what evidence of the defendant's wealth invites—unaided speculation about the defendant's conduct in other cases.
>
> [B]asing retribution on the defendant's wealth is normatively objectionable. . . . Punishment based on the characteristics of the actor must be viewed with suspicion. . . . [P]unishment based on the characteristics of the actor invites erratic and random responses to concerns that have nothing to do with specific misconduct.

Arlen, Should Defendants' Wealth Matter?, 21 J. Legal Stud. 413 (1992), challenges Abraham and Jeffries' analysis with an economic model wherein defendants' wealth is a relevant factor in setting standards of care and assessing compensatory and punitive damages if actors are risk averse rather than risk neutral.

Does anything prevent the plaintiff from discovering evidence about the defendant's net wealth to argue for an increase in the level of punitive damages? Most states list wealth of the defendant as a relevant factor in the determination of a punitive damages award. See, e.g., Cal. Jury Instr.—Civ. §14.71 (Comm. on Cal. Civil Jury Instr. 2023), *available at* WL BAJI 14.71; N.Y. Pattern Jury Instr.—Civ. §2:278 (Comm. on Pattern Jury Instr. Ass'n of Sup. Ct. Justices 2023), *available at* WL NY PJI 2:278. Few states, however, instruct the jury on the proper use of wealth evidence in the calculation of punitive damages awards, which creates a risk that wealthy defendants could be punished because of their financial status. The U.S. Supreme Court may take up the issue in the future; for now, it has left the matter with its cryptic statement that "wealth of a defendant cannot justify an otherwise unconstitutional punitive damages award." State Farm Mut. Auto. Ins. Co. v. Campbell, 538 U.S. 408, 427 (2003), *infra* at 676.

3. *Taxation and Insurability of Punitive Damage Awards.* Unlike compensatory damages, punitive damages, which are viewed more as a windfall, are taxable. In *O'Gilvie v. United States, 519 U.S. 79, 83 (1996)*, the Supreme Court interpreted I.R.C. §104(a)(2), which exempts from taxation damages received "on account of personal injuries. . . ." The Court excluded punitive damages on the ground that they "[are] not 'received . . . on account of' the personal injuries [of a plaintiff], but rather [are] awarded 'on account of' a defendant's reprehensible conduct and the jury's need to punish and deter it." I.R.C. §104(a)(2) was later amended to explicitly exclude punitive damages from exemption.

Several states, including California and New York, prohibit insurance for directly assessed punitive damages on public policy grounds. See Sharkey, Revisiting the Noninsurable Costs of Damages, 64 Md. L. Rev. 409 (2005). Corporate defendants can, however, deduct punitive damages awards from their taxes under I.R.C. §162. Does the federal policy of deductibility undermine the public policy choices of states that prohibit insurance coverage for punitive damages?

4. *Statutory and Common Law Reform of Punitive Damages.* The extensive common law litigation on punitive damages has brought forth a wide range of legislative reforms that either cap or ban punitive damages, or else limit admissible evidence as to them. New Hampshire's law provides simply: "No punitive damages shall be awarded in any action, unless otherwise provided by statute." N.H. Rev. Stat. Ann. §507:16 (2023). Other states have capped punitive damages as a multiple of actual damages, at least in some areas. For example, Conn. Gen. Stat. Ann. §52-240b (2023) caps punitive damages at twice compensatory damages in products liability cases. In addition, some states have ordered bifurcated trials of liability and damages in punitive damages cases. See Cal. Civ. Code §3295(d) (2023), where on the application of the defendant, the court shall not admit evidence of the defendant's "profits or financial condition" until the jury has made an award of actual damages. See also Kan. Stat. Ann. §60-3701(a)–(b) (2023), under which the trier of fact determines the defendant's liability for punitive damages and the court determines its amount.

On another front, eight states have enacted split-recovery statutes that direct a portion of punitive damages awards away from the plaintiff, either to the state treasury or to a designated fund. For example, Or. Rev. Stat. §31.735 (2023) provides that 60 percent of all punitive damage awards go to a Criminal Injuries Compensation Account and 10 percent to a court facilities fund. That law was upheld against takings and other state constitutional challenges in DeMendoza v. Huffman, 51 P.3d 1232 (Or. 2002). See also Dardinger v. Anthem Blue Cross & Blue Shield, 781 N.E.2d 121, 146 (Ohio 2002), where Pfeifer, J., on his own initiative directed that two-thirds of a $30 million punitive damages award against a health-plan provider should be paid to the Esther Dardinger Fund at the Cancer Hospital and Research Center at Ohio State University, where she was treated:

> The final net amount remaining after the prescribed payments [to Dardinger, and various fees] should go to a place that will achieve a societal good, a good that can rationally offset the harm done by the defendants in this case. Due to the societal stake in the punitive damages award, we find it most appropriate that it go to a state institution. In this case we order that the corpus of the punitive damages award go to a cancer research fund, to be called the Esther Dardinger Fund, at the James Cancer Hospital and Solove Research Institute at the Ohio State University.

Similarly, Klein, J., in Sundquist v. Bank of Am., N.A., 566 B.R. 563, 616–17 (Bankr. E.D. Cal. 2017), also sua sponte, directed that $40 million of a $45 million punitive damages award against Bank of America should be distributed among seven different California law schools and consumer advocacy organizations, such as the National Consumer Bankruptcy Rights Center:

> It follows that the public purpose of the societal component of punitive damages against Bank of America in this case should be focused on consumer law in the form of better education in consumer law and more robust resources for leading public service consumer law organizations. . . . By channeling to . . . public academic and consumer advocacy institutions the societal portion of legitimate punitive damages . . . this court is able to fashion a punitive damages remedy that addresses the enormity of the situation.

However, the parties later settled for an undisclosed amount, with the Sundquists voluntarily donating $300,000 to the seven organizations. Sundquist v. Bank of Am., N.A. (In re Sundquist), 580 B.R. 536, 543 (Bankr. E.D. Cal. 2018). Can split-recovery schemes achieve their purpose if parties can settle and cut out the portion designated for the state or alternative recipient? For a discussion of split-recovery schemes and the potentially expansive reach of *Dardinger*, see Sharkey, Punitive Damages as Societal Damages, 113 Yale L.J. 347, 422–28 (2003). Given the presence of some statutory reforms, should constitutional limitations be imposed on punitive damage awards?

State Farm Mutual Automobile Insurance Co. v. Campbell

538 U.S. 408 (2003)

Kennedy, J. We address once again the measure of punishment, by means of punitive damages, a State may impose upon a defendant in a civil case. The question is whether, in the circumstances we shall recount, an award of $145 million in punitive damages, where full compensatory damages are $1 million, is excessive and in violation of the Due Process Clause of the Fourteenth Amendment to the Constitution of the United States.

I

In 1981, Curtis Campbell (Campbell) was driving with his wife, Inez Preece Campbell, in Cache County, Utah. He decided to pass six vans traveling ahead of them on a two-lane highway. Todd Ospital was driving a small car approaching from the opposite direction. To avoid a head-on collision with Campbell, who by then was driving on the wrong side of the highway and toward oncoming traffic, Ospital swerved onto the shoulder, lost control of his automobile, and collided with a vehicle driven by Robert G. Slusher. Ospital was killed, and Slusher was rendered permanently disabled. The Campbells escaped unscathed.

In the ensuing wrongful death and tort action, Campbell insisted he was not at fault. Early investigations did support differing conclusions as to who caused the accident, but "a consensus was reached early on by the investigators and witnesses that Mr. Campbell's unsafe pass had indeed caused the crash." 65 P.3d 1134, 1141 (Utah 2001). Campbell's insurance company, petitioner State Farm Mutual Automobile Insurance Company (State Farm), nonetheless decided to contest liability and declined offers by Slusher and Ospital's estate (Ospital) to settle the claims for the policy limit of $50,000 ($25,000 per claimant). State Farm also ignored the advice of one of its own investigators and took the case to trial, assuring the Campbells that "their assets were safe, that they had no liability for the accident, that [State Farm] would represent their interests, and that they did not need to procure separate counsel." To the contrary, a jury determined that Campbell was 100 percent at fault, and a judgment was returned for $185,849, far more than the amount offered in settlement.

At first State Farm refused to cover the $135,849 in excess liability. Its counsel made this clear to the Campbells: "'You may want to put for sale signs on your property to get things moving.'" Nor was State Farm willing to post a supersedeas bond to allow Campbell to appeal the judgment against him. Campbell obtained his own counsel to appeal the verdict. During the pendency of the appeal, in late 1984, Slusher, Ospital, and the Campbells reached an agreement whereby Slusher and Ospital agreed not to seek satisfaction of their claims against the Campbells. In exchange the Campbells agreed to pursue a bad faith action against State Farm and to be represented by Slusher's and Ospital's attorneys. The Campbells also agreed that Slusher and Ospital would have a right to play a part in all major decisions concerning the bad-faith action. No settlement could be concluded without Slusher's and Ospital's approval, and Slusher and Ospital would receive 90 percent of any verdict against State Farm.

In 1989, the Utah Supreme Court denied Campbell's appeal in the wrongful-death and tort actions. State Farm then paid the entire judgment, including the amounts in excess of the policy limits. The Campbells nonetheless filed a complaint against State Farm alleging bad faith, fraud, and intentional infliction of emotional distress. [State Farm defended on the ground that it had made an honest mistake. At trial, the plaintiff received an award of $2.6 million in compensatory damages and $145 million in punitive damages. The trial judge reduced those figures to $1 million and $25 million respectively. The Utah Supreme Court affirmed the $1 million award for compensatory damages and reinstated the $145 million in punitive damages on the ground that "State Farm's decision to take the case to trial was a result of a national scheme to meet corporate fiscal goals by capping payouts on claims company wide. This scheme was referred to as State Farm's 'Performance, Planning and Review,' or PP & R, policy. To prove the existence of this scheme, the trial court allowed the Campbells to introduce extensive expert testimony regarding fraudulent practices by State Farm in its nation-wide operations" over a 20-year period. It pointed to State Farm's "massive wealth," and the low probability of detection—estimated at one case in 50,000—for actions that each carried various criminal and civil penalties, "including $10,000 for each act of fraud, the suspension of its license to conduct business in Utah, the disgorgement of profits, and imprisonment."] We granted certiorari.

II

We recognized in Cooper Industries, Inc. v. Leatherman Tool Group, Inc., 532 U.S. 424 (2001), that in our judicial system compensatory and punitive damages, although usually awarded at the same time by the same decisionmaker, serve different purposes. Compensatory damages "are intended to redress the concrete loss that the plaintiff has suffered by reason of the defendant's wrongful conduct." By contrast, punitive damages serve a broader function; they are aimed at deterrence and retribution.

While States possess discretion over the imposition of punitive damages, it is well established that there are procedural and substantive constitutional limitations on these awards. The Due Process Clause of the Fourteenth Amendment prohibits the imposition of grossly excessive or arbitrary punishments on a tortfeasor. The reason is that "[e]lementary notions of fairness enshrined in our constitutional jurisprudence dictate that a person receive fair notice not only of the conduct that will subject him to punishment, but also of the severity of the penalty that a State may impose." To the extent an award is grossly excessive, it furthers no legitimate purpose and constitutes an arbitrary deprivation of property.

Although these awards serve the same purposes as criminal penalties, defendants subjected to punitive damages in civil cases have not been accorded the protections applicable in a criminal proceeding. This increases our concerns over the imprecise manner in which punitive damages systems are administered. We have admonished that "[p]unitive damages pose an acute danger of arbitrary deprivation of property. Jury instructions typically leave the jury with wide discretion in choosing amounts, and the presentation of evidence of a defendant's net worth creates the potential that juries will use their verdicts to express biases against big businesses, particularly those without strong local presences." Honda Motor [Co. v. Oberg, 512 U.S. 415, 432 (1994)]. Our concerns are heightened when the decisionmaker is presented, as we shall discuss, with evidence that has little bearing as to the amount of punitive damages that should be awarded. Vague instructions, or those that merely inform the jury to avoid "passion or prejudice," do little to aid the decisionmaker in its task of assigning appropriate weight to evidence that is relevant and evidence that is tangential or only inflammatory.

In light of these concerns, in [BMW of North America v. Gore, 517 U.S. 559 (1996)], we instructed courts reviewing punitive damages to consider three guideposts: (1) the degree of reprehensibility of the defendant's misconduct; (2) the disparity between the actual or potential harm suffered by the plaintiff and the punitive damages award; and (3) the difference between the punitive damages awarded by the jury and the civil penalties authorized or imposed in comparable cases. We reiterated the importance of these three guideposts in *Cooper Industries* and mandated appellate courts to conduct *de novo* review of a trial court's application of them to the jury's award. Exacting appellate review ensures that an award of punitive damages is based upon an "'application of law, rather than a decisionmaker's caprice.'"

III

Under the principles outlined in BMW of North America, Inc. v. Gore, this case is neither close nor difficult. It was error to reinstate the jury's $145 million punitive damages award. We address each guidepost of *Gore* in some detail.

A

"[T]he most important indicium of the reasonableness of a punitive damages award is the degree of reprehensibility of the defendant's conduct." We have instructed courts to determine the reprehensibility of a defendant by considering whether: the harm caused was physical as opposed to economic; the tortious conduct evinced an indifference to or a reckless disregard of the health or safety of others; the target of the conduct had financial vulnerability; the conduct involved repeated actions or was an isolated incident; and the harm was the result of intentional malice, trickery, or deceit, or mere accident. The existence of any one of these factors weighing in favor of a plaintiff may not be sufficient to sustain a punitive damages award; and the absence of all of them renders any award suspect. It should be presumed a plaintiff has been made whole for his injuries by compensatory damages, so punitive damages should only be awarded if the defendant's culpability, after having paid compensatory damages, is so reprehensible as to warrant the imposition of further sanctions to achieve punishment or deterrence.

Applying these factors in the instant case, we must acknowledge that State Farm's handling of the claims against the Campbells merits no praise. The trial court found that State Farm's employees altered the company's records to make Campbell appear less culpable. State Farm disregarded the overwhelming likelihood of liability and the near-certain probability that, by taking the case to trial, a judgment in excess of the policy limits would be awarded. State Farm amplified the harm by at first assuring the Campbells their assets would be safe from any verdict and by later telling them, postjudgment, to put a for-sale sign on their house. While we do not suggest there was error in awarding punitive damages based upon State Farm's conduct toward the Campbells, a more modest punishment for this reprehensible conduct could have satisfied the State's legitimate objectives, and the Utah courts should have gone no further.

This case, instead, was used as a platform to expose, and punish, the perceived deficiencies of State Farm's operations throughout the country. The Utah Supreme Court's opinion makes explicit that State Farm was being condemned for its nationwide policies rather than for the conduct directed toward the Campbells. This was, as well, an explicit rationale of the trial court's decision in approving the award, though reduced from $145 million to $25 million. . . .

A State cannot punish a defendant for conduct that may have been lawful where it occurred. Nor, as a general rule, does a State have a legitimate concern in imposing punitive damages to punish a defendant for unlawful acts committed outside of the State's jurisdiction. Any proper adjudication of conduct that occurred outside Utah to other persons would require their inclusion, and, to those parties, the Utah courts, in the usual case, would need to apply the laws of their relevant jurisdiction.

Here, the Campbells do not dispute that much of the out-of-state conduct was lawful where it occurred. They argue, however, that such evidence was not the primary basis for the punitive damages award and was relevant to the extent it demonstrated, in a general sense, State Farm's motive against its insured. This argument misses the mark. Lawful out-of-state conduct may be probative when it demonstrates the deliberateness and culpability of the defendant's action in the State where it is tortious, but that conduct must have a nexus to the specific harm suffered by the plaintiff. A jury must be instructed, furthermore, that it may not use evidence of out-of-state conduct to punish a defendant for action that was lawful in the jurisdiction where it occurred. A basic principle of federalism is that each State may make its own reasoned judgment about what conduct is permitted or proscribed within its borders, and each State alone can determine what measure of punishment, if any, to impose on a defendant who acts within its jurisdiction.

For a more fundamental reason, however, the Utah courts erred in relying upon this and other evidence: The courts awarded punitive damages to punish and deter conduct that bore no relation to the Campbells' harm. A defendant's dissimilar acts, independent from the acts upon which liability was premised, may not serve as the basis for punitive damages. A defendant should be punished for the conduct that harmed the plaintiff, not for being an unsavory individual or business. Due process does not permit courts, in the calculation of punitive damages, to adjudicate the merits of other parties' hypothetical claims against a defendant under the guise of the reprehensibility analysis, but we have no doubt the Utah Supreme Court did that here. Punishment on these bases creates the possibility of multiple punitive damages awards for the same conduct; for in the usual case nonparties are not bound by the judgment some other plaintiff obtains.

The same reasons lead us to conclude the Utah Supreme Court's decision cannot be justified on the grounds that State Farm was a recidivist. . . .

. . . The Campbells attempt to justify the courts' reliance upon this unrelated testimony on the theory that each dollar of profit made by underpaying a third-party claimant is the same as a dollar made by underpaying a first-party one. For the reasons already stated, this argument is unconvincing. The reprehensibility guidepost does not permit courts to expand the scope of the case so that a defendant may be punished for any malfeasance, which in this case extended for a 20-year period. In this case, because the Campbells have shown no conduct by State Farm similar to that which harmed them, the conduct that harmed them is the only conduct relevant to the reprehensibility analysis.

B

Turning to the second *Gore* guidepost, we have been reluctant to identify concrete constitutional limits on the ratio between harm, or potential harm, to the plaintiff and the punitive damages award. We decline again to impose a bright-line ratio which a punitive damages award cannot exceed. Our jurisprudence and the principles it has now established demonstrate, however, that, in practice, few awards exceeding a single-digit ratio between punitive and compensatory damages, to a significant degree, will satisfy due process. In [Pacific Mutual Life Insurance Co. v.] Haslip[, 499 U.S. 1, 23–24 (1991)], in upholding a punitive damages award, we concluded that an award of more than four times the amount of compensatory damages might be close to the line of constitutional impropriety. We cited that 4-to-1 ratio again in *Gore*. The Court further referenced a long legislative history, dating back over 700 years and going forward to today, providing for sanctions of double, treble, or quadruple damages to deter and punish. While these ratios are not binding, they are instructive. They demonstrate what should be obvious: Single-digit multipliers are more likely to comport with due process, while still achieving the State's goals of deterrence and retribution, than awards with ratios in range of 500 to 1, or, in this case, of 145 to 1. . . .

In sum, courts must ensure that the measure of punishment is both reasonable and proportionate to the amount of harm to the plaintiff and to the general damages recovered. In the context of this case, we have no doubt that there is a presumption against an award that has a 145-to-1 ratio. The compensatory award in this case was substantial; the Campbells were awarded $1 million for a year and a half of emotional distress. This was complete compensation. The harm arose from a transaction in the economic realm, not from some physical assault or trauma; there were no physical injuries; and State Farm paid the excess verdict before the complaint was filed, so the Campbells suffered only minor economic injuries for the 18-month period in which State Farm refused to resolve the claim against them. The compensatory damages for the injury suffered here, moreover, likely were based on a component which was duplicated in the punitive award. Much of the distress was caused by the outrage and humiliation the Campbells suffered at the actions of their insurer; and it is a major role of punitive damages to condemn such conduct. . . .

[Kennedy, J., rejects the specific justifications that the Utah Supreme Court offered to justify the 145 multiple: State Farm's massive wealth and the rate of concealment.]

C

The third guidepost in *Gore* is the disparity between the punitive damages award and the "civil penalties authorized or imposed in comparable cases." We note that, in the past, we have also looked to criminal penalties that could be imposed. The existence of a criminal penalty does have bearing on the seriousness with which a State views the wrongful action. When used to determine the dollar amount of the award, however, the criminal penalty has less utility. Great care must be taken to avoid use of the civil process to assess criminal penalties that can be imposed only after the heightened protections of a criminal trial have been observed, including, of course, its higher standards of proof. Punitive damages are not a substitute for the criminal process, and the remote possibility of a criminal sanction does not automatically sustain a punitive damages award.

Here, we need not dwell long on this guidepost. The most relevant civil sanction under Utah state law for the wrong done to the Campbells appears to be a $10,000 fine for an act of fraud, an amount dwarfed by the $145 million punitive damages award. The Supreme Court of Utah speculated about the loss of State Farm's business license, the disgorgement of profits, and possible imprisonment, but here again its references were to the broad fraudulent scheme drawn from evidence of out-of-state and dissimilar conduct. This analysis was insufficient to justify the award.

IV

[Reversed and remanded for a redetermination of punitive damages by the Utah courts.]

Scalia, J., dissenting. I adhere to the view expressed in my dissenting opinion in [*Gore*] that the Due Process Clause provides no substantive protections against "excessive" or " 'unreasonable' " awards of punitive damages. I am also of the view that the punitive damages jurisprudence which has sprung forth from [*Gore*] is insusceptible of principled application; accordingly, I do not feel justified in giving the case *stare decisis* effect. I would affirm the judgment of the Utah Supreme Court.

[In *Gore*, Scalia, J., had written in dissent: "What the Fourteenth Amendment's procedural guarantee assures is an opportunity to contest the reasonableness of a damages judgment in state court; but there is no federal guarantee a damages award actually *be* reasonable."]

Thomas, J., dissenting.

I would affirm the judgment below because "I continue to believe that the Constitution does not constrain the size of punitive damages awards." Accordingly, I respectfully dissent.

Ginsburg, J., dissenting. . . .

In *Gore*, I stated why I resisted the Court's foray into punitive damages "territory traditionally within the States' domain." I adhere to those views, and note again that, unlike federal habeas corpus review of state-court convictions under 28 U.S.C. §2254, the Court "work[s] at this business [of checking state courts] alone," unaided by the participation of federal district courts and courts of appeals. It was once recognized that "the laws of the particular State must suffice [to superintend punitive damages awards] until judges or legislators authorized to do so initiate system-wide change." I would adhere to that traditional view.

NOTES

1. *Punitive Damages in the Supreme Court.* *State Farm* represents the most authoritative Supreme Court decision on the appropriate constitutional standards for evaluating punitive damages. Sharkey, State Farm v. Campbell (2003): The Misguided Legacy of Proportionality, *in* Landmark Cases in the Law of Punitive Damages (Goudkamp & Katsampouka eds., 2023), argues that the Supreme Court planted the seeds of a particular type of "proportionality" jurisprudence of punitive damages, focused narrowly on the ratio of punitive-to-compensatory damages, with a profound impact upon courts and scholars, both in the United States and abroad.

Three tugboats (right) push the oil tanker *Exxon San Francisco* (center) into place beside the crippled tanker *Exxon Valdez* (left) in Prince William Sound on March 30, 1989, to begin off-loading the remainder of crude oil in the *Valdez*.

Source: Chris Wilkins / AFP / Getty Images

The Court waded back into the punitive damages waters in Exxon Shipping Co. v. Baker, 554 U.S. 471 (2008), where the Court imposed a firm limit on permissible punitive-compensatory ratios in the context of maritime law. In 1989, the *Exxon Valdez* spilled eleven-million gallons of crude oil into Prince William Sound when it ran aground on

Bligh Reef while under the command of Captain Hazelwood, a "relapsed alcoholic." A jury awarded $5 billion in punitive damages, which the Ninth Circuit eventually reduced to $2.5 billion (about five times compensatory damages). The Supreme Court took the case under its admiralty jurisdiction, and then reviewed the award below under common law excessiveness standards. The Court criticized "the stark unpredictability of punitive awards," relying on its interpretation of recent statistical analyses of punitive damages awards. It then concluded "that a 1:1 ratio [between the two] . . . is a fair upper limit in such maritime cases." In a provocative footnote, the Court suggested that "[i]n this case, . . . the constitutional outer limit may well be 1:1." In dissent, Justice Ginsburg expressed dismay that "the Court [will] rule, definitively [on next opportunity], that 1:1 is the ceiling due process requires in all of the States, and for all federal claims." For critiques of the empirical and theoretical foundations of the Court's imposition of a 1:1 ratio, see Eisenberg et al., Variability in Punitive Damages: An Empirical Assessment of the U.S. Supreme Court's Decision in *Exxon Shipping Co. v. Baker*, 166 J. Institutional & Theoretical Econ. 5 (2010), and Sharkey, The Exxon Valdez Litigation Marathon: A Window on Punitive Damages, 7 U. St. Thomas L.J. 25 (2009).

2. *Harm to "Nonparties."* In Philip Morris USA v. Williams, 549 U.S. 346, 355 (2007), the Court vacated a jury award of $79.5 million in punitive damages in a wrongful death action that awarded the plaintiff $800,000 in noneconomic damages. Breyer, J., wrote:

> In our view, the Constitution's Due Process Clause forbids a State to use a punitive damages award to punish a defendant for injury that it inflicts upon nonparties or those whom they directly represent, i.e., injury that it inflicts upon those who are, essentially, strangers to the litigation. . . . [A] defendant threatened with punishment for injuring a nonparty victim has no opportunity to defend against the charge, by showing, for example in a case such as this, that the other victim was not entitled to damages because he or she knew that smoking was dangerous or did not rely upon the defendant's statements to the contrary.
>
> For another, to permit punishment for injuring a nonparty victim would add a near standardless dimension to the punitive damages equation. How many such victims are there? How seriously were they injured? Under what circumstances did injury occur? The trial will not likely answer such questions as to nonparty victims. The jury will be left to speculate. And the fundamental due process concerns to which our punitive damages cases refer—risks of arbitrariness, uncertainty and lack of notice—will be magnified.

He refused to pass on the question of whether the 100-to-1 ratio was excessive, preferring to await the outcome on remand. Breyer, J., did allow the use of harm to third parties to assess the level of reprehensibility of the conduct in the case at bar; however, in his dissent, Stevens, J., wrote, "This nuance eludes me. When a jury increases a punitive damages award because injuries to third parties enhanced the reprehensibility of the defendant's conduct, the jury is by definition punishing the defendant—directly—for third-party harm." Is there a meaningful difference between punishing someone for their past conduct toward third parties and punishing someone because their past conduct toward third parties made their conduct more reprehensible in the case at bar?

The case then took a curious turn back in the hands of the Oregon Supreme Court, which reaffirmed the $79.5 million punitive damages verdict on "an independent and adequate state ground." Williams v. Philip Morris Inc., 176 P.3d 1255, 1260 (Or. 2008). Under Oregon law, parties may appeal the rejection of a proposed jury instruction only if it was "clear and correct in all respects," and the Oregon Supreme Court held that Philip Morris did not meet that standard. In the face of this federal-state court standoff, the U.S. Supreme Court "blinked" by dismissing certiorari as improvidently granted after accepting an appeal from the Oregon court's state law–based decision. See Sharkey, Federal Incursions and State Defiance: Punitive Damages in the Wake of *Philip Morris v. Williams*, 46 Willamette L. Rev. 449 (2010). What opportunities remain open to lower state and federal courts for awarding punitive damages in excess of single-digit multipliers?

3. *Punitive Damages in the Lower Courts.* The recent Supreme Court decisions have had important effects on the behavior of both state and lower federal courts. In Romo v. Ford Motor Co., 122 Cal. Rptr. 2d 139 (Ct. App. 2002), the court dealt with a 1993 rollover accident involving a used 1978 Ford Bronco that killed three passengers and injured three more. Ford paid nearly $5 million in actual damages for its share of the actual damages and was assessed $290 million in punitive damages on the ground that the Bronco's roof, which was steel in the front and weaker fiberboard in the rear, had been designed to look sturdier than it was. Vartabedian, P.J., refused to reduce a punitive award that was 48 times compensatory damages, holding that the false appearance of sturdiness counted as "'malicious or despicable' conduct." After *State Farm*, the Supreme Court vacated the judgment and remanded the case to the California appellate court "for further consideration in light of [*State Farm*]." Ford Motor Co. v. Romo, 538 U.S. 1028 (2003). Thereafter, an award of $23.7 million in punitive damages, about five times total compensatory damages, was upheld on appeal. Romo v. Ford Motor Co., 6 Cal. Rptr. 3d 793 (Ct. App. 2003).

Courts after *Williams* have found jury instructions to be deficient if they do not clearly delineate between using the evidence of harm to third parties to impermissibly punish and using the evidence to permissibly determine the conduct's level of reprehensibility. See, e.g., Schwarz v. Philip Morris Inc. (Estate of Schwarz), 235 P.3d 668, 675 (Or. 2010); Riley v. Volkswagen Grp. of Am., Inc., 51 F.4th 896, 901 (9th Cir. 2022). Compare GEICO v. Gonzalez, 403 P.3d 1153, 1165–66 (Alaska 2017) (distinguishing *Williams* by noting that the plaintiff's lawyer there had improperly asked the jury to consider harm to a "market share" of smokers), with R.J. Reynolds Tobacco Co. v. Neff, 325 So. 3d 872, 881–82 (Fla. Dist. Ct. App. 2021) (determining statements by plaintiff's lawyer referring to "millions of family members" sufficient to warrant a new trial). If a jury no longer can consider the impact of the defendant's behavior on nonparties, will the defendant be underdeterred? See, e.g., Hylton, Reflections on Remedies and *Philip Morris v. Williams*, 27 Rev. Litig. 9, 31 (2007). Some courts have found that the impact of the defendant's behavior on nonparties can be considered when determining reprehensibility, but only when those nonparties are members of the general public. See McLawhorn v. Ocwen Loan Servicing, LLC, No. 4:14-CV-02745-RBH, 2017 WL 624539, at *4 (D.S.C. Feb. 15, 2017).

The effects in the lower courts of the Court's decision to impose a 1:1 cap on punitive damages in *Baker* are even more difficult to predict. Most courts seem content to limit the scope of its 1:1 ratio to maritime cases. See, e.g., Hardy v. City of Milwaukee, 88 F. Supp. 3d 852, 856 (E.D. Wis. 2015) (setting a punitive damage award nine times actual damages); Colombo v. BRP US Inc., 179 Cal. Rptr. 3d 580, 608 (Ct. App. 2014), (upholding a 3:1 punitive-compensatory damages ratio); Cote v. Philip Morris USA, Inc., 985 F.3d 840 (11th Cir. 2021) (upholding a nearly $27 million award with a 3.3-to-1 punitive-compensatory damages ratio while rejecting *Baker*'s limit). Other courts have applied its limits beyond the realm of admiralty law. See, e.g., Tolbert v. Gallup Indian Med. Ctr., 555 F. Supp. 3d 1133, 1152 (D.N.M. 2021) (noting that *Baker*'s bright-line ratio may be instructive for "substantial" compensatory awards consisting of purely economic damages). Any reason for different standards?

4. *Deterrence and Reputational Effects.* In Mathias v. Accor Economy Lodging, Inc., 347 F.3d 672, 677–678 (7th Cir. 2003), Posner, J., affirmed a 37:1 punitive-compensatory damages ratio, where the jury awarded $5,000 in compensatory damages and $186,000 in punitive damages to each of two guests at defendant's bedbug-infested hotel.

> The award of punitive damages in this case . . . serves the additional purpose of limiting the defendant's ability to profit from its fraud by escaping detection and (private) prosecution. If a tortfeasor is "caught" only half the time he commits torts, then when he is caught he should be punished twice as heavily in order to make up for the times he gets away.

Posner, J., further observed: "All things considered, we cannot say that the award of punitive damages was excessive, albeit the precise number chosen by the jury was arbitrary. It is probably not a coincidence that $5,000 + $186,000 = $191,000/191 = $1,000: i.e., $1,000 per room in the hotel."

How important is the threat of punitive damages in forcing Accor Economy Lodging and similar actors to prevent harms arising from bedbugs in the future? What about regulatory and/or criminal penalties? Or nonlegal economic incentives? See Shavell, On the Proper Magnitude of Punitive Damages: *Mathias v. Accor Economy Lodging, Inc.*, 120 Harv. L. Rev. 1223 (2007), which argues: "The need for punitive damages—and, for that matter, for compensatory damages—to accomplish deterrence is of a much lower order when victims are the customers of a firm than when they are not."

SECTION E. COLLATERAL BENEFITS

Plaintiffs may receive additional funds for their injuries from parties other than tortfeasors, such as insurance companies or the government. These payments are called collateral benefits. When plaintiffs receive collateral benefits prior to trial, may the defendant introduce evidence of those benefits to reduce its own damage payments? See RST §920A, stating the general rule in the negative. Although the collateral source rule is in tension with the fair compensation goal of tort law between the victim and the tortfeasor, it is arguably more just to allow the plaintiff to benefit from any windfall. However, the modern trend has been toward allowing defendants to introduce evidence of collateral benefits at trial.

Harding v. Town of Townshend
43 Vt. 536 (1871)

[The plaintiff sued for injuries caused "by reason of an insufficiency of a highway of the defendant." The plaintiff had received payment of $130 from an insurance policy that he purchased for $7. The court charged the jury that it should reduce the amount of recovery by the net proceeds of the insurance, $123.]

Peck, J. There is no technical ground which necessarily leads to the conclusion that the money received by the plaintiff of the accident insurance company should operate as a defense, or enure to the benefit of the defendant. The insurer and the defendant are not joint tortfeasors or joint debtors so as to make a payment or satisfaction by the former operate to the benefit of the latter. Nor is there any legal privity between the defendant and the insurer so as to give the former a right to avail itself of a payment by the latter. The policy of insurance is collateral to the remedy against the defendant, and was procured solely by the plaintiff and at his expense, and to the procurement of which the defendant was in no way contributory.

It is in the nature of a wager between the plaintiff and a third person, the insurer, to which the defendant was in no measure privy, either by relation of the parties or by contract or otherwise. It cannot be said that the plaintiff took out the policy in the interest or behalf of the defendant; nor is there any legal principle which seems to require that it be ultimately appropriated to the defendant's use and benefit.

But it is urged, on the part of the defense, that the plaintiff is entitled to but one satisfaction for the injury he has sustained. If we assume this to be a correct proposition, the question arises whether the defendant stands in a condition to make this objection. This depends on the question who, as between the insurer and the defendant, ought to pay the damage—which of the two ought primarily to make compensation to the plaintiff and ultimately to bear the loss? If the insurer ought ultimately to bear the loss, the defendant is entitled in this action to have the benefit of that payment; but if the defendant should ultimately bear the loss, then the payment by the insurer and the collection of the entire damage of the defendant only creates an equity between the plaintiff and the insurer, to be ultimately adjusted between them, in which the defendant has no interest, and with which he has no concern. . . . [A]s between the insurer and the wrong-doer, in reason and justice the burden of making compensation to the injured party ought to be ultimately borne by the party thus in fault. . . . It would seem to be a perversion of justice to subrogate the wrong-doer, who has caused the loss, to the rights of the injured party as to his remedy against the insurer. But it is not uncommon that the insurer, who has paid the loss, is put in place of the insured and subrogated to his rights in respect to his remedies against others for the injury.

Judgment of the county court reversed, and judgment for the plaintiff for the amount of the verdict, and the $123 to be added thereto.

NOTES

1. ***Varieties of Collateral Benefits.*** In addition to insurance payouts made directly to the plaintiff (as in *Harding*, above), collateral source payments also include a variety of other compensation mechanisms, including salary, Motts v. Michigan Cab Co., 264 N.W. 855 (Mich. 1936); payments from the Welfare Fund of the United Mine Workers, Conley v. Foster, 335 S.W.2d 904 (Ky. 1960); and sick or vacation pay, Davidson v. Vogler, 507 S.W.2d 160 (Ky. 1974). The principle has been hotly contested in those instances where an injured plaintiff receives a discount from list price from Medicare, Medicaid, or some private insurer, only to claim that the tort recovery for these Medicaid expenditures should be calibrated by the list and not the discounted price—arguing in effect that under the collateral source rule neither the defendant nor its insurer is entitled to the benefit of plaintiff's market prowess or good fortune. The cases are split, with some parties allowing the plaintiffs to recover the list price, others a reduced price, and still others a blend. For the full recovery option, see Kenney v. Liston, 760 S.E.2d 434, 444–45 (W. Va. 2014). For the amount actually paid approach, see Bozeman v. State, 879 So. 2d 692, 705–06 (La. 2004), and Patchett v. Lee, 60 N.E.3d 1025, 1032 (Ind. 2016). How should the value be computed if health care providers routinely accept these discounts? If different prices for identical services are charged to government and private insurers?

2. ***Government Benefits and the Collateral Source Rule.*** The collateral source rule gives rise to special complications when the government is both a tortfeasor liable under the Federal Tort Claims Act and the supplier of first-party benefits under, for example, Social Security and veterans' benefits programs. With mixed success, the government typically claims that payments under other government programs do not count as collateral payments, and hence should be used to reduce the government's tort obligation. In Steckler v. United States, 549 F.2d 1372, 1379 (10th Cir. 1977), the government sought to set off both veterans' benefits and Social Security from the tort award. The court deducted veterans' benefits to prevent the plaintiff from recovering "double payment" for the same injury from the same source. The court refused, however, to allow the government a total setoff for Social Security. "The part contributed by the worker and the employers has the aspects of social insurance and as such is collateral to monies contributed by the government." The part of Social Security from general government contributions, however, was not collateral, and hence was set off against tort damages, like veterans' benefits. *Steckler* then placed the burden on the plaintiff to determine what fraction of the Social Security payment counted as a nondeductible collateral source.

Steckler was modified by Berg v. United States, 806 F.2d 978, 985 (10th Cir. 1986):

> We are now convinced that it is in fact impossible to distinguish accurately which part of a fund that has been produced by millions of contributors is attributable to the government and which part is attributable to a particular injured party. Therefore, we require that the plaintiff bear the burden of showing only that he or she contributed to a special fund that is separate and distinct from general government revenues.

The court held that Medicare benefits, funded under Social Security, so qualified as collateral sources. That approach was followed in Molzof v. United States, 6 F.3d 461, 465, 466 (7th Cir. 1993), in which Cudahy, J., applying Wisconsin law, refused to allow the government to set off benefits it paid out through its Veterans Administration program against damages awarded against it under the Federal Tort Claims Act, on the ground that the two funds were different sources even if the defendant was the same. What if the Social Security or veterans' benefits were by statute or by agreement explicitly set off from tort awards?

3. ***Statutory Modification of the Collateral Source Rule.*** The ongoing expansion of tort liability has ushered in many statutory exceptions to the collateral source rule, especially for health care providers.

CALIFORNIA CIVIL CODE (2023)

§3333.1. Negligence of Health Care Provider; Evidence of Benefits and Premiums Paid; Subrogation

(a) In the event the defendant so elects, in an action for personal injury against a health care provider based upon professional negligence, he may introduce evidence of any amount payable as a benefit to the plaintiff as a result of the personal injury pursuant to the United States Social Security Act, any state or federal income disability or worker's compensation act, any health, sickness or income-disability insurance, accident insurance that provides health benefits or income-disability coverage, and any contract or agreement of any group, organization, partnership, or corporation to provide, pay for, or reimburse the cost of medical, hospital, dental, or other health care services. Where the defendant elects to introduce such evidence, the plaintiff may introduce evidence of any amount which the plaintiff has paid or contributed to secure his right to any insurance benefits concerning which the defendant has introduced evidence.

What should be done with the information once introduced? A New York statute, N.Y. C.P.L.R. §4545(a) (2023), reduces recovery for any present or future payment, subject to reasonable estimation. That amount recoverable is increased by an amount equal to (1) the cost of keeping the benefit in place during the previous two years, plus (2) the projected contractual cost of keeping the benefits in place in the future. The purpose of the New York statute is to return the plaintiff to the same position she would have been in if she had not acquired any collateral coverage at all.

What role does the Affordable Care Act (ACA) play in modifying collateral source payouts? Ann S. Levin, Comment, The Fate of the Collateral Source Rule After Healthcare Reform, 60 UCLA L. Rev. 736 (2013), looks at how the ACA affects the traditional rationales that undergird the collateral source rule, arguing that because the ACA is both making insurance coverage well-nigh universal through its individual mandate and because it also makes it so that insurance contracts are more standardized, there is less of a need for the collateral source rule. It then advocates for a scheme much like the one in New York state. For a contrasting view that the ACA should not affect the tort system at all, see Andrew F. Popper, The Affordable Care Act Is Not Tort Reform, 65 Cath. U. L. Rev. 1 (2015).

Benjet, A Review of State Law Modifying the Collateral Source Rule: Seeking Greater Fairness in Economic Damages Awards, 76 Def. Couns. J. 210 (2009), provides a summary of state modifications of the collateral source rule. For an attack on the various statutory exceptions to the collateral source rule, see Marshall & Fitzgerald, The Collateral Source Rule and Its Abolition: An Economic Perspective, 15 Kan. J.L. & Pub. Pol'y 57, 58 (2005). For an analysis of the corrective justice underpinning of the collateral source rule and a discussion of how the abolition of the rule would challenge the fundamental nature of American tort law, see Krauss & Kidd, Collateral Source and Tort's Soul, 48 U. Louisville L. Rev. 1 (2009).

4. *Subrogation and Reimbursement.* A second way to avoid the double recovery possible when collateral benefits are present is to allow the collateral source to receive repayment of its expenses from the successful tort claim, or in some cases take control over that tort litigation (i.e., subrogation to the collateral source). In many instances, third-party insurers base their rates in part on their ability to recover those funds. Knowing this, plaintiffs may seek to enter into collusive settlements with defendants, whereby they claim that all or a disproportionate part of the recovery is allocated to pain and suffering, to which no subrogation rights attach. In Westendorf v. Stasson, 330 N.W.2d 699, 702 (Minn. 1983), the tort settlement provided that all "payments to be made hereunder are solely attributable to the pain and suffering and permanent injury" of the plaintiff and the loss of consortium to her spouse. But the court held that this settlement did not bind the insurance company whose rights it sought to cut off. That result is supported in Sykes, Subrogation and Insolvency, 30 J. Legal Stud. 383, 386 (2001), on the ground that if the injured party bore, as against the insurer, the risk of pain and suffering when no third-party tortfeasor was present, the "fortuitous presence of an injurer liable for the insured's losses" should not alter that balance.

5. *Subrogation and the Independent Cause of Action.* As a matter of contract law, a subrogee's claim is an assignment, which means that the claim is subject to all defenses that the defendant can raise against the injured party. "Where the insured has no right of recovery, the insurer has no enforceable right of subrogation." Gibbs v. Hawaiian Eugenia Corp., 966 F.2d 101, 106 (2d Cir. 1992). That rule prevents any health plan from recovering its costs in treating a smoker's lung cancer from a tobacco company if the smoker's claims were blocked by the defense of assumption of risk. To circumvent these subrogation limitations, many insurers assert "direct" or "independent" claims against the tobacco defendants. These independent claims were allowed to state Medicaid programs by courts that have held that Medicaid's public duty to provide care to tort victims authorizes direct actions for their own expenses, free of defenses that could be asserted against the tobacco smokers. In contrast, private labor unions and health plans have been generally rebuffed when they have sought to unhinge their reimbursement claims that stem from RICO claims for racketeering and fraudulent misrepresentation from the underlying tort actions.

6. *Litigation Financing.* One large question lurking behind tort damages is how to finance litigation when some portion of the recovery has to compensate the lawyer for services rendered. The challenge is to use a payment device that imposes the smallest net tax on the plaintiff. Possible options include hourly fees, contingent fees, class actions, fee shifting, sales of mature and unmatured tort claims, and litigation insurance. Below is the briefest of surveys.

a. ***Contingent Fees.*** Today, the plaintiff's attorney typically receives compensation from a contingency fee that is payable only out of the money that plaintiff receives, either by settlement or judgment. Their terms may vary, but the standard agreement generally specifies two conditions of payment. First, the proceeds of recovery will first repay the attorney dollar-for-dollar for certain out-of-pocket costs (such as expenses for investigation or experts). Second, usually between one-third to one-half of the remaining proceeds goes to the lawyer as the contingent fee (unless otherwise limited by local statute). Virtually all plaintiff tort litigation is financed this way. This system has a built-in agency cost conflict, as the lawyer may be tempted to encourage settlement too soon to minimize costs even if the plaintiff stands to gain otherwise. Thus if it takes an additional $100 to recover $240 more dollars in total, the lawyer (with a one-third contingent fee) may not wish to incur that cost ($100) if he only obtains an additional $80 in contingent fees, even if the client's gain ($160) more than offsets the lawyer's loss. Plaintiffs may find it difficult to monitor their lawyers directly, so the stronger social sanction is reputational. Conversely, some clients may prefer lawyers to pursue weak claims, as when another $100 in expenditures produce $75 in net gain.

The contingent fee is far less common on the defense side, where hourly fees tend to dominate, in part because it is exceedingly difficult to agree on the baseline from which contingent fees would be determined. For the plaintiff, that number is zero. For the defendant, it is necessary to find a number to serve as that baseline, given the difficulties of valuation. But if such a number is found, the contingent fee is some fraction of the savings that comes from a lower settlement or judgment.

Scholars have debated whether the contingent fee system is ultimately good for tort law. For a defense of contingent fees, see Kritzer, Seven Dogged Myths Concerning Contingency Fees, 80 Wash. U. L.Q. 739 (2002). Dana & Spier, Expertise and Contingent Fees: The Role of Asymmetric Information in Attorney Compensation, 9 J.L. Econ. & Org. 349 (1993), likewise extols the virtues of the contingent fee system. For concerns that the contingent fee overcompensates lawyers in mass torts cases, where group settlements can reduce litigation costs, see Brickman, O'Connell & Horowitz, Rethinking Contingency Fees: A Proposal to Align the Contingency Fee System with Its Policy Roots and Ethical Mandates (1994).

b. ***Class Actions.*** Class actions are commonly used to aggregate large numbers of relatively small cases with common elements, each of which may be too small to bring in its own right. An attorney will often try to settle cases on behalf of the class, subject to certification by a judge that the fees are proper and the settlement terms are favorable to class members. These cases raise the risk to a defendant of "bet your company" cases where damages awards could bankrupt a company. The Class Action Fairness Act of 2005, 28 U.S.C. §§1332(d), 1453, 1711–1715, was passed to allow defendants to remove many such cases into federal courts, where the perceived risk is lower. Nonetheless, class actions remain a powerful tool for individual plaintiffs.

c. ***Fee Shifting.*** The traditional American rule is that each side bears its own cost, regardless of whether they win or lose. In contrast, under the English rule, the loser pays the fees for both sides. The choice of compensation system influences the strategies that parties choose on whether to bring or defend suits. Usually, parties are willing to take larger risks when they know that the high probability of loss will not increase their overall legal bills. See generally Shavell, Suit, Settlement and Trial: A Theoretical Analysis Under Alternative Methods for the Allocation of Legal Costs, 11 J. Legal Stud. 35, 58–60 (1982). One consequence of the difference in fee systems is that riskier claims, including those based on novel legal theories, are more likely to be brought in the United States than in England. See Prichard, A Systemic Approach to Comparative Law: The Effect of Cost, Fee, and Financing Rules on the Development of the Substantive Law, 17 J. Legal Stud. 451 (1988).

d. ***Sale of Tort Claims.*** Today, tort law forbids the outright assignment of damages claims not yet adjudicated. While total assignment of damages is prohibited, the contingent fee contract effectively constitutes a partial sale. Academic opinion tends to favor the lifting of all restrictions on sale, which reduces delay and uncertainties of litigation for injured plaintiffs. See Shukaitis, A Market in Personal Injury Tort Claims, 16 J. Legal Stud. 329, 329–30, 339–40 (1987).

e. ***Litigation Insurance.*** Litigation insurance is yet another way to cover legal fees. These contracts are legal today, but they face the serious moral hazard risk that only parties who expect to litigate are likely to purchase this coverage. This market has emerged in Germany, where contingent fees are prohibited.

f. ***Litigation Financing.*** More controversial is the rise of third-party litigation funding, by entities, not law firms, that specialize in handling these claims. Such financing has gained wide acceptance in the United Kingdom and Australia and has gained a foothold in some U.S. jurisdictions, despite an apparent ban on such a practice. For a thorough vetting of the pros and cons of alternative litigation financing structures, see Symposium, A Brave New World: The Changing Face of Litigation and Law Firm Finance, 63 DePaul L. Rev. 193 (2014).

TABLE OF CASES

Principal cases are indicated by italics.
Alphabetization is letter-by-letter
(e.g., "Indiana Harbor" precedes "Indian Towing").

B

C

G

H

I

J

L

M

N

O

P

Q

R

S

T

U

V

TABLE OF RESTATEMENT SECTIONS

Restatement of Torts (RT)

Restatement (Second) of Torts (RST)

Restatement (Third) of Torts—Apportionment of Liability (RTT: AL)

Restatement (Third) of Torts—Intentional Torts to Persons (Tentative Draft, Approved 2021) (RTT: IT)

Restatement (Third) of Torts—Liability for Physical and Emotional Harm (RTT: LPEH)

Restatement (Third) of Torts—Miscellaneous Provisions (Tentative Draft, Released 2023)

Restatement (Third) of Torts—Products Liability (RTT: PL)

Restatement (Third) of Torts—Remedies (Tentative Draft No. 2, Approved 2023) (RTT: Remedies)

Restatement (Second) of Agency (RSA)

Restatement (Second) of Contracts (RSC)

TABLE OF SECONDARY AUTHORITIES

C

D

H

M

T

U

INDEX

R

S

T